HANDBOOK OF LATIN AMERICAN STUDIES: No. 43

A Selective and Annotated Guide to Recent Publications in Anthropology, Economics, Education, Geography, Government and Politics, International Relations, and Sociology

VOLUME 44 WILL BE DEVOTED TO THE HUMANITIES: ART, FILM, HISTORY, LANGUAGE, LITERATURE, MUSIC, AND PHILOSOPHY

EDITORIAL NOTE: Comments concerning the *Handbook of Latin American Studies* should be sent directly to the Editor, *Handbook of Latin American Studies*, Hispanic Division, Library of Congress, Washington, D.C. 20540.

HANDBOOK OF LATIN AMERICAN STUDIES: NO. 43

SOCIAL SCIENCES

Prepared by a Number of Scholars
for the Hispanic Division of The Library of Congress

Edited by DOLORES MOYANO MARTIN

1981

UNIVERSITY OF TEXAS PRESS   *Austin*

International Standard Book Number 0-292-73022-5
Library of Congress Catalog Card Number 36-32633
Copyright © 1982 by the University of Texas Press
Printed in the United States of America

Requests for permission to reproduce material from this work should be sent to
Permissions, University of Texas Press,
Box 7819, Austin, Texas 78712.

First Edition, 1982

CONTRIBUTING EDITORS

SOCIAL SCIENCES

Andrés Suárez, *University of Florida*, GOVERNMENT AND POLITICS
Antonio Ugalde, *University of Texas at Austin*, SOCIOLOGY
Nelson P. Valdés, *University of New Mexico, Albuquerque*, SOCIOLOGY
Carlos H. Waisman, *University of California, San Diego*, SOCIOLOGY
Alan C. Wares, *Summer Institute of Linguistics, Dallas*, ANTHROPOLOGY
Jan Peter Wogart, *World Bank*, ECONOMICS
Gary Wynia, *University of Minnesota*, GOVERNMENT AND POLITICS

HUMANITIES

Earl M. Aldrich, Jr., *University of Wisconsin, Madison*, LITERATURE
Joyce Bailey, *New Haven, Conn.*, ART
Jean A. Barman, *University of British Columbia*, HISTORY
Roderick J. Barman, *University of British Columbia*, HISTORY
Bruce-Novoa, *Yale University*, LITERATURE
David Bushnell, *University of Florida*, HISTORY
Edward E. Calnek, *University of Rochester*, HISTORY
D. Lincoln Canfield, *Southern Illinois University at Carbondale*, LANGUAGES
Donald E. Chipman, *North Texas State University, Denton*, HISTORY
Don M. Coerver, *Texas Christian University*, HISTORY
Michael L. Conniff, *University of New Mexico, Albuquerque*, HISTORY
Edith B. Couturier, *Chevy Chase, Md.*, HISTORY
Ethel O. Davie, *West Virginia State College*, LITERATURE
Lisa E. Davis, *York College*, LITERATURE
Maria Angélica Guimarães Lopes Dean, *University of Wisconsin, Parkside*, LITERATURE
Ralph E. Dimmick, *Organization of American States*, LITERATURE
Roberto Etchepareborda, *Organization of American States*, HISTORY
Rubén A. Gamboa, *Mills College*, LITERATURE
Naomi M. Garrett, *West Virginia State College*, LITERATURE
Cedomil Goić, *University of Michigan*, LITERATURE
Roberto González Echevarría, *Yale University*, LITERATURE
Richard E. Greenleaf, *Tulane University*, HISTORY
Oscar Hahn, *University of Iowa*, LITERATURE
Michael T. Hamerly, *Seattle, Wash.*, HISTORY
John R. Hébert, *Library of Congress*, BIBLIOGRAPHY AND GENERAL WORKS
Carlos R. Hortas, *Yale University*, LITERATURE
Randal Johnson, *Rutgers University*, FILM
Djelal Kadir, *Purdue University*, LITERATURE
Franklin W. Knight, *Johns Hopkins University*, HISTORY
Pedro Lastra, *State University of New York at Stony Brook*, LITERATURE
Asunción Lavrin, *Howard University*, HISTORY
William Luis, *Dartmouth College*, LITERATURE
James B. Lynch, Jr., *University of Maryland, College Park*, ART
Murdo J. MacLeod, *University of Arizona*, HSTORY
Wilson Martins, *New York University*, LITERATURE
Carolyn Morrow, *University of Utah*, LITERATURE
Gerald M. Moser, *Pennsylvania State University*, LITERATURE
Robert J. Mullen, *University of Texas at San Antonio*, ART
John V. Murra, *Cornell University*, HISTORY
José Neistein, *Brazilian American Cultural Institute, Washington*, ART
Betty T. Osiek, *Southern Illinois University at Edwardsville*, LITERATURE
José Miguel Oviedo, *University of California, Los Angeles*, LITERATURE
Margaret S. Peden, *University of Missouri*, LITERATURE

CONTENTS

EDUCATION

GEOGRAPHY

GOVERNMENT AND POLITICS

INTERNATIONAL RELATIONS

SOCIOLOGY

INDEXES

EDITOR'S NOTE

I. GENERAL TRENDS

The growing interest of Europeans in Latin American studies noted in previous volumes of *HLAS* is evident in the contributions on Mexican geography by the Puebla/Tlaxcala Project, a joint German/Mexican research program. According to one geographer, "the success of the Puebla-Tlaxcala Project demonstrates the value of long-term funding and close international cooperation in regionally based research" (p. 452). As evident as European interest is the growing sophistication of Latin American scholarship, especially in economics, a field in which notable progress has been made in the last five years. One economist attributes the "quality and diversity" of economic research in Latin America to the discipline's maturity (p. 328). Another believes the trend is due to the increasing number and greater appreciation of rigorous and productive research institutions (p. 247), a fact attributed by other economists to a now well-established Latin American tradition of government support for research in the social sciences (p. 271). The lead taken by Latin Americans over foreign scholars in economics is also evident in archaeology, a field in which "nationals continue to account for more than 80 percent" of works on Argentina, Brazil, and Chile (p. 61). In some countries, nationals have turned into regional scholars, a trend exemplified by Brazil, where "the high quality of research on the problems of the Northeast" is generated chiefly by Northeasterners (p. 372).

The volume of literature devoted to the study of women is, in the words of one contributor, "astonishing" (p. 754) even if much of it has not "outgrown the polemical state" (p. 754). Exceptions are some studies of female political participation (p. 583) and women's economic role (p. 323). Studies of the elderly, a new topic for Latin America, is welcomed by two sociologists in this volume (p. 740 and 754).

The intense preoccupation with cities and their problems so evident in recent years has subsided with the resurgence of interest in more traditional areas of research such as population, social classes, inequality, and rural society (p. 119, 740 and 754). Rural poverty, in particular, is a leading theme in this volume, with many authors attributing the rise of a rural proletariat to the mechanization of agriculture and the effects of minimum wage laws (p. 283, 372 and 483). According to an ethnologist, these two factors as well as other aspects of "modernization," have had an adverse demographic impact by reinforcing or even increasing the desire for children among the rural proletariat (p. 104).

The large number of works published on the subject of energy underscores the magnitude of the problem for Latin America, as a number of economies enter an era of expensive energy and slower growth requiring major structural readjustments (p. 371 and 483). And yet, while much attention is devoted to the economic aspects of energy there is little written on the politics of energy as revealed, for example, in the relationship between petroleum revenues and democratic rule

(p. 567). The fact that "studies of how government decision-making on a particular issue relates to the wider polity are still few and far between" is deplored by one contributor (p. 323).

To complement the excellent study of the breakdown of democratic rule annotated last year (see *HLAS 42:1920*), we need a comparable analysis of the breakdown of totalitarian regimes, particularly in South America. However, an "excellent history of military politics" appeared in 1980 (p. 618) in addition to a number of good bibiographies and descriptive articles on the subject (p. 4).

The fastest growing field in anthropology today is medical or epidemiological anthropology and this reflects "the growing awareness of the importance and significance of Latin America for the investigation of human evolution, adaptation and biological variation" (p. 203). And indeed, the discovery in Ecuador of what is believed to be "the earliest human fossil known in the New World" (p. 203) underscores this significance.

II. REGIONAL TRENDS

Mexico

Political events in Central and South America continue to force the emigration of many social scientists to Mexico, a development of the last 10 years which has contributed not only to the enhancement of Mexican research but to the country's overall "intellectual enrichment" (p. 726). Mexico's rising international status as an energy-rich country is reflected in the growing literature on two topics: Mexico's foreign relations (p. 644) and the question of energy resources (p. 271).

Caribbean and Central America

In the Caribbean, anthropological and sociological research continues to flourish, with Haiti as the area receiving the most attention (p. 119) and migration as the topic commanding the most interest (p. 740). The volume of literature on Cuba continues to grow in some of the social sciences but to decline in others. Studies of Cuban foreign policy, for example, have been "growing rapidly, reflecting Castro's greater activism in recent years," (p. 644) while studies of the Cuban economy have declined to an "appalling" extent (p. 306), especially in view of the increasing availability and regularity of statistical material published in Cuba (p. 306). The slight decline in the number of studies of another island economy, Puerto Rico, is attributed to the recession and to the "political changing of the guard" (p. 311). There is a consensus that the notable increase of publications on Central America—an area much neglected in the past—is a direct consequence of the Nicaraguan revolution, violence in El Salvador, the Panama Canal treaties, and related political tensions throughout the region (p. 645).

Andean Countries

Implicit in many works on Venezuela by national and foreign scholars is an effort to understand the consolidation of democracy (p. 567). There are also several studies that explore the "survivability" of democracy in Colombia (p. 567), especially in view of the problems posed by the nation's "clandestine economy" (p. 323). The direct consequence of the enormous demand of a US clandestine drug market, this underground world is the subject of serious study at last (p. 323). The excess of foreign exchange generated by this clandestine economy seriously threatens Colombia's monetary policy, and one study suggests that "a better solution would be to incorporate it into the legal economy to the extent possible" (p. 323).

In many works about Peru there is a new tone of "universal disillusionment with Velasco Alvarado's Peruvian revolutionary experiment" (p. 339), and especially with his claim of achieving development through "neither communism nor capitalism" (p. 339). A sense of "crisis" pervades most studies of the Peruvian economy (p. 339), and a deep pessimism is evident in most works on the country's politics (p. 583). The volume of literature on Peru notwithstanding, most contributing editors agree that the Andean country to register the most impressive gains in recent years is Bolivia. An economist speaks of "a notable improvement in quality" that makes "a real contribution towards understanding the complex and fragmented economy of Bolivia" (p. 352). Likewise, a political scientist emphasizes the "much higher quality" of studies of Bolivian politics and government (p. 584). And finally, the ethnologist singles out Bolivia as the leading example of the "increased level of research and publication on the Andean countries" (p. 168).

In contrast to the highly charged and polemical literature on Chile discussed in previous volumes, "openly anti-Junta and anti-Allende articles form a distinct minority" in this one (p. 339). The more reflective tone of the literature on Chilean politics noted in *HLAS 41* has given way to one of deep pessimism, not unlike Peru's, especially in studies "coming from the center and center-left" (p. 582).

The River Plate Countries

In Argentina, a country with one of the largest and most productive academic communities in Latin America, years of political terrorism, upheaval, and repression have led to cultural decline. There has been a similar decline in Uruguay and Paraguay, where only the least controversial sociological research such as descriptive demography is conducted at present (p. 764). However, in contrast to the shriveling of sociology and political science, research on the economies of the region is thriving. In Argentina, for example, one economist notes that "economic literature has flourished recently in terms of both quantity and quality," (p. 361) while another points to the excellent studies of Uruguay's agricultural sector, a development he attributes to the return of numerous foreign-trained economists (p. 352).

Brazil

In *HLAS 41* (p. xv), we noted that in contrast to other countries of the southern cone, Brazil's political *abertura* had created a climate of free discussion favoring the public examination of issues. The result has been "a body of political science literature of exceptional quality and scope" generated in Brazil in the last few years (p. 622). For example, the history of ideas and of political movements is "stimulating some of the best scholarly research" (p. 623). Important research is also being done in sociology, a field in which Brazilians have excelled in recent years (p. 772), and in ethnology, a discipline in which field research is yielding novel interpretations of the country's tropical forest and savannah cultures. Unfortunately, sophisticated understanding of these cultures is emerging just as they are succumbing to "progress," their members shunted aside as "ignorant savages," and their environment rapidly being developed into "grasslands" (p. 143).

III. OBITUARIES

CLIFFORD EVANS (1920–1981)

On January 9, 1981, Clifford Evans died of heart failure in Washington, D.C. A contributing editor to the ARCHAEOLOGY: SOUTH AMERICA Section of *HLAS* for more than 24 years, Evans' first contribution to *HLAS 19* appeared in 1957. He was a specialist in the prehistory of the Amazonian forest and lowlands, a region largely neglected until his pioneer studies. Evans and his wife, Betty Meggers, were one of the most productive teams in South American archaeology. Together they trained numerous Brazilian scientists and cooperated with the Brazilian National

Research Council in a program which in the last 15 years greatly expanded knowledge of the prehistory of Brazil. In Ecuador, Evans and Meggers' pioneer studies documented stylistic links between Ecuadorian and Japanese pottery suggesting evidence of Japanese contact with coastal Ecuador as early as 3000 BC. Evans received a BA degree from the University of Southern California in 1941 and a PhD from Columbia University in 1950. In the same year, he was appointed Curator for South American Archaeology of the Smithsonian Institution, where he worked until his death. In 1956 he received the Washington Academy of Sciences Award for Scientific Achievement and in 1966, the Gold Medal of the 37th International Congress of Americanists as well as the Order of Merit from the Government of Ecuador. Evans will be deeply missed not only by the staff of *HLAS* but by all of us in the field of Latin American studies who were familiar with his unflagging enthusiasm and deep affection for the peoples and cultures of Latin America.

JAMES R. SCOBIE (1929–1981)

On January 4, 1981, James R. Scobie died of heart failure in La Jolla, California. A contributing editor to the HISTORY: ARGENTINA, PARAGUAY, AND URUGUAY Section of *HLAS* for more than 10 years, Scobie's first contribution to *HLAS 28* appeared in 1966. He also served on the *HLAS* Advisory Board for 10 years (1971–81). Scobie's major contributions were in Argentine social and economic history. His early study of the agrarian evolution of Argentina, *Revolution in the Pampas: a social history of Argentine wheat, 1860–1910* (1964), led him to study one of its consequences, the spectacular growth of the city of Buenos Aires, splendidly portrayed in his fourth and last book: *Buenos Aires: plaza to suburb, 1870–1910* (1974). Scobie received a BA degree from Princeton University in 1950 and a PhD from Harvard University in 1954. He taught history at the University of Maryland Overseas Program (1956–57), University of California at Berkeley (1957–64), Indiana University (1964–77), and the University of California at San Diego (1977–81). He received numerous fellowships from the Guggenheim, Doherty, and Tinker Foundations and from the Social Science Research Council-American Council for Learned Societies. During the years in which he served as contributing editor to *HLAS* and later, as a member of the Advisory Board, Scobie became an invaluable advisor and trusted friend. None of us will forget his loyal devotion to *HLAS* and his wise counsel to its staff.

IV. SPECIAL DEVELOPMENTS

A pilot effort established in 1978, the Hispanic Acquisitions Project of the Library of Congress was formally incorporated into the Exchange and Gift Division as an ongoing Hispanic Acquisitions Program in late 1981. As noted in previous volumes, HAP has become an invaluable asset to the *Handbook of Latin American Studies* by continuing to add important new research publications to the Library's collections. In 1981–82, the HAP staff made notable gains in improving the Library's coverage of publications from Panama, Venezuela, Colombia, and the Dominican Republic. The non-Spanish speaking Caribbean remains a high priority for future efforts.

V. CHANGES IN VOLUME 43

Anthropology
William T. Sanders (Pennsylvania State University) collaborated with Norman Hammond in the preparation of the section on Mesoamerican archaeology. Waud H. Kracke (University of Illinois, Chicago-Circle) annotated the material on ethnology

of the South American Lowlands. William E. Carter (Library of Congress) reviewed the literature on ethnology of the South American highlands.

Economics

Clark W. Reynolds (Stanford University) prepared the section on Mexico. David D. Denslow (University of Florida) and Dennis J. Mahar (World Bank) annotated the literature on Brazil.

Government and Politics

Because of the increasing volume of the literature in the field, the section on South America: East Coast was subdivided as follows: Venezuela was assigned to David Dent (Towson State College) together with Colombia and Ecuador; Gary W. Wynia (University of Minnesota) annotated the literature for Argentina, Paraguay, and Uruguay; and Margaret Daly Hayes (US Senate Committee on Foreign Relations) prepared the section on Brazil.

Sociology

Antonio Ugalde (University of Texas-Austin) reviewed materials for Mexico and Central America. Shirley J. Harkess (University of Kansas) annotated the literature on Brazil.

Subject Index

As noted in *HLAS 42* (p. xviii), the policy of the *HLAS* Subject Index is to use the Library of Congress subject headings as much as possible, but when necessary, to adapt them to terms that predominate in the literature as familiar and useful ones to Latin Americanists. As in previous volumes, the index continues to expand geographic terms and to further cross reference them as well as subject terms.

Numbering

The standardized numbering system adopted for the social sciences in *HLAS 39* (see p. xiii) has been modified for the following disciplines:

GEOGRAPHY 5001-6000
GOVERNMENT AND POLITICS ... 6001-7000
INTERNATIONAL RELATIONS ... 7001-8000
SOCIOLOGY 8001-9000

Other Changes

Changes in the editorial staff of the *Handbook*, the administrative officers of the Library of Congress, and membership in the Advisory Board are reflected in the title page of the present volume.

Washington, December 1981   Dolores Moyano Martin

HANDBOOK OF
LATIN AMERICAN STUDIES:
No. 43

BIBLIOGRAPHY AND GENERAL WORKS

JOHN R. HÉBERT, *Hispanic Division, Library of Congress*

A FULL RANGE OF BIBLIOGRAPHIES, reference tools, and general works appeared last year of which only a certain number were selected for this section and are so identified in this essay. The quality of works produced in this period is of high caliber and includes some unique and very useful tools for the researcher.

It is encouraging to note the development and continued publication of national bibliographies or tools providing timely information on recent national publishing similar to that of national bibliographies. Indeed, the number of such tools has increased over the past few years. Worthy of mention are the *Anuario Bibliográfico Colombiano Rubén Pérez Ortíz* for 1977–78 and 1979 (items **3** and **4**), the Brazilian *Boletim Bibliográfico da Biblioteca Nacional* with issues for 1980 (item **6**), and the *Bibliografía Chilena, 1976–1979* (item **8**) which contains separate listing by year of publications and titles submitted for legal deposit. Publishing in the English-speaking Caribbean is well covered by the national bibliographies of Guyana, Jamaica, Trinidad and Tobago, and Barbados. We note in this section the appearance of the *Guyanese National Bibliography* (1980, item **9**) and the *Jamaican National Bibliography* (1979, item **11**) available in quarterly supplements and in annual cumulations. For a broad overview in 10 years of national research and publication, one should consult the cumulative *Jamaican National Bibliography 1964–1974* (1980, item **10**) compiled by the Institute of Jamaica, and available from G. K. Hall Co. of Boston. Other nations have compiled listings of publications submitted for copyright or legal deposit as supplemental tools or alternatives to the timely appearance of national bibliographies. One such example is the Bolivian *Boletín Bibliográfico* (item **7**) of its Depositorio Nacional which provides full description of each bibliographic entry.

Among the significant bibliographies and general research/reference tools that have appeared since *HLAS 42* is Sara de Mundo Lo's initial volume of the *Index to Spanish American collective biography* (item **44**). Vol. 1 cites works of biography on Bolivia, Chile, Colombia, Ecuador, Peru, and Venezuela, that are available in US and Canadian libraries. José Marcial Ramos Guédez's *Bibliografía afrovenezolana* (item **49**) and *Black Latin America: a bibliography* by the Latin American Studies Center at California State University in Los Angeles (item **25**) are significant additions to the scholarship on the subject, thus complementing works by Benjamín Núñez and others identified in this section in recent years. Enrique Florescano's *Bibliografía general del desarrollo económico de México 1500–1976* (item **20**), in two volumes, is an impressive compilation containing more than 4600 citations covering the entire historical range of Mexican economic development from the colonial period to the present. Finally, the *Research guide to Andean history: Bolivia, Chile, Ecuador, and Peru* (item **152**), edited by John TePaske, is a cooperative effort by fellow historians of the Andes designed to identify collections and trends in research.

The wide variety of subject bibliographies and reference works published in the last two years can be roughly divided into the following major topics: women's studies, agriculture, international relations, and the military. The field of women's studies is a leading topic for the entire region and exemplified by works such as Elba Siqueira de Sá Barretto's *Bibliografia anotada sobre a mulher brasileira* (item **16**); Carmen D. de Herrera's *Bibliografía de obras escritas por mujeres panameñas 1970–1974* (item **19**); the Inter-American Center for Documentation and Agriculture Information's *Bibliografía: participación de la mujer en el desarrollo rural de América Latina y el Caribe* (item **8204**); and Joycelin Massiah's *Women in the Caribbean: an annotated bibliography* (item **42**). These are just a few recent works that effectively supplement Meri Knaster's previous compilation on women in Spanish America (see *HLAS 39:9040*).

The following noteworthy works on agricultural topics contain information related to agricultural practices in a country or region as well as social aspects such as land reform or settlement patterns: the Instituto Colombiano Agropecuario's *Bibliografía agropecuaria de Colombia 1977–1978* (item **15**); *Contribuciones del IICA a la literatura de las ciencias agrícolas* (item **27**) which contains nearly 5900 references on the topic; the Honduran Centro de Documentación e Información Agrícola's *Bibliografía agrícola nacional: suplemento 1972–1977* (item **26**); Carmen Villegas' *Bibliografía sobre colonización de América Latina* (item **56**); Angela Hernández de Caldas' *Historia de las bibliotecas agrícolas, pecuarias y forestales de Colombia* (item **141**); and Donald H. Dyal and David Chapman's thoughtful article in the *Revista Interamericana de Bibliografía*, "Periodical Literature of Hispanic American Agricultural History: a Bibliographical Research Problem" (item **168**).

Researchers interested in current works on international relations or 20th-century border problems should consult the following: Jorge Bustamante's *México-Estados Unidos: bibliografía general sobre estudios fronterizos* (item **23**) which contains mainly post-1960 publications; Hélène LeDoare's "Le Brésil et la Cone Sud: les Conflits Frontaliers; Bibliographie Commenté" in *Cahiers des Amériques Latines* (item **38**); and María de Lourdes Urbina and Javier Rodríguez Piña's *La migración de trabajadores mexicanos a Estados Unidos: referencia bibliográfica* (item **7200**).

Several new guides and catalogs to collections will provide improved access to materials. An ambitious project at the Arizona State Museum in Tucson, the Documentary Relations of the Southwest project, continues to identify manuscript documents related to the colonial experience in the internal provinces of New Spain (i.e., current US southwest and Mexico's northeast and northwest). The initial guide to the project, *Northern New Spain: a research guide* was prepared by Thomas C. Barnes *et al.* (see *HLAS 42:121*); the indexes and catalog of the project, *Documentary relations of the Southwest: master indexes* (item **95**) available only on microfiche, have appeared and contain citations to several thousand documents. Other publications of note include Lawrence H. Feldman's *Colonial manuscripts of Jalapa, Jutiapa and Santa Rosa Departments in the Republic of Guatemala* (item **100**); Julio González's *Catálogo de mapas y planos de La Florida y La Luisiana: Archivo General de Indias* (item **103**); and the *Catálogo descriptivo de la Colección de Manuscritos del Museo Histórico Nacional* (item **111**) produced by the Uruguayan Museo Histórico Nacional and consisting mainly of references to 19th-century papers.

An interesting development among recent works is the publication of a number of bibliographies and state-of-the-art articles on military studies which are cited below. The most notable are Mauricio Días David's article "El Estado en América Latina y los Militares en la Política Latinoamericana" (item **30**); Herbert E. Gooch's *The military and politics in Latin America* (item **32**); and Ron Seckinger's "The Central American Militaries: a Survey of the Literature" (item **52**).

In brief, the volume and caliber of bibliographies and general works issuing from or written about Latin America have been high with only the more significant examples being annotated in this section. Likewise, useful works such as indexes to current periodicals, accessions lists of recent acquisitions, new glossaries and dictionaries, and new serial titles continue to provide improved access to the growing literature on a varied range of themes.

GENERAL BIBLIOGRAPHIES

1   **Delorme, Robert.** Latin America: social science information sources, 1967–1979. Santa Barbara, Calif.: ABC–Clio Press; Oxford, Eng.: Clio Press, 1980. 262 p.; indexes.
    Unannotated listing of books and articles published between 1967–79. Majority of 5600 citations are in English and by country. Includes author and subject index.

2   **Piedracueva, Haydée.** Annual report on Latin American and Caribbean bibliographic activities 1981. Madison, Wisconsin: SALALM Secretariat, 1981. 46 p. (XXVI SALALM working paper; A-2) (mimeo)
    Contains a selected list of recent bibliographies on Latin American and Caribbean topics, arranged in broad subject categories. Includes author and subject indexes. Lists 444 books and articles. Submitted to the XXVI Seminar on the Acquisition of Latin American Library Materials, Tulane University, New Orleans, Louisiana, April 1–4, 1981.

NATIONAL BIBLIOGRAPHIES

3   **Anuario Bibliográfico Colombiano Rubén Pérez Ortiz:** 1977–1978. Compilado por Francisco José Romero Rojas. Bogotá: Instituto Caro y Cuervo, Departamento de Bibliografía, 1980. 803 p.
    Vol. 16 of the *Anuario* provides listing of works published in Colombia in 1977–78. Presents publications in order by subject. Provides separate listings of translations, new periodical titles, and editorial houses and bookstores.

4   ———: 1979. Compilado por Francisco José Romero Rojas. Bogotá: Instituto Caro y Cuervo, Departamento de Bibliografía, 1981. 524 p.
    Vol. 17 of the *Anuario* presents publications in order by subject. Includes separate listings of translations, new periodicals, and editorial houses.

5   **Bibliografía nacional en curso, 1977** (PEBN/B, 21/22:73/76, 1975/1976, p. 63–87)
    Lists works in Dewey Decimal Classification order.

6   *Boletim Bibliográfico da Biblioteca Nacional.* Biblioteca Nacional. Vol. 25, Nos. 1/3, 1980– . Rio de Janeiro.
    Listing in three issues of 5475 Brazilian publications mainly from 1979, arranged in order by Dewey Decimal Classification. Includes author index and listing of acronyms used.

7   *Boletín Bibliográfico.* Instituto Boliviano de Cultura. Instituto Nacional de Historia y Literatura. Depositorio Nacional. Año IV, Nos. 8/9, enero–feb./oct. 1981– . La Paz.
    Annotated records of Bolivian works published in 1979–80 and deposited in Bolivia. Titles appear in alphabetical order by author. Provides author and subject indexes.

8   **Chile. Biblioteca Nacional.** Bibliografía chilena, 1976–1979. Santiago: Ministerio de Educación Pública, Dirección de Bibliotecas, Archivos y Museos, 1981. 355 p.
    Lists books, pamphlets, new journals and newspapers and all other publications produced in Chile during period; includes official publications. Material is presented by date of publication, with general subject indexes for each year's grouping. Includes items deposited for legal deposit.

9 *Guyanese National Bibliography.* National Library of Guyana. Jan./Dec. 1980– . Georgetown.

Subject list of new books printed in Guyana, based on books and non-book material deposited at the National Library, classified and arranged by Dewey Decimal Classification. Includes author/title index and separate listing of publishers.

10 Institute of Jamaica, *Kingston.* The Jamaican national bibliography, 1964–1974. Millwood, N.Y.: Kraus International Publications, 1981. 439 p.; index.

Consists of cumulation of entries in the Jamaican National Bibliography 1964–70 and titles of Jamaican publications acquired and catalogued by the West Indian Reference Library, Institute of Jamaica, between 1971–74. Includes books, articles, pamphlets and microforms. Notes publications by Jamaican authors published abroad and works about Jamaica published anywhere. Entries appear in subject arrangements. Includes general index, list of periodicals and newspapers, current maps, and bibliographic works on manuscript collections.

11 *Jamaican National Bibliography.* National Library of Jamaica, Institute of Jamaica. Jan./Dec. 1979– . Kingston.

Subject list of Jamaican material received in the National Library arranged according to the Dewey Decimal Classification. Author/title/series index and a list of Jamaican publishers appear.

SUBJECT BIBLIOGRAPHIES

12 Alzamora C., Lucía. Planificación regional en América Latina. Quito: Junta Nacional de Planificación y Coordinación Económica (JUNAPLA), Instituto Latinoamericano de Investigaciones Sociales (ILDIS), 1977. 55 p. (Materiales de trabajo; 13)

Lists 442 references in works on the theory, methodology of regional diagnosis, spatial planning and regional studies (on Ecuador, Latin America, and general) pertaining to the general theme of regional planning.

13 Anderson, Víctor D. Bibliografía municipal geográfica puertorriqueña. Río Piedras, P.R.: Editorial Universitaria, Universidad de Puerto Rico, 1980. 147 p.

Materials are presented in two sections related to general works on Puerto Rican municipalities and specific works on particular municipalities respectively. Works on subjects related to each of 78 Puerto Rican municipalities appear with heaviest emphasis on San Juan.

14 *Bahia Acervo Bibliográfico.* Fundação Centro de Pesquisas e Estudos. Vol. 2, Nos. 1/2, jan./dez. 1979– . Salvador, Brazil.

Provides references to official publications of Bahia state. Includes author index.

Bayart, Jean-François. L'analyse des situations autoritaires: étude bibliographique. See item **6006**.

Beretta, Pier Luigi. Contribuição para uma bibliografia geográfico do Rio Grande do Sul, Brasil. See item **5320**.

15 Bibliografía agropecuaria de Colombia, 1977–1978. Bogotá: Ministerio de Agricultura, Instituto Colombiano Agropecuario, 1980. 208 p.; indexes.

Cites 2100 works on various aspects of the theme, including agricultural sciences, agricultural extension, rural sociology, vegetable production, plant protection, animal production, and natural resources. Provides key work, author and institutional indexes.

16 Bibliografia anotada sobre a mulher brasileira: história, família, grupos étnicos, feminismo. Coordenadora: Elba Siqueira de Sá Barretto. São Paulo: Departamento de Pesquisas Educacionais da Fundação Carlos Chagas, 1977. 219 p.

Separate sections on history, family, ethnic groups, and feminism appear, each with separate introductory essays. Each entry receives extensive descriptive annotations. Additional publications on Brazilian women in the arts, law, education, public health, sociology, psychology, demography, and communications are planned. See also item **8366**.

17 Bibliografia Carioca: 1977. Rio de Janeiro: Departamento Geral de Cultura, Divisão de Documentação e Biblioteca, 1978. 31 p.

Alphabetical listing, by author, of selected works on the folk culture of the Carioca and Rio de Janeiro. Title index, library location, and location symbols for regional libraries are included. Intended for the informal reader.

18   **Bibliografia de dados estatísticos de Pernambuco.** Suplemento à edição de 1976. Governo do Estado de Pernambuco, Secretaria de Planejamento, Instituto de Desenvolvimento de Pernambuco-CONDEPE. Compilação, Maria do Perpétuo Socorro Barbalho Prazeres. Recife: O Instituto, 1979. 53 p.; indexes.

Identifies works on a wide range of topics in which statistical data on Pernambuco appears. Publications cited are found in the library of the Instituto de Desenvolvimento de Pernambuco (CONDEPE). Author and subject indexes are given.

19   **Bibliografía de obras escritas por mujeres panameñas, 1970–1974.** Colaboradores, Carmen D. de Herrera et al. Panamá: Asociación Panameña de Bibliotecarios, 1976. v, 112, 52 leaves; indexes.

Lists in separate sections, theses presented by Panamanian women at the Universities of Panama and Santa María la Antigua during period 1970–74. Another section gives works by women for same period. Includes author index.

20   **Bibliografía general de desarrollo económico de México: 1500–1976.** v. 1/2. Indice de autores. Coordenador: Enrique Florescano. México: Departamento de Investigaciones Históricas, Instituto Nacional de Antropología e Historia, 1980. 2 v. (1177 p.) (Colección Científicas, bibliografías; 76)

Provides over 4600 annotated citations on the theme. Identifies both statistical as well as documents and interpretative essays on economic development divided into seven main arrangements (i.e., bibliographies, general works, general works on specific sectors of economics, pre-colonial, colonial, 19th century and 20th century). This work designed as a guide to the non-specialist as well as the serious researcher, lists primarily material contained in Mexico City collections, although references to works in the collections of the University of California, University of Texas and the Library of Congress appear. Includes separate author index. Complements Florescano's *Ensayos sobre el desarrollo económico de México y América Latina: 1500–1975* (México: Fondo de Cultura Económica, 1979).

21   **Bibliografía geopolítica.** v. 1, 1897–1980. Montevideo: GEOSUR (Asociación Sudamericana de Estudios Geo-

políticos e Internacionales), 1980. 31 p. (Fascículos; 12)

Cites 317 titles related to the theme of geopolitics and international relations appearing between 1858–1980. This selected listing includes subject index.

22   *Bibliografía Médica Venezolana.* Ministerio de Sanidad y Asistencia Social. 1968/1970–   . Caracas.

This issue constitutes the 7th installment of the bibliography and covers publications in Venezuela appearing between 1968–70. Over 7000 author and title/subject entries appear. Publications are arranged in alphabetical order by author and subject (i.e., disease, anatomy, etc.).

Bibliografía sobre el Mercado Común Centroamericano. See item 8142.

23   **Bustamante, Jorge.** México-Estados Unidos: bibliografía general sobre estudios fronterizos. México: Colegio de México, 1980. 251 p. (Colección Frontera norte)

Contains primarily current (i.e., post-1960) monographs, books, articles, theses, and papers on a wide range of themes related to the study of the Mexican-US border. Publications appear in alphabetical order in each of 14 thematic categories (e.g., migration, US Mexican population, history, bibliography, demography and urbanism, literature, sociopolitical movements, ecology). Brief introductory article provides information on borderland studies.

24   **Butler, Janet L.** A guide to African, Hispanic, and Native American films. Compiled by Janet L. Butler, Gerald R. Belton, and Clarence Smith; cover design, E. Michael Gay. Buffalo, N.Y.: Regional Development Media Service, 1978? ca. 100 p.; indexes.

Consists of listing of non-commercial films produced by minority filmmakers and about minority concerns presented in alphabetical order by film title. Each entry has title, designation of film length, whether in color or black-and-white and a brief description of the film. Material related to Latin America and Hispanics interspersed throughout the list. Lacks index to themes or geographical areas of films.

25   **California State University,** *Los Angeles.* **Latin American Studies Center.** Black Latin America: a bibliography. Los An-

geles: Latin American Studies Center, California State University, 1977. 73 p. (Latin America bibliography series; 5)

Extensive but unannotated list of books and articles, mostly available in US collections, about blacks in Latin America. Breakdown by country. [M. D. Hayes]

26 Centro de Documentación e Información Agrícola, *Tegucigalpa.* Bibliografía agrícola nacional: suplemento, 1972–1977. Secretaría de Recursos Naturales, Centro de Documentación e Información Agrícola. Tegucigalpa: El Centro, 1978. 51 p.; indexes.

Contains references to publications produced by Hondurans and by foreigners on Honduras agricultural themes. Notes location of material and includes author and subject indexes. Lists 946 unannotated citations.

Centro de Estudios para el Desarrollo e Integración de América Latina. Complemento a la bibliografía. See item **6014.**

Commonwealth Institute, *London.* Guyana and Belize: a teacher's guide to study resources. See item **5256.**

27 Contribuciones del IICA a la literatura de las ciencias agrícolas. Ed. rev. y ampl. Turrialba, Costa Rica: Centro Interamericano de Documentación e Información Agrícola, 1977. 411 p. (Bibliotecología y documentación no. 12)

This revised edition of 1972 publication contains nearly twice as many contributions as previous work. This growth reflects present world trends whereby the literature of the scientific and technological sector, including socioeconomic works almost doubles every five years. Total 5,866 references appear. Provides author and subject indexes.

Cubas Alvariño, Ana M. Reforma agraria: bibliografía, catálogo colectivo, 1962–1972. See item **3516.**

28 Dahlin, Therrin C.; Gary P. Gillum; and **Mark L. Grover.** The Catholic Left in Latin America: a comprehensive bibliography. Boston: G. K. Hall, 1981. 410 p.

After an introduction on the Catholic Left which briefly describes movements over the past 25 years, more than 3950 citations appear arranged by country and subjects within country arrangements. General section on Latin America includes sections on

Hélder Câmara and Camilo Torres; general subjects (e.g., agrarian reform, communism, liberation, Marxism, violence) appear within each country listing. Primarily lists publications appearing between 1960–78. Separate author and title indexes appear.

29 Debien, Gabriel. Chronique bibliographique de l'histoire des Antilles françaises (SHG/B, 35, 1. trimestre, 1978, p. 11–46)

Bibliographical essay of recent (1974–77) publications that provide access to materials on the French Antilles or new publications on various aspects of the history of the French in the Antilles.

30 Días David, Mauricio. El estado en América Latina y los militares en la política latinoamericana (LI/IA, 7:2/8:1, 1978, p. 133–160, bibls.)

Author presents two distinct bibliographies with one on the role of the state in Latin America with specific sections on Brazil, Chile, Mexico, and Peru and the military in Latin American politics with specific sections on Argentina, Brazil and Chile in the period 1964–76. Both are selected bibliographies with monographs separated from articles and papers. For political scientist's comment, see item **6032.**

31 Domingos Neto, Manuel. Indicações bibliográficas sobre o Estado do Piauí. Teresina: Governo do Estado do Piauí, Secretaria de Planejamento, Fundação Centro de Pesquisas Econômicas e Sociais do Piauí, 1978. 50 leaves; index (Estudos diversos—Fundação Centro de Pesquisas Econômicas e Sociais do Piauí; 3)

Contains nearly 100 annotated entries on the history, colonization, economy, society, natural setting, and planning of Piauí.

Ferrari, Gustavo. La política exterior argentina a través de la bibliografía general. See item **7397.**

Fundação Cultural do Maranhão. Departamento de Assuntos Culturais. Indios do Maranhão: bibliografia. See item **1109.**

Glazier, Stephen D. Bibliografía del medium espiritista y la posesión: pt. 2. See item **984.**

32 Gooch, Herbert E. The military and politics in Latin America. Los Angeles: Latin American Studies Center, California State University, 1979. 76 p. (Latin

America bibliography series; no. 7)

Provides selected listing of citations on the study of the military institution in Latin America and its role in development. Includes works on civil-military relations in Latin America, histories of Latin American militaries and relations with civilian institutions, institutional development and political roles of militaries and relevant dissertation and theses research on the subject. No index or annotations of selections are provided. For political scientist's comment, see item **6041**.

Graber, Eric S. An annotated bibliography of rural development and levels of living in Guatemala. See item **3085**.

33 Hernández de Caldas, Angela. El carbón a través de la documentación: un catálogo colectivo. Bogotá? Colombia: Fundación Mariano Ospina Pérez, 1979. 94 p.; indexes.

Publication designed to provide information to those engaged in studies pertaining to coal and energy in Colombia. However, the 1067 entries in the bibliography also list works on coal elsewhere. Notes library locations of titles and includes author, geographic, and subject indexes. Publications appear in alphabetical order.

34 Instituto Colombiano para el Fomento de la Educación Superior. Centro de Documentación. ICFES, diez años de producción bibliográfica. Compilado por Victoria Galofre Neuto y Maria Cristina de Arango. Bogotá, Colombia: División de Documentación e Información de ICFES, Sección de Documentación en Educación Superior, 1979. 59 p.; index (Serie bibliográfica/Ministerio de Educación Nacional, Instituto Colombiano para el Fomento de la Educación Superior, División de Documentación e Información, Centro de Documentación, 0120-0259; v. 4, no. 1)

Includes references to works prepared for seminars, conferences, meetings organized by ICFES; notes documents in the bibliographic and published documents series of the institute; and publications of the various divisions of ICFES (e.g., documentation, technical and occupational education, university training). Contains subject index. Updates earlier compilation by Dora Susana Rozo entitled *Colección ICFES: 1969–1976*.

Inter-American Center for Documentation and Agriculture Information. Bibliografía, participación de la mujer en el desarrollo rural de América Latina y el Caribe, enero 1980. See item **8204**.

35 Inter-American Children's Institute. Library. Bibliografía sobre drogas. 3. ed. aumentada. Montevideo, Uruguay: Instituto Interamericano del Niño, 1980. 101 p.

Presents, in alphabetical order by author, works related to drug use and children. Work was compiled from material in the library of the Institute in response to request for information on essential works for the protection of children. Lacks indexes.

36 Inter-American Development Bank. Institute for Latin American Integration. Documentation Service. Bibliografía selectiva sobre integración/Selective bibliography on integration. Buenos Aires: Instituto para la Integración de América Latina, Banco Interamericano de Desarrollo, 1977. 106 leaves in various foliations; index (Serie bibliográfica—Servicio de Documentación, Instituto para la Integración de América Latina, Banco Interamericano de Desarrollo; no. 1)

Selected bibliography on integration contains three sections devoted to Latin American themes (i.e., general studies, integration schemes, and sectorial subjects). Works on the theme related to Europe, Asia, and Africa appear. Contents of some key works on the Latin American aspect of integration are outlined. Includes author index.

37 Junta del Acuerdo de Cartagena. Biblioteca. Bibliografía económica de los países miembros. v. 1, Bolivia, Colombia, Ecuador. Lima: 1979. 316 p.

Selected listing of 2833 references of monographs, reports, official documents, statistics, legislation, articles, etc., published between 1969–79 on themes of economic and social development in the countries mentioned; these materials are contained in the collections of the Library of the Junta. Vol. 2 devoted to Peru, Venezuela and the general themes affecting all member countries is forthcoming.

Latin American Centre for Economic and Social Documentation. Interpretaciones sociológicas y sociopolíticas del desarrollo de América Latina: bibliografía de 25 años. See item **8032**.

38 Le Doare, Hélène. Le Brésil et le Cone
Sud: les conflits frontaliers; bibliographie commentée (CDAL, 18, 1978, p. 215 – 225)

Underlying interest in this selected annotated bibliography is the rivalry between Argentina and Brazil in the Southern Cone of South America. Includes articles and monographs dealing separately with the La Plata basin, Itaipú, the Beagle Channel conflict, Bolivia's access to the sea and the Brazilian-Bolivian border. For geographer's comment see item **5363**.

39 LeoGrande, William M. Two decades
of socialism in Cuba (LARR, 16:1, 1981, p. 187–206)

Author evaluates eight current works on Cuba since 1959.

Levine, Robert M. Race and ethnic relations in Latin America and the Caribbean: an historical dictionary and bibliography. See item **8210**.

40 Lidmilová, Pavla. A situação dos estudos Luso-Brasileiros na Tchecoslováquia (ASB/PP, 23:1, 1980, p. 6–13, bibl.)

Bibliographical essay which identifies primary works, mainly in the post World War II period, on Luso-Brazilian linguistics studies in Czechoslovakia. Major researcher in the field is Zdenek Hampl whose works appear in the essay and in the selected bibliography accompanying the article.

41 Lifschitz, Edgardo. Bibliografía analítica sobre empresas transnacionales/
Analytical bibliography on transnational corporations. México, D.F.: Instituto Latinoamericano de Estudios Transnacionales, 1980. 607 p.

Contains publications devoted to transnational corporations regardless of their geographic area of concentration. Bibliography cites 3815 publications, in alphabetical order, published through July 1978. Provides separate subjects: economic sector (agriculture, mining, industry, banking); geographic aspects; firms; institutions indexes; and English equivalent terms. Bibliographic entries include listing of table of contents of works, in Spanish. Notes location of material cited in the bibliography in Mexico.

42 Massiah, Joycelin. Women in the Caribbean: an annotated bibliography: a guide to material available in Barbados.

Compiled by Joycelin Massiah, with the assistance of Audine Wilkinson, Norma Shorey. Cave Hill, Barbados: Institute of Social and Economic Research (Eastern Caribbean), University of the West Indies, 1979. 133 leaves; index (Occasional bibliography series; no. 5)

This is an annotated bibliography which contains over 400 citations related to women in the English, Spanish, French and Dutch speaking Greater and Lesser Antilles. Entries include works in books, chapters, articles, theses, pamphlets, government documents, addresses, and newspaper articles found in nine Barbados repositories; repository location of publications appear. Material is presented by country within 11 subject groups, including general works, role and status of women, law and politics, family and fertility, education, literature and the arts, religion, women's organizations, biography and autobiography, general reference works, and economics and employment. Cites Meri Knaster's *Women in Spanish America: an annotated bibliography from Pre-Conquest to contemporary times* (G.K. Hall, 1977) as the stimulus for this publication.

43 Morales Padrón, Francisco. Guía bibliográfica general sobre historia de
América (EEHA/HBA, 22, 1978, p. 63–129)

Annotated listing of publications, periodicals useful to the study of the history of the Americas. Separate sections are devoted to general bibliographies, guides to collections, reference works, general historical works and key works on the prehispanic, discovery and conquest, colonial, independence, and national periods.

44 Mundo Lo, Sara de. Index to Spanish
American collective biography. v. 1, The Andean countries. Boston, Mass.: G.K. Hall, 1981– . 1 v. (Unpaged); indexes.

Vol. 1 in a contemplated five-volume series, this selected annotated bibliography provides access to information about the lives of individuals associated with Bolivia, Chile, Colombia, Ecuador, Peru, and Venezuela. Contains about 3200 entries of works available in the US or Canada. Sections are devoted to individual countries and each section has author, short title, biographies, and geographical indexes. Future volumes of the series will be devoted to Mexico, the River Plate, Central America and the Caribbean, and general Spanish American sources.

45 Parada Caicedo, Jorge Humberto. Bibliografía comentada sobre migraciones en Colombia. Bogotá, Colombia: Instituto Colombiano para el Fomento de la Educación Superior, División de Documentación e Información, Centro de Documentación, 1980. 86 p.; indexes (Serie bibliográfica, 0120-0259; v. 5, no.1)

Contains 156 annotated entries on migration in Colombia and on the subject in Latin America. Prepared as part of ICFES' program on human resources and employment in higher education. Includes subject and author indexes. For sociologist's comment, see item **8277.**

46 Pease G.Y., Franklin. Perú, una aproximación bibliográfica. México: Centro de Estudios Económicos y Sociales del Tercer Mundo, 1979. 244 p.; indexes.

Excellent partially annotated bibliography of selected works on Peru. Includes chapters on geography, history, education, economy, society, Andean and Peruvian culture, and international relations, each preceded by an introductory bibliographical essay. Provides names index.

47 Philipps, Beverly and **Barbara Saupe.** Peru: land and people; a bibliography. Madison: University of Wisconsin, Land Tenure Center Library, 1980. 73 p. (Training and methods; 15. Supplement; 2)

Provides all of the Center's Library references to monographs, conference papers, theses, and articles on Peru. Work is divided into sections on land tenure and agrarian conditions. No index appears.

Pinheiro, Neusa Catarina. Bibliografia sobre espécies florestais nativas. See item **5398.**

48 Polgár, László. Bibliographia de historia Societatis Iesu (AHSI, 49:98, luglio/dic. 1980, p. 551–664)

Lists over 1000 recent (1974–79) publications on the history of the Jesuit Order and on individual Jesuits. Provides separate sections on cultural history, Jesuit activities in the Americas, and individual Jesuit leaders. Includes author and personal name indexes.

49 Ramos Guédez, José Marcial. Bibliografía afrovenezolana. Caracas: Instituto Autónomo, Biblioteca Nacional y de Servicios de Bibliotecas, 1980. 125 p. (Serie bibliográfica; 2)

Provides references to over 900 bibliographies, books and pamphlets, and articles on Afro-Venezuelans and Afro-Venezuelan literature. Includes author index.

50 Reátegui G., Mirca. Bibliografía sobre antropología y arqueología de la selva del Perú (PEBN/B, 21/22:73/76, 1975/1976, p. 5–58)

Contains over 250 annotated citations to works on the subjects collected from libraries in Lima. Each main subject (i.e., anthropology and archaeology) is divided into subcategories, with entries appearing in alphabetical order by author. Includes author index.

51 Rodríguez Flores, Emilio. Zacatecanos en la cultura. s.l.: Impr. del Gobierno del Estado, 1979. 167 p.; bibl.; ill.

Provides biographical sketches for 43 noted Zacatecan musicians, artists, and writers of the 19th and 20th centuries.

52 Seckinger, Ron. The Central American militaries: a survey of the literature (LARR, 16:2, 1981, p. 246–258)

A bibliographical essay with references to general studies and individual country studies on the theme. Only current works, i.e., since 1962, are considered.

53 Souza, Yvonne Coelho de. Bibliografia de Mato Grosso e Mato Grosso do Sul. Campo Grande, MS: Associação Profissional de Bibliotecários de Mato Grosso do Sul, 1979. 18, 3, 15 leaves.

Lists, in alphabetical order, more than 200 works on the states. Includes repository location of works cited.

54 Topete, María de la Luz. Bibliografía antropológica del Estado de Oaxaca, 1974/1979. Oaxaca, México: Centro Regional de Oaxaca, Instituto Nacional de Antropología e Historia, 1980. 168 p. (Estudios de antropología e historia; no. 22)

Provides citations on published and unpublished works, working papers, typewritten studies and theses appearing since 1974. Contains nearly 1000 entries divided into sections and anthropological, botanical/geological, and miscellaneous studies. Includes location of items and onomastic index.

55 Universidad de Cuenca. Instituto de Investigaciones Sociales. Fichas bibliográficas de la historia del Ecuador y del Azu-ay. v. 1, Obrás generales, precolonia, colonia, independencia y Gran Colombia. v. 2, República, estructura del estado. Cuenca, Ecuador, 1978. 2 v. (117, 122 p.)

Identifies material in the university's several libraries and in the Casa de Cultura Ecuatoriana (in Azuay) on the theme. Citations are presented in alphabetical order by author within each greater historical category, i.e., general works, colonial, precolonial, independence and Gran Colombia, and republic periods.

Urbina, María de Lourdes and **Javier Rodríguez Piña.** La migración de trabajadores mexicanos a Estados Unidos: referencia bibliográfica. See item **7220.**

56   **Villegas, Carmen.** Bibliografía sobre colonización de América Latina. Turrialba, Costa Rica: Centro Interamericano de Documentación, Información y Comunicación Agrícola, Biblioteca y Terminal de Servicios, 1980. 122 p.; indexes (Documentación e información agrícola; no. 80 0301-438X)

Provides references to 1539 publications on agricultural colonization in Latin America that have appeared since 1947. Includes books, theses, pamphlets, journal articles, and papers. Entries appear in alphabetical order in separate country sections. Provides author and subject indexes.

Wagner, Erika and **Walter Coppens.** Sexta bibliografía antropológica reciente sobre Venezuela. See item **1216.**

Women in the Caribbean: a bibliography. See item **1064.**

Zumaeta Z., Héctor. Bibliografía introductoria para el estudio de la cultura mapuche. See item **1307.**

Zuvekas, Clarence, Jr., A partially annotated bibliography of agricultural development in the Caribbean region. See item **3199.**

COLLECTIVE AND PERSONAL BIBLIOGRAPHIES

Bonich Fernández, Georgina. Ernesto (Che) Guevara, estudio bibliográfico. See item **6252.**

Castellanos V., Rafael Ramón. El Presidente Carlos Andrés Pérez: bibliografía. See item **6392.**

57   **De Antonio Pompa y Pompa.** México: Instituto Nacional de Antropología e Historia, SEP, 1979. 91 p.; bibl.; ill.

Contains brief articles on the impact of an outstanding scholar of Mexican history in his field. Includes articles on Pompa y Pompa and archaeology, provincial archives, anthropology, regional history, and periodical collections.

58   **Rama, Angel.** Los productivos años setenta de Alejo Carpentier: 1904–1980. (LARR, 16:2, 1981, p. 224–245)

Provides a useful review of the contributions of the Cuban writer.

59   **Rivas Dugarte, Rafael Angel.** Simón Bolívar en publicaciones periódicas del exterior: materiales para una hemeroteca. Caracas: Centro de Estudios Latinoamericanos Rómulo Gallegos, 1980. 238 p.; index (Colección Manuel Landaeta Rosales)

Contains over 1900 citations to articles; book reviews; and references to correspondence, monographic studies, speeches, and anecdotes about Bolívar that have appeared in non-Venezuelan journals. Entries appear in alphabetical order. Includes list of journals reviewed and index.

60   **Román-Lagunas, Jorge.** Obras de Pedro de Oña y bibliografía sobre él (RIB, 31:3, 1981, p. 345–365)

Identifies 145 works by and about the noted late 16th-century and early 17th-century Chilean poet and includes brief historical essay on him.

61   **Verani, Hugo J.** Hacia la bibliografía de Octavio Paz (CH, 343/345, enero/marzo 1979, p. 752–791)

Identifies all published works by Paz with editions, translations, and works about him and his writings.

62   **The Written works of Pál Kelemen:** a bibliography. Compiled by Bernard L. Fontana. Tucson, Arizona: Southwestern Mission Research Center, 1981. 7 p.

Lists works published between 1937–79 by the noted art historian who wrote on precolombian art, Baroque and Rococo art of Latin America, and the art and archaeology of the US Southwest.

rativa de Colón/der Pan American
, Washington (IAA, 5:4, 1979,
—371)

Succinct description of the 250,000
e Columbus Memorial Library of the
which originated at the turn of the cen-
rough contributions of printed materi-
m all member states of the old Pan
ican Union. The Library is an impor-
enter for Latin American research, es-
ly in the field of inter-American docu-
, official gazettes, and periodicals in
umanities from 1910—1960s. [G.M.

Contreras Cruz, Carlos. Fuentes históricas para el estudio de Puebla (*in*
ntro de Historiadores Latinoameri-
y del Caribe, 2d, Caracas, 1977. Los
s históricos en América Latina: po-
s, acuerdos y resoluciones: Caracas,
de marzo de 1977. Caracas: Universi-
ntral de Venezuela, Facultad de Hu-
ades y Educación, Escuela de Historia,
v. 1, t. 1, p. 317—324)

Describes various holdings of materi-
the study of 19th- and 20th-century
. Of particular note was information
judicial archives and the Biblioteca
ua of the Universidad Autónoma de
.

*Documentary Relations of the South-
west: Master Indexes.* Arizona State
m. Jan. 1981—   . Tucson.

First efforts of the Documentary Rela-
f the Southwest (DRSW) Project. This
che publication includes descriptive
ns to several thousand documents
contain information relevant to the
h in the Southwest Borderlands region
US and Northern Mexico. Access to
uments is provided by several indexes
y word, place name, personal names,
al location, ethnic groups, general in-
ion/subject). Invaluable source of in-
ion on colonial period materials of the
. For information on the documentary
, see Thomas C. Barnes *et al.*'s *North-
w Spain: a research guide* (Tucson:
sity of Arizona Press, 1981) annotated
AS *42:121.*

Documentos producidos por el Fondo
Simón Bolívar. San José, Costa Rica:
Centro Interamericano de Documenta-
Información Agrícola, 1980. 24 leaves;

index (Documentación e información agrícola, 0301-438X; no. 84)

The 107 documents included represe
the major portion of works on rural develop
ment in Latin America and the Caribbean
produced by the Fondo since 1976. Provides
separate author, subject and key word
indexes.

97   **Documentos relativos** a la historia co
lonial hondureña existentes en el Archivo General de Centroamérica, Guatemala
(Boletín del Sistema Bibliotecario de la
UNAH [Universidad Nacional Autónoma de
Honduras, Tegucigalpa] 8:3, julio/sept. 1980
p. 29—33)

Lists manuscript items in the Guatemalan archive related to the Casa de Res-
cates in Tegucigalpa. Documents are mainly
from the 18th century, although items from
1621—1802 are given.

98   **Documentos relativos** a la independencia de Norteamérica existentes en
archivos españoles. v. 2, Archivo Histórico
Nacional, expedientes: años 1801—1820. Por
Pilar León Tello con la colaboración de Concepción Menéndez y Carmen Torroja. v. 4,
Archivo General de Indias, sección papeles de
Cuba: correspondencia y documentación oficial de los gobernadores de Luisiana, años
1777—1803. Por Reyes Siles Saturino, bajo la
dirección de Rosario Parra Cala. Madrid:
Ministerio de Asuntos Exteriores, Dirección
General de Relaciones Culturales, 1980. 2 v.;
indexes.

Vol. 2 includes an inventory of Legajos
5537—5565 of la Sección de Estado del
Archivo Histórico Nacional (AHN). Among
the early 19th-century papers are found materials related to the Spanish colonial movements for independence, the intrigues of
Aaron Burr, plans of Francisco Miranda for
revolt in Venezuela, and Andrew Jackson's
activities in West Florida. Much material of
commercial interest (e.g., tribute payments,
ship movements, pirate attacks) is found in
this compilation. Vol. 4 consists of references
to 2044 documents in Legajos 1—40 of the
Papeles de Cuba. Primarily covers years
1780—97 and includes correspondence of Bernardo de Gálvez, Esteban Miró, and Barón de
Carondelet and their activities in Louisiana
and West Florida during final years of 18th
century. Provides useful analytical index.

LIBRARY SCIENCE AND SERVICES

63   **Alamo de Torres, Daisy.** Directorio de
bibliotecas de Puerto Rico. Río Piedras, P.R.: Asociación Estudiantes Graduados
de Bibliotecología, Universidad de Puerto
Rico, 1979. 100 p.

Simple listing of academic, institutional, public, prison, and specialized libraries on the island.

64   **Avila, Jorge A.** Bibliofilia y bibliografía
en Honduras (Boletín del Sistema Bibliotecario de la UNAH [Tegucigalpa] 8:3,
julio/sept. 1980, p. 16—18)

Notes historical efforts to provide national bibliographic information on Honduran publications. Particular references are
made to the work of Rafael Heliodoro Valle,
Jorge Fidel Durón, and Miguel Angel García.

65   **Buenos Aires. Universidad. Instituto
Bibliotecológico.** Guía de escuelas y
cursos de bibliotecología y documentación
en América Latina. Buenos Aires, Argentina:
Universidad de Buenos Aires, Instituto Bibliotecológico, 1979. 145 p. (Publicación Instituto Bibliotecológico; no. 57)

This updated edition of a work that appeared in 1974 provides information on
schools, course curriculum, faculty size, and
degrees offered by library science faculties in
Latin American universities.

66   **Buonocore, Domingo.** Pedro N. Arata:
bibliófilo, bibliofilia y bibliomania
(Bibliotecología y Documentación
[Asociación de Bibliotecarios Graduados de la
República Argentina, Buenos Aires] 1:1, ene-
ro/junio 1979, p. 5—9)

Pedro Arata (1849—1922) was an Argentine bibliophile and medical doctor
whose 32,000 volume library on science included works on magic, alchemy, and Leonardo Da Vinci. His library was later given to
the Argentine Academy of Medicine and the
Faculty of Agronomy and Veterinary Science
in Buenos Aires.

67   **Cámara Nacional de la Industria Editorial Mexicana.** México Editor 1979.
Anuario. México: 1979. 307 p.

Lists 4700 titles published in Mexico
in 1978 by ISBN number, author, and title.
Also gives information on publishers, book
stores, and principal public libraries. Publication includes brief articles on the ISBN in

Mexico, book fairs, the 6th National Book-
mans Convention, libraries and publishing
industry, rights of authors, the editor and
writer, and an analysis of the Mexican publishing industry, with statistical data.

68   **Chan, Graham K.L.** Third World libraries and cultural imperialism (Assistant
Librarian [London] 72:10, Oct. 1979,
p. 134—140)

Based on his personal experiences in
Jamaica, author pleads for the development
of librarianship in developing countries, according to their needs and solutions rather
than on techniques borrowed from the developed world.

69   **Congreso Bolivariano de Archiveros,**
2d, Lima, 1974. II [i.e. Segundo] Congreso Bolivariano de Archiveros. Lima: Universidad Nacional Mayor de San Marcos,
1979. 202 p.; bibl.; ill.

Contains the program, list of participants, and presentations made at the II Congress held in Lima in late Nov. 1974.

70   **Cortés Alonso, Vicenta.** Archivos de
España y América; materiales para un
manual. Madrid: Editorial de la Universidad
Complutense, 1979. 382 p.

This manual attempts to provide examples of the wide range of activities engaged in by archivists in fulfillment of their
obligations. Includes specific references to
situations in Spain and Latin America. Provides sections on the relations between Spanish and American archives, reports on the
Archivo Histórico del Guayas (Ecuador), and
development of archives in Brasília, and descriptions of Hispanic archives (e.g., San
Agustín de Santa Fé de Bogotá, Archivo Nacional de Colombia).

71   **Fernández, Stella Maris.** La enseñanza
de la bibliotecología en la Facultad de
Filosofía y Letras (Bibliotecología y Documentación [Asociación de Bibliotecarios Graduados de la República Argentina, Buenos
Aires] 1:2, julio/dic. 1979, p. 5—30)

Reviews initiatives since the 19th
century, precursors, teachers and plans of
study, signaling the distinct stages through
which library science education moved in
Argentina.

72   **Guia das bibliotecas brasileiras.** 2. ed.
Rio de Janeiro: Secretaria de Planeja-

mento da Presidência da República, Fundação Instituto Brasileiro de Geografia e Estatística, Directoria Técnica, 1979. 1017 p.

Directory of all types of libraries by city and state. Indicates size of collections.

73   Guia de bibliotecas universitárias brasileiras. v. 1/2. Brasília: Ministerio da Educação e Cultura, Departamento de Assuntos Universitários, Coordenação do Aperfeiçoamento de Pessoal de Nível Superior, 1979. 2 v. (294, 272 p.)

Vol. 1 refers to libraries in the north, northeast, central west and south region; vol. 2 to libraries in the southeast region. This survey contains basic administrative data concerning 488 university libraries in Brazil (e.g., information about library systems, central libraries, departmental and/or isolated libraries in Brazilian universities).

74   IREBI. Indices de revistas de bibliotecología. Oficina de Educación Iberoamericana. Nos. 22/23, mayo/sept. 1980– . Madrid.

This joint publication (three times a year) of the Oficina de Educación Iberoamericana (Madrid), the Instituto Bibliográfico Hispánico (Madrid), and the Centro de Documentación Bibliotecológica (Argentina), is an essential source of information on current publishing on library science. Contains tables of contents of library science journals published throughout the world and a list of journals reviewed.

75   Mareski, Sofía. Práctica de documentación y archivo. Asunción, Paraguay: Ministerio de Relaciones Exteriores, Academia Diplomática y Consular, 1978. 80 leaves; bibl.; ill.

Work designed to serve as a manual for archivists handling materials in the Paraguayan Foreign Ministry. Includes basic terminology for types of documents and formats to be used for archive materials.

76   Martínez Baeza, Sergio. Sistema nacional de bibliotecas públicas: Chile (Revista CERLAL [Bogotá] 28 dic. 1980, p. 19–22)

Notes the development of public libraries in Chile since 1977 and the projection for future growth in construction. Notes major readership increases.

77   Penna, Carlos Victor. Preplanificación de un sistema de información cien-

tífica y tecnológica (Bibliotecología y Documentación [Asociación de Bibliotecarios Graduados de la República Argentina, Buenos Aires] 1:2, julio/dic. 1979, p. 31–58)

Describes a plan for developing a system of scientific and technical information control, retrieval, and dissemination in Venezuela.

78   Rojas L., Octavio G. Hacia una nueva conciencia de la información: un enfoque diferente en la enseñanza de bibliotecología (PUJ/UH, 10, 1979, p. 99–113, ill.)

Suggests curriculum reform for the teaching of library science in Latin America, Colombia, and author's university, Universidad Javeriana in Bogotá.

79   Sabor, Josefa E. Planeamiento bibliotecario en América Latina (Bibliotecología y Documentación [Asociación de Bibliotecarios Graduados de la República Argentina, Buenos Aires] 1:1, enero/junio 1979, p. 75–118)

Notes the post World War II meetings and congresses devoted to library planning in Latin America, out of which emerged, since 1968, publications on the theory and methodology of library planning.

80   Saracević, Tefko. Training and education of information scientists in Latin America (UNESCO/JIS, 2:3, July/Sept. 1980, p. 170–179)

Briefly analyzes problems in acquiring qualified human resources for information science work in Latin America. Calls for the creation of better opportunities in formal, academic education in information science.

81   Sosa de Maciel, Ramona. Bibliografía bibliotecológica paraguaya. Asunción: Escuela de Bibliotecología, Universidad Nacional de Asunción, 1980. 37 leaves.

Lists 577 publications (i.e., books, pamphlets, articles in journals and newspapers) in the field of library science.

82   Suaiden, Emir José. Biblioteca pública brasileira: desempenho e perspectivas. São Paulo: Livros Irradiantes; Rio?: Instituto Nacional do Livro, Ministério da Educação e Cultura, 1980. 82 p.; forms.

This published thesis contains a brief history of the development of public libraries in Brazil and concludes with a suggested policy for future development.

ACQUISITIONS, COLLECTIONS AND CATALOGS

83   Andrade, Diva and Alba Costa Maciel. Dissertações e teses defendidas na FFLCH/USP: 1939–1977. São Paulo: Universidade de São Paulo, Faculdade de Filosofia, Letras e Ciências Sociais, 1977. 206 p. (Boletim especial, 1)

Lists theses and dissertations in the fields of the social sciences, philosophy, geography, history, classics, modern letters, and oriental languages and linguistics. Includes statistics of degrees by department in five-year intervals and author index.

84   Argueta, Mario. Documentos relativos a la historia colonial hondureña existentes en el Archivo General de Centroamérica en Guatemala (Boletín del Sistema Bibliotecario de la UNAH [Universidad Nacional Autónoma de Honduras, Tegucigalpa] 9:1, 1981?, p. 41–44)

Lists documents related to the establishment of settlements on the north coast of Honduras and the Bay Islands, including settlement of Río Tinto and Trujillo.

85   Bahamian reference collection: bibliography. Compiled by Paul G. Boultbee. Nassau: College of the Bahamas Library, 1981. 57 p.

Lists nearly 500 items in Bahamian Reference Collection housed at Oakes Field Library of the College of the Bahamas. Collection includes monographs, articles, journals, official documents, and maps.

86   Bazant, Jan. Los archivos de nortarías de Zacatecas (CM/HM, 30:1, julio/sept. 1980, p. 134–136)

Brief description and location of the notary archives of Zacatecas. Author notes the recent improved access to notarial records.

87   Boletím Bibliográfico. Secretaria das Minas e Energia, Coordenação da Produção Mineral. Vol. 1, No. 2, abril/junho 1979– . Bahia, Brazil.

This serial provides material on geology acquired by the agency's documentation center. Lists books, technical reports, periodical articles, new serials, and maps. Maps listed are primarily those produced by the Coordenação da Produção Mineral.

88   Casa de Chile [...] Documentació[...] logo, 1977/1978. Méx[...]

The Casa de C[...] in Mexico is devoted [...] Chilean history, parti[...] catalog lists in subjec[...] als fr[...] tions available from [...]

89   Catálogo bibli[...] 3. Medellín, C[...] tegración Cultural, 1 [...]

Vol. 3 of mult[...] union catalog of pub[...] contains citations to [...] phlets, and theses. V[...] journal articles. Vols [...] This union catalog p[...] contents for each cit[...] publications in 30 A[...] Items appear in sepa[...] cludes author index [...]

90   Catálogo de M[...] Catarina exis[...] cional (BRBN/A, 98[...]

Identifies 369[...] subject and general [...]

91   Central Ame[...] University of [...] partment for Spain, [...] ica. No. 1, Nov. 198[...]

Irregular pub[...] len Brow, bibliogra[...] order by author rec[...] Central America in [...]

92   Centro de D[...] Antropológi[...] materiales del Inst[...] Verano sobre grupo[...] 1955–1980: micro[...] C.D.A. Editor resp[...] Paz, Bolivia: Institu[...] Instituto Nacional [...] de Documentación [...] 47 p.; indexes (Ser[...] lógica; 1)

Describes 1 [...] Lingüístico de Ver[...] groups, available [...] vian research cent[...] ethnic group inde[...]

93   Cohnen, Ils[...] morial Libr[...]

IICA, [...] ción e [...]

mem[...] Unio[...] p. 36[...]

volu[...] OAS, [...] tury, [...] als fr[...] Amer[...] tant c[...] pecial[...] ments[...] the hu[...] Dorn[...]

94 [...]

Encue[...] canos[...] estudi[...] nencii[...] 20–2[...] dad C[...] manio[...] 1979,[...]

als for[...] Puebl[...] on the[...] Lafrag[...] Puebl[...]

95 [...]

Muse[...]

tions [...] micro[...] citatio[...] which[...] Spanis[...] of the[...] the do[...] (i.e., k[...] archiv[...] forma[...] forma[...] region[...] projec[...] ern N[...] Unive[...] in HL[...]

96 [...]

99   Elizondo Elizondo, Ricardo. Fuentes documentales y bibliográficas que para el estudio de la Reforma, Segundo Imperio y triunfo de la República, posée la Biblioteca Cervantina del I.T.E.S.M. (Revista Coahuilense de Historia [Colegio Coahuilense de Investigaciones Históricas, Saltillo, México] 2 : 12, marzo/abril 1980, p. 30–49)

Lists materials on Maximillian's intervention contained in the state archives of Nuevo León and in the Cervantina Library of the Technical Institute of Monterrey. Includes letters, testimonies, illustrations, general works, and archival collections for period 1859–73. Material is generally of regional interest (i.e., Nuevo León de Coahuila).

100   Feldman, Lawrence H. Colonial manuscripts of Jalapa, Jutiapa and Santa Rosa Departments in the Republic of Guatemala. Columbia, Missouri: 1981. 650 p. (Informe; 2)

This is vol. 2 in an OAS funded project "Indice del Pasado, Guía para el Futuro." Provides brief listings and cross references to every manuscript known to exist in the departments given in the title, written prior to 1822, and located in the public archives of Central America as well as a sizeable sampling of those in Seville's Archivo de Indias. Includes description of archives, listing of documents in alphabetical order by department/township and chronology and indexes by subject and type. Plans subsequent volume for the departments of El Progreso, Chiquimula, and Zacapa.

101   Flores, María G. Mexican American archives at the Benson Collection: a guide for users. Edited by Laura Gutiérrez-Witt. Austin: University of Texas at Austin, General Libraries, 1981. 74 leaves.

Provides useful information on the varied collections of Mexican American manuscript materials at the Benson Library. Includes references to literary manuscripts organizational archives (e.g., the Carlos Villalongin Dramatic Co., 1848–1930; League of United Latin American Citizens, 1929–1980), and personal papers (e.g., Carlos Eduardo Castañeda, 1926–58; and Romulo Munguía (1911–75). Guide serves to document first phase of continuing program to strengthen and develop Mexican American materials and research resources at the University of Texas, Austin.

102   Glass, John B. The Boturini collection and the Mexican National Museum and General Archive, 1821–1826. Lincoln Center, Mass.: Conmex Associates, 1977. 25 p.; bibl. (Contributions to the ethnohistory of Mexico; no. 5)

Description of the founding of the museum and the general archives between 1821–26 and disposition of the Lorenzo Boturini Benaducci Collection as their basis. Author refers to existing inventories of the collection made in 1823 and 1826 and the notice of items missing in each inventory.

103   González, Julio. Catálogo de mapas y planos de la Florida y la Luisiana. Madrid: Dirección General del Patrimonio Artístico, Archivos y Museos, 1979. 92 p.; indexes.

Lists 245 manuscript maps found in various collections of the General Archives of the Indies in Seville (e.g., Patronato, Indiferente, Audiencias of Santo Domingo and México, Papeles de Cuba) related to southeastern US' borderlands. Majority of maps (74 percent) were prepared in the 18th century. Includes geographic names index.

104   Haigh, Roger M. South American holdings of the Genealogical Society of Utah Microfilm Collection (Center for Historical Population Studies Newsletter [University of Utah, Salt Lake City] 3, Spring 1981, p. 3–6)

Provides brief description of the microfilm holdings of the Society. Great strengths are found in Argentine, Brazilian, and Chilean materials, mainly good runs of parish and civil register records. Work in Bolivia, of late, has been significant, with 2556 reels of microform available by Dec. 1980.

105   Herrera Canales, Inés and **Margarita Urías Hermosillo.** Fondos antiguos documentales y bibliográficos que se conservan en la Biblioteca Pública del Estado de Tabasco (MAGN/B, 3 : 1[7], 3. serie, enero/marzo 1979, p. 39–45)

Describes various documental collections, including notarial records and Acts of the Cabildo (1814–15, 1818–20, 1830, and 1846), 18th- and 19th-century documents from Tabasco.

106   Kula, Marcin. Fuentes relativas a Cuba en los archivos de Polonia (PAN/ES, 3, 1976, p. 283–288)

Brief record of Cuban materials in Poland. Consists mainly of 20th-century consular reports found in Warsaw's Archive for Recent Documents.

107 Luquiens, Frederick Bliss. Venezuela: bibliografía de su literatura en la Biblioteca de la Universidad de Yale (VANH/B, 61:243, julio/sept. 1978, p. 541–581)

Complete cataloging information is provided; table of contents of some anthologies appear.

108 Manigat, Max. Haitiana 1971–1975 [i.e. dix-neuf-cent soixante-et-onze-dix-neuf-cent soixante-quinze]; bibliographie haïtienne. LaSalle, Qué.: Collectif Paroles, 1980. 83 p.; 21 p.

Lists nearly 600 books by date of imprint authored by Haitians on Haiti, Hispaniola and other subjects and by foreigners on Haiti and Hispaniola. Includes author and subject index. This represents a useful supplement to Max Bissainthe's *Dictionnaire de bibliographie haïtienne* (Metuchen: Scarecrow, 1973).

109 Mendoza, Argentine Republic (city). **Universidad Nacional de Cuyo.** Catálogo de publicaciones de la Universidad Nacional de Cuyo, 1939–1979: adhesión al 40° aniversario de la fundación de la Universidad. v. 2. Compilador: Hebe Pauliello de Chocholous. Mendoza: Universidad Nacional de Cuyo, Rectorado, Biblioteca Central, 1979. 429 p.; plates (Cuadernos de la Biblioteca— Universidad Nacional de Cuyo, Biblioteca Central; 8-1979)

Publications are arranged by faculty and by departments within faculties. Works on philosophy, history, and literature were most popular. Provides indexes to periodical publications, authors, and abbreviations.

110 México. Archivo General de la Nación. Catálogo del ramo correspondencia diversas autoridades. v. 1/8. Elaborado por Enrique Villavicencio. México, D.F.: Archivo General de la Nación, 1978/1979. 8 v. (Serie Guías y catálogos)

The Ramo is composed of 70 volumes divided into two parts: 1) consists of 62 volumes for the years 1755–1810, containing correspondence of the viceroys with governors, military authorities, administrators, naval officers in Veracruz, Havana, and Yucatán; 2) consists of eight volumes for years 1823–55, containing correspondence of the administrators of the Contaduría Mayor del Tribunal with the Executive ministers in Mexico City. Items appear by volume in chronological order.

111 Montevideo. Museo Histórico Nacional. Catálogo descriptivo de la Colección de Manuscritos del Museo Histórico Nacional. v. 7. Montevideo: Impr. Nacional, 1978. 289 p.; ill.; index.

Serves as a guide to over 2150 manuscript collections in the *Museo*, primarily private and public papers of noted 19th-century Uruguayans, among them are Ramón and Manuel Artagaveytia, Hugo Barbagelata, Carmelo Cabrera, Benjamín Fernández y Medina, José Pedro Massera, Raúl Montero Bustamante, and Alfredo Vásquez Acevedo. Also includes indexes for personal and geographic names, ships, periodicals, and donors.

112 Oliveira, Daíse Apparecida et al. Catálogo geral de manuscritos do Arquivo Histórico Municipal 'Washington Luís' (AM/R, 41:191, jan./dez. 1978, p. 55–496)

Provides information on the contents of the manuscript section of the archives and is related to the history of the city of São Paulo. A separate alphabetical index by subject or governmental function provides location numbers; separate catalog is presented for materials on Santo Amaro and was prepared by Daíse Apparecida Oliveira and Carlos G.F. Cerqueira.

113 Organization of American States. Administration. Documentos oficiales de la Organización de los Estados Americanos: lista general de documentos. v. 20, Enero-diciembre 1979. Washington, D.C.: 1980. 144 p.

Provides listing of official records, in numerical order within each document group, of OAS documents issued in 1979. Includes list of meetings held.

114 ———. General Secretariat. Catálogo de informes y documentos técnicos de la OEA. Washington, D.C.: 1981. 81 p. (SG/Ser. A/III.1/Supl. 1978)

Cites technical reports and studies which are not included in the OAS' official records series or offered for sale in the *Catalog of Publications*. This publication is the second supplement produced since the

1974–76 cumulative edition of the *Catálogo de Informes*. Includes technical reports, studies resulting from missions, final reports of seminars and workshops, papers presented by staff members, extended surveys and technical reports, theses or studies prepared by OAS fellowship holders. Provides author, English-Spanish glossary, and title listings.

115   Pleasonton, Ghislaine. French and Spanish colonial archives in Louisiana (*in* Cultural traditions and Caribbean identity: the question of patrimony. Edited by S. Jeffrey K. Wilkerson. Gainesville: Center for Latin American Studies, University of Florida, 1980, p. 211–216)

Brief description of the types of material relevant to colonial history of Louisiana found in the Louisiana State Museum in New Orleans; of particular interest are the judicial records of the French Superior Council (1714–69) and the Spanish Supreme Council (Cabildo to 1803). The collection is often called the Cabildo Archives or the Black Boxes Archives.

116   Registro Nacional de Derechos de Autor certificados de depósitos (PEBN/B, 21/22:73/76, 1975/1976, p. 103–176)

Records printed and non-printed texts of Peruvian authors in alphabetical order deposited for copyright from Jan. 1975–Dec. 1976.

117   Reich, Peter L. Algunos archivos para el estudio de la historia eclesiástica mexicana en el siglo XX (CM/HM, 30:1, julio/sept. 1980, p. 126–133, bibl.)

Describes four archives in the Federal District of Mexico in which useful materials for the study of the 20th-century Mexican Catholic Church can be found (i.e., libraries of the Conciliar Seminary, Mexican Social Secretariat, Archive of Plutarco Elías Calles, and Center for Studies of the History of Mexico, Condumex).

118   Rosenbach Museum & Library. The Viceroyalty of New Spain and early independent Mexico: a guide to original manuscripts in the collections of the Rosenbach Museum & Library. Compiled by David M. Szewczyk; edited by Catherine A. Barnes and David A. Szewczyk. Philadelphia: The Museum and Library, 1980. 139 p.; a–j p. of plates; ill.

Describes about 360 documents in the Rosenbach Museum and Library related to the theme. Documents are presented in alphabetical order by main author and each document is annotated. Includes chronological and general indexes. Contains materials of and by Cortés as well as material from throughout the colonial and early independence period. A major portion of the documents are from the 18th century.

119   van Soest, Jaap. Archival sources to the history of the Netherlands Antilles: a challenge for archivists and historians (NWIG, 54:2, juli 1980, p. 73–93)

Provides brief survey of main archival collections, both governmental and private, in Netherlands Antilles, the Netherlands, and elsewhere. Mentions descriptions of and source publications from those collections, and discusses historical research completed and to be done.

REFERENCE WORKS AND RESEARCH

120   Allis, Jeanette B. West Indian literature: an index to criticism, 1930–1975. Boston: G.K. Hall, 1981. 353 p. (A Reference publication in Latin American studies)

Excellent listing of works and criticism of major West Indian English-speaking writers. Separate citations of works by authors, by critics and reviewers, and by articles appear in this work. Information is derived from 77 journals and five essay collections appearing between 1930–75.

121   Archives de la Martinique. Guide des Archives de la Martinique. Liliane Chauleau. Fort-de-France, Martinique: Archives départementales, 1978. 68 p.

Provides information on the resources, services and history of the archives of Martinique and in France relevant to the island's study. Includes descriptions of contents of Martinique's various archives (e.g., communal, ecclesiastical and hospital) as well as the French national archives.

122   Archivo Histórico de Jalisco. Guía de los archivos históricos de Guadalajara. Guadalajara, Jalisco, México: Gobierno de Jalisco, Secretaría General, Unidad Editorial, 1979. 68 p.; 1 fold. leaf of plates; bibl.; ill.

(Colección Textos Jalisco. Serie Bibliografías y catálogos; no. 1)

Describes 17 historical archives in the city providing information on the thematic, chronological, and geographic content of the collections and the availability of indexes, catalogs, inventories, and card files in each.

123 Bergquist, Charles. What is being done? Some recent studies on the urban working class and organized labor in Latin America (LARR, 16:2, 1981, p. 203–223)

Author provides a coherent bibliographical essay based on 11 current works on the Latin American working class. Useful review of current scholarship.

124 *Bibliographie Latinoamericaine d'Articles.* Institut des Hautes Études de l'Amérique Latine, Centre de Documentacion. No. 10, mai 1981– . Paris.

Contains citations from more than 200 journals related to the study of Latin America. Articles appear by country and by subjects within each country. Lacks index.

125 Blasier, Cole. The Soviet Latin Americanists (LARR, 16:1, 1981, p. 107–123)

Brief review of current state of Soviet Latin American scholarship, examines resources, individual scholars, foreign ties, field work, professional life, scholarly climate, and public impact of the professionals.

126 Bolivia. Ministerio de Industria, Comercio y Turismo. Directorio Industrial 1979/1980. La Paz: Departamento de Estadística Industrial, 1979. 238 p.

Lists first and second order manufacturing plants run by state, private and mixed groups. Identifies individual companies by product in alphabetical order and within each department of the country. Provides name of company, owner, date of initiation of operations, and products produced. Statistics show numbers of plants in each industry by department from 1975–79. List was compiled to serve as a base for the preparation of the document *Sector industrial manufacturero en cifras.*

127 Brazil. Instituto Joaquim Nabuco de Pesquisas Sociais. Indice do Boletim Joaquim Nabuco de Pesquisas Sociais: 1953–1971. Recife, 1979. 42 p.

Provides access to material in 18 issues of the journal through information on volume, page, and year of publication.

128 Briggs, Donald C. and Marvin Alisky. The historical dictionary of Mexico. Metuchen, N.J.: Scarecrow Press, 1981. 259 p.; bibl. (Latin American historical dictionaries; no. 21)

Provides brief description of terms, individuals and events related to Mexican culture, history and politics. Although strongly oriented towards the 20th century, it includes much earlier material. Provides bibliographies of pre-1910 era and the modern period, primarily comprised of English language publications.

129 Cámara de Comercio de Bogotá. Centro de Información Económica. Red Colombiana de Información y Documentación Económica (RECIDE). Directorio. Bogotá: 1981. 45 p.

Lists institutions, libraries, and directors involved in economic information and documentation network in Colombia.

130 Centro Internacional de Agricultura Tropical. Catálogo de publicaciones periódicas unidad de servicios de documentación del CIAT. Cali. Colombia: 1980. 129 p. (Serie CIAT 01CI-1)

Listing of journals received at the center includes holdings and subject index.

131 Confederación Universitaria Centroamericana (CSUCA) and **Centro de Documentación Económica y Social de Centroamerica** (CEDESC). Documentación socioeconómica centroamericana. No. 2, junio 1979; No. 3, diciembre 1979; No. 4, junio 1980. San José, Costa Rica: 1979–1980. 3 v. (237, 255, 262 p.)

Provides references to approximately 900 additional entries on the subject since issue no. 1 appeared in 1978. Multiple indexes enhance access to specific documents (e.g., author, institutional, geographic, meeting, series, subject). Useful publication for Central American economic and social research.

132 Consejo Episcopal Latinoamericano (CELAM). Guía eclesiástica latinoamericana 1981. Bogotá: Secretariado General del CELAM, 1981. 184 p.

Provides names and addresses of the Roman Catholic Church's hierarchy in Latin America and the Caribbean. Includes membership of various CELAM committees and names index.

133   Conte Porras, Jorge. Diccionario bio-gráfico de Panamá (Boletín de la Academia Panameña de la Historia [Panamá] 21/22, 3. época, enero/junio 1980, p. 169–222)

Second edition of biographical dictionary that will list 2500 Panamanians from the 16th century to the present. First portion of listing provides coverage for personages in the letters a–c. It is assumed that the rest of the dictionary will appear in subsequent issues of the *Boletín*.

134   Contenido y autores de los números anteriores de la revista *Estudios Sociales* (CPU/ES, 18:4, 1978, p. 165–169)

Listing identifies wide number of contributors to the first 17 issues of this Chilean publication.

135   Costa Rica. Ministerio de Cultura, Juventud y Deportes. Dirección General de Bibliotecas. Indice de diarios y seminarios de Costa Rica: julio/agosto 1980. San José: Imprenta Nacional, 1981. 64 p.

Index of principal articles appearing during indicated months in *Contrapunto, Extra, La Nación, La Prensa Libre, La República*, and *Seminario Universidad*. This bimonthly publication features separate author/title, subject, and name indexes. It is available through the Biblioteca Nacional.

136   Duport, Claude. Catalogue des thèses et memoires sur l'Amérique Latine soutenus en France entre 1975 et 1978 (CDAL, 19, 1979, p. 5–78)

Lists theses in alphabetical order by author. Theses on general Latin American topics appear in separate order by subject as do works on individual countries.

137   Echevarría Caselli, Evelio. Indice general del *Repertorio Americano*. t. 1, A–B. San José: Editorial Universidad Estatal a Distancia, 1981. 381 p.

This work is vol. 1 in a 21,700 citation, 2475 page-index to the noted Costa Rican journal for its 40-year history (i.e., 1919–59). A general index will be provided in the last volume of the publication.

138   Fundação Instituto Brasileiro de Geografia e Estatística. Boletim Bibliográfico. v. 9/11, no. 1/4 (1976/1978). Rio de Janeiro: IBGE, 1980. 294 p.

This analysis of 34 Brazilian periodicals includes the appearance of 467 annotated citations. Issues of publications are mainly from 1973–78. Includes combined author/subject index.

139   Guia das editoras brasileiras. v. 17. 2. ed. rev. e aum. Rio de Janeiro: Sindicato Nacional dos Editores de Livros, 1980. 104 p.

This new revised edition contains details about 481 publishers. Entries are arranged in alphabetical order by state. Provides publisher and subject indexes as well as name, address and subject of publications for each publisher.

Guía de investigaciones en curso en la Universidad de Buenos Aires. See item **4375**.

140   Handbuch der deutschen Lateinamerika-Forschung Institutionen, Wissenschaftler und Experten in der Bundesrepublik Deutschland und Berlin (West): neuere veröffentlichungen. Zusammengestellt von Renate Ferno und Wolfgang Grenz. Hamburg; Bonn: Deutscher Akademischer Austauschdienst, 1980. xvii, 483 p.; indexes.

Describes levels of research on Latin America in West Germany. Provides information on institutions—libraries, archives, documentation and information centers, and academic institutes—and individuals engaged in the study of the area. Includes names of Latin Americans and other Europeans involved in such research in West Germany and Berlin. Indexes provide access to information by discipline, geographic area, institutions, and personal names. Very useful addition to the literature on Latin American research.

141   Hernández de Caldas, Angela. Historia de las bibliotecas agrícolas, pecuarias y forestales de Colombia: documento presentado al Sistema Nacional de Información de COLCIENCIAS. Prólogo por Armando Samper Gnecco. Bogotá, Colombia: Ministerio de Educación Nacional, Fondo Colombiano de Investigaciones Científicas y Proyectos Especiales Francisco José de Caldas, 1980. 125 p.; bibl.; ill.

Brief history of special agricultural libraries in the 19th and 20th centuries; primary emphasis is on the post-1950 development.

142 *Indice de Ciências Sociais.* Boletim bibliográfico semestral. Instituto Universitário de Pesquisas do Rio de Janeiro. Ano I, No. 2, feb. 1980– . Rio de Janeiro.

Provides abstracts of articles appearing in 16 Brazilian social science journals issued between 1977–79. Includes subject and key word indexes.

143 **Instituto Brasileiro de Informação em Ciências e Tecnologia.** Siglas de entidades brasileiras: versão preliminar. Rio de Janeiro: Conselho Nacional de Desenvolvimento Científico e Tecnológico, Instituto Brasileiro de Informação Ciência e Tecnologia, 1979. 788, 115 p.

Provides an extensive listing of acronyms of 5436 Brazilian scientific and technical institutions. Two separate listings appear: one contains acronyms in alphabetical order, the other consists of names of entities in alphabetical order.

144 **Inventario de investigación socioeconómica en el Perú.** Elaborado por Centro de Documentación, Escuela Administración de Negocios para Graduados. Lima: Agrupación para la Integración de la Información Socio-Económica, 1980. 96, 8 leaves; bibl.; ill.; indexes.

Record of results of survey conducted in 1980 in which 96 institutions replied. Indicates works published and research in progress on the theme. Includes indexes for acronym, director, researcher, research area, and research in progress.

145 **Investigaciones en curso y terminadas** (RIB, 31:3, 1981, p. 425–442)

Research, whether in progress or completed, on varied themes related to Latin American studies is listed separately and in alphabetical order.

146 **Latin America and the Caribbean, II:** a dissertation bibliography. Editor: Marian C. Walters. Ann Arbor, Mich.: University Microfilms International, 1980, 78 p.

Compilation of 1868 doctoral dissertations and 100 masters theses. Serves to update University Microfilms International 1977 publication, *Latin America and the Caribbean: a dissertation bibliography.* Each entry includes author, title, degree earned, date of degree, school name, number of text pages, and publication number for University Microfilms.

147 **Latin American Studies in the Universities of the United Kingdom 1981.** Staff research in progress or recently completed in the humanities and the social sciences. No. 12. London: Institute of Latin American Studies, University of London, 1981. 42 p.

Presents research and publishing activities of British Latin Americanists by subject of research. Includes author index.

Lauer, Wilhelm. Puebla-Tlaxcala: a German-Mexican research project. See item **5119.**

148 **México en 500 libros.** Enrique Florescano, coordinador. Herman Bellinghausen et al., colaboradores. México, D.F.: Editorial Nueva Imagen, 1980. 187 p.; bibl.; index (Serie Historia)

Selection of readings that serve as a guide to those who seek a general image of the historical and present development of the country. Each work cited is described. Selections cover, in separate sections, works on history, geography, economics, society, politics, sciences, social sciences and humanities; only relatively current literature, or facsimilies, appear. Includes author index.

Norton, Augustus R. and **Martin H. Greenberg.** International terrorism: an annotated bibliography and research guide. See item **7093.**

Organismos interamericanos. See item **7101.**

149 **Pereira, Marília Mesquita Guedes** and **Norma Maria Fernandes Nogueira.** Catálogo de teses defendidas na UFPb, 1970/1979. João Pessoa: Universidade Federal de Paraiba, Biblioteca Central, 1980. 318 p.

Catalogue of dissertations accepted at the University of Paraiba, Brazil. Provides title, date of defense, subject, abstracts in Portuguese and English, and whether or not indexes to author, title and/or subject are included. Covers dissertations in the fields ranging from engineering to education and sociology.

150 **Pérez López, Abraham.** Diccionario biográfico hidalguense. San Salvador: Pérez López, 1979. 527 p.

Contains biographical and historical description of various individuals and offices in the state. Entries appear in alphabetical order; no indexes are given.

151 Quién es quién en el Uruguay. Editado por Central de Publicaciones S.R.L.; promoción de Panamérica Uruguaya S.A. Montevideo: Central de Publicaciones, 1980. 688 p.; ill.; index.

Covers persons and businesses in the arts, banking and commerce, sciences, industry, and professions. Separate descriptions of businesses and institutions appear. Work is preceded by introductory sketches on the history, economy, literature, architecture, education, music, and industry of Uruguay.

152 Research guide to Andean history: Bolivia, Chile, Ecuador, and Peru. Contributing editors, Judith R. Bakewell et al.; coordinating editor, John T. TePaske. Durham, N.C.; Duke University Press, 1981. 346 p.; bibl.; index.

Useful guide to the contents of major archives, research libraries, and collections in the four countries. Contains over 50 articles which describe collections or provide sources in the country for a particular type of historical analysis. The Bolivian segment concentrates on the description of collections, the Chilean, Ecuadorian and Peruvian contributions provide a combined description of collections/libraries/archives and essays on sources for the study of particular themes or chronologies of history.

153 Roa Santana, Manuel de Jesús. Indice de publicaciones periódicas de universidades dominicanas. v. 2. Santo Domingo: Instituto Tecnológico de Santo Domingo, 1980. 177 p. (Serie bibliográfica; no. 1, 3)

Analyzes articles in 13 serial titles with presentation of citations by subject arrangement. All issues of journals appeared before July 1979. Includes author index.

154 Romero Flores, Jesús. Biografías de nicolaítas distinguidos. Morelia: Gobierno del Estado de Michoacán, 1980. 154 p.; 21 leaves of plates; ports.

Provides brief biographical sketches of 193 noteworthy alumni of the Colegio de San Nicolás de Hidalgo, founded in Pátzcuaro in 1540 by Vasco de Quiroga. Among its illustrious students were Miguel Hidalgo y Costilla, José María Morelos, Melchor Ocampo, and Nicolas León.

155 Rossi, Ernest E. and Jack C. Plano. The Latin American political dictionary. Santa Barbara, Calif.: ABC-Clio, 1980. 261 p.; index.

Provides definitions and significance of frequently used terms in Latin American political, economic, sociological, geographical, and historical studies. A basic listing which includes general index.

156 Sable, Martin Howard. The Latin American studies directory. Detroit: Blaine Ethridge Books, 1981. 124 p.

Identifies organizations, institutions, associations, research and information centers, government agencies, foundations, libraries and data banks, and publishers and dealers in books related to Latin American studies. Intended for the neophyte.

157 Silvestrini-Pacheco, Blanca and María de los Angeles Castro Arroyo. Sources for the study of Puerto Rican history: a challenge to the historian's imagination (LARR, 16:2, 1981, p. 156–171)

Provides useful insights on the sources for the study of the history of Puerto Rico, both on the island and in foreign archives and collections. A description of the municipal and notarial holdings of the Archivo General de Puerto Rico is included. Documentary sources in the Puerto Rican collection of the José M. Lázaro Library at the University of Puerto Rico appear in an appendix.

158 *Social and Economic Studies:* author and keyword index. v. 1/26, 1953/1977. Compiled by Rievé Robb. Mona, Jamaica: Institute of Social and Economic Research (ISER), University of the West Indies, 1980. 280 p.

This first cumulative index to the journal contains all items in the journal except for publication announcements, notes on contributors, obituaries, and annual reviews of projects. The index is arranged by single author and keyword in alphabetical sequence. Each entry contains author, title, date of publication.

159 Souza, Antonio Loureiro de. Baianos ilustres: 1567–1925. Capa de Carlos Cezar. 3. ed. rev. São Paulo: Instituição Brasileira de Difusão Cultural, 1979. 358 p.; bibl. (Biblioteca Literatura moderna; 51)

Provides biographical description of 151 Baianos of the 16th to the 20th century. Majority of those listed lived in the 19th century. Little change has been made since the second edition.

160   Statistical Abstract of Latin America.
v. 21. Edited by James W. Wilkie and
Stephen Haber. Los Angeles: UCLA Latin
American Center, 1981. 671 p.

Provides a wealth of socioeconomic
data on Latin America with cumulative indexes to vols. 17–21 of the publication. Includes the following analytical articles:
Mexico's population history in the 19th century by John Kicza; Bolivian public expenditure and the role of decentralized agencies by
Thomas Millington; Mexican community
studies in a historical framework 1930–70
by Stephen Haber; a quantification of the
class structure of Mexico 1895–1970 by
James Wilkie and Paul Wilkins; Latin American fisheries 1938–78 by Manuel Moreno
Ibáñez; a comparison of the populations of
Mexico and Argentina in 1980 by Richard
Wilkie; and quantitative data sets on Latin
America by Carl Deal. An invaluable reference tool.

161   Sumários do *Mensário do Arquivo Na-*
cional (MAN, 12:2, fev. 1981,
p. 5–72)

Reproduces tables of contents of the
Brazilian national archive publication from
May 1975 to Dec. 1980.

162   Theses in Latin American studies at
British universities in progress and recently completed. No. 14, 1981. London: Institute of Latin American Studies, University
of London, 1981. 1 v.

Lists theses completed and in progress
since the academic year 1978–79. Includes
title, field of study, author, name of supervisor, university, expected date of completion
and degree sought or awarded for each thesis.
Author and subject indexes appear.

163   Universidade Federal de Goiás. Biblio-
teca Central. Seção de Periódicos.
Catálogo de periódicos. Goiânia: 1980. 218 p.

Lists journals by subject, with holdings included. Alphabetical list of titles appear. Also provides location of titles in one of
four university libraries.

164   Uruguay. Biblioteca Nacional. Centro
Nacional de Documentación Cien-
tífica, Técnica y Económica. Directorio de
servicios de información y documentación
en el Uruguay. Montevideo: 1980. 132 p.

Alphabetical listing of 1976 public and
private institutions, each entry containing

information on collection size, subject areas,
types of service, available copying equipment, involved in information science in
Uruguay. Subject, institutional, acronymic,
and geographic indexes appear.

165   Valenzuela de Garay, Carmen. Indices
de los veinticuatro volúmenes de la revista *Folklore Americano,* por autor y por
título: noviembre de 1953–diciembre de
1977 (CIF/FA, 25, junio 1978, p. 17–42)

Index provides separate author and title access to the articles in this important
inter-American journal.

166   Zettel, Francine M. *Revista del Museo*
Nacional, Instituto Nacional de Cultura, Lima, Peru: a bibliography of volumes
30–40, 1961–1974 (UNC/ED, 3:2, July 1978
[i.e. Dec. 1979] p. 74–85)

A listing by volume of the tables of
contents of the journal. No index is provided.

GENERAL WORKS

América Latina. See item **5003.**

167   Cozean, Jon D. Latin America 1980.
Washington, D.C.: Stryker-Post Publications, 1980. 107 p.

Provides brief historico-political
sketches on each country of Latin America;
work is intended for the layman.

Documento uno: una selección de prensa sobre la problemática universitaria. See item
4537.

168   Dyal, Donald H. and **David L. Chap-**
man. Periodical literature of Hispanic
American agricultural history: a bibliographical research problem (RIB, 31:2,
1981, p. 215–226)

Calls for the preparation of a bibliography of periodical literature on Hispanic
American agricultural history which could
serve as a catalyst to the preparation of a general history on the theme. Authors note
marked paucity of general Latin American
and even national histories on agricultural
development.

169   Emmanuel, Patrick A.M. Problems of
research and data collection in small
islands without a social science faculty
(UN/ISSJ, 32:3, 1980, p. 560–563)

Author focuses on the problems of research and data collection in non-campus territories affiliated with the University of the West Indies, mainly the seven Leeward and Windward Islands. It is noted that with independence there has been a decline in the amount of systematic data generated by official sources.

170 García Cabrera, Manuel. Folios. San Juan, Puerto Rico: Biblioteca de Autores Puertorriqueños, 1979. 118 p.

A collection of essays that includes articles on the bookstores in San Juan at the beginning of the 20th century, the history of printing in Puerto Rico, the writing of Luis Palés Matos, the Indian novel in Spanish America (written by Concha Meléndez), and the publications of the Biblioteca de Autores Puertorriqueños.

171 Greene, J. E. Research and information support systems (UN/ISSJ, 32:3, 1980, p. 555–559)

Identifies main developments in contemporary social science research in the English-speaking Caribbean, the range of available information support systems, and varied rationale for mixing research and support systems. Limitations on financial and physical resources decisive factor in development of support systems.

Hanke, Lewis. The early development of Latin American studies in the U.S.A. See item **4329.**

172 Inotainé Bonifert, Mária. Az aranyrög tetején üldögélö koldus. Budapest: Gondolat, 1979. 406 p.; ill. (Világjárók; 125)

General book on Peru, describing the history, landscape, customs, and intellectual life. Integrates quotes and the work of past and present literary figures and intellectuals into contemporary Peruvian reality. Author traveled widely through the highlands, the *selva*, and the coast. Attractive photographs depicting Peru's many facets enhance the text. [G. M. Dorn]

173 Lemmo Brando, Angelina. Esquema de estudio para la historia indígena de América. Caracas: Facultad de Humanidades y Educación, Universidad Central de Venezuela, 1980. 165 p.

Provides an outline for the study of the history of indigenous peoples of America. Includes guide to historical sources for the study of American ethnohistory.

174 Lottman, Herbert R. Argentina: a book world, a world away (Publishers Weekly [New York] 220:12, Sept. 18, 1981, p. 100–113; 116–119)

Author describes current commercial book publishing scene in Argentina. Concludes that in spite of economic and political difficulties, the Argentines still have a vigorous publishing market; publication of translations is a major facet of the current output. Problems of censorship after publication still beset well-intentioned Argentine publishers.

175 Manigat, Max. Le livre haïtien en diaspora: problèmes et perspectives (Études Littéraires [Press de l'Université Laval, Québec] août 1980, p. 335–345)

Overview of Haitian publishing, outside of Haiti, by exiled Haitians in the past 10 years. Publishers and distributors of Haitian publications outside of Haiti are listed. Political science and literary works of criticism published by Haitians outside of Haiti rival in numbers of titles of works produced in Haiti.

176 Méndez, Jesús. The origins of *Sur*, Argentina's elite cultural review (RIB, 31:1, 1981, p. 3–16)

Useful account of the beginnings of the famous Argentine journal and the roles that Waldo Frank, Samuel Glusberg, and Victoria Ocampo each played in its development.

177 Muriel, Guadalupe. Los estudios de historia de Hispanoamérica en México (UNAM/L, 13, 1980, p. 361–370)

Provides a review of secondary, primary, and university level study of Spanish America in Mexico.

Oppenheimer, Robert. Chile. See item **6569.**

178 Rama, Carlos M. Visión crítica del estado actual del latinoamericanismo europeo (*in* Encuentro de Historiadores Latinoamericanos y del Caribe, 2d, Caracas, 1977. Los estudios históricos en América Latina: ponencias, acuerdos y resoluciones: Caracas, 20–26, de marzo de 1977. Caracas: Universidad Central de Venezuela, Facultad de Humanidades y Educación, Escuela de Historia, 1979, v. 1, t. 2, p. 734–747)

Briefly reviews the state of Latin American studies in Europe. Major centers of research are identified in France, England,

West Germany and Italy, and in the rest of the continent.

179 Rodrigues, Olao. História da imprensa de Santos. s.l.: Gráfica A Tribuna, 1979. 277 p.; ill.

Covers 130 years of printing in Santos (i.e., since 1849) when first periodical, *Revista Comercial*, appeared. Lists periodicals, newspapers, and publications of fraternal, social religious, sport and school organizations of Santos with brief descriptions of each publication. Personal names index appears.

180 Shatunóvskaya, Irina. Una casa para todo el continente (URSS/AL, 1, 1980, p. 106–116, plates)

Provides a glowing account of the activities of the Casa de las Américas (Havana) since its founding in 1959.

181 *United States Views of Mexico.* A quarterly review of opinion from the United States press and *The Congressional Record*. Banamex Cultural Foundation. No. 1, First Quarter 1981–   . Washington, D.C.

Purpose of publication is to monitor public opinion in the US for those who are interested in the way Mexico is perceived north of the border. First issue includes articles on diplomacy; Mexican officials and elections; immigration; energy; agriculture; trade; business; transportation; tourism; health; and culture. Annual subscription rate: $150.00. Available from Banamex Cultural Foundation, 2010 Massachusetts Avenue, N.W., Washington, D.C. 20036.

182 Urbanski, Edmund Stephen. Latin American studies and bibliography in Poland (LARR, 15:3, 1980, p. 175–179)

Provides overview of Latin American and Iberian interest in Poland, especially in post-World War II period. Polish interest and translations of Latin American works were influenced by early 20th-century migrations to Latin America. Post-World War II study of Latin America developed at the University of Warsaw and in the Institute of History of the Polish Academy of Science.

183 Yucatán, a world apart. Edited by Edward H. Moseley and Edward D. Terry. University: University of Alabama Press, 1980. 335 p.; bibl.; ill.; index.

This informative work consists of 11 essays that survey the geography, history, anthropology, sociology, politics, literature, and economy of Yucatán. Includes Gilbert Joseph's article on the Mexican Revolution in Yucatán 1910–40, Edward Terry's essays on literature in Yucatán and Alfredo Barrera Vásquez' bibliographical essay on Yucatecan archaeology.

NEW SERIAL TITLES

184 *Argos.* División de Ciencias Sociales y Humanidades, Universidad Simón Bolívar. No. 1, 1980–   . Caracas.

Sections of the serial cover: Political and International Relations; Sociology; History; Literature and Linguistics; and Bibliographies. Contributing authors are from Venezuela or other South American countries, however, all contributors to the first issue are faculty members of the Universidad Simón Bolívar. Also includes book reviews of publications in Spanish as well as translations. The Director of the University's División de Ciencias Sociales y Humanidades is Dino Garber.

185 *Boletín del Instituto de Estudios Sociales de la Universidad de Guadalajara.* No. 1, enero/marzo 1980– Guadalajara, México.

First issue of quarterly publication is a result of four years of research on the part of the Institute. Major sections include summaries of projects and research underway in the Institute, articles, documents and sources on the history of Jalisco, and news items. The Institute's Director is Manuel Rodríguez Lapuente.

186 *Colección Estudios CIEPLAN.* Corporación de Investigaciones Económicas para Latinoamérica. No. 1, julio 1979– Santiago.

The Colección de Estudios CIEPLAN replaces the Estudios CIEPLAN monographic series, of which 32 titles have already been published. This publication will appear irregularly, but with a minimum of two issues per year, and might also include the Notas Técnicas y Apuntes CIEPLAN. Address is Avenida Cristóbal Colón 3494, Santiago, Chile. Executive Committee President: Alejandro Foxley.

187 *Defensa Nacional.* Revista del Centro de Altos Estudios Militares. Año 1,

No. 1, oct. 1980–   . Lima.

The publisher's address is: Centro de Altos Estudios Militares, Avenida Escuela Militar, s/n Chorrillos, Lima, Peru. Director is Gen. Luis Vásquez Duclos.

Economía Mexicana: Análisis y Perspectivas. Centro de Investigación y Docencia Económicas (CIDE). No. 1, 1979–   . See item **2992**.

188   *Educação e Sociedade.* Revista quadrimestral de ciencias da educação. Centro de Estudos Educação e Sociedade. No. 1, set. 1978 through No. 3, maio 1979–   . São Paulo.

189   *Equinoxe.* Revue guyanaise d'histoire et de geographie. Association des Professeurs d'Histoire et de Géographie (A.P.H.G.) de la Guyane avec le concours du Centre Départemental de Documentation Pédagogique (C.D.D.P.) de Cayenne. Cayenne, Guyane.

190   *Historia.* Revista/libro trimestral. Buenos Aires.

Foreign subscription rates of this quarterly publication are: $US 60.00 per year, $US 15.00 per issue. Within Argentina: $120.00 annually. Address: Maipú 621, 4°C, 1006 Buenos Aires, Argentina. Director: Armando Alonso Piñeiro.

191   *Mesoamérica.* Revista del Centro de Investigaciones Regionales de Mesoamérica. Año 1, No. 1, enero/junio 1980–   . La Antigua, Guatemala.

First issue of the Centro's journal serves as a preview to the types of material that the journal seeks to publish (i.e., articles and reports focused on the broadly based interpretations of past and present activities in Mesoamerica). Contains articles on colonial and national periods of Central American nations, demographic history, travel accounts, research resources, projects and book reviews. Copies of the new publication are available from: Centro de Investigaciones Regionales de Mesoamérica (CIRMA), 5a Calle Oriente 5, (Apartado Postal 336), La Antigua, Guatemala.

192   *Revista Colombiana de Sociología.* Departamento de Sociología, Universidad Nacional. Bogotá.

Address of this journal is: Apartado Aéreo 058443, Universidad Nacional, Bogotá, Colombia. Director: Gabriel Restrepo F.

193   *Revista de Ciencia Política.* Instituto de Ciencia Política, Pontificia Universidad Católica de Chile. No. 2, 1980–   . Santiago.

Primary focus of the articles is on Chile, however, some incorporate other areas of the world. Includes a lengthy summary of the academic activities of the Institute, as well as their new publications. Mailing address: Avenida Vicuña Mackenna 4860, Edificio No. 10, tercer piso, Santiago de Chile. Director: Gustavo Cuevas Farren.

194   *Revista Universidad de Sonora.* Departamento de Extensión Universitaria, Sección de Publicaciones, Edificio de la Rectoría. Vol. 1, No. 1, feb. 1977–   . Hermosillo, Sonora, México.

Published three times per year. Director: Carlos Gámez López.

195   *La Torre de Papel.* Revista bimestral de literatura, arte, ciencia y filosofía. No. 1, junio/julio 1980–   . Buenos Aires.

Sections include short stories, essays, poems, interviews, arts and shows, and bibliographic notes. Committee of contributors has correspondents in Barcelona, Caracas, Frankfurt, London, Madrid, México, New York, Paris, and Rome. Translations are included in the short stories and poetry sections. Major Latin American and other writers appear (e.g., Borges, Updike, Jorge Onetti, Manuel Puig).

196   *The Writings.* A journal of the Young Socialist Movement. Young Socialist Movement. Vol. 2, 1979–   . Georgetown.

Journal is divided into four sections: On Guyana; Poems and Verse; On Theory and Youth; and International. Publication reflects theoretical contributions of the Young Socialist Movement of Guyana.

JOURNAL ABBREVIATIONS BIBLIOGRAPHY AND GENERAL WORKS

AHSI   Archivum Historicum Societatis Iesu. Rome.

AM/R   Revista do Arquivo Municipal. Prefeitura do Município de São Paulo, Depto. Municipal de Cultura. São Paulo.

ASB/PP   Philologica Pragensia. Academia Scientiarum Bohemoslovenica. Praha.

BRBN/A   Anais da Biblioteca Nacional. Divisão de Obras Raras e Publicações. Rio de Janeiro.

CDAL   Cahiers des Amériques Latines. Paris.

CH   Cuadernos Hispanoamericanos. Instituto de Cultura Hispánica. Madrid.

CIF/FA   *See* IPGH/FA.

CM/HM   Historia Mexicana. El Colegio de México. México.

CPU/ES   Estudios Sociales. Corporación de Promoción Universitaria. Santiago.

EEHA/HBA   Historiografía y Bibliografía Americanista. Escuela de Estudios Hispano-Americanos de Sevilla. Sevilla.

IAA   Ibero-Amerikanisches Archiv. Ibero-Amerikanisches Institut. Berlin, FRG.

IPGH/FA   Folklore Americano. Instituto Panamericano de Geografía e Historia, Comisión de Historia, Comité de Folklore. México.

LARR   Latin American Research Review. Univ. of North Carolina Press *for the* Latin American Studies Association. Chapel Hill.

LI/LA   *See* NOSALF/IA.

MAGN/B   Boletín del Archivo General de la Nación. Secretaría de Gobernación. México.

NOSALF/IA   Ibero Americana. Scandinavian Association for Research on Latin America. Stockholm.

NWIG   Nieuwe West-Indische Gids. Martinus Nijhoff. The Hague.

PAN/ES   Estudios Latinoamericanos. Polska Akademia Nauk (Academia de Ciencias de Polonia), Instytut Historii Instituto de Historia). Warszawa.

PEBN/B   Boletín de la Biblioteca Nacional. Lima.

PUJ/UH   Universitas Humanistica. Pontificia Univ. Javeriana, Facultad de Filosofía y Letras. Bogotá.

RIB   Revista Interamericana de Bibliografía (Inter-American Review of Bibliography). Organization of American States. Washington.

SHG/B   Bulletin de la Société d'Histoire de la Guadeloupe. Archives Départementales *avec le concours du* Conseil Général de la Guadeloupe. Basse-Terre, W.I.

UN/ISSJ   International Social Science Journal. United Nations Educational, Scientific, and Cultural Organization. Paris.

UNAM/L   Latinoamérica. Anuario de estudios latinoamericanos. Univ. Nacional Autónoma de México, Facultad de Filosofía y Letras, Centro de Estudios Latinoamericanos. México.

UNC/ED   El Dorado. Univ. of Northern Colorado, Museum of Anthropology. Greeley.

UNESCO/JIS   UNESCO Journal of Information Science, Librarianship and Archives Administration. United Nations Educational, Scientific and Cultural Organization. Paris.

URSS/AL   América Latina. Academia de Ciencias de la URSS (Unión de Repúblicas Soviéticas Socialistas). Moscú.

VANH/B   Boletín de la Academia Nacional de la Historia. Caracas.

ANTHROPOLOGY

GENERAL

251 Alcina, José. L'art précolombien. Paris: Editions d'Art Lucien Mazenod, 1978. 613 p.; bibl.; ill.; index; map; plates; tables.

Contains 177 color plates and 594 b/w photographs (with brief captions) of Mesoamerican and Andean masterpieces, the great majority of which were well known from other publications. Includes descriptions, illustrations, and plans of the major archaeological sites. Comprehensive, scholarly text on cultural development, with little concern for iconography. [HvW]

252 La Antropología americanista en la actualidad; homenaje a Raphael Girard. Edited by the Comité del Libro. Homenaje a R. Girard; Francis Polo Sifontes, Presidente [and] Jorge Luis Villacorta, Secretario. México: Editores Mexicanos Unidos, 1980. 2 v.; bibl.; ill.; tables.

Articles by 82 authors, mostly in Spanish and English, on anthropology, art, mythology, and related subjects, covering the entire continent south of the US. Issued on the occasion of Girard's 80th birthday. [HvW]

252a Butterworth, Douglas and John K. Chance. Latin American urbanization. Cambridge; New York: Cambridge University Press, 1981. 243 p.: bibl.; index; map (Urbanization in developing countries)

Well researched, general treatment of urbanization in contemporary Latin America. One of the major conclusions is that, at least in the case of Latin America's major cities, dependent capitalism, high rates of population growth, and massive movements of people from rural to urban areas have resulted in urban growth *without* development. The coverage ranges from Argentina and Chile in the south to Mexico in the north. [W.E. Carter]

253 Congreso Peruano: El Hombre y la Cultura Andina, *3d, Lima, 1977.* El hombre y la cultura andina: actas y trabajos. v. 3/5. Editor: Ramiro Matos M. Lima: Editora Lasontay, 1978/1980. 3v. (1076 p.) (Continuous pagination); bibl.; ill.; maps; plates; tables.

For vols. 1/2 of the proceedings of this congress (published 1978), see *HLAS 41:782.* Vols. 3/5 (published 1980) also consist of papers delivered at the congress, held under the auspices of the Programa Académico de Arqueología, Universidad Nacional Mayor de San Marcos. All individual papers included in vols. 3/5 are annotated separately according to discipline (archaeology, ethnology, history, etc.) and entered under author's name in this volume, *HLAS 43,* or in the humanities volumes, *HLAS 42* or *HLAS 44.* [Ed.]

Huizer, Gerrit. Ciencia social aplicada y acción política: notas sobre nuevos enfoques. See item **8026.**

254 Humboldt, Alexander, *Freiherr von.* Vistas de las Cordilleras y monumentos de los pueblos indígenas de América. Palabras preliminares, José López Portillo; prólogo, Miguel S. Wionczek; traducción e introducción, Jaime Labastida. México: Secretaría de Hacienda y Crédito Público, 1974. 373 p.; 69 leaves of plates; bibl.; ill. (some col.).

Spanish translation of 1810 French edition, with reproduction of original plates. Contains geographical and archaeological studies, primarily from Mexico and South America. Original French title: *Vues des Cordillères et monuments des peuples indigènes de l'Amérique.* [HvW]

255 International Congress of Americanists, *42d, Paris, 1976.* Actes. v. 6, Los dioses titulares étnicos y los héroes deificados. v. 7, La déchiffrement des écritures mésoaméricaines. v. 8, Mesoamerican communities from proto-historic to colonial times: models for culture change. v. 9a, Prehistória brasileira. v. 9b, La huasteca à la frontière Nord-Est de la Mésoamérique. v. 10, Problemas de iconología en el arte hispanoamericano: 1500–1800. v. au sèrie, Etnohistoire de la Vallé de México d'après les chroniques indigènes en langua Nahuatl. Paris: Société des Américanistes, Musée de l'Homme, 1977/1978. 6 v.; bibl.; ill.; maps; tables.

For vols. 1/5 of the proceedings of this congress (a total of 11 vols.), see *HLAS 41:255*. Papers delivered at this congress are annotated individually and entered under the author's name. For papers on archaeology, ethnology, linguistics, biological anthropology, etc., see the social sciences volume, *HLAS 41* and this one, *HLAS 43*. For contributions to ethnohistory, history, art, etc., see the humanities volumes, *HLAS 42* and *HLAS 44*. [Ed.]

Marino Fores, Anselmo. Bibliografía de antropología americana: temas generales; antropología social y aplicada; arqueología; arte y prehistoria; etnología y etnohistoria; antropología física; lingüística; varios. See *HLAS 42:52*.

Meggers, Betty J. Conexiones y convergencias culturales entre Norte América y América del Sur. See item **8037**.

Mundkur, Balaji. The alleged diffusion of Hindu divine symbols into precolumbian Mesoamerica. See *HLAS 42:992*.

———. The cult of the serpent in the Americas: its Asian background. See *HLAS 42:993*.

Pollak-Eltz, Angelina. Cultos afroamericanos: vudú y hechicería en las Américas. See *HLAS 42:995*.

255a Peasant livelihood: studies in economic anthropology and cultural ecology. Rhoda Halperin, James Dow, editors. New York: St. Martin's Press, 1977. 332 p.; bibl.; index.

Using the analytical framework of Karl Polanyi, this series of articles deals with Peru, Mexico, India, Africa, and peasants in general. Chapters dealing with Latin American issues include: Benjamin Orlove's "Against a Definition of Peasantries: Agrarian Production in Andean Peru;" William P. Mitchell's "Irrigation Farming in the Andes: Evolutionary Implications;" Stephen B. Brush's "The Myth of the Idle Peasant: Employment in a Subsistence Economy;" Rhoda Halperin's "Redistribution of Chan Kom: a Case for Mexican Political Economy;" Frances F. Berdan's "Distributive Mechanisms in the Aztec Economy;" Madeline Barbara Leons' "The Economic Networks of Bolivian Political Brokers: Revolutionary Road to Fame and Fortune;" Carol A. Smith's "How Marketing Systems Affect Economic Opportunity in Agrarian Societies;" Lee A. Parson's and Barbara Price's "Mesoamerican Trade and its Role in the Emergence of Civilization;" Benjamin Orlove's "Inequality among Peasants: the Forms and Uses of Reciprocal Exchange in Andean Peru;" James Dow's "Religion in the Organization of a Mexican Peasant Economy;" and Anthony Leeds' "Mythos and Pathos: Some Unpleasantries on Peasantries." [W.E. Carter]

255b Taussig, Michael T. The devil and commodity fetishism in South America. Chapel Hill: University of North Carolina Press, 1980. 264 p.; bibl.; index.

Proposes the thesis that beliefs and rituals associated with the devil are intricate symbolic manifestations of the loss of control over means of production. Using a Marxist theoretical framework, the thesis is tested with two case studies: black sugar plantation workers living in the Cauca Valley of Colombia and Indian and Mestizo highland Bolivian miners. [W.E. Carter]

255c Valderrama, Mariano. Aportes para una bibliografía del problema indígena (*in* Campesinado e indigenismo en América Latina [see item **1229**] p. 231–251)

Consists of 207 items focusing on ethnicity and the indigenous movement. Omitted is most basic ethnography. [W.E. Carter]

ARCHAEOLOGY: Mesoamerica

NORMAN HAMMOND, *Associate Professor of Archaeology, Douglass College, Rutgers University*
WILLIAM T. SANDERS, *Professor of Anthropology, Pennsylvania State University*

THERE CONTINUES TO BE MUCH interest in the ecology and economy of the Maya Area. The detailed study of climatic change in northeastern Peten, based on cores from the Yaxha-Sacnab basin, spans five millenia and indicates an essentially similar environment throughout (item **268**), with an initial human occupation in the early formative. Studies more directly concerned with the economic landscape include the recent use of radar mapping to detect large areas of canals and raised fields in Peten and Belize, with ground checks indicating late formative dates for some areas (item **255d**); the belated formal publication of the late Dennis Puleston's study of *ramón* (*Brosimum alicastrum*) as a putative tree crop is welcome (item **305**).

There has been progress in settlement pattern studies as is apparent in a symposium volume (item **295**) based on a 1977 gathering. Adams' radar-mapping paper also rationalizes wetland-margin site locations, while several papers on the Peten savannas (items **255d, 375** and **376**) indicate that their settlement was marginal and late. A general survey of savanna environments in tropical American prehistory includes an examination of Maya Area data using a definition wider than merely that of grasslands. The northeastern Peten continues to yield settlement studies such as an assessment of whether political rather than ecological factors were the determinant ones (item **377**), and a negative evaluation of a concentric-zone model for Tikal (item **313**).

Settlement-pattern data have been used as the basis for studies of political and social organization, including one at macro-scale by Folan (item **273**) that postulates interacting coastal and inland polities, and a micro-scale analysis by Fry (item **333**) of the regional marketing system servicing Tikal with pottery. The major program of fieldwork and publication at Kaminaljuyu (see *HLAS 41:347*) has produced a detailed study by Michels (item **301**) in which a chiefdom level of organization and a conical clan structure are axiomatic.

The artistic and intellectual superstructure of Maya civilization is relatively underrepresented in 1979–80 publications, but the ambitious linking of planets with deities, on the basis of a new correlation and early beginning for the Mesoamerican calendar, by Kelley (item **405**) is certain to arouse controversy. Another useful contribution is Coggins' adoption (item **265**) of a vertical-circle model to explain quadridirectionality (see *HLAS 41:275*), which if correct reduces the utility of horizontal circle models linked to hypothesized settlement patterns.

Within the time-span of ancient Maya culture, there have been rapid and dramatic developments in knowledge of the Archaic period from 10000–2000 BC. Numerous aceramic sites have been located in the western highlands of Guatemala (item **320**) including one with a Folsom-like point (item **347**) indicating occupation by 10000–6000 BC. In Belize, a seriated sequence spanning the period 9000–2000 BC has been claimed on the basis of comparative lithic technology (item **360**); subsequent unpublished (as of 31 Dec. 1980) discoveries indicate occupation of Belize from the early Holocene onwards. Discoveries at Loltun Cave, in northern Yucutan, have been briefly reported but also suggest a long preceramic period before the first pottery-using occupation ca. 1800 BC. The Maya Area, which as recently as 1975 lacked a firmly documented occupation prior to 1000 BC, is now perceived as having a post-Pleistocene occupation comparable with any in the New World, including long-distance resource procurement by the end of the Archaic (item **368**).

Further work has been done on the early formative (2000–1000 BC) occupation at Cuello, Belize (items **343** and **344**) and a late early formative occupation has been confirmed stratigraphically at nearby Colha (item **325**). Recent publications pay little attention to the middle formative, although the recognition of it as the period in which the developmental momentum of Maya culture began to accelerate should ensure specific research in the future. In contrast, the late formative (after 400 BC) has been the subject of several studies and yielded important data on the emergence of complex society: at Lamanai (item **370**) and Mirador (item **361**) colossal pyramids have been attributed to this period, together with smaller but still impressive constructions at Cuello (item **344**), Cerros and Komchen (still in press), and a peaking of production in the huge chert factory site at Colha (item **325**). There is growing recognition of the early classic period as the second phase of Maya civilization, its first phase beginning around or before the time of Christ. This developmental trajectory makes the volcanic diffusionism of one school of thought (e.g., item **385**) less relevant than it previously appeared.

Several major studies on classic period sites have appeared, including the map of Dzibilchaltun (item **392**), vol. 1 of the Tonina report (item **318**), and two substantial preliminary reports on Colha (items **324** and **325**). Preliminary reports have also appeared on the projects at Copan and Quirigua, the two major sites of the southeastern lowlands (items **317** and **373**). The existence at both sites of stelae of earlier dates than hitherto known constitutes an enticing indication of importance preceding their noted late classic florescenes. Pollock's monumental study of the Puuc sites (item **371**) is a substantial reminder of the merits of Carnegie archaeology.

Little has appeared on the history of Maya archaeology, a subject overdue for serious and detailed consideration, but the second edition of Willey and Sabloff's *History of American archaeology* (1980) places the important developments within a continental perspective, and Bernal's *History of Mexican archaeology* (item **257**) within a Mesoamerican one. The republication of Catherwood's scarce 1844 lithographs in a usefully annotated edition (item **262**) is a welcome addition to the source material for the historiography of Maya studies.

The present and future concerns of Mayanists, ethical rather than academic, are brought out by several publications dealing with looting and the rescue of monuments and information: Mayer's list (item **364**) of looted monuments in US collections is a bitter reminder of what has been lost already; Hairs' description of the Naranjo rescue operation (item **342**), although old, is an indication of concern in Guatemala; and the latest fascicule of Ian Graham's *Corpus of Maya hieroglyphic inscriptions* (item **404**) constitutes an example of what needs to be done. Realization that infinitely more useful and important than looted materials are excavated ones because of their information content is evident in the corpus of vases presented by Foncerrada de Molina and Lombardo de Ruiz (item **332**).

Overall, the most important developments in Maya archaeology in 1979–80 have been the widespread recognition of the Archaic, the developed nature of late formative society, and the continued emphasis on the relationship between environment, settlement, and subsistence. [NH]

The period from April 1977 to April 1979 was characterized by a number of ongoing research projects in northern and western Mesoamerica in various stages of completion. This is reflected only in part by the literature annotated below. Unfortunately, much of the research published in the form of papers and in professional journals such as *World Archaeology*, *Field Archaeology*, and *American Antiquity*, or presented at national or international meetings, is not well represented in this bibliography.

Field projects completed and in the publishing stage, as of December 1980, include Millon's (University of Rochester) Teotihuacan Mapping Project; Flannery's (University of Michigan) Valley of Oaxaca Human Ecology Project; Sanders (Pennsylvania State University) and Parsons' (University of Michigan) various survey projects in the Basin of Mexico; the Puebla-Tlaxcala Project sponsored jointly by the German and Mexican governments; several field projects in the Basin of Mexico and Valley of Toluca sponsored by the National University of Mexico; the Chalcatzingo Project in Morelos, directed by David Grove (University of Illinois at Urbana); Richard Diehl's (University of Missouri) and Eduardo Matos' (INAH) separate but coordinated projects at Tula; Barbara Voorhies' Chiapas Project; the various field projects of the New World Archaeological Foundation in Chiapas, directed by Gareth Lowe; and the Tehuacan Project of the Peabody Foundation, directed by Richard MacNeish. Field projects in progress during this period included Blanton (Purdue University) and Kowaleski's (University of Georgia) surveys in the Valley of Oaxaca; Sanders' (Pennsylvania State University) studies of prehispanic agricultural systems in the Basin of Mexico; ongoing extensions of the original Peabody Foundation project in the Tehuacan Valley, directed by Drennan; and the very impressive and exciting excavations of the Templo Mayor in the Zocalo at Mexico City sponsored by INAH and directed by Eduardo Matos M.

Two well-established trends in research in Mesoamerica continued to be of strong interest during this period: i.e., settlement archaeology and ecology. More recent trends in the archaeological literature, only partly reflected in this bibliography, are an increasing interest in the reconstruction of trade networks by trace element analysis, and the application to archaeological problems of spatial models drawn from geography along with analogic models from ethnography and ethnohistory.

This bibliography does reflect some of those trends, most particularly a strong revival of interest in the archaeology of the postclassic period, in which archaeological and ethnohistoric sources of information are being combined to present a detailed picture of life in Mesoamerica in postclassic times.

A number of major meetings took place during the period which dealt with the archaeology of Mesoamerica, aside from the annual meetings of the Society for American Archaeology. These include a Mesa Redonda in Guanajuato, Mexico, called Procesos de Cambio in 1977; a conference, in honor of the late Dennis Puleston, on Maya Subsistence, held at Minneapolis in 1979; a colloquium of the American Ethnohistoric Society on Highland Guatemalan Demography, 1979, at Albany; a meeting sponsored by Dumbarton Oaks on Highland-Lowland Interaction in Mesoamerica, in Washington, in 1980; a Wenner-Gren conference at Burg Wartenstein, Austria, held in 1980, on Settlement Patterns, as a Festschrift in honor of Gordon Willey. [WTS]

Several items included in this bibliography were annotated by a former contributor to this section, Hasso von Winning, and are identified by his initials. [Ed.]

GENERAL

255d Adams, Richard E.W. Swamps, canals and the locations of ancient Maya cities (AT/A, 54, 1980, p. 206–214, ill., maps)

Reports results of radar mapping in Maya lowlands. Location of canalized areas in swamps suggests intensive wetland manipulation, and rationalizes site locations near swamp margins. [NH]

256 Benavides C., Antonio and **Anthony P. Andrews.** Ecab; poblado y provincia del siglo XVI en Yucatán. México: Instituto Nacional de Antropología e Historia, 1979. 71 p.; ill.; maps; tables (Cuadernos de los centros regionales; sureste)

Definitive report on church and conventual building at the first Spanish landfall in the Maya area, with a discussion of the 16th-century polity of Ecab. [NH]

257 Bernal, Ignacio. A history of Mexican archaeology: the vanished civilizations of Middle America. Translated by Ruth Malet. New York: Thames and Hudson Ltd., 1980. 208 p.; bibl.; facsim.; ill.; maps; plates.

Excellent description of the emergence of antiquarianism and practical archaeology in Mexico until 1950. Especially strong on the 16th- through 18th-century material and the intellectual milieu underlying early archaeological work in Mexico. [NH]

258 Biese, L.P. and **E. Iannuccillo.** The reduction of Maya Long Count dates and Calendar Round position to their Gregorian equivalents (SAA/AA, 44:4, 1979, p. 784–791)

Describes basic program to accomplish specified aims on a microcomputer; another program gives possible Long Count dates for any given Calendar Round position. [NH]

259 Braun, Barbara. Sources of the Cotzumalhuapa style (MV/BA, 26:1, 1978, p. 159–232, bibl., ill.)

Author concludes from the detailed study of themes and compositions of Cotzumalhuapa sculptures that the style is derived primarily from various Mesoamerican sources (e.g., Olmec, "colonial Olmec," Dainzú as in item **319**) to no small degree from the Andean area (e.g., Chavín, Recuay, San Agustín), and possibly also from the Atlantic Watershed of Costa Rica. [HvW]

260 Broda, Johanna. Cosmovisión y estructura de poder en el México prehispánico (FAIC/CPPT, 15, 1978, p. 165–172, bibl.)

Interpretative synthesis of the role of cult practices and cosmology in political and socioeconomic development from the early classic period to the Conquest. [HvW]

261 Carlson, John B. The case for geomagnetic alignments of precolumbian Mesoamerican sites: the Maya (UNC/K, 10:2, June 1977, p. 67–88, bibl., plate, tables)

Evidence for lodestone compass and transmission of highland alignments to lowlands as cultural imports is assessed, with comparative reference made to oriental geomancy. [NH]

262 Catherwood, Frederick. Visión del mundo maya. Introducción, Alberto Ruz Lhuillier; biografía del artista, Dolores Plunket. Edición privada de Cartón y Papel de México. México: s.n., 1978. ca. 100 p.; bibl.; ill. (some col.)

Lavish reedition of the scarce color lithographs originally issued by Catherwood in 1844 as *Views of ancient monuments in Central America, Chiapas and Yucatan*. Contains a critical introduction and summary of the Stephens-Catherwood expeditions illustrated with reduced-size copies of the monochrome engravings from Stephens' 1841 and 1843 books. A valuable resource for study. [NH]

263 Codex Wauchope: a tribute roll. Edited by Marco Giardino, Barbara Edmonson, Winifred Creamer. Festschrift in honor of Robert Wauchope. New Orleans: Human Mosaic, 1978. 184 p.; bibl.; ill.

Amusing and affectionate *Festschrift* for Robert Wauchope. Papers on the Chamula cargo system, syncretic elements in colonial Chiapas town planning, classic Maya warfare, and possible identification of Maya matrilineal glyphs, and trade in formative Central Mexico, and Costa Rica. Originally issued as vol. 12 of *Human Mosaic* in 1978. [WTS]

264 Coe, Michael D. The Maya. London: Thames and Hudson, 1980. 180 p.; ill.

Revised second edition of an excellent popular work, first published in 1966. Takes into account the new view of Maya agriculture and society. [NH]

265 Coggins, Clemency. The shape of time: some political implications of a four-part figure (SAA/AA, 45:4, 1980, p. 727–739)

Four-part figures represent the vertical circle of the sun's diurnal path, rather than the horizontal circle of the cardinal directions. Teotihuacán solar cycle ritual introduced at Tikal in the early classic was institutionalized as the *katun* cycle, and the iconography of *katun* celebration is quadripartite. The non-historic stelae erected at *katun* endings drew emphasis away from the historic commemorative stelae of purely dynastic function, thereby making rituals publicly relevant and broadening the role of the ruler. [NH]

266 Comunicaciones: proyecto Puebla-Tlaxcala. Edited by Wilhelm Lauer and Konrad Tyrakowski. Número especial para el 2. Simposio: 2 al 7 de Oct. 1978. Puebla, México: Fundación Alemana para la Investigación Científica, 1978. 248 p.; bibl.; fold. maps; fold. tables; illus.; maps; plates; tables.

Symposium volume of 25 papers covering a variety of topics, from the ecology and geography of the Puebla-Tlaxcala area to contemporary urban Puebla. Includes papers on the prehispanic, Conquest, colonial, Independence, and modern periods, and on agriculture, industry, demography, cosmology, and other problems. [WTS]

267 Cultural evolution: Maya highlands and lowlands. Edited by R.E.W. Adams (*in* International Congress of Americanists, 42d, Paris, 1976. Actes [see item **255**] v.8, p. 125–209, bibl., ill., maps, tables)

Vol. 8 of the Congress' proceedings entitled *Mesoamerican communities from protohistoric to colonial times: models of culture change*, contains seven symposium papers and commentary on diverse topics by R.E.W. Adams; R.L. Rands; S.M. Ekholm; J.W. Michels; J.A. Graham; J. Quirarte; N. Hammond; and G.R. Willey. For titles of vols. 1/5 of these proceedings, see *HLAS* 41:255, for vols. 6/11, see item **255**. [NH]

268 Deevey, E.S. and others. Maya urbanism: impact on a tropical karst environment (AAAS/S, 206, 1979, p. 298–306, maps, tables)

Examines human effect on the Yaxha-Sacnab lake basins of Peten over the past five millenia on the basis of sediment cores and lakeshore studies. Initial early formative occupation confirms other Maya lowland evidence for this phase. Very high phosphorus budget suggests surprisingly high organic inflow to lakes. For geographer's comment, see item **5089**. [NH]

269 Dickson, D.B. Ancient agriculture and population at Tikal, Guatemala: an application of linear programming to the simulation of an archaeological problem (SAA/AA, 45:4, 1980, p. 697–712)

Uses simulated agricultural carrying capacity with varying combinations of *milpa*, intensive cultivation, and *ramón* arboriculture to infer population potentials for Tikal. *Ramón* and roots would give the highest potential: 70–77,000 people in the late classic. [NH]

270 Doty, D.C. A new Mayan Long Count-Gregorian Conversion Computer Program (SAA/AA, 44:4, 1979, p. 780–783)

FORTRAN-G program converts Maya to Gregorian dates and also prints Julian Day Number, Sacred Round position and Lord of the Night. Secondary Series can also quickly be computed. [NH]

271 Dütting, Dieter. Aspects of classic Maya religion and world view (Tribus [Linden Museum, Stuttgart, FRG] 29, Sept. 1980, p. 107–167, bibl., ill.)

Interprets the symbolism of the Palenque Tablets, in particular the squint eye/spiral eye contrast expressed on them and elsewhere. Discusses other topics (e.g., Cauac monster) and graphemes (spirals, God K's forehead element 617a, etc.) that elucidate underworld scenes on painted vases and other ideological concepts. [HvW]

272 Epstein, Jeremiah F. Precolumbian Old World coins in America: an examination of the evidence with comment (UC/CA, 21:1, Feb. 1980, p. 1–20, bibl., tables)

Catalogs the available numismatic data and examines its contents, concluding that no firm evidence for Old World prehispanic contact exists. [NH]

273 Folan, William J. The political and economic organization of the lowland Maya (Mexicon [Berlin, FRG] 2:5, 1980, p. 72–77, map)

Advances a model of southern, central and northern inland core polities surrounded by an arc of coastal jurisdictions, the latter possessing capitals located at their inland borders to facilitate exchange. The systems of northern and southern lowland Maya are more alike than different, with the major difference resulting from the north's greater resource and bulk transport potentials. [NH]

274 Fox, John W. Lowland to highland mexicanization processes in southern Mesoamerica (SAA/AA, 45:1, Jan. 1980, p. 43–54, ill., map, plates)

Gulf Coast lowlands frontier area between Mexican and Maya zones was a critical focus for several waves of Maya Mexicanization, beginning in the epiclassic period (AD 800–1000). These influences appear first in lowland areas and subsequently in the Guatemala highlands, with the ethnohistoric Quiché and Cakchiquel. Author suggests the Río Negro and Río Motagua Basins as major transmission routes. [WTS]

275 Gann, Thomas. Thomas Gann's report on Lubaantun: *Visit to ruins on the Columbia Branch of the Rio Grande* (BISRA/BS, 8:6, 1980, p. 25–29)

Publication of a 1903 report of the first exploration of this classic Maya site (see also *HLAS 41:293*). [NH]

276 García Quintana, Josefina and **José Rubén Romero Galván.** México Tenochtitlan y su problemática lacustre. México: UNAM, 1978. 132 p.; bibl.; ill. (Serie histórica; no. 21. Cuaderno—Instituto de Investigaciones Históricas)

Discusses the role of the lake system in the cultural evolution of the Basin of Mexico, with emphasis on the Aztec period. Treats irrigation, diking, rechannelling of streams, chinampas, and other means of water control as well as the problem of flooding and the role of the lakes in providing non-agricultural food resources. [WTS]

277 Garza, Mercedes de la. El hombre en el pensamiento religioso náhuatl y maya. México: Universidad Nacional Autónoma de México, 1978. 141 p.; bibl. (Cuaderno—Centro de Estudios Mayas; 14)

Cosmological study of postclassic Nahua and Maya myths of successive cyclical creations of the universe and man. Man's fundamental nature is seen as determined by his relationships to the gods, whom he has created to serve and nourish in

the world they created for him. Dualisms of free-will/determinism, life/death, light/darkness, good/evil are related to this dual nature of man. [WTS]

278 Grayson, Donald K. and **Payson D. Sheets.** Volcanic disasters and the archaeological record (*in* Volcanic activity and human ecology. Edited by Payson D. Sheets, Donald K. Grayson. New York: Academic Press, 1979, p. 623–632, bibl.)

Archaeology can be used to document the human impact of eruptions. [NH]

279 Gutiérrez Solana, Nelly and **Daniel G. Schávelzon.** Corpus bibliográfico de la cultura olmeca. México: Universidad Nacional Autónoma de México, 1980. 135 p.

Lists 850 titles, each with numerical prefix to indicate type, context, or region. [HvW]

280 Hamblin, Robert L. and **Brian L. Pitcher.** The classic Maya collapse: testing class conflict hypotheses (SAA/AA, 45:2, April 1980, p. 246–267, ill., tables)

Resurrection of Thompson's "peasant revolt" model for the collapse, using escalation, collective learning, and dialectic formulations. Probably partially correct, like the original idea. [NH]

281 Hammond, Norman. Prehistoric human utilization of the savanna environments of Middle and South America (*in* Human ecology in savanna environments. Edited by D.R. Harris. London: Academic Press, 1980, p. 73–105, map)

Survey of archaeological evidence from non-arid and non-wet environments of the New World tropics. [NH]

282 Harrison, P.D. Prehispanic Maya agriculture (*in* International Congress of Americanists, 42d, Paris, 1976. Actes [see item 255] v.8, p. 297–453)

Consists of 11 symposium papers and commentary by Harrison; B. Dahlin; D.S. Rice; N. Hammond; T.P. Culbert *et al.*; F.M. Wiseman; A.H. Siemens; W.T. Sanders; D.E. Puleston; B.L. Turner, II; O. Stavrakis; and G.R. Willey. Most papers are original versions of those published in Harrison and Turner's *Pre-hispanic Maya agriculture* (see *HLAS 41:296*). [NH]

283 Heyden, Doris. El "signo del año" en Tehuacan [sic, = Teotihuacan], su supervivencia y el sentido sociopolítico del símbolo (in Mesoamérica. Homenaje a Paul Kirchhoff. Edited by Barbro Dahlgren. México: INAH, 1979, p. 61–68, bibl., ill.)

Revised version of author's 1977 article in English (see *HLAS 41:302*). [HvW]

284 Hicks, Frederic. "Flowery war" in Aztec history (AAA/AE, 6:1, Feb. 1979, p. 87–92)

Questions interpretations of Aztec "flowery wars" as either true wars of conquest or as intended to procure captives for ritual sacrifice. Suggests instead that this institution provided practice exercises in military training. [WTS]

285 Highland culture contacts in the lowland Maya area: recent data and implications. Edited by A.G. Miller (in International Congress of Americanists, 42d, Paris, 1976. Actes [see item 255] v.8, p. 211–295)

Contains five symposium papers and commentary by Miller; E.W. Andrews, V; C. Coggins; J.W. Ball; L. Schele; and G.R. Willey. [NH]

287 Ichon, Alain *et al.* Rabinal et la Vallée Moyenne du Rio Chixoy, Baja Verapaz, Guatemala. Paris: Centre National de la Recherche Scientifique, Institut d'Ethnologie, 1979. 230 p.; ill. (Cahiers de la R.C.P. 500; no. 1)

General summary of the geology, history, and ethnography of a sector of the valley studied in advance of flooding by a new dam. [NH]

288 Jiménez Moreno, Wigberto. Sincretismo, identidad, y patrimonio en Mesoamérica (in Cultural traditions and Caribbean identity: the question of patrimony. Edited by S. Jeffrey K. Wilkerson. Gainesville, Center for Latin American Studies, University of Florida, 1980, p. 353–372)

Postulates a circum-Caribbean oikoumene called Mexiamerica which, despite its environmental and cultural diversity was characterized in the mid-19th century by widespread religious, artistic, and linguistic syncretism, of which the cult of the Virgin of Guadalupe is a notable instance. Discusses the role of syncretic concepts in the forging of a national identity and consciousness in colonial and republican Mexico. [WTS]

289 Karen, Ruth. Feathered serpent: the rise and fall of the Aztecs. New York: Four Winds Press, 1979. 184 p.; 1 leaf of plates; bibl.; ill.; index.

Discusses Aztec society, cosmology, history, and myth—in a rather uncritical and often inaccurate adaptation of selected ethnohistorical sources, superficially written for high school students. Pt. 1 is a short story set during the Conquest; pt. 3, a brief survey of major archaeological sites and sources. [WTS]

290 Krowne, C.M.; R.V. Sidrys; and S.K. Cooperman. A lowland Maya Calendar Round-Long Count Conversion Computer Program (SAA/AA, 44:4, 1979, p. 775–780)

FORTRAN program converts Calendar Round to Long Count dates and *vice versa*. [NH]

291 Kurbjuhn, Kornelia. Die Sitze der Maya, eine ikonographische Untersuchung. Neustetten, FRG: Spengler, 1980. 348 p.; bibl.; ill.; maps; tables.

Thorough examination of the significance of seats (benches, thrones, etc.) in Mayan art, with reference to their occupants, rituals, foreign influences, and linguistic connotations. Author's dissertation at Universität Tübingen. [HvW]

292 Lamb, W. The sun, moon, and Venus at Uxmal (SAA/AA, 45:1, 1980, p. 79–86)

Suggests that counts of mosaic façade elements in the Monjas embody astronomical periodicity information, and that depictions of "Chac" are really Venus. Puuc style façades should be seen as coded signals, not as purely decorative constructions. [NH]

293 Lee, Thomas A., Jr. Early colonial Coxoh Maya syncretism in Chiapas, Mexico (CEM/ECM, 12, 1979, p. 93–109, bibl., ill., maps plates)

Iconography and material culture of this group show fusion of Maya and Spanish traits in the 17th century. [NH]

294 Lincoln, Charles Edward. Izamal, Yucatan, Mexico: un reconocimiento breve, descripción preliminar y discusión (Boletín de la Escuela de Ciencias Antropológicas de la Universidad de Yucatán [Mérida, México] 8:43, 1980, p. 24–69)

Useful summary of the extant archaeological and documentary data. [NH]

295 Lowland Maya settlement patterns. Edited by W. Ashmore. Albuquerque: University of New Mexico Press, 1981. 465 p.; bibl.; ill.; index.

Consists of 15 papers and summary review by 16 authors. Historical introduction and time-space framework are followed by five papers containing problem-oriented discussion and considerations of analytical units and definitions. Seven papers present regional data synthesis from the Copan Valley north to Yucatan; three papers discuss models to explain settlement patterns. Includes an extensive bibliography up to 1980. Likely to remain the standard source on this topic for a generation. [NH]

296 Macazaga Ordoño, César. Ritos y esplendor del Templo Mayor. México: Editorial Innovación, 1978. 159 p.; bibl.; ill.; index.

Plan and contents of the Templo Mayor complex reflect the mythology and ritual of several cults linked by a number of crosscutting dualities: sun/moon; sun/rain; life (fertility)/death (war, sacrifice). Includes brief review of relevant ethnohistoric and iconographic materials. [WTS]

297 McClung de Tapia, Emily. Ecología y cultura en Mesoamérica. México: UNAM, Instituto de Investigaciones Antropológicas, 1979. 1 v.; fold. maps; ill. (Cuadernos Serie antropológica; 30)

Discussion, within a broad systems framework, of ecological, agricultural, demographic, and cultural potential of the basin of Mexico, the Teotihuacan and Oaxaca valleys, and the humid lowlands of the Maya area. [NH]

298 Matos Moctezuma, Eduardo. Muerte a filo de obsidiana: los nahuas frente a la muerte. México: Instituto Nacional de Antropología e Historia, 1978. 190 p.; bibl.; ill.

A concept of duality—of death generating the rebirth of life—underlies the Aztec concept of human sacrifice. A brief review of comparative and diachronic parallels to these beliefs, chosen on the basis of comparability of political economy, and linked specifically to the double economic base of Tenochtitlan (agriculture and conquest/tribute). Gives ethnohistoric and archaeological evidence of concepts of death and afterlife. [WTS]

299 ———. El Templo Mayor de Tenochtitlán; economía e ideología (BBAA, 1, junio 1980, p. 7–19, plates)

Tenochtitlán's Templo Mayor and its context consistently reflect a political economy based jointly upon agriculture (Tlaloc) and conquest/tribute (Huitzilopochtli). Ethnohistorical accounts of associated myths (e.g., the defeat of Coyol by Huitzilopochtli) and rituals, along with the contents of offerings, confirm the relation of the symbolism to the material conditions of life. [WTS]

300 Maya archaeology and ethnohistory. Edited by Norman Hammond and G.R. Willey. Austin: University of Texas Press, 1979. 292 p.; bibl.; ill.; index; maps.

Consists of 14 papers from the 1976 Cambridge Mesoamerican Archaeology Symposium which covered wide range of materials and orientations. Volume is divided into three sections: 1) *Theoretical Interpretations*: essays by M.J. Becker; B.H. Dahlin; C. Coggins; G.L. Cowgill; and D.E. Puleston; 2) *Data Presentations*: by G.R. Willey and R.M. Leventhal; B.L. Turner, II; J. Quirarte; M. Greene Robertson; and S.M. Ekholm; and 3) *Ethnohistoric Approaches*: by P.D. Harrison; T.A. Lee, Jr.; A.G. Miller and N.M. Farriss; and G. Brotherston. Introduction by Willey and Hammond discusses the papers. [NH]

301 Michels, J.W. The Kaminaljuyu chiefdom. University Park: Pennsylvania State University Press, 1979. 278 p.; ill.; maps.

Discusses the evolution of the Kaminaljuyu chiefdom in terms of the new archaeological data, but without allowing for other interpretations. Uses conical clan model, with five postulated sub-chiefdoms of differing status. Interesting illustration of limits reached by ethnographic analogy and inference. [NH]

302 Morales Fernández, Rafael. Reformas institucionales para alcanzar efectivamente la protección del patrimonio cultural (SGHG/A, 46:1/4, enero/dic. 1973, p. 154–165)

Proposes organization reforms for Guatemala's Instituto Nacional de Antropología e Historia including the expansion of its component agencies, as a means by which the government may address the problem of theft and destruction of archaeological monuments. Suggests new taxes for funding protection and conservation of both cultural and natural (endangered species) heritage of Guatemala. [WTS]

303 **Nations, J.D.** Snail shells and maize preparation: a Lacandon Maya analogy (SAA/AA, 44:3, 1979, p. 568–571)

Suggests that *Pomacea flagellata* was widely used as much for the lime in the shells (for processing maize) as for the animal's protein. Notes Lacandon ethnographic data that supports this view. [NH]

304 **Prem, Hanns J.** Methodische Forderungen an den Nachweis transpazifischer Kulturkontakte (MVW/AV, 33, 1979, p. 7–14, bibl.)

Outlines stringent methodological requirements for evaluating proposed evidence of transpacific contacts. [HvW]

305 **Puleston, Dennis Edward** and **Peter Oliver Puleston.** El ramón como base de la dieta alimenticia de los antiguos mayas de Tikal: nuevos datos sobre subsistencia alimenticia en el maya clásico (IAHG/AHG, 2:1, 1979, p. 55–69, bibl., plates)

Published version of a 1968 paper summarizing D.E. Puleston's influential theories on *ramón* as a Maya staple. [NH]

306 **Rounds, J.** Lineage, class, and power in the Aztec state (AAA/AE, 6:1, Feb. 1979, p. 73–86)

Describes problems of political integration in Tenochtitlán, given the conflict between traditional lineage heads and the emerging central government. Tribute from wars of conquest enhanced the relative strength of the central government, and underwrote an increasingly stratified social and political structure. [WTS]

307 **Schávelzon, Daniel G.** El complejo arqueológico Mixteca-Puebla: notas para una redefinición cultural. México: UNAM, 1980. 65 p.; bibl.

Compilation of copious published data concerning Mixtec origins and the far-ranging distribution of their artifacts. Proposes nine socioeconomic hypotheses, but arrives at no final conclusion. [HvW]

308 **Sheets, Payson D.** Maya recovery from volcanic disasters (AIA/A, 32:3, 1979, p. 32–42, ill., maps)

Reports fieldwork in El Salvador, argu-

ing for the non-permanent nature of volcanic eruption damage. [NH]

309 **Tunnicliffe, K.C.** Aztec astrology. Romford, England: L.N. Fowler, 1979. 98 p.

How to cast a horoscope in the Aztec calendar: contains Aztec and Christian calendar correlations, with symbolism of the months, weeks, and days of the Aztec solar and tonalpohualli cycles. [WTS]

310 **Valencia, Ariel.** Perspectivas sobre el patrimonio cultural en México (*in* Cultural traditions and Caribbean identity: the question of patrimony. Edited by S. Jeffrey K. Wilkerson. Gainesville: Center for Latin American Studies, University of Florida, 1980, p. 17–35)

Author maintains that enforcement of UNESCO policies concerning conservation of national patrimony is the responsibility of individual nations. Describes US-Mexican negotiations to protect Mexican archaeological materials that are the property of the Mexican state and a significant component of its national identity. [WTS]

311 **von Winning, Hasso.** The "Binding of the Years" and the "New Fire" in Teotihuacan (IAI/I, 1979, p. 15–32, bibl., ill.)

Iconographic evidence suggests that the Aztec "New Fire" ceremony to initiate a 52-year cycle had its origin in early classic Teotihuacan, where it is represented by firewood bundles. [HvW]

312 **Willey, Gordon R.; Richard M. Leventhal;** and **William L. Fash, Jr.** El asentimiento maya del Valle de Copán (YAXKIN, 2:2, dic. 1977, p. 99–116, ill., maps, plates)

Spanish version of conclusions and data also presented in English (see item **300**). [NH]

EXCAVATIONS AND ARTIFACTS

313 **Arnold, J.E.** and **A. Ford.** A statistical examination of settlement patterns of Tikal, Guatemala (SAA/AA, 45:4, 1980, p. 713–728)

Authors test computed labor investment for residential groups at Tikal and their locations against a concentric-zone model of residence in which high-status families lived closer to the ceremonial precinct. They find that the evidence does not support the model, and suggests instead a mosaic pattern, with some low-status groups being close in and high-status ones on the edges of the mapped area. Article indicates there existed a more complex relationship between family status and dwelling location than the one provided by the accepted model. [NH]

314 El Arte del Templo Mayor. México: Museo del Palacio de Bellas Artes, 1980. 83 p.; bibl.; ill.; map.

Exhibition catalog of the spectacular finds in the center of Mexico City during excavations of the Great Temple. These include Olmec and Teotihuacan masks; Mezcala and Aztec sculptures; gold, obsidian and shell ornaments; inlaid human skulls; and fine pottery. See also *HLAS 41:373* and items **359** and **362**. [HvW]

315 Ball, Joseph W. The archaeological ceramics of Becan, Campeche, Mexico. New Orleans: Middle American Research Institute, Tulane University, 1977. 190 p; bibl.; ill. (Publication—Middle American Research Institute, Tulane University; 43)

Consists of type-variety analysis of Becan ceramics to assess that site's chronology and changing regional relations. Initial occupation (Acachen complex) shows close ties with the Mamom of Petén; the Río Bec zone retains Petén influence throughout its local development through Sabucan (Tzakol 2–3) times. The late classic shows an increased regionalism, and the Xcocom complex (Tepeu 3) is characterized by new types. Unlike the architecture, the ceramic ties of the site are largely Petén. [WTS]

316 Barrera Rubio, Alfredo. Trabajos de conservación en el Chichán Chob de Chichén Itzá (UY/R, 20:120, nov./dic. 1978, p. 36–46)

Practical and theoretical reconstruction of the Chichán Chob. The twin roof-combs were decorated with Chac-masks and *grecas*. [NH]

317 Baudez, Claude F. Investigaciones arqueológicas en Copán, 1979 (YAXKIN, 3:1, junio 1979, p. 69–75)

Summarizes work on acropolis, Great Plaza and site-periphery. Discoveries include fragments of early classic stela (No. 35, dated early 5th century AD) related to Petén;

which indicates earlier florescence and more distant links with Copán than hitherto suspected. [NH]

318 Becquelin, P.; C.F. Baudez *avec la collaboration de* **Marie-Charlotte Arnauld** et al. Tonina, une cité Maya de Chiapas. v. 1. México: Misión Archéologique et ethnologique française au Mexique, 1979. 1 v.; ill.; maps.

Vol. 1 of the final report on excavations at Tonina in an upland Chiapas valley. Occupation sequence begins in protoclassic, with peak occupation in late and terminal classic, and minor postclassic use. Ceramics are analyzed by modes and explicit criticism of Type: variety classificatory system; they can be integrated into the lowland type: variety framework. Vol. 2 will cover architecture, monuments, artifacts, settlement. [NH]

319 Bernal, Ignacio and **Andy Seuffert.** The ballplayers of Dainzú. Graz, Austria: Akademische Buch- und Verlagsanstalt, 1979. 31 p.; bibl.; map; plates (Artes Americanae; 2)

Detailed descriptions of the ballplayer, probable deity figures, and petroglyphs on over 40 elaborately carved low-relief slabs and stones at Dainzú (east of Oaxaca city) and nearby sites. The style of these sculptures is related to Monte Albán II and the end of Olmec art. Excellent large drawings. [HvW]

320 Brown, K.L. A brief report on paleo-indian-archaic occupation in the Quiché Basin, Guatemala (SAA/AA, 45:2, 1980, p. 313–324)

Reports 117 aceramic sites containing basalt tools from north of Los Tapiales, and discusses environmental influence on possible Archaic settlement pattern. [NH]

321 Bruhns, K.O. Plumbate origins revisited (SAA/AA, 45:4, 1980, p. 845–848)

Aberrant Plumbate types from Cihuatán, El Salvador, date to the early postclassic of AD 850–1200 (carbon dates), and have links with Veracruz ceramics. Wider production of Plumbate pottery than hitherto supposed seems likely. [NH]

322 Chiu, B.C. and **Philip Morrison.** Astronomical origins of the offset street grid at Teotihuacan (Archaeoastronomy [Supplement to *Journal for the History of Astronomy*, v. 11, Giles, England] 2, 1980, p. S55–S64)

Notes the 89° angle between the North-South and East-West streets of the Teotihuacan grid, and links it to observation of the Aug. 21 sunset from two locations, one in center city and the other on Cerro Gordo to the North-East. Authors suggest connection with Aug. 13th, 3114 BC, as the initial date of the Maya Long Count. [NH]

323   Clark, John E. and **Thomas A. Lee, Jr.**
A behavioral model for the obsidian industry of Chiapa de Corzo (CEM/ECM, 12, 1979, p. 33–51, bibl., tables)

Documents change from late formative importation of macrocores and tanged macroblades, to middle classic importation of large polyhedral cores, and even later finished bifaces. The behavioral models match those of other Maya highland sites studied to date. [NH]

324   The Colha Project, 1979: a collection of interim papers. Edited by Thomas R. Hester. San Antonio: Center for Archaeological Research, University of Texas at San Antonio, 1979. 1 v.; ill.

Data-based collection of reports on the first season's work at an important Maya lowland chert-working center. Amplifies earlier work by Hammond and others showing a Mamom-to-postclassic sequence and numerous chert workshops, and emphasizes production technology and debitage analysis. [NH]

325   The Colha Project: second season, 1980 interim report. Edited by Thomas R. Hester, Jack D. Eaton, and Harry J. Shafer. San Antonio: Center for Archaeological Research, University of Texas at San Antonio, 1980. 353 p.; ill.; map.

Collection of data-based papers reporting on work at a Maya lowland chert-working center, where many workshop mounds are being studied. Site use begins in late early formative, peaks in late formative and late classic before ending in postclassic. Late preclassic ball court underlies later one. Other sites in the region have also yielded Archaic lithics indicating much earlier occupation. [NH]

326   *Comunicaciones Proyecto Puebla-Tlaxcala*. Fundación Alemana para la

Investigación Científica. No. 15, 1978– Puebla, México.

Special issue for the Segundo Simposio, 2–7 Oct. 1978. Edited by Wilhelm Lauer and Konrad Tyrakowski. Contains following articles on archaeology: Marta Foncerrada de Molina's "Reflexiones en Torno a la Pintura de Cacaxtla" (see *HLAS 41:392*); Franz Tichy's "El Calendario Solar como Principio de Organización del Espacio para Poblaciones y Lugares Sagrados" (p. 153–163, see item **394**); Johanna Broda's "Cosmovisión y Estructura de Poder en el México Prehispánico" (p. 165–172, see item **260**); Angel García Cook's "Tlaxcala: Poblamiento Prehispánico" (p. 173–187, see item **336**). [HvW]

327   ——. ——. No. 16, 1979–   .
Puebla, México.

Proceedings of the Segundo Simposio, 2–7 Oct. 1978. Edited by Wilhelm Lauer and Konrad Tyrakowski. Contains commentaries on some of the articles in *Comunicaciones* No. 15 (see item **326**) and the following articles on archaeology: William Lauer's "Síntesis y Perspectivas tras 17 Años de Investigación Científica de la Región Puebla-Tlaxcala" (p. 17–25); Horst Hartung's "El Ordenamiento Espacial de los Conjuntos Arquitectónicos Mesoamericanos: el Ejemplo de Teotihuacán" (p. 89–103), which refers to pecked crosses as orientation markers, and urban renewal due to population growth as evidence for deliberate planning to distribute mass in space; Diana López de Molina's "Excavaciones en Cacaxtla: Tercera Temporada" (p. 141–148); Sonio Lombardo de Ruiz's "Contribución del Estudio de la Forma a la Iconografía de los Murales de Cacaxtla, Puebla" (see item **358**); and Peter J. Schmidt's "Investigaciones Arqueológicas en la Región Huejotzingo, Puebla: Resumen de los Trabajos del Proyecto Arqueológico Huejotzingo" (p. 169–181). [HvW]

328   ——. ——. No. 17, 1979–   .
Puebla, México.

Contains the following articles on archaeology: Mark Swanson's "La Lítica del Area de Huejotzingo" (p. 35–45), a classification of obsidian tools; Monika Tesch's "Breve Resumen de los Resultados del 'Proyecto Walter' (Proyecto Acatepec)" (p. 47–56), which describes ceramics of a late preclassic site; and Fernando C. de Brasdefer's "Un Palación de Acoluiztli Nezahualcóyotl en el Extremo Norte de la Sierra Nevada" (p. 65–86), reporting on exploration of a fortified hilltop ruin at Yehualica, Sierra de Calpulalpán, identified by historical data as one of the palaces of Nezahualcóyotl (1418–72), king of Texcoco. [HvW]

329   Domínguez Chávez, Humberto. Arqueología de superficie en San Cristóbal Ecatepec, Estado de México: un estudio del desarrollo de las fuerzas productivas en el México prehispánico. Apéndices del Wilfrido Du Solier; prefácio por William T. Sanders. México: Biblioteca Enciclopédica del Estado de México, 1979. 236 p.; 8 leaves of plates [1 fold.]; ill. (Biblioteca enciclopédica del Estado de México; 70)

Surface survey of sites near Ecatepec that span the range of formative through postclassic occupations, with excavations at a formative settlement. Discussion of salt manufacture and trade as economic specializations of the lakeshore communities draws on both archaeological and ethnohistoric evidence. [WTS]

330   Estudios preliminares sobre los mayas de las tierras bajas noroccidentales. Edited by Lorenzo Ochoa. México: UNAM, Instituto de Investigaciones Filológicas, Centro de Estudios Mayas, 1978. 129 p.; bibl.; ill.; maps.

Results of four seasons of archaeological research in the region of the Usumacinta and San Pedro Rivers, including three chapters on Chontal languages. [HvW]

331   Feuchtwanger, Franz. Ikonographische Ursprünge einiger mesoamerikanischer Gottheiten (MV/BA, 2, 1978 [i.e. 1979] p. 241–280, ill.)

Observes morphological similarities among classic/postclassic gods and select preclassic figurines from central highland Mexico. Notes that these deity precursors are personified by ritual dancers and by masks, not by statuettes with determinative attributes. [HvW]

332   Foncerrada de Molina, Marta and **Sonia Lombardo de Ruiz.** Vasijas pintadas mayas en contexto arqueológico: catálogo. México: UNAM, Instituto de Investigaciones Estéticas, 1979. 364 p.; bibl.; ill. (Estudios y frentes del arte de México; 39)

Convenient manual of 534 painted classic Maya vessels scientifically excavated at 50 sites. Gives brief descriptions of motifs, technical data, and present location, with line drawings (including roll-outs) and color plates. [HvW]

333   Fry, Robert E. The economics of pottery at Tikal, Guatemala: models of exchange for serving vessels (SAA/AA, 44:3, 1979, p. 494–512)

Tikal was supplied with service pottery through a complex regional marketing network including a probable central market near the main ceremonial precinct. Central and northern Tikal received goods of better quality than other sectors of the settlement. The exchange mechanism is the same one postulated for utilitarian ceramics; analysis was carried out by multidimensional scaling. [NH]

334   Fuente, Beatriz de la and **Nelly Gutiérrez Solana.** Escultura huasteca en piedra: catálogo. México: UNAM, Instituto de Investigaciones Estéticas, 1980. 465 p.; bibl.; ill. (Cuadernos de historia del arte; 9)

Consists of a detailed descriptive catalog of 392 sculptures in Mexico and abroad that were carefully researched and classified. Includes 367 good photographs. Distinguishes between proper Huastec style sculptures (10th–12th centuries) and others from the Huastec area with Toltec or Aztec traits. [HvW]

335   Gallegos Ruiz, Roberto. El señor 9 [i.e. Nueve] Flor en Zaachila. México: Universidad Nacional Autónoma de México, 1978. 144 p.; 16 leaves of plates; bibl.; ill.; maps.

Excavation of two tombs under the patio of Mound A, Zaachila. Burial of Nine Flower indicates Mixtec influence at Zaachila, beginning perhaps as early as 900 AD and peaking at around 1250. Identifies Nine Flower with the Nine Serpent depicted in Codex Nuttall, a Mixtec noble who married a Zapotec princess of Zaachila, and thereby suggesting a mechanism for the introduction of Mixtec traits into a Zapotec town. [WTS]

336   García Cook, Angel. Tlaxcala: poblamiento prehispánico (FAIC/CPPT, 15, 1978, p. 173–178, bibl.)

Cultural sequence (including regional maps and detailed chronological chart) of settlements and of their political and technological aspects. [HvW]

337 **García Moll, Roberto.** Un relieve Olmeca de Tenosique, Tabasco (CEM/ECM, 12, 1979, p. 53–59, bibl., ill., map, plates)

Reports on incised elaborate mask on flat subcircular slab, from Emiliano Zapata *ejido* near Usumacinta. [NH]

338 **González C., Marcelino.** La restauración de los centros arqueológicos prehispánicos de Guatemala: un enfoque crítico (SGHG/A, 46:1/4, enero/dic. 1973, p. 127–153, bibl.)

Difficulties and limitations of restoration projects at seven major Guatemalan sites (Quirigua, Uaxactun, Zaculeu, Tikal, Mixco Viejo, Iximche, Seibal) which posed quite different ecological and architectural challenges to this aspect of site preservation, and in which criteria for restoration varied widely. [WTS]

339 **Graham, E.A.; L. McNatt; and M. Gutchen.** Excavations in footprint cave, Caves Branch, Belize (Journal of Field Archaeology [Boston University, Boston, Massachusetts] 7, 1980, p. 153–172, ill., maps)

Useful summary of recent work in a large limestone cave in the Maya Mountains. [NH]

340 **Graham, John A.** and **Rainer Berger.** Fechamientos por radiocarbono provenientes de Copan (YAXKIN, 2:2, dic. 1977, p. 117–120, bibl.)

Samples collected in 1936 by Stromsvik from Mound 26 a Copan yielded dates in the early classic, fitting ceramic data, and early late classic; hieroglyphic date from the same structure complex (Stela M) of 9.16.5.0.0. fits these dates on the 11.16 but not the 12.9 correlation. [NH]

341 **Gussinyer, Jordi.** Proposición de un sistema de excavación dentro de una gran ciudad: México (UB/BA, 29, 1979, p. 83–118, bibl., col. plates)

Discusses salvage archaeology of 1967–71 that accompanied construction of the 42 km subway system in Mexico City. Concentrates on problems of organizing the course of fieldwork, and of cataloguing the artifacts recovered. [WTS]

342 **Hairs, Joya.** La operación rescate: un recurso de emergencia para salvar el patrimonio arqueológico de Guatemala (SGHG/A, 46:1/4, enero/dic. 1973, p. 166–168)

Describes work of the Tikal Association in 1970–71 to rescue 19 stelae from the site of Naranjo, Peten, and remove them for safekeeping in the face of serious threat of vandalism and theft. A plea for both government and private support for such rescue and protection work. [WTS]

343 **Hammond, Norman.** Cuello, 1979: a summary of the season (BISRA/BS, 8:3, 1980, p. 33–44, ill.)

Summary of excavations at an early through late formative site in northern Belize, including recovery of carbonized maize and successive plaster-faced buildings. [NH]

344 ———. Early Maya ceremonial at Cuello, Belize (AT/A, 54, 1980, p. 176–190, ill., map)

Reports on 1980 excavations at early through late formative Maya lowland site. Early buildings, stela of ca. AD 100, and mass sacrifice of ca. 400 BC are among important finds. [NH]

345 **Hartung, Horst.** Maquetas arquitectónicas precolombinas de Oaxaca (MV/BA, 25, 1977 [i.e. 1978] p. 387–400, bibl., ill.)

Descriptions of architectural features of small monolithic temple models from Oaxaca. These were not intended as preliminary construction models, but may have had a symbolic significance. [HvW]

346 ——— and **Anthony F. Aveni.** Reconsideration on a circular tower in the Central Yucatan region (IAA, 5:1, 1979, p. 1–18, ill., map, plates)

Cylindrical building at Puerto Rico, Campeche, near Xpuhil, resembles the first state of the Caracol at Chichen Itza. Horizontal shafts transecting the tower halfway up could indicate astronomical alignments and function. [NH]

347 **Hayden, B.** A fluted point from the Guatemalan highlands (UC/CA, 21, 1980, p. 702)

A Folsom-like obsidian point from the Villatoro site near Huehuetenango suggests occupation of the region 12,000-8000 years yrs. ago; extinct fauna in the vicinity may be evidence of human impact. [NH]

348 Healy, Paul F. and Heather McKillop.
Moho Cay, Belize: a preliminary report on the 1979 archaeological season (BISRA/BS, 8:6, 1980, p. 10–16)

Mangrove island site off Belize City has middle classic and early postclassic occupations, and dual role as trading port and manatee-hunting base. Bone carvings indicate links with Altun Ha on the mainland, 40 km northwest, and exotic goods show contacts south to highland Guatemala. [NH]

349 Henderson, John S. Atopula, Guerrero, and Olmec horizons in Mesoamerica.
New Haven: Department of Anthropology, Yale University, 1979. 256 p.; bibl.; (Yale University publications in anthropology; no. 77)

Two horizons—one earlier blackware and another later whiteware—characterized the spread of the Olmec style. As an elite manifestation with restricted associations, Olmec style may reflect the movement of high-status, pochteca-like groups, for whom these ceramic markers constituted statements of ethnic identity. Author considers militarism, and religion, and especially trade to explain the Olmec expansion. [WTS]

350 ——. El noroeste de Honduras y la frontera oriental maya (YAXKIN, 2:4, dic. 1978, p. 241–254, bibl.)

Discusses the archaeology of the Naco Valley in the light of recent fieldword and the extant documentary evidence. The La Sierra site may be the classic precursor of Naco; occupation earlier than late classic is sparse. [NH]

351 Ichon, Alain. Rescate arqueológico en la cuenca del Río Chixoy: pt. 1, informe preliminar. Guatemala: Editorial Santa Piedra *for* Centre National de la Recherche Scientifique (CNRS), Paris, n.d. 49 p.; ill.

Results of survey and excavations at Los Encuentros and Cauinal. Major periods of occupation are middle formative-early classic, epiclassic, and postclassic. [NH]

352 —— *et al.* Archéologie de sauvetage dans la Vallée du Rio Chixoy: 2. Cauinal. Guatemala: Editorial Santa Piedra *for* Centre National de la Recherche Scientifique (CNRS), Paris, 1980. 220 p.; ill.

The major postclassic site in the middle Chixoy drainage, Cauinal, lies athwart the Río Cala a few km from the confluence with the Chixoy. Middle formative occupa-

tion on the south bank of the Cala does not include any identified structures. One large and four smaller ceremonial precincts are surrounded by extensive settlement. Its architecture is characteristic of the highland postclassic. A useful report on well-conducted excavations. [NH]

353 Kampen, M.E. An early classic sculpture from El Tajin, Veracruz, Mexico (SEM/E, 1:2, 1978, p. 91–97, ill.)

Describes ball-player stela (Tajin Sculpture No. 1) comparing it to other later examples of Tajin ball game-associated relief art and to early classic Maya styles of depiction of the human figure. [WTS]

354 León y Gama, Antonio de. Descripción histórica y cronológica de las dos piedras: reproducción facsimilar de las primeras ediciones mexicanas, primera parte 1832. México: M.A. Porrúa, 1978. 116, 148 p.; 8 leaves of plates: ill. (Colección Tlahuicole; no. 1)

Facsimile edition of Pt. 1 (1792) and Pt. 2 (1832) of León y Gama's work. Describes the "Calendar Stone" and the monumental Coatlicue, stone sculptures recovered from the Zócalo of Mexico City, and discusses calendrical and astronomical systems of the Aztecs, making a disclaimer that none of this is really heretical. [WTS]

355 Lind, Michael. Postclassic and early colonial Mixtec houses in the Nochixtlan Valley, Oaxaca. Nashville, Tennessee: Vanderbilt University, 1979. 74 p.; 1 leaf of plates; bibl.; ill. (Publications in anthropology; no. 23)

Reports on excavations of poorly-preserved houses, identified as "noble" on the basis of their multiroom arrangements, each spanning the late postclassic-early colonial periods. Author postulates that the observed rebuildings represent continuity of domestic groups through time, based on ethnohistorically-derived models of the Mixtec kingdoms. [WTS]

356 Lischka, Joseph J. Reconocimiento arqueológico de algunos sitios en la Sierra de los Cuchumatanes (IAHG/AHG, 2:1, 1979, p. 11–19, bibl., ill., maps)

Surface survey of two sites (Agua Blanca and El Cedro) in the municipio de Chiautla, dept. of Huehuetenango, Guatemala. Both are above 3200 m altitude, and both have mound architecture, neither has confirmed dating, although the classic period is tentatively suggested. [WTS]

357   Littman, E.R. Maya Blue: a new perspective (SAA/AA, 45:1, 1980, p. 87–100)

Reviews work to date on identification of this pigment, suggesting that several clays besides attapulgite could have formed its basis, and that mineral coloring as well as indigo could have been used. [NH]

358   Lombardo de Ruiz, Sonia. Contribución del estudio de la forma a la iconografía de los murales de Cacaxtla (FAIC/CPPT, 16, 1979, p. 149–160, bibl., ill.)

Author doubts Marta Foncerrada's interpretations (see *HLAS 41:390–392*), i.e., that the Cacaxtla murals represent actual battle scenes. Recognizes a strong Maya tradition, and concludes that the paintings are allegorical, expressing the glorification of a lineage through human sacrifice. See also Diana López de Molina's "Los Murales Prehispánicos de Cacaxtla" in *Antropología e Historia* (INAH, México, 3:20, Dec. 1977, p. 2–8, bibl., ill.). [HvW]

359   López Austin, Alfredo. Iconografía mexica; el monolito verde del Templo Mayor (UNAM/AA, 16, 1979, p. 133–153, bibl., ill.)

Outlines an ethnohistorical and semantic approach to interpreting the relief carving spread over three sides of the monument. A male *pulque* god emerges from the breast of the *pulque* goddess Mayahuel after her death when she continues her astral course as the Moon. [HvW]

360   MacNeish, Richard S.; S. Jeffrey K. Wilkerson; and Antoinette Nelken-Terner. First annual report of the Belize Archaic Archaeological Reconnaissance. Andover, Massachusetts: Robert S. Peabody Foundation for Archaeology, 1980. 72 p.; fold. tables; ill.; maps.

Presents seriated preceramic sequence for the east-central Maya lowlands, with five phases spanning the period 9000–2000 BC (radiocarbon years). Dating is presently based on comparative lithic typology, including fishtailed points from the earliest phase, but shifting exploitation patterns are adumbrated that lead into the sedentary agricultural

mode known from Cuello (see *HLAS 41:404–405*). [NH]

361   Matheny, R.T. El Mirador, Peten, Guatemala: an interim report. Provo, Utah: New World Archaeological Foundation, 1980. 99 p.; ill. (Papers of the New World Archaeological Foundation; 45)

Describes the 1979 field season at the colossal late formative site in northern Peten. [NH]

362   Matos Moctezuma, Eduardo. Una máscara olmeca en el Templo Mayor de Tenochtitlan (UNAM/AA, 16, 1979, p. 11–19, bibl., ill., map)

Description of an intact Olmec greenstone mask (ca. 10th century BC) discovered among the offerings in the Great Temple (15th century AD). It probably originated in the Guerrero-Puebla-Oaxaca border region. [HvW]

363   ———. El proyecto Templo Mayor (INAH/B, 3:24, dic. 1978, p. 3–17, bibl., ill.)

Outlines objectives and procedures of the excavations and reconstruction conducted by INAH. This issue (92 p.) contains six additional articles on related topics, in particular, the large Coyolxuahqui sculpture. [HvW]

364   Mayer, Karl Herbert. Maya monuments: sculptures of unknown provenance in the United States. Ramona, California: Acoma Books, 1980. 86 p.; bibl.; plates.

Catalog of 70 stelae, lintels, panels, etc. in museums and private collections. Contains carefully researched descriptions of motifs of glyphic inscriptions, and 83 full-page photographs and line drawings. For monuments of unknown provenance in Europe, see *HLAS 41:417*. [HvW]

365   Moser, Christopher L. The head-effigies of the Mixteca Baja (UNC/K, 10:2, June 1977, p. 1–18, bibl., ill., map, tables)

Head-effigy (cabecita colosal) figurines of the Mixteca Baja may be of Nuine (middle-late classic) style, of which they have been considered diagnostic, but no direct associations substantiate this chronological placement. Classification of such figurines is presented, along with suggestions that they constitute features of a trophy-head cult. [WTS]

366 Müller, Florencia. La cerámica del centro ceremonial de Teotihuacan. México: INAH, 1978. 263 p.; appendix; bibl.; ill.; map; table.

Description of pottery types, by phases, from 200 BC to AD 1521. Although completed in 1968 and scantily illustrated, it is yet unsurpassed. For an abridged version, see *HLAS 31:1108*. [HvW]

367 Mundkur, Balaji. The alleged diffusion of Hindu divine symbols into precolumbian Mesoamerica: a critique (UC/CA, 19:3, Sept. 1978, p. 541–583, bibl., ill., plates, tables)

Author criticizes use of transpacific contacts to explain presumed similarities between Hindu and Mesoamerican calendarics. Maintains that they are based upon erroneous interpretation of the Hindu corpus, a misleading comparative methodology, and incompatibility with the known chronology of Hindu-Buddhist expansion. [WTS]

368 Nelson, F.W. and **B. Voorhies.** Trace element analysis of obsidian artifacts from three shell midden sites in the littoral zone, Chiapas, Mexico (SAA/AA, 45:3, 1980, p. 540–550)

Neutron-activation analysis indicates procurement of obsidian in the Chantuto Zone from Tajumulco (72 percent) and El Chayal (28 percent) during the period 3000–2000 BC, while at a later period, including the early classic, San Martín Jilotepeque largely replaced Chayal as a source, and Pachuca obsidian from central Mexico was also imported. [NH]

369 Parsons, Lee A. Precolumbian art: the Morton D. May and the Saint Louis Art Museum collections. New York: Harper & Row, 1980. 320 p.; bibl.; col. plates; ill.; index; maps; tables.

Contains good illustrations and descriptions of 468 fine examples of prehispanic art, including many outstanding specimens (331 from Mesoamerica, 43 from Lower Central America, 94 from Andean area). [HvW]

370 Pendergast, D.M. Lamanai—Indian Church: cross-section of Belize's past (BISRA/BS, 8:3, 1980, p. 19–32, ill.)

Short summary of work done since 1974 at a large preclassic through postclassic Maya center in north-central Belize. Settlement through the mid-19th century and massive late preclassic buildings are among many important findings. [NH]

371 Pollock, Harry Evelyn Dorr. The Puuc: an architectural survey of the hill country of Yucatan and northern Campeche, Mexico. Cambridge, Massachusetts: Peabody Museum of Archaeology and Ethnology, Harvard University, 1980. 600 p.; bibl.; ill.; index; envelope of 8 leaves of plates (5 fold.) (Memoirs of the Peabody Museum; v. 19)

Solid data-based report on extensive fieldwork, admirably illustrated. A basic source for the study of florescent sites and their architecture. [NH]

372 Prehistoric social, political, and economic development in the area of the Tehuacan Valley: some results of the Palo Blanco project. Edited by Robert D. Drennan; with contributions by John R. Alden et al.; Spanish text translated by Verónica Kennedy. Ann Arbor: Museum of Anthropology, University of Michigan, 1979. 259 p.; bibl.; ill. (Research reports in archaeology; contribution 6. Technical reports—Museum of Anthropology, University of Michigan; no. 11)

Consists of: papers on the construction sequence of the Purron dam, including commentary on its relation to carrying capacity (Spencer); on results of surface survey of an early Palo Blanco phase ceramic workshop (Redmond); preliminary reports on text excavations and surface surveys of the sites of Zuachilco (Alden) and Cuayucatepec (Drennan), and of the formative and classic periods of the Cuicatlan Canada (Spencer and Redmond); and a preliminary summary of botanical remains from the mentioned sites (Smith). All papers include summaries in Spanish. [WTS]

373 Quirigua reports. v. 1, Papers 1–5, site map. Robert J. Sharer, general editor. Philadelphia: University Museum, University of Pennsylvania, 1979. 1 v.; bibl.; ill. (University Museum monograph; no. 37)

Five papers presenting overall research goals and preliminary results of 1973–76 field seasons, emphasizing the clarification of the stratigraphic relations of major architectural groups at the site. Includes papers on

ington, D.C.: Dumbarton Oaks, Trust-
or Harvard University, 1978. 2 v.; bibl.;
plates (Studies in precolumbian art and
aeology; 19)

Pt. 1 identifies four stylistic phases of
-relief *danzantes*, spanning Monte Albán
nd possibly extending into Monte Albán
he last phase is Izapan-influenced and
ws probable ties with the site of Dainzu.
plores stylistic links of the carvings with
ramics, and of the Monte Albán materials
th others of Southern Mesoamerica. Pt. 2
an exhaustive illustrated catalogue of all
own *danzante* carvings, including frag-
ents. [WTS]

83 ———. El Mesón, Veracruz, and its
monolithic reliefs (MV/BA, 25:1, 1979
i.e. 1978) p. 83–138, bibl., ill.)

Investigations of the site and region,
and a comparative iconographic study of
three late preclassic/protoclassic monuments, with reference to pottery and figurines. Discusses their cultural context and
the survival and revival of older Olmec features. [HvW]

384 **Seven rock art sites** in Baja California.
Edited by Clement W. Meighan and
V.L. Pontoni. Socorro, N.M.: Ballena Press,
1978. 236 p.; bibl.; ill. (Ballena Press publications on North American rock art; no. 2)

A series of papers, each one dealing
with a different site and including an index
of motifs and tables of frequency of motifs of
rubbed, pecked, incised, or painted petroglyphs. Cites problems of chronology, attempting seriation and some obsidian hydration dating. Ethnographic analogies, often
necessarily attenuated, suggest functional
linkage with shamanism; geographic ties
with the rock art of the Great Basin, California, and the Southwest are also explored.
[WTS]

385 **Sheets, Payson D.** Environmental and
cultural effects of the Ilopango eruption in Central America (*in* Volcanic activity
and human ecology. Edited by Payson D.
Sheets, Donald K. Grayson. New York: Academic Press, 1979, p. 525–564, bibl., ill.,
maps, plates, table)

The Ilopango eruption in AD 260 ±
114 disrupted an established peasant-farming
society and enforced some migration to the
Maya lowlands, a phenomenon which is ar-
chaeologically detectable at sites such as Bar-

ton Ramie. Contains useful material on the
Joya de Ceren house, buried by the sixth-
century Laguna Caldera eruption. [NH]

386 **Shook, Edwin M.** and **Marion Popenoe
Hatch.** The ruins of El Balsamo, Department of Escuintla, Guatemala. Los Angeles: Institute of Archaeology, University of
California, Los Angeles, 1978. 37, 1 p.; 1 leaf
of plates; bibl.; ill. (*Journal of New World
Archaeology*; v. 3, no. 1)

Preliminary ceramic study of middle
preclassic site with ties to Monte Alto. Site
also contains monumental architecture, a
possible reservoir, and stone sculpture. Author explores ties with highland and coastal
Guatemala. [WTS]

387 **Sidrys, Raymond V.** and **John M. An-
dresen.** A second round structure from
Northern Belize, Central America (RAI/M,
13:4, Dec. 1978, p. 638–650)

Circular plastered platform at Chan
Chen, almost 11 m in diameter and 2 m
high, dates to late formative (based on carbon
dating and ceramics). Surface bears only
small stakeholes, which are likely to have
been structural, not astronomical. [NH]

388 **Simoni, Mireille.** Mexique précolombien: janvier–mars 1979, Ville du
Mans Musée de Tessé: catalogue de l'exposition. Le Mans, France: Jupilles, 1979. 40 p.;
ill.

Catalogue of exhibition at the Musée
de Tessé, Le Mans. Contains brief chronology
of Mesoamerica and descriptions and illustrations of 57 pieces from Central and West
Mexico, Veracruz, Oaxaca, and Maya area,
plus one each from Casas Grandes and Panama. [WTS]

389 **Solís Olguín, Felipe R.** Catálogo de la
escultura mexica del Museo de Santa
Cecilia Acatitlan. México: INAH, 1976. 41
p.; bibl.; ill.

Describes and illustrates 92 mostly
unpublished Aztec sculptures in a regional
museum near Mexico City. [HvW]

390 **Solórzano, Federico A.** Gancho de atlatl del occidente de México. Guadalajara: I.N.A.H., Centro Regional de Occidente,
Museo Regional de Guadalajara, 1976. 89
[i.e.150] p.; 59 ill.; bibl.; map (Cuadernos de
los museos)

Description and analysis of 47 bone
artifacts identified as atlatl hooks, from

the control of mosses and algae on monuments, and on a suggested earlier dating for Altar L. [WTS]

374 Rattray, Evelyn Childs. La cerámica de Teotihuacan: relaciones externas y cronología (UNAM/AA, 16, 1979, p. 51–70, bibl., ill.)

Presents an overview of the ceramic sequence from late Tlamimilolpa to Metepec phases (AD 300–750), distinguishing local wares from foreign ceramics from the Gulf coast, Oaxaca and Maya region, which are identified by style, and petrographic and neutron activation tests. Teotihuacan controlled the pottery trade, and increasingly imitated foreign wares using local clays. [HvW]

375 Rice, Don S. and **Prudence M. Rice.** Home on the range: aboriginal Maya settlement in the Central Petén Savannas (AIA/A, 32:6, 1979, p. 16–25, ill., maps)

Describes Maya use of Petén grasslands, mainly in late classic; same content as the formal report (see item **376**) but with good color illustrations. [NH]

376 ——— and ———. Introductory archaeological survey of the Central Petén Savannas, Guatemala: 1978 (*in* Studies in ancient Mesoamerica. Edited by J.A. Graham. Berkeley: University of California, Archaeological Research Facility, 1979, v. 4, p. 231–277, bibl., ill., maps)

Reports presence of mainly late classic site primarily near savanna/forest margins. Overspill and hunting seem likely factors in savanna settlement. [NH]

377 ——— and ———. The Northeast Petén revisited (SAA/AA, 45:3, July 1980, p. 432–454, maps, tables)

Study of settlement data based on the Yaxha-Sacnab survey suggests that patterns were initially determined by ecological factors, but that the impact of political and organizational factors increased through time as Maya society became more complex. [NH]

378 Rodríguez, François. Participación de la Misión Arqueológica y Etnológica Francesa en México en el proyecto del Departamento de Salvamento Arqueológico del I.N.A.H. en Guanajuato (Gto.), 1978: reporte de campo. s.l.: s.n., 1978 or 1979. 62, 22 leaves; ill.

Detailed diary of fieldwork done in

1978 at La Gavia and La P juato, with descriptions of of ceramic, lithic, and othe liminary report that draws [WTS]

379 Sanders, William T. T Huasteca archaeologic excavation: 1957 field season. Dept. of Anthropology, Univei souri-Columbia, 1978. 210 p.; plates; bibl.; ill. (University of monographs in anthropology; n

Archaeological informati date geological features in a regi terized by complex sequences of erosion, and shifting river channe tions interpretation of the Huaste ological sequence as a series of dis distinctive periods, preferring to er developmental continuities in cera [WTS]

380 Schele, Linda and **Peter Math** bodega of Palenque, Chiapas, Washington, D.C.: Dumbarton Oaks, 180 p.; bibl.; ill.

Catalogue of over 900 objects fr Palenque, photographed and drawn, ar according to provenience data that is re corded or could be reconstructed. Gives tensive treatment to glyphic material, st tablets, stucco work, and figurines; exclu ceramics or jade objects previously published. [WTS]

381 Schoeninger, Margaret J. Dietary reconstruction at Chalcatzingo, a formative period site in Morelos, Mexico. Ann Arbor: Museum of Anthropology, University of Michigan, 1979. 97 p.; bibl.; ill. (Contributions in human biology; no. 2. Technical reports—Museum of Anthropology, the University of Michigan; no. 9)

Confirms ranked society at this middle formative site on the basis of observation that status burials (defined as such on the basis of grave goods) have significantly less silicon as a bone component. This indicates the probability of higher-meat, lower-vegetable content in the childhood diets of these individuals. Neutron activation analysis and atomic absorption spectrometry confirm the results of chemical analysis. [WTS]

382 Scott, John F. The *danzantes* of Monte Albán. pt. 1, Text. pt. 2, Catalogue.

Michoacan and Jalisco, recovered from tombs but without provenience or associations. [WTS]

391 Stresser-Péan, G. San Antonio Nogalar; la Sierra de Tamaulipas et la frontière Nord-Est de la Mésoamérique. Mexico: Mission archéologique et ethnologique française au Mexique, 1977. 905 p.; bibl.; ill.; index (Etudes mésoaméricaines; v. 3)

Site report of excavations at San Antonio Nogalar, Tamaulipas, a site with Panuco III-early Panuco IV (Pitahaya-Zaquil) period occupation, with ceramic relationships with the Huasteca and, more distantly, with Teotihuacan. Implications for connections of Tamaulipas to the Huasteca. Chapters on Tamaulipas ethnohistory (16th century-present), on distribution of Indian populations and languages, and of modes of production from hunting-gathering to agriculture in the state. [WTS]

392 Stuart, G.E.; J.C. Scheffler; E.B. Kurjack; and J.W. Cottier. Map of the ruins of Dzibilchaltun, Yucatan, Mexico. New Orleans, Louisiana: Middle American Research Institute, Tulane University, 1979. 1 v. (Publication—Middle American Research Institute, Tulane University; 47)

Boxed sectional map of major Maya ceremonial precinct and settlement in northwestern Yucatan that complements Kurjack's 1974 settlement monograph (see *HLAS 37:643*) and the forthcoming excavation reports. Also provides a valuable data base for further work on Maya settlement structure. Overall key map contained in Kurjack. [NH]

393 Taladoire, Eric. Ball-game scenes and ball courts in West Mexican archaeology: a problem in chronology (IAI/I, 5, 1979, p. 33–44, bibl., map, table)

Discusses the distribution, typology, and dating of ball courts and ceramic models of western Mexico as well as their relationship to those of southern and northern Mexico. [HvW]

394 Tichy, Franz. El calendario solar como principio de organización del espacio para poblaciones y lugares sagrados (FAIC/CPPT, 15, 1978, p. 153–163, bibl., ill.)

Explains the interrelationship of astronomy, time, and space as a guiding principle for the orientation of ceremonial structures and the layout of large and small settlements. [HvW]

395 Turner, B.L., II and W.C. Johnson. A Maya dam in the Copan Valley, Honduras (SAA/AA, 44:2, 1979, p. 299–305)

Probable classic period masonry dam in the Quebrada Petapilla seems to have impounded a spring, providing a small pond and perhaps a head of water for canal irrigation. [NH]

396 von Winning, Hasso. Betrachtungen zu einem gefälschten polychromen Maya-Gefäss (MV/BA, 26:2, 1978 [i.e. 1979] p. 233–240, bibl., ill.)

Demonstrates that the spurious polychrome design on a genuine Maya vase is a misinterpreted copy of a published vase from Tikal. [HvW]

397 Warren, John R. and Ricardo J. Warren. Petroglyphs in five rock shelters near Tegucigalpa, Honduras (UNC/K, 10:2, June 1977, p. 89–93, plates)

Describes and illustrates petroglyph motifs—zoomorphic, anthropomorphic, and geometric. [WTS]

398 Webster, D. Spatial bounding and settlement history at three walled northern Maya centers (SAA/AA, 45:4, 1980, p. 834–844)

Defensive walls at Chacchob, Dzonot Ake, and Cuca mark fortified elite enclaves that housed community ritual and administrative functions together with high-status households. [NH]

NATIVE SOURCES

399 Barthel, Thomas S. Enigmatisches im Codex Vaticanus 3773: Kosmogramm un Eschatologie; ein Beitrag zur Indo-Mexikanistik (MLV/T, 28, Nov. 1979, p. 83–122, bibl., ill.)

Interpretation of folios Nos. 13–16, which depict temples with ring-eyed birds, owls, scolopenders, and serpents, in combination with day signs. These are analyzed in terms of structural composition, calendric sequence, contrasts and parallels, and their cosmological significance (dealing with the fate of the soul after death). Pt. 2 discusses correspondences with East Indian literature, and pt. 2 applies these to specific iconographic features to explain a disguised underlying Hinduistic cosmological model. [HvW]

400 ———. "Tollan" aus palencanischer Sicht (IAI/I, 5, 1979, p. 111–143, bibl.)

Interpretations of hieroglyphic texts at Palenque and Piedras Negras indicate that the term *tollan* has been applied to different classic period metropolises, the first being Teotihuacan (in the northern quadrant); the second, Tikal (east); and the third, Palenque (west). Comments also on successive epi-classic and postclassic designations (e.g., Tollan Xicocotitlan = Tula), and their location. [HvW]

401 Dütting, Dieter. "Bats" in the Usumacinta-Valley: remarks on inscriptions of Bonampak and neighboring sites in Chiapas, Mexico (DGV/ZE, 103:1, 1978, p. 1–56, bibl., ill.)

Suggests that "bat" glyphs in inscriptions refer to late classic military intruders in the Lower Usumacinta basin. [NH]

402 ———. On the hieroglyphic inscriptions of three monuments from Piedras Negras, Guatemala (DGV/ZE, 104:1, 1979, p. 17–63, bibl., ill., plates, tables)

Attempted decipherment of Stelae 1 and 3 and Lintel 3. [NH]

403 ———. Sustina gratia, an inquiry into the Farmer's Almanacs of the Codex Dresden (IAI/I, 5, 1979, p. 145–170, bibl., ill.)

The heliacal disappearance of the Pleiades signals the beginning of the rainy season and of the agricultural cycle with its "sustaining grace," the maize plant or sustenance. Author discusses this topic in terms of passages in Codex Dresden and epigraphic texts, with explicit interpretations of phonetic values of various graphemes and reference to deities, including God K. [HvW]

404 Graham, Ian. Corpus of Maya hieroglyphic inscriptions. v. 2, pt. 3: Ixkun, Ucanal, Ixtutz, Naranjo. Cambridge, Massachusetts: Peabody Museum of Archaeology and Ethnology, Harvard University, 1980. 1 v.; ill.; map.

Continuation of ambitious project to publish all Maya inscriptions, with the best drawings and photographs now available. A basic research tool and invaluable record. [NH]

405 Kelley, David H. Astronomical identities of Mesoamerican gods (Archaeoastronomy [Supplement to *Journal of the History of Astronomy*, v. 11, 1980, Giles, England] 1980, p. S1–S54)

Ambitious and radical assertion that most planets (including Mercury, Mars, Jupiter, and Saturn) were observed and linked with Mesoamerican deities. Time measured from a base date 12 Lamat 1 Pop (Maya Calendar Round) gives intervals that match synodic periods of the planets of lunar phases. The calendar is unitary and early. [NH]

406 Prem, Hanns J. Aztec writing considered as a paradigm of Mesoamerican scripts (*in* Mesoamérica. Homenaje a Paul Kirchhoff. Edited by Barbro Dalhgren. México: INAH, 1979, p. 104–118, bibl., ill.)

Systematic analytical exposition of the structure, function, and scope of Mesoamerican hieroglyphic writing includes comparison between Aztec and Maya script. [HvW]

407 Reina, R.E. and **R.M. Hill.** Lowland Maya subsistence: notes from ethnohistory and ethnography (SAA/AA, 45:1, 1980, p. 74–79)

Colonial documentary description of Alta Verapaz subsistence suggests smoking of maize, perhaps for *chultun* storage, and use of *ramón*. [NH]

ARCHAEOLOGY: Caribbean Area

W. JERALD KENNEDY, *Associate Professor of Anthropology, Florida Atlantic University*

IN *HLAS 41* (see p. 56–57), I remarked that, in contrast with the previous two years, there was a growing volume of published works in both the Caribbean and Central America. At this writing, the rate of publications has diminished somewhat yet archaeological research in both regions remains viable as this bibliography attests.

CARIBBEAN ISLANDS: While this bibliography makes no claim to be comprehensive it is evident that research is being conducted on many of the islands in the Caribbean. For example, there are articles dealing with the archaeology of Antigua, the Bahamas, St. Kitts, Trinidad, Barbados, Martinique, Cuba, Hispaniola, Puerto Rico, and the Turks and Caicos. Of the published reports in this area several trends are apparent: 1) an interest in historical archaeology is evident. Seven monographs and articles deal with archaeology of the colonial period. Findings related to the early historic period are reported from the Dominican Republic (items **414** and **446–448**), Haiti (item **432**), and Barbados (items **429** and **430**); 2) Taino art and mythology are frequent themes and subjects of six monographs in which relevant artifactual and ethnohistoric data are brought to bear in the presentations; and 3) a number of articles describe and analyze rock art, both pictographs and petroglyphs, in the Dominican Republic (items **441, 445, 449** and **450**).

The serious student and scholar working in this area will find Badillos' Anthropological/Caribbean bibliography (1977) a valuable reference tool (item **413**). While several articles of theoretical importance are cited one should note the important works of Veloz (item **461**) and Koslowski (item 437), both of which are bound to provoke lively discussions.

Two important meetings were held. The Second Bahamas Conference on Caribbean Prehistory was held at Molloy College, Rochville Centre, New York, October, 1978. The proceedings have been published by the *Florida Anthropologist* (see item **422**).

The Eighth International Congress for the Study of Precolumbian Culture in the Lesser Antilles convened in July 1979 on St. Kitts. Over 125 scientists, representing 24 nations, attended. The proceedings from this conference were published by the Arizona State University (see item **434**).

Archaeological research continues in the Caribbean where excavations in Haiti on the historic site of Puerto Real are being conducted by Ray Willis (University of Florida) and several projects are underway in the Dominican Republic.

Louis Allaire (University of Manitoba) continues his archaeological work on the island of Martinique. Shaun Sullivan (Ph.D. candidate, University of Illinois) conducted excavations on the Middle Caicos Islands.

R. Christopher Goodwin (Smithsonian Institution) directed an Archaeological Field School in the summer of 1980, on St. Kitts and Nevis (for further comments, see "Current Research Section," *American Antiquity*, 46: 1, 1981, p. 200).

CENTRAL AMERICA: The review of Olga Linares (item **481**) constitutes a timely examination of much of the recent significant research in Lower Central America. The author comments on the need for additional research beyond the descriptive level of this region.

While much research is descriptive, the subjects are varied and range from site reports to analyses of ceramics and stone sculpture. Also, publications indicate that research is being conducted in every Central American country. The book by Mary Helms (item **477**) is a fine example of the successful combination of archaeological data, ethnohistoric documents, and the author's creativity. Indeed, she goes far beyond the level of description as she examines many facets of sociopolitical complexity in precolumbian Panama.

The Forty-third International Congress of Americanists met in Vancouver, B.C., Canada, in August, 1979. It should also be noted that an advanced seminar in Central American archaeology was held at the School of American Research, Santa Fe, N.M. in April, 1980. Publication of the symposia papers is planned.

Oscar Fonseca (University of Costa Rica) conducted excavations at the Guayabo site in Costa Rica and Michael Snarskis (Nacional Museum of Costa Rica) continues his ongoing research in Highland and the Atlantic Watershed regions of Costa Rica.

Two unpublished but highly significant doctoral dissertations should also be mentioned:

Drolet, Robert. Cultural settlement along the moist Caribbean slopes of eastern Panama. University of Illinois, 1980.

Goodwin, R. Christopher. The prehistoric cultural ecology of St. Kitts, West Indies. Arizona State University, 1979.

ANTILLES

408   Alegría, Mela Pons. Taino Indian art (AIA/A, 33:4, 1980, p. 8–15, ill.)

Discusses Taino Indian art from the Greater Antilles including ritual and ceremonial objects (e.g., duhos, spatulas, zemis) as well as petroglyphs and ceremonial structures.

409   Alegría, Ricardo E. Apuntes en torno a la mitología de los indios taínos de las Antillas Mayores y sus orígenes suramericanos. Santo Domingo: Centro de Estudios Avanzados de Puerto Rico y el Caribe, Museo del Hombre Dominicano, 1978. 178, 1 p.; ill.

Delightful discussion of four Taino mythological themes in early historical sources. Compares myths dealing with the creation of man, the origin of women, the divine twins, and great flood myths with similar but variant South American versions.

410   ———. Etnografía taína y los conquistadores (in International Congress for the Study of the Precolumbian Cultures of the Lesser Antilles, 8th, St. Kitts, 1979. Proceedings [see item **434**] p. 430–446)

Author notes that many Taino objects were brought to Europe by returning conquistadors. Archaeological excavations have recovered many objects similar to those mentioned in early historical documents. Contains illustrations.

411   Allaire, Louis. On the historicity of Carib migrations in the Lesser Antilles (SAA/AA, 45:2, April 1980, p. 238–245, ill., map)

Interesting article that seriously questions data on historical expansion of the Caribs from Northeastern South America to West Indies. Suggests reevaluation of archaeological and ethnohistorical data.

412   Armstrong, Douglas V. Shell fish gatherers of St. Kitts: a study of archaic settlement and subsistence patterns (in International Congress for the Study of the Precolumbian Cultures of the Lesser Antilles, 8th, St. Kitts, 1979. Proceedings [see item **434**] p. 152–167)

Presents a model of archaic subsistence practices and settlement patterns on St. Kitts and discusses utilization of this model for predicting site locations.

413   Badillo, Sued Jalil. Bibliografía antropológica para el estudio de los pueblos indígenas en el Caribe. Santo Domingo: Ediciones Fundación García-Arévalo, 1977. 579 p.

Excellent bibliographic reference work, despite many omissions, book is conveniently arranged into two parts: 1) Subject: general works, archaeology, ethnography, geography, history, linguistics; and 2) Areas: insular Caribbean and wider Circum-Caribbean region.

414   Borrell B., Pedro J. Arqueología submarina en la República Dominicana. Fotografías, Federico Schad y Pedro J. Borrell B. Santo Domingo: Comisión de Rescate Arqueológico Submarino, Grupo de Investigaciones Submarinas, 1980. 138 p.; ill.

Describes formation of underwater salvage archaeology program (GIS) in the Dominican Republic. Descriptive summaries acquaint reader with important finds and ongoing projects (e.g., the salvage operations of two important 18th-century galleons, the "Nuestra Señora de Guadalupe," and the "Conde de Tolosa" in the Bay of Samana). Well illustrated with pictures of artifacts recovered from various underwater sites.

415   Carbone, Víctor. The paleoecology of the Caribbean area (The Florida Anthropologist [Florida Anthropological Society,

Gainesville] 33 : 3, Sept. 1980, p. 9–119)

Presents paleoecological data in support of a series of abrupt climatic shifts during the Holocene in the Caribbean. Suggests further study of cultural-environmental relationships, and reaffirms need for more systematic and thorough collection of pollen, plants, and macro/micro faunal remains. See item **422.**

416   Caro Alvarez, José A. La coboba. Fotografías de Max Pou, V. Krantz, Leonel Castillo. Santo Domingo: Museo del Hombre Dominicano, 1977. 29 p.; chiefly ill.

Brief discussion of a Taino ritual, the Coboba ceremony, is followed by illustrations of a small number of zemis, duhos and vomit spatulas associated with this rite.

417   Chanlatte-Baik, Luis and **Yvonne Narganes.** La Hueca Vieques: nuevo complejo cultural agroalfarero en la arqueología antillana (*in* International Congress for the Study of the Precolumbian Cultures of the Lesser Antilles, 8th, St. Kitts, 1979. Proceedings [see item **434**] p. 501–523)

Preliminary report on the La Hueca site on Vieques Island. Authors note site and region will provide many answers to Caribbean cultural history especially regarding the Saladoid series in the Greater and Lesser Antilles. Illustrated.

418   Daggett, Richard E. The trade process and the implications of trade in the Bahamas (The Florida Anthropologist [Florida Anthropological Society, Gainesville] 33:3, Sept. 1980, p. 143–151)

Examination of various types of precolumbian trade followed by a consideration of its presence and impact in the Bahamas. See item **422.**

419   Dittert, Alfred E.; Elisabeth S. Sipe; and **Christopher Goodwin.** The conservation of shell and shell artifacts from archaeological contexts (*in* International Congress for the Study of the Precolumbian Cultures of the Lesser Antilles, 8th, St. Kitts, 1979. Proceedings [see item **434**] p. 218–236)

Very useful paper dealing with the treatment, cleaning, and stabilization of molluscan shells.

420   Faught, Michael. Better than tree rings? (*in* International Congress for the Study of the Precolumbian Cultures of the Lesser Antilles, 8th, St. Kitts, 1979. Proceedings [see item **434**] p. 214–217)

Preliminary investigation and discussion of the utilization of bivalve species (Donax Denticulatus) shell ring growth as a potential chronologic marker.

421   Fernández Méndez, Eugenio. Arte y mitología de los indios taínos de los Antillas Mayores. San Juan, Puerto Rico: Ediciones CEMI, 1979. 109 p.; 17 leaves of plates; bibl.; ill.

Discussion of the art and mythology of the Tainos in the Caribbean area. Writer presents evidence that Taino cosmological belief system can be linked to precolumbian cultures in the intermediate area and Mesoamerica. Many similarities appear more evident to author than to this reviewer.

422   *The Florida Anthropologist.* Florida Anthropological Society. Vol. 33, No. 3, Sept. 1980–   . Gainesville.

Contains seven papers delivered at the Second Bahamas Conference on Caribbean Prehistory in Oct. 1978, at Molloy College, Rockville Centre, New York. See items **415, 418, 424, 428, 435** and **460.**

423   Fortuna, Luis. El maíz en La Indígena (MHD/B, 9:13, 1980, p. 159–164)

Author considers the available evidence supporting the appearance of maize in precolumbian Hispaniola.

424   Glazier, Steven D. Aboriginal Trinidad in the 16th century (The Florida Anthropologist [Florida Anthropological Society, Gainesville] 33 : 3, Sept. 1980, p. 152–159)

Utilizing historic, archaeological, and linguistic data, author concludes that during the 16th century there were various Carib-speaking groups sharing island of Trinidad and others, including true Arawaks. Findings also support view that aboriginal populations of 16th-century Trinidad share more cultural features with tropical forest mainland groups. See item **422.**

425   ———. Theoretical approaches to the study of Trinidad's prehistory (Journal of the Virgin Islands Archaeological Society [Frederickstad, St. Croix, Virgin Islands] 5, 1978, p. 32–55)

Brief description of various theoretical approaches taken in Trinidadian archaeological research.

426 Goodwin, R. Christopher. Demographic change and the carib-shell dichotomy (*in* International Congress for the Study of the Precolumbian Cultures of the Lesser Antilles, 8th, St. Kitts, 1979. Proceedings [see item **434**] p. 45–68)

Utilizing demographic change model, author examines subsistence and settlement pattern changes on St. Kitts during Saladoid series. Concludes that shift from crabs and terrestrial fauna to shallow water, and finally to deep-sea fishing was part of overall intensification of food production prompted by rapid growth of island's population.

427 ——. The Lesser Antillan Archaic: new data from St. Kitts (Journal of the Virgin Islands Archaeological Society [Frederickstad, St. Croix, Virgin Islands] 5, 1978, p. 6–16, plates)

Report on the discovery of two Archaic-period shell middens on St. Kitts. Author notes radiocarbon dates of 2123 BC and 198 BC and suggests possibility that they represent two distinct Archaic traditions.

428 Granberry, Julian. A brief history of Bahamian archaeology (The Florida Anthropologist [Florida Anthropological Society, Gainesville] 33:3, Sept. 1980, p. 83–93)

Historical sketch of archaeological investigations in the Bahamas, Turks, and Caicos Islands. Noting that systematic work has just begun, author suggests that systematic and methodical excavations be conducted over all the Bahamian Archipelago. See item **422.**

429 Handler, Jerome S. and **Frederick W. Lange.** Plantation slavery on Barbados, West Indies (AIA/A, 32:4, July/August 1979, p. 45–52)

One of the most complete archaeological and historical studies of New World slave populations to date. Authors discuss their findings from a project on Barbados (1971–73) that was specifically designed to yield information on domestic life and mortuary practices in slave villages which is not available from written sources. Information was gathered from excavations and surface collections representing 14 sugar plantations and a slave cemetery. Data from 92 burials ranging in date from late 17th century to first decade of the 19th were also recorded. Results show early pervasive influence of West African traditions with increased European influences through time.

430 ——; ——; and **Charles Oser.** Carnelian beads in necklaces from a slave cemetery in Barbados, West Indies (Ornament [A quarterly of jewelry and personal adornment, Los Angeles] 4:2, 1979, p. 15–20)

Brief discussion of results from excavations of a slave cemetery in Barbados, West Indies (see item **429**). Includes artifact inventory, especially glass beads and two unique (for the New World) carnelian beads, most likely from India. Since there were no direct trade routes, authors speculate that carnelian beads were transported to Barbados directly from Southeast Africa. They also reconstruct aspects of 17th- and 18th-century social systems.

431 Harris, Peter. Excavation report: lovers' retreat period IV, Tobago (*in* International Congress for the Study of the Precolumbian Cultures of the Lesser Antilles, 8th, St. Kitts, 1979. Proceedings [see item **434**] p. 524–552)

Report on Lovers' Retreat site reveals admixture of two pottery traditions. Author believes they represent confirmation of Carib men/Arawakan women integration, as recorded by early chronicles.

Helms, Mary W. Succession to high office in precolumbian circum-Caribbean chiefdoms. See item **995.**

432 Hodges, William. Puerto Real: excavation dans la Plaine de Limonade (IFH/C, 147, déc, 1979, p. 37–52, ill., plates)

Account of preliminary archaeological excavations at Puerto Real, Plains of Limonade, Haiti. Discovery of Meillac ceramics established a precolumbian component at this site. Subsequent excavations consisted of test trenches that defined several structures believed to be early colonial Spanish settlement of Puerto Real.

433 Hoffman, Charles A. The outpost concept and the Mesoamerican connection (*in* International Congress for the Study of the Precolumbian Cultures of the Lesser Antilles, 8th, St. Kitts, 1979. Proceedings [see item **434**] p. 307–316, bibl.)

Thoughtful article utilizing the "outpost" social-unit/port-of-trade concept in an effort to explain the origins of cultural florescene in the Greater Antilles with respect to the Meso American interaction sphere. Uses the southwest Casa Grande site and the Mexican trader class, the Pochteca as comparative examples. Author suggests steps which might be taken to verify his propositions.

434 International Congress for the Study of the Precolumbian Cultures of the Lesser Antilles, *8th, St. Kitts, 1979.* Proceedings. Edited by Suzanne M. Lewenstein. Tempe: Arizona State University, 1980. 623 p.; bibl.; ill.; maps; plates; tables.

Consists of 42 articles dealing with many facets of Caribbean prehistory (e.g., island biogeography, Antillean Archaic, symbolism, organic remains, trade, ethnohistory, methodology, theory). For individual annotations of articles, see items **410, 412, 417, 419–420, 426, 431, 433, 436, 439, 443–444, 452, 454, 457–459, 464, 466–467, 655, 732, 823** and **829–830.**

435 Irving, Rouse. The concept of series in Bahamian archaeology (The Florida Anthropologist [Florida Anthropological Society, Gainesville] 33 : 3, Sept. 1980, p. 94–98)

Significant discussion of confusion surrounding series concept in Caribbean prehistory. Using examples from Bahamian archaeology author notes that his ceramic units are to be understood as series of ceramic styles while others treat series as ceramic types. In final analysis, the two approaches complement one another, with the former used primarily to study population groups and the latter more appropriate for dealing with the temporal dimension. See item **422.**

436 Jones, Alick R. Animal food and human population at Indian Creek, Antigua (*in* International Congress for the Study of the Precolumbian Cultures of the Lesser Antilles, 8th, St. Kitts, 1979. Proceedings [see item **434**] p. 264–273)

Results of three excavations at Indian Creek, Antigua. Identifies and analyzes for their subsistence potential 55 species of invertebrates. Author estimates population was less than 50 persons.

437 Koslowski, Janusz K. In search of the evolutionary pattern of the preceramic cultures of the Caribbean (MHD/B, 9 : 13, 1980, p. 61–79)

Excellent article utilizing recent data to argue that previous classificatory systems applied to Caribbean prehistory are inadequate. Considers Paleoindian and Mesoindian modes of adaptation.

438 López-Baralt, Mercedes. El mito taíno: raíz y proyecciones en la Amazonia continental. Mapas y fotografías, Bolívar Aparicio. Río Piedras, Puerto Rico: Ediciones Huracán, 1976. 108 p.; bibl.; ill. (Colección Semilla)

Interesting book on Taino mythology examines relationships that existed between Arawakans of the Antilles and of Northeast South America.

439 Lundberg, Emily R. Old and new problems in the study of Antillean ceramic traditions (*in* International Congress for the Study of the Precolumbian Cultures of the Lesser Antilles, 8th, St. Kitts, 1979. Proceedings [see item **434**] p. 131–138)

Consideration of Caribbean preclassic complexes in light of recent archaeological data. These data indicate the likelihood that several aceramic cultures entered the Caribbean. Author suggests that revisions are due in the treatment of Paleo-Indians as distinct traditions.

440 Mattioni, Mario. Finaltés culturelles de la recherche archéologique aux Antilles (*in* Cultural traditions and Caribbean identity: the question of patrimony. Edited by S. Jeffrey K. Wilkerson. Gainesville: Center for Latin American Studies, University of Florida, 1980, p. 139–156)

Writer considers the cultural aims of archaeological research in the Caribbean, suggesting that we can better understand the present by looking at the past. Discusses elements such as the geographical sphere, cultural "space," and current ethnic order.

441 Morbán Laucer, Fernando A. El arte rupestre de la República Dominicana: petroglifos de la Provincia de Azua. Santo Domingo: Fundación García-Arévalo, 1979. 93 p.; 1 fold. leaf of plates; bibl.; ill. (Serie Investigaciones—Fundación García-Arévalo; no. 9)

Well illustrated monograph on rock art in the Dominican Republic. Chap. 1 deals with general features and varied motifs and techniques employed in this media. Chap. 2 considers petroglyphs found at different locations in Azua province.

442 ———. Los figurines de arcilla en la prehistoria (MHD/B, 9:13, 1980, p. 81–115)

Writer discusses large number of clay figurines found in the Dominican Republic and the New World and offers various interpretations.

443 **Myers, Robert A.** Archaeological materials from Dominica in North American and European museums (*in* International Congress for the Study of Precolumbian Cultures of the Lesser Antilles, 8th, St. Kitts, 1979. Proceedings [see item **434**] p. 473–480)

Brief list of various museum collections possessing archaeological specimens from the Island of Dominica.

444 **Nicholson, Desmond.** The atlatl-spur: a newly identified artifact from the Lesser Antilles (*in* International Congress for the Study of the Precolumbian Cultures of the Lesser Antilles, 8th, St. Kitts, 1979. Proceedings [see item **434**] p. 394–405)

Compares probable atlatl spurs found at the Indian Creek site on Antigua with atlatl spurs from California and other New World cultures.

445 **Olmos Cordones, Hernán** and **Abelardo Jiménez Lambertus.** Primer reporte de petroglifos de los sitios Palma Caña y El Palero, Provincia La Vega (MHD/B, 9:13, 1980, p. 125–152)

Preliminary report on petroglyphs found at Palma Caña and El Palero sites in La Vega Province, Dominican Republic, includes interpretation of their design motifs.

446 **Ortega, Elpidio** and **Carmen Fondeur.** Arqueología de la Casa del Cordón. Dibujos en portada de Aida Ripley de Mencía. Santo Domingo: Fundación Ortega Alvarez, 1979. 97 p.; bibl.; ill. (Serie científica; 2)

Brief but interesting study of artifacts found at historic site, Casa del Cordón, Santo Domingo. Built in 1503, it was one of first stone buildings constructed in 16th century. Authors provide information about customs, preferences, and social positions of numerous occupants of house over 400 years. The 35,318 artifacts, principally ceramic, found therein were not excavated stratigraphically but studied as collection. One of more interesting findings are five sherds of Chicoid series, suggesting early servants were slaves taken from indigenous population.

447 ——— and ———. Arqueología de los monumentos históricos de Santo Domingo. San Pedro de Macorís: Universidad Central del Este, 1978. 244 p.; bibl.; ill. (Serie científica; 7)

Summary of 16 houses and monuments in the Dominican Republic that have been partially excavated and studied over past 10 years. Analysis of ceramic material found at these sites adds to our knowledge of colonial-period ceramics in the Caribbean.

448 ——— and ———. Estudio de la cerámica del período indo-hispano de la Antigua Concepción de la Vega. Santo Domingo: Fundación Ortega Alvarez, 1978 [i.e. 1979]. 101 p.; bibl.; ill. (Serie científica; 1)

Detailed analysis of 896 ceramics excavated from the early colonial-period city of La Concepción de la Vega, Dominican Republic, which reached its maximum size between 1510–26. Prime concern of this study is to demonstrate that new ceramics from La Vega Vieja are products of local Indian potters who absorbed European influences rather than of Central American origin. Well illustrated.

449 **Pagán Perdomo, Dato.** Aspectos zooarqueológicos y geográficos en el arte rupestre de Santo Domingo (MHD/B, 9:13, 1980, p. 49–60)

Author reports on the 77 recorded examples of rock art in the Dominican Republic. Analysis of petroglyphs focuses on the frequency of zoomorphic motifs, geographic distribution, and relationship of petroglyphs with specific precolumbian populations in the Dominican Republic.

450 ———. Nuevas pictografías en la Isla de Santo Domingo: las Cuevas de Borbón. Santo Domingo: Museo del Hombre Dominicano, 1978. 130 p.; bibl.; ill. (Colección Estudio y arte; no. 4)

Excellent and well-illustrated book examines remarkable cave art of recently discovered Borbón Cave, San Cristóbal province, Dominican Republic. General section is followed by chapters which contain illustrations of many of the 963 pictographs. Relates specific symbols to Taino mythology, deities, rituals, sexual scenes, as well as island fauna and flora.

451 ——— and **Manuel García Arévalo.** Notas sobre las pictografías y petroglifas de las Guacaras de Comedero Arriba y el Hoyo de Sanabe, República Dominicana (MHD/B, 9:14, 1980, p. 13–56)

Discussion of rock art found at two cave sites in Sánchez Ramírez province, Dominican Republic. Guacaras site was C14 dated 2775 ± 215 BP.

452 Pantel, Agamemnon G. Canejas Cave site excavations, Fort Buchanan Military Reservation, San Juan, Puerto Rico (in International Congress for the Study of the Precolumbian Cultures of the Lesser Antilles, 8th, St. Kitts, 1979. Proceedings [see item **434**] p. 363–393)

Discussion of cultural resource survey of Canejas Cave site, Puerto Rico.

453 Petitjean Roget, Henry. L'art des Arawak et des Caraïbes des Petites Antilles: analyse de la décoration des céramiques. Fort de France: Centre d'études régionales Antilles-Guyane, 1978. 60, 105 p.; bibl.; ill. (Les Cahiers du CERAG; no. 20)

Discussion and analysis of selected design motifs on Carib and Arawakan ceramics in the Lesser Antilles. Copiously illustrated.

454 ———. Faragunaol, Zemi du Miel Chez les tainos des Grandes Antilles (in International Congress for the Study of the Precolumbian Cultures of the Lesser Antilles, 8th, St. Kitts, 1979. Proceedings [see item **434**] p. 195–205)

Utilizing an ethnolinguistic approach to works of Brother Ramon Pané, author attempts to analyze a Taino myth which deals with the discovery of wild honey and the initial domestication of Melipona bees.

455 Rimoli, Renato. Restos de fauna en el sitio arqueológico de Escalera Abajo, provincia Puerto Plato (MHD/B, 9:13, 1980, p. 171–192)

Discusses in some detail zooarchaeological data from two cave sites in Escalera Abajo, Dominican Republic.

456 Ripley, George. El Cemi taino de algodón (MHD/B, 9:13, 1980, p.115–124)

Detailed examination of famous cotton Zemi, now in Turin. Author concludes it represented an important personage, perhaps a participant in the Cohoba ceremony.

457 Robinson, Linda Sickler. The crab motif in aboriginal West Indian shell-work (in International Congress for the Study of the Precolumbian Cultures of the Lesser Antilles, 8th, St. Kitts, 1979. Proceedings [see item **434**] p. 187–194)

Author isolates and identifies the crab as a design motif on shell artifacts from the Folmer Andersen Collection, St. Croix, Virgin Islands.

458 Robol, M.J. and **A.L. Smith.** Archaeological implications of some C14 dating on Saba and St. Kitts (in International Congress for the Study of the Precolumbian Cultures of the Lesser Antilles, 8th, St. Kitts, 1979. Proceedings [see item **434**] p. 168–176)

Recent studies of Mt. Miserys' pyroclastic stratigraphy on St. Kitts suggest a more varied and active history than has been assumed. Considers likelihood of this activity influencing population at northern end of island. Shell artifacts found overlying most recent pyroclastic flow at Saba date from 3155 ± 65 BP.

459 Ruppe, Reynold J. Sea level rise and Caribbean prehistory (in International Congress for the Study of the Precolumbian Cultures of the Lesser Antilles, 8th, St. Kitts, 1979. Proceedings [see item **434**] p. 331–337)

Discusses rising sea levels and their implications in the drowning of terrestrial archaeological sites in the Circum-Caribbean region. Expresses optimism about ability to locate many of these sites, and stresses their importance in better understanding New World population movements.

460 Sullivan, Shaun D. An overview of the 1976 and 1978 archaeological investigations in the Caicos Islands (The Florida Anthropologist [Florida Anthropological Society, Gainesville] 33:3, Sept. 1980, p. 120–142)

Summary of 10-month survey (1976–78) in Turks and Caicos Islands, in which 41 sites were recorded. Most sites (35) were found on Middle Caicos; occupation dates for those sites studied are from AD 750–AD 900. Preliminary findings of the survey are significant. Other sites (26) had only imported (Meillacoid) ceramics, and one site (M-6) appears to be a planned community exhibitinig plazas, a ball court, and distinct residential zones. Author considers important questions regarding trade and colonization. See item **422**.

Vega, Bernardo. Los cacicazgos de la Hispaniola. See item **5433**.

461   Veloz Maggiolo, Marcio. Medioambiente y adaptación yumana en la prehistoria de Santo Domingo. v. 2. 2. ed. Santo Domingo: Ediciones de Taller, 1976–1977. 2 v.; bibl.; ill. (Biblioteca Taller; 63. v. 2: Colección Historia y sociedad; no. 30. v. 2: Publicaciones de la Universidad Autónoma de Santo Domingo; v. 200)

   Second monograph by specialist in Antillean culture history focuses on modes of production and subsistence orientation of precolumbian populations in the Dominican Republic. Volume treats beginnings of agriculture and presents considerable data based on recent archaeological findings in Cuba, Puerto Rico, and especially the Dominican Republic. Notes great variety of subsistence adaptation and argues for a revision of earlier models.

462   ——— and Elpidio Ortega. Nuevos hallazgos arqueológicos en la costa norte de Santo Domingo (MHD/B, 9:13, 1980, p. 11–48)

   Interesting summary article in which authors discuss preliminary findings from a 1978 reconnaissance along the north coast of the Dominican Republic. Article plots distribution of 16 sites and attempts initial temporal ordering of sites. Authors' long range goal is to analyze stylistic differences in ceramics found in this area in order to redefine the geopolitical boundaries of precolumbian chiefdoms on the island.

463   ———; Fernando Luna Calderón; and Renato O Rímoli. Investigaciones arqueológicas en la Provincia de Pedernales, Rep. Dominicana. San Pedro de Macorís, República Dominicana: Universidad Central del Este, 1979. 99 p.; 2 fold. leaves of plates; bibl.; ill. (Serie científica; 8)

   Consists of three preliminary reports on archaeological findings at four sites in Pedernales province, south coast of Dominican Republic, adjacent to Haitian border: 1) Veloz briefly describes the four sites as three pre-ceramic sites of Archaic period Río Pedernales, Cueva Roja, and Jinagosa (Río Pedernales appears to be a stratified site C14 dated 2590 BC, Cueva Roja has large quantities of human and animal bone as well as considerable lithic materials, and Jinagosa has lithic artifacts related to Mordan culture)

a fourth site (Las Mercedes with Chicoid series ceramics) is of late occupation; 2) Fernando Luna discusses various aspects of physical anthropology, especially the paleopathology of the Cueva Roja population; and 3) Renato Rímoli considers the zooarchaeology from the Cueva Roja site.

464   Walker, Jeff. Analysis and replication of lithic artifacts from the Sugar Factory Pier sites, St. Kitts (in International Congress for the Study of the Precolumbian Cultures of the Lesser Antilles, 8th, St. Kitts, 1979. Proceedings [see item **434**] p. 69–79, ill.)

   Author discusses the manufacture and use of lithic artifacts from the Sugar Factory Pier site, a Saladoid component site on St. Kitts. Illustrated.

465   Wilkerson, S. Jeffrey K. The question of Caribbean patrimony (in Cultural traditions and Caribbean identity: the question of patrimony. Edited by S. Jeffrey K. Wilkerson. Gainesville: Center for Latin American Studies, University of Florida, 1980, p. 3–16)

   After defining "patrimony," author discusses its implications and importance for both national and regional identity in the Caribbean.

466   Wing, Elisabeth S.; Alfred E. Dittert; J. Collins; and Christopher Goodwin. The preservation and study of prehistoric coral and coral artifacts: a case study from St. Kitts, West Indies (in International Congress for the Study of Precolumbian Cultures of the Lesser Antilles, 8th, St. Kitts, 1979. Proceedings [see item **434**] p. 246–263)

   Informative paper on material excavated in St. Kitts describes care, cleaning, and stabilization of coral specimens and artifacts.

467   ——— and Sylvia Scudder. Use of animals by the prehistoric inhabitants of St. Kitts, West Indies (in International Congress for the Study of the Precolumbian Cultures of the Lesser Antilles, 8th, St. Kitts, 1979. Proceedings [see item **434**] p. 237–245)

   Investigators examine the faunal assemblage from the Sugar Factory Pier and Cayon sites on St. Kitts. Data confirms that terrestrial species associated with archaeological sites are sparse, while aquatic species are abundant. Through time, faunal assemblages change notably, with earlier occupations reflecting a greater number of reef-dwelling fishes and later occupations showing more pelagic (i.e. dwelling close to the surface) species. Authors suggest that this reflects acquisition of new fishing skills required for taking advantage of offshore resources.

CENTRAL AMERICA

468   Arellano, Jorge Eduardo. La colección "Squier-Zapatera," pt. 1, estudio de estatuaria prehispánica (BNBD, 32/33, nov. 1979/feb. 1980, p. 3–137, fasc., ill., maps, plates)
Lengthy article describes the Squier-Zapatera monumental stone collection at the Central American College in Grenada, Nicaragua. Also recounts nine archaeological expeditions by Squier to Zapatera island beginning in 1849.

469   ———. Introducción al arte precolombino de Nicaragua. Managua: Departamento de Historia de la Cultura, Universidad Centroamericana, 1978. 36 p.; bibl.; ill.
Short monograph presenting the precolumbian art of Nicaragua. Sections deal with petroglyphs found in various regions, ceremonial architecture, stone sculptures, and ceramics.

470   Boggs, Stanley Harding. Apuntes sobre varios objetos de barro procedentes de "Los Guapotes" en el Lago de Güija. San Salvador, El Salvador: Ministerio de Educación, Dirección de Publicaciones, 1977. 9, 3 p.; 2 leaves of plates; bibl.; ill. (Colección Antropología e historia; no. 9)
Brief comments about clay artifacts found at Los Guapotes, Hacienda San Juan, Lake Guija, El Salvador. Describes 12 ceramic fragments, principally effigy heads and vessel supports. Author concludes the ceramic of Mexican style were made locally. Stylistically these artifacts are placed in the general Tula-Mazapa horizon, approximately 14th century.

471   Earnest, Howard H., Jr. Proyecto de Rescate "Cerrón Grande;" excavaciones-interpretaciones, Hacienda Santa Barbara. San Salvador: Administración del Patrimonio Cultural, 1977. 67 p.; bibl.; map; plates (Colección Antropología e historia; 7)

Preliminary report on the Cerrón Grande salvage archaeology program, an energetic project directed by Stanley Boggs. Focussing on the Central Valley of Río Lempa, author summarized findings from seven sites recorded since 1975.

472   Ferrero, Luis. La Gran Nicoya: vínculo cultural de América (BNBD, 27, enero/feb. 1979, p. 1–23, bibl., ill.)
Summary review of the archaeology and chronological placement of cultures in Costa Rica's Greater Nicoya sub-area.

473   Fowler, William R., Jr. Proyecto de Rescate "Cerrón Grande:" excavaciones-interpretaciones, Hacienda Los Flores. San Salvador: Administración del Patrimonio Cultural, 1977. 49 p.; bibl.; ill.; maps; plates (Colección Antropología e historia; 6)
Site report and interpretation of results from salvage excavations at two late preclassic period sites: Hacienda Los Flores and Río Grande. Data provides evidence of large populations and intensive agricultural production among inhabitants, most likely Mayan, during late preclassic times. Data also suggests long-distance exchange networks between El Salvador's Lempa Valley and Valley of Mexico during this period. Both sites appear to have been abandoned during early classic due to volcanic eruptions in the vicinity.

474   Furletti, René and **Joaquín Matilló Vila.** Piedras Vivas. Fotografía, Ulrico Richters. Managua, Nicaragua: Gurdian, División Editorial, 1977. 152 p.; bibl.; ill. (Serie arqueológica; no. 1. Colección Biblioteca Banco Central)
First volume in new series, published by Banco Central of Nicaragua, with focus on Nicaraguan archaeology. Book is divided into two parts: 1) very brief background on Nicaragua's geography, prehistoric cultures, native languages, and material culture; and 2) well illustrated section describes lithic sculpture and petroglyphs and attempts to classify stone sculptures stylistically into three categories (i.e., pre-Mayan, Chontales, and Mayan-Aztecan).

475   Haberland, Wolfgang. La Cueva del Espíritu Santo (Anales [Administración del Patrimonio Cultural, San Salvador] 49, 1976, p. 93–106, ill., maps, plates)
Preliminary report and discussion of

cave art found by author in Northeastern El Salvador.

476 ——. Marihua rojo sobre beige y el problema pipil (Marijua red-on-buff and the Pipil question). San Salvador, República de El Salvador: Administración del Patrimonio Cultural, 1978. 34, 1 p.; bibl.; ill. (Colección Antropología e historia; no. 13. Arqueología)

Reprint of article published in 1964 concerning author's archaeological investigations in Western and Central El Salvador in 1953–54 and 1958. Analyzes locally-made Marihua Red on Beige ware and certain design motifs, and compares it with similar wares from Central Mexico. Concludes that similarities attest to Pipil migration. The latter may have been involved in dispersal of Toltec tribe in Central Mexico.

477 Helms, Mary W. Ancient Panama: chiefs in search of power. Austin: University of Texas Press, 1979. 228 p.; bibl.; ill.; index (The Texas Pan American series)

Important and well-written monograph that goes far beyond its stated aims to reconstruct and subsequently analyze precolumbian chiefdoms of Panama circa AD 1500. Treats regional power elites, long distance trade networks, and sumptuary goods in detail.

478 Ichon, Alain. Archéologie du sud de la péninsule d'Azuero, Panama. Mexico: Mission archéologique et ethnologique française au Mexique, 1980. 521 p.; 36 leaves of plates (2 fold.); bibl.; ill. (some col.) (Études mésoaméricaines: Série 2; 3)

A tour de force in which author presents results of three field seasons in Tonosi region, Azuero Peninsula, Panama. Summarizing data gathered from 79 sites, Ichon presents excellent treatment of the ceramics, funerary practices, and settlement patterns associated with the Bucaro, El Indio, La Cañaza, and Bijaguales cultural phases (100 BC–AD 1300). Covers diffusion vectors and extra areal contact. Well illustrated.

479 Lange, Frederick W. Costa Rica y el arqueólogo de subsistencia (YAXKIN, 2:2, dic. 1979, p. 125–130, bibl.)

Brief article describes recent developments since passage of legislation regarding precolumbian antiquities in Costa Rica.

480 —— and **Richard M. Accola.** Metallurgy in Costa Rica (AIA/A, 134, Sept./Oct. 1979, p. 26–33, ill.)

Metal artifacts have been recovered in recent excavations at sites in Northwestern Costa Rica (Nacascola, Ruiz, and Guacamaya). Copper bell found at Nacascola in burial cache associated with known ceramic types date metal artifacts toward end of Middle Polychrome period AD 1000–AD 1200. While direction of diffusion remains unclear tear-shaped copper bell suggests metallurgical relationships existed between Lower Central America, southern Maya region, and Western Mexico. At Ruiz site, a lost wax mold fragment of the Late Polychrome Period (AD 1200–AD 1520) attests to presence of local metallurgical industry in Guanacaste. While Mexico used both copper and silver, native Costa Rican metallurgists utilized copper only as an alloy with gold (Tumbaga). Authors feel that Nacascola bell and other copper artifacts from region were most likely northern rather than local trade goods.

481 Linares, Olga F. What is Lower Central American archaeology? (Annual Review of Anthropology [Annual Review, Inc., Palo Alto, California] 8, 1979, p. 21–43, bibl.)

Linares provides succinct, excellent summary of recent archaeology conducted in Lower Central America. Outlining the variety of research efforts, she laments the abundance of descriptive work, and makes a plea for more analytical and problem-oriented research. Author also argues in favor of a cultural basis that will consider the Intermediate area as a whole instead of the "parochial" view which restricts one solely to Lower Central America.

482 López, Manuel R. Informe preliminar sobre una excavación de rescate arqueológico realizado en la Hacienda La Presita, Departamento de San Miguel (Anales [Administración del Patrimonio Cultural, San Salvador] 50, 1977, p. 21–29, bibl., ill., maps, plates)

Description of excavations on the Hacienda La Presita in the Department of San Miguel, El Salvador. Preliminary tests and analysis of artifacts suggest this to be a small site contemporaneous with occupational phases of the early classic period ceremonial site, Quelepa.

483 Véliz, Vito. Análisis arqueológico de la cerámica de Piedra Blanca. Tegucigalpa: Instituto Hondureño de Antropología e Historia, 1978. 63 p.; bibl.; ill. (Estudios antropológicos e históricos; 1)

Analysis of a ceramic collection excavated by Herbert Spinden in 1920. Artifacts are from the site of Piedra Blanca (Peña Blanca) in Northeastern Honduras. Author utilized contemporary ceramic classifications and places them in the Cocal Horizon of the postclassic period. A number of vessel handles and supports suggest influence from the highlands and Greater Nicoya archaeological zones in Costa Rica.

ARCHAEOLOGY: South America

BETTY J. MEGGERS, *Research Associate, Department of Anthropology, Smithsonian Institution*
CLIFFORD EVANS, *Curator, South American Archaeology, Department of Anthropology, Smithsonian Institution*

BIENNIAL REVIEW OF THE LITERATURE on archaeology of South America offers an opportunity to observe oscillations and trends in the number and authorship (national versus foreign) of publications. Although many brief contributions have been omitted for lack of space, the number of entries for this volume is about 20 percent greater than for *HLAS 41*. Again, Peru has a commanding lead; this time Argentina and Chile are next, followed by Brazil, Ecuador, and Colombia. The only country unrepresented is French Guiana. In *HLAS 41*, Peru was followed by Brazil, which had more than twice the number of entries as Argentina. Chile, Colombia, and Venezuela were in fourth place and there were no items for Guyana or Paraguay.

When the proportions of national and foreign authors are compared, some variation is also evident. As usual, foreigners outnumber nationals in Peru, but the preponderance this time is even greater for Ecuador. This is largely a consequence of the appearance of reports on multi-year field programs by Spanish and German archaeologists. In Argentina, Brazil, and Chile, nationals continue to account for more than 80 percent of the entries. The increase in the proportions of Colombian nationals from about 61 to 79 percent reflects the funding for fieldwork by the Fundación de Investigaciones Arqueológicas Nacionales of the Banco de la República and its publication of the results in a series of scientifically competent and well-printed monographs. Another noteworthy event is the inception of the *Journal of the Walter Roth Museum of Archaeology and Anthropology* (vol. 1, 1977), where 10 of the 11 entries for Guyana appeared.

Three major monographs on early ceramic complexes of Venezuela, one on the Barrancoid tradition of the lower Orinoco (item **828**), one on a Saladoid tradition site on the eastern coast (item **831**), and one on the Saladoid tradition and its successors on the middle Orinoco (item **826**), provide the first detailed descriptions of these important archaeological cultures. The authors reach different conclusions about the origins and relative antiquities of the two traditions, as well as on their absolute dates.

Another set of major monographs presents the results of intensive excavations at rockshelters occupied between 8000 and 10,000 years ago in the highlands of Colombia (items **664–665** and **679**) and Peru (items **767** and **976**). Specialized reports on plant and animal remains, paleoclimatic reconstructions, and artifacts offer insight into aspects of adaptation by these early hunter-gatherers, such as initial steps toward domestication of plants and responses to climatic oscillations. Preliminary results of similar investigations in other parts of South America attest to growing interest in the problem of man's arrival.

The mystery of the Nazca lines continues to provoke outlandish theories. An overview of Morrison in *Pathways to the gods* (item **781**) is balanced, comprehensive, authoritative, and readable. A similar approach to reconstructing Ecuadorian prehistory by Turolla in *Beyond the Andes* (item **722**) is sensational, misleading, and replete with errors. Serious scholars should consult Porras' *Arqueología del Ecuador* (item **713**), the most up-to-date summary available.

GENERAL

484   Encuentro de Arqueología del Litoral,
    5th, Fray Bentos, Uruguay, 1977. Encuentro de Arqueología del Litoral. Río Negro, Uruguay: Museo Municipal de Historia Natural de Río Negro, 1977. 276 p.

Papers presented at the fifth regional meeting on the archaeology of southern Brazil, Uruguay, and adjacent parts of Argentina. Except for reports on sites near Salto Grande on the Río Uruguay, most deal with surface collections.

485   García Reinoso, Marta Ottonello de.
    Tipos de instalación humana y ciudades en América precolombina (*in* La Ciudad a través del tiempo. Buenos Aires: Universidad de Buenos Aires, Facultad de Filosofía y Letras, 1978, p. 83–96, bibl.)

Review of variables explaining why urban centers emerged among some agriculturalists while others failed to expand beyond the village level of complexity.

486   The Junius B. Bird Pre-Columbian
    Textile Conference, *Washington, D.C., 1973.* Proceedings. Edited by Ann Pollard Rowe; Elizabeth P. Benson; and Anne-Louise Schaffer. Washington, D.C.: The Textile Museum and Dumbarton Oaks, 1979. 287 p.; bibl.; ill.; tables.

Consists of 13 papers detailing aspects of precolumbian Peruvian textiles from Chavín to Inca periods. One paper discusses textile impressions from the Valdivia culture of coastal Ecuador, and another summarizes non-Maya Mesoamerica. Employs technological, functional, and iconographic approaches, providing a useful introduction to current research on this aspect of material culture.

487   Lynch, Thomas F. Presencia y adaptación post-glacial del hombre en los Andes Sudamericanos (Chungara [Universidad del Norte, Departamento de Antropología, Arica, Chile] 8, 1980, p. 96–123, bibl.)

Review of the evidence indicates that man arrived in South America no earlier than about 11,000 years ago.

488   Marschall, Wolfgang. Influencias asiáticas en las culturas de la América Antigua: estudios de su historia. Diseño de la portada, Amei Marschall; translation by Beatriz Medina. México: Ediciones Euroamericanas, 1979. 201 p.; 4 leaves of plates; bibl.; ill.; index.

After reviewing history of Transpacific controversy, Marschall presents data on four categories of resemblances between Asia and America: 1) blowguns; 2) cult of the dead; 3) wheeled toys; and 4) loom-made textiles. In each case, evidence obtained by comparative method supports an introduction from Asia. Concludes with review of watercraft available. A reasoned, non-polemic presentation, which includes assessment of arguments against the feasibility of Transoceanic contacts and of the validity of cultural comparisons for establishing origins.

489   Ottolenghi, Aldo. Civilizaciones americanas prehistóricas. Buenos Aires: Hachette, 1980. 190 p.; ill. (Los Enigmas del universo)

Author argues that writing ancestral to the oldest Middle Eastern script existed in Brazil, Paraguay, and Chile, and that immigrants from South America settled in the eastern Mediterranean. His thesis has no scientific basis.

490 Perdomo, Lucía R. de. La dispersión de la cerámica "Mocasín" (ICA/RCA, 20, 1976, p. 497–505, bibl., ill., map)

"Shoe-shaped" vessels are distributed from southwestern US to central Chile, along the west, suggesting they may reflect commercial activities not yet recognizable from other kinds of archaeological remains.

491 Pistilli S., Vicente. Vikingos en el Paraguay: la aldea vikinga-guaraní en la Cuenca del Plata. Asunción: Ediciones Comuneros, 1978. 57, 27 p.; bibl.; ill.

Notes similarities between fortified Guaraní villages and Viking settlements, and concludes the former result from Viking influence.

492 Pre-Columbian Metallurgy of South America. A conference at Dumbarton Oaks, October 18th and 19th, 1975. Elizabeth P. Benson, editor. Washington, D.C.: Dumbarton Oaks Research Library and Collections, Trustees for Harvard University, 1979. 207 p.; bibl.; ill.

Six papers presented at a two-day conference discuss aspects of precolumbian metallurgy in Colombia, Peru, Chile, and Argentina: Heather Lechtman's "Issues in Andean Metallurgy;" Alicia Dussán de Reichel's "Some Observations on the Prehistoric Goldwork of Colombia;" Julie Jones' "Mochica Works of Art in Metal: a Review;" Julius B. Bird's "The 'Copper Man:' a Prehistoric Miner and his Tools from Northern Chile;" Alberto Rex González's "Precolumbian Metallurgy of Northwest Argentina: Historical Development and Cultural Process;" and Luis I. Rodríguez Orrego's "A Site of Metallurgical Activity in Northwest Argentina."

493 Sanoja Obediente, Mario. Origen de los sistemas agrarios (BBAA, 40:49, 1978, p. 9–24, bibl.)

Contrary to common emphasis on technological innovation represented by agriculture, Sanoja calls attention to interaction between environment, technology, and socioeconomic organization in explaining agriculture's evolution. A review of these interactions in Old and New World contexts suggests why food production based on grain affords more potential for cultural expansion than that based on vegeculture.

ARGENTINA

494 Aguerre, Ana M. Observaciones sobre la industria toldense (Sapiens [Museo Arqueológico Dr. Osvaldo F.A. Menghin, Chivilcoy, Provincia Buenos Aires] 3, 1979, p. 35–54, bibl., ill.)

Comparison of lithic technology and habitat of sites of the Toldense complex with those of the Magallanes (Fell's) suggests they represent two contemporary Paleo-Indian populations adapted to different environments.

495 ———. A propósito de un nuevo fechado radiocarbónico para la "Cueva de Las Manos," Alto Río Pinturas, Provincia de Santa Cruz (SAA/R, 11, 1977, p. 129–142, bibl., ill.)

New date from layer 6 of 9300 ± 90 BP coincides with earlier result. General description of stratigraphy is supplemented with detailed list of lithic materials from layer 5 and upper, middle, and lower sections of layer 6.

496 Alfaro, Lidia C. Arte rupestre en la cuenca del Río Doncellas, Provincia de Jujuy, República Argentina (SAA/R, 12, 1978, p. 123–146, bibl., ill.)

Description of human and animal figures on the walls of rock shelters, caves, and outcrops at about 3600 m elevation.

497 ——— and **Margarita Gentile.** Los mates pirograbados de la cuenca del Río Doncellas (Antiquitas [Boletín de la Asociación Amigos del Instituto de Arqueología, Facultad de Historia y Letras, Universidad del Salvador, Buenos Aires] 26/27, 1978, p. 1–11, bibl., ill.)

Description of 15 gourds, 12 with pyroengraved designs, from an archaeological cemetery. Associated artifacts include textiles, bows and arrows, coarse pottery, and other characteristic "puna culture" elements.

498 Antecedentes de santuarios de altura conocidos hasta junio de 1978 (Revista del Centro de Investigaciones Arqueológicas de Alta Montaña [San Juan, Argentina] 3, 1978, p. 50–71, tables)

Lists 55 mountains on which archaeological remains (principally Inca) have been reported, with name and date of visitors, type of remains, and elevation. Identifies hearths, stone constructions, mummies, pottery, figurines, metal and other elements. Useful summary.

499 Bárcena, J. Roberto. Informe sobre recientes investigaciones arqueológicas en el noroeste de la provincia de Mendoza, Argentina (*in* Congreso de Arqueología Chilena, 7th, Altos de Vilches, Chile, 1977. Actas [see item **613**] v. 2, p. 661–692, bibl., ill., map)

Investigations in the Valle de Uspallata permitted mapping of Inca highway through region and excavation in two associated tambos and structure that appears to have served as hunting lodge. C14 date of AD 1560 ± 90 agrees with the chronological position inferred from ceramics.

500 Belelli, Cristina. La decoración de la cerámica gris incisa de Patagonia, República Argentina (MP/R, 27, 1980, p. 199–225, bibl., map, graphs)

Analysis and quantification of decorative motifs on incised gray pottery from northern and central Patagonia based on 75 specimens from 17 sites. Infers north to south diffusion.

501 Berberián, Eduardo E. and Elsa Argüello de Dorsch. Alfarería con impresiones de cesta procedente de "El Cadillal," Provincia de Tucumán, Rep. Argentina (UNCIA/R, 6, 1978, p. 7–14, bibl., ill., map)

Impressions of coiled basketry on pottery dating about AD 1000. Pottery of Santa María complex is associated.

502 ——— **and Francisco Massidda.** Investigaciones arqueológicas en Las Barrancas, Departamento Belén, Catamarca: nuevas contribuciones para el estudio de la cultura Condorhuasi del noroeste Argentino (UNTIA/R, 2:3, 1975, p. 7–47, bibl., ill., maps, plates, tables)

Description of pottery from two tombs, which appear to represent Condorhuasi I, dated about beginning of Christian era. Finds are compared with data and interpretations by other archaeologists.

503 ———; **Jorgelina García Azcárate; and Marcelino Caillou.** Investigaciones arqueológicas en la región del Dique El Ca-

dillal, Tucumán, República Argentina: los primeros fechados radiocarbónicos (SAA/R, 11, 1977, p. 31–53, bibl., ill., map)

C14 samples from two burial urns from different cemeteries gave nearly identical dates of 910 ± 100 and 910 ± 130 years ago, which are compatible with their placement in early Santa María period.

504 Cabezas, Osvaldo Alfredo; Juan Carlos Joaquín; and David Jorge Casas. Yacimiento de Tabladitas, Puna Jujeña (Revista del Museo de Historia Natural de San Rafael [San Rafael, Argentina] 3 : 1/4, 1976, p. 89–94, bibl.)

Agricultural village of late period composed of 15–20 houses associated with cemetery and terraced fields. Architecture, pottery, metal, and stone artifacts are briefly described.

505 Caggiano, María Amanda. Análisis de rasgos decorativos en algunos sitios pertenecientes a la provincia de Buenos Aires, Argentina (*in* Encuentro de Arqueología del Litoral, 5th, Fray Bentos, Uruguay, 1977. Encuentro . . . [see item **484**] p. 31–51, bibl., ill.)

Description of paste, surface, form, and decoration of pottery from three locations in northern Buenos Aires province; the principal decorative technique is drag-and-jab.

506 ———; **Olga Beatriz Flores; Marta Graciela Méndez; and Susana Alicia Salceda.** Nuevos aportes para el conocimiento antropológico del Delta del Paraná (SAA/R, 12, 1978, p. 155–74, bibl., ill., tables)

Description of excavations, faunal remains, pottery, bone artifacts, and human skeletons at the habitation site Paraná Ibicuy I, Gualeguaychú Dept. Pottery decoration is by red painting and drag-and-jab.

507 Calandra, Horacio Adolfo; María Amanda Caggiano; and María Beatriz Cremonte. Dispersión de la técnica corrugada en el ámbito del Noroeste Argentino (Sapiens [Museo Arqueológico Osvaldo F.A. Menghin, Chivilcoy, Provincia Buenos Aires] 3, 1979, p. 61–68, bibl.)

Corrugated surface treatment occurs in low frequency on pottery from the lower formative at sites in Salta and Jujuy dating 620 BC or earlier.

508 Cardich, Augusto and **Nora Flegenheimer.** Descripción y tipología de las industrias líticas más antiguas de Los Toldos (SAA/R, 12, 1978, p. 225–242, bibl., ill.)

Description of lithics from Level 11, with a C14 date of 12,600 BP. Specimens from this level tend to be larger and broader than those from Levels 10 and above; they are predominantly formed on flakes, with marginal retouch only on one surface and pronounced bulbs of percussion. Complex in Level 11 is compatible with hypothesis of local evolution of the more elaborated Toldense industry.

509 ———; E.P. Tonni; and **N. Kriscautzky.** Presencia de *Canis familiaris* en restos arqueológicos de Los Toldos, Provincia de Santa Cruz, Argentina (SAA/R, 11, 1977, p. 115–119, bibl., ill.)

Description of dog remains from the Casapedrense levels in Cave 3 at Los Toldos, C14 dated between 7260 ± 350 and 4840 ± 300 BP.

510 Casamiquela, Rodolfo M. Temas patagónicos de interés arqueológico (SAA/R, 12, 1978, p. 213–223, bibl., ill.)

Description of the manufacture and use of scrapers of glass and the relevance of the observations to interpreting archaeological lithic remains.

511 Cione, Alberto L. and **Eduardo P. Tonni.** Paleoethnozoological context of a site of Las Lechiguanas Islands, Paraná Delta, Argentina (UNV/ED, 3:1, April 1978, p. 76–86, bibl., map, table)

Identification of faunal remains reveals fish and land vertebrates (no birds). From species represented, authors infer that fish were harpooned, that site was occupied seasonally, and that during occupation, environment was as today.

512 Congreso Nacional de Arqueología Argentina, *4th, San Rafael, Argentina, 1976. Actas* y memorias. San Rafael, Argentina: Museo de Historia Natural de San Rafael, 1976. 3 v. (*Revista de Museo de Historia Natural de San Rafael;* vols. 1/3, nos. 1/4)

For individual annotations of papers delivered at this congress, see items **639, 645** and **650.**

513 Fernández, Jorge. Los chichas, los lipes y un posible enclave de la cultura de San Pedro de Atacama en la zona limítrofe argentino-boliviana (Estudios Atacameños [Universidad del Norte, Museo de Arqueología, San Pedro de Atacama, Chile] 6, 1978, p. 19–35, bibl., ill., map)

Linguistic affiliations of the chichas and lipes on the border between Bolivia and Argentina are disputed; archaeology is poorly known but provides indications of relationships with complexes in adjacent Chile that deserve investigation.

514 ———. La población pre-araucana del Neuquén: intento reconstructivo a través del arte rupestre (*in* Congreso de Arqueología Chilena, 7th, Altos de Vilches, Chile, 1977. Actas [see item **613**] v. 2, 1977, p. 617–630, bibl., ill., maps)

Classification of motifs at 62 sites distributed throughout Neuquén province permits differentiation of four regional styles, designated as parallel lines, tracks, frets, and Guaiquivilo (a variant of parallel lines). Track and fret styles intruded from the south, whereas parallel lines dominate in northwest. Occasional superpositions provide chronological information. Patagonian styles are associated with prolongations of that environment and northern expansion of groups adapted to its exploitation.

515 Fernández Distel, Alicia A. Nuevos hallazgos de estólicas en el borde de la Puna Jujeña, Argentina (*in* Congreso de Arqueología Chilena, 7th, Altos de Vilches, Chile, 1977. Actas [see item **613**] v. 1, p. 131–165, bibl., ill., map)

Two complete spear throwers were encountered associated with a burial in one rockshelter dated 1450 BC; fragments in another dated 2130 BC. These are described and illustrated, along with numerous hooks from the region. Table gives details on seven of most complete examples from Northwest Argentina.

516 ———. Nuevos hallazgos precerámicos en la región de las Salinas Grandes, Puna de Jujuy, Argentina (UNCIA/R, 6, 1978, p. 15–62, bibl., ill., map, tables)

Analysis of material from surface collections supports recognition of two lithic industries proposed by Cigliano: Tres Morros and Saladillo. Latter appears to be a local phenomenon.

517 ———. Tiuiyaco: un asentamiento
agroalfarero de características tempranas en el norte de la Quebrada de Humahuaca, Jujuy (Revista del Museo de Historia Natural de San Rafael [San Rafael, Argentina] 4 : 1/4, 1976, p. 55–73, bibl., ill., table)

Small (diameter 2–3 m), semi-subterranean, circular, stone walled dwellings were excavated. Associated tricolor pottery indicates a dating about AD 700.

518 **Gambier, Mariano.** Ecología y arqueología de los Andes Centrales argentino-chilenos (Revista del Museo de Historia Natural de San Rafael [San Rafael, Argentina] 3 : 1/4, 1976, p. 185–199, bibl.)

Detailed description of environment provides basis for interpreting changes in human occupation; local variations in climate appear correlated with changes in subsistence emphasis, population density, settlement pattern, and external influence.

519 ———. Excavaciones arqueológicas en los valles interandinos de la Alta Cordillera (in Congreso de Arqueología Chilena, 7th, Altos de Vilches, Chile, 1977. Actas [see item **613**] v. 2, p. 519–530, bibl., ill.)

Investigations at two sites in Argentina near the Chilean border reveal that in the past, as today, region was exploited by pastoral groups from both sides of cordillera. C14 dates range from AD 180–1000.

520 ———. Investigaciones arqueológicas en las Sierras Centrales, Provincia de San Luis, Argentina. San Juan, Argentina: Universidad Nacional de San Juan, Instituto de Investigaciones Arqueológicas y Museo, 1979, p. 1–10; bibl. (Publicaciones; 5)

Suggests that spread toward east after about AD 500 was in response to reduced subsistence resources resulting from climatic change in Andean foothills.

521 **Gómez, Roque Manuel.** Contribución al conocimiento de las industrias líticas tempranas de Santiago del Estero (UNTIA/R, 2 : 3, 1975, p. 171–188, ill., map)

Classification of 38 projectile points from surface collections by shape and size. Three periods appear to be represented: Ayampitin, Intihuasi II–III, and agro-ceramic.

522 **González, Alberto Rex.** El Noroeste Argentino y el área andina septentrional (ANC/B, 52 : 3/4, marzo 1978, p. 373–404, bibl., ill.)

The spatial and temporal distributions of 24 traits (dental mutilation, neck rests, burial urns, ocarinas, monolithic axes, etc.) reported from the northern Andes (Colombia-Ecuador) and Northwest Argentina, but rare or absent in the intervening highlands are reviewed. Arbitrariness of traits makes independent development unlikely; dispersion along eastern margin of Andes is proposed as a working hypothesis.

523 **González, Sergio P.E. and Eduardo A. Crivelli Montero.** Excavaciones arqueológicas en el Abrigo de Los Chelcos, Departamento San Alberto, Córdoba (SAA/R, 12, 1978, p. 183–206, bibl., ill., map, tables)

Excavation revealed lower nonceramic occupation and later one with pottery. Describes lithics, pottery, fauna, and human skeleton remains. Typological comparisons with Intihuasi and Ongamira suggest dating between 3000 and 1000 BC for Component I and AD 500–1000 for Component II.

524 **Gradin, Carlos J.** Grabados de la Angostura del Río Deseado, provincia de Santa Cruz, Argentina (in Congreso de Arqueología Chilena, 7th, Altos de Vilches, Chile, 1977. Actas [see item **613**] v. 2, p. 595–616, bibl., ill., map)

Describes group of petroglyphs in form of circles with radiating short lines, a widespread motif that appears to die out with introduction of pottery about 7th century AD.

525 ———. Parapetos de piedra y grabados rupestres de la Meseta del Lago Buenos Aires (Revista del Museo de Historia Natural de San Rafael [San Rafael, Argentina] 3 : 1/4, 1976, p. 315–337, bibl., ill., map)

Three localities with petroglyphs and a site with small circular stone-walled rooms were encountered on the pampa in northwestern Santa Cruz province. Region is habitable only during summer, and remains are assigned dates within Christian era. Proposes three-period chronology for petroglyphs based on differences in technique and motif.

526 ———. Las pinturas del Cerro Shequen (UNCIA/R, 6, 1978, p. 62–92, bibl., ill., map)

Five pictograph locations in south-central Chubut province feature stepped lines, diamonds, frets, and other geometric motifs; similar designs on local pottery imply a relatively recent date.

527 ——. Pinturas rupestres del Alero Cárdenas, Provincia de Santa Cruz (SAA/R, 11, 1977, p. 143–158, bibl., ill., map)

Nine categories of motifs are described and interpreted in context of known distributions. Results suggest cultural continuity from Uruguay to Patagonia, and possibility that Río Negro and Chubut provinces were center for dispersal of the fret style.

528 —— and **Carlos A. Aschero.** Cuatro fechas radiocarbónicas para el Alero del Cañadón de las Manos Pintadas, Las Pulgas, Provincia del Chubut (SAA/R, 12, 1978, p. 245–248)

Evaluation of six C14 dates from excavations, which extend between 1380 BC and AD 250.

529 **Gramajo de Martínez Moreno, Amalia.** Los estudios antropológicos y arqueológicos de Santiago del Estero. Tucumán: Ediciones NOA-Cultural, 1977. 69 p.; 20 leaves of plates; bibl.; ill. (Ediciones Noa-Cultural; s/n: Serie roja, bibliografía y compilaciones especiales)

History of archaeological investigation, including skeletal studies, in Santiago del Estero, from its inception in 1856. Useful bibliographical and historical source.

530 **Krapovickas, Pedro.** El tránsito entre la puna argentina y los valles orientales (III/AI, 39[39]:4, oct./dic. 1979, p. 681–695, bibl.)

Prior to Inca expansion, archaeological sites adjacent to the puna change from agricultural villages at lower elevations to more concentrated and heavily defended settlements at higher elevations. Presumably, this reflects changes in relations between puna and quebrada populations, but their nature remains speculative.

531 **Lagiglia, Humberto A.** La cultura de Viluco del centro oeste argentino (Revista del Museo de Historia Natural de San Rafael [San Rafael, Argentina] 3:1/4, 1976, p. 227–265, bibl., ill., map)

Viluco culture evolved in Mendoza and San Juan provinces from local antecedents influenced from central Chile. Maize and other cultigens were supplemented by hunting. Pottery is described in detail; other

characteristics more briefly. Phase II is marked by integration into Inca empire.

532 ——. Dinámica cultural en el centro oeste y sus relaciones con áreas aledañas argentinas y chilenas (in Congreso de Arqueología Chilena, 7th, Altos de Vilches, 1977. Actas [see item **613**] v. 2, p. 531–560, bibl., ill., tables)

Review of cultural development in west central Argentina from Paleo-Indian to Inca times shows influences from central Chile and northwest Argentina. However, a distinctive pattern emerged because of the marginal environment.

533 **Lancha Packewaia,** arqueología de los canales fueguinos: primer informe. Por Luis Abel Orquera et al. Buenos Aires: Editorial Huemul, 1977. 248 p.; 4 leaves of plates; bibl.; ill.; index (Colección Temas de arqueología; 1)

Excavations in shell midden on Beagle Channel's north shore revealed two components, differentiated by types of tools, raw materials, and techniques of manufacture. Recent Component dates between AD 870 and 1663; Early Component between about 3000 and 2200 BC. Provides detailed descriptions of excavations, artifacts, and other data. Appendixes give petrographic characteristics of flakes and observations of Yámana diet. Important contribution to archaeology of Tierra del Fuego.

534 **Lorandi, Ana María.** El desarrollo cultural prehispánico en Santiago del Estero, Argentina (SA/J, 65, 1978, p. 63–85, bibl., ill.)

Interprets Chaco-Santiagueña cultural tradition (between AD 800–1600) as outcome of adaptation by populations of different origins to local environmental resources.

535 ——. Significación de la fase Las Lomas en el desarrolo cultural de Santiago del Estero (SAA/R, 11, 1977, 69–77, bibl., ill.)

Recent fieldwork affirms that Las Lomas phase is the incipient expression of the Chaco-Santiagueña Tradition and transitional between the preceding Las Mercedes phase and fully developed Chaco-Santiagueño.

536 **Lorenzi, Mónica de** and **Pío Pablo Díaz.** La ocupación incaica en el sector septentrional del Valle Calchaquí (Revista del Museo de Historia Natural de San Rafael [San Rafael, Argentina] 3:1/4, 1976, p. 75–88, bibl.)

Information on sites, roads, and artifacts associated with Inca occupation in Salta province.

537 Madrazo, Guillermo B. Los cazadores a larga distancia de la región pampeana (Prehistoria Bonaerense [Olavarría, Argentina] 1979, p. 11–67, bibl.)

Review of ethnohistorical and archaeological evidence from Argentine pampas in ecological context suggests hypothesis that diversity of lithic industries masks general uniformity in subsistence patterns and social organization. Two major cultural and climatic periods are recognized: terminal Pleistocene hunters using stone projectile points and subsequent hunters employing bolas. Article is a notable attempt to interpret confusing, sporadic, and poorly dated archaeological remains.

538 Nardi, Ricardo L.J. Observaciones sobre las manoplas de la Argentina y Chile (MEMDA/E, 23/24, enero/dic. 1976, p. 36–53, bibl., ill.)

Broad, elongated, bracelet-like objects of wood and bronze from archaeological contexts are reexamined. A typology is presented using morphological criteria. Various functions are reviewed and problems of their verification discussed. Author suggests that three groups differentiated by form may have also had different functions.

539 Ochoa de Masramón, Dora. Contribución al estudio del arte rupestre de las Sierras Centrales de San Luis. San Juan, Argentina: Universidad Nacional de San Juan, Instituto de Investigaciones Arqueológicas y Museo, 1980. 79 p.; bibl.; ill. (Publicaciones; 7)

Systematic description of 21 localities, including characteristics of the rock, associated artifacts, and details of the petroglyphs and pictographs.

540 Palanca, Floreal and Gustavo Politis. Los cazadores de fauna extinguida de la Provincia de Buenos Aires (Prehistoria Bonaerense [Olavarría, Argentina] 1979, p. 69–91, bibl., chart)

Remains of glyptodon and other extinct fauna are associated with flakes of crystalline quartz and quartzite at La Moderna; investigations at the site since 1972 are summarized.

541 Podestá, Clara and Elena B. de Perrota. Desarrollo cultural del Valle Santa María durante el período tardío o de desarrollos regionales (Revista del Museo de Historia Natural de San Rafael [San Rafael, Argentina] 3:1/4, 1976, p. 43–54, bibl., ill.)

Absence of significant change in settlement pattern and cultural complexity, after AD 1000, implies that by that date an equilibrium adaptation to the habitat had been achieved.

542 Raffino, Rodolfo Adelio. Las aldeas del formativo inferior de la Quebrada del Toro, Salta, Argentina (Estudios Atacameños [Universidad del Norte, Museo de Arqueología, San Pedro de Atacama, Chile] 5, 1977, p. 64–108, appendix, bibl., map, tables)

Summary of evidence from six sites representing lower formative period (600 BC–AD 400) and evaluation of evidence for local development and outside influence. During this period, llama herding overtook hunting as the principal subsistence activity, supplemented by cultivation of maize and squash. Faunal remains are described in an appendix by Eduardo P. Tonni and José H. Laza.

543 ———. La ocupación Inka en el Noroeste Argentino: actualización y perspectivas (SAA/R, 12, 1978, p. 95–121, bibl., map, tables)

Architectural elements are divided into three categories: typically Inca, locally developed, and general. Presence or absence of resulting 34 elements is recorded for 34 excavated Inca sites; 86 additional sites are examined for more general traits. It was found that 96 percent of sites are one day's march apart; 87 percent are associated with rock art; 75 percent with mining; only nine percent are fortified. Other differences between Inca and Inca-influenced sites shed light on nature of Inca presence in Northwestern Argentina.

544 ——— and Eduardo Mario Cigliano. Un modelo de poblamiento en el Noroeste Argentino (in Congreso Peruano: El Hombre y la Cultura Andina, 3rd, Lima, 1977. El hombre y la cultura andina [see item 756] v. 2, p. 673–707, bibl., ill.)

Archaeological investigations at Tastil and other sites in Quebrada del Toro (Salta), ethnohistorical data, and present land use provide basis for a model of urban-rural relations during Regional Development Period. Exploitation of a range of ecological zones, craft specialization, status differentiation, exchange, population size, and political organization are among aspects considered.

545 ——— and ———. Nota sobre una nueva instalación agrícola en el Noroeste Argentino (UNCIA/R, 6, 1978, p. 93–104, bibl., ill., table)

La Campana, representing the late Santa María tradition, is a complex of agricultural terraces for intensive production not associated directly with a major settlement; this pattern of land use is well suited to the local environment.

546 ———; ———; and **María E. Manzur.** El Churcal: un modelo de urbanización tardía en el Valle Calchaquí (Revista del Museo de Historia Natural de San Rafael [San Rafael, Argentina] 3:1/4, 1976, p. 33–42, ill.)

Preliminary information on investigations at a large site covering some 230,000 m², dated between AD 1100–1350 on the basis of predominance of Santa María style pottery. About 750 features, including houses, patios, streets, and refuse deposits, were mapped, as well as 300 tombs of adults.

547 ———; **Eduardo P. Tonni;** and **Alberto L. Cione.** Recursos alimentarios y economía en la región de la Quebrada del Toro, Provincia de Salta, Argentina (SAA/R, 11, 1977, p. 9–30, bibl., ill., map)

Analysis of faunal remains from sites extending from 600 BC to European contact shows primary emphasis on domesticated llama-alpaca, supplemented by hunting of vicuña. Relative frequencies of principal species are shown by site and period. Cultigens represented at Tastil and ethnohistorical accounts provide additional evidence for the inference that a balanced diet was achieved.

548 **Romero, Carlos Alfredo** and **María Alejandra Uanini.** Los grabados rupestres del sitio Ampiza 1, Aguas de Ramón, Departamento Minas, Provincia de Córdoba (UNCIA/R, 6, 1978, p. 111–133, bibl., ill., map, tables)

Group of petroglyphs in a rockshelter near the northwestern boundary of Córdoba province, featuring abstract motifs composed of concentric circles and straight lines.

549 **Schlegel, Mary Luz; Esther Margarita Soto;** and **Adan Hajduk.** Yacimientos arqueológicos en el curso superior del Río Limay, provincia de Neuquén (Revista del Museo de Historia Natural de San Rafael [San Rafael, Argentina] 3:1/4, 1976, p. 365–381, bibl., ill., map)

Survey located 13 sites, representing rock shelters and open locations. Five produced pottery. General descriptions are given of the sites and materials obtained from surface collections.

550 **Schobinger, Juan.** Nuevos lugares con arte rupestre en el extremo sur de la provincia de Mendoza (SAA/R, 12, 1978, P. 175–182, bibl., ill., map)

Review of 14 locations with petroglyphs; the style suggests dating within the Christian era.

551 **Sempé de Gómez Llanes, María Carlota.** Las culturas agroalfareras prehispánicas del Valle de Abaucán, Tinogasta-Catamarca (SAA/R, 11, 1977, p. 55–68, bibl.)

Summary of regional cultural development of pottery making agriculturalists from 450 BC to AD 1690. Early, Middle, and Hispano-Indigenous periods are divided into chronological phases, and diagnostic features are listed for each.

552 **Tarragó, Myriam Noemí.** La localidad arqueológica de Las Pailas, provincia de Salta, Argentina (*in* Congreso de Arqueología Chilena, 7th, Altos de Vilches, Chile, 1977. Actas [see item **613**] v. 2, p. 499–517, bibl., ill.)

Preliminary results of test excavations in a large settlement 14 km northwest of Cachi, assigned to the Regional Developmental Period, but with occupation continuing into Inca times.

553 ——— and **Mónica de Lorenzi.** Arqueología del Valle Calchaquí (MEMDA/E, 23/24, enero/dic. 1976, p. 1–35, bibl., plates)

Although archaeological work began nearly a century ago in the Calchaquí Valley (Cachi dept.) the cultural sequence remains poorly known and no C14 dates are available. This summary of existing knowledge is divided into stages and periods, extending from

Paleo-Indian to colonial. Information on each period includes site distribution, settlement pattern economy, technology, art, social organization, and ritual, as these can be inferred from the archaeological remains.

BOLIVIA

554 Berberián, Eduardo E. and **Jorge Arellano López.** Desarrollo cultural prehispánico en el altiplano sur de Bolivia: primera aproximación (MP/R, 27, 1980, p. 259–281, bibl., ill., map)

First attempt to define cultural periods on Bolivia's southern altiplano (Potosí dept.). Three are Paleo-Indian, each with two subdivisions. Diagnostic artifacts, possible affiliations, and estimated dating are provided. There is a haitus from 1500 BC to AD 1300, when the post-Tiahuanaco Mallku chiefdom developed.

555 Boero Rojo, Hugo. La increíble ciudadela prehispánica de Iskanwaya, Aucapata y Maukallajta (La Ciudad del Oro). Prólogo, Carlos Ponce Sanginés; nota científica, Jorge Arellano López. La Paz: Editorial Los Amigos del Libro, 1977. 8, 90 p.; 13 leaves of plates; ill. (some col.) (Colección Bolivia mágica)

Popular account of the discovery of a large ruin perched on the edge of a precipice as Machu Picchu, but attributed to the pre-Inca Mollo culture between AD 1200 and 1485. Includes a plan of the ruins and numerous photographs of architectural details.

556 ——— and **Oswaldo Rivera Sundt.** El fuerte preincaico de Samaipata. La Paz: Editorial Los Amigos del Libro, 1979. 144 p.; bibl.; ill. (Colección Bolivia mágica)

About 120 km southwest of Santa Cruz, Bolivia, is a large archaeological site dominated by a sandstone outcrop 200 by 60 m, completely covered with niches, steps, benches, channels, rectangular pits, zoomorphic figures, and other features carved into the stone. Pottery from nearby habitation sites is attributed to Tiahuanaco through Inca periods. Details of the carved elements are illustrated, as well as complete pottery vessels.

557 Browman, David L. The temple of Chiripa, Lake Titicaca, Bolivia (in Congreso Peruano: El Hombre y la Cultura Andina, 3rd, Lima, 1977. El hombre y la cultura andina [see item **756**] p. 807–813)

Recent excavations at Chiripa permit differentiating occupational phases extending from 1300 BC to present. Cultural, plant, and animal remains were collected for all phases, and should permit reconstruction of cultural development and directions of interchange with other regions.

558 Dougherty, Bernard and **Horacio A. Calandra.** Nota preliminar sobre investigaciones arqueológicas en los Llanos de Moxos, Departamento del Beni, República de Bolivia (UNLPM/R, 8, 1981, p. 87–106, bibl., ill., map)

Reports preliminary results of three seasons of archaeological investigation in Bolivia's northeastern lowlands. No artificially constructed mounds were found, nor evidence of large population density. The Masicito complex shares features with formative pottery of Northwestern Argentina, and appears to be earlier than Nordenskiold believed.

559 Linares Málaga, Eloy. Cómo inventariar arte rupestre en los Andes meridionales. La Paz, Bolivia: Casa Municipal de la Cultura Franz Tamayo, 1979. 124 p.; bibl.; ill.

Details relevant to complete description of petroglyphs are specified as a basis for collecting uniform data throughout the hemisphere. Description of motifs is illustrated using Petroglyph No. 26 from the Majes Valley of Arequipa. Zoomorphic figures account for 60 percent of the representations.

560 Portugal Ortiz, Max. La arqueología de la región del Río Beni. La Paz: s.n., 1978. 135 p.; bibl.; ill.; maps.

Describes pottery vessels, figurines, and other artifacts from collections but offers minimal scientific documentation. Serves mainly to demonstrate the need for systematic archaeological investigation in Bolivia's eastern lowlands.

561 Ruiz Estrada, Arturo. Exploraciones arqueológicas en Cabanillas, Puno (in Congreso Peruano: El Hombre y la Cultura Andina, 3rd, Lima, 1977. El hombre y la cultura andina [see item **756**] v. 2, p. 791–806, bibl., ill.)

Description of four chullpas of probable Inca date constructed of stone, with a surface coating of clay.

BRAZIL

562 Abrahao Schorr, María Helena. Análisis de los restos de alimentos de las grutas del Proyecto Paranaiba (*in* Encuentro de Arqueología del Litoral, 5th, Fray Bentos, Uruguay, 1977. Encuentro . . . [see item **484**] p. 3–10, graphs, table)

Faunal remains from three rockshelters in the state of Goiás, Brazil, were classified into mammals, reptiles, fish, birds, and mollusks. Calculation of relative frequencies by excavation level shows the decline in relative frequencies of mammal and bird bones as mollusks increase; at the upper end of the sequence, proportion of mammal bones again increases. These changes in subsistence emphasis correlate with three cultural phases extending from Paleo-Indian to ceramic occupations of the region.

563 Andreatta, Margarida Davina. Projecto arqueológico Anhanguera, Estado de Goiás, Missão 1977 (MP/R, 25, nova série, 1978, p. 47–64, bibl., maps, plates)

Brief description of fieldwork at two ceramic and one preceramic sites, including listing of kinds of cultural remains encountered.

564 Araújo, Adauto José Gonçalves de. Contribuição ao estudo de helmintos encontrados em material arqueológico do Brasil. Rio de Janeiro: s.n., 1980. 55 p.; bibl.; ill.; map.

Coprolites from four archaeological sites in Minas Gerais were examined for parasites. Those from Gruta do Gentio II, with C14 dates between 3490 and 430 years ago establish the existence of ancilostomids among prehistoric populations. Incompatibility of this organism with cold climates supports hypothesis of Transoceanic migrations.

565 Bryan, Alan L. and Ruth Gruhn. Results of a test excavation of Lapa Pequena, MG, Brazil (Arquivos do Museu de História Natural [Universidade Federal de Minas Gerais, Belo Horizonte, Brazil] 3, 1978, p. 261–325, bibl., ill., map)

Excavations in a small rock shelter northwest of Montes Claros revealed lithic debris and hearths. Shaped tools were not encountered and the industry shows stability throughout the period of occupation.

566 Chmyz, Igor. Projeto Arqueológico Itaipú: quarto relatório das pesquisas realizadas na área de Itaipú, 1978/1979. Curitiba, Brazil: Projeto Arqueológico Itaipú, 1979. 109 p.; bibl.; charts; ill.; glossary; maps.

Vol. 4 describes results of salvage archaeology on Rio Paraná's left bank: 19 sites represent two preceramic and four ceramic complexes; one preceramic and one ceramic complex were not previously encountered. See also item **567**.

**567 ———. Projeto Arqueológico Itaipú: terceiro relatório das pesquisas realizadas na área de Itaipú, 1977/1978. Curitiba, Brazil: Projeto Arqueológico Itaipú, 1978. 141 p.; bibl.; charts; ill.; maps.

Vol. 3 reports on results of salvage archaeology in the region to be flooded by the Itaipú dam on Rio Paraná's left bank: 40 sites were studied, representing several preceramic and ceramic phases and traditions. Lithic and pottery descriptions are presented by phase, accompanied by illustrations and charts. Brief conclusion discusses affiliations with previously reported phases from adjacent regions. Basic reference for the archaeology of southern Brazil.

568 Dias, Ondemar. Dados para o povoamento não Tupiguarani do Estado do Rio de Janeiro: relações arqueológicas e etnográficas (Boletim do Instituto de Arqueologia Brasileira [Rio de Janeiro, Brazil] 8, 1979, p. 18–40, bibl.)

Suggests a correlation between groups speaking languages of the Marco-Je stock and pottery of the Una tradition.

569 ——— and Eliana Carvalho. Uma habitação semi-subterrânea em Minas Gerais, dados arqueológicos (Arquivos do Museu de História Natural [Universidade Federal de Minas Gerais, Belo Horizonte, Brazil] 3, 1978, p. 239–257, bibl., ill., tables)

Depressions visible on three adjacent sites proved on excavation to represent semi-subterranean houses. Pottery represents the Jaraguá phase, of non-Tupiguarani affiliation, C14 dated about AD 1000.

570 ——— and ———. A pré-história da Serra Fluminense e a utilização das grutas no Estado do Rio de Janeiro (IAP/P

[Antropologia] 31, 1980, p. 43–86, bibl., ill.)
Archaeological evidence for the coexistence of groups with distinct ceramic traditions, settlement patterns, and burial practices accords with ethnohistorical accounts. Groups with the same cultural tradition exhibit differences attributable to adaptation to distinct local environments.

571 Garcia, Caio del Rio. Nova datação do sambaqui Maratuá e considerações sobre as flutuações eustáticas propostas por Fairbridge (Revista de Pré-História [Universidade de São Paulo, Instituto de Pré-História, São Paulo] 1, 1979, p. 15–30, bibl., tables)
Recently obtained date for the Maratuá shell-midden is 3865±95 years, contrasting with earlier results of 7327±1300 BP. Sea level reconstructed by Fairbridge for this time does not conform with site's location. Dates for other shell-middens are also compared with the curve, leading to conclusion that contradictions are too numerous to be resolved without further fieldwork.

572 Guidon, Niède *et al.* Art rupestre préhistorique et actual de l'Amérique du Sud (*in* International Congress of Americanists, 42, Paris, 1976. Actes [see item **255**] v. 9-B, p. 239–407, bibl., ill., map)
Consists of 17 papers presented at a symposium during the 42nd International Congress of Americanists, Paris, 1976. Topics: methodological considerations for the study of rock art; elaboration of relative chronologies and typologies; stereophotography; analysis of themes and structure. Description of petroglyphs from upper Río Apaporis, Colombia; Vale do São Francisco, Brazil; new sites in Venezuela; upper Río Pinturas, Argentina; Checta, Lima Dept., Peru; southeastern Piauí, Brazil; Mato Grosso, Brazil; and Surinam.

573 Hilbert, Peter Paul and Klaus Hilbert. Archäeologische Untersuchungen am Rio Nhamundá, unterer Amazonas (Beiträge zur Allgemeinen und Vergleichenden Archäologie [Deutsches Archäologisches Institut, Berlin, FRG] 1, 1980, p. 439–450, ill., map)
Summarizes decorative techniques associated with pottery of the Pocó phase with C14 dating about the beginning of the Christian era. Assemblage includes punctation, rocker stamping, fingernail marking, braid impression, modelling, incision, and polychrome painting.

Instituto Histórico e Geográfico de Alagoas. Museu. Catálogo ilustrado da Coleção Arqueológica. See *HLAS 42:145.*

574 Jungueira, Paulo Alvarenga. Pinturas e gravações rupestres das Lapas Pequena e Pintada, Município de Montes Claros, Minas Gerais (Arquivos do Museu de História Natural [Universidade Federal de Minas Gerais, Belo Horizonte, Brazil] 3, 1978, p. 327–341, bibl., ill.)
Description of geometric and zoomorphic (realistic) depictions on the walls of two rockshelters.

575 ———— and Ione Mendes Malta. Sítios cerâmicos da região de Lagoa Santa (Arquivos do Museu de História Natural [Universidade Federal de Minas Gerais, Belo Horizonte, Brazil] 3, 1978, p. 117–182, bibl., ill., map, table)
Survey in the Lagoa Santa region located 45 sites with pottery, 16 of them in rockshelters. Open sites had sufficient pottery for quantitative analysis, permitting construction of a seriated sequence. Of the pottery 97.3 percent is undecorated; vessel shapes are simple rounded forms.

576 Kneip, Lina Maria; Antônia M.F. Monteiro; and Giraldo Seyferth. A aldeia pré-histórica de Três Vendas, Ararauma, Estado do Rio de Janeiro (MP/R, 27, 1980, p. 283–338, bibl., ill., map, tables)
Description of intensive excavation at a protohistoric habitation site of the Tupiguarani Tradition (Brushed Subtradition), estimated to have had a population of 150.

577 Laming-Emperaire, Annette. Missions archéologiques franco-brésiliennes de Lagoa Santa, Minas Gerais, Brésil: le Grande Abri de Lapa Vermelha (Revista de Pré-História [Universidade de São Paulo, Instituto de Pré-História, São Paulo] 1, 1979, p. 53–89, bibl., ill.)
Four field seasons, concentrating on excavation of the Grand Abri de Lapa Vermelha, produced evidence of human occupation in the form of skeletal remains, charcoal, coprolites, and pictographs. Reliable C14 dates extend back to 11,680±500 BP; an earlier date of 25,000 years is problematical. Summarizes history of archaeology in Lagoa Santa region.

578 Laroche, Armand François Gaston. Arqueologia do baixo Açu e notícias sôbre culturas líticas do Rio Grande do Norte. Natal, Brazil: Universidade Federal do Rio Grande do Norte, Museu Câmara Cascudo, Departamento de Arqueologia, 1981. 1 v.; bibl.; ill. (Suplemento; 7)

Preliminary description of lithic (lanceolate and stemmed points) and ceramic (Papeba Tradition) complexes from sites on the Rio Piranhas-Açu encountered in survey preliminary to flooding of the basin.

579 ———; **Adjelma Soares;** and **Silvia Laroche.** Um sítio epipaleolítico microlítico do Nordeste brasileiro? Chã de Caboclo Bj. 10, Pernambuco. Recife, Brazil: Fundação Joaquim Nabuco, 1980. 83 p.; bibl.; charts; ill. (Série monografias; 17)

Open site, 90 km northwest of Recife, produced lithic and ceramic remains extending from about 11,000 years ago to Neobrazilian period. Although the deposit is shallow, several lithic and ceramic complexes can be differentiated and correlated with numerous C14 dates. This report summarizes data obtained during four seasons between 1975–78. Important reference for Paleo-Indian in northeastern Brazil.

580 **Maranca, Silvia.** Pinturas rupestres da Toca da Entrada do Pajaú, Estado do Piauí: análise das figuras zoomorfas (MP/R, 27, 1980, p. 157–197, bibl., ill., map)

Typological, quantitative, and positional analyses of the zoomorphic depictions, which constitute 29.96 percent of the 504 figures recorded from a rockshelter in southeastern Piauí. Primary division was between dominant (10 percent or more in relative frequency) and complementary (less than 10 percent frequency) animals. Deer, emu, and birds are in the first category; rodents, frogs, armadillos, capivaras, jaguars, and tapirs in the second. No habitation refuse was associated.

581 **Meggers, Betty J.** Climatic oscillation as a factor in the prehistory of Amazonia (SAA/AA, 44, 1979, p. 252–266, bibl., ill.)

Conflicting interpretations of prehistoric cultural development in the Amazon basin and Brazilian coast are assessed in the context of climatic oscillations reconstructed from data on soils, geomorphology, palynology and paleoclimatology.

582 ——— and **Silvia Maranca.** Uma reconstituição experimental de organiza-

ção social, baseada na distribuição de tipos de cerâmica num sítio habitação da tradição Tupiguarani (IAP/P [Antropologia] 31, 1980, p. 227–247, bibl., charts, tables)

Surface and sub-surface samples of pottery from 12 generally oval patches arranged in ring, corresponding to a prehistoric village of the Tupiguarani tradition in southern Piauí, were classified into types. Analysis showed that red slipping was confined to the samples from seven locations, six of them on the eastern half of the ring. Red-on-white painting was confined to samples from the western half. These differences suggested a moiety division with matrilocal residence. Ethnographic and ethnohistoric accounts of Tupi social organization are compatible with this interpretation.

583 **Miranda, Avelino Fernandes de.** Notas sobre o habitat dos horticultores do centro-sul de Goiás (IAP/P [Antropologia] 31, 1980, p. 165–183, bibl., map, tables)

Groups representing three different ceramic-agricultural traditions moved into southern Goiás, the Tupiguarani and Aratu traditions from the south and the Uru tradition from the west. All sites are in forest, but nearby cerrado was probably exploited by hunting and gathering. Pottery of the Uru tradition has griddles, implying use of bitter manioc; their absence in the pottery of the Aratu tradition may indicate only sweet manioc was grown.

584 **Morais, José Luis de.** Inserção geomorfológica de sítios arqueológicos do alto Paranapanema, SP (MP/R, 25, nova série, 1978, p. 65–86, bibl., ill., maps, tables)

Discussion of kinds of information from geomorphology relevant to interpreting the location and characteristics of archaeological sites and evaluating disturbance subsequent to habitation.

585 **Pallestrini, Luciana.** O espaço habitacional em pré-história brasileira (MP/R, 25, nova série, 1978, p. 11–30, bibl., plates)

Generalized discussion of kinds of inferences about prehistoric societies obtainable from archaeological remains in southern Brazil.

586 ——— and **Philomena Chiara.** Indústria lítica de Três Vendas, Município de Araruama, Estado do Rio de Janeiro (MP/R, 27, 1980, p. 133–144, bibl., charts)

General types and relative frequencies of debitage and artifacts at a ceramic site of the Tupiguarani tradition. Among artifacts, 48 percent were side scrapers.

587 Prous, André. Première information sur les maisons souterraines de l'état de São Paulo (Revista de Pré-História [Universidade de São Paulo, Instituto de Pré-História, São Paulo] 1, 1979, p. 127–145, bibl., ill., map)

Four locations with pithouses extend the distribution of this type of construction to the north. Undecorated pottery and ground stone celts are associated.

588 ———; Ana Lúcia Duarte Lanna; and **Fabiano Lopes de Paula.** Estilística e cronologia na arte rupestre de Minas Gerais (IAP/P [Antropologia] 31, 1980, p. 121–146, bibl., ill., map)

Three regional traditions are defined in Minas Gerais: 1) Planalto tradition emphasizes monochrome representations of animals, especially deer; 2) São Francisco tradition features bichrome or polychrome depictions of snails, birds, and fish, deer being rare; and 3) Sumidouro tradition is geometric. Each tradition is divided into regional styles.

589 Ribeiro, Pedro Augusto Mentz. Casas subterrâneas no planalto meridional, município de Santa Cruz do Sul, Rio Grande do Sul, Brasil (Revista de CEPA [Associação Pró-Ensino em Santa Cruz do Sul, Brasil] 9, 1980, p. 1–52, bibl., ill., map, tables)

Complete excavation of two adjacent pit houses revealed earth benches, a ramp for access, and occupational debris. Pottery belongs to Eveiras Phase of Taquara tradition. Charcoal sample from House B gave a date of AD 1035.

590 ———. A cerâmica Tupiguarani do vale do Rio Pardo e a redução jesuítica de Jesus Maria (*in* Congreso de Arqueología Chilena, 7th, Altos de Vilches, Chile, 1977. Actas [see item **613**] v. 2, p. 637–647, bibl., chart, map)

Survey of the Pardo and Pardinho Rivers permitted identification of two contemporary phases of the Tupiguarani tradition and the subsequent Reduções phase associated with the Jesuit mission of Jesus Maria. Identification of iron working installations at the latter places the initial date for

this technology 64 years earlier than previously believed.

591 ———. Indústrias líticas do sul do Brasil: tentativa de esquematização (PUC/V, 24:96, 1979, p. 471–493, bibl., map, table)

Two general lithic traditions have been distinguished in Paraná, Santa Catarina, and Rio Grande do Sul. Complexes lacking stone projectile points belong to Humaitá tradition; those possessing them to Umbú tradition. Existing C14 dating suggests Humaitá tradition expanded from west to east, Umbu tradition from north to south. Possible affiliations with shell-middens and petroglyphs are discussed. A useful general summary of recent research.

592 ———. Sobre uma pedra gravado na Vale do Rio Pardo, RS, Brasil (SAA/R, 12, 1978, p. 147–154, bibl., ill.)

A flat oval stone, 12.3 by 9.3 cm, found in southern Brazil, has incised designs similar to engraved plaques from Patagonia and the middle Rio Uruguay.

593 ——— and Itala de Silveira. Sítios arqueológicos da tradição Taquara, fase Erveiras, no Vale do Rio Pardo, RS, Brasil (CEPA/R, 8, 1979, p. 3–60, bibl., ill., map, tables)

Pottery from surface collections and tests at 30 sites defines a new phase of the Taquara tradition of southern Brazil. Pottery indicating contact with the Tupiguarani tradition occurred at nine sites. Lithic artifacts and pottery are described and illustrated.

594 Schmitz, Pedro Ignacio. A evolução da cultura no sudoeste de Goiás (IAP/P [Antropologia] 31, 1980, p. 185–225, bibl., ill.)

Rock shelters in southwestern Goiás have been occupied for the past 11,000 years. Paranaíba Phase, ending about 9000 BP, correlated with end of Pleistocene; it is characterized by a unifacial lithic industry and bone points. Serranópolis Phase, extending from 9000 to about 5000 BP, correlated with warmer temperatures and variable rainfall; the lithic industry is nondescript. The Jataí Phase, representing pottery making agriculturalists, begins about 1000 BP when the present-day climate prevailed. Iporá Phase of Tupiguarani tradition concludes the sequence.

595 ———, Indústrias líticas en el sur de Brasil (FFCL/EL, 14:47 [ano 13] 1978, p. 103–129, bibl., map)

Review of distribution of principal lithic traditions of southern Brazil suggests they may reflect specialization to different subsistence and environmental resources. Sites with C14 dates are shown on a map, and names and dates of sites are grouped by tradition in a table.

596 ———; Silvia Moehlecke; and Altair Sales Barbosa. Sítios de petroglifos nos projetos Alto-Tocantins e Alto-Araguaia, Goiás (IAP/P [Antropologia] 30, 1979, 73 p.; bibl., ill., maps)

Description of five petroglyph locations representing three different styles: 1) abstract anthropomorphic; 2) geometric; and 3) naturalistic anthropomorphic and zoomorphic. Authors believe third correlates with horticultural groups. Large fold-outs show associations; tables permit analysis of motifs by site.

597 Simões, Mário F. Coletores-pescadores ceramistas do litoral do Salgado, Pará (MPEG/B, 78, 1981, 26 p.; bibl., ill., map)

Surface and stratigraphic excavations in 43 shell-middens on the Atlantic coast, Pará state, provide data for defining Mina Phase. Ground and chipped stone, bone, shell, and pottery artifacts are described. Pottery is tempered with shell and decorated rarely with red wash, brushing, unobliterated coils, or incision. C14 dates extend between 3000 and 1500 BC. Both dating and characteristics of pottery suggest affiliation with Alaka Phase of Guyana, and more remotely with early formative pottery of north coastal Colombia.

598 Simonsen, Iluska and Acary de Passos Oliveira. Modelos etnográficos aplicados à cerâmica de Miararré. Goiânia, Brazil: Editora da Universidade Federal de Goiás, 1980. 114 p.; bibl.; ill.

Pottery type description based on 141 specimens from the bottom of Lake Miararré, upper Xingú. Temper is predominantly cauixi; decoration by incision, punctuation, applique, and modeling. Hypotheses concerning origin, ethnographic affiliation, and use of pottery are considered. English summary (19 p.) provides principal details of method of analysis.

599 Uchôa, Dorath P. and Caio del Rio Garcia. Resultados preliminares do projeto de pesquisas arqueológicas no baixo curso do Rio Ribeira, Cananéia-Iguape: litoral sul de São Paulo, Brasil (Revista de Pré-História [Universidade de São Paulo, Instituto de Pré-História, São Paulo] 1, 1979, p. 91–113, bibl., chart, ill., map)

Describes 75 shell middens encountered in area about 600 km². Table gives dimensions, composition, condition, and C14 dates. Latter extend between 5900±520 and 840±80 BP, with majority between 5000 and 3000 BP.

CHILE

600 Aldunate del Solar, Carlos. Cultura mapuche. Santiago: Ministerio de Educación, 1978. 56 p.; ill. (Serie El Patrimonio cultural chileno. Colección Culturas aborígenes)

General description of the environment and culture of the Mapuche (Araucanian) Indians of north central Chile, and their role in the history of the country.

601 Ampuero Brito, Gonzalo. Cultural diaguita. Santiago: Ministerio de Educación, 1978. 54 p.; bibl.; ill.; map (Serie El Patrimonio cultural chileno. Colección Culturas aborígenes)

Summary of history of investigation and present status of knowledge of the Diaguita culture, dating between about AD 1000–1500 on the Chilean coast (Norte Chico). Illustrated in color.

602 Barthel, Thomas S. The eighth land: the Polynesian discovery and settlement of Easter Island. Translated from the German by Anneliese Martin. Honolulu: University Press of Hawaii, 1978. 372 p.; bibl.; index.

Final publication of ethnohistorical data and oral traditions collected on Easter Island in 1957–58 and previously partially communicated in a series of essays. Important reference for specialists. Translated from the German: Das achte Land.

603 Bird, Junius. "El Hombre de Cobre," un minero prehistórico del Norte de Chile y sus herramientas (Boletín [Museo Arqueológico de La Serena, Chile] 16, 1977/1978, p. 77–106, bibl., ill.)

Description of circumstances of discovery of the body of a copper miner near Chuquicamata in 1899 and its subsequent history, terminating with the deposit of the mummy and some of the artifacts at the American Museum of Natural History. Others are at the National Museum of Natural History. Stone hammers, wooden sticks, baskets, a skin bag, and several woolen textiles are described. C14 dates indicate an antiquity of about 1400 years.

604 Bittmann, Bente. Fishermen, mummies and balsa rafts on the coast of Northern Chile (UNC/ED, 3:3, 1978, p. 60–103, bibl., ill.)

Presents a case for examining more carefully the possibility that cultural developments on the northern coast of Chile were influenced by groups to the north, where evidence for sea travel dates back to early formative times.

605 ——— and Juan R. Munizaga. Algunas consideraciones en torno al "complejo Chinchorro," Chile (in Congreso de Arqueología Chilena, 7th, Altos de Vilches, Chile, 1977. Actas [see item 613] v. 1, p. 119–129, bibl., ill.)

Review of procedure of artificial mummification practiced by populations of the "Chinchorro complex" distributed between Arica and Antofagasta. The pattern, involving evisceration, restoration of the living form, and wrapping, appears in conjunction with other innovations that imply an external origin, as yet unknown.

606 ———; R.P. Gustavo Le Paige; and Lautaro Núñez A. Cultura atacameña. Santiago: Ministerio de Educación, 1978. 64 p.; col. ill.; map (Serie El Patrimonio cultural chileno. Colección Culturas aborígenes)

Chronological review of prehistory of the puna of Atacama from Paleo-Indian to Spanish colonial times; excellent, well illustrated summary of adaptation to this marginal environment.

607 Brito, Oscar; Angel Deza; Alvaro Román; and Guido Concha. Fechamiento por termoluminiscencia de cerámicas del sitio Toconce 2 B (in Congreso de Arqueología Chilena, 7th, Altos de Vilches, Chile, 1977. Actas [see item 613] v. 1, p. 53–58)

Results of age determination of thermoluminescence of five potsherds did not differ from C14 dates by more than 10 percent, indicating this method can be successfully employed in Chile.

608 Campbell, Ramón. Eventual proyección de la cultura de Tiwanaku en el Pacífico Oriental, Isla de Pascua (in Congreso de Arqueología Chilena, 7th, Altos de Vilches, Chile, 1977. Actas [see item 613] v. 2, p. 575–594, bibl., ill.)

Review of distribution in central Andes of five elements of Easter Island architecture and sculpture leads to conclusion that there was contact between the two regions; the time and method of communication, and whether it initiated from the mainland or the island are not yet established.

609 Castillo G., Gastón and Arturo Rodríguez O. Excavaciones preliminares en el sitio "La Fundación:" una industria tipo Cárcamo (Boletín [Museo Arqueológico de La Serena, Chile] 16, 1977/1978, p. 125–144, bibl., ill., map)

Preliminary report on results of excavations at a site northeast of La Serena with a lithic industry characterized by projectile points with tapering stems.

610 Castro R., Victoria; José Berenguer R.; and Carlos Aldunate del S. Antecedentes de una interacción altiplano-área atacameña durante el período tardío: Toconce (in Congreso de Arqueología Chilena, 7th, Altos de Vilches, Chile, 1977. Actas [see item 613] v. 2, p. 477–498, bibl., ill., map)

Site in the Rio Loa drainage, consisting of an agglutinated settlement, rock shelters used for burial, and chullpas, represents intrusion of a population from the altiplano and adaptation to a transitional habitat.

611 Cervellino Giannoni, Miguel and Francisco Tellez Cancino. Emergencia y desarrollo en una aldea prehispánica de Quillagua, Antofagasta. Copiapó, Chile: Museo Regional de Atacama, 1980. 276 p.; bibl.; ill. (Contribución Arqueológica; 1)

Describes results of excavations at a late period settlement in Río Loa Valley, about 65 km from shore. Emphasis is on evaluating the adaptation to the special environment of this desert "oasis" and relations with highlands and coast. Maize and algarroba were principal staples and appear to have sustained a stable population; absence of significant alternation in technology implies successful adaptation was achieved.

612 Checura Jeria, Jorge. Funebria incaica en el cerro Esmeralda, Iquique, I Region (Estudios Atacameños [Universidad de Norte, Museo de Arqueología, San Pedro de Atacama, Chile] 5, 1977, p. 125–141, bibl., ill., map)

Description of two female sacrifices interred together inland from Iquique at 905 m elevation. Ages were about nine and 19 years. They were accompanied by 104 items (pottery, metal, shell, textiles) of Imperial Inca style.

613 Congreso de Arqueología Chilena, 7th, *Altos de Vilches, Chile, 1977.* Actas. Santiago: Sociedad Chilena de Arqueología, 1979? 2 v.

Papers from this Chilean archaeological Congress are annotated separately in this section and entered under authors' names (see items **499, 514–515, 519, 524, 532, 552, 590, 605, 607–608, 610, 614, 627, 630, 634, 642, 652** and **750**). For ethnohistorical papers, see *HLAS 42:1593–1594* and *HLAS 42:1754.* [Ed.]

614 Durán S., Eliana. El yacimiento de María Pinto, sus correlaciones y ubicación cultural (*in* Congreso de Arqueología Chilena, 7th, Altos de Vilches, Chile, 1977. Actas [see item **613**] v. 1, p. 261–275, bibl., ill.)

Description of pottery and stone objects from five tombs in a cemetery of the late Diaguita culture in central Chile.

615 Falabella G., Fernanda and **Teresa Planella O.** Sequencia cronológica-cultural para el sector de desembocadura del Río Maipo (Revista Chilena de Antropología [Universidad de Chile, Departamento de Antropología, Santiago] 3, 1980, p. 87–107, bibl., ill.)

Excavations in four sites permit establishment of a local sequence of three ceramic complexes. The Llolleo Complex has two C14 dates placing its inception about AD 200. The Aconcagua Complex is estimated to extend between about 800–1400. The third complex is Colonial. No preceramic occupations were encountered.

616 Ferrando, Caludio Cristino and **Patricia Vargas Casanova.** Prospección

arqueológica de Isla de Pascua (Anales [Universidad de Chile, Santiago] 161/162, 1980, p. 193–225, bibl., ill.)

Systematic survey begun in 1968 has covered 40 percent of the island, with documentation of 3,552 sites. This progress report explains procedures, categories of data, and methods of analysis.

617 Focacci, Guillermo. Síntesis de la arqueología del extremo Norte de Chile (Chungara [Universidad del Norte, Departamento de Antropología, Arica, Chile] 8, 1980, p. 3–23, bibl.)

Review of cultural development from about 5000 BC to European contact.

618 Gambier, Mariano. La cultura de Ansilta. San Juan, Argentina: Universidad Nacional de San Juan, Instituto de Investigaciones Arqueológicas y Museo, 1977. 272 p.; appendixes, bibl., ill., tables.

First detailed monograph on this little-known culture of the central valley of Chile, dating between about 1300 BC and AD 900. Investigations were conducted in 14 caves, five rockshelters, seven semisubterranean houses, and seven open sites. Stone, bone, and pottery are described in detail, as well as ornaments and bone tools. Appendixes by specialists discuss textiles, plant remains (maize, quinoa, beans) and human skeletons. Basic reference for specialists.

619 Grove, Robert Bruce. Investigaciones acerca del complejo Chuqui (Estudios Atacameños [Universidad del Norte, Museo de Arqueología, San Pedro de Atacama, Chile] 6, 1978, p. 5–18, bibl., ill., map)

Careful excavations in four sites of the Chuqui complex, defined by Lanning and assigned by him an age of 16,000 years, shows the "artifacts" to be of natural origin, attributable to impact of metal animal shoes, cartwheels, or llama hoofs.

620 Hidalgo L., Jorge. Incidencias de los patrones de poblamiento en el cálculo de la población del Partido de Atacama desde 1752 a 1804: las revistas inéditas de 1787–1792 y 1804 (Estudios Atacameños [Universidad del Norte, Museo de Arqueología, San Pedro de Atacama, Chile] 6, 1978, p. 53–76, bibl., charts, maps)

Census figures for the population of the Atacama region of North Chile must be interpreted in the context of evidence for transhumance and simultaneous control of distinct environments among historic and prehistoric groups, as well as the allowances reflecting depopulation after European contact.

621 Iribarren Charlin, Jorge. Complejos culturales líticos en Atacama y Coquimbo, Chile (Revista de Pré-História [Universidade de São Paulo, Instituto de Pré-História, São Paulo] 1, 1979, p. 115–126, bibl., ill., map)

Brief summary of characteristics of three complexes dating about 5000–6000 BC: the Huentelauquén complex, the Shell Fishhook complex, and the Cárcano complex.

622 ———. La cultura Huentelauquen y sus proyección a otra del litoral de California (in Congreso Peruano el Hombre y la Cultura Andina, 3rd, Lima, 1977. El hombre y la cultura andina [see item **756**] v. 2, p. 708–733, bibl., ill., maps)

Review of the locations from which cogged stones have been collected on the coast of Chile south of La Serena. Recent finds in the vicinity of Antofagasta expand the distribution and provide new data on context.

623 Kaltwasser P., Jorge; Alberto Medina R.; and Juan R. Munizaga V. Cementerio del período arcaico en Cuchipuy (Revista Chilena de Antropología [Universidad de Chile, Departamento de Antropología, Santiago] 3, 1980, p. 109–123, bibl., ill.)

Excavations in a cemetery on the beach of the former Lake Taguatagua revealed burials representing at least four occupations extending from Paleo-Indian through archaic into ceramic periods. The preceramic population was dolicocephalic, the ceramic population brachycephalic.

624 Kuzmanic P., Ivo and Gabriel Cobo C. Excavación en Las Pircas (Boletín [Museo Arqueológico de La Serena, Chile] 16, 1977/1978, p. 145–188, bibl., ill., map)

Excavations in a rockshelter containing pictographs near La Serena revealed a single occupation corresponding to hunter-gatherers and/or herders. Pottery of Molle types occurred sparsely. C14 date of 440 AD is compatible with the ceramic association.

625 Le Paige, Gustavo. Vestigios arqueológicos incaicos en las cumbres de la zona atacameña (Estudios Atacameños [Universidad del Norte, Museo de Arqueología, San Pedro de Atacama, Chile] 6, 1978, p. 36–52, ill., map)

Brief text recounts visits to several Inca installations on the summits of volcanoes; plans and photographs show details of architecture and associated cultural remains.

626 Llagostera Martínez, Agustín. 9,700 (i.e. Nine thousand seven hundred) years of maritime subsistence on the Pacific: an analysis by means of bioindicators in the North of Chile (SAA/AA, 44, 1979, p. 309–324, bibl., ill.)

Differences in the presence and relative frequencies of shellfish and fish in archaeological sites are compatible with oscillations in climate and water temperature reconstructed for the north coast of Chile during the past 10,000 years. They also make intelligible such cultural innovations as shell fishhooks and maritime transport by rafts, the latter introduced about 1700 BP.

627 ———. Ocupación humana en la costa norte de Chile asociada a peces local-extintos y litos-geométricos: 9680±160 BP (in Congreso de Arqueología Chilena, 7th, Altos de Vilches, Chile, 1977. Actas [see item **613**] v. 1, p. 93–113, bibl., ill., map)

Analysis of fish remains from the shell-midden of Quebrada Las Conchas near Antofagasta revealed species now locally extinct. Among artifacts are cogged stones. Two C14 samples from the base of the midden dated 9400 and 9680 BP, indicating subsistence adaptation to marine resources was achieved by this time.

628 McCoy, Patrick C. Stone-lined earth ovens in Easter Island (AT/A, 52:206, Nov. 1978, p. 204–216, bibl., ill., map, tables)

One or more stone-lined pits for cooking were encountered at 361 of 1315 habitation sites. Outline is variable, but breadth concentrated between 50–70 cm. They occur in a variety of contexts, and duration of use ranges from a few weeks to permanently. The only other occurrence in Polynesia is on Hawaii. Geographical, stylistic, frequency, and other methods of clustering are employed for deducing social and behavioral patterns.

629 Madrid de Colin, Jacqueline. El área andina meridional y el proceso agroalfarero en Chile Central (Revista Chilena de Antropología [Universidad de Chile, Departamento de Antropología, Santiago] 3, 1980, p. 25–39, bibl., chart, map)

Correlation of the complexes from the coast, central valley, and cordillera environmental zones of central Chile by preceramic and ceramic periods (both divided into early, middle, and late subperiods), provides a basis for preliminary assessment of the relationship between environment and cultural history.

630 Massone Mezzano, Mauricio. Aconcagua Rojo Engobado, un tipo cerámico del complejo cultural Aconcagua (*in* Congreso de Arqueología Chilena, 7th, Altos de Vilches, Chile, 1977. Actas [see item **613**] v. 1, p. 247–260, bibl., ill.)

Description of a type of pottery associated with burials at sites of Diaguita affiliation, which appears to originate just prior to Inca influence.

631 ———. Nuevas consideraciones en torno al complejo Aconcagua (Revista Chilena de Antropología [Universidad de Chile, Departamento de Antropología, Santiago] 3, 1980, p. 75–85, bibl., ill., map, table)

Comparative analysis of the occurrence of four pottery types at 13 sites of the Aconcagua Complex in central Chile reveals regional variation; cultural and chronological implications are reviewed.

632 Muñoz Ovalle, Iván. Investigaciones arqueológicas en los túmulos funerarios del Valle de Azapa, Arica (Chungara [Universidad del Norte, Departamento de Antropología, Arica, Chile] 8, 1980, p. 57–78, bibl., table)

Resume of excavations of two burial mounds of the Alto Ramírez phase, dated between about 400 BC and AD 500. Plant and animal remains, pottery, basketry, and textiles were associated. Skull deformation was practiced.

633 Niemeyer F., Hans. La cueva con pinturas indígenas del Río Pedregoso, Departamento de Chile Chico, Provincia de Aysén, Chile (Revista del Museo de Historia Natural de San Rafael [San Rafael, Argentina] 3:1/4, 1976, p. 339–364, appendix, bibl., ill., map)

Cavern in Chilean Patagonia, close to the Argentine border, is ornamented with painted lines, dots, and outlines of human hands (beautifully shown in color plates). Lithic artifacts from surface are described by L. Bate in an appendix and assigned to the Patagoniense.

634 ——— and **Virgilio Schiappacasse F.** Investigación de un sitio temprano de cazadores-recolectores arcaicos en la desembocadura del Valle de Camarones, I región de Chile (*in* Congreso de Arqueología Chilena, 7th, Altos de Vilches, Chile, 1977. Actas [see item **613**] v. 1, p. 115–118, bibl., ill.)

Lower levels of the site Camarones-14 represent the Quiani I phase, of Shell Fishhook complex. Circular hooks in various stages of manufacture are illustrated; compound hooks, weights, bifacial projectile points, mortars, cordage, netting, and faunal remains were also represented. Three C14 dates range from 5470 to 4665 BC.

635 Núñez A., Lautaro. Emergencia y desintegración de la sociedad tarapaqueña: riqueza y pobreza en una quebrada del Norte Chileno (UC/AT, 439, 1. semestre, 1979, p. 163–213, bibl., ill., maps)

Traces changing human exploitation of the Quebrada de Tarapacá from preagricultural to modern times, interweaving environmental, social, and economic factors of local or external origin.

636 ——— and **Cora Moragas W.** Ocupación arcaica temprana, en Tiliviche, Norte de Chile: informe de avance (Boletín [Museo Arqueológico de La Serena, Chile] 16, 1977/1978, p. 53–76, bibl., ill., map)

Stratigraphic data from 20 pits and a series of C14 dates permit defining three chronological zones: 1) Early Zone dates between 7810 and 5900 BC; 2) Intermediate Zone between 5900 and 4955 BC; and 3) Late Zone between 4955 and 4110 BC. Site is 40 km from shore and subsistence pattern reflected in plant and animal remains indicates exploitation of marine and interior resources. Climatic change may have led to increased emphasis on marine resources, which characterizes later complexes on this part of Chilean coast.

637 ——— and ———. Una ocupación con cerámica temprana en la secuencia del distrito de Cáñamo, costa desértica del Norte de Chile (Estudio Atacameños [Universidad del Norte, Museo de Arqueología, San Pedro de Atacama, Chile] 5, 1977, p. 21–49, bibl., ill., map, tables)

Investigations at 15 sites on peninsula 60 km south of Iquique provide basis for a five-stage local sequence extending from about 2000 BC to Inca conquest. Pottery, maize, and cotton are adopted about 860 BC. Presence or absence of 117 traits (bone, shell, wood, basketry, textiles, cordage, lithics, pottery, plants, fauna, burials) is tabulated to show their continuity and discontinuity between stages.

638   Núñez Henríquez, Patricio and **Vjera Zlatar Montan.** Actividades en la comuna de Pisagua, período precerámico (Boletín [Museo Arqueológico de La Serena, Chile] 16, 1977/1978, p. 42–52, bibl., map)

Archaeological evidence and dating suggest that hunter-gatherer sites previously interpreted as reflecting transhumance are probably contemporary populations that retained their identities in spite of similar habitats and spatial proximity.

639   ——— and ———. Radiometría de Aragón-1 y su implicancia en el precerámico costero del Norte de Chile (*in* Congreso Nacional de Arqueología Argentina, 4th, San Rafael, Argentina, 1976. Actas y memorias [see item 512] pt. 1, p. 105–117, bibl., ill., map, tables)

Description of stratigraphy and artifacts from a habitation site representing a seasonal camp of hunter-gatherers. Three C14 dates bracket its occupation between about 6700 and 2500 BC.

640   ——— and ———. Tiliviche-1b y Aragón-1 [Estrato-V]; dos comunidades precerámicas coexistentes en Pampa del Tamarugal, Pisagua, Norte de Chile (*in* Congreso Peruano: el Hombre y la Cultura Andina, 3rd, Lima, 1977. El hombre y la cultura andina [see item 756] v. 2, p. 708–733, bibl., ill., maps)

Comparison of plant, marine fauna, and artifacts of fiber, wood, bone, shell, and stone from sites six km apart in similar locations and occupied between 6000 and 4000 BC shows significant differences, implying distinct patterns of adaptation to the same potential resource base.

641   Ortiz-Troncoso, Omar R. Punta Santa Ana et Bahía Buena: deux gisements sur une ancienne ligne de rivage dans le Détroit de Magellan (SA/J, 66, 1979, p. 133–204, bibl., ill., map, tables)

Describes stratigraphic excavations in two habitation sites, with refuse less than 85 cm deep, dating between about 4500 and 3000 BC, when sea level was higher than at present. Three occupational levels were recognized; stone and bone artifacts are described and tabulated by level. Faunal remains attest to importance of land mammals and birds in the diet; marine resources were also exploited.

642   Pino Quivira, Mario and **Juan Varela Barbagelata.** Aplicación del método de datación por hidratación de obsidiana al sitio arqueológico de Laguna de Taguatagua, Provincia de O'Higgins (*in* Congreso de Arqueología Chilena, 7th, Altos de Vilches, Chile, 1977. Actas [see item 613] v. 1, p. 25–52, bibl., map, tables)

C14 dates and measurements of soil temperature are used to establish two rates of hydration for obsidian from archaeological contexts in the vicinity of Laguna de Taguatagua. Cooler temperatures between 11500 and 6500 BP are reflected in a rate slower than that obtained for the period since 6500 BP.

643   Pollard, Gordon C. El complejo cerámico Vega Alta del Río Loa Medio, Antofagasta, Chile (UCC/NG, 6, 1978/1979, p. 95–113, bibl., ill., tables)

Sites on the middle Rio Loa with pottery decorated by incision, punctation, corrugation, and applique represent a previously undescribed complex. The sample was classified into 14 wares using criteria of paste and surface treatment. Seriation using wares was unsuccessful, but rim forms and techniques of decoration provided a basis for recognizing early, middle and late periods with the Vega Alta complex. C14 date of 200 BC is considered terminal; inception is estimated about 800 BC.

644   Rivera D., Mario A. Cronología absoluta y periodificación en la arqueología chilena (Boletín [Museo Arqueológico de La Serena, Chile] 16, 1977/1978, p. 13–41, bibl., charts, tables)

Availability of 158 C14 dates for Chile warrants attempt to recognize periods of general significance. Four regions are defined: Arid North, Semi-arid North, Central, and South. Tables give date, site, excavator, lab number, material dated, and cultural type. Correlations with the Arid North and Semiarid North indicated by this framework are shown on charts.

645 ———. Desarrollo cultural en el Norte árido y semi-árido de Chile: proposición de un modelo de periodificación (*in* Congreso Nacional de Arqueología Argentina, 4th, San Rafael, Argentina, 1976. Actas y memorias [see item **512**] pt. 1, p. 95–104, bibl., tables)

Suggests traditional separation of Norte Grande and Norte Chico has impeded recognition of similarities in cultural development. Chronological scheme of Early, Initial, Intermediate, and Late periods is proposed for entire region, and its utility demonstrated by insertion of 114 C14 dates. Tables give provenience of dates and compare the chronologies of arid and semi-arid subregions.

646 **Santoro V., Calogero.** Estratigrafía y secuencia cultural funeraria; fases Azapa, Alto Ramírez y Tiwanaku: Arica, Chile (Chungara [Universidad del Norte, Departamento de Antropología, Arica, Chile] 8, 1980, p. 24–44, bibl., ill.)

Excavations in a cemetery revealed three periods spanning some 2000 years. Burials of the earlier phase (Azapa) were associated with engraved gourds, stone mortars, wood bags, necklaces of shell, stone, and bone beads, and snuff taking apparatus. Burials of intermediate phase (Alto Ramírez) had crude pottery and remains of maize, quinoa, manioc and sweet potato. Tiwanaku burials constituted only six percent; maize, quinoa, gourds, and baskets were associated, as well as textiles. Three C14 dates for the Azapa phase range from 990 to 560 BC.

647 ———. Fase Azapa, transición del arcaico al desarrollo agrario inicial en los valles bajos de Arica (Chungara [Universidad del Norte, Departamento de Antropología, Arica, Chile] 8, 1980, p. 46–56, bibl.)

Characteristics of settlement pattern and material culture of Azapa phase sites indicate it represents the final state in transition from wild food to agricultural subsistence on the north coast of Chile. Five C14 dates range from 905 to 610 BC.

648 **Serracino, George** and **Frank Pereyea.** Tumbre: sitios estacionales en la industria tambilliense (Estudios Atacameños [Universidad del Norte, Museo de Arque-

ología, San Pedro de Atacama, Chile] 5, 1977, p. 5–20, bibl., ill., map)

The Tambilliense industry is represented by 43 sites on the eastern part of the Salar de Atacama in Northern Chile. Bifaces and scrapers were the only shaped artifacts.

649 **Silva Galdames, Osvaldo.** Consideraciones acerca del período inca en la Cuenca de Santiago, Chile Central (Boletín [Museo Arqueológico de La Serena, Chile] 16, 1977/1978, p. 211–243, bibl.)

Disagreement over location of Inca empire's southern frontier can be resolved by reexamination of early documents. Author interprets evidence as indicating that Santiago basin was colonized by the ruler and not by the state, with resulting differences in nature and strength of impact on local society.

650 **Stehberg L., Rubén.** El cementerio alfarero temprano de Chacayes, interior del Cajón del Maipo (*in* Congreso Nacional de Arqueología Argentina, 4th, San Rafael, Argentina, 1976. Actas y memorias [see item **512**] pt. 1, p. 277–295, bibl., ill., map)

Salvage excavations at a cemetery southeast of Santiago produced remains of 14 individuals, analyzed by J. Munizaga. Pottery and other artifacts represent the Molle complex. Single C14 date is AD 430.

651 ——— and **Andrés Pinto.** Ocupaciones alfareras tempranas en Quebrada El Salitral del Cordón de Chacabuco (Revista Chilena de Antropología [Universidad de Chile, Departamento de Antropología, Santiago] 3, 1980, p. 57–73, apendices, bibl., ill.)

Pottery encountered in excavations in a rockshelter indicates its use by three successive pottery-making groups during the first millennium AD. These movements reflect pattern of exploitation combining marine and inland resources.

652 ——— and **Keith Fox.** Excavaciones arqueológicas en el Alero Rocoso de Los Llanos, interior del Arrayan, provincia de Santiago (*in* Congreso de Arqueología Chilena, 7th, Altos de Vilches, Chile, 1977. Actas [see item **613**] v. 1, p. 217–241, bibl., ill., map)

Rockshelter northeast of Santiago contained brief preceramic occupation, followed around AD 400 by intermittent use of pottery-making groups up to colonial times.

Stratigraphy, faunal remains, pottery and stone artifacts are described and their significance in the broader chronology of the region discussed.

653 Tarragó, Myriam Noemí. Relaciones prehispánicas entre San Pedro de Atacama, Norte de Chile, y regiones aledañas: la Quebrada de Humahuaca (Estudios Atacameños [Universidad del Norte, Museo de Arqueología, San Pedro de Atacama, Chile] 5, 1977, p. 50–63, bibl., ill.)

Five pottery vessels encountered in cemetery excavations near San Pedro de Atacama are assigned to the Isla complex of the Quebrada de Humahuaca, implying communication between these environmentally distinct regions by the Middle Period.

654 Thomson, W.J. Te Pito Te Henua o Isla de Pascua (Anales [Universidad de Chile, Santiago] 161/162, 1980, p. 31–160, ill.)

Translation into Spanish of the report by Paymaster Thomson of his visit to Easter Island in 1886, including introduction by Gonzalo Figueroa and original illustrations and photographs of objects in the National Museum of Natural History, Smithsonian Institution.

COLOMBIA

655 Angulo Valdés, Carlos. Concheros tardíos en el norte de Colombia (*in* International Congress for the Study of the Pre-Columbian Cultures of the Lesser Antilles, 8th, St. Kitts, 1979. Proceedings [see item 434] p. 80–87, bibl., ill., map)

Excavations in eight shell-middens on the margins of the Ciénaga Grande de Santa Marta demonstrate persistence of emphasis on marine food resources up to European contact.

656 Bird, Junius. Legacy of the stingless bee (AMNH/NH, 88:9, Nov. 1979, p. 49–52, plates)

Casting gold by using lost-wax process is rare in Peru but common in Colombia, perhaps because of ease in obtaining wax produced by stingless bees restricted to tropical forests.

657 Bouchard, Jean-François. Investigaciones arqueológicas en la costa pac-

ífica meridional de Colombia: el Proyecto Tumaco (ICA/RCA, 21, 1977/1978, p. 283–314, bibl., ill., map)

Preliminary analysis of pottery from excavations at sites southeast of Tumaco suggests three periods: 1) earlier is characterized by red-banded painting sometimes combined with incision, tripods, and figurines of the Tumaco style; 2) intermediate marks beginning of mound construction and change in ceramics, implying hiatus in sequence; and 3) latest emphasizes incised decoration in complex geometric patterns and vessel shapes not previously reported from region.

658 Bray, Warwick. The gold of El Dorado. London: Times Newspapers Ltd., 1978. 240 p.; bibl.; ill.

Catalog designed to accompany exhibition of 582 precolumbian objects, mostly gold, from Colombia. Author reviews development of El Dorado legend and efforts to locate treasure; provides information on miners, goldsmiths, technology, styles and dates; and includes ethnohistorical accounts of nine principal regions represented by specimens. Objects, including a few pottery, stone, and textile specimens, are illustrated and briefly described.

659 Cardale de Schrimpff, Marianne. Investigaciones arqueológicas en la zona de Pubenza, Tocaima, Cundinamarca (ICA/RCA, 20, 1976, p. 335–496, bibl., ill., maps, plates, tables)

Potsherds obtained from stratigraphic excavations in habitation site Pubenza III were classified into three groups, all sherd tempered. Pubenza Rojo Bañado, decorated mainly by zoned and unzoned incising and zoned punctation, comprises 93 percent or more of sample from lowest stratum. Upper stratum is dominated by Pubenza Polícromo and Pubenza Impresión de Estera (griddles with mat impressions on the underside). Based on three C14 dates, period I is estimated from AD 750–1150 and period II from AD 1150–1550. Detailed descriptions of form and decoration, together with tabulations of provenience, make this report significant for specialists.

660 ———. Textiles arqueológicos de Nariño (ICA/RCA, 21, 1977/1978, p. 245–282, bibl., glossary, ill.)

Rare examples of textiles from south highlands, one group preserved as impressions on metal, the other with surviving fibers. Structural details are described and diagrammed. Cotton and camelid wool were identified. C14 date of AD 1250 was obtained from one tomb.

661 Chaves Mendoza, Alvaro. Panorama prehistórico de la costa caribe colombiana (PUJ/UH, 10, 1979, p. 11–49, bibl.)

Brief review of prehistoric sequence, based mainly on Reichel-Dolmatoff's work, followed by descriptions of coastal groups as described by 16th and 17th-century chroniclers.

662 ——— and **Mauricio Puerta.** Entierros primarios de Tierradentro. Bogotá: Fundación de Investigaciones Arqueológicas Nacionales del Banco de la República, 1980. 160 p.; bibl.; ill.; maps; plates; tables.

Shaft tombs containing primary burials were investigated in two localities in the Tierradentro region, Cauca Dept., 16 at San Francisco and eight at Santa Rosa. Contents are described and supplemented with plans and illustrations of pottery. Skeletal remains were seldom well preserved. C14 date of AD 630 was obtained from one of the Santa Rosa tombs.

663 Correal Urrego, Gonzalo. Apuntes sobre el paleolítico en Colombia (AGH/BHA, 65:722, julio/sept. 1978, p. 331–356, bibl., plate)

Useful summary of the present status of knowledge of Paleo-Indian occupation in Colombia, including climatic reconstruction, artifacts, and human skeletal remains. Earliest C14 date is 12,460 years ago.

664 ——— *et al.* Investigaciones arqueológicas en abrigos rocosos de Nemocón y Sueva. Bogotá: Fundación de Investigaciones Arqueológicas Nacionales, Banco de la República, 1979. 262 p.; ill.

Detailed report on excavations in two rock shelters in Cundinamarca Dept., including stratigraphy, palynology, faunal remains, and artifacts of stone and bone. Copious illustrations, tables, and graphs supplement written information. Principal occupation of Nemocón dates between 7500 and 6800 years ago; date of 10,090 years ago was obtained from Sueva. Debitage abounds; artifacts are restricted to hammerstones, scrapers of stone and bone, and perforators of bone. Significant contribution to knowledge of earliest occupants of the region.

665 ——— *et al.* Investigaciones arqueológicas en los abrigos rocosos del Tequendama: 12.000 años de historia del hombre y su medio ambiente en la altiplanicie de Bogotá: with an extensive English abstract, Archaeological investigations in the Tequendama rock shelters: 12,000 years of history of man and his environment on the high plain of Bogotá. Bogotá: Fondo de Promoción de la Cultura del Banco Popular, 1977. 194 p.; bibl.; ill. (Premios de arqueología; b. 1. Biblioteca Banco Popular)

Final report on excavations in a rock-shelter on southwestern margin of the plain of Bogotá. Nine stratigraphic layers were defined, extending from Pleistocene to modern. Four cultural zones correspond to layers 5, 7a, 8b and 9 (top); Zones I–III are preceramic; Zone IV, ceramic. In addition to detailed descriptions of cultural remains (bone and stone artifacts and burials), fauna, human skeletal remains are analyzed. Palynology and soil studies previously conducted permit correlation of cultural and paleoclimatological sequences. Decline in population between about 5000 and 2500 BP appears attributable to a dry interval, which reduced local subsistence resources. Essential reference for specialists on early man in the Americas.

666 Cubillos, Julio César. Arqueología de San Agustín: El Estrecho, El Parador y Mesita C. Bogotá: Fundación de Investigaciones Arqueológicas Nacionales, 1980. 230 p.; bibl.; ill.; tables (Publicación de la Fundación de Investigaciones Arqueológicas Nacionales; 6)

Description of excavations at three sites of San Agustín culture, with C14 dates extending from 10 BC to AD 255. Detailed plans of tombs and contents are supplemented by photographs. Variety of pottery is indicated by detailed type descriptions, rim profiles and corresponding vessel shapes. Tabulation of occurrences by excavated levels provides basis for observing chronological changes. An important contribution to archaeology of this famous but still enigmatic culture.

667 Fajardo, Julio José. San Agustín: una cultura alucinada. Bogotá: Plaza & Janés, 1977. 1 p.; bibl.; ill. (Realismo fantástico)

Departing from hypothesis that Colombia's San Agustín culture can be interpreted only by identifying with the original population and with use of local hallucinogens, author convinces himself by self-experiment.

668 Falchetti de Sáenz, Ana María. Arqueología de Sutamarchán, Boyacá. Bogotá: Biblioteca Banco Popular, 1976. 268 p.; bibl.; ill.

Pottery collected from four sites in the Municipio of Ráquira and 14 in the Municipio of Sutamarchán permitted differentiating three local complexes, which are described in detail. One of the latter sites presented characteristics indicative of workshop, where pottery was manufactured for use elsewhere. A single date of AD 1004 was obtained by C14. In addition to descriptions of region, sites, excavations, and pottery, author made technological observations on present-day potters. Extremely useful report for specialists in Colombian archaeology.

669 ———. Colgantes "Darién:" relaciones entre áreas orfebres del occidente colombiano y Centroamérica (Boletín [Museo del Oro, Banco de la República, Bogotá] 2, enero/abril 1979, p. 1–55, appendix, bibl., ill., map, plate, table)

"Darién" pendants are stylized anthropomorphic figures cast in gold by the lost-wax process. Their diagnostic characteristics are defined from study of 135 examples, supplemented by 62 related specimens. They have been encountered in all major regions of Colombia, as well as Panama, Costa Rica, and Yucatán. In spite of their stylistic unity, pendants appear to be of local manufacture, raising the question of their cultural significance. Variations in details of execution are provided in an appendix.

670 Franco de S., María Victoria. Escultura agustiana: sociedad matriarcal y patriarcal (UPB, 35:123, abril 1979, p. 13–24, plates)

Analysis of elements of San Agustín sculptures, together with archaeological data, leads to hypothesis that religion emphasizing the moon and female attributes gave way to emphasis on the sun and male attributes during 4th and 5th centuries AD.

671 Grass, Antonio. Animales mitológicos: diseño precolombino colombiano. Bogotá: Litografía Arco, 1979. 250 p.; ill.

More than half the volume consists of 500 depictions of animals on objects of gold, stone, pottery, and bone, arranged by kind of animal and by archaeological culture. Brief text speculates on their significance to the artists.

672 Grupo de Investigación de Arqueología y Prehistoria. Investigación arqueológica y prehistórica de un yacimiento conchal en la costa atlántica colombiana, Turbo, Antioquia. Medellín, Colombia: Universidad de Antioquia, Facultad de Ciencias y Humanidades, Departamento de Antropología, 1980. 200 p.; bibl.; ill; tables.

Detailed report on stratigraphy, burials, pottery, stone, bone, and shell artifacts from two shell-middens on opposite sides of a small quebrada on the right margin of the Golfo de Urabá. Two cultural phases were distinguished: Phase I equates with a layer of shells and cultivation of yuca; Phase II corresponds to a black clay layer without shells and cultivation of maize; C14 date of 1530 BP may mark beginning of Phase II. Two dates of 2175 and 2300 BP are from beginning of Phase I. Interpretations place this site in context of previous investigations from general region.

673 Herrera de Turbay, Luisa Fernanda and Mauricio Londoño Paredes. Reseña de un sitio arqueológico en el Magdalena Medio, Puerto Serviez (ICA/RCA, 19, 1975, p. 139–197, ill., map)

Shaft tomb with two chambers contained 63 complete urns containing human and animal bones, and 63 other vessels. Decoration emphasized incision; lids were adorned with human figures seated on benches or birds. Vessels and decorative motifs are extensively illustrated.

674 Marwitt, John P. Investigaciones arqueológicas en los llanos orientales de Colombia (UNV/ED, 3:1, abril 1978, p. 42–61, bibl., map)

Survey between headwaters of Ariari and Meta Rivers in east-central Colombia located 24 large habitation sites. Tests at eight revealed refuse containing potsherds, to a depth of 30 cm. Two cultural phases are tentatively recognized. Puerto Caldas Phase is characterized by sherd-tempered pottery with rare incised and modeled decoration; red slip and surface brushing are common. Single C14 date obtained from atypical cariape-tempered pottery is 760 BC. Granada Phase has predominantly sand-tempered pottery, rare adornos and white-on-red painting. Date obtained from cariape temper is AD 810. Long time span indicated by dates is incompatible with slight variation in pottery and settlement pattern.

675 Osborn, Ann. La cerámica de los tunebos: un estudio etnológico. Bogotá: Fundación de Investigaciones Arqueológicas Nacionales, Banco de la República, 1979. 81 p.; bibl.; ill.

Detailed description of process of pottery making among Tunebo of northern Boyacá, followed by observations on use and disposal of vessels. Conclusions note some of sources of error in making inferences from archaeological pottery remains about social organization, domestic-versus-ceremonial function, and relative frequencies of types of vessels made. Tunebo custom of dispersed disposal of broken pieces may be a survival of earlier practices, and explain paucity of potsherds in archaeological habitation sites in region.

676 Perdomo, Lucía R. de. Excavaciones arqueológicas en Zona Panche, Guaduas-Cundinamarca (ICA/RCA, 19, 1975, p. 247–289, bibl., ill., map)

Describes stratigraphic tests and tombs in site attributed to the Panche. Pottery is decorated by zoned crosshachure; folded-over, finger-pressed rims are characteristic. Skulls were deformed.

677 Plazas de Nieto, Clemencia. Orfebreía prehispánica del altiplano nariñense, Colombia (ICA/RCA, 21, 1977/1978, p. 197–244, bibl., ill., tables)

Stylistic analysis of 1194 metal objects from Nariño province reveals two distinct groups, one associated with the Capulí phase and the other with the Piartal-Tuza phases (see item 685). Capulí phase pieces can be related to other parts of Colombia and Ecuador; Piartal-Tuza style is wholly southern in its affiliations.

678 ———— and Ana María Falchetti de Sáenz. Technology of ancient Colombian gold (AMNH/NH, 88:9, Nov. 1979, p. 37–48, map, plates)

Popular discussion of the principal techniques for working gold in precolumbian times.

679 The Quaternary of Colombia. Edited by T. Van der Hammen (Palaeogeography, Palaeoclimatology, Palaeoecology [Elsevier Scientific Publishing Co., New York] 25, 1978, p. 1–190, bibl., charts, ill.)

Contains four papers presenting detailed information on deposits in a rock shelter on the Sabana de Bogotá: E.J. Schreve-Brinkman's "A Palynological Study of the Upper Quaternary Sequence;" T. Van der Hammen's "Stratigraphy and Environments of the Upper Quaternary of the El Abra Corridor and Rock Shelters;" G.F. Ijzereef's "Faunal Remains from the El Abra Rock Shelters;" and T. Van der Hammen's and G. Correal Urrego's "Prehistoric Man on the Sabana de Bogotá." Three major climatic episodes can be reconstructed. First and second predate human occupation. Dramatic fluctuations in climate and vegetation occurred during past 10,000 years and affected human adaptation, as shown by changes in population density, tool types, and subsistence emphasis. Maize agriculture was introduced about 2500 BC. This is one of the most comprehensive studies of remains of early man in South America; essential for the specialist.

680 Rodríguez Lamus, Luis Raúl. El alfarero. Fotografías, Eduardo González. Bogotá: C. Valencia Editores, 1978. 198 p.; ill.

Beautiful photographs of pottery vessels, stamps, and figurines selected to show the skill and artistry exercised by prehistoric potters of Colombia.

681 Rojas de Perdomo, Lucía. Muisca: alfarería y decoración. Bogotá: Ediciones Zazacuabi, 1977. 51 p.; bibl.; ill. (Colombia: Arte y cultura)

General discussion of Muisca pottery by categories of use (funerary, ceremonial, commerce, domestic). The dominant combinations of geometric motifs in painted designs are shown on 14 pages. Style is dated between AD 310 and 1305 on the basis of nine C14 determinations.

682 Sutherland, Donald R. and **Carson N. Murdy.** Adaptaciones prehistóricas al ambiente litoral en la isla de Salamanca, costa norte de Colombia (PUJ/UH, 10, 1979, p. 51–75, maps, plates, tables)

Fieldwork (1973–74) located 21 shell-middens representing four types of accumulations. All contained pottery; time span is estimated between AD 500 and Spanish contact. Analysis of faunal remains indicates an equilibrium adaptation to local resources. Tables show mollusk and vertebrate species represented at two excavated sites.

683 Thiemer-Sachse, U. Vorspanisches Gold aus Kolumbien (UR/L, 31 : 12, Herbstsemester 1978, p. 73–88)

First description of five gold objects of various highland styles.

684 Uribe Alarcón, María Victoria. Asentamientos prehispánicos en el altiplano de Ipiales, Colombia (ICA/RCA, 21, 1977/1978, p. 57–195, bibl., fig., maps, plates)

Survey and stratigraphic excavation at four sites established a chronological sequence for the intermontane basin straddling the Colombia-Ecuador frontier. Three phases are differentiated by ceramic types and correspond to those recognized by Francisco for the Ecuadorian portion of the basin. Seven C14 dates indicate that two phases, Capuli and Piartal, are contemporary rather than sequential; latter develops into Tuza phase. Detailed descriptions of ceramics, excavations, and shaft tombs; numerous illustrations; and systematic comparative analysis make this a basic reference for the archaeology of the region.

685 ———. Relaciones pre-hispánicas entre la costa del Pacífico y el altiplano nariñense, Colombia (ICA/RCA, 20, 1976, p. 11–24, bibl., plates)

Brief resumé of objects from tombs of the Capuli style, dated about AD 1080, and comment on evidence for communication with the coast.

686 von Hildebrand, Elizabeth H.R. Levantamiento de los petroglifos del Río Caquetá entre La Pedrera y Araracuara (ICA/RCA, 19, 1975, p. 303–370, bibl., foldout map, ill.)

Describes 14 locations with petroglyphs which are copiously illustrated. They provide a basis for comparison with other occurrences.

687 ———. Resultados preliminares del reconocimiento del sitio arqueológico de La Pedrera, Comisaría del Amazonas, Colombia (ICA/RCA, 20, 1976, p. 145–176, bibl., map, plates)

Detailed description of pottery from the surface of a site on the lower Caquetá, 45 km from the Brazilian frontier. Temper is cariapé; decoration features negative painting, incision, and biomorphic adornos. T-shaped stone axes and cylindrical pottery stamps are associated.

ECUADOR

688 Alcina Franch, José. La arqueología de Esmeraldas, Ecuador: introducción general. Madrid: Ministerio de Asuntos Exteriores, Dirección General de Relaciones Culturales, 1979. 200 p.; bibl.; ill. (Memorias de la Misión Arqueológica Española en el Ecuador; 1)

Team of Spanish archaeologists conducted archaeological, ethnographic, ethnohistoric, linguistic, and geological investigations on Esmeraldas Province's north coast (1971–75). Vol. 1 of planned 13 reports results and gives history of project, geography of region, theoretical assumptions, history of fieldwork, and summary of cultural phases defined and their interrelations. Chronological sequence covers Regional Developmental and Integration periods, C14 dates between about 500 BC and European contact. Only one site of the late formative period was encountered.

689 Athens, John Stephen, II. El proceso evolutivo en las sociedades complejas y la ocupación del período Tardío-Cara en los Andes septentrionales del Ecuador. Otavalo, Ecuador: Instituto Otavaleño de Antropología, 1980. 307 p.; bibl.; ill. (Serie arqueología)

After reviewing hypotheses accounting for origin of complex society, Athens rejects them because they do not allow prediction. Departing from the thesis that evolution of social complexity will result from several classes of selective pressures, he frames five hypotheses relevant to the spatial, environmental, social, and subsistence conditions conducive to this result in the provinces of Imbabura and northern Pichincha in highland Ecuador. Archaeological and ethnohistorical data on the period from AD 1250–1525 are cited in support of the validity of this approach.

690 ———. Teoría evolutiva y montículos prehistóricos de la sierra septentrional del Ecuador (Sarance [Revista del Instituto Otavaleño de Antropología, Otavalo, Ecuador] 7, 1979, p. 29–44)
Speculations on the function of large earth platforms and their implications for explaining the development of complex societies.

691 **Barriuso Pérez, María Angeles.** Sistemas de enterramiento en Atacames, Esmeraldas (in International Congress of Americanists, 42nd, Paris, 1976. Actes [see item 255] v. 9-B, p. 245–257, bibl., ill.)
Description of several types of burials encountered during excavations at the Atacames site, including primary inhumations directly in the earth and cremations in large pottery cylinders or jars with offerings around the exterior.

692 **Berenguer R., José** and **José Echeverría A.** Propuesta metodológica para el registro de sitios arqueológicos en los Andes septentrionales de Ecuador: sistema regional de designación y ficha de prospección (Sarance [Revista del Instituto Otavaleño de Antropología, Otavalo, Ecuador] 7, 1979, p. 5–28, bibl., ill.)
Standardized method of numbering archaeological sites is presented, using abbreviations for province, canton, parroquia, along with a sample site registration form.

693 **Bischof, Henning.** La Fase Engoroy: períodos, cronología y relaciones (Bonner Amerikanistische Studien [Seminar für Volkerkunde, Bonn, FRG] 3, 1975, p. 11–37, bibl., ill., map)
Description of pottery from the central coast of Guayas Province, Ecuador, assigned to the Engoroy phase, a local representative of the Chorrera Tradition. Author assigns an initial date about 900 BC and rejects hypothesis of Mesoamerican influence presented by Coe, Evans, and Meggers.

694 ———. El Machalilla Temprano y algunos sitios cercanos a Valdivia (Bonner Amerikanistische Studien [Seminar für Volkerkunde, Bonn, FRG] 3, 1975, p. 39–67, bibl., ill., tables)

On the basis of pottery excavated at Palmar on the coast of Guayas Province, Ecuador, author assesses origins and affiliations of the Machalilla complex. Proposes an evolution on northern coast of Ecuador from regional variant of Valdivia around 3500–3700 years ago.

695 ———. San Pedro und Valdivia—Frühe Kermikkomplexe an der Küste Südwest-Ekuadors (Beiträge zur Allgemeinen und Vergleichenden Archäologie [Deutsches Archäologisches Institut, Berlin, FRG] 1, 1980, p. 335–389, bibl., ill., map)
Description with good illustrations of the San Pedro ceramic complex, considered to precede the Valdivia complex on the coast of Ecuador. Decoration is by straight and undulating incisions of variable width on a slightly polished surface. Standardization of execution implies a long period of development, but no antecedents are known as yet in the western hemisphere.

696 **Bogin, Barry.** Recent climate change and human behavior on the southwest coast of Ecuador: a model for archaeological reconstruction (UNC/ED, 3:3, 1978, p. 43–59, bibl., map)
Changes in local subsistence activities on the Santa Elena Peninsula following heavy rains in 1971 serve as a model for interpreting the discontinuous archaeological record as a reflection of oscillating rainfall patterns.

697 **Bonifaz, Emilio.** Cazadores prehistóricos del Ilalo. Quito: s.l., 1979. 117 p.; ill.; map.
Author, a big-game hunter, applies his hunting experience to the problem of reconstructing weapons and hunting methods of Paleo-Indians in central highlands of Ecuador. Interesting contribution to a controversial topic.

698 **Damp, Jonathan E.; Deborah M. Pearsall; and Lawrence T. Kaplan.** Beans for Valdivia (AAAS/S, 212, 1981, p. 811–812, ill.)
Carbonized remains of beans of the genus *Canavalia* indicate this domesticate was grown on the coast of Ecuador by beginning of Valdivia culture, around 3300 BC.

699 **Estudios sobre la arqueología del Ecuador.** Editado por Udo Oberem. Bonn: Bonner Amerikanistische Studien,

1976. 129 p.; 3 leaves of plates (6 fold.); bibl.; ill. (Bonner amerikanistische Studien; 3)

Five papers deal with various aspects of the archaeology of coastal and highland Ecuador (see items 693–694 and 710–712).

700 Gardner, Joan S. Pre-Columbian textiles from Ecuador: conservation procedures and preliminary study (Technology and Conservation Magazine [The Technology Organization, Inc., Boston, Massachusetts] 4:1, 1979, p. 24–30, bibl., ill.)

General description of methods of cleaning, conserving, and mounting textiles from a late Milagro period burial on coast of Ecuador.

701 Guinea, Mercedes and Jesús Galván. Relaciones comerciales en Esmeraldas como resultado del análisis de las cerámicas por difracción de rayos X y microscopía electrónica (in International Congress of Americanists, 42nd, Paris, 1976. Actes [see item 255] v. 9-B, p. 259–272, bibl., tables)

Difference in the mineralogy of decorated pottery from sites in Atacames region permitted identification of non-local origin. Two patterns of exchange were detected. During Tiaone phase of Regional Developmental Period, network was terrestrial and local; during Atacames phase of Integration Period, it was coastal and part of regional system extending from south.

702 Hartmann, Roswith. Ecuador: Alt-Amerikas Einfallator? (WM, 8, Aug. 1979, p. 58–69, 94, plates)

Well illustrated popular review of principal cultural periods of coastal Ecuador and problems of influences from Asia, Mesoamerica, and Amazonia on precolumbian groups.

703 Holm, Olaf. Hachas monedas del Ecuador (in Congreso Peruano: el Hombre y la Cultura Andina, 3rd, Lima, 1977. El hombre y la cultura andina [see item 756] v. 1, p. 347–361, ill., map)

Discussion of the general characteristics of the "ax money" from late period of south coastal Ecuador and its significance in implying a precolumbian capitalist economy.

704 Idrovo Uригüen, Jaime and Napoleón Almeida D. La cerámica en Ingapirca. Cuenca: Comisión de Ingapirca, 1977. 102 p.

Illustration and description of examples of complete vessels and fragments from

excavations around Ingapirca. Authors assert occupation extends from about 2000 BC to European contact, and divide the sequence into several traditions. Pieces are not described by type or period, nor is relative frequency of decorative techniques or vessel shapes provided. Report is thus of minimal value for archaeologists.

705 Ledergerber, Paulina. Comparación entre la cerámica bruñida Guangala del Ecuador y Nasca del Perú (EANH/B, 62:133/134, 1979, p. 291–360, bibl., ill.)

Comparison of motifs represented in decoration produced by burnishing of samples of pottery from the Guangala phase of coastal Ecuador and the Nasca culture of south coastal Peru reveals close similarities. Paste, texture, surface finish, color, and vessel size and form are also similar, raising the question whether communication may have existed between two populations. Numerous illustrations show the closeness of the resemblances.

706 López y Sebastián, Lorenzo Eladio and Chantal Caillavet. La fase Tachina en el contexto cultural del horizonte Chorrera (in International Congress of Americanists, 42nd, Paris, 1976. Actes [see item 255] v. 9-B, p. 199–215, bibl., ill., map)

Preliminary description of pottery and obsidian flakes from La Cantera on the right bank of the delta of the Río Esmeraldas, which indicate Chorrera influence or occupation of the north coast of Ecuador.

707 Marcos, Jorge G. Intercambio a larga distancia en América: el caso del Spondylus (Boletín de Antropología Americana [Instituto Panamericano de Geografía e Historia, México] 1, junio 1980, p. 124–129, bibl., ill.)

Reviews ritual importance of Spondylus shells in Mesoamerica and the Andean area and suggests that Ecuador served as center of distribution beginning in formative period. This traffic may have facilitated interchange of cultural elements, accounting for some unexplained cultural similarities between the Nuclear Areas.

708 Martín Acosta, María Emelina. Dos piezas típicas de la cultura Valdivia (Cuadernos Prehispánicos [Seminario Americanista de la Universidad, Casa de Colón, Valladolid, Spain] 6, 1978, p. 77–98, ill.)

General summary of Valdivia cultural characteristics and detailed description of types of figurines and their possible significance. Two new examples of Valdivia type, one a head and the other a body, are illustrated.

709 Meggers, Betty J. Did Japanese fishermen really reach Ecuador 5,000 years ago? (Early Man [Northwestern Archaeology, Inc., Evanston, Illinois] 2:4, 1980, p. 15−19, glossary, ill., map)

Acceptance of hypothesis of a connection between Middle Jomon pottery of Japan and Valdivia pottery of Ecuador depends on whether complicated inventions are believed easily repeated, rather than on objective comparisons.

710 Meyers, Albert. La cerámica de Cochasquí (Bonner Amerikanistische Studien [Seminar für Volkerkunde, Bonn, FRG] 3, 1975, p. 81−111, bibl., charts, tables)

Pottery from stratigraphic excavations in one pyramid, one burial mound, and one habitation area is classified into 35 rim forms. Relative frequencies were computed by level and seriated to show changes through time. Of the sherds, 90 percent were undecorated. Only distinction considered reliable is predominance of shoe-shaped vessels in earlier levels and amphoras in later ones.

711 ———.; Udo Oberem; Jürgen Wentscher; and Wolfgang Wurster. Dos pozos funerarios con cámera lateral en Malchingui, Provincia de Pichincha (Bonner Amerikanistische Studien [Seminar für Volkerkunde, Bonn, FRG] 3, 1975, p. 113−139, ill.)

Detailed description of two shaft and chamber tombs: 35 percent of the pottery in Tomb I and 83 percent in Tomb II was decorated by negative painting or burnishing. C14 date from Tomb II was AD 150. Tomb I is considered to date about 800 BC.

712 Oberem, Udo. Informe de trabajo sobre las excavaciones de 1964/1965 en Cochasqui, Ecuador (Bonner Amerikanistische Studien [Seminar für Volkerkunde, Bonn, FRG] 3, 1975, p. 69−81, map)

Preliminary information on excavations in and around a complex of platform mounds with ramps and burial mounds 50 km. north of Quito. No metal objects were encountered, but stone artifacts and pottery were abundant. Two chronological periods can be recognized, Cochasquí I from AD 950−1250 and Cochasquí II from AD 1250−1550.

713 Porras G., Pedro I. Arqueología del Ecuador. Quito: The Author, 1980. 326 p.; bibl.; ill.; map.

Revision of *Ecuador prehistórico* (published 1976, see *HLAS 39*: 898) incorporating recent unpublished data. Organized by periods (preceramic, formative, regional developmental, integration), subdivided by geographical region. All named phases are described using a standard format. Most complete and reliable summary available for Ecuadorian prehistory.

714 Rivera Dorado, Miguel. Ensayo de tipología de la cerámica Tiaone (*in* International Congress of Americanists, 42nd, Paris, 1976. Actes [see item **255**] v. 9-B, p. 229−244, bibl., ill.)

Description of pottery from La Propicia site on Tiaone River, Esmeraldas Province, by types and varieties. Principal decoration is parallel red bands. Several C14 dates extend from AD 50 to 260.

715 Salazar, Ernesto. Análisis tipológico de las colecciones de superficie de los sitios de Pucará, sierra del Ecuador (UC/A, 34, abril 1979, p. 9−84, ill., map, tables)

Morphological classification of obsidian and basalt specimens from the surface of two open sites in the vicinity of El Inga, which represent the same complex, tentatively correlated with El Inga III.

716 ———. El hombre temprano en la región del Ilalo, sierra del Ecuador. Cuenca, Ecuador: Departamento de Difusión Cultural, Universidad de Cuenca, 1979. 113 p.; bibl.; ill.; map; tables.

Classification and quantitative analysis of surface collections at four sites, in the vicinity of El Inga, show similar patterns. Tables give frequencies by type and raw material (obsidian or basalt). Important contribution to Paleo-Indian knowledge.

717 ———. Talleres prehistóricos en los altos Andes del Ecuador. Cuenca, Ecuador: Departamento de Difusión Cultural, Universidad de Cuenca, 1980. 133 p.; bibl.; ill.; map.

Six quarry-workshop sites were encountered on the páramo associated with obsidian flows in the Ilaló zone. Lithic samples were classified into functional types; shaped artifacts were not encountered.

718 Salvador Lara, Jorge. La huella del primer hombre ecuatorial: problema de investigición interdisciplinaria (BBAA, 34:48, 1977, p. 109–126, bibl.)

Useful review of evidence from paleontology, physical anthropology, archaeology, and obsidian dating relating to the antiquity of man in highland Ecuador.

719 Sánchez Montañés, Emma. Precisiones sobre un estilo de figurillas del norte del Ecuador (IGFO/RI, 37:147/148, enero/junio 1977, p. 277–285, bibl., ill.)

Classification of 91 "Atacames type" pottery figurines in the Museo de América in Madrid. Suggests they are a variety of the Jama-Coaque complex, produced in southwestern Esmeraldas province during the regional developmental period.

720 ———. Un tipo de placa ritual de la cultura Tumaco-Tolita (in International Congress of Americanists, 42nd, Paris, 1976. Actes [see item **255**] v. 9-B, p. 273–281, bibl., ill.)

Review of the evidence for chronology and distribution shows that plaques showing bound persons are contemporary on the north coast of Ecuador and the Colima-Jalisco-Nayarit region of Mexico, making direction of diffusion uncertain. It is suggested they represent significant stages during the life cycle.

721 Stothert, Karen E. La prehistoria temprana de la Península de Santa Elena, Ecuador: una interpretación preliminar (MNCR/V, 5:1/2, 1979, p. 73–87, bibl., ill., map)

Comparison of 28 technological variables represented in lithic materials of two preceramic phases, Vegas and Achallan, and two occupations of the pottery-making Valdivia phase shows continuity. A discontinuity exists between Valdivia and Machalilla lithic traditions, implying arrival of a different population.

722 Turolla, Pino. Beyond the Andes: my search for the origins of pre-Inca civilization. New York: Harper and Row, 1980. 364 p.; bibl., ill.

Personal account by an enthusiastic but uninformed explorer of his adventures in pursuing evidence for reconstructing the prehistory of Ecuador. Readable but very misleading; archaeological data and procedures are ignored; speculations are unscientific. An unfortunate example of popularization of archaeology.

723 Ubelaker, Douglas H. The Ayalán cemetery; a late integration period burial site on the south coast of Ecuador. Washington, D.C.: Smithsonian Institution, 1981. 175 p.; appendixes, bibl.; ill.; tables (Smithsonian contributions to anthropology; 29)

First detailed analysis of skeletal remains from secondary urn burials in a cemetery of the Milagro Phase, dating AD 730–1550. Up to 25 individuals of various ages and both sexes were placed in a single urn accompanied by objects of metal, stone, shell, and pottery. Cultural materials are described. Skeletal remains yielded data on stature, infant mortality, life expectancy, disease, fracture, and skull deformation. In addition to 54 Milagro Phase urns, 25 primary and two secondary non-urn burials were encountered. These represent an earlier occupation dated between 500 BC and AD 1155. Appendix gives identification of fauna associated with the burials.

724 Usera Mata, Luis de. Ensayo de tipología de la cerámica de Balao, Esmeraldas (in International Congress of Americanists, 42nd, Paris, 1976. Actes [see item **255**] v. 9-B, p. 217–227, bibl., ill.)

Description of pottery from a site near the town of Esmeraldas; decoration is by deep incision or narrow red bands. Four C14 dates range from AD 940 to 1370.

THE GUIANAS

725 Boomert, Aad. The analysis of the ceramic finds from Itabru, Berbice River (Archaeology and Anthropology [Journal of the Walter Roth Museum of Archaeology and Anthropology, Georgetown, Guyana] 2:1, 1979, p. 78–86, appendix, bibl., ill., tables)

Description of pottery from two stratigraphic excavations at a habitation site of the Koriabo phase. Three sherds of Taruma phase affiliation were collected from the surface.

726 ———. Prehistoric habitation mounds
in the Canje River area? (Archaeology
and Anthropology [Journal of the Walter Roth
Museum of Archaeology and Anthropology,
Georgetown, Guyana] 1 : 1, 1978, p. 44–51,
bibl., ill.)
Review of evidence for raised fields on
the coast of Surinam as a basis for interpreting reports of "elevations" in the coastal
swamps of Guyana.

727 ———. The prehistoric stone axes of
the Guianas: a typological classification (Archaeology and Anthropology [Journal
of the Walter Roth Museum of Archaeology
and Anthropology, Georgetown, Guyana]
2 : 2, 1979, p. 99–124, bibl., chart, ill., maps)
Six general types of axes are recognized, each subdivided into two to seven
variations, based on a sample of more than
400 from Surinam. Occurrences elsewhere in
the Guianas, Amazonia, and the West Indies
are noted. Characteristic Amazonian forms
predominate over those from the West
Indies.

728 **Dubelaar, C. N.** and **Jevan P. Berrangé.**
Some recent petroglyph finds in south-
ern Guyana (Archaeology and Anthropology
[Journal of the Walter Roth Museum of Ar-
chaeology and Anthropology, Georgetown,
Guyana] 2 : 1, 1979, p. 60–77, ill., maps)
Description of petroglyphs on the
Kuyuwini and upper Essequibo Rivers, and
on the southern Rupununi savanna; liberally
illustrated.

729 **Meggers, Betty J.** and **Clifford Evans.**
An experimental reconstruction of
Taruma village succession and some implications (in Brazil, anthropological perspectives;
essays in honor of Charles Wagley [see item
1081] p. 39–60, ill.)
Hypothetical reconstruction of the settlement history of the prehistoric Taruma on
the upper Essequibo River, based on the scri-
ated ceramic sequence, calls attention to
seldom recorded ethnographic information
useful to archaeologists.

730 **Versteeg, A. H.** Archaeological investigations at Kwamalasamoetoe, south
Surinam (Stichting Surinaams Museum [Pa-
ramaribo] 30, June 1980, p. 23–46, bibl., ill.,
map)
Four sites with pottery of the Taruma
Phase of southern Guyana are reported. A

few sherds of Koriabo Phase types were associated, as well as ground stone axes of unusual shape. These are inferred to precede
the Taruma Phase occupation.

731 ———. The first C14 datings of ar-
chaeological material from Surinam.
Paramaribo: Surinaams Museum, 1979. 1 v.
(Mededelingen der Surinaamse Musea;
no. 29)
Evaluation of a group of C14 dates ob-
tained from sites of the Hertenritz and
Koriabo phases of the coast of Surinam.

732 ———. Prehistoric cultural ecology of
the coastal plain of western Surinam
(in International Congress for the Study of
the Pre-Columbian Cultures of the Lesser
Antilles, 8th, St. Kitts, 1979. Proceedings [see
item 434] p. 88–97, bibl., ill.)
Two stages of the construction of
mounds and raised fields may correlate with
recent changes in sea level, which would
have affected the suitability of coastal land
for agriculture.

733 **Williams, Denis.** Controlled resource
exploitation in contrasting neotropical
environments evidenced by Meso-Indian petroglyphs in southern Guyana (Archaeology
and Anthropology [Journal of Walter Roth
Museum of Archaeology and Anthropology,
Georgetown, Guyana] 2 : 2, 1979, p. 141–148,
bibl., ill.)
On the Rupununi savanna, geometric
motifs account for 73.6 percent of the elements represented by petroglyphs whereas
fishtraps constitute 84.5 percent of those
from the adjacent forest. This suggests different attitudes toward exploitation of subsistence resources, reflecting the more readily
exhaustible resources of the savanna.

734 ———. A Mazaruni-type handaxe? (Archaeology and Anthropology [Journal
of the Walter Roth Museum of Archaeology
and Anthropology, Georgetown, Guyana]
1 : 1, 1978, p. 32–33, ill.)
Curved, blunt-ended, ground stone objects with a slight constriction close to the
butt could have functioned as hand-held
weapons.

735 ———. Petroglyphs at Marlissa: Berbice River (Archaeology and Anthropology [Jounal of the Walter Roth
Museum of Archaeology and Anthropology,

Georgetown, Guyana] 1 : 1, 1978, p. 24–31, bibl., ill.)

Description of petroglyphs normally submerged; two general groups can be distinguished, one typical of the south Rupununi savanna and the other characteristic of eastern Guyana.

736 ———. Preceramic fishtraps on the upper Essequibo: report on a survey of unusual petroglyphs on the upper Essequibo and Kassikaityu Rivers, 12–28 March, 1979 (Archaeology and Anthropology [Journal of the Walter Roth Museum of Archaeology and Anthropology, Georgetown, Guyana] 2 : 2, 1979, p. 125–140, bibl., ill., map, table)

Describes 161 elements recorded at 32 petroglyph sites and classified into fishtrap, anthropomorphic, zoomorphic, and miscellaneous motifs. Fishtrap group constituted 84.5 percent of the total; occurrence of many examples below normal low-water level suggests execution when the climate was drier, which occurred at the end of the Pleistocene.

737 ———. A report on preceramic lithic artifacts in the south Rupununi savannas (Archaeology and Anthropology [Journal of the Walter Roth Museum of Archaeology and Anthropology, Georgetown, Guyana] 2 : 1, 1979, p. 11–53, bibl., ill., map, tables)

Description of petroglyphs, associated stone tools, polishing depressions on boulders, and rock alignments encountered during three seasons of survey. Details are provided on condition and type of rock, motifs, and methods of execution of petroglyphs. Systematic data and liberal illustration make this a model for describing this form of archaeological evidence.

PERU

738 **Alarco, Eugenio.** Dos temas norteños. Lima: Editorial Ausonia-Talleres Gráficos, 1975. 27 p.; bibl.; ill.

Suggests that the figures represented at Sechín, which have been interpreted as warriors and captives, are instead priests and ghosts and souls of the dead.

739 **Amat Olazábal, Hernán.** Los yaros: destructores del Imperio Wari (in Congreso Peruano del Hombre y la Cultura Andina, 3rd, Lima, 1977. El hombre y la cultura andina [see item 756] v. 2, p. 614–640, bibl., ill., map)

Archaeological survey in the Ancash and Huánuco regions reveals numerous sites of varying magnitudes attributable to the ethnohistoric Yaro. Evidence is presented for the hypothesis that the Yaro achieved a political organization that put an end to Wari domination in the highlands and established their own empire, which lasted for about 200 years.

740 **Anders, Martha B.** Sistema de depósitos en Pampa Grande, Lambayeque (PEMN/R, 43, 1977, p. 243–279, bibl., ill., map)

Rows of contiguous, uniform-sized, rectangular rooms are a common feature of construction at Pampa Grande. Excavations in several rooms in various units established their function for storing maize and beans. Absence of storage facilities of this kind and magnitude prior to Moche V implies significant change in socioeconomic organization at this time, but none of the explanations suggested can be verified without further investigation.

741 **Arqueología peruana.** Compiled by Ramiro Matos Mendieta. Lima: 1979. 214 p.; ill.

Consists of 15 papers delivered at a seminar on "Investigaciones Arqueológicas en el Perú, 1976," presenting results of recent unpublished fieldwork by Peruvian and US archaeologists. Noteworthy is Bonavía's demonstration that the much publicized Chivateros complex represents workshop sites rather than an early lithic tradition.

742 **Arte precolombino:** Museo Nacional de Antropología y Arqueología, Lima. pt. 1, Arte textil y adornos. Textos de la introducción, Luis Guillermo Lumbreras; asesoría artística, Sara de Lavalle; fotografía, Werner Lang. Lima: Banco de Crédito del Perú, 1977. 1 v.; bibl., chiefly col. ill. (Colección Arte y tesoros del Perú)

Excellent photographs in color and black-and-white of outstanding textiles and metal ornaments plus a few objects of other materials arranged by time period, beginning with "origins" (prior to 6th century BC); chapters cover Paracas, classic cultures, Wari, late cultures, and Inca.

743 **Banco Popular del Perú, Lima.** El arte y la vida vicús. Texto de Luis Guillermo Lumbreras. Lima: Banco Popular del Perú, 1979. 180 p.; bibl., ill. (some col.)

Excellent illustrations of pottery vessels, in the Banco Popular del Perú, from the upper valley of the Río Piura, north coastal Peru, are placed in context by Lumbreras, who draws upon dating and chronology in adjacent regions and characteristics of local environment. Pottery dates between about 500 BC–AD 500, and combines realistic modeling with white-on-red and negative painting to produce a distinctive style. The environment is transitional between typical Peruvian coastal desert and Ecuadorian forest, and the Vicús pottery reflects influences from both directions. Pottery is classified into categories that shed light on environment, subsistence, technology, war, houses, tombs, deities, and some activities. Excellent overview of this little-known culture.

744 Begler, Elsie B. and Richard W. Keatinge. Theoretical goals and methodological realities: problems in the reconstruction of prehistoric subsistence economies (World Archaeology [Routledge & Kegan Paul, London]11, 1979, p. 208–226, bibl., figs., tables)

Plant remains from two Peruvian coastal sites associated with irrigation agriculture serve to illustrate variables affecting representation. Authors conclude that quantification provides no better indication of diet than presence/absence notation.

745 Bird, Robert McK. and Junius B. Bird. Gallinazo maize from the Chicama Valley, Peru (SAA/AA, 45, 1980, p. 325–332, bibl., ill., tables)

Analysis of maize from the site of Huaca Prieta representing the Gallinazo period shows discontinuity with both earlier Salinar and later Moche types; the closest resemblances are with modern types grown/north and east of the Chicama Valley.

746 Bonavía, Duccio and Alexander Grobman. Sistema de depósitos y almacenamiento durante el período precerámico en la costa del Perú (SA/J, 66, 1979, p. 21–44, bibl., maps, table)

Investigations at Los Gavilanes site, near Culebras, revealed 47 shallow (0.50–1.75 cm) circular and oval pits ranging from three m diameter to 20 by 12.50 m. C14 dates of 4140 and 3750 BP are congruent with its identification with preceramic period. Both maize remains and information from local residents describing storage of maize in pits in the sand indicate this to be a central storage facility for the valley. Estimates are made of possible amount of maize that might have been stored, the population this would feed, and amount of land required to produce it. Existence of intensive maize cultivation at this time makes it necessary to reconsider inferences about the subsistence economy and relations between coast and highlands.

747 Bouchard, Jean-François. Patrones de agrupamiento arquitectónico del Horizonte Tardío del Valle del Urubamba (PEMN/R, 42, 1976, p. 97–111, bibl., ill.)

Several kinds of groupings of rectangular rooms are examined to explore relationships between arrangement and function, and various hypotheses are considered.

748 Burger, Richard L. and Frank Asaro. Análisis de rasgos significativos en la obsidiana de los Andes centrales (PEMN/R, 43, 1977, p. 281–325, bibl., map, tables)

Combining neutron activation and X-ray fluorescence permitted differentiating 13 types of obsidian from sources in Peru and Bolivia. Their archaeological distribution in time and space allows identification of interaction spheres, whose validity is supported by other kinds of evidence. Major changes in patterns of distribution correlated with spread of Chavín and Hauri. These results indicate that more attention to this source of data will aid in reconstructing prehistoric patterns of exchange and interaction.

749 ———— and Lucy Salazar Burger. Ritual and religion at Huaricoto (AIA/A, Nov./Dec. 1980, p. 26–32, ill.)

Recent excavations at a ceremonial site 55 km from Chavín de Huantar reveals the existence of an earlier and contemporary cult, termed the Kotosh Religious Tradition, because of similarities to structures previously encountered at Kotosh. Dating from about 2000 to 200 BC, the site functioned during the period of Chavín fluorescence, but although innovations were adopted the pre-Chavín tradition was not disrupted.

750 Cané, Ralph E. Algunas ideas sobre los dibujos gigantes y grupos de líneas, principalmente de la zona de Palpa-Nasca en el Perú (in Congreso de Arqueología Chilena, 7th, Altos de Vilches, Chile, 1977. Actas [see item **613**] p. 561–573, bibl., ill.)

Describes five major types of figures

found in deserts of southern Peru and theo-ries about their function. An experiment by Explorers Club in constructing a hot-air bal-loon and flying it with passengers over the area raises questions whether prehistoric population used this method to view the figures.

751 Cárdenas M., Mercedes. A chronology of the use of marine resources in an-cient Peru. Lima: Pontificia Universidad Católica del Perú, Instituto Riva-Agüero, Seminario de Arqueología, 1979. 30 p.; ill. (Publicación del Instituto Riva-Agüero; no. 104)

Chronological sequences from lithic (initiating 7000–4000 BC) to contact periods are provided from the valleys of Piura, Chao, Santa, Huaura, and Rimac. The 993 sites sur-veyed are classified by function and period. Illustrations of landscapes and sites include aerial views; text is a generalized resumé.

752 Cardich, Augusto. Origen del hombre y de la cultura andinos (*in* Historia del Perú. v. 1, Perú antiguo. Lima: Editorial Juan Mejía Baca, 1980, v. 1, p. 31–156, bibl., ill.)

Up-to-date resumé of knowledge of late Pleistocene environment as basis for re-viewing evidence for human settlement in highlands and coast. Author's long personal involvement in research on this problem makes his assessments of archaeological evi-dence worthy of careful consideration.

753 Chauchat, Claude. El Paijanense de Cupisnique: problemática y metodo-logía de los sitios líticos de superficie (PEMN/R, 43, 1977, p. 13–26, bibl.)

C14 date of 10,200 ± 180 BP from bur-ial attributed to Paijan projectile point com-plex agrees with dating from other sites. Shallowness of most sites makes definition of this early industry difficult, and sugges-tions are offered to overcome this problem.

754 ———. Sitio del complejo de Chiva-teros en la Palma de los Fósiles—zona de Cupisnique—y su significado (Purun Pacha [Instituto Andino de Estudios Ar-queológicos, Lima] 1, 1979, p. 1–3)

Bifaces and other lithics from a quarry site fit description of Chivateros "industry," but locale is unsuitable for habitation. Pres-ence of workshops for production of Paiján points implies same population was responsi-ble for both. Similarly, Chivateros could be

the source of materials for manufacture of artifacts of the Luz complex, rather than an independent tradition.

755 Choy, Emilio. Antropología e historia. Lima: UNMSM, 1979. 1 v.; bibl.; ill.

Posthumous republication of 10 arti-cles on aspects of the origin and evolution of civilization in the Americas, with emphasis on Peru. Written between 1955–67, the facts are somewhat out of date. Collection is of historical interest for its insight into the mind of an unusual self-taught archaeologist. Introduction reviews Choy's contribution to the formation of Peruvian archaeologists and his moderating influence.

756 Congreso Peruano: El Hombre y la Cultura Andina, 3rd, Lima, 1977. El hombre y las cultura andina. v. 1/5. Edited by Ramiro Matos M. Lima: Comisión del Congreso Peruano, Secretaría General, 1978/1980. 4 v.; bibl.; ill.; maps; tables.

Consists of several hundred papers and abstracts, in five volumes, dealing with all aspects of Andean man and culture, includ-ing archaeology, ethnology, peasants, colonial history, physical anthropology, folklore, and linguistics. Vols. 1/2 (see *HLAS 41:782*) con-tain mainly archaeological papers, the most detailed of which are annotated separately in this section (see items **544, 557, 561, 622, 640, 703, 739, 763, 782, 800–801** and **803**).

757 Conrad, Geoffrey W. Cultural material-ism, split inheritance, and the expan-sion of ancient Peruvian empires (SAA/AA, 46, 1981, p. 3–26, bibl.)

Argues that the legal principle of split inheritance (by which principal heir assumed state office but none of the deceased func-tionary's possessions) was the driving force behind Chimu and Inca expansion because it required each new ruler to amass his own fortune in lands and other wealth. This sys-tem generated stresses that ultimately led to the empire's collapse. Isbell (p. 27–30) and Paulsen (p. 31–37) criticize Conrad's thesis which prompts him to make a few revisions (p. 38–42) but to maintain his opposition to a cultural materialist explanation.

758 Cordy-Collins, Alana. The dual di-vinity concept in Chavín art (UNC/ ED, 3:2, July 1978 [.e. Dec. 1979] p. 1–31, bibl., ill., plates)

Discusses elements of Chavín art indicating that the concept of male-female complimentarity was a fundamental religious principle.

759 Custred, Glynn. Hunting technologies in Andean culture (SA/J, 66, 1979, p. 7–19, bibl.)

Outlines Andean hunting practices and their changing role in subsistence from Paleo-Indian through Inca times.

760 Day, Kent G. Pozos de agua y manejo del agua en Chan Chan, Perú (Puran Pacha [Instituto Andino de Estudios Arqueológicos, Lima] 1, 1979, p. 26–36, bibl.)

Discussion of system of wells that furnished water to population of Chan Chan, its management, and its implications for reconstructing city's social and administrative structure.

761 Donnan, Christopher B. and **Donna McClelland.** The burial theme in Moche iconography. Washington: Dumbarton Oaks, Trustees for Harvard University, 1979. 46 p.; bibl.; ill. (Studies in pre-Columbian art & archaeology; no. 21)

Analysis of complex scenes portrayed on seven vessels of late Moche (ca. AD 600) origin depicting rituals associated with burial of real or fictitious person of importance.

762 Eisleb, Dieter and **Renate Strelow.** Altperuanische Kulturen. v. 3, Tiahuanaco. Berlin, FRG: Museums für Völkerkunde, 1980. 396 p.; bibl.; ill. (Veröffentlichungen des Museums für Völkerkunde Neue Folge; 38. Abeitlung Amerikanische Archäologie; 5)

Detailed and well illustrated catalog of objects of the Tiahuanaco style in the Museum für Völkerkunde. Pottery, stone, metal, bone, and textiles are included, giving an excellent representation of the material culture.

763 Eling, Herbert H., Jr. Interpretaciones preliminares del sistema de riego antiguo de Talambo en el Valle de Jequetepeque, Perú (in Congreso Peruano: El Hombre y la Cultura Andina, 3rd, Lima, 1977. El hombre y la cultura andina [see item **756**] v. 2, p. 401–419, bibl., map)

The Talambo irrigation canal extends for 60 km, carrying water north into the margin of the Jequetepeque Valley. The existence of archaeological settlements at the point of origin and various branches implies local control, which differs from systems described for other valleys and highlights danger of generalizing from few examples.

764 Fung Pineda, Rosa and **Carlos Williams León.** Exploraciones y excavaciones en el Valle de Sechín, Casma (PEMN/R, 43, 1977, p. 111–155, appendixes, bibl., ill., map)

Survey and excavation at several locations in the Casma Valley revealed occupations dating in Intermediate Period, not previously observed. Plans and descriptions are provided for settlements of the initial ceramic, Early Horizon, and Middle Horizon as well. Site of Sechín Alto (dating from 1200 BC) is largest ceremonial center of that age in Peru.

765 Gasparini, Graziano and **Luise Margolies.** Inca architecture. Translated by Patricia J. Lyon. Bloomington: Indiana University Press, 1980. 350 p.; bibl.; glossary; ill.; index.

Basic reference for students of Inca architecture, liberally illustrated with plans, photographs, and drawings reconstructing aspects of roofing and other features not preserved. Formal architectural elements are few and standardized, giving Inca buildings an austere aspect, which is compensated by the variety in shape and contour of the stones. The perfection of the massive stone walls contrasts with the gabled pole and thatch roofs, providing a combination incongruous to European-oriented viewers. First-hand descriptions are supplemented by numerous quotations from chroniclers and more recent visitors. For ethnohistorian's annotation of Spanish original, see *HLAS 42:1639*.

766 Goetzke-Ricault, Mark A. Le jaguar moyen: espace et sens dans l'iconographie de Chavin (EHESS/C, 29, 1978, p. 71–91, bibl., ill.)

Suggests that the jaguar depicted in Chavín art serves as a medium of articulation or codification of beliefs and its significance should be sought here rather than in the character of the animal depicted.

767 Guitarrero Cave: early man in the Andes. Edited by Thomas F. Lynch. New York: Academic Press, 1980. 328 p.; bibl.; ill.; index (Studies in archaeology)

Guitarrero Cave, in the central Callejón de Huaylas, contains occupation refuse dating from about 10,000 to about 8,000 years ago. This final report provides first detailed descriptions of a succession of cultural complexes reflecting evolution of human adaptation to the Andean environment and transition from wild food subsistence to incipient domestication. Specialized reports on pollen, present vegetation, archaeological plant remains, faunal remains, and fabrics constitute a major part of the volume; Lynch describes the stratigraphy and stone, bone, and wood tools. Significant results include evidence for domesticated beans in lowest levels and maize by fourth millennium BC. Wild plants from a variety of micro environments exploited seasonally, remained the focus of subsistence for millennia, however. Comparisons with data from sites of similar age throughout the Andes place the Guitarrero sequence in the broader framework and reveal paucity of concrete information on which to base interpretations.

768 Gutiérrez Pareja, Salustio. Ciudades ocultas del Cusco milenario. Cuzco, Perú: Editorial Andina, 1979? 90, 10 p.; bibl.; ill.

Information on seven little known late period sites north of Cuzco, including descriptions of the topography, ruins, present inhabitants, and personal observations. Illustrations include sketch maps, drawings and photos of structures, and typical artifacts.

769 Hyslop, John. El área lupaca bajo el dominio incaico: un reconocimiento arqueológico (PUCP/H, 3 : 1, julio 1979, p. 53–80, bibl., maps)

Investigation of 15 archaeological sites occupied after incorporation of the Lupaca into the Inca empire supports information from early historical documents about social, political, and economic situation; in addition, investigation reveals aspects not recorded by chroniclers important for interpreting stability and change.

770 Isbell, William H. Environmental perturbations and the origin of the Andean state (in Social archaeology: beyond subsistence and dating. New York: Academic Press, 1978, p. 303–313, bibl.)

Argues that environmental diversity of Andean region favored specialization and exchange to offset effects of fluctuations in local productivity, leading to centralization of decision-making and to the emergence of states as the most effective mechanisms for maintaining stable adaptation.

771 Kano, Chiaki. The origins of the Chavín culture. Washington: Dumbarton Oaks, Trustees for Harvard University, 1979. 87 p.; bibl.; ill. (Studies in pre-Columbian art & archaeology; no. 22)

Proposes correlation between, on the one hand, the evolution of the feline cult, central to the development of Chavín culture, from animal deity to anthropomorphic deity to ancestral god and, on the other, the transition from village to chiefdom to state. Similar correlations in Asian societies and Mesoamerican parallels are noted but a decision as to the existence of influences is avoided.

772 Kauffman Doig, Federico. El Perú antiguo. Manual de arqueología peruana. Dibujos, E. Chumpitaz et al.; fotografías, principalmente de A. Guillén et al. 6. ed. Lima, Perú: Peisa, 1978. 798 p.; bibl.; ill.; indexes.

General introduction to Peruvian archaeology expanded and up-dated to 1977, but with few references to recent data; most useful for its numerous illustrations.

773 ———. Sechín: ensayo de arqueología iconográfica (Arqueológicas [Museo Nacional de Antropología y Arqueología, Lima] 18, 1979, p. 101–142, bibl., ill., map)

Groups representations in Sechín sculpture into three categories: a) "dignitaries;" b) human sacrificial victims; and c) non-anatomical elements.

774 ———. Sexualverhalten im alten Peru. Lima: Kompaktos, 1979. 189 p.; ill.

Inventory, liberally illustrated with drawings and color photographs, of the varieties of sexual activities represented on pre-columbian Peruvian pottery.

775 Kendall, Ann. Descripción e inventario de las formas arquitectónicas Inca: patrones de distribución e inferencias cronológicas (PEMN/R, 42, 1976, p. 13–96, bibl., ill.)

Detailed measurements were made of architectural features at 61 Inca and 22 pre-Inca sites in Ecuador, Peru, and Bolivia in the effort to define features useful for chronological assignment. Short time period and margin of error make C14 dates of little value. Features selected are defined and often sketched. Problems of interpretation are reviewed.

776 Lavallée, Danièle. La ocupación formativa del abrigo de Telarmachay, Junín (III/AI, 39[39]:4, oct./dic. 1979, p. 669–679)

Summary of features, faunal, lithic, and ceramic remains from stratigraphic excavation in levels of the Telarmachay rockshelter attributable to formative period (1800–100 BC). Evidence suggests the shelter was used seasonally by groups with mixed herding and agricultural subsistence.

777 ———. Telarmachay: campamento de pastores en la puna de Junín del período formativo (PEMN/R, 43, 1977, p. 61–110, bibl., ill., map, tables)

Description of excavations in a rock shelter occupied between 1500 and 200 BC. Detailed analysis of lithic and bone, both very abundant, revealed high degree of homogeneity throughout deposit. Pottery was rare and predominantly plain. Small area of shelter implies occupation by single family or group of hunters; relationship between this way of life and agricultural settlements at lower elevations in region remains to be established.

778 Miasta Gutiérrez, Jaime. El Alto Amazonas: arqueología de Jaén y San Ignacio, Perú. Lima: Universidad Nacional Mayor de San Marcos, Dirección de Proyección Social, Seminario de Historia Rural Andina, 1979. 213 p.; bibl.; ill.; map; tables.

Excavations were conducted at three sites in drainage of Río Chinchipe, tributary of the Marañón, near Ecuadorian border. Detailed pottery type descriptions and numerous illustrations of decorated sherds provide concrete information on this little-known region. Affiliations with early formative complexes in Ecuador and Peru are discussed in somewhat rambling fashion.

779 Morris, Craig. The archaeological study of Andean exchange systems (in Social archeology: beyond subsistence and dating. New York: Academic Press, 1978, p. 315–327, bibl.)

Review of kinds of archaeological evidence relevant to reconstructing nonmarket exchange systems in central Andean region.

780 ——— and **Idilio Santillana.** Perspectiva arqueológica en la economía incaica (PUCP/H, 2:1, julio 1978, p. 63–81, bibl.)

Discussion of evidence for intensive production of textiles at the Inca center of Huánuco Viejo.

781 Morrison, Tony. Pathways to the gods: the mystery of the Andes lines. Incorporating the work of Gerald S. Hawkins. New York: Harper & Row, 1978. 208 p.; bibl.; ill.; index.

Intelligent, readable review of the history of investigation of the lines and figures on the desert of Nazca. Author has visited area, discussed various interpretations with Reiche, Hawkins, and other experts. His search took him to Cuzco and the Titicaca basin, where similar lines occur. Astronomical and calendrical associations have not been supported by computerized tests. Ethnohistoric accounts and surviving traditions support conclusion that lines connect sacred places and this view is favored by the author. Includes excellent photographs of Nazca patterns, as well as of seldom illustrated lines on Bolivian altiplano.

782 Parsons, Jeffrey R. and **Ramiro Matos Mendieta.** Asentamientos pre-hispánicos en el Mantaro, Perú: informe preliminar (in Congreso Peruano: El Hombre y la Cultura Andina, 3rd, Lima, 1977. El hombre y la cultura andina [see item 756] v. 2, p. 539–555, bibl., ill.)

Survey of 400 by 500 km zone in Mantaro Valley permitted definition of cultural history from about 900 BC to Inca period. Significant changes in population size, settlement pattern, and architecture are summarized.

783 Paul, Anne. Paracas textiles: selected from the museums collections. Göteborg: Göteborgs Etnografiska Museum, 1979. 56 p.; ill.; 39 of plates (Etnologiska studies; 34)

Describes and illustrates 24 textile specimens acquired in 1935 and alleged to belong to a single mummy bundle. Data include dimensions, fiber, technique, and arrangement and description of motifs.

784 Pozorski, Shelia G. Late prehistoric llama remains from the Moche Valley, Peru (Annals [Carnegie Museum of Natural

History, Pittsburgh, Pennsylvania] 48:9, 1979, p. 139–170, bibl., ill., tables)

Detailed analysis of llama remains from three sites extending from Early Intermediate into the Late Intermediate Period. Information is provided on number of individuals, burned and unburned bones, age at death, frequency of each type, butchering marks, as a basis for cultural interpretations.

785 ———. Prehistoric diet and subsistence of the Moche Valley, Peru (World Archaeology [Routledge & Kegan Paul, London] 11, 1979, p. 163–184, bibl., map, tables)

Analysis of plant and animal remains from excavations at 11 sites extending from preceramic (2500 BC) to contact (AD 1532) times revealed three major subsistence patterns: 1) marine resources and wild plants; 2) irrigation agriculture and domesticated animals; and 3) intervalley food distribution.

786 ——— and **Thomas Pozorski.** Alto Salaverry: a Peruvian coastal preceramic site (Annals [Carnegie Museum of Natural History, Pittsburgh, Pennsylvania] 48:9, 1979, p. 337–375, bibl., ill., map, tables)

Description of domestic and nondomestic architecture, burials, and other features excavated at a site at the mouth of the Moche River. Artifacts and plant remains are described. Subsistence emphasized marine resources and wild plants, as well as cultivated beans, squash, pepper, avocado, and guava. Site belongs to Cotton preceramic (2500–1800 BC).

787 **Pozorski, Thomas.** The Las Avispas burial platform at Chan Chan, Peru (Annals [Carnegie Museum of Natural History, Pittsburgh, Pennsylvania] 48:8, 1979, p. 119–137, bibl., ill., tables)

Excavations in one of the large platforms at Chan Chan allow description of the construction and verification of the mortuary function of these structures. Some 300 individuals are estimated from skeletal remains to have been sacrificed, all females, mainly between ages 18–25.

788 **The Prehistory of the Ayacucho Basin, Peru.** v. 3, Nonceramic artifacts. Richard S. MacNeish et al. Ann Arbor: Published *for the* Robert S. Peabody Foundation for Archaeology *by* University of Michigan Press, 1980. 1 v.; bibl.; ill.; index.

Large-scale multidisciplinary project

of archaeological survey and excavation in Ayacucho Basin, central Peruvian highlands, permitted reconstructing a cultural sequence from prior to 13,000 BC to European contact. Some 20,000 nonceramic artifacts, mainly lithics, are described using a typology derived by detailed analysis of attributes and computerized clustering. Initial separation is unifaces and bifaces; 25 types with temporal significance were identified among haftable bifaces, 11 among nonhaftable bifaces. Terminally worked unifaces also exhibited chronological variation. Ground stone tools, bone, wood, textiles, and cordage are described. Details of the lithic attributes and coding are provided, permitting use of the same classification by others. Tables show frequences of types by phase and site.

789 **Radicati di Primeglio, Carlos.** El sistema contable de los incas: yupana y quipu. Lima, Perú: Librería Studium, between 1976 and 1980. 116 p.; bibl.; ill.

Detailed discussion of manner in which two kinds of devices were used for making mathematical calculations and recording numbers in precolumbian Peru. The *yupana* is a rectanguloid board of stone, bone, or pottery with its surface covered by square depressions, which the author considers to have been assigned values in standardized increments; the *quipu* is a set of cords with knots having numerical values.

790 **Ramos, Luis J.** and **María Concepción Blasco.** Las representaciones de "aves fantásticas" en materiales nazcas del Museo de América de Madrid (IGFO/RI, 37: 147/148, enero/junio 1977, p. 265–276, ill.)

Of 1035 Nazca vessels in the Museo de América, 107 depict "real" birds and 72 "fantastic" birds. Characteristics of latter depictions are described and their interpretation reviewed.

791 ——— and ———. Los tejidos y las técnicas textiles en el Perú prehispánico. Con un complemento de analogías terminológicas de María Flor Portillo. Valladolid: Seminario Americanista de la Universidad, 1977. 94 p.; 7 leaves of plates; bibl.; ill. (Bernal, serie americanista; v. 10)

General remarks on precolumbian textiles precede description of the most common techniques represented in the collections of the Museo de América in Madrid by Ramos and Blasco. A chapter by Portillo attempts to correlate English and French terminology with that used by the authors.

792 Ravines, Rogger. El cuarto de rescate de Atahualpa (PEMN/R, 42, 1976, p. 113–143, bibl., ill.)

Combines descriptions by Spanish chroniclers of Inca city of Cajamarca with more recent plans of the building where it is considered that Atahualpa was imprisoned. Includes photographs of building's present condition.

793 ———. Prácticas funerarias en Ancón: pt. 1 (PEMN/R, 43, 1977, p. 327–397, ill.)

Systematic description of 28 burials, all in rectangular pits, the majority adults. Burial position is sketched and offerings are listed and illustrated.

794 ——— and **Karen Stothert.** Un entierro común del Horizonte Tardío en la costa central del Perú (PEMN/R, 42, 1976, p. 153–206, appendixes, bibl., ill.)

Inventory and description of items included in a burial of the Late Horizon at Ancón. Body was wrapped in cloth, inserted in a net, and covered with a totora mat. Three gourd containers and two pottery vessels contained plant remains; another vessel once contained liquid. Plant remains are identified and constitute one of the largest samples from central coast during Inca period. Excellent photographs show netting, cordage, weaving implements, and details of wrapping.

795 Reategui G., Mirca. Bibliografía sobre antropología y arqueología de la selva del Perú (PEBN/R, 73/76:21/22, 1975/1976, p. 5–58)

Annotated bibliography of works on the eastern lowlands of Peru, includes references from adjacent regions relevant to broader interpretations. For bibliographer's comment, see *HLAS 42:60.*

796 Rick, John W. Prehistoric hunters of the high Andes. New York: Academic Press, 1980. 360 p.; bibl.; ill.; index (Studies in archaeology)

Hypothesis that "benevolent" environments, such as the Peruvian puna, lead to sedentary human populations and equilibrium exploitation of wild food resources is examined by using evidence from excava-

tions at Pachamachay cave and a smaller cave, Pampacancha. The social organization and population density of vicuña herds make them uniquely suited to long-term exploitation, accounting for nearly exclusive representation of camelid bones in the archaeological deposit. Amount and character of cultural débris from Pachamachay imply it was a base camp, whereas Pampacancha was used for temporary hunting expeditions. Projectile point types are inferred to differentiate social groups, such as bands, rather than cultural horizons or time periods. These and other novel interpretations make this volume an important if controversial contribution to reconstruction of early human adaptation to the high Andes.

797 Ríos, Marcela and **Enrique Retamozo.** Objetos de metal procedentes de la Isla de San Lorenzo. Lima: Instituto Nacional de Cultura, Museo Nacional de Antropología y Arqueología, 1978. 97 p.; bibl.; ill. (Arqueológicas; 17)

In 1906, Uhle excavated tombs on San Lorenzo island, opposite the port of Callao. Several hundred metal objects (predominantly silver) were among objects encountered. Representative vessels, ornaments, and utensils are described. Date is late pre-Inca or Inca. One appendix lists all objects from the Uhle collection; a second describes 10 textiles from San Lorenzo.

798 Rivera Dorado, Miguel. La cerámica inca de Chinchero, Perú (IAI/I, 4, 1977, p. 139–170, bibl., ill., map)

Some 20,000 sherds from excavations at Chinchero, dating from about AD 1200 to Spanish contact, were classified into two plain and two decorated (painted) types on the basis of ware and decoration. Each type is described systematically, providing data useful for comparison.

799 Roe, Peter G. Recent discoveries in Chavin art: some speculations on methodology and significance in the analysis of a figural style (UNV/ED, 3:1, April 1978, p. 1–41, bibl., ill.)

Brief response to criticism of author's elaboration of Rowe's chronology of Chavín style, and a longer discussion of validity and approach of qualitative seriation, precede interpretation of changes in elements and groupings of this elaborate artistic corpus.

800 Rosselló Truel, Lorenzo. Sistemas astronómicos de campos de rayas (*in* Congreso Peruano: El Hombre y la Cultura Andina, 3rd, Lima, 1977. El hombre y la cultura andina [see item 756] v. 2, p. 521–534, bibl., ill.)

Lines similar to those of Nazca occur in the lower Rímac and Chillon regions. They appear to date from formative period and to have had an astronomical significance.

801 ———. Sobre un motivo de Kotosh identificado como maíz (*in* Congreso Peruano: El Hombre y la Cultura Andina, 3rd, Lima, 1977. El hombre y la cultura andina [see item 756] v. 2, p. 435–442, bibl., ill.)

Design on pottery vessel of pre-Chavín date from Kotosh, interpreted by Coe and others as depicting an ear of maize in typical Olmec style, is shown to incorporate symbols associated with feline representations. This identification is more consistent with total stylistic context of vessel.

802 Ruiz Estrada, Arturo. Arqueología de la ciudad de Huancavelica. Lima: Servicios de Artes Gráficas, 1977. 61 p.; bibl.; ill.

Brief resumée of prehistory of Huancavelica (south-central Peruvian highlands) from Paleo-Indian to colonial times.

803 Saco, María Luisa. Algunos aspectos de los tejidos de Paracas (*in* Congreso Peruano: El Hombre y la Cultura Andina, 3rd, Lima, 1977. El hombre y la cultura andina [see item 756] v. 2, p. 401–419, bibl., ill.)

Motifs and colors of Paracas textile elements illuminate view of real world as well as concept of the supernatural held by the population associated with Paracas culture.

804 ———. Fuentes para el estudio del arte peruano precolombino. Lima: Retablo de Papel Ediciones, 1978. 261 p.; indexes (Retablo de Papel Ediciones; 27)

Description of principal sources on precolumbian monuments and art, divided into three general categories; 1) chroniclers of the 16th and 17th centuries; 2) travelers and scholars of the 18th and 19th centuries; and 3) archaeologists of the 20th century. Indexed by author, place name, and culture or style.

805 Shady, Ruth and Arturo Ruiz. Evidence for interregional relationships during the Middle Horizon on the north-central coast of Peru (SAA/AA, 44, 1979, p. 676–684, bibl., ill., map)

Pottery of two regional styles associated with a burial suggests hypothesis that several powerful independent but interacting centers rather than single political "empire" are reflected by spread of Huari tradition.

806 ——— and ———. Huaura, Costa Central: interacción regional en el período intermedio temprano (Arqueológicas [Museo Nacional de Antropología y Arqueología, Lima] 18, 1979, p. 1–99, appendixes, bibl., ill., map)

Description of excavations at Végueta representing occupation during the first part of the Early Intermediate Period, including faunal remains, pottery, and environmental characteristics. Three C14 dates are AD 165, AD 400 and AD 735. Comparison with pottery from other regions reveals uniformities that imply considerable interaction among diverse populations.

807 Smith, John W. Recuay gaming boards: a preliminary study (IAI/I, 4, 1977, p. 111–138, bibl., ill.)

"Tablets" with square compartments are interpreted as gamingboards; for a different interpretation see item 789.

808 Stat, Daniel K. Ancient sound: the whistling vessels of Peru (SAF/P, 85:2, Summer 1979, p. 2–7, bibl., ill., plates)

Acoustical study of precolumbian whistling bottles revealed that those of the same culture differed by less than half an octave, and that their interacting frequencies when played simultaneously produced changes in the state of consciousness of listeners, described as a "Zen-like state of clarity."

809 Stothert, Karen E. and Rogger Ravines. Investigaciones arqueológicas en Villa el Salvador (PEMN/R, 43, 1977, p. 157–225, bibl., ill.)

Salvage excavations at a site 25 km south of Lima, representing a platform topped by rooms, later used as a cemetery. Ceramics place it in little-known period between end of Early Horizon and beginning of the Early Intermediate Horizon. Data are provided on 87 burials.

810 Tee, Garry J. Evidence for the Chinese origin of the jaguar motif in Chavín art

(Asian Perspectives [University Press of Hawaii, Honolulu] 21, 1980, p. 27–29, bibl., ill.)

Comparison of feline-shaped vessels of Chavín and those of early Chou manufacture shows such close similarities as to imply a Transpacific influence.

811 Tello, Julio C. and T. Mejía Xesspe. Paracas. pt. 2, Cavernas y necrópolis. Lima: Universidad Nacional Mayor de San Marcos, Dirección Universitaria de Biblioteca y Publicaciones, 1979. 502 p.; glossary; ill.; maps.

This volume continues publication of materials in the archives of Julio C. Tello, pt. 1 having appeared in 1959 (see *HLAS* 23:522). Includes investigations on the Paracas peninsula during 1925–30, studies of art based on the contents of mummy bundles opened after 1931 as well as information on central Andean languages, religion, and mythology.

812 Terada, Kazuo. Excavation at La Pampa in the north highlands of Peru, 1975. Tokyo: University of Toyko Press, 1979. 194 p.; figures; maps; 129 plates; tables (Japanese Scientific Expedition to Nuclear American; report 1).

Excavations at La Pampa, Ancash Dept., provide information on two formative complexes. Yesopampa Period, C14 dated between 1400 and 970 BC, is characterized ceramically by neckless globular jars with brushed, polished red, or plain surface and decoration by appliqué fillets. Succeeding La Pampa Period, with date of 670 and 540 BC, corresponds to classic Chavín culture. A late local style and an Inca occupation are also represented. Architectural plans and reconstructions, illustrations of pottery and other artifacts, and tables showing provenience of pottery, stone, metal, bone, and shell materials make this report essential for specialists.

813 Trimborn, Hermann. Excavaciones en Sama, Departamento Tacna, Perú (IAI/I, 4, 1977, p. 171–178, ill.)

Brief account of archaeological investigations at Sama, a Lupaca settlement destroyed by earthquake in 1604.

814 Tsunoyama, Yukihiro. Textiles of the Andes: catalogue of the Amano Collection. San Francisco: Heian International, Inc., 1979. 248 p.; 183 col. plates.

Magnificent presentation of textiles in the collection of Lima's Amano Museum, principally from Chancay culture. Also includes specimens from Santa Cruz, Paracas, Nazca, Chavín, and other localities. Valuable for excellent color plates.

815 von Breunig, Georg A. Nazca: a gigantic sports arena? a new approach for explaining the origin of the desert markings in the basin of Río Grande in southern Peru (UNC/ED, 3:3, 1978, p. 1–42, bibl., ill.)

Author departs from hypothesis that use of patterns on desert of south coastal Peru as courses for foot races would have caused displacement of soil toward the outer edge at sharp curves. Finding this configuration, he considers other features compatible with their interpretation as sports facilities. An interesting example of the manner in which selected information can be used to create a convincing argument, as long as other kinds of data are ignored.

816 von Schuler-Schömig, Immina. Die "Fremdkrieger" in Darstellungen der Moche-Keramik (MV/BA, 27, Neue Folge, 1979, p. 135–213, bibl., ill.)

Detailed iconographic analysis of depictions on pottery indicates that the so-called "foreign soldiers" are probably a distinct group within Moche society.

817 Waisbard, Simone and Jack Waisbard. Les pistes de Nazca: pour qui, pourquoi . . . et comment? Paris: R. Laffont, 1977. 349 p.; 6 leaves of plates; bibl.; ill. (Les Enigmes de l'univers)

Extensive review of explanations for the patterns produced on the desert floor between Palpa and Nazca on the south coast of Peru; no consensus exists concerning their use or significance.

818 West, Michael. Early watertable farming on the north coast of Peru (SAA/AA, 44, 1979, p. 138–144, bibl.; ill.)

Investigations at two nearby sites at the mouth of the Virú Valley are interpreted as functionally differentiated segments of one community, one part of which was engaged in fishing, the other in farming sunken plots accessible to the watertable. Dating is Puerto Moorin Phase of the Early Intermediate Period, about 2000 BP.

URUGUAY

819 **Bosch, Ademar; Mabel Moreno de Bosch; Juan Campos;** and **Jorge Femenias.** Técnicas y motivos decorativos de la cerámica arqueológica de los Ríos Tacuarembó Grande, Chico y Río Negro Medio (in Encuentro de Arqueología del Litoral, 5th, Río Negro, Uruguay, 1977. Encuentro . . . [see item **484**] p. 245–261, bibl., ill., map, tables)

Description of decorated sherds from surface collections at 11 sites in north central Uruguay. Techniques are punctation, incision, corrugation, and fingernail marking. Rim profiles correspond to simple vessels with vertical to outsloping walls.

820 **Centros de Estudios Arqueológicos.** Investigaciones arqueológicas en el área de Salto Grande: tres primeros radiocarbonos (in Encuentro de Arqueología del Litoral, 5th, Río Negro, Uruguay, 1977. Encuentro . . . [see item **484**] p. 69–88, bibl., ill., map)

C14 dates were obtained from three excavations on two islands in the Salto Grande region of Río Uruguay. Dates of 400 and 420 BC appear associated with preceramic occupations; a date of AD 810 correlated with pottery decorated with simple incised patterns.

821 **Taddei, Antonio; Juan Campos;** and **Ademar Bosch.** Las industrias líticas de los Ríos Tacuarembó Grande y Chico (in Encuentro de Arqueología del Litoral, 5th, Río Negro, Uruguay, 1977. Encuentro . . . [see item **484**] p. 225–243, bibl., ill., map, table)

Description and classification of lithic materials from surface collections at seven sites in north central Uruguay. Stemmed and unstemmed projectile points are represented. Pottery was encountered at five sites, as well as European objects, providing terminal dating.

VENEZUELA

822 **Boulton, Alfredo.** El arte en la cerámica aborigen de Venezuela. Caracas: The Author, 1978. 254 p.; bibl.; ill.

Author aims to present precolumbian ceramics of Venezuela as artistic expression of aboriginal population, and succeeds admirably. Excellent photographs of hundreds of complete vessels or fragments from public and private collections are identified by cultural provenience and present location; measurements are usually provided.

823 **Nieves de Galicia, Fulvia.** Población prehispánica de la región de Cupira: sector oriental de la Ensenada de Higuerote, Venezuela (in International Congress for the Study of the Pre-Columbian Cultures of the Lesser Antilles, 8th, St. Kitts, 1979. Proceedings [see item **434**] p. 290–306, bibl., ill., map)

Early accounts of Tomuza Indians, who inhabited coast east of Caracas, are compatible with inferences derived from late archaeological sites in the region.

824 **Perera, Miguel A.** Arqueología y arqueometría de las placas líticas aladas del occidente de Venezuela. Caracas: Universidad Central de Venezuela, Facultad de Ciencias Económicas y Sociales, 1979. 146 p.; bibl.; ill.; map; tables.

Classifies nearly 300 winged plaques from western Venezuela into eight types based on form. Analyzes raw materials, technique of manufacture, geographical distribution, and function. Constitutes a thorough review of existing data and interpretation, with application of statistical methods to establish correlations among variables.

825 **Roosevelt, Anna Curtenius.** La Gruta: an early tropical forest community of the Middle Orinoco Basin (in Unidad y variedad. Ensayos en homenaje a José M. Cruxent. Edited by Erika Wagner and Alberta Zucchi. Caracas: Instituto Venezolano de Investigaciones Científicas, 1978, p. 173–201, bibl., ill., map)

Describes pottery associated with first of three phases of Saladoid Tradition recognized at sites on Middle Orinoco and assigned an initial date of about 2100 BC. Describes low population density and tropical forest agriculture based on bitter manioc. If dating is correct, this is the earliest known occurrence of manioc cultivation, and of the Saladoid ceramic tradition.

826 ———. Parmana: prehistoric maize and manioc subsistence along the Orinoco and Amazon. New York: Academic Press, 1980. 1 v.; index (Studies in archaeology)

Archaeological sequence on middle Orinoco serves as a point of departure for reviewing theories about cultural development in Amazonia and assessing their validity. Interpretations of environmental potential proposed by Steward, Meggers, Carneiro, Lathrap, and Gross are summarized, and "prime movers" of technological change are reviewed. Chap. 3 presents data from ethnohistorical accounts and contemporary biological research on agricultural potential of tropical forest and floodplain soils, hunting and fishing resources, and nutritional value of staple cultigens. When these considerations are applied to the Parmana archaeological sequence, they suggest hypothesis that demographic intensification resulted from the change from manioc cultivation and a terra firme orientation to intensive maize cultivation on the floodplain. This is a useful compilation of recent data on subsistence potential of tropical lowlands of South America and a provocative interpretation of cultural development on the middle Orinoco.

827 Rouse, Irving. The La Gruta sequence and its implications (*in* Unidad y variedad. Ensayos en homenaje a José M. Cruxent. Edited by Erika Wagner and Alberta Zucchi. Caracas: Instituto Venezolano de Investigaciones Científicas, 1978, p. 203–229, bibl., charts, ill.)

Sequence of nine phases representing three traditions: La Gruta, Corozal, and Camoruco, provides basis for reconstructing routes of migration and diffusion to and from the Middle Orinoco. La Gruta is the earliest known phase of the Saladoid Tradition, but whether it entered the Orinoco from Amazonia or the west cannot be established yet; Rouse favors Amazonia. Corozal is a local transitional manifestation. Camoruco belongs to the Arauquinoid series and is seen as a development within Venezuela. Justification is presented for accepting C14 dates placing La Gruta at beginning of second millenium BC.

828 Sanoja Obediente, Mario. Las culturas formativas del Oriente de Venezuela; la Tradición Barrancas del Bajo Orinoco. Caracas: Biblioteca de la Academia Nacional de la Historia, 1979. 518 p.; bibl.; charts; ill.; maps; tables (Serie Estudios, monografías y ensayos; 6)

Detailed report of results of stratigraphic excavations in sites of the Barrancoid Tradition at the mouth of the Orinoco.

Two regional phases are differentiated by the presence and relative frequency of pottery types. Tables and graphs give frequencies of pottery and other remains, and seriated chronological sequences for each phase. Three periods are defined: preclassic, classic, and postclassic. Review of distribution of preclassic features indicates this tradition is related to early formative complexes of the central and northern Andean region. Evidence points to immediate origin in northern Colombia, linked with emergence of cultivated root crops. This is first comprehensive monograph on this important early ceramic tradition of eastern Venezuela (for annotation of preliminary version of this study, see *HLAS 41:868*).

829 ———. Los recolectores tempranos del Golfo de Paria, Estado Sucre, Venezuela (*in* International Congress for the Study of the Pre-Columbian Cultures of the Lesser Antilles, 8th, St. Kitts, 1979. Proceedings [see item **434**] p. 139–151, bibl., ill.)

Excavations in two shell-middens produced lithic artifacts and C14 dates indicating they constitute horizon about a millennium earlier than the Manicuaroide complex of the Paria peninsula.

830 Vargas Arenas, Iraida. La tradición cerámica pintada del Oriente de Venezuela (*in* International Congress for the Study of the Pre-Columbian Cultures of the Lesser Antilles, 8th, St. Kitts, 1979. Proceedings [see item **434**] p. 276–289, bibl., ill.)

Recent excavations at sites with white-on-red pottery on the middle Orinoco and the east coast of Venezuela produced C14 dates indicating that the tradition spread from the Orinoco to the coast; the distribution of decorative elements and vessel morphology becomes intelligible within this time-space framework.

831 ———. La tradición Saladoide del Oriente de Venezuela; la Fase Cuartel. Caracas: Biblioteca de la Academia Nacional de la Historia, 1979. 326 p.; bibl.; ill.; tables (Serie Estudios, monografías y ensayos; 5)

Although the Saladoid or White-on-Red tradition is well known in archaeological literature, this monograph presents the first detailed systematic description of artifacts from a representative site. Ten 2 × 2 stratigraphic pits provide basis for seriated ceramic sequence, which in turn allows recognition of chronological differences in less common artifacts of stone and shell. C14 dates extend from AD 290 to 1055. Comparison with sites of this tradition on the middle Orinoco supports hypothesis of migration from that region about beginning of Christian Era to east coast, where hybridization with Barrancoid tradition of lower Orinoco occurred. Subsequently, Saladoid tradition dispersed westward along the coast and northeastward to the Lesser Antilles. An essential reference for all archaeologists working in the Caribbean area.

832 Zucchi, Alberta. La variabilidad ecológica y la intensificación de la agricultura en los llanos venezolanos (in Unidad y variedad. Ensayos en homenaje a José M. Cruxent. Edited by Erika Wagner and Alberta Zucchi. Caracas: Instituto Venezolano de Investigaciones Científicas, 1978, p. 349–365, bibl., maps)

Origin and subsequent expansion of Arauquinoid tradition is interpreted in context of environment and potential for intensification of subsistence on the Middle Orinoco.

833 ——— and William M. Denevan. Campos elevados e historia cultural prehispánica en los llanos occidentales de Venezuela. Caracas: Universidad Católica Andrés Bello, Instituto de Investigaciones Históricas, 1979. 178 p.; appendixes; bibl.; figures; maps; plates; tables.

Detailed discussion of raised fields covering an area of about 15.5 km^2 along Caño Ventosidad, southeastern Barinas. Nine test pits were excavated; soil samples, pollen, as well as archaeological material, are described and tabulated. Two C14 dates from one excavation are AD 855 and 885, a few centuries earlier than expected from ages obtained for related pottery from region. This is the most complete analysis yet produced for this type of precolumbian agricultural technology.

ETHNOLOGY: Middle America

JOHN M. INGHAM, *Associate Professor of Anthropology, University of Minnesota*

IT IS TEMPTING TO LIKEN MIDDLE AMERICA to the Tower of Babel: the area embraces not only a profusion of languages and traditions, but also many local scenarios of social change. Unlike in the Tower, however, there is in Middle America order amid the cacophony. It consists of the cultural patterns and dynamic processes that underlie the manifest diversity. Our knowledge of both of these is clearly advancing, as the following compilation demonstrates. Studies of cultural symbolism and pattern are moving us closer to formulations of deep structure, for broad areas of Middle America as well as for particular ethnic traditions (items **854** and **858**). At the same time, research on change has begun to delineate some of its underlying mechanisms.

Among other things, Middle Americanists are on the verge of making a significant contribution to the theory of demographic transition by offering a partial explanation for the failure of that transition to occur. Several studies show that modernization reinforces or even increases the desire for children among peasants. Another recurrent pattern described in the literature is population growth rendering land scarce and forcing peasants to make economic adjustments by undertaking truck farming, craft production for tourist markets, or wage labor. Because all of these activities can absorb more labor than a small corn field, they increase the economic value of children. Consequently, peasants may realize larger families through higher birth rates or simply by maintaining traditionally high rates in the face of falling infant and child mortality (see *HLAS 39:1038* and items **884, 894** and **937**). Researchers also suggest that population growth and the economic adjustments associated with it may have far-reaching implications for traditional social organization and culture (items **834, 842** and **894**).

Continuing attention is focused on the problem of ethnicity. There is interesting discussion of the cultural meanings of "Indian" and "ladino" (item **841**) and of the relationship of these categories to social class (items **837, 893** and **929**). Also noteworthy is the research that demonstrates that ethnicity and traditional culture are not necessarily barriers to economic development (items **835, 858** and **863**). A related phenomenon is the continuing criticism of the integrationist policies of Aguirre Beltrán, the former director of Mexico's INI (Instituto Nacional Indigenista) (items **836, 889, 917, 932** and **936**). In fact, to a considerable extent these policies have been discredited; some government branches even seem disposed toward actively encouraging ethnic pluralism (item **897**).

834 Abrams, Ira R. Modernization and changing patterns of domestic group development in a Belizean Maya community: the usefulness of the diachronic approach (*in* Family and kinship in Middle America and the Caribbean: proceedings of the 14th seminar of the Committee on Family Research of the International Sociological Association, Curaçao, September 1975. Edited by Arnaud F. Marks, René A. Römer. Willemstad, Netherlands: Institute of Higher Studies in Curaçao, 1977?, p. 19–50, bibl., map, tables)

Thoughtful study of developmental cycle of domestic groups demonstrates that a trend away from subsistence agriculture and wage labor toward small-scale cane farming promoted a rise in the proportion of extended family arrangements.

835 Barabas, Alicia Mabel. Trabajo propio y trabajo de la gente: articulación económica y etnicidad entre los Chatinos de Oaxaca. Oaxaca, México: Centro Regional de Oaxaca, Instituto Nacional de Antropología e Historia, 1978. 56 p.; bibl.; map; plates; tables (Estudios de antropología e historia; 13)

Solid account of roles of two types of labor—self-employment in the milpa and migratory labor for cash on nearby coffee fincas—in the maintenance of Chatino ethnicity. Cash income has reinforced the mayordomía system and reciprocal exchanges between compadres. The ethnographic discussion is prefaced with a criticism of the notion that economic change inevitably implies the disappearance of ethnic groups.

836 ———— and Miguel Bartolomé.
Hydraulic development and ethnocide: the Mazatec and Chinantec people of Oaxaca, Mexico. Copenhagen, Denmark: International Work Group for Indigenous Affairs, 1973. 20 p.; bibl.; maps (IWGIA Document; 15)

Critical assessment of Mazatec relocation and planned Chinantec relocation.

837 Bartolomé, Miguel Alberto and **Alicia Mabel Barabas.** La resistencia maya: relaciones interétnicas en el oriente de la península de Yucatán. México: SEP, Instituto Nacional de Antropología e Historia, Centro Regional del Sureste, 1977. 133 p.; bibl.; ill. (Colección científica—Instituto Nacional de Antropología e Historia; 53: Etnología)

Stimulating investigation of the dynamics of Maya ethnicity, from colonial period to present. Drawing on ideas of Barth and Cardoso de Oliveira, authors examine interrelation of class and ethnicity, finding that class relations have been the seedbed of Maya rebellion but that continuing resistance to Ladinos has been phrased in terms of cultural values and symbols.

838 Becquelin-Monod, Aurore and **Alain Breton.** El Carnaval de Bachajón: cultura y naturaleza, dinámica de un ritual Tzeltal (CEM/ECM, 12, 1979, p. 191–239, bibl., tables)

This detailed analysis of a Tzeltal Carnival elucidates its relation to the organization of the *kalpules* and historical events.

839 Bozzoli de Wille, María Eugenia. Localidades indígenas costarricenses. 2. ed. aumentada y corr. San José, Costa Rica: Editorial Universitaria Centroamericana, 1975. 231 p.; bibl.; ill. (Colección Aula)

First part reproduces first edition (1969) while a second and longer part gives account of recent changes, including dispossession of peasants, migration, and disappearance of refuge regions.

840 Brandes, Stanley H. Dance as metaphor: a case from Tzintzuntzan, Mexico (UCLA/JLAL, 5:1, Summer 1979, p. 25–43, bibl.)

Thorough, perceptive description shows that the *Danza* (a devil dance) of Tzintzuntzan, Michoacán, expresses key features of world view.

841 Brintnall, Douglas E. Race relations in the southeastern highlands of Mesoamerica (AAA/AE, 6:4, Nov. 1979, p. 638–652, bibl.)

Takes issue with the tendency of Middle Americanists to characterize the Indian-Ladino distinction in terms of ethnicity. Among Guatemalans themselves the distinction is more racial than ethnic. Author says that the emphasis on ethnicity in discussions of Indian-Ladino relations tends to distort the social situation in several ways: it underestimates importance of descent in ethnic designation; it obscures Ladino racism; and it leads researchers to confuse Indian economic development with Ladinoization.

842 ———. Revolt against the dead: the modernization of a Maya community in the highlands of Guatemala. New York: Gordon and Breach, 1979. 199 p.; bibl.; ill.; maps; plates; tables (Library of Anthropology)

Brintnall essays a panoramic view of the changes occurring in a Guatemalan community and clarifies their interrelations. Shows how population growth and changes in labor laws have encourged cash cropping. The latter, in turn, has given young men more economic independence, thus undermining the traditional gerontocracy, in both the family and civil-religious hierarchies. The revolt against the dead, in other words, was also a revolt against the authority of the elders. Brintnall's description and analysis of social process is excellent; one might wish, however, that he had given somewhat more attention to the symbolism of the ancestors.

843 Carmack, Robert M. Historia social de los quichés. Guatemala, C.A.: Editorial José de Pineda Ibarra, Ministerio de Educación, 1979. 455 p.; bibl.; ill. (Publicación - Seminario de Integración Social Guatemalteca; no. 38)

Valuable collection of 13 essays on the Quiché, ranging from ethnohistorical studies of the prehispanic and colonial Quiché to papers on contemporary ethnography and social change. Most of the papers were published previously.

Castillo Robles, Soledad and **Blanca Irma Alonso Tejeda.** La Semana Santa en San Lucas Tecopilco, Tlax. See *HLAS 42:1314.*

844 Chapman, Anne MacKaye. Les enfants de la mort: univers mythique des indiens Tolupan (Jicaque). México: Mission archéologique et ethnologique française au Mexique, 1978. 520 p.; 17 leaves of plates; bibl.; ill. (Études mésoaméricaines; v. 4)

Presentation of myths in Spanish and French is followed by a brief ethnography of the Jicaque and some analytical remarks.

845 Chemin Bassler, Heidi. Sobrevivencias precortesianas en las creencias de los pames del Norte, Estado de San Luis Potosí, México. San Luis Potosí: Academia de Historia Potosina, 1977. 13 p.; 2 leaves of plates; bibl.; ill. (Biblioteca de historia potosina: Serie Cuadernos; 54)

Paper in two sections: 1) cites colonial commentary on the Pames which describes them as people who worshipped the Sun, kept small idols of their gods, and made offerings to spirits that resided in rocks; and 2) describes similar beliefs and practices of contemporary Pames.

846 Climo, Jacob J. Capitalism and unemployment on a collective farming—ejido—development project in southern Yucatan, Mexico (SAA/HO, 38:4, Winter 1979, p. 395–399, bibl., tables)

Argues that government-supported capitalist priorities were responsible for an ejido development project's failure to eliminate unemployment.

847 ———. Underemployment and unemployment on a collective farming—ejido—development project in Southern Yucatan, Mexico (*in* Papers in Anthropology [see item **910**] p. 23–37)

Gives an informative overview of present situation of Mexico's collective ejidos and presents detailed case study of one commercially successful cattle-ranching and cash-cropping ejido in southern Yucatan. Concludes that project failed to eliminate unemployment because it operated under constraints imposed by capitalist funding and fiscal management.

848 Coberly, Russell W. Maternal and marital dyads in a Mexican town (UP/E, 19:4, Oct. 1980, p. 447–457, bibl., table)

Assesses relative importance of maternal and marital dyads in Socoltenango, Chiapas. Although literature on the Mexican family portrays the mother-child relationship as being more important than the husband-wife relationship, data on household composition adduced here imply that in cases of remarriage the marital dyad dominates the maternal dyad.

849 Cognitive studies of Southern Mesoamerica. Editor on the field, Helen L. Neuenswander; consultant editor, Dean E. Arnold. Dallas, Texas: Museum of Anthropology, Summer Institute of Linguistics, 1977. 283 p.; bibl.; ill.; index; maps; tables (Publication - Sil Museum of Anthropology; 3)

Volume contains series of excellent papers: Harry S. McArthur's "Releasing the Dead: Ritual and Motivation in Aguacatec Dances" shows that the dance itself is but one element in a system of activities whose purpose it is to release the dead from bondage and thus secure their good will toward the living. Ruth Carlson's and Francis Eachus' "The Kekchi Spirit World" has some interesting implications for the comparative study of concepts of the soul in Middle America. Marilyn G. Henne's "Quiche Food: Its Cognitive Structure in Chichicastenango" examines cultural categories for meals and food; for the Quiche, only corn is "real food." Helen L. Neuenswander's and Shirley D. Sounder's "The Hot-Cold Wet-Dry Syndrome Among the Quiche of Joyabaj: Two Alternative Cognitive Models," among the Quiche there are two models of health, an ideal model which postulates that health requires a balance of hot and cold and an actual model according to which health is associated with warmth. Dennis and Jean Stratmeyer's "The Jacaltec Nawal and the Soul Bearer in Concepción Huista," this is one of the best descriptive treatments of the *nagual* in the literature. David F. Oltrogge's "The Ethnoentomology of Some Jicaque (Tol) Categories of the Order Hymenoptera," the presence of at least 40 names for bees and wasps

indicate their cultural importance. James Butler's and Dean E. Arnold's "Tzutujil Maize Classification in San Pedro La Laguna" examines maize classification in relation to the growing season. Judith J. Oltrogge's and Helen L. Neuenswander's "Colineality in Jicaque Cosmological, Socio-Political, and Kin Structures," cosmology, socio-political organization, and kinship are shown to evince homologous patterns of colineality; Ray Elliot's "Nebaj Ixil Unitary Kin Terms," a highly technical analysis of Nabaj kin classification delineates its features and shows that it does not conform to any single Murdockian type.

850 Colín, Mario. Instantáneas sobre los mazahuas. Toluca: Gobierno del Estado de México, Dirección del Patrimonio Cultural y Artístico del Estado de México, 1977. 64 p. (Testimonios de Atlacomulco; 3)

Brief articles describe the social, economic, and cultural importance of present-day Mazahua.

851 Collier, George A. The determinants of highland Maya kinship (NCFR/JFH, 3:4, Winter 1978, p. 439–453, bibl.)

Subordination of close-corporate Indian communities to dominant mestizo nationals may render Indian kinship organization more responsive to local economic conditions. In Zinacantan, corn farming encourages gerontocracy, the securing of family labor through manipulation of bride-wealth and inheritance, and formation of localized descent groups. In Amatenango, where wage labor and pottery making are more important than farming, kinship is bilateral.

852 Collier, Jane F. Stratification and dispute handling in two highland Chiapas communities (AAA/AE, 6:2, May 1979, p. 305–328, bibl.)

This excellent comparative study highlights role of dispute-handling techniques in elaboration and perpetuation of cultural values. In Tzotzil-speaking Zinacantan, disputes are resolved through mediation; in bilingual San Felipe, wrong-doers are punished. Difference may be due to importance of corn farming in Zinacantan. Successful farmers recruit their labor force among patrilineal kin and neighbors; they thus have vested interests in both mediation of disputes among kin and neighbors and in maintenance of norms that reinforce debt and servitude. In San Felipe, wage labor is the rule and incentives for mediation are correspondingly less. In Zinacantan, disputes raise questions of legal philosophy and ultimate religious values, whereas in San Felipe they merely involve perpetrators and their victims.

853 Collin, Laura and Félix Báez-Jorge. El patrimonio cultural de los grupos étnicos: nativismo o conciencia para sí? (III/AI, 39:3, p. 587–599, bibl.)

Expresses reservation that newly devised programs for supporting and even promoting ethnic pluralism in Mexico may have the unfortunate effect of encouraging reactionary forms of nativism. Urges that such programs should also impart anthropological knowledge concerning relations between rural communities and national society.

854 Cordry, Donald Bush. Mexican masks: their uses and symbolism. Austin: University of Texas Press, 1980. 280 p.: ill.; maps; plates.

Definitive work and essential reading for the student of Mexican religion. Extraordinary series of chromatic and black-and-white plates illustrate useful chapters on iconography, mask makers, materials, local styles, symbolism, and social uses. Throughout Cordry demonstrates unusual knowledge of regional variation and a keen perception of prehispanic influence.

855 Cosminsky, Sheila. Childbirth and midwifery on a Guatemalan finca (Medical Anthropology [Redgrave, Pleasantville, New York] 1:3, Summer 1977, p. 69–104, bibl., plates, table)

Contains interesting description of traditional beliefs and practices concerning care of the mother before and after birth, delivery, and children's illnesses. Author evaluates medical efficacy of traditional practices, finding in many instances that they are beneficial or at least harmless.

856 ———. The evil eye in a Quiché community (in The Evil eye. Edited by Clarence Maloney. New York: Columbia University Press, 1976, p. 163–174, bibl., plate)

Examines evil-eye belief in Santa Lucia Utatlán, Guatemala, and speculates that it may offer an explanation for unintended harm.

857 Crumrine, N. Ross. The evaluation of structural explanations of myth and ritual especially in regard to Mayo revitalization, Sonora, Mexico (UNC/K, 9:4, Feb. 1977, p. 72–79, bibl.)

Structural model, according to which oppositions are systematically inverted, is said to fit data from various domains of Mayo culture. Author claims that his structural formulation satisfies several tests of validity. However, its application appears to be somewhat arbitrary.

858 ———. Mayo Indian myth and ceremonialism, northwest Mexico: the dual ceremonial cycle (UNC/K, 10:2, June 1977, p. 44–66, bibl.)

Mayo ceremonial system has proven more persistent than techno-economic sphere, which has been more affected by modernization. Ceremonial system seems to be a variant of Uto-Aztecan pattern postulated by Edward Spicer in 1964.

859 ———. A transformational analysis of Mayo ceremonialism and myth (UCLA/JLAL, 4:2, Winter 1978, p. 231–242, bibl., ill.)

Attempts to show that Mayo myth and ritual exhibit a phrase structure involving elements of "birth," "life," "death," and "resurrection."

860 Dehouve, Danièle. Parenté et mariage dans une communauté Nahuatl de l'état de Guerrero, Mexique (SA/J, 65, 1978, p. 173–208, bibl., ill., tables)

Detailed analysis of family, lineage, kinship terminology, and marital alliance in a Nahuatl-speaking community.

861 DeWalt, Billie R. Alternative adaptive strategies in a Mexican ejido: a new perspective on modernization and development (SAA/HO, 38:2, Summer 1979, p. 139–143, bibl., ill., table)

Suggests that notion of adaptive strategy is less ethnocentric and more descriptive of actual change than concept of modernization. In a community in northwest part of Mexico state, families have responded differently to innovations offered by development agents. Policy implications are discussed.

862 ———. Drinking behavior, economic status, and adaptive strategies of modernization in a highland Mexican commu-

nity (AAA/AE, 6:3, August 1979, p. 510–530, tables)
Multivariate analysis of data from a community in Mexico state shows that immoderate drinking among males does not necessarily interfere with agricultural innovation.

863 ——. Modernization in a Mexican ejido: a study in economic adaptation. Cambridge; New York: Cambridge University Press, 1979. 303 p.; bibl.; ill.; maps; plates; tables (Cambridge Latin American studies; 33)
Evidence for diverse economic circumstances and strategies among households in central highlands community is said to challenge notion that peasant communities are homogeneous and conservative. Results of author's multivariate analyses also question commonplace assumption that participation in religious fiestas and drunkenness preclude agricultural innovation.

864 Dewey, Kathryn G. The impact of agricultural development on child nutrition in Tabasco, Mexico (Medical Anthropology [Redgrave, Pleasantville, New York] 4:1, Winter 1980, p. 21–54, bibl., tables)
Concludes that agricultural development in Plan Chontalpa, Tabasco, has not improved diet and nutrition among preschool children.

865 Finkler, Kaja. Applying econometric techniques to economic anthropology (AAA/AE, 6:4, Nov. 1979, p. 676–681, bibl.)
Traditional sharecropping arrangements in the Mezquital Valley, Hidalgo, are shown to provide more economic gain to sharecropper than one would predict from economic analysis based on Cobb-Douglas functions. Methodological exercise aims at illustrating opportunities for econometric analysis in anthropology.

866 Foster, George M. Methodological problems in the study of intracultural variation: the hot/cold dichotomy in Tzintzuntzan (SAA/HO, 38:2, Summer 1979, p. 179–183, bibl.)
Years of field work experience demonstrate inter-informant variability in use of the categories "hot" and "cold." Discusses reasons for cultural inconsistency and explores their methodological and theoretical implications.

867 ——. Tzintzuntzan: Mexican peasants in a changing world. 2. ed. rev. New York: Elsevier/North Holland, 1979. 392 p.; bibl.; plates; tables.
Revised edition of Tzintzuntzan (1967), see HLAS 29:1349), already a classic in Middle American literature. Text remains unaltered, except for a new preface and the addition of an epilogue. Latter chronicles the recent changes, including rising standard of living, an erosion of the image of Limited Good, and, remarkably, a revitalization of the fiesta system. Foster also defends his concept of Limited Good, noting that it was never intended to serve as a description of world view in today's modernizing Mexico.

Furst, Jill Leslie. The tree birth tradition in the Mixteca, Mexico. See HLAS 42:1320.

868 García Ruiz, Jesús F. Eléments pour une analyse de la représentation et de la conception de la personne chez les Mam (CDAL, 19, 1979, p. 167–183)
Examines role of symbolic and social constitution of the individual in Mam cultural persistence.

869 Gatti, Luis María; Delia Cuello; and Graciela Alcalá. Historia y "espacios sociales:" ensayo de una regionalización "de clases" de la Plantación Citrícola de Nuevo León (BBAA, 41:50, 1979, p. 23–37.)
Argues that the region is a social and ideological construction which draws on experience of the house and varies according to social class.

870 Genti di laguna: ideologia e istituzioni sociali dei Huave di San Mateo del Mar. Edited and compiled by Italo Signorini. Milano, Italy: Franco Angeli Editore, 1979. 283 p.; bibl.; tables.
Este conjunto de estudios representa el primer resultado tangible de una misión etnológica italiana a México cuyo objetivo fué el estudio de los huave de San Mateo del Mar, con especial referencia a actividades de subsistencia, parentescos natural y social y sistema político. Contiene asimismo un análisis de Carla Maria Rita sobre concepción y nacimiento; estudios de Tranfo sobre nagualismo y tonalismo; de Signorini y Tranfo sobre enfermedades y de Giorgio Raimondo Cardona sobre categorías gnoseológicas y lingüísticas. [M. Carmagnani]

Gossen, Garry H. Translating Cuscat's War: understanding Maya oral history. See *HLAS 42:1325*.

871 Gross, Joseph J. Marriage and family among the Maya (*in* Family and kinship in Middle America and the Caribbean: Proceedings of the 14th seminar of the Committee on Family Research of the International Sociological Association, Curaçao, September 1975. Edited by Arnaud F. Marks, René A. Römer. Willemstad, Netherlands: Institute of Higher Studies in Curaçao, 1977?, p. 51–86, bibl.)

Takes issue with notion that patrilineal-extended family is traditional in Maya household organization; actually, evidence indicates that the nuclear family has been the norm from preconquest times to present.

872 Gudeman, Stephen. Mapping means (*in* Social anthropology of work. Edited by Sandra Wallman. London: Academic Press, 1979, p. 229–247, bibl., tables)

Provocative analysis of the language used to designate and "map" land sites in Panamanian countryside shows that the language changes with transformations of subsistence regime. Under traditional conditions of absentee ownership and swidden argriculture, emphasis on natural power of land concealed real control of means of production; with land reform and increasing land scarcity, rights were couched in more personal terms; finally, with advent of a government sugar-cane refinery, assertion of personal rights ended. Concludes that maps are not merely cognitive phenomena or reflections of material given; they also are expressions of social allocation and use of the means of production.

873 Halperin, Rhoda. Administración agraria y trabajo: un caso de la economía política mexicana. Traducción de Antonieta S.M. de Hope. México: Instituto Nacional Indigenista: Secretaría de Educación Pública, 1975. 228 p.; 8 leaves of plates; bibl.; ill.; plates; tables (Colección SEP-INI; no. 36)

In this rather pedantic discussion of political theory and anthropological economics, author shows need for more concern with political factors in Mexico's agrarian economy. Point is illustrated with a reading of the literature on Chan Kom.

874 Hartwig, Vera K. de. Integrationsprozesse der indigenen Bevölkerung Mexikos im Rahmen der landwirtschaftlichen und handwerklichen Produktion in Chiapas und Tabasco, Mexiko (EAZ, 20:2, 1979, p. 279–294, bibl., map, plates)

Consideration of integration of indigenous populations into Mexico's national economy as seen through coffee and folk textile production in Chiapas and sombrero production in Tabasco.

875 ———. Los yaquis y la integración en México (UNAM/AA, 15, 1978, p. 95–108, bibl.)

Among Mexico's ethnic groups, the situation of the Yaqui has some unique features, the subject of this paper. A history of armed resistance has secured their land titles and won them certain rights of self-determination; meanwhile, credit and marketing arrangements integrate their agriculture into the national economy.

Helms, Mary W. Iguanas and crocodilians in tropical American mythology and iconography with special reference to Panama. See *HLAS 42:1168*.

876 Herrera Porras, Tomás. Cuna cosmology: legends from Panama. Collected and translated from Cuna into Spanish by Tomás Herrera Porras; translated into English, edited, and discussed by Anita G. McAndrews; photographs by Ann Parker. Washington: Three Continents Press, 1978. 105 p.; bibl.; ill.; map (on lining papers)

Fascinating series of Genesis-like legends collected from the bilingual Herrera Porras. Unfortunately, lack of exegesis and ethnographic context seriously detract from the volume's scholarly value. For folklorist's comment, see *HLAS 42:1169*.

877 Horstman, Connie and **Donald V. Kurtz.** Compadrazgo and adaptation in sixteenth-century central Mexico (UNM/JAR, 35:3, Fall 1979, p. 361–372, bibl.)

Argues that compadrazgo became popular in the postconquest period as an adaptation to social stress and disintegration. Offers no new data and relies on somewhat questionable theoretical and empirical assumptions.

878 Howard, Michael C. Ethnicity and economic integration in southern Belize (Ethnicity [Academic Press, New York] 7, 1980, p. 119–136, bibl., map)

With increasing interaction with non-Maya, Kekchi and Mopan have become more self-conscious about their ethnicity and more resistant to exploitation. Along with overview of present situation of the Maya in southern Belize, paper includes interesting material on patron-client compadrazgo.

879 Howe, James. The effects of writing on the Cuna political system (UP/E, 18:1, Jan. 1979, p. 1–16, bibl.)

Chronicles a remarkable series of changes in Cuna society and political organization brought about by the introduction of writing. Writing has been used to expand alliances, to record ritual participation, and to verify ritual competence; it has played a part in the elaboration of communal labor arrangements and in the systemization of law; and it has made political procedures more routine, impersonal, ambiguous, and official. In effect, a literate Cuna society has taken on many of the characteristics of state-level polities. Of course, introduction of writing in traditional societies does not always have such consequences. Author suggests that Cuna's history of communal organization and self-determination also influenced their recent social evolution.

880 ———. How the Cuna keep their chiefs in line (RAI/M, 13:4, Dec. 1978, p. 537–553, bibl.)

Insightful examination of customary restraints on Cuna chiefs with implications for general problem of how political power is exercised and circumscribed in traditional societies.

881 Hurtado Vega, Juan José. La "Mollera caída:" una subcategoría cognitiva de las enfermedades producidas por la ruptura del equilibro mecánico del cuerpo (BBAA, 41:50, 1979, p. 139–148, bibl., plates, table)

Describes Cackchiquel explanations of and treatments for "fallen fontanel."

882 Kearney, Michael. A world-view explanation of the evil-eye (in The Evil eye. Edited by Clarence Maloney. New York: Columbia University Press, 1976, p. 175–192, bibl., plates)

Argues that belief in the evil eye in Mexico is an expression of paranoia.

883 Kehoe, Alice B. The Sacred Heart: a case for stimulus diffusion (AAA/AE, 6:4, Nov. 1979, p. 763–771, bibl., ill.)

In this paper a scholarly examination of the available evidence leads to the inference that the Catholic symbol of the Sacred Heart may have diffused from Mexico.

884 Kelly, Phyllis B. A model of population increase in the Mazahua region, Mexico (III/AI, 34[35]:2, abril/junio 1979, p. 371–380, bibl., ill., table)

Cybernetic, demographic model suggests that population pressure leads in turn to resource scarcity, migration and wage labor, higher value of children, and more population growth. This cycle, however, may be on the verge of being broken as opportunities for wage labor diminish and interest in birth control rapidly mounts (see also item **894** and HLAS 39:1038).

885 Krantz, Lasse. Marketing, brokerage and stratification in peasant societies (BBAA, 1, junio 1980, p. 86–105, bibl., ill.)

Discusses conditions favoring local traders in Guanajuato.

886 Lagarriga Attias, Isabel. Explicaciones causales de la autoidentificación étnica dadas por los habitantes de la región otomí del norte del estado de México (INAH/A, 6:54, 1976, 7. época, p. 43–70, bibl., tables)

Author's previous work had shown the importance of economic factors in Otomí marginality. This paper shows that the Otomí themselves offer cultural reasons for their ethnic identity.

887 ——— and Juan Manuel Sandoval Palacios. Ceremonias mortuarias entre los otomíes del norte del Estado de México. Toluca: Gobierno del Estado de México, 1977. 122 p.; appendixes; bibl.; ill. (Serie de antropología social; 1)

Describes concept of the soul, funerary ritual, and the celebration of Todos Santos among the Otomí. Concluding remarks concern implications for discussions about the meaning of death in Mexican culture.

888 ——— and ———. Otomíes del norte del Estado de México: una contribución al estudio de la marginalidad. Edición preparada por Mario Colin. México: Biblioteca Enciclopédica del Estado de México,

1978. 222 p.; ill. (Biblioteca enciclopedica del Estado de México; 63)

Statistical analysis of census data from various municipalities finds a relation between Otomí marginality and agriculture.

889 León-Portilla, Miguel. Etnias indígenas y cultura nacional mestiza (III/AI, 39:3, 1979, p. 601–621)

Reviews history of Mexico's Indianist policies, giving special attention to their foundations in the work and ideas of Manuel Gamio, who wanted to help Indians emerge from their backwardness. Subsequent applications of Gamio's policies were aimed at the material betterment of the Indians and note, as some critics have claimed, at the destruction of traditional culture. Nonetheless, León-Portilla concedes that Indianist policies have tended to have this effect despite actual intentions and ends by calling for a greater effort to encourage the preservation of Indian languages and culture.

890 Littlefield, Alice. The expansion of capitalist relations of production in Mexican crafts (JPS, 6:4, July 1979, p. 471–488, bibl.)

Comprehensive review of recent developments in Mexico's rural crafts documents increasing control of production by entrepreneurial middlemen and the spread of putting-out systems.

891 Logan, Michael H. Anthropological research on the hot-cold theory of disease: some methodological suggestions (Medical Anthropology [Redgrave, Pleasantville, New York] 1:4, Fall 1977, p. 87–112, bibl.)

Undertakes comprehensive review of extant literature on hot-cold humoral medicine. Among other things, author notes need for more historical research and faults the literature for an assumption of cultural uniformity.

892 ——— and Warren T. Morrill. Humoral medicine and informant variability: an analysis of acculturation and cognitive change among Guatemalan villagers (AI/A, 74:5/6, 1979, p. 785–802, bibl., tables)

Notes that there is considerable interinformant variation in the use of the categories "hot" and "cold" in highland Guatemala. Finds that ladinos and acculturated Indians are more apt to use a neutral catagory along with the categories "hot" and "cold" in the classification of foods and medicines. Indian preference for a binary rather than triadic classification may reflect the greater salience of malnutrition and illness in Indian experience.

893 Lomnitz-Adler, Claudio. Clase y etnicidad en Morelos: una nuevo interpretación (III/AI, 39:3, 1979, p. 439–475, bibl., map, tables)

Neither class stratification nor geographical remoteness is sufficient to explain the persistence of Nahuatl. Presence of barrio communal lands and use of Nahuatl in political process have also been significant. This paper deserves attention as a serious attempt to bring a comparative approach to the problem of the relation between ethnicity and class. However, the aggregation of data by municipality is a methodological weakness inasmuch as important variations occur at the community/hamlet level in Morelos.

894 Loucky, James. Production and the patterning of social relations and values in two Guatemalan villages (AAA/AE, 6:3, Aug. 1979, p. 702–722, tables)

This significant contribution to cultural ecology suggests that economic specialization in Guatemalan highlands may be a response to land scarcity: San Pablo, a land-scarce community, has specialized in rope making; San Juan, less land-scarce, has remained agricultural. In San Pablo the critical resource (maguey fiber) is readily available, production is more a function of labor input, and labor is more seasonally continuous and generally less demanding than in San Juan. Consequently, rope makers of San Pablo rely more on child and female labor, marry earlier, and have higher birth rate. Less dependant on inheritance for means of production, they form separate households sooner. They also have a stronger work ethic than those of San Juan, which may explain a greater propensity to convert to Protestantism. For similar observations on the Chiapas highlands, see Collier's study (*HLAS 39:1038*) and item **884** in this section.

895 McGoodwin, James Russell. Mexico's marginal inshore Pacific fishing cooperatives (CUA/AQ, 53:1, Jan. 1980, p. 39–47, bibl.)

Describes various factors, including corrupt officialdom, population growth, and government-imposed conservation measures, which have undermined inshore fishing co-operatives in northwest Mexico.

896 ———. Pelagic shark fishing in rural Mexico: a context for cooperative action (UP/E, 18:4, Oct. 1979, p. 325–336, bibl., map)

Observes that shark fishermen cooperate while working in order to minimize risks of injury. Author thus suggests that lack of cooperation which seems so pervasive among peasants may be as much a function of socio economic context as an expression of cultural norm or social character.

Mexico. Instituto Nacional de Antropología e Historia. Proyectos Especiales de Investigación. See HLAS 42:154.

897 *México Indígena.* Organo de Difusión del Instituto Nacional Indigenista. Distribuidor: Porrúa Hnos. No. 20, nov. 1978– . México.

This important article summarizes the Mexican government's intention to depart from the integrationist policies of the past and to emphasize instead cultural pluralism.

898 Miller, Frank C. and Cynthia A. Cone. Alternative paths to fuller employment in Mexico (*in* Papers in Anthropology [see item **910**] p. 47–58)

In this stimulating paper, authors compare three rural situations: publicly owned industrial town, private enterprise in a market town, and an Indian community. In the first two, economic development failed to keep pace with population growth. In Indian town, a combination of out-migration, successful INI-sponsored projects, and land acquisition by community led to fuller employment. Drawing on their research experiences in these three situations, authors consider the desirability of promoting dispersed, small-scale, labor-intensive development projects in the countryside.

899 Moore, Alexander. Initiation rites in a Mesoamerican cargo system: men and boys, Judas and the Bull (UCLA/JLAL, 5:1, Summer 1979, p. 55–81, bibl., map)

Argues that in the Guatemalan community of Atchalán, the recruit's first year of service in civil-religious cargo system prefigures pattern of later service in system. Al-though application of van Gennep's schema to sequence of events in the initial year is a bit awkward, article includes some intriguing material, particularly with regard to "symbolic lessons" involving Judas, the Bull, and alcohol. For folklorist's comment, see HLAS 42:1177.

900 Morales Chua, Hilda Nelida. Bibliografía antropológica de Guatemala: 1975–1978 (BBAA, 40:49, 1978, p. 79–86)

Includes over 70 Guatemalan publications dealing with folklore, social anthropology, and linguistics.

901 Morales Hadalgo, Italo A. El pavo real y el árbol de la vida: dos diseños en los tejidos indígenas de Guatemala (IAHG/AHG, 2:1, 1979, p. 23–39, bibl., ill., plates)

Examines symbolism of quetzal/peacock and tree of life motifs in Guatemalan Indian textiles.

902 Motta Sánchez, José Arturo. Publicaciones del Departamento de Etnología y Antropología Social del Instituto Nacional de Antropología e Historia, 1974–1975: México (BBAA, 34:48, 1977, p. 103–108)

Lists publications and annotations.

903 Nolasco Armas, Margarita. Oaxaca indígena: problemas de aculturación en el Estado de Oaxaca y subáreas culturales. Prólogo, Gonzalo Aguirre Beltrán. México: Instituto de Investigación e Integración Social del Estado de Oaxaca, 1972. 338 p.; 3 fold. leaves of plates; bibl.; maps (Serie Investigaciones - Instituto de Investigación e Integración Social del Estado de Oaxaca; no. 1)

Statistical data, aggregated by language and socioeconomic area, purports to document presence and characteristics of "refuge regions."

904 Nutini, Hugo G. The systematic and exocentric dimensions of compadrazgo in rural Tlaxcala, Mexico (PMK, 24, 1978, p. 231–246)

Covers much of the same ground as item **905**.

905 ——— and **Douglas R. White.** Community variations and network structure in the social functions of compadrazgo in rural Tlaxcala, Mexico (UP/E, 16:4, Oct. 1977, p. 353–384, bibl., ill., tables)

Notes ways in which some types of

compadrazgo lead to or result from other types, thus forming long-lasting systematic networks. Comparative study indicates that elaboration of compadrazgo types is related to acculturation, viz., compadrazgo networks are less important in communities in which kinship is still a strong organizing principle.

906 Ochoa Zazueta, Jesús Angel. La muerte y los muertos: culto, servicio, ofrenda y humor de una comunidad. México: Secretaría de Educación Pública, 1974. 167 p.; bibl.; ill. (SepSetentas; 153)

The cult of the dead is central feature of folk Catholicism of Mizquic, a Chinampa community in Federal District of Mexico. Book describes cult, including beliefs about naguales, La Muerte, the dead, life after death, and the festivities of All Saints' and All Souls' days.

907 Ogien, Ruwen. Culture de la pauvreté: Oscar Lewis et sa critique (FS/CIS, 25:65, juillet/déc. 1978, nouvelle série, p. 285–314, bibl.)

Critique of Oscar Lewis' "culture of poverty" concept which faults it for failing to take account of the changing meanings of poverty in different social contexts and for making the poor responsible for their situation.

908 O'Nell, Carl W. and **Arthur J. Rubel.** The development and use of a gauge to measure social stress in three Mesoamerican communities (UT/E, 19:1, Jan. 1980, p. 111–127, bibl., tables)

This study employs an index of social stress (based on measures of socioeconomic insecurity and problems in role performance) to demonstrate a relation between stress and occurrence of susto.

909 Orellana, Sandra L. Aboriginal medicine in highland Guatemala (Medical Anthropology [Redgrave, Pleasantville, New York] 1:1, Winter 1977, p. 113–156, bibl., maps)

Compiles medical beliefs and practices described by priests and chroniclers during the early colonial period.

910 *Papers in Anthropology.* Department of Anthropology, University of Oklahoma. Vol. 21, No. 1, Spring 1980– Norman, Oklahoma.

The entire issue is devoted to two symposia on Mexico: 1) *Rural Unemploy-*

ment and Underemployment in Mexico, Problems and Proposed Solutions: Jacob J. Climo's "Introduction;" Juan Jesús Arias "Underemployment and Survival in Baca, Yucatan, Mexico" (p. 5–10) documents unreported unemployment among Henequengrowing peasants and describes their various alternative economic strategies; Rodney Carlos Kirk's "Agrarian Reform and Designed Unemployment" (p. 11–21) argues that the failure of Mexico's land reform program to provide for more than bare subsistence needs is partly responsible for high unemployment/underemployment; Jacob J. Climo's "Underemployment and Unemployment on a Collective Farming (Ejido) Development Project in Southern Yucatan, Mexico" (see item **847**); Raymond E. Wiest's "The Interrelationship of Rural, Urban, and International Labor Markets: Consequences for Rural Mexican Community" (p. 39–46) examines causes and consequences of labor migration in rural Michoacán; Frank C. Miller's and Cynthia A. Cone's "Alternative Paths to Fuller Employment in Mexico" (see item **898**); Jacob J. Climo's "Summary." 2) *People of Mexico, Problems and Potential*: John L. Aguilar's "Shame and Conformity: Psychological Determinants of Indian Conformity in Inter-ethnic Deference Rituals" (p. 67–77) is a well-written and insightful discussion of role of shame in Indian compliance with inter-ethnic deference rituals in highland Chiapas; George Agogino's and Ann Bennett's "The Rapid Acculturation of the Huasteca" is a cursory summary of distribution and situation of present-day Huasteca (p. 79–89); John L. Gwaltney's "Darkly through the Glass of Progress" (p. 91–100) gives overview of Chinantec, with emphasis on problem of filarial disease-induced blindness; George Agogino's and Bobbie Ferguson's "Investigation of a Mexican-Indian Jewish Community: Hidalgo, Mexico" (p. 101–104) is a brief note on small Jewish community in mestizo town; and Thomas McCorkle's and Margery McCorkle's "Observations on Early Childhood Learning in a Mexican Community" (p. 105–109) describes upper and lower-class socialization practices in Uruapan, Michoacán.

911 Peña, Guillermo de la. Herederos de promesas: agricultura, política y ritual en los Altos de Morelos. México: Centro de Investigaciones Superiores del INAH, 1980.

391 p.; bibl.; maps; tables (Ediciones de La Casa Chata; no. 11)

Criticizes undue emphasis on the closed-corporate community in Middle American studies and argues instead for historical and regional analysis, taking for its subject matter north-central Morelos. The history is well done but in this case advantages of regional analysis are not convincingly demonstrated; indeed, book is somewhat disjointed. One suspects that lack of corporateness and coherence which author attributes to village society and culture may be as much a function of author's perspective as of ethnographic reality.

Pérez Estrada, Francisco. Ensayos nicaragüenses. See *HLAS 42:2388.*

912 Pérez Kantule, Néle and **Rubén Pérez Kantule.** Picture-writings and other documents. New York: AMS Press, 1979. 75 p.; 8 leaves of plates; bibl.; ill.

Texts written by Cuná Indians in Cuná, Spanish, and English, originally published in two volumes in 1928–30. Includes material on religious beliefs and customs along with explanation of Cuná picture writing.

913 Petterson, John S. Fishing cooperatives and political power: a Mexican example (CUA/AQ, 53:1, Jan. 1980, p. 64–74, bibl.)

Discusses historical and social reasons for the success of fishing cooperatives in Ensenada, Baja California.

914 Prem, Hanns J. Milpa y hacienda, tenencia de la tierra indígena y española en la cuenca del Alto Atoyac, Puebla, México: 1520–1650. Con contribuciones de Ursula Dyckerhoff y Günter Miehlich. Wiesbaden: Steiner, 1978. 325 p.; bibl.; index (Das Mexiko-Projekt der Deutschen Forschungsgemeinschaft = El Proyecto México de la Fundación Alemana para la Investigación Científica; 13)

A major contribution to knowledge of early colonial period; makes exhaustive use of documentary sources to trace the transformations in land tenure associated with emergence of the hacienda. For historian's comment, see *HLAS 42:1562.*

915 Reck, Gregory G. In the shadow of Tlaloc: life in a Mexican village. Har-

mondsworth, England; New York: Penguin Books, 1978. 224 p.; ill.

Some fine writing and a certain amount of poetic license have gone into this evocation of life in the Sierra Norte of Puebla. Writing like a novelist, Reck gives us an intimate portrait of a Nahua Indian subjected to the dislocation and trauma of rapid social change. Caught between Indian communalism and mestizo greed, the Indian's thinking becomes a contradictory mixture of modern aspirations for economic betterment and nostalgia for the way things were. Portraying his subject with wit and sensitivity, Reck has us empathize with the Indian's hopes and fears, with the promise and absurdity of his situation. Focus here is on artistically recreated experience, not on objective fact but book is not lacking in skillful ethnography. Descriptions of Indian-mestizo interaction and the machismo of mestizos and would-be mestizos are particularly well done.

916 Reifler de Bricker, Victoria. Movimientos religiosos indígenas en Los Altos de Chiapas (III/AI, 39:1, enero/marzo 1979, p. 17–46)

With impressive control of historical evidence, author shows that expansion of festival cycle in 18th and 19th centuries and chapel-building movement in the 20th century were Indian inspired. Thus, one cannot say, as Marvin Harris has, that the proliferation of saints' cults among New World Indians is simply or primarily a function of clerical greed. In fact, in two cases reported here, Indian uprisings were precipitated by Spanish and ladino efforts to suppress new cults.

917 Reina, Rubén E. and **Robert M. Hill, II.** The traditional pottery of Guatemala. Austin: University of Texas Press, 1978. 299 p.; bibl.; ill.; maps; plates; tables (The Texas Pan American series)

With unusual ethnographic precision, author examines molding and firing techniques in 25 rural aldeas and pueblos. Authors, however, are not merely concerned with technicalities of production; they also make interesting observations about social relations of production, cultural significance of craft production, and regional marketing system.

918 Religión y sociedad. México: Departamento de Etnología y Antropología Social, Instituto Nacional de Antropología e Historia, 1977. 72 p. in various pagings; bibl. (Estudios—Departamento de Etnología y Antropología Social, I.N.A.H.; 17. Cuadernos de trabajo—Departamento de Etnología y Antropología Social, I.N.A.H.; 17)

Contains several worthwhile papers: Tim Knab's "Talocan Tlamanic: 1, 2, Supernatural Beings of the Sierra de Puebla;" Isabel Lagarriga Attias' "Un Ejemplo de Religiosidad de los Marginales de México: El Espiritualismo Trinitario Mariano;" and Kaja Finkler's "Spiritualism in Rural Mexico."

919 Rubenstein, Robert A. The cognitive consequences of bilingual education in northern Belize (AAA/AE, 6:3, Aug. 1979, p. 583–601, bibl., tables)

Examination of the impact of Spanish-English bilingualism on children's cognitive processes suggests that bilingualism learned in a stressful situation may result in linguistic and, perhaps, cognitive disabilities.

920 Salinas Pedraza, Jesús and Russell Bernard. Rc Hnychnyu (The Otomí). v. 1, Geography and fauna. Albuquerque: University of New Mexico, 1978. 1 v.; ill.; map.

This bilingual book, product of joint effort by Otomí villager and American linguist, describes in parallel English and Otomí texts empirical knowledge, beliefs, and attitudes of Otomí about their environment and its fauna. The presentation, which is richly laden with anecdotes and folklore, reveals empirical perceptiveness and poetic sensitivity of the Otomí people.

921 San Salvador. Museo Nacional David J. Guzmán. Exploración etnográfica, Departamento de Sonsonate. San Salvador: Ministerio de Educación, Dirección General de Cultura, Juventud y Deportes, Dirección de Publicaciones, 1975. 415 p.; 63 leaves of plates; bibl.; ill. (Etnografía salvadoreña; 2. Colección Estudios y documentos; no. 4)

Contains introductory overview of region followed by ethnographic vignettes of its 16 municipios. Style of presentation is rather cursory and extremely empirical but data are sufficiently detailed to indicate ethnographic richness of the region.

922 Schaedel, Richard P. The anthropological study of Latin American cities in intra- and interdisciplinary perspective. Austin: The University of Texas at Austin, Institute of Latin American Studies, 1974. p. 139–170; bibl. (Offprint series; 170)

Attempts to place study of Latin American cities in context of archaeological knowledge about urbanism, and argues that major cities grow because infrastructural investments tend to be greater in cities than in the countryside.

923 Schuman, Malcolm K. When a house is not a home: fieldworkers and landlords in a Mayan village, Yucatan, Mexico (SAA/HQ, 38:4, Winter 1979, p. 400–404, bibl.)

Engagingly written cautionary tale describes political and legal difficulties encountered by unsuspecting fieldworkers as they tried to build houses for themselves in a Maya town.

924 Schwartz, Norman B. and Kenneth W. Eckhardt. Values, ethnicity, and acculturation in Petén, Guatemala (UCL/CD, 11:2, 1979, p. 219–246, bibl., tables)

In a Petén town, ethnic distinction between Indian and Ladino is still maintained, although in name only; in matters of language, dress, and culture, Indians are almost fully acculturated. In view of reported differences in socialization practices, authors expected differences in value orientation between the two groups; however, administration of Kluckhohn-Strodtbeck Value-Orientation Schedule failed to support this expectation.

Smith, Kenneth W. *Todos los Santos*: spirits, kites, and courtship in the Guatemalan Maya highlands. See *HLAS 42:1187.*

925 Sokolovsky, Jay. The local roots of community transformation in a Nahuatl Indian village (BBAA, 40:49, 1978, p. 49–60, bibl., table)

Provides an informative account of religious and civil offices in a Nahuatl-speaking community and examines use of civil offices by those persons seeking to promote change (article also appeared in the *Anthropological Quarterly*, 51:3, 1977, p. 163–173).

926 Studies of the Yaqui Indians of Sonora, Mexico. By W. C. Holden et al. New York: AMS Press, 1979. 142 p.; bibl.; ill.; index (Scientific series; no. 2)

Reprinted from 1936 ed.

927 Suárez, Cruz. La ceremonia pro-piciatoria del Popocatepetl, Volcán Santiago, de Nicaragua (BNBD, 25, sept./oct. 1978, p. 10–19, bibl., maps)

Nahuatl toponyms and evidence of the Tlaloc cult argue for inclusion of western part of Nicaragua in culture area of Mesoamerica.

928 Swetnam, John J. An ethnographic test of class and pluralist models of Guatemalan ethnicity (UNM/JAR, 35:3, Fall 1979, p. 350–360, bibl., tables)

Urban/rural variable predicts alloca-tion of urban market stalls better than eth-nicity, suggesting that class provides a more powerful model of Guatemalan society than ethnic pluralism.

929 ———. Interaction between urban and rural residents in a Guatemalan mar-ketplace (UA, 7:2, Summer 1978, p. 137–153, bibl., tables)

Rural Indian vendors in Antigue mar-ket adopt features of urban ladino lifestyle and establish mutually supportive relations with ladino vendors. Inter-ethnic solidarity is phrased in terms of shared poverty and the virtues of being poor. Author believes that his research illustrates importance of class stratification in Guatemalan society and pro-poses a program of anthropological research which would look at other situations in which poor ladinos and Indians might per-ceive themselves as having common bonds.

930 Taggart, James M. Men's changing im-age of women in Nahuat oral tradition (AAA/AE, 6:3, Aug. 1979, p. 723–724, bibl., tables)

Delightful paper brings commendable methodological rigor to interpretation of folktales in two Sierra Nahuat commu-nities. In one, an historical trend toward bi-lateral inheritance has improved status of women. In the other, land scarcity and re-moteness from tax office have been associ-ated with less impact of the Juárez Reform Laws and more persistence of patrilineal in-heritance and male dominance. Difference is reflected in cognate tales about Adam and Eve: in the land-scarce/patrilineal commu-nity folktales depict women as being more sexually wanton and less competent. Docu-mentation of secular trend in inheritance strongly implies influence of social form on

biblical story rather than a mere insomor-phism of the two.

931 *Tlalocan.* Revista de fuentes para el conocimiento de las culturas indígenas de México. UNAM, Instituto de Investiga-ciones Antropológicas, Instituto de Investiga-ciones Históricas. Vol. 17, 1977– . México.

Contains the following articles: Fer-nando Horcasitas' "Para la Historia de la Re-vista *Tlalocan;*" Miguel León-Portilla's "Una Denuncia en Náhuatl, 1595;" Luis Reyes Garcí's "Genealogía de Doña Francisca de Guzmán, Xochimilco, 1610;" Jon Ek's "A Witchcraft Trial in Guerrero;" Karen Dakin's "Pedro Cuaresma and Other Nahuatl Sto-ries;" Artemisa Echegoyen's and Catalina Voigtlander's "Peregrinación a la Laguna y en Busca de Trabajo en la Carretera;" Cornelia Mak's "Picturesque Mixtec Talk;" Cornelia Mak's "Maguey Tapping in the Highland Mixteco;" Elena E. de Hollenbach's "El Ori-gen del Sol y de la Luna;" Allan R. Jamie-son's "El Origen del Nombre del Pueblo de Chiquihuitlan, Oaxaca;" Benjamín Pérez González's "La Fundación de Tuxta: una Leyenda Chontal;" Sandra L. Orellana's "El Negro del Volcán y El Origen del Lago de Atitlán;" Don Burgess' "El Origen del Ma-rrano en Tarahumara;" Mauricio F. Mixco's "Textos para la Etnohistoria en la Frontera Dominicana de Baja California;" Pedro Ca-rrasco's "Los Señores de Xochimilco en 1548;" Guillermo Foladori's "Un Documento Histórico de Zongólica, Veracruz;" J. Eric S. Thompson's "Hallucinatory Drugs and Hobgoblins in the Maya Lowlands;" Wil-liam H. Fellowes' "The Treatises of Her-nando Ruiz de Alarcón;" Noemí Quezada's "La Danza del Volador y Algunas Creencias de Temporal en el Siglo XVIII;" Thomas A. Lee, Jr.'s "El Origen del Lago Jécameyá Mes-calapa, Chiapas;" Stephen A. Colston's "A Comment on Dating the 'Cronica X';" and Fernando Horcasitas' "Indice de la Revista *Tlalocan*: vols. I-IV."

932 Varese, Stefano. Defender lo múltiple: nota al indigenismo. Oaxaca, México: Centro Regional de Oaxaca, Instituto Nacio-nal de Antropología e Historia, 1978. 22 p.; bibl. (Estudios de antropología e historia; 16)

Blistering critique of forced accultura-tion and passionate defense of cultural pluralism.

933 ———. Una dialéctica negada: notas sobre la multietnicidad mexicana (*in* Seminario de Historia de la Cultura Nacional, Instituto Nacional de Antropología e Historia, 1976. En torno a la cultura nacional. Héctor Aguilar Camín et al. México: Instituto Nacional Indigenista, Secretarí de Educación Pública, 1976, p. 137–158, bibl.)

Dominance of so-called national culture—that of the ruling class—has blocked the natural creativity of ethnic diversity. Argues that ethnicity should be defined in terms of language rather than cultural practices, which have a contingent relation to the social strategies that characterize given historical periods.

934 **Velasco Toro, José.** Indigenismo y rebelión totonaca de Papantla: 1885–1896 (III//AI, 39:1, enero/marzo 1979, p. 81–106)

Abolition of communal land among the Totonac in the latter half of the 19th century produced a militant revitalization movement; a leader of the first uprising advocated a return to Catholic practice, reduction of taxes, expulsion of foreigners, and rights to land.

935 **Vigueira, Carmen.** Percepción y cultura: un enfoque ecológico. Portada, Miguel Angel Guzmán. México: Centro de Investigaciones Superiores del INAH, 1977. 319 p.; bibl.; ill. (Ediciones de la Casa Chata; 4)

Criticizes evolutionary and psychodynamic approaches in cross-cultural studies of perception and argues that perception-test results can be best understood as learned patterns of response to local ecology. Presentation and analysis of Rorschach protocols collected among the Tajín Totonac purport to illustrate the thesis.

936 **Warman, Arturo.** Los indigenistas y el modelo de país (Nexos [Centro de Investigación y Científica, Prado Norte, México] 2, feb. 1978, p. 1–6)

Reviews essential trends of *indigenismo* from early colonial period to present, and concludes that observations on recent criticisms of the development-oriented indigenismo of Aguirre Beltrán.

937 ———. . . . Y venimos a contradecir: los campesinos de Morelos y el Estado Nacional. México: Centro de Investigaciones Superiores del INAH, 1976. 351 p.; bibl.; maps (Ediciones de la Casa Chata; no. 2)

Warman reconstructs historial expansion of Morelos' capitalist economy and shows that, at every stage, the peasant has adopted defensive strategies. In the recent period, peasants have adopted truck-farming and Green Revolution technology, despite their financial costs and risks, as means of coping with inflation. Warman disputes Boserup's theory that population growth is a cause of intensification of agriculture; in Morelos, at least, he thinks population increase should be understood as response to modern labor-intensive agriculture. He is maintaining, in other words, that reproduction is an element in the peasant's most recent strategy of self-defense.

938 **Wilken, Gene C.** Whistle speech in Tlaxcala, Mexico (AI/A, 74:5 6, 1979, p. 881–888, bibl., map)

Whistle speech is a fascinating and widespread but little studied phenomenon in Mexico. This paper provides a clear account of the Tlaxcalan version of the technique and briefly considers its function and origin.

939 **Woods, Clyde M.** Alternative curing strategies in a changing medical situation (Medical Anthropology [Redgrave, Pleasantville, New York] 1:3, Summer 1977, p. 25–54, bibl., tables)

Describes changes which are occurring in the traditional medical practices of a Guatemalan community. Modern medicine is increasingly favored because it is effective, but many people combine traditional and modern forms of treatment.

940 **Young, James C.** A model of illness treatment decisions in a Tarascan town (AAA/AE, 7:1, Feb. 1980, p. 106–131, bibl., ill., tables)

Systematic eliciting procedures are used to construct a formal model of treatment selection. Choice of treatment (e.g., self-treatment, curer, or doctor) is influenced by gravity of illness, knowledge of home remedies, "faith," and accessibility of treatment.

ETHNOLOGY: West Indies

LAMBROS COMITAS, *Professor of Anthropology and Education, Teachers College, Columbia University, and Director, Institute of Latin American and Iberian Studies, Columbia University*

FOR THIS VOLUME OF *HLAS*, I have reviewed publications in social and cultural anthropology and related areas for 28 distinct Caribbean territories: Antigua, Aruba, Bahamas, Barbados, Barbuda, Belize, Bermuda, Bequia, Carriaçou, Cuba, Curaçao, Dominican Republic, Grenada, Guadeloupe, Guyana, Haiti, Jamaica, Martinique, Montserrat, Puerto Rico, St. Kitts, St. Lucia, St. Vincent, Surinam, Terre-de-Haut (Les Saintes), Trinidad and Tobago, United States Virgin Islands and Venezuela. Also included are annotations of an unusually large number of publications that appeared during the current review period on the Commonwealth Caribbean or the Caribbean region as a whole, as well as a few on Caribbean people abroad.

In terms of geographic distribution, the number of annotated publications on the Caribbean as a region is larger than that for any single territory within the region. Haiti is the territory receiving the most attention followed closely by Jamaica and Guyana, and then by Surinam and Belize. Other territories relatively well-represented are Barbados, Guadeloupe, Puerto Rico, and Trinidad and Tobago.

As usual, the publications cited in this section cover a very wide range of subject matter. Nevertheless, the bulk of the items can be divided into the following categories:

I. CLASS AND ETHNICITY

Interest in ethnicity, in aspects of social stratification, and in the study of elites has dramatically increased. For publications that deal with the region as a whole or the Commonwealth Caribbean, see Cross on urbanization (item **970**), Hall on pluralism, race, and class (item **993**), and Layng on stereotypes and ethnic relationships (item **1014**). On Jamaica, Austin has written on symbols (item **947**), Bell and Stevenson on changing attitudes of political leaders (item **952**), Bell and Robinson on changing cultural identity of political leaders (item **953**), Gordon on working class radicalism (item **986**), Holzberg on economic elites (item **999**), Kuper on race, class and culture (item **1007**), Post on the 1938 disturbances and their aftermath (item **1039**), Reid on economic elites (item **1043**), and St. Pierre on the 1938 disturbances (item **1045**). Works that deal with Guyana include Bartels on ethnicity and class struggle (item **950**), Cross on colonialism and ethnicity (item **969**), Jayawardena on culture and ethnicity (item **1002**), Manley on post-independence (item **1021**), and Silverman on dependency and class formation (item **1048**). For Surinam, see De Bruijne on the Lebanese (item **972**), Dew on ethnicity and politics (item **975**), and Speckmann on ethnic relations (item **1051**). Henriques and Manyoni deal with ethnic relations in Barbados and Guyana (item **997**); Layne with race and class in Barbados (item **1013**); Abraham Van Der Mark with Sephardic Jews in Curaçao (item **1056**); Bonniol with the "petits blancs" of Terre-de-Haut (item **958**); Brathwaite with occupational elites in Trinidad and Tobago (item **962**); Cole with the impact of the revolution on Cuban racism (item **967**); and Gregory on Indian identity in Belize (item **987**).

II. RELIGION AND MAGIC

Among the noteworthy publications on the Jonestown tragedy are Baechler (item 948), Gutwirth (item 989), Hall (item 992), and Lewis (item 1015). Haitian vodun is covered by Isaac (item 1001) and Laguerre (items 1010 and 1012) and Rastafarianism by Campbell (item 963) and Cashmore (item 964). Pollak-Eltz describes two Afro-Venezuelan *fiestas* (item 1037); Brana-Shute and Brana-Shute deal with ritual therapy in Paramaribo (item 961); and Glazier provides bibliography on the spiritualist medium and possession (item 984). For broader treatments of Black religious experience in the New World, see Simpson (item 1049) and Walker (item 1058). From a historical perspective, Posern-Zielinski analyzes Amerindian religious ferment in 19th-century British Guiana (item 1038); Schuler examines Jamaican Myalism (item 1047); and Mathews describes aspects of African participation in 17th-century Puerto Rican religious life (item 1026). Histories of Protestantism are provided by Pressior for Haiti (item 1041); and by Abénon (item 941) and Lafleur (items 1008 and 1009) for Guadaloupe.

III. HEALTH AND MEDICINE

On Haiti, Charles (item 965), Philippe and Romain (item 1033) and Weidman (item 1059) deal with *indisposition*, a culture-bound disorder; and Coreil evaluates medical responses to an anthrax epidemic (item 968). Dressler analyzes beliefs and treatment in St. Lucia (item 978); Stevenson deals with medicinal plants and hypertension in St. Kitts (item 1053); and Halberstein and Davies examine changing health patterns on Bimini (item 991). Koss deals with a Puerto Rican therapist-spiritist training project (item 1006), and Sandoval with *santería* as a mental health care system (item 1046).

IV. MATING, MARRIAGE, HOUSEHOLD, AND FAMILY

The publications dealing with these traditionally popular anthropological topics include Adams on work opportunity and household organization among Barama River Caribs (item 943); Alexander on stratification and the family (item 944); Besson on tenure and transmission of land and the cognatic descent group (item 955); Higman on the slave family in Trinidad (item 8202); Laguerre on a Haitian extended family (item 1011); Manyoni on extra-marital mating patterns (item 1022); Midgett's critique of Rubenstein (item 1027); Rubenstein in parental roles in St. Vincent (item 1044); R.T. Smith on the family in the Caribbean (item 1050); and Whitehead on residence, kinship, and mating as adaptive strategies (item 1063).

V. IMMIGRATION AND EMIGRATION

The movement of the Caribbean people continues to be of importance to the anthropologist. Chaney and Sutton write on Caribbean migration to New York (item 1000); Locher on rural-urban migration and the Haitian extended family (item 1016); Marshall on illegal Haitian migration to the Bahamas (item 1024); and Philpott on the migration dependency of Montserrat (item 1034).

Two other areas that appear to be developing rapidly are scientific studies of the expressive arts (i.e., festivals, dance, music and theatre) exemplified by publications such as items 956, 971, 976, 982, 1020, 1030 and 1060. The second area is women's studies with two bibliographic efforts by Cohen Stuart (item 1064) and Massiah (item 1065), as well as substantive articles by Gussler (item 988) and Henney (item 996).

The contextual studies of Barbuda provided by Berleant-Schiller (item 954) and

Lowenthal and Clarke (items **1017** and **1018**) deserve special attention, in light of Antigua's independence and Barbuda's antipathy toward continuing its subservient relationship to that new island-nation.

In closing, I note the great loss suffered by all Caribbeanists in the recent passing of Chandra Jayawardena, Douglas Taylor and Eric Williams and the assassination of Walter Rodney.

I am indebted to Ellen Schnepel for her valuable contribution to the preparation of this section.

941 Abénon, Lucien. Les protestants de la Guadeloupe et la communauté réformée de Capesterre sous L'Ancien Régime (SHG/B, 32:2, 1977, p. 25–62)

Author deals with origin of Protestants in Guadeloupe, their social situation, problem of property, and maintenance of Protestantism into 18th century. Rather than history of Protestantism in Guadeloupe, this is an essay on its importance within religious affairs of island during Ancient Regime. Utilizing available source material, discusses origin (geographic and socioeconomic) of Protestants, how they responded to revocation of Elicit of Nantes, and how Protestantism remained a vital force in Guadeloupe into 18th century, despite authorities.

942 Adams, John E. From landsmen to seamen: the making of a West Indian fishing community (PAIGH/G, 88, dic. 1978, p. 151–166, bibl., maps)

Author traces beginning, growth, and final dominance of fishing in a Bequia community formerly populated by slaves and sharecroppers. Series of factors are cited to explain this phenomenon: environmental conditions, restrictive immigration policies, economic pressures, etc. Although, majority of fishermen do not find occupation of fishing attractive, community's economic base remains fishing (i.e., occupation a man turns to when no other jobs are available).

943 Adams, K.J. Work opportunity and household organization among the Barama River Caribs of Guyana (AI/A, 74:1/2, 1979, p. 219–222)

Analysis of economic factors affecting household organization of those Caribs while employed in mining, as well as prior to such employment, and following cessation of mining activities in area. Concludes that pattern of cooperation among adult individuals from different households in same settlement was eroded by introduction of wage work, markets, and money economy. Nevertheless, individuals continued to seek subsistence as a member of a household, although composition of household was extended beyond the earlier nuclear family organization.

944 Alexander, Jack. A note concerning research on the relation between stratification and the family in the Caribbean (UPR/CS, 15:1, April 1975, p. 123–129, bibl., table)

Posits utility of formulating theories concerning family and stratification in the Caribbean so that they focus on the interrelation between various aspects of stratification and various aspects of family life and which can be tested quantitatively. Includes useful table itemizing stratification variables related to family variations in 53 Caribbean family studies.

Alexis, Gerson. Voudou et quimbois: essai sur les avatars du voudou à la Martinique. See *HLAS 42:1253.*

945 The Amerindians in Guyana, 1803–73: a documentary history. Edited by Mary Noel Menezes; with a foreword by Donald Wood. London: Cass; Totowa, New Jersey: Biblio Distribution Centre, 1979. 314 p.; bibl.; index; map.

Selection of documents from London's Public Record Office, Guyana's National Archives, and archives of several missionary societies, which depict Amerindian culture in Guyana and illustrate attitudes and policies of metropolitan and local governments towards them in 1803–73. Volume is divided into eight sections devoted to different topics and introduced by editor: 1) Amerindians— their appearance, characteristics, customs and beliefs, diseases, attitudes towards other tribes and races; 2) present policy toward Amerindians; 3) officials for the protection of

Indians; 4) legal jurisdiction over Indians; 5) Indians and boundaries; 6) Indian slavery, industrial employment, Indians and their land; 7) conversion of Indians; and 8) government policy towards Indian civilization. Interesting and useful collection.

946 Anderson, Alan B. Recent acculturation of Bush Negroes in Surinam and French Guiana (CRCA/A, 22:1, 1980, p. 61–84, bibl., map)

Relatively short but useful review of published evidence dealing with acculturation of Bush Negroes by the urbanized coastal society. Author sketches relevant historical context and then discusses degree of African influence on Bush Negro culture. With specific reference to aspects of culture retention or change, deals with social organization and kinship, religious beliefs and practices, the arts, and language. With regard to motivation for culture change, treats trade with coast, temporary work on coast, changing values and appearances, economic development of interior, impact of tourism, education and emigration, urbanization, and politicization. Author concludes that many pressures on Bush Negro culture may lead to its eventual disappearance.

947 Austin, Diane J. History and symbols in ideology: a Jamaican example (RAI/M, 14:3, Sept. 1979, p. 497–514, bibl., ill.)

Author uses Maurice Bloch's distinction between ritual and normal communication, while casting doubt on whether that distinction should have been tied to a distinction between ideology and knowledge. Based on a case involving a Jamaican working-class woman, analyzes Jamaican class ideology and argues "that ritual communication as an aspect of social control, pervades even 'practical' activity, and therefore should be seen as a possible dimension in all thought, whatever the type of society." For historian's comment, see *HLAS 42:2501*.

948 Baechler, Jean. Mourir à Jonestown (AES, 20:2, 1979, p. 173–210)

Explanation of Jonestown suicide/massacre is not to be sought in literature on sects or revolutionary movements—it is a unique case. Author concentrates on Jim Jones, dealing with his reasons for killing himself, why he felt it necessary or good to take the whole community with him, and

why the community acquiesced. Interprets Jones' suicide as the apocalypse sanctioning the ultimate failure of a life plan centered on power and directed against the entire world. Jones took sect with him because he no longer distinguished himself from it and followers acquiesced because thought of sect's destruction was unbearable to them.

949 Barrow, Christine and **J.E. Greene.** Small business in Barbados: a case of survival. Cave Hill, Barbados: University of the West Indies, Institute of Social and Economic Research, 1979. 125 p.; bibl.; tables.

Reports on project aimed at monitoring changes in performance and attitudes that occurred in small business sector between 1974–76, paying particular attention to impact of Small Business Development Project sponsored by Barbados Institute of Management and Productivity. Based on survey data, volume outlines political sociology of small business people in Barbados. Authors define small business in context of Barbados, discuss origins and persistence of white elite, delineate demographic and operational characteristics of small businessmen in Barbados, their business attitudes, values, and institutional supports, and questions size and survival. Welcome addition to literature.

950 Bartels, Dennis. Ethnicity, ideology, and class struggle in Guyanese society (CRCA/A, 22:1, 1980, p. 45–60, bibl.)

Author argues that ethnic boundaries, as defined by F. Barth, are critical in understanding ideology of class and ethnic conflict that developed in colony of British Guiana. Historically, allocation of disproportionate economic benefits and burdens to ruling class led to development of social and economic differences among ethnic groups. In contemporary Guyana, disproportionate allocation and racist ideology continue, as does conflict between Indo- and Afro-Guyanese working people. Based on the 1973 election, author views this discrimination as result of deliberate policy on the part of Burnham's PNC in order to retain Afro-Guyanese political support, a policy made possible by US government support of PNC.

951 Bébel-Gisler, Dany. La langue créole force jugulée: étude sociolinguistique des rapports de force entre le créole et le français aux Antilles. Paris, France: Editions l'Harmattan, 1976. 255 p.; bibl.

Guadeloupean author is concerned with structural relationships between French and Creole languages at heart of Antillean society, more specifically place of language within contexts of power, politics, and ideology. One of book's goals is to determine economic, political and cultural importance of linguistic forces at hand and to unveil their concrete strategies, within phenomena of colonialism and assimilation. Beginning with discussion of theoretical and methodological problems, author describes advent of domination of French language and dependency of Creole in Antilles (Guadeloupe and Martinique) in context of sociohistorical situation and educational system as well as through treatment of relationship of both languages in social and political arenas. Concludes that functioning of (arbitrary) symbolic power of French is, in fact, a question of political power.

952 Bell, Wendell and **David L. Stevenson.**
Attitudes toward social equality in independent Jamaica: twelve years after nationhood (CPS, 11:4, Jan. 1979, p. 499–532, bibl., tables)
Restudy of Jamaican leaders, 12 years after political independence, describes changes in their attitudes toward equality. Authors test earlier explanation of causes and consequences of egalitarian attitudes and explore new developments in elite attitudinal patterns. Results are summarized in a path model designed to demonstrate causal linkages between key theoretical variables.

953 —— and **Robert V. Robinson.** European melody, African rhythm, or West Indian harmony?: changing cultural identity among leaders in a new state (SF, 58:1, Sept. 1979, p. 249–279, bibl., tables)
Restudy of Jamaican leaders in 1974, 12 years after political independence, explores changes in their orientations toward cultural identity since 1962, date of first study. Interviews with 83 leaders reveal dramatic changes such as their becoming more favorable to Jamaican and West Indian life styles.

954 Berleant-Schiller, Riva. The failure of agricultural development in post-emancipation Barbuda: a study of social and economic continuity in a West Indian community (CEDLA/B, 25, Dec. 1978, p. 21–36)

Analyzes Barbudian community's success in preserving its system of shifting cultivation and communal land tenure against challenges of outsiders with considerable political power. Author considers reasons for Barbudian cultural continuity, discussing Swidden cultivation and Barbudian ideology of common ownership in light of three attempts at development of commercial cultivation (Codrington period—export crops and livestock in 1860s; Barbuda Island Company—plantation crops in 1890s; and, Crown tenancy—cotton in early 20th century).

955 Besson, Jean. Symbolic aspects of land in the Caribbean: the tenure and transmission of land rights among Caribbean peasantries (*in* Peasants, plantations and rural communities in the Caribbean [see item **1031**] p. 86–116)
After short but elegant review and critique of literature on cognatic descent and descent groups, Caribbean kinship systems, and cognatic descent group in the Caribbean, author offers alternative interpretation on the latter to the one proposed by Solien and Otterbein. She claims that cognatic descent group in the Caribbean is, and always has been "an unrestricted, dispersed, non-residential descent group operating in relation to a specific resource only (family land); and that in this case the 'specific resource' is symbolic rather than economic. The viability of family land as a symbolic resource is enabled by the sacrifice of its viability as an economic resource. Thus the majority of co-heirs who do remain on family land, efficient land use is subordinated to the inalienable claims of the numerous absentee heirs."

956 Bettelheim, Judith. Jamaican Jonkonnu and related Caribbean festivals (*in* Africa and the Caribbean: the legacies of a link [see *HLAS 42:2499*] p. 80–100)
Author discusses artistic geography of Jamaican Jonkonnu and context of its development, and delineates European and African elements in festival. Also considers possible artistic relationship between Jamaica's Christmas festival and others in Bermuda, Nassau, St. Kitts, Nevis, and Belize. For folklorist's comment, see *HLAS 42:1258*.

957 Bolland, O. Nigel. Labour control in post-abolition Belize (JBA, 9, Dec. 1979, p. 21–35, bibl.)

Author argues need to reevaluate meaning of "emancipation" by examining constraints imposed on British Honduran workers after abolition. Provides an outline of colony's economic situation between 1830–70 and discusses systems of labor control and its consequences. Also treats consequences of changes in economic situation since 1850: "To the extent that labourers remained dependent and coerced, emancipation, properly defined as the realm of freedom, was not achieved. The transition was not from slavery to freedom but, rather from one system of labour control to another and the old struggle between former masters and slaves continued, although in new forms."

958 Bonniol, Jean-Luc. Terre-de-Haut des Saintes: contraintes insulaires et particularisme ethnique dans La Caraïbe. Paris, France: Editions Caribbéennes, 1980. 377 p.; bibl.; maps; plates; tables.

Community study of Terre-de-Haut, small island of Les Saintes, occupied primarily by population of "petits blancs." Author's aim is to provide a study which is both historical and anthropological, and in which relationship between local community and larger Caribbean and European context is not lost. He focuses on how ecological constraints led to emergence of distinct ethnic identity and cultural specificity and to an island history quite different from that of more typical Caribbean plantation societies. In essence, an investigation of the nature of a population on an island without sugar, where majority must earn their livelihood through fishing. A contribution to the literature on migration, population movement, and ethnicity.

959 Brana-Shute, Gary. On the corner: male social life in a Paramaribo Creole neighborhood. Assen, The Netherlands: Van Gorcum, 1979. 123 p.; bibl.; ill.

Study of social organization of lower-class Creole neighborhood in Paramaribo, Surinam, based on two-years' field work (1972–74). Author concentrated on group of about 20 adult male Creoles ranging in age from 24 to 62 who congregated at neighborhood pub or *winkel*. Besides discussing male barroom behavior as both a symbolic and leisure-time activity, author uses the males as a point of departure from earlier "family" research in the Caribbean. "The street-corner behavior demonstrated by these men is in large part a response to a system that demands little else from them. Given their circumstances, the mating system, household organization, and the men's status in the occupational hierarchy—all relationships characterized by loose, shifting, and irregular interaction—these men need the compensation that their shop sanctuary provides."

960 Brana-Shute, Rosemary and **Gary Brana-Shute.** Crime and punishment in the Caribbean. Gainesville: University of Florida, Center for Latin American Studies, 1980. 146 p.; figures; index; tables.

Anthology of articles on various aspects of crime and punishment including: Delroy Chuck's "The Role of the Sentencer in Dealing with Criminal Offenders;" Dudley Allen's "Urban Crime and Violence in Jamaica;" Dudley Allen's "Crime and Treatment in Jamaica;" Kenneth Pryce and Daurius Figueira's "Rape and Socio-Economic Conditions in Trinidad and Tobago;" Rafael Santos del Valle's "Reflections on the Problem of Urban Crime and Violence in Puerto Rico;" Max Carre's "A Profile of the State of Criminology in Haiti;" Michael Parris' "Urban Crime and Violence in Guyana;" Michael Parris' "A Survey of the Guyanese Prison Population: a Research Note;" A. Leerschool-Liong A. Jin's "Planned Research into the Criminological Consequences of the Mass Transmigration of the Bush Negroes in Suriname;" and J.M.M. Binda's "Women and Violent Crime in Suriname."

961 —— and ——. Death in the family: ritual therapy in a Creole community (KITLV/B, 135:1, 1979, p. 59–82)

Rich and informative description of rituals carried out by traditional Paramaribo Creoles of lower socioeconomic status after young woman's accidental death. Details ceremonies and attendant ritual paraphernalia, identifies participants, gives specific reasons why certain ceremonials were undertaken, and discusses social and spiritual interactions of principals. Valuable contribution to the literature.

962 Brathwaite, Farley S. Race, social class and the origins of occupational elites in Trinidad and Tobago (CEDLA/B, 28, June 1980, p. 13–29, tables)

Based on results of surveys of five occupational/professional groups (doctors, lawyers, accountants, secondary teachers, and nurses), author argues the following: that both race and class played a decisive role in occupational elite origins; that each factor exerted influence on the process independently of the other; that social class exerted greater influence than race; and that sex and time of birth, when introduced as control variables, each played an important role in the process. Results did not support the position that African socioeconomic opportunities were better than those of the East Indians. Study is placed in the context of theoretical discussion of the nature of Caribbean society.

Brereton, Bridget. Race relations in colonial Trinidad, 1870–1900. See *HLAS 42:2555*.

———. The Trinidad Carnival, 1870–1900. See *HLAS 42:1260*.

Cabrera, Lydia. Reglas de Congo: Palo Monte Mayombé. See item **8178**.

963 Campbell, Horace. Rastafari: culture of resistance (IRR/RC, 22:1, Summer 1980, p. 1–22)

Author contends that academic research on Rastafarianism has been preoccupied with cults, millenarianism, and metaphysics "without prior and accompanying study of production relations . . ." In the latter context, he summarizes the development of Rastafarianism in Jamaica, its international ideological linkages, Garvey and Jamaica, the struggle for political independence, the Rodney intervention, and Rastafari as the people's culture. Notes: "Rastafari culture remains an indelible link between the resistance of the Maroons, the Pan-Africanist appeal of Marcus Garvey, the materialist and historical analysis of Walter Rodney, and the defiance of reggae."

Casal, Lourdes. Race relations in contemporary Cuba. See item **8180**.

964 Cashmore, Ernest. Rastaman: the Rastafarian movement in England. London: George Allen and Unwin, 1979. 263 p.; bibl.

Serious and detailed treatment of Rastafarianism in England, based on two years of field and archival research. Author explores foundations of the movement in Jamaica, paying specific attention to Marcus Garvey; post-war Jamaican migration to England and early patterns of adaptation; the emergence and developmental trajectory of English Rastafarianism; etc. A welcome addition to the growing literature on Rastafarianism and its diaspora.

965 Charles, Claude. Brief comments on the occurrence, etiology and treatment of *indisposition* (Social Science and Medicine [New York] 13B:2, April 1979, p. 135–136)

Haitian social anthropologist based in Miami offers his impressions of this culture-bound syndrome. *Indisposition* is far more prevalent among females and is associated with three types of blood conditions (i.e., the blood is too rich, the blood is "coming up," and the blood is too poor).

966 Chibnik, Michael. Working out or working in: the choice between wage labor and cash cropping in rural Belize (AAA/AE, 7:1, Feb. 1980, p. 86–105, tables)

Utilizing data generated in two predominantly Creole villages in east central Belize, author argues utility of "statistical behavior" approach to investigation of economic decision-making. Such an approach permits statistical analyses of relationship between the observed characteristics of economic actors and the choices they make. Author maintains that statistical analysis of how males in the two villages allocate their time between wage labor and cash cropping generates information that cannot be derived from a "natural decision-making approach" to elicit the rules governing choice.

967 Cole, Johnnetta B. Race toward equality: the impact of the Cuban Revolution on racism (The Black Scholar [Black World Foundations, Sausalito, California] 1980, p. 2–24, bibl.)

Author argues that racism in its institutionalized forms has been eliminated in Cuba. Although a number of specific conditions conducive to the elimination of racism under a socialist form of government existed in pre-Revolutionary Cuba, specific government actions were required to accomplish that objective in post-Revolutionary Cuba.

Author describes the impact of socialism on racism; the proclamations, laws, and other early moves; education; and internationalist involvement or the African-Cuba full circle. Article ends with a discussion of the racial problems that remain unresolved in Cuba. See also item **8180**.

968 Coreil, Jeannine. Traditional and Western responses to an anthrax epidemic in rural Haiti (Medical Anthropology [Redgrave, Pleasantville, New York] 4:1, Winter 1980, p. 79–105, bibl., map)

Analyzes response to a localized but severe anthrax epidemic for its implications regarding pluralistic health care systems. Villagers coped by resorting to multiple treatment modes. The differential responses of modern and traditional health practitioners reveal the practical and conceptual problems of cross-cultural practitioner collaboration.

969 Cross, Malcolm. Colonialism and ethnicity: a theory and comparative case study (ERS, 1:1, Jan. 1978, p. 37–59, tables)

Author sees ethnicity as a complex phenomenon composed of two analytically separable processes, rather than a single invariate identity. Distinguishes between conditions which heighten awareness of ethnic divide (termed by author *ethnic salience*) and those which increase intensity of attachment to group's putative culture (i.e., *ethnic allegiance*). Argues that conditions producing latter phenomenon are endemic to colonial situation. Within this context of interethnic contact, author compares Trinidad and Tobago with Guyana.

970 ———. Urbanization and urban growth in the Caribbean: an essay on social change in dependent societies. Cambridge, England: Cambridge University Press, 1979. 174 p.; bibl.; index; tables.

Argues that, unlike some parts of the world, the Caribbean has been denied power and autonomy of action necessary to control process of urbanization and urban growth. In this context, author examines theories and problems of urbanization and dependence, economic order in the Caribbean, population structure and change, social structure and social organization, race, class, education, and politics. He then considers consequences of these processes and solutions posed by policy makers and planners. Uses data from Commonwealth Caribbean, Puerto Rico, Cuba, and Haiti.

971 Daniel, Yvonne. The potency of dance: a Haitian examination (The Black Scholar [Black World Foundation, Sausalito, California] 11:8, Nov./Dec. 1980, p. 61–73, bibl. plates)

Gives a stylistic movement analysis of Petro, voodoo dance, in order to define the role of dance in Haitian society. Author provides background information on dance in general, dance within Haitian voodoo literature, the origin of Petro within voodoo mythology, and voodoo dance in Haitian social structure. She concludes that dance becomes a potent symbol which makes some sense of the Haitian experience to those affected by the inconsistencies in that economically poor nation.

972 De Bruijne, G.A. The Lebanese in Suriname (CEDLA/B, 26, June 1979, p. 15–37, tables)

Ground-breaking study of smallest, but economically important "trade minorities" of Surinam. Author deals with Lebanese in Surinam from turn of 20th-century (origins in Lebanon, process of migration, early period of settlement; development into a dominant textile-trade group; reasons for their success in textiles; early group cohesion and economic success; economic development after World War II; position and status in contemporary urban Paramaribo; and recent diversification in choice of occupations). Welcome addition to very scant literature on Lebanese diaspora to the New World.

973 Debien, Gabriel. Les esclaves des plantations Mauger à Saint-Domingue: 1763–1802 (SHG/B, 43/44:1/2, 1980, p. 31–164, tables)

Beginning with brief portrait of two planters in Artibonite region of Saint-Domingue, author offers a history of a sugar and an indigo/cotton plantation (1763–1802). Relies on existing rich source of plantation papers but acknowledges unreliability of some of these sources such as reports written by plantation managers to absentee proprietors.

974 Deive, Carlos Esteban. Notas sobre la cultura dominicana (MHD/B, 8:12, enero 1979, p. 293–305, bibl.)

Short listing of elements of Taino culture which survived and were incorporated into Dominican culture. Also gives more detailed enumeration of cultural contributions of republic's black and mulatto populations (those coming directly from Africa; fugitive slaves from French Hispaniola; those from Lesser Antilles; black workers from English-speaking Caribbean; ex-slaves from North America; and numerous manual workers imported from Haiti). Author discusses relevance of Caribbean cultural concepts to Dominican reality.

975   Dew, Edward. The difficult flowering of Surinam: ethnicity and politics in a plural society. The Hague, The Netherlands: Martinus Nijhoff, 1978. 234 p.; bibl.; index; tables.

Political history details development and course of ethnic politics in Surinam from 1942 to the final struggle for independence in 1975. Author contends "that ethnic politics in a democratic plural society need not degenerate into dictatorship or anarchy." While this optimistic note does not ring true in light of recent events in Surinam, author's meticulous recording of key political events in that largely ignored territory over a period of three and a half decades—particularly in the elections of 1949, 1951, 1955, 1958, 1963, 1967, 1969, and 1973—is a welcome and valuable addition to the Caribbean literature. For political scientist's comment, see item **6337.**

976   Dirks, Robert. The evolution of a playful ritual: the Garifuna's John Canoe in comparative perspective (*in* Forms of play of native North Americans. Edited by Edward Norbeck and Claire R. Farner. St. Paul, Minnesota: West Publishing Co., 1979, p. 89–109, bibl.)

Comparison of John Canoe as practiced by Black Caribe Belize with John Canoe in West Indies, and English sword dance and mumming in Northern Ireland and Newfoundland. Study's objectives are to examine derivation and significance of this "playful ritual," motivating factors and reasons why its threats are delivered playfully rather than in earnest.

977   Dodd, David J. The role of law in plantation society: reflections on the development of a Caribbean legal system (International Journal of the Sociology of Law [London] 7, 1979, p. 275–296, bibl.)

Essay traces continuities in role of law in Guyana from time of slave plantations to present. Author argues that kadi-justice was developed early for purposes of social control within the plantation. Purpose of plantation system was to mobilize large groups of laborers for routine tasks to be performed collectively in the cultivation of a single crop. No dramatic shift in the role of law accompanied emancipation of slaves and introduction of indenture system. In contemporary Guyana, a cooperative socialist polity, the law remains an instrument of state power that manipulates government's managers (judges, lawyers, etc.) into decisions and actions consistent with the government's position. As a result, legal and judicial systems are weak and ineffectual in guarding citizens from governmental excess.

978   Dressler, William W. Ethnomedical beliefs and patient adherence to a treatment regimen: a St. Lucian example (SAA/HO, 39:1, Spring 1980, p. 88–91)

Brief communication reports research on 40 hypertensive St. Lucians. Study was designed to test hypothesis that, within mixed medical setting, the greater an individual's commitment to an ethnomedical belief system, the less likely it is that the individual will adhere to treatment regimen prescribed within Western medical setting. Partial support for hypothesis was found in that the higher an individual's acceptance of personalistic beliefs (i.e., illness explained as the active aggression of some human, non-human, or supernatural agent), the lower their compliance.

979   Elkins, W.F. The black princes of Jamaica (UPR/CS, 15:1, April 1975, p. 117–122)

Describes actions of two Jamaicans who spuriously claimed royal identities (Royal Prince Thomas Isaac Makarooroo of Ceylon and Shervington Mitcheline, Crown Prince and Heir Apparant of the Abyssinian Empire) during early decades of this century: "The Black Princes of Jamaica, like countless other persons of African descent, thought of Ethiopia as a nation of freedom and dignity. Biblical references to the ancient empire bolstered this image. Shervington seems to have utilized this popular conception mainly for self-advancement. But Makarooroo had broad social concerns. Through his efforts to revitalize black culture in Jamaica, he helped stimulate the growth of national consciousness, a prerequisite for independence."

980   Étude ethno-socio-psychologique et linguistique du milieu haitien, en vue d'une reforme de l'Université d'Etat preparée sous la direction du Professeur J.B. Romain. San Juan, Puerto Rico: Association of Caribbean and Research Institutes (UNICA) [and] Organization of American States, Washington, D.C., 1979. 130 p.; bibl.; tables (Series on university structure and organization)

Quantitative study of university structural reform divided into sections: 1) a study of Haitian cultural milieu deals with the people's material, social, and spiritual life; and 2) study of nation's State University, prepared by university and nonuniversity personnel, discusses hypotheses, methodology of questions such as role and mission of the university. Study uses four approaches (sociological, psychological/psycho-pedagogical, ethnological/cultural, and linguistic) represented by four questionnaires, included in the volume, and whose results are tabulated and analyzed.

981   Everyday life in Barbados: a sociological perspective. Edited by Graham M.S. Dann. Leiden, The Netherlands: Royal Institute of Linguistics and Anthropology, Department of Caribbean Studies, 1979. 190 p.

Contains seven substantive essays on contemporary Barbados, and an introductory, theoretical/methodological article by editor on understanding everyday Barbadian life. Essays are arranged by age of subjects studied, from childhood to old age: Ernestine Jackman's "Barbadian Village Games of Yesterday;" Annette Woodroffe's "The Bajan Sunday School;" Barbara Corbin's "Picnics in Barbados;" Winston Crichlow's "The Nutseller;" Janet Stoute and Kenneth Ifill's "The Rural Rum Shop: A Comparative Case Study;" and Glennis Nurse's "The Elderly." Provides interesting material for both Barbadian specialist and comparative studies.

982   Fouché, Franck. Voudou et théâtre. Montréal, Canada: Les Editions Nouvelles Optique, 1976. 123 p.; bibl.

Author attempts to study vodun phenomenon in its dual aspect: as pre-theatre and theatre. If vodun is indeed pre-theatre with myth, ritual, and symbolism, Haitian author believes it, too, can be considered theatre, or what he refers to as théâtre-histoire, a kind of living theatre of Haitian history. As such, he attributes to vodun another role—revolutionary theatre—in which art and poli-

tics are merged into a popular form of expression which will serve the Haitian people towards a definition of their cultural identity and in their struggle against neocolonialism.

983   Gaspar, David Barry. Runaways in seventeenth-century Antigua, West Indies (CEDLA/B, 26, June 1979, p. 3–13)

Examination of marronage on small and relatively flat sugar island of Antigua before 1700. Before and after passage of a comprehensive act in 1680 concerning runaway slaves, many temporarily abandoned their plantations in "a form of slave resistance which has been called petit marronage." Author deals primarily with those involved in grand marronage, slaves who absconded with no intention of returning. Despite scanty data, author offers interesting example of slave resistance under very unfavorable geographical and ecological conditions.

Gilfond, Henry. Voodoo, its origins and practices. See HLAS 42:1272.

984   Glazier, Stephen D. Bibliografía del medium espiritista y la posesión: pt. 2 (MHD/B, 7:9, enero 1978, p. 137–159)

Part 2 (M–Z) of an unannotated bibliography on the spiritualist medium and possession. While it contains a number of Caribbean-related references to the Caribbean, it's main focus is topical rather than geographical.

985   González, Nancie L. Sex preference in human figure drawings by Garifuna—Black Carib—children (UP/E, 18:4, 1979, p. 355–364, bibl., tables)

To test possible effects of father-absence among Garifuna children in Livingston, Guatemala, author analyzes figure drawings by 146 boys and 172 girls. Girls drew figures of their own sex significantly more than did boys. Analysis of percentages of self-sex drawings by age and sex reveal interesting and possibly significant complexities. While it is difficult to explain findings in their entirety, author concludes that certain aspects of drawings are consistent with existing descriptions and interpretations of Garifuna social organization.

986   Gordon, Derek. Working-class radicalism in Jamaica: an exploration of the privileged worker thesis (UWI/SES, 27:3, Sept. 1978, p. 313–341, bibl., figures, tables)

Based on a sample of 346 industrial workers in factories located in Kingston Metropolitan Area, author examines privileged-worker hypothesis, which attributes working-class conservatism or reformism to special conditions enjoyed by a section of industrial workers. Concludes that there are serious flaws in argument presented by privileged worker theorists: e.g., sample gave little evidence of expected negative effect of "special conditions" on working-class consciousness; and with few exceptions, factors associated with large-scale machine industry increased receptivity of workers to radical and socialist ideas.

987 Gregory, James R. On being Indian in southern Belize: a research note (BISRA/BS, 8:4, July 1980, p. 1–9)

Brief report on emerging sense of pride in Indian identity among the Mopan Indians of southern Belize. Unlike Indians in predominantly Hispanic societies, a growing sense of being Indian is accompanying the modernization process among indigenous people of this non-Hispanic region.

988 Gussler, Judith D. Adaptive strategies and social networks of women in St. Kitts (*in* A World of women: anthropological studies of women in the societies of the world. Edited by Erika Bourguignon. New York: Praeger, 1980, p. 185–209)

Among strategies developed by lower-class females in St. Kitts for survival in harsh economic environment of that society is the effective use of networks. Author briefly describes different forms these networks take over the life cycle, and examines their implications for social and geographic mobility of Kittitian females.

989 Gutwirth, Jacques. Le suicide-massacre de Guyana et son contexte (CNRS/ASR, 24[47]:2, avril/juin 1979, p. 167–188)

Based primarily on two works by American journalists (Charles Krause's *Guyana massacre*, and Marshal Kilduff's and Ron Javers' *The suicide cult*), author analyzes context and sources of Jonestown tragedy. Although viewing it as an exceptional aberration, he attributes its apocalyptic and utopian elements to US religious history. Perceives the People's Temple to be part of American Christian mosaic rather than an exotic cult, a fact which accounts for the lack of attention given it until 1977–78. Hypothesizes that Jones and his People's Temple promulgated such contradictory notions—communalism and arbitrary totalitarianism; financial exploitation and socialist claims; theology of liberation and a revival of traditional styles—that the explosive mixture eventually was set off by Jones' paranoia and particular conditions of Guyanese isolation.

990 Guyanese sugar plantations in the late nineteenth century: a contemporary description from the 'Argosy.' Edited by Walter Rodney. Georgetown, Guyana: Release Publishers, 1979, 97 p.; plates.

Edited and introduced by the late Walter Rodney, this small book reproduces series of articles entitled "Our Sugar Estates," which appeared in the *Argosy*, "a planter newspaper," in British Guiana from Feb./Sept. 1883. The unnamed journalist responsible for series provides descriptions and accounts of sugar estates starting with those on Essequibo coast and islands, and continuing eastward to those in Demerara and on Corentyne coast of Berbice. Invaluable source for social scientists interested in plantation systems, sugar estates, or socioeconomic history of Guyana.

991 Halberstein, Robert A. and **John E. Davies.** Changing patterns of health and health care on a small Bahamian island (Social Science and Medicine [New York] 13B:2, April 1979, p. 153–167, bibl., figures, tables)

Careful reconstruction of changing profile of health and disease on Bimini in the Bahamas. Utilizing wide variety of data, author assesses relative importance of numerous biocultural elements in evolution of health care on this island. Three major health problems, hypertension, hemoglobinopathies, and excessive infant mortality, are influenced by a wide assortment of biosocial factors. Improved water supply has contributed to the epidemiologic transition of the population, as has the introduction of standard, primary health care in 1970. "Traditional" and "new" medical systems have effectively interacted: "Data reveal a complex and dynamic picture of health and disease affected by multiple biocultural and ecological forces."

992 Hall, John R. Apocalypse at Jonestown (SO, 16:6, Sept./Oct. 1979, p. 52–61, bibl.)

Author affirms that "Mass suicide united the divergent public threads of meaningful existence at Jonestown—those of political revolution and religious salvation. It was an awesome vehicle for a powerful statement of collective solidarity by the true believers among the people of Jonestown—that they would rather die together than have the life that was created together subjected to gradual decimation and dishonor at the hands of authorities regarded as illegitimate."

993 Hall, Stuart. Pluralism, race and class in Caribbean society (in Race and class in post-colonial society: a study of ethnic group relations in the English-speaking Caribbean, Bolivia, Chile and Mexico. Paris: UNESCO, 1977, p. 150–182)

Concentrating on non-Hispanic Caribbean and in context of critical examination of M.G. Smith's plural society concept, author uses a "typological" approach in order to explore role of "race" and "color" in structuring group relations across Caribbean society. After discussion of variations and typological shifts, recommends analysis which would pay close attention to ethnic, cultural and ideological factors at play in contemporary Caribbean societies in their "national-bourgeois" stage. Such a study should not abandon class analysis of these societies in favor of what author calls a less powerful "plural" or a more loosely defined "ethnic" analysis.

994 Harrison, David. The changing fortunes of a Trinidad peasantry: a case study (in Peasants, plantations and rural communities in the Caribbean [see item 1031] p. 54–85, tables)

Study of community of agriculturalists near Toco, northeast Trinidad, in 1860–1972. Couched in Caribbean social sciences terms of "peasantry" issue, study indicates that community of "Demsay" has continually been dependent on wider administrative unit of Trinidad and Tobago and, until formal independence in 1962, on the United Kingdom, despite initial attempts in late 19th century to develop peasant mode of agriculture.

995 Helms, Mary W. Succession to high office in pre-Columbian circum-Caribbean chiefdoms (RAI/M, 15:4, Dec. 1980, p. 718–731, bibl., figures)

Describes rules for succession to high offices and their implications in chiefdoms of Panama, parts of northern Colombia, and the Greater Antilles, as noted by European observers in early 16th century. Many of these rules appear to have been "determinate" (i.e., successor to the incumbent was automatically predetermined). These patterns do not appear to have conflicted with other political and symbolic aspects of the societies.

996 Henney, Jeannette H. Sex and status: women in St. Vincent (in A World of women: anthropological studies of women in the societies of the world. Edited by Erika Bourguignon. New York: Praeger, 1980, p. 161–183)

Describes activities of Spiritual Baptist congregation during typical service: differential behavior of male and female worshippers in dissociational states; differential gratification that accrues to men and women through participation in dissociation; similarities between behavior of individuals in an altered state and that of individuals involved in sexual intercourse; and differential opportunities and status available to lower-class males and females in larger Vincentian society. Author argues that since lower-class Vincentian women have better opportunities than men to gain financial stability through petty trading, it is the men rather than the women who have greater compensation and status in the Spiritual Baptist cults.

997 Henriques, Fernando and Joseph Manyoni. Ethnic group relations in Barbados and Grenada (in Race and class in post-colonial society: a study of ethnic group relations in the English-speaking Caribbean, Bolivia, Chile and Mexico. Paris: UNESCO, 1977, p. 55–110)

While Barbados and Grenada share a common heritage of slavery, and have similar patterns of inter-ethnic relationships, their differences apparently are due to political and economic history, differences of scale in each society, demographics, physical features and different economies. Nevertheless, authors believe "the fundamental factor which provides unity in any assessment of this area of relationships in the Caribbean is the persistence of the 'white bias.'" By 'white bias,' authors mean conscious and unconscious desire on the part of a majority of Caribbean people of African descent to approximate the European as closely as possible.

Higman, Barry W. African and Creole slave family patterns in Trinidad. See item **8202**.

998   Hoetink, Harry. The cultural links (*in* Africa and the Carribbean: the legacies of a link [see *HLAS 42:2499*] p. 20–40)

Delineation of three types of cultural influence and innovation involved in formation of Afro-American societies: "1) The influences from African anthrocultures, blended and molded in the New World, and traditionally labeled 'Africanisms,' varying from very change-resistant perceptions and behavior of an ego- and body-oriented nature, to vehicles for social and supernatural communication such as language and religion stressing their variety and their diffusion over many functional strata and population groups; 2) Those cultural and social forms of acting and perception, created primarily in the New World as a product of given functional strata and called sociocultures and whose links with Africa or Europe were ephemeral or at least very indirect, and the span of their variety possibly being determined by certain 'grammars' common to the cultures of origin . . . ; 3) Those forms of thought and behavior, created in the New World and most prominent in the United States of America owing to its predominantly creole Afro-American population, and the slaves came to occupy as an 'ethnic group' within the society at large."

999   Holzberg, Carol S. Strategies and problems among economic elites in Jamaica: the evolution of a research focus (CRCA/A, 22:1, 1980, p. 5–23, bibl.)

Discussion of the development of an appropriate research focus for studying economic elites in Jamaica. Author comments on personal problems and conflicts of female researcher conducting field study of an economically superordinate segment of a basically poor population. Pays particular attention to problems of entry into the field and issues of holism, chronic culture shock, and presentation of self; and isolates situational ambiguities and conflicts as specific methodological problems of elite research.

1000   *International Migration Review*. Center for Migration Studies. No. 13, Summer 1979– . New York.

Special issue, edited by Elsa M. Chaney and Constance L. Sutton, consists of eight articles written primarily by anthropologists and sociologists and dealing with various aspects of Caribbean migration to New York City.

1001   Isaac, Acelius E. The influence of voodoo on the lives of the Haitian people (IJ/JJ, 9:4, 1975, p. 2–4, 6–7, 9–11)

Author dispels popular misconceptions about voodoo created by foreign writers and journalists and attacks attitude of some Haitians who try to deny or cover up the existence of voodoo in Haiti. Like African religions, voodoo is "a way of life for the Haitian people. It is anchored in their culture, in their beliefs, and in their philosophy of life." Author does not confine himself to what has already been written about voodoo but to what he understands it to be all about. Touches upon relationship of voodoo with: African religion, Haitian history, politics, Catholicism, Protestantism, and finally, family life, commerce, and agriculture; concluding that "no one is able to write a full and worthwhile account on Haitian voodoo without an understanding of the Haitian people themselves."

1002   Jayawardena, Chandra. Culture and ethnicity in Guyana and Fiji (RAI/M, 15:3, Sept. 1980, p. 430–50, bibl., table)

Exploration of factors leading to contrasting developments of Indian culture in Guyana and Fiji despite fact that East Indians came to both colonies from same areas of India under same indenture system, and both remained predominantly rural in polyethnic societies. Author identifies three main factors in the development of ethnicity: class, social status, and power. "Political processes arising from these fields of action transform ethnic identity into that self-conscious phenomenon one may term 'ethnicity.' However, it is a process that occurred in Guyana but hardly in Fiji because of historically determined and crucial differences in these fields. Thus, despite other similarities, divergent patterns were created out of what was once the same culture derived from India."

1003   Johnson, Howard and **Edwin Jones.** The political uses of Commissions of Enquiry: pt. 1, The imperial-colonial West Indies, context, the Forster and Moyne Commissions; pt. 2, The post-colonial Jamaican context (UWI/SES, 27:3, Sept. 1978, p. 256–283, bibl.)

Two-part article analyzes reasons that led to establishment of important Commissions of Enquiry in British West Indies prior to World War II (Forster Commission of 1937 investigated oilfield disturbances in Trinidad; Moyne Commission of 1938, social and economic conditions in British West Indian colonies). Author argues that they were designed to facilitate introduction of defensive reforms and used by Colonial Office as mechanism for introducing change along desired lines "without appearing to impose Colonial Office solutions." Pt. 2 examines more recent ones: Mordecai Sugar Commission (1966), Maffessanti Enquiry (1968), DaCosta Commission (1973), and Mills Local Government Enquiry (1974).

1004 Kahn, Morton Charles. Djuka, the bush Negroes of Dutch Guiana. With an introduction by Blair Niles; and a foreword by Clark Wissler. New York: AMS Press, 1979. 233 p.; 44 leaves of plates; bibl.; ill.; index.

Welcome reprint of Kahn's 1931 study of the Djuka. This almost classic work touches on aspects of group's history; ecology; settlement pattern; dance; economy; social organization, marriage and the family; medicine and magic; language; West African survivals; and art.

1005 Knight, Franklin W. and Margaret E. Crahan. The African migration and the origins of an Afro-American society and culture (*in* Africa and the Caribbean: the legacies of a link [see *HLAS 42:2499,* p. 1–19)

Introductory chapter by editors of interdisciplinary collection of linkages between Africa and Caribbean. Authors touch on problems related to transatlantic slave trade (including impact of this forced movement on Africa itself); process of Afro-Americanization; estimation of indigenous Amerindian populations in Antilles at time of conquest; analysis of forms of cultural transmission; designation and identification of African ethnic groups; nature of slave importation over time; demographic profiles of Caribbean colonies; etc.

1006 Koss, Joan D. The therapist-spiritist training project in Puerto Rico: an experiment to relate the traditional healing system to the public health system (Social Science and Medicine [New York] 14B:4, Nov. 1980, p. 255–266, bibl.)

Description of project designed to bring together Spiritist healers with mental health workers and other medical and health professionals in Puerto Rico by providing opportunity for continuous contact. Training curriculum makes available new skills to members of both Spiritist and community mental-health systems. One goal of project is beginning to be realized: practitioners of each system have started referring patients to each other.

1007 Kuper, Adam. Race, class and culture in Jamaica (*in* Race and class in postcolonial society: a study of ethnic group relations in the English-speaking Caribbean, Bolivia, Chile and Mexico. Paris: UNESCO, 1977, p. 111–149)

After critical examination of theories related to the nature of Jamaican society and question of race, author concludes by stating that color is no longer relevant to legal status of Jamaicans and that color is of very limited importance to employment prospects—but that it continues to be a factor in politics, in self-image, and in assessment of social status. "In all these areas however, colour—in the complex Jamaican sense—intermingles, as it has always done, with notions of style and culture and personal attitude . . . Therefore, although race or colour is certainly an issue in Jamaica, and a very complex one, it is true to say—as the smug like to say in Jamaica—that there are very few societies in the world in which it is of such limited relevance to social mobility, to self-image, to the perception of others."

1008 Lafleur, Gérard. L'origine des Protestants de Guadeloupe au XVIIᵉ siécle (SHG/B, 37:3, 1978, p. 49–57)

Article represents part of the growing literature on Protestantism in the Antilles. Author believes that knowledge of the origin of this minority of the island of Guadeloupe will help elucidate the reactions of this group to their emigration. Touches upon the areas of their origin in the Metropole, their relationship with the economic and politcal interests of France and her Antillean colonies, and their place of settlement on Guadeloupe in the 17th century. He questions whether the coherence of the Protestant group resulted from their common religion or their common regional origin.

1009 ———. Le pouvoir et les Protestants de la Guadeloupe aux XVIIᵉ et XVIIIᵉ siécles (SHG/B, 39:1, 1979, p. 27–39)

Author briefly treats Protestantism in France prior to 17th century, and then discusses settlement of Protestants (Huguenots) in Antilles, with emphasis on island of Guadeloupe. Following chronological treatment (using letters, code, and laws of period), shows how relations between Protestants and authorities, in Guadeloupe as well as in France, fluctuated during two centuries in response to situation in and orders issuing from France. Concludes that strong Protestant minority became established in Guadeloupe by playing the game of being faithful to power and by participating actively and sincerely in public life without submitting totally to royal demands.

1010 Laguerre, Michel S. Bizango: a voodoo secret society in Haiti (*in* Secrecy: a cross-cultural perspective. Edited by Stanton K. Tefft. New York: Human Sciences Press, 1980, p. 147–160, bibl.)

Description and analysis of Bizango, a secret society operating in western and southern regions of Haiti. Describes recruitment, ritual of initiation, monthly rallies, symbols, secret signs, etc. Author argues that Bizango society had its roots in Haitian Maroon communities, and is not an entirely post-independence phenomenon. Article emphasizes how cells of Maroon communities continued to exist after independence in 1804 through formation of secret societies. Author views these societies as institutional mechanisms by which "maroons" of contemporary Haiti protect their personal and communal interests.

1011 ———. Ticouloute and his kinfolk: the study of a Haitian extended family (*in* Extended family in black societies. By Demitri B. Shimkin et al. The Hague: Mouton Publishers, 1978, p. 407–445, figures, tables)

After a useful review of Haitian kinship studies, author describes and analyzes structure and functioning of a Haitian extended family, using a sample of 10 households, all linked by kinship but physically separated in four different environments—

fully rural, village, urban in Haiti, and urban in Brooklyn, US.

1012 ———. Voodoo heritage. Beverly Hills, California: Sage Publications, 1980. 231 p.; bibl.; figures; plates.

Detailed study of relationships between voodoo and island's ecology through sociological analysis of songs and prayers of a vodun congregation in Belair, a slum in the northeastern part of Port-au-Prince. Introductory chapter deals with the origin, content, functions, characteristics, classification, and transmission of voodoo songs. Two long substantive chapters deal with songs directly related to living spirits in Haitian environment (Legba, Aizan, Marasa, etc.), and with ecology of human-spirit strategic interactions (preparation songs; salutation songs; orientation songs, greeting songs, litany of saints, voodoo spirits, and ancestors; possession/trance; and relaxation and recessional songs). Interesting and useful materials and analyses.

1013 Layne, Anthony. Race, class, and development in Barbados (UWI/CQ, 25:1/2, March/June 1979, p. 40–51, tables)

Analyzes distribution of occupational opportunities among Negroes, whites, and coloreds in Barbados: "During the DLP regime, Barbadians witnessed a period of educational expansion and absolute occupational gains for Negroes. They also saw the white population strengthen its grip on the key positions in the occupational structure . . . While the Barbadian racial-class structure has undergone some modification over the years, the historical roots of this brake on development have not been tackled in any fundamental way."

1014 Layng, Anthony. Stereotypes and ethnic relationships in the Caribbean (UPR/CS, 15:1, April 1975, p. 130–134, bibl.)

Citing importance but lack of cross-cultural functional analysis of etiology of ethnic images in Caribbean, author offers model of analysis based on ethnocentrism work by Robert LeVine and Donald Campbell. Argues this model provides orderly beginning for study of Caribbean ethnic stereotypes.

1015 Lewis, Gordon K. "Gather with the saints at the river:" the Jonestown Guyana holocaust of 1978; a descriptive and interpretative essay on its ultimate meaning from a Caribbean viewpoint. Río Piedras: Institute of Caribbean Studies, University of Puerto Rico, 1979. 50 p.

Informed, provocative, and sweeping examination of Jonestown holocaust and its relevance for understanding messianic cultism in the region; American religious incursions; nature of US relations with Caribbean territories; contemporary American society; and direction of Caribbean socialism. Particularly useful for Caribbean specialists. For historian's comment, see *HLAS 42:2609.*

1016 Locher, Uli. Rural-urban migration and the alleged demise of the extended family: the Haitian case in comparative perspective. Montreal: Centre for Developing Area Studies, McGill University, 1977. 14 leaves (Working papers—Center for Developing Area Studies, McGill University; no. 20 0384-59X)

On basis of data collected in 1973 in three types of Port-au-Prince settlements (squatter, inner city slum, and middle-class) author details dynamics of rural-urban migration and places it into wider context of Haitian migration and emigration. Data from inner city slum (336 respondents) is used to delineate social participation and maintenance of rural ties.

1017 Lowenthal, David and **Colin G. Clarke.** Common lands, common aims: the distinctive Barbudan community (*in* Peasants, plantations and rural communities in the Caribbean [see item **1031**] p. 142–159)

Focusing on post-emancipation Barbuda, authors explain "how the descendants of (Barbudan) slaves kept their communal ties and more or less successfully coped with the vicissitudes of a meagre environment and a succession of misinformed if not hostile proprietors, managers and colonial administrators." Authors stress geographical constraints, historical stability, common ownership of land, shifting cultivation, open-range livestock, emigration, and communal solidarity as factors leading to unique pattern of Barbuda's social and economic life.

1018 ——— and ———. Island orphans: Barbuda and the rest (ICS/JCCP, 18, 1980, p. 298–307, bibl.)

Illuminating article explains Barbudan fear of domination by Antigua, after latter achieves political independence, and offers full discussion of complex problems of insularity and autonomy.

1019 Lundahl, Mats. Peasants and poverty: a study of Haiti. New York: St. Martin's Press, 1979. 699 p.; bibl.; figures; index; tables.

Book provides well-documented analysis of peasant economy of Haiti (early 1950s–early 1970s), and is of particular value to anthropologists interested in the "peasant" sectors of Caribbean society.

1020 Macdonald, Annette C. The big drum dance of Carriacou (RRI, 8:4, Winter 1978/1979, p. 570–576, bibl., plate)

Short but thorough description of origin, context, musical style, dancing, and functions of the Big Drum Dance, "probably the most extensive dance complex retained from early slave times . . ."

1021 Manley, Robert H. Guyana emergent: the post-independence struggle for nondependent development. Boston: G.K. Hall & Co. [and] Shenkman Publishing Co., Cambridge, Massachusetts, 1979. 158 p.; index.

Study of the strategies pursued by Guyanese political leadership during country's first post-independence decade, and of Guyanese role in Caribbean integration, decolonization, and ideological reorientation in general. Author argues that Guyanese accomplishments during first 10 years of national life were considerable but that potential for ethnic conflict remains a major unresolved problem, one which probably cannot be solved by Burnham and Jagan, nor by their parties, PNC and PPP.

1021a Manning, Frank E. Tourism and Bermuda's black clubs: a case of cultural revitalization (*in* Tourism—passport to development?: perspectives on the social and cultural effects of tourism in developing countries. Edited by Emanuel de Kadt. Oxford, England: Oxford University Press for the World Bank and UNESCO, 1979, p. 157–178)

Bermuda, unlike many other areas, has benefitted socioculturally and materially from tourism. It is argued that Bermuda, in this regard, has three distinctive features: 1) a cultural revitalization was achieved through the fusion of Black racial and cultural consciousness with glamor, opulence and stylistic sophistication (best exemplified in the Black clubs of the island); 2) a system of planning and control that has developed tourism without substantially altering the natural or social environment and that has allowed the material benefits of the industry to be widely distributed among the island's population; and 3) a tourist-native relationship that has become a positive symbol of cultural identity and national pride.

1022 Manyoni, Joseph R. Extra-marital mating patterns in Caribbean family studies: a methodological excursus (CRCA/A, 22:1, 1980, p. 85–118, bibl., tables)

Author argues that contemporary West Indian sexual attitudes, behavior, and mating patterns, family structures, and value systems originated in plantation system of 17th to 19th centuries and disputes "African derivation thesis." Maintains that most studies of Caribbean mating and family have relied on either traditional "survey/interview" or "selected case-study" methods. Few have systematically utilized region's extensive archival data (e.g., the official Registers of Marriages and Births) or examined sexual behavior, mating, and marriage in context of value system shared by entire society. Utilizing data drawn largely from Barbados, author examines mating patterns in historical perspective and presents short case studies for Barbados, Antigua, Montserrat, Demarara, Trinidad, and St. Vincent.

1023 Marks, Arnaud F. Intergroup relationships in the Caribbean: a field of long-range sociological research (CEDLA/B, 26, June 1979, p. 39–66, bibl.)

Author argues that study of intergroup relationships in Caribbean area is particularly rewarding for sociology and social policy. Such relationships are embedded in small but complex societies with specific colonial plantation histories characterized by slavery and indenture (i.e., foundations for extreme economic, political and cultural dependence). Author proposes theoretical approach influenced by criticism of M.G. Smith's pioneering work on plural society. Presents outline of sociological theory of groups, inequality, and conflict, followed by sets of empirical questions and testable hypotheses.

1024 Marshall, Dawn I. "The Haitian problem:" illegal migration to the Bahamas. Mona, Jamaica: University of the West Indies, Institute of Social and Economic Research, 1979. 239 p.; bibl.; maps; tables.

Based primarily on survey data collected in New Providence, Bahamas (1969–71), this comprehensive monograph deals with problems of Haitian illegal entry into the Bahamas. Describes both areas of origin and destination, with specific emphasis on factors that contribute to migration. A case study of Haitians in the Carmichael area of New Providence provides useful comparisons with lower-income Bahamians.

1025 Massajoli, Pierleone and Mario Mattioni. Elementi amerindiani nella cultura creola della Martinica (IGM/U, 59:3, maggio/giugno 1979, p. 561–588, bibl., plates)

Authors deal with several aspects (house types, food stuffs, fishing, pottery, basket-making, medicinal plants) of Amerindian culture in the formation and evolution of the Creole culture of Martinique.

1026 Mathews, Thomas G. African presence in 17th-century Puerto Rican religious ceremonies (in Cultural traditions and Caribbean identity: the question of patrimony. Edited by S. Jeffrey K. Wilkerson. Gainesville: Center for Latin American Studies, University of Florida, 1980, p. 157–176)

Utilizing materials dealing with celebration of Corpus Christi religious holiday, author notes prominent participation of Africans and descendants in social and religious life of San Juan.

1027 Midgett, Douglas. Revisions in West Indian family studies: a critique of Rubenstein's contribution (UWI/SES, 27:4, Dec. 1978, p. 507–513, bibl., tables)

Author criticizes Rubenstein's contention that conventional interpretation of West Indian lower-class conjugal patterns is false (i.e., West Indians tend to mate extra-residentially when young, then settle into co-residential consensual unions, and delay legal marriage into middle age). Rubenstein, on basis of data from St. Vincent and from Vincentian migrants, argues that early marriage occurs frequently and that many marry before the age of 40. Midgett claims that the Rubenstein argument is incorrect on three counts: 1) major contention is not unambiguously demonstrated; 2) there is critical error of omission in data selection; and

3) Vincentian population analyzed is so anomalous as to make any general statements from the study suspect.

1028 Olwig, Karen Fog. National parks, tourism, and local development: a West Indian case (SAA/HO, 39:1, Spring 1980, p. 22–31, bibl.)

Study of development of Virgin Islands National Park on island of St. John and the impact of this park on the local population. ". . . the most important role of the anthropologists in park planning and tourism would seem to be that of pointing out the inherent conflicts in projects which propose to preserve local resources in order to further tourism. Indigenous peoples, under present circumstances, are not likely to receive the greatest benefit of such developments."

Ortiz Fernández, Fernando. Historia de una pelea cubana contra los demonios. See *HLAS 42:2520.*

1029 Otterbein, Keith F. Transportation and settlement pattern: a longitudinal study of South Andros (Anthropology [State University of New York, Department of Anthropology, Stony Brook] 2:2, Dec. 1978, p. 35–45, bibl., figures)

Study of changes in settlement pattern and orientation of houses on largest island of Bahamas brought about by changes in local transportation. "As the mode of transportation changed from small boats, to footpaths, to a road, the houses came to be built near and facing the major means of travel."

1030 Pearse, Andrew. Music in Caribbean popular culture (RRI, 8:4, Winter 1978/1979, p. 629–639)

Schematically explores popular culture, or cultural manifestations of non-elite strata in class societies of Trinidad, Tobago, Grenada, and Carriacou (from emancipation of slaves until 1950s, when commercial, mechanically reproduced music began to exert overwhelming influence). Author notes association of music with particular social institutions is important for understanding process of musical change under conditions of cultural pluralism. Lists 31 kinds of music and institutions associated with each kind, starting with "Congo" and ending with "Steel Band."

1031 Peasants, plantations and rural communities in the Caribbean. Edited by Malcolm Cross and Arnaud Marks. Guilford, England: University of Surrey, Department of Sociology [and] Royal Institute of Linguistics and Anthropology, Department of Caribbean Studies, Leiden, 1979. 304 p.

Eight of 10 papers were written for 3rd Caribbean Colloquium, organized by Universities of Surrey and Sussex in cooperation with Royal Institute of Linguistics and Anthropology, held in Leiden, Dec. 1977: Gad. J. Heuman's "The Struggle for the Settler Vote: Politics and Franchise in Post-Emancipation Jamaica;" David Nicholls' "Rural Protest and Peasant Revolt in Haiti: 1804–1869;" David Harrison's "The Changing Fortunes of a Trinidad Peasantry" (see item 994); Jean Besson's "Symbolic Aspects of Land in the Caribbean: the Tenure and Transmission of Land Rights among Caribbean Peasantries" (see item 955); Wout van den Bor's "Peasantry in Isolation: the Agrarian Development of St. Eustatius and Saba;" David Lowenthal's and Colin Clarke's "Common Lands, Common Aims: the Distinctive Barbudan Community" (see item 1017); Eric Hanley's "Mechanized Rice Cultivation: the Experience of an East Indian Community in Guyana;" Henk Luning and Prakash Sital's "The Economic Transformation of Small Holder Rice Farming in Surinam;" Michael Allen's "Sugar and Survival: the Retention of Economic Power by White Elites in Barbados and Martinique;" and Jan van Huis' "Marketing Problems and Agricultural Extension in Nickeria (Surinam): a Stimulant to an Alternative Strategy."

1032 Phalen, John H. Aloe cultivation and industrialization on Aruba: a symbolic interlude (SOCIOL, 30:1, 1980, p. 52–65, map, tables)

Study views present-day cultivation of cash crop *aloe vera* as sociologically significant persistence of an Aruban sociocultural and economic tradition. Author argues that advent of oil refinery and steady work enabled this particular tradition to survive and to provide a supplementary source of income. Beyond the purely economic value of aloe cultivation, however, activity has become "symbolic of a prideful continuity with the past and of being Aruban."

1033 Philippe, Jeanne and **Jean Baptiste Romain.** *Indisposition* in Haiti (Social Science and Medicine [New York] 13B:2, April 1979, p. 129–133, bibl.)

Study of culturally-influenced Haitian syndrome authors describe as halfway between psychic and somatic ailment. Reports results of clinical and questionnaire study of 69 individuals in Port-au-Prince area. Of sample, 43 percent experienced *indisposition* more than once. Based on Rorschach responses of sub-sample, subjects were considered normal. Haitians believe sickness to be caused by conditions and actions of blood and by magic, and do not think it curable by medical doctors. Authors argue that *indisposition* is one of several types of dissociative states commonly referred to by Haitians.

1034 Philpott, Stuart B. The Montserratians: migration dependence and the maintenance of island ties in England (*in* Between two cultures: migrants and minorities in Britain. Edited by James L. Watson. Oxford, England: Basil Blackwell, 1977, p. 90–119, bibl.)

It is argued that Montserrat's dependency on migration and its migrants should be regarded as relatively successful adaptation thus far but it has produced a particularly vulnerable social system. Author deals with Montserrat's early migrant history; post-emancipation period; migration to Britain as of early 1950s; social implications of migration; its effect on class structure, remittances and agricultural mobilization of passage money; fostering of children; and remittance obligations. With regard to Montserratians in Britain, author touches on residence patterns, occupation, churches and credit associations, social activities, and social sanctions and remittance obligations.

1035 Pillot, Didier. Croyances populaires et systèmes agricoles traditionnels en Haiti (IFH/C, 145/146, nov. 1979, p. 17–28, ill.)

Study, conducted by group of students of Haiti's State University's Faculty of Ethnology, explores beliefs and practices of traditional peasant farmers in Haiti. Of interest to researchers are importance of lunar cycle, women's role, and beliefs in protection of garden. However, it is difficult to discern importance attached by peasants to such beliefs and practices.

1036 Piquion, René. Ébène: essai. Port-au-Prince: Impr. H. Deschamps, 1976. 283 p.

Essay contributes to literature reflecting on major themes of Black Diaspora: culture, identity, collectivity. Focusing on such topics as négritude, African personality, New World and African culture, oral traditions, and religion, it encompasses what is referred to as "le monde noir."

Poggie, John J., Jr. Small-scale fishermen's beliefs about success and development: a Puerto Rican case. See item **8230.**

1037 Pollak-Eltz, Angelina. Tradiciones africanas en Chuao, estado Aragua (MHD/B, 8:12, enero 1979, p. 307–325, bibl., plates)

After very brief description of history, setting, population, economy, social system, fiesta calendar, religiosity, and curanderism of Afro-Venezuelan community, author describes two fiestas which have preserved an African cast: Corpus Christi, or the Fiesta of the Devils, and San Juan, or the Fiesta of the Saint of the *Negros*.

1038 Posern-Zieliński, Aleksander. Religious ferment among the Indians of British Guiana at the turn of the 19th century (PAN/ES, 4, 1978, p. 97–125)

Very useful paper for those interested in syncretic religious behavior and/or the acculturation of Amerindians in The Guianas. Author demonstrates that syncretic Hallelujah religion did not surface in British Guiana suddenly, but was generated by religious ferment that embraced Carib-speaking tribes of Guianese interior as early as mid-19th century. This ferment took different forms: escapist movements preaching transformation of existing interethnic relations, and mass movements striving for speedy conversion of Christianity as a precondition for status advancement of Indians.

1039 Post, Ken. Arise ye starvelings: the Jamaican labour rebellion of 1938 and its aftermath. The Hague: Martinus Nijhoff, 1978. 502 p.; bibl.; index; tables (Institute of Social Studies. Series on the development of societies; v. 3)

Marxist study of key period and event in Jamaican and West Indian history. Bringing to analysis considerable valuable data, author attempts to trace "the links between the economic and the political, the 'concentration' of the one into the other, and in doing so has also posed the problem of how to relate theory to data in the writing of history."

A most interesting description and interpretation of the behavior of Jamaican workers and peasants immediately prior to the outbreak of World War II, particularly in light of contemporary sociopolitical conditions in Jamaica.

1040 Powers, Ann Marie and **John H. Phalen.** Some aspects of reciprocal exchange: economic organization in Aruba, Netherlands Antilles (AI/A, 75, 1980, p. 620–625, bibl., diagrams)

Analysis of food crop cultivation and the reciprocal or exchange system of labor (i.e., *paga lumba*) on Aruba. Relationships necessary for traditional food crop production and distribution were kinship relations, created and perpetuated by complementary *paga lumba* marriage system (i.e., brother/sister exchange or sister exchange).

1041 Pressoir, Catts. Le protestantisme haïtien . . . Port-au-Prince: Imprimerie de la Société Biblique et des Livres Religieux d'Haïti, 1945/77. 2 v.

Written by evangelist, these two books represent pt. 2 of work with same title on history of Protestantism in Haiti. Following opening chapter on immigration of Black Americans to Haiti, author covers various Protestant churches on the island, each in a separate chapter: Methodist, Anglican, Apostolic Orthodox, Protestant Episcopal, Free Methodist, various Baptist churches, Adventist. Aside from treating each church—its location, history, important pastors, duties, etc.—author focuses on evangelizing missions, ending with discussion of Bible Societies and their attempt to translate the Bible into Creole and to teach peasants to read.

1042 Price, Richard. Kwasimukamba's gambit (KITLV/B, 135:1, 1979, p. 151–169, bibl., plates)

Uses materials drawn from two quite different historical traditions to examine aspects of the life of Kwasi "one of the most extraordinary black men in Surinam, or perhaps in the world." The African-born Kwasi, who lived in 18th century, was a man of many parts (curer, diviner, intermediary in dealings with runaway slaves), and was admired by whites. Author compares materials and traditions on Kwasi, first presenting him as depicted by whites in written sources at time when his life intersected with Saramaka

history, and then as depicted by contemporary Saramaka in their oral tradition. Author maintains that "it seems clear that the contrastive accounts together, define a richer field of psychological possibilities, and enhance our understanding of the dynamics of the situation, far better than either source would alone." Examined in juxtaposition, these two accounts do, in fact, shed interesting light on the extremely brittle relations between the Bush Negroes and the coastal plantation society of the time.

1043 Reid, Stanley. Economic elites in Jamaica: a study of monistic relationship (CRCA/A, 22:1, 1980, p. 25–44, bibl., figures)

In context of neo-Weberian position that economic organizational forms are deeply rooted in social system, author examines economic elites in Jamaica over time. He then deals specifically with foreign investment; elite activity and the state; ownership of corporate enterprises; interlocking directorships and influence; and legal firms as institutional links between polity and family group. Concludes that evolution of specialized economic institutions in Jamaica has not meant structural differentiation of the functions the elite family grouping performs. He does note that "what is however noticeable is that the 'extended' family or what Zeitlin (1974) has called the 'Konecon' group where kinship ties, occupational roles and economic interests form a complex network, is the dominant social formation in Jamaican economy."

1044 Rubenstein, Hymie. Conjugal behaviour and parental role flexibility in an Afro-Caribbean village (The Canadian Review of Sociology and Anthropology [Canadian Sociology and Anthropology Association, Montreal] 17:4, Nov. 1980, p. 330–337)

Author contends that explanations of lower-class, black West Indian family organization based on independent variables, either diachronically or synchronically rooted, have sometimes prematurely preceded detailed ethnographic studies of Afro-Caribbean family system. In this context, folk systems have not been given the attention they deserve in Caribbean family studies. Based on field research (1969, 1972) in peasant community, St. Vincent, author provides qualitative description of extra-residential mating and parental roles this form of mating creates. His description reveals folk system that permits wide variety of behaviors for parents, a system in which actors are constantly being replaced. Utilizing, in part, Rodman's concept of "stretched" value system, author argues that variable and malleable pattern of mating and parenting in St. Vincent permits adjustment to changing circumstances and is, therefore, an appropriate adaptive mechanism to the marginal socioeconomic condition of most villagers.

1045 St. Pierre, Maurice. The 1938 Jamaica disturbances: a portrait of mass reaction against colonialism (UWI/SES, 27:2, June 1978, p. 171–196, bibl., tables)

Description and analysis of 1938 disturbances in Jamaica, focusing on events that occurred at Frome Estate in Westmoreland. Author examines political nature of mass violence and question of leadership, arguing that Jamaican society of that time generated serious economic strains for the masses with no opportunity to deal with these pressures in socially acceptable ways. Strikes, looting, damage to property and person, and loss of life resulted. Concludes that despite need that developed for middle-class individuals to mediate and negotiate with authorities, and increasing irrelevance of continuing mass violence, it was the masses that made the initial attack against colonialism and paved the way for future politicization of mass discontent by middle-class leaders.

1046 Sandoval, Mercedes C. *Santería* as mental health care system: a historical overview (Social Science and Medicine [New York] 13B:2, April 1979, p. 137–151, bibl.)

Quite useful review of *santería*, an Afro-Cuban cult organization. Author describes its heterogeneous belief structure and pantheon of god/saints; historical process that led to its introduction in Cuba and its effect on religions and health-seeking behavior on the island; problems of Cubans in Dade Co., Florida; and function of *santería* in North American setting. Contemporary *santería*'s "intrinsic flexibility, eclecticism and heterogeneity have been advantageous in helping ensure functional, dogmatic and ritual changes which enable it to meet the different needs of its many followers." This explains its spread among migrant Cubans and others, and its current vitality and dyna-

mism as a religious form and a mental health care system.

1047 Schuler, Monica. Myalism and the African religious tradition in Jamaica (*in* Africa and the Caribbean: the legacies of a link [see *HLAS 42:2499*] p. 65–79)

Useful description and analysis of Myalism, Afro-Jamaican religious movement that appeared in 1760s. Myalism first emerged as a pan-African religious society to protect slaves from European sorcery; in early 19th century adopted Christian elements. Myalists were leading slave rebellions by 1831–32; during the post-slavery period the movement gained converts despite official persecution; and by the 1840s it challenged Christian missionaries. Driven underground by authorities, it reappeared in strength in early 1860s. Author argues that Myal tradition was the core of strong and self-confident counter-culture that guaranteed that no evils of post-slavery period would be accepted passively.

1048 Silverman, Marilyn. Dependency, mediation, and class formation in rural Guyana (AAA/AE, 6:3, Aug. 1979, p. 466–490)

While based on premise that West Indian economies are dependent, paper suggests that macroprocesses, chiefly discussed by economists, have obscured vital microprocesses within dependent economies that are critical for understanding the dynamic of such societies. In context of review of relevant literature on West Indian dependency, plantations and peasants in the Caribbean, and concept of mediation, author presents ethnographic data on Rajgahr, an East Indian village. Data permit generalizations of peasants, plantations, occupational multiplicity, the nature of mediation, and factionalism and class formation. Author concludes that "Rajgahr Village is not an encapsulated structure that has stood on the edges of Guyanese history and society. It has been, and is, an integral part of this historical process."

1049 Simpson, George Eaton. Religious cults of the Caribbean: Trinidad, Jamaica and Haiti. Río Piedras: University of Puerto Rico, Institute of Caribbean Studies, 1980. 347 p.; bibl.; figures; index; plates.

Second revision and enlargement of well-known and important collection of writings by the most indefatigable investigator of

Caribbean religious behavior. Contains 13 articles on Trinidad, Jamaica and Haiti found in the 1970 version plus two additional articles: "Afro-American Religions and Religious Behavior" (*Caribbean Studies*, 12:2) and "The Kele—Chango—Cult in St. Lucia" (*Caribbean Studies*, 13:3).

1050 Smith, Raymond T. The family and the modern world system: some observations from the Caribbean (NCFR/JFH, 3:4, 1978, p. 337–360, bibl.)

Reviews West Indian family studies focusing on approaches that utilize synchronic class analysis; community analysis; culture-historical analysis; family and cultural differences, hierarchy, and marriage and family religions. Author argues, partly on basis of his own and colleagues' data on Guyana, that "structures—of social categorization, of relations between social groups, of marriage, kinship, and domestic life—developed very early in the formation of these societies and have continued to exercise a profound influence in the constitution and processes of social life. The peoples of the Caribbean are neither African, East Indian, Asiatic, nor European, even though these labels are attached to elements in the local structures . . ." Contends that West Indian structures are Creole.

1051 Speckman, John D. Ethnicity and ethnic group relations in Surinam (UPR/CS, 15:3, Oct. 1975, p. 5–15, tables)

Brief exploration of relationships among East Indians, Creoles, and Javanese in Surinam. Author emphasizes importance of ethnicity in that new nation and explicitly draws same conclusions as Leo Despres did for Guyana or that ethnicity rather than social class is the dominant variable in order of inequality.

1052 Steins, Martin. La négritude: un second souffle? (UCL/CD, 12:1, 1980, p. 3–43)

Attempt to trace the progression of Senghor's interpretation and modification of his concept of *négritude* since its inception more than 40 years ago. *Négritude* encompasses such notions as race, âme, civilization, nationalism, African socialism, culture ideology, and politics. Interestingly, even 30 years after the first attack of *négritude*, the debate continues, and it is Stein's belief that as long as African societies remain economically, technically, and politically dependent, the concept of *négritude* will continue to be of importance.

1053 Stevenson, David R. Intervillage preference of high blood pressure medicinal plants on St. Kitts, West Indies (Medical Anthropology [Redgrave, Pleasantville, New York] 3:4, Fall 1979, p. 503–524, bibl., figures, tables)

Overall intervillage preference of high blood pressure medicinal plants is for "maiden apple" (Momordica charantia) and "breadfruit bush" (Artocarpus altilis), both known to contain reserpine and other potentially effective hypotensive agents.

1054 Sued Badillo, Jalil. Bibliografía antropológica para el estudio de los pueblos indígenas en el Caribe. Santo Domingo: Ediciones Fundación García-Arévalo, 1977. 579 p. (Série investigaciones; no. 8)

Substantial bibliography on the Caribbean's indigenous people is divided into two parts: 1) by subject matter (e.g., general works, archaeology, ethnography, etc.); and 2) by area (e.g., Bahamas, Cuba, Jamaica, etc.). For bibliographer's comment, see *HLAS 41:48.*

1055 Sullivan, Paul. The founding and growth of Bullet Tree Falls (BISRA/BS, 6:6, Nov. 1978, p. 1–22, bibl., maps)

Description of present ethnic, economic, and residential characteristics of a small village in western half of Cayo District, Belize. Second part of article reconstructs its early history, with particular reference to various categories of migrants.

1056 Van Der Mark, Abraham E. Marriage and the family in a white Caribbean elite: the impact of descent for the ethnic persistence of the Sephardic Jews in Curaçao (CRCA/A, 22:1, 1980, p. 119–134, bibl.)

Although Sephardic Jews in Curaçao are declining dramatically in number, they still maintain high status positions that are out of proportion to their size as a group. Author argues that even though it is a small elite, it has preserved its ethnic identity longer than comparable groups in the Americas. Author offers descent as the factor that contributed most of this ethnic persistence. In this context, he examines endogamy; demography; and the state of business; the value of women in the past; concubinage and illegitimacy; and current patterns of inter-marriage and hypogamy.

1057 Veloz Maggiolo, Marcio. Sobre cultura dominicana . . . y otras culturas: en-sayos. Santo Domingo: Editora Alfa y Omega, 1977. 219 p.; bibl.

Essays by a Dominican archaeologist and social anthropologist on a wide range of subjects (e.g., precolumbian art, Dominican culture during the First Republic, etc.).

1058 Walker, Sheila S. African gods in the Americas: the black religions con-tinuum (The Black Scholar [Black World Foundation, Sausalito, California] 11:8, Nov./Dec. 1980, p. 25–36, bibl., plates)

Religion is a major element of African culture that survived slavery and the post-emancipation period in the New World. Vary-ing sociohistorical circumstances, however, have led to the different forms of African reli-gious structures, styles, and attitudes in the New World. "A common unifying feature that manifests itself in differing ways along this continuum is the existence of spirit possessions as the supreme religious act ex-pressing the fundamental nature of the re-lationship between human beings and their deities. The possession of the faithful by spir-itual beings is the ultimate sacramental ex-pression in the African cults of Haiti, Cuba, Brazil, and Trinidad, as well as in black Christian churches in New York, Chicago, Oakland, and especially in the southern United States."

1059 Weidman, Hazel Hitson. Falling-out: a diagnostic and treatment problem viewed from a transcultural perspective (So-cial Science and Medicine [New York] 13B:2, April 1979, p. 95–112, bibl.)

Description of a "culture-bound," sei-zure-like disorder called *falling-out* by black Americans, *blacking-out* by Bahamians and *indisposition* by Haitians in Miami area. The afflicted collapses without warning, without convulsions, tongue-biting, or incontinence, usually hears and understands what is hap-pening, but is powerless to move and al-though eyes are open, tends not to see. Author considers prevalence as well as prob-lems of diagnosis from both emic and etic perspectives. Reviews a number of therapeu-tic approaches that require both trans-disciplinary and transcultural orientations.

1060 Wells, Marilyn. Circling with the an-cestors: hugulendii symbolism in eth-nic group maintenance (BISRA/BS, 8:6, Nov. 1980, p. 1–9)

Description of the *hugulendii* circular dance of the black Caribs and analysis of the symbolic aspects of the dance in relationship to black Carib world view.

1061 Wessman, James W. The demographic structure of slavery in Puerto Rico: some aspects of agrarian capitalism in the late nineteenth century (JLAS, 12:2, Nov. 1980, p. 271–289, tables)

Analysis of the demographic structure of slavery in 32 *barrios* of the Jurisdiction of San Germán in 1872, based on a fiscal regis-ter of slaves. Gives basic demographics, in-cluding number of slaves by municipality and *barrio*, sex of slaves, number of owners, mean number of slaves per owner, median age, and sex ratio. In addition, details types of slave holding, division of slave labor, slave marital status, mortality, manumission, and purchase of freedom. Data "contradict some of the commonly heard statements about the benign character of slavery in Puerto Rico."

1062 ———. Division of labour, capital ac-cumulation and commodity exchange on a Puerto Rican sugar-cane hacienda (UWI/SES, 27:4, Dec. 1978, p. 464–480, bibl.)

Production and circulation of sugar as a commodity on the *hacienda* San Francisco in southwestern Puerto Rico during 1911. Author's aim is to complement Mintz's cul-tural history of a Puerto Rican sugar cane *hacienda* and to add aspects of Marxist eco-nomic theory to questions of capital com-position, surplus value generation, and *hacienda* viability. Deals specifically with di-vision of labor, capital accumulation, and commodity exchange for the *hacienda* San Francisco.

1063 Whitehead, Tony L. Residence, kin-ship, and mating as survival strategies: a West Indian example (WRU/JMF, 40:4, Nov. 1978, p. 817–828, bibl., tables)

Based on data from an ethnographic community study carried out in Jamaica in 1974, author explores applicability of model whose basic premise is that economic mar-ginality leads to specific adaptive responses in residential, kinship, and mating patterns.

Strategies for survival are discussed (e.g., "scuffling," female-headed households and consanguinity, mating flexibility, polygynous unions, dependents as links in domestic networks, and residential flexibility).

1064 Women in the Caribbean: a bibliography. Compiled by Bertie A. Cohen Stuart. Leiden, The Netherlands: Royal Institute of Linguistics and Anthropology, Department of Caribbean Studies, 1979. 163 p.; index.

Bibliography of 651 annotated references to publications on women in the Caribbean region is divided into five sections: 1) family and household; 2) cultural factors, 3) education; 4) economic factors; and 5) politics and law. Includes useful section on biographies of individual women and list of women's organizations by territory. For bibliographers comment, see *HLAS 42:39*.

1065 Women in the Caribbean: an annotated bibliography. Compiled by Joycelin Massiah. Cave Hill, Barbados: University of the West Indies, Institute of Social and Economic Research (Eastern Caribbean), 1979. 133 p.; index (Occasional bibliography series; no. 5)

Bibliography contains 408 annotated references to publications available in Barbados dealing with women in Caribbean region. Work is organized into 11 categories: general, role and status; law and politics; family and fertility; economics and employment; education; literature and the arts; religion; women's organization, biography and autobiography; and general reference works. Each category is sub-divided by individual territory or group of territories.

ETHNOLOGY: South America, Lowlands

WAUD H. KRACKE, *Associate Professor of Anthropology, University of Illinois, Chicago Circle*

THIS IS A PERIOD OF CONTRASTS. It is an exciting time in the evolution of anthropological research in lowland South America, as new field research now reaching publication generates novel concepts appropriate to these tropical forest and savannah cultures and a distinctive regional conceptual pattern begins to emerge. Accumulating research has made it timely for new regional syntheses (items **1088, 1136, 1144, 1156,** and **1183**), surveys of the literature (items **1135, 1192, 1196,** and **1211**) and regionally or topically focused bibliographies (items **1109, 1216** and San Roman and Riester in item **1067**).

The times, however, are grim for these tropical forest societies. Invasions of their lands by prospectors, ranching interests, oil and mining companies, and national road-building programs are more flagrant than ever (items **1082, 1096, 1099–1100, 1108, 1110, 1122, 1150, 1165, 1174, 1190, 1201, 1220–1222,** and **1224**). Brazilian Indians have been threatened with "emancipation" from government protection and dissolution of their reservations (items **1066, 1096,** and **1168**). Reports are coming out that several FUNAI (Brazilian Indian Service) projects that were very well conceived but short-lived were terminated as they began to succeed (items **1123, 1172, 1179,** and see also *HLAS 41:1183*). Recent resignations and firings of FUNAI's experienced Indianists and their replacement by less qualified personnel has injured the agency's effectiveness and credibility. On the other hand, indigenous movements such as those in Ecuador and Colombia (items **1132** and **1189**) are growing elsewhere, the catalyst in Brazil being CIMI, Indigenist Missionary Council (items **1155** and **1176**). A highlight of this development was the 1977 Barbados conference of indigenous leaders (item **1131**). Unfortunately, the pattern of violence against CRIC leaders in Colombia (item **1132**) is being repeated in Brazil, where several Indian leaders were assassinated in 1980. The best general overview of the situation in Brazil to 1977 is provided by Davis (item **1099**). More recent developments are covered in Cultural Survival's special reports on Brazil (item **1096**) and, more controversially, on Paraguay (item **1161**). Regular reports on the situation of South American Indians are carried by the newsletters of IWGIA, Cultural Survival, Survival International and the Anthropological Resource Center (ARC), and intermittently by *Akwesasne Notes*.

It is ironic that as the richness and complexity of these indigenous societies are being revealed by anthropological studies, the societies themselves are succumbing to "progress;" their members shunted aside as "ignorant savages" or worse. Recent research emphasizes the complexity of their social organization, their artistic creativity, ritual, mythology, and cosmological thought and, even more to the point, the depth of understanding these cultures have of the delicate ecological balance of the tropical forest, an environment in which they have lived for centuries, now rapidly being "developed" into grasslands (items **1126**, **1181**, **1188**, and **1220**).

The last few years have seen several important contributions to the ethnography of the Northwest Amazon (items **1129–1130**, **1134**, and **1136**; see also items **1068** and **1080**) and the Chaco (items **1077**, **1079**, and **1166**), each showing in a different way the complexity these societies attain in their social organization. On the Gê, the long-awaited summation of the Harvard Central Brazil project (item **1101**) has been closely followed by Seeger's probing study of the Suyá (item **1193**; see also items **1095** and **1112–1113**). Two of these ethnographies are noteworthy for attempting to probe the symbolism underlying the social structures, (items **1129** and **1193**), while others consist of searching studies of ritual and its iconography (items **1068**, **1098**, and **1130**). Mourning and its ceremonies have attracted special attention, some studies discussing its psychological as well as social aspects (items **1094**, **1098**, **1140**, **1149**, **1153**, and **1214**). Two recent ethnographies highlight headmanship (items **1105** and **1142**), the latter being a psychological study of the dynamics of leadership in the social structure of a Tupi-speaking society. Another study examines a revitalization movement and its leadership (item **1166** and see also *HLAS 35:1295*).

In the realm of theory, one notes that after decades of preoccupation with theories of "environmental limitation" on the development of Amazonian cultures, there is a more positive interest in the structures and world views of the cultures themselves. The distinctive features of South American native cultures are finally coming into focus, especially the complex symbolic structures that permeate their social and ritual organization.

A repeatedly voiced concern is the inadequacy of traditional anthropological models, derived from Africa and elsewhere, to explain the special features and problems of lowland South American social organization (items **1098**, **1101**, **1135**, **1169**, and **1192**). The conference held in Brazil in 1978 on "the Construction of the Person in Indigenous Societies" offers important new directions in this respect by proposing a set of analytic concepts issuing from studies of Brazilian societies (items **1084**, **1097**, **1198**, and **1214**). Four recent ethnographies provide especially good examples of this type of analysis, highlighting body and reproductive imagery in the representation of the social order (items **1098**, **1129–1130**, and **1193**; see also items **1094** and **1181**, and *HLAS 41:1205*). Naming systems also have an important place (items **1152**, **1178**, and **1214**). Several studies debate the nature of taxonomy in these tropical forest cultures, some raising issues concerning the ethnoscientific theory of classification (items **1074** and **1206**), others using modes of classification as a key to the thought processes implicit in the social forms of these cultures (items **1083**, **1093**, **1181**, and **1206**). Brent Berlin's ethnobiological study (see *HLAS 39:1299*) has been anthologized in Ronald Casson's *Language, culture and cognition* (London: MacMillan, 1981).

The recent growth of interest in symbolism has led to a flowering of studies of art forms as channels for self expression by artists (items **1092**, **1186–1187**, **1194**, and see *HLAS 41:1162*) and for collective expression of social identity and values (items **1124**, **1127**, **1180**, **1195**, **1203**, and **1213**). These works include studies of music (items **1074**, **1128**, **1194–1195**, and **1203**), ceramics (items **1092**, **1127**, **1170**, **1184–1185**, and **1219**), basketry weaving (items **1124** and **1170**), body painting (items **1078** and **1213**), painted fabrics (items **1186** and **1187**) and designs drawn on paper for the ethnographers (items **1092**, **1180**, and **1186**). One should also note methodologically innovative study of aesthetic judgments of feather art by Kensinger and others (see *HLAS 41:1162*). Several studies (items **1092**, **1124**, and **1186–1187**) deal with the impact on art style of the availability of a commercial market for it.

Cosmology is another recent subject of interest. Several studies (items **1067**, **1146–1147**, **1180**, **1182**, and **1203**) describe the cosmos as it relates to the experience of the shaman in his hallucinatory perception of the "other side" of reality. For a bibliography of such studies, one should consult the piece by San Román and Riester in item **1067**; see also items **1073**, **1116**, **1166**, **1191**, and *HLAS 39:1306*, now expanded into a book: Marc de Civrieux's *Religión y magia kari'ña* (Caracas: Universidad Católica Andrés Bello, 1974). Another group deals with the mythological dimensions of the cosmos (items **1072**, **1075**, **1089**, **1125**, and **1223**).

In studies of social structure, there is much interest in the prevalence of uxorilocality in tropical forest societies (see *HLAS 41:1185*), with theories advanced on its frequency in these societies (items **1143**, **1160**, and **1209**) and its consequences for social organization (items **1093**, **1102**, and **1208**). A few papers on kinship terminology bear out the prevalence of two-line systems in these societies (items **1106**, **1133**, and **1202**), and some interesting systems of marriage exchange have been brought to light (items **1077**, **1129**, and **1162**). Reflecting current concerns in our own society, a number of authors debate the power relations between the sexes (items **1072**, **1104**, **1117**, **1177**, and, **1199**), several stressing the effect of uxorilocality in enhancing the position of women (items **1092–1094**, **1177**, **1187**, and **1218** but contrast item **1104**).

Psychological research in the lowlands, hitherto represented primarily by the work of Laurence C. Watson and (earlier) Jules Henry, has been augmented by several publications using depth psychology in field research, two on the psychodynamics of mourning (items **1140** and **1149**) and three on dreams (items **1140–1141** and **1217**). One book focuses on the psychology of leadership in a Tupi tribe, exploring new ways of relating personalities and psychological processes with the social organization and social processes (item **1142**). A new strain of anthropological interest in the experience of field work and its epistomological implications for anthropology is represented in a small but significant contribution by Roberto Da Matta (item **1159**) and an interesting self-reflective ethnography by Jean-Paul Dumont (item **1105**). An article of my own touches on similar concerns (item **1140**).

Cultural materialist "environmental limitation" theories continue to generate bitter controversy. Most recently, a presumed scarcity of protein resources has been invoked to explain anything from food taboos (see *HLAS 41:1192*) to warfare (item

1120), eliciting numerous rebuttals on the extensive availability of animal and vegetable protein (items **1076, 1086** and see also the debate, which includes added data, in *Current Anthropology*, 20:1, 1979, p. 150–155; and 21:4, 1980, p. 540–546). Ruddle (item **1188**) attributes the decline of big game animals to recent destruction of forests. Gross has turned to Carneiro's circumscription hypothesis to explain the large size of Gê villages and their complexity of organization (item **1118**). Other studies draw on the profound native knowledge of the environment (items **1076** and **1126**), some researchers finding that the preservation of the ecological balance is rooted in deep religious conviction (item **1181** and see *HLAS 39:1376*).

With a growing library of research publications, the ethnography of lowland South America is assuming an increasingly significant place in world anthropology. A distinctive point of view is emerging, shaped by South American anthropologists together with North American, British, French and other European contributions. This growth is reflected also in the appearance of several new journals and periodicals devoted primarily or significantly to ethnography of the area. The *Anuário Antropológico*, founded by Roberto Cardoso de Oliveira at the Universidade de Brasília, has come out with three volumes, of which the first is reviewed here (items **1162, 1178** and **1206**) and two volumes of the *Working papers on South American Indians* have appeared, edited by Kenneth M. Kensinger at Bennington College (items **1202** and **1204**). The recently established journals *Amazonia Peruana* (item **1067**) and *El Dorado* both continue publication.

Finally, although it has not been customary to list dissertations on lowland South American cultures, two recent theses whose contents have not yet found their way to publication have been cited by other authors. Thomas Langdon's *Food restrictions in the medical system of the Barasana and Taiwano Indians of the Colombian Northwest Amazon* (Tulane University, 1975), which deals with shamanism and cure as well as food taboos, is repeatedly cited in literature on the Northwest Amazon. Gregory Urban's *A model of Shokleng social reality* (University of Chicago, 1978) attempts a logical analysis of Southern Gê social categories and discusses genetic relationships among the Gê tribes. Also worth noting is an interesting study of child development by Joan Abelove, *Pre-verbal learning of kinship behavior among Shipibo Indians of Eastern Peru* (CUNY, 1978).

1066 Agostinho, Pedro. Emancipação do índio (SBPC/CC, 32:2, fev. 1980, p. 173–183)

Legal discussion of the Draft Act promulgating the policy of "emancipation" (termination of reservations and protected status for Indians) in relation to the requirements of the Constitution and the Indian Statute, concluding that the Draft Act did not conform with the constitutional and statutory obligations of the government.

1067 *Amazonia Peruana.* Centro Amazónico de Antropología y Aplicación Práctica. Vol. 2, No. 4, enero 1979– . Lima.

Special issue on shamanism, with articles by Gerhar Baer on "Religión y Chamanismo de los Matzigenka" (Machiguenga); J. and J.P. Chaumeil on "Chamanismo

Yagua;" Jesús Victor San Roman on four Peruvian curanderos ("Visiones, Curaciones y Brujerías: Hablan los Brujos"); and an article by Anthony Stocks (reviewed separately) on music in a hallucinogenic curing ritual (Tendiendo un Puente entre el Cielo y la Tierra en Alas de la Canción"). A short bibliography by J.V. San Roman and Jürgen Riester closes the volume.

1068 Århem, Kaj. Observations on life cycle rituals among the Makuna (Arstryck [Göteborgs Etnografiska Museum, Göteborgs, Sweden] 1978, p. 10–47)

Makuna (Northwest Amazon) life-cycle rituals from birth through death are presented as "a total system of ideas and ritual behavior," each ritual carefully described and compared with the others to reveal the system of transformations between them, and relating them to life cycle rituals of related tribes. Rebirth of a soul in an infant grandchild makes the rituals of a life cycle part of a larger cycle of a soul. See item **1130**.

1069 Aspelin, Paul. The ethnography of Nambicuara agriculture (KITLV/B, 135, 1979, p. 18–58, bibl.)

In continued debate, author provides evidence to show that Nambicuara agriculture was more important and constant a part of the food supply than Lévi-Strauss credited, but defends Lévi-Strauss against criticism by Price (see *HLAS 41:1184*) by finding reasonable explanations for Lévi-Strauss' observations (see *HLAS 39:1288*).

1070 Baldus, Herbert. Ensaios de etnologia brasileira. Pref. de Afonso d'E. Taunay; apresentação à 2a. ed. de Egon Schaden. 2. ed. São Paulo: Companhia Editora Nacional, 1979. 214 p.; bibl.; ill.; indexes (Brasiliana; v. 101)

Discursive ethnographic notes on tribes studied by this wide-ranging Brazilian ethnographer, including papers on the Kaingang "cult of the dead," chiefly succession among the Tereno (alleging primogeniture), and Tapirapé feast groups and work groups. Begins with a brief history of German ethnology in Brazil, and closes with a survey of the current cultural condition of the Kaingang, Tapirapé, Bororo and Karajá Indians.

1071 Bamberger, Joan. Exit and voice in Central Brazil: the politics of flight in Kayapó society (*in* Dialectical societies [see item **1101**] p. 130–146)

Within Kayapó social structure, conflicts are channelled into the men's societies. Village fission following a collective duel was the dominant traditional mode of expressing dissent. Current contact conditions no longer permit unlimited fission and are beginning to encourage individual political expression.

1072 ———. The myth of matriarchy: why men rule in primitive society (*in* Women, culture and society. Edited by Michelle Zimbalist Rosaldo and Louise Lamphere. Stanford, California: Stanford University Press, 1974, p. 263–280)

Analyzes myths that portray an ancient period of female dominance in society (including Bachoven's *Mutterrecht*) and argues that in Amazonian cultures such myths constitute a social charter for the male initiation ceremony which transfers a boy from the female-dominated domestic circle to the male-dominated ceremonial sphere.

1073 Bartolomé, Miguel Alberto. Shamanismo y religión entre los avá-katú-eté del Paraguay. México: Instituto Indigenista Interamericano, 1977. 153 p.; 3 leaves of plates; bibl.; ill. (Serie Antropología social; 17)

With the object of "showing how mythology and shamanism influence Guaraní cultural life," this book sketches Avá-Katú-eté beliefs in spiritual beings and souls and describes the central role of shamans in their society, beginning with a summary of the Twin Cycle of myths.

1074 Bastos, Rafael José de Menezes. A musicológica Kamayurá: para uma antropologia da comunicação no Alto Xingú. Brasília: Fundação Nacional do Indio (FUNAI), Departamento Geral de Planejamento Comunitário, Divisão de Estudos e Pesquisas, 1978. 1 v.; bibl.; charts; figures; maps; plates.

Exposition of the conceptual system of classification of Kamayurá vocal and instrumental music, based on five and a half months of field work in the Xingú, with a discussion of the relation of music to ritual and the symbolism of the sacred flutes. Music is seen as central in ethnography of communication (see also items **1194** and **1195**).

1075 Becher, Hans. A lua e a reencarnação; a criação do homem na imaginação dos índios Surára, Noroeste do Brasil (IAI/I, 2, 1974, p. 227–237, plates)

Yanomamö sprang from drops of the moon's blood when it was pierced by an arrow. When a corpse is cremated its soul rises up to the moon but eventually returns by coming down in a drop of water that enters a man's penis and becomes another child.

1076 Beckerman, Stephen. The abundance of protein in Amazonia: a reply to Gross (AAA/AA, 81:3, Sept. 1979, p. 533–560, bibl., tables)

Taking issue with Daniel Gross' (*HLAS 39:1331*) and Marvin Harris' (item **1120**) theories explaining Amazonian social structure on the basis of limited protein supply, this article points out the abundance of vegetable protein available in the tropical forest diet. Author has done fieldwork with the Bari of the Maracaibo Basin in Colombia.

1077 Bernand-Muñoz, Carmen. Les Ayoré du Chaco septentrional: étude critique à partir des notes de Lucien Sébag. Paris: Mouton, 1977. 291 p.; bibl.; index.

This "Ethnography" of the Ayoré was reconstructed from field notes left by Lucien Sébag, is supplemented by published sources and includes comparisons with the Chamacoco and other Zamuco cultures. The Ayoré and Chamacoco are especially interesting because their asymmetrical moiety system is composed of seven exogamous patrilineal clans which are paired in preferential alliances and stratified somewhat like the Bororo "subclans" system proposed by Lévi-Strauss. Named after trees, the clans "own" various natural species and cultural properties that are described in detail. Book includes extensive discussion of sources on Zamuco tribes and their history; chapters on life cycle, ecology and warriors, chiefs and shamans; and much on mythology. See also item **1079**.

1078 Bisilliat, Maureen. Xingu: tribal territory. Photos by Maureen Bisilliat; text by Orlando Villas-Bôas, Cláudio Villas-Bôas. London: Collins, 1979. 31, 15 p.; 80 leaves of plates: chiefly col. ill.

Beautiful photo essay on role played by body painting and decoration in daily and ritual contexts of Xinguan cultures. Also includes glimpses of visually and texturally related features of everyday life. Introductory essay on Xingú life and terrain.

1079 Bórmida, Marcelo and **Mario Califano.** Los indios ayoreo del Chaco Boreal: información básica acerca de su cultura. Buenos Aires: Fundación para la Educación, la Ciencia y la Cultura, 1978. 188 p.; 6 leaves of plates; ill.

This ethnography of the Ayoré, based on three field trips, stresses the economy, material culture and aspects of daily life and complements the more abstract approach of Bernand-Muñoz's book (item **1077**). Includes brief description of a complex clan system that is somewhat different from the one proposed by Bernand-Muñoz, and suggests the non-exogamous linkages of clans into covert ceremonial moieties. Clan adoptions complicate picture. Also includes accounts of religious beliefs.

1080 Bourgue, François. Los caminos de los hijos del cielo: estudio socioterritorial de los Kawillary del Cananarí y de Apaporis (ICA/RCA, 20, 1976, p. 101–144, bibl., maps)

Brief but interesting ethnographic sketch of (nearly extinct) Arawakan member of the multilingual Vaupés region. They participate in marriage alliances with neighboring Tucanoan groups with whom they share the pattern of five-fold clan subdivisions (see item **1129**) and linguistic exogamy. Most of the article focuses on the myth of settlement of the region and its attendant cosmology.

1081 Brazil, anthropological perspectives: essays in honor of Charles Wagley. Maxine L. Margolis and William E. Carter, editors. New York: Columbia University Press, 1979. 443 p.; bibl.; ill.; index.

Festschrift for Charles Wagley consists of articles by his students representing all aspects of his wide-ranging interest in the anthropological study of Brazil (ethnography of indigenous societies, study of rural Brazil and Amazonian folk society, the anthropology of Brazilian national culture, etc.). All articles on Brazilian Indian cultures are annotated separately in this section and entered under author's name (see items **1095, 1110, 1117–1118, 1120, 1169,** and **1200**).

1082 Carelli, Vincent and **Milton Severiano.** Mão branca contra o povo cinza. Apresentação de Dom Tomás Balduino. São Paulo: Centro de Trabalho Indigenista, 1980. 24 p. (Brasil debates)

Documents the destruction of the Guaporé Valley Nambicuara groups, initially by ranchers using defoliants related to Agent Orange to clear grazing lands, and now by the impending rerouting of the Cuiabá-Porto Velho highway which will pass near their villages.

1083 Castro, Eduardo B. Viveiros de. Alguns aspectos do pensamento Yawalapiti; Alto Xingú: classificações e transformações (BRMN/B, 26, nova série, abril 1978, p. 1–41, bibl.)

After sketching Xinguan (perhaps pan-Amazonian?) classificatory modifiers, author discusses Yawalapiti categories of living things and ingestibles (food, emetics, tobacco) as elements in a "logique du sensible." "Natural" (*kanupa*) things endanger processes of transformation (growth in infancy, puberty seclusion). Metamorphosis (illness, cure) is brought about by shamanic contact with spirits through tobacco smoke. Important contribution to the understanding of thought and religion in Amazonian cultures, as well as to theory of food taboos.

1084 ———. A fabricação do corpo na sociedade Xinguana (BRMN/B, 32, nova série, maio 1979, p. 40–48, bibl.)

Discusses ritual seclusion in the Xingú and the "bodily changes or exchanges" that are brought about during seclusion. Part of the symposium on "the construction of the self in indigenous societies" (see item **1198**).

1085 Chagnon, Napoleon A. Yanomamö, the fierce people. 2d. ed. New York: Holt, Rinehart and Winston, 1977. 174 p.; 1 leaf of plates; bibl.; ill.; index (Case studies in cultural anthropology)

Popular ethnology of the Venezuelan Yanomamö reissued with concluding chapter on acculturation to Western society. Includes amusing anecdotes some of which portray missionary (especially Protestant) contempt for Yanomamö culture. Author describes how he defied one such missionary by taking hallucinogens during a ritual ceremony. Includes list of the Yanomamö film series.

1086 ——— and **Raymond B. Hames.** Protein deficiency and tribal warfare in Amazonia: new data (AAAS/S, 203:4383, 2 March 1979, p. 910–913, bibl., ill., tables)

Marshalls data on Yanomamö hunting to show that they have an abundant supply of game, countering Marvin Harris' and Daniel Gross' explanation of Yanomamö warfare as caused by limited protein availability/population control. For Harris' reply, see item **1120**; note further exchange of views with Ross in the "Letters Column" of *Science* (204:4431, 8 Feb. 1980, p. 590–593, bibl.).

1087 Chapelle, Richard. Les hommes à la ceinture d'écorce. Photos de Carméla Chapelle. Paris: Flammarion, 1979. 252 p.; 14 p. of plates (some col.); ill.

Consists of adventures of French cinematographer in search of newly contacted Cintas Largas Indians. Describes two-week stay in Cinta Larga village and attempts generalizations about their culture, and gives account of brief contact with Surui. Offers idealized version of Apoena Meireles' controversial pacification expeditions. These early descriptions of newly contacted groups are of interest but readers should beware of serious inaccuracies, such as including both groups under "Kawahib."

1088 Chiara, Vilma. Brésil (in Anthropologie regionale. v. 2, Asie, Amérique, Mascareignes. Edited by Jean Poirier. Paris: Editions Gallimard, 1978, v. 2, p. 1618–1714)

Excellent overview, written in a lively and engaging style, of the indigenous cultures of Brazil, beginning with a précis of the history of contact with pointed comments on FUNAI's Indian policy, and a history of early Brazilian ethnography. Brief survey of tribes, organized regionally, is followed by a 64-page generalized summary of Amazonian culture. Comprehensive and reasonably up to date, despite inevitable omissions, this is an admirable substitute for the outdated general articles in Steward's *Handbook*. Recommended as excellent introductory reading for a course on South American Indians. Closes with four pages on Afro-Brazilian culture.

1089 ———. Do cru ao cozido: ensaio sobre o tempo mítico dos Krahô (USP/RA, 22, 1979, p. 29–38, bibl.)

Essay on Kraho mythical time which uses Lévi-Straussian structural analysis. Discusses the sequential alternation of fire and water, raw and cooked in Kraho myths and in their religious thought.

1090 Cognat, André. Antecume: ou, Une autre vie: récit. Recueilli par Claude Massot. Paris: R. Laffont, 1977. 337 p.; 6 leaves of plates; ill. (Collection Vécu)

Consists of the tale of the French adventurer André Cognat. In 1961, he began living with the Wayana and in 1972 took a Wayana wife (to whom the book is dedicated). The dramatic narrative of his experience includes scattered observations of the culture, "collected" (transcribed?) by Claude Massot. Illustrated with excellent plates, some in color.

1091 Cohen, Bill. Biochemical determinants of visual phenomena in the Amazonian Yage ceremony (UNC/ED, 3:2, July 1978 [i.e. Dec. 1979] p. 32–64, bibl.)

Uses ethnographic descriptions of *banisteriopsis* use, experiments with harmaline, and descriptions of successive stages of intoxication in order to describe the visual phenomena produced by ayahuasca. While acknowledging that drug-induced visions may be determined by cultural expectations, author suggests that the appearance of snakes and felines may be products of the drug's psycho-pharmacological effects and may account for the importance of such figures in South American mythology.

1092 Costa, Maria Heloisa Fénelon. A arte e o artista na sociedade Karajá. Brasília: Fundação do Indio, Departamento Geral de Planejamento Comunitario, Divisão de Estudos e Pesquisas, 1978. 1 v.; bibl.; charts; col. plates; plates.

A study of Karajá artistic styles and the sources of change in them. Compares the media of body painting and ceramic figurines, the former (also used on figurines) conservative, using geometric figures and designs representing animals of accentuating body parts. Stylistic change in ceramic figurines, from geometric toward increasing naturalism, is attributed to commercialization as well as the introduction of firing. Women's status, already high in this uxorilocal society, is enhanced by their taking over the once male production of ceramics, now income producing. Free drawings obtained from children and adolescents yield interesting comparisons by sex and age in style and subject matter.

1093 Crocker, J. Christopher. My brother the parrot (in The Social use of mataphor: essays on the anthropology of rhetoric. Edited by J. David Sapir and J. Christopher Crocker. Philadelphia: University of Pennsylvania Press, 1977, p. 164–192)

"Investigates the social nature of cosmological metaphor" through a discussion, based on author's field work, of the question: in what sense do Bororo men mean "We are red macaws?" Dismisses Lévy-Bruhl's view that it implies substantial identity, but also Lévi-Strauss' purely metaphorical interpretation. Rather, men are macaws because both temporarily serve as the abode of clan spirits (aroe); men when they embody spirits of the opposite moiety in ritual, thus temporarily overcoming matrilineal domination by women, and macaws when spirits enter their bodies for carnal purposes. Argument also draws on beliefs about the soul after death,

habitats of spirits and birds, and the nature of relationships of "totem" spirits to clans.

1094 ———. Selves and alters among the Eastern Bororo (in Dialectical societies [see item **1101**] p. 249–300, bibl.)

Discussion of the intricate balance of agnatic and matrilineal bonds in Bororo social structure, culminates in a description of the "dialectical inversions" in postmortuary ritual. In the latter, the soul and social personality of the deceased are ritually represented by a member of the deceased's father's clan. Author details complex internal structure of clans and concludes with a discussion of the dialectics of Bororo social organization.

1095 Crocker, William H. Canela kinship and the question of matrilineality (in Brazil, anthropological perspectives: essays in honor of Charles Wagley [see item **1081**] p. 225–249, map)

After brief ethnographic introduction to the Gê and Canela, author questions whether at one time the Canela had the exogamous matrilineal moieties described by Kurt Nimuendaju but no longer in existence even though households are uxorilocal. Author suggests hypothesis that the Canela may once have had corporate exogamous matrilineages that now survive only in the rules of transmission of rights to certain ceremonies.

1096 Cultural Survival. Brazil. Cambridge, Massachusetts: Cultural Survival, 1979. 1 v. (Cultural survival special report; no. 1)

Collection of articles and documents on the threat to Indian survival in Brazil, translated from Brazilian publications of the Comissões pró-Indio of São Paulo and Rio de Janeiro. Include statements by Indians, anthropologists and Church leaders on "emancipation" (see item **1066**) and on other issues (see item **1174**). For more on this subject, see items **1082, 1099, 1150, 1165, 1173–1174,** and **1179.**

1097 Cunha, Manuela Carneiro da. De amigos formais e pessoa: de companheiros, espelhos e identidades (BRMN/B, 32, maio 1979, p. 31–39, bibl.)

Discusses the Krahó institution of the "companion." Personally chosen but ritually important, the "companion" contributes to the definition of the person who selects him by establishing similarity between them. Part of the symposium on "the construction of the person in indigenous societies" (see item **1198**).

1098 ———. Os mortos e os outros: uma análise do sistema funerário e da noção de pessoa entre os índios Krahó. São Paulo: Editora HUCITEC, 1978. 152 p.; 8 leaves of plates; bibl.; ports (Linguagem)

This perceptive and probing structural study of death in Krahó society, based on two months of fieldwork supplemented by extensive bibliographic research, seeks to elucidate the Krahó concept of the person as implicit in their ideas about death and in their funeral and mourning rituals. The key concept of "the other"—apparent in the role *affines* play in burial as well as in the institution of "the ceremonial friend" who represents the deceased in funerary ritual—culminates in a belief on which Krahó society is founded: that there is an absolute opposition between the living and the dead. Also includes interesting discussion of ancestral cults and their absence in Krahó and other Gê societies which author explains in terms of the social basis of personal identity. For more on the subject of mourning, see items **1140** and **1149**.

1099 Davis, Shelton H. Victims of the miracle: development and the Indians of Brazil. New York: Cambridge University Press, 1977. 205 p.; bibl.; index; map.

Best general treatment available in English of relations between Brazilian Indians and the nation's society and the threats to their survival. Documents development of Indian policy since 1940, especially since the 1964 coup, with special attention to developments after 1970. Details the effects of agribusiness, mining and other commercial concerns involved in development of the Amazon, and the undermining of effective development of parks and reservations for Indians. See also items **1082, 1096, 1165, 1172–1173,** and **1179.**

1100 Despojo y reivindicación. Lima: Centro de Investigación y Promoción Amazónica, 1978. 76 p.; bibl.

Six short, mimeographed essays: Richard Smith's "Los Amuesha: una Minoría Amenazada;" Alberto Chirif's "La Cuestión de las Tierras y del Desarrollo Económico de las Comunidades Nativas;" Richard Smith's "Extracto de 'Las Muchachas Indias son las Mejores Domésticas:' Otro Aspecto de Etnocidio;" Tulio Mora's, Carlos Mora's and Alberto Chirif's "Apreciaciones Socio-Culturales de los Grupos Etnolingüísticos Aguaruna y Huambiza;" Alberto Chirif's "La Ley Forestal y de Fauna y su Importancia para las Comunidades Nativas," and "En Torno a la Titulación de las Comunidades Nativas y a los Recursos Forestales y de Fauna Silvestre." [W.E. Carter]

1101 Dialectical societies: the Gê and Bororo of central Brazil. Edited by David Maybury-Lewis; contributors, Joan Bamberger et al. Cambridge: Harvard University Press, 1979. 340 p.; bibl.; ill.; index (Harvard studies in cultural anthropology; 1)

Long awaited synthesis of the Harvard Central Brazil Project, a joint study of Gê and Bororo social structures by Brazilian and US ethnographers under David Maybury-Lewis. After Maybury-Lewis' brief introductory sketch of the project, Jean Carter Lave and Julio Melatti discuss Krikati and Krahó name transmission, Melatti suggesting that "cross transmission" of names balances uxori-locality by "returning" men's names to their natal households (see items **1148** and **1163**). Roberto Da Matta connects Apinaje relationship terminology with their ideology of social relations, contrasting the consubstantial nuclear family with public ceremonial relationships (see item **1158**). Joan Bamberger examines Kayapó conflict, showing new modes of expressing dissent (see item **1071**). In a pair of articles at the heart of the book, Terence Turner sets forth a general model of Gê societies and applies it to the Kayapó, stressing uxorilocal residence as a means for one man to achieve domination over another. Gê moiety systems are seen as superstructural integrative institutions which order the principles of control embodied in uxorilocality and age-grade hierarchy (see items **1209** and **1210**). Maybury-Lewis' contribution sketches Sherente political factions, still organized around otherwise defunct moieties. He proposes an alternative theory of Gê and Bororo societies based on opposition between a female domestic sphere and a central male ceremonial order (see item **1160**). Only in Central Gê societies do moieties themselves embody political opposition. These opposing theories are followed by J. Christopher Crocker's view from the Bororo (see item **1094**) accommodating elements of both. His discussion of the balance of agnatic and matrilineal bonds in Bororo society reaches a fitting conclusion in the most explicit discussion of dialectics in the book. Maybury-Lewis closes the volume by showing the inapplicability of traditional kinship concepts (descent, alliance or componential analysis) to lowland South American societies.

1102 Dietschy, Hans. Graus de idade entre os karajá do Brasil central (USP/RA, 21, 1. parte, 1978, p. 69–85, bibl.)

Outlines stages of Kayapó life cycle and their ceremonial articulation with suggestion that they follow natural phases of psychological and biological development. Author notes that generational principle in kin terminology and alternating generational emphasis in naming (by grandparent) are related to the problem of dysharmonic uxorilocal residence rule and patrilineal recruitment in men's groups. These are referred to ambiguously as "dual descent." (Also seems to equate age grades with generational terminology.)

1103 Diniz, Edson Soares. Uma reserva indígena no centro-oeste paulista: aspectos das relações interétnicas e intertribais. São Paulo: Fundo de Pesquisas do Museu Paulista de Universidade de São Paulo, 1978, 158 p.; bibl.; ill. (Série de etnologia; v. 3. Coleção Museu Paulista)

Succinct presentation of facts on population, agriculture, employment, kinship, religious beliefs and interethnic relations of the Ñandeva Guaraní and Terêna on the Araribá Reservation in São Paulo state. Includes demographic and economic statistics on both groups and on neighboring population.

1104 Dole, Gertrude. The marriages of Pacho: a woman's life among the Amahuaca (*in* Many sisters: women in cross-cultural perspective. Edited by Carolyn J. Matthiessen. New York: Free Press, 1974, p. 3–34)

Through a detailed ethnographic account of a girl's attempts at marriage, Dole illuminates aspects of Amahuaca social structure, kin ties and interpersonal relationships, and especially the role and position of women in Amahuaca society.

1105 Dumont, Jean Paul. The headman and I: ambiguity and ambivalence in the fieldworking experience. Austin: University of Texas Press, 1978. 211 p.; bibl.; ill.; index (Texas Pan American series)

Combines a basic ethnography of the Panaré with a reflective account of field work, complementing the more structuralist approach of his earlier book (see *HLAS 39:1318*). Pt. 1 details ethnographer's entry into the field and formation of key relationships, pt. 2 provides context of naming, kinship and marriage rules (which permit grandparent-grandchild unions) and a description of drama of succession to headmanship, showing how author's relationships in the settlement fit into this political process; pt. 3 is a structural analysis of Panaré communication with outsiders (Creoles, national society, and the anthropologist as outsider) depicting compadrazgo as the negative equivalent of marriage which encapsulates relations with Creoles. Book closes with discussion of national and missionary attempts to "civilize"/subjugate the Panaré, and their response to the progressive incursions of Western culture.

1106 Fields, Harriet L. and **William R. Merryfield.** Mayoruna (Panoan) kinship (UP/E, 19:1, Jan. 1980, p. 1–28, bibl., figures, tables)

Description of marriage practices (cross-cousin marriage or capture of alien women) and a formal genealogical analysis of Mayoruna kin terms, which constitute a two-line system with certain asymmetries.

1107 Frič, Alberto V. Indiáni Jižní Ameriky. Praha: Orbis, 1977. 252 p.

New and revised edition of the notes of well-known Czech explorer and traveler, Josef Václav Frič who visited South America in the 1920s, especially the Chaco. His account includes many first-hand observations of the Guaykurú, Araucanians, Macicuí, etc. Includes about 50 remarkable period photographs of individuals. [G.J. Kovtun]

1108 Friede, Juan. Processo de aculturación del indígena en Colombia (CBR/BCB, 16:1, enero 1979, p. 9–27, bibl.)

Describes history of relations between Colombian Indians and the dominant colonizing elements from 16th century to conditions which led to the establishment of

CRIC in 1971, stressing the "policy of violent acculturation" and its consequences.

1109 Fundação Cultural do Maranhão. Departamento de Assuntos Culturais. Indios do Maranhão: bibliografia. São Luis: Fundação Cultural do Maranhão, Departamento de Assuntos Culturais, 1977. 19 p.; index.

Annotated bibliography, not exhaustive but with some interesting items.

1110 Galvão, Eduardo. The encounter of tribal and national societies in the Brazilian Amazon (in Brazil, anthropological perspectives: essays in honor of Charles Wagley [see item **1081**] p. 25–38)

Historical review of the acculturation process of Amazonian Indians in Brazil, illustrated by a detailed survey of the process in the Rio Negro region. Delineates stages of acculturation and the historical, social and ecological factors that affect it.

1111 Giaccaria, Bartolomeu. Significado da água na cultura Xavánte (USP/RA, 21:1, 1978, p. 95–108)

Concerns the meaning of ritual bathing. "Living" (running) water is the abode of good spirits, "dead" (still) water of bad. Baths in river water, for life and strength, occur in several rites of passage. "The bath of children" which cements a betrothal is described in detail, and other ceremonial baths are sketched more briefly.

1112 ——— and Adalberto Heide. Jerônimo xavante sonha: contos e sonhos. Campo Grande, Brasil: Casa da Cultura, 1975. 239, 53 p.; 8 leaves of plates; ill. (Publicação da "Casa da Cultura:" no. 2. Publicações do Museu Regional "Dom Bosco;" 5)

Collection of stories, myths and dreams told by Geronimo, an elderly Shavante, taped by his younger compatriots (see item **1113**), and translated into Portuguese. Also includes smaller corpus of stories told by Raimundo and typed in Shavante with interlinear literal Portuguese translation.

1113 ——— and ———. Xavante (Auwẽ uptabi; povo autentico): pesquisa historico-etnográfica. São Paulo: Editorial Dom Bosco, 1972. 304 p.; fold. tables; ill.; maps; plates; tables.

Detailed and careful ethnographic description of Shavante society, especially strong on details of ritual, by a Salesian missionary with 10 years of work experience with them, and illustrated with fine photos by A. Heide. Nine years of direct observation are supplemented by an interesting experiment in ethnographic method to minimize the distorting influence of an outside investigator: four young Shavante tape-recorded the instruction they received on tribal lore while serving as "disciples" to two old Shavante men.

1114 Giacone, Antonio. Trentacinque anni fra le tribù del Rio Uaupés (Amazzonia-Brasile). A cura di Pietro Ambrosio. Roma: LAS, 1976. 239 p.; 6 leaves of plates; bibl.; ill.; indexes (Pubblicazioni del CSSMS: Diarie memorie; 1)

Condescending treatise on cultures of the Vaupes by Salesian missionary of some evangelistic fervor. Though he distinguishes the different language groups and has compiled dictionaries of three Tucanoan languages and Macú, he offers generalized, somewhat superficial description of Vaupés culture including sketches of rites of passage, social structure, religious beliefs and myths and legends, some of which contain useful observations. Pt. 2 tells history of Vaupés Salesian mission and account of its successes in converting Indians. Pt. 3 consists of phrase-list and 40-page Italian-Tucanoan word list.

1115 Goldman, Irving. The Cubeo Indians of the Northwest Amazon. 2. ed. Urbana: University of Illinois Press, 1979. 315 p.; bibl.; ill.; index (Illini books edition)

Reissue of classic ethnography, first complete one published on a Northwest Amazon culture. Includes five-page "Afterword" sketching developments since 1963 (as seen in visits back to the Cubeo in 1968 and 1979), and results of new policy at the Mitú mission of encouraging native traditions. Also has four-page bibliography of works on Northwest Amazon which have appeared in 16 years since original publication of the monograph.

1116 Gómez-Perasso, José Antonio. La concepción Kom Lyk y Mak'a del Cosmos (UCNSA/SA, 12:1/2, dic. 1977, p. 25–44, ill.)

Brief outline of layered cosmology of these two groups derived from their mythologies, with sketches by a Mak'a shaman, followed by a Mak'a vocabulary.

1117 Gregor, Thomas. Secrets, exclusion, and the dramatization of men's roles (*in* Brazil, anthropological perspectives: essays in honor of Charles Wagley [see item 1081] p. 250–269)

Describes Mehinaku secret men's cult and men's house. Argues that the secrecy serves to draw a social boundary between the sexes, but that men's obtrusive "secret" rituals dramatize the male role for a hidden audience of women, and that the men's house serves as a stage for a dramatization of aggressive masculinity.

1118 Gross, Daniel R. A new approach to Central Brazilian social organization (*in* Brazil: anthropological perspectives: essays in honor of Charles Wagley [see item 1081] p. 321–342)

Gross describes Gê adaptive pattern of exploiting varied habitats in rotation in seasonal treks and attributes large seasonal village size to a conjectured instability of food resources unique to the cerrado region, and to endemic warfare. The strategy of dispersal which is frequent Amazonian response to warfare is precluded by the restricted areas of gallery forest available for cultivation. Based on field work conducted by author and four students in different Gê cultures.

1119 ——— *et al.* Ecology and acculturation among native peoples of Central Brazil (AAAS/S, 206:4422, 30 Nov. 1979, p. 1043–1050, map, plate, tables)

Statistical study of Mekranotire Kayapó, Shavante, Bororo and Canela subsistence activity and time spent producing goods for market, argues that the more impoverished the soil, the more a tribe will be forced into trading for manufactured goods. (Unfortunately, in their sample, time spent producing market items correlated just as well with length of contact of the culture.)

1120 Harris, Marvin. The Yanomamö and the causes of war in band and village societies (*in* Brazil, anthropological perspectives: essays in honor of Charles Wagley [see item 1081] p. 121–132)

Harris uses Chagnon's data to attack his theory that Yanomamö intervillage politics can be attributed to the villages' desire to preserve their sovereignty. Instead, Harris proposes his theory that warfare can be explained as a population control mechanism

required by increased pressure on the protein supply. See item **1086**.

1121 Hartmann, Günther. Masken der Pau d'Arco-Kayapo, Brasilien (MLV/T, 26, Nov. 1977, p. 103-108, bibl., ill., plates)

Consists of notes on Pau d'Arco masks and the dances they appear in and Kayapó names and their animal-name dance societies. Work is based on Kissenbarth's 1908–09 field notes and masks he collected for the Berlin Ethnographic Museum, and on an unpublished treatise on the Pau d'Arco by Nimuendajú.

1122 Helm, Cecília Maria Vieira. Identidade étnica entre os índios Kaingáng do Paraná (UFP/EB, 4[4]:7, junho 1979, p. 71–91)

After introductory discussion on ethnic identity, article describes the Kaingang of the Posto Apucarana, problems caused by their seasonal harvest employment, and their perception of themselves as Indians in relation to their employers.

1123 ——— and **Jussara Maria Marcondes Carneiro.** O Projeto Kaingáng (UFP/EB, 3[3]:6, 1978, p. 207–213, bibl.)

Describes 1975 Kaingáng Indians Project which generated the following proposals (never put into effect by FUNAI): reducing the Indians' economic dependence on labor which interfered with their own subsistence activities, ending the encroachment on Indian lands by outside enterprises, and encouraging development of native leadership. See also items **1172** and **1179**, and *HLAS 41:1183*.

Hemming, John. Red gold: the conquest of the Brazilian Indians. See *HLAS 42:3581*.

1124 Henley, Paul and **Marie-Claude Mattéi-Müller.** Panaré basketry: means of commercial exchange and artistic expression (FSCN/A, 49, 1978, p. 29–130, ill., map, plates, tables)

Thorough and interesting study of development of production of decorative baskets for commercial sale. Details effects of this development on Panaré communities involved, and on quality of basketry and relationship of Panaré artisans to their work. Authors' slightly updated Spanish version is entitled: *Wapa, la comercialización de la artesanía indígena y su innovación artística* (Caracas: Litografía Technicolor, 1978) and contains beautiful illustrations of 121 basket designs and of the basket-weaving process.

1125 Herrera Angel, Leonor. El nacimiento de los Matapi (ICA/RCA, 20, 1976, p. 201–280, bibl., figure)

Version of a culture-hero epic which explains the origin of many natural and cultural features with commentary on the myth's form, and ecology, and cosmology implicit in it.

1126 The Héta Indians: fish in a dry pond. Vladimír Kozák; David Baxter; Laila Williams; and Robert L. Carneiro. New York: American Museum of Natural History, 1979. p. 351–434; bibl., ill. (Anthropological papers of the American Museum of Natural History; v. 55, pt. 6 0065-9452)

Valuable and careful documentation of Heta economic activities and material culture assembled by Baxter and Williams from Kozák's notes and photographs of 20 visits in 19 years to this small, Tupi-speaking hunting and gathering group, "before the disappearance of the Heta and their culture." Includes 65 fine photographs, some of which document the manufacture and use of stone tools. Closes with observations by Junius Bird on their weaving.

1127 Hildebrand, Elizabeth R. von. La manufactura del budare entre la tribu Tinimuka: Amazonia, Colombia (ICA/RCA, 20, 1976, p. 177–200, ill., plates)

Describes "the technique of constructing a *budare*, a high-sided [ceramic] griddle for toasting *casabe* [manioc cakes] . . . and some of the associated conceptions, values and cosmological visions, showing how for an Indian woman to make a budare is to make an object which reflects the whole of her culture, representing it and obligating her to follow it."

1128 Hill, Jonathan. Kamayurá flute music; a study of music as meta-communication (Ethnomusicology [Society of Ethnomusicology, Middletown, Connecticut] 23 : 3, Sept. 1979, p. 417–432, bibl., figures)

Secondary study based on published accounts of Xingú ritual and Kamayurá music (see item **1074**) and on a few selections from one published record of Xingú music. This small sample of music supports a rather elaborate structural analysis of symbolic relationship among musical instruments, their melodies, and ceremonies that include them.

1129 Hugh-Jones, Christine. From the Milk River: spatial and temporal processes in northwest Amazonia. Cambridge: Cambridge University Press, 1979. 302 p.; ill.; index (Cambridge studies in social anthropology; 26)

Analyzes conceptual structure of Vaupés Tucanoan society and cosmology, beginning with fivefold hierarchical series of sib specializations within phratries (chiefs, dancers, warriors, shamans and servants). Author correlates them with series of same-generation kin terms and with major modes of social relations both within clans and on an interclan level. The child's birth and social development constitute a central metaphor which links these social processes with Vaupes (particularly Barasana) cosmology, in a symbolic analysis of cosmological imagery and space-time dimensions which offers interesting comparisons to Reichel-Dolmatoff's controversial suggestions on Desana cosmology. An interesting feature is the analysis of the symbolic meaning of the process of manioc preparation. An important contribution to structural theory.

1130 Hugh-Jones, Stephen. The palm and the Pleiades: initiation and cosmology in northwest Amazonia. Cambridge: Cambridge University Press, 1979. 332 p.; 2 leaves of plates; bibl.; ill.; index (Cambridge studies in social anthropology; 24)

Detailed description and exegesis of the Barasana Yurupari (*he*) initiation rite, in which author participated, and related rites, with an analysis that systematically relates them to myths, in a "test" of Lévi-Strauss' *Mythologiques*. Ancestors and mythic times, cyclicity, menstruation and rebirth of initiates are central referents of the ritual symbolism.

1131 Indianidad y descolonización en América Latina: documentos de la Segunda Reunión de Barbados. México: Editorial Nueva Imagen, 1979. 407 p.; bibl.; maps (Serie interétnica)

Following the 1st Barbados Conference of Anthropologists (1971) which produced the important Declaration of Barbados (see *HLAS 37 : 1400* and *HLAS 39 : 1391*) a second conference was held in July 1977, which also included indigenous and indigenist leaders. The "Documents" of the conference include statements of problems and programs by leaders of indigenous movements including

CRIC (see item **1132**) and Ecuador's Shuar Federation's and statements by indigenous community leaders in various countries, and descriptions of projects, and analyses by anthropologists.

1132 Indígenas y represión en Colombia. Juan Friede et al. Bogotá: Centro de Investigación y Educación Popular, 1979. 93 p. (Serie Controversia; no. 79 [i.e. 80])

Report on the condition of Indians in Colombia focuses on the Consejo Regional Indígena del Cauca (CRIC), with articles by anthropologists, indigenists and CRIC leaders. Juan Friede and Orlando Fals-Borda sketch CRIC's development in historical context, Adolfo Triana discusses new "indigenous statute," and other articles describe assassinations and imprisonments of CRIC leaders, current state of the organization and the situation it confronts.

1133 Jackson, Jean. Bará zero generation terminology and marriage (Ethnology [Plenum, New York] 16:1, Jan. 1977, p. 83–104, bibl., figures, maps, tables)

Sketch of componential analysis of cousin terms of the Bará relates them to marriage patterns. They are analyzed from three perspectives considered as three intersecting semantic domains: genealogical, alliance and sociogeographic distance. Matrilateral/patrilateral distinctions implicitly recognize a third group, not directly involved in marriage exchange (affines of affines) who are of maximum social, geographic and linguistic distance.

1134 ———. Language identity of the Colombian Vaupés Indians (in Explorations in the ethnography of speaking. Edited by R. Bauman and J. Sherzer. Cambridge, England: Cambridge University Press, 1974, p. 50–64, bibl., maps, tables)

Discusses Vaupés multilingualism and social organization, concentrating on the social importance of languages as badges of social identity and markers of kin-group membership.

1135 ———. Recent ethnography of indigenous northern lowland South America (Annual Review of Anthropology [Palo Alto, California] 4, 1975, p. 307–340, bibl.)

Definitive review of social anthropological research in the Amazon and Orinoco Basins, covering 264 items from 1960 to

1973. Covers items in English, French, Spanish and Portuguese.

1136 ———. Vaupés marriage: a network system in the Northwest Amazon (in Regional analysis. v. 2, Social systems. Edited by Carol A. Smith. New York: Academic Press, 1976, p. 65–93, bibl., figures, maps, tables)

Integrative view of multilingual regional society of the Vaupés, stressing interconnectedness of varied language groups. Lineages and sibs (language groups), grouped into exogamous phratries, are scattered among affinally related groups in "neighborhoods" along rivers. Regional analysis focuses on network of marriage links and the clustering of such links between certain groups within each other's "field of movement."

1137 Jank, Margaret. Culture shock. Chicago: Moody Press, 1977. 208 p.

Missionary account describes process of deculturating Yanomamö Indians in years of missionary work, but also provides scattered ethnographically useful information about the same villages where William Smole (see *HLAS 39:1388*) did his field work. Offers a variety of human interest information about Yanomamö life not usually given in ethnographies.

1138 Johnson, Orna R. The social context of intimacy and avoidance: a videotape study of Machiguenga meals (Ethnology [Plenum, New York] 19:3, July 1980, p. 353–366, bibl., chart, table)

Videotape study during field work reveals that most food exchanges at Machiguenga meals are between spouses or between unmarriageable kinsmen, almost never between opposite sex cross cousins, potential sex partners, in accordance with the rule of avoidance between relatives of this category.

Jouanen, José. Los jesuítas y el Oriente ecuatoriano, 1868–1898: Monografía histórica. See *HLAS 42:3048.*

1139 Kloos, Peter. The Akuriyo of Surinam: a case of emergence from isolation. Copenhagen: IWGIA, 1977. 1 v.; bibl. (IWGIA document; 27)

Documents contact of this hunter-gatherer group (1968–71) and the problems of adaptation to settled agricultural village life. High mortality is traced to change in diet and life style as well as influenza. Factors undermining traditional male role have promoted assimilation to Trio culture. Points out crucial services which missionaries provide as well as culturally disruptive aspects of evangelization.

1140 Kracke, Waud H. Amazonian interviews: dreams of a bereaved father (Annual of Psychoanalysis [Yale University Press, New Haven, Connecticut] 8, 1980, p. 249–267, bibl.)

Presents series of depth interviews with Kagwahiv Indian father who had recently lost two children and traces the mourning process. Notes instances when ethnographer's countertransference and cultural presuppositions temporarily impeded communication.

1141 ———. Dreaming in Kagwahiv: dream beliefs and their psychic uses in an Amazonian Indian culture (in Psychoanalytic study of society. v. 8. Edited by Warner Muensterberger; Aaron Esman; and L. Bryce Boyer. New Haven, Connecticut: Yale University Press, 1979, p. 119–171, bibl.)

Sketches complex set of dream beliefs among the Kagwahiv (Parintintin) and shows how dreamers use dream beliefs to describe and explain their dreams and to deal with emotional conflicts expressed in them. Shows how dream beliefs explain the phenomena of dreaming, and how different individuals habitually use different beliefs selected from a complex system. Based on indepth interviews carried out during field work.

1142 ———. Force and persuasion: leadership in an Amazonian society. Chicago: University of Chicago Press, 1978. 322 p.; 4 leaves of plates; bibl.; ill.; index.

Fieldwork-based account of leadership among the Kagwahiv (Parintintin) Indians, combines psychological and social anthropological research strategies in order to explain the nature of leadership and its relationship to Kagwahiv social structure. Social analysis includes discussion of norms of leadership, and structural basis for leader's power in uxorilocal residence and bride service. Psychological analysis, based on depth interviews with leaders and followers, probes emotional satisfactions and tensions in leader-follower relationships, as well as motives and personality characteristics of successful and unsuccessful leaders. Suggests that flexible norms stress consensual leadership but permit emergence of strong, authoritarian leaders in time of crisis.

1143 ———. Uxorilocality in patriliny: Kagwahiv filial separation (Ethos [Society for Psychological Anthropology, Washington, D.C.] 4:3, Fall 1976, p. 295–310)

Examination of the problem of dystonicity in the Kagwahiv social organization in which uxorilocal residence is combined with patrilineal moieties, as in many societies in lowland South America (see HLAS 41:1158), showing how, in Kagwahiv society, uxorilocal residence provides a basis for authority (see item **1101**). An account of one marriage which deviates from the pattern suggests that uxorilocality also helps young men to separate from their parents and attenuate Oedipal ties.

1144 Laming-Emperaire, Annette and **Luisa María Gutiérrez Amaro.** L'Amérique australe (in Anthropologie régionale. v. 2, Asie, Amérique, Mascareignes. Edited by Jean Poirier. Paris: NFF - Gallimard, 1978, p. 1714–1864)

Survey of cultures of southern South America. Brief introduction by Annette Laming-Emperaire comments on historical sources that are the primary basis for this section. Gutiérrez Amaro's "Les Indiens du Bassin Moyen et Inférieur du Rio de la Plata" (p. 1722–1797) covers an area extending from the Chaco to Uruguay and Rio Grande do Sul, reconstructs the cultures of "canoe Indians," Chaco "foot Indians," and (briefly) Arawakan horse-riding tribes. Laming-Emperaire's "Chile and Argentina" (p. 1798–1864) deals with Atacameñans, hunters of Patagonia and Tierra del Fuego and southern Argentina, the Araucanians, and some cultures of the Argentine Chaco, closing with the extermination of the last.

1145 Langdon, E. Jean. Siona clothing and adornment, or, you are what you wear (in Fabrics of culture: anthropology of clothing and adornment. Edited by Justine Cordwell and Ron Schwartz. The Hague: Mouton, 1979, p. 298–307, bibl., ill., plates)

Siona *cusmas*, decorated with patterns, represented an attempt to emulate the powerful *yagé* people encountered in *yagé*-induced visions. Adoption of Western clothing represents a change in perception of the locus of "power" in the universe.

1146 ———. The Siona hallucinogenic ritual: its meaning and power (*in* Understanding religion and culture: anthropological and theoretical perspectives. Edited by John H. Morgan. Washington, D.C.: University Presses of America, 1979, p. 58–85, notes)

Vivid account effectively integrates Siona religious beliefs and experience. Presented in terms of Geertz's model of religion as a cultural system, article argues that hallucinogenic ritual convincingly dramatizes the spiritual "other side" of reality. Visions produced by *yagé* (banisteriopsis) in a ritual allow the shaman to enter the "other side," where, using his *dau* (substance of knowledge of power) he negotiates with spirits to preserve or restore the health of the patient or the world.

1147 ———. Yagé among the Siona: cultural patterns in visions (*in* Spirits, shamans and stars: perspectives from South America. Edited by David Browman and Ron Schwarz. The Hague: Mouton, 1979, p. 63–80, bibl.)

The now declining Siona religion is centered on attaining contact with spirits on four levels of the universe via yagé-induced visions in a ceremony conducted by a master shaman. Training for the shamanic role involves being led by a master shaman through a series of patterned visions, increasing knowledge and power (*dau*) for contacting new spirits. Power may also be damaged in bad visions. A text of each type of vision is presented and analyzed.

1148 Lave, Jean Carter. Cycles and trends in Krīkati naming practices (*in* Dialectical societies [see item **1101**] p. 16–44)

Name transmission has replaced the age-set system as the primary organizing principle of Krīkati society.

1149 Levak, Milena Maselli. Motherhood by death among the Bororo Indians of Brazil (Omega [Journal of death and dying. Baywood Publishing Co., Farmingdale, New York] 10:4, 1979/1980, p. 323–334)

A dying Bororo is tended by his mother—or a consanguineal ritual mother if (as likely) his real mother is dead—and after death. For different views of these institutions, see items **1094** and **1214**. For a similar

paper discusses the psychological as well as social functions of these roles in repairing or undoing the mother-child separation at death. For different views of these institutions, see items **1101** and **1214**. For a similar view of Krahó role, see chap. 6 of item **1098**.

1150 Lisbôa, Thomaz de Aquino. Entre os índios münkü: a resistência de um povo. São Paulo: Edições Loyola, 1979. 83 p.; bibl.; ill. (Coleção Missão aberta; 1)

Vivid chronicle by a culturally sensitive Jesuit father of the contacting and pacification of the Münkü of Western Mato Grosso and the struggles against illness, road builders and bureaucracy in order to achieve a minimum of security and living space for the tribe.

1151 Lizot, Jacques. Le cercle des feux: faits et dits des Indiens Yanomami. Paris: Éditions du Seuil, 1976. 248, 8 p.; bibl.; ill. (Recherches anthropologiques)

Weaves a picture of Yanomamö life with narratives from daily life interspersed with expositions of beliefs, practices and culture patterns. Pt. 1 describes day-to-day life in the shapuno, has chapters on death ("on cinders and tears"), "tales of love," and "women's lives." Pt. 2, "Magical Powers," brings out the relationship between shamans and *hekura* spirits, closing with a shamanic attack on an enemy village ("Devourers of Souls"). Pt. 3, "War and Alliance," relates hunting and warfare. This study provides a very different perspective on Yanomamö life from the familiar one presented by Napoleon Chagnon (item **1085**).

1152 ———. Onomastique Yanomami (L'Homme [Paris] 13:3, 1973, p. 60–71, bibl., charts, tables)

Semantic and social analysis of Yanomamö names. Asserts that names are not secret, but that their public use is prohibited and insulting, especially if the names are those of dead people. Hunters also avoid uttering the names of prey species, which would alarm the prey. See also item **1178**.

1153 ——— and **Hélène Clastres.** La muerte y la idea del canibalismo entre los Yanomami (VMJ/BIV, 18:14, 1978, p. 107–142, plates)

Yanomamö cremation and drinking of the ashes and their prohibition to utter the name of the dead are explained in Hertzian terms as an affirmation of society's continuity and collectivity. Uses myths and details of their practice to show how Yanomamö strain to differentiate themselves from the "cannibalistic" Caribs.

1154 Lobo, Eulália María Lahmeyer. Les Indiens du nord et centre de l'Amérique du Sud (*in* Anthropologie régionale. v. 2, Asie, Amérique, Mascareignes. Edited by Jean Poirier. Paris: NRF, Gallimard, 1978, p. 1449–1547, bibl. [Encyclopédie de la Pléiade; v. 22])

Condensed survey of the Indians of Colombia, Venezuela and the Guianas chiefly based on secondary sources such as Steward's *Handbook of South American Indians*, especially his "Circum-Caribbean Chiefdoms," other publications of the same period, and a few more recent ones.

1155 Lorscheiter, Vendelino. A Igreja e os índios no Brasil: *Pastoral indigenista ontem o hoje* (*in* Colóquio de Estudos Luso-Brasileiros, Tokyo, 1976. Anais. Tokyo: Associação Japonesa de Estudos Luso-Brasileiros, 1976, v. 10, p. 74–104)

Recounts gradual change in Catholic missionary efforts as they evolved from catechization to *conscientização* (consciousness-raising) concludes with the statement of the "Indigenist Missionary Assembly" which proposed a program in defense of Indian lands and self determination. See also item **1176**.

1156 Margolies, Luise and **María Matilde Suárez.** Historia de la etnología contemporánea en Venezuela. Caracas: Universidad Católica Andrés Bello, Instituto de Investigaciones Históricas, Centro de Lenguas Indígenas, 1978. 48 p.; bibl. (Colección de leguas indígenas: Serie menor; 4)

History of recent developments in Venezuelan anthropology. Argues that Acosta Saignes and Johannes Wilbert mark transition from period of "precursors," dominated by Koch-Grünberg and others, to 'la etnología contemporánea.' Discusses work of ethnographers who have worked in Venezuela, concluding with an 11-page bibliography.

1157 Márquez V., María Elena. Los tunebo. Fotografías, Francisco Penagos. Medellín, Colombia: Editorial Copymundo, 1979. 253 p.; 18 leaves of plates; bibl.; ill.

Ethnographic account by Teresite sister who spent 19 years of missionary work among the Tunebo. Simply presented description, sometimes rather abbreviated, includes some detailed information on religious ritual and beliefs such as numerous ritual song texts and several myths, all in translation, in addition to one version of the origin myth in Tunebo with line-by-line translation. Also provides brief notes on family and marriage practices. Presents kin terminology in series of idiosyncratic charts somewhat difficult to follow.

1158 Matta, Roberto Da. The Apinayé relationship system: terminology and ideology (*in* Dialectical societies [see item **1101**] p. 83–127)

Article analyzes relational terminology in terms of the ideology of social relations. The consubstantiality of the nuclear family, expressed in "couvade" food restrictions and kin/affine avoidance, is contrasted with the public, structural character of ceremonial relationships and moiety membership, which are transmitted with names through the mediation of adoptive ritual "parents."

1159 ———. Ofício de etnólogo, ou como ter "anthropological blues" (BRMN/B, 27, maio 1978, p. 1–12)

Anthropology, the transformation of the exotic into the familiar (or in the studies of our own society, of the familiar into the exotic), entails an emotional involvement with the subject of study which includes feelings of loneliness and unexpected human contact, triumphs of discovery which cannot be shared, and nostalgia after departure from the field. This affective process of fieldwork, for which anthropological training does not prepare us, is here encompassed in the phrase "anthropological blues."

1160 Maybury-Lewis, David. Cultural categories of the Central Gê (*in* Dialectical societies [see item **1101**] p. 218–248, bibl.)

Though most Sherente communities are still organized in factions centered on lineages of opposite moieties, exogamy and other moiety functions are largely defunct. Uxorilocal residence is explained as a consequence of assigning the female domestic domain to the periphery in contrast to the central male ceremonial domain. In Central Gê, political opposition is embodied in patrilineal moieties rather than relegated to peripheral domestic groups as in other Gê societies, while integrative forces are provided by age sets.

1161 ———— **and James Howe.** The Indian peoples of Paraguay: their plight and their prospects. Cambridge, Massachusetts: Cultural Survival, 1980. 1 v. (Cultural survival special report; no. 2)

Report on an investigation into the conditions of indigenous peoples of Paraguay, carried out in two brief survey trips (in Nov. 1978 and Jan. 1979, totaling five months). Includes 15-page controversial discussion of earlier allegations of genocide carried out against the Ache by the Paraguayan government (see *HLAS 39:1279*) and a survey of "Indianist organizations" working with indigenes in Paraguay.

1162 Melatti, Júlio Cézar. Estrutura social Marubo: um sistema australiano na Amazônia (Anuário Antropológico [Edições Tempo Brasileiro, Rio de Janeiro] 1976 [i.e. 1977] p. 83–120, bibl., ill., tables)

Preliminary investigation of Panoan Marubo Indians established existence of a system of matrilineally transmitted alternating generation exogamous kin groups. These are compared with the Kariera four-section system of Australia and also with other Panoan systems, notably the Cashinahua system described by Kensinger (see *HLAS 41:1161*) which is even more clearly similar to a Kariera system.

1163 ————. The relationship system of the Krahó (*in* Dialectical societies [see item **1101**] p. 46–79)

Crow terminology matches matrilineal transmission of men's names, but neglects corresponding patrilineal transmission of women's names. Matrilineal name transmission counterbalances uxorilocality by permitting a man to bestow his name on his sister's son, returning his name to his natal household which he himself has left.

1164 Menget, Patrick. Temps de naître, temps d'être: la couvade (*in* La fonction symbolique. Edited by Isard and P. Smith. Paris: Gallimard, 1979, p. 245–264)

"Couvade" (food and work avoidances around birth) is considered in the context of Txicao beliefs about conception, biological development, and health. Author takes issue with Van Gennep's and Malinowski's views of couvade as emulating maternity and af-

firming social paternity: *both* parents observe the restrictions, and so do "cogenitors." Rather, the avoidances help maintain in the child a balance of active or "strong" ("hot") principles by "weak" ("cold") ones, and prevent a dangerous mixing of parent's and child's substances, a separation maintained later on in the parent-child incest taboo. The last point is substantiated by comparing the attitudes expressed in myth toward different kinds of incest.

1165 Migliazza, Ernesto. The integration of the indigenous peoples of the territory of Roraima, Brazil. Copenhagen: International Work Group for Indigenous Affairs, 1978. 29 p.; bibl.; ill. (IWGIA document; 32)

Brief survey of various language groups in the Brazilian territory of Roraima, including Yanomamö, Carib, Arawak, Uruak and Maku speakers, and their situation vis-à-vis land development, road building and other pressures of expanding national society (see also item **1199**).

1166 Miller, Elmer S. Harmony and dissonance in Argentine Toba society. New Haven, Connecticut: Human Relations Area Files, 1980. 167 leaves; bibl.; ill. (Ethnography series. HRAFlex books; SI12-001)

Description, based on extensive fieldwork, of a Toba revitalistic movement, addresses the following questions: "Why did Pentecostalism provide the creative synthesis which sparked the Toba movement when other religions failed?;" and "Why did the movement emerge at this particular time in Toba history?" (p. 6). Also discusses traditional Toba cosmology and shamanism of the "steady-state adaptive system," historical events and economic changes that disrupted the harmonic balance, and successive efforts to restore cosmic and social harmony.

1167 Miller, Tom O., Jr. Tecnologia cerámica dos caingang paulistas. Curitiba, Brazil: Governo do Paraná, Secretaria de Estado de Educação e da Cultura, Diretoria de Assuntos Culturais, 1978. 51 p.; ill. (Arquivos do Museu Paranaense, Nova série: Etnologia; no. 2)

Attempt to identify some non-Tupian archaeological potsherds found in São Paulo led author to investigate pottery-making among the Kaingang. His study, besides cataloguing functions and techniques for producing various types of pottery, confirmed identification of "Casa de Pedra" ware as ancestral Kaingang.

1168 Moser, Rudolf. Zur heutigen Lage der Indianer in brasilianisch-Amazonien (SSA/B, 43, 1979, p. 7–20, map, plates)

Thoughtful overview of current situation of Amazonian Indians in Brazil based on critical review of Brazilian daily press. Discusses recently contacted groups, the role of FUNAI and religious missions, recent threats to the integrity of Xingú Park, and, in special detail, issue of "emancipation" (i.e., termination of reservations for Indians). Author mentions a visit to a Shavante village (see also items **1066** and **1096**).

1169 Murphy, Robert F. Lineage and lineality in lowland South America (*in* Brazil, anthropological perspectives: essays in honor of Charles Wagley [see item **1081**] p. 217–224)

Argues that lack of genealogical depth in South American Lowland societies limits or precludes development of African-style lineages, perhaps because land is a relatively free (not scarce) resource (see also items **1101** and **1198**).

1170 Myazaki, Nobue; Helda Bullotta Barracco; and Yolanda Lhullier dos Santos. Elementos simbólicos na cerâmica, tortuais e trançados do Alto Rio Xingú, Estado de Mato Grosso (MP/R, 25, 1978, p. 31–46, bibl., ill.)

Brief exegesis of designs on baskets, storage jars and spindles among the Yawalapití, Kamayurá, and Waurá, based on brief field work.

1171 Nimuendajú, Curt. The Šerente. Translated, from the manuscript, by Robert H. Lowie. New York: AMS Press, 1979. 106 p.; 4 leaves of plates; bibl.; ill.

While this classic account of the Sherente has been corrected by Maybury-Lewis, who found them uxorilocal instead of patrilocal (see item **1160**), the work of the founder of Brazilian anthropology should be kept available. Its reissue in the same year as the Harvard Gê Project's report which is dedicated to him, is timely.

1172 Oliveira, João Pacheco de. O projeto Tükuna: uma experiência de ação indigenista (BRMN/B, 34, nov. 1979, p. 1–39, bibl.)

Account of one of six action projects

undertaken by FUNAI in brief period of diligence (1975–77). Project used model of indigenist action, elaborated in the publication, stressing indigenous involvement in decision making and execution of project plan. By revising originally envisaged project down to certain restricted goals, project was able to achieve some success before FUNAI's policy reversal withdrew support from pro-Indian action projects (see also items **1123** and **1179**).

1173 Oliveira, Roberto Cardoso de. A sociologia do Brasil indígena. 2. ed. Rio de Janeiro: Tempo Brasileiro, 1978. 222 p.; bibl.; ill. (Biblioteca Tempo universitária; 31)

Nine essays (written 1960–69) on problems of contact of indigenous groups with Brazilian national society. First three are based on author's research with Tukuna and urbanized Terêna. Chap. 7 develops model of inter-ethnic friction based on demographically defined contact regions. Others are historical, programmatic or general discussions of the problems.

Paul Rivet, 1876–1976: selección de estudios científicos y biográficos. See *HLAS 42:3052.*

Perrin, Michel. Le chemin des indiens morts: myths et symboles goajiro. See *HLAS 42:1430.*

1174 A Política de genocídio contra os índios do Brasil. Trabalho elaborado por um grupo de antropólogos patriotas brasileiros que não podem revelar os seus nomes por agora, dado o regime fascista existente no Brasil. Lisboa?: Associação de Expresos Políticos Antifascistas, 1976. 42 p.; ill.

Area by area catalogue of conditions and histories of contact of recently contacted tribes in Brazil, by a group of anthropologists who maintain their anonymity, documenting government failures to provide promised and legally required protection for Indian lands, lives and livelihood, with a section on menaces to Xingú Park. Closes with an indictment of corruption and conflict of interest in FUNAI, and of the government's policy of genocide.

Powlison, Paul. Bosquejo de la cultura yagua. See *HLAS 42:1411.*

1175 Price, P. David. Comercio y aculturación entre los nambikuara (III/AI, 37:1, enero/marzo 1977, p. 123–135, bibl.)

Describes Southern Nambicuara system of exchange and problems introduced when they are forced to bargain in order to trade their artifacts for manufactured goods. Concludes with a critique of FUNAI's Artindia program and suggestions for improving it which were carried out by Projeto Nambicuara personnel.

1176 Prien, Hans Jürgen. Indianerpolitik und katolische Mission in Brasilien im 19. und 20. Jahrundert (AIA/I, 3, 1975, p. 155–181, bibl.)

Sketches history of Indian policy and its abuses and injustices dating from Brazil's independence (1822). Describes shift of Catholic missions after Vatican II from a policy of acquiescence and complicity with Indian subjugation to one of active championing of Indian rights (see also item **1155**).

1177 Ramos, Alcida Rita. On women's status in Yanoama societies (UC/CA, 20:1, March 1979, p. 185–187, bibl.)

From the perspective of Sanumá subgroup, among whom she conducted 26 months of field work, Ramos takes issue with Shapiro's and Chagon's portrayal of Yanoama women as subservient, arguing that they take an active part in political life and are respected for their knowledge.

1178 ———. O público e o privado: nomes pessoais entre Sanumá (Anuário Antropológico [Edições Tempo Brasileiro, Rio de Janeiro] 1976 [i.e. 1977] p. 13–38, bibl.)

After outlining Sanumá sib and lineage structure, relates system of names distinguishing "patronymics" (sib and lineage names, after their founders) from "personal names" acquired at birth from an animal killed in a ritual hunt or from a personal characteristic. Personal names are avoided in etiquette, to prevent embarrassment, but not as thoroughly as among other Yanoama groups (see item **1152**). No special avoidance attaches to names of the dead.

1179 ——— and **Kenneth I. Taylor.** The Yanoama in Brazil 1979 and Committee for the Creation of the Yanomami Park. The Yanomami Indian Park, proposal and justification. Copenhagen: International Work Group for Indigenous Affairs (IWGIA), 1979. 1 v.; appendixes; bibl.; maps; plates; tables (IWGIA Document; 37)

Survey of current threats to physical and cultural survival of Yanoama Indian cultures documents effects of disease, community disorganization and depletion of food resources resulting from road construction and illegal mining. Since this survey was written, the situation has deteriorated further due to a massive gold rush in the heart of Yanoama territory in the fall 1980. Document describes how a short-lived action project to aid Yanoama with medical and other assistance was terminated after six months by withdrawal of FUNAI support. Also reviews proposal for an integral Yanomami Park, contrasting it with the inadequate FUNAI proposal for 21 small, separated areas.

1180 Reichel-Dolmatoff, Gerardo. Beyond the Milky Way: hallucinatory imagery of the Tukano Indians. Los Angeles: UCLA Latin American Center Publications, 1978. 159 p.; bibl.; ill.; index (UCLA Latin American studies; v. 42)

Includes color plates of Vaupés Indian paintings, some as executed traditionally on houses or implements, others consisting of pictures of yagé visions drawn on paper by informants (mostly Barasana) for the author, each one with artist's commentary. Accompanying text summarizes the yagé origin myth and describes ritual use of banisteriopsis, the hallucinatory experience, the iconography of traditional designs, and their origins in hallucinatory visions which the author traces to "phosphenes."

1181 ———. Desana animal categories, food restrictions, and the concept of color energies (UCLA/JLAL, 4:2, Winter 1978, p. 243–291, bibl., ill., tables)

Discussion of Desana food classification serves as take-off point for tour of Desana cosmology. Classifications of animals by habitat, color, odor (big game has rank, "estrous" smell related to menstruation), etc., related to edibility, are parallel to classifications of women by clan (marriageability). Rank smelling (sexual) red and black (large) game animals are dangerous to people in conditions of being "cooked," (gestation, sexual maturity) and avoided by them (see item **1129**). These rules also contribute to the population balance of game species, as evidenced by rapid depletion of game in areas where rules have broken down.

1182 ———. Desana Shamans' rock crystals and the hexagonal universe (UCLA/ JLAL, 5 : 1, Summer 1979, p. 117–128, bibl., plates)

Detailed exegesis of the hexagonal crystal which is the source of the Desana shaman's power, identified with the normative order and imbued with transformative power equated with cooking and gestation.

———. The loom of life: a Kogi principle of integration. See *HLAS 42 : 1238.*

1183 Ribeiro, Darcy and **Mary Ruth Wise.** Los grupos étnicos de la Amazonia Peruana. Lima, Perú: Ministerio de Educación: Instituto Lingüístico de Verano, 1978. 237 p.; bibl.; index; map (Comunidades y culturas peruanas; no. 13)

Useful reference work compiled for the missionary group of the Summer Institute of Linguistics. Includes following: 1) map and table providing linguistic classifications or all Indian groups in the Peruvian Amazon; 2) tables of contact situation and demographic statistics for Indian groups of Peruvian Amazon; 3) alphabetical list of these tribes giving for each its location, population, history, present state, the Summer Institute team working with it, and brief bibliographic references (not very complete); 4) comments on the language groups and their interrelations; 5) six-page bibliography; and 6) an index of tribal and language group names.

1184 Roe, Peter G. Aboriginal tourists and artistic exchange between the Pisquibo and the Shipibo: "trade ware" in the ethnographic setting (*in* Trade and transport in lowland South America. Edited by Peter Francis. Calgary, Canada: University of Calgary, Department of Archaeology, 1971, 1 v. [Occasional papers; no. 6])

The Shipibo, sophisticated ceramic artists, acquire Pisquibo pots for their "quaintness" as "primitive" productions by Shipibo standards. The structure of Shipibo and Pisquiboo designs are compared using an approach for design analysis devised by the author.

1185 ———. Archaism, form and decoration: an ethnographic and archaeological case study from the Peruvian montaña (IAS/ÑP, 14, April 1976, p. 78–98, bibl., charts, figures, plates)

Shipibo potter's copying of the form, but not the surface decoration, of an ancient Cumancaya (ancestral Shipibo) ceramic vessel excavated by the author provides the basis for a discussion of artistic innovation through archaism. Roe challenges traditional archaeological assumptions about stylistic borrowing, offering a more complex formulation based on the nature of the ceramic tradition as "art" or "craft."

1186 ———. Art and residence among the Shipibo Indians of Peru: a study in microacculturation (AAA/AA, 82 : 1, March 1980, p. 42–71, ill., plate)

Using method he developed for precise description of stylistic patterns in the highly geometric Shipibo designs, Roe studied mutual stylistic influences among textile artists, the matrilineal and uxorilocal Shipibo, testing comon archaeological hypothesis of mother-daughter transmission of style in female crafts. While, in general, stylistic continuity within a local group corresponded to mother-daughter transmission, an exceptional case of virilocal residence provided the test case which showed that co-residence can sometimes override descent in style transmission.

1187 ———. Marginal men: male artists among the Shipibo Indians of Peru (Anthropologica [Research Center for Amerindian Anthropology, University of Ottawa, Ottawa, Canada] 21 : 2, 1979, p. 189–221, bibl., charts, figures, plates)

Among the uxorilocal Shipibo, textile painting is a female art form. The very few men who practice it do so strictly for the tourist trade and are highly conventional in their designs; their innovation is in choosing the role of artist. Author documents their conventionality by stylistic analysis comparing their designs to women's.

1188 Ruddle, Kenneth. El sistema de auto-subsistencia de los indios yukpa. Caracas: Universidad Católica Andrés Bello, Instituto de Investigaciones Históricas, 1978. 142 p.; bibl.

For English original of this translation, see *HLAS 39 : 1382.*

1189 Salazar, Ernesto. An Indian federation in lowland Ecuador. Copenhagen: IWGIA, 1977. 68 p.; bibl.; ill. (IWGIA document; 28)

History of Shuar (Jívaro and Achuara) contact and an account of the development since 1964 of the earliest and most successful indigenous movement in Northern Lowland South America, the Shuar Federation, recently in the news on account of its conflict with a major film director.

1190 Schindler, Helmut. Los guayabero en el Oriente de Colombia (IAI/I, 3, 1975, p. 127–132)

The Guayabero, decimated 30 years ago by an epidemic, have been increasing in population since 1970 (per field work in 1970–74), but now face problems of invasion of their lands (even guaranteed reservations), dependence on trade, and health.

1191 ——. Informaciones sobre la religión guayabera: Oriente de Colombia)IAI/I, 4, 1977, p. 213–244, map)

Describes the various named supernatural beings that exist in Guayabera belief, the earth and other levels of the cosmos, recounts a series of myths, and closes with the quoted "reflections of a shaman" on Guayabera cosmology vis-á-vis that of missionaries and other whites.

1192 Seeger, Anthony. Os índios e nós: estudos sobre sociedades tribais brasileiras. Capa, AG Comunicação Visual Assessoria e Projeto Ltda., foto do autor. Rio de Janeiro: Editora Campus, 1980. 181 p.; bibl.; ill. (Contribuições em ciências sociais; 6)

Collection of essays, translated from the English and based on author's field work, all but two published for the first time. Introductory reflections on his field work, "Uma Criança no Mundo," are followed by a paper on "The Significance of Body Ornaments" (previously published in English, see *HLAS 39:1385*) which points out the central place held by the faculties of hearing and speaking in Suyá conceptions of thought. An essay on old men explores the bawdy clowning that is part of their role, and an important study of leadership stresses the contrast between secular faction leaders and conciliatory ceremonial leaders. Concludes with remarks on what distinguishes lowland South American social groups from African descent groups, and a useful bibliographic essay on recent South American ethnography.

1193 ——. Nature and society in central Brazil: the Suya Indians of Mato Grosso. Cambridge, Massachusetts: Harvard University Press, 1981. 1 v.; bibl.; charts; maps; tables (Harvard studies in cultural anthropology; no. 4)

Highly important ethnography of a Northern Gê society in the Xingú, stresses the cosmological opposition between nature and society ("animals and "Suya") as the central organizing principle of the society—an interpenetrating opposition, since nature is a source of power and creativity in society. Senses of hearing, vision and smell are important modalities expressing this opposition, hearing being associated with social virtues and strong smell with power in nature (and also with faction leaders and women). These principles are worked out in the domains of social space and time, the life cycle, kinship, leadership, myths, chants and omens and predictive dream symbols. Association of sexuality with hunting as expressed in some predictive dreams is reminiscent of some of Reichel Dolmatoff's contentions for the Desana.

1194 ——. Por que os indios suyá cantam para as suas irmãs? (*in* Arte e sociedade: ensaios de sociologia da arte. Edited by Gilberto Velho. Rio de Janeiro: Zahar Editores, 1977, p. 34–63, bibl.)

Description and analysis of the Suyá *akia* form, individual songs sung simultaneously in certain ritual contexts, to be heard by the singers' sisters. The place of these songs in ritual explains aspects of their form and Suyá singing style, and is related to the social structure through the hypothesis that music (like love songs in our society) bridges distances in social space.

1195 ——. What can we learn when they sing? Vocal genres of the Suyá Indians of Central Brazil (Ethnomusicology [Society of Ethnomusicology, Middletown, Connecticut] 23:3, Sept. 1979, p. 373–394, bibl., charts)

Discussion of the two major Suyá musical forms, communal *ngere* sung in unison and individual *akia* sung simultaneously, analyzing the musical structure of each type and its relationship to Suyá culture.

1196 —— and **Eduardo Viveiros de Castro.** Resenha bibliográfica: pontos de vista sobre os índios brasileiros; um ensaio bibliográfico (BIB [Boletim Informativo e Bibliográfico de Ciências Sociais, Suplemento de

Dados No. 16, Instituto Universitário de Pesquisas, Rio de Janeiro] 2, 1977, p. 11–35, bibl.)

A general survey of literature on Brazilian Indians, with a 13-page bibliography. Stresses recent work (since about 1960), but not limited to it. Major sections on "basic sources," "the Indians and the state," "cultural materialism," "social organization," "religion and cosmology," and "contact and social change." Excellent in balance and coverage, but especially valuable in relating research on Brazilian Indians to current theoretical and political issues. See also item **1135** and *HLAS 42:63.*

1197 ———— and ————. Terras e territórios indígenas do Brasil (Encontros com a Civilização Brasileira [Rio de Janeiro] 12, June 1979, p. 101–109, bibl.)

Brief discussion of the relations of Brazilian Indian societies with their surrounding territory, stressing diversity of ecological relations with different environments and the general absence of a concept of land as "property" or of circumscribed tribal territory. Discusses effect of confinement by settlers and enterprises and the problems that must be faced to prevent destruction of the Indians.

1198 ————; **Roberto da Matta;** and **Eduardo B. Viveiros de Castro.** A construção da pessoa nas sociedades indígenas brasileiras (BRMN/B, 32, maio de 1979, p. 2–19)

Thematic paper presented in a conference on "The Construction of the Self in Indigenous Societies" organized by Yonne de Freitas Leite and held on 21–23 June 1978, offers a new paradigm to replace inappropriate "African models" in analyzing lowland South American societies. Argues that the focal organizing metaphor of indigenous Brazilian societies is not lineage and ancestors—genealogies are shallow and social groups are defined by shared symbolic properties—but the person, in both bodily and social aspects. "The concepts of name and substance, soul and blood, predominate over an abstract language of rights and duties." Physiological processes, names and bodily adornment are key vehicles for expressing the social order and its relationship with nature. For additional symposium papers illustrating these themes, see items **1084, 1097** and **1215.**

1199 **Shapiro, Judith.** Sexual hierarchy among the Yanomama (*in* Sex and class in Latin America: women's perspectives on politics, economics and the family in the Third World. Edited by June Nash and Helen Icken Safa. Brooklyn, New York: J.F. Bergen Publishers, Inc., 1980, p. 86–101, index)

Discussion of the role of women in Yanomamö society, based on field work, and argues that the society promotes a higher level of integration among men than women (e.g., in the highly articulated relations between brothers-in-law and in more highly formalized male roles in ritual). The closest female relationships are those between mother and daughter, who are separated on the daughter's marriage; also women, are peripheral in ritual. Article stresses importance of comparative study of sexual hierarchy.

1200 ————. The Tapirapé during the era of reconstruction (*in* Brazil, anthropological perspectives: essays in honor of Charles Wagley [see item **1081**] p. 61–85)

Briefly traces the contact history of the Tapirapé, "one of the best documented groups in Brazil," and thoughtfully analyzes the relationships between the Tapirapé and neighboring Indian tribes (especially the Karajá), local Brazilians, several anthropologists who have visited them, and the Little Sisters of the Poor. Discusses the effects of each group on the cultural vitality of the Tapirapé.

1201 **Smith, Richard Chase.** The multinational squeeze on the Amuesha people of central Peru. Copenhagen: International Working Group for Indigenous Affairs, 1979. 1 v.; bibl.; map; tables (IWGIA document 35)

Documents renewed threat posed by multinational mining firms to Amuesha rights to their land after they successfully disputed a Franciscan mission for land rights. Author's extensive analysis of international economic networks, the national political scene, and Japan's dependence on external sources of minerals provides an unusually broad picture of the source of pressures on a single Amazonian tribe. Appendices discuss relevant national laws.

1202 **Social correlates of kin terminology.** David John Thomas, issue editor. Kenneth M. Kensinger, series editor. Bennington, Vt.: Bennington College, 1978. 1 v. (Working papers on South American Indians; 1)

Consists of six papers—presented at a symposium held by the American Anthropological Association in Houston, Dec. 1977—and concerning systems which, with the exception of the Pemon, have cross-cousin marriage rules and corresponding two-line terminologies. The Pemon separate cross and parallel terms for *same* sex cousins, but not opposite sex ones, thus suppressing affinal relationships. Other papers stress variability and negotiability of kin terms, and Adams emphasizes the contrast of male and female perspectives. The papers are: Kathleen J. Adams' "Barama River Carib Kinship: Brother-Brother and Mother-Daughter, Identity Merging in a Two-Section System" (p. 3–12, bibl.); Gertrude E. Dole's "Pattern and Variation in Amahuaca Kin Terminology" (p. 13–36, bibl.; charts); Robert A. Hahn's "Negotiated Kinship among the Rikbakca" (p. 37–53, bibl.; charts); Orna R. Johnson's "Kinship Decisions among the Machiguenga: the Dravidian System in a Small-Scale Society" (p. 54–62, bibl., chart); David J. Thomas' "Pemon Zero Generation Terminology: Social Correlates" (p. 63–81, bibl.); Kenneth M. Kensinger's "Comments" (p. 82–85).

1203 Stocks, Anthony. Tendiendo una puente entre el cielo y la tierra en alas de la canción: el uso de la música en un ritual alucinógeno de curación en el bajo Huallaga, Loreto, Perú (CAAAP/AP, 2:4, enero 1979, p. 71–100, music, tables)

Describes and analyzes shamanic curing ritual in Lagunas, Eastern Peru, using Van Gennep's classic framework, but with special focus on the communicative significance of the music in it as a "psychological bridge between ordinary and non-ordinary reality." Chart summarizes argument, and 12 songs are reproduced (without words), followed by a musical chart of the range of each song and the scale used in it. Appendix discusses cosmological context of the ceremony. Although this is a study of Amazonian Peruvian folk culture, it is annotated in this section because of the indigenous origin of the ritual.

1204 Studies in hunting and fishing in the neotropics. Raymond B. Hames, issue editor. Bennington, Vt.: Bennington College, 1980. 137 p.; bibl.; ill. (Working papers on South American Indians; no. 2)

Papers selected from a symposium held at the 43rd International Congress of Americanists, Vancouver, Aug. 1979. All stress the abundance of protein sources in Amazonian societies and criticize theories purporting to explain all Amazonian social order on the basis of protein scarcity (see item **1120**). The papers are: William T. Vickers' "An Analysis of Amazonian Hunting Yields as a Function of Settlement Age" (p. 7–30, bibl., graph, table); Raymond B. Hames' "Game Depletion and Hunting Zone Rotation among the Ye'kwana and Yanomamö of Amazonas, Venezuela" (p. 31–66, bibl., map, graphs, tables); Stephen Beckerman's "Fishing and Hunting by the Barí of Colombia" (p. 67–109, bibl., graphs, tables); Napoleon Chagnon's "Highland New Guinea Models in the South American Lowlands" (p. 112–130, bibl.); and Bernard Nietshmann's "The Limits to Protein" (p. 132–137, bibl.).

1205 Taylor, Kenneth I. Body and spirit among the Sanumá (Yanoama) of North Brazil (*in* Pre-Congress Conference on Medical Anthropology, Stritch School of Medicine, 1973. Medical anthropology. Edited by Francis X. Grollig, Harold B. Haley. The Hague: Mouton; Chicago: distributed in the USA and Canada by Aldine, 1976, p. 27–48, bibl. [World anthropology])

Describes the animal *hekula* spirits which aid Sanumá shamans, emphasizing their helpful and cooperative nature.

1206 ———. Sistemas de classificação e a ciência do concreto (Anuário Antropológico [Edições Tempo Brasileiro, Rio de Janeiro] 1976 [i.e. 1977] p. 121–148, bibl., tables)

Contrasts the "arranging classification" of the Sanumá hierarchical taxonomy of fauna with the "codifying classification" of the Tukuna totemic clan system, and criticizes Lévi-Strauss' confusion of the two in his discussion of the "science of the concrete."

1207 Thomas, David John. Demografía, parentesco y comercio entre los indios pemón: pt. 3, Comercio (VMJ/BIV, 18:15, enero/junio 1979, p. 99–154, bibl., tables)

Last part of three-part article (for pt. 2, "*Parentesco*," see *HLAS 41:1201*) presents author's University of Michigan dissertation in Spanish translation. Detailed account of Pemon income-producing activities and trade with their neighbors, noting items traded and social aspects of trade partnerships and distribution. Values are established by tradi-tional equivalences, not by supply and demand, (which only affects intensity of trade) nor by labor value.

1208 ———. Sister's daughter marriage among the Pemon (UP/E, 18:1, Jan. 1979, p. 61–70)

Sister's daughter marriages are re-garded as verging on incestuous among the Pemon, but are practiced as a limiting case. Their advantage is minimization of obliga-tions to the wife's father, who is also sister's husband.

Torre López, Fernando. Notas etnográficas sobre el grupo anti o campa de la Amazonía peruana. See *HLAS 42:1416.*

1209 Turner, Terence. The Gê and Bororo societies as dialectical systems: a gen-eral model (*in* Dialectical societies [see item **1101**] p. 147–178, bibl.)

Uxorilocal residence offers an effective by limited range means for a man to achieve dominance over another (his son-in-law) in the absence of land scarcity (see items **1142** and **1143**). It is the formal principle through which dominance is exercised by older men over younger ones, mirrored at a higher structural level in the age-grade hierarchy. The moiety systems which pervade Gê so-cieties are interpreted as superstructural inte-grating institutions which reflect and order the same principles of control, and the trek as a situation in which such control can be demonstrated.

1210 ———. Kinship, household and com-munity among the Kayapó (*in* Dialec-tical societies [see item **1101**] p. 179–218, bibl.)

Details process of separation from natal family and integration into procreative family for both sexes. Describes the man's coming under his father-in-law's dominance and ultimately dominating his own sons-in-law, showing how the age-graded series of Kayapó moieties model and determine these processes. Naming by "marginal relatives" (mother's brother, etc.) is shown to be a transformation of primary intra-family rela-tionships of the natal family into inter-family relationships of the procreative family.

1211 Vásquez, Juan Adolfo. The present state of research in South American

mythology (IAHR/N, 25:3, Dec. 1978, p. 240–276)

Excellent region-by-region review of publications on mythology in South Ameri-can cultures, following Steward's culture area divisions. Curious omission of any refer-ence to Lévi-Strauss' *Mythologiques* may reflect highly ethnographic-folkloristic emphasis. All references are in footnote form; a general bibliography, organized alphabetically, would have enhanced the study's value.

1212 Verswijver, Gustaaf. Séparations et migrations des Mekrãgnoti: groupe Ka-yapo du Brésil Central (SSA/B, 42, 1978, p. 47–59, bibl., map, plates)

Ethnohistorical account of migrations, wars and segmentations since 1900 of the Mẽkranoti Kayapó and process of contact, based on oral accounts by elderly informants and published accounts by *sertanistas* who contacted them. Besides clarifying relation-ships among four current Mẽkranoti Kayapó groups (including Tchukahamai), article pro-vides fascinating reconstruction of growth of factions and the process of village segmenta-tion through 77 years.

1213 Vidal, Lux Boelitz. A pintura corporal entre índios brasileiros (USP/RA, 21:1, 1978, p. 87–94)

Consists of description of significant dimensions of contrast in Kayapó body paint-ing and social states which are marked by body painting, in comparison with two other Gê tribes (Xikrĩ, Xavante) and one Tupi group (Kamayurá).

1214 Viertler, Renate Brigitte. O estudo de parentesco e as práticas de nominação entre os índios borôro: os nomes de caça pela morte de um borôro, iebio-mage (USP/RA, 21, 1. parte, 1978, p. 61–68, bibl.)

Explication of the bestowal and struc-ture of "hunting names" for a deceased Bo-roro, according to the Bororo's own ideology rather than preconceived anthropological kinship concepts—an important project more fully worked out in author's recent book on Bororo villages (see *HLAS 41:1205*). "Kinship" is established not by genealogical ties but through the mediation of "titles" handed down through clans, and through the complex set of substitutions occurring at the death of a Bororo (see also items **1101** and **1149**).

1215 ———. A noção de pessoa entre os bororo (BRMN/B, 32, maio 1979, p. 20–30, bibl.)

Relates Bororo concepts of life force, breath and shadow/soul (*aroe*), and various categories of name which a Bororo bears, with their concept of person. Part of symposium on "The Construction of the Person in Indigenous Societies" (see item **1198**).

1216 Wagner, Erika and **Walter Coppens.** Sexta bibliografía antropológica reciente sobre Venezuela (FSCN/A, 45, 1976, p. 71–85)

This sixth installment in annual series of bibliographies of recent anthropological publications on Venezuela, covers books published 1976–78. Includes separate listing of doctoral dissertations. For summary of previous numbers in this series, see authors' "Bibliografía Antropológica" in *Boletín Indigenista Venezolano* (Ministerio de Justicia, Comisión Indigenista, Caracas, 18:15, enero/junio 1979, p. 7–52).

1217 Watson, Lawrence C. and **Maria-Barbara Watson-Franke.** Spirits, dreams and the resolution of conflict among urban Guajiro women (Ethos [Society for Psychological Anthropology, Washington] 5:4, Winter 1977, p. 388–408, bibl.)

Interviews with migrant Guajiro women in Maracaibo, show that manifest dreams are used to resolve personal conflicts arising from the stresses of urban life and the absence of cultural supports. Three cases are summarized in which a dream of a spirit (*yoluha*) proferred a resolution to a conflict (see also item **1141**).

1218 Watson-Franke, Maria Barbara. Social pawns or social power? the position of Guajiro women (FSCN/A, 45, 1976, p. 19–39)

Argues that, in matrilineal Guajiro society, the woman plays an active and powerful role in family, lineage and public affairs, and takes an active part in decision making, leadership, and shamanism.

1219 Whitten, Dorothea S. and **Norman E. Whitten, Jr.** Ceramics of the Canelos Quichua (AMNH/NH, 87:8, Oct. 1980, p. 90–99, col. plates)

This thoughtful article on pottery making by Canelos Quichua women describes types of vessels made, techniques for forming and decorating them, and places pottery making within the potter's social, cultural and personal world.

1220 Whitten, Norman E., Jr. Amazonian Ecuador: an ethnic interface in ecological, social and ideological perspectives. Copenhagen: International Working Group for Indigenous Affairs, 1978. bibl., maps, plates (IWGIA document; 34)

Survey of Ecuadorian tropical forest societies sketches their cultures and current situations with respect to the nation's society. Covers jungle Quichua, "Jivaroans" and the Shuar Federation, and smaller groups severely oppressed by petroleum exploration, invasion of settlers, and intensive evangelization by North American missionaries (see item **1224**).

1221 ———. Ecuadorian ethnocide and indigenous ethnogenesis: Amazonian resurgence amidst Andean colonialism. Copenhagen: International Working Group for Indigenous Affairs, 1976. 1 v.; bibl.; maps (IWGIA document; 23)

Account of the struggle of Canelos Quichua swidden agriculturalists against the internal colonialism of Ecuadorian society.

1222 ———. Jungle Quechua ethnicity: an Ecuadorian case study (*in* International Congress of Anthropological and Ethnological Sciences, 9th, Chicago, 1973. Western expansion and indigenous people: the heritage of Las Casas. Editor, Elias Sevilla-Casas. The Hague: Mouton; Chicago: distributed in the USA and Canada by Aldine, 1977, p. 161–191, bibl. [World anthropology])

Discusses ethnic identity of the jungle Quechua and their relations with neighboring peoples, Quechua and non-Quechua, in the context of Ecuadorian internal colonialism.

1223 Wilbert, Johannes. Geography and telluric lore of the Orinoco Delta (UCLA/JLAL, 5:1, Summer 1979, p. 129–150, bibl., plates)

Following brief introduction to Orinoco delta geography and sketch of Warao, describes their "mythical geography" (beliefs about the earth's surface and residences of earth gods) and "mythical ecology" (explanations of seasonal faunal variations and sequences in mythology of man-animal relationships) and "shamanistic geography" to do with acquisition of quartz crystals and other shamanic paraphernalia.

1224 Yost, Jaime A. El desarrollo comunitario y la supervivencia étnica: el caso de los huaorani, Amazonía ecuatoriana. Quito: Instituto Lingüístico de Verano, 1979. 29 p.; bibl. (Cuadernos etnolingüísticos; no. 6)

Description of a project by the Summer Institute of Linguistics missionary organization to organize the Huao community against outside pressures, especially from the discovery of oil on their territory. Stresses the importance of securing adequate land reserves to guarantee continued protein supply. Provides no indication that one of the most intense pressures on Huaorani ("Auca") culture has been that of evangelization by North American missionaries (see item **1220**).

ETHNOLOGY: South America, Highlands

WILLIAM E. CARTER, *Chief, Hispanic Division, Library of Congress*

IN SPITE OF THREATS TO CURTAIL research funds, Andean ethnology continues to flourish. By contrast with 109 items annotated for *HLAS 41* (1979), 181 are annotated here. Although in part this may be due to a change in contributing editors, it also probably reflects an increased level of research and publication in the Andean countries themselves. Bolivia is a case in point; there the number of items annotated has risen from 18 to 54. Increases in the other countries have occurred, but have been far less dramatic. For Ecuador, which one would think would be of almost equal interest to ethnologists, only 14 items have been annotated. And for Chile, Colombia, and Venezuela, there have been even fewer.

The best of the research tends to be more focused than it was in the past. Even where it follows in the tradition of the general community study, it is placed in some specific theoretical framework, as in the case of Billie Jean Isbell's ecologically oriented *To defend ourselves* (item **1363**). An increasing number of studies are interpreting local situations within larger national or international contexts. Thus Taussig (item **255b**) sees devil worship in Colombia's Cauca Valley and Bolivia's tin mines as related to international capitalism, and calls it commodity fetishism; Butterworth (item **252a**) sees urban growth without development as a product of dependent capitalism; Guillet (item **1357**) sees the increase of rural reciprocal labor relationships as a response to the pressures of overexploitation on the part of industrialized countries; Judith María Buechler (item **1252**) sees peasant mestizo markets as directly influenced by government policy and activity; June Nash (item **1279**) sees Bolivian miners as the pawns of dependency and international exploitation; and Campaña and Rivera (item **1338**) see the highland Peruvian agriculturalist as a key, but exploited, factor in the national economy of Peru ever since conquest.

Ethnologists have not been alone in tracing these larger relationships. An important, growing trend has been for representatives of working class and indigenous groups themselves to give descriptions and interpretations of their plight. The most outstanding example presented here is Domitila Barrios de Chungara's *Let me speak* (item **1247**). Collected, transcribed, and edited by Moema Viezzer, a Brazilian anthropologist, Domitila's testimony graphically describes the impact of decisions made at the national and international level on the households and family life of miners. A similar, though less politicized, view may be found in another autobiographical work: *Dos mujeres indígenas* (item **1260**). That we are now being provided such insights speaks well for the impact of female researchers and for the increasing levels of education available to the working classes of the Andes.

Three special topics appear to have been the object of growing interest. There has been increasing realization that native Andean agricultural techniques are both complex and well adapted to the climate and soils in which they are used. Stephen Brush (item **1335**) has published a short, but masterful study of potato varieties in highland Peru, and has given public vent to his concern that professional developers are threatening a unique gene pool of cultigens developed over millenia. Sánchez Farfán (item **1389**), following in the same vein, has documented native potato taxonomies based on size, taste, texture, color, and time of use.

Traditional coca use has been another subject of considerable interest—an understandable response to national and international pressures to control the production and shipment of cocaine. Catherine Allen (item **1328**) has described the ceremonial uses of coca in highland Peru, William Carter and his colleagues have completed two major studies (items **1254** and **1255**) of traditional coca use throughout Bolivia, and a major symposium on coca and cocaine (item **1234**) was held at Lima (July 1979). The proceedings of that conference are testimony to some of the problems plaguing the issue. Most of the papers focus on psychological damage resulting from use, but their conclusions can hardly be taken seriously, for they are marred by an almost total absence of scientific controls and methodology. Some papers purporting to be reports of social science research are little more than diatribes by narcotics control officers. One of the few voices clamoring for objective, physiological research continues to be that of Roderick Burchard (item **1253**).

A third topic of special interest has been the changing nature of the indigenous movement. In Ecuador a new official policy (item **1316**) encourages indigenous leaders to take a direct role in decision making; in Peru (items **1346** and **1347**) the indigenous movement has been seen in its larger political context, and in Bolivia an Aymara Indian (items **1285** and **1286**) has attempted to develop an Amerindian philosophy, and a major symposium has been held on the worthiness of cultural pluralism (item **1273**).

Lamentably, many US and Andean researchers continue to fail to communicate. A large number of publications totally ignore previous and very similar work produced by a small number of Andean research centers and by a handful of independent US researchers. CIPCA in La Paz, the Allpanchis group in Cuzco, and the Instituto de Estudios Peruanos in Lima have been the most outstanding of the Andean groups, and all three have brought new insights to their research by involving native speakers of Aymara and Quechua as researchers. Among US researchers, monographs by Billie Jean Isbell (item **1363**), Ted Lewellen (item **1366**), June Nash (item **1279**), Joseph Bastien (item **1250**), and David Guillet (item **1357**) have already become important, permanent contributions to the literature. The same could be said of a collection of articles produced by the Colombian anthropologists, Gerardo and Alicia Reichel-Dolmatoff, and focussing on the ideologies of the native peoples of Colombia (item **1310**).

Clearly the wave of the future is to move away from the study of strange customs and structures and toward the holistic study of real people in real situations. Cooperation across national boundaries, still in its infancy, will probably increase. And the "specialists" will have to learn that they are accountable to the "natives," for the natives themselves are now part of the research effort.

GENERAL

1225 Association française pour l'étude et la recherche sur les pays andins. La Forêt dans ses confins andins: la ceja de montaña: actes. Du 3e colloque, Association française pour l'étude et la recherche sur les pays andins . . . Grenoble, 3, 4, et 5 déc. 1977. Grenoble: Université des langues et lettres de Grenoble, Centre d'études et de recherches sur le Pérou et les pays andins (C.E.R.P.A.), 1977. 224 p.; 9 leaves of plates; bibl.; ill.

Papers presented at 3rd colloquium of Association Française pour l'Étude et la Recherche sur les Pays Andins (AFERPA). Includes: Philippe et Anne-Marie Descola's "Contacts Inter-Etniques dans l'Oriente Equatorien: un Exemple d'Acculturation Médiatisée;" Gabriel Judde's "La Nature dans l'Oriente Equatorien aux Confins des Cordillères, d'après les Récits de Trois Voyageurs Français au 19ème Siècle;" Abdon Yaranga Valderrama's "Neo-Genocidio y Etnocidio en la Selva Andina;" Carlos Peñaherrera del Aguila's "Características Geográficas de la Ceja de la Selva en el Perú y sus Cambios Ecológicos por Acción del Hombre;" J. Brisseau-Loaiza's "Les Problèmes de la Mise en Valeur du Versant et du Piémont Amazoniens dans le Sud du Pérou;" Baltazar Caravedo Molinari's "La Selva en la Formación del Mercado Nacional Peruano: 1920–1972;" Claude Collin Delavaud's "Esquisse d'un Bilan du Collaque;" and Guy Martinière's "Aux Frontières des Pays Andins: la Politique du Brésil et l'Intégration de l'Amérique Latine."

1226 Bonfil Batalla, Guillermo. Las nuevas organizaciones indígenas: hipótesis para la formulación de un modelo analítico (SA/J, 65, 1978, p. 209–219)

Theoretical discussion of meaning and direction of the indigenous movement. Although one of the models that is most staunchly defended is that of a separate ethnic identity within the framework of a plural society, the argument is simultaneously made that indigenous groups cannot be understood today wthout constant reference to international forces. Author would seem to want us to believe that indigenous groups should, at one and the same time, be both part of and separate from the modern world.

1227 Brush, Stephen B. The environment and native Andean agriculture (III/AI, 40:1, enero/marzo 1980, p. 161–172)

General discussion of the complexity of the traditional Andean agricultural system, accompanied by a statement of concern that the gene pool of basic cultigens such as potatoes is being seriously eroded.

1228 Cadorette, Raimundo. Perspectivas mitológicas del mundo aymara (IPA/A, 10, 1977, p. 115–136)

An approach to Aymara belief systems through the most common of public rituals. Argues that, among the Aymara, "Catholic" rituals have meanings and functions substantially different from those found in the Catholicism of dominant, Western cultures.

1229 Campesinado e indigenismo en América Latina. Enrique Valencia et al. Lima: Ediciones CELATS, 1978. 279 p.; bibl.

Proceedings of symposium sponsored jointly by Centro Latinoamericano de Trabajo Social (CELATS) and Centro Peruano de Estudios Sociales (CEPES) Cuzco, March 1978. Treats four major topics: 1) The indigenous problem and the national problem; 2) Thought on the indigenous problem; 3) Indigenous action; and 4) Class and ethnic identification. Though some papers are excellent, the whole is, as tends to be the case with symposia, uneven.

1230 Gallegos A., Luis. Previsión del clima entre los aymaras (III/AI, 40:1, enero/marzo 1980, p. 135–141)

Short, "folk-wisdom" version of Aymara weather forecasting, based on water levels, vegetative cycles, winds, cloud cover, and the behavior of animals and birds.

1231 García Tamayo, Eduardo. Estructura y función del compadrazgo: dos aproximaciones antropológicas (PUCP/DA, 4, feb. 1979, p. 95–118, bibl., ill.)

Consideration of structural and functional approaches to godparentage, as illustrated by comparative materials from Europe and various parts of Latin America. Particular attention is paid to Bolivian data taken from the writings of Xavier Albó and Hans Buechler. While not a major contribution to general field of fictive kin studies, article can be used as a good Spanish language introduction to the subject.

1232 **Guillet, David.** Land tenure, ecological zone, and agricultural regime in the central Andes (AAA/AE, 8:1, Feb. 1981, p. 139–156)

Through a series of community studies, communal land tenure is found to be associated with grazing and sectorial fallowing, while private land tenure is found to be associated with permanent irrigation, specialized horticulture, and long-term fallowing.

1233 ———. Reciprocal labor and peripheral capitalism in the Central Andes (UP/E, 19:2, April 1980, p. 151–168)

Argues that reciprocal labor is increasing in the central Andes and that this is related, at least in part, to a pattern of over-exploitation imposed by core (i.e.. industrialized countries) in their search for surplus accumulation.

1234 **Inter-American Seminar on Medical and Sociological Aspects of Coca and Cocaine,** Lima, 1979. Proceedings. Edited by F.R. Jeri. Lima: Pacific Press, 1980. 264 p.; bibl.; ill.; indexes; plates; tables.

Papers presented at symposium jointly sponsored by the Pan American Health Office/World Health Organization and the Bureau of International Narcotics Matters of the US Department of State. The quality of the papers is exceedingly uneven and the translations from the Spanish originals abysmal. Reports of laboratory studies, most of which, because of methodological sloppiness, could at the best be called pseudo-science, are honored with the term "research," while reports of ethnographic studies are called simply "national reports." In spite of such serious problems and biases, the book is a must for researchers interested in the coca question.

Kaba, Román. Fish, peasants, and state bureaucracies: the development of Lake Titicaca. See item **6459.**

1235 **Mariscotti de Görlitz, Ana Maria.** Pachamama Santa Tierra: contrib. al estudio de la religión autóctona en los Andes centro-meridionales. Berlin: Mann, 1978. 430 p.; 5 leaves of plates; bibl.; ill.; index; map (Indiana: Beiheft; 9)

Full ethnography and ethnohistory of beliefs and rituals related to the Pachamama. Ranging from Peru to northern Argentina, and from the Chavín horizon to the mod-

ern day, the author exhaustively examines both diachronic and synchronic variations. Though containing relatively little analysis, the work should be considered a basic one for Andeanists.

1236 **Robbins, Michael C.** and **Linda Coffman Robbins.** A stochastic process model of conflict and cooperation in Andean communities (AAA/AE, 6:1, Feb. 1979, p. 134–142, tables)

Using as a base a 1975 article by W.F. Whyte, "Conflict and Cooperation in Andean Communities" authors attempt, through mathematical models, to deduce the future distribution of communities if present trends continue as well as the general nature of overall, long-term processes of community evolution. Of analytic more than ethnographic importance, the Robbins' treatment of the problem is avowedly speculative, but demonstrates the potential that mathematics have to reveal processes obscured by theoretical summaries and abstractions of observed facts.

1237 **Vickers, William T.** Ethnological methods, results, and the question of advocacy in Andean research (LARR, 15:3, 1980, p. 229–239)

Perceptive defense of the legitimacy of advocacy by Andean ethnologists. Vickers argues that most social scientists are less ivory tower than they are believed to be, and through examples demonstrates that the ethnological community study remains a viable approach to problems of sociocultural evolution.

1238 **Wiedemann, Inga.** The folklore of coca in the South American Andes coca pouches, lime calabashes and rituals (DGV/ZE, 104:2, 1979, p. 278–308, bibl., plates)

Naive and superficial treatment of the traditional use of coca. Contains a comparative description of the shape and designs of coca bags through the Andes but no satisfying details on a single one. In all, a very minor addition to the burgeoning literature on use of the leaf.

ARGENTINA

1239 **Cagliotti, Carlos.** Some considerations about the chewing of coca leaf in the

Argentine Republic (in Inter-American Seminar on Medical and Sociological Aspects of Coca and Cocaine, Lima, 1979. Proceedings [see item 1234] p. 137–144)

Alarmist evaluation of the effect of coca chewing on the Argentine population. In the absence of field research, conclusions reached are that coca chewing is harmful to psychological, physical, and social health, and that it is universally considered as drug addiction.

1240 **Consideraciones clínicas** sobre el efecto de la masticación de hoja de coca en el ser humano. Autores, José Antonio et al. s.l.: Instituto de Patología Regional de Salta, 1979? 74 p.; bibl.; ill. (Monografías médicas del I. de P.R.; no. 13)

Report of important research into alleged physiological and psychological effects of coca chewing: 28 chronic chewers were subjected, under clinical conditions, to lengthy battery of tests and observations, and conclusions were reached that coca chewing produces no detectable damage to the organism, no psychic alterations, does not lead to malnutrition, has little effect on the central nervous system, and does not lead to physical dependence.

1241 **Gerula, Ricardo Luis.** Situación, vida y cultura de los indios mapuches. Buenos Aires: Centro de Investigación y Acción Social, 1975. 32 p. (Revista del Centro de Investigación y Acción Social; año 24, no. 241)

Laconic and unsatisfactory description of Argentine Mapuche society and culture. Treatment is uneven, major emphasis being given to beliefs and rituals. Concludes with call for protective measures.

1242 **Whiteford, Scott.** Marginalidad asociacional: los trabajadores temporales y un sindicato (UP/EA, 4:2, 1973/1976, p. 43–52)

Exposition of the disillusionment of migrant cane workers in northwestern Argentina with regards to the cane workers' union. That union, deriving its power from the central government, suffered considerable retrenchment with the fall of Perón.

BOLIVIA

1243 **Albó, Javier.** Khitïpxtansa?, quienes somos?: Identidad localista, étnica y clasista en los aymaras de hoy. La Paz, Bolivia: Centro de Investigación y Promoción del Campesinado, between 1976 and 1979. 52 p.; 1 leaf of plates; bibl.; diagr. (Cuadernos de investigación - CIPCA; no. 13)

Pioneer attempt to document self perception and ethnic identification among the Bolivian Aymara. The point is made that the contemporary Aymara are many things and that their perceptions are multiple. Ethnic pride is seen as growing rather than diminishing.

1244 ———. La paradoja aymara: ¿solidaridad y faccionalismo? (UP/EA, 4:2, 1974/1976, p. 67–109)

Argues that Aymara communal solidarity is born of the coordination of many individual interests. Differential access to strategic resources is seen as the omnipresent motive in factionalism, and factionalism itself is seen to increase with proximity to or involvement in major urban centers. A provocative article.

1245 **Los Aymaras** dentro de la sociedad boliviana. La Paz: Centro de Investigación y Promoción del Campesinado, 1976. 85 p.; bibl.; ill. (Cuadernos de investigación - CIPCA; no. 12)

Papers presented at 1974 conference, held in La Paz, on the role of the aymara in Bolivian society. Includes: Josep M. Barnadas' "Cultura, Alienación, Desalienación;" Mario Montaño A.'s "Panorama de las Culturas Indígenas en Bolivia;" Javier Albó's "La Paradoja Aymara: Comunitario e Individualista;" Eduardo Bracamonte's "Relaciones de la Nación Aymara con la Comunidad Boliviana;" Jimmy Zalles' "La Iglesia Aymara dentro de la Iglesia Boliviana;" Yolanda Bedregal's "Literatura y Arte Aymaras dentro de la Cultura Boliviana; and Paz Jiménez's "Nosotros, los Aymaras, en la Sociedad Boliviana."

1246 **Ayni ruway:** educación y desarrollo en América nativa: evaluación. L. Rojas et al. Cochabamba, Bolivia: s.n., 1978. 93 p. (Ediciones América profunda; 1)

Series of brief essays analyzing the intent and results of the Waykhuli rural development project in the high valley of Cochabamba. Essays are heavy on philosophy and polemics and light on concrete data.

Barnadas, Josep María. Apuntes para una historia aymara. See *HLAS 42:3138.*

1247 **Barrios de Chungara, Domitila** and **Moema Viezzer.** Let me speak!: testimony of Domitila, a woman of the Bolivian mines. Translated by Victoria Ortiz. New York: Monthly Review Press, 1978. 235 p.; ill.

One of the truly exceptional books to emerge from Andean studies in recent years. Consists of personal account of a Bolivian miner's wife, recorded and edited by a Brazilian anthropologist. Domitila Chungara is anything but typical, but her experience encapsulates the multiple problems faced by the Andean masses today.

1248 **Bastien, Joseph William.** Feminine ritualist and symbols in the Andes (BBAA, 40:49, 1978, p. 61–77, bibl.; ill.)

Detailed description of a misfortune/cleansing ritual conducted by a Bolivian Quechua speaking female diviner. Solid ethnography but weak analysis.

1249 ———. Matrimonio e intercambio en los Andes (UP/EA, 8:15, 1979, p. 33–55)

Reports result of analysis of 205 marriages in the hamlets that compose Kaata, in northwestern Bolivian highlands. Marriage is seen as a means for linking households from different ecological zones.

1250 ———. Mountain of the condor: metaphor and ritual in an Andean ayllu. St. Paul: West Pub. Co., 1978. 227 p.; bibl.; ill.; index (Monograph - The American Ethnological Society; 64)

A breakthrough in the study of Andean belief and ritual. Working in the village of Kaata, in the Bautista Saavedra province of Bolivia, Bastien succeeded in discovering and documenting how the local inhabitants relate cosmology to the surrounding terrain, and how metaphysical concepts permeate the productive process.

1251 **Bedregal, Yolanda.** Literatura y arte aymaras dentro de la cultura boliviana (*in* Los aymaras dentro de la sociedad boliviana [see item **1245**] p. 57–72)

Short, superficial article on Aymara art forms. Of greatest value and interest are the few poems that are reproduced.

Beltrán, Heredia, Augusto and others. Carnaval de Oruro: Tarabuco y Fiesta del Gran Poder. See *HLAS 42:1039.*

1252 **Buechler, Judith-Maria.** The dynamics of the market in La Paz, Bolivia (UA, 7:4, Winter 1978, p. 343–359, maps)

Capsule analysis of changes in the La Paz marketing system over a 10-year period. The market is seen as a system in constant flux and as one directly affected by government policy and activity. Important article for an understanding of markets in the Andes.

1253 **Burchard, Roderick E.** On coca chewing and the polycythemia hypothesis (UC/CA, 21:1, Feb. 1980, p. 108–109)

Research note suggesting, on the basis of new data from highland Bolivia, that the chewing of coca leaf does not protect Andean peoples living under the hypoxic conditions of high altitudes from polycythemia. Note is challenged by Andrew Fuchs of the University of Pennsylvania's Department of Anthropology.

1254 **Carter, William E.** and **Mauricio Mamani P.** Traditional use of coca in Bolivia. La Paz, Bolivia: Museo Nacional de Etnografía y Folklore, 1978. 269 p.; bibl.; tables.

Report based on random sample of 2991 households living in Bolivia's five highland departments. The amount of coca needed for traditional consumers in these departments is estimated as 11,164,482 kilograms, greater than the production estimates that existed at the time the study was carried out.

1255 ———; ———; **José V. Morales;** and **Philip Parkerson.** Coca in Bolivia. La Paz, Bolivia: Tutapi, 1980. 762 p.; appendixes; bibl.; tables.

Results of 30 months of research on traditional coca use, encompassing seven community case studies and a nationwide survey that was statistically representative of 96 percent of Bolivia's rural and small town dwellers. The most exhaustive study of traditional coca use to date.

1256 ———; **Philip Parkerson;** and **Mauricio Mamani P.** Traditional and changing patterns of coca use in Bolivia (*in* Inter-American Seminar on Medical and Sociological Aspects of Coca and Cocaine, Lima, 1979. Proceedings [see item **1234**] p. 159–164)

Disjointed article, cut and pasted from

a larger report without authors' permission, describing incidence of use, socialization to use, reasons for use, levels of use, and reactions to programs of control.

1257 Centro de Investigación y Promoción del Campesinado. Coripata, tierra de angustias y cocales. Equipo CIPCA. La Paz: Centro de Investigación y Promoción del Campesinado, 1977. 192 p.; 8 leaves of plates (6 fold.); bibl.; ill. (Cuadernos de investigación - CIPCA; 15)

Descriptive study focusing on social structure, patterns of production, and linkages with the larger society. Agents of change such as unions, schools, churches, and "narcotics" control are treated realistically and seen as part of the total picture.

1258 ———. Yungas, los "otros" Aymaras: diagnóstico económico-socio-cultural de Sud Yungas. Equipo CIPCA. La Paz: Centro de Investigación y Promoción del Campesinado, 1976. 79 p.; 4 fold. leaves of plates; bibl.; maps (Cuadernos de investigación - CIPCA)

Generalized statements and analyses regarding the economic and social structure of Sud Yungas. Monograph's basic value lies in the fact that it was prepared by a team that had intimate knowledge of altiplano Aymara society. On the basis of that knowledge, constant and convincing comparisons are made.

1259 Dandler H., Jorge. Campesinado y reforma agraria en Cochabamba, 1952–1953: dinámica de un movimiento campesino en Bolivia. La Paz: Centro de Investigación y Promoción del Campesinado, 1975. 40 p.; 3 leaves of plates; bibl.; ill. (Cuadernos de investigación - CIPCA; 9)

Cursory review of events leading up to and following the Revolution of 1952, with special emphasis on activities of peasant leaders. Author has given much fuller treatment to the subject in previous publications.

1260 Dos mujeres indígenas. México: Instituto Indigenista Interamericano, 1976. 184 p.; 2 leaves of plates; ill. (Serie Antropología social; 14)

Welcome addition to the sparse bibliography on Latin American working class women. The story of Basilia, a Quechua speaking mining woman, was collected by June Nash and that of Facunda, a Chiriguano Chaco dweller of northern Argentina, by Manuel María Rocca. Most of the book is in the words of the women themselves, though the first chapters of the Basilia section are biographical reconstruction and interpretation by June Nash. Includes a translation from English of Basilia by J. Nash.

1261 Eckstein, Susan. El capitalismo mundial y la revolución agraria en Bolivia (UNAM/RMS, 41[41]:2, abril/junio 1979, p. 457–478, bibl.)

Historical analysis of Bolivian economic development since 1952. The revolution of that year is seen as opening the floodgates for foreign penetration and control, and the country is seen today as at least as dependent and marginal as it had been before. Although marred by some questionable judgments of a general nature, the article does present a convincing argument that both internal and external forces have contributed to Bolivia's continuing dependency and marginality.

1262 Fortún, Julia Elena. Integración o coexistencia cultural? (in Mesa Redonda sobre Expresiones de la Cultura Boliviana en el Lapso 1925–74, La Paz, Bolivia, 1975. Dualismo o pluralismo cultural en Bolivia [see item **1273**] v. 1, p. 99–113)

Proposes political and economic integration but at the same time maintenance of a culturally plural society.

1263 Girault, Luis. La cultura kallaway (in Mesa Redonda sobre Expresiones de la Cultura Boliviana en el Lapso 1925–74, La Paz, Bolivia, 1975. Dualismo o pluralismo cultural en Bolivia [see item **1273**] v. 1, p. 59–72)

Important contribution to our understanding of the nature and role of the Kallawaya. Author questions their antiquity, yet offers evidence that they once had a distinct language.

1264 Grieshaber, Erwin P. Survival of Indian communities in nineteenth-century Bolivia: a regional comparison (JLAS, 12:2, Nov. 1980, p. 223–269, tables)

For period 1838–77, compares persistence of Indian communities in departments of La Paz, Oruro, and Potosí with their decline in department of Cochabamba. Attributes difference to altiplano's low agricultural potential and Cochambamba

Valley's high cash crop potential. Ignores crucial variables of population density.

1265 Harris, Olivia. Laymis y machas: temas culturales del norte Potosí (*in* Mesa Redonda sobre Expresiones de la Cultura Boliviana en el Lapso 1925–74, La Paz, Bolivia, 1975. Dualismo o pluralismo cultural en Bolivia [see item **1273**] v. 1, p. 73–83)

Concise, informative article that not only adds an important dimension to the ethnography of Potosí, but that addresses the knotty historical problems of the quechuaization of Aymara speaking populations.

1266 ——— and Javier Albó. Monteras y guardatojos: campesinos y mineros en el norte de Potosí. La Paz, Bolivia: Centro de Investigación y Promoción del Campesinado, 1976. 77, 15 p.; bibl.; ill. (Cuadernos de investigación - CIPCA; no. 7)

Unusual study, comparing and contrasting peasants and miners both structurally and in terms of social protest movements and reforms. Although brief, atheoretical, and published in an ephemeral format, the monograph constitutes something of a breakthrough in our understanding of rural Bolivian society.

1267 Heath, Dwight B. Justicia de contrabando: los juzgados revolucionarios de los campesinos bolivianos (UP/EA, 4:2, 1974/1976, p. 53–58)

Documents alienation of Bolivia's rural population from the national court system. Argues that a dual legal system, whereby rural disputes are mostly handled locally, has grown since the 1952 Revolution.

1268 Iriarte, Gregorio. El cooperativismo y la comunidad indígena: crítica al cooperativismo desde una perspectiva aymara. La Paz, Bolivia: Puerta del Sol, 1979. 97 p.; bibl. (Colección Luces y sombras; 2)

Proposes the thesis that cooperativism should adjust to traditional structures of mutual help found in indigenous communities, and not viceversa. Presentation is marred by lack of knowledge of published sources, by lack of detailed analysis of customs described, by a great deal of spurious history, and by a lack of specificity in describing how the cooperative movement can accommodate itself to indigenous traditions.

1269 Larson, Brooke. Rural rhythms of class conflict in eighteenth-century Cochabamba (HAHR, 60:3, Aug. 1980, p. 407–430, map, tables)

Major article on peasant-landlord relations in 18th-century Cochabamba. Comparisons are made with central Mexico, and the conclusion is reached that opportunitites for profit were far greater there than they were in Cochabamba. The Cochabamba elite perceived their land to be not so much a factor of production as a source of rent, collateral, and unremunerated labor.

1270 Léons, Madeline Barbara. Race, ethnicity, and political mobilization in the Andes (AAA/AE, 5:3, Aug. 1978, p. 484–494)

On the basis of a case study of blacks, Indians, and *mistis* in the Yungas region of Bolivia, the conclusion is reached that ethnicity is emphasized when it can lead to extralocal support. Because such support is not available for blacks, the long-range goal they envision for their family line is assimilation into the mestizo mainstream. By contrast, Indians in the same region build political strength on the basis of ethnicity.

1271 Leons, William. Las relaciones étnicas de una comunidad multiracial en los yungas bolivianos (UP/EA, 4:2, 1974/1976, p. 161–177)

Description of plight of a small enclave of blacks in the Bolivian yungas. Because of their peculiar situation, these blacks are said to be the most anxious of any local residents to modify their culture, and the males are alleged actively to seek mates from other ethnic groups.

1272 Me vendí, me compraron: análisis socio-económico, en base a testimonios, de la zafra de caña en Santa Cruz de la Sierra. Bárbara y Juergen Riester et al. Santa Cruz de la Sierra, Bolivia: s.n., 1979. 86 p.; 15 leaves of plates; bibl.; ill. (Cuaderno para no-campesinos)

Inside view of the life of sugarcane migrant workers in eastern Bolivia. Although short on analysis, the descriptions fill an important void in our understanding of the impact of "development" on the working masses.

1273 Mesa Redonda sobre Expresiones de la Cultura Boliviana en el Lapso

1925–74, *La Paz, Bolivia, 1975.* Dualismo o pluralismo cultural en Bolivia: trabajos presentados a la Mesa Redonda sobre Expresiones de la Cultura Boliviana en el Lapso 1925–74. La Paz: Casa Municipal de la Cultura Franz Tamayo, 1975. 2 v.; bibl. (Biblioteca Paceña: Nueva serie)

Consists of works presented at a round table held in La Paz, 1974. Of direct interest to ethnologists are the following (six of which are annotated separately in this section, see item number after title): Félix Eguino Zaballa's "Educación y Cultura;" Carlos Urquizo Sossa's "Cultura y Turismo;" Wagner Terrazas Urquidi's "Recursos Naturales y Desarrollo de Bolivia;" Julio Díaz Arguedas "Nuestra Cultura Social, Política y Militar;" Mario Montaño Aragón's "Antropología e Historia;" Carlos Ponce Sanginés' "Origen del Dualismo Cultural en Bolivia;" Alfonso Finot's "El Pluralismo Cultural en Bolivia;" Mario Montaño Aragón's "Transculturación y Contraculturación en Bolivia" (see item **1277**); Luis Girault's "La Cultura Kallawaya" (see item **1263**); Olivia Harris' "Laymis y Machas: Temas Culturales del Norte de Potosí" (see item **1265**); Marcelo Sanginés Uriarte's "Un Enfoque Sociológico de la Educación Rural" (see item **1290**); Julia Elena Fortun's "Integración o Coexistencia Cultural" (see item **1262**); Max Portugal Ortiz's "Antecedentes Precolombinos;" Max Portugal Zamora's "Aportes Precolombinos a la Civilización Occidental;" Mario Rolón Anaya's "La Cultura Kechwa" (see item **1287**); Walter Hermosa Virreira's "Las Tribus Selvícolas en la Cultura Boliviana;" and Beatriz Rossels' "Influencias Foráneas en las Culturas Nativas."

1274 Montaño Aragón, Mario. Antropología cultural boliviana. La Paz: Casa Municipal de la Cultura Franz Tamayo, 1977. 262 p.; bibl.; ill. (Biblioteca paceña; nueva serie)

Popular level prehistory, ethnohistory, and ethnology of the many cultures of Bolivia, filled with factual errors, outmoded analytical approaches, and unfounded conjecture. By trying to encompass everything, the book succeeds in accomplishing practically nothing.

1275 ———. Panorama de las culturas indígenas en Bolivia (*in* Los aymaras

dentro de la sociedad boliviana [see item **1245**] p. 13–23)

Unsophisticated attempt to reconstruct Bolivian culture history.

1276 ———. Raíces semíticas en la religiosidad aymara y kichua. La Paz, Bolivia: Biblioteca Popular de Ultima Hora, 1979. 192 p.; bibl.; ill. (Colección Historia)

Spurious argument that Aymara and Quechua religions have Semitic roots. Author falls into the same isolated culture trait trap that destroyed the Kulturkreiss school. As a result, the book is destined to become an almost instant curiosity.

1277 ———. Transculturación y contraculturación en Bolivia (*in* Mesa Redonda sobre Expresiones de la Cultura Boliviana en el Lapso 1925–74 [see item **1273**] v. 1, p. 47–58)

Brief discussion of cuture change in Bolivia, disjointed and of questionable logic.

1278 Nash, June C. Conflicto industrial en los Andes: los mineros bolivianos del estaño (UP/EA, 4:2, 1974/1976, 219–257)

Describes struggles of Bolivian miners' union, and suggests that their experience can serve as a model for workers in those advanced industrialized countries from which capital is fleeing in search of cheap labor and low taxes. Bolivian miners are alleged to have concluded that their major hope lies in political power.

1279 ———. We eat the mines and the mines eat us: dependency and exploitation in Bolivian tin mines. New York: Columbian University Press, 1979. 363 p.; bibl.; ill.; index.

Excellent study of mine workers around the city of Oruro. Much valuable verbatim interview material is included, as are also raw economic data and an account of the nature and role of union activities. Dependency and exploitation are the leitmotiv from beginning to end.

1280 Nordenskiöld, Erland. The changes in the material culture of two Indian tribes under the influence of new surroundings. New York: AMS Press, 1979. 245 p.; bibl.; ill.

Reprint of 1920 edition dealing with changes in the material culture of the Chiriguano and Chané of southern Bolivia and northern Argentina. Book is a classic for its time and stands as an example of the enormous changes that have occurred in the ethnological approach over the last 60 years.

Paredes, M. Rigoberto. Mitos, supersticiones y supervivencias populares de Bolivia. See *HLAS 42:1046.*

1281 Paredes de Salazar, Elssa. Presencia de nuestro pueblo. La Paz: s.n., 1976. 137 p.; 32 leaves of plates; bibl.; ill.

Superficial work in the tradition of descriptive folklore. Though marred by the argument that traditional dress is the cause of Bolivia's plural society, prejudices, and discrimination, book does have some useful photographs and watercolors of folk and festive costumes.

Peñaranda de Guillén Pinto, Natty. Espíritu eterno, *Pacha Ajayu.* See *HLAS 42:1052.*

1282 Platt, Tristán. Espejos y maíz: temas de la estructura simbólica andina. La Paz, Bolivia: Centro de Investigación y Promoción del Campesinado, 1976. 56 p.; 12 leaves of plates; bibl.; ill. (Cuadernos de investigación - CIPCA; 10)

Structural analysis of symbolism in northern Potosí. A superior work that merits far better treatment than the highly acidic, mimeographed paper it was given. Author is British and has spent the better part of a decade in the Bolivian highlands.

1283 Preston, David A. Explotación o simbiosis: las relaciones pueblo-campo en América andina (CDAL, 17, 1978, p. 113–131, bibl., map)

On the basis of a comparison of Pucarani, an old mestizo town, and Batallas, a new peasant dominated market center, Preston argues that Latin American rural dwellers can benefit from reform. At the same time, he documents the continuation of power by mestizo townsmen through their domination of provincial politics. Conclusion is reached that, to consolidate their gains, more peasants will have to become permanent town residents.

1284 Rabaj, Serafín and Víctor Campos. Profiles of the problems of coca in Bolivia: data about production of coca according to a survey done in 1977 (in Inter-American Seminar on Medical and Sociological Aspects of Coca and Cocaine, Lima, 1979.

Proceedings [see item **1234**] p. 154–158)

Totally garbled English version of Spanish language report on Bolivia's 1977 coca producers' census. Both production and traditional consumption seem drastically underreported, but the reasons for the underreporting are unclear since the sampling procedures are nowhere discussed.

1285 Reinaga, Fausto. Indianidad. La Paz: Ediciones Partido Indio de Bolivia, 1978. 124 p.; bibl.

Personal statement of philosophy by one of the leaders of Indian power in Bolivia. Both Christianity and Marxism are repeatedly attacked, and a call is made for humanity to turn to the wisdom of the Andes, characterized by an all pervading respect for and balance with nature.

1286 ——. El pensamiento amáutico. La Paz: Ediciones Partido Indio de Bolivia, 1978. 173 p.; bibl.

Glorification of the Amerindian heritage accompanied by denunciations of the Spanish Empire, racism, European culture, Marxism, and even Che Guevara. The theme is similar to that found in author's book *Indianidad* (see item **1285**).

1287 Rolón Anaya, Mario. La cultura kechwa (in Mesa Redonda sobre Expresiones de la Cultura Boliviana en el Lapso 1925–74, La Paz, Bolivia, 1975. Dualismo o pluralismo cultural en Bolivia [see item **1273**] v. 1, p. 149–159)

Proposes that cultural integration be reciprocal, rather than of a subordinating or destructive nature.

1288 Sandagorda, Armando E. Coca production in Bolivia (in Inter-American Seminar on Medical and Sociological Aspects of Coca and Cocaine, Lima, 1979. Proceedings [see item **1234**] p. 165–169)

General, superficial description of coca growing that ends with production estimates that are over three times as great as those given in the Rabaj and Campos article published in the same volume (see item **1284**). A monument to the confusion existing on the matter!

1289 ——. Sociocultural aspects of coca use (in Inter-American Seminar on Medical and Sociological Aspects of Coca and Cocaine, Lima, 1979. Proceedings [see item **1234**] p. 150–153)

Plagiarized article drawn from the Carter, Mamani, et al. report: "Traditional Use of Coca Leaf in Bolivia," published through the National Museum of Folklore and Ethnology in La Paz, Bolivia, 1978.

1290 Sanginés Uriarte, Marcelo. Un enfoque sociológico de la educación rural (*in* Mesa Redonda sobre Expresiones de la Cultura Boliviana en el Lapso 1925–74, La Paz, Bolivia, 1975. Dualismo o pluralismo cultural en Bolivia [see item **1273**] v. 1, p. 85–98)

Research report on rural education in Tarija, of worth basically because of the dearth of information on that part of Bolivia.

1291 Sandoval, Godofredo and **Javier Albó.** Ojje por encima de todo: historia de un centro de residentes ex-campesinos en La Paz. La Paz, Bolivia: Centro de Investigación y Promoción del Campesinado, 1978. 114 p.; 2 leaves of plates; bibl.; maps (Cuadernos de investigación - CIPCA; 16)

Brief study of social and economic relations between Ojje, a Titicaca island community of the Bolivian-Peruvian border, and community's migrants presently living in the city of La Paz. Data are welcome addition to our knowledge of rural-urban migration in Bolivia, but the analysis is weak.

1292 Stearman, Allyn Mac Lean. The highland migrant in lowland Bolivia: multiple resource migration and the horizontal archipelago (SAA/HO, 37:2, Summer 1978, p. 180–185)

Description and analysis of migration to Santa Cruz that appears to be a preliminary version of a more complete treatment of the subject published in *América Indígena* (abril/junio 1979). Emphasis is placed here on multiple resource use, and the general discussion is illustrated at the end of the article with family case studies.

1293 ———. Migrants andinos en el Oriente Boliviano: el caso de Santa Cruz (III/AI, 34[34]:2, abril/junio 1979, p. 381–400, bibl., maps)

Excellent summary and analysis of migration to the Department of Santa Cruz over the past 28 years. Article places this migration in its historical context, chronicles the impact of changing agricultural systems on the movement, and documents the interethnic conflicts to which it has given rise.

For a capsule view of migration to Santa Cruz, there is hardly a better source.

1294 Viezzer, Moema. El Comité de Amas de Casa de siglo XX: an organizational experience of Bolivian women (LAP, 6[22]:3, Summer 1979, p. 80–86)

Brief natural history of the Housewives' Committee out of which came Domitila Barios de Chungara, the woman whose testimony formed the basis of the book, *Si me permiten hablar* (see item **1247**). Written by the Brazilian who collected and edited Domitila Chungara's testimony, article discusses how the committee began, its forms of action and struggle, repercussions resulting from its formation, its successes and limitations, and the possibilities of generalizing from its experience. Conclusion is reached that the experience of the committee was quite unique.

1295 Widerkehr, Doris E. Autonomy overshadowed: a Bolivian cooperative within the nationalized mining industry (SAA/HO, 39:2, Summer 1980, p. 153–160)

Case study that explores degree of local autonomy that exists within a cooperative that is nationalized, aspects of cooperative organization that reinforce an egalitarian ideology, and miners' role in setting the economic priorities of the enterprise and handling other managerial decisions. Conclusion is reached that the nationalized mining company (COMIBOL) is perceived by the members of the cooperative as more of an adversary than a partner, and that the cooperative organization itself is leading to incipient stratification.

1296 Zalles, Jimmy. La iglesia aymara dentro de la Iglesia boliviana (*in* Los aymaras dentro de la sociedad boliviana [see item **1245**] p. 47–56)

Popular level description of religious syncretism among the Aymara.

CHILE

1297 Böning, Ewald F. Das *kultrún*, die *machi*-Trommel der Mapuche (AI/A, 73, 1978, p. 817–844, bibl., ill.)

Detailed description of the history, form, and use of the *kultrún* drum among the Mapuche. The drum is still employed by curers for magical, therapeutic, and ritual purposes. Article is a classic example of the obsolete material culture approach.

1298 Castro Gatica, Omar. Escultura mapuche. Ilus. de Guillermo Meriño Pedreros. Temuco, Chile: Impr. Alvarez, 1976. 28 leaves; bibl.; ill.

Simple introduction to the wood and stone carvings of the Mapuche, illustrated with line drawings.

1299 Espinosa Ojeda, Bernarda. La emigración en una comunidad mapuche (III/AI, 34[35]:2, abril/junio 1979, p. 401–416, bibl.)

Minor contribution to the study of Mapuche rural-urban migration. Drawn basically from a case study in the Chol-Chol district of southern Chile, article adds little to our understanding of either the push or pull factors accounting for Mapuche migration. Weak analysis is given based on demographics and economics, but accommodation in the new urban setting is ignored.

1300 Hartwig, Vera. Die Indianer-Agrarfrage in Chile bis 1970 [i.e. neunzehnhundertsiebzig]. Berlin: Akademie-Verlag, 1976. 258 p.; 8 leaves of plates; appendix; bibl.; ill. (Veröffentlichungen des Museums für Völkerkunde zu Leipzig; 30)

Marxist treatise by East German scholar focusing on social organization, agricultural production, and land tenure of the Chilean Mapuche. The Chilean and US capitalist bourgeois systems are properly chastised, and the Communist Party is praised as the Indian's best friend.

1301 Kay, Cristóbal. Reforma agraria y movilización campesina en Chile (CLASCO/ERL, 1:3, sept./dic. 1978, p. 94–124)

Macro-study of Chilean agrarian reform, focusing on global statistics and political action.

1302 Kurteff, Aída. Los araucanos en el misterio de los Andes. Fotografías, Arlette Neyes; tapa, Kitty L. de Passalia. Buenos Aires: Editorial Plus Ultra, 1979. 157 p.; bibl.; ill. (Colección Argentina indígena)

Undocumented, general treatment of Mapuche belief and ritual, accompanied by considerable unsubstantiated speculation regarding the origin of Mapuche culture.

1303 Mas, María Rosa. General aspects on licit control, undue use and illicit traffic of cocaine in Chile (in Inter-American Seminar on Medical and Sociological Aspects of Coca and Cocaine, Lima, 1979. Proceedings [see item 1234] p. 185–187)

Brief description of the legal situation in Chile with regard to cocaine use, followed by an appeal for control of coca leaf production in Peru and Bolivia.

1304 Provoste Fernández, Patricia. Diferenciación e integración social en el altiplano chileno (III/AI, 39[39]:4, oct./dic. 1979, p. 795–811, bibl.)

Description of social hierarchy based on rotating fiesta sponsorship among the Aymara of northern Chile. Author argues that historical factors have led to a basic egalitarianism and that integration into Chilean national society seems to be on the horizon, threatening both pauperization and disintegration of the ethnic group. Article is short on both data and analysis, but important for the comparative perspective it gives on a little known enclave of Aymara.

1305 San Martín M., René. Algunos antecedentes para una catequesis del niño mapuche de las zonas agrícolas (Stylo [Revista de ciencia, arte y literatura. Pontificia Universidad Católica de Chile, Temuco, Chile] 12:16, 1977, p. 8–15)

Overly simplistic description of child rearing practices among the Mapuche. A far better job would have been done by simply referring readers to the works of Sister Inés Hilger.

1306 ván Kessel, Juan. Muerte y ritual mortuorio entre los aimaras (UCC/NG, 6, 1978/1979, p. 77–93, bibl., map)

Description, accompanied by minimal analysis, of death ritual among Aymara llama herders of northern Chile. Some customs and beliefs differ significantly from those previously described for the Bolivian Aymara, but most are either similar or identical. Article is marred by total lack of reference to major published sources that deal with Bolivian Aymara death ritual.

1307 Zumaeta A., Héctor. Bibliografía introductoria para el estudio de la cultura mapuche (Stylo [Revista de ciencia, arte y literatura. Pontificia Universidad Católica de Chile, Temuco, Chile] 12:16, 1977, p. 16–27)

Short bibliography limited to items on the Mapuche available through the following: Centro de Estudios Regionales, Biblioteca Central, Pontificia Universidad Católica, Sede Regional Temuco; Biblioteca Municipal de Temuco; and Biblioteca del Museo Araucano. Listing fails to include some sources as obvious as the *Handbook of South American Indians*.

COLOMBIA

1308 Estupiñan, L.F. and H. Tamayo. Differential study between coca and cocaine in Colombia (*in* Inter-American Seminar on Medical and Sociological Aspects of Coca and Cocaine, Lima, 1979. Proceedings [see item **1234**] p. 175–184)

Basically pharmacologic study, concluding with observations on Colombia's international cocaine traffic.

1309 Friedemann, Nina S. de and Richard Cross. Mangombe: guerreros y ganaderos en Palenque. Bogotá: C. Valencia Editores, 1979. 228 p.

Deals with the history of blacks in San Basilio del Palenque.

1310 Reichel-Dolmatoff, Gerardo and Alicia Reichel-Dolmatoff. Estudios antropológicos. Bogotá: Instituto Colombiano de Cultura, 1977. 584 p.

Collection of articles produced over many years by two outstanding researchers, focusing on the ideological accomplishments of the native peoples of Colombia. Of particular interest to specialists on the Andean highlands are those dealing with the Sierra Nevada de Santa Marta.

1311 Schorr, Thomas S. Las motivaciones sicodinámicas de la violencia en poblaciones campesinas del Valle del Cauca Central, Colombia (UP/EA, 4:2, 1974/1976, p. 59–66)

Examines the relationship between values and behavior, focusing on concepts such as machismo, pendejismo, motherhood, and the Virgin.

1312 Sevilla Casas, Elías. Economía y dominación en una comunidad indígena colombiana (CLACSO/ERL, 1:3, sept./dic. 1978, p. 125–166)

Detailed study of the changing economy of a community of Paez, located on the eastern slopes of the Cordillera Central of Colombia. They are seen as victimized by the encroachment of capitalism, and on the verge of total extinction.

1313 Watson-Franke, María Barbara. Social pawns or social powers? the position of Guajiro women (FSCN/A, 45, 1976, p. 19–40)

Describes socialization practices for girls, and asserts that Guajiro women share responsibilities and rights equally with men. The claim is made that girls receive a more concentrated and accentuated education than boys.

ECUADOR

1314 Archetti, Eduardo P. and Kristi Anne Stolen. Burguesía rural y campesinado en la sierra ecuatoriana (UTIEH/C, 34, 1980, p. 58–82, bibl., tables)

Solid study of agrarian reform in highland Ecuador. Concrete data are given as to the effect of the reform on different landholding and structural systems. Participants in the mixed economy of the dairy industry are described as those who have most benefitted from the changes, and who today occupy the enviable position of "campesinos ricos."

1315 Bernand, Carmen. La machisme piège: maladie, malheur et rapports de sexe dans les Andes méridionales de l'Equateur (EPHE/H, juillet/déc. 1979, p. 189–203, tables)

Argues that, among peasants of the Equadorian Andes, concepts of disease are related to and conditioned by concepts of sex and age. Certain diseases are common to children, others to women, and others to men. Alcoholism falls into the latter category; although commonly associated with male dominance, it results in the exact opposite (i.e. in women taking effective command of households when their men have become incapacitated through drink).

1316 Burgos-Guevara, Hugo. La autodeterminación de las poblaciones indígenas del Ecuador: nuevo rumbo del indigenismo ecuatoriano (BBAA, 34:48, 1977, p. 61–77)

General statement of a new indigenous policy for Ecuador, accompanied by specific position statements regarding land, indigenous organizations, the responsibility of the anthropologist, suffrage, ethnocide, and the responsibility of the state. Autodetermination is to be the hallmark of the new policy, with indigenous leaders taking direct part in decision making and ceasing to be mere observers.

1317 Donoso, H. Coca use in Ecuador (*in* Inter-American Seminar on Medical and Sociological Aspects of Coca and Cocaine, Lima, 1979. Proceedings [see item **1234**] p. 188–190)

Brief note on the history of coca use in Ecuador, accompanied by a description of present Ecuadorian anti-coca legislation.

1318 Gallardo Moscoso, Hernán. Presencia de Loja y su Provincia: antropología social. Loja, Ecuador: Editorial Casa de la Cultura, Núcleo de Loja, 1976, cover 1978. 510 p.

Motley collection of facts, figures, and impressions. Census data, a glossary of terms, a list of proverbs, riddles, verses, and strange customs are but part of what the reader can find here. The book's author calls all this social anthropology.

1319 Gangotena G., Francisco. La feria y el mercado: tres formas de producir y comercializar (Antropología Ecuatoriana [Casa de la Cultura Ecuatoriana, Quito, Ecuador] 1, 1978, p. 46–64)

Attempt, meeting with limited success, to establish a tripart typology of markets. Ecuador is implicit, though ethnographic data are absent.

1320 Mena P., J. Vicente. Breves anotaciones sobre el arco iris o cuichig (Antropología Ecuatoriana [Casa de la Cultura, Quito, Ecuador] 1, 1978, p. 65–71)

Informative note documenting the Ecuadorian variation of this pan-Andean concept.

1321 Moore R., Bruce R. El cambio cultural entre los colorados de Santo Domingo. Quito: Instituto Lingüístico de Verano, 1979. 51 p.; map (Cuadernos etnolingüísticos; no. 5)

Cursory and old fashioned ethnography of the Colorados. Considered are material culture, economic activities, social structure, the life cycle, and change.

1322 Muñoz-Bernard, Carmen. Tradition orale, histoire populaire et indianité dans une sociéte paysanne de la sierra mérid-

ionale (UTIEH/C, 34, 1980, p. 83–98)

Comparison of the myth of the three ages (father, son, and holy ghost) with others found in the Ecuadorian highlands, followed by a discussion as to how such myths may be used to reinforce the "Indian" self concept.

1323 Punín de Jiménez, Dolores. La cerámica de Cera, Ecuador: un estudio socioeconómico y cultural (IPGH/FA, 25, junio 1978, p. 125–161, maps, plates, tables)

Superficial report in the old style of skeletal or outline description and no analysis. First 18 p. are devoted to an unsatisfactory account of ecology, demography, and customs of the region, and final 12 p. to cursory survey of ceramic techniques and products.

1324 Rhon D., Francisco. Lucha étnica o lucha de clases: Ecuador (*in* Campesinado e indigenismo en América Latina [see item **1229**] p. 71–85)

Generalities about social class and ethnic traditions, ending with the unrealistic hope that indigenous society can recuperate its own elements and cultural values.

1325 Social Science Centers in Quito (LARR, 14:2, 1979, p. 209–212)

Brief description of the activities of four social centers in Quito: the Centro de Planificación y Estudios Sociales (CEPLAES), the Fundación de Investigación y Asesoría para el Desarrollo (FIAD), the Facultad Latinoamericana de Ciencias Sociales (FLACSO), and the Instituto Latinamericano de Investigaciones (ILDIS).

1326 Walter, Lynn. Social strategies and the fiesta complex in an Otavaleño community (AAA/AE, 8:1, p. 172–185)

Analysis of the relationship between family and cargo festivals in Ahuango, an Otavaleño community of northern highland Ecuador.

1327 Whitten, Norman E., Jr. Ecological imagery and cultural adaptability: the Canelos Quichua of Eastern Ecuador (AAA/AA, 80:4, Dec. 1978, p. 836–859, plate)

More condensed analysis and interpretation of data than those found in author's book: *Sacha Runa: ethnicity and adaptation of Ecuadorian jungle Quichua* [see HLAS 39:1407]. Whitten argues convincingly that there is an inherent complementarity of cultural continuity and cultural change, just as there is an inherent complementarity of ecology and symbolism. Though he lauds Gerardo Reichel-Dolmatoff for equating cosmology with real infrastructure, he challenges that author's implicit conclusion that indigenous cosmology will fragment in the face of radical change.

PERU

Alarco, Rosa. Danza de "Los Negritos de Huánuco." See *HLAS 42:1388.*

1328 Allen, Catherine J. To be Quechua: the symbolism of coca chewing in highland Peru (AAA/AE, 8:1, 1971, p. 157–171)

Argues that ceremonial uses of coca involve standardized forms of behavior, the observance of which orients the actors spatially, socially, and religiously.

1329 *Apacheta.* Revista de las tradiciones populares del Perú. Francisco Iriarte Brenner. Vol. 1, 1977– . Lima.

Journal devoted to studies of Peruvian folklore. Traditional fiestas, magic, traditional medicine, oral literature, music, dance, costuming, and folklore and education are the topics treated in the first volume.

1330 Aramburú, Carlos E. Las migraciones a las zonas de colonización en la selva peruana: perspectivas y avances (PUCP/DA, 4, feb. 1979, p. 81–94, bibl., tables)

Treatment of migration to the *ceja de la selva* Huallaga region of Peru. Article compares this migration with that to Lima and to other Peruvian cities, and concludes that economic considerations and movement of entire families characterize rural-rural more than they do rural-urban migration. Comparisons suffer from a lack of data, from unicausal thinking and from erroneous interpretation of fact.

1331 El área de antropología de la Pontificia Universidad Católica: sus memorias y tesis de grado, 1968–1978. Compiled by Jorge P. Ostering (PUCP/DA, 4, feb. 1979, p. 121–127)

Short history of anthropology at the Catholic University of Lima accompanied by a list of theses produced in 1971/78.

1332 Arguedas, José María. Dos estudios sobre Huancayo. Huancayo: Universidad Nacional del Centro del Perú, Departamento de Publicaciones, between 1977 and 1978. 143 p.; bibl. (Serie estudios andinos del Centro; 2. Cuadernos universitarios)

Two short ethnographic studies produced by well-known Peruvian novelist at a time when he was heavily influenced by North American cultural anthropology. First study is entitled "Evolución de las Comunidades Campesinas," and the second "Estudio Etnográfico de la Feria de Huancayo."

Bolton, Charlene and **Ralph Bolton.** Rites of retribution and restoration in Canchis. See *HLAS 42:1394.*

1333 Bracco Dieckman, Mercedes. La migración eventual a la ceja de selva. Lima, Perú: Centro de Investigaciones Socio-Económicas, Universidad Nacional Agraria la Molina, 1979 or 1980. 58, 3 p.; bibl. (Serie Documento de trabajo - CISE; no. 24)

Cursory review of temporary migration to higher altitude of forests of eastern Peru. Migrants are seen as choosing this as one of several options, but not necessarily as a permanent one.

1334 Bradfield, Stillman and **Leila Bradfield.** Migrant receiving centers in developing countries: the case of Chimbote, Peru (*in* Internal migration systems in the developing world. Edited by Robert H. Thomas and John M. Hunter. Boston: G.K. Hall; Cambridge, Mass.: Schenkman Publishing Co., 1980, p. 62–81, map)

Perceptive natural history of migration to Chimbote from time of its founding in the 1760s to 1970s. Analysis is unusual in that it encompasses elites as well as the working class. One of major conclusions is that Chimbote must be seen as an integral part of national and international systems.

Brown, Michael F. Notas sobre la chonguinada de Junín. See *HLAS 42:1395.*

1335 Brush, Stephen B. The myth of the idle peasant: employment in a subsistence economy (*in* Peasant livelihood: studies in economic anthropology and cultural ecology [see item **255a**] p. 60–78, graph, tables)

On the basis of work in the Chachapoyas region of northeastern Peru, Brush argues that the concept of underemployment is fallacious in noncapitalistic situations, because it assumes definitions and methods of analysis appropriate to measuring unemployment only in capitalist market economies, and because it ignores the nature of work as defined in peasant economies.

1336 ———; **Heath J. Carney;** and **Zósimo Huamán.** Dynamics of Andean potato agriculture (SEB/EB, 35:1, 1981, p. 70–88)

Definitive study of native potato varieties in highland Peru. Conclusion is reached that maintenance of numerous varieties is neither causal nor random, but is rather based on a complex taxonomic system.

1337 Cáceres, Baldomero. Coca y realidad: aula sin muros. Lima: Universidad Nacional Mayor de San Marcos, Dirección de Proyección Social, Seminario de Historia Rural Andina, 1979. 57, 5 p.; bibl.

Defense of role of coca in traditional Peruvian society and attack on proposals to eradicate the plant. Based on articles previously published in *La Prensa* and *La Voz de Huancayo*, this slim, mimeographed volume brings important historical sources on coca to the attention of the Peruvian public, but is marred by emotional polemics.

1338 Campaña, Pilar and **Rigoberto Rivera.** Campesinado y migración en una sociedad de enclave (PUCP/DA, 4, feb. 1979, p. 51–80, bibl., tables)

Diachronic, structural-functional analysis of highland Peruvian rural society that sees the agriculturalist as a key factor in the national economy of Peru since time of conquest. Using a Marxist analytical framework, author traces historical changes in exploitative structures and concludes that Peru's recent agrarian reform merely reflects the passing of power from the agrarian to the industrial elite and does nothing to redress the long standing extractive bias of the Peruvian economy.

1339 ——— and ———. El proceso de descampesinización en la Sierra Central del Perú (CLACSO/ERL, 1:2, mayo/agosto 1978, p. 71–100)

Studies the relationship between eight rural communities and the nearby Cerro de Pasco mine.

1340 Carnival and coca leaf: some traditions of the Peruvian Quechua Ayllu.

Edited and translated by Douglas Gifford, Pauline Hoggarth. Edinburgh: Scottish Academic Press; London: Distributed by Chatto and Windus, 1976. 111 p.; 16 p. of plates; bibl.; ill.; index; maps (on lining papers)

Account, provided by two native Quechua speakers, of the rituals and customs of a highland Peruvian community. Original Spanish and Quechua text appears parallel to an English translation. Concluding chapter consists of a brief, generalized ethnography.

1341 Contreras H., Jesús. El compadrazgo y los cambios en la estructura de poder local en Chinchero, Perú (UB/BA, 29, 1979, p. 5–29, bibl.)

Simplistic view of functions of godparentage in Urubamba province, Cuzco dept. Argument presented is that godparentage has basically economic and political functions, and that it both reflects and serves as an indicator for social change. Ties established through baptism and marriage are the only ones seriously considered.

1342 Crónica. La coca: sus productores, consumidores y la Ley 22095 (Antropología Andina [Centro de Estudios Andinos, Cuzco, Perú] 3, 1979, p. 89–99)

Critique of plans to control coca production and use in Peru, accompanied by a resolution from the Primer Congreso Nacional de Antropología del Hombre del Altiplano Puneño.

1343 Custred, Glynn. Symbols and control in a high altitude Andean community (AIA/A,m 74:3/4, 1979, p. 379–392, bibl.)

Major analysis of crop fertility rites among the Peruvian Quechua. Formal treatment of structure of ritual offering is exceptionally perceptive; functional analysis that follows, rather than breaking new ground, reinforces analyses previously made for other highland Peruvian and Bolivian groups.

1344 De Wind, Adrian. De campesinos a mineros: El origen de las huelgas en las minas peruanas (UP/EA, 4:2, 1974/1976, p. 1–32)

Historical analysis of the conversion of peasants into Cerro de Pasco miners. Major emphasis is on lack of resources in the communities of origin and on the failure of paternalism on the part of the Cerro de Pasco Corporation.

1345 Deere, Carmen Diana. The differentiation of the peasantry and family structure: a Peruvian case study (NCFR/JFH, 3:4, Winter 1978, p. 422–438, bibl.)

Pedestrian analysis of transition from the hacienda system to agrarian capitalism in Cajamarca, Peru. Argument is made that the destruction of the traditional hacienda system has led to increased differentiation among peasants, and that poor peasant households tend to be nuclear in structure whereas rich peasant households tend to be extended. The line between data and conclusions is, however, tenuous and weak.

1346 Degregori, Carlos Iván. Indigenismo, clases sociales y problema nacional (in Indigenismo, clases sociales y problema nacional: la discusión sobre el "problema indígena" en el Perú [see item 1362] p. 17–68)

Political analysis of the development of the indigenous movement in Peru.

1347 ———. Ocaso y replanteamiento de la discusión del problema indígena, 1930–1977 (in Indigenismo, clases sociales y problema nacional: la discusión sobre el "problema indígena" en el Perú [see item 1362] p. 227–251)

Discusses recent indifference and popular resistance to the indigenous movement in Peru, as well as frustrated attempts to revive antiquated liberal myths.

Erasmus, Charles J.; Solomon Miller; and **Louis C. Faron.** Contemporary change in traditional communities of Mexico and Peru. See HLAS 42:3073.

1348 Escobar, Gabriel and **Glorida Escobar.** Observaciones etnográficas sobre la crianza y los usos del cuye en la región del Cuzco (Antropología Andina [Centro de Estudios Andinos, Cuzco, Perú] 1/2, 1976, p. 34–49)

One of the few detailed descriptions of the raising of cuyes. Authors insist that the process is complex, though the data hardly support such a conclusion.

1349 Figueroa, Adolfo. La economía de las comunidades campesinas: el caso de la sierra sur del Perú (in Campesinado e indigenismo en América Latina [see item 1229] p. 181–228)

Results of a comparative survey of seven rural communities in southern Peru.

1350 Flores Galindo, Alberto. Movimientos campesinos en el Perú: balance y esquema (in Seminario La Investigación en Ciencias Sociales en el Perú—Reseña y Avances, Lima, 1976. La investigación en ciencias sociales en el Perú: economía, historia social, ciencia política, problemática laboral, problemática rural [see item 1390] p. 226–240)

Superficial comparison of colonial with 20th-century peasant movements. Comparison is short on data and long on definition and polemic.

1351 Flores Ochoa, Jorge A. Distorsiones en el uso del ecosistema de la puna y los programas de cooperación técnica (Antropología Andina [Centro de Estudios Andinos, Cuzco, Perú] 3, 1979, p. 14–20)

Argues that development agencies should encourage expansion of alpaca, rather than sheep herding, since the latter represents a distortion of the puna ecosystem.

———. Enqa, Enqaychu, Illa y Khuya Rumi: aspectos mágico-religiosos entre pastores. See HLAS 42:1402.

1352 ———. Pastoralists of the Andes: the alpaca herders of Paratía. Ralph Bolton, translator. Philadelphia: Institute for the Study of Human Issues, 1979. 134 p.; bibl.; ill.; index.

Translation of Los pastores de Paratía (1968, see HLAS 35:1397). Presents perceptive and well rounded picture of a group that has successfully adapted to one of the most difficult environments on earth.

1353 Francke Ballve, Marfil. El movimiento indigenista en el Cuzco: 1910–1930 (in Indigenismo, clases sociales y problema nacional: la discusión sobre el "problema indígena" en el Perú [see item 1362] p. 107–166)

Student thesis, presented here in published form, and chronicling the transition from ideology to political action in the emergence of the indigenous movement of Cuzco.

1354 Fuenzalida Vollmar, Fernando. Poder, etnia y estratificación social en el Perú rural (in Perú, hoy. Por José Matos Mar et al. 3. ed. México: Siglo Veintiuno Editores, 1975, p. 8–86 [El Mundo del hombre: sociología y política])

Provocative description and analysis,

based on four case studies, of the modernization of Peruvian society. The argument is cogently made that Peru should no longer be conceptualized as composed of stagnant ethnic groupings such as the white, the mestizo, and the Indian. It rather should be seen as a single continuum in which the basic distinguishing variables are economic and occupational.

1355 Gow, David D. Símbolo y protesta: movimientos redentores en Chiapas y en los Andes peruanos (III/AI, 39:1, enero/marzo 1979, p. 47–80, bibl.)

Thought-provoking analysis that tries to explain why Hispanic Catholic mythical beings became the symbols of revitalization movements in Chiapas, whereas in Peru symbols of such movements tended to be Amerindian. Conclusion is reached that the selection of dominant religious symbols by post-conquest society depended largely on exogenous events.

1356 Grondín N., Marcelo. Comunidad andina: explotación calculada. Santo Domingo, República Dominicana: Unidad de Divulgación Técnica de la Secretaría de Estado de Agricultura de la República Dominicana, 1978. 279 p.; bibl.; ill.

Major restudy of Muquiyauyo, Peru, by student of Richard N. Adams. Benefitting substantially from Adams' previous work both in the same community and in Guatemala, book traces changes in community structure and power manipulation from 1900–73. Conclusion is reached that, both at the local and the national level, ideology is and has been used to facilitate acceptance by peasant masses of their own exploitation.

1357 Guillet, David. Agrarian reform and peasant economy in southern Peru. Columbia: University of Missouri Press, 1979. 227 p.; bibl.; ill.; index (University of Missouri studies; 69)

Detailed study of impact of agrarian reform on Pampa de Anta region of southern Peru. Conclusion is reached that reform has succeeded in removing basis of power of former landed elite, and that this has brought about considerable structural change to the juridical, political, and communications institutions of the region.

Gushiken, José. Tuno: el curandero. See *HLAS 42:1404.*

1358 Hickman, John M. Control social y la adaptación de los Aymares [sic] urbanos y rurales en la zona de Chucuito, Perú (UP/EA, 4:2, 1974/1976, p. 111–130)

Examines effect of mestizo hegemony on Aymara attitudes and culture change. Concludes that presence of mestizos reinforces traditional Aymara patterns.

1359 Horna Ramírez, Rubén. Coca production in Peru (*in* Inter-American Seminar on Medical and Sociological Aspects of Coca and Cocaine, Lima, 1979. Proceedings [see item **1234**] p. 202–205)

Brief description of patterns of coca production in Peru, estimating total production to have been 8,300,416 kilograms in 1978.

1360 Houdart-Morizot, Marie-France. Intégration et domination à Cuenca: communauté indienne paysanne du Pérou (UTIEH/C, 31, 1978, p. 135–148)

Description and analysis of intraethnic domination in the central highlands of Peru. Mechanisms used by a minority to dominate the majority are traditional ones such as endogamic moiety organization, godparentage (*compadrazgo*), and the fiesta system. Tradition is seen by author not only as means of repression but also as guarantor of values.

1361 ———. Tradition et pouvoir à Cuenca: communauté andine. Lima: Institut français d'études andines, 1976. 279 p.; 1 leaf of plates; bibl.; ill.; index (Recherche interdisciplinaire sur les populations andines [projet A.C.L.] v. 2. Travaux de l'Institut français d'études andines; t. 15)

Study emphasizing the dynamic nature of community structure in the Huancavelica area of Peru. The ideal is juxtaposed to the real, and conclusion is reached that Cuenca society rests on an obligatory disequilibrium, and that it experiences a perpetual struggle between order and protest and old and new forms.

1362 Indigenismo, clases sociales y problema nacional: la discusión sobre el "problema indígena" en el Perú. Carlos Iván Degregori et al. Lima: Centro Latinoamericano de Trabajo Social, 1978 or 1979. 251 p.; bibl.

Series of essays dealing with the context, origins, and development of the indigenous movement in Peru. Years 1919–23 are looked upon as the apex of the movement and the last 20 years are seen as representing a movement to the right, accompanied by a restoration of Hispanicism.

1363 Isbell, Billie Jean. To defend ourselves: ecology and ritual in an Andean village. Austin: Institute of Latin American Studies, University of Texas at Austin: distributed by University of Texas Press, 1978. 289 p.; bibl.; ill.; index (Latin American monographs; no. 47)

While not really an ecological study, this is destined to become a basic book for Andean studies. Major foci include social and political structure, reciprocity, and ritual. Work is prefaced by an unusually perceptive introduction based on the author's personal experience.

——— and **Fredy Amilcar Roncalla Fernández.** The ontogenesis of metaphor: riddle games among Quechua speakers seen as cognitive discovery procedures. See *HLAS 42:1406*.

1364 Kapsoli, Wilfredo. En torno a los movimientos campesinos en el Perú contemporáneo (*in* Seminario La Investigación en Ciencias Sociales en el Perú—Reseña y Avances, Lima, 1976. La investigación en ciencias sociales en el Perú: economía, historia social, ciencia política, problemática laboral, problemática rural [see item **1390**] p. 246–249)

Brief analysis of peasant movements that attempts to establish five major periods from 1879 to present. In that each period is treated in a single short paragraph, analytical categories are hardly convincing.

1365 Laite, A.J. Industrialisation, migration and social stratification at the periphery: a case study of mining in the Peruvian Andes (UK/SE, 26:4, Nov. 1978, p. 859–885)

Argues that, in countries such as Peru, mine workers tend not to sever ties with their rural past; rather they maximize alternatives across a number of economic sectors. One is reminded of the multi-ecology or archipelago theory of John Murra. Analysis, though marred by excesses of Marxist rhetoric, is a fairly perceptive one.

1366 Lewellen, T.C. Peasants in transition: the changing economy of the Peruvian Aymara: a general systems approach. Boul-

der, Colo.: Westview Press, 1978. 195 p.; bibl.; ill. (A Westview replica edition)

Lucid but at times overly facile analysis of economic, social, and cultural change among the Peruvian Aymara. The importance of religious conversion to change and leadership is repeatedly stressed. While basically sound, book is marred by numerous misreadings of the analysis and conclusions of previous research.

1367 Lima. Universidad de San Marcos. Seminario de Investigación Antropológica. La SAIS Cahuide y las comunidades campesinas. Universidad Nacional Mayor de San Marcos, Programa Académico de Ciencia Social, Seminario de Investigación Antropológica. Lima: El Seminario, 1978. 85 p.; bibl.; map.

Case study of agrarian reform in the central highlands of Peru, presented in a technical report format with a minimum of analysis. Useful only as a source of raw data.

1368 Maletta, Héctor. Cuatrocientas tesis doctorales norteamericanas sobre el Perú (Estudios Andinos [Universidad del Pacífico, Lima, Perú] 8:15, 1979, p. 57–134)

Valuable listing and analysis of doctoral thesis on Peru, written at North American universities from 1969–76. From 1955 on, a larger number appeared in anthropology than in any other single discipline.

1369 Martínez, Héctor and Carlos Samaniego. La política indigenista (*in* Campesinado e indigenismo en América Latina [see item **1229**] p. 149–177)

Summary review of major indigenously oriented programs in Peru. Discussed are the Peruvian indigenist Institute, the Cornell-Peru Project, the Puno-Yambopata Program, the National Plan for the Integration of the Aboriginal Population, and Community Development and Popular Cooperation.

1370 Marzal, Manuel Maria. Funciones religiosas del mito en el mundo andino cuzqueño (PUCP/DA, 4, feb. 1979, p. 11–22, bibl.)

Superficial functional analysis of four myths from the Cuzco area: the myth of the three eras of creation; the myth of the Pachamama; the myth of the Christ of Huanca; and the myth of the Cigurinocochal lagoon. Theoretical framework for the analysis is drawn from Clifford Geertz's *Religion as a cultural system.*

1371 Mayer, Enrique. Consideraciones sobre la indígena (*in* Perú, identidad nacional. César Arróspide de la Flor *et al.* Lima: Centro de Estudios para el Desarrollo y la Participación, 1979, p. 79–109, ill. [Serie Realidad nacional])

Innovative look at the pejorative aspects of traditional classifications of indigenous Peruvians. Argument is made that anthropologists themselves are largely to blame for negative images of indigenous populations, and that instead of there being an "Indian problem," there is a "non-Indian problem." Mayer concludes by appealing for a "desacralization" of the distinction between the descendent of native Peruvians and the descendent of immigrants.

1372 Millones, Luis. Sociedad indígena e identidad nacional (*in* Perú, identidad nacional. César Arróspide de la Flor *et al.* Lima: Centro de Estudios para el Desarrollo y la Participación, 1979, p. 57–77 [Serie Realidad nacional])

Essay, based largely on conjecture, describing in the most general way three historic periods of Indian hegemony: the Inca Empire, the messianic reign of Juan Chocne, and the Indian republic of Tupac Amaru. Author himself admits that the essay format allows him to speculate on the paucity of data and frees him from the obligation to do serious research. Need more be said?

1373 Mitchell, William P. Inconsistencia de status y dimensions de rangos en los Andes Centrales del Perú (Estudios Andinos [Universidad del Pacífico, Lima, Perú] 8:15, 1979, p. 21–31)

Asserts that prestige and stratification are multi-dimensional in the Central Andes, and provides a listing of criteria for determining both.

1374 Moles, Jerry A. What does one say to a naked lady?: validity, variability, and data collection, a Peruvian example (UNM/ JAR, 34:2, Summer 1978, p. 263–290, bibl., tables)

The results of testing, on the basis of forms of address and using the Multitrait-Multimethod Matrix developed by Campbell and Fisk, the validity of informant responses in an ethnographic interview situation. The

conclusion is reached that the Multitrait-Multimethod Matrix provides an acceptable tool for evaluating the accuracy of ethnographic data. Problem, of course, lies in going from highly restricted sets of data, such as those used here, to the enormous complexity of the full round of culture.

1375 Montoya V., Beatriz G. Los minifundios en al altiplano peruano (III/AI, 39[39]:4, oct./dic. 1979, p. 773–793, tables)

Poor and inadequate treatment of the subject of small holdings on the Peruvian altiplano. Based on data from five case study households, article adds no new insights to our knowledge of land tenure and agricultural production for this part of the world. At the most it indicates that these differ little from what has been amply described for neighboring Bolivia.

1376 Oliver-Smith, Anthony. Disaster rehabilitation and social change in Yungay, Peru (SAA/HO, 36:1, Spring 1977, p. 5–13)

On the basis of the Yungay experience, the argument is made that disaster victims want a return to normalcy—not an adventure in social change. Their felt needs thus conflict with the intentions of most disaster relief organizations.

1377 Orlove, Benjamin S. Ricos y pobres: la desigualdad en las comunidades campesinas (Estudios Andinos [Universidad del Pacífico, Lima, Perú] 8:15, 1979, p. 5–20)

Study of both upward and downward social mobility in rural communities in the Canchis province, Cuzco department. The implied rather than stated conclusion is that Andean society is less egalitarian and less unchanging than is commonly believed.

1378 ———. Two rituals and three hypotheses: an examination of solstice divination in southern highland Peru (CUA/AQ, 52:2, April 1979, p. 86–98, bibl.)

Review of three sets of explanations of Andean ritual: historical, sociological, and actor-based. The three are applied to two solstice divination rituals in Canchis province, Peru, and conclusion is reached that the actor-based hypothesis produces a more thorough and detailed explanation than do the other two.

1379 Ortiz Rescaniere, Alejandro. Huarochirí, cuatrocientos años después: informe preliminar. Lima: Departamento de Ciencias Sociales, Pontificia Universidad Católica del Perú, 1977. 140 p.; bibl.; ill.

Comparison of contemporary Huarochiri mythology with that collected in the same locale by Francisco de Avila at the close of the 16th century. Conclusion is reached that mythological motifs and traditions have remained basically intact, in spite of changes in detail. A work that deserves a format better than the mimeographed, highly acidic paper that it was given.

1380 Ossio, Juan M. Los mitos de origen en la comunidad de Andamarca, Ayacucho, Perú (IPA/A, 10, 1977, p. 105–113)

Short, general discussion of the nature of myths collected in the community of Andamarca, Ayacucho, Peru. Some are said to define the origin of certain families, some to explain the association of certain families with specific agricultural zones of the community, and some to explain the origin of the community itself. One complete example is given.

1381 Osterling, Jorge P.; Jaime de Althaus; and Jorge Morelli S. Los vendedores ambulantes de ropa en el cercado: un ejemplo del sector económico informal en Lima metropolitana (PUCP/DA, 4, feb. 1979, p. 23–41, bibl., ill., table)

Preliminary analysis of ambulatory clothes salespeople in Lima. The major part of the article is devoted to developing a hierarchical taxonomy that rises from those who are constantly on the move (*marchantes*), through those who display their wares on squares of plastic (*paracaídas*) to those who display them on make-shift tables (*tableros*), and finally to those who own wheeled kiosks (*carretas*). Social structure and process rather than quantitative economic analysis constitute the primary focus of the discussion that follows.

Peasant cooperation and capitalist expansion in central Peru. See *HLAS 42:3105.*

1382 Quijano, Aníbal. Dominación y cultura; Lo cholo y el conflicto cultural en el Perú. La Paz: Mosca Azul Editores, 1980. 119 p.

Think piece that argues that the rapid growth of the cholo group in Peru reflects a change in occupational roles on the part of large segments of the Indian masses and points the way toward a future Peru that will be different from anything known to date. Though marginal today, cholos are seen as basic to a new nationalism that will demand economic-political independence and that will emphasize those cultural values that are peculiarly Peruvian.

1383 Quiroz, Haydée; Elena Rivas; and Gladys Guerra. La artesanía textil en San Miguel de Pallaques. Lima: Universidad Nacional Mayor de San Marcos, Seminario de Historia Rural Andina, 1978. 91, 26 p.; 17 leaves of plates; bibl.; ill.

Study of the production and commercialization of crafts in Cajamarca, northern Peru. Emphasis is primarily on weaving for the urban market, and the study includes some survey data drawn from 80 producers and offering rare insight into costs of production and profit margins.

1384 Ramírez, Yonel and Pedro Ruiz. The illicit traffic and use of coca and cocaine in Peru in 1978 (*in* Inter-American Seminar on Medical and Sociological Aspects of Coca and Cocaine, Lima, 1979. Proceedings [see item **1234**] p. 196–201)

Basic interest in this short article lies in its references to the increasing use of cocaine paste.

1385 Revista a Pucará. J. Sabogal W., compilador. Huancayo, Perú: Instituto de Estudios Andinos, 1978. 46 p.; 1 leaf of plates; bibl.; map (Cuadernos del IEA; 2)

Verbatim, recorded and transcribed statements by native residents of Pucará, focusing on the impact of outside agents of change. A simplistic but worthwhile contribution to Andean oral history.

Rodríguez Pastor, Humberto. Una rebelión de culíes chinos Pativilca, 1870. See *HLAS 42:3116.*

1386 Roe, Peter G. Art and residence among the Shipibo Indians of Peru (AAA/AA, 82:1, 1980, p. 42–71)

Testing of the archaeological hypothesis that a group of coresiding females produces relatively homogeneous art, through an analysis of painted textile samplers produced by Shipibo women of the Peruvian montaña.

1387 **Sabella, James C.** José Olaya: analysis of a Peruvian fishing cooperative that failed (CUA/AQ, 53:1, Jan. 1980, p. 56–63, bibl.)

Solid analysis of the failure of a cooperative of Peruvian artisanal fishermen. Variables used to explain the failure range from family structure to values, natural ecology, capital formation, and national level government policy. The conclusion is reached that the best guarantee of continued reasonable fish prices lies with artisanal fishing.

1388 **Sabogal Wiesse, José R.** Vernacular art in the Andes before modernization: Ayacucho (UNESCO/CU, 6:2, 1979, p. 96–105, bibl.)

Low level description of the folk art tradition of Ayacucho. The author makes an appeal for preservation of the tradition and for recognition that quantity can never substitute for quality.

1389 **Sánchez Farfán, Jorge.** Papas y hombres (Antropología Andina [Centro de Estudios Andinos, Cuzco, Perú] 3, 1979, p. 51–74)

Valuable listing, accompanied by tables, of native Andean potato classifications that are based on size, taste, texture, color, and time of use.

1390 **Seminario La Investigación en Ciencias Sociales en el Perú—Reseña y Avances,** *Lima, 1976.* La investigación en ciencias sociales en el Perú: economía, historia social, ciencia política, problemática laboral, problemática rural. Javier Iguíñiz E. et al. Lima: Tarea, Centro de Publicaciones Educativas, 1979. 268 p.; bibl.

Proceedings of a symposium held in 1976. Four papers deal directly with Andean ethnology: Alberto Flores Galindo's "Movimientos Campesinos en el Perú, Balance y Esquema;" Manuel Burga's "Movimientos Campesinos en Jequetepeque en el Siglo XX: Estructura y Coyuntura Agrarias;" Wilfredo Kapsoli's "En Torno a los Movimientos Campesinos en el Perú Contemporáneo;" and Mario Valderrama's "Enfoques y Perspectivas de Clase en el Análisis de la Problemática Agraria."

1391 **Seminario sobre la Situación y los Derechos Políticos del Analfabeto en Perú,** *Lima, 1978.* Situación y derechos políticos del analfabeto en el Perú: documentos del Seminario realizado entre el 13 y 16 de Noviembre de 1978. Lima, Perú: Departamento de Ciencias Sociales, Pontificia Universidad Católica del Perú, 1978. 180 p.; bibl.; ill.

Proceedings of a 1978 seminar organized by the Department of Social Science of the Catholic University of Lima to deal with the problems of illiteracy in Peru. Included are Rolando Ames Cobián's "Derecho al Voto; Democracia y Capitalismo;" Sinesio López's "De la Sociedad Andina al Campesinado pobre Actual;" Julio Cotler's "Comentarios a las Ponencias de R. Ames y S. López;" Orlando Plaza's "Situación y Derechos Políticos de los Analfabetos en el Sector Rural;" Narda Henríquez A.'s "Condición de Analfabetismo en el Perú;" Alejandro Camino D.C.'s "Reflexiones Respecto a la Palabra y la Escritura Frente al Problema del Multilingüismo en el Perú;" Pedro Patrón Faura's "El Sistema Electoral en el Perú;" Alfonso Camacho P.'s "Mecanismo de Organización del Voto a los Analfabetos—el Caso Boliviano;" René Beoteguy Elio's "El Proceso Electoral del 9 de julio de 1978;" and Alex Noriega's and Silvera Luque's "Testimonio de Dirigentes Populares Respecto a la Situación y Derechos Políticos de los Analfabetos."

1392 **Silverblatt, Irene** and **John Earls.** Mito y renovación: el caso de moros y los aymaras (IPA/A, 10, 1977, p. 93–104, bibl.)

Case study of the merging of history and myth, emanating from a claim by the inhabitants of Auquilla, Peru, that they be officially recognized as an indigenous community. Intriguing questions of interpretation and analysis are suggested but not clearly posed or answered.

1393 **Smith, Gavin A.** Socio-economic differentiation and relations of production among rural-based petty producers in central Peru: 1880 to 1970 (JPS, 6:3, April 1979, p. 286–310, bibl.)

An antidote to easy generalities. Smith traces changing production relations among the Huasicanchinos of Central Peru over a 90-year period. He concludes that the process of economic differentiation found there can be understood only within the context of a specific system of production. Those who adhere to the natural history approach of Franz Boas will be happy; those who try to interpret everything in terms of dialectical materialism will not. For historian's comment, see *HLAS 42:3122*.

1394 Thompson, Stephen I. Assimilation and nonassimilation of Asian-Americans and Asian Peruvians (CSSH, 21:4, Oct. 1979, p. 575–588, bibl.)

Attempt to explain, culturally and historically, differences in assimilation of Asians in the United States and Peru. The problem posed is that: 1) Chinese in Lima are heavily assimilated to Peruvian society; 2) Chinese in New York are relatively unassimilated; and 3) Japanese in Lima are far less assimilated than are Japanese in the United States. Historical circumstances, demographics, and the values of immigrant groups themselves are seen as greater determinants than are the dominant cultures of the host countries. For historian's comment, see *HLAS 42:3124*.

1395 Torres Adrián, Mario. Formas de adaptación económica de la población en las comunidades compesinas del Perú: un análisis contextual. Lima: Pontificia Universidad Católica del Perú, Departamento de Ciencias Sociales, Centro de Investigaciones Sociales, Económicas, Políticas y Antropológicas, 1977. 40 p.

Mimeographed working paper prepared for the VI meeting of the Working Group on Internal Migration of the Population and Development Commission of CLASCO. On the basis of statistics drawn from the National Community Development Office, the hardly earth shaking conclusion is reached that rural Peru is highly complex and conditioned by a variety of developmental levels and demographic profiles.

1396 Torres Rodríguez, Oswaldo. Reforma agraria y cooperativización en la sierra central peruana (III/AI, 39[39]:4, oct./dic. 1979, p. 813–829, tables)

Argues that, despite the fact that successive governments have promoted cooperatives in highland Peru, relatively few have been successful. They have been plagued with internal organizational problems, divisions between leaders and members, mismanagement of funds, lack of adequate credit, and a paucity of technical support. Perhaps because no serious attempt is made in the article to relate these failures to structural or cultural constraints, the outlook for the cooperative movement in the area is seen by the author as being fairly dismal.

Urquiaga, José. Indios: Puno, 1916. See *HLAS 42:3127*.

1397 Uzzell, Douglas. "Cholos" y agencias gubernamentales en Lima: antecedentes y análisis (UP/EA, 4:2, 1974/1976, p. 33–42)

Brief description of how drivers in Lima came to perceive the government bureaucracy as adversary rather than facilitator, and of the way that they shifted their strategies accordingly. The author sees this as a harbinger of things to come.

1398 Valderrama, Mariano. Enfoques y perspectivas de clase en el análisis de la problemática agraria (in Seminario La Investigación en Ciencias Sociales en el Perú—Reseña y Avances, Lima, 1976. La investigación en ciencias sociales en el Perú: economía, historia social, ciencia política, problemática laboral, problemática rural [see item **1390**] p. 250–256)

Critique of previous Marxist analysis of rural Peruvian society, accompanied by a call for detailed, Marxist studies of social class in specific urban and small town situations.

1399 ———. Los planteamientos de Haya de la Torre y de José Carlos Mariátegui sobre el problema indígena y el problema nacional (in Indigenismo, clases sociales y problema nacional: la discusión sobre el "problema indígena" en el Perú [see item **1362**] p. 187–225)

In this comparative treatment of the ideas of Haya de la Torre y Mariátegui, emphasis is given to the paternalistic nature of APRA doctrine.

1400 ——— and Agusta Alfajeme. El surgimiento de la discusión de la cuestión agraria y del llamado problema indígena (in Indigenismo, clases sociales y problema nacional: la discusión sobre el "problema indígena" en el Perú [see item **1362**] p. 53–68)

Brief history of the emergence of the indigenous movement in Peru, including references to the role of novelists.

1401 ——— and ———. Viejas y nuevas fracciones dominantes frente al problema indígena: 1900–1930 (in Indigenismo, clases sociales y problema nacional: la discusión sobre el "problema indígena" en el Perú [see item **1362**] p. 69–106)

Discusses the relation of Peruvian thought to the development of the indigenous movement. Set aside for special treatment are Manuel Vicente Villarán, Francisco García Calderón, José de la Riva-Agüero, and Victor Andrés Belaúnde.

1402 Valencia Espinoza, Abraham. Nombres del maiz y su uso ritual por los K'anas (Antropología Andina [Centro de Estudios Andinos, Cuzco, Perú] 3, 1979, p. 75–88)

Maize taxonomy of a puna dwelling population of the department of Cuzco, particularly valuable for its insight into perceptual categories.

Vassallo, Manuel. Rumi Maqui y la nacionalidad quechua. See *HLAS 42:3128.*

1403 Velaochaga Dam, Carlos. Religión y cultura en los Andes (Antropología Andina [Centro de Estudios Andinos, Cuzco, Perú] 3, 1979, p. 40–50)

Attempt to establish basic metaphysical concepts of the Peruvian Quechua. The attempt is marred by an almost total neglect of research produced by foreign ethnographers.

1404 Webster, Steven. Factores de posición social en una comunidad nativa quechua (UP/EA, 4:2, 1974/1976, p. 131–159)

Asserts that indigenous communities

in the southern Andes should be seen as ethnic components of a plural society rather than as lower class clusters within a regional class system. Wealth and prestige are seen as equally important in determining status.

VENEZUELA

1405 Gonzáles-Carrero, A. and **A. Mancilla.** Considerations about the problem of coca and cocaine in Venezuela (*in* Inter-American Seminar on Medical and Sociological Aspects of Coca and Cocaine, Lima, 1976. Proceedings [see item **1234**] p. 206–212)

For those looking for a description of coca and cocaine use in Venezuela, this will be a disappointment. Generalities and polemics predominate.

1406 Pollak-Eltz, Angelina. Semejanzas estructurales en la religiosidad popular entre Africa occidental y Venezuela (Cuadernos Afro-Americanos [Instituto de Antropología e Historia, Universidad Central de Venezuela, Caracas, Venezuela] 1975, p. 124–134)

Relates elements in Venezuelan folk Catholicism to African precedents, emphasizing the re-interpretation of Catholic doctrine, the cult of María Lionza, and magical beliefs and practices.

Wagner, Erika and **Walter Coppens.** Sexta bibliografía antropológica reciente sobre Venezuela. See item **1216.**

LINGUISTICS

ALAN C. WARES, *Summer Institute of Linguistics*

ONE OF THE MOST FASCINATING ASPECTS of linguistics is the description of languages. Even though all languages have a great deal in common (i.e., a system of sounds produced by the human voice, combinations of those sounds into minimum meaningful units, and combinations of those units into more complex groupings that make communication possible between speaker and hearer), each one is unique. No two languages are exactly alike, even though they may have developed from a common ancestral form as, for example, Spanish and Portuguese did from Latin. Because it is unique, each language merits a careful description in terms of its own structure rather than in terms of another, whether it be the investigator's own or a revered classical language no longer in common use. Describing an Amerindian language in terms of Latin grammar is like using Newtonian physics to explain the behavior of subatomic particles. This kind of description is not, however, a total loss; we can still appreciate the work of 16th-century scholars who first analyzed some of the New World languages. Nevertheless, for 20th-century linguists modern descriptive techniques are preferable (item **1444**).

Many of the items included in this section are texts in the native language (items **1407**, **1425**, **1427**, and **1438**). A noteworthy example is the Tzotzil dictionary compiled by Alfa Delgaty (item **1451**), which illustrates the usage of words and expressions and also includes a grammar of the language. Also valuable are a number of articles on the analysis of discourse which were written at a workshop on the subject held several years ago in Colombia (items **1436–1440**).

The mystical books of *Chilam Balam* (items **1420** and **1426a**) and *Popol Vuh* (items **1412**, **1445** and **1466**) continue to arouse interest, as do hitherto unpublished manuscripts (items **1469**, **1426a–b** and **1478a**)

One doesn't generally associate Polynesian languages with Latin America, but inasmuch as Easter Island is a possession of Chile, the dictionary of Rapanui (item **1433a**) has its place here. Linguistic studies in Chile have been advanced by the establishment of linguistic departments in institutes of higher learning and the continuing work on the linguistic atlas of southern Chile (item **1423**). Similar atlases exist for the speech of Nicaragua (item **1408**) and the Portuguese spoken in Minas Gerais, Brazil (item **1434**). Other sociolinguistic studies deal with attitudes toward language, generally the indigenous language spoken in the particular area (items **1411**, **1428**, **1448**, and **1455**).

On the subject of bilingualism, there are pages and pages of statistics (item **1460**), but these hold little significance without a satisfactory measure of the degree of bilingualism, just as statistics on literacy mean little unless accompanied by a standard measurement of literacy. It is interesting to note (item **1435**) that cultures can coexist for centuries in a given location without giving rise to bilingualism.

Other topics among the wide variety covered in the works listed below are lexical borrowing (items **1413** and **1443**) and syntactic borrowing (item **1474**), ethnobotany (items **1419** and **1421**), comparative studies (item **1468**), and typology (item **1478b**).

It is regrettable that some groups feel threatened by the presence in Latin America of members of the Summer Institute of Linguistics (SIL), an organization devoted to linguistic research and to human betterment through the promotion of literacy and literature in the vernacular tongues. Motivation for such research is the opportunity to translate the Bible into those languages.

Chester Bitterman, a member of the SIL, was preparing to study an Indian language of Colombia when he was kidnapped and held hostage by terrorists who demanded the immediate expulsion of the Summer Institute of Linguistics from that country, where its members have worked since 1962 under the aegis of the Colombian Ministry of Government. The Institute had long before decided not to capitulate to the demands of international terrorists groups, so there was no question of leaving except at the request of the government of Colombia. When the terrorists realized that their demands would not be met, they murdered their captive.

There is no way of knowing what Chester Bitterman might have accomplished as a linguist and a translator. We pay tribute to him as a colleague and pray for a speedy end to the international lawlessness that brought about his death.

Abrahams, Roger D. The training of the man of words in talking sweet. See *HLAS 42:1252.*

1407 Albisetti, César and **Angelo Jayme Venturelli.** Enciclopédia bororo. v. 1, Vocabulários e etnografía. v. 2, Lendas e antropônimos. v. 3, pt. 1, Textos dos cantos de caça e pesca. Campo Grande, Brazil: Faculdade Dom Aquino de Filosofia Ciência e Letras, Instituto de Pesquisas Etnográficas, 1962/1976. 3 v. (1047, 1269, 277 p.) ill. (Publicação do Museu Regional Dom Bosco; 1/3)

The Bororo Indians, numbering about 500, live in Central Mato Grosso, Brazil. Vol. 1 of this encyclopedia on the Bororos is reviewed in *HLAS 27:1197.* Vol. 2 includes Bororo legends with interlinear and free translation, and copious notes. Illustrated with photographs, and includes about 100 p. of Bororo names. Vol. 3 includes song texts used by Bororo Indians of Brazil before going hunting or fishing.

1408 Alemán Ocampo, Carlos. Distribución de las lenguas habladas de Nicaragua (BNBD, 26, nov./dic. 1978, p. 25–30)

A necessary first step in the study of the speech of the inhabitants of Nicaragua, is a survey of the country's languages and their locations. Nicaraguan Spanish has an abundant lexicon of words borrowed from Nahuatl as well as from English and French, reflecting historical contact with these cultures. English is still the dominant language of Creoles in Bluefields and adjacent areas. Larger segment of the population speaks Miskito, which has become the trade language of the lowlands. Other indigenous languages have been known to exist, but their present status is indeterminate.

1409 Almeida, Ileana. Códigos culturales y movilidad semántica en el kechua (III/AI, 39[39]:4, oct./dic. 1979, p. 721–731, bibl.)

As an example of how words change in meaning from one era to another, author cites case of *indi*, a falcon considered sacred by ancient Incas. In course of time it became a totem, and with emergence of sun-worship it became identified with *inti*, the sun itself. In modern Quechua the suffix *-nti* signifies interrelatedness. The thesis is that such a diachronic linguistic change reflects change in the social structure of the Inca Empire during the course of time.

1411 ———. Leticia: estudios lingüísticos sobre la Amazonia colombiana. Con una monografía etnográfica de Elena Alvar. Bogotá: Instituto Caro y Cuervo, 1977. 558 p.; bibl.; ill.; index (Publicaciones del Instituto Caro y Cuervo; 63)

Study of the speech (phonology and lexicon) of inhabitants of Leticia, a rural community in the southernmost tip of Colombia near the Brazil and Peru borders. Includes report of linguistic attitudes of area Indians.

1412 Andueza, María. Pervivencia del *Popol Vuh* (Thesis [Nueva revista de filosofía y letras, UNAM, México] 2:5, abril 1980, p. 20–28, ill.)

Myth and history are combined in the *Popol Vuh*, a work supposedly of Quiché origin. It is a book in which wisdom is a community affair in which everyone can participate. As literary work it exhibits a dualism which is complementary rather than oppositional; it is also a mythic history. First two parts deal with mythological and theological themes, and last two trace genealogy of Quiché rulers. This brief article provides insights into a work that has been somewhat of a mystery since its publication a century ago (see *HLAS 39:1639*).

An annotated glossary of folk medicines used by some Amerindians in Guyana. See *HLAS 42:1295.*

Araya, Guillermo. Algunos aspectos del ALESUCH. See *HLAS 42:1194* and *1336.*

1413 Arrom, José Juan. Arcabuco, cabuya y otros indoamericanismos en un relato del Padre José de Acosta (MHD/B, 8:12, enero 1979, p. 277–292)

With the discovery and conquest of the New World in the 16th century, Spaniards found their language lacking in words for items that were peculiar to New Spain, so they borrowed terms from indigenous languages. An early Spanish priest stationed in Lima wrote about the adventures of a fictitious colleague and sent the manuscript to Rome in 1586. It was published 80 years later as a genuine biography which attracted little notice until recently, when it was seen to be a work of fiction. It contains many words now common in Spanish, but unknown in Spain until the 16th century. Author lists 20 of these, but discusses only two or three in detail.

1414 Asociación de Lingüística y Filología de América Latina. Lingüística y educación: actas del IV Congreso Internacional de la ALFAL, Lima (6–10 enero, 1975). Lima: Universidad Nacional Mayor de San Marcos, Dirección Universitaria de Biblioteca y Publicaciones, 1978. 691 p.; bibl.; ill.

Consists of 61 papers presented at 4th International Congress of Asociación de Lingüística y Filología de la América Latina (ALFAL) in 1975. These cover a wide range of subjects (e.g., child speech, bilingualism, linguistic interference, jargon, and language teaching programs).

1415 Aulie, H. Wilbur. Diccionario chól-español, español-chól. Compilado por H. Wilbur Aulie y Evelyn W. de Aulie, con la colaboración de César Menéses Díaz y Cristóbal López Vázquez. México: Instituto Lingüístico de Verano, 1978. 215 p.; 4 leaves of plates; ill. (Vocabularios indígenas; 21)

Dictionary of Chol, a Mayan language of Chiapas, Mexico, spoken by about 80,000 speakers. Includes grammatical categories, examples of usage, and dialect variants, as well as a brief description of the language. Chol-Spanish section has well over 3,000 entries.

Bébel-Gisler, Dany. La langue créole force jugulée: étude sociolinguistique des rapports de force entre le créole et le français aux Antilles. See item **951**.

Beyond the codices: the Nahua view of colonial Mexico. See *HLAS 42:5126*.

1417 Boremanse, Didier. Magic and poetry among the Maya: northern Lacandon therapeutic incantation (UCLA/JLAL, 5:1, Summer 1979, p. 43–53, bibl.)

In the belief that the Creator gave them not only their common ills but also therapeutic incantations to cure them, the northern Lacandón Indians of Chiapas, Mexico, are very careful to learn the correct pronunciation of their esoteric lore which not many of their number understand. Includes example of an incantation with a brief analysis of its structure.

1418 Briggs, Lucy Therina. A critical survey of the literature on the Aymara language (LARR, 14:3, 1979, p. 87–106, bibl., table)

Excellent detailed study of works on Aymara, an indigenous language of Peru, Bolivia, and northern Chile used by some two million speakers. See *HLAS 41:19*.

1419 Brown, Cecil H. Growth and development of folk botanical life forms in the Mayan language family (AAA/AE, 6:2, May 1979, p. 366–385, map, tables)

Reconstructs life-form systems for earlier stages of the Mayan language on the basis of names occurring in modern Mayan languages. Discusses principles underlying botanical nomenclature development.

1420 Burmann García, Lee. Aproximación a las obras *El libro de Chilam Balam de Chumayel* y *La tierra del faisán y del venado* (UY/R, 20:119, sept./oct. 1978, p. 67–96)

Study of the *Book of Chilam Balam* (see *HLAS 39:1705*) and *The land of the pheasant and the deer*, the former written originally in Maya and the latter in Spanish, but with a strong Mayan flavor.

1421 Butler, James and **Dean E. Arnold.** La clasificación Tzutujil del maíz en San Pedro La Laguna (GIIN/GI, 13:1/2, jan./junio 1978, p. 75–102, bibl., map, table)

Tzutujil farmers (Tzutujil is a Mayan language of Guatemala) refer to the corn plant by different names, depending on the type of corn (grown at high elevation or at low) on its stage of growth (young or mature). Subclassification depends on other factors, such as size of the ear of corn, its hardness, and the season in which it was grown.

1422 Campbell, Lyle. Quichean linguistic prehistory. Berkeley: University of California Press, 1977. 132 p.; bibl.; ill. (University of California Publications in linguistics; v. 81)

Considers Quichean subgroup of Mayan languages to consist of Quiché, Achí, Cakchiquel, Tzutujil, Pokomam, Pokomchí, Uspantec, and Kekchí. He holds Achí to be a dialect of Quiché, and Pokomam and Pokomchí to be dialects of a single language, which he calls Pokom. Presents 245 cognate sets, reconstructs Proto-Mayan phonemes, and discusses sub-grouping, diffusion, and Quichean philology (see *HLAS 37:1825*).

1423 Cartagena, Nelson. Los estudios lingüísticos en Chile durante la decada, 1964–1974 (IAA, 6:1, 1980, p. 53–78, bibl.)

With the establishment of a linguistics department at the University of Chile at Valparaíso, the Institute of Language and Literature at the Catholic University of Valparaíso, and the Linguistic Society of Chile, founded in 1971, Chile has become an area of increasing linguistic interest and study. Author expects study of Mapuche in the province of Cautín to continue. Another notable linguistic project is the Atlas lingüístico-etnográfico del sur de Chile (see *HLAS 41:1336*).

1424 Cerrón-Palomino, R. Cambios gramaticalmente condicionados en quechua: una desconformación de la teoría neogramática del cambio fonético (PUC/L, 1:2, dic. 1977, p. 163–186, bibl.)

Cites examples from several dialects of Quechua to support the contention that sound change may be morphologically conditioned, that it is not a purely phonetic phenomenon.

1425 Chumap Lucía, Aurelio and **Manuel García-Rendueles.** "Duik múun . . . :" universo mítico de los aguaruna. Carátula, Bárbara Simón R. y Xiligrafía Aguaruna. Lima, Perú: Centro Amazónico de Antropología y Aplicación Práctica, 1979. 2 v. (866 p.); ill. (Serie Antropológica; 2)

Consists of 100 texts of Aguaruna folklore, with Spanish translation. Aguarunas are a Jivaroan group of northern Peru, numbering about 22,000.

1426 Civeira Taboada, Miguel. Yucatán visto por Fray Alonso Ponce, 1588–1589, Vocabulario de palabras mayas que figuran en la obra de Fray Alonso Ponce por Domingo Mártinez Paredez. Mérida, México: Universidad de Yucatán, 1977. 130 p.

Describes Yucatan, Mexico, as it appeared to Fray Alonso Ponce in the 16th century, and lists a vocabulary of Mayan words that occur in his diary.

1426a The Codex Pérez and the Book of Chilam Balam of Maní. Translated and edited by Eugene R. Craine and Reginald C. Reindrop. Norman: University of Oklahoma Press, 1979. 209 p.: bibl.; ill.; index (The Civilization of the American Indian series)

Translation of a compilation of manuscripts written in Yucatec Mayan over a century ago by Juan Pío Pérez, a native speaker of the language. The *Codex* is a mixture of astrology, Roman Catholic tradition, and Mayan lore, and includes within it the *Book of Chilam Balam* (see *HLAS 39:1705*).

1426b El Códice de Huichapan. v. 1, Relato otomí del México prehispánico y colonial. Editor: Manuel Alvarado Guinchard. México: Instituto Nacional de Antropología e Historia, SEP, Departamento de Lingüística, 1976– . 1 v.: bibl.; facsims. (Colección científica—Instituto Nacional de Antropología e Historia; 48: Lingüística)

Facsimile reproduction of pages of a manuscript written in Otomi (central Mexico), with the writing deciphered, phonemicized, and translated into Spanish.

1427 *Comunidades y Culturas Peruanas.* Instituto Lingüístico de Verano. Vol. 16, 1979– . Yarinacocha, Perú.

Issue devoted to the following topic: "Initik Augmatbau: Historia Aguaruna." Consists of 12 language texts with Spanish translation of legends about the history of the Aguarunas, a Jivaroan language group numbering 22,000 speakers located in the Upper Marañón River area of Peru. Compilers of the texts were: Timías Akuts Nugkai, Arturo Paati Dusiya, Alejandro Shwit Piitug, and Jeanne Grover.

1428 Congreso de Lenguas Nacionales, *3d, Cochabamba, Bolivia, 1976.* Lingüística y educación: Tercer Congreso de Lenguas Nacionales. La Paz: Instituto Boliviano de Cultura, 1977. 285 p.; bibl.

Papers presented at a conference held in Cochabamba, Bolivia on national, indigenous languages. Topics are: problems of translation, literacy, teaching of Spanish, and attitudes toward language as they relate to Aymara, Quechua, Guaraní, and other languages of South America.

Cuentos folklóricos de los achual. See *HLAS 42:1400.*

1429 Dahlin de Weber, Diana. Presuposiciones de preguntas en el quechua de Huánuco. s.l.: Instituto Lingüístico de Verano, 1976. 14 p.; bibl. (Documento de trabajo—Instituto Lingüístico de Verano; no. 8)

Interrogative suffixes -*raq* and -*taq* in Húanuco Quechua differ slightly in meaning, the former being used when the interrogator is not sure the person addressed knows the answer, and the latter when he believes he does.

D'Ans, André-Marcel. La verdadera biblia de los cashinahua. See *HLAS 42:1401.*

1430 Dennis, Ronald K. and **Ilah Fleming.** La lengua tol-jicaque: los sustantivos (YAXKIN, 1:3, julio 1976, p. 2–7, bibl.)

Jicaque phonology includes three series of stops and affricates (simple, aspirated, and glottalized), two fricatives, three nasals, one liquid, four semivowels, and six vowels—a total of 29 phonemes. Article summarizes noun classification and use of suffixes and pronouns.

1431 ———; Margaret Royce de Dennis; and **Ilah Fleming.** El alfabeto tol: jicaque (YAXKIN, 1:1, oct. 1975, p. 12–22, tables)

Describes practical orthography of Jicaque, a Hokan language of Honduras, which required 32 symbols to represent the 29 phonemes of the language which native speakers call Tol. Article includes 200-word vocabulary (the so-called Swadesh list).

1432 Dietrich, Wolf. Las categorías verbales, partes de la oración, en tupí-guaraní (IAI/I, 4, 1977, p. 245–261)

One of the most extensive language families of South America is Tupí-Guaraní, whose migrations from Paraguay across the Gran Chaco into Bolivia and Brazil have been documented from the early 16th century. Tupí is considered the more archaic language, characterized by having closed syllables in contrast to open syllables in Guaraní cognates. Using Chiriguano as a typical Guaraní language, author uses linguistic markers to classify verbs in that language.

Educación bilingüe: una experiencia en la Amazonía peruana: antología. See item **4539.**

1433 Elliott, Ray. Términos de parentesco unitarios de los ixiles de Nebaj (GIIN/GI, 13:1/2, jan./junio 1978, p. 103–149, bibl., map, tables)

The way one individual is expected to behave toward another in Ixil culture (Ixil is a Mayan language of Guatemala) depends on the relationship between the two. Kinship terms define such relationships and depend on sex (of ego, of referent, and of referent relative to ego), age of referent relative to age of ego, generation distance, lineality, and consanguinity.

1433a Englert, Sebastián. Idioma rapanui: gramática y diccionario del antiguo idioma de la Isla de Pascua. Santiago: Universidad de Chile, 1978 [c1977]. 287 p.

The author describes Rapanui phonology and grammar in terms of Latin; besides making nouns fit a pattern of declensions, he states that the language lacks the verbs "to have" and "to be." About two-thirds of the book is a dictionary of the language, which is spoken by some 2,000 inhabitants of Easter Island, a possession of Chile.

1434 Esboço de um atlas lingüístico de Minas Gerais. José Ribeiro et al. Rio de Janeiro: Ministério da Educação e Cultura, Fundação Casa de Rui Barbosa, 1977. 1 v.; bibl.; glossaries; maps (some col.)

Discusses procedures for gathering language data directly and spontaneously from interviews, and indirectly by means of questionnaires. Maps of the state of Minas Gerais, Brazil, indicate the localities visited and the varieties of usage in Portuguese noted for the linguistic atlas of this state.

1435 Escobar, Alberto. El problema de la lengua y la identidad nacional (*in* Perú, identidad nacional. César Arróspide de la Flor. Lima: Centro de Estudios para el Desarrollo y la Participación, 1979, p. 169–189, bibl., table [Serie Realidad nacional])

Speakers of Spanish, Quechua, and Aymara have coexisted in Peru for more than four centuries without having developed extensive bilingualism, although contact with the indigenous languages has modified Peruvian Spanish to some degree, especially outside of the capital. Migration from rural to urban areas led to population increase and to new language use reflecting socioeconomic changes that profoundly affect national identity.

1436 Estudios chibchas. t. 1, Tunebo, Ica. Lomalinda, República de Colombia: Editorial Townsend, 1976. 1 v. (153 p.): bibl. (Serie sintáctica; no. 1)

Three articles dealing with Chibchan languages of Colombia, including a language text in Tunebo and Ica. Individual entries are: Paul Headland's and Stephen H. Levinsohn's "Prominencia y Cohesión dentro del Discurso en Tunebo" (p. 1–40); Edna Headland's "Distribución de Información en Tunebo" (p. 41–75); and Hubert P. Tracy's and Stephen H. Levinsohn's "Referencia a los Participantes en los Discursos Expositivos de Ica" (p. 77–104).

1437 Estudios en cacua, jupda y sáliba. Lomalinda, República de Colombia: Editorial Townsend, 1976. 185 p.; (Serie sintáctica; no. 3)

Studies of three indigenous languages of eastern Colombia, which are as yet unclassified. Narrative discourse in Cacua is basically time-oriented, with logical or locative linkages within the paragraphs, as illustrated by a lengthy analyzed text. Three genres of Jupda Macú discourse (narrative, procedural, and expository) are analyzed and illustrated. Study of a Sáliba text shows 23 paragraph types, with six degrees of embedding.

1438 Estudios en camsá y catio. Lomalinda, República de Colombia: Editorial Townsend, 1977. 206 p.; ill. (Serie sintáctica; no. 4)

Discourse analysis applied to text material in two languages of Colombia: Camsá, an isolated language of 2,500 speakers in the south, and Catío, a Carib language of 10,000 speakers in the north. The articles are: Linda Howard's "Esquema de los Tipos de Párrafo en Camsá" (p. 1–67); Mareike Schöttelndreyer's "La Narración Folclórica Catía como un Drama en Actos y Escenas" (p. 95–153). The remainder of the book consists of language text.

1439 Estudios en inga. Lomalinda, República de Colombia: Editorial Townsend, 1976. 207 p.; bibl.; ill. (Serie sintáctica; no. 2)

Four articles on Inga, the northernmost language of the Quechua family, spoken by over 6,000 inhabitants of the Caquetá and Putumayo River area of Colombia. Individual articles are: Alonso Maffla Bilbao, "Estructura Fonológica, y Estructura del 'vbl' del Inga, lengua del Putumayo" (p. 3–50); and three studies by Stephen H. Levinsohn, "Perspectiva de la Oración Funcional en Inga" (p. 51–105), "Progresión y Digresión Respecto al Hilo Central de los Discursos en Inga" (p. 107–139), and "Referencia al Participante en el Discurso Narrativo Inga" (p. 141–190).

1440 Estudios tucanos. Lomalinda, República de Colombia: Editorial Townsend, 1977? 1 v.; bibl.; graphs (Serie sintáctica; no. 5)

Consists of analyzed discourse from nguage texts in Southern Barasano, Core-

guaje, Cubeo, Guanano, Tatuyo, Tucano, and Tuyuca, all of them Tucanoan languages of Colombia. Divisions and subdivisions of the discourse are clearly indicated. Free translation of the text follows interlinear literal translation.

1441 Folk literature of the Gê Indians. Johannes Wilbert, editor, with Karin Simoneau; contributing authors, Horace Banner et al. Los Angeles: UCLA Latin American Center Publications, University of California, Los Angeles, 1978. 1 v.; bibl. (A book on lore. UCLA Latin American studies; v. 44)

The 177 tales in this volume in the Folk Literature series published by UCLA (see *HLAS 39:1179–1780*) originally appeared in English, French, German, and Portuguese). Apanyekua, Apinaye, Cayapo, Craho, Crenye and Ramkokamekra, in which these tales originated, are Gê languages of Brazil. Volume includes motif analyses.

1442 García de León, Antonio. Pajapan, un dialecto mexicano del Golfo. México: SEP, Instituto Nacional de Antropología e Historia, Departamento de Lingüística, 1976. 149 p.; bibl.; ill. (Colección Científica— Instituto Nacional de Antropología e Historia; 43: Lingüística)

Sociolinguistic study of the Gulf of Mexico dialect of Nahuatl, spoken in the southern part of the state of Veracruz, Mexico. Includes lexicostatistical data from various dialects, texts with Spanish translation, and Spanish-Nahuatl vocabulary.

García González, José. Algunas consideraciones lingüísticas a propósito de un nuevo cuento afrocubano. See *HLAS 42:1268*.

1443 ——— and Gema Valdés Acosta. Restos de lenguas bantues en la región central de Cuba (UCLV/I, 59, enero/abril 1978, p. 7–50)

Expressions from Bantu languages of Africa are heard in common use in certain parts of Cuba. Article includes Bantu phonology, morphology, and vocabulary.

1444 Gerzenstein, Ana. Lengua chorote. Buenos Aires: Universidad de Buenos Aires, Facultad de Filosofía y Letras, Instituto de Lingüística, 1978. 1 v. (Archivo de lenguas precolombinas; v. 3)

Careful description of the phonology, morphology, and grammar of Chorote, a language of the Chaco area of Argentina which belongs to the Mataco-Maya language family.

1445 Girard, Rafael. Esotericism of the Popol Vuh. Translated from the Spanish with a foreword by Blair A. Moffett. Pasadena, Calif.: Theosophical University Press, 1979. 359 p.; ill.; index.

Assuming the *Popul Vuh* to be an authentic Quiche document, writer interprets it as an account of Mayan metaphysics, with parallels in present-day indigenous culture. This is a translation of the Spanish edition of 1948.

1446 González Casanova, Pablo. Estudios de lingüística y filología nahuas. Ed. y estudio introductorio, Ascensión H. de León-Portilla. México: Universidad Nacional Autónoma de México, 1977. 289 p; 5 leaves of plates; bibl.; ill.; index.

Studies of the Aztec (Mexicano or Nahuatl) language by Pablo González Casanova (1889–1936), a Mexican linguist and philologist. Extensive introduction includes biography. Among articles are texts and vocabularies, studies of influence of Nahuatl on Mexican Spanish, and of Spanish on Nahuatl.

1447 Good, Claude. Diccionario triqui de Chicahuaxtla: triqui-castellano, castellano-triqui. México: Instituto Lingüístico de Verano, 1978. 104 p.; ill. (Serie de vocabularios indígenas Mariano Silva y Aceves; no. 20)

Five phonemic levels of tone are indicated in Triqui words listed in this dictionary, which also contains grammatical notes, kinship terms and salutations, and a list of number names. Trique (the more common spelling) is a Mixtecan language of the state of Oaxaca, Mexico, used by 15,000 speakers; 5,5000 of these speak the dialect of San Andrés Chicahuaxtla.

Granda, Germán de. Formulas mágicas de conjuro en el departamento del Chocó, Colombia. See *HLAS 42:1232.*

1448 Hasler, Juan A. Un sondeo en tres áreas de bilinguismo rural en México (UNAM/RMS, 39:3, julio/sept. 1977, p. 985–999)

Describes attitudes of indigenous peoples of three different areas of Mexico—Totonac, Tlapanec, and Tarascan—towards their mother tongue and Spanish.

Herrera Porras, Tomás. Cuna cosmology: legends from Panama. See item **876** and *HLAS 42:1169.*

1449 Herrero, Joaquín and Federico Sánchez de Lozada. Gramática quechua: estructura del quechua boliviano contemporáneo. Cochabamba: Editorial Universo: distribuye, C.E.F. Co., 1978. 520 p.; index.

Describes Bolivian Quechua in terms of morphemes and morphemic clusters. Contains an abundance of illustrative sentences, but lacks succinct description of the language structure. Well indexed.

Hilton, Ronald. El Padre Las Casas, el castellano y las lenguas indígenas. See *HLAS 42:5085.*

1450 Holt, Dennis and William Bright. La lengua paya y las fronteras lingüísticas de Mesoamérica (YAXKIN, 1:2, enero 1976, p. 35–42, bibl., graphs)

Mesoamerican languages in general are distinguished from Central American by glottalized stops and affricates in the former, and voiced stops and labialized velars in the latter. As a result of cultural interaction and borrowings, Paya, a Chibchan language of Central America, exhibits features of both types.

1451 Hurley viuda de Delgaty, Alfa and Agustín Ruiz Sánchez. Diccionario tzotzil de San Andrés con variaciones dialectales: tzotzil-español, español-tzotzil. México: Instituto Lingüístico de Verano, 1978. 481 p.; bibl.; ill. (Serie de vocabularios y diccionarios indígenas "Mario Silva y Aceves;" no. 22)

At least four dialects of Tzotzil are represented in this dictionary in addition to that of San Andrés. Sense distinctions are indicated as well as examples of usage, making this a most valuable dictionary for the study of a Mayan language. Includes fairly detailed study of the grammar of the language (72 p.).

1452 Instituto Indigenista Nacional, *Guatemala.* Alfabeto de las lenguas mayances. Guatemala: Editorial Universitaria, Universidad de San Carlos de Guatemala, 1977. 125 p.

Compilation of alphabets of 19 Mayan languages of Guatemala and one Arawakan language. Alphabets, based on modern phonemic analyses, are recognized as "official" by the Guatemala Ministry of Education.

Jackson, Jean. Language identity of the Colombian Vaupés Indians. See item **1134**.

————. Vaupés marriage: a network system in the Northwest Amazon. See item **1136**.

1453 Landaburu, John. El tratamiento gramatical de la verdad en la lengua andoque (ICA/RCA, 20, 1976, p. 79–100, bibl., tables)

Describes phonology of Andoque, a Witotoan language of Colombia, spoken by about 150 inhabitants of the Aduche river area. In addition to the segmental phonemes (nine vowels, 13 consonants), the language exhibits nasalization and tone. A notable syntactic element, termed "assertive," is obligatorily present in every assertive sentence, in contrast to statements based on inference or on testimony of someone other than the speaker.

1454 The Languages of native America: historical and comparative assessment. Edited by Lyle Campbell and Marianne Mithun. Austin: University of Texas Press, 1979. 1034 p.; bibl.; index; map.

Contains studies by 15 authors discussing early language classification systems of North American Indian languages, and summarizing more recent comparative linguistic studies in this area. A good, comprehensive treatment.

1455 Lastra de Suárez, Yolanda and **Fernando Horcasitas.** El Náhuatl en el norte y el occidente del estado de México (UNAM/AA, 15, 1978, p. 185–250, bibl., maps, tables)

Third in a series of reports of studies on the use of and attitude toward Nahuatl in various parts of Mexico (see *HLAS 39:1680*)

1456 Lionnet, Andrés. Los elementos de la lengua cahita: yaqui-mayo. México: Universidad Nacional Autónoma de México, 1977. 91 p. (Serie antropológica; 29)

Concise analysis and comparison of Yaqui and Mayo, two distinct but related Uto-Aztecan languages whose speakers (about 19,000 Yaqui, 30,000 Mayo) are located chiefly in the state of Sonora, Mexico, with about 5,000 Yaqui in Arizona. Includes synopsis of morphology and grammar, and a vocabulary list of words, stems, and affixes.

1457 López Austin, Alfredo. Intento de reconstrucción de procesos semánticos del Náhuatl (UNAM/AA, 15, 1978, p. 165–184, ill.)

Proposes tentative rules for reconstruction of semantic development in Nahuatl with *ix* and *mal* taken as examples of elements that are rich in significance.

1458 Loukotka, Čestmír. Classification of South American Indian languages. Edited by Johannes Wilbert. Los Angeles: UCLA, Latin American Center, 1968. 453 p.; bibl.; fold. map (Reference series; 7)

Standard work on the subject of South American Indian languages. There are three main divisions: 1) languages of Paleo-American tribes; 2) languages of tropical forest tribes; and 3) languages of Andean tribes. Each is subdivided geographically, and each subdivision includes list of language stocks or isolates. Includes a large map of South America showing language locations, and a bibliography of 123 p. Excellent reference work.

1459 Manelis Klein, Harriet E. Una gramática de la lengua toba: morfología verbal y nominal. Montevideo: Universidad de la República, División Publicaciones y Ediciones, 1978. 185 p.; bibl.; ill.

Phonology and grammar of Toba, a Guaicuran language of more than 15,000 speakers in northern Argentina and Bolivia. Appendixes include list of noun and verb roots and list of affixes.

Marcuschi, Luiz Antonio. Linguagem e classes sociais: introdução crítica à teoria dos códigos lingüísticos de Basil Bernstein. See item **8381**.

1460 Martínez Ruíz, Jesús. Densidad territorial de los monolingües y bilingües de México en 1960–1970: estadísticas del Proyecto Sociolingüístico. México: Instituto de Investigaciones Sociales, Universidad Nacional Autónoma de México, 1977. 228 p.; maps; tables.

Statistics on monolingualism and bilingualism in Mexico, by states and *municipios*. Includes maps and tables.

1461 Mayan texts. Edited by Louanna Furbee-Losee. Chicago: University of Chicago Press, 1976/1979. 2 v.; bibl. (Native American texts series; v. 1, no. 1 0361-3399. v. 2: IJAL-NATS monograph; no. 3)

Consists of analyzed texts from Mayan languages of Mesoamerica. Vol. 1 contains texts in languages of Guatemala: Kekchi, Quiché, Tzutujil, Pocomán, Mam, Jacaltec, and Kanjobal; and one text in Huastec, which is spoken in Mexico; vol. 2 consists of texts in languages of Mexico: Chol, Lacandón, Yucatec Maya, Tzeltal, and Tzotzil. Although format of the text and quality of reproduction vary from text to text, these volumes should prove excellent source material for discourse analysis and comparative studies of Mayan languages.

Migliazza, Ernesto. The integration of the indigenous peoples of the territory of Roraima, Brazil. See item **1165**.

1462 Montes Giraldo, José Joaquín. Fitónimos de sustrato en el español del altiplano cundiboyacense y dialectos muiscas (ICC/T, 33 : 1, enero/abril 1978, p. 41–54, maps, table)

Certain plant names in Spanish of the Colombian central highlands exhibit a *ch* ~ *rr* variation (e.g., a flowering tree called *chaque* ~ *raque*) which is attributed to their having been borrowed from different dialects of the now extinct Muisca language. On the basis of place names in the same region, writer posits that a phonological change *rr* > *ch* occurred in Muisca at some period.

1463 La oficialización del Quechua (SGL/B, enero/junio 1975, p. 5–10)

Discusses proposed official alphabet for Quechua and the areas of bilingualism and monolingualism in Peru. Appended is the Decree of 27 May 1975 which recognized Quechua as an official language of Peru, along with Spanish.

1465 Ortega Ricaurte, Carmen. Los estudios sobre lenguas indígenas de Colombia: notas históricas y bibliografía. Bogotá: Instituto Caro y Cuervo, 1978. 443 p.; 16 leaves of plates; bibl.; ill.; indexes (Publicaciones del Instituto Caro y Cuervo: serie bibliográfica; 13)

Approximately half of this book (p. 245–406) is a bibliography of works in or about indigenous languages of Colombia, including extensive historical notes to give perspective to the bibliographical data. Contributors to this linguistic knowledge include 16th-century Catholic priests, 20th-century evangelical linguists, and European, North American, and Colombian investigators.

Parodi, Claudia. Algunos aspectos léxicos relativos al repartimiento forzoso o cuatequitl del centro de México, 1575–1599. See *HLAS* 42 : 2074.

Pérez Kantule, Nele and **Rubén Pérez Kantule.** Picture-writings and other documents. See item **912**.

1466 Porro, Antonio. O anão do uxmal e os gêmeos do *Popol Vuh* (MP/R, 24, nova série, 1977, p. 7–21, bibl.)

Comparison of the themes of two Maya texts, the *Legend of the dwarf of Uxmal* and the *Popol Vuh*, shows structural and cultural analogy in prehispanic mythological literature from highland and lowland Mayan areas.

1467 Programa Interamericano de Lingüística y Enseñanza de Idiomas (PILEI), *5th, São Paulo, 1969.* Atas. São Paulo: Universidad de São Paulo, 1979. 406 p.; bibl.; ill.; tables.

Papers presented at the 5th symposium of PILEI in 1969 deal with a variety of themes such as sociolinguistics, computational linguistics, language teaching, and literacy. The following is a list of individual contributions: Heles Contreras' "La Revolución Chomskyana" (p. 77–85); Nelson Rossi's "Os Falares Regionais do Brasil" (p. 87–98); Norman A. McQuown's "O Papel da Língua Materna na Educação Nacional" (p. 99–104); Juan M. Lope-Blanch's "Tareas más Urgentes de la Lingüística Iberoamericana" (p. 105–112); Madeleine Mathiot's "Reseña Crítica de la Sociolingüística Norteamericana Actual" (p. 113–122); Paul L. Garvin's "La Experiencia Checa y el Trabajo de la Escuela de Praga" (p. 125–131); Evangelina Arana de Swadesh's "El Español de México en las Zonas de Contacto" (p. 133–139); Joseph E. Grimes' "La Computación en Lingüística ¿Deshumanización o Liberación del Espíritu Investigador?" (p. 141–146); Mervin C. Alleyne's "National Languages and Creole Languages" (p. 147–151); Gilles-R. Lefebvre's "Les Aspects Sociaux de la Dualité Linguistique au Canada" (p. 153–171); Leopoldo Wigdorsky's "Una Investigación Piloto sobre la Eficacia Comparada del 'Método de Gramática y Traducción' y el 'Enfoque Oral' en la Enseñanza de una Lengua Extranjera" (p. 175–181); Xavier Albo's "Sociolingüística del Valle de Cochabamba, Bolivia" (p. 183–200); Frederick B. Agard's "Pronúncia e Ortografia do Inglés para Falantes de Espanhol e Português" (p. 201–209); Eric Lenneberg's "Fundamentos Biológicos da Linguagem" (p. 211–217); Yolanda Lastra's "El Habla y la Educación de los Niños de Origen Mexicano de Los Angeles" (p. 219–228); Sarah C. Gudschinsky's "The Role of the Linguist in the Preparation of Materials" (p. 229–236); Norman P. Sacks' "El Programa Intensivo del Español en el Verano" (p. 241–248); Robert B. Kaplan's "On Camels and Intensive English Programs" (p. 249–255); Adriana Gandolfo's "La Publicación de una Antología Interamericana de Lingüística Aplicada: Actividad en la Argentina" (p. 257–262); Mervin C. Alleyne's "Problems of an Archives Center for Creole Languages" (p. 265–269); Donald F. Solá's "Un Archivo de Lengua Quechua" (p. 271–275); Wolfgang Wölck's "Especificación y Foco en Quechua" (p. 277–286); Vládimir Honsa's "Características Fonológicas de los Tipos Dialectales del Español en la República Dominicana" (p. 289–297); Ivan Lowe's "Os Trabalhos de Lingüística Computacional do Summer Institute of Linguistics" (p. 301–307); Ernesto Zierer's "Lingüística Matemática en la Universidad Nacional de Trujillo" (p. 309–310; María Beatriz Fontanella de Weinberg's "Los Auxiliares Españoles" (p. 313–318); and Eunice Pontes' "Os Possessivo de Segunda Pessoa do Plural em Belo Horizonte" (p.319–322).

1468 Rensch, Calvin R. Situación actual de los estudios lingüísticos de la lenguas de Oaxaca. Oaxaca, México: Instituto Nacional de Antropología e Historia, Centro Regional de Oaxaca, 1977. 21 p.; bibl. (Estudios de antropología e historia; 17)

Almost 100 indigenous languages are spoken in the state of Oaxaca, Mexico, many of them exhibiting unusual features such as five tones of Trique or the three degrees of vowel length of Mixe of Coatlán. Author mentions studies in typology, and comparative and descriptive studies, and suggests topics for further linguistic study.

1469 Riese, Berthold and **Günter Zimmermann.** Weitere Schritte zur Lösung des Rätsels der Mayasprachigen Solana/o-Worterbücher (SA/J, 65, 1978, p. 103–119, bibl., ill.)

Describes manuscript dictionaries of Cakchiquel (Mayan, Guatemala) in an effort to identify the compiler of the original from which other manuscript copies were made. Task was complicated by the fact that the name was given variously as Francisco Solano, Félix Solana, and F. Alonso Solana. Authors conclude that the compiler was a Franciscan friar named Félix Solano.

1470 Rivas, Pedro Geoffroy. Toponimia nahuat de Cuscatlán. 2. ed. San Salvador: Ministerio de Educación, Dirección de Cultura, Dirección de Publicaciones, 1973. 163 p.

Many place names in El Salvador have been misinterpreted, partly owing to an inadequate knowledge of Nahuat. In this revised edition of his 1961 publication, author attempts to correct this situation, citing five rules for proper analysis and listing 16 locative elements.

Robledo, Tey Diana. La poesía náhuatl de Machilxóchitl. See *HLAS 42:5105.*

Salinas Pedraza, Jesús and **H. Russell Bernard.** Rc Hnychnyu (The Otomí). v. 1, Geography and fauna. See item **920.**

1471 Schuhmacher, W.W. On the linguistic aspect of Thor Heyerdahl's theory: the so-called non-Polynesian number names from Easter Island (AI/A, 71:5/6, 1976, p. 806–847, bibl., tables)

Discusses evidence for the hypothesis that Easter Island language and culture had its origin on the American continent (North and South), noting especially the number names used in various languages.

1472 Sherzer, Joel. Namakke, sunmakke, kormakke: three types of Cuna speech event (*in* Explorations in the ethnography of speaking. Edited by Richard Bauman and Joel Sherzer. Cambridge, UK: Cambridge University Press, 1974, p. unavailable)

Chanting, speaking, and shouting characterize three kinds of speech usage among the Cuna of San Blas, Panama. The first of these is used in formal gatherings (congresses), the second in curing ceremonies, and the last at girls' puberty rites.

——. Strategies in text and context: *Cuna kaa kwento.* See *HLAS 42:1186.*

1473 Straight, Henry Stephen. The acquisition of Maya phonology: variation in Yucatec child language. New York: Garland

Pub., 1976. 255 p.; bibl. (Garland studies in American Indian linguistics)

Detailed discussion of results of a study of the speech of 22 children of Yucatec Maya households, ranging in age from three and a half to 14 years. Subjects were asked to imitate recorded sounds, and their responses were recorded on another tape. Tests administered were: Phonological Imitation (in which the stimuli were syllables, one set being vowels only, the other CV syllables); Imitation (words); Imitation (sentences); and two Language Dominance, in which the stimuli were body parts and pictures of familiar objects. All testing was done using the Maya language.

1474 Suárez, Jorge A. La influencia del español en la estructura gramática del náhuatl (UNAM/AL, 15, 1977, p. 115–164, bibl.)

Borrowing of Spanish words into Nahuatl has as its corollary, the influence of Spanish syntactic structure on the same language. Bulk of this article deals with simple borrowings and transpositions, or the extension of functions of an indigenous item by analogy with Spanish. Includes many illustrations from various dialects of Nahuatl.

1475 Sullivan, Thelma D. Compendio de la gramática náhuatl. México: Universidad Nacional Autónoma de México, Instituto de Investigaciones Históricas, 1976. 382 p.; bibl.; index (Serie de cultura náhuatl: Monografías; 18)

Grammar of classical Nahuatl, with illustrations from 16th-century codices, by an outstanding scholar in the field of Uto-Aztecan studies.

1476 Summer Institute of Linguistics. Bibliografía del Instituto Lingüístico de Verano en el Perú, 1946–1976. Recopilación de Mary Ruth Wise y Ann Shanks. Lima: Instituto Lingüístico de Verano, 1977, i.e. 1978. 305 p.; index.

Bibliography of the Summer Institute of Linguistics in Peru, representing 30 years of linguistic and ethnographic publications dealing with indigenous groups of Peru, as well as literary materials and literature in the vernacular languages. Includes items in press and on microfiche.

1477 Villalón, María Eugenia. Aspectos de la organización social y la terminología de parentesco e'ñapa (vulg. panare).

Caracas: Universidad Católica Andrés Bello, Instituto de Investigaciones Históricas, Centro de Lenguas Indígenas, 1978. 40 p.; bibl.; ill. (Colección de lenguas indígenas: Serie menor; 5)

Analysis of Panare kinship terms with ethnographic data. The Panare, who call themselves e'ñapa, are an indigenous group of 1200 inhabitants of Venezuela whose language is a member of the Carib family.

1478 Villamañán, Adolfo de. Vocabulario barí comparado: comparación de los vocabularios del Fr. Francisco de Catarroja (1730) y Fr. Francisco Javier Alfaro (1788) con el barí actual. Caracas: Universidad Católica Andrés Bello, Centro de Lenguas Indígenas, 1978. 61 p. (Colección Lenguas indígenas: Serie menor; 1)

Author compares two vocabulary lists of Bari words taken from 18th-century manuscripts with a list of the same expressions in modern usage, but makes no attempt at reconstruction. Known also as Motilon, this is a Chibchan language of 3,000 speakers, not to be confused with Carib Motilon, which is also known as Yukpa.

1478a El Vocabulario Kekchi: español de Fray Eugenio de Gongora, O.P., 1739. Presentación: Agustín Estrada Monroy (IAHG/AHG, 2:1, 1979, p. 149–193)

Transcription of a manuscript vocabulary of Kekchi compiled by an 18th-century Dominican friar. Brief discussion of problems of paleography and pecularities of abbreviation. Orthography of text has been modernized.

1478b Vrhel, František. Sobre la fonología tipológica del Maya (UCP/IAP, 10, 1976, p. 77–86)

Of three phonological types (Atlantic, with well developed vocalic and nasal systems like Guaraní; Pacific, with weak vocalic and strong oral consonant systems like Chontal Maya [Chontal of Tabasco]; and Central, with traces of both these systems like Quechua), Yucatec Maya has been considered Pacific. It lacks voiced stops, however (with the exception of *b*) and has only one liquid (*l*). Author considers this a typical Indian language of the New World.

1479 Wölck, W. Un problema ficticio: ¿lengua o dialecto quechua? (PUC/L, 1:2, dic. 1977, p. 151–162, bibl.)

Popular notion of dialect and languag

derives from distinction between standard language necessary for government administration and varieties of local speech, or between sociopolitical and ethnocultural languages. Prior to the Spanish conquest Quechua was in the former class, but many Spanish speakers of the mestizo culture consider it a dialect.

BIOLOGICAL ANTHROPOLOGY

R.A. HALBERSTEIN, Associate Professor, Department of Anthropology and Department of Epidemiology and Public Health, University of Miami

THE PAST DECADE WITNESSED A VIRTUAL explosion of new research on biological anthropology in Latin America and the Caribbean. The entire region has now fully emerged as a proven testing ground suitable for all phases of anthropological field and laboratory work. The ever-accelerating increase in publications during this period reflects the growing awareness of the importance and significance of Latin America for the investigation of human evolution, adaptation, and biological variation. Future scientists will benefit greatly from the extensive theoretical and practical research that is currently underway.

The present review focuses upon materials published in 1978–80. As in the last volume, *HLAS 41*, annotated references are categorized under the following headings: Paleoanthropology; Population Studies: Biodemography; Population Studies: Genetics; Human Adaptation and Variation; Human Development; and Epidemiological Anthropology.

PALEOANTHROPOLOGY

The items in this section are based upon prehistoric fossilized and mummified human remains discovered in Mexico, Peru, Ecuador, Brazil, Argentina, Chile, Panama, Costa Rica, and the Dominican Republic. Methods include physical measurement of the specimens, X-rays, histology, electron microscopy, computerized statistical tests, and biomechanical analysis. A variety of topics are addressed, such as burial customs, age and ethnic variations in anatomical characteristics, sexual dimorphism, ancient medical and dietary practices, pathologies and artificial deformation, and paleodemography. The possible functional and nutritional significance of cannibalism and human sacrifice in ancient Mexico is re-examined by Ortiz de Montellano (item **1503**). Convincing osteological evidence for syphilis in precolumbian Dominican Republic is provided by Luna Calderón (item **1499**).

Two extremely important sites have been recently uncovered. The skeleton from Otavalo, Ecuador, reported by Davies (item **1490**) is at least 25,000 years of age and may be as old as 36,000 BP. If the latter date is verified, it would be the earliest human fossil known in the New World. Beynon and Siegel (item **1482**) describe specimens which are among the oldest ever found in Peru (10,000 BP).

The First Americans, edited by Laughlin and Harper (item **1492**) is an especially noteworthy contribution to Latin American paleoanthropology. The authors in this collection tackle such controversial issues as the origins of New World populations, biological variability and evolutionary affinities of prehistoric groups, the possibility of transoceanic migration and culture contact, dental and skeletal morphology of early Americans, paleopathology, and the relationship between physical and cultural evolution in America. The monograph by Stone (item **1513**) is an effective case study of human evolution in Costa Rica based upon abundant fossil and archaeological evidence.

POPULATION STUDIES: BIODEMOGRAPHY

The references compiled here represent the results of research conducted in 17 different Latin American and Caribbean countries. These works focus upon variations in fertility, mortality, mate selection, family and household structure, migratory behavior, and urbanization.

Patterns of reproductive performance, population growth, and fertility control have been closely monitored in Latin America because of the persistent threats of overpopulation and resource depletion throughout the region. The field study by Halberstein (item **1539**) in the Bahamas illustrates the interaction of a complex assortment of biosocial factors involved in population control on a small island. Stycos (item **1565**) has authored an insightful review of the current trends, problems, and prospects in human fertility in Latin America.

Several articles have appeared on numerical changes in indigenous Indian populations. While Land and De Almeida (item **1543**) and Shankman (item **1562**) discuss the decimation and cultural decline of Indian groups in Brazil and Paraguay, Mayer and Masferrer (item **1549**) bring forth ample data showing that the overall Indian population of North, Central, and South America actually doubled in size between 1962–78. The bibliography compiled by Edmonston (item **1536**) is a very useful general reference source on Latin American and Caribbean biodemography. The selection by Gujral (item **1538**) is probably the best statistical overview of Caribbean demography that is presently available.

POPULATION STUDIES: GENETICS

Contained in this section are both descriptive and theoretical studies on population genetics. The field data augment the growing stockpile of evidence on microevolution and biological variability in Latin America. The model-building and computer similation, on the other hand, utilize collected data in order to help diagnose and predict trends in genetic structures in real populations.

The following genetic polymorphisms are reported or statistically tested: blood groups, red cell proteins (e.g., hemoglobin) and enzymes (e.g., G-6PD), serum proteins, immunoglobin allotypes, HLA antigens, digestive enzymes (e.g., intestinal lactose and liver aconitase), salivary and milk proteins, dermatoglyphics, color vision, inherited dental traits, and well-marked genetic disorders (hemophilia, brachydactyly, etc.). This body of information is employed to explore such areas as mutation rates, estimates of genetic admixture and "genetic distance," racial and ethnic variations, genetic correlates of geographic and linguistic diversity, and models of genetic equilibrium and heterozygosity.

A number of individual studies deserve special recognition. The series of papers by Azevedo and associates (items **1571–1575**) are the successful products of indepth population genetics research in a well-defined community in Brazil. Crawford and co-workers (items **1584–1586**) accurately reconstruct evolutionary processes and microdifferentiation among Indian and Mestizo populations in Central Mexico from the analysis of a wide range of genetic characteristics. The study by

Leslie *et al.* (item **1593**) is an instructive example of the association between mating patterns and genetics in an isolated population. Neel (item **1600**) incisively appraises the current status of the large-scale multidisciplinary investigation of the Yanomama Indians of South America that has been carried out over the past 14 years. Chakraborty (item **1583**) and Mestriner (item **1596**) use genetic data from Latin America to formulate new statistical models of genetic and population structure.

HUMAN ADAPTATION AND VARIATION

Latin America has served for many years as a fruitful site for research on human adaptation to different environments and stresses because of its varied ecological mosaic. Adaptation to tropical, desert, and high altitude climates has been facilitated by the evolution of distinctive biological traits and behaviors.

The relative efficiencies of different hunting techniques in tropical South America are compared by Hames (item **1631**) and Werner *et al.* (item **1653**). Methods of resource utilization and ecosystem management by populations inhabiting the Mexican desert are comprehensively described by Toledo *et al.* (item **1652**).

Significant new field work on high altitude adaptation has taken place in the Andes mountains of South America. Monge (item **1639**) perceptively reviews recent findings on physiological and anatomical features, typical pathologies and illnesses, and acclimatization processes. The other items concerning high altitude environments are ecologically oriented and deal with such topics as hemoglobin characteristics (items **1620** and **1625**), growth (items **1629, 1645** and **1651**), and health (item **1624**). An excellent series of investigation on lung function at high altitude was conducted by Mueller and associates (items **1640–1644**).

Also included in this section are publications on quantitative biological variations—dental traits, anthropometric dimensions, physiological systems, etc. Halberstein (item **1630**) summarizes recent evidence on variability across Caribbean island nations.

HUMAN DEVELOPMENT

Research on growth, nutrition, and human development in Latin America involves several different methodological approaches and data sources—anthropometric measurements, X-rays, clinical examinations and medical histories, biochemical analyses of blood and urine, age of menarche, studies of metabolism and hair structure, and dietary evaluations.

Of central concern in this section are the biological and social effects of malnutrition and undernutrition. Convincing evidence is brought forward to illustrate the profound impact of protein-calorie malnutrition and specific nutrient deficiencies upon physical growth and maturation (items **1670, 1678, 1684** and **1686**), cognitive development and scholastic achievement (items **1669, 1673** and **1691**), child health and mortality (items **1685, 1698** and **1704**) and family size and structure (items **1656, 1668** and **1699**).

Blasco's monograph (item **1657**) is an outstanding general review of the multiple problems and variables associated with nutritional stress throughout Latin America. Nationwide multidisciplinary case studies have been carried out in Jamaica (item **1683**), Brazil (item **1697**), El Salvador (item **1696**), and Colombia (item **1702**).

Valiente Berenguer (item **1700**) has compiled a comprehensive bibliography on nutritional research in Chile. The nutrient content of actual diets sampled in Latin America have been assessed (items **1694–1695** and **1702**). More specialized topics range from the possible nutritional correlates of warfare (item **1661**) to ethnic differences in food consumption and dietary behaviors (items **1663** and **1664**).

The prospects for the future of human development in Latin America are positive and encouraging. Several studies have suggested that new advances in agriculture, the rise of urbanization and technology, and other features of Latin America's rapid modernization are leading to substantial dietary and nutritional improvements.

EPIDEMIOLOGICAL ANTHROPOLOGY

Probably the fastest growing field in Latin American anthropology today is medical (or epidemiological) anthropology, and this is reflected in the steady increase in volume of publications over the past decade. A useful general summary of research on traditional medicine in native populations was written by Anzures y Bolaños (item **1707**). The collection edited by Kidd (item **1709**) is an up-to-date synthesis of current scientific findings regarding personal, public, and environmental health. López Hermosa (item **1734**) has assembled an extensive bibliography on Latin American medical anthropology. Naranjo's (item **1742**) absorbing ethnohistorical analysis of the medical systems in Guatemala covers the evolution of health-related materials and activities from prehistoric times to the present.

A variety of individual research problems are explored in the presently annotated items: disease epidemiology, traditional curing and healing practices, uses of herbal medicine and hallucinogenic drugs, the role of magic and religion in health and illness, medical acculturation and modernization, and public health problems and "Westernized" health services.

New studies have been published on "folk" illnesses in Latin America. *Susto*, a well-documented culturally influenced disorder throughout Latin America, has been re-analyzed by Klein (item **1729**) and Rubel and O'Nell (item **1748**). *Indisposition*, a previously unrecognized disease peculiar to Haiti, is described by Philippe and Romain (item **1744**). A special issue of *América Indígena* (Vol. 38, No. 4, 1978, see item **1706**) is devoted to coca use in South America—its history, medicinal applications, economic aspects, non-medical usage, magico-religious functions, and biological and psychological effects.

RECENT DOCTORAL DISSERTATIONS
Biological Anthropology in Latin America (1978–1980)

Coreil, Jeannine. Disease prognosis and resource allocation in a Haitian mountain community. Univ. of Kentucky, 1979.

Corno, Robert B. Migrant adjustment in Bogotá, Colombia: occupation and health care. Brown Univ., 1979.

Crankshaw, Mary E. Changing faces of the Achachilas: medical systems and cultural identity in a highland Bolivian village. Univ. of Massachusetts, 1980.

DeWalt, Kathleen M. Nutritional strategies and agricultural change in a Mexican communtiy. Univ. of Connecticut, 1980.

Dolan, Peter M. Predicting Indian alcohol consumption from sociocultural data: an anthropological model and field study. UCLA, 1979.

Dressler, William W. Hypertension in St. Lucia: social and cultural dimensions. Univ. of Connecticut, 1979.

Fan, Margaret Y. Socioeconomic status effects and ethnicity effects on fertility of Mexican Americans. UCLA, 1980.

Gamble, George R. Natality, contraception, and family patterns in a Caracas barrio. Univ. of North Carolina, 1979.

Gordon, Kathleen D. A scanning electron microscope study of dental attrition. Yale Univ., 1980.

Jenkins, Carol L. Patterns of protein-energy malnutrition among preschoolers in Belize. Univ. of Tennessee, 1980.

Lubin, Arthur N. The influence of a natural disaster on human fertility. Univ. of Georgia, 1980.

Massara, Emily B. ¡Que gordita! a study of weight among women in a Puerto Rican community. Bryn Mawr College, 1979.

Millard, Ann V. Corn, cash, and population genetics: family demography in rural Mexico. Univ. of Texas, 1980.

Mitchell, Mary F. Class, therapeutic roles, and self-medication in Jamaica. University of California, Berkeley, 1980.

Nations, James D. Population ecology of the Lacandon Maya. Southern Methodist University, 1979.

Ober, Carole L. Demography and microevolution on Cayo Santiago. Northwestern Univ., 1979.

Pebley, Anne R. The age at first birth and the timing of the second birth in Costa Rica and Guatemala. Cornell Univ., 1980.

Pillet, Bernard D. Fertility changes in the early decades of rapid socioeconomic development: a statistical description of the recent Mexican experience. Stanford Univ., 1980.

Pinal, Roger del. The use of maternity histories to study the determinants of infant mortality changes in ladino communities of Guatemala. Univ. of California, Berkeley, 1980.

Place, Dorothy M. The effect of modernization on fertility in Mexico. Univ. of California, Davis, 1980.

Poats, Susan. The Mojui Project: the role of an applied anthropologist in a Central Amazon health and nutrition project. Univ. of Florida, 1979.

Porter, Elaine G. Social-psychological and communication factors in birth control use in the Dominican Republic. Pennsylvania State Univ., 1980.

Rosenberger, Alfred. Phylogeny, evolution, and classification of New World monkeys. City Univ. of New York, 1979.

Stavrakis, Olga. Effect of agricultural change upon diet in a village in northern Belize. Univ. of Minnesota, 1979.

Stevenson, David A. Medicinal plant use and high blood pressure on St. Kitts, West Indies. Ohio State Univ., 1979.

Stier, Frances R. The effect of demographic change on agriculture in San Blas, Panama. Univ. of Arizona, 1979.

Townsend, John W. The effect of food supplementation on the cognitive development of rural Guatemalan children. Univ. of Minnesota, 1978.

Vance, Carole S. Female employment and fertility in Barbados. Columbia Univ., 1979.

Wagner, Catherine A. Coca, chicha, and trago: communal rituals in a Quechua community. Univ. of Illinois, 1978.

PALEOANTHROPOLOGY

1480 Agrinier, Pierre. A sacrificial mass burial at Miramar, Chiapas, Mexico. Provo, Utah: Brigham Young University, New World Archaeological Foundation, 1978. (52 p.; bibl.; ill.; map; tables)

Descriptive study of prehistoric skeletal remains from multiple burial site in Chiapas, Mexico. Cause of death of several individuals attributed to ritualized sacrifice.

1481 Allison, Marvin J. Paleopathology in Peru (AMNH/NH, 88:2, 1979, p. 74–83, bibl., ill., plates)

Colorful description of results of author's extensive research on paleopathology in prehistoric Peruvian mummies. Cycles of disease and injury charted for 5,000 year period. Nutritional, gastro-intestinal, and infectious diseases are discussed. Average ages at death are calculated. Article is effectively punctuated photographically.

Atúnez de Mayolo R., Santiago E. La alimentación en el Tawantinsuyu. See *HLAS 42:1587.*

1482 Beynon, Diane E. and **M.I. Siegel.** Ancient human remains from central Peru (SAA/AA, 46:1, Jan. 1981, p. 167–176, bibl., tables)

Descriptive summary of four naturally mummified human bodies and four nearly complete skeletons 6,000–10,000 years old from four sites in the highlands and coastal areas of Central Peru. Age, sex, stature, general pathology, and archaeological context are discussed. These remains are among the oldest human fossils ever discovered in South America.

1483 Borgognini Tarli, S.M. *et al.* Blood group determination in ancient Peruvian material (Journal of Human Evolution [Academic Press, London] 8:6, Sept. 1979, p. 589–595, bibl., tables)

Thirty-three mummified skeletons from prehistoric Peru were tested chemically for evidence of ABO blood group antigens. Type O was only one detected.

1484 Bradbury, Ray and **A. Lieberman.** The mummies of Guanajuato. New York: Harry N. Abrams, Inc., 1978. 95 p.; plates.

Popular, non-scientific photo-illustrated narrative on 115 ancient mummies housed in a museum in Guanajuato, Mexico. Text is disjointed and photographs are only of medium quality.

1485 Brewbaker, James L. Diseases of maize in the wet lowland tropics and the collapse of the classic Maya civilization (SEB/EB, 33:2, April/June 1979, p. 101–118, bibl., maps, tables)

Sustained and persistent crop failure of maize (*Zea mays*) due to virus epidemic is proposed as primary contributing factor in decline of Maya culture in ninth century AD. The suspected virus probably originated in northern South America when maize was first brought into the Caribbean around the year O AD.

1486 Catalogue of fossil hominids. pt. 3, the Americas, Asia, Australia. Editors: Kenneth Page Oakley and Bernard Grant Campbell. London: British Museum of Natural History, 1975. 1 v.; bibl.; map.

One volume in set of three catalogues fossil discoveries throughout the world, including site location, chronological age, associated artifacts, flora and fauna, physical measurements, photographs, etc. This volume contains data on prehistoric fossils from Argentina, Brazil, Chile, Ecuador, Mexico, Panama, and Peru.

1487 **Chapman, Florence E.** Dental paleopathology at Florianopolis, Brazil (Yearbook of Physical Anthropology [Wenner Gren Foundation for Anthropological Research, New York] 20, 1977, p. 347–348, bibl.)

Pathological characteristics described for dentitions of 57 prehistoric hunters buried on an island off the coast of Brazil. Dental attrition, abrasion, and inflammation were detected in most of the sample. Abcessed teeth and jawbone regression were also found. Dietary materials and customs are reconstructed.

1488 **Chávez Velásquez, Nancy A.** La materia médica en el Incanato. Lima: Editorial Mejía Baca, 1977. 426 p.; bibl.; ill.; indexes.

Archaeological and historical reference work on medical systems in precolumbian populations of Peru. Ancient Inca and related cultures are studied for period 300 BC–1000 AD. Activities of physicians, types of diseases and methods of diagnosis, forms of treatment, and therapeutic medicinal substances are all outlined. Common and scientific names of drug plants are indexed, as are treatment regimens and published references.

1489 **Cocilovo, José A.** Estudio de dos factores que influencian la morfología craneana en una colección andina (UNTIA/R, 2:3, 1975, p. 197–212, bibl., tables)

Re-study of series of 118 prehistoric skeletons from northeastern Peru. Material was subjected to 28 anthropometric measurements and seven indices. Sexual dismorphism and racial variations are documented. Cranial deformations, both artificial and pathological, are numerous and well-marked. Simple statistics are applied to results.

1490 **Davies, David M.** Some observations on the Otavalo skeleton from Imbabura Province, Ecuador (in Early man in America. Edited by A.L. Bryan. Edmonton, Alberta, Canada: University of Alberta, Department of Anthropology, Archeological Researches International, 1978, p. 273–274, bibl., table [Occasional papers; 1])

Description of skull, mandible, teeth, and assorted post-cranial bones of prehistoric man found near Otavalo, Ecuador. Radiocarbon dating and thermoluminescence suggest individual is between 25,000 and 36,000

years old. Provides several measurements and notes physical characteristics of the fossil remains. If above chronology is confirmed, this specimen may be oldest human fossil so far discovered in the New World.

1491 **El-Najjar, M.Y.** Maize, malaria and the anemias in the pre-Columbian New World (Yearbook of Physical Anthropology [Wenner Gren Foundation for Anthropological Research, New York] 20, 1977, p. 329–338, bibl., tables)

Series of 3,361 precolumbian crania from seven distinct geographic areas in New World were examined for presence of pathologies. High incidence of porotic hyperostosis discovered in populations that had been dependent upon maize as a staple, and author speculates this is result of nutritional properties of maize treatment with alkali leading to iron and protein deficiency.

1492 **The First Americans:** origins, affinities, and adaptations. Edited by William S. Laughlin and Albert B. Harper. New York: G. Fischer, 1979. 340 p.; bibl.; ill.; index.

Collection of 15 diverse chapters dealing with origins and biological evolutions of earliest New World populations. Genetic affinities and evolutionary relationships are reconstructed for past and present New World groups and possible antecedent regions in the Eastern Hemisphere. Latest theories are provided on ancestry of most ancient Americans and timing of their earliest migrations.

1493 **Gasque López, Fernando.** La obstetricia maya en la época precolombiana (UY/R, 21:123/124, mayo/agosto 1979, p. 54–65, plates, tables)

Customs associated with childbirth in ancient Maya are briefly outlined. Beliefs and actions regarding virginity, pubescence, pregnancy, and delivery are deduced from written accounts and other historical sources. Obstetrical practices are described.

1494 **Jiménez Lambertus, Abelardo.** Estudio del esqueleto de las excavaciones de la Villa de la Concepción (MHD/B, 8:12, enero 1979, p. 261–276, tables)

Study of complete skeleton minus phalanges perhaps 5,000 years old from prehistoric Dominican Republic. Describes characteristics of site, burial, and associated artifacts. Outlines physical traits and pathological features of fossil remains.

1495 ———. Paleopatología ósea columnar en esqueletos indígenas precolombinos de la Isla de Santo Domingo (MHD/B, 7:9, enero 1978, p. 111–124, ill.)

Bone pathologies in the vertebral column studied in a sample of 27 precolumbian skeletons from Santo Domingo. Age differences are significant, especially with respect to type of vertebra affected. All specimens over 40 years of age at death exhibited degenerative changes.

1496 Klepinger, Linda L. Paleodemography of the Valdivia III phase at Real Alto, Ecuador (SAA/AA, 44:2, April 1979, p. 305–309, bibl., tables)

Paleodemographic analysis of prehistoric Ecuadorian population, based upon 72 burials dating to 3,500–5,400 years ago. Author reconstructs life expectancy and life tables, fertility rates and family size, generation length, and mortality patterns. Sample represents an entire population rather than a ritual burial.

1497 ———. Prehistoric dental calculus gives evidence for coca in early coastal Ecuador (NWJS, 269, Oct. 1977, p. 506–507, bibl., table)

Heavy accumulation of dental calculus (tartar) found in sample of 27 skulls 2,800 years old from Ecuador. Chewing of coca leaves with lime may have been partially responsible, and author's X-ray fluorescence study seems to support this hypothesis.

1498 Kowalenski, Stephen A. Population-resource balances in Period I of Oaxaca, Mexico (SAA/AA, 45:1, Jan. 1980, p. 151–164, bibl., tables)

Analysis of human ecology and environmental adaptation in prehistoric Mexico. Population size changes and resource utilization and management are reconstructed from skeletal and artifactual evidence.

1499 Luna Calderón, Fernando. Primeras evidencias de sífilis en las Antillas precolombinas. Santo Domingo, R.D.: Universidad Autónoma de Santo Domingo, 1977. 18 p.; 3 leaves of plates; bibl.; ill. (Cuadernos del CENDIA; no. 2. Publicaciones de la UASD; v. 243)

Evidence presented for presence of syphilis in prehistoric osteological remains

from Caribbean area. Prehispanic human fossils from Dominican Republic exhibit cranial and skeletal lesions and deformations characteristically associated wtih syphilis. Photographs are unfortunately of relatively poor quality.

1500 Morbán Laucer, Fernando; Rafael Acta; and Emil Acta. Enfermedades en los niños aborígenes de la Isla de Santo Domingo (MHD/B, 4:8, enero/marzo 1976, p. 163–175)

Paleopathological study of 372 skeletons approximately 900 years old from Santo Domingo. Dental and osteological disorders are described. Evidence indicates high frequency of caries, cranial deformation, tetanus, parasitic infections, and spontaneous abortion.

1501 Ochoa, Lorenzo. Historia prehispánica de la Huaxteca. Presentación de Ignacio Bernal. México: Universidad Nacional Autónoma de México, 1979. 178 p.; 56 p. of plates; ill. (Serie Antropología. Instituto de Investigaciones Antropológicas; 26)

Prehistory of Huaxteca Indians of east-central Mexico integrates archaeological and physical anthropological data. Describes physical characteristics and pathological conditions based upon large sample of fossil remains. Reconstructs burial procedures, artificial deformation and ritual mutilation, and surgical practices. Discusses medical and funerary artifacts with the aid of excellent illustrations.

1502 Olmos Cordones, Hernán and Abelardo Jiménez Lambertus. Estudio de los restos biológicos de las excavaciones arqueológicas realizadas en el antigue Colegio de Gorjón (MHD/B, 8:12, enero 1979, p. 225–256, ill., plates, table)

Catalogues several hundred human fossils and artifacts from 22 levels at ancient site in Dominican Republic. Provides simple descriptive statistics on listed materials.

1503 Ortiz de Montellano, Bernard R. Aztec cannibalism: an ecological necessity? (AAAS/S, 200:4342, May 1978, p. 611–617, bibl., tables)

Examines previously published hypothesis that ancient Aztec cannibalism and sacrifice served nutritional functions in a protein-deficient diet. Author's analysis of typical foods and consumption patterns in Aztec society indicates that protein intake was generally adequate and that cannibalism occurred mainly during harvest times. This evidence points more to ritual and religious functions of Aztec sacrifice and cannibalism.

1504 Pearsall, Deborah. Paleoethnobotany in western South America: progress and problems (*in* The Nature and status of ethnobotany. Edited by R.I. Ford. Ann Arbor: University of Michigan, Museum of Anthropology, 1978, p. 389–416; bibl., map, tables [Anthropological papers; 67])

Archaeological analysis of prehistoric plant/people relationships in eight South American countries. Fossilized pollen and other ancient botanical remains dating from 13,000 years ago are described and compared. Archaeological sites and palynological data are effectively arranged in a single large table.

1505 Ramos Rodríguez, Rosa María. Algunas observaciones sobre los enterramientos humanos en el sitio "El Rey," Can Cun (UNAM/AA, 15, 1978, p. 251–265, bibl., ill., tables)

Study of 53 human burials at prehistoric (postclassic) Maya site in Quintana Roo, Yucatán. Burials are described with respect to spatial distribution, position and orientation of the corpses, tomb structure, associated burial artifacts, and morphological characteristics. Several cases of cranial deformation and dental mutilation were discovered.

1506 Röseler, Peter H. Klinische und radiologische Analyse von Gesichtsveränderungen einer peruanischen Mumie (IAI/I, 3, 1975, p. 199–224, bibl., plates)

Well-illustrated radiographic study of prehispanic mummy nearly 10,000 years old from Peru. Anthropometric and X-ray data reveal a number of unique clinical characteristics and pathologies.

1507 Schoeninger, Margaret J. Diet and status at Chalcatzingo: some empirical and technical aspects of strontium analysis (AJPA, 51:3, Sept. 1979, p. 295–310, bibl., ill., tables)

Levels of trace element strontium in prehistoric bones used to determine diet and biomedical characteristics of early Mexicans from state of Morelos 2,000–3,000 years ago. Bone strontium content and social status within the community were compared in 91 mortuary skeletons and associated arti-

facts. Study revealed evidence of less meat in diet of individuals from lower social classes.

1508 ——. Dietary reconstruction at Chalcatzingo, a Formative period site in Morelos, Mexico. Ann Arbor: Museum of Anthropology, University of Michigan, 1979. 97 p.; bibl.; ill. (Contributions in human biology; no. 2. Technical reports—Museum of Anthropology, the University of Michigan; no. 9)

Reconstructs past diets and nutritionally-related behavior at prehistoric site in Morelos, Mexico. Evidence is derived from chemical assays of fossil bones, especially of strontium content, and analyses of burials and associated mortuary items.

1509 Scott, Eugenie C. Increase of tooth size in prehistoric Coastal Peru, 10,000 BP–1,000 BP (AJPA, 50:2, Feb. 1979, p. 251–258, bibl., tables)

Increase in tooth size discovered in sample of 65 fossil specimens dating 10,000–1,000 BP from Peru. Increase may be related to changes in cranial and facial structure and unusual attrition patterns.

1510 —— and B.R. DeWalt. Subsistence and dental pathology etiologies from prehistoric coastal Peru (Medical Anthropology [Redgrave, Pleasantville, N.Y.] 4:2, Spring 1980, p. 272–289, bibl., tables)

Employs path analysis to assess possible association between form of subsistence economy and characteristic types of dental pathology in series of 53 museum specimens age 1,000 through 10,000 years old from coastal Peru. While statistical treatment indicates significant correlation, small sample size precludes firm conclusions.

1511 Seggiaro, Luis A. Medicina indígena de América. 3. ed. Buenos Aires: Editorial Universitaria de Buenos Aires, 1977. 78 p.; 8 leaves of plates; bibl.; ill. (Cuadernos de EUDEBA; 182)

Brief coverage of prehispanic and traditional medicine of aboriginal and indigenous Indian groups in Central and South America. Devotes special attention to ancient Maya, Aztec, and Inca. Surveys curing procedures, surgical practices, and use of drug plants.

1512 Somolinos d'Ardois, Germán. Capítulos de historia médica mexicana. México: Sociedad Mexicana de Historia y Filosofía de la Medicina, 1978. 1 v.; bibl.; ill.

Explores prehistoric medical practices in Mexico through archaeological, fossil, and historical evidence. Reconstructs diseases, illnesses, and accidents in ancient times from numerous varied sites. Tools, implements, art objects, and other prehispanic artifacts are logically and effectively interpreted in this well-illustrated work.

1513 Stone, Doris. Precolumbian man in Costa Rica. Cambridge, Mass.: Harvard University, Peabody Museum Press, 1977. 238 p.; bibl.; ill.; maps; plates; tables.

Well-illustrated synthesis and review of published research on prehistory of Costa Rica. Analyzes geographic, archaeological, and physical anthropological evidence dating back to earliest settlers in 300 BC. The 292 high quality photos of artifacts and human remains greatly enhance the work.

1514 Stothert, Karen E. Unwrapping an Inca mummy bundle (AIA/A, 32:4, July/Aug. 1979, p. 8–17, bibl., ill., maps, plates)

Popular exposition and high-quality photographs of 500-year old mummy discovered on central coast of Peru. Adult female had been ceremoniously buried along with spectacular array of grave goods and artifacts.

1515 Torres Mazzucchi, María del Huerto. Estudio antropológico de esqueletos aborígenes de Río Segundo: Pcia de Córdoba, Rep. Argentina (UNTIA/R, 2:3, 1975, p. 147–170, bibl., plates, tables)

Thorough metrical analysis of three fossil skeletons from prehistoric Argentina. Craniometry, sexual dimorphism, age at death, cause of mortality, stature and weight, and osteopathology were all determined through anthropometric techniques.

1516 Turner, Christy G. Dental caries and early Ecuadorian agriculture (SAA/AA, 43:4, Oct. 1978, p. 694–697)

Sample of 90 teeth obtained from two prehistoric sites in Ecuador exhibits noticeable lack of dental caries. Absence of decay in 4,000-year old teeth is unusual since populations practiced maize agriculture, an activity that has long been associated with extensive dental caries.

1517 Ubelaker, D.H. Skeletal evidence for kneeling in prehistoric Ecuador (AJPA, 51:4, Nov. 1979, p. unavailable, bibl., ill., plates, tables)

Describes prehistoric foot and leg bones from 62 burials from cemetery on southern coast of Ecuador. Modifications in surface of several foot bones along with the presence of "squatting facets" on femora suggest habitual kneeling posture. Compares results with five other New World skeletal populations.

1518 Uhle, Max. La momia peruana: de las obras póstumas (IAI/I, 3, 1975, p. 189–197, bibl.)

Practice of ritual mummification of the dead in prehispanic Peru is discussed in general terms based upon a few studies published a number of years ago. Describes procedures and methods, locations, associated artifacts, and magico-religious aspects. Author suggests that cultism surrounding death and its aftermath was a form of ancestor worship among ancient Peruvians.

1519 Weinstein, Robert S. *et al.* Ancient bone disease in a Peruvian mummy revealed by quantitative skeletal histomorphometry (AJPA, 54:3, March 1981, p. 321–326, bibl., plates, tables)

Skeletal pathologies detected in prehistoric Peruvian mummy using histological techniques and microradiographs. Reduction in bone mass suggests metabolic disorder at time of death.

1520 Weisman, Abner Irving. Medicine before Columbus: as told in pre-Columbian medical art. New York: Pre-Cortesian Publications, 1979. 152 p.; bibl.; ill.; maps; tables.

Lively and colorful account of evolution of prehistoric medical systems in Latin America. Main sources of data and evidence include wall paintings, sculpture, engravings, medical-surgical artifacts, and other ancient art forms.

POPULATION STUDIES: BIODEMOGRAPHY

Acuña B., Olda M. and **Carlos F. Denton L.** La familia en Costa Rica. See item **8137.**

Alba-Hernández, Francisco. La población de México: evolución y dilemas. See item **8074.**

1521 Allman, James and **John May.** Fertility, mortality, migration and family planning in Haiti (LSE/PS, 33:3, Nov. 1979, p. 505–521, tables)

Population dynamics on Haiti are described from CELADE demographic survey data. Compares national trends with observations from selected component subpopulations. Fertility, mortality, and migration all have an impact on population structure and evolution. Discusses family planning programs.

1522 Arreto, Carmen and **Hernán Orellana.** Bolivia, proyección de la población por sexo y grupos de edad, 1950–2000. La Paz: Instituto Nacional de Estadística, between 1976 and 1979. 22 p.; bibl.; 2 graphs.

Brief computer-based study of future population trends in Bolivia. National population doubled between 1950–75, and it is predicted to double again to over 10 million residents by the year 2000.

1523 Balakrishnan, T.R. Probability of conception, conception delay, and estimates of fecundability in rural and semi-urban areas of certain Latin American countries (Social Biology [Society for the Study of Social Biology, New York] 26:3, Fall 1979, p. 226–231, bibl., tables)

Analyzes fertility and associated parameters through data from national surveys conducted in rural and urbanizing areas of Mexico, Costa Rica, Colombia, and Peru. Relatively early entry into sexual unions, high probability of conception, and substantial fecundity characterize these regions.

1524 Bartlema, Johannes. Bolivia: diferenciales de fecundidad según la muestra censal 1976 en comparación con los resultados de la encuesta demográfica. La Paz: Instituto Nacional de Estadística, 1977. 39 p.; bibl; graphs.

Reviews national and regional fertility statistics for Bolivia, based upon 1976 census and supplementary demographic questionnaires. Describes urban-rural differences. Linguistic, educational, and socioeconomic variables also strongly influence fertility throughout the country.

1525 Black, Francis L. et al. Birth and survival patterns in numerically unstable proto-agricultural societies in the Brazilian Amazon (Medical Anthropology [Redgrave, Pleasantville, N.Y.] 2:3, Summer 1978, p. 95–127, bibl., map, tables)

Presents demographic structure for eight "unacculturated" Indian tribes in Brazil. Compares fertility and mortality trends with other native populations in South America and Africa.

Browner, Carole. Toma de decisiones sobre el aborto: algunos hallazgos en Colombia. See item **8262.**

1526 Carvajal, Manuel and **P. Burgess.** Socioeconomic determinants of fetal and child deaths in Latin America: a comparative study of Bogotá, Caracas, and Rio de Janeiro (Social Science and Medicine [New York] 12C:3/4C, Nov. 1978, p. 89–98, bibl., tables)

Statistical evaluation of published data concerning cultural influences on prenatal and childhood mortality in three South American cities. Marriage forms, income and educational levels, and migrations all helped to account for intrapopulational variations.

1527 Carvalho, José Alberto de and **C.H. Wood.** Mortalidad, distribución del ingreso y residencia rural-urbana en Brasil (ACEP/EP, 3:7/12, julio/dic. 1978, p. 7–19, bibl., tables)

Regional and cultural variations in mortality in Brazil are effectively assessed from 1930–1970 census materials. Data from 10 separate geographic zones indicate urbanization is associated with mortality reductions, especially in younger age groups, and increased life expectancy. Wide variations were found among the 10 zones in mortality rates and level of economic development. Authors conclude that modernization is strongly and increasingly influencing mortality trends in Brazil.

1528 Cavanaugh, Joseph A. Is fertility declining in less developed countries? An evaluation and analysis of data sources and population programme assistance (LSE/PS, 33:2, July 1979, p. 283–293, tables)

Analysis of recent fertility rates in 30 developing countries including 16 Latin American and Caribbean nations. Discusses problems in data sources and concludes that some of the supposed fertility declines are actually more apparent than real.

1529 Chackiel Z., Juan. La fecundidad y la mortalidad diferencial en Costa Rica: 1963–1973 (in Seminario Nacional de Demografía, 6th, Heredia, Costa Rica, 1976. Informe. San José: Universidad Nacional de

Costa Rica, 1976, v. 2, p. 456–497, tables)

Reviews fertility and mortality rates in Costa Rica for period 1963–73. Notes regional variations. Census statistics contained in 30 tables indicate wide differentials which may increase opportunity for natural selection. Achieved reproduction was influenced by rural or urban residence and mother's age, educational level, and marital status. Factors affecting infant mortality include urbanization, socioeconomic status, and level of unemployment.

1530 Cisa Rodríguez, Agustín. Evolución demográfica de la población mundial. Montevideo: Acali Editoria, 1979. 36 p.; bibl. (Cuadernos de estudios sociales; 3)

Charts world-wide demographic and populational trends with emphasis upon Latin America. Compares "developed" and "developing" nations with respect to fertility and population growth, mortality, and future population estimates. Data are presented in 20 separate tables.

1531 Costa Rica. Dirección General de Estadística y Censos. Encuesta mundial de fecundidad de la República de Costa Rica. San José: Dirección General de Estadística y Censos, 1978. 369 p.; appendices; bibl.; ill.

Demographic profile of Costa Rica emphasizes fertility, population growth, and future trends. Mate selection, age at marriage, divorce, family planning programs, contraception, and mortality have all profoundly affected population size in recent years. Two-thirds of volume consists of detailed tables (184 p.) and sample questionnaires (50 p.).

1532 Cross, Malcolm. Urbanization and urban growth in the Caribbean. New York: Cambridge University Press, 1979. 174 p.; bibl.; maps; tables.

Up-to-date treatment of urbanization process and demographic-cultural ramifications throughout the Caribbean. Describes attendant changes in population structure, social organization, and ethnic group composition. Reviews population policies.

1533 Denton, E. Hazel. Economic determinants of fertility in Jamaica (LSE/PS, 33:2, July 1979, p. 295–305, tables)

Census data suggest that birth rates in Jamaica are related to, and affected by, marital status and type of marriage union, level of female employment, income, and educational attainment. Outlines fertility variations within the country.

1534 Díaz-Briquets, Sergio and Lisandro Pérez. Cuba: the demography of Revolution. Washington: Population Reference Bureau, 1981. 43 p.; bibl.; map; plates; tables (Population Bulletin; 36:1)

Thorough analysis of demographic transition in Cuba based upon censuses, statistical data, and vital records dating from 1899. Population size doubled twice and increased 650 percent overall since the turn of this century. Birth rates have fluctuated since 1954, however fertility actually declined between 1973–79, and mortality and migration have decreased or remained stable. Author examines socioeconomic and political determinants of demographic changes and considers possible role of Cuban Revolution. For geographer's comment, see item **5041**.

1535 Downing, Douglas C. and David Yaukey. The effects of marital dissolution and re-marriage on fertility in urban Latin America (LSE/PS, 33:3, Nov. 1979, p. 537–547, tables)

CELADE (UN) survey data on adult females from seven Latin American capital cities are used to determine the effects of divorce and remarriage on fertility rates. Reproductive time lost through marital dissolution commonly causes an overall fertility reduction, but many variables, such as educational level, age, and socioeconomic status may influence final reproductive output.

1536 Edmonston, Barry. Population research in Latin America and the Caribbean, a reference bibliography. Ann Arbor, Mich.: Published for the International Population Program and the Latin American Studies Program, Cornell University, by University Microfilms International, 1979. 161 p. (Monograph publishing: Sponsor series)

Catalog of recent publications on demographic and anthropological research in Latin American and Caribbean populations. References are arranged by country and topic. Headings include: General Population Studies; Population Distribution; Mortality; Fertility, Marriage, and the Family; Migration; and Demographic Interrelations.

——— and **Frank Wm. Oechsli.** Fertility decline and socioeconomic change in Venezuela. See item **3385**.

Fox, Robert W. and Jerrold W. Huguet. Tendencias demográficas y de urbanización en América Central y Panamá. See item **8150**.

1537 Gómez B., Miguel. Algunos datos preliminares de la Encuesta Nacional de Fecundidad (*in* Seminario Nacional de Demografía, 6th, Heredia, Costa Rica, 1976. Informe. San José: Universidad Nacional de Costa Rica, 1976, v. 1, p. 100–110, tables)

Results of nationwide fertility survey conducted in Costa Rica in 1976. Report consists mainly of raw statistics, and rural-urban differences are emphasized in the discussion.

1538 Gujral, Surinder S. Recent demographic trends in the Caribbean with special reference to Barbados, Jamaica, Trinidad and Tobago, and Guyana (*in* The Caribbean issues of emergence: socioeconomic and political perspectives. Edited by Vincent P. MacDonald. Washington, D.C.: University Press of America, 1980, p. 249–264, bibl., tables)

Reviews demographic changes throughout the Caribbean for period 1950–79 including evaluation of impact of various population policies that have been established. Topics covered include population growth and fertility, migration and mortality, and fluctuations in population density and distribution. Presents in-depth case studies for four disparate Caribbean island nations.

1539 Halberstein, Robert A. Population regulation in an island community (WSU/HB, 52:3, Sept. 1980, p. 479–498, bibl., ill., map, tables)

Anthropological field investigation of fertility control and other aspects of population size regulation in a small island community in the Bahamas. Survey data and analyses of written records reveal a complex assortment of factors leading to reproduction regulation including late age of menarche, increased use of contraceptives, pronounced childhood mortality, extensive emigration, and reproductive wastage.

1540 Herold, Joan M. Female migration in Chile: types of moves and socioeconomic characteristics (PAA/D, 16:2, May 1979, p. 257–277, bibl., ill., tables)

Internal migration of females in Chile examined for period 1965–70. Age, educational level, and socioeconomic status all influence migration patterns in this country.

Older females of higher educational and socioeconomic rank were more likely to be "repeat" and "non-return" migrants.

1541 Johnston, Francis E. *et al.* An analysis of environmental variables and factors associated with growth failure in a Mexican village (WSU/HB, 52:4, Dec. 1980, p. 627–637, bibl., tables)

Analyzes principal component and discriminant function of factors associated with nutritional status in sample of 276 malnourished and well-nourished children from a rural Mexican community. Socioeconomic conditions, demographic characteristics, morbidity, and anthropometric traits of parents were all important variables.

1542 Kelly, Phyllis B. A model of population increase in the Mazahua region, Mexico (III/AI, 34:2, abril/junio 1979, p. 371–380, bibl., tables)

Population growth investigated in a region of rural Mexico where there is a high value and great emphasis placed on children. Data for period 1933–74 indicate that rapid population increase led to changes in social and biodemographic characteristics of the community including migration rates, socioeconomic level, mortality patterns, and age-sex composition. Author believes present case is representative for rural Mexico as a whole.

1543 Land, Ney and Arilza Nazareth de Almeida. População e depopulação em grupos indígenas (III/AI, 34[34]:2, abril/junio 1979, p. 339–370, bibl.)

Reviews factors contributing to the depopulation of indigenous Indian populations of Brazil. Mentions migration, interbreeding, extermination, social disintegration, loss of territories and contagious diseases. Closely scrutinizes two Indian tribes as case studies.

1544 Livingstone, Mario. Modelos causales para explicar la mortalidad neo y postneonatal (CPU/ES, 17, 3. trimestre, 1978, p. 103–124, table)

Examines infant and childhood mortality in Chile to uncover contributing factors. Constructs models of causation and possible alternative future directions. Studies various health and economic problems.

1545 Logan, Kathleen. Migration, housing, and integration: the urban context of

Guadalajara, Mexico (UA, 8:2, Summer 1979, p. 131–148, bibl., tables)

Anthropological analysis of rapidly growing migration flow into Guadalajara, Mexico. Reports social, economic, and biomedical problems in large immigrant populations.

1546 Machado, Giovanna. En defensa del aborto en Venezuela. Diseño portada, Aracelys Ocante; fotos, Ana Amundaray. Caracas: Editorial Ateneo de Caracas, 1979. 177 p.; annexes; bibl.; ill. (Colección F)

Thorough and well-documented investigation of abortion in Venezuela including historical practices, methods, and legal-political-religious aspects. Examines statistical correlation of abortion with such variables as church affiliation, sexual activity, and socioeconomic status. Considers pros and cons of abortion legalization in Venezuela.

1547 Martins, José de Souza. *O estudo da fertilidade humana no distrito de São Paulo*: notas e informações sobre o transbordamento temático e o descompasso teórico (SBPC/CC, 31:5, maio 1979, p. 494–498)

Reviews recent book on fertility in São Paulo, Brazil and critically assesses data on demography, biology, and socioeconomic characteristics of fertility trends.

1548 Mauldin, W. Parker and **Bernard Berelson.** Condiciones del descenso de la fecundidad en los países en desarrollo, 1965–1975 (ACEP/EP, 3:1/6, Jan./June 1978, p. 3–107, bibl., ill., maps, tables)

Large-scale macroscopic review and comparison of recent changes in natality in 94 developing countries around the world including 20 Latin American and Caribbean nations. Simple statistical tests are employed to investigate possible correlations between observed birth rates and 21 different biocultural and demographic variables.

1549 Mayer, Enrique and **Elio Masferrer.** La población indígena de América en 1978 (III/AI, 34[34]:2, abril/junio 1979, p. 211–337, tables)

Massive quantity of census data compiled to estimate the size of the Indian populations of North, Central, and South America in 1978. Over five million New World Indians reside in urbanized metropolitan areas. Provides extensive demographic histories for Indian constituents of a number of Latin American nations.

1550 Merrick, Thomas W. Fertility and land availability in rural Brazil (PAA/D, 15:3, Aug. 1978, p. 321–336, bibl., tables)

Discovers fertility differentials between agricultural and residential rural areas in southern Brazil. Multivariate analysis of census data indicates that besides land availability, literacy and childhood mortality are statistically associated with fertility rates.

1551 Morris, Leo *et al.* Frecuencia anticonceptiva en Paraguay (ACEP/EP, 3:7/12, July/Dec. 1978, p. 35–47, bibl., tables)

Evaluation of contraceptive usage in Paraguay including discussion of the management and distribution of birth control devices, their effects on actual fertility rates, and their influence on the incidence of abortion. Survey data indicate 15.5 percent of females age 15–44 use contraceptives in Paraguay, and frequency of occurrence is nearly three times higher among urban residents.

1552 Mosher, William D. The theory of change and response: an application to Puerto Rico, 1940–1970 (LSE/PS, 34:1, March 1980, p. 45–58, bibl., ill., tables)

Demonstrates fertility decline in Puerto Rico between 1940–70 with statistical data. Worldwide trend in developing countries of "demographic transition" and "demographic response" is well-established in Puerto Rico.

1553 Müller, María S. La mortalidad en la Argentina: evolución histórica y situación en 1970. s.l.: Centro de Estudios de Población, 1978. 111 p.; bibl.; graphs.

Comprehensive statistical appraisal of mortality in Argentina including review of historical trends. Age, sex, geography, and linguistic differentials are well-summarized. Compares data from other countries with present materials. Volume features 60 p. of tabular data.

1554 Nicosia M., Julia. Encuesta demográfica de Panamá. Panamá: República de Panamá, Contraloría General de la República, Dirección de Estadística y Censo, 1978. 1 v.; bibl.; ill.

Summary and description of recent national demographic census statistics from Panama, with emphasis upon fertility and population growth, mortality, and migration. Work is enhanced by 38 tables, maps and census tracts, and sample of complete census survey form.

1555 Palloni, Alberto. A new technique to estimate infant mortality with an application for El Salvador and Colombia (PAA/D, 16:3, Aug. 1979, p. 455–473, bibl., tables)

New model to estimate infant mortality is developed using data from Colombia and El Salvador for period 1950–70. Explores effects of recent fertility changes and mortality decline in these countries.

1556 Porras F., Celso A. Costa Rica: evolución de la mortalidad infantil en los últimos 25 años (*in* Seminario Nacional de Demografía, 6th, Heredia, Costa Rica, 1976. Informe. San José: Universidad Nacional de Costa Rica, 1976, v. 2, p. 385–427, bibl., tables)

Statistical demographic study of recent mortality trends in Costa Rica based upon census and survey data. Regional and socio-economic differences in mortality rates are well-marked. Authors utilize multivariate and regression analyses to ascertain and measure importance of factors determining level of infant mortality.

1557 Reutlinger, Shlomo and Harold Alderman. The prevalence of calorie-deficient diets in developing countries (WD, 8:5/6, May/June 1980, p. 399–411, bibl., ill., tables)

Extent of malnutrition, as measured by protein-calorie deficiency, is estimated for numerous countries including 17 from Latin America. In 65 percent of surveyed nations, the population consumes less than minimal worldwide standards for daily calorie and protein ingestion.

1558 Riedel, Osvaldo Hugo Montenegro. A fecundidade feminina no Nordeste: tendéncias e diferenciais (BNB/REN, 8:3, julho/set. 1977, p. 445–4571, bibl., tables)

Explores fertility differentials for regional Brazilian populations during period 1950–70. Significant economic variables across different states are related to contrasting fertility levels. Recommendations for future fertility reductions are based upon observations from low-fertility regions of the country. For geographer's comment, see item **5402.**

1559 Roberts, George W. Fertility and mating in four West Indian populations: Trinidad and Tobago, Barbados, St. Vincent, Jamaica. With an introduction by D.V. Glass. Mona, Jamaica: Institute of Social and Economic Research, University of the West Indies, 1975. 341 p.; bibl.; ill.; index.

Quantitative statistical analysis of fertility rates in Barbados, Trinidad and Tobago, Jamaica, and St. Vincent. Fertility differentials were discovered by type of marital union, educational attainment, religious preference, geographic area, and degree of urbanization. Historical and current population trends are well-demonstrated by extensive published and original data.

1560 Rodríguez V., Virginia. La investigación de la fecundidad en Costa Rico a través de encuestas (*in* Seminario Nacional de Demografía, 6th, Heredia, Costa Rica, 1976. Informe. San José: Universidad Nacional de Costa Rica, 1976, v. 1, p. 71–99, tables)

Descriptive research on fertility patterns in Costa Rica is based upon 1976 nationwide survey. Includes census and interview data in 25 tables. Reconstructs recent trends from historical documents.

1561 Ruíz de Zárate, Mary. Planificación familiar o exterminio masivo de la población borinqueña (OCLAE, 1, 1980, p. 17–28, plates)

Critical analysis of sterilization and family planning practices in Puerto Rico. Author investigates controversial evidence suggesting that large-scale sterilization of women age 15–19 may be a form of political genocide in this country.

1562 Shankman, Paul. The denouement of the South American Indians (Journal of Ethnic Studies [College of Ethnic Studies, Western Washington State College, Bellingham, Wash.] 7:3, Fall 1979, p. 87–94, bibl.)

Review essay of two recent books on the decimation of Indian populations in Brazil and Paraguay. Depopulation of native peoples in South America is due mainly to urbanization and resulting hybridization, genocide, and the destruction of traditional cultures.

1563 Singh, Susheela. Demographic variables and the recent trend in fertility in Guyana: 1960–1971 (LSE/PS, 33:2, July 1979, p. 313–327, tables)

Reviews general demographic structure of Guyana and recent fertility trends. Birth rate and natality reductions during period 1960–71 are due mainly to voluntary and involuntary fetal mortality, contraception, and changing mate selection and marriage patterns and customs.

1564 Stinner, William F. and Klaus de Albuquerque. Urban-rural variations in household size and membership in Puerto Rico: 1950 to 1970 (Journal of Caribbean Studies [Association of Caribbean Studies, Coral Gables, Fla.] 1:2/3, Spring/Autumn 1980, p. 184–197, bibl., tables)

Household size and structural changes are charted for Puerto Rico during the period 1950–70. Demographic transitions, especially in conjunction with urbanization, have produced modifications in household composition. For example, both economic stress and recent demographic trends are responsible for a decline in average household size. See also items 3233–3234.

1565 Stycos, J. Mayone. Recent trends in Latin American fertility (LSE/PS, 31:3, Nov. 1978, p. 407–425, tables)

Demographic overview of factors contributing to fertility decline in several selected Latin American and Caribbean countries. Evidence points directly to increasingly dominant role and widespread influence of birth control and family planning programs, but changes in agriculture and literacy rates are also important.

Techa, Siegfied H. and Raymond Ph. Römer. Fertility trends in the Netherlands Antilles. See item 8247.

1566 Terra, Juan Pablo. Situación de la infancia en América Latina y el Caribe (ACEP/EP, número especial, abril 1980, p. 45–80, tables)

Reports on infantile population of Latin America and the Caribbean including demography, nutrition, and health characteristics. Considers population growth, family structure, and mortality patterns.

1567 Trussell, T.J. and K. Hill. Fertility and mortality estimations from the Panama retrospective demographic survey, 1976 (LSE/PS, 34:3, Nov. 1980, p. 551–563, bibl., tables)

Preliminary analysis of fertility and mortality profiles of Panama based on UN and CELADE survey data. High fertility and childhood mortality persist in Panama, especially in rural areas.

1568 Uthoff, Andras. Fecundidad y desarrollo económico y social en Chile: 1952–1970 (UC/EE, 12, 2. semestre 1978, p. 35–81, tables)

Regards fertility changes in recent years in Chile as manifestations of nation's broader economic and social change. New forms of household structure, migration, educational and religious institutions, and female employment have all rapidly and profoundly influenced differential fertility in Chile.

1569 Zavala de Cosío, María Eugenia. Problèmes de population au Mexique (CDLA, 17, 1978, p. 89–111, bibl., tables)

Insightful review of Mexico's demographic history and ongoing evolution. Population growth accelerated sharply after 1940 due mainly to mortality reductions, especially in younger age groups, and subsequent development of younger overall population and increased fertility. Although family planning has been coordinated nationally since 1973, the potential reproductive capabilities of the Mexican population remains enormous for the immediate future.

POPULATION STUDIES: GENETICS

1570 Ashcroft, M.T. and G.R. Sergeant. Body habitus of Jamaican adults with sickle cell haemoglobin C (SC) disease (West Indian Medical Journal [University of the West Indies, Mona, Jamaica] 28:4, Dec. 1979, p. 219–221, bibl., tables)

Presents anthropometric measurements for 52 Jamaican adults age 19–87 with haemoglobin SC. Subjects exhibited significantly smaller dimensions than national averages.

1571 Azevedo, Eliane S. Características antropogenéticas da população da Bahia, Brasil (OAS/CI, 19:3/4, julio/agosto 1978, p. 28–35, bibl., plates, tables)

Analyzes and compares population genetics of different ethnic and racial groups in state of Bahia, Brazil. Electrophoretic studies of several blood groups, serum proteins, and enzymes permitted reconstruction of evolutionary relationships and process of tri-racial hybridization among five sub-populations.

1572 ———. Inbreeding in a Brazilian general hospital (UCGL/AHG, 43:3, Feb. 1980, p. 255–264, bibl., tables)

Compares sample of 925 adult inpatients in Bahia, Brazil, hospital with 925 matched controls to determine possible relationships between disease incidence and levels of racial admixture. Hospital patients found to disproportionately represent relatively inbred family lines.

1573 ———. Subgroup studies of black admixture within a mixed population of Bahia, Brazil (UCGL/AHG, 44:1, July 1980, p.55–60, bibl., tables)

Traditional racial classifications are checked with genetic and epidemiological data from Bahia, Brazil. Admixture and inbreeding rates are calculated utilizing dermatoglyphic data and an analysis of family name distribution.

1574 ——— et al. Distribution of abnormal hemoglobins and glucose-6-phosphate dehydrogenase variants in 1,200 school children of Bahia, Brazil (AJPA, 53:4, Nov. 1980, p. 509–512, bibl., tables)

Examines hemoglobin variations in 1,200 Brazilian school children and studies G-6-PD polymorphisms in a sub-sample of 369 males. Hemoglobin AS and AC were more frequent than statistically expected, but they were the only abnormal genotypes encountered. No interrelation found between the hemoglobin and G-6-PD polymorphisms.

1575 ——— et al. Human aconitase polymorphism in three samples from Northeastern Brazil (UCGL/AHG, 43:1, July 1979, p. 7–10, bibl., tables)

Tests livers from 358 newborns from two Brazilian states for variation in enzyme aconitase. Uses genetic polymorphisms to determine degree of racial admixture in subsamples.

1576 Barbosa, S. and **H. Krieger.** The effects of inbreeding and of some genetic polymorphisms on blood pressures, pulse rate and hematocrit in Northeastern Brazil (HH, 29:2, 1979, p. 106–110, bibl., tables)

Studies possible roles of inbreeding and pleiotropic effects of blood protein polymorphisms on hematology of northern Brazilians. Inbreeding seemed to have its greatest impact on pulse rate among the 7,642 subjects.

1577 Barrantes, R. and **Francisco M. Salzano.** Genetic and nongenetic influences on the ABH and Lewis antigen levels of saliva and milk (HH, 29:4, 1979, p. 230–235, bibl., tables)

ABH and Lewis antigens checked in saliva and milk of 250 women immediately following childbirth in Porto Alegre, Brazil. Amount of Lewis substance depended upon ABH secretor status in both secretions.

1578 Baume, R.M. and **Michael H. Crawford.** Discrete dental trait asymmetry in Mexican and Belizean groups (AJPA, 52:3, March 1980, p. 315–321, bibl., tables)

Compares tooth size and asymmetry in 982 dental casts collected in four Mexican Indian and two Afro-Belizean populations. Significant populational and ethnic differences suggest important role of genetics, although environmental influences are considered.

1579 Black, Francis L. Restriction and persistence of polymorphisms of HLA and other blood genetic traits in the Parakana Indians of Brazil (AJPA, 52:1, Jan. 1980, p. 119–132, bibl., ill., tables)

Reports results of tests for polymorphisms in HLA and 22 other blood genetic systems for 129 Parakana Indians of northern Brazil. Limited heterogeneity and unusual variants characterize sample.

1580 Buschang, Peter H. and **R.M. Malina.** Brachymesophalangia-V in five samples of children: a descriptive and methodological study (AJPA, 53:2, Aug. 1980, p. 189–195, bibl., tables)

The incidence of Brachymesophalangia-V (BMP-V), a simply inherited anatomical anomaly of the finger, was studied in five samples of children from disparate ethnic backgrounds including 383 individuals from Mexico. Results are compared with published data from nine other Latin American countries.

1581 Callegari, Jacques; M. Sidia; and Francisco M. Salzano. Demography and genetics of the Kraho and Gorotire Indians of Brazil (Journal of Human Evolution [Academic Press, London] 8:5, July 1979, p. 513–522, bibl., tables)

Demographic data collected from three Brazilian Indian populations in order to help elucidate previously obtained genetic information. Mate selection patterns, reproductive histories, and mortality statistics indicate the populations differ in potential for natural selection and genetic drift.

1582 Cantu, J.M. *et al.* Partial mispairing and crossing-over between Beta and Gama genes as the origin of the Gama-Beta thalassemia gene (Human Genetics [Excepta Medica Foundation, Amsterdam] 49:2, 1979, p. 191–198, bibl., ill.)

Studies genetic basis of thalassemia in two siblings and their parents from Mexico. Reviews distrubution of hemoglobinopathies in Mexico.

1583 Chakraborty, Ranajit. Relationship between single- and multi-locus measures of gene diversity in a subdivided population (UCGL/AHG, 43:4, May 1980, p. 423–428, bibl., ill., tables)

Develops mathematical measures of genetic diversity and equilibrium with the aid of field data from several South American Indian populations. Examines enzyme polymorphisms to test models and methodology.

1584 Crawford, Michael H. and **E.J. Devor.** Population structure and admixture in transplanted Tlaxcaltecan populations (AJPA, 52:4, May 1980, p. 485–490, bibl., map, tables)

Calculates admixture estimates, genetic distances, and average heterozygosity for eight populations which historically originated in the state of Tlaxcala, Mexico. Discusses genetic composition of populations in the context of known historical events which shaped gene flow and hybridization with outside groups.

1585 —— *et al.* The Black Caribs (Garifuna) of Livingston, Guatemala: genetic markers and admixture estimates (WSU/HB, 53:1, Feb. 1981, p. 87–103, bibl., map, tables)

Documents variations and polymorphisms for 24 inherited blood proteins and enzymes in transplanted Black Carib population of Guatemela. Uses data from 206 blood specimens to estimate degree of genetic admixture and to reconstruct precise evolutionary ancestry of population.

1586 —— *et al.* Gene flow and genetic microdifferentiation of a transplanted Tlaxcaltecan Indian population: Saltillo (AJPA, 50:3, March 1979, p. 401–412, bibl., map, plate, tables)

Uses blood specimens from 302 subjects to reconstruct effects of hybridization in transplanted urban Indians in northern Mexico. Gene frequency distributions obtained on 29 blood genetic systems suggest triracial ancestry with Indian, Spanish, and African contributions.

1587 Cruz-Coke, Ricardo and **Lucia Rivera.** Genetic characteristics of Hemophilia A in Chile (HH, 30:3, 1980, p. 161–170, bibl., tables)

Genetic and demographic investigation of 40 kindreds containing 113 cases of Hemophilia A from Chile. Derives gene frequencies by segregation analysis. Presents fertility and life expectancy of hemophiliacs and their siblings along with estimates of mutation rates.

1588 Daltabuit, Magalí and **María Elena Sáenz.** Hábitos de consumo de leche y deficiencia de lactasa intestinal en el Valle de Mezquital (UNAM/AA, 15, p. 267–292, bibl., tables)

Investigates lactase deficiency and milk consumption patterns in 117 youngsters from state of Hidalgo, Mexico. 77 percent of sample were deficient in the enzyme, and this is similar to high frequencies previously discovered elsewhere in Mexico. Sample children exhibit extensive variation in milk-drinking habits and ability to tolerate lactose. Authors recommend reconsidering use of milk in nutritional improvement programs in Mexico.

1589 Escobar, V. *et al.* Genetic structure of the Queckchi Indians: dental microdifferentiation (HH, 29:3, 1979, p. 134–142, bibl., tables)

Investigates and compares nine traits of dental morphology in 540 Queckchi Indians from Guatemala with other populations to determine their exact position in American Indian phylogeny. Authors question validity of dental characteristics in calculating genetic distance.

1590 Freire-Maia, N. and **I.J. Cavalli.** Genetic investigations in a northern Brazilian island: pt. 1, Population structure (HH, 28:5, 1978, p. 386–396, bibl., maps, tables)

Presents genetic demography for small (307 inhabitants) Brazilian island population. Authors calculate sex ratio, migration rates, effective breeding population size, mate selection distances and consanguinity, inbreeding coefficient, standard mortality and fertility rates, and frequency of twinning.

1591 ——— *et al.* Mohr-Wriedt (A₂) brachydactyly: analysis of a large Brazilian kindred (HH, 30:4, 1980, p. 225–231, bibl., ill., tables)

Studies 117 individuals with Mohr-Wriedt brachydactyly from a large Brazilian kindred of German ancestry. Describes segregation analyses, fertility data, and dermatoglyphic anomalies.

1592 Henke, J. and **E. Spieker.** Population genetic studies in Aymara-speaking people of Bolivia (ZMA, 70:2, Okt. 1979, p. 181–184, tables)

Screens blood specimens from 67 unrelated Aymara-speaking Indians of Bolivia by electrophoresis to assess blood group antigens, immunoglobin allotypes, and red cell enzymes. Compares findings with previously published data on other Indian groups, and reports several unusual genetic variants for this sample.

1593 Leslie, Paul W. *et al.* Genetic implications of mating structure in a Caribbean isolate (ASHG/J, 33:1, Jan. 1981, p. 90–104, bibl., tables)

Studies mate selection patterns on St. Barthelemy, historically a relatively isolated Caribbean island. Explores genetic and evolutionary effects of consanguinity, emigration, and celibacy. Because many individuals never reproduce, effective breeding population size is greatly reduced, and there is increased opportunity for the action of genetic drift.

1594 Li, F.H.F. *et al.* A second study of the survival of a neutral mutant in a simulated Amerindian population (American Naturalist [Essex Institute, Lancaster, Pa.] 112:983, 1978, p. 83–96, bibl., tables)

Applies statistical techniques to population genetics data from South American Indian groups in order to calculate mean survival time of new mutants. Authors revise previously published estimates.

1595 Lisker, Ruben *et al.* Double blind study of milk lactose intolerance in a

group of rural and urban children (ASCN/J, 33:5, May 1980, p. 1049–1053, bibl., tables)

Investigates lactose intolerance in 240 rural and 101 urban children in Mexico. Finds significant differences, due partly to genetics and due partly to higher rate of gastrointestinal infections in rural areas.

1596 Mestriner, A. *et al.* New studies on the Esterase D polymorphism in South American Indians (AJPA, 52:1, Jan. 1980, p. 95–101, bibl., map, tables)

Presents esterase and carbonic anhydrase enzyme polymorphisms for 2490 South American Indians from 10 different tribes. Finds wide variations generally correlated with linguistic differences. Reviews geographic aspects of tribal diversity.

1597 Mohrenweiser, Harvey *et al.* Electrophoretic variants in three Amerindian tribes: the Baniwa, Kanamari, and Central Pano of western Brazil (AJPA, 50:2, Feb. 1979, p. 237–246, bibl., ill., map, plates, tables)

Describes 25 polymorphic genetic systems for sample of 812 individuals representing three Brazilian Indian tribes. Tabulates and utilizes common and rare electrophoretic variants for evolutionary comparisons of the different tribes.

1598 Mueller, William and **K.M. Weiss.** Colour-blindness in Colombia (Annals of Human Biology [Taylor and Francis Publishers, London] 6:2, March/April 1979, p. 137–145, bibl., tables)

Presents data on frequency of colour-blindness in two neighboring mestizo villages in Andes mountains of Colombia. Results show similarity to other populations in Latin America having European admixture. Discusses effects of various economic factors and possible action of natural selection of colour-blindness with reference to other published articles.

1599 Munan, Louis and **Anthea Kelly.** Frequency of fatal congenital anomalies of the nervous system: association with geographic latitude (Social Biology [Society for the Study of Social Biology, New York] 26:4, Winter 1979, p. 335–340, bibl., map, tables)

Epidemiological data on lethal genetic disorders of the nervous system reveal significant statistical association with geographic location in the New World. Gradient of different frequencies of inherited defects was found in comparing one city in North America, one in the Caribbean, and six diverse cities in South America.

1600 Neel, James V. The population structure of an Amerindian tribe: the Yanomama (Annual Review of Genetics [Palo Alto, Calif.] 12, 1978, p. 365–413, bibl., ill., maps, tables)

Extensive and thorough review of large-scale multidisciplinary research on Yanomama Indians of Brazil and Venezuela. Topics include population size and demographic characteristics, inbreeding and migration, gene frequency distribution, mutation and genetic drift, and natural selection. Includes 118-item bibliography, an especially useful feature.

1601 ——— and **E.D. Rothman.** Indirect estimates of mutation rates in tribal Amerindians (NAS/P, 75 : 11, 1978, p. 5585–5588, bibl., tables)

Employs three different methods to estimate mutation rates in 12 South American Indian populations. Uses electrophoresis to detect mutations in 28 inherited proteins. Derives an "average" estimate from the three separate approaches.

1602 ——— et al. Genetic studies on the Ticuna, an enigmatic tribe of Central Amazons (UCGL/AHG, 44 : 1, July 1980, bibl., ill., maps, plates, tables)

Presents data on 37 polygenic genetic systems for sample of 1,763 Ticuna Indians of Brazil, Peru, and Colombia. Low intervillage variability was encountered. Describes new polymorphisms and rare private alleles.

1603 O'Rourke, D.H. and **Michael H. Crawford.** Odontometric microdifferentiation of transplanted Mexican Indian populations: Cuanalan and Saltillo (AJPA, 52 : 3, March 1980, p. 421–434, bibl., map, tables)

Documents dental variations for four Mexican Indian populations of related genetic background. Evolutionary microdifferentiation is manifested in odontometric data comparisons, due mainly to differing levels of African and European admixture.

1604 Petzl, M.L. and **E.A. Chautard-Freire-Maia.** Additional information on the recombination fraction between Beta hemoglobin and MNSs loci (HH, 29 : 3, 1979, p. 177–180, bibl., table)

Possible genetic linkage between hemoglobin and MNSs loci examined with blood specimens from 40 nuclear families residing in a southern Brazilian city. Results of the lod score method suggest independent segregation.

1605 Plato, C.C. et al. Total and lateral digital and a-b palmar interdigital ridge counts among northern and southern Peruvian Quechua (WSU/HB, 52 : 4, Dec. 1980, p. 639–640, bibl., tables)

Evaluates dermatoglyphic samples for ridge counts in 523 males from Quechua Indian populations of Peru. Finds regional variations and discovers significant differences when comparing present results with published reports on Quechua of Bolivia.

1606 Saenz, G.F. et al. Hemoglobin Suresnes in a Costa Rican woman of Spanish-Indian ancestry (Hemoglobin [Marcel Dekker Journals, New York] 2 : 4, 1978, p. 383–387, bibl., table)

New hemoglobin variant detected in adult Costa Rican female of mixed Spanish-Indian ancestry. Authors detail chemical and genetic aspects of variant and identify exact location of mutation responsible for molecular change.

1607 Salzano, Francisco M. and **S.M. Callegari Jacques.** Genetic demography of the central Pano and Kanamari Indians of Brazil (WSU/HB, 51 : 4, Dec. 1979, p. 551–564, bibl., map, tables)

One segment of ongoing anthropological investigation of four populations of Brazilian Indians. Age-sex composition, migration, hybridization, and population size changes help to explain patterns of genetic microdifferentiation observed in nine genetic systems analyzed in blood samples from 427 individuals.

1608 ——— et al. Ag groups of the Kraho Indians of Brazil (HH, 31 : 1, 1981, p. 61–64, bibl., tables)

Examines Ag lipoprotein system for polymorphisms in 73 blood samples obtained in two villages of Brazilian Kraho Indians. Gene frequencies contrast with those in three populations of different racial and ethnic background.

1609 —— *et al.* The Caingang revisited: blood genetics and anthropometry (AJPA, 53:4, Nov. 1980, p. 513–524, bibl., plate, tables)

Ascertains population genetics of Caingang Indians of Brazil through study of 23 genetic polymorphisms in 248 blood samples and collection of 11 anthropometric measurements from 400 additional subjects. Genetic distances calculated among four populations are compared with geographic and linguistic distances.

1610 —— *et al.* Genetic demography of the Amazonian Ticuna Indians (Journal of Human Evolution [Academic Press, London] 9:3, March 1980, p. 179–191, bibl., map, tables)

Demographic analysis of eight villages of Ticuna (Tukuna) Indians of Brazil. Migration and fertility rates are high, while sterility and mortality rates are low in these groups. Population structure suggests low opportunity for natural selection.

1611 Serrano, Carlos and **Julieta Aréchiga.** Estudio bioantropológico del surco palmar transverso en los mayas yucatecos (CEM/ECM, 12, 1979, p. 15–32, bibl., ill., map, tables)

Well-executed genetic investigation of dermatoglyphic traits in Maya Indians of Yucatan. Authors make effective use of charts, illustrations, and nine tables of data collected from 552 males and 409 females from this population. Transverse palmar line receives special attention and analysis.

1612 Silva, Rosilda S. *et al.* Rare and common types of phosphoglucomutase in two Brazilian populations (WSU/HB, 53:2, May 1981, p. 227–238, bibl., plates, tables)

Determines polymorphisms of the PGM enzyme system in 695 white and 1,032 black subjects from Porto Alegre, Brazil and in 38 Xikrin Indians of Northeastern Brazil. Discovers rare phenotypes and extensive heterozygosity.

1613 Tchen, P.; F. Fonval; and **E. Bois.** Genetic study of the Cuiva Indians of Venezuela (Annals of Human Biology [Taylor and Francis Publishers, London] 6:3, May/June 1979, p. 231–240, bibl., map, tables)

Researches genetic variation in sample of 200 Cuiva Indians of southern Venezuela. Discovers low degree of polymorphic vari-

ability in serum and red blood cell protein markers. Population structure and demographic characteristics suggest the operation of genetic drift.

1614 —— *et al.* Blood group antigens in the Emerillon, Wayampi, and Wayana Amerindians of French Guiana (HH, 31:1, 1981, p. 47–53, bibl., map, tables)

Genetic polymorphisms in 13 different red blood cell protein systems are tabulated for three Indian populations from French Guiana. Frequencies are compared with other American Indian populations, and unusual distribution of alleles in the Diego blood group system is observed.

1615 Vieira Filho, João Paulo Botelho. O diabetes mellitus entre os índios dos Estados Unidos e os do Brasil (USP/RA, 21, 1. parte, 1978, p. 53–60, bibl.)

Statistical comparison of diabetes incidence and prevalence among North American Indians and Brazilian Indians. Diabetes is a common disorder in native Americans in both countries and is historically higher in the more inbred populations. Author compiles valuable bibliographic material.

1616 Yoshihara, Corinne M. and **H.W. Mohrenweiser.** Characterization of an electrophoretic variant of erythrocyte acid phosphatase restricted to the Ticuna Indians of Central Amazonas (ASHG/J, 32:6, Nov. 1980, p. 898–907, bibl., ill., plates, tables)

Reports new genetic variant of the red cell enzyme acid phosphatase for Ticuna Indians of Brazil. Electrophoretic mobility and thermostability of this enzyme are different from previously discovered polymorphisms in this system.

1617 Yunis, E. *et al.* Partial trisomy 3q (Human Genetics [Excerpta Medica Foundation, Amsterdam] 48:3, 1979, p. 315–320, bibl., plates, tables)

Discovers partial trisomy 3q in chromosome analysis of a five-year-old female from Bogotá, Colombia. Reports severe congenital malformations and psychomotor retardation. Compares clinical characteristics with 11 other similar cases.

1618 Zavala, Carlos *et al.* Complex segregation analysis of diabetes mellitus (HH, 29:6, 1979, p. 325–333, bibl., tables)

Statistical analysis of sample of 1,293

nuclear families containing at least one diabetic patient. Reports evidence for recessive inheritence and an especially high risk in families with affected mothers.

HUMAN ADAPTATION
AND VARIATION

1619 Almroth, Stina G. Water requirements of breast-fed infants in a hot climate (ASCN/J, 31:7, July 1978, p. 1154–1157, bibl., tables)

Uses urine samples from 16 Jamaican infants to determine water requirements. Results suggest breast-fed babies in hot climates manage well without additional water.

1620 Arnaud, J. et al. Methaemoglobin and erythrocyte reducing systems in high altitude natives (Annals of Human Biology [Taylor and Francis Publishers, London] 6:6, Nov./Dec. 1979, p. 585–592, bibl., tables)

Examines metabolic activity of red blood cell in 169 male Aymara Indians living under conditions of hypoxic stress in high altitude Bolivia. Compares enzyme levels and methaemoglobin content with control groups of same ethnic background. Also records red blood cell count, haemoglobin, and haematocrit in two sample populations.

1621 Bolton, Ralph. Guinea pigs, protein, and ritual (UP/E, 18:3, July 1979, p. 229–252, bibl., tables)

Explores relationship between environmental and economic constraints, nutritional requirements, timing of communal fiestas, and raising of guinea pigs in high altitude Peru. Finds cyclic pattern of ritual behaviors to be closely tied to the even, year-round distribution of protein in the population.

1622 ———. High altitude sex ratios: how high? (Medical Anthropology [Redgrave, Pleasantville, New York] 4:1, Winter 1980, p. 107–138, bibl., tables)

Genealogical and census data suggest that sex ratios in high altitude areas in Andean South America are only slightly higher than worldwide averages. Data from Ecuador, Peru, and Bolivia are compared.

1623 Casteel, Richard W. Human population estimates for hunting-and-gathering groups based on net primary production data: examples from the central desert of Baja, California (UNM/JAR, 35:1, Spring 1979, p. 85–98, bibl., map, tables)

Derives maximum population density estimates for hunting-and-gathering groups from quantitative models based upon published demographic and economic data from six Indian populations in central desert of Baja, California. Population sizes and densities predicted from models compared favorably with actual figures from the region.

1624 Dutt, James S. and **P.T. Baker.** Environment, migration and health in Southern Peru (Social Science and Medicine [New York] 12:1B, Jan. 1978, p. 29–38, bibl., tables)

Sex, altitude, and migratory behavior all found to be associated statistically with disease symptoms reported in Peru. Takes varying cultural backgrounds into account.

1625 Ferrell, Robert E. et al. The multinational Andean genetic and health program: pt. 9, Gene frequencies and rare variants of 20 serum proteins and erythrocyte enzymes in the Aymara of Chile (ASHG/J, 32:1, Jan. 1980, p. 92–102, bibl., map, tables)

Compares gene frequencies and distribution among 2,096 Aymara Indian, mestizo, and Spanish subjects from northern Chile using data on 20 serum proteins and two red cell enzymes. Reports several unique electrophoretic variants. Discusses possible role of the polymorphisms in high altitude adaptation.

1626 Fleischen, Mark L. An unusual distribution for height among males in a Warao Indian village: a possible case of lineal effect (AJPA, 53:3, Sept. 1980, p. 397–405, bibl., ill., map, tables)

Field investigation of environmental and cultural factors responsible for bimodal distribution of height among males of the Warao Indian populations of Venezuela. Restricted gene flow across villages and across family lines has probably led to the unusual distribution of height because of the "lineal effect," a form of genetic drift.

1627 Gautier du Defaix, H. et al. Liver storage iron in normal populations of Cuba (ASCN/J, 33:1, Jan. 1980, p. 133–136, bibl., tables)

Records liver storage iron values for sample of 161 liver specimens taken from

Cuban subjects who died acutely traumatic deaths. Describes age and sex differences. Authors believe this is a good method to assess normal hepatic storage iron variations.

1628 Gross, Daniel R. *et al.* Ecology and acculturation among native peoples of Central Brazil (AAAS/S, 206:4422, Nov. 1979, p. 1043–1050, bibl., maps, tables)

Study of multifaceted relationship of Central Brazilian Indians to their natural environment and how this affects their economic activities. Population size and degree of acculturation found to influence market involvement and other adaptive subsistence behaviors. Food energy yields are calculated for different cultivated crops in the four study communities.

1629 Haas, J.D. *et al.* Altitude, ethnic and sex difference in birth weight and length in Bolivia (WSU/HB, 52:3, Sept. 1980, p. 459–477, bibl., ill., tables)

Reports birth weight and length for 105 healthy newborns from high altitude and 77 babies from low altitude in Bolivia. Discusses ethnic variations and effects of mother's anthropometric characteristics upon pregnancy outcomes.

1630 Halberstein, Robert A. Physical anthropology in the Caribbean (Journal of Caribbean Studies [Association of Caribbean Studies, Coral Gables, Fla.] 1:2/3, Spring/Autumn 1980, p. 104–118, bibl.)

Topical and bibliographic survey of recent trends in physical anthropological research in the Caribbean, with special emphasis on the past decade. Publications are reviewed in the following areas: Paleoanthropology, Biodemography, Human Biological Variation, and Medical and Nutritional Anthropology. Future directions are charted.

1631 Hames, Raymond B. A comparison of the efficiencies of the shotgun and the bow in neotropical forest hunting (Human Ecology [Plenum, New York] 7:3, Sept. 1979, p. 219–252, bibl., tables)

Comparison of hunting efficiency of shotgun and bow in controlled experiments in Indian populations in southern Venezuela. The shotgun has rapidly replaced the bow in this area, and it has had a profound impact on hunting behavior, economic activities, and the size and composition of local animal populations.

1632 Harris, Edward F. and **M.T. Nweeia.** Dental asymmetry as a measure of environmental stress in the Ticuna Indians of Colombia (AJPA, 53:1, July 1980, p. 133–142, bibl., tables)

Dental symmetry described for sample of 57 Ticuna Indians from Colombia. Variation was partitioned by sex, tooth, arcade, and dimension. Explores possible relationships with dietary practices.

1633 —— and ——. Tooth size of Ticuna Indians, Colombia, with phenetic comparisons to other Amerindians (AJPA, 53:1, July 1980, p. 81–92, bibl., ill., maps, tables)

Examines dental traits, especially tooth size variations, in 57 Ticuna Indians age 17–30 from Colombia. Comparisons with other South American Indians and non-Indian groups are facilitated by multivariate statistics.

1634 Jaén, María Teresa; Carlos Serrano; and **Juan Comas.** Data antropométrica de algunas poblaciones indígenas mexicanas: aztecas, otomís, tarascos, coras, huicholes. México: Universidad Nacional Autónoma de México, Instituto de Investigaciones Antropológicas, 1976. 112 p.; 16 leaves of plates; bibl.; ill. (Serie antropológica; 28)

In-depth cross-cultural anthropometric comparison of five indigenous Indian groups (Huichols, Coras, Aztecs, Tarascans and Otomis) from five different Mexican states. In addition to height, weight, and 50 individual physical dimensions, 16 anthropometric indices were calculated for the 680 total subjects. References cited are dated, and two-thirds of the volume are devoted to raw data.

1635 Johnston, Francis E. and **L.M. Schell.** Anthropometric variation of native American children and adults (*in* The First Americans: origins, affinities, and adaptations [see item **1492**] p. 275–291, bibl., tables)

Review of published research on morphological variability of children and adults in native American Indian populations. Compares 11 separate indigenous cultural groups from Central and South America with respect to seven anthropometric measurements. Extensive heterogeneity discovered in physical growth and development among sample populations. Native American Indians tend to be smaller than people from Europe or US. Authors point out methodological and technical problems with research works under review.

1636 Kroeger, Axel. Housing and health in the process of cultural adaptation: a case study among jungle and highland Indians from Ecuador (DGV/ZE, 104:1, 1979, p. 79–104, bibl., ill., map, plates, tables)

Explores relationship between housing facilities and incidence of certain diseases through the administration of 727 family interviews in four Indian populations from lowland and high-altitude Ecuador. Well-illustrated article provides evidence of correlation between three basic house types and family health. Modernization of housing has brought certain epidemiological problems to these communities. Cites 95 references.

1637 Lasker, Gabriel W. and **H. Womack.** An anatomical view of demographic data: biomass, fat mass, and lean body mass of the United States and Mexican human populations (in Physiological and morphological adaptation and evolution. Edited by W.A. Stini. The Hague: Mouton, 1979, p. 369–378, bibl., tables [World anthropology])

Calculates average biomass of US and Mexico by multiplying mean body weight times the number of individuals in the populations. Also estimates relative amounts of fat and muscle in the populations. Discusses nutritional and evolutionary implications.

1638 López Alonso, Sergio. Antropometría de una muestra de población escolar de Cholula, Pue. (INAH/A, 6:54, 179–190, bibl., plates, tables)

Descriptive anthropometric study of 911 school children age seven–16 from Cholula, Puebla, Mexico. Stature, weight, sitting height, cephalic index, and ponderal index are tabulated. Notes age, sex, and ethnic differences within the sample.

1639 Monge C., Carlos. High altitude research (in Biomedical research in Latin America: background studies. Edited by Charles V. Kidd. Washington, D.C.: U.S. Department of Health, Education, and Welfare, Public Health Service, National Institutes of Health, 1980, p. 189–203, bibl. [NIH publication no. 80-2051])

Reviews research areas and accomplishments in high altitude regions of Latin Amer-

ica. Describes physiological and anatomical adaptations, characteristic pathologies and illnesses, and acclimatization processes based upon studies conducted in Bolivia, Ecuador, Peru, Colombia, and Mexico. History of high altitude studies, methodological problems, and future research prospects are briefly mentioned.

1640 Mueller, William H. *et al.* The Aymara of western Bolivia: pt. 5, Growth and development in an hypoxic environment (WSU/HB, 52:3, Sept. 1980, p. 529–546, bibl., tables)

Compares anthropometric age changes of Aymara Indians of high altitude areas of Bolivia and Chile to coastal peoples. While ethnicity and permanence of residence were important variables, hypoxia was mainly responsible for development of certain adaptive modifications unique to high altitude groups. Despite possessing smaller body sizes, high altitude samples exceed lowlanders in chest measurements.

1641 —— *et al.* Genes and epidemiology in anthropological adaptation studies: familial correlations in lung function in populations residing at different altitudes in Chile (Medical Anthropology [Redgrave, Pleasantville, N.Y.] 4:3, Summer 1980, p. 367–384, bibl., tables)

Studies lung function and height for concordance among 1,476 pairs of relatives in Chile's Aymara Indian population. Heritability of lung function was lower than height in the sample. Assesses effects of altitude variations.

1642 —— *et al.* A multinational Andean genetic and health program: pt. 6, Physiological measurements of lung function in an hypoxic environment (WSU/HB, 50:4, Dec. 1978, p. 489–513, bibl., ill., tables)

Studies lung function in 614 Aymara Indians, permanent residents of high altitude areas in northern Chile. Anthropometric measurements, other physical characteristics, age, ethnicity, and various environmental features all were associated with certain physiological indicators of vital capacity and other expressions of lung function.

1643 —— *et al.* A multinational Andean genetic and health program: pt. 7, Lung function and physical growth—multivariate analyses in high and low altitude populations (Aviation, Space, and Environmental Medicine [Aerospace Medical Association, Washington, D.C.] 49:10, Oct. 1978, p. 1188–1196, bibl., tables)

Relationship between lung activity and physical dimensions was discovered in high altitude children from northern Chile. Uses principal components and other multivariate statistical tests to assess importance of body size and proportions in physiological efficiency in younger people.

1644 —— *et al.* A multinational Andean genetic and health program: pt. 8, Lung function changes with migration between altitudes (AJPA, 51:2, Aug. 1979, p. 183–196, bibl., ill., tables)

Studies lung function in 377 individuals who migrated to new altitudes in northern Chile. Examines effects on lung function of ethnic background, altitude, age, sex, exercise and physical conditioning, occupation, migration, and physical traits. Heredity, developmental adaptation, and environmental variables all contributed significantly to changes in lung size and activity in the sample.

1645 Palomino, Hernán *et al.* Altitude, heredity and body proportions in Northern Chile (AJPA, 50:1, Jan. 1979, p. 39–50, bibl., ill., tables)

Ongoing investigation of effects of hypoxia on growth and development in high altitude Chile. Assesses body proportions of 2,096 individuals age 0–97 from different altitudes and ethnic groups. Finds significant differences in comparing Aymara and Spanish sub-samples, but altitude was correlated with developmental changes in head, chest, and overall growth configuration.

1646 Ramírez, María Eugenia. Cambios morfométricos en los otomís (UNAM/AA, 15, 1978, p. 311–322, bibl., tables)

Anthropometric comparison of four Otomí Indian populations from state of Hidalgo, Mexico sampled between 1933–76 (504 individuals). Statistical tests indicate significant gains over the years in height, weight, and several physical dimensions, although face and head measurements remained relatively constant. Since study populations are closely related genetically, author suggests changes are probably due to environmental factors such as improved nutrition and health facilities.

1647 Schutz, Yves *et al.* Energy expenditures and food intakes of lactating women in Guatemala (ASCN/J, 33:4, April 1980, p. 892–902, bibl., tables)

Examines and compares total energy intake and expenditure in 18 lactating women with non-lactating control women from same rural village in highland Guatemala. Heart rate, oxygen consumption, and nutrient intake were all quantified. Finds no significant differences between the two groups in energy intake or expenditure.

1648 Shuman, Malcolm K. Culture and deafness in Maya Indian society: an examination of illness roles (Medical Anthropology Newsletter [Society for Medical Anthropology, Washington, D.C.] 11:3, May 1980, p. 9–13, bibl.)

Anthropological analysis of deafness among Maya Indian villages in Yucatan, Mexico. Roles, behaviors, expectations, and cultural influences related to deafness are studied through case studies.

1649 Souza, Antonio Carlos Araújo de *et al.* Influencia ecológica sobre doenças geriátricas (PUC/V, 24:95, 1979, p. 371–385, bibl., maps, tables)

Using published census data, public health reports, and demographic survey results, authors attempt to ascertain environmental influences upon health and disease of elderly in state of Rio Grande do sul, Brazil. Special emphasis is placed upon the epidemiology of cardiovascular diseases and cancers. Eight separate maps illustrate the sharp geographic variations in several disorders.

1650 Staudt, Frits J. *et al.* Physical working capacity of male inhabitants from upper Surinam (Journal of Human Evolution [Academic Press, London] 8:3, March 1979, p. 399–405, bibl., map, tables)

Tests 20 black males from Surinam for aerobic power with a bicycle ergometer. Sample characterized by comparatively low values. Heart rates and oxygen utilization were measured.

1651 Stinson, Sara. The physical growth of high altitude Bolivian Aymara children (AJPA, 52:3, March 1980, p. 377–385, bibl., ill., map, tables)

Describes ontogenetic patterns for 510 Aymara Indian children age six–20 living at altitudes between 3,800 and 4,000 m. in Bolivia. Delayed growth, development, and maturity characterize sample. Compares results with Quechua Indian and North American children.

1652 Toledo, Víctor M. *et al.* Los puré-
pechas de Patzcuaro: una aproximación ecológica (III/AI, 40:1, Jan./March 1980, p. 17–56, bibl., tables)

Interdisciplinary research among the Purépecha (Tarascan) Indians of Mexico focuses upon ecosystem management and utilization of resources. Population makes effective use of soils, weather patterns, plants, and animals in adapting to the hot climate conditions.

1653 Werner, Dennis *et al.* Subsistence productivity and hunting effort in native South America (Human Ecology [Plenum, N.Y.] 7:4, Dec. 1979, p. 303–306, bibl., tables)

Concise discussion of hunting techniques in a number of contemporary South American Indian populations. Hunting has evolved to a sophisticated level of efficiency and productivity, and this applies both to groups that employ traditional weapons (bow-and-arrow, spear, traps, etc.) as well as groups with more modern weapons (rifles, high-power scopes, etc.).

HUMAN DEVELOPMENT

1654 Alleyne, S.I. *et al.* Menarcheal age among girls attending school in urban and rural Jamaica (West Indian Medical Journal [University of the West Indies, Mona, Jamaica] 29:4, Dec. 1980, p. 254–260, bibl., tables)

Age at first menstruation ascertained in 1,148 girls from four schools in Jamaica. Socioeconomic and anthropometric factors are probably responsible for relatively late age of menarche.

1655 Anderson, Mary Ann. Comparison of anthropometric measures of nutritional status in preschool children in five developing countries (ASCN/J, 32:11, Nov. 1979, p. 2339–2345, bibl., tables)

Weight, height, and upper arm circumference were measured in 7,304 children age 1–5 from five developing countries including Colombia, Costa Rica, and the Dominican Republic. The three dimensions are com-

pared for accuracy in evaluating nutritional status. Good agreement in malnutrition diagnosis was found between height and weight.

1656 Aspelin, Paul L. Food distribution and social bonding among the Mamainde of Mato Grosso, Brazil (Journal of Anthropological Research [University of New Mexico, Albuquerque] 35:3, Fall 1979, p. 309–327, bibl., ill., tables)

Quantitative evaluation of distribution of foodstuffs among Indian populations of northwestern Brazil. Family size and social-economic network structure were important variables in food distribution patterns.

1657 Blasco, Juan Carlos. Indicadores sobre la situación de la infancia en América Latina y el Caribe/Indicators on the situation of children in Latin America and the Caribbean. Trabajo realizado por Juan Carlos Blasco, bajo la supervisión y apoyo técnico de la División de Estadística y Análisis Cuantitativo de la CEPAL; traducción, Marjorie Casassus; dirección de arte, Mary Ann Streeter Prieto. s.l.: UNICEF; s.l.: CEPAL, 1979,. 279 p.; bibl.; ill.

Elaborate interdisciplinary UN-supported investigation of child health and development in Latin America. Childhood mortality, nutrition, and health status were found to correlate directly with urbanization, socioeconomic and educational levels, ethnic group differences, and the distribution of food and health resource services. Includes general demographic characteristics of several sample populations.

1658 Bogin, Barry A. Monthly changes in the gain and loss of growth in weight of children living in Guatemala (AJPA, 51:2, Aug. 1979, p. 287–292, bibl., tables)

Monthly weight increments followed in sample of 246 children age 5–18 from Guatemala City. No seasonal patterns of rhythms in weight changes were observed.

1659 ——— and Robert B. MacVean. Growth in height and weight of urban Guatemalan primary school children of low and high socioeconomic class (WSU/HB, 50:4, Dec. 1978, p. 477–487, bibl., ill., tables)

Increments in height and weight monitored in 155 urban Guatemalan children age 7–13 of low socioeconomic status and compared with 155 control subjects of high socioeconomic status. Significant differences found across two sub-samples. Growth in height and weight showed a statistically significant correlation with each other.

1660 ——— and ———. Nutritional and biological determinants of body fat patterning in urban Guatemalan children (WSU/HB, 53:2, May 1981, p. 259–268, bibl., tables)

Nutritional status and physique compared in 981 children age 7–14 from low and high socioeconomic classes in urban Guatemala. Body fat patterning was especially variable in the samples and is probably closely related to health.

1661 Chagnon, Napoleon A. and R.B. Hames. Protein deficiency and tribal warfare in Amazonia: new data (AAAS/S, 203:4383, March 1979, p. 910–913, bibl., tables)

Although previous anthropological studies suggested that warfare among many native Amazonian peoples stems from competition over scarce food resources, the present data on Yanomama Indians from Brazil and Venezuela reveal their protein intake and nutritional status are actually more than adequate, due mainly to successful hunting and fishing activities. Data on seven other tribal populations also indicate no correlation between protein ingestion and warfare intensity. For ethnologist's comment, see item **1086**.

1662 Cohen, Florence S. El parto y el rol de comadrona en una aldea garifuna de Honduras (YAXKIN, 3:1, junio 1979, p. 27–46, bibl.)

Examination of childbirth and the role of the midwife in small village in northern Honduras. Author personally assisted in the delivery of four babies and interviewed three "professional" midwives. Data collected on pregnancy, labor and delivery procedures, infant care, feeding practices, and health precautions.

1663 Desai, I.D. *et al.* Food habits and nutritional status of agricultural migrant workers in southern Brazil (ASCN/J, 33:3, March 1980, p. 702–714, bibl., ill., tables)

Migrant farm workers from 100 families from urban slums in Brazil were studied with respect to food habits and nutrition. Rice and bean based diet found to be generally inadequate in quality and quantity. Carbonated drinks, alcohol, and starchy foods added further problems to dietary insufficiency.

1664 DeWalt, Kathleen M. *et al.* Nutritional correlates of economic microdifferentiation in a highland Mexican community (*in* Nutritional anthropology: contemporary approaches to diet and culture. Edited by N. Jerome; R. Kandel; and G. Pelto. Pleasantville, N.Y.: Redgrave Pub. Co., 1980, p. 205–222, bibl., tables)

Wide variations in dietary patterns found in Indian-mestizo agricultural village in central Mexico. While economic differences account for much of the nutritional variation, authors' data show that cultural differences are also important, especially customs and traditions of food use. Conclusions are unfortunately not supported by sufficient statistical quantification.

1665 Dewey, Kathryn G. The impact of agricultural development on child nutrition in Tabasco, Mexico (Medical Anthropology [Redgrave, Pleasantville, N.Y.] 4:1, Winter 1980, p. 21–55, bibl.)

Evaluates effects of agricultural development project on childhood nutrition in rural Mexican community. Assesses impact of new dietary behaviors in 149 preschool children using anthropometry, biochemical tests, and clinical examinations. New agricultural project did not appreciably improve nutritional status in the sample children. For ethnologist's comment, see item **864**.

1666 Faulhaber, Johanna. El crecimiento diferencial en algunas regiones del cuerpo (UNAM/AA, 16, 1979, p. 457–485, bibl., tables)

Growth and developmental changes documented in a longitudinal study of 523 Mexico City children age one month through 11 years. Numerous body measurements were statistically correlated with chronological age. Age changes in physical development showed significant sexual differences.

1667 Fierro-Benítez, Rodrigo. Desnutrición, subdesarrollo y dependencia (AI/I, 4:3, May/June 1979, p. 164–169)

General article on nutritional problems and their relation to economic conditions throughout Latin America. Research by author and other scientists indicates some improvement in certain areas such as iodine deficiency and chronic protein-calorie malnutrition, but nutrient shortages still are impeding economic progess in Latin America.

1668 **Franklin, David L.** and **Isabel Vial de Valdés.** Desnutrición infantil y su relación con el tiempo y las habilidades de la madre (UCC/CE, 16:49, dic. 1979, p. 343–358, bibl., tables)

Data from Chile and Colombia are analyzed in order to maximize improvements and minimize economic costs of nutritional programs. Childhood nutrition is shown to be the product of numerous factors including mother's lifestyle and work habits, caloric demands, household structure, diet, and allocation of time and resources.

1669 **Freeman, Howard E.** *et al.* Nutrition and cognitive development among rural Guatemalan children (APHA/J, 70:12, Dec. 1980, p. 1277–1285, bibl., tables)

Longitudinal investigation of nutritional supplements administered to women and children from four rural Guatemalan Indian villages. Anthropometric measurements and cognitive tests were repeated over period of seven years. Statistical analyses suggest inadequate nutritional intake adversely affects cognitive development irrespective of social factors. Proteins, minerals, and vitamins were all regulated in sample groups.

1670 **Frisancho, A. Roberto.** Nutritional influence on childhood development and genetic control of adolescent growth of Quechuas and mestizos from the Peruvian lowlands (AJPA, 52:3, March 1980, p. 367–375, bibl., tables)

Relative contributions of genetics and nutrition in childhood growth and development evaluated from data on 1,202 Quechua and mestizo children age 6–19 from lowland Peru. Heredity and environment were found to be alternately more important at different periods during growth.

1671 **Gehlert Mata, Carlos.** Algunos aportes para la mejor comprensión del problema nutricional de la niñez guatemalteca (URL/ES, 14, oct. 1979, p. 17–26, bibl.)

Series of 10 important questions and possible answers regarding serious and persistent problem of malnutrition among Guatemalan children. Offers recommendations.

1672 **Graham, George G.** *et al.* Urban-rural differences in the growth of Peruvian children (ASCN/J, 33:2, Feb. 1980, p. 338–344, bibl., tables)

Growth and development patterns compared between samples of children age 2–19 from rural villages and poor urban areas in northern Peru. Sexual and rural-urban differences are pronounced, especially during certain age periods.

1673 **Grantham-McGregor, S.M.** *et al.* A new look at the assessment of mental development in young children recovering from severe malnutrition (Developmental Medicine and Child Neurology [National Spastics Society, Medical Education and Information Unit, London] 20:6, Dec. 1978, p. 773–778, bibl., tables)

Compares 17 malnourished and 15 adequately nourished hospitalized Jamaican children age 6–24 months with respect to brain and mental development. Rapid improvements followed nutritional recuperation among malnourished individuals, but some developmental damage may have permanent effects.

1674 **Halberstein, Robert A.** Age at menarche on a small Bahamian island (Annals of Human Biology [Taylor and Francis Publishers, London] 6:6, Nov./Dec. 1979, p.593–594, bibl., table)

Descriptive report on mean age at first menstruation in sample of females from island of Bimini, Bahamas. The relatively delayed menarcheal age that was discovered is a contributing factor to the trend of fertility reduction, especially among younger women, documented in this population.

1675 **Higman, Barry W.** Growth in Afro-Caribbean slave populations (AJPA, 50:3, March 1979, p. 373–386, bibl., ill., tables)

Historical data studied on height in African slave populations in Trinidad, Guyana, and other British colonies in 19th-century Caribbean. Compares information on several thousand individuals with black populations in Cuba and US. Considers differences in menarche and other growth indicators. Afro-Caribbean adults today are about 10 cm taller than their direct ancestors of a century and a half ago.

1676 **Hunt, Isabelle F.** Dietary zinc intake of low income pregnant women of Mexican descent (ASCN/J, 32:7, July 1979, p. 1511–1518, bibl., tables)

Zinc intake was monitored in 344 pregnant Mexican women of low socioeconomic status through 24-hour dietary recalls. Of the sample, 85 percent exhibited zinc intake levels well below the recommended MDR.

1677 Kohn de Brief, Fritzi. Age at menarche in Venezuelan students residing in metropolitan Caracas (*in* Physiological and morphological adaptation and evolution. Edited by W.A. Stini. The Hague: Mouton, 1979, p. 349–362, bibl., tables)

Weight, height, and age at menarche recorded for 1,260 female students in Caracas, Venezuela. Average age at first menstruation is 12.7 years according to the probit method. Sample variation correlated well with nutritional status and nutrient intake.

1678 Koopman, James S. *et al.* Food, sanitation, and the socioeconomic determinants of child growth in Colombia (APHA/J, 71:1, Jan. 1981, p. 31–37, bibl., tables)

In Cali, Colombia, 228 *barrios* were scored with respect to 50 nutritional indicators. Influences of diet, anthropometric measurements, and socioeconomic conditions upon child growth and development are presented. Food availability seemed to be more correlated with overall child health than with growth and maturation.

1679 Lejarraga, H. *et al.* Age of menarche in urban Argentinian girls (Annals of Human Biology [Taylor and Francis Publishers, London] 7:6, Nov./Dec. 1980, p. 680–682, bibl., table)

Cross-sectional data on age at first menstruation among sample of 6,494 schoolgirls from La Plata City, Argentina. Probit analysis revealed a mean menarcheal age of 12.5 years, which is relatively early compared to other Latin American groups.

1680 Lowry, M.F. and R. Bailey. The size of Jamaican newborns from 27–42 weeks gestation (West Indian Medical Journal [University of the West Indies, Mona, Jamaica] 27:3, Sept. 1978, p. 137–146, bibl., tables)

Correlates measurements of 1,230 newborns in Jamaican hospital with gestational age. Nutritional status was not considered.

1681 Malina, Robert M. *et al.* Growth of rural and urban children in the Valley of Oaxaca, Mexico (AJPA, 54:3, March 1981, p. 327–336, bibl., ill., map, tables)

Height, weight, and upper arm dimensions presented for 1,410 school children age

6–14 from two urban and four rural populations in Oaxaca, Mexico. Significant differences discovered between Indian and ladino samples, but the effects of urbanization are unclear.

1682 —— *et al.* Growth status of school children in a rural Zapotec community in the Valley of Oaxaca, Mexico in 1968 and 1978 (Annals of Human Biology [Taylor and Francis Publishers, London] 7:4, July/Aug. 1980, p. 367–374, bibl., map, tables)

Mixed-longitudinal investigation of growth and development in Zapotec Indian children from Oaxaca, Mexico. Compares anthropometric data collected in 1968 on 361 children age 6–14 with 363 subjects of the same ages examined in 1978. Height, weight, and arm skinfold and muscle circumference measurements reveal little improvement in growth status over the 10-year study period.

1683 Marchione, Thomas J. Factors associated with malnutrition in the children of western Jamaica (*in* Nutritional anthropology: contemporary approaches to diet and culture. Edited by N. Jerome; R. Kandel; and G. Pelto. Pleasantville, N.Y.: Redgrave Publishing Co., 1980, p. 223–274, bibl., map, tables)

Well-quantified computerized study of cultural variables influencing malnutrition in Jamaica featuring factor analysis of a large stockpile of census, survey, and published demographic data. Demonstrates how 31 separate variables (household size, income, diet, accessibility of health facilities, etc.) differentially affect nutritional status among Jamaican children of all ages.

1684 Martorell, R. *et al.* Malnutrition, body size, and skeletal maturation: interrelationships and implications for catch-up growth (WSU/HB, 51:3, Sept. 1979, p. 371–389, bibl., tables)

Field study in four rural Guatemalan villages on the effects of malnutrition on body size and skeletal maturation of the hand and wrist. Nutritional stress seemed to depress body size development moreso than skeletal maturation. Comparisons are provided with well-nourished populations from Guatemala and the US.

1685 Mena de Godínez, Carolina. Evaluación biológica de un aislado proteínico de soya en niños de edad pre-escolar. Guatemala: Universidad de San Carlos de Guatemala, Facultad de Ciencias Químicas y Farmacia, Instituto de Nutrición de Centro América y Panamá, 1977. 51 leaves.

Descriptive research on physical, nutritional, and health effects of dietary improvement in eight nutritionally stressed children age 27–44 months from Guatemala. Subjects responded favorably to high-protein food supplement and exhibited rapid gains in height and weight. However, small sample size prevents firm conclusions.

1686 Mueller, William H. Fertility and physique in a malnourished population (WSU/HB, 51:2, May 1979, p. 153–166, bibl., tables)

Examines relationship between body build and reproductive performance in 704 adults from a moderately malnourished population in the Andes mountains of Colombia. Achieved fertility is higher among fatter individuals, but socioeconomic status is also important. Discusses possible operation of natural selection.

1687 Murguía, Raúl. Diferenciación social, crecimiento y desarrollo corporal (Boletín de Antropología Americana [Instituto Pan-Americano de Geografía e Historia, México] 1, junio 1980, p. 52–61, bibl., ill.)

Popular account of relationship between social class and growth and development in Mexico. Anthropometric characteristics of contemporary Mexicans are discussed without benefit of statistical data. Author attempts to sort out genetic and environmental influences upon human development from published sources.

1688 Nigh, Ronald B. El ambiente nutricional de los grupos mayas de Chiapas (III/AI, 40:1, Jan./March 1980, p. 73–92, bibl., map, tables)

Field investigation of demographic and environmental causes of malnutrition among Maya Indians of Mexico and Yucatan. Sharp reduction in natural resource availability in recent years has contributed more to lowering of nutritional quality than has population growth. Secondary nutritional sources, particularly collected foods, constitute an essential supplement to agricultural products in sustaining the population.

1689 Pardo, Lucía. Efectos de las variaciones económicas en la fecundidad: Chile,

1952–1972 (UC/EE, 14:2, 1979, p. 75–132, bibl., tables)

Elaborate and exhaustive comparative study of fertility trends in Chile. Economic variables are directly tied to fertility levels and fecundity during period 1952–72. Sophisticated statistics enhance successful treatment of data.

1690 Paredes-López, O. La alimentación: ¿penuria social en América Latina? (AI/I, 3:5, sept./oct. 1978, p. 282–284, tables)

General review of nutritional problems throughout Latin America. Agriculture and labor difficulties have compounded nutritional stress in region by decreasing per capita food production rates. As a result, Latin America has experienced a rapid increase in the importation of basic foods.

1691 Powell, C. and **S.M. Grantham-McGregor.** The associations between nutritional status, school achievement and school attendance in twelve-year-old children at a Jamaican school (West Indian Medical Journal [University of the West Indies, Mona, Jamaica] 29:4, Dec. 1980, p. 247–253, bibl., tables)

Nutritional status is related to school performance in Jamaica, but study of 1,721 students disclosed that school attendance is also an extemely important factor.

1692 Rogoff, Barbara. Etnografía del desarrollo del niño en una comunidad maya de proceso de modernicación: San Pedro la Laguna, Sololá, Guatemala (GIIN/GI, 12:3/4, julio/dic. 1977, p. 207–224, bibl.)

Anthropological investigation of growth and development of children in Mayan Indian community of 5,000 inhabitants in the altiplano of Guatemala. Pregnancy and childbirth, infancy, childhood, adolescence, and maturation are discussed within their cultural contexts. Physical and behavioral development of children in this population are likely to undergo substantial modifications in the future.

1693 Romain, J.B. Research on puberty in Haiti (in Physiological and morphological adaptations and evolution. Edited by W.A. Stini. The Hague: Mouton, 1979, p. 255–261, bibl., tables)

Age at menarche investigated in a sample of 1,729 females age 10–18 from

Port-au-Prince and several towns in western Haiti. Racial and socioeconomic class differences are noted. Age at first menstruation averaged 13.6–15.0 years in the various groups studied.

1694 Santos, José E. dos *et al.* Relationship between the nutritional efficacy of a rice and bean diet and energy intake in preschool children (ASCN/J, 32:7, July 1979, p. 1541–1544, bibl., tables)

Diet and food intake studied for nutritional quality and effectiveness in sample of Brazilian children age 4–6 receiving a rice and bean diet. Nitrogen balance and urea excretion were measured.

1695 Santos, Walter J. Problema alimentar e nutricional da infáncia brasileira (INEP/RBEP, 62:143, jan./abril 1979, p. 233–252, tables)

Investigation of causes and outcomes of dietary and nutritional stress among Brazilian children. Author's statistics indicate nutritional deficiencies are directly responsible for country's excessive infant mortality rates. Assays nutrient content of typical diets and suggests possible modifications.

1696 Seminario Nacional sobre Alimentación y Nutrición, *1st, Sonsonate, El Salvador, 1977.* Nutrición humana y sistema alimentario en El Salvador: compilación de estudios presentados ante el I Seminario Nacional sobre Alimentación y Nutrición, que tuvo lugar en el Hotel Cerro Verde, septiembre 12–14, 1977. San Salvador: Editorial Universitaria, Universidad de El Salvador, 1978. 166 p.; bibl.; ill.

Problem-oriented monograph on nutrition and human ecology in El Salvador. Discusses production systems and their economic and political aspects with recommendations for dietary and nutritional improvements. Briefly explores relationship of nutrition and disease.

1697 Sgarbieri, Valdemiro Carlos. A nutrição em transição: novas descobertas e tendências (SBPC/CC, 31:3, março 1979, p. 262–279, bibl., table)

General treatment of the multiple cultural, biological, and environmental factors contributing to human nutrition in Brazil. Nutritional problems and their possible solutions are placed in an ecological context. Data are compared from Brazil, Ghana, India, and the US.

1698 Sheffer, M.L. *et al.* The social environment of malnourished children compared with that of other children in Jamaica (Journal of Biosocial Science [Blackwell Scientific Publications, Oxford, U.K.] 13:1, Jan. 1981, p. 19–30, bibl., tables)

Compares Jamaican children hospitalized for severe protein-calorie malnutrition with 20 well-nourished control subjects also being hospitalized. Notes significant differences between two samples in weight, head circumference, and several other anthropometric characteristics. Considers numerous cultural and economic factors but largely overlooks biomedical variations.

1699 Stinson, Sara. Child growth and the economic value of children in rural Bolivia (Human Ecology [Plenum, N.Y.] 8:2, June 1980, p. 89–104, bibl., tables)

Houehold size and composition, economic contributions of children, and physical growth patterns show a complex interrelationship in rural Bolivian population. Uses five anthropometric measurements to assess developmental phenomena.

1700 Valiente Berenguer, Sérgio. Bibliografía chilena relacionada con políticas de alimentación y nutrición, 1960–1975. Edición a cargo de Sérgio Valiente Berenguer, Sylvai Anabalón Casas. Santiago: Universidad Nacional de Chile, Instituto de Nutrición y Tecnología de los Alimentos, Unidad de Políticas de Alimentación y Nutrición, 1978. 161 p.

Large annotated bibliography of food, nutrition, and related research in Chile. References, published between 1960–76, are classified according to sub-area headings and also arranged chronologically and by author. Topics include food supplies, consumption patterns, health and nutrition, nutrition policies and programs, and current reasearch.

1701 Van Wering, Elizabeth R. The secular growth trend on Aruba between 1954 and 1974 (WSU/HB, 53:1, Feb. 1981, p. 105–115, bibl., tables)

Cross-sectional growth study involving 2,559 children age 0–14 from Aruba. Secular growth changes during 1954–74 found for height, weight, and sitting height, but values continue to lag behind Dutch children.

1702 Vélez Trujillo, Luis Guillermo. Barreras del hambre: comentarios sobre economía campesina. Prólogo de Julio César

Turbay Ayala. Bogotá: distribuidor, Futura, 1978. 224 p.; ill.

General overview of problems of nutrition and human development in Colombia. Topics range from nutrient-calorie content of typical diets to utilization of land space, depletion of natural resources, and energy demands of increased agricultural productivity.

1703 Villanueva, María. Adiposidad, muscularidad, y linearidad en un grupo de niños mexicanos de distintos niveles socioeconómicos (UNAM/AA, 16, 1979, p. 407–432, bibl., tables)

Comparative anatomy and anthropometry of 819 Mexican school children representing contrasting socioeconomic backgrounds. Children from the lower socioeconomic levels were shorter, lighter, and less muscular. Compares findings with published data from other Mexican groups and interprets them in terms of dietary and nutritional factors.

1704 Ward, John O. and **John H. Sanders.** Determinantes nutricionais e migração no Nordeste brasileiro: um estudo de caso nas áreas rural e urbana no Ceará (BNB/REN, 11:2, abril/junho 1980, p. 293–324, tables)

Evaluates nutrition in Northeastern Brazil in order to eliminate certain well-defined nutritional deficiency disorders. Migration, urbanization, and the establishment of nutritional improvement programs have all had an impact on nutritional levels in the region. High fertility and relatively low standard of living have historically compounded nutritional problems in this area. For sociologist's comment, see item **8406.**

EPIDEMIOLOGICAL ANTHROPOLOGY

1705 Allen, Catherine J. To be Quechua: the symbolism of coca chewing in highland Peru (AAA/AE, 8:1, Feb. 1981, p. 157–171, bibl., tables)

Coca is observed to be an integral element of culture of Quechua Indians of southern Peru. In addition to its biomedical uses the plant serves as a symbol of cultural identity even in young children. Ceremonial and social "rules" governing coca leaf chewing are described without statistical data.

1706 America Indígena. Instituto Indigenista Interamericano. Vol. 38, No. 4, oct./dec. 1978– . México.

Special issue devoted to coca leaf use in South America. Ten separate articles deal with history, medical applications, economic implications, and magico-religious aspects. Data from high altitude Peru and Bolivia are featured. See also item **1234.**

1707 Anzures y Bolaños, María del Carmen. Medicinas tradicionales y antropología (UNAM/AA, 15, 1978, p. 131–164, bibl.)

Broad overview of traditional non-Western medical systems with emphasis upon Latin American populations. Examines roles of magic and religion in healing and therapeutic practices. Author recommends additional research and publications on curing and related activities in native populations in Central and South America.

Azeredo, Paulo Roberto de. Classe social e saúde na cidade no Rio de Janeiro: primeira metade do século XIX. See *HLAS 42:3509.*

1708 Baruzzi, R.G.; L.F. Marcopito; and **M. Iunes.** Programa médico preventivo da Escola Paulista de Medicina no Parque Nacional do Xingú (USP/RA, 21, 2. parte, 1978, p. 155–170, bibl., map, plates)

Survey of recent medical acculturation in Xingu Indian tribes of Brazil. Sociocultural impact of modern medicine is analyzed. Biomedical status of populations have been improved by thorough checkups, vaccinations, and direct treatments.

1709 Biomedical research in Latin America: background studies. Edited by Charles V. Kidd. Washington, D.C.: U.S. Department of Health, Education, and Welfare, Public Health Service, National Institutes of Health, 1980. 239 p.; bibl.; ill.; tables [NIH publication no. 80-2051]

Extensive and thorough coverage of biomedical research theories, methods, and findings in Latin American countries. Chapters (13) deal with latest work on public and personal health problems including parasitic diseases, environmental health, cancer, diabetes, mental illness, climatic and altitude stress, government health support systems, health manpower migration and availability, and biomedical impact of earthquakes and other natural disasters.

1710 Bolton, Ralph. Agresión e hipoglicemia entre los qolla: un estudio de antropología sicobiológica (IBEAS/EA, 4[2]:4, 1974/76, p. 179–218, tables)

Possible relationship between hypoglycemia and various types of aggressive behavior is explored among Qolla Indians of Peru. Author uses written records and clinical data to demonstrate inverse correlation between blood glucose levels and different forms of aggression.

Burchard, Roderick E. On coca chewing and the polycythemia hypothesis. See item **1253**.

1711 Butt Colson, Audrey. Oposiciones binarias y el tratamiento de la enfermedad entre los Akawaio. Caracas: Universidad Católica Andres Bello, Instituto de Investigaciones Históricas, Centro de Lenguas Indígenas, 1978. 41 p. (Colección de lenguas indígenas: Serie menor; 2)

Anthropological investigation of traditional medical diagnosis and treatment among the Akawaio, a Carib-speaking Indian population numbering 5,000 in Venezuela. Outlines categories of disease, medicinal substances, and healing treatments.

1712 Bye, Robert A. Hallucinogenic plants of the Tarahumara (Journal of Ethnopharmacology [Elsevier Sequoia, Lausanne, Switzerland] 1:1, 1979, p. 23–48, bibl., tables)

In anthropological and ethnobotanical terms, analyzes plants used by Mexican Tarahumara Indians to alter perceptions and induce hallucinations. Reviews historical accounts and classifies previously unidentified hallucinogenic plants.

1713 Campos Rey de Castro, Jorge. La situación de salud y la enseñanza de la medicina en América Latina (UUAL/U, 76, abril/junio 1979, p. 239–250)

General overview of public health problems and health services in Latin America. Special attention is devoted to medical education and facilities.

1714 Castillo Ríos, Carlos. Remedios y capitalismo: fármacos, leches en polvo y transnacionales. Lima: Ediciones Realidad Nacional, 1979. 96 p.; bibl.

General review of drugs and other medicinal products and their distribution in Latin America. Focus is on improper advertising, false or exaggerated claims, inadequate testing, and undesired drug side effects. Recommendations are offered to alleviate problems associated with rapid spread of modern synthetic prescription medications in Latin America.

Caycho Jiménez, Abraham. Folklore médico y fitoalucinismo en el Perú. See *HLAS 42:1397.*

1715 Coreil, Jeannine. Traditional and Western responses to an Anthrax epidemic in rural Haiti (Medical Anthropology [Redgrave, Pleasantville, N.Y.] 4:1, Winter 1980, p. 79–104, bibl., map)

In 1977, the Anthrax epidemic in Haiti stimulated a variety of adaptive responses from traditional healers and "modern" health care providers. Coping strategies differed but were equally effective throughout the population. For ethnologist's comment, see item **968**.

1716 Cosminsky, Sheila and **M. Scrimshaw.** Medical pluralism on a Guatemalan plantation (Social Science and Medicine [New York] 14B:4, Nov. 1980, p. 267–278, bibl., tables)

Compares alternate medical systems, resources, and behaviours in small (690 individuals) rural Guatemalan community. Population utilized both traditional and modern health services or various combinations thereof. Describes roles of health seekers and healers.

1717 Deltgren, Florian. Culture, drug, and personality: a preliminary report about the results of field research among the Yebamasa Indians of Rio Piraparana in the Colombian Comisaria del Vaupes (Ethnomedicine [Arbeits Gemeinschaft Ethnomedizin and H. Buskerverlag, Hamburg, FRG, 5:1/2, 1978/1979, p. 57–82, bibl., tables)

Rural Colombian Indians use *caji*, a hallucinogenic drink brewed from vines in the genus *Banisteriopsis*. Author's data suggest individual drug reactions are conditioned by learning cultural expectations. Ceremonial context of drug ingestions lends social significance to spiritual matters in the community. Consumption is strictly regulated, but repeated doses are required to "qualify" for communication with spiritual entities.

1718 Dobkin de Ríos, Marlene. Socioeconomic characteristics of an Amazon urban healer's clientele (Social Science and Medicine [N.Y.] 15B:1, Jan. 1981, p. 51–63, bibl., tables)

Field study of success of traditional healing in a Peruvian city. Interviews with 95 clients of one folk healer reveal close correspondence between patient and healer with respect to views of disease etiology and treatment.

1719 Domínguez, Jorge Alejandro. Conocimientos médicos de los mayas, aztecas, tarascos y la herbolaria médica mexicana (GIIN/GI, 13:1/2, enero/junio 1978, p. 220–238, bibl., tables)

Outlines medical knowledge, practices, and medicinal plants of prehispanic and modern Indian populations in Mexico. Charts historical trends and tabulates medicinal plants according to taxonomic and common names, applications, and chemical components.

1720 Evans, Alfred S. *et al.* A case-control study of Hodgkin's disease in Brazil: pt. 2, Seroepidemiologic studies in cases and family members (American Journal of Epidemiology [Johns Hopkins University, Baltimore, Md.] 112:5, Nov. 1980, p. 609–618, bibl., tables)

Compares 70 individuals with Hodgkin's disease with 70 with non-malignant tumors and 128 normal siblings in rural Brazil. Genetic and serological studies reveal significant differences in blood characteristics and disease histories in the three sample groups.

1721 Fábrega, Horacio and **J.E. Hunter.** Judgements about disease: a case study involving ladinos of Chiapas (Social Science and Medicine [New York] 12:1B, Jan. 1978, p. 1–10, bibl., tables)

Theories of disease causation and proper treatment elicited from informants residing in rural Chiapas, Mexico. Explores with statistics association between emotions, personality characteristics, and 24 specific types of "folk" diseases.

1722 Finkler, Kaja. Non-medical treatments and their outcomes (Culture, Medicine, and Psychiatry [D. Reidel Dordrecht, The Netherlands] 4:3, Sept. 1980, p. 271–310, bibl., tables)

Investigates through series of follow-up studies outcomes of treatments at Spiritualist temple in rural region of Mexico. Spiritualist treatments failed more often than succeeded, and healings tended to occur in a restricted number of disease categories. Healings emphasized patient's cleansing and purification.

Gade, Daniel B. Inca and colonial settlement, coca cultivation and endemic disease in the tropical forest. See *HLAS 42:1638.*

1723 Grell, G.A.C. Clinical aspects of the management of hypertension in the Caribbean (West Indian Medical Journal [University of the West Indies, Mona, Jamaica] 29:3, Sept. 1980, p. 163–174, bibl., tables)

Up-to-date review article on hypertension research in the Caribbean. Estimates drug and medication effectiveness from hospital data. Case studies from Jamaica, Virgin Islands, Bahamas, St. Kitts, Guyana, and Barbados.

1724 Guerra, Francisco. La evaluación farmacológica de las fuentes históricas sobre la medicina precolombina (GIIN/GI, 13:1/2, enero/junio 1978, p. 175–185, bibl.)

Interesting account of origins and evolution of medicinal plant usage in Guatemala and other Central American countries. Work is based on chronicles and records kept by colonists dating from the early sixteenth century.

1725 Halberstein, Robert A. and **J.E. Davies.** Changing patterns of health and health care on a small Bahamian island (Social Science and Medicine [New York] 13B:2, April 1979, p. 153–167, bibl., ill., map, tables)

Interdisciplinary field research on rapidly changing epidemiological profile of small island in the Bahamas. Ascertains past and current health problems through analysis of census data, clinical examinations, church records and vital registers, and an anthropological survey administered to 85 percent of the population. Medical modernization, traditional healing system, and usage of local medicinal plants receive special attention. For ethnologist's comment, see item **991.**

1726 Harwood, Allan. Rx—spiritist as needed: a study of a Puerto Rican community health resource. New York: Wiley-Interscience, 1977. 251 p.; bibl.; tables.

Results of ethnographic research and participant observation in 79 households and six Spiritualist "churches" (*centros*) in urban Puerto Rico. Various reasons for consulting a spiritist were elicited from informants. Healing and therapeutic functions are illustrated with case studies.

1727 Hernández Colón, Sandra. The traditional use of medicinal plants and herbs in the province of Pedernales, Santo Domingo (Ethnomedicine [Arbeits Gemeinschaft Ethnomedizin and H. Buskeverlag, Hamburg, FRG] 4:1/2, 1976/1977, p. 139–166, bibl., tables)

Unusual field study of traditional healing and medical modernization in rural Santo Domingo. Author discusses aspects of "hot-cold" theory, humoral medicine, and problems associated with rapid medical acculturation. Chart containing charcteristics and usages of 65 medicinal plants is featured.

Inter-American Seminar on Medical and Sociological Aspects of Coca and Cocaine, *Lima, 1979.* Proceedings. See item **1234**.

1728 Kirchhoff, Louis W. *et al.* A case-control study of Hodgkin's disease in Brazil: pt. 1, Epidemiological aspects (American Journal of Epidemiology [Johns Hopkins University, Baltimore, Md.] 112:5, Nov. 1980, p. 595–608, bibl., tables)

Studies genetic, cultural, and environmental factors influencing distribution of Hodgkin's disease in rural Brazil. Discovers significant sex, socioeconomic, and demographic variation in comparing afflicted and normal individuals.

1729 Klein, Janice. *Susto*: the anthropological study of disease of adaptation (Social Science and Medicine [New York] 12:1B, Jan. 1978, p. 23–28, bibl., tables)

Susto, a type of fright-related soul loss found throughout Latin America, has well-defined psychological and physical aspects. Other culturally-specific, fright-related diseases of adaptation are compared with *susto*.

1730 Lacassie, M.D. *et al.* Poor predictability of lactose malabsorption from clinical symptoms for Chilean populations (ASCN/J, 31:5, May 1978, p. 799–804, bibl., tables)

Data on 436 Chileans used to calculate predictive value of clinical symptoms

and age in diagnosing lactose intolerance. Regression analysis showed poor predictability of malabsorption from clinical symptoms.

1731 Larrick, James W. *et al.* Patterns of health and disease among the Waorani Indians of eastern Ecuador (Medical Anthropology [Redgrave, Pleasantville, N.Y.] 3:2, Spring 1979, p. 147–190, bibl., ill., maps, tables)

Health, disease, and health care are changing rapidly among Waorani Indians, a tribe totaling 612 idividuals from the Amazon jungle in eastern Ecuador. Population's health profile reflects increasing contact with outside cultures.

1732 Lind, Ulf. Natur und Tierherren bei den Lengua-Indianern in Paraguay (Ethnomedicine [Arbeits Gemeinschaft Ethnomedizin and H. Buskeverlag, Hamburg, FRG] 5:3/4, 1978/1979, p. 447–459, bibl., tables)

Biocultural research on healing practices and behaviors of shamans in Lengua Indian population of Paraguay. Medical system is strongly influenced by religious rituals designed to combat malevolent or angered spirits which can cause disease.

Logan, Michael H. Anthropological research on the hot-cold theory of disease: some methodological suggestions. See item **891**.

1733 ——. Variations regarding *susto* causality among the Cakchiquel of Guatemala (Culture, Medicine, and Psychiatry [D. Reidel Dordrecht, The Netherlands] 3:2, June 1979, p. 153–167, bibl., table)

Investigates in Guatemala possible causes of *susto*, a culturally-defined ("folk") illness found throughout Latin America. Discovers variations in theories of etiology among Cakchiquel Indian informants.

1734 López Hermosa, Luis. Bibliografía histórica médica mexicana, 1970–1974. México: Sociedad Mexicana de Historia y Filosofía de la Medicina, between 1975 and 1979. 51 p.; indexes.

Bibliographic compilation of references dealing with historical and traditional medicine in Mexico. The 491 items, published between 1970–74, are arranged chronologically and alphabetically.

1735 Maués, Raymundo Heraldo. Aplicação combinada dos modelos etnocientífico e de tomada-de-decisão ao estudo da medicina popular (SBPC/CC, 31:10, out. 1979, p. 1155–1160, bibl., ill.)

Models employed to illustrate various aspects of folk medicine in small fishing community in state of Pará, Brazil. Uses folk taxonomy to classify diseases and experience of illness. Examines diagnostic categories from emic point of view.

1736 Messer, Ellen. Present and future prospects of herbal medicine in a Mexican community (in The Nature and status of ethnobotany. Edited by R.I. Ford. Ann Arbor: University of Michigan, Museum of Anthropology, 1978, p. 137–161, bibl., tables [Anthropological papers; no. 67])

Persistence of herbal medicine investigated in Oaxaca, Mexico, in small, agriculturally-based Indian population which is undergoing rapid modernization. Extensive medicinal plant classification is provided including applications, preparation methods, and "humoral quality" (hot or cold). Traditional botanical medicaments have gradually been supplemented by factory-made prescription drugs and patent medicines available in local pharmacies. Author also briefly discusses indigenous notions of disease etiology, symptoms, and healing philosophies.

1737 Mihalik, Gary J. Guyanese ethnomedical botany: a folk pharmacopoeia (Ethnomedicine [Arbeits Gemeinschaft Ethnomedizin and H. Buskeverlag, Hamburg, FRG] 5:1/2, 1978/1979, p. 83–96, bibl., tables)

Studies medicinal substances traditionally used in Guyana through informant reports and analysis of collected plant specimens. Compares mixed ancestry populations in country's "Westernized" areas with local Indian populations. Identifies 25 medicinal plants by popular and taxonomic names, botanical characteristics, and healing applications. Researches origins of Guyanese folk medicine.

1738 Morós Ghersi, Carlos Alberto. La situación de salud y la enseñanza de la medicina en América Latina (UUAL/U, 76, abril/junio 1979, p. 319–365, bibl.)

General assessment of public health situation in Latin America containing evaluation of medical education and facilities. Topics include demography and disease epidemiology, mortality and life expectancy, environmental factors, technological changes, and utilization of alternative medical resources.

1739 Morrill, Richard L. and **Juan J. Angulo.** Spatial aspects of a smallpox epidemic in small Brazilian city (AGS/GR, 69:3, July 1979, p. 319–330, tables)

Reexamines, with the aid of statistical models, epidemiology, spatial patterns, and spread of 1956 smallpox epidemic in Brazil. Contagion was well-marked and stemmed largely from direct physical contact among children at schools. For geographer's comment, see item **5383**.

1740 Morton, Julia F. Brazilian pepper: its impact on people, animals and the environment (SEB/EB, 32:4, Oct./Dec. 1978, p. 353–359, bibl.)

Brazilian pepper (*Schinus terebinthifolius*) is native to Brazil but has wide distribution in Florida, Hawaii, and the Bahamas. Certain of its chemical components are toxic to humans and other animals, while other constituents are of medicinal value.

1741 Naranjo, Plutarco. Hallucinogenic plant use and related indigenous belief systems in the Ecuadorian Amazon (Journal of Ethnopharmacology [Elsevier Sequoia, Lausanne, Switzerland] 1:2, April 1979, p. 121–145, bibl.)

Survey of historic and recent use of hallucinogenic plants in native populations of Ecuador. Archaeological evidence shows that the ingestion of hallucinogenic substances, especially those derived from species of the genus *Banisteriopsis*, dates from prehistoric times. It is directly tied to the particular belief systems in the culture under study.

1742 ———. Medicina indígena y popular de América Latina y medicina contemporánea (GIIN/GI, 13:1/2, enero/junio 1978, p. 187–219, bibl.)

Well-documented examination of evolution of medical systems in Guatemala. Precolumbian medicine is reconstructed with archaeological evidence from different cultural groups including ancient Maya, Aztec, and Inca. Describes various facets of gradual confluence of traditional "magical" medicine and more modern "empirical" medicine. Aboriginal medical systems continue to influence healing and other health-related activities in Guatemala.

Orellana, Sandra L. Aboriginal medicine in highland Guatemala. See item **909**.

1743 Palma, Néstor Homero. La medicina popular del noroeste argentino: sus implicancias médico-sanitarias. Prólogo, José Alberto Mainetti. Buenos Aires: Editorial Huemul, 1978. 341 p.; bibl.; ill. (Colección Temas de antología; 2)

Anthropological account of indigenous medical systems of Indian populations in Argentina. Disease classifications and etiologies are outlined, as are treatments, ritual activities of healers, medicinal plant usage, and research directions.

1744 Philippe, Jeanne and **J.B. Romain.** Indisposition in Haiti (Social Science and Medicine [New York] 13B:2, April 1979, p. 129–133, bibl., tables)

Clinical and epidemiological profile of folk illness in Haiti based upon interviews with 69 patients. The syndrome is believed to be not curable by modern medicine. For ethnologist's comment, see item **1033**.

1745 Pieh, Samuel H. The Caribbean: a proving ground for environmental health in developing nations (Journal of Environmental Health [National Association of Sanitarians, Denver, Colo.] 42:3, Nov./Dec. 1979, p. 139–141, bibl.)

Brief essay on status of environmental health research in the Caribbean. Findings from the WHO and related organizations are cited regarding chronic ailments in the region and methods for their control.

Rabaj, Serafín and **Víctor Campos.** Profiles of the problems of coca in Bolivia: data about production of coca according to a survey done in 1977. See item **1284**.

1746 Reichel-Dolmatoff, Gerardo. Beyond the milky way: hallucinatory imagery of the Tukano Indians. Los Angeles: UCLA Latin American Center, 1978. 386 p.; bibl.; ill.; plates; tables (UCLA Latin American Center publications; 42)

Artistic and ethnographic analysis of graphic art work of Tukano Indians of Brazil. Contains 60 illustrations and 15 color plates of paintings produced by Tukano artists under the influence of the hallucinogenic vine *yajé* (two species of genus *Banisteriopsis*). Offers anthropological interpretations.

1747 Rivero Serrano, Octavio. La situación de salud y la enseñanza de la medicina en América Latina (UUAL/U, 77, julio/sept. 1979, p. 663–677, bibl.)

Brief discussion of public health conditions and medical systems operating throughout Latin America. Provides neither quantitative data nor statistics.

1748 Rubel, Arthur J. and **C.W. O'Nell.** Difficulties of presenting complaints to physicians: *susto* illness as an example (PAHO/B, 13:2, 1979, p. 134–138, bibl.)

Susto, a folk illness in Mexicans and Mexican-Americans, is characterized by soul-loss, reduction in appetite and weight, and lowered motivation and activity. Epidemiological data suggest that *susto* sufferers are significantly "less healthy" than control subjects. Authors cite organic and psychological problems experienced in this "culturally defined" disease.

1749 Salgado, João Amilcar. Políticas de población en América Latina: políticas de población y escuelas de medicina (UUAL/U, 76, abril/junio 1979, p. 389–408, tables)

Interrelationships among political structure, availability of medical facilities, and population dynamics are explored for several Latin American countries. Local policies limiting population growth are outlined.

1750 Sandstrom, Alan R. The image of disease: medical practices of Nahua Indians of the Huasteca. Columbia: Department of Anthropology, University of Missouri-Columbia, 1978. 60 p.; 1 leaf of plates; bibl.; ill. (Monographs in anthropology; 3)

Brief monograph on responses to illness in Nahua Indian community in Veracruz, Mexico. Places treatment procedures and preventive measures within cultural context of local beliefs regarding disease etiology. Describes spirit entities as intimately involved in processes of becoming ill and getting healed.

1751 Sarkís, Alia and **Víctor Manuel Campos.** Curanderismo tradicional del costarricense. San José: Editorial Costa Rica, 1978. 176 p.; ill.

Analysis of ancient and traditional medical practices and healing materials in

Costa Rica, many of which are still in use today. Separate chapters (35) describe treatments and medicinal substances for some 60 different conditions ranging from asthma to heart disease to malaria to alcoholism. Magical and religious aspects of curing are closely scrutinized.

1752 Shimada, Akio *et al.* Regional differences of death from chronic diseases in Rio Grande do Sul, Brazil from 1970 to 1976 (Social Science and Medicine [New York] 15D:1, Feb. 1981, p. 187–198, bibl., maps, tables)

Epidemiological investigation of cancer and cardiovascular disease in Brazilian state. Significant differences related to economy and geographic location (coastal vs. inland). Certain dietary habits may be responsible for high cancer prevalence and mortality rates.

1753 Stevenson, David R. Intervillage preference of high blood pressure medicinal plants on St. Kitts, West Indies (Medical Anthropology [Redgrave, Pleasantville, New York] 3:4, Fall 1979, p. 503–524, bibl., ill., maps, tables)

Reports successful utilization of medicinal plants to combat hypertension in Caribbean island of St. Kitts. Interviews with several hundred adult sugarcane workers showed different preferences for a variety of curative plants. For ethnologist's comment, see item **1053**.

1754 Takemoto, T. *et al.* The human impact of colonization and parasite infestation in subtropical lowlands of Bolivia (Social Science and Medicine [New York] 15D:1, Feb. 1981, p. 133–139, bibl., tables)

High rates of parasitic infections discovered in tropical Bolivia. Regional variations attributed to agricultural development, differences in living conditions, and sanitation.

Torres Bruno, Ofelia. Sanidad en el Uruguay: información bibliográfica, 1804–1976. See *HLAS 42:68.*

1755 Trotter, Robert T. Evidence of an ethnomedical form of aversion therapy on the United States-Mexico border (Journal of Ethnopharmacology [Elsevier Sequoia, Lausanne, Switzerland] 1:3, Oct. 1979, p. 279–284, bibl.)

Ethnographic and botanical data concerning usage of species of genus *Hura* to discourage excessive alcohol consumption by problem drinkers in northern Mexico and Mexican-American populations in Texas. Exact chemical components or psychophysiological mechanisms involved in the development of alcohol aversion are as yet unknown.

1756 Viveros Jarry, Elena. Sea su propio médico: un nuevo énfasis en la educación de adultos con medio de prevención de enfermedades (Horizonte [Universidad Federal de Paraíba, João Pessoa, Brasil] 3:7, abril/junho 1978, p. 188–194, table)

Brief article on disease prevention and intervention programs in Brazil. Author discusses increasing occurrence of self-medication in the country.

1757 Ward, Colleen and **M.H. Beaubrun.** Trance induction and hallucination in Spiritualist Baptist mourning (Journal of Psychological Anthropology [Association of Psychohistory, New York] 2:4, Fall 1979, p. 479–488, bibl., table)

Trance and hallucinatory behavior studied in context of ritual healing and mourning in Trinidad. Many associated customs have been directly imported from outside but have been effective nevertheless in adaptation to disease and death.

1758 Yawney, Carole. Drinking patterns and alcoholism in Trinidad (*in* Beliefs, behaviors, and alcoholic beverages. Edited by M. Marshall. Ann Arbor: University of Michigan Press, p. 94–107)

Social and economic influences on alcoholism in Trinidad compared in different ethnic groups. East Indians (Hindu) and blacks contrasted sharply in drinking patterns. Describes organized treatment programs.

1759 Young, James C. A model of illness treatment decisions in a Tarascan town (AAA/AE, 7:1, Feb. 1980, p. 106–131, tables)

Examines alternative reactions and behavioral responses to illness and its treatment in small Indian community in west-central Mexico. Model of typical decisions and decision-making process is built employing data on 323 actual illness episodes recorded in the population.

1760 Zschock, Dieter K. Health care financing in Central America and the Andean region (LARR, 15:3, 1980, p. 149–168, bibl., tables)

Report from workshop on health care facilities and management in Central and South America. Evaluates cost effectiveness of recently emerging programs.

JOURNAL ABBREVIATIONS
ANTHROPOLOGY

AAA/AA American Anthropologist. American Anthropological Association. Washington.

AAA/AE American Ethnologist. American Anthropological Association. Washington.

AAAS/A *See* AAAS/S.

AAAS/S Science. American Association for the Advancement of Science. Washington.

ACEP/EP Estudios de Población. Asociación Colombiana para el Estudio de la Población. Bogotá.

ACH/BHA Boletín de Historia y Antigüedades. Academia Colombiana de la Historia. Bogotá.

AES Archives Européennes de Sociologie. Paris.

AGH/BHA *See* ACH/BHA.

AGS/GR The Geographical Review. American Geographical Society. New York.

AI/A Anthropos. Anthropos-Institut. Psoieux, Switzerland.

AIA/A Archaeology. Archaeological Institute of America. New York.

AJPA American Journal of Physical Anthropology. American Association of Physical Anthropologists and the Wistar Institute of Anatomy and Biology. Philadelphia, Pa.

AMNH/NH Natural History. American Museum of Natural History. New York.

ANC/B Boletín de la Academia Nacional de Ciencias. Córdoba, Argentina.

ASHG/J American Journal of Human Genetics. The American Society of Human Genetics. Baltimore, Md.

AT/A Antiquity. A quarterly review of archaeology. The Antiquity Trust. Cambridge, England.

BBAA Boletín Bibliográfico de Antropología Americana. Instituto Panamericano de Geografía e Historia, Comisión de Historia. México.

BISRA/BS Belizean Studies. Belizean Institute of Social Research and Action and St. John's College. Belize City.

BNB/REN Revista Econômica do Nordeste. Fortaleza, Brazil.

BNBD Boletín Nicaragüense de Bibliografía y Documentación. Banco Central de Nicaragua, Biblioteca. Managua.

BRMN/B Boletim do Museu Nacional. Compôsto e impresso na Oficina Gráfica da Univ. do Brasil. Rio.

CAAAP/AP Amazonía Peruana. Centro Amazónico de Antropología y Aplicación Práctica, Depto. de Documentación y Publicaciones. Lima.

CBR/BCB Boletín Cultural y Bibliográfico. Banco de la República, Biblioteca Luis-Angel Arango. Bogotá.

CDAL Cahiers des Amériques Latines. Paris.

CEDLA/B Boletín de Estudios Latinoamericanos. Centro de Estudios y Documentación Latinoamericanos. Amsterdam.

CEM/ECM Estudios de Cultura Maya. Univ. Nacional Autónoma de México, Centro de Estudios Mayas. México.

CEPA/R *See* CEPAL/R.

CEPAL/R CEPAL. Review/Revista de la CEPAL. Naciones Unidas, Comisión Económica para América Latina. Santiago.

CLACSO/ERL Estudios Rurales Latinoamericanos. Consejo Latinoamericano de Ciencias Sociales, Secretaría Ejecutiva y de la Comisión de Estudios Rurales. Bogotá.

CLASCO/ERL *See* CLACSO/ERL.

CNRS/ASR Archives de Sociologie des Religions. Centre Nationale de la Recherche Scientifique. Paris.

CPS Comparative Political Studies. Northwestern Univ., Evanston, Ill. and Sage Publications, Beverly Hills, Calif.

CPU/ES Estudios Sociales. Corporación de Promoción Universitaria. Santiago.

CRCA/A Anthropologica. Canadian Research Centre for Anthropology. St. Paul Univ. Ottawa.

CSSH Comparative Studies in Society and History. An international quarterly. Society for the Comparative Study of Society and History. The Hague.

CUA/AQ Anthropological Quarterly. Catholic Univ. of America, Catholic Anthropological Conference. Washington.

DGV/ZE Zeitschrift für Ethnologie. Deutschen Gesellschaft für Völkerkunde. Braunschweig, FRG.

EANH/B Boletín de la Academia Nacional de Historia. Quito.

EAZ Ethnographisch-Archäologische Zeitschrift. Deutscher Verlag Wissenschaften. East Berlin.

EHESS/C Communications. École des Hautes Études en Sciences Sociales, Centre d'Études Transdisciplinaires. Paris.

EPHE/H L'Homme. Revue française d'anthropologie. La Sorbonne, l'École Pratique des Hautes Études. Paris.

ERS Ethnic and Racial Studies. Routledge & Kegan Paul. London.

FAIC/CPPT Comunicaciones Proyecto Puebla-Tlaxcala. Fundación Alemana para la Investigación Científica. Puebla, México.

FFCL/EL Estudos Leopoldenses. Faculdade de Filosofia, Ciências e Letras. São Leopoldo, Brazil.

FS/CIS Cahiers Internationaux de Sociologie. La Sorbonne, École Pratique des Hautes Études. Paris.

FSCN/A Antropológica. Fundación La Salle de Ciencias Naturales, Instituto Caribe de Antropología y Sociología. Caracas.

GIIN/GI Guatemala Indígena. Instituto Indigenista Nacional. Guatemala.

HAHR Hispanic American Historical Review. Duke Univ. Press *for the* Conference on Latin American History of the American Historical Association. Durham, N.C.

HH Human Heredity. Basel, Switzerland.

IAA Ibero-Amerikanisches Archiv. Ibero-Amerikanisches Institut. Berlin, FRG.

IAHG/AHG Antropología e Historia de Guatemala. Instituto de Antropología e Historia de Guatemala. Guatemala.

IAHR/N Numen. International review for the history of religions. International Association for the History of Religions. Leiden, The Netherlands.

IAI/I Indiana. Beiträge zur Volker-und Sprachenkunde, Archäologie und Anthropologie des Indianischen Amerika. Ibero-Amerikanisches Institut. Berlin, FRG.

IAP/P Pesquisas. Anuário do Instituto Anchietano de Pesquisas. Porto Alegre.

IAS/ÑP Ñawpa Pacha. Institute of Andean Studies. Berkeley, Calif.

IBEAS/EA Estudios Andinos. Instituto Boliviano de Estudio y Acción Social. La Paz.

ICA/RCA Revista Colombiana de Antropología. Ministerio de Educación Nacional, Instituto Colombiano de Antropología. Bogotá.

ICC/T Thesaurus. Boletín del Instituto Caro y Cuervo. Bogotá.

ICS/JCCP Journal of Commonwealth and Comparative Politics. Univ. of London, Institute of Commonwealth Studies. London.

IFH/C Conjonction. Institut Français d'Haïti. Port-au-Prince.

IGFO/RI Revista de Indias. Instituto Gonzalo Fernández de Oviedo and Consejo Superior de Investigaciones Científicas. Madrid.

IGM/U L'Universo. Rivista bimestrale dell'Istituto Geografico Militare. Firenze, Italy.

III/AI América Indígena. Instituto Indigenista Interamericano. México.

IJ/JJ Jamaica Journal. Institute of Jamaica. Kingston.

INAH/A Anales del Instituto Nacional de Antropología e Historia. Secretaría de Educación Pública. México.

INAH/B Boletín del Instituto Nacional de Antropología e Historia. Secretaría de Educación Pública. México.

INEP/RBEP Revista Brasileira de Estudos Pedagógicos. Instituto Nacional de Estudos Pedagógicos. Centro Brasileiro de Pesquisas Educacionais. Rio de Janeiro.

IPGH/FA Folklore Americano. Instituto Panamericano de Geografía e Historia, Comisión de Historia, Comité de Folklore. México.

IRR/RC Race and Class. A journal for black and Third World liberation. Institute of Race Relations and The Transnational Institute. London.

JBA Journal of Belizean Affairs. Belize City, Belize.

JLAS Journal of Latin American Studies. Centers or institutes of Latin American studies at the universities of Cambridge, Glasgow, Liverpool, London and Oxford. Cambridge Univ. Press. London.

JPS The Journal of Peasant Studies. Frank Cass & Co. London.

KITLV/B Bijdragen tot de Taal-, Land- en Volkenkunde. Koninklijk Instituut voor Taal-, Land- en Volkenkunde. Leiden, The Netherlands.

LAP Latin American Perspectives. Univ. of California. Riverside.

LARR Latin American Research Review. Univ. of North Carolina Press *for the* Latin American Studies Association. Chapel Hill.

LSE/PS Population Studies. London School of Economics, The Population Investigation Committee. London.

MEMDA/E Etnía. Museo Etnográfico Municipal Dámaso Arce. Municipalidad de Olavarría, Provincia de Buenos Aires, Argentina.

MHD/B Boletín del Museo del Hombre Dominicano. Santo Domingo.

MLV/T Tribus. Veröffentlichungen des Linden-Museums. Museum für Länder- und Völkerkunde. Stuttgart, FRG.

MNCR/V Vínculos. Revista de antropología. Museo Nacional de Costa Rica. San José.

MP/R Revista do Museu Paulista. São Paulo.

MPEG/B Boletim do Museu Paraense Emílio Goeldi. Nova série: antropologia.

Conselho Nacional de Desenvolvimento Científico e Tecnológico, Instituto Nacional de Pesquisas da Amazônia. Belém, Brazil.

MV/BA Baessler-Archiv. Museums für Völkerkunde. Berlin.

MVW/AV Archiv für Völkerkunde. Museum für Völkerkunde in Wien und von Verein Freunde der Völkerkunde. Wien.

NAS/P Proceedings of the National Academy of Sciences. Washington.

NCFR/JFH Journal of Family History. Studies in family, kinship and demography. National Council on Family Relations. Minneapolis, Minn.

NMJS Nature. A weekly journal of science. Macmillan & Co. London.

OAS/CI Ciencia Interamericana. Organization of American States, Dept. of Scientific Affairs. Washington.

OCLAE OCLAE. Revista mensual de la Organización Continental Latinoamericana de Estudiantes. La Habana.

PAA/D Demography. Population Association of America. Washington.

PAHO/B Bulletin of the Pan American Health Organization. Washington.

PAIGH/G Revista Geográfica. Instituto Panamericano de Geografía e Historia, Comisión de Geografía. México.

PAN/ES Estudios Latinoamericanos. Polska Akademia Nauk (Academia de Ciencias de Polonia), Instytut Historii (Instituto de Historia). Warszawa.

PEMN/R Revista del Museo Nacional. Casa de la Cultura del Perú, Museo Nacional de la Cultura Peruana. Lima.

PMK Paideuma. Mitteilungen zur Kulturkunde. Deutsche Gesellschaft für kulturmorphologie von Frobenius Institut au der Johann Wolfgang Goethe—Universität. Wiesbaden, Germany.

PUC/L Lexis. Revista de lingüística y literatura. Pontificia Univ. Católica del Perú. Lima.

PUC/V Veritas. Revista. Pontifícia Univ. Católica do Rio Grande do Sul. Porto Alegre, Brazil.

PUCP/DA Debates en Antropología. Pontificia Univ. Católica del Perú, Depto. de Ciencias Sociales. Lima.

PUCP/H Histórica. Pontificia Univ. Católica del Perú, Depto. de Humanidades. Lima.

PUJ/UH Universitas Humanistica. Pontificia Univ. Javeriana, Facultad de Filosofía y Letras. Bogotá.

RAI/M Man. A monthly record of anthropological science. The Royal Anthropological Institute. London.

RRI Revista/Review Interamericana. Univ. Interamericana, San Germán, Puerto Rico.

SA/J Journal de la Société des Américanistes. Paris.

SAA/AA American Antiquity. The Society for American Archaeology. Menasha, Wis.

SAA/HO Human Organization. Society for Applied Anthropology. New York.

SAA/HQ *See* SAA/HO.

SAA/R Relaciones de la Sociedad Argentina de Antropología. Buenos Aires.

SAR/P El Palacio. School of American Research, the Museum of New Mexico, and the Archaeological Society of New Mexico. Sante Fe.

SBPC/CC Ciência e Cultura. Sociedade Brasileira para o Progresso da Ciência. São Paulo.

SEB/EB Economic Botany. Devoted to applied botany and plant utilization. *Published for* The Society for Economic Botany *by the* New Botanical Garden. New York.

SEM/E Ethnos. Statens Ethnografiska Museum. Stockholm.

SF Social Forces. *Published for the* Univ. of North Carolina Press *by the* Williams & Wilkins Co. Baltimore, Md.

SGHG/A Anales de la Sociedad de Geografía e Historia de Guatemala. Guatemala.

SGL/B Boletín de la Sociedad Geográfica de Lima. Lima.

SHG/B Bulletin de la Société d'Histoire de la Guadeloupe. Archives Départementales *avec le concours du* Conseil Général de la Guadeloupe. Basse-Terre, West Indies.

SO Society. Social science and modern society. Transaction, Rutgers—The State Univ. New Brunswick, N.J.

SOCIOL Sociologus. Zeitschrift für empirische Soziologie, sozialpsychologische und ethnologische Forschung (A journal for empirical sociology, social psychology and ethnic research). Berlin.

SSA/B Bulletin. Société Suisse des Américanistes. Geneva.

UA Urban Anthropology. State Univ. of New York, Dept. of Anthropology. Brockport.

UB/BA Boletín Americanista. Univ. de Barcelona, Facultad de Geografía e Historia, Depto. de Historia de América. Barcelona.

UC/A Anales de la Universidad de Cuenca. Cuenca, Ecuador.

UC/AT Atenea. Revista de ciencias, letras y artes. Univ. de Concepción. Concepción, Chile.

UC/CA Current Anthropology. Univ. of Chicago. Chicago, Ill.

UC/EE Estudios de Economía. Univ. de Chile. Facultad de Ciencias Económicas y Administrativas, Depto. de Economía. Santiago.

UCC/CE Cuadernos de Economía. Univ. Católica de Chile. Santiago.

UCC/NG Norte Grande. Revista de estudios integrados referentes a comunidades humanas del Norte Grande de Chile, en una perspectiva geográfica e histórica-cultural. Univ. Católica de Chile, Instituto de Geografía, Depto. de Geografía de Chile, Taller Norte Grande. Santiago.

UCGL/AHG Annals of Human Genetics (Annals of Eugenics). Univ. College, Galton Laboratory. London.

UCL/CD Cultures et Développement. Revue internationale des sciences du dévellopement Univ. Catholique de Louvain *avec le concours de la* Fondation Universitaire de Belgique. Louvain, Belgium.

UCLA/JLAL Journal of Latin American Lore. Univ. of California, Latin American Center. Los Angeles.

UCLV/I Islas. Univ. Central de las Villas. Santa Clara, Cuba.

UCNSA/SA Suplemento Antropológico. Univ. Católica de Nuestra Señora de la Asunción, Centro de Estudios Antropológicos. Asunción.

UFP/EB Estudos Brasileiros. Univ. Federal do Paraná, Setor de Ciências Humanas, Centro de Estudos Brasileiros. Curitiba, Brazil.

UK/SE *See* UK/SR.

UK/SR The Sociological Review. Univ. of Keele Staffordshire, England.

UNAM/AA Anales de Antropología. Univ. Nacional Autónoma de México, Instituto de Investigaciones Históricas. México.

UNAM/AL Anuario de Letras. Univ. Nacional Autónoma de México, Facultad de Filosofía y Letras. México.

UNAM/RMS Revista Mexicana de Sociología. Univ. Nacional Autónoma de México, Instituto de Investigaciones Sociales. México.

UNC/ED El Dorado. Univ. of Northern Colorado, Museum of Anthropology. Greeley.

UNC/K Katunob. Univ. of Northern Colorado, Museum of Anthropology. Greeley.

UNCIA/R Revista del Instituto de Antropología. Univ. Nacional de Córdoba. Córdoba, Argentina.

UNESCO/CU Cultures. United Nations Educational, Scientific and Cultural Organization. Paris.

UNLPM/R Revista del Museo de La Plata. Univ. Nacional de La Plata, Facultad de Ciencias Naturales y Museo. La Plata, Argentina.

UNM/JAR Journal of Anthropological Research. Univ. of New Mexico, Dept. of Anthropology. Albuquerque.

UNTIA/R Revista del Instituto de Antropología. Univ. Nacional de Tucumán. San Miguel de Tucumán, Argentina.

UNV/ED *See* UNC/ED.

UP/E Ethnology. Univ. of Pittsburgh. Pittsburgh, Pa.

UP/EA Estudios Andinos. Univ. of Pittsburgh, Latin American Studies Center. Pittsburgh, Pa.

UPB Universidad Pontificia Bolivariana. Medellín, Colombia.

UPR/CS Caribbean Studies. Univ. of Puerto Rico, Instituto of Caribbean Studies. Río Piedras.

UR/L Lateinamerika. Univ. Rostock. Rostock, GDR.

URL/ES Estudios Sociales. Univ. Rafael Landívar, Instituto de Ciencias Políticas y Sociales. Guatemala.

USP/RA Revista de Antropologia. Univ. de São Paulo, Faculdade de Filosofia, Letras e Ciências Humanas and Associação Brasileira de Antropologia. São Paulo.

UT/E *See* UP/E.

UTIEH/C Caravelle. Cahiers du monde hispanique et luso-brésilien. Univ. of Toulouse, Institut de'Études Hispaniques, Hispano-Americaines et Luso-Brésiliennes. Toulouse, France.

UUAL/U Universidades. Unión de Universidades de América Latina. Buenos Aires and México.

UWI/CQ Caribbean Quarterly. Univ. of the West Indies. Mona, Jamaica.

UWI/SES Social and Economic Studies. Univ. of the West Indies, Institute of Social and Economic Research. Mona, Jamaica.

UY/R Revista de la Universidad de Yucatán. Mérida, México.

VMJ/BIV Boletín Indigenista Venezolano. Ministerio de Justicia, Comisión Indigenista. Caracas.

WD World Development. Pergamon Press. Oxford, U.K.

WM Westermann Monatschefte. Georg Westermann Verlag. Braunschweig, FRG.

WRU/JMF Journal of Marriage and the Family. Western Reserve Univ. Cleveland, Ohio.

WSU/HB Human Biology. Official publication of the Human Biology Council. Wayne State Univ., School of Medicine. Detroit, Mich.

YAXKIN Yaxkin. Instituto Hondureño de Antropología e Historia. Tegucigalpa.

ZMA Zeitschrift für Morphologie und Anthropologie. E. Nägele. Stuttgart, Germany.

ECONOMICS

GENERAL

JOHN M. HUNTER, *Director, Latin American Studies Center, Michigan State University*

IT IS MOST DIFFICULT TO CHARACTERIZE each of these biennia in a few sensible and satisfying words. There is no doubt that the literature expands rapidly in quantity and probably even more so in quality and that Latin Americans have contributed in a major way to both trends. An important factor in these advances is the increasing number and greater appreciation of stable, serious research institutions in Latin America.

It is also difficult to know how to utilize these few words in order to best cover the material reviewed. In this volume I concentrate on four topics: 1) agriculture; 2) employment and the labor force; 3) consumers; and 4) private foreign lending.

1) AGRICULTURE: Agriculture, as a major "problem," receives increasing attention in the literature, reflecting the increasing professional and specialized attention being given it. The coverage is extremely wide; some of the more noteworthy items follow. ILPES (UN Latin American Institute of Economic and Social Planning) devoted a 600-page volume to planning for the sector (item **2902**). Ernest Feder (item **2808**) devotes 500 pages to examining the structure of agriculture. Danilo Astori (item **2757**) reviews various interpretations of the agricultural sector. Alain de Janvry and Lynn Ground (item **2845**) treat "land reform" especially, and William Thiesenhusen (item **2951**) characterizes changes in the sector in the last decades. Both R. Albert Berry and William Cline (item **3335**) and Dennis Anderson and Mark Leiserson (item **2752**) have written interesting empirical, quantitative studies, the former dealing with the relation of farm-size to output and the latter with non-farm employment. Gerson Gomes and Antonio Pérez (item **2824**) deal with the process of modernization and inadequate agricultural response. Solon Barraclough and Jacques Goethals (item **2761**) deal with problems of peasant training—as does Guillermo Bedregal and Franco Tradardi (item **2762**). Roger Burbach and Patricia Flynn (item **2770**) present a strong indictment of "agrobusiness." The USDA (item **2963**) annually provides otherwise inaccessible current data on agricultural production and trade.

2) EMPLOYMENT AND THE LABOR FORCE: Juan Buttari, as ECIEL's compiler and editor, is responsible for two major volumes (item **2805**) that are important sources of data and analysis. Patricio Meller (item **2875**) examines several models to study industrial output/employment changes. Victor Tokman (item **2954**) is concerned with the effects of employment on income redistribution to the poor. Joachim Singelman and Marta Tienda (item **2939**) note a declining proportion of females in industrial employment. Two useful compendia of employment policies were produced, by Humberto Pereira (item **2907**) and International Labour Office, PREALC (item **2913**); the latter is specifically analytic. Two pieces give specific

attention to the informal urban sector, about which much is assumed and little known: Tokman (item **2955**) and Ray Bromley and Chris Gerry (item **2776**).

3) CONSUMERS: Considerable information is beginning to appear on various aspects of individual economic behavior. In a broad sense, John Kenneth Galbraith's thesis (item **2818**) fits this category. Much of ECIEL's work in this area came to published fruition in this period: see the work edited by Robert Ferber on consumption and income distribution (item **2791**); Philip Musgrove on household income and consumption (item **2885**), household size, employment and poverty (item **2884**); and Musgrove and Ferber on the urban poor (item **2886**). Alberto Baltra Cortés (item **2759**) examines the Duesenberry effect at the individual and national levels with respect to its influence on development.

4) PRIVATE FOREIGN LENDING: This is a new topic, perhaps presciently. Robert Devlin explores the increasing role of private foreign banks in lending to Latin America (item **2797**). Charles Lipson (item **2865**) examines this phenomenon on a worldwide basis, and Jonathan Aronson (item **2753**) and Susan Strange (item **2942**) analyze some of its consequences, including the repercussions from default and the politics of renegotiation.

The disadvantage of organizing by topics as I have done is the exclusion of excellent material which does not fall into the chosen categories. To mention just a few such omissions: Vicente Galbis, in two pieces (item **2816** and **2817**) does pioneering empirical work on the relationships between interest rate policy/behavior and inflation; Alfredo Roldán (item **2923**) analyzes and compares eight inflation models—Harberger, Diz, et al.; Nathaniel Leff (item **2859**) treats entrepreneurship in order to examine its current role as a development constraint. Finally, Jere Behrman and James Hanson (item **2787**) have edited a fine volume resulting from a NBER/IPES and Republic of Panama conference on planning. Its main feature is the examination of the utility of various models to explain and forecast in Latin America.

2751 La Agricultura en la integración latinoamericana. Obra editada bajo la dirección de José Garrido Rojas. Santiago de Chile: Editorial Universitaria, 1977. 183 p.; bibl. (Nuevas perspectivas de la integración latinoamericana; v. 2. Estudios internacionales)

Covers a wide range of topics related to agriculture in integration: LAFTA and the Andean Group are given specific attention (see also items **2839** and **2952**).

2752 Anderson, Dennis and **Mark W. Leiserson.** Rural nonfarm employment in developing countries (UC/EDCC, 28:2, Jan. 1980, p. 227–248, tables)

Explores empirically non-farm employment and finds it substantial in rural areas. Explores policy implications and needs for further research.

2753 Aronson, Jonathan David. The politics of private bank lending and debt renegotiations (*in* Debt and the less developed countries. Edited by Jonathan David Aronson. Boulder, Colorado: Westview Press, 1979, p. 283–315, tables)

Not Latin America-specific but covers Mexico-Brazil as cases with others. Banks have political power but less than might be expected. They have considerable impact, however, on relations among nations although they frequently do not realize it.

2754 Ary, Gláucio and **Dillon Soares.** The web of exploitation: state and peasants in Latin America (RU/SCID, 12:3, Fall 1977, p. 3–24)

Industrialization by import substitution occurred as export expansion is occurring only by systematically keeping agricultural prices (wages, earnings) low.

2755 Assael, Hector. The internationalization of Latin American economies: some reservations (CEPAL/R, April 1979, p. 41–55)

The internationalization of large- and medium-sized economies has been analyzed, mostly seeking out the benefits. Assael focuses on *problems* associated with channeling development and internal demand/supply with internal price structures and income distribution (UN Sales No. E.79.II G2).

2756 The Assault on world poverty: problems of rural development, education, and health. With a preface by Robert S. McNamara. Baltimore: Published for the World Bank by the Johns Hopkins University Press, 1975. 425 p.; bibl.

Convenient collection of sector papers dealing primarily with the rural poor: rural development, agricultural credit, land reform, education, health.

2757 Astori, Danilo. Algunas interpretaciones sobre el proceso económico de la agricultura en la América Latina (FCE/TE, 47[2]:186, abril/junio 1980, p. 335–376)

Review of interpretations of the agricultural sector: structural; neo-classical, with and without dualism; historic-structural. Approaches are then contrasted with respect to methodology, categories of analysis, historical periods covered, and policy recommendations.

The Automotive industry in Latin America. See item **7008**.

2758 Balassa, Bela. La reforma de las políticas económicas en los países en desarrollo. México: Centro de Estudios Monetarios Latinoamericanos (CEMLA), 1979. 269 p.; tables.

Translation of *Policy reform in developing countries* (New York: Pergamon, 1977). The first essay is general dealing with incentive systems in LCD's (with industrial bases) and those remaining are a collection of policy recommendations on this theme to Mexico, Venezuela, Chile, Andean Group, Egypt, Portugal, Korea—when Balassa had served as consultant, 1973–1976.

2759 Baltra Cortés, Alberto. El efecto Duesenberry y las economías en desarrollo (BCV/REL, 14:56, 1979, p. 65–77)

Duesenberry effect at individual and national levels helps account for high consumption and low savings.

2760 La Banca de interés social en América Latina. San José, Costa Rica: CEDAL, 1977. 141 p. (Seminarios y documentos; 28)

Consists of 12 articles (some country cases) on aspects of popular or labor-owned banks (i.e., financial institutions to help poor save and to provide them credit short of usury).

2761 Barraclough, Solon and **Jacques Goethals.** Capacitación para el desarrollo rural (BCV/REL, 11:44, p. 125–158)

Discusses problems in the practice of peasant training and demonstrates with Latin American examples, closes with a "revolutionary strategy" of rural training.

2762 Bedregal, Guillermo and **Franco Tradardi.** Liberación rural desarrollo desde abajo. México: Extemporáneos, 1978. 131 p.; bibl. (Colección Latinoamericana: Serie Ensayo; 7)

Most "development" plans deal with specific "needs" to be filled by some governmental or supergovernmental agency. This model starts at the bottom—with the poor and seeks ways to involve them and to release their energies collectively. General, descriptive, and purports to be region-wide.

2763 Behar, Jaime. Una interpretación crítica de la integración latinoamericana (BNCE/CE, 30:5, mayo 1980, p. 423–432)

Careful analysis of current facts of integration against the arguments for it of the 1960s.

2764 Bell, R.T. Theories of the terms of trade of less developed countries: a critical survey (IEI/EI, 32:2/3, maggio/agosto 1979, p. 200–217, tables)

Excellent review of terms-of-trade theory dealing mostly with Prebisch, Emmanuel, W.A. Lewis, their critics and defenders.

Berry, R. Albert and **William R. Cline.** Agrarian structure and productivity in developing countries: a study prepared for the International Labour Office within the framework of the World Employment Programme. See item **3335**.

2765 Binswanger, Hans P.; Vernon W. Ruttan; and Uri Ben-Zion. Induced innovation: technology, institutions, and development. Baltimore: Johns Hopkins University Press, 1978. xiv, 423 p.; bibl.; graphs; index.

Seeks to incorporate innovations, both technical and institutional, into growth theory (i.e., to treat them endogenously). "Cases and tests" include chapters on Argentina by Alain de Janvry (item **3671**) and on Brazil by Sanders and Ruttan (item **3781**).

2766 Bird, Graham. The terms of trade of developing countries: theory, evidence and policy (IEI/EI, 32:4, nov. 1979, p. 399–413, table)

Carefully examines terms of trade deterioration (empirical evidence unclear) and its implications. Suggests that "drawing" arrangements be adjusted for changes in terms of trade.

2767 Bitar, Sergio. Los oligopolios internacionales en la industria: algunos efectos sobre las economías latinoamericanas (*in* Bitar, Sergio. Corporaciones multinacionales y autonomía nacional. Caracas: Monte Avila Editores, 1977, p. 9–41)

Careful presentation concludes that the degree of oligopoly in international manufacturing is incompatible with developmental objectives: satisfying basic needs, income redistribution, and full employment.

2768 Boĭko, Pavel Nikolaevich. América Latina: expansión del imperialismo y crisis de la vía capitalista de desarrollo. Moscú: Progreso, 1977. 258 p.; bibl. (Progreso, problemas de los países en desarrollo)

Russian view of the economic history of post-World War II Latin America. Treatment is regional except for interesting chapter on Cuba (see item **3204**).

2769 Briones, Alvaro. Economía y política del fascismo dependiente. México: Siglo Veintiuno Editores, 1978. 326 p.; bibl. (Economía y demografía)

The nature of capital accumulation is such that it has intense political implications—tending to dependent dictatorships.

Bruce, David C. The impact of the United Nations Economic Commission for Latin America: technocrats as channels of influence. See item **7012**.

2770 Burbach, Roger and **Patricia Flynn.** Agribusiness in the Americas. New York: Monthly Review Press: North American Congress on Latin America, 1980. 1 v.; bibl.

Comprehensive indictment of "agribusiness" (broadly defined to include Coca

Cola, Wrigley, Ford). Major chapters are case studies of particular firms in specific places, trade practices, a particular firm internationally.

Business International Corporation, *New York.* Latin American forecasting study 1979–83. See *HLAS 42:125.*

2771 Campos, Roberto de Oliveira. The New International Economic Order: aspirations and realities (*in* World change and world security. Edited by Norman C. Dahl and Jerome B. Wiesner. Cambridge, Mass.: MIT Press, 1978, p. 73–116)

A balanced, wise "elder statesman's" view of the NIEO.

Cardoso, Fernando Henrique. Current theses on Latin American development and dependency: a critique. See *HLAS 42:1923.*

2772 Carnoy, Martin. Can educational policy equalise income distribution in Latin America? With the collaboration of José Lobo, Alejandro Toledo, Jacques Velloso. Westmead, Eng.: Published on behalf of the International Labour Office by Saxon House, 1979. 110 p.; bibl.

Considers empirical evidence: Brazil, Mexico, Cuba, Peru, Chile. Conclusion: educational policy can help in that direction (supply side) but only likely to be effective if there is appropriate income distribution policy on demand side.

2773 Casas González, Antonio. Las inversiones extranjeras y las empresas transnacionales de Estados Unidos y Canada en América Latina (BCV/REL, 12:48, 1977, p. 35–54)

Interesting review of policy and its evolution toward foreign investment by the US government, the Canadian government, and recipient governments.

2774 ———. Reflexiones sobre el futuro de la ALALC (INTAL/IL, 4:40, Oct. 1979, p. 7–34)

Review of LAFTA's experiences, changed world conditions, suggestions for a modification of its form and objectives.

2775 Castellanos, Diego Luis and **Guillermo D. Márquez.** La Ley de Comercio Exterior de los Estados Unidos: 1974 (BCV/REL, 11:42, 1975, p. 35–83, tables)

After an excellent review of US trade policy from 1974, analyzes US Trade Act of

1974 from the point of view of the world economy and specifically that of Venezuela. Highly critical.

2776 Casual work and poverty in Third World cities. Edited by Ray Bromley and Chris Gerry. Chichester, Eng.; New York: Wiley, 1979. 323 p.; bibl.; indexes.

Seeks understanding of a very large portion of the urban labor force about which little is known and about which much is assumed. Brazil, Colombia, Mexico are the specific subjects of the Latin American chapters. Important contribution.

2777 Cecelski, Elizabeth; Joy Dunkerley; and **William Ramsey.** Household energy and the poor in the Third World. With an appendix by Emmanuel Mbi. Washington: Resources for the Future, 1979. 152 p.; bibl. (RFF research paper; R-15)

Topic is of considerable interest. Latin America gets little attention. Useful bibliography.

2778 Centro de Estudios Monetarios Latinoamericanos (CEMLA), *Mexico.* Vinculación entre las políticas fiscal y monetaria: avances y experiencias recientes (*in* Vinculación entre las políticas fiscal y monetaria: reuniones y seminarios. México: CEMLA, 1979, p. 3–65, bibl., tables)

Objectives are distributive justice, growth, employment. Fiscal and monetary policy must be used together and in delicate balance. Discusses models and experiences of Argentina, Brazil, Chile, Colombia, Mexico.

2779 CEPAL (Comisión Económica para América Latina). ALALC: el programa de liberación comercial y su relación con la estructura y las tendencias del comercio zonal (INTAL/IL, 4:40, Oct. 1979, p. 48–69)

Fine critique of experiences under LAFTA.

2780 ———. La evolución económica y social de América Latina durante 1979 (Economía Colombiana [Contraloría General de la República, Bogotá] 125:4, feb./marzo 1980, p. 18–37, tables)

Review of 1979. Salient findings: growth, expanded external deficit, growing investment from abroad but in the form of credits, inflationary pressures.

2781 Chapparo Alfonzo, Julio. Metodología para el estudio de la empresa multina-

cional andina (BCV/REL, 13:49, 1977, p. 37–90, bibl., table)

Legal bases for organization and existence of multinational firms within the Andean group area.

2782 Chiriboga Villagómez, José Ricardo. El BID, instrumento del desarrollo. Quito: Artes Gráficas, 1978. 190 p.

Interesting personal memoir from 18 years service in the Bank. Covers wide range of topics.

2783 Choncol, Jacques. L'agriculture et le problème de l'emploi en Amérique Latine (FDD/NED [Problèmes d'Amérique Latine, 51] 4517/4518, 22 juin 1978, p. 126–146, tables)

Rural population continues to expand rapidly without commensurate increase in employment for several reasons. This situation leads to various types of migration.

2784 ———. Alternativas para América Latina: un nuevo tipo de desarrollo rural con reforma agraria o la aceleración de la desintegración social (NSO, 41, marzo/abril 1979, p. 5–13, ill.)

Priorities: 1) plan agriculture including growth poles; 2) food production preferred to export production; 3) industrialization should emphasize agricultural-support activities (e.g., fertilizers); 4) industry should concentrate on products for low-income families; 5) increased rural services (e.g., health, education).

2785 *Cladindex.* Resumen de documentos CEPAL/ILPES. Organización de las Naciones Unidas. Comisión Económica para América Latina (CEPAL). Centro Latinoamericano de Documentación Económica y Social (CLADES). Vol. 1/3, 1977/1980– . Santiago.

Extremely useful bibliographic tool that will be brought up to date semiannually. Includes meetings, drafts, studies, reports, books, texts, articles. Nearly 1000 items. Pt. 1 provides complete document description; pt. 2, referral indexes: author, institutions, titles, series, etc. Vol. 2 (1979) updates the index and covers items 972–1304. Vol. 3 (1980) includes items 1305–1718. For bibliographer's comment on vols. 1/2, see *HLAS 41:102* and *HLAS 42:130.*

2786 ¿Como evaluar las particularidades y el nivel de desarrollo del capitalismo en América Latina?: polémica entre especialistas soviéticos (Estudios Contemporáneos [Universidad Autónoma de Puebla, México] 1:1, enero/marzo 1980, p. 99–133, table)

Interesting exchange among Latin American specialists of the USSR concerning the development of Latin American economies. Original version appeared in *América Latina* (June 1978).

2787 Conference on Planning and Short-Term Macroeconomic Policy in Latin America, *Isla Contadora, Panama, 1975.* Short-term macro-economic policy in Latin America. Edited by Jere Behrman, James Hanson. Cambridge, Mass.: Published for the National Bureau of Economic Research by Ballings Pub. Co., 1979. 370 p.; bibl.; ill.; index (Other conference series; no. 14)

Remarkable volume, outcome of a conference jointly sponsored by ILPES, NBER, and the government of Panama. Main feature is the exploration of the utility of various econometric models to explain and forecast various aspects of Latin American economies: monetary vs. fiscal policy; export effects; prices and employment; etc.

2788 Conferencia de Facultades y Escuelas de Economía de América Latina, *6th, Guadalajara, Mexico, 1974.* Economía y desarrollo en América Latina. México: UDUAL, Secretaría General, 1977. 214 p.; bibl.

Principally of interest as proceeds of a series of conferences begun in 1953 by schools of economics, Union of Latin American Universities. This volume reports 1974 meeting.

2789 Congreso Nacional de Economistas (México), *2d, México? 1977.* Financiamiento e inversión para el desarrollo: memoria. México: Colegio Nacional de Economistas, between 1977 and 1979. 556 p.; bibl.; ill.; index.

More than 100 presentations on a wide variety of subjects. Serious pieces with a good deal of attention to Mexico. Organized around major topics. Merits attention.

2790 Consumer markets in Latin America. London: Euromonitor Publications, 1978. 297 p.

Convenient reference work reports by country (except for CACM) items such as

"basic marketing parameters;" "finance and investment;" "resources;" "industrial development;" "trade;" etc. Second section provides information by commodity groups for each country.

2791 Consumption and income distribution in Latin America. Edited by Robert Ferber. Introduction and overview by Joseph Grunwald. Washington: ECIEL, Organization of American States, 1980. 484 p.; tables.

Published papers from the 10th anniversary (1973) conference of ECIEL submitted by remarkable set of authors and discussants. Major topic divisions: consumption and savings; income distribution and growth; prices, welfare, and integration; micro-data for international comparisons.

2792 Corbo, Vittorio. Comercio exterior y empleo: algunas experiencias de países en desarrollo (UCC/CE, 16:47, abril 1979, p. 23–34, bibl., tables)

Empirically notes that more open economies experience greater growth rates; manufacturing for export generates more employment than import substitution manufacturing.

2793 Correa, Carlos. Main issues in the regulation of license arrangements on foreign trademarks: the Latin American experience (WD, 7:7, July 1979, p. 705–712)

There are several negative aspects to extensive use of foreign trademarks. Latin American experience to limit these has been largely experimental.

Crowe, Brian G. International public lending and American policy. See item **7025.**

2794 Currie, Laughlin. Is there an urban bias? Critique of Michael Lipton's *Why poor people stay poor: urban bias in world development* (Journal of Economic Studies [Glasglow, Scotland] 6:1, May 1979, p. 88–105)

Perceptive review article which holds the Lipton global study against the Latin American experience. Currie (evidently) finds the Lipton work to merit considerable attention, but he finds little in Latin America to support either argument or conclusions.

2795 Davydov, Vladimir. Interacción de la ciencia y la producción en la periferia del sistema capitalista (URSS/AL, 26:2, 1980, p. 63–83, plates)

The need for Latin American countries to develop their own "science" and avoid dependency on transnationals.

2796 *Desarrollo Rural en las Américas.* Organización de los Estados Americanos. Instituto Interamericano de Ciencias Agrícolas. Vol. 11, edición especial, dic. 1979– . Bogotá.

Reproduces papers given at 1979 seminar sponsored by IICA on "Strategy and Policy for Rural Development for the Decade of the 80's." Also commemorates 50 years of the Kellogg Foundation.

2797 Devlin, Robert. External finance and commercial banks: their role in Latin America's capacity to import between 1951 and 1975 (CEPAL/R, first half, 1978, p. 63–97, tables)

Considers the major shift to commercial banking (as opposed to official institutions) and lending to LDC's and for development which has occurred since the mid-1960s. Evaluates this phenomenon and examines some solutions to problems outlined.

2798 Díaz Alejandro, Carlos F. Algunas vicisitudes históricas de las economías abiertas en América Latina (IDES/DE, 19:74, julio/sept. 1979, p. 147–159, tables)

Takes a careful look at the decade of the 1930s for small/passive and large/active economies—a crucial period in industrialization. Experience of the 1970s is then examined in these terms.

2799 ———. Inversión extranjera directa por latinoamericanos (INTAL/IL, 1:4, julio 1976, p. 3–17, table)

Surveys various kinds of direct Latin American foreign investments, reasons for them, and possible outcomes.

2800 Diercksens, Wim. La reproducción de la fuerza de trabajo bajo el capital. Pt. 3, La reproducción a nivel global y la emancipación de la clase trabajadora. San José: Universidad de Costa Rica, Facultad de Ciencias Sociales, Instituto de Investigaciones Sociales, 1978. 222 p.; bibl. (Avances de investigación; 4:31)

Final pt. 3 of study of labor force and its development. Pts. 1/2 dealt with this at the family and class level. Pt. 3, at the national and international level, is based largely on historical analysis. Frankly Marxist.

2801 Donelson, Stuart; Jorge E. Hardoy; Susana Schkolnik; and Ana M. Hardoy. Los programas de ayuda de las agencias multilaterales para los asentamientos humanos en la América Latina (FCE/TE, 46[3]:183, julio/sept. 1979, p. 677–714, tables)

Descriptive account of lending by eight multinational agencies (World Bank, IDB, etc.) related to human settlements. Compares to total lending, categories of use, countries of destination.

2802 Dussel, Enrique D. De Medellín a Puebla: una década de sangre y esperanza, 1968–1979. México, D.F.: Edicol: Centro de Estudios Ecuménicos, 1979. 615 p.; bibl.; ill. (Colección Religión y cambio social)

Excellent study of the relationship between Church, State and economic development throughout Latin America during the 1968–79 period. [M. Mamalakis]

2803 Eckaus, R.S. La regulación financiera como medio de orientar la política de desarrollo en la América Latina (BCV/REL, 11:44, p. 93–124, bibl., tables)

Discussion of the efficacy of regulation through control by the rate(s) of interest and by modification of portfolios.

2804 *Economía de América Latina.* Revista de información y análisis de la región. Centro de Investigación y Docencia Económicas (CIDE). Semestre No. 1, sept. 1978– . México.

Impressive new semi-annual journal. This particular issue concentrates on problems of stabilization and experiences with stabilization policies of a number of countries. A final section treats two unrelated topics: Cuban economic policy, external debt of Latin America. Sets high standards for itself.

2805 Employment and labor force in Latin America: a review at national and regional levels. Edited by Juan J. Buttari. Washington: ECIEL Study, Organization of American States, 1979. 2 v. (566 p.) (Continuous pagination) fold. tables; tables.

ECIEL began research on employment in 1972, and this has taken its institutions in several directions. These volumes (hopefully, more are to follow) reflect the first line of research: a survey of the variables relevant to the study of labor supply and demand. These volumes have an introductory chapter and conclude with a summary/regional chapter. Those between report studies on Central America, Argentina, Brazil, Costa Rica, Chile, Peru.

2806 Estabilidad y flexibilidad en el ordenamiento jurídico de la integración. Obra editada bajo la dirección de Rodrigo Díaz Albonico. Santiago de Chile: Editorial Universitaria, 1977. 172 p.; bibl. (Nuevas perspectivas de la integración latinoamericana; v. 1. Estudios internacionales)

Anthology concerned with the legal aspects and processes of LAFTA.

2807 Fajnzylber, Fernando. Sobre la restructuración del capitalismo y sus repercusiones en la América Latina (FCE/TE, 46[4]:184, oct./dic. 1979, p. 889–914, tables)

Analyzes the "project for global restructuring" along classical economic lines as not likely to serve the needs of Latin America; nor is it likely to be saleable elsewhere.

2808 Feder, Ernest. La lucha de clases en el campo: análisis estructural de la economía agrícola latinoamericana. México: Fondo de Cultura Económica, 1975. 520 p.; bibl.; tables (Lecturas; 14)

Although published sometime ago (1973, in German), this is a solid anthology on agriculture in Latin America. Divided into four major sections: 1) overview of the agrarian problem; 2) socio-political structure; 3) resource use; and 4) agrarian reform and other strategies for development. Several "country" cases.

2809 Ferrer, Aldo. La viabilidad de la integración latinoamericana (NSO, 37, julio/agosto 1978, p. 64–74, ill.)

Reality of integration is industrial or manufacturing integration. This is very complex for each nation to deal with economically and politically.

2810 Ferris, Elizabeth G. Foreign investment as an influence on foreign policy behavior: the Andean Pact (IAMEA, 33:2, Autumn 1979, p. 45–69, bibl., tables)

Finds that countries with more foreign investment are less supportive of general restrictions on it. The reasons therefore are not entirely clear.

2811 Ffrench-Davis M., Ricardo. Distribución de beneficios y eficiencia en la integración económica. Santiago de Chile: Corporación de Investigaciones Económicas para Latinoamérica, 1977. 48 p.; bibl. (Estudios CIEPLAN; 18)

Investigates cost effectiveness of integration, in general and on a regional basis, and discusses distributive mechanisms. Concludes with recommendations to promote efficiency and equity.

2812 ———. Eficiencia y equidad en la integración económica de países en desarrollo: el caso de la programación regional de inversiones (IDES/DE, 18:72, enero/marzo 1979, p. 467–484, bibl.)

Suggests that distortions and disequilibria inherent in underdevelopment permit regional planning of investment (for example) to intervene and improve both efficiency and equity results as compared to results expected from customs union theory.

2813 The Financing of education in Latin America. Washington, D.C.: Inter-American Development Bank, 1980? 382 p.; tables.

See also item **2937** under Seminario sobre Financiamiento. Edited papers from a second seminar (1978) to continue exploration of the topic. Excellent coverage, useful volumes.

2814 Frenkel, Roberto and **Guillermo O'Donnell.** The stabilization programs of the International Monetary Fund and their internal impacts (*in* Capitalism and the state in US-Latin American relations. Edited by Richard R. Fagen. Contributors, Cynthia Arnson and others. Stanford, Calif.: Stanford University Press, 1979, p. 171–216, tables)

Combination of economics and politics. Stabilization plans of the IMF are based on false assumptions, damage the poor, fail, assure continuity in power of those who began to implement them in the first place.

2815 Furtado, Celso. Les nouvelles sources de pouvoir dans l'Ordre Economique International (UP/TM, 21:81, jan./mars 1980, p. 11–20)

Discusses five sources of international economic power and the means of utilizing them to reduce the burdens of dependence.

2816 Galbis, Vicente. Inflation and interest rate policies in Latin America:

1967–76 (IMF/SP, 26:2, June 1979, p. 334–366, tables)

Reconstructs policy measures regarding interest rates, presents data on interest rate behavior in 19 countries, evaluates effects of those policies. Pioneer work in this area.

2817 ———. Money, investment, and growth in Latin America, 1961–1973 (UC/EDCC, 27:3, April 1979, p. 423–443)

Econometric investigation of a "neo-liberal" proposition that inflation and low interest rates tend to retard investment and growth. Results do not support the view that inflation was detrimental to growth either because it lowered investment or misallocated resources.

2818 Galbraith, John Kenneth. The nature of mass poverty. Cambridge: Harvard University Press, 1979. 150 p.

A remarkable little book which should be read by those interested in development. An equilibrium at levels of destitution arises from mass accommodation to poverty. Industrialization, migration, socialism, are examined as means of escape from the accommodation.

2819 Garay, Luis J. Grupo Andino y proteccionismo: contribución a un debate. Prólogo de Carlos Lleras Restrepo. Bogotá: Editorial Pluma, 1979. 414 p.; bibl. (Pluma universitaria; 2)

Serious theoretical analysis of the present situation and proposals regarding the Andean group. Considerable attention is given the common external tariff.

2820 Genberg, Hans and **Kenryk Kierskowski.** Impact and long-run effects of economic disturbances in a dynamic model of exchange rate determination (CAUK/WA, 115:4, 1979, p. 653–669, bibl., tables)

Econometric study of price instability related to the structural composition of imports. Mexico and Brazil are included among seven countries with data drawn from the 1960s to mid-1970s.

2821 Gerardi, Ricardo Eugenio. Posibles tendencias del intercambio comercial de América Latina y la CEE (BNCE/CE, 30:5, mayo 1980, p. 463–472, tables)

Careful estimate of reversing the de-creasing share of Latin American exports to the European Economic Community.

2822 Gilbert, Alan. The state and regional income disparities in Latin America (in Studying Latin America: essays in honor of Preston E. James. Edited by David J. Robinson. Ann Arbor, Mich.: Published for Department of Geography, Syracuse University, by University Microfilms International, 1980, p. 215–244, table)

Immense regional inequalities that exist in Latin America are made worse by: 1) misspecified development policies, and 2) lack of welfare programs which have reduced inequalities elsewhere.

2823 Glade, William P. El papel de las empresas del sector público en la integración de la estructura industrial latinoamericana: algunas observaciones preliminares; difusión de los esfuerzos de integración en América Latina. Austin: The University of Texas at Austin, Institute of Latin American Studies, 1975? 54 p. (Offprint series; 175)

Reprinted from *Revista de la Integración* (BID/INTAL, 19/20, May/Sept. 1975). Public enterprises have been important change elements and offer special opportunities as integration elements. Little is found in the literature, and attention should be turned in this direction, in particular to limiting factors.

2824 Gomes, Gerson and **Antonio Pérez.** The process of modernization in Latin American agriculture (CEPAL/R, 8, Aug. 1979, p. 55–74)

Latin American agriculture is not a traditional "backward" sector, yet it does not react adequately to demands placed upon it. Causes are not shortage of material, human resources, or technology but the structure of the sector and the form modernization seems to take.

2825 Gómez Arango, Gilberto and **Ernesto Parra Escobar.** El Nuevo Orden Económico Internacional y la Trilateral. Bogotá: Centro de Investigación y Educación Popular, 1978. 150 p.; bibl.; diagr. (Serie Controversia; no. 68–69)

Examines evolution of the NIEO and particularly the trilateral (Europe, North America, Japan) response to it. The latter group is seen as a device to maintain the present power structure and to expand the markets and investment opportunities of the industrialized, capitalistic countries.

2826 González Cano, Hugo. Tax incentives for the promotion of non-traditional exports in Latin America (Development Financing [Semiannual review of the Public Sector Program. Organization of American States, General Secretariat, Washington] 3:1/2, June/Dec. 1979, p. 3–74)

Comprehensive study of the topic including measures, country summaries, comments on means of evaluating effectiveness.

2827 Goyer, Doreen S. The international population census bibliography, revision and update, 1945–1977. New York: Academic Press, 1980. 576 p. (Studies in population. Texas bibliography; 2)

Worldwide but enormously useful to Latin Americanists. Cites documents in published language and in English, name and address of official publisher, and description of publication.

2828 Graciarena, Jorge. The basic needs strategy as an option: its possibilities in the Latin American context (CEPAL/R, 8, Aug. 1979, p. 39–54)

"Poverty (treated as anomaly in present system) alleviation" is seen as antithetical to "basic needs" (redesigning systems so that poverty would be excluded as a possibility). Analyzes the implications of the latter with respect to its implementation in Latin America.

2829 Grosfeld, Jan. Les perspectives des coopératives agricoles en Amérique Latine (IIDC/C, 29:1/2, 1979, p. 42–55)

Outlines functions and types of agricultural cooperation and indicates that they have been disappointing in their impacts.

2830 Grosse, Robert. Foreign investment regulation in the Andean Pact: the first ten years (IAMEA, 33:4, Spring 1980, p. 77–94, table)

Early years saw reduced investment but this tendency has reversed.

2831 Grunwald, Joseph. Industrialización e integración económica en América Latina (BCV/REL, 11:44, p. 57–92, tables)

Reviews the results of two studies and concludes that there are great gains from integration but that small, poor countries will

gain least. Sectorial distribution of gains is modified when an exchange-saving criterion is added to trade-creation and trade-diversion. Closes with suggestions for specific policies to overcome some obstacles.

2832 Halty Carrere, Máximo. ¿Hacia un nuevo orden tecnológico? (Ciencia, Tecnología y Desarrollo [Fondo Colombiano de Investigaciones Científicas y Proyectos Especiales Francisco José de Caldas, Bogotá] 3:2, 1979, p. 320–343, ill., table)

Argues for "technologization" of middle income countries along specific lines as opposed to (or in addition to) "industrialization."

2833 Hanson, James A. The short-run relation between growth and inflation in Latin America: a quasi-rational or consistent expectations approach (AEA/AER, 70:5, Dec. 1980, p. 972–989)

Studies econometrically Brazil, Chile, Colombia, Mexico, Peru. Among other conclusions: significant and small relation between growth and unexpected inflation; 10 percentage points of inflation produce about one *extra* percentage point of growth.

2834 Helleiner, G.K. Structural aspects of Third World trade: some trends and some prospects (JDS, 15:3, April 1979, p. 70–107, tables)

In NIEO excitement, we should not overlook structural changes that are occurring in Third World trade: importance of transnational firm trade, new protectionism, system of flexible exchange rates and their significance.

2835 Herrera, Felipe. Development and cultural policies: prospects of the area (UNESCO/CU, 5:3, 1978, p. 129–145)

Much of the recent change in Latin America has been regionally exogenous, and little has been done to preserve national culture, much less the regional cultural heritage. Much can be done; SELA is an example in the economic field of what might be done culturally.

2836 Herrou-Aragón, Alberto A. Inflación y balanza de pagos: la experiencia de algunos países latinoamericanos (UCC/CE, 17:50, abril 1980, p. 41–60, tables)

Econometric study of effects of monetary disequilibria on balances of payments— Argentina, Colombia, Costa Rica, Guatemala. Results depend on elasticities of substitution between traded and non-traded goods in production, consumption, and shares of each.

2837 Hirschman, Albert O. Auge y ocaso de la teoría económica del desarrollo (FCE/TE, 47:188, Oct./Dec. 1980, p. 1055–1077)

Perceptive sketch of the "rise and fall" of development theory with analysis of the reasons therefore.

2838 ——. La matriz social y política de la inflación: elaboración sobre la experiencia latinoamericana (PCE/TE, 47[e]:187, julio/sept. 1980, p. 679–709)

Describes the social-political *ambiente* in which Latin American inflations have prospered as economic phenomena. Then analyzes the social and political *effects* of inflations.

2839 La Industria en la integración latinoamericana. Obra editada bajo la dirección de Raimundo Barros Charlín. Santiago de Chile: Editorial Universitaria, 1977. 149 p.; bibl. (Nuevas perspectivas de la integración latinoamericana; v. 3. Estudios internacionales)

Industry and integration with particular attention to complementarity (see also items **2751** and **2952**).

2840 Inflation and stabilisation in Latin America. Edited by Rosemary Thorp and Laurence Whitehead. New York: Holmes and Meier, 1979. 285 p.; tables.

Collaborative effort through a seminar series of the editors, Guido di Tella, Henry Finch, Valpy Fitzgerald, John Wells. Case study countries include Mexico, Chile, Peru, Uruguay, Argentina, Brazil. Most concern experience only in the 1970s.

2841 Instituto Chileno del Acero. Evaluación del posible impacto ocupacional del programa metalmecánico y de las propuestas automotriz y petroquímica del Grupo Andino. v. 1, Resumen y conclusiones. v. 2, Análisis detallado. Preparado por el Instituto Chileno del Acero. Santiago de Chile?: Organización Internacional del Trabajo, Programa Regional del Empleo para América Latina y el Caribe, 1975. 2 v. (Documento de trabajo—PREALC: 89)

This study is interesting in itself, and it also suggests others which may exist or should be undertaken. Analyzes the expected impacts of integration proposals in the Andean Group with respect to three industrial groups (petrochemicals, automobile, and metal-works).

2842 Inter-American Development Bank, Buenos Aires. Institute for Latin American Integration. The Latin American integration process in 1978. Buenos Aires: 1978. 348 p.; tables.

Annual publication treating general topics, specific ones such as the Andean group, documentation, and summaries of special studies (in this volume, multinationals). See also *HLAS 39:2839–2840*. Excellent source of information.

2843 International Bank for Reconstruction and Development. World tables, 1980, from the data files of the World Bank. Baltimore: Published for the World Bank [by] Johns Hopkins University Press, 1980. 1 v.; index.

Follows 1976 edition. A marvelous source of data of 140 countries in four series: population, national accounts, prices; international sector and central government finances; comparative economic data; social indicators.

2844 International trade and agriculture, theory and policy. Edited by Jimmye S. Hillman and Andrew Schmitz. Boulder, Colorado: Westview Press, 1979. 333 p.; bibl.; ill.; index (Westview special studies in international economics and business)

Not specifically related to Latin America and only one chapter deals particularly with developing countries, the topic is an important one and the coverage good.

2845 Janvry, Alain de and **Lynn Ground.** Types and consequences of land reform in Latin America (LAP, 5[4]:19, Fall 1978, p. 90–112, tables)

Analyzes the process through which land reform occurs within the dynamics of the social system and then seeks to classify various reforms according to a consistent model. Discuss impacts of each type.

Jiménez, Roberto and **P. Zeballos.** América Latina y el mundo desarrollado: bibliografía comentada sobre relaciones de dependencia. See *HLAS 42:47*.

2846 Jiménez Cabrera, Edgar. Las empresas multinacionales y el sistema político latinoamericano. San Salvador, El Salvador: UCA Editores, 1979. 213 p. (Colección Estructuras y procesos; v. 6)

Descriptive, comprehensive treatment of the role of foreign investment in the economic and political structures of Latin America. Intends to add considerable understanding of dependency.

2847 ———. El funcionamiento de la economía latinoamericana: crítica a las recomendaciones de la Escuela de Chicago (UJSC/ECA, 35:375/376, enero/feb. 1980, p. 39–54, tables)

Much broader than the title implies although the Chicago "school" attracts considerable attention. The level of generalization is high which detracts from country-specific applicability of the argument.

2848 Karnes, Thomas L. Tropical enterprise: Standard Fruit and Steamship Company in Latin America. Baton Rouge: Louisiana State University Press, 1978. 332 p.

Business history of a family firm from the turn of the century until its acquisition by Castle and Cooke in 1968. Mainly an integrated banana seller, it operated in Mexico, Central America, Ecuador. Fascinating and instructive reading but not primarily an evaluation of the firm's impact in host countries.

2849 Kornevall, Christian. Efectos sobre el empleo de un cambio del modo de financiamiento de la seguridad social (*in* Oficina Internacional del Trabajo. Programa Regional del Empleo para América Latina y el Caribe [PREALC]. Investigaciones sobre empleo. Santiago: Oficina Internacional del Trabajo, 1980, p. 25–38, tables)

Examines employment effects of shifting social security financing from a payroll tax to a value added tax. Results are positive for employment, production, and the distribution of income between covered and non-covered sectors.

2850 Kronish, Rich and **Ken Mericle.** Latin America: wheels, deals and class struggle (NACLA, 12:4, July/Aug. 1979, p. 10–21, plates)

The history of the automobile industry in Mexico, Brazil, Argentina—the role and treatment of the working class as a part of its development.

2851 Kuznetsov, Viacheslav. La cooperación multilateral en la esfera cambiaria y financiera (URSS/AL, 2, 1979, p. 17–34)

Soviet survey of regional financial institutions, their functions and effects. The IDB gets prime attention as an imperialist organ for the US and, since incorporation of other lenders, an imperialist organ for a consortium of capitalistic countries.

2852 Lage, Gerald M. and **Frank K. Kiang.** The potential for mutually beneficial trade negotiations between the United States and advanced LDCs (CAUK/WA, 115:2, 1979, p. 297–314, bibl., tables)

Seeks to determine if there are mutually beneficial tariff reductions possible between the US and major LDC trading partners. Ten countries include Colombia, Brazil, and Mexico. Findings: such bargaining could usefully supplement other policies.

2853 Lagos, Gustavo. De *La riqueza de las naciones* de Adam Smith a la pobreza de las naciones de la IV UNCTAD (INTAL/IL, 1:6, sept. 1976, p. 4–19, tables)

Uses Smith as point of reference to indicate classical economics predicted narrowing of international income gaps, but that this did not happen. Sketches background, evolution and components of NIEO.

2854 Landau, Georges D. El BID y el financiamiento de desarrollo en América Latina (BNCE/CE, 30:4, abril 1980, p. 330–338)

Gives major attention to the changing roles of *national* development banks.

2855 Latin America and the New International Economic Order. Edited by Jorge Lozoya & Jaime Estevez. New York: Pergamon Press, 1980. 1 v.; bibl.; index (Pergamon policy studies in the New International Economic Order)

Of considerable interest: political systems, trade, industrialization are major topics. Starts with premise that major problems stem from capitalism's internationalization and the changes which have occurred in the LDC's in the process of development.

2856 Latin America/Japan Business Cooperation Symposium, *Washington, D.C., 1979.* Sponsored by Inter-American Development Bank and the Export-Import Bank of Japan. Washington, D.C.: Inter-American Development Bank, 1979. 272 p.

Reports a 1979 symposium covering wide range of subjects. Includes several background papers and a rapporteur's summary. Increasingly important topic.

2857 Latin American-European Business Cooperation Symposium, *Montreaux, Switzerland, 1977.* Latin American-European business cooperation. Buenos Aires: Inter-American Development Bank, 1978? 340 p.

Record of 1977 symposium in Switzerland of 1200 participants—government officials, international civil servants, businessmen. Plenary sessions covered general and country topics; special sessions, some rather technical business-economic topics; sectoral sessions, such items as mining, automobile manufacture. There are approximately 70 articles—a good deal of information but hard to dig out.

Latin American shipping 1979. See *HLAS 42:148.*

2858 Ledesma, Joaquín R. La teoría de la integración y la Asociación Latinoamericana de Libre Comercio. Buenos Aires: Fundación para el Estudio de los Problemas Argentinos (FEPA), 1979. 31 p.; bibl.; tables (Documento de trabajo; 18)

If integration is to facilitate growth substantially, the complexity of the Latin American economies needs to be understood and the theory should include them.

2859 Leff, Nathaniel H. Entrepreneurship and economic development: the problem revisited (The Journal of Economic Literature [American Economic Association, Nashville, Tenn.] 17:1, March 1979, p. 46–64, bibl.)

Excellent summary of the title theme with entrepreneurship being rather narrowly viewed. It does not now appear to be the constraint it was once thought to be.

2860 ———— **and Kazuo Sato.** La inestabilidad macroeconómica, el crecimiento económico a corto plazo y la dependencia externa de los países en desarrollo (FCE/TE, 47[1]:85, enero/marzo 1980, p. 193–318, bibl., tables)

Fairly simple macro model which concerns itself especially with the effects of dependency on foreign capital and the savings-reactions to price changes. Analyzes the instability in the short-run of six countries

studied which include Brazil, Argentina, Chile, and Costa Rica.

2861 Lewerenz, Jürgen. Labour banks in Latin America and the Caribbean. Frankfurt, FRG: Bank für gemeinwirtschaft Aktiengesellschaft, 1979. 60 p.; tables (Series Commonwealth economy; no. 21)

Review of the nature of relatively new "laborers" banks, the predominant type being that of the "OAS" variety stemming from the Alliance for Progress. Part of a series of labor banks.

2862 Lewis, W. Arthur. Evolución del Orden Económico Internacional. Traducción de José Treviño Botti. México: Centro de Estudios Económicos y Demográficos, El Colegio de México, 1980. 91 p. (Jornadas; 92)

Two 1977 Princeton lectures honoring J. Schumpter analyzing the evolution of the current world order over 150 years—puts "new order" in that perspective.

2863 Lietaer, Bernard A. Europe + Latin America + the multinationals: a positive sum game for the exchange of raw materials and technology in the 1980s. Farnborough: Saxon House, 1979. 273 p.; bibl.; ill. (ECSIM publications)

Startling—from publisher-sponsor to format to objective. Seeks to describe the decade of the 1980s with particular attention to European-Latin American relations but in their larger contexts. Expects "negative sum game" which may be turned around if European labor and industry modify policies with respect to Latin America with benefits accruing to both areas.

2864 Lim, David. Industrial processing and location: a study of tin (WD, 8:3, March 1980, p. 205–212, tables)

Little reason is found for further processing tin in producing countries because they use so little of it themselves and because it is used almost entirely with other products (e.g., steel for tin plate) which they do not have.

2865 Lipson, Charles. The IMF, commercial banks, and Third World debts (*in* Debts and the less developed countries. Edited by Jonathan David Aronson. Boulder, Colorado: Westview Press, 1979, p. 317–333)

Commercial banks became recipients of petro-dollars and loaned them to better-off LDCs. Debt management now becomes problem jointly for banks and LDCs and former press for stronger World Bank and IMF funding to assist in balance of payments difficulties.

2866 Llamazares, Juan. Cómo vender en Africa: oportunidades comerciales para América Latina. Bogotá: Organización de los Estados Americanos, Centro Interamericano de Promoción de Exportaciones, 1972. 387 p.; 1 leaf of plates; bibl.; maps.

Basically a commercial atlas of Africa, becoming badly dated but still with a good deal of useful information.

2867 Love, James. Trade concentration and export instability (JDS, 15:3, April 1979, p. 60–69, tables)

By a new technique, finds both product and market concentration do contribute to instability. This is contrary to most other empirical evidence.

2868 Love, Joseph L. Raul Prebisch and the origins of the doctrine of unequal exchange (LARR, 15:3, 1980, p. 45–72)

Readable account which traces the empirical, pragmatic development of Prebisch's ideas as precursors of dependency doctrine.

2869 McNall, Scott G. and Sally O. Margolin. Multinational corporations in Latin America: the search for consumers and raw materials (RU/SCID, 12:3, Fall 1977, p. 65–85, bibl., tables)

Analysis of why multinational corporations go where they do (advanced LDCs with large populations and resource-rich LDCs) and the impacts of the relationships.

2870 Mahler, Vincent A. Dependency approaches to international political economy: a cross-national study. New York: Columbia University Press, 1980. 218 p.; bibl.; index.

Distills testable hypothesis from dependency theorists and then tests them in 70-country, cross-sectional correlation analysis. In general, the hypotheses stand up.

2871 Mamalakis, Markos. La teoría mineral del crecimiento: la experiencia latinoamericana (FCE/TE, 45[4]:180, oct./dic. 1978, p. 841–878)

Sketches a "mineral" theory of growth which includes elements of production, income distribution, capital formation. Enumerates those elements relevant to mineral "type" countries. Draws on Latin American countries as examples: Chile, Venezuela, Bolivia are "mineral" types; Mexico and Peru, "semimineral."

Martinière, Guy. Les Amériques latines: une histoire économique. See *HLAS 42:1795.*

2872 Martz, Mary Jeanne Reid. SELA: the Latin American economic system ploughing the seas? (IAMEA, 32:4, Spring 1979, p. 33–64)

Traces the development of Sistema Económico Latinoamericano, its brief activities, and considers its possible future. Very informative.

2873 Massad, Carlos. Cartera de inversiones de los países exportadores de petróleo: diversificación orientada hacia América Latina (UC/EE, 12, 2. semestre 1978, p. 147–172, tables)

Written for publication in Kuwait. Basically analyzes non-petroleum exporting Latin America as a possible recipient of petro-dollars to diversity oil producing countries' portfolios.

2874 Mattos, Carlos A. de. Plans versus planning in Latin American experience (CEPAL/R, 8, Aug. 1979, p. 75–90)

Reviews two decades of planning in Latin America and the disappointments attendant upon it. Gradually, newer more pragmatic means have been adopted.

2875 Meller, Patricio. El patrón de concentración industrial de América Latina y de Europa occidental (IDES/DE, 18:72, enero/marzo 1979, p. 559–577, tables)

Compares industrial concentration in Latin America with Western Europe. Finds similar patterns among other important results.

2876 Menon, Bhashkar P. Bridges across the south: technical cooperation among developing countries. New York: Pergamon Press, 1980. 144 p.; bibl.; ill.; index (Pergamon policy studies on the new International Economic Order. Pergamon policy studies)

Journalist's account of UN Conference on Technical Cooperation among Developing Countries with considerable attention to the background. One of a series on NIEO.

2877 Mercado y dependencia. Ursula Oswald, coordinadora; con ponencias de Celso Cartas et al.; y comentarios de Jorge Alonso et al.; portada, Kurtycz. México: Centro de Investigaciones Superiores del Instituto Nacional de Antropología e Historia: Editorial Nueva Imagen, 1979. 409 p.; bibl.

Papers and comments from 1977 seminar. Deals largely with Mexico and in general with agriculture. Application of Marx to a set of relevant sub-problems.

2878 Monografía de la CEPAL (Ciencia, Tecnología y Desarrollo [Fondo Colombiano de Investigaciones Científicas y Proyectos Especiales Francisco José de Caldas, Bogotá] 3:2, 1979, p. 242–319)

Carefully prepared document which seeks to set out a Latin American position for a UN conference on science and technology for development.

2879 Monografía del Grupo Andino (Ciencia, Tecnología y Desarrollo [Fondo Colombiano de Investigaciones Científicas y Proyectos Especiales Francisco José de Caldas, Bogotá] 3:2, 1979, p.217–242, tables)

Presentation covers two principal points: 1) fundamentals relating technology to socioeconomic development and how this becomes a matter of concern to the international community; and 2) financial problems and arrangements (see also item **2878**).

2880 Morales Crespo, Eddle and **Asdrúbal Aguiar Aranguren.** De la integración colonial a la desintegración republicana (BCV/REL, 14:53, 1979, p. 109–159)

Traces political-economic history of regions and compares, finally, the experiences of LAFTA and the Andean Pact seeking to explain differences in their relative successes.

2881 Moreno, Fernando. La integración latinoamericana. Santiago de Chile: Instituto Chileno de Estudios Humanísticos, 1978. 289 p.; bibl.

In considerable detail covers the historical background; industrialization, integration and LAFTA; the experience of LAFTA through the Andean Pact.

2882 Muñoz Gomá, Oscar. Debates sobre la teoría del capital y del crecimiento. Santiago, Chile: Corporación de Investigaciones Económicas para Latinoamérica, 1978.

28, 2 leaves; bibl.; graph (Notas técnicas—CIEPLAN; no. 6)

Competent review of capital theory and the role of capital in growing economies.

2883 ———. Dualismo, organización industrial y empleo. Santiago de Chile: Corporación de Investigaciones Económicas para Latinoamérica, 1977. 49 p.; bibl. (Estudios CIEPLAN; 19)

Examines the causes and explanation of dualism from the general analytical approach to specific explanations of Latin American situations.

2884 Musgrove, Philip. Household size and composition, employment, and poverty in urban Latin America (UC/EDCC, 28:2, Jan. 1980, p. 249–266, tables)

Further examination of ECIEL-study involving data on households in 10 Andean cities, 1967–69. Striking conclusions: household poverty is not highly associated with low average income (but with large family size and low employment rates) nor is it highly associated with low employment rates among adults. Important implications are explored.

2885 ———. Permanent household income and consumption in urban South America (AEA/AER, 69:3, June 1979, p. 355–368, bibl., tables)

Econometric study of household incomes (Peru, Colombia, Ecuador—1967–69) and its determinants. Transitory variation in income is negligible; permanent income can be predicted from a few variables; average elasticity of consumption with respect to income is less than one.

2886 ——— and Robert Ferber. Identifying the urban poor: characteristics of poverty households in Bogotá, Medellín and Lima (LARR, 14:2, 1979, p. 25–54, plate, tables)

An extensive study of 1967–69 survey data from Bogotá, Medellín, Lima to define the "poor" and to find reasonable approaches to welfare. Some policy implications are explored.

2887 Mytelka, Lynn Krieger. Regional development in a global economy: the multinational corporation, technology, and Andean integration. New Haven: Yale University Press, 1979. 233 p.; bibl.; ill.; index.

Careful and up-to-date study of the Andean Pact and the role of foreign investment in member countries. Equity in distribution of gains remains a key issue.

2888 Naim, Moíses. Transfer pricing by multinational corporations and its regulations by host countries (AI/I, 5:3, May/June 1980, p. 166–171, bibl., tables)

Argues that host government regulations to control *transfer pricing* (intra-firm transfers) are likely to be ineffective since prices in intra-firms transactions are nearly irrelevant.

2889 Nairn, Ronald C. Wealth of nations in crisis. Houston, Tex.: Bayland Pub., 1979. 289 p.; bibl.; index.

Libertarian treatise argues that much of the world's agricultural ills are caused by policies and structures which inhibit growth and production—and that concentration on incentives and the human factor would increase agricultural productivity immensely.

2890 New York Times Information Service Inc. Investment and development in Latin America: a survey of business trends and prospects. Parsippany, N.J.: New York Times Information Service, 1977. 1 v. (Corporate information series)

Contains thousands of news item summaries from some 60 periodicals, chiefly from 1976–77, without plans to up-date. Most entries are by country with comparatively few for region as a whole. The Information Bank *is* current, however, and specific searches can be requested.

2891 Ominami, Carlos. Critique des théories du développment en Amérique latine (UP/TM, 20:80, oct./déc. 1979, p. 725–746)

Reviews critically development theory (Prebisch, evolutionist, Frank, Chicago school). Suggests some elements for an alternative approach.

2892 Organization of American States. Synthesis of economic performance in Latin America during 1979. Washington: 1979? 40 p.; tables.

OAS publication which seeks to fill a particular void: summary information for the region for a year with short-term projections for the following year. World trends are related to Latin American economies and major trends in Latin America are viewed—both by region and by country. Timeliness is critical to the value of the projections for the year following that summarized.

2893 ———. General Secretariat. Methods for evaluating Latin American export operations: a manual for new exporters. Washington: General Secretariat, Organization of American States, 1978. 113 p.; bibl.; ill.

Far from the beaten track! An elementary manual for potential Latin American exporters to the US. Combines description, case studies, and useful data regarding other information sources.

2894 ———. Programa del Sector Público. Inflación y tributación: análisis de los efectos de la inflación y de los sistemas de ajustes empleados para corregir sus distorsiones en los países de América Latina. Washington: Secretaria Ejecutiva para Asuntos Económicos y Sociales, Secretaría de la Organización de los Estados Americanos, 1978. 167 p. (Documentos ocasionales—Programa del Sector Público, Organización de los Estados Americanos)

Technical topic concerned primarily with the impact of inflation on taxation rather than the reverse. General discussion liberally sprinkled with case material. Sample chapters: adjustments in personal income taxes, incorporate profits taxes, capital gains taxation, etc.

2895 Orlandi, Alberto. Prices and gains in the world coffee trade (CEPAL/R, first half, 1978, p. 161–197, tables)

A careful study of coffee costs, production and marketing. Colombia is given considerable attention. The final market price and production costs are included with analysis of the distribution of value-added from producer to retailer.

2896 Owen, A.D. Purchasing power parity theory: some empirical results for the LAFTA countries (IEI/EI, 32:4, nov. 1979, p. 462–473, bibl., tables)

Seeks to "explain" the ratio of the official exchange rates to purchasing power parities for the 11 LAFTA countries. "Openess," resource endowments, and tourist revenue were found to be relevant explanatory variables.

2897 Pacto Andino: carácter y perspectivas. Ernesto Tironi, compilador; colaboradores, Augusto Aninat et al. Lima: Instituto de Estudios Peruanos, 1978. 390 p.; bibl. (América-problema; 9)

Eight articles by well-known authors on aspects of the Pact. Generally broad in scope.

2898 Pérez Brignoli, Héctor. The economic cycle in Latin American agricultural export economies, 1880–1930: a hypothesis for investigation (LARR, 15:2, 1980, p. 3–33, tables)

Argues that ECLA and dependency theorists take too simple a view of cyclical behavior in export economies. Seeks empirical evidence and a model with particular emphasis on the Argentine agricultural economy and Costa Rican coffee production. For historian's comment, see *HLAS 42:1937.*

2899 Peru. Ministerio de Integración. Dirección General de Asuntos Especiales y de Investigación. Situación económica de los países andinos en el marco de la economía internacional, 1976. Lima: Ministerio de Integración, Dirección de Asuntos Especiales y de Investigación, Oficina de Comunicaciones e Información, 1977. 368 p. (Informe de coyuntura—Ministerio de Integración; no. 3, ed. extraordinaria)

Data and description of general economic situations for Andean Pact countries.

Petras, James F. Critical perspectives on imperialism and social class in the Third World. See item **8050.**

————. The Latin American agrotransformation from above and outside and its social and political implications. See item **6068.**

2900 Pinto, Aníbal. La apertura al exterior en la América Latina (PCE/TE, 47[3]:187, julio/sept. 1980, p. 533–578, tables)

Examines the "opening" of Latin American economies as a development strategy and in the context of integration of the world's economies. Carefully considered conclusions.

2901 ————. Una visión latinoamericana de la inflación en los países industrializados (BCV/REL, 11:45, p. 157–197)

Seeks to find in the "forgotten" Latin American inflations lessons for the indus-

trialized economies as they begin to experience their mid-1970s inflations.

———— and **Armando Di Filippo.** Desarrollo y pobreza en la América Latina: un enfoque histórico-estructural. See *HLAS 42:1805.*

2902 La Planificación del desarrollo agropecuario: un enfoque para América Latina. v. 2, pts. 3/4. Por Jesús González M. et al. México: Siglo Veintiuno Editores, 1977. 1 v.; bibl.; ill. (Economía y demografía. Textos del Instituto Latinoamericano de Planificación Económica y Social)

This large treatise concentrates entirely on the agricultural sector and seems largely independent of vol. 1 (pts. 1/2, see *HLAS 41:2928*). Pt. 3 deals with policy for agricultural development (seven chapters), and pt. 4 treats regional development or agriculture (one chapter). A useful effort.

Planidex. Vol. 1, 1980– . See *HLAS 42:159.*

2903 Platt, D.C.M. Dependency in nineteenth century Latin America: an historian objects (LARR, 15:1, 1980, p. 113–130)

Examines generalizations of "dependistas" regarding post-colonial Spanish America as Platt interprets the facts. The piece's usefulness is increased by a Stein and Stein examination of Platt (see item **2941**) and his brief rejoinder (p. 147–149). For Spanish version of article, see *Desarrollo Económico* (Instituto de Desarrollo Económico y Social, Buenos Aires, 19:76, enero/marzo 1980, p. 435–451).

2904 La política monetaria y el ajuste de la balanza de pagos: tres estudios. Santiago: Naciones Unidas, Comisión Económica para América Latina (CEPAL), 1979. 67 p.; bibl.; tables (Cuadernos de la CEPAL; 29)

Consists of the following econometric studies: Valeriano García's "The Demand for Imports" and "Balance of Payments Adjustments, Credit Policy, and External Debt;" and Alvaro Saieh's "Monetary Aspects of the Exchange Rate."

2905 Political economy of food. Edited by Vilho Harle. Farnborough, Eng.: Saxon House; Brookfield, Vt.: distributed by Renouf USA, 1978. 438 p.; bibl.

Papers presented at a conference in Tampere, Finland (Tampere Peace Research

Institute). A substantial portion of the book deals with Latin America. Generally unfamiliar authors and another perspective make it interesting volume.

2906 Políticas de empleo al alcance de los Ministerios del Trabajo (in Oficina Internacional del Trabajo. Programa Regional del Empleo para América Latina y el Caribe [PREALC]. Investigaciones sobre empleo. Santiago: Oficina Internacional del Trabajo, 1980, p. 7–24, tables)

Reviews employment policies for employment-oriented Ministries of Labor and suggests some new functions to increase effectiveness.

2907 Políticas de empleo en América Latina: los casos de Venezuela, Colombia, Ecuador y Centroamérica. Por Humberto Pereira, coordinación; Boris Chacón et al. Bogotá: Siglo Veintiuno Editores, 1977. 253 p.; bibl. (Economía y demografía)

Series of country studies include Venezuela, Colombia, Ecuador, Central America, and Panama.

2908 Porzecanski, Arturo C. A comparative study of exchange rate policy under inflation (JDA, 12:2, Jan. 1978, p. 133–152, tables)

Studies Argentina, Brazil, Chile, Uruguay—selected because of persistent rates of inflation of over 30 percent for two decades. Policies depended on development philosophy, attitude toward inflationary effects of devaluation, estimates of trade price elasticities.

2909 Prebisch, Raúl. Introducción al estudio de la crísis del capitalismo periférico (FCE/TE, 46[3]:183, julio/sept. 1979, p. 547–567)

A critical fault of "liberal" economies of the periphery is their tendency to persistent inequality in their distribution of income. "Trickling down" does not occur because much of the surpluses of the rich find their way into consumption rather than further investment. Neo-classical theories are not of much help.

2910 Prewo, Wilfried. The structure of transport costs on Latin American exports (CAUK/WA, 114:2, 1978, p. 305–327, tables)

Summarizes data in transport cost functions from Latin America since much is expected of exports. Functions also indicate important variables, suggest rate of monopolistic exploitation by shipping conferences.

2911 El problema ocupacional en América Latina. v. 2, Concentración industrial, tecnología y empleo. Coordinado y compilado por Juan J. Buttari. Buenos Aires: Programa de Estudios Conjuntos sobre Integración Económica Latinoamericana (ECIEL) [and] Ediciones SIAP, 1978. 302 p.; tables.

This companion volume to *HLAS 39:2923* is descriptive and analytic with three principal objectives: 1) determination of the relative importance changes in labor productivity, changes in sectoral composition of the product, and changes in the size distribution of firms have on employment opportunity; 2) characteristics of structure and size distribution of manufacturing in Latin America; and 3) labor absorption by industry. Includes some regional analysis but much is country analysis.

2912 Problemas económicos y sociales de América Latina. Raúl Prebisch et al. Bogotá?: Ediciones Universidades Simón Bolivar y Libre de Pereira, 1979. 358 p. (Colección Universidad y pueblo; 38)

In order to commemorate the publication of *Desarrollo Indoamericano*'s 50th issue, this volume reprints significant articles on the title theme. Major complaint: no dates or places where pieces first appeared.

2913 Programa Regional del Empleo para América Latina y el Caribe. Acción de los Ministerios de Trabajo en la política del empleo del Grupo Andino. Santiago, Chile: PREALC, 1975. 111 p. in various pagings; bibl.; graphs (Documento de trabajo— PREALC; 87)

Prepared for a meeting called by the Ministers of Labor of the Andean Group, covers three topics: employment policies usually available at ministerial level and their effects, employment effects of changing the social security system, policies suitable for modifying rural employment.

2914 ———. Archivo de datos ocupacionales sobre América Latina y el Caribe. Santiago, Chile: PREALC, 1979. 15 leaves; tables (Documentos de trabajo— PREALC; 168)

Data for 24 countries.

2915 ———. Asalariados de bajos ingresos y salarios mínimos en América Latina. Santiago, Chile: PREALC, 1979. 126 p.; bibl. (Documentos de trabajo—PREALC; 170)

Considers low-wage earners and the significance of minimum wage provisions in Latin America.

2916 ———. Una nueva dimensión de la OIT: interrelaciones entre empleo, población y distribución del ingreso. Santiago, Chile: PREALC, 1978. 20 leaves, 2 leaves of plates; diagrs. (Documento de trabajo—PREALC; 157)

Considers the BACUE model in Latin America which has been employed elsewhere and which relates population, employment, income distribution.

2917 Puentes, Mirta Beatriz. La teoría de la información como modelo de análisis estructural en la ciencia económica (BCV/REL, 12:48, 1977, p. 141–204, bibl., tables)

Exposition of an information model as an aid to understanding dependency both on country and regional levels.

2918 Ranis, G. ¿Existe un arquetipo de desarrollo latinoamericano y cuáles son sus problemas actuales? (BCV/REL, 11:43, 1975, p. 219–243)

Review of development policy and relationships in Latin America with objectives of increasing employment, expanding distributive justice, and enlarging the growth rate.

2919 Reca, Lucio G. Uso de recursos públicos e investigación agropecuaria en América Latina (UCC/CE, 16:49, dic. 1979, p. 359–371, bibl.)

Notes the need to expand agricultural research and explores what needs to be done and how the tasks should be shared.

2920 Reynolds, Clark W. Bankers as revolutionaries in the process of development (in Debt and the less developed countries. Edited by Jonathan David Aronson. Boulder, Colorado: Westview Press, 1979, p. 129–156, tables)

Considerable attention to flow-of-funds analysis in examining the transfer of rents from sector to sector to attain social objectives. Suggests little evidence that private foreign finance has been effective in reducing income inequality, for example, but that it is possible for it to be so.

2921 ———. Uso del análisis de flujo de fondos para estudiar el desarrollo del mercado de capitales en la América Latina (BCV/REL, 10:38, 1974, p. 167–217, bibl., tables)

Methodologically significant. Discusses benefits and weaknesses and preliminary results from three studies: Colombia, Brazil, Peru. May be more accessible in OAS, Third Annual Assembly on Capital Market Programs, 1973.

2922 Rietti Matheu, Mario. Moneda y banca: su evolución en América Latina. Prólogo de Antonio Ortíz Mena. Bogotá: Gráficas Fepar, 1979. 280 p.; bibl.; tables (Biblioteca Felaban)

An organized examination of the expanded and changing monetary sector (broadly viewed) in Latin America since 1960 both as a contributor to growth and as affected by it. Concentrates on changes from the traditional—e.g., regional financial institutions, financing development, banking integration. For English version, see *Money and banking in Latin America* (New York: Praeger Publishers, 1979).

2923 Roldán, Alfredo E. Estudios econométricos de la inflación en algunos países latinoamericanos (CEMLA/M, 11:3, julio/sept. 1979, p. 309–346, bibl.)

Summarizes eight studies of inflation (Harberger, Diz, Díaz Alejandro, etc.) and compares them. Finds them all valuable but none exhaustive (i.e., verification of *a* theory is not enough when causes and *cures* are at issue).

2924 Root, Franklin R. and **Ahmed A. Ahmed.** Empirical determinants of manufacturing direct foreign investment in developing countries (UC/EDCC, 27:4, July 1979, p. 751–767, tables)

Utilizes 58 countries and tests 38 variables suggested as important in the literature—economic, social, political. Six variables (with some collinearity) were discovered to be important.

2925 Rosenberg, Emily S. The exercise of emergency controls over foreign commerce: economic pressure on Latin America (IAMEA, 31:4, Spring 1978, p. 81–96)

Historical article emphasizes World War I experiences as backdrop to discuss subsequent use of emergency powers by the executive in international economic situations.

2926 Rosenburg, Hernán. Transferencia tecnológica a la América Latina a través de inversiones extranjeras directas: algunos costos y problemas no visibles (BCV/REL, 14:53, 1978, p. 201–243, bibl., tables)

For various reasons considers benefits of technological transfers overvalued and costs undervalued. Seeks to demonstrate validity of these points.

2927 Salazar Carrillo, Jorge. Comparisons of construction costs in Latin America (LARR, 14:2, 1979, p. 202–207, tables)

Studies most LAFTA countries in 1960 and 1968 with costs broken down into infrastructure, housing, non-residential construction.

2928 ———. Estructura de los salarios industriales en América Latina. Con la colaboración de Juan J. Buttari y la participación de Francisco J. Ortega y Adalberto García Rocha. Buenos Aires: Ediciones SIAP [Sociedad Interamericana de Planificación], 1979. 244 p.; tables (ECIEL: Programa de estudios conjuntos sobre integración latinoamericana)

Pioneering study and by-product of ECIEL's comparative cost studies. Data are for 1960s and include only manufacturing.

2929 Salgado, Germánico. The Latin American regional market: the project and the reality (CEPAL/R, April 1979, p. 85–132)

A careful look at integration, the objectives of LAFTA, obstacles, and a reformulation of concepts and objectives necessary if LAFTA is to be revitalized (UN Sales No. E.79. II.G.2).

2930 San Miguel, Manuel. Hacia un nuevo orden económico mundial (ANCE/A, 22, 1977, p. 42–76)

General, competent background to the NIEO, some of the history of thought, particularly with respect to trade, and the issues involved in reaching the objectives.

2931 Sánchez, Fernando. Producción e industrialización de granos en América Latina (OAS/CI, 20:3/4, abril 1979, p. 15–20, tables)

Study of recent data on grain produc-

tion and consumption with projections to 1990 under various assumptions.

2932 Sandilands, Roger James. Monetary correction and housing finance in Colombia, Brazil, and Chile. Farnborough, Eng.: Gower, 1980. 492 p.; bibl.; diagrs.; index.

Examines problems of long-term finance in inflation and the alleviation of at least some through indexing. Argues that single sector indexing need not cause pernicious distortions.

2933 Santos, Theotonio dos. La tecnología y la restructuración capitalista: opciones para América Latina (BNCE/CE, 29:12, dic. 1979, p. 1361–1370)

Explores the capitalist crisis, the tendency toward monopoly control of technology, the means toward technological dependence. Suggests policies to alleviate.

2934 Schydlowsky, Daniel M. Política de comercio internacional en la crecimiento económico de la América Latina (BCV/REL, 11:41, 1975, p. 103–148, tables)

A 1972 paper. Thesis: Manufacturing in Latin America has not ceased to be an exchange user, nor has it generated employment as expected; both disappointments are the result of policy decisions.

A select bibliography of economic development: with annotations. See *HLAS 42:64.*

2935 Seminario Internacional sobre el Ecuador y las Políticas de Fomento Industrial, *Quito, 1976.* Fomento industrial en América Latina. Marcelo Avila et al. Bogotá: Ediciones Internacionales, 1977. 205 p.; bibl.; ill.

Compendium of serious pieces on industrialization policy. Ffrench-Davis has general article and others deal with countries: Avila Orguela on Ecuador; Espinosa Bedoya on Peru; Katz on Argentina; Nolff on Venezuela; Poveda Ramos on Colombia.

2936 Seminario Producción y Transferencia de Tecnología Administrativa para el Sector Público en América Latina, *Caracas, 1975.* Seminario Producción y Transferencia de Tecnología Administrativa para el Sector Público en América Latina. Caracas: Centro Latinoamericano de Administración para el Desarrollo, 1975. 10 pamphlets; bibl.; ill.

Collection of papers which ranges beyond administrative technology. The general material (e.g., Katz) is probably more accessible elsewhere. The material on administrative technology may not be.

2937 Seminario sobre Financiamiento de la Educación en América Latina, *1st, Washington, D.C., 1976.* Financiamiento de la educación en América Latina. Compiladores, Mario Brodersohn y María Ester Sanjurjo. México: Fondo de Cultura Económica, Banco Interamericano de Desarrollo, 1978. 654 p.; bibl.; index (Sección de obras de economía)

Very useful compilation from a high-level conference held in 1976 by the Inter-American Development Bank. Covers wide range of topics and provides considerable data. The material was clearly well prepared. See also item **2813**.

2938 Seselovsky, Ernesto R.; Sergio R. Di Pietro; and Walter A.R. Perino. Los precios de transferencia en las empresas transnacionales: políticas para anular sus efectos en las economías dependientes (BCV/REL, 11:41, 1975, p. 85–102)

Authors propose a series of policies to deal with multinational pricing policies for international transfers, especially overinvoicing, and other defects (e.g., bias toward imported components).

Sheahan, John. Market-oriented economic policies and political repression in Latin America. See item **6082**.

2939 Singelman, Joachim and **Marta Tienda.** Changes in industry structure and female employment in Latin America: 1950–1970 (USC/SSR, 63:4, July 1979, p. 745–769, tables)

Data are from seven countries (1950–70). With increased industrialization, rates of women in industrial labor force have fallen. Yet changes have occurred which favor expansion of employment of women (e.g., greater proportion of service industries).

Smith, Tony. The underdevelopment of development literature: the case of dependency theory. See item **7139**.

2940 *Statistical Abstract of Latin America.* University of California, Latin American Center. Vol. 20, 1980– . Los Angeles.

Annual publication continues to improve and expand. Contains wide range of carefully documented data and five specialized chapters (e.g., James W. Wilkie's "The Rural Population of Argentina to 1970").

2941 Stein, Stanley J. and **Barbara H. Stein.** D.C.M. Platt: the anatomy of autonomy (LARR, 15:1, 1980, p. 131–146)

See item **2903**.

2942 Strange, Susan. Debt and default in the international political economy (*in* Debt and the less developed countries. Edited by Jonathan David Aronson. Boulder, Colorado: Westview Press, 1979, p. 7–26)

Credit in trouble threatens default. Looks historically at default and creditors' reactions. Needs to be viewed with cool eyes by both creditors and debtors and with anticipation.

2943 Street, James H. Los ajustes de la América Latina ante la crisis de la OPEP y la recesión mundial (FCE/TE, 46[4]:184, oct./dic. 1979, p. 867–888, bibl.)

Impacts on inflation, growth, debt service and reaction thereto. Most problems remain unsolved; most solutions must be internal ones.

2944 The Structure of the world economy and prospects for a New International Economic Order. Edited by Ervin Laszlo and Joel Kurtzman. New York: Pergamon Press, 1980. 1 v.; bibl.; index (Pergamon policy studies on the new international economic order)

One of 17 books on NIEO topics. This one has a heavy Latin American flavor with Ferrer, Oteiza, Wionczek contributing— among others.

2945 Swift, Jeannine. Economic development in Latin America. Cover design, Mies Hora. New York: St. Martin's Press, 1978. 154 p.; diagrs.

Useful text in introduction to Latin American economics.

Symposium on Equality of Opportunity in Employment in the American Region, *Panama, 1973.* Equality of opportunity in employment in the American region: problems and policies: report and documents of a regional symposium (Panama, 1–12 October 1972). See item **8061**.

2946 Symposium on the Use of Socioeconomic Investment Criteria in Project Evaluation, *Inter-American Development*

Bank, 1973. Social and economic dimensions of project evaluation: proceedings and papers of the Symposium on the Use of Socioeconomic Investment Criteria in Project Evaluation, held at the Inter-American Development Bank on March 28–30, 1973. Editors, Hugh Schwartz, Richard Berney. Washington: IDB, 1977. 338 p.; ill.

Full report on a symposium devoted to project evaluation. Important discussion of two basic works: Little-Mirrles and UNIDO guidelines. Discussion documents are included. Illuminating.

2947 Tait, Alan A.; Wilfrid L.M. Grätz; and Barry J. Eichengreen. International comparisons of taxation for selected developing countries; 1972–1976 (IMF/SP, 26:1, March 1979, p. 123–156)

Brings up-to-date and refines measure of taxing effort and capacity (see also *HLAS 39:2781*).

2948 Tami, Felipe S. Reflexiones sobre las experiencias de integración económica en América Latina (ANCE/A, 22, 1977, p. 11–41)

Traces the development of theory on integration and then the history of Latin American integration. Finds conventional theory too narrow to apply comfortably to integration of developing countries.

2949 Technological progress in Latin America: the prospects for overcoming dependency. Edited by James H. Street and Dilmus D. James. Boulder, Colorado: Westview Press, 1979. 257 p.; tables.

Pt. 1 comprises four essays on the nature of technological dependence, and pt. 2, eight case studies (Colombia, Mexico, Brazil, Argentina, Puerto Rico) in internal technological diffusion. Editors' contribution is considerable; among other authors are David Felix, Samuel Morley, Gordon Smith, and Paul Strassmann.

2950 Teitel, Simón. Productividad, mecanización y calificaciones: una prueba de la hipótesis de Hirschman para la industria latinoamericana (PCE/TE, 47[3]:187, julio/sept. 1980, p. 613–650, bibl., tables)

Employing data from seven countries, explores the Hirschman proposition that in certain capital intensive industries ("process-centered," "machine paced") Latin American economies may have a comparative advantage.

2951 Thiesenhusen, William C. Current development patterns and agrarian policy in Latin America (*in* The process of rural transformacion: Eastern Europe, Latin America, and Australia. Edited by Ivan Volgyes, Richard E. Lonsdale, and William P. Avery. New York: Pergamon Press, 1979, p. 128–139, tables)

Discusses the state of agriculture and, although there has been neither "evolution or revolution," it has changed in the last decades.

2952 Tironi, Ernesto. Estrategias de desarrollo e integración: divergencias en el caso andino. Santiago, Chile: Corporación de Investigaciones Económicas para Latinoamérica, 1977. 49 p.; bibl. (Estudios Cieplan; 7)

Deals with political and economic strategies for integration. Issues related to the Andean Group get special attention (see also items **2751** and **2839**).

2953 ———. Políticas nacionales alternativas respecto al comercio de productos básicos (BCV/REL, 57/58, 1979, p. 179–219, tables)

Traces history of primary product exportation with recent changes. Policy alternatives refer to stabilization, balance of payments, factor income stability.

2954 Tokman, Víctor E. Distribución del ingreso, tecnología y empleo: análisis del sector industrial en el Ecuador, Perú y Venezuela. Santiago de Chile: Instituto Latinoamericano de Planificación Económico y Social, 1975. 177 p.; bibl. (Cuadernos del Instituto Latinoamericano de Planificación Económica y Social; no. 23)

Separate studies of Peru, Ecuador, Venezuela. Central hypothesis tested: redistributions of income to the poor causes shifts of industrial employment to more traditional and labor-intensive production—a "virtuous circle." Note date. Methodology and data of interest.

2955 ———. Tecnología para el sector informal urbano. Santiago de Chile: Programa Regional del Empleo para América Latina y el Caribe, 1978. 15 leaves; bibl. (Documentos ocasional—PREALC; 4)

Notes prevalence of subutilized urban labor and the existence of an informal industrial sector. Outlines this sector's technological needs, efficiency, and means of improving the acquisition of the desired technology.

2956 Torres Adrián, Mario. Los recursos humanos y la desigualdad social en la dinámica demográfica de América Latina (UNAH/RCE, 1:1, sept. 1979, p. 5–31, tables)

Relates population and development. The former is more than a problem of growth; the latter more than a problem of population.

2957 Trubek, David M. Unequal protection: thoughts on legal services, social welfare, and income distribution in Latin America (Texas International Law Journal [University of Texas, School of Law, Austin] 13:2, Spring 1978, p. 243–262)

Improved delivery systems for legal representation could increase equality in the distribution of income in Latin America. Analyzes types of cases in which this might be done, current impediments, and offers some suggestions.

United Nations. Agency for International Development. Directorio de recursos para el desarrollo. See *HLAS 42:170.*

2958 ———. Comisión Económica para América Latina (CEPAL). Estudio económico de América Latina, 1978. v. 1. México: 1979. 636 p. (E/CEPAL/G.1103. 8 nov. 1979)

Vol. 1 consists of four short essays: 1) introduction, 2) growth, 3) external sector; and 4) inflation (p. 1–36) and then country reviews (Argentina, Jamaica). A third part (presumably appearing in vol. 2 of this preliminary and mimeo version) deals with the internationalization of Latin American and the world economies. A rich source of data.

2959 ———. Economic and Social Council. Report of the Latin American conference on human settlements (CEPAL/R, 28 Feb. 1980, p. 1–35)

Summary and resolutions of 1979 ECLA conference. Was a regional response and an effort to participate in the UN Habitat: Centre for Human Settlements.

2960 ———. ———. Report of the Second Regional Conference on the Integration of Women into the Economic and Social Development of Latin America: Macuto, Venezuela, 12–16 Nov. 1979 (CEPAL/R, 26 Feb. 1980, p. 1–49)

Summary and resolution of 1979 Venezuela conference. List of documents prepared for the conference will also be of interest.

2961 ———. ———. Report of the seminar on styles of development and environment in Latin America (CEPAL/R, 4 Jan. 1980, p. 1–77, bibl.)

Report of very interesting seminar. Contains a summary report and commission reports: styles of development and the environment, agriculture and forestry modernization, industrialization and energy, planning. Bibliography of documents presented.

———. **Economic Commission for Latin America.** Series históricas del crecimiento de América Latina. See *HLAS 42:1949.*

2962 ———. ———. Library. Bibliografía sobre pobreza. Santiago de Chile: CEPAL, 1978. 141 p.; indexes.

Prepared as part of an interinstitutional project on "critical poverty" from sources found in six libraries in Santiago. The majority of entries seem to be from English-language journals.

2963 United States. Department of Agriculture. Economics, Statistics, and Cooperatives Service. Western hemisphere agricultural situation: review of 1979 and outlook for 1980. Washington: 1980. 49 p.; tables (Supplement No. 5 to WAS-21)

Excellent source (annual) for information on western hemisphere agriculture. There is a one-page summary, but most (p. 1–34) of the text is descriptive material by country, including Canada but not the US. Includes hard-to-get data on agricultural production and trade (p. 35–49).

2964 Vaitsos, Constantino V. Comercialización de tecnología, inversión extranjera y la decisión 24 de la Comisión del Acuerdo de Cartagena (BCV/REL, 11:43, 1975, p. 185–217, tables)

Concentrates on those aspects of Decisión 24 related to the importation of technology. Three subtopics: characteristics of the technology market, empirical studies of Andean technology imports, policies incorporated in Decisión 24.

2965 ———. Intercountry income distribution and transnational enterprises. Oxford: Clarendon Press, 1974. 198 p.; bibl.; index.

Careful, analytic effort to assess some MNC effects. Develops methodology and some empirical results. Deals with Andean Pact countries.

2966 Valdés, Alberto. Liberalización del comercio en países desarrollados y sus beneficios potenciales a los países pobres: el caso de agricultura (UCC/CE, 16:49, dic. 1979, p. 323–341, bibl.)

Examines gains (magnitude and distribution) to LDC's of 50 percent reduction in tariffs on 80 commodities by OECD countries.

2967 Vega-Centeno, Máximo and Néride Sotomarino. Niveles y estructuras de precios en el Grupo Andino: realidad e implicaciones (PUCP/E, 2:3, junio 1979, p. 147–184, tables)

One of the ECIEL studies on comparative prices and purchasing power parity. Heavy methodological emphasis. Prices compared are from 1973 and 1968 sampling.

2968 Vilas, Carlos. El populismo como estrategia de acumulación: América Latina (UNAH/RCE, 1:1, sept. 1979, p. 54–87)

Traces development of European "populism," and compares to Latin America—Vargas, Perón. Analyzes role and impediments in Latin America.

2969 Vusković, Pedro. Latin America and the changing world economy (NACLA, 14:1, Jan./Feb. 1980, p. 2–15, ill., plate)

Discusses implications for Latin America of what he sees are two major recent developments: internationalization of production and a new notion of "interdependence" on part of developed, capitalistic nations.

2970 White, Eduardo and Jaime Campos. Elementos para el estudio de las empresas conjuntas latinoamericanas (INTAL/IL, 1:3, junio 1976, p. 11–30, table)

Analyses of joint national ownership in Latin America as an emerging phenomenon—why it occurs and its probable effects.

2971 Wionczek, Miguel S. Ciencia y tecnología y relaciones de dependencia en América Latina (BCV/REL, 13:54, 1978, p. 89–105)

Discusses a strategy for technological independence or autonomy against an historical sketch of the technological development of the region.

2972 ———. El contexto más amplio de los arreglos bilaterales para la explotación de los recursos entre los países desarrollados y los menos desarrollados (FCE/TE, 45[4]: 180, oct./dic. 1978, p. 879–902)

Asks four questions and explores the answers to raw materials, access, world objectives, expanding world economy.

2973 ———. Crecimiento y estrategias comerciales de Latinoamérica durante el período de postguerra (BCV/REL, 11:42, 1975, p. 85–134, tables)

Review of trade of Latin American countries and the nature of the shift from import substitution policies to export promotion policies and the establishment of priorities therefore.

2974 ———. Problemas centrales de la planificación científica y tecnológica en los países en desarrollo (AI/I, 4:3, May/June 1979, p. 132–139)

Discusses a framework for developing a domestic and autonomous scientific and technological capacity. In general, this should be underplanned rather than overplanned.

2975 ———. Problemática política y económica de las transnacionales en el contexto latinoamericano (BCV/REL, 12:47, 1977, p. 77–100)

Discusses primarily 10 principles elaborated in Latin America for the behavior of foreign firms. Gives attention to the differences in points of view in the U.S. and in recipient nations.

2976 World Bank Research Program: abstracts of current studies. Washington, D.C.: World Bank, 1978. 126 p.

Valuable listing of 85 research projects being undertaken by the Bank at printing. They fall in eight categories: 1) Development Policy; 2) International Finance and Trade; 3) Agriculture and Rural Development; 4) Industry; 5) Transportation; 6) Public Utilities; 7) Urbanization and Regional Development; 8) Population and Human Resources.

2977 Záitsev, Nikolái. Las empresas multinacionales latinoamericanas (URSS/AL, 1, 1980, p. 60–78)

Discusses the Latin American multinational as one means of economic collaboration, provisions for it by the Andean Group, SELA, etc.

MEXICO

CLARK W. REYNOLDS, *Professor of Economics, Food Research Institute, Stanford University*

A WELCOME CHANGE NOTED IN THE ECONOMIC literature on Mexico reviewed for this *Handbook* is its increasingly technical, policy-oriented nature. Several factors are responsible for this new trend, namely, the expanding role of formal economic analysis in planning and policy-making in Mexico, and the proliferation of Mexican institutions dedicated to social science research. In addition, Mexico's second great petroleum boom is attracting the attention of foreign scholars to this "middle-income developing country," although the quality of the oil-related research has yet to match its quantity. Given this "rediscovery" of Mexico, the present section cannot possibly be comprehensive. Furthermore, the reader should keep in mind that much of the literature on Mexico is interdisciplinary, and is therefore annotated in other sections of the *Handbook* (e.g., Sociology, History, Government and Politics, International Relations, etc.). Mexico, as much as any Latin American country, illustrates the impossibility of engaging in meaningful economic analysis without also attending to political, historical, and institutional factors. This fact, which represents a challenge to scholarship, necessarily creates problems for bibliographical guides organized along narrow disciplinary lines. The pending automation of the *Handbook* and its subject index should alleviate this problem and facilitate interdisciplinary research at the Library of Congress.

The "conjunctural" character of Mexican economic literature is evident from a glance at the titles of the works listed below. For example, there is an abundance of articles that deal with the 1976 crisis from a variety of perspectives. Most regard this period as a watershed in Mexican economic development (items **2996–2997, 3027–3030, 3038** and **3044**) and consider its inflation, fiscal and balance-of-payments deficits, capital flight, and peso devaluation as symptomatic of more fundamental problems of economic growth and distribution. Even the more conventional technical literature on the recent cyclical behavior of the economy relates peso overvaluation and fiscal imbalance to the political pressures that forced recent administrations to delay tax reform and assign a lower priority to distributional policies, forestalling the day of reckoning (item **3023**). At the same time, the emerging new technical literature which analyzes the economic process in direct distributional terms has led to a closer relationship between national economic policy and the government's social goals (item **3034**).

Political microeconomic studies such as those by Fagen and Nau on Mexican gas relations with the US (item **2994**), and by Bennett and Sharpe on international policy implications of automobile industry development in Mexico (item **2984**) clearly demonstrate the complexity introduced by the changing "rules of the game" into bilateral bargaining between the two nations and between the private and public sectors in each. These studies, along with the forthcoming works by Steve Sanderson on cattle, and David Mares on export crops such as tomatoes, suggest that adjustment to market forces is influenced by intricate political and institutional pressures that are themselves conditioned by previous and predicted economic behavior. Such studies constitute harbingers of the need to place economic analysis (both micro and macro) within a broader analytical framework in which the axiomatic structure of economic modelling will be responsive to social and political pressures, and viceversa. This trend—already evident in the works on

Brazil, by Bacha, Baer, Cardoso, etc., and in the "Plantation School" of the Caribbean—represents the start of a new era in Mexico. What is still lacking in the country, however, is for these new micro studies to influence macroeconomic analysis.

US-Mexican interdependence is another area that has attracted scholarly attention recently, as trade, migration, investment, and technology transfer between the two countries expand at an unprecedented rate. Most of the works to date on this "North-South" problem have appeared in the US (items **3015**, **3029** and **3040–3041**), although Mexican institutions such as CIDE, CEESTEM, Colegio de México, CENIET, and UNAM are also publishing more on the subject. The US literature generated by the recent hydrocarbon boom (item **3045**) generally has not contained much technical economic analysis. This situation is beginning to change, however, as a more sophisticated monographic literature emerges from energy research centers at US universities and in Mexico (item **3031**). Most researchers writing on the political and social consequences of oil are non-economists. One hopes that this issue will stimulate more interdisciplinary collaboration in the future. Migration is another field of emerging scholarship that is studied primarily by non-economists— for that reason, the best research on the subject, works by CENIET, Jorge Bustamante, Wayne Cornelius and others, are not annotated in this section, e.g., see item **2079**, *HLAS 41:9609*, etc.—notwithstanding the important economic factors for undocumented workers involved in the supply and demand in the migration process.

Interest in the agricultural sector, which had declined over the past decade, is once again on the rise. Several micro studies examine the reasons for differential supply response, both by type of holding and by crop, as well as the social consequences for the rural population of poor productivity. The fact that Mexico has turned increasingly to the US and other foreign markets for basic grains has sparked debate about international agricultural imperialism. This dependence on foreign markets led to the questioning of government policies that favor the use of cash crop exports from irrigated regions to finance urban growth. The literature abounds with criticism of these policies and of their adverse impact on rainfed agriculture. Such criticism was partly responsible for the current Mexican Agricultural System (SAM), which uses petroleum revenues to increase production and productivity of basic grains and to augment commodity subsidies to the rural and urban poor. Description and analysis of the SAM program and of the earlier integrated rural development program (PIDER) are beginning to appear, although much of the information on the two programs is contained in restricted documents of the Federal Government and the World Bank (a major supporter of PIDER). Due to this inaccessibility of the relevant data, there is very little solidly based macroeconomic analysis of contemporary Mexican rural development available in either Spanish or English (except for a few major works, such as the one by Hewitt de Alcántara).

This review does not cover the numerous sectoral plans or the *Plan Global* of the current administration, central as they are to the policy process, and to the unpublished professional research that often anticipates published analysis. For reasons of space, works on economic history are relegated to the history section. Also excluded are technical papers, available in limited circulation from the research programs of Banco de Mexico, CENIET, CIDE, CESTEM, Colegio de Mexico, UNAM, and US-Mexican study programs at such US universities and research centers as the University of California (San Diego, Los Angeles, Berkeley, and other campuses), Harvard, University of Wisconsin, University of Texas (Austin and El Paso), San

Diego University, Stanford University, and the Overseas Development Council in Washington, D.C. Current economic affairs in Mexico are described in *Comercio Exterior* (Banco Nacional de Comercio Exterior), *Review of the Economic Situation of Mexico* (Banco Nacional de México), and other periodicals. *El Trimestre Económico* and *Economía y Demografía* remain the two major professional journals of economics in Mexico, but political economic issues are being covered with greater frequency in *Foro Internacional*, the CIDE periodicals, and the publications of UNAM, as well as its new journal *Economía Mexicana* (item **2992**).

Finally, one should note those areas that call for additional research. They include employment, wages and labor organization, service and related tertiary sectors as major absorbers of urban underemployed, wealth distribution (as opposed to income distribution) and its relationship to social and institutional structure, entrepreneurship and the investment process in the private sector, technology transfer, non-tariff trade barriers and the formulation of commercial policy, and the political economy of Mexico's changing international power relations. Also requiring further analysis is the role of programs such as INFONAVIT (housing program), CONASUPO (food distribution system of the Federal Government), IMSS (social security system). The political economy of interdependence between the US and Mexico is another key area only beginning to be explored.

2978 Acedo Valenzuela, Carlos. El campo mexicano: mito y realidad (ISTMO, 109, marzo/abril 1977, p. 5–18, plates)

Argues that Mexican agriculture should be organized on the basis of market induced productivity. Attacks the use of Mexican agricultural policy as an instrument for rural welfare.

2979 Alvarez Soberanis, Jaime. The need to establish a policy restricting the use of foreign trademarks in developing countries: the case of Mexico (WD, 7:7, July 1979, p. 713–726, tables)

Shows some of the negative effects of the use of foreign trademarks in the developing countries, taking into account the Mexican experience. Contains statistical data concerning the licensing agreement registered in the Mexican Registry for Transfer of Technology, which demonstrate the importance of the use of foreign trademarks, its cost, and the type of restrictive business clauses that such agreements include.

2980 Angelier, Jean-Pierre. Le secteur de l'énergie au Mexique (FDD/NED [Problèmes d'Amérique Latine, 52] 4523/4524, 20 juillet 1979, p. 106–145, map, tables)

Traces the development of the petroleum industry and its effect on national development policy from the "Porfiriato" to the present.

2981 Appendini, Kirsten A. de and **Vania Almeida Salles.** Algunas consideraciones sobre los precios de garantía y la crisis de producción de los alimentos básicos (CM/FI, 19:3, enero/marzo 1979, p. 402–429)

General discussion of trends in Mexican agricultural policy in the 1970s, especially with respect to the policy of subsidizing agricultural inputs and imposing a price ceiling on agricultural output. Concludes that as a result of cost pressures and price ceilings, modern capitalist enterprises have shifted from the production of basic grains to the export market.

2982 Ayala, José *et al.* La crisis económica: evolución y perspectivas (*in* México, hoy. Por José Ayala *et al.* Coordinado por Pablo González Casanova y Enrique Florescano. México: Siglo Veintiuno Editores, 1979, p. 19–96, tables)

This first section of *México, hoy* on "The Economic Crisis" offers an extensive international, empirical, and structural analysis of the causes of the 1976 economic crisis by some of Mexico's leading social critics. First section places the Mexican situation in the perspective of the development of the international economic system after World War II. Second section deals with growing government deficits and international indebtedness. Final section attempts to explain the disequilibrium in the economy as a result of concentration of wealth and power leading to a narrow economic base and underutilized capacity. An important work.

2983 Barkin, David and **Gustavo Esteva.** Inflación y democracia: el caso de México. México: Siglo Veintiuno Editores, 1979. 167 p.; bibl. (Economía y demografía)

Examines the issue of inflation in Mexico in terms of political clashes among competing socioeconomic groups. Provides a structuralist critique of both monetarist and Keynesian approaches by emphasizing the distributional causes and consequences of inflation.

2984 Bennett, Douglas C. and **Kenneth E. Sharpe.** Agenda setting and bargaining power: the Mexican state versus transnational automobile corporations (PUCIS/WP, 32:1, Oct. 1979, p. 57–89, table)

This article uses a case study of the development of automobile production within Mexico to analyze international power relationships. Authors identify points of conflict between the companies and the Mexican state and then describe mobilization of power resources and the strategies by either side to obtain their goals as a process that is more flexible than conventional bargaining power approaches might suggest. For political scientist's comment, see item **7168.**

2985 ——— and ———. La industria automotriz mexicana y la política económica de la promoción de exportaciones: algunos problemas del control estatal de las empresas transnacionales (FCE/TE, 46[3]:183, julio/sept. 1979, p. 715–746, tables)

Examines the debate about import substitution versus export promotion, and persuasively argues for caution against too enthusiastic endorsement of export promotion given industry-specific export capabilities and international market demand. Using the example of the Mexican auto industry, authors argue that export promotion would be carried out by foreign firms and have unexpected political and distribution effects.

2986 ——— and ———. The state as banker and entrepreneur: the last-resort char-

acter of the Mexican state's economic intervention, 1917–76 (CUNY/CP, 12:2, Jan. 1980, p. 165–189)

Presents the Mexican state as ultimate guarantor of national economic sovereignty and promoter of capitalist development through its entrepreneurial and financial policy since the Revolution. This approach is traced historically from the ideology of ruling groups in the north that evolved from the Revolution given the practical problems of late-industrializing market economies.

2987 Burke, Robert V. Green Revolution technologies and farm class in Mexico (UC/EDCC, 28:1, Oct. 1979, p. 135–154, tables)

Analyzes the sources of segmentation caused by "green revolution" technologies. Cobb-Douglas production function estimation drawn from census data shows significantly different coefficients for small and large private holdings and ejidos with fertilizer productivity being higher on more modern farms as a result of higher level capital intensity and quality. Institutional constraints which lead to economies of scale result from lack of capital and equipment rental to smaller farms, which would in turn raise the productivity of agricultural inputs. Although the debate about inaccessibility of "green revolution" technology to small farmers has been well covered, this article gives clear empirical evidence and focuses specifically on the Mexican case.

Capetillo, Ileana Cid. Apuntes para el análisis de un proceso internacional: la crisis del petróleo y el caso de México. See item **7171.**

2988 Coatsworth, John H. Indispensable railroads in a backward economy: the case of Mexico (EHA/J, 39:4, Dec. 1979, p. 939–960, tables)

This article, based on a Ph.D. dissertation at the University of Wisconsin, assesses the impact of railroads on 19th-century Mexico. Social savings are estimated to determine direct benefits. While passenger savings are said to have been negligible (owing to an assumed low social opportunity cost of time), freight savings and indirect benefits are said to have accounted for over half of the increase in productivity of the economy prior to 1910. Author argues that railroad savings went mainly to stimulate the export sector, while unlike the US experience backward linkages to Mexican industry failed to develop, foreign exchange costs were high, and the effects of land tenure, social structure and institutions were negative. Study concludes that railroads promoted both growth and underdevelopment in Mexico.

2989 Coloquio sobre Economía Mexicana, *México, 1979.* Memoria: panorama y perspectivas de la economía mexicana. Edited by Nora Lustig. México: El Colegio de México, 1980. 609 p.

Useful collection of essays from a 1979 colloquium on the Mexican economy including survey works on contemporary agriculture, industrial concentration, international trade, and finance by some of Mexico's leading policymakers, academics, and critics.

Congreso Nacional de Economistas (Mexico), *2d, Mexico? 1977.* Financiamiento e inversión para el desarrollo: memoria. See item **2789.**

2990 Cordera, Rolando and **Carlos Tello.** Mexico: la disputa por la nación; perspectivas y opciones del desarrollo. México: Siglo Veintiuno Editores, 1981. 149 p.

Non-technical political statement of two alternative orientations for the Mexican state in the coming decades. The "Nationalist Project" envisages populist interventionism with capitalist, mixed-enterprise economy serving broad social goals. It is contrasted favorably with a hypothetical "neo-Liberal project" based on free market principles and favoring national and foreign capitalist development which, authors argue, has dominated Mexican policies since World War II and which they fear may continue, not withstanding goals of the Constitution of 1917. Further empirical analysis and counterfactual modeling along political-economic lines might help to sharpen this important debate.

2991 Díaz Serrano, Jorge. Informe de Petróleos Mexicanos, 1979 (BNCE/CE, 30:4, abril 1980, p. 386–394, tables)

Summary of the 1979 annual report given by the Director of Pemex with useful information about the Mexican oil industry reflecting official views of issues such as the Ixtoc oil spill and Mexican natural gas.

2992 *Economía Mexicana: Análisis y Perspectivas.* Centro de Investigación y Docencia Económicas (CIDE). No. 1, 1979– . México.

New annual publication by one of Mexico's most important research institutions. Edited by Jaime Ros. Issue No. 1 offers applied economic papers on key issues such as the 1976 devaluation, inflation, the balance of payments deficit, and alternative future development models.

2993 Egüez Solís, José and **Antonio Martín del Campo.** Las fuentes del crecimiento de la producción agrícola en la parte central de El Bajío: 1954–1974 (AGRO, 32, 1978, p. 79–92, bibl., tables)

Estimates production functions for irrigated and non-irrigated private and ejido farms of El Bajío to estimate the sources of productivity growth in the four agricultural units. Authors find that the productivity growth in non-irrigated units is due mainly to increased inputs, while productivity increases in irrigated units is due mainly to technological change and unexplained factors.

2994 Fagen, Richard R. and **Henry R. Nau.** Mexican gas: the northern connection (*in* Capitalism and the State in the U.S.-Latin American relations. Edited by Richard R. Fagen. Contributors, Cynthia Arnson et al. Stanford, California: Stanford University Press, 1979, p. 382–427, tables)

Important article is a detailed analysis of the motivation and strategies of the national actors who negotiated the ill-fated *Gasoducto* Plan to export natural gas from the oil fields in southern Mexico to the US natural gas transmission system. Authors set out the different alliances formed between interests in Mexico and the US, disaggregating from the usual US vs. Mexico approach to analyzing interdependent power relationships. This case study demonstrates the degree of political communication inherent in even the most obviously economic transactions.

2995 Fairchild, Loretta G. Performance and technology of U.S. and national firms in Mexico (*in* Technological progress in Latin America: the prospects for overcoming dependency [see item **2949**] p. 129–148, tables)

Survey compares profitability and technological innovativeness of Mexican domestic firms and multinational subsidiaries in the city of Monterrey, Mexico, and finds that although both types of firms were competitive as far as profits, exports, and growth, the Mexican national firms were found to rely more heavily on domestic technology and labor intensive techniques.

2996 FitzGerald, E.V.K. Stabilisation policy in Mexico: the fiscal deficit and macroeconomic equilibrium, 1960–77 (in Inflation and stabilisation in Latin America [see item **2840**] p. 23–64)

Argues that Mexico's "stabilizing development" in the 1960s depended less on rigid control of money and aggregate demand than on favorable conditions in domestic and foreign markets plus acceptance by the banking system of the Central Bank's diversion of their deposit base to fund modest fiscal deficits. It analyzes the crises of Echeverría's "shared development" program in the 1970s in the terms of the contention that internal and external shocks to the economy required larger government deficits and eventual devaluation (in an earlier paper he suggests that fiscal reform might have been an alternative path). Imaginative exploration of the political and institutional issues underlying stabilization policy in Mexico.

2997 ———. The state and capital accumulation in Mexico (JLAS, 10:2, Nov. 1978, p. 263–282)

This is an excellent, well-documented review of contradictions which result from the Mexican state's perceived role as motivator of growth and protector of national sovereignty. FitzGerald traces the changing financial role of the state from the beginning of the "Mexican miracle" to the present and argues that it cannot continue to subsidize and restructure the development process without more fiscal resources and associated autonomy to promulgate structural change. Continued use of the financial system to support the growing fiscal deficit diverts funds from private investment and leads to foreign debt and domestic inflation.

2998 Garza, Gustavo and Martha Schteingart. Mexico City: the emerging megalopolis (in Metropolitan Latin America: the challenge and the response [see *HLAS 41:9016*] p. 51–85, bibl., maps, tables)

Discusses the historical and economic reasons for the primacy of Mexico City in the urban development of Mexico. The authors' analysis of the failure of national policies for decentralization and the continuing economic and political advantages of the capital city lead them to conclude that Mexico

City will continue to grow at a very rapid rate through the rest of the century.

Gatti, Luis María and Graciela Alcalá. Los trabajadores asalariados de la zona citrícola de Nuevo León. See item **8090**.

George, Pierre. La relève mexicaine. See item **5112**.

2999 Gollás, Manuel. Tamaño y crecimiento de las empresas industriales de México (FCE/TE, 46[2]:182, abril/junio 1979, p. 285–310)

Uses a number of measures to indicate a positive relationship between concentration of industry and firm size in Mexico.

3000 González Casanova, Pablo. México: el desarrollo más probable (in México, hoy. Por José Ayala et al. Coordinado por Pablo González Casanova and Enrique Florescano. México: Siglo Veintinuo Editores, 1979, p. 405–419)

Closing work of the collection, *Mexico, hoy*, which projects a continuation of the development of monopoly capital and liberal economic policy arguing that it can only be countered by a coalition of the democratic left. Of particular interest is the author's analysis of the composition of the Mexican left, their different goals and possible areas of cooperation.

3001 Green, Rosario. Cambios recientes en la política de deuda externa del gobierno mexicano (CM/FI, 19:3, enero/marzo 1979, p. 453–470)

Descriptive treatment of IMF austerity program and growing dependence of Mexico on US private bank lending, despite increased petroleum revenues.

3002 Hernández Herrera, Javier *et al.* El minifundio en la agricultura mexicana (AGRO, 26, 1976, p. 3–20, bibl., tables)

Estimates the relative efficiency of farms of different size, land tenure and quality from data obtained from the states of Querétaro and Michoacán. Smaller farms are shown to be more productive per hectare, but are not more efficient with respect to total inputs, especially labor. Irrigation increased the productivity of all inputs.

3003 Hernández Laos, Enrique. Economías externas y el proceso de concentración regional de la industria en México (FCE/TE, 47[1]:185, enero/marzo 1980, p. 119–158, map, tables)

Finds that external economies are important to industrial location in Mexico. High levels of industrial efficiency are shown to be correlated with regions of greatest industrialization. Author projects continued concentration of industry due to external economies, despite rising social costs and congestion in these areas.

3004 ——— and **Jorge Córdova Cháves.** Estructura de la distribución del ingreso en México (BNCE/CE, 29:5, mayo 1979, p. 505–520, tables)

Reports and analyzes data on distribution of income and consumption gathered from the 1977 National Survey of Household Incomes and Expenditure carried out by the Secretary of Planning and Budget. Authors compare data on the distribution of income by decile (1950–77) to show the regressive distributional effects of modern Mexican development on the lower income groups. Numerous charts display results of the 1977 survey and relate national and regional distribution of income with sources of income, expenditure, and household characteristics.

3005 **Hewitt de Alcantara, Cynthia.** Modernizing Mexican agriculture: socio-economic implications of technological change, 1940–1970. Geneva: United Nations Research Institute for Social Development, 1976. 350 p.; bibl.; graph (UNRISD studies on the "green revolution"; no. 11)

One of the most complete works on recent development of Mexican agriculture and agricultural policy containing much data on output, value, and distribution of crop production. Work is critical of Mexico's neglect of its agricultural sector through early 1970s and deals with social consequences of this neglect with hard facts and analysis. Especially useful are the extensive bibliography and footnotes.

3006 **James, Dilmus D.** Mexico's recent science and technology planning (SAGE/JIAS, 22:2, May 1980, p. 163–193)

Reviews the role of science and technology policy on growth and employment and suggests means of improving the effectiveness of the Mexican program for promoting scientific and technological independence and advancement.

3007 **Jenkins, Rhys.** The export performance of multinational corporations in Mexican industry (JDS, 15:3, April 1979, p. 89–107, tables)

Confronts the debate about the contribution of multinational firms to national development in middle income developing countries. Finds that multinationals and their subsidiaries in Mexico do not necessarily have a higher import content or send a higher share of exports to regional markets than do national firms. Author's balanced treatment of the subject and ample bibliography make this an important contribution to the debate.

3008 **King, Jonathan.** Interstate migration in Mexico (UC/EDCC, 27:1, Oct. 1978, p. 83–101, tables)

Migration data from the 1970 Mexican census is used to test for determinants of migration. Roughly paralleling the results of other studies, the author finds urbanization, unemployment, literacy, population density, and an established migrant stream to be positively correlated with out-migration.

3009 **Kraft, Joseph.** A reporter at-large: the Mexican oil puzzle (The New Yorker [New York] Oct. 15, 1979, p. 152–181, ill.)

An essay on the implications of Mexico's newfound oil wealth. Interviews head of Pemex, Jorge Díaz-Serrano; Carlos Tello, Minister of Planning and Budget at the beginning of the López-Portillo sexenio; and Pedro Ojeda Paullada, current Minister of Labor. These give the reader an inside view of the political and philosophical conflicts revolving around Mexico's petroleum and its national development plans. Article's second half reconstructs the debate between the US and Mexico about the sale of natural gas. For political scientist's comment, see item **7188**.

3010 **Lebas-Tubiana, Laurence** and **François Lerin.** Intentions et contraintes de la politique agricole mexicaine, 1976–1980 (FDD/NED [Problèmes d'Amérique Latine, 57] 4579/4580, 28 juillet 1980, p. 127–202, tables)

Reviews Mexican agricultural policy in the latter half of the 1980s with respect to the constraints imposed on prior agricultural policy, current inflation, rising domestic demand, and fluctuation in the international market. Authors examine President López Portillo's shift from land redistribution to technical and financial assistance under the Sistema Alimentario Mexicano (SAM).

3011 López Cervantes, Ernesto and **Antonio Martín del Campo.** Especificidades del modelo de capital financiero en el desarrollo agrícola del distrito de Riego Num. 10, en Sinaloa: consideraciones de sus impactos por tipo de unidad (AGRO, 32, 1978, p. 29–50, bibl., tables)

Examines the effect of credit offered by the different types of financial institutions on agricultural production in Sinaloa. Private and international credit favors larger, more capitalized farms, while smaller farms and ejidos are dependent on non-private sources of credit which carry with them a significant amount of influence over the farmer's decision-making process.

3012 Lustig, Nora. Distribución del ingreso, estructura del consumo y características del crecimiento industrial (BNCE/CE, 29:5, mayo 1979, p. 535–543, bibl., tables)

This article, based on the author's Ph.D. dissertation at the University of California, Berkeley, tests the hypothesis that the concentration of income stimulates production in the durable goods industries in the modern sector of the economy. Results support this and conversely that redistributing income to the poorer consumers in general would stimulate demand for basic goods produced by the traditional sector. The model applies estimated income elasticities by commodity groups to assumed changes in the relative income by deciles. It also shows that increments of income redistributed to poorer households in the major urban areas are likely to be spent on modern sector durable goods and not on basic consumption goods due to the demonstration effect. Since the durable goods sector is import intensive, income concentration results in increased trade dependence.

————— and **Teresa Rendon.** Female employment, occupational status, and socioeconomic characteristics of the family in Mexico. See item **8108**.

3013 Mancke, Richard B. Mexican oil and natural gas: political, strategic, and economic implications. New York: Praeger, 1979. 163 p.; bibl.

Useful geological, historical and institutional overview of petroleum in Mexico setting the context for current debates on petroleum policy and Mexican development.

3014 Márquez, Viviane B. de. Organizational structure and innovativeness in the pulp and paper industry of Mexico (in Technological progress in Latin America: the prospects for overcoming dependency [see item **2949**] p. 149–172, tables)

Review of the debate about the developmental role of transnational firms in Mexico. Author surveyed firms in the pulp and paper industry and found that transnational firms tended to be more innovative than their national counterparts.

El Medio ambiente en México y América Latina. See item **8111**.

México. Comisión Nacional de los Salarios Mínimos. Estados Unidos Mexicanos, zonas económicas para la fijación de los salarios mínimos 1977: división municipal por zonas económicas actualizado a diciembre de 1977. See item **5525**.

3015 Mexico and the United States: energy, trade, investment, tourism, immigration. Edited by Robert H. McBride. Englewood Cliffs, New Jersey: Prentice-Hall, 1981. 197 p.

Collection of essays presented at the 1980 binational meeting of the American Assembly on Mexican-American Relations. An uneven representation of viewpoints on major issues in US-Mexican relations such as energy, trade, and immigration. Weakest areas are the work on trade, the absence of major commentaries on macroeconomic behavior, structural interdependence of the two economies, or future dimensions of policy. For political scientist's comment, see item **7192**.

3016 Mexico's foreign trade in 1978 and future prospects (BNCE/CE, 25:4, April 1979, p. 127–133, tables)

General review prepared by the Banco Nacional de Comercio Exterior analyzes changes in the 1978 International Trade and Balance of Payments Accounts, and reviews the goals of the Global Development Plan and the National Industrial Development Plan with respect to Mexico's projected development path.

3017 Mixon, J. Wilson; Barry W. Poulson; and **Myles S. Wallace.** The political economy of devaluation in Mexico: some new evidence (IAMEA, 33:2, Autumn 1979, p. 71–85, bibl.)

Authors test the strength of the impact of changes in the US and Mexican money supply on Mexican income and price levels and find that the US presence is significant, but not dominant. The analysis suggests that floating the Mexican peso would give the government more domestic monetary control and autonomy from the US economy.

3018 Montañez, Carlos and **Horacio Aburto.** Maíz, política institucional y crisis agrícola. Portada, Alberto Diez. México: Centro de Investigaciones del Desarrollo Rural: Editorial Nueva Imagen, 1979. 249 p.; bibl.

Examines the public sector role in recent Mexican agricultural development performance and relates guaranteed price policy to the current crisis in terms of contemporary agricultural development policy modeling.

3019 Murphy, Ewell E., Jr. Decision 24, Mexicanization, and the New International Economic Order: the anatomy of disincentive (Texas International Law Journal [University of Texas, School of Law, Austin] 13 : 2, Spring 1978, p. 289–308)

Reviews the nationalistic trends of the Latin American countries of the 1970s as manifested by Decision 24 of the Andean Common Market Commission, the Mexicanization Laws of the Echeverría administration, and the UN Resolution on the New International Economic Order. These developments are cast as impediments to further technology transfer and long-term investments by the industrialized countries in Latin America. Author also sees these events as barriers to communication and sociocultural exchange.

3020 Nguyen, D.T. and **M.L. Martínez Saldivar.** The effects of land reform on agricultural production, employment and income distribution: a statistical study of Mexican states, 1959–1969 (RES/EJ, 355 : 89, Sept. 1979, p. 624–635, tables)

Compares the productivity of the land reform sector (ejidos) to the private sector using state data for 1959 and 1969 to attempt to prove the economic viability of land reform. Authors find that total factor productivity is greater in the land reform sector than in the private sector. This result, however, is reversed when ejidal labor is costed at market

wage rates and not as its social opportunity cost. Evidence presented by authors corroborates results from other studies in different countries that the high productivity of peasant agriculture is due to intensive use of family labor. A good coverage of the state of the art on peasant productivity.

3021 Opciones de política económica en México después de la devaluación. Gerardo M. Bueno, coordinador; Saúl Trejo et al.; prólogo, David Ibarra. México: Editorial Tecnos, 1977. 245 p.; bibl.; 5 graphs.

Written after the devaluation crisis of 1976, important essays offer balanced, informed political-economic perspectives by several of Mexico's top professions on the lessons learned as background for future policy. Still timely and relevant to post-petroleum Mexico.

3022 Ortiz Martínez, Guillermo. Acumulación de capital y crecimiento económico: perspectivas financieras en México. México: Centro de Estudios Monetarios Latinoamericanos, 1979. 176 p.; ill.

Based on a Stanford Ph.D. dissertation, the book develops an innovative general equilibrium model of the Mexican economy and financial system to analyze the effects of the international economy on the domestic accumulation of capital. The model serves to measure the capacity of the government to control the economy through monetary and fiscal policy. Ortiz gives a dynamic view of the development of the Mexican financial system along with a rigorous discussion of current issues which is the best to date.

3023 —— and **L. Solís.** Financial structure and exchange rate experience Mexico: 1954–1977 (JDE, 6, 1979, p. 515–548)

Excellent discussion of Mexican experience regarding exchange rate policy and development of the financial market since the 1950s. The unique structure of Mexican financial institutions is described, updating the earlier work by Brothers and Solís, with emphasis on how they have conditioned possibilities for monetary and exchange rate policy intervention. Calls for "correct alignment of the exchange rate" against dangers of overvaluation from oil revenues. Important article.

3024 Pinto Aguilar, Gerardo J. and **Antonio Martín del Campo.** Adopción y diferencia de tecnología agrícola en dos regiones de economía campesina en México (AGRO, 32, 1978, p. 51–70, bibl., tables)

Compares the structure and technology of peasant farmers in the two regions of Puebla and Tlaxcala. Comparing irrigated with rainfed agriculture in the two areas, authors find greater difference in technology and structure between the two regions than between the two types of agriculture.

3025 Programa Regional del Empleo para América Latina y el Caribe (PREALC). Opciones de políticas y creación de empleo productivo en México. Santiago de Chile: Oficina Internacional del Trabajo, Programa Regional del Empleo para América Latina y el Caribe, 1978. 84 p. (Investigaciones sobre empleo; 9)

This solid study models the effects of policies for the adoption of labor-using technologies, the promotion of labor-intensive exports, and the redistribution of income on employment growth and income distribution in Mexico. Authors find that such policies and especially promotion of labor-using technologies would jointly favor employment, income distribution, and economic growth.

3026 Revel-Mouroz, Jean. La politique économique mexicaine, 1976–1980 (FDD/NED [Problèmes d'Amérique Latine, 57] 4579/4580, 28 juillet 1980, p. 73–126, tables)

Review of Mexican economic policy during the first four years of President López Portillo's administration by a leading French scholar.

3027 Reynolds, Clark W. Growth, distribution and structural change in Mexico: recent trends and future prospects (in The Future of Mexico. Edited by Lawrence E. Koslow. Tempe: Center for Latin American Studies, Arizona State University, 1977, p. 19–33, bibl., tables)

This article discusses some of the changes in the political and economic structure of Mexico in the third quarter of this century and suggests new areas for research under the topics of employment and sectoral transformation in economic development.

3028 ———. Labor market projections for the United States and Mexico and current migration controversies (Food Research Institute Studies [Stanford University, Stanford, Calif.] 17:2, 1979, p. 121–155)

Projects the growth of the labor force and labor demand in Mexico and the US and finds that unless Mexico grows at a rate of at least seven percent a year through the year 2000, and unless the US is willing to sacrifice potential economic growth, Mexico will be a labor surplus and the US will be a labor deficit country though the year 2000. Stresses potential complementarity of two way migration under bilateral control.

3029 ———. The structure of the economic relationship (in Mexico-United States relations [see item **7193**] p. 125–135)

Examines the implications of "full exchange" (free trade, investment, migration, and technology transfer) between the US and Mexico in terms of consequences for the level and distribution of wages and patterns of economic growth. Hypothesizes that convergence of real wage levels for unskilled labor might benefit Mexican workers but would be resisted by US labor. Restructuring of both economies along the lines of dynamic comparative advantage would require far more than "full exchange" and the latter would almost certainly lead to severe political and social instability in both countries. Calls for a joint approach to development short of "full exchange" reflecting the different nature and goals of the two economies and societies notwithstanding their great potential complementarity.

3030 ———. Why Mexico's stabilizing development was actually destabilizing: with some implications for the future (WD, 6:7/8, July/August 1978, p. 1005–1018, bibl., tables)

Apparent successes of Mexican economy during the 1960s caused deferral of difficult solutions to fiscal, financial, and social problems. Echeverría's administration policies heightened the instability of the economy by avoiding tax reforms, postponing peso devaluation and by failing to implement measures to reduce social inequalities. For Spanish version of this article, see HLAS 41:2970.

3031 Rizzo, Sócrates and **Leopoldo Solís.** Opciones de política económica, 1979–1982. México: Bank of Mexico, 1979. 1 v. (Research document series; 12)

Treats the growth perspectives for Mexico under the new circumstances of oil and gas generated revenues relieving the foreign exchange constraint. Focuses on current constraints on growth represented by skilled labor, capacity to formulate and implement investment projects, and the need to restrain the monetization of petroleum surplus revenues for purposes of monetary and financial stability. Calls for absorption of growth in labor force and replacement of hydrocarbon reserves with expansion in productive capacity of the economy, requiring a growth rate of 7.9 percent in 1980, 1981, and 1982, the entire surplus of oil exports directed to investment (rather than other current expenditure programs). Provides an analytical framework to justify a rapid growth strategy though one consistent with rising savings and investment rates and reasonable rates of inflation. This optimistic projection contains indicators of output, inputs, and data on the gross and net projected returns from hydrocarbons of great value to real and financial analysis of contemporary Mexico.

3032 Sepúlveda Amor, Bernardo. México: perspectivas de un país de desarrollo intermedio sobre la economía internacional (*in* Simposio sobre México hoy, 1978. Visión del México contemporáneo. México: El Colegio de México, 1979, p. 57–68)
    This is a general overview of the middle-income countries' development prospects in the next decade. Author singles out the problems of increased protectionism by the developed countries, and the increase in middle income countries' needs to borrow from private capital markets at market rates as the most important barriers to growth.

3033 ——— and Antonio Chumacero. La inversión extranjera en México. México: Fondo de Cultura Económica, 1977. 262 p.; tables (Sección de Obras de Economía)
    Reasonably balanced, well-documented report on the composition of, especially US, direct foreign investment in Mexico. The Statistical Appendix collects data on direct foreign investment and multinationals from a variety of sources.

3034 Serra Puche, Jaime. Políticas fiscales en México: un enfoque de equilibrio general. México: El Colegio de México, 1981. 161 p.
    Based on Yale Ph.D. dissertation, this is a skillful general equilibrium analysis of the impact of the value added tax (IVA) on income distribution and resource allocation.

The study is pathbreaking and innovative in its Mexican application. It makes use of a comparative static model relying on 1968 data under alternative assumptions about the fiscal and balance of payments deficits. The model permits disaggregation of the effects of alternative fiscal policies on "poor," "low income," and "rich households" with very suggestive results notwithstanding the restrictive assumptions on which the essentially static model is based.

3035 Serrón, Luis A. Scarcity, exploitation, and poverty: Malthus and Marx in Mexico. With foreword by Irving M. Zeitlin. Norman: University of Oklahoma Press, 1980. 279 p.; bibl.; index.
    Author uses Mexico as a case study to show that the social and political aspects of wealth distribution are more relevant to the explanation of poverty than are simple concepts of overpopulation.

3036 Solís M., Leopoldo. External equilibrium and fuller uses of productive resources in Mexico (*in* The Future of Mexico. Edited by Lawrence E. Koslow. Tempe: Center for Latin American Studies, Arizona State University, 1977, p. 35–40)
    Nontechnical survey of trends in the Mexican economy in the first half of the 1970s by one of Mexico's leading economists. Deals with stop-go issues of balance of payments stability versus growth.

3037 Tancer, Robert S. Regulating foreign investment in the seventies: the Mexican approach (*in* The Future of Mexico. Edited by Lawrence E. Koslow. Tempe: Center for Latin American Studies, Arizona State University, 1977, p. 191–222, table)
    Discussion of the history and development of Mexican legal control on foreign investment, especially examining the laws of nationality and ownership and the institutions created to enforce these laws. For political scientist's comment, see item **7217.**

3038 Tello, Carlos. La política económica en México, 1970–1976. México: Siglo Veintiuno Editores, 1980. 1 v.
    Analysis of the political and economic situation in Mexico, pointing to restrictionist monetary policy, concentration of wealth, and world recession as major causes of the 1976 economic crisis. His analysis, which takes a sanguine view of the growing inter-

ventionist role of the Mexican state, provides a framework for projection into the future, suggesting further problems if major structural reforms are not undertaken to deconcentrate wealth and broaden the basis of tax and expenditure policy. These themes are developed still further in his joint work with Rolando Cordera, the best-selling *México: la disputa por la nación* (México: Siglo Veintiuno Editores, 1981) in which both authors call for a "proyecto nacional" in which labor would play a more prominent political and economic role and more nationalist policies would be pursued with respect to external dimensions of the economy.

3039 United States. Department of Housing and Urban Development. Office of International Affairs. Housing and urban development planning in Mexico: a bibliography. Washington, D.C.: The Office, 1980. 54 p.

Comprehensive annotated bibliography of Mexican and American documents on Mexican urban development.

3040 U.S.-Mexico economic relations. Edited by Barry W. Poulson and T. Noel Osborn; introduction by Hugo B. Margáin. Boulder, Colorado: Westview Press, 1979. 442 p.; bibl.; ill.; index (Westview special studies in international economics and business)

Collection of papers on particular aspects of US-Mexican economic relations ranging from theoretical studies to applied econometric models. Tending to appear out of historical or political-economic context, are interesting academic exercises.

3041 Views across the border: the United States and Mexico. Edited with an introduction by Stanley R. Ross. Albuquerque: University of New Mexico Press, 1978. 456 p.; bibl.; index.

Useful essays by both Mexican and American authors presented at a 1975 conference on border relations. Objective is to provide an integrated view of the region. Despite assymetry of topics chosen and dirth of economic analysis, one of best works on the issue of interdependence to date. For political scientist's comment, see *HLAS 41:8647.*

3042 Villar, Samuel I. del. El manejo y la recuperación de la economía mexicana en crisis: 1976–1978 (CM/FI, 14:4, abril/junio 1979, p. 540–575)

Valuable contribution to the literature on the 1976 Mexican crisis. It is a description of events more than an analysis of structural causes or conflicts, and derives its material from primary official sources. A good historical monograph to complement the more analytical work on the crisis of 1976.

3043 Villarreal, René. El desequilibrio externo en la industrialización de México, 1929–1975: un enfoque estructuralista. México: Fondo de Cultura Económica, 1976. 280 p.; bibl.; ill.

Drawn from author's Yale Ph.D. dissertation, this is a very well-documented analysis of Mexico's industrialization policy, especially the stages of import substitution, from the beginning of the Great Depression to the present. Calls for a new era of export-promoting industrialization with greater efficiency of domestic industry, eliminating a number of import barriers, which he argues will also favor the expansion or producer goods manufacturing for both domestic and foreign markets. His approach to a more flexible exchange rate policy is particularly relevant during the post-petroleum discovery era of an overvalued peso.

3044 Whitehead, Laurence. La política económica del sexenio de Echeverría: ¿qué salió mal y por qué? (CM/FI, 20: 3, enero/marzo 1980, p. 484–513)

In-depth political economic analysis of the maneuvers of the Echeverría administration in its attempts to resolve the conflicts resulting from 15 years of "stabilizing development." Focuses on still-unresolved issues of reconciling stability, growth, and distribution.

3045 Williams, Edward J. Mexican hydrocarbon export policy: ambition and reality (*in* International energy policy. Edited by Robert M. Lawrence and Martin O. Heisler. Lexington, Mass.: Lexington Books, 1980, p. 65–79 [Policy Studies Organization series])

This article surveys the changes in Mexico's petroleum policy through the 1970s reflecting a broader resource base. The latter allows Mexico greater degrees of freedom to debate the goals of rapid industrial growth versus national self-reliance.

3046 ———. The rebirth of the Mexican petroleum industry: developmental directions and policy implications. Lexington, Mass.: Lexington Books, 1979. 218 p.; bibl.; ill.; index.

Surveys Mexico's domestic and international petroleum policies since the 1976 discoveries. Final chapter discusses the potential of Mexico's petroleum wealth for dealing with long-standing structural problems facing the Mexican society. For political scientist's comment, see item **7223**.

3047 Young, Frank W.; Donald K. Freebairn and Reuben Snipper. The structural context of rural poverty in Mexico: a cross-state comparison (UC/EDCC, 27:4, July 1979, p. 669–686, tables)

Techniques of factor analysis employed to identify the following structural indicators of poverty in Mexico: urban differentiation, commercial agricultural development, extensive ranching, rigid institutions, and the subsistence/market town complex.

CENTRAL AMERICA, PANAMA AND THE CARIBBEAN
(except Cuba and Puerto Rico)

MANUEL J. CARVAJAL, *Associate Professor of Economics, Florida International University and Nova University*

ALTHOUGH THE SURFACE AREA of this region totals only about one million square kilometers (i.e., approximately the size of the states of Texas and New Mexico combined), the three dozen or so countries comprising it present an intractable case in economic development because of their geographic, historic, and cultural diversity. The socioeconomic problems of these countries are partly due to their relatively small size and to their failure to make substantial progress toward fuller integration, as economic and political independence become increasingly more difficult to reconcile with marginally viable production and marketing structures. It is not surprising, therefore, that a great deal of the literature annotated below concerns the integration experience (items **3049–3052, 3056, 3061, 3070, 3080, 3170** and **3175**).

The two major integration movements in the region are the Central American Common Market (CACM) and the Caribbean Community (CARICOM). CACM, established formally in 1960, has withstood with various degrees of success numerous crises arising out of petty jealousy, misconceived national pride, and perceived inequalities in the distribution of benefits and costs among member nations. In addition, natural disasters (item **3155**) and political instability (item **3075**) have slowed its much-needed restructuring. Nevertheless, the governments of the five Central American republics seem to share a genuine commitment to attaining total social and economic integration, as evidenced by the declarations and accords of the economic affairs ministers in Guatemala (Jan. 1979) and the planning and foreign relations ministers in Costa Rica (Jan. and March 1980, respectively).

CARICOM is composed by 12 British Commonwealth territories: five independent countries (Barbados, Grenada, Guyana, Jamaica, and Trinidad and Tobago); five associated states (Antigua, Dominica, St. Kitts-Nevis, St. Lucia, and St. Vincent); and two colonies (Belize and Montserrat). They possess a common heritage and language but their similarities do not extend much further, ranging in population from 13,000 in Montserrat to over 2 million in Jamaica, in density from 3.8 persons per square kilometer in Guyana to 616.4 in Barbados, and in per capita income from $440 in Grenada to $1,600 in Trinidad and Tobago. There are also significant differences in patterns of economic activity and resource endowment: while Barbados, Belize, and the seven Eastern Caribbean Islands (the latter eight are commonly referred to as the less developed countries, or LDCs) depend heavily upon agricultural exports and tourism, raw and processed minerals (alumina, bauxite, and petroleum) are much more important in the economies of Guyana, Jamaica, and Trinidad and Tobago. Furthermore, because of their small size and high production costs, Barbados and the LDCs have relied on guaranteed markets provided by the other three countries, which have achieved a greater degree of independent decision-making due to their more diversified resource base. Although this situation has repeatedly strained relations among members of CARICOM, and endangered its integrity, there seems to be a consensus in the community that integration is the only viable way of coping with limited markets, economic fragmentation, and overdependence on extraregional trade.

An important focus of the integration literature is the role of foreign investment (items 3062, 3172, 3182, 3184 and 3192). The indigenous attitude takes the form of an approach-avoidance conflict—approach toward generation of employment and contribution to growth; avoidance of its connotations of political and economic imperialism. Both foreign and domestic investors are intimidated by the region's political instability, and research and other aspects of the development effort are hampered by ideological polarization and fear of reprisal.

Another major topic in recent publications is poverty (items 3071, 3073, 3089, 3096, 3117 and 3145), especially in rural areas (items 3054, 3081, 3090, 3111, 3160 and 3187) and the small-farm sector (items 3064–3065, 3102, 3107, 3118, 3162, 3164, 3167, 3183, 3189 and 3200). Economists have finally begun to realize that poverty is conditioned not only by economic factors, but by noneconomic elements such as education, health and nutrition (items 3114, 3119, 3147 and 3156), housing (items 3131, 3143 and 3197), morbidity and mortality (item 3121), transportation (item 3079), family planning, and migration (items 3125, 3134 and 3136). Even more important is the implicit acceptance of these variables as endogenous and their automatic inclusion in any serious economic model. Although a significant portion of the literature on poverty—especially that prepared by domestic scholars—is descriptive and institutionally-oriented (items 3080, 3094, 3098, 3100, 3137, 3148–3149, 3163 and 3188), the influence of young foreign-trained economists and of international researchers is apparent in recent empirical studies, some of which utilize rather sophisticated methodologies (items 3072, 3074, 3103–3104, 3113, 3123, 3146 and 3168).

Interesting enough, the public and international organization sectors continue to generate some of the most scientifically rigorous studies. The academic community should not lose sight of the fact that, ultimately, it behooves these organizations to cope with the cruel resource allocation realities and cannot afford the luxury of building models which, albeit theoretically elegant and methodologically flawless, may rest on impertinent foundations. Many ministries, autonomous and semiautonomous agencies, and other public and quasipublic institutions are rising to this challenge beyond all expectations (items 3076, 3092, 3099, 3129–3130, 3140–3141 and 3177). Regional organizations such as the *Secretaría Permanente del Tratado General de Integración Económica Centroamericana* (SIECA) (items 3053, 3055 and 3059), the CARICOM Secretariat, and the Caribbean Development Bank (CDB) (items 3167 and 3168) also are actively investigating issues affecting the welfare of their members. Finally, international institutions such as the US

Agency for International Development (USAID) (items **3063, 3069, 3085–3086, 3113–3121, 3127, 3131, 3133, 3138–3139, 3143, 3153–3154, 3156, 3159, 3161, 3165–3166, 3169, 3171, 3178, 3187, 3189, 3195–3197** and **3199–3200**), Canadian International Development Agency (CIDA); Inter-American Development Bank (IDB) (items **3066–3067, 3088** and **3194**); World Bank (IBRD) (items **3079, 3122, 3158** and **3198**); *Programa Regional del Empleo para América Latina y el Caribe* (PREALC) (items **3097, 3106, 3126** and **3151**); Inter-American Institute of Agricultural Sciences (IICA) (items **3095** and **3181**); Organization of American States (OAS) (items **3132, 3152, 3185** and **3186**); International Labor Office (ILO) (item **3101**); and various United Nations organizations, e.g., FAO (items **3078, 3157** and **3194**); ECLA (items **3112** and **3155**) and UNDP (item **3157**) are either producing or financing numerous in-depth studies on project feasibility, economic sector assessment, agricultural and industrial development planning, etc. Joint research seems to be gaining popularity, as evidenced by several multiagency publications (items **3091, 3124** and **3128**).

The present section has been organized in a new, and presumably one hopes more meaningful, fashion. The first grouping, containing 16 regional publications, is followed by an extensive category consisting of 60 entries related to individual Central American countries (Costa Rica, El Salvador, Guatemala, Honduras, and Nicaragua). Panama, with 11 entries, forms a separate category. Although geographically Panama is the continuation of Central America, there are significant differences between it and the other five nations with respect to ethnic composition, historical development, socioeconomic structures, and other fundamental aspects. The island of Hispaniola, shared by the Dominican Republic and Haiti, constitutes the fourth grouping, which contains 27 items. The fifth and last category encompasses the British Caribbean, and includes all the CARICOM members, including noninsular Belize and Guyana; it contains 40 publications.

The items included in the section are a cross-sectional representation of the literature published on the region during 1977–80. In addition to meeting the *HLAS*'s permanent-value criterion, they either have contributed or have the potential of contributing to the formulation of public policies. This potential for changing and, hopefully, improving the system is, in my opinion, the best measure of their value.

GENERAL

3048 Agricultural development and economic progress in the Caribbean basin. E.T. York et al. Tallahassee: Presidential Mission on Agricultural Development in Central America and the Caribbean, 1980. 137 p.

Report on Mission appointed by President Carter notes that many difficulties experienced by Caribbean countries are related to unfavorable balances of trade and that the solution of these difficulties depends on the revitalization of agriculture. Concludes that the great potential of Caribbean countries for expanding their agricultural sectors, as well as for increasing their productivity and economic viability, will be contingent on an explicit US commitment to this endeavor.

3049 Argueta Figueroa, Hugo. La supranacionalidad en la comunidad económica y social centroamericana (CSUCA/ESC, 12, feb. 1979, p. 63–93)

Exposition of constraints that impede greater economic and social integration among Central American countries.

3050 Cáceres, Luis R. Economic integration and export instability in Central America: a portfolio model (JDS, 15 : 3, April 1979, p. 141–153)

Paper investigates effects of economic integration on the export sectors of Central American countries by using a portfolio model to ascertain whether or not trade flows are a stabilizing force. Evidence shows that for Costa Rica and Nicaragua interregional trade has smoothed fluctuations caused by their traditional exports.

3051 ———. Integración económica e inflación en Centroamérica: un modelo espacial (FCE/TE, 45:4, oct./dic. 1978, p. 811–839)

Develops an econometric model in order to test hypothesis that inflation in Central America is fostered by common market structures.

3052 Deans, Robert H. Commodity and geographical concentration in the CACM countries and implications for economic development (UPR/CS, 16:3/4, Oct. 1976/Jan. 1977, p. 171–205)

Paper concludes that Central American countries are forced to specialize in the production and export of more limited range of goods than larger countries. This specialization gives rise to a high degree of commodity and geographical concentration of exports and a low degree of commodity concentration and a high degree of geographical concentration of imports. CACM countries are not significant contributors to the trade of their trading partners even though the major share of their trade is with a limited number of countries. CACM members continue to rely heavily on their exports as a basis for expanding their foreign exchange earnings.

3053 Gabuardi Lacayo, Carlos. El desarrollo agrícola y la integración económica centroamericana. Guatemala: Secretaría Permanente del Tratado General de Integración Económica Centroamericana, 1977. 139 p.

Study of the role of the agricultural sector in Central American integration efforts. It focuses on agricultural credit, institutional aspects, agricultural policies, employment, income distribution, nutrition, mobility of human resources, and agroecologic considerations.

3054 Hoffmann, Helga and **Angel J. Sciara.** Diagnóstico de las estadísticas y bibliografía sobre el empleo rural en Centroamérica y Panamá. Santiago: Programa Regional del Empleo para América Latina y el Caribe, 1979. 1 v.

Summary and evaluation of statistical and bibliographical data and studies on rural employment, female participation in the agricultural labor force, policies toward agricultural diversification, land distribution patterns, application of technology, and migration flows.

3055 Leiva, Gustavo. El dualismo económico del sector agrícola centroamericano: ensayo de descripción, origen histórico y principales opciones de políticas en torno al empleo. Guatemala: Secretaría Permanente del Tratado General de Integración Económica Centroamericana, 1979. 85 p.

Historical analysis of the evolution of Central American production and agrarian structures. It contends that the basic needs of the rural population can be satisfied only through long-term developmental programs that generate rural employment.

3056 Lizano Fait, Eduardo. Cooperación monetaria e integración económica en el Mercado Común Centroamericano. México: Centro de Estudios Monetarios Latinoamericanos, 1978. 235 p.; bibl.

Major research questions raised are: 1) whether or not economic integration has resulted in greater monetary cooperation among member countries; 2) the extent to which member countries are willing to give up some of their monetary autonomy; and 3) whether or not the future of the integration movement depends upon even greater monetary cooperation.

3057 Moncarz, Raúl. Moneda y banca en América Central. Tegucigalpa, Honduras: Escuela Bancaria Superior Centroaméricana, 1978. 291 p.; bibl.

Comprehensive analysis of the role and behavior of money and banking in Central America, with emphasis on financial development, money markets, liquidity, central banking, inflation, and monetary policy.

3058 Ohiorhenuan, John F. Dependence and non-capitalist development in the Caribbean: historical necessity and degrees of freedom (SS, 43:4, Winter 1979/1980, p. 386–408)

Attempts to broaden the theory of noncapitalist development—a recent contribution of Soviet bloc scholars on development strategy—by examining the interplay of ideas and material circumstances in the Caribbean. Argues that the decolonization process was accompanied by a broad alliance of progressive forces under the leadership of the national petite bourgeoisie. The concentration of capital in foreign hands and the weakness of the working classes constituted additional factors in the emergence of a coalition of all national groups against foreign capital.

3059 Pomareda, Carlos. Política agrícola, comercio exterior y los problemas del empleo rural en Centroamérica. Guatemala: Secretaría Permanente del Tratado General de Integración Económica Centroamericana, 1979. 50 p.

Study contends that Central American agriculture is characterized by a dual structure—a commercial export subsector existing alongside traditional minifundia devoted to staples. Land tenure patterns contribute to rural unemployment, low income levels, and rural-to-urban migration. Analysis is based on a mathematical programming model.

3060 Real, Blas and **Mario Lungo.** El problema regional en Centro América (Economía Política [Facultad de Ciencias Económicas, Universidad Autónoma de Honduras, Tegucigalpa] 16, julio 1978/marzo 1979, p. 53–80)

Article suggests that regional development should be analyzed within a social-division-of-labor framework and not be limited to the study of spatial effects of the technical division of labor.

3061 Shaw, Royce Q. Central America: regional integration and national political development. Boulder, Colo.: Westview Press, 1978. 242 p.; bibl. (A Westview replica edition)

Study of domestic politics and the role political leadership plays in the integration movement is based on the premise that the key to understanding failure of the integration programs lies not in advanced economic or regional integration theory, but in the domestic politics of the member states. Author analyzes major events and processes comprising the history of the integration movement and examines roles and goals of major actors. Also challenges hypothesis that external penetration of the common market by the US was a major cause of its ultimate failure.

3062 Task Force on Private Sector Activities. Measures to promote the role of the private sector in Caribbean development.

Washington, D.C.: Caribbean Group for Cooperation in Economic Development, 1980. 46 p.

Report which identifies major obstacles and facilities for private activities and recommends measures for stimulating private sector development.

3063 United States. Agency for International Development. Secondary mortgage market development. Washington, D.C.: 1979. 82 p.; appendix (ROCAP project paper—CA)

Purpose of this project is to establish a viable secondary mortgage market program in the Central American Bank for Economic Integration (CABEI), capable of and dedicated to supporting housing finance institutions and housing projects for the poor in Central America. The funds will be invested by CABEI through the purchase of mortgages and mortgage-backed securities from national housing finance institutions such as savings and loan associations, housing banks, cooperatives, and housing trust funds.

CENTRAL AMERICA

3064 Alvarez, José and **Chris O. Andrew.** Actividades de producción y distribución de granos básicos en fincas pequeñas de Guatemala (Estudios Sociales [Instituto de Ciencias Político-Sociales, Universidad Rafael Landívar, Guatemala] 14, oct. 1979, p. 1–15)

Describes basic grain production and distribution patterns in 1,548 small farms located in five different regions. Includes analysis of input utilization and output markets.

3065 An analysis of project feasibility and potential impact of credit and technical assistance to small scale rural enterprises in Guatemala. Samuel Daines; Raymond Manhoff; Mack McLendon; and William Roach. Washington, D.C.: Agency for International Development, 1978. 130 p.; appendix; bibl.

Offers thorough analysis of the impact of credit and technical assistance on 45,000 target-group families earning their livelihood from small-scale rural enterprises. Provides profile of the target group (income and employment); a benefit-cost analysis; an evaluation methodology; and an examination of credit policies, practices, and institutions.

3066 Banco Interamericano de Desarrollo; Banco Internacional de Reconstrucción y Fomento; and Agencia para el Desarrollo Internacional. Informe general sobre el desarrollo agropecuario y rural de Costa Rica. Washington, D.C.: 1977. 88 p.

Inquiry into Costa Rica's economic evolution, including agricultural exports, price structure, fiscal policy, public investment, agrarian structure and land distribution, rural employment and occupational structure, income distribution, productivity trends and use of technology, planning and administration, and infrastructure. Study pays special attention to policy-related issues and identification of programming alternatives.

3067 ———; ———; and ———. Informe general sobre el desarrollo agropecuario y rural de Guatemala. Guatemala: 1977. 3 v.; appendixes.

Three-volume report recommends strategies, policies, and programs for increasing agricultural production and raising standards of living. Vol. 1 contains the report itself and a summary; vols. 2/3 are appendixes.

3068 Bolaños Zamora, Rodrigo. Inflación en Costa Rica, 1953–1977: una interpretación. Heredia, Costa Rica: Instituto de Estudios Latinoamericanos, Universidad Nacional, 1979. 31 p.; appendix; bibl. (Instituto de Estudios Latinoamericanos; no. 7)

Attempt to identify economic variables which contribute significantly to inflationary pressures.

Boletín Bibliográfico. Banco Central de Nicaragua. No. 9, abril/oct. 1979– . See *HLAS* 42:97.

3069 Bufete Acosta Bonilla y Asociados. Estudio sobre la participación de la mujer en el desarrollo económico y social de Honduras. Tegucigalpa: Agencia para el Desarrollo Internacional, 1977. 195 p.; appendix; bibl.

Massive study of the country's socioeconomic structure and the contribution (both actual and potential) of women to its growth and improvement. Virtually all social and economic indicators are analyzed. Also contains a comprehensive statistical appendix.

3070 Camacho, Daniel. Notas introductorias al conocimiento de la sociedad costarricense y de los efectos de la integración centroamericana. San José: Universidad de Costa Rica, 1978. 126 p. (Avances de investigación; no. 32)

Study concludes that economic integration has increased the degree of dependence of Costa Rican industry on foreign goods and services. Also contends that the industrial sector has not been effective in reducing the unemployment rate.

3071 Carvajal, Manuel J. Bibliography of poverty and related topics in Costa Rica. Washington, D.C.: Rural Development Division, Bureau for Latin America and the Caribbean, Agency for International Development, 1979. 329 p. (Working document series Costa Rica. General working document; no. 1)

Comprehensive bibliography contains 2,056 entries covering 1960–78. Entries are classified according to 17 academic-discipline and 10 type-of-document categories. Also contains topical, institution, and geographic location indices.

3072 ——— and **David T. Geithman.** Income distribution and economic development: some intra-country evidence (Southern Economic Journal [University of North Carolina, Chapel Hill] 44:4, April 1978, p. 922–928)

Article analyzes influences of several structural elements on income inequalities in Costa Rica using 1963 Population Census data. Empirical results are summarized as follows: 1) Greater interregional variation in proxies for regional human capital stock—years of education and age—leads to greater regional wage-and-salary inequalities; 2) greater regional absorption of labor employed in agriculture leads to more equitable regional labor income distribution; 3) higher level of regional development, as measured by a higher level of wage-and-salary earnings, results in more inequality in the size distribution of labor income; 4) when regional human-capital variation and unemployment and migration differences are controlled, increases in average regional wages and salaries lead to less inequality; 5) broader participation in the social security system (one key measure of public sector's redistributive activity) decreases regional income inequality;

6) extensive migration into a region generates inequality in wage-and-salary distribution; 7) rising unemployment results in greater income inequality; and 8) regional income inequality is relatively inelastic with respect to the variables analyzed in the study, thus implying that the distribution of labor income cannot be greatly affected by a change in any single independent variable.

3073 ——; ——; and **Patrick R. Armstrong.** Pobreza en Costa Rica. San José: Dirección General de Estadística y Censos, 1977. 330 p.; bibl.; graphs.

Study of poverty in Costa Rica based on a household-level match of the 1973 Population, Housing, and Agricultural Censuses. Estimates Gini coefficients to be 0.44 for urban families, 0.43 for rural nonfarm families, and 0.66 for farm families. Also estimates poverty incidence to be 13.8 percent among urban households, 34.2 percent among rural nonfarm households, and 27.6 percent among farm households. Consists of seven chapters: 1) presents theoretical framework, focusing on conceptualization, historical perceptive, determinants (genetic potential, education, age, employment, occupation, migration, urban-rural residence, fertility, and discrimination), and criteria of poverty; 2) discusses methodology for matching three censuses; 3/6) present empirical results—Chap. 3 focuses on income, poverty, and labor; Chap. 4 deals with education (illiteracy and schooling index); 5) analyzes fertility, mortality, and internal migration; and 6) refers to housing (structural condition of the dwelling, tenancy, availability of services, and exposure to mass media); 7) contains summary, conclusions, and recommendations on priorities; short-term *versus* long-term solutions; tax policy; government expenditures; and monetary, credit, population, and urban and regional policy.

3074 **Casey Gaspar, Jeffrey.** Limón, 1880–1940: un estudio de la industria bananera en Costa Rica. Diseño de portada, Osvaldo Salas. San José: Editorial Costa Rica, 1979. 324 p.; 2 fold. leaves of plates; bibl.; ill.

In-depth study examines evolution of the banana industry in the Atlantic coast and its impact on demographic characteristics, socioeconomic conditions, and political influences.

3075 **Comité Nacional de Unidad Sindical.** Fascismo en Guatemala: un vasto plan represivo antipopular y antisindical. Guatemala: 1977. 36 p.

Document denounces extreme-right groups allegedly seeking to destroy the labor union movement, increase political repression, and assassinate leaders associated with the popular movement.

3076 **Costa Rica. Oficina de Planificación Nacional y Política Económica.** Plan Nacional de Desarrollo 1979–1982 Gregorio José Ramírez. San José: 1979. 5 v.

Five-volume publication contains the National Development Plan. Vol. 1 consists of an analysis of major socioeconomic problems and issues; vol. 2 presents the plan's objectives and policies; and vols. 3/5 focus on specific programs in areas of population, science, technology, money and banking, administrative reform, agriculture and industry, education, health and sanitation, housing, energy, transportation, and irrigation.

3077 ——. Secretaría Ejecutiva de Planificación Sectorial Agropecuaria y de Recursos Naturales Renovables. Características de la ganadería de carne y lineamientos de política. San José: 1980. 187 p.; appendix; bibl.

Comprehensive study of production, marketing, and consumption of beef. Pays special attention to land use, employment generation, prices, technology, research activities, and animal health.

3078 **Costa Rica:** asistencia técnica para la identificación de alternativas concretas para el desarrollo forestal de la zona norte. José R. Torres; Jaime Agudelo; Jon Tellun; and Mats Schartau. Roma: Organización de las Naciones Unidas para la Agricultura y la Alimentación, 1980. 39 p.

Project consists of five parts: 1) Selection of a minimum area of 100,000 hectares for forest development; 2) field study to identify availability and types of resources; 3) management for potential industrial use; 4) determination of the best way of extracting wood; and 5) identification of alternatives for industrial utilization of wood. Recommends that forest resources in the Northern Zone be developed within an integral framework.

3079 **Costa Rica:** San José Urban Transport Project. C. Madavo et al. Washington,

D.C.: World Bank, 1977. 35 p.; appendixes.

Major objective of this project is to improve travel conditions in San José, especially for users of public transport. Major components are improvement to radial routes in seven corridors; intersection and subarea improvements, dispersal schemes, pedestrian crossings, and a Central Business Traffic Signal System; equipment for road maintenance, traffic management and regulation enforcement, and for a bus inspection facility; technical assistance in the form of advisers on project management, traffic planning, public transport development, enforcement, traffic signals, and bus maintenance; and training for Ministry of Public Work and Transport's Staff in traffic engineering, bus operations and regulation, and traffic surveillance and enforcement.

3080 Dada Hirezi, Héctor. La economía de El Salvador y la integración centroamericana 1945–1960. San Salvador: UCA Editores, 1978. 107 p.; bibl. (Colección Estructuras y procesos; v. 3)

Book attempts to test hypothesis that evolution of the Central American Common Market is not merely the result of ECLA-US collision of views, but was influenced as well by the interaction of foreign interests and the interests of the domestic bourgeoisie.

3081 Daines, Samuel. Analysis of small farms and rural poverty in El Salvador. San Salvador: Agency for International Development, 1977. 100 p.; appendix.

Document focuses on land availability, distribution, tenure, use, and productivity; credit demand, access, and use; marketing and transportation systems; yield patterns; application of technology; and employment patterns in small farms and labor productivity, farm and nonfarm income, and crop profitability for the rural poor. Appendix contains numerous tables prepared by the author and Dwight Steen of USAID/El Salvador.

3082 De Franco, Mario A. and María Hurtado de Vijil. Algunos aspectos del funcionamiento socio-económico de Nicaragua (Revista del Pensamiento Centroamericano [Publicidad de Nicaragua, Managua] 159, abril/junio 1978, p. 38–104)

Economic analysis of Nicaragua in the aftermath of the 1972 earthquake. Focuses on agricultural investment, urban growth, aggregate demand, and government expenditures.

3083 El Salvador. Ministerio de Planificación y Coordinación del Desarrollo Económico y Social. Plan operativo institucional 1980. San Salvador: 1980. 4 v.

Massive, multivolume exposition of the National Development Plan. Vol. 1 summarizes goals, objectives, and basic strategies; vol. 2 addresses development of infrastructure (various forms of transport, telecommunications, mail, and energy); vol. 3 (pts. 1/2) deals with urban and regional development (housing, waste disposal systems, and public administration); and vol. 4 focuses on social development (health, education, and community development).

3084 Gómez Barrantes, Miguel and Carlos Quintana. Estimaciones del consumo de granos básicos en Costa Rica: 1976. San José: Universidad de Costa Rica, 1977. 115 p.; appendix.

In-depth study of rice, bean, and corn consumption according to a 1974 urban survey and a 1976 rural survey. Also focuses on farm consumption.

3085 Graber, Eric S. An annotated bibliography of rural development and levels of living in Guatemala. Washington, D.C.: Agency for International Development, 1979. 81 p.

Comprehensive bibliography includes publications since 1955 in the fields of economics, sociology, anthropology, political science, agriculture, nutrition, and history. Consists of 547 entries which are classified according to four subject matters: general development, social conditions, and levels of living; agriculture; rural life and organization; and small farm development, technology, and marketing.

3086 ———. Income distribution, employment and social well-being in Guatemala: a survey. Washington, D.C.: Agency for International Development, 1980. 1 v.

Summary and evaluation of both quantitative and qualitative information on income distribution, with special reference to rural development. Incorporates information on asset distribution and nonmarket goods and services. Also suggests guidelines for additional research.

3087 Guatemala. Secretaría General del Consejo Nacional de Planificación Económica. Plan nacional de desarrollo 1979/1982. Guatemala: 1978. 20 v.

Colossal work consists of 20 volumes containing description and analysis of programs and projects comprising the National Development Plan.

3088 Guzmán Fabián, Miguel. Informe socioeconómico de Costa Rica. Washington, D.C.: Banco Interamericano de Desarrollo, 1977. 75 p.; appendix.

Evaluation of the capability and performance of the Costa Rican economy, focuses on population growth, natural resources, income distribution, employment, infrastructure, public finance, prices and salaries, balance of trade, and external debt. Recommends top priority for diversification-oriented agricultural projects leading to production of export or import-substitution goods, industrial projects which utilize domestic raw materials, and infrastructure projects linked with productive employment.

3089 Herrick, Bruce and Barclay Hudson. Urban assessment of San José, Costa Rica: focus on poverty. San José: Agency for International Development, 1977. 1 v.

Urban sector analysis describes urban poverty in Costa Rica at various levels of disaggregation; suggests broad priorities for policy formulation, based on analysis of constraints bearing on improvements of poor communities; and tests usefulness of recently developed USAID Guidelines for Urban and Regional Analysis. Analyzes nature, location, and causes of poverty, and stresses different needs of people slightly below minimum income levels and those close to absolute despair. Study notes poverty in Costa Rica where poor and rich are relatively mixed together, is not defined by geographic areas. Some slums are geographically well defined but their income profiles are not as dramatically different from other urban areas as in other countries. Study stresses need for poverty intervention strategies that are more specific than broad. Authors attribute country's success in avoiding sharp differences between rich and poor to its progressive social structure and government programs. In recent decades, however, lowest two income deciles have been gaining less than the upper deciles. Study consists of 13 chapters: 1) in-

troduction; 2) summary and conclusions; 3) country sketch; 4) urban functional analysis; 5) migration; 6) poverty; 7) social analysis of the poor and community organization; 8) employment; 9) urban administration and finance; 10) housing; 11) urban policy planning and program coordination; 12) external assistance to the urban sector; and 13) urban development strategies and priorities.

3090 Honduras. Información básica sobre el area rural y la reforma agraria en Honduras. Tegucigalpa: 1979. 108 p.; bibl.

Document contains Honduras' contribution to the World Conference on Agrarian Reform and Rural Development, held in Rome under FAO auspices. Addresses availability of physical and human resources, education, employment, income distribution, agrarian reform instruments, incidence of rural poverty, health and nutrition, and productivity of small farmers.

3091 ———. Instituto Hondureño de Desarrollo Rural and Catholic Relief Services. 84 [i.e. Ochenta y cuatro] meses de Reforma Agraria del Gobierno de las Fuerzas Armadas de Honduras. Tegucigalpa: 1980. 280 p.; appendix.

Study describes the structure of the agricultural sector prior to agrarian reform, analyzes the change of structure occurring with the reform, and recommends courses of action to raise the institutional capacity of both public and private sectors.

3092 ———. Ministerio de Recursos Naturales. Consejo Superior de Planificación Económica y Agencia para el Desarrollo Internacional. Compilación de los estudios básicos del diagnóstico del sector agrícola. Tegucigalpa: 1978. 562 p.

Honduras' agricultural sector assessment was based on these 10 different studies: farmers' organizations and cooperatives; agricultural marketing; supply of and demand for human resources; macroeconomic analysis of the agricultural sector; prices of basic grains; agricultural credit; agricultural planning, and infrastructure.

3093 ———. ———. ———. Desarrollo y aprovechamiento de los recursos humanos. Tegucigalpa: 1979. 128 p.; appendix.

Important component of the 1979–83 National Development Plan focuses on demographic analysis, labor force characteristics, internal migration, education, health, and nutrition as forms of human-capital investment.

3094 Hurtarte, Víctor Hugo. Control del exceso de liquidez en El Salvador. San Salvador: Banco Central de Reserva de El Salvador, between 1977 and 1979. 47 p.

Inquiry into income-consumption-savings relationships and major determinants of liquidity expansions and contractions between 1973–76. Also proposes measures for absorbing excess liquidity and analyzes both their short-term and long-term consequences.

Información Documental Costarricense y Centroamericana. Serie A, No. 2, enero/junio 1980– . See *HLAS 42:144.*

3095 Instituto Interamericano de Ciencias Agrícolas, *Turrialba, Costa Rica.* La etapa de instrumentación de la ejecución del proceso de planificación agrícola en Honduras. Tegucigalpa: 1979. 68 p.

Consists of evaluation of agricultural policy implementation and analysis of major obstacles encountered. Contains a chapter with recommendations for facilitating and expediting policy implementation.

3096 Inversiones y Estudios Económicos, S. de R.L. Las condiciones de empleo e ingresos en el sector rural pobre de Honduras. Tegucigalpa: 1980. 4 v.; appendixes.

Four-volume report on employment and income conditions of the rural poor, sponsored by USAID. Vol. 1 consists of a review of the literature and data sources; vol. 2 is a quantitative analysis of labor force utilization and salaries paid by the export-oriented agricultural subsector, which includes cotton, bananas, coffee, wood, cattle, and sugar; vol. 3 focuses on the socioeconomic conditions of the rural poor; and vol. 4 deals with regional distribution of the population, employment, and income.

3097 Jarvis, Lovell and Emilio Klein. Generación de empleo y la conservación de los recursos naturales: un programa para El Salvador. Santiago: Programa Regional del Empleo para América Latina y el Caribe, 1979. 39 p.

Pt. 1 of this study analyzes the agrarian structure, forms of land tenure, employment, and seasonality. Pt. 2 focuses on deterioration of natural resources. Pt. 3 evaluates the impact of the agricultural soil conservation program on technology, employment, income, and production.

3098 Manjívar, Rafael. Crisis del desarrollismo: caso El Salvador. San José: Editorial Universitaria Centroamericana, 1977. 139 p.; bibl. (Colección Añil)

Social, political, and economic development in El Salvador are viewed as a series of attempts by the ruling oligarchy to channel the process in favor of the traditional political structure and additional foreign dependency. Fiscal, monetary, and agrarian reforms are systematically opposed by the agricultural-exporting bourgeoisie, whose members seek to maintain their status quo and attract foreign investment.

3099 Nicaragua. Ministerio de Planificación. Programa de Reactivación económica en beneficio del pueblo. Managua: 1980. 142 p.

Exposition of the Revolutionary National Development Plan for Reconstruction. After defining goals and objectives, it addresses the various programs which comprise it, including role of the State, agricultural and industrial production, foreign trade, investment, fiscal policy, income and employment, and social services.

3100 Núñez Soto, O. Somocismo: desarrollo y contradicciones del modelo capitalista agroexportador en Nicaragua 1950–1975. Managua: Universidad Nacional Autónoma de Nicaragua, 1978. 110 p.

Study contends Somoza's regime served as the catalyst for the agricultural-export capitalist model. Analyzes capital deepening in Nicaragua as an expression of world capital accumulation and views domestic production in terms of world market demands.

3101 Organización Internacional del Trabajo. Construcción de caminos rurales con tecnologías de mano de obra intensiva en Guatemala. Guatemala: 1979. 314 p.

Study examines transport in Guatemala and related aspects: infrastructure; availability of and demand for labor; socioeconomic conditions of communities that perceive the most benefits from construction of rural roads; capability of local industry to produce machinery and equipment; specifications for designing and building roads; required resources; and alternatives to labor-intensive approaches.

3102 O'Sullivan-Ryan, J. Rural development programs among marginal farmers in the western highlands of Guatemala. Stanford: Institute for Communication Research, 1978. 112 p.

Study reports effect of information and extension services on the lives of 600 subsistence highland farmers, based on data gathered from them. Contends that government information and credit programs have little impact. Empirical findings indicate that location frequently determines whether or not farmers receive extension assistance and that larger farmers receive more assistance than smaller farmers. Although formal education does not influence productivity, it determines the level of investment among larger farmers.

3103 Planning and Development Collaborative International (PADCO), **Inc.** Acciones específicas relacionadas con la elaboración del Plan Nacional de Vivienda para Honduras. Washington, D.C.: PADCO, n.d. 2 v.; appendixes.

Two-volume publication contains five specific studies in support of the National Housing Plan. Studies consist of an investigation into the nature and dimensions of the informal housing sector; a probe into land-market operations; an analysis of the financial situation in the housing sector; and two feasibility studies, one proposes establishing a land bank, the other, a social fund for housing.

3104 La Pobreza en Costa Rica: problemas metodológicos para determinar algunas de sus características. Víctor H. Céspedes et al. San José: La Academia de Centro América, 1977. 1 v.

USAID-sponsored study examines poverty incidence and determinants in Costa Rica. Also analyzes size of family, fertility, migration, land use and tenure, unemployment, illiteracy, dwelling conditions, and availability of infrastructure services.

3105 Poitevin, René. El proceso de industrialización en Guatemala. San José: Editorial Universitaria Centroamericana, 1977. 321 p.; appendix; bibl. (Colección Seis)

Historical study of Guatemalan power structures and conflicts between the indus-trial and government sectors. Includes important analysis of the Central American Common Market.

3106 Programa Regional del Empleo para América Latina y el Caribe (PREALC). La aplicación del Convenio Centroamericano de Incentivos Fiscales y sus efectos sobre el empleo y el desarrollo del sector industrial en El Salvador. Santiago de Chile: Organización Internacional del Trabajo, 1977. 126 p.; bibl.; graphs (Documento de trabajo—PREALC; 115)

In-depth analysis of the impact, in terms of employment generation, of the Central American Fiscal Incentive Agreement. Focuses on productivity, foreign exchange, and level of industrial output.

3107 Promoción y Capacitación Campesina para la Reforma Agraria (Honduras). Las empresas campesinas comunitarias en el desarrollo político, social, económico y cultural de Honduras. Instituto Nacional Agrario, PROCCARA, Promoción y Capacitación para la Reforma Agraria. Tegucigalpa, Honduras: PROCCARA, 1979. 33, 9 leaves.

Analysis of the impact of farmers' community enterprises on the country's development process, with emphasis on land tenure and distribution patterns.

Revista Centroamericana de Economía. Año 1, No. 1, sept. 1979– . See *HLAS 42:229.*

3108 Rothschuh Villanueva, Guillermo and **Eddy Matute Ruiz.** Notas sobre acumulación de capital, control natal y desarrollo del estado en Nicaragua. Managua: Universidad Centroamericana, 1977. 141 p.; bibl.

Comprehensive socioeconomic analysis of 1945–75 developments that have shaped the political system. Deals with income distribution, savings; land tenure; population density; agricultural and industrial production; unemployment; foreign investment; impact of the Common Market; and public administration.

3109 Seligson, Mitchell A. Peasants of Costa Rica and the development of agrarian capitalism. Madison: University of Wisconsin Press, 1980. 220 p.; bibl.; ill.; index.

Comprehensive study contends that the introduction of coffee radically altered the Costa Rican peasant's social status by forcing many yeoman farmers off their lands and turning them into rural proletarians on large coffee *haciendas*. Author focuses on the historical evolution of the country's peasantry and examines rural social stratification, squatting, and the government's response to land-tenure problems.

3110 Smith, Carol A. Beyond dependency theory: national and regional patterns of underdevelopment in Guatemala (AAA/AE, 5:3, agosto 1978, p. 574–617)

Author argues that Guatemala's underdevelopment cannot be traced to its long-standing export dependency but to uneven expansion of export-generated capital and its varying impact on relations of production in different parts of the economy. Evidence in support of this position consists of census data on changing patterns of urban growth and occupational characteristics of economic cores and peripheries. Author measures this evidence using explicit models of dependency structures and underdevelopment, as well as field and historical data on changing patterns of relations of production.

3111 Torres, James F. Income levels, income distribution and levels of living in rural Honduras: a summary and evaluation of quantitative and qualitative data. Washington, D.C.: Agency for International Development, 1979. 73 p.

Topics analyzed in this study include rural income and wealth distribution, nutrition, literacy and education, life expectancy, housing, physical quality of life, and income distribution policy. Also contains five case studies: San Lorenzo, the Southern Zone, Ajuterique and Lejamani, Yarumela, and Monjarás.

3112 United Nations. Economic Commission for Latin America. Nicaragua: economic repercussions of recent political events. New York: 1979. 131 p.; appendix.

Document seeks to facilitate mobilization of international technical and financial cooperation requested by the Nicaraguan Government of National Reconstruction. Provides information on recent events and the magnitude of social damage caused by the earthquake and civil war. Also describes priorities of the new government with respect to organization of the financial system, reactivation of productive capacity, generation of foreign exchange, and aims of social developments.

3113 United States. Agency for International Development. Agricultural sector assessment: El Salvador. San Salvador: 1977. 87 p.; appendix.

In-depth study shows that continued reliance on basic grains alone offers little hope for increasing the incomes of those living on small farms. Proposes that programs be designed to increase land productivity because of its scarcity and increase labor intensity because of its abundance. Other conclusions are: 1) land tenure pattern is extremely skewed which leads to land overutilization for small farms; 2) severe unemployment exists both on and off the farm, for the rural target group; 3) small farms do not utilize multiple cropping as much as they should; 4) small farmers do not emphasize planting of permanent crops or improvement of livestock operations; 5) availability of small-farm production credit is very limited; 6) there is a need for technicians and institutions to assist small farmers in several capacities; 7) data collection and management are deficient; 8) agroindustry is almost twice as labor intensive as all other industries; and 9) stimulation of agroindustrial output would directly expand the demand for small-farm products and provide new markets for labor-intensive crops.

3113a ——. ——. An assessment of the agricultural sector in Costa Rica. San José: 1977. 1 v.

USAID/Costa Rica's first agricultural assessment, prepared for meeting program analytic requirements and as a program and strategy document useful to the government of Costa Rica. Contains four sections: 1) overview of the Costa Rican economy and a macroeconomic analysis of the agricultural sector; 2) description of the target group, including resource endowment, income, market orientation, production, and socioeconomic characteristics of small farmers and the nonfarm rural poor; 3) description and analysis of overall sector and major subsectors includes overview of land and climate, land tenure, infrastructure, and public and private institutions and production and market situation for various groupings of commodity systems; and 4) specific suggestions for programs and policies to resolve constraints imply that limiting factors to development are areas which could be emphasized by USAID and the government of Costa Rica. Suggests strategy for USAID assistance in the agricultural sector, stressing rational utilization of natural resources, employment, resolution of marketing problems, agroindustry, sectoral planning, crop diversification, land settlement, and export promotion.

3114 ———. ———. Assessment of the public health sector in Honduras (1975–1985). Tegucigalpa: 1980. 147 p.

Report focuses on policy-formulation and resource-allocation issues. Analyzes health sector programs, selected health problems and diseases (diarrhea, immunopreventable diseases, malaria, tuberculosis, malnutrition, and pregnancy and birth related problems), and selected issues in program support (administration, logistics, maintenance of facilities and equipment, budgetary procedures, training of human resources, and data collection and processing).

3115 ———. ———. Costa Rica: urban employment and community improvement. Washington, D.C.: 1978. 112 p.; appendix.

Project is designed to assist the government of Costa Rica in developing a coordinated approach concerning problems of the urban poor through interagency collaboration at policy, management, and operational levels, including shared outreach programs. Goals are employment and productivity (8,000 workers productively employed); living conditions (shelter and infrastructure); and planning, policy, and program coordination.

3116 ———. ———. El Salvador Project Paper—Agrarian Reform Credit. Washington, D.C.: 1980. 46 p.; appendix.

Project designed to increase both availability of credit to the agrarian reform sector and the capacity of the Agricultural Development Bank to provide such credit. Analyzes the Salvadorian agrarian reform and the structure of the agricultural sector.

3117 ———. ———. El Salvador project paper: small producer development. Washington, D.C.: 1980. 88 p.; appendix.

Project attempts to develop and expand profitable small-scale enterprises owned and operated by the Salvadorian poor.

It is designed to increase economic opportunities and employment and lead to higher income levels by alleviating technological, market, and credit constraints through the establishment of cooperatives.

3118 ———. ———. Guatemala: small farmer marketing. Washington, D.C.: 1977. 92 p.; appendix.

Reports on project designed to use Guatemala's comparative advantage in the production of temperate climate fruits and vegetables. The project would also achieve significant small-farmer income increases and provide more job opportunities in the Western Highlands by virtue of establishing a Cooperative Marketing Association in conjunction with the cooperative movement. Project's geographical area contains 136,000 rural families who are subsistence or small-market oriented farmers. Per-capita annual income for three-fourths of the target population is under US$90. Most are of Indian origin, socially and economically excluded from the rest of society, and suffer from such easily preventable diseases as respiratory illness, diarrhea, malnutrition, and parasites.

3119 ———. ———. Health sector assessment. Guatemala: 1977. 343 p.

Comprehensive overview of the Guatemalan health sector, with emphasis on health planning, extension of services (maternal and child health, family planning, communicable disease control, and community participation), human resources, nutrition, and environmental sanitation.

3120 ———. ———. Nicaragua: a country profile. Washington, D.C.: 1977. 82 p.; bibl.

Prepared by the Office of Foreign Disaster Assistance, this publication presents an overview of the country. Includes sections on ethnic and sociocultural groups, languages, education, religions, currency exchange rate, treaties and agreements, government, disaster preparedness, population, health and nutrition, GNP, balance of payments, land use, and power and communications.

3121 ———. ———. Population strategy paper: El Salvador. San Salvador: 1978. 50 p.

Paper develops strategy for assisting the government of El Salvador in designing, implementing, and coordinating family planning as well as development policies that would have a greater impact upon fertility during 1978/82 and beyond. Specifically, the paper defines target groups among which the impact would be greatest and intensifies motivational campaigns and services not only in family planning, but also through population-related activities in the health, nutrition, education, agricultural, and industrial sectors. Also studies government commitment, community participation, role and status of women, and attitudes and roles of elites.

Who's who in Costa Rica 1979–1980. See *HLAS 42:174.*

3122 World Bank, *Washington.* Guatemala: current economic and social position and prospects. Washington, D.C.: 1977. 92 p.; appendix.

Unrestricted-circulation report which recommends that tax reforms be undertaken to strengthen the government's basic fiscal position. Topics include land and mineral resources; infrastructure; population; income distribution; social services; growth patterns; prices; the external sector; money and banking; public finance and investment; agriculture; and manufacturing.

PANAMA

3123 Borts, G.H. and J.A. Hanson. El enfoque monetario de la balanza de pagos con aplicación empírica al caso de Panamá (UCC/CE, 15:44, abril 1978, p. 91–120)

Development of an econometric model for the Panamanian balance of payments, with special reference to the effects of external shocks.

3124 Chapman, Guillermo O. Factores que afectan la demanda por mano de obra en Panamá. Panamá: Ministerio de Planificación y Política Económica [and] Agencia para el Desarrollo Internacional, 1979. 184 p.

Document which examines unemployment and underemployment in relation to other economic variables, projects labor force participation and unemployment rates into the future, identifies labor demand determinants, and proposes courses of action for creating sources of employment.

3125 Gandásegui, Marco A. Las migraciones internas en Panamá. Panamá: Ministerio de Salud, Oficina de Estudios de Población, 1978. 94 p.; bibl. (Avances de investigación; v. 1, no. 2)

Research into migration flow determinants, including sex and age. It also identifies volume and direction of migration patterns.

3126 García Huidobro, Guillermo. Panamá: instrumentos de incentivo al desarrollo industrial y su efecto en el empleo. Santiago: Programa Regional del Empleo para América Latina y el Caribe, 1980. 126 p.

Study which analyzes 1960–1975 industrial development's output, employment, and contribution to exports; evaluates the extent to which certain firms should continue to enjoy protection from foreign competition; and delineates a policy of fiscal incentives for promoting investment.

3127 Investigación y Desarrollo, S.A. Situación de la pequeña empresa en Panamá. Panamá: Agencia para el Desarrollo Internacional, 1980. 84 p.

Comprehensive study of small manufacturing, commerce, and service enterprises. It focuses on credit facilities, market size, distribution channels, determination of prices, advertising, and government's economic policy.

3128 Jordan, Gloria M. Informe sobre las actividades que realizan las organizaciones de cuatro communidades en el area metropolitana. Panamá: Ministerio de Planificación y Política Económica [and] Agencia para el Desarrollo Internacional, 1980. 72 p.; appendix.

Evaluation of institutional performance in four poor communities of the metropolitan area: El Chorrillo, Pan de Azúcar, Cativá, and Barrio Norte de Colón.

3129 Panamá. Ministerio de Desarrollo Agropecuario. Plan trienal de desarrollo agropecuario. Santiago de Veraguas: 1979. 2 v.

Formulation of the Panamanian Agricultural Development Plan in two volumes: volume 1 focuses on goals, objectives, and strategies of agricultural development, including employment, income distribution, agroindustry, agrarian reform, agricultural cooperatives, institutional development, marketing, land use and availability, factors of production, and capital accumulation; vol. 2 analyzes agricultural development instruments and policies concerning prices, credit, small farmers, training, production, and investment.

3130 ———. **Ministerio de Planificación y Política Económica.** Algunos problemas, perspectivas y lineamientos del desarrollo económico y social de Panamá. Panamá: 1980. 91 p.

Exposition of the goals, objectives, strategies, and policies of the National Development Plan with emphasis on the agricultural, industrial, and transport sectors and social development.

3131 Panama shelter sector assessment. Ted Priftis et al. Washington, D.C.: Agency for International Development, 1977. 88 p.; appendix.

Study which recommends improvements in housing finance, rent control legislation, and development of new programs to meet the country's housing needs. It emphasizes the necessity for urban planning, data collection and distribution, and review and monitoring of the environmental impact of the shelter sector.

3132 Proyecto de desarrollo integrado de la región oriental de Panamá-Darién. Estudio realizado por la Unidad Técnica del Proyecto Panamá-Darién durante el período 1975–1978, Gobierno de la República de Panamá, Programa de Desarrollo Regional. Washington: Secretaría General de la Organización de los Estados Americanos, 1978. 308 p.; ill.; portfolio (5 fold. maps)

The strategy proposed by this study revolves around the relationship among the region's human, physical, and financial resources in an attempt to complement the Pan-American Highway under construction. Sectoral investment programs and projects of productive, infrastructure, and social service nature are analyzed in the areas of agriculture and agroindustry, forestry, fishing, highways, energy, telecommunications, housing, education, and health.

3133 United States. Agency for International Development. Panama: rural growth and service centers. Washington, D.C.: 1978. 94 p.; appendix.

Project seeks to implement the government of Panama's decentralized growth

policies aimed at stimulating development in the populous Western and Central regions. It is based on an integrated approach to urban and rural development and draws heavily upon central-place and growth-pole theory. It consists of three major activities: strengthening the government's capacity to plan development centers, fostering viable productive and supporting enterprises, and providing housing and town infrastructure.

DOMINICAN REPUBLIC and HAITI

3134 Ahlers, Theodore H. Haitian rural-urban migration: a case study of four small towns. Port-au-Prince: Inter-American Institute of Agricultural Sciences, 1978. 54 p.; bibl.; ill.

Study indicates that inmigrants to small towns are likely to be of rural origin, younger and less educated than nonmigrant population in towns. They also are likely to reside in households of above-average economic level, which suggests that they come from wealthier rural households. Out-migrants, in turn, tend to move to larger urban areas and be younger but better educated than the nonmigrant population. Chain migration is important as urban contacts reduce the cost of urban information and provide support during the search for employment.

3135 Aquino González, Carlos. Fundamentos para una estrategia de desarrollo agrícola. Santo Domingo: Centro de Investigaciones Económicas y Alimenticias, Instituto Superior de Agricultura, 1978. 190 p.; bibl.

Thorough analysis of the agricultural sector focuses on production; poverty; price control; imports; marketing; credit; technology; agroindustry; human resources; availability of energy; economies of scale; and agrarian reform.

3136 Bretón, Minerva; Nelson Ramírez; and **Pablo Tactux** [sic]. La migración interna en la República Dominicana. Santo Domingo: Fondo para el Avance de las Ciencias Sociales, 1977. 311 p.; appendix; ill.

Consists of in-depth inquiry into internal migration patterns, demographic and socioeconomic differentials between migrants and nonmigrants, and determinants of various types of migration based on the 1971

National Demographic Survey. Education, occupational mobility, sex, and employment are among the variables analyzed.

3137 Charles, Gérard P. Modernisation et développementisme en Haiti (IFH/C, 144, juillet 1979, p. 5–28)

Survey of the Haitian economy, focuses on foreign aid, industrialization, credit, agriculture, and exports.

3138 Conrad, Joseph H. Agricultural sector assessment livestock subsector for Haiti. Port-au-Prince: Agency for International Development, 1978. 55 p.; appendix.

Assessment of livestock as an integral part of complex animal-crop farming systems. Five alternative strategies are suggested to the Government of Haiti: 1) determine actual role of different types of livestock; 2) improve nutrition and management by emphasizing utilization of crop residues and by-products; 3) initiate long-range genetic improvement and selection programs; 4) conduct adaptive research for identifying appropriate technology; and 5) provide technical assistance and supervised credit to producers of livestock on small farms.

3139 Defay, Jacques. Financial and human resources limitations in Haiti's agricultural sector during the period 1977–1981. Port-au-Prince: Agency for International Development, 1978. 56 leaves.

Study probes the extent to which Haiti's agricultural agencies could absorb additional external financial and technical assistance. Examines availability of local financial and human resources necessary to implement development projects underway or in the pipeline.

3140 Dominican Republic. Oficina Nacional de Planificación. Plan trienal de inversiones públicas 1980–1982. Santo Domingo: 1980. 91 p.; appendix.

Exposition of a three-year national public investment plan. After an assessment of economic conditions in the aftermath of hurricanes David and Frederick, study identifies the 1980–82 development goals and objectives and projects macroeconomic activity. Sectoral programs included in the plan are in agriculture and industry; health; education; potable water; housing; transport and communications; energy; and tourism.

3141 ———. Secretaría de Estado de Agricultura. Aspectos del empleo rural en la República Dominicana. Santo Domingo: 1977. 65 p.

Rural employment aspects analyzed in this study are labor supply and demand; family vs. hired labor; seasonality; disguised unemployment; income differentials by region, size of farm, and crop; and the impact of credit. Study's major conclusion is that since smaller farms use relatively more labor than larger farms, agrarian reform would result in greater labor absorption.

3142 ———. ———. Plan de desarrollo agropecuario 1980–1982. Santo Domingo: 1979. 232 p.

Consists of agricultural development plan based on extensive research on soil erosion; water availability and management; transfer of technology; agricultural credit; qualified human resources; institutional rigidities; nutrition and food consumption; marketing; foreign trade; employment; and agrarian reform. Also contains a detailed list and discussion of specific projects.

3143 Dominican Republic shelter sector assessment. Washington, D.C.: Office of Housing, Agency for International Development, 1980. 2 v.

Thorough analysis of the shelter sector presented in two volumes. Vol. 1 studies housing demand and potential target groups, housing institutions, main sources for financing and credit policies, and inter-institutional relationships. Includes recommendations for planning and financing housing and basic services, complementary policy measures to support improvements in housing finance mechanisms, and specific institutional responsibilities. Vol. 2 contains six annexes: 1) characteristics of internal migration; 2) household income and expenditure; 3) powers and responsibilities of principal housing-related institutions; 4) effects of varying interest rates on proposed housing solutions; 5) current economic situation and trends; and 6) statistical annex.

3144 Doré y Cabral, Carlos. Problemas de la estructura agraria dominicana. Santo Domingo: Editoriales de Taller, 1979. 122 p.; bibl. (Biblioteca Taller; 112)

Marxist analysis of the agricultural sector, consisting of six articles appearing in the journal *Impacto Socialista*. Topics covered are: land use, productivity, and tenure; latifundia and minifundia; agrarian reform; etc.

3145 Gow, David D. The rural poor in Haiti: a social analysis. Port-au-Prince: Agency for International Development, 1977. 38 leaves; bibl.

Analytical view of landholdings and tenure, income, employment, rural consumption patterns, basic services, noneconomic restraints, target population's perceptions of its problems, and the role of women.

3146 Haiti. Institut Haitien de Statistique.
Travaux macro-économiques pour le Plan Quinquennal 1976–1981. Port-au-Prince: 1977. 167 p.; appendix.

Publication consisting of three macroeconomic models of the Haitian economy. First model analyzes aggregate supply (agriculture, manufacturing, services, and imports) and aggregate demand (exports, consumption, investment, and cost of living); second model projects gross domestic product by economic sector; and third model focuses on imports and changing nature of aggregate demand.

3147 ———. Secretairerie d'Etat du Plan.
Bases et propositions pour une politique nationale d'alimentation et de nutrition. Port-au-Prince: 1980. 2 v.

In-depth two-volume analysis of nutrition and malnutrition, focusing on underproduction and underconsumption, morbidity, and the adverse effects of rapid population growth. Vol. 1 contains recommendations for improvement of the overall nutrition situation; vol. 2 deals with specific policies of various nutrition-related sectors.

3148 Herrera Miniño, Fabio. Una estrategia para el desarrollo dominicano. Santiago de los Caballeros: Universidad Católica Madre y Maestra, 1977. 131 p.; bibl.

Recommendations for an integrated development strategy encompass: changes in the agrarian structure; increase in agricultural output; development of agricultural industries; mining, and tourism; education and fiscal reforms; and greater involvement by the armed forces in the development process.

Joachim, Benoît. Aux sources d'un blocage du développement: la dependance néocoloniale d'Haïti vue à travers les problèmes de la terre du capital: XIXe.—début XXe. siécles. See *HLAS 42:2573*.

3149 ———. Les racines du sous-développement en Haiti. Port-au-Prince: Imprimerie Henri Deschamps, 1980. 257 p.; bibl.

Historical analysis of the Haitian economy and its underdevelopment. Focuses on the evolution of the nation's social structures that followed the revolution of slaves, the emergence of neocolonialism, and foreign dependence.

Lacerte, Robert K. The evolution of land and labor in the Haitian Revolution, 1791–1820. See *HLAS 42:2574*.

3150 Maguire, Bob. Bottom-up development in Haiti. Rosslyn, Va.: The Inter-American Foundation, 1979. 63 p.

Identification of underdevelopment patterns in Haiti, including land distribution, tenure, and duality.

Nicholls, David. Prosperous state of unrest: Dominican Republic under pressure. See item **5048.**

3151 Programa Regional del Empleo para América Latina y el Caribe (PREALC). Tecnología, empleo y distribución de ingresos en la industria azucarera de la República Dominicana. Organización Internacional del Trabajo, Programa Mundial del Empleo, Programa Regional del Empleo para América Latina y el Caribe. Prepared by C.D. Scott. Santiago, Chile: PREALC, 1978. 74, 18 p.; 6 leaves of plates; bibl.; ill. (Documento de trabajo—PREALC; 158)

In-depth study of the sugar industry emphasizes management-labor relations; presence of economies of scale; operation efficiency of sugarmills; employment structure; income distribution; and research-and-development efforts.

3152 Proyecto DELNO. Unidad Técnica.
Plan de acción para el desarrollo regional de la Línea Noroeste: estudio, Llevado e cabo por la Unidad Técnica del Proyecto DELNO durante el período 1973–1975, Gobierno de la República Dominicana, Programa de Desarrollo Regional. Washington: Secretaría General de la Organización de los

Estados Americanos, 1977. 487 p.; 1 leaf of plates; ill.; maps (4 fold. in pocket).

Massive report delineating development priorities, strategies, and projects in the Northwestern portion of the Dominican Republic. Contains description, analysis, and recommendations for 22 different projects.

3153 Roe, Terry L. An economic evaluation of the Haitian agricultural marketing system. St. Paul, Minn.: The Author, 1978. 202 leaves; bibl.

Consists of brief discussion of the role of marketing and a description of consumption, production and market characteristics. Includes analysis of marketing channels for domestically produced and consumed agricultural commodities, marketing channels of major export crops, and marketing of agricultural inputs. Also considers market interdependencies, storage needs, and price dimensions of market performance. Final discussion focuses on transportation, weights and measures, grades and standards, information needs, concessional food grain imports, and a description of donor programs in the marketing area.

3154 Smucker, Glenn R.; Leslie Delatour; and Yvan Pinchinat. Food aid and the problem of labor intensive rural development. Port-au-Prince: Agency for International Development, 1979. 81 p.; appendix; bibl.

Investigation identifies problems and clarifies issues commonly raised in the use of food aid, labor-intensive approaches to public works, and community development. Report deals with creation of employment, building low infrastructures of benefit to rural poor, redistribution of resources to the benefit of rural poor, provision of incentives for voluntary labor, and improvement of nutrition and provision of relief to food-deficit situations.

3155 United Nations. Comisión Económica para América Latina. Repercusiones de los huracanes David y Federico sobre la economía y las condiciones sociales de la República Dominicana. México: 1979.

Assessment of short-term and long-term damages caused by both hurricanes. Surveys infrastructure; agricultural, industrial, commerce, energy, and tourism sectors; balance of trade; and foreign assistance.

3156 United States. Agency for International Development. Dominican Republic: health sector II. Washington, D.C.: 1978. 58 p.; appendix.

Project designed to extend the Basic Health Services Program established in 1974 to an additional 100 rural communities with an estimated population of 200,000 inhabitants. Also includes upgrading 100 rural clinics and 20 small hospitals through staff training and provision of equipment. Moreover, seeks to provide potable water, sewage disposal, and health education services to approximately 160,000 inhabitants of the rural areas served by the Basic Health Services Program.

3157 Wiggin, C.B. Nutrition apliquée et développement rural: Haiti. Rome: Programme des Nations Unies pour de Développement et Organisation des Nations Unies pour l'Alimentation et l'Agriculture: 1977. 31 p.; appendix.

Final report of the activities of a joint UNDP-FAO mission. Specific recommendations concern administrative organization, extension services, irrigation, credit, erosion, and nutrition policy.

3158 World Bank, *Washington.* República Dominicana: problemas principales del desarrollo económico. Washington, D.C.: 1979. 468 p.

In-depth analysis of the performance of economic indicators such as prices; marketing; competitiveness of agricultural products; credit; public expenditures; irrigation; balance of trade; energy sources; crop diversification; wages; employment; and private investment.

3159 Zuvekas, Clarence, Jr. Agricultural development in Haiti: an assessment of sector problems, policies, and prospects under conditions of severe soil erosion. Prepared for USAID/Haiti by Clarence Zuvekas, Jr. Washington, D.C.: Agency for International Development, 1978. 355 p.; bibl.; ill.

Report proposes that USAID efforts concentrate on consolidation and improvement of existing programs and on institutional building, including a variety of short- and long-term training programs. Recommends specific projects and programs in areas of erosion control and irrigation, coffee production and marketing, and rural road construction.

3160 ——. Land tenure, income, and employment in rural Haiti: a survey. Secretarial assistance, Mary T. Carter, María E. Reed. Washington: Rural Development Division, Bureau for Latin America, Agency for International Development, 1978. 123 p.; bibl.; graphs (Working document series: Haiti; general working document 2)

In-depth analysis of the rural sector focuses on land tenure and distribution, levels of living (per-capita income estimates and regional income differentials), income distribution, labor force participation and employment, migration, and public policy.

BRITISH CARIBBEAN

3161 Assessment of the information processing needs for agricultural sector planning in Guyana. Rupert Ambrose et al. Washington, D.C.: Agency for International Development, 1979. 55 p.

Study based on in-depth interviews with officials of various public agencies attempts to determine need for an information-processing system. Also seeks to establish what manpower and other resources are needed to support said system and proposes alternative options for acquiring such resources.

Berleant-Schiller, Riva. The failure of agricultural development in post-emancipation Barbuda: a study of social and economic continuity in a West Indian community. See *HLAS 42:2553.*

3162 Bernstein, Richard H. and **Robert W. Herdt.** Towards an understanding of milpa agriculture: the Belize case (JDA, 11:3, April 1977, p. 373–392)

Recommendations on how to increase the productivity of the subsistence *milpa* sector.

3163 Best, Simon J. World inflation and the St. Lucian economy 1970–1978 (Bulletin of Eastern Caribbean Affairs [University of the West Indies, Institute of Social and Economic Research, Cave Hill, Barbados] 4:4, Sept./Oct. 1978, p. 1–22)

Article contends that world economic situation after the energy crisis disrupted almost every sector of the domestic economy. Also examines measures adopted to broaden country's economic base for its eventual independence from Great Britain.

Bolland, O. Nigel and **Assad Shoman.** Land in Belize, 1765–1871. See *HLAS 42:2374.*

3164 Brierley, John S. Fragmentation of holdings: a study of small farms in Grenada (Tropical Agriculture [University of the West Indies, Imperial College of Tropical Agriculture (and) IPC Science and Technology Press Ltd., Surrey, England] 55, April 1978, p. 135–140)

Study analyzes individual fragments with respect to their size, area cultivated, tenure, and distance from farmer's residence, with indices of vegetable and tree-crop occurrence denoting specific land-use characteristics. Author concludes that fragmentation is not justified either economically or agriculturally.

3165 Burke, B. Meredith. A discussion of needed inputs to foster employment generation in Barbados and LDC's. Washington, D.C.: Agency for International Development, 1979. 46 p.; appendix.

Report based on five weeks of interview held with civil servants, development bankers, management trainers, and business people in Barbados, Antigua, St. Lucia, and St. Kitts. Consensus of those interviewed was that the scarcity and low quality of human resources available for business training and lack of credit constitute the prime obstacle to the growth of viable business.

3166 Buvinić, Mayra; Nadia H. Youssef; and **Barbara von Elm.** Women-headed households: the ignored factor in development planning. Washington, D.C.: Agency for International Development, 1978. 113 p.; bibl.

Discussion of female household heads in the Caribbean includes case study which provides a model for the kind of data that can be drawn from national censuses. Study provides evidence of the disadvantaged position of female household heads as compared both to the female population in general and to the male household head population.

3167 Campbell, Lewis G.; A.H. Cruickshank; and **J. Bernard Yankey.** Agricultural credit in general, rural development, and the credit strategy for small farmers in the less developed countries of the English-speaking Caribbean. Bridgetown: Caribbean Development Bank, 1976. 32 p.

Study of institutional features of credit agencies which serve small farmers and of the Caribbean Development Bank. Focuses on absorption and availability of credit and the ratio of disbursement to commitment. Also provides recommendations for channeling agricultural credit toward improving rural community life.

3168 Caribbean Development Bank. Country investment plans (CIPs) for integrated agricultural development projects in the less developed member states of the Caribbean Development Bank. Bridgetown: 1977. 59 p.

Study describes economic conditions of the islands, identifies major obstacles to their development, estimates future activity under the farm improvement credit scheme, and evaluates agricultural development proposals and their respective capital requirements.

3169 Clapp and Mayne, Inc. Evaluation of industrial estate loans provided by the Caribbean Development Bank. Washington, D.C.: Agency for International Development, 1979. 86 p.

Analysis includes Antigua, Barbados, Belize, Dominica, Montserrat, St. Kitts-Nevis, and St. Lucia. Recommends that these countries develop a uniform system of economic rental rates, provide incentives for the participation of private investors in the creation of industrial facilities, strengthen and improve external promotion programs, and prepare annual rolling five-year projections of demand for factory space and its costs.

3170 DeCastro, Steven. A technological policy for petrochemicals in CARICOM (UWI/SES, 28:1, March 1979, p. 283–336)

Policies proposed by this paper include: aiding governments in their negotiation with multinational corporations and other sources of technology for petrochemical plants; formulating strategies for capital-goods import substitutions in said plants as done by the Andean Group; resolving potentially destructive competition among territories for new petrochemical plants by implementing an effective depolarization strategy based on priorities; allowing for in-

digenous design of and procurement for such plants to insure better maintenance, pooling of spare parts, and designs that are flexible and suited to the feedstocks and markets of the region.

3171 Erickson, Frank A. and Elizabeth B. Erickson. A review of agricultural marketing in Jamaica. Washington, D.C.: Agency for International Development, 1980. 82 p.; bibl.

Inquiry into major issues and problems of agricultural marketing, especially those affecting the livelihood and income of small farmers and marketers. Also reviews recent major studies of marketing in Jamaica and addresses question of whether or not marketing margins are excessive.

3172 Farrell, Trevor M. A tale of two issues: nationalization, the transfer of technology and the petroleum multinationals in Trinidad-Tobago (UWI/SES, 28:1, March 1979, p. 234–281)

Inquiry into the transfer of technology by multinational companies and the feasibility and desirability of nationalizing their local subsidiaries.

3173 Graham, Douglas H. and Compton Bourne. Agricultural credit and rural progress in Jamaica: a development dilemma. Columbus: Ohio State University, 1979. 1 v. (Economics and sociology occasional paper; no. 633)

Paper consists of five parts: 1) establishes macroeconomic context of growth and stagnation for recent years in Jamaica; 2) discusses how economic decline affected the financial sector; 3) examines growth, institutional features, and performance of agricultural credit; 4) evaluates specific credit institutions and programs; 5) reviews major agricultural credit supply strategies.

Guyanese sugar plantations in the late nineteenth century: a contemporary description from the *Argosy.* See *HLAS 42:2571.*

3174 Hope, Kempe R. Development policy in Guyana: planning, finance, and administration. Boulder, Colorado: Westview Press, 1979. 260 p.; bibl. (A Westview replica edition)

Main hypothesis is whether or not Guyana government's development policy has been used as an instrument of postwar economic growth to achieve the following:

direct development planning toward increasing productive investment levels; bring about optimal allocation of resources; utilize various planning tools to raise funds for financing growing development expenditures; and provide the necessary inputs for implementing policy goals.

3175 ———. A macro-economic overview of the trade impact of CARICOM: a study of selected Caribbean countries (IEI/EI, 32:4, nov. 1979, p. 436–447)

Inquiry into the impact of the Caribbean Community (CARICOM) on the trade of Barbados, Guyana, Jamaica, and Trinidad and Tobago. Concludes that the larger the market the greater the scope of specialization. Also notes member countries have succeeded in combining their resources to bolster both the region's overall development and that of each member country.

3176 ———. The post-war planning experience in Guyana. Tempe: Center for Latin American Studies, Arizona State University, 1978. 43 p.; bibl. (Special studies— Center for Latin American Studies, Arizona State University; no. 16)

Traces evolution of development planning in Guyana, and suggests that a reversal of the techniques from top-bottom to bottom-up might prove beneficial. [R.A. Berry]

3177 Jamaica. Ministry of Agriculture. Five year development plan 1978–83: agricultural sector plan. Kingston: 1977. 2 v.

Two-volume inquiry examines availability of resources; major obstacles to agricultural development; and present and potential courses of action for land reform, soil conservation, and irrigation and drainage projects. Also includes projections and development guidelines for coconut, coffee, cocoa, sugar, bananas, spices, fruit trees, forestry, citrus, and tobacco as well as livestock and its derivates. Pays special attention to credit, domestic food markets, certified seed production, and agricultural cooperation and research.

3178 Jameson, Kenneth P. and Frank J. Bonello. A macroeconomic assessment of the economy of Guyana. Washington, D.C.: Agency for International Development, 1978. 84 p.; appendix.

Comprehensive report which examines the country's basic structure within a historical context since Guyana's independence from Great Britain, evaluates its performance, and projects interplay of economic variables in the future.

3179 Johnson, Caswell L. Emergence of political unionism in economies of British colonial origin: the cases of Jamaica and Trinidad (AJES, 39:2, April 1980, p. 151–163)

Main hypothesis of this paper states that the political activities of trade unions played a role in the economic development process by helping to achieve first political independence and then economic growth. When political unionism became incompatible with needed acceleration of growth rates, social and economic conditions deteriorated producing a crisis. A consequence of the latter was that unions offered their support to a particular political party in exchange for union control over certain economic and social policy issues. This trade-off altered the character and direction of the labor movement.

3180 Jones-Hendrickson, S.B. The disassociation factor in revenue production: St. Kitts-Nevis-Anguilla, 1950–1973 (UWI/SES, 27:3, Sept. 1978, p. 237–255)

Study identifies revenue share determinants and their explanative power in revenue production by using two macroeconomic models, one comparative static and one dynamic. Concludes that in St. Kitts-Nevis-Anguilla revenue share is determined by the vitality of the external trade sector and not by the level of economic development as conventionally measured.

3181 Locher, Uli. The marketing of agricultural produce in Jamaica. Kingston: Inter-American Institute of Agricultural Sciences, 1977. 78 p.

Report recommends support for the higgler marketer and coordination of government services (transport, credit, and physical market facilities) to improve the traditional system.

3182 Long, Frank. Is size a disadvantage in dealing with transnational corporations? (IAMEA, 33:4, Spring 1980, p. 61–75)

Study of foreign investment policies in Guyana shows that neither small size nor poverty prevents a country from controlling economic activity or striking hard bargains with transnationals, even when the latter provide most of the technology.

3183 Mills, Frank L. Production relationships among small-scale farmers in St. Kitts (UWI/SES, 25:2, June 1976, p. 153–167)

Article shows that breakeven analysis is relevant in searching for the optimal level of input use and combination. Concludes that constant returns to scale appear to prevail over input range studied; that production can be increased by moving more land and labor into the cash-tenants region, and more labor and capital into the share-tenants region; and that the small-scale agricultural production system operates much more efficiently than is generally realized.

3184 Odle, Maurice A. Technology leasing as the latest imperialist phase: a case study of Guyana and Trinidad (UWI/SES, 28:1, March 1979, p. 189–233)

Article concludes that policies must be devised to insure a significant reduction on the direct and indirect costs of leasing of technology and for developing indigenous technological capability. Perceives leasing of technology as contributing to income maldistribution, distortion of tastes, inflation, shortage of foreign exchange, and unemployment.

3185 Organization of American States, *Washington.* Economic study of Grenada. Washington, D.C.: 1977. 1 v.

Analysis of recent macroeconomic trends, focuses on a 25 percent decline in 1970–76 real GDP. Contends that the tax structure is income inelastic.

3186 ———, ———. Executive Secretariat for Economic and Social Affairs. Short term economic reports. v. 6, Trinidad and Tobago. Prepared by Martha F. Lynch. Washington, D.C.: General Secretariat, Organization of American States, 1979. 55 p.; appendix.

Economic survey consists of six parts: 1) recent economic trends; 2) external sector; 3) public sector; 4) monetary and financial situation; 5) prices, wages, and employment; and 6) growth prospects.

3187 Robert R. Nathan Associates, Inc. The income and production of Guyana rural farm households. Washington, D.C.:

Agency for International Development, 1980. 1 v.; appendix.

Report based primarily on 1979 Survey-of-Rural-Farm-Households data conducted by the government of Guyana. Focuses on low-income target groups, acreage and production of crops and livestock, and use and potential of various agricultural programs.

3188 Sackey, James A. Dependence, underdevelopment and socialist-oriented transformation in Guyana (IAMEA, 33:1, Summer 1979, p. 29–50)

Article contends that Guyana's development strategy and its accompanying difficulties cannot be explained without reference to its state of dependence, class formation, and the conceptual ambivalence of the ruling government. Stresses the interrelationship of internal and external inequalities and how domestic class formation is part of the periphery of the world capitalist economy.

3189 The Small farmer in Jamaican agriculture: an assessment of constraints and opportunities. David Sarfaty et al. Kingston: Ministry of Agriculture; Washington; Department of Agriculture [and] Agency for International Development, 1978. 274 p.; appendix; bibl.

Examination of economic, social, administrative, and cultural constraints pressing upon small farmers and performance of the agricultural sector. Includes development of a small farmer profile.

3190 Stone, Carl. An appraisal of the co-operative process in the Jamaican sugar industry (UWI/SES, 27:1, March 1978, p. 1–20)

Study based on survey of 200 community residents and 400 cooperators, conducted on four coop farms. Focuses on the nature of the sugar industry, the cooperative process as a mechanism of change, and group and political conflicts reflected in coop policies developed.

3191 Thompson, B.P. Current economic situation and prospects: Belize. Bridgetown: British Development Division in the Caribbean, 1977. 46 p.

Study which attributes the 1975–76 lull in economic activity to low sugar prices, high import prices, and the effects of world recession. Projects an improvement in economic conditions.

3192 Tramm, Madeleine L. Multinationals in Third World development: the case of Jamaica's bauxite industry (UWI/CQ, 23:4, Dec. 1977, p. 1–16)

Paper concludes that the bauxite industry's activities and interests in Jamaica have fostered economic growth and created opportunities for social mobility but failed to generate significant social progress. The industry is large in scale, vertically integrated, and capital intensive. Its extensive use of land removes resources usable for agriculture, disrupts the natural environment, and promotes further overcrowding.

3193 Trinidad and Tobago. Central Statistical Office. The gross domestic product of the Republic of Trinidad and Tobago, 1966–1976. Port-of-Spain: 1977. 49 p.; appendix.

Sec. 1 of this study discusses coverage, data sources, and methods of estimation; sec. 2 presents overview of the economy; and sec. 3 consists of sectoral reviews of the following: agriculture; sugar; petroleum; manufacturing; construction; distribution services and restaurants; hotels and guest houses; transport and communications; government; education; and personal services.

3194 United Nations. Food and Agriculture Organization and **Inter-American Development Bank,** *Washington.* Preparation of parish markets project. Washington, D.C.: 1977. 69 p.; appendix.

Review of Jamaican agricultural marketing policies and distribution system. Project intends to replace 16 parish markets and construct a new one, provides space for wholesaling and small-processing equipment facilities.

3195 United States. Agency for International Development. Caribbean regional project paper: employment investment promotion II. Washington, D.C.: 1979. 183 p.; appendix.

Project's goal is to increase employment and income levels of the poor in the English-speaking Caribbean by stimulating investment in small and medium business through the provision of credit. Project activities consist of direct lending by the Caribbean Development Bank for industrial purposes, on-lending to small and medium business enterprises through financial intermediaries, and technical assistance.

3196 ——. ——. Jamaica: integrated rural development. Washington, D.C.: 1977. 68 p.; appendix.

Development of an agricultural production model that can be replicated on small hillside farms throughout Jamaica. Model is based on continuous, multiple-cropping techniques suitable for land that has been terraced and otherwise treated with appropriate soil conservation measures. Major components are: erosion control, demonstration and training centers, farmer organizations and services, agricultural extension, and rural infrastructure.

3197 ——. ——. **Office of Housing.** Jamaica shelter sector assessment. Washington: 1977. 156 p.; bibl.; ill.

In-depth analysis which includes country background (location and physical description, economic conditions, and political overview and national government structure); the target population (sociocultural characteristics and income distribution); dimensions of the shelter program (population characteristics and housing practices); housing delivery systems; and constraints.

3198 World Bank, *Washington.* Regional economic survey of East Caribbean Common Market countries. Washington, D.C.: 1978. 118 p.; appendix.

Comprehensive analysis focuses on output, investment, and growth; prices and wages; the external sector; public finances; economic integration; and the agriculture, industry, tourism, and transportation sectors.

3199 Zuvekas, Clarence, Jr. A partially annotated bibliography of agricultural development in the Caribbean region. Washington: Rural Development Division, Bureau for Latin America and the Caribbean, Agency for International Development, 1978. 202 p.; indexes (Working document series: Caribbean regional; general working document; no. 1)

Comprehensive bibliography contains 1,908 entries. Also provides crop and topical indexes.

3200 ——. A profile of small farmers in the Caribbean region: Antigua, Barbados, Belize, British Virgin Is., Cayman Is., Dominica, Grenada, Monserrat, St. Kitts-Nevis-(Anguilla), St. Lucia, St. Vincent, Turks & Caicos Is. Washington: Rural Development Division, Bureau for Latin America and the Caribbean, Agency for International Development, 1978. 101 p.; bibl. (Working document series: Caribbean region; general working document; no. 2)

Analysis of statistical information bearing on small-farming and small-farmer characteristics in the Caribbean Region. Covers household characteristics (age and sex distribution, size, and multiple job-holding); level-of-living indicators (income and income distribution, employment, education, housing, water supply, toilet facilities, electricity, infant mortality, life expectancy, and nutrition); land (distribution, fragmentation, and tenure); technology; and government services (extension, credit, and marketing).

CUBA

JORGE F. PEREZ-LOPEZ, *Bureau of International Labor Affairs, United States Department of Labor*

THE REVIEW OF RECENT ECONOMIC LITERATURE ON CUBA indicates an appalling decline in the number of meaningful analyses by Cuban economists despite the increasing availability and regularity of statistical materials published in the island by the Comité Estatal de Estadísticas (items **3208–3213**). While such a decline may be partly attributed to difficulties in obtaining materials from Cuba, it appears that there has been a substantial reduction in production as well. The leading economic journal, *Economía y Desarrollo*, is being received with a time lag of about 12 months; a review of issues for the second half of 1978 and the first three quarters of 1979 turned up only two articles (items **3202** and **3229**) suitable for mention here, and one of them is by Soviet authors (item **3202**). The continued deterioration of *Economía y Desarrollo* is partly counterbalanced by the publication by the Comité Estatal de Estadísticas of a promising new journal, *Revista Estadística*, since December 1978 (item **3227**).

Two documents issued in 1980 are essential for students of the Cuban economy. The first is the proposed guidelines for the second five-year plan 1981–85 (item **3226**). The second is Castro's report to the Second Congress of the Cuban Communist Party held in Dec. 1980 (item **3207**). When read together, these two documents provide a good basis for understanding performance and problems encountered in the 1976–80 plan and prospects for 1981–85.

With reference to economic literature published outside of Cuba, a positive development is the reappearance, beginning in 1978, of a regular chapter on the Cuban economy in CEPAL's annual *Estudio Económico de América Latina* (items **3215** and **3232**). As noted in the introduction to this section in *HLAS 41* (p. 266–267), CEPAL last considered Cuba in its regular publications in 1963. An important 1978 CEPAL study on the Cuban socioeconomic model (see *HLAS 41:3082*), previously available only in mimeographed form, has been published commercially and received wide distribution (item **3231**).

3201 Banco Nacional de Cuba, *La Habana.* Cuba: economic development and prospect. La Habana: 1978. 35 p.

Important work reviewing economic developments through 1977. Follows general format of report published in 1975 (see *HLAS 39:3104*), though this report is much briefer. Contains sections on the overall economic situation, agriculture, industry, foreign trade, and a brief note on the preliminary objectives for the 1981–85 plan.

3202 Becarevich, Anatoli; V. Borodayev; K. Leino; and A. Mansilla. La creación de la base técnico-material del socialismo en Cuba (UH/ED, 51, enero/feb. 1979, p. 58–83)

Analyzes economic development strategy adopted by Cuba in the mid-1960s, in which agriculture dominates. States that this strategy is the optimal one for Cuba given its resource base and the advantages of the socialist division of labor, and criticizes earlier policies, such as the "industrialization fever" of the early 1960s. Authors are associated with the Latin American Institute of the Soviet Academy of Sciences.

3203 Bernstein, Richard E. and Robert H. Deans. Farm size and tenancy in prerevolutionary Cuba (IAA, 4:3, 1978, p. 217–235)

Clever empirical piece relating farm size and tenancy to agricultural output in pre-revolutionary Cuba. Authors estimate a series of Cobb-Douglas production functions using cross-section data from the National Agricultural Census of 1946. Results suggest that land redistribution would have lead to output gains, and support the type of agrarian reform policies instituted in 1959.

Bondarchuk, Vladimir. El tránsito al socialismo: algunos aspectos socioeconómicos de la experiencia cubana. See item **6251.**

3204 Boïko, P. Agudización de la crisis socioeconómica en Cuba: la Revolución cubana; carácter semicolonial de la estructura económica de la Cuba prerevolucionaria (*in* Boïko, P. América Latina: expansión del imperialismo y crisis de la vía capitalista de desarrollo [see item **2768**] p. 150–179, tables)

Soviet author of this unusual work selectively uses materials written in the 1950s by Cuban and US economists in order to paint an extraordinarily bleak picture of the economy of pre-revolutionary Cuba.

3205 Brundenius, Claes. Measuring income distribution in pre- and post-revolutionary Cuba (UP/CSEC, 9:2, July 1979, p. 29–44)

Using fragmentary data, author constructs income distribution figures for 1953,

1960, 1962, and 1973. Tentatively concludes that income distribution has become more equitable since the Revolution.

3206 Carnoy, Martin and Jorge Werthein. Cuba: economic change and education reform 1955–1974. Washington: The World Bank, 1979. 152 p.; tables (Staff working paper; no. 317)

Chapter 2 (p. 21–52) is a superficial review of Cuban economic development and policies since 1959.

3207 Castro, Fidel. Informe Central al Segundo Congreso (Bohemia [La Habana] 72:52, dic. 26, 1980, p. 34–67)

Lengthy report by Fidel Castro to the Second Congress of the Cuban Communist Party, held in Dec. 1980. Pt. 1 (p. 36–46) reviews aggregate and sectoral economic performance and the pitfalls that prevented the accomplishment of goals of the 1976–80 plan; summarizes aspects of the proposed plan for 1981–85; and lays out general guidelines for long-term development plan to the year 2000. Pt. 8 (p. 60–62) reviews the international economic situation and its impact on Cuba's development. Should be read in conjunction with the guidelines for the 1981–85 plan (see item **3226**). Essential for researchers and students of the Cuban economy. For English version of this report, see *FBIS Daily Reports—Latin America* (vol. 6, 22 Dec. 1980, p. Q1–Q81).

3208 Cuba. Comité Estatal de Estadísticas. Anuario estadístico de Cuba 1978. La Habana: 1980?. 326 p.

Statistical yearbook similar to earlier yearbooks published by JUCEPLAN (see *HLAS 39:3110–3111* and *HLAS 41:3053*). Main section contains over 240 tables showing data for 1978 and earlier (in the case of foreign trade, latest reported data is for 1976). Yearbook is divided into 15 subsections: 1) territory and climate; 2) population; 3) global indicators; 4) labor and wages; 5) agriculture; 6) industry; 7) construction; 8) transportation and communications; 9) domestic commerce; 10) foreign trade; 11) education; 12) culture and art; 13) sports; 14) public health; and 15) tourism and recreation. Includes a new section of 46 tables on international comparisons (Cuba, COMECON members and Latin American and Caribbean nations). Contains subject index.

3209 ——. ——. Atlas demográfico de Cuba. La Habana: Instituto Cubano de Geodesia y Cartografía, 1979. 99 p.

This useful demographic atlas, the first of its kind, is aimed at non-specialists. Of particular interest are maps on geographic distribution of the population and urbanization, characteristics of the population in 1977, vital statistics, and internal and external migration. Handsomely produced. For geographer's comment, see item **5040**.

3210 ——. ——. La economía cubana: 1978. La Habana: 1979. 17 p.

Review of chief economic accomplishments of 1978, as compared to those of 1977. Contains chapters on global indicators; industry; construction and investment; agriculture; transportation and communications; foreign trade; and standard of living. Represents a notable improvement in quality over earlier issues (see *HLAS 41:3050–3051*).

3211 ——. ——. La economía cubana: primer semestre 1979. La Habana: 1979. 17 p.

Compares economic developments in the first half of 1979 with those in first half of 1978. Similar in contents to item **3210**.

3212 ——. ——. Guía estadística 1979. La Habana: 1980? 20 p.

First issue of pocket-sized compendium of selected economic and social statistics. Most of the data is for 1979; for foreign trade, latest reported data is for 1977.

3213 ——. ——. Statistical yearbook compendium of the Republic of Cuba 1976. La Habana: n.d. 70 p.

English-language statistical abstract for 1976 contains selected series from the *Anuario* (see item **3208**), arranged in 79 tables. Most series run through 1976; for foreign trade, latest reported data is for 1975.

3214 ——. Instituto Cubano de Investigaciones y Orientación de la Demanda Interna. Investigaciones científicas de la demanda en Cuba. La Habana: Editorial Orbe, 1979. 161 p.

Collection of seven papers describing research activities of the Internal Demand Institute, by staff members in 1976. Particularly interesting are the descriptions of the on-going monthly national consumption survey and efforts to estimate national consumption norms for food, clothing, and shelter.

3215 **Cuba** (*in* Estudio económico de América Latina, 1978. New York: United Nations, Consejo Económico y Social, Comisión Económico para América Latina, 1979, v. 1, p. 306–337)

Excellent survey of Cuban economic development in the 1970s divided into two time periods, 1971–75 and 1976–78. Sections on foreign trade and on economic relations with the Soviet Union are especially useful. Contains 13 tables based on official Cuban data. Also appeared under the title "La Economía Cubana en los Años Setenta" in Mexico's journal *Comercio Exterior* (29:11, nov. 1979, p. 1262–1272) and as an appendix to *Cuba: estilo de desarrollo y políticas sociales* (see item **3231**).

3216 **Eckstein, Susan.** Capitalist constraints on Cuban socialist development (CUNY/CP, 12:3, April 1980, p. 253–274)

Author attempts to show that despite Cuba's two decades of revolution and its close economic and political ties with the Soviet Union, its economy continues to be significantly affected by market economies.

Economía de América Latina. Semestre No. 1, sept. 1978– . See item **2804**.

3217 **Flora, Jan L.** Agricultura: sector líder de la Revolución Cubana (Estudios Rurales Latinoamericanos [Bogotá] 3:1, enero/abril 1980, p. 25–50, bibl., tables)

Useful review of Cuban development strategy, in which agriculture predominates. Using interesting case studies on sugarcane production, cattle raising, and participation by small private farmers, study emphasizes the impact and implications of such growth strategy on human resources.

García-Baquero González, Antonio. Estados Unidos, Cuba y el comercio de neutrales. See *HLAS 42:2568*.

García Martínez, Orlando. Estudio de la economía cienfueguera desde la fundación de la colonia Fernandina de Jagua hasta mediados del siglo XIX. See *HLAS 42:2569*.

3218 **González Rodríguez, Lázaro.** La introducción de los principios básicos de la organización científica del trabajo en la economía cubana. La Habana: Editorial de Ciencias Sociales, 1977. 70 p.

Presents theoretical rationale for the introduction in Cuba, following a directive of the Party's First Congress, of a series of measures rationalizing labor (e.g., relating wages to work performed). These measures fall under the rubric of "scientific organization of labor."

3219 Hagelberg, G.B. Cuba's sugar policy (in Revolutionary Cuba in the world arena. Edited by Martin Weinstein. Philadelphia: Institute for the Study of Human Issues, 1979, p. 31–50)

Good overview of Cuba's domestic and international sugar policies through 1976. Analyzes Cuban sugar exports to the Soviet Union, Eastern Europe, and the world market during 1960–76, and discusses Cuba's role in the early negotiations of an International Sugar Agreement. Article is based on a paper originally presented at a conference sponsored by the Center for Latin America and the Caribbean of New York University in the fall of 1975, and updated in May 1978.

3220 Hewett, Edward A. Cuba's membership in the CMEA (in Revolutionary Cuba in the world arena. Edited by Martin Weinstein. Philadelphia: Institute for the Study of Human Issues, 1979, p. 51–76)

Insightful article prepared by well-known expert on Soviet and COMECON economic affairs for a conference sponsored in the fall of 1975 by New York University's Center for Latin America and the Caribbean. Author analyzes motivation and conditions of Cuba's entrance in COMECON in 1972 in an effort to determine whether that membership best served the interests of Cuba or of the Soviet Union and COMECON. Concludes that in the short run Cuba could benefit from the association; however, in the long run, the country could bear a considerable cost if membership perpetuates the export structure. Unfortunately, the paper was not updated for publication.

3221 Losman, Donald. International economic sanctions. Albuquerque: University of New Mexico Press, 1979. 152 p.; bibl.; index.

Comparative study of the economic impact of international economic sanctions, based on case studies of the US boycott of Cuba, the Arab boycott of Israel, and international sanctions against Rhodesia. Chapter

on the US boycott of Cuba is an expanded version of author's earlier article (see *HLAS 41:3062*).

3222 Marrero y Artiles, Leví. Cuba: economía y sociedad. v. 6/7, Del monopolio hacia la libertad comercial: 1701–1763, pts. 1/2. Madrid: Editorial Playor, 1978. 2 v. (234, 251 p.) ill.; maps; tables.

Two new volumes in projected 14-volume work on Cuban economic history, begun by the author in 1972 (for vol. 1, see *HLAS 37:4421*; vol. 2, *HLAS 39:3123*; and vols. 3/5, *HLAS 41:3063*). Vols. 6/7 cover the first half of the 18th century. Vol. 6 studies population, foreign influences, the land grant system, and cattle raising; vol. 7 covers the sugar and tobacco industries, foreign trade, and contraband. Volumes contain many illustrations, maps, tables, and a subject index.

3223 Martell, Raúl. La empresa socialista. La Habana: Editorial de Ciencias Sociales, 1978. 172 p.; index.

Collection of six essays published by the author in 1976–77 in the weekly magazine *Bohemia*. They deal with the role of enterprises in the new economic management and planning system.

3224 Morawetz, David. Economic lessons from some small socialist developing countries (WD, 8:5/6, May/June 1980, p. 337–369, tables)

Provocative study attempting to assess the economic performance of small socialist LDCs with a view of developing a model which may be relevant to other small LDCs following the socialist path. Serious questions arise concerning results—even though author warns they are preliminary—because of the diversity of the sample (e.g., Cuba, Tanzania, Sri Lanka, Burma, Portugal, and Chile under Allende) and data limitations. As expected, in comparison to the other countries, Cuba's performance is good on redistribution areas but poor on growth.

3225 Pavón González, Ramiro. El empleo femenino en Cuba: aspectos económicos, demográficos y socioculturales. La Habana: Editorial de Ciencias Sociales, 1977. 104 p.; tables (Demografía)

After a lengthy discussion of female labor-force participation in Western economies and the Soviet Union, author finally begins on p. 55 to deal with economic, demographic, and social aspects of female employment in Cuba. Analysis is limited since it was completed before official data from the 1970 population census became available.

3226 Proyecto de los lineamientos económicos y sociales para el quinquenio 1981–1985 (Granma [La Habana] 14 julio 1980, p. 4–5; 15 julio 1980, p. 4–5; 16 julio 1980, p. 4–5; 17 julio 1980, p. 4–5)

Contains guidelines for second five-year plan (1981–85) made public in mid-July 1980. Guidelines for the first five-year plan (1976–80) were never published. Lists 542 objectives to be accomplished, nearly 500 of which are directly related to the economy. In the majority of cases, no specific planned growth rates are indicated. Plan emphasizes growth through more efficient use of existing resources, and gives high priority to the implementation of the economic management and planning system. Preamble includes brief review of economic performance in 1976–80. Should be read in conjunction with Castro's report to the Party's Second Congress (see item **3207**). For English version of this work, see *Foreign Broadcast Information Service, Latin America Report* (No. 2184, 5 Sept. 1980. p. 15–113).

3227 *Revista Estadística.* Comité Estatal de Estadísticas. No. 1, dic. 1978– . La Habana.

Biannual publication of the Comité Estatal de Estadísticas is devoted to statistical theory and applications and serves primarily as a medium to disseminate staff work. No. 1 (Dec. 1978) contains articles on the economic management and planning system, a sample design of a household income survey for the city of Havana, and the organization of statistics in Cuba. No. 2 (July 1979) examines the development of Cuba statistics within the framework of COMECON, the 1981 housing and population census, and economic classification systems. Each issue includes book reviews and statistical briefs sections; articles are summarized in Russian and English.

3228 Roca, Sergio. Economic aspects of Cuban involvement in Africa (UP/CSEC, 10:2, julio 1980, p. 55–80)

Well-documented attempt to analyze the economic implications of Cuban involvement in Africa using the methodology of cost-benefit analysis. Positive results of African activities are listed as: increased leverage with the Soviet Union, income from services performed abroad, diversification of foreign trade markets, potential new supply of petroleum, and opportunity for the exportation of surplus labor. Negative results are: domestic opportunity costs (in fishing, social services, construction, transportation), postponement in normalization of relations with the US, and loss of financial assistance from Western countries. Author tentatively concludes that the economic cost-benefit ratio has been unfavorable to Cuba. The same issue of *Cuban Studies/Estudios Cubanos* includes relevant comments by Pérez-Lopez (p. 80–85) and Eckstein (p. 85–90, see item **7302**). For political scientist's comment, see item **7344**.

3229 Rodríguez García, José L. Política económica de la Revolución Cubana 1959–1960 (UH/ED, 54, julio/oct. 1979, p. 128–153)

Important article that reviews economic programs of anti-Batista groups prior to the revolutionary takeover in 1959, and compares them with actual policies implemented in 1959–60.

3230 Theriot, Lawrence H. and **JeNelle Matheson.** Soviet economic relations with non-European CMEA: Cuba, Vietnam and Mongolia (*in* United States. Congress. Joint Economic Committee. Soviet economy in a time of change: a compendium of papers submitted to the Joint Economic Committee. Washington, D.C.: GPO, 1979, v. 2, p. 551–581)

Section on Cuba (p. 551–67) reviews trends in Soviet trade with and aid to Cuba, through 1978. Study's main contribution is a careful estimate of Soviet economic assistance, in the form of repayable aid and of trade subsidies resulting from below-market prices of Soviet oil sold to Cuba and above-market prices of Cuban sugar and nickel purchased by the Soviet Union.

United Fruit Company, un caso del dominio imperialista en Cuba. See *HLAS 42:2625.*

3231 United Nations. Consejo Económico y Social. Comisión Económica para América Latina. Cuba: estilo de desarrollo y políticas sociales. México: Siglo XXI Editores, 1980. 195 p.

Reproduces two important CEPAL documents: *Apreciaciones sobre el estilo de desarrollo y sobre las principales políticas sociales en Cuba* (see *HLAS 41:3082*), and the section on Cuba from the *Estudio económico de América Latina, 1978* (see item **3215**).

3232 ———. ———. ———. Cuba: notas para el estudio económico de América

Latina, 1979. México: 1980. 25 p. (CEPAL/ NEX/1030/Rev.1)

Preliminary version of economic survey for 1979 that will be included in *Estudio económico de América Latina, 1979*. Follows general format of earlier study (see item **3215**) but refers only to 1979.

AN ANNOTATED BIBLIOGRAPHY ON THE ECONOMY OF PUERTO RICO: 1976–1980

FUAT M. ANDIC and SUPHAN ANDIC, *Professors of Economics, University of Puerto Rico, Río Piedras*

THE HARMFUL EFFECTS THAT THE RECESSION of 1973–75 had on the Puerto Rican economy lasted throughout the five years covered by this bibliography. True, there was a moderate rate of growth in 1976, 1977, and 1978, but this trend was not sustained in 1979 and 1980. The island's dependence on imported oil and external funds on the one hand, and the general stagflation in Western Europe and the US on the other, pulled the economy persistently downwards in 1979 and 1980. Hence, it is not surprising that economists dealing with Puerto Rico have once again turned their attention to the analysis of general economic conditions.

Another significant event was the political "changing of the guard" that took place in 1976. The political philosophy of the New Progressive Party, voted into power at that time, is drastically different from that of the Popular Democratic Party, which had governed the island almost without interruption since the early 1950s. One major difference is that the New Progressive Party stresses statehood for Puerto Rico. As a result, during the last five years, it has taken certain policy measures towards this end, including changes in the tax incentives program and greater reliance on federal transfers.

The impact of these two factors on Puerto Rican economic research is clearly demonstrated in the brief list of works annotated for this bibliography. Of a total of 104 entries, almost one-fourth (i.e., 24) deal with Puerto Rico's development process and the island's general economic conditions. The 1973–75 recession forced economists to evaluate not only the strategy and forms of development, but also the changing economic conditions of the island. The report prepared by the Committee to Study Puerto Rico's Finances, under the chairmanship of Professor James Tobin (see *HLAS 39:3197*) has sparked much discussion, both scientific and polemic. The so-called Tobin report has its counterpart in the present bibliography in the report prepared for the President by the US Department of Commerce under the title of "Economic Study of Puerto Rico" known as the Kreps Report (item **3319**). Like its predecessor, the Kreps Report gave rise to numerous controversies and stimulated writings on general economic conditions, economic structure and development.

Twenty-three entries can be grouped under the subject of public finance (i.e., taxation and expenditures). Interest in these matters reflects the tightening of

Puerto Rico's industrial incentives program since 1976 and the simultaneous rise in federal transfers, including payments under the Food Stamps Program. This group of studies concentrates on the drastic changes in the tax incentives, the impact of federal transfers, and, to a lesser extent, the impact of funds accumulated as a result of changes in federal statutes relating to what are commonly known as 936 corporations.

The concern with declining productivity and other labor problems, which caused the reactivation of the Governor's Council on Labor Policy, is the focus of 16 items in the section. It is interesting to note that among these only one deals with the problems of women in the labor force.

Demographic issues, such as the changing composition of the island's population, and especially return migration to Puerto Rico from the mainland were also favorite subjects and comprise 10 entries.

Puerto Rico's agricultural problems continue to preoccupy the island's economists. The 11 entries in this category include micro studies of sugar cane, dairy products, and experimental crops such as rice.

Topics given less attention recently are those concerning problems of the industrial sector. There are only five entries dealing specifically with manufacturing and two with construction, a sector that has been experiencing grave difficulties since 1974. However, one should not conclude from this fact that industrial problems are neglected since many individual sector issues are discussed in great detail in the general studies, specially the Kreps Report mentioned above.

Two other areas that are losing the fascination they previously held for economists are income distribution and international trade/import substitution. There are only five entries on the former and four on the latter. Environmental studies, natural resources, and economics of education received even less attention in this volume, a total of four entries.

Finally, it is worth emphasizing that the Kreps Report, besides containing a wealth of information and statistics, also has a fairly good bibliography on the economy of Puerto Rico in its entirety as well as its individual sectors, and on the factors of production. Anybody who is interested in the Puerto Rican economics cannot afford to miss this very valuable study.

3233 Albuquerque, Klaus de; Paul D. Mader; and William F. Stinner. Metropolitan dominance and fertility change in Puerto Rico: 1950–1970 (UWI/SES, 24:4, Dec. 1975, p. 433–443)

Measures the correlation between fertility and access and proximity to metropolitan areas. Concludes that the decline in fertility in the first decade was largely caused by migratory movements, but in the second decade it was positively correlated to modernization variables, such as education, diffusion of contraceptive methods, and sterilization.

3234 ———; ———; and ———. Modernization, delayed marriage and fertility in Puerto Rico: 1950–1970 (UWI/SES, 25:1, March 1976, p. 55–65)

Analyzes the possible correlation between three modernization variables (urbanization, industrialization, and education) and delayed marriage, and between the latter and fertility.

3235 Alvarado, Arcilio. La planificación y la rama legislativa (UPR/P, 8:1/2, junio/dic. 1974, p. 97–108)

Discussion of current economic, social, and physical planning and its relation to the legislative branch.

3236 Andic, Suphan and Parimal Choudhury. The impact of the Food Stamp Program in Puerto Rico. San Juan, P.R.: Department of Social Services, 1977. 180 p.; appendix; graphs; tables.

Based on surveys of food retailers,

wholesalers, and households, authors assess the impact of food stamps by investigating the food distribution system and consumer behavior before and after the implementation of the program.

3237 Asmar, Alejandro. Análisis breve del informe Tobin. Río Piedras: Universidad de Puerto Rico, Departamento de Economía, 1976. 12 p. (mimeo) (Serie de ensayos y monografías; 1)

Briefly summarizes the major points in the Tobin Report (see *HLAS 39:3197*), and discusses the various criticisms of it.

3238 Ason, Elías R. Comentarios sobre las recomendaciones del uso de los fondos de las corporaciones 936. Río Piedras: Universidad de Puerto Rico, Departamento de Economía, 1977. 12 p. (mimeo) (Serie de conferencias y foros; 7)

Analyzes Section 936 of the Federal Internal Revenue Code and its impact on credit in Puerto Rico; makes recommendations for the most appropriate use of the funds generated by that section.

3239 Badillo Veiga, Américo. Apuntes para una crítica de los estudios de migración en Puerto Rico (*in* Crisis y crítica de las ciencias sociales en Puerto Rico. Edited by Rafael L. Ramírez and Wenceslao Serra Díaz. Río Piedras: Universidad de Puerto Rico, Centro de Investigaciones Sociales, 1980, p. 231–246)

3240 Bergad, Laird W. Agrarian history of Puerto Rico, 1870–1930 (LARR, 13:3, 1978, p. 63–94)

Historical survey of sugar, coffee, and tobacco crops which shaped the island's economy in the period under consideration. Author concludes that agroindustrial complexes at the turn of the century were totally different from their 19th-century counterparts, and that the factors of production were organized in a totally different manner when the plantation replaced the *hacienda*. The complete reorganization of the agrarian structure resulting from sovereignty change had adverse effects on sugar and coffee. For historian's comment see *HLAS 42:2552*.

3241 Borges, Sheila. Report on governmental regulation and its impact on productivity in Puerto Rico. Prepared for the Sub-Committee on Government Regulation of the Governor's Advisory Council on Labor

Policy. San Juan, P.R.: 1976. 229 p.; appendix.

A minutely detailed study that identifies and evaluates the government regulation affecting productivity, and provides specific recommendations. Author's general recommendation is the revision or elimination of obsolete or inflexible legislation in order to achieve maximum flexibility for industry without loss of job security for the worker.

3242 Bruckman, Walter H. Rechazo y atracción como causas de la migración interna en Puerto Rico: un modelo econométrico (UPR/RCS, 20:2, sept. 1978, p. 145–162)

Attempts to prove that migration is the result of economic and sociological elements and is explained more fully by "push" than by "pull" factors. Defines variables that affect internal migration.

3243 Bryce, Murray. The development of import-substitution industries in Puerto Rico. Prepared for the Economic Development Administration. San Juan, P.R.: s.n., 1977. 1 v. (mimeo) appendixes; tables.

Summarizes the increasing number of problems facing Puerto Rican industrial development, and suggests ways to embark on a comprehensive import-substitution effort while continuing to give priority to export development.

3244 Cabarrouy de Elías, Luisa M. and **Salvador Lugo.** Trends and problems of the local Puerto Rican owned manufacturing industries. Prepared for the Inter Agency Strategy Committee of the Finance Council. San Juan, P.R.: 1975. 16 p. (mimeo) appendixes; figures; glossary; tables.

Assesses trends and problems in local manufacturing industries so that limited government funds can be allocated to obtain the highest multiplier effect. Finds that the apparel and knitting industries offer the most promising growth trends, and recommends measures for promoting their growth.

3245 Caldari, Luigi; Tomás Cardona Morales; and Víctor Cardona Sánchez. La lucha por Puerto Rico o como no desarrollar una isla (UPR/P, 7:1/2, junio/dic. 1973, p. 1–17, figures)

Critical analysis of the island's economic development strategy which entails increased energy requirements with subsequent negative environmental consequences.

3246 Cardona Sánchez, Víctor. Los altos precios del petróleo y el desarrollo económico de Puerto Rico (UPR/P, 7:1/2, junio/dic. 1973, p. 33–40, graphs)

Author suggests a restructuring of the economy so as to reduce the high energy input coefficient of many activities.

3247 Cestero, Hermán; Antonio A. Llorens; José D. Rivera; and Guillermo Serra. Efecto económico de la aplicación de la tecnología en la producción de leche. Río Piedras: Universidad de Puerto Rico, Estación Experimental Agrícola, 1974. 14 p.; tables (Publicación; 85)

Examines economic impact on a dairy of intensive pasture and rational feeding of concentrate supplements.

3248 Choudhury, Parimal. The Food Stamp Program and unemployment in Puerto Rico. San Juan, P.R.: Department of Social Services, 1978. 189 p.; appendix; tables.

Based on a 1976 survey encompassing the entire island, work assesses the impact of the program upon employment and unemployment. Concludes that the high level of unemployment among participants is not a consequence of the program, but rather of Puerto Rico's socioeconomic problems.

3249 ——— and Angel Luis Ruiz. The impact of the Food Stamp Program on the Puerto Rican economy: an input-output approach. Río Piedras: Universidad de Puerto Rico, Departamento de Economía, Unidad de Investigaciones Económicas, 1978. 20 p. (mimeo) statistical appendix; tables (Serie de ensayos y monografías; 7)

Using an input-output approach, concludes that the program has increased the output and employment in food production both in Puerto Rico and the US and the nutritional level of lower-income classes.

3250 Cook, Larry H. Inter-industry linkages in Puerto Rico. San Juan, P.R.: Economic Development Administration, Office of Economic Research, 1979. 29 p. (mimeo) appendix; tables.

Presents some standard measurements of industry linkages, based on the 1972 input-output table, and warns against the danger of using them to identify key sectors for development without also considering supply constraints.

3251 Corrada Guerrero, Rafael. Crítica del desarrollo económico de Puerto Rico (in Crisis y crítica de las ciencias sociales en Puerto Rico. Edited by Rafael L. Ramírez and Wenceslao Serra Deliz. Río Piedras: Universidad de Puerto Rico, Centro de Investigaciones Sociales, 1980, p. 191–214, tables)

Critique of the present economic development of the island and a call to study the applicability of a Cuban-style strategy.

3252 Costas Elena, Luis P. Exenciones contributivas de ingresos en Puerto Rico (CAPR/RCA, 38:3, agosto 1977, p. 307–440)

Critique of the island's industrial incentive program offers some "romantic," almost "utopian," alternatives for its replacement.

3253 ———. History of federal income taxation in Puerto Rico: analysis of the possessions corporation in comparison with other modes of business operations in Puerto Rico; an insight into tax exemption in Puerto Rico (CAPR/RCA, 36:2, mayo 1975, p. 477–582)

Detailed history and description of the structure of federal income taxation in Puerto Rico.

3254 Cruz Báez, Angel David. "Nueva era agrícola" o síndrome de deterioro agrícola: el comportamiento de la agricultura en Puerto Rico en los últimos años (UPR/RCS, 18:3/4, sept./dic. 1974, p. 9–39, bibl., ill., tables)

Examines briefly the deterioration of the agricultural sector in Puerto Rico as a result of the openness of the political-economic system and the tenancy structure of the agricultural resources. Concludes that if the sector is to be strengthened, a new and real agricultural reform must be introduced rapidly, and on a massive scale.

3255 Duncan, Cameron. Beneficios marginales en el sector manufacturero en Puerto Rico, 1976. San Juan, P.R.: Consejo Asesor del Gobernador sobre Política laboral, 1978. 58 p.; tables.

Based on surveys of manufacturing establishments, collects and interprets statistical data on the existing wide variety of employee benefits in Puerto Rican industry.

3256 Duncan, Egerton W. Current planning with foreign subsidiaries: WHTCs,

Puerto Rico, possession exclusion (JT, 34:6, June 1976, p. 366–369)

Discusses current uses of Western Hemisphere Trade Corporations and possessions corporations, with special emphasis on Puerto Rico and its Industrial Incentives Act.

3257 Espinet Colón, Gabriel R. and **Edgardo González Villafañe.** Análisis económico de la producción de yautías, Puerto Rico, 1975. Río Piedras: Universidad de Puerto Rico, Estación Experimental Agrícola, 1977. 11 p.; tables (Boletín, 249)

Analysis of the costs and return of tanier production. Concludes that farmers operate near the break-even point and attributes low production per-*cuerda* to climatic variations, disease, and large labor requirements.

3258 Freyre, Jorge F. El modelo económico de Puerto Rico. San Juan, P.R.: Inter American University Press, 1979. 270 p.; appendixes; graphs; tables.

Claims to be the first step toward revising and perfecting the existing econometric model of the Puerto Rican economy.

3259 Galvin, Miles. The organized labor movement in Puerto Rico. Rutherford, N.J.: Fairleigh Dickinson University Press [and] Associated University Presses, 1980. 241 p.

Traces Puerto Rican trade unionism from the times of Spanish rule to the current industrial era.

3260 García Santiago, Ramón. La situación actual y las perspectivas de la planificación (UPR/P, 8:1/2, junio/dic. 1974, p. 65–78)

Description of current planning with a view to the future.

3261 Goldman, Max. History of the industrial incentives program: 1948 to date (FBA/FBJ, 33:4, Fall 1974, p. 345–349)

Brief description of the industrial incentives program in Puerto Rico and its development from 1948 to date.

3262 Gómez Acevedo, L. Organización y reglamentación del trabajo en el Puerto Rico del siglo XIX: propietarios y jornaleros. San Juan, P.R.: Instituto de Cultura Puertorriqueña, 1970. 502 p.; appendixes.

Monograph of the economic and social history of labor (1838–77), emphasizing the introduction, implementation, and final disappearance of the so-called "libreta" system. For historian's comment, see *HLAS 34:2161.*

González Vales, Luis E. Alejandro Ramírez y su tiempo: ensayos de historia económica e institucional. See *HLAS 42:2570.*

3263 González Villafañe, Edgardo. Análisis de la organización y operación de los matadores regionales de Puerto Rico. Río Piedras: Universidad de Puerto Rico, Estación Experimental Agrícola, 1976. 19 p.; tables (Boletín; 242)

Analysis of the organization and performance of regional slaughterhouses and of their functioning and inspection norms. Deficiencies in organization and the strictness of federal regulations are cited as factors for their improper operation.

3264 Gray, H. Peter. The economics of business investment abroad. New York: Grane, Russak, 1972. 249 p.; bibl.; tables.

Chap. 5 contains a section (p. 158–66) on Puerto Rico illustrating the role foreign (US) investments have played in the economic development of the island (1948–70). Concludes that the costs of reducing such investments would be cataclysmic.

3265 Griggs, Robert S. Current tax climate favors dealing with affiliates in Puerto Rico (JT, 35:6, Dec. 1976, p. 376–378)

Reviews current state of affairs regarding product pricing by subsidiaries, as established under Section 482 of the regulations and under a special procedure applicable only to manufacturing affiliates in Puerto Rico and their treatment by the IRS.

3266 Herrero, José A. La economía de Puerto Rico: el presente crítico. Río Piedras: Universidad de Puerto Rico, Departamento de Economía, Unidad de Investigaciones Económicas, 1976? 32 p. (mimeo) (Serie de conferencias y foros; 1)

Analyzes briefly the 1974–75 recession and suggests encouraging labor intensive industries for the generation of internal capital. Such a plan requires a drastic change in policies, attitudes, and ultimately, ideology.

3267 Holbrook, Robert S. A study of the characteristics, behavior and implications of "Possessions Corporations" in Puerto Rico. Washington, D.C.: The Department of the Treasury, 1977. 69 p. (mimeo) notes; tables.

Describes the characteristics of the "Possessions Corporations," and of federal and Puerto Rican tax laws that have given rise to them, paying particular attention to the corporations' responses to the 1976 changes in these laws.

3268 Kiefer, Donald W. Treating Puerto Rico as state under federal tax and expenditure programs: a preliminary economic analysis. Washington, D.C.: Library of Congress, Congressional Research Service, 1977. 44 p.

If Puerto Rico were to be fully treated as a state, its overall gains from increased transfers would compensate for its overall losses in increased federal taxes. However, this would imply a redistribution of personal income from upper to lower incomes. Moreover, the impact on investment would be negative.

3269 López, Alicia and Michael Rosenberg. Tax treatment of conducting business in Puerto Rico (CCH/TTM, 55:8, Aug. 1977, p. 498–505)

Paper concentrates primarily on the tax consequences of US manufacturing subsidiaries operating in Puerto Rico. Takes into account the relevant changes of the 1976 Tax Reform Act.

3270 Maldonado, Rita Margarita. Analyzing Puerto Rican migration: reply (USDL/MLR, 100:8, Aug. 1977, p. 34–55)

Reply to Steven Zell's criticism (see item **3333**).

3271 ———. Why Puerto Ricans migrated to the United States in 1947–73 (USDL/MLR, 99:9, Sept. 1976, p. 7–14, appendix, tables)

By means of regression analysis, author determines the factors in the "economic opportunity" concept that have been most instrumental in the post-war migration of Puerto Ricans to the US. Concludes that they are the changes in relative wages and relative unemployment rates between Puerto Rico and the US. For criticism of paper and author's reply, see items **3333** and **3270.**

3272 Mann, Arthur J. Sobre la medición de desembolsos públicos en especie (UPR/RCS, 20:1, March 1976, p. 51–89, tables)

Assesses money value of the benefits

derived from public spending and finds public expenditure favors low-income families.

3273 ——— and **William C. Ocasio.** La distribución del ingreso personal en Puerto Rico: una nueva dimensión (UPR/RCS, 19:1, March 1975, p. 1–23, tables)

Adds depth to the economic studies on the distribution of personal income in Puerto Rico. The use of municipal and regional distribution data sheds new light on the subject. Finds a trend towards equality during 1949–69, without significant variation in the distribution between municipalities and regions.

3274 ——— and ———. Patterns of income concentration over time in Puerto Rico: a curvilinear regression model (Eastern Economic Journal [Eastern Economic Association, Bloomsbury State College, Department of Economics, Bloomsburg, Pa.] 4:3/4, July/Oct. 1978, p. 177–184)

Statistical test of the Kuznets hypothesis on the relationship between income concentration and economic growth. Logarithmic regressions which best account for cross-section and over-time variations do not validate the expected inverted U-pattern.

3275 Martin, Gary and Alan Udall. Structural change in Puerto Rican industry (GDB/BR, 4:8, Aug. 1979, p. 2–7, 19, tables)

Outlines the major overall and industry-by-industry changes in manufacturing employment, wage levels, value added per worker, and labor's share in value added during the period 1972–73. Finds little overall change in average manufacturing wages, an increased productivity, a decline in labor's share, and a remarkably stable industrial structure. Paper assesses the use of this knowledge for targeting future growth in industry.

3276 Muler Manzanares, Luis. Nivel de vida y condiciones de la vivienda en las comunidades aisladas del Centro Las Marías. Río Piedras: Universidad de Puerto Rico, Estación Experimental Agrícola, 1976. 42 p.; tables (Boletín; 247)

Analysis of the socioeconomic conditions of the isolated communities in the Las Marías Center. Overall results indicate extreme poverty.

3277 —— and José E. Santini. Estudio socioeconómico de 29 fincas individuales de Título IV de la Ley de Tierras distribuidas de 1967 a 1970. Río Piedras: Universidad de Puerto Rico, Estacíon Experimental Agrícola, 1976. 53 p.; tables (Boletín; 241)

Compares socioeconomic characteristics of families to whom farms were distributed between 1941–67.

3278 Muñoz, Nicolás. Estructura ocupacional y distribución del ingreso de Puerto Rico: 1959–1969 (UPR/CS, 16:2, July 1976, p. 156–183, tables)

Based on census data and using Lorenz curves and Gini coefficients, study concludes that the change in the occupational structure (1959–69) has meant a better overall distribution on family incomes, although in the more developed regions the redistribution has worsened.

3279 ——. Perfil de la fuerza laboral de Puerto Rico. Preparado para el Consejo Asesor del Gobernador sobre Política Laboral, Oficina del Gobernador, San Juan, P.R.: 1977. 46 p.; appendixes; graphs; tables.

Compilation of statistics on the labor force of Puerto Rico with analysis and interpretation.

3280 Navas Dávila, Gerardo. Algunos apuntes sobre la planificación del desarrollo en Puerto Rico (UPR/P, 9:1/2, junio/dic. 1975, p. 49–59)

Brief analysis of development planning efforts.

3281 New York (state). City University of New York. The History Task Force. Centro de Estudios Puertorriqueños. Labor migration under capitalism: the Puerto Rican experience. New York: Monthly Review Press, 1979. 287 p.; tables.

Radical analysis of Puerto Rico's capitalist development from the abolition of slavery in 1873 up to the present, with an accompanying study of migration and industrialization since 1930. Uses a politico-economic perspective which incorporates several interrelated factors, including population growth, class struggle, political status, bureaucracy, and the demand for labor in the US.

3282 Oliveras, Cándido. La ampliación del ámbito de la planificación en Puerto Rico (UPR/P, 8:1/2, junio/dic. 1974, p. 59–64)

Brief description of economic planning in Puerto Rico.

3283 Paolo, Gordon A. di. Marketing strategy for economic development: the Puerto Rican experience. New York: Dunellen, 1976. 144 p.; bibl.; index.

Examines the problem of attracting foreign investment to a relatively underdeveloped area. Focuses on the Puerto Rican experience during the third quarter of this century, particularly its attempt to import investment capital from the US. Indicates that Puerto Rico's efforts conform essentially to the view of the development problem as one of "marketing." Discusses the applicability of Puerto Rico's lessons to other less-developed nations.

3284 Picó, Hernández Isabel. Estudio sobre el empleo de la mujer en Puerto Rico (UPR/RCS, 19:2, junio 1975, p. 139–166, graphs)

Considers the problem of women's employment within the context of general employment scarcity, abundant labor force, and a large amount of employment. Finds that the female labor force is insufficiently represented, under-utilized, and receives lower salaries.

3285 Picó, Rafael. Los primeros años de la planificación en Puerto Rico (UPR/P, 8:1/2, junio/dic. 1974, p. 25–57)

Describes the historical development of the Puerto Rico Planning Board during the first years of its creation.

3286 ——. Puerto Rico: un ejemplo de planificación integral (UPR/P, 8:1/2, junio/dic. 1974, p. 1–24)

Analysis of the Puerto Rico Planning Board and its effectiveness in reaching its goals of reform and progress.

3287 Podwin, Horace J. de; Glenn D. Meyers; Federico Córdero; and José Sánchez. The labor relations experience of selected Puerto Rican operations: a guide to productivity improvement. San Juan, P.R.: s.n., 1976. 58 p.

Based on interviews with representatives of industrial operations, authors identify barriers to productivity improvement, and make recommendations for developing sophisticated managers capable of adapting work processes to rapidly evolving technologies.

3288 Puerto Rico. Administración de Fomento Económico. Oficina de Estudios Económicos. Análisis económico del programa de incentivos industriales de Puerto Rico. Prepared for the Industrial Incentives Committee. San Juan, P.R.; 1978. 335 p. (mimeo)

Analysis of the subsidies received by industrial operations under the industrial incentives program. Concludes that despite the successful industrialization the program has given rise to, it has failed to expand the tax base. Recommends a new program with limited incentives, estimating the additional public revenue that can be expected from it.

3289 ———. The Commission on an Integral Social Security System. Report to the Governor and the Legislative Assembly, Commonwealth of Puerto Rico. San Juan, P.R.: 1976. 126 p.; appendixes; tables.

Evaluates Puerto Rico's Social Security Programs individually and as a whole, and makes recommendations to integrate more fully the existing disability insurance programs, to establish a Central Disability Agency, to improve the existing public assistance programs, and to create a Commission on Employment to give immediate attention to the problems of high unemployment and low labor force participation.

3290 ———. Consejo Asesor del Gobernador sobre Política Laboral. Las garantías de compensación semanal mínima. San Juan, P.R.; 1978. 38 p.; appendixes; tables.

Analysis of the reaction of labor leaders and employer representatives to guaranteed minimum weekly wage.

3291 ———. ———. Neither at work nor in school: structural unemployment among youth in Puerto Rico; causes, consequences and remedies. By Millard Hansen and María S. Ortiz de Martínez. San Juan, P.R.: 1979. 104 p.

Authors criticize the efforts to upgrade the skills of the structurally unemployed, proposing instead the shaping of jobs and training to fit the capacities of the structurally unemployed. They propose setting up school programs on work opportunities, and recommend the creation of an agency to assist youth in the transition from school to work.

3292 ———. ———. Plan de Acción para Aumentar la Productividad en la Economía de Puerto Rico: diagnóstico y recomendaciones, informe final. By Nicolás Muñoz Muñoz and José. H. Colón Villanueva. San Juan, P.R.: 1979. 284 p.; tables.

Exhaustive study of the various aspects of productivity. Provides recommendations to prevent its declining rate, e.g., the establishment of a Productivity Center.

3293 Puerto Rico Development Group, Inc. An appraisal of industrial incentives in Puerto Rico. Prepared for the Economic Development Administration. San Juan, P.R.: 1976. 39 p.; graphs; maps; tables.

Study of industrial incentives in Puerto Rico in the context of its industrial promotion experience during the past decade and the present competitive position of its manufacturing industries, especially vis-à-vis the US.

3294 Puerto Rico y el mar: un programa de acción sobre asuntos marinos, informe al Gobernador. Río Piedras: Universidad de Puerto Rico [and] San Juan, P.R.: Administración de Fomento Económico, 1974. 131 p.; ill.

Spanish version of *HLAS 39:3211.*

3295 Quintero Rivera, Angel G. La clase obrera y el proceso político en Puerto Rico (UPR/RCS, 18:3/4, Sept./Dec. 1974, p. 61–103, graphs, tables)

Socialist analysis of the development of the working class into a supposedly conscious and combatant force in Puerto Rico on the basis of the changing agricultural structure from 1898 onwards.

3296 Ramos Mattei, Andres A. Apuntes sobre la transición hacia el sistema de centrales en la industria azucarera: contabilidad de la Hacienda Mercedita: 1861–1900. Río Piedras: Centro de Estudios de la Realidad Puertorriqueña, 1975. 30 p. (mimeo) annex; graphs; tables (Cuaderno; 4)

Study of the transition from the traditional sugar plantations to a system of "centrales" based on the 19th-century records and accounting books of the Hacienda Mercedita in Ponce. Concludes that the sugar industry was well advanced into the mechanized "central" system when the North Americans arrived in 1898.

3297 ———. Las inversiones norteamericanas en Puerto Rico y la ley Foraker, 1898–1900 (UPR/CS, 14:3, Oct. 1974, p. 53–69, graphs, ill., tables)

Explores the type and magnitude of economic relations that have made feasible the political control of the island by the US. Concludes that the events of the period merely served to accelerate the gradual assimilation of the Puerto Rican economy to the commercial and financial interests of the US.

3298 **Rohena, Santos, Jr.** Los desperdicios sólidos como un recurso natural (UPR/P, 7:1/2, junio/dic. 1973, p. 115–121)

Analyzes the possibilities and advantages of recycling solid waste as energy source and land reclamation.

3299 **Rohrlich, George F.** Problems of social insurance coordination: the case of Puerto Rico (ARIAI/JRI, 45:2, June 1978, p. 239–259)

Analyzes the present state and problem areas in the social insurance and related programs. Discusses obstacles to inter-program coordination, concluding that its persistent lack results in waste. Suggests alternative courses for the consolidation of the programs.

3300 **Rosado Cotto, Juan Carlos.** Fondos federales y la política pública del Estado Libre Asociado de Puerto Rico (UPR/RAP, 6:2, marzo 1974, p. 105–139, tables)

Critical analysis of the inefficient and ineffective use of federal funds.

3301 **Ross, David F.** Political status and economic development: will the dependent variable please stand up? (IAUPR/RI, 6:1, Spring 1976, p. 7–17)

Essay on the economics of the political options (independence, commonwealth, and statehood) open to Puerto Rico.

3302 **Ruiz, Angel Luis.** Análisis de la productividad en la industria de centrales y refinerías de azúcar en Puerto Rico. Río Piedras: Universidad de Puerto Rico, Departamento de Economía, Unidad de Investigaciones Económicos, 1977. 21 p. (mimeo) tables (Serie de ensayos y monografías; 5)

Examines labor productivity in sugar refining during the last 20 years, and concludes that its decline has reduced the sector's employment generating impact and its contribution to value added.

3303 ———. Análisis estructural de la industria de la construcción, años 1962–63 al 1971–72. Río Piedras: Universidad de Puerto Rico, Departamento de Economía, Unidad de Investigaciones Económicos, 1978. 10 p. (mimeo); tables (Serie de ensayos y monografías; 6)

Analyzes structural changes in the construction industry during the last 15 years. Discusses its impact on employment and production in other sectors, particularly during 1971–72 to 1976–77, when the industry experienced a strong recession. Concludes that the sector increased its use of intermediate inputs, reduced its use of labor and its degree of integration with other sectors. The industry recession thus had the effect of curtailing production and employment in other sectors.

3304 ———. La demanda por recursos humanos en la economía de Puerto Rico: requisitos actuales y proyecciones para 1985. Prepared for Consejo Asesor del Gobernador sobre Política Laboral. San Juan, P.R.: 1978. 68 p.; tables.

Simple quantitative projection of labor force requirements assuming alternative rates of GNP growth and no change in the inter-industry and occupational employment structure.

3305 ———. Enfoque de insumo-producto para determinar una política de substitución de importaciones en Puerto Rico. Río Piedras: Universidad de Puerto Rico, Departamento de Economía, Unidad de Investigaciones Económicas, 1977. 20 p. (mimeo); tables (Serie de ensayos y monografías; 3)

Uses the input-output technique to set guidelines for an import-substitution policy considered to hold great potential for sectors with low capital/labor ratios.

3306 ———. The impact of the economic recession on the Puerto Rican economy: an input-output approach (UPR/CS, 16:3/4, Oct. 1976/Jan. 1977, p. 125–148, tables)

Estimates the change in the various components of final demand during the recession of 1973–76 and its repercussion on output and employment levels.

3307 —— and **Fernando Zalacaín.** La medición de la productividad en Puerto Rico. Prepared for P. R. Governor's Advisory Council on Labor Policy. San Juan, P.R.: 1976. 190 p. (mimeo); graphs; tables.

Measures and analyzes partial and total productivity. Partial analysis shows differences by sector, while total productivity analysis indicates declines comparable to those of underdeveloped countries.

3308 **Sánchez, Víctor M.** El impacto en la administración pública de la ley que fija la política pública ambiental del Estado Libre Asociado (UPR/RAP, 6:1, Oct. 1973, p. 67–77)

Stresses the importance of resource conservation and notes the contradictions between the law and the technological development policy, industrial growth, and urban expansion.

3309 **Santiago Meléndez, Jaime A.** Objectives and strategy for economic development: a challenge. Río Piedras: Universidad de Puerto Rico, Departamento de Economía, Unidad de Investigaciones Económicas, 1976. 14 p. (Serie de conferencias y foros; 3)

Brief analysis of the 1974–75 recession and of cooperative development as a viable solution.

3310 ——. One step forward (Wilson Quarterly [The Wilson Center, The Smithsonian Institution, Washington, D.C.] 4:2, Spring 1980, p. 132–140)

Overview for the layman of Puerto Rico's politico-economic development since the 1930s.

3311 ——. El presupuesto ejecutivo: reto al poder legislativo. Río Piedras: Universidad de Puerto Rico, Departamento de Economía, Unidad de Investigaciones Económicas, 1977. 57 p. (mimeo) (Serie de temas relacionados; 4)

Provides a brief description of the changes in the budgetary process in Puerto Rico.

3312 ——. La situación presupuestaria de 1976 y 1977 y sus efectos sobre la economía (PRNP/BGA, 25:230, marzo/junio 1976, p. 2–7, tables)

Analyzes government budget situation for 1976–77 and the prevailing economic conditions affecting forecasting future economic activity in Puerto Rico. Concludes that although a severe recession is still present, one can be optimistic concerning recuperation in the basic sectors.

3313 **Santini, José Emilio.** Características socio-económicas de las familias participantes en el estudio del arroz de grano corto producido localmente. Río Piedras: Universidad de Puerto Rico, Estación Experimental Agrícola, 1977. 12 p.; tables (Boletín; 251)

Part of a study to investigate the economic feasibility of growing short-grain rice in Puerto Rico. Provides an analysis of the socioeconomic characteristics and the change in the patterns of consumption of rice and other food of families participating in the Food Stamp Program.

3314 **Sierra, Ralph J., Jr.** El nuevo trato contributivo federal de las corporaciones norteamericanas dedicadas a industria o negocio en Puerto Rico (CAPR/RCA, 38:2, May 1977, p. 235–249)

Reviews the new norms established by Law No. 94-455 (1976) governing taxable earnings of US corporations operating in US possessions and discusses the degree to which they affect US corporations in Puerto Rico.

3315 ——. Tax advantages available to U.S. companies doing business in Puerto Rico (JT, 38:5, May 1973, p. 310–314)

Focusing on US taxation of Puerto Rico's resident individuals and corporations, its domicile corporations, and its income tax, author discusses how to obtain maximum benefits by coordinating the Industrial Incentives Act with the Puerto Rico Income Tax Act. Also treats planning and problem areas.

3316 **Tirado de Alonso, Irma G.** Equity and efficiency considerations concerning higher education in Puerto Rico. Río Piedras: Universidad de Puerto Rico, Departamento de Economía, 1977. 10 p. (mimeo) appendixes (Serie de conferencias y foros; 8)

Analyzes the inequities and inefficiencies in the present (1977) state of provision and financing of higher education. Suggests alternative arrangements to achieve equity and efficiency.

3317 Toro Calder, Jaime. Estudio sobre ubicación ocupacional de graduados de bachiller en ciencias sociales para los años 1969–1973 (UPR/RCS, 19:2, June 1975, p. 194–225)

Data on the relationship between college education in social sciences and the job market in a country developing from a rural to an industrial and urban society. Reveals that social sciences graduates play an important role in satisfying the society's needs in social services.

3318 Torres Román, Samuel. La problemática económica de Puerto Rico. Río Piedras: Universidad de Puerto Rico, Departamento de Economía, 1976. 29 p. (mimeo) (Serie de ensayos y monografías; 2)

Examines past strategy of economic development in Puerto Rico. Because of structural changes, it is currently impossible to maintain the high growth rate achieved in the past.

3319 United States. Department of Commerce. Economic study of Puerto Rico: Report to the President. Prepared by the Inter-Agency Task Force coordinated by the U.S. Department of Commerce. Washington, D.C.: GPO, 1979. 2 v.; appendixes; tables.

Study consists of three parts: Pt. 1 provides a macroeconomic overview containing analyses of production, income, employment, external trade, inflation, investment and the public sector; pt. 2 analyzes federal programs and policies; and pt. 3 analyzes the structure and operation of the economic sectors, and presents policy and program options.

3320 ———. Department of Health, Education and Welfare. Report of the Under-Secretary's Advisory Group on Puerto Rico, Guam and Virgin Islands. Washington, D.C.: 1976. 1 v. (Various paginations) (mimeo); tables.

Provides information on current economic conditions and their impact on public assistance needs. Summarizes treatment under the Social Security Act, and explores the fiscal implications of alternative funding arrangements.

3321 Vicente-Chandler, José et al. Cultivo intensivo y perspectivas del arroz en Puerto Rico. Río Piedras: Universidad de Puerto Rico, Estación Experimental Agrícola, 1977. 71 p.; graphs; tables (Boletín; 250)

Describes an intensive management system for rice production in Puerto Rico, and evaluates the prospects for commercial rice production.

3322 Wagenheim, Kal. A survey of Puerto Ricans on the U.S. mainland in the 1970s. New York: Praeger *in cooperation with the* Metropolitan Applied Research Center, 1975. 133 p.

Comparison between Puerto Ricans on the mainland and total population, blacks, other Hispanic groups, and Puerto Ricans in Puerto Rico. Despite significant gains in some socioeconomic areas, a relatively high rate of unemployment, low level of education, and low level of income characterize the Puerto Ricans as compared to other socioeconomic groups.

3323 Wanninski, Jude. The way the world works. New York: Basic Books, 1978. 295 p.

Last chapter describes briefly the tax history and the present economic condition of Puerto Rico in the light of its political and economic relations with the US.

3324 Wasow, Bernard. Dependent growth in a capital importing economy: the case of Puerto Rico (OU/OEP, 30:1, March 1978, p. 117–129)

Explores long-range implications of externally financed growth under alternative assumptions of domestic saving behavior. Concludes that the current growth pattern will be difficult to sustain.

3325 Watlington Linares, Francisco. El reto del desempleo y la política de distribución de tierras en Puerto Rico (UPR/RCS, 19:4, dic. 1975, p. 371–392, tables)

Analyzes the "back-to-the-land" movement alternative as a way of reducing unemployment.

3326 Weisskoff, Richard. Income distribution and export promotion in Puerto Rico (*in* Advances in input-output analysis. Edited by K. Polenske and J. Skelks. Cambridge, Mass.: Ballinger Publisher, 1976, p. 205–228, appendix, graphs, tables)

Study directed toward investigating the sources of rapid changes in employment and income distribution in Puerto Rico during a decade of extraordinary growth

(1953–63). Also evaluates the impact on the island economy both of continuing its so-called successful growth strategy and of departing from this historical path. Concludes that the termination of export promotion strategy may be a practical alternative in the search for real job creation. For Spanish version, see *Distribución del ingreso* (Edited by Alejandro Foxley. Mexico: Fondo de Cultura Económica, 1974, p. 90–110).

3327 ――――. A multi-sector simulation model of employment, growth, and income distribution in Puerto Rico: a re-evaluation of successful development strategy. With the assistance of Richard Levy, Laurie Nisonoff, and Edward Wolff. Washington, D.C.: U.S. Department of Labor, Manpower Administration, 1972. 1 v. (mimeo) appendixes; charts; graphs; tables.

Measures the historical trend in employment, and discusses different development strategies for the coming decades. Concludes that "modern" industrialization strategy discriminated against the employment objective in favor of the income objective. Recommends a strategy based on import substitution of consumer goods maximizing local employment while income levels remain stable. One appendix concludes that food income elasticity is slightly higher in Puerto Rico than in developing countries, although still less than unity, while elasticity for other goods is strikingly similar.

3328 ―――― and **Edward Wolff.** Development and trade dependence: the case of Puerto Rico 1948–1963 (HU/RES, 57:4, Nov. 1975, p. 470–477)

Measures net effects of the industrialization process on the structure of import flows, and examines the resulting changes in dependence on imports. Concludes that despite income increases, prices decline. Induced imports declined because of the overwhelming imports saving effect on the technical structure.

3329 ―――― and ――――. Linkages and leakages: industrial tracking in an enclave economy (UC/EDCC, 25:4, July 1977, p. 607–628, tables)

Analysis of the linkages between local sectors and leakages to the world economy in the process of creating new industries and displacing others. Concludes that the important linkages to household demand are lost in the "criss-cross" enclave, that the openness of the economy blocks import substitution, and that a "franchising mentality" undermines local entrepreneurship and makes production for the local market almost impossible.

3330 Wells, Henry. Development problems of the 1970s in Puerto Rico (IAUPR/RI, 7:2, Summer 1977, p. 169–192)

Reviews policies toward economic and social development and their consequences (1940–70); examines the development process since 1970; and comments on its implications for Puerto Rico's future political relationship with the US.

3331 Wolff, Edward. The rate of surplus value in Puerto Rico (JPE, 83:5, Oct. 1975, p. 935–949, bibl., tables)

Using a Marxian frame of reference, offers an algebraically consistent and empirically operational estimation of the rate of surplus value and of the impact of technological change on it. Finds the rate of surplus value to be relatively stable and its level surprisingly high despite massive industrialization and radical transformation of the society during 1948–53.

3332 Zalacaín, Fernando. Sustitución de importaciones industriales: la experiencia internacional y el caso de Puerto Rico. San Juan, P.R.: s.n., 1975. 97 p.; appendix; graphs; tables.

Technical background paper for *HLAS 39:3150.*

3333 Zell, Steven. Analysing Puerto Rican migration: problems with the data and the model (USDL/MLR, 100:8, Aug. 1977, p. 29–34, tables)

Criticizes item **3271** stating that its model is predictive of net migration flows, and does not present their structure. For response to Zell's criticism, see item **3270.**

COLOMBIA AND ECUADOR

R. ALBERT BERRY, *Professor of Economics, University of Toronto*

COLOMBIA: THE RAPID ECONOMIC GROWTH that has been taking place for over a decade combined with the resulting widening gap in incomes has stimulated scholarly interest in problems of income distribution, low-income occupations, small-scale industry, and related subjects. Important studies of income distribution are those of Fields and Schultz (item **3343**), who highlight the association across persons between educational level and income; Selowsky (item **3357**), whose study of the incidence of the benefits of government expenditures breaks new methodological ground; and Thirsk (item **3360**), who reviews information on the extent of rural poverty. Roa (item **3355**) presents a more general critique of contemporary Colombia as a non-egalitarian society. The Swansea University project on the urban informal sector of Cali has generated a number of revealing studies, such as those by Birkbeck and Bromley (items **3336** and **3337**). Moser's very detailed look at a group of self-employed small-scale traders is helpful (item **3352**). Huddle finds high savings rates among the group of artisans he surveyed (item **3346**). Small and medium-sized manufacturing industry, a step or two up the economic hierarchy from the informal sector, is analyzed by Gómez and Villaveces (item **3345**).

The coffee and drug bonanzas that dramatically increased dollar revenues in the mid-1970s ended, at least for the time being, Colombia's chronic foreign exchange shortage. This phenomenon is one of the subjects discussed in the volume edited by Wiesner (item **3358**). Two factors, the drug sector and the inflation that was partially caused by an excess of foreign exchange, helped create Colombia's large "clandestine economy," which operates alongside the legal one. Junguito (item **3347**) discusses the difficulties the existence of this clandestine economy has posed for monetary policy; and Child (item **3338**) maintains that the attempt to crush it has failed, suggesting that a better solution would be to incorporate it into the legal economy to the extent possible.

The state of the industrial sector became a source of concern in the late 1970s, as investment had dropped to a disturbingly low level. Misas (item **3351**) argues that the López government's important liberalization strategy failed to promote growth and efficiency. Ocampo's study (item **3353**) of the attitudes of prominent businessmen and others emphasizes the lack of consensus on the problems facing the country. Of special interest in connection with industrial development is Lombard's review of the screening system for foreign investment applications that was established by Law 444 in 1967 (item **3349**). However, studies of how government decision-making on a particular issue relates to the wider polity and society are still few and far between.

The economic history of Colombia is still in many ways unexplored, but there are encouraging signs of increasing activity in this area. Two examples are Bergquist's study (item **3334**) of the political economy of coffee at the turn of the century, a particularly important contribution, and Uribe's work which offers an interesting broader review of the subject (item **3361**).

Colombia's agrarian reform program may now also be considered history; the studies by Galli (item **3344**) and Skoczek (item **3359**) emphasize its failure to challenge seriously the evolution of the rural economy towards large scale capitalistic units. Vélez (item **3362**) blames sluggish food production on this trend. The study of rural electrification by Saunders et al. (item **3356**) identifies what will probably be an increasingly important policy concern in the future.

The economic role of women in Colombia is a relatively new area of research. A noteworthy contribution on this subject is the study by León de Leal and Deere (item **3348**) on the sexual division of labor in Colombian agriculture.

ECUADOR: A number of themes of common concern in Latin America—among them the issues of dependency and inequality—emerge in the current literature on Ecuador. The chapters by Salgado (item **3370**) and Moncada (item **3367**) in the book *Ecuador, hoy*, edited by G. Drekonja, provide a useful overview of the past and the present, as well as presenting options for the future. Recognition that the current oil boom will not last forever is reflected in the studies concerned with industrial development. Agosin (item **3365**) critically evaluates Ecuador's Ley de Fomento Industrial, and Pfaller (item **3368**) reflects more generally on industry's options and probable future problems. Former Agriculture Minister Maldonado articulately describes the aftermath of the 1973 attempt at agrarian reform and the groups that sabotaged it.

COLOMBIA

Administración López Michelsen, 74–78: una gestión con proyecciones hacia el año dos mil. See item **6339**.

Arango, Mariano. Café e industria, 1850–1930. See *HLAS 42:2971*.

Bejarano, Jesús Antonio. El fin de la economía exportadora. See *HLAS 42:2973*.

3334 Bergquist, Charles W. Coffee and conflict in Colombia, 1886–1910. Durham, N.C.: Duke University Press, 1978. 277 p.; bibl.; ill.; index.

Important analysis of a crucial transitional period in Colombian history. Author relates upper class ideological and economic interests to the political history of the time. For historian's comment, see *HLAS 42:2971*.

Bernal Pinilla, Luis Darío. Siglo XIX: los comerciantes vs. Colombia. See *HLAS 42:2975*.

3335 Berry, R. Albert and **William R. Cline.** Agrarian structure and productivity in developing countries: a study prepared for the International Labour Office within the framework of the World Employment Programme. Baltimore: Johns Hopkins University Press, 1979. 248 p.; bibl.; graphs; index.

Systematic study of the relationship of farm-size to output. Conclusion: small farms usually make better use of scarce factor (land) as well as generate higher social factor productivity. Policy conclusions point to land reform if there is land to divide and providing small farmers with various kinds of assistance even where there is not. Brazil and Colombia are among major case studies. [J. M. Hunter]

3336 Birkbeck, Chris. Self-employed proletarians in an informal factory: the case of Cali's garbage dump (WD, 6:9/10, Sept./Oct. 1978, p. 1173–1186)

In-depth study of the organization of work among the scavengers at the garbage dump in Cali, Colombia.

Boletín de Coyuntura Socioeconómica. No. 1, mayo 1980– . See *HLAS 42:199*.

Brasseur, Gérard. La Guyane, Française: un bilan de trente années. See item **5255**.

3337 Bromley, Ray. Organization, regulation and exploitation in the so-called "urban informal sector:" the street traders of Cali, Colombia (WD, 6:9/10, Sept./Oct. 1978, p. 1161–1172)

Useful analysis of street traders as an example of the "urban informal sector." Points out that many traders operate illegally, and emphasizes their fairly frequent interaction with large enterprise and the negative official attitudes they confront.

3338 Child Vélez, Jorge. Detrás del dinero (Economía Colombiana [Contraloría General de la República, Bogotá] 125, 4. epoca, feb./marzo 1980, p. 46–52)

Expresses rather common point of view in Colombia that the attempt to do away with the "clandestine" economy (especially the drug trade) has backfired, and that a better strategy would be to effect a rational incorporation of many of these activities into the legal economy.

3339 Dent, David W. Urban development and governmental response: the case of Medellín (*in* Metropolitan Latin America: the challenge and the response [see *HLAS 41:9016*] p. 127–153, bibl., map, tables)

Medellín's administration has responded with unusual concern and dynamism to the problems associated with growth. However, this response has led to a concentration of political and other power in Medellín that is detrimental to nearby, secondary cities.

3340 Economic policy and income distribution in Colombia. Edited by R. Albert Berry and Ronald Soligo. Boulder, Colo.: Westview Press, 1980. 269 p. (A Westview replica edition)

Highly informative, clear and logically written book that could be easily adapted to the classroom. Provides a comprehensive description of the effects of various fiscal policies—particularly those governing taxes and expenditures—on income distribution in Colombia. This important contribution to the literature on Colombia is highly recommended for researchers as well as teachers. [J. Salazar-Carrillo]

3341 Fernández, Javier. Colombia y el Grupo Andino: análisis de estrategias (CEDE/DS, 3, enero 1980, p. 13–50, tables)

Concludes that Colombia has achieved some moderate benefits from participation in the Andean Group, but fewer than its partners. Maintains that Colombia would benefit considerably more if trade barriers among the members were reduced. Thoughtful article.

Fernández, Raúl A. Imperialist capitalism in the Third World: theory and evidence from Colombia. See item **6346.**

3342 Fields, Gary S. Migración permanente en Colombia: prueba de la hipótesis del ingreso esperado (CEDE/DS, 3, enero 1980, p. 97–116, bibl., tables)

Analysis of interdepartmental migration in Colombia on the basis of the 1973 population census. Concludes that economic opportunities are the dominant cause of migration flows.

3343 ——— and T. Paul Schultz. Regional inequality and other sources of income variation in Colombia (UC/EDCC, 28:3, April 1980, p. 447–467, tables)

Analysis based on the 1973 population census finds that education is the strongest single correlate of income levels, and that regional differences, while substantial, are relatively unimportant.

Galindo, Aníbal. Estudios económicos y fiscales. See *HLAS 42:2979.*

3344 Galli, Rosemary E. Colombia: el desarrollo rural como mecanismo de control social (UNAM/RMS, 41[41]:2, abril/junio 1979, p. 545–572)

Insightful interpretation of government support for rural development programs in Colombia (most of which are designed for purposes of social control rather than social change).

García, Antonio. Colombia: medio siglo de historia contemporánea. See *HLAS 42:2980.*

3345 Gómez Buendía, Hernando and **Ricardo Villaveces Pardo.** La pequeña y mediana industria en el desarrollo colombiano. Carátula diseñada por Hugo Zapata. Bogotá: Inéditos, 1979. 175 p.; bibl.

Studies the role that small and medium-scale industry has played in Colombia's development, analyzes their problems and prospects, and makes policy suggestions for increasing their contribution to the economy.

3346 Huddle, Donald L. An analysis of the saving behaviour of a group of Colombian artisan entrepreneurs (WD, 7:8/9, Aug./Sept. 1979, p. 847–864, tables)

Study showing that an important low-income Colombian subgroup—the artisan—has high and rising marginal savings rates. This is explained by "own" investment opportunities and high rates of return on simple capital equipment, inventories and educational services.

3347 Junguito Bonnet, Roberto. La economía subterránea y la política monetaria (Economía Colombiana [Contraloría General de la República, Bogotá] 125, 4. época, feb./marzo 1980, p. 57–64, tables)

Points out the dramatic increase in the importance of the "underground" economy during the 1970s, specifically the coffee and drug bonanzas. The latter have created problems in the control of the money supply and in tax collection. Furthermore, the high level of inflation has increased the incentive to engage in clandestine economic activities.

3348 León de Leal, Magdalena and Carmen Diana Deere. Estudio de la mujer rural y el desarrollo del capitalismo en el agro colombiano (CM/DE, 12:1[34], 1978, p. 4–36)

Attempt to determine how the development of capitalist agriculture in Colombia has affected the sexual division of labor. Hypothesizes that women play the role of a "reserve army" to be recruited or dismissed according to demand.

3349 Lombard, François J. The foreign investment screening process in LDCs: the case of Colombia, 1967–1975. Foreword by Covey T. Oliver. Boulder, Colo.: Westview Press, 1979. 171 p.; bibl. (A Westview replica edition)

Important initial look at the functioning of the Colombian system for screening foreign investment applications that was instituted in 1967. Emphasizes the role of domestic politics in the process.

3350 López Arias, César Augusto. Empresas multinacionales. Bogotá?: Ediciones Universidades Simón Bolívar, Libre de Pereira y Medellín, 1977. 195 p.; bibl. (Colección Universidad y pueblo; 17)

Responsible study of the presence, impact, importance of foreign investment in Colombia. From the outset, though, his "contra" position is clear. [J. M. Hunter]

3351 Misas Arango, Gabriel. La politique industrielle du gouvernement López: 1974–1979 (FDD/NED [Problèmes d'Amérique Latine, 52] 4523/4524, 20 juillet 1979, p. 90–104, tables)

Argues that the López government's import liberalization strategy failed to induce growth and efficiency in manufacturing because the country's oligopolistic structure constituted a barrier which could only be broken down by aggressive government involvement.

3352 Moser, Caroline O. N. Why the poor remain poor: the experience of Bogotá market traders in the 1970s (SAGE/JIAS,

22:3, Aug. 1980, p. 365–387, bibl., tables)

Examines self-employed small-scale traders in a Bogotá plaza and analyzes the reasons for their failure to make economic progress by capital formation during 1970–78. Personal life crises, such as illness, and the incursion of large-scale capital (e.g., supermarkets) are cited as key factors.

Musgrove, Philip and Robert Ferber. Identifying the urban poor: characteristics of poverty households in Bogotá, Medellín and Lima. See item **2886.**

3353 Ocampo Zamorano, Alfredo. Hacia un nuevo compromiso del empresario con Colombia: estudio sociológico. Cali: Fundación para la Educación Superior, 1978. 338 p.; bibl.; ill. (Ediciones FES-Tercer Mundo; v. 1)

On the basis of a large number of interviews, author concludes that there is a serious lack of consensus on Colombia's problems and goals among prominent businessmen, politicians, and administrators, as well as lack of will and social discipline. Believes this situation gives cause for serious concern.

Orlandi, Alberto. Prices and gains in the world coffee trade. See item **2895.**

Palacios, Marco. Coffee in Colombia, 1850–1970: an economic, social, and political history. See *HLAS 42:2989.*

3354 Peláez V., Santiago. La industria de la confección, Valle de Aburrá, 1977: estructura productiva, financiera y evolución reciente. Medellín: Centro de Investigaciones Económicas, 1978. 261 p.; bibl.; graphs.

Very detailed study of the clothing industry in the Medellín region.

3355 Roa Suárez, Hernando. Colombia: dependiente y no participante; aspectos económicos, sociales, culturales y políticos de la participación. Aproximación a un análisis crítico. 2. ed. Bogotá: Universidad Jorge Tadeo Lozano, 1974. 143 p.; bibl.; tables.

Economic, social, cultural, and political indicators reveal how far Colombia is from being a truly democratic participatory society.

3356 Rural electrification and development: social and economic impact in Costa Rica and Colombia. John Saunders et al. Boulder, Colo.: Westview Press, 1978. 180 p.; bibl.; ill. (A Westview replica edition)

Useful analysis of the effects of rural electrification projects. This recent development in Latin America deserves more study.

3357 Selowsky, Marcelo. Who benefits from government expenditure?: a case study of Colombia. New York: Published for the World Bank by Oxford University Press, 1979. 186 p.; bibl.; index.

Important study of income redistribution through government expenditures. Study is strong methodologically because it uses per-capita family income rather than family income to measure economic welfare, and because its benefit incidence estimates are based on a survey specifically designed for that purpose. Expenditures on health, public utilities, and education (primary education in particular) were found to be progressive.

3358 Simposio sobre Financiamiento Externo, 2d, *Medellín, Colombia, 1978.* Política económica externa de Colombia, 1978. Eduardo Wiesner, editor. Bogotá?: Asociación Bancaria de Colombia, 1978. 349 p.; bibl.; graphs (Biblioteca Asociación Bancaria de Colombia)

Valuable set of essays by Colombian economists on topics concerning Colombia's external sector and related policy (e.g., devaluation, capital movements, and the coffee bonanza).

3359 Skoczek, Maria. La reforma agraria y las transformaciones de la agricultura en Colombia y Venezuela (PAN/ES, 4, 1978, p. 181–203, maps)

Argues that the agrarian reform agencies in Colombia and Venezuela have created many facilities that benefit larger farms, while having practically no direct effect on the mass of small farmers and landless workers. They have thus accelerated the development of capitalistic relationships in the countryside.

Temas Económicos. See HLAS 42:235.

3360 Thirsk, Wayne R. Some facets of rural poverty in Colombia. Washington: Agency for International Development, Bureau for Latin America and the Caribbean, Rural Development Division, 1978. 77 p.; tables (General working document; 2)

Thorough and useful review of the facts on rural poverty in Colombia. Concludes that the distribution of rural income

is highly concentrated, the bottom six deciles may reasonably be considered poor, and the poor have received some of the fruits of rural growth.

3361 Uribe Garros, Carlos. Panorama de la economía colombiana. Bogotá: Universidad Externado de Colombia, 1975. 322 p.; bibl.; index.

Sweeping but interesting review of Colombia's economic history from the Spanish conquest to the present.

Urrutia, Miguel. El sindicalismo durante el siglo XIX. See *HLAS 42:2997.*

3362 Vélez M., Hugo E. Factores de inflación en la economía colombiana, 1971–1977. Bogotá: Inéditos, 1979. 204 p.; bibl.

Attributes the rapid inflation of the 1970s in Colombia to sluggish food production, which is, in turn, caused by the advance of capitalistic relationships in the agricultural sector.

3363 Vidales, Luis. Historia de la estadística en Colombia. Recolectaron los datos y el material bibliográfico, José Luis Díaz Granados y Alfredo Leguízamo Motto. Bogotá: Banco de la República, 1978. 594 p.; bibl.

Worthwhile compilation of the history and present state of socioeconomic statistics in Colombia. Will be a time-saver for many researchers.

3364 Wolff, Juergen H. Reflexiones sobre el control fiscal en Colombia (PUJ/U, 53, dic. 1977, p. 33–51)

Argues that the fiscal scandals Colombia has suffered with some frequency are due to certain defects in its fiscal procedures, and suggests changes.

Zambrano Pantoja, Fabio. La economía colombiana en la primera mitad del siglo 19, 1820–1850. See *HLAS 42:2999.*

ECUADOR

3365 Agosin, Manuel R. An analysis of Ecuador's industrial development law (JDA, 13:3, April 1979, p. 263–273, tables)

Case study of the development laws that Ecuador has used to further the growth of its industrial sector. Although the *Ley de Fomento Industrial* may have played a role in expanding manufactured exports, its effects on overall economic development have been ambiguous. A more vigorous strategy is needed to stimulate employment and raise the incomes of the poor.

Luzuriaga C., Carlos and **Clarence Zuvekas, Jr.** An annotated bibliography of income, income distribution, and levels of living in rural Ecuador. See *HLAS 42:51.*

3366 Maldonado Lince, Guillermo. La reforma agraria en el Ecuador (UTIEH/C, 34, 1980, p. 33–56)

Former Minister of Agriculture describes the Agrarian Reform Law of 1973, which was decreed by the military government of the day despite opposition from dominant social groups. He then traces the way in which these groups work, by and large successfully, to impede application of the law.

3367 Moncada, José. Las perspectivas de evolución del Ecuador hacia fines del presente siglo: pt. 1 (in Ecuador, hoy. Por Gerhard Drekonja et al. Apéndice documental, Gustavo Jarrín Ampudia. Bogotá: Siglo Veintiuno Editores, 1978, p. 91–33, tables)

Interesting review of Ecuador's socioeconomic evolution during the last 25 years and the options for the rest of this century. Focuses on demographic, technological, industrial, and agricultural developments.

3368 Pfaller, Alfred. Estrategia de industrialización: reflexiones al caso del Ecuador (in Ecuador, hoy. Por Gerhard Drekonja et al. Apéndice documental, Gustavo Jarrín Ampudia. Bogotá: Siglo Veintiuno Editores, 1978, p. 134–165, bibl.)

Author is optimistic about the industrial advances Ecuador may achieve in the near future with the assistance of the Andean Pact. At the same time, he is rather pessimistic concerning the more distant future, mainly because of a predicted absence of a coherent policy to develop a national or regional technological capacity. He expects an accentuation of industrial dualism and a resulting aggrevation of social tensions.

3369 Redclift, M. R. The influence of the Agency for International Development (AID) on Ecuador's agrarian development policy (JLAS, 21:1, May 1979, p. 185–201)

This insightful article makes the very important point that without identifying the "development context" in which agencies like AID operate, it is impossible to explain the variability in its programs and results. To illustrate point, author performs the kind of analysis that he recommends. Study deserves to be widely read. [Q. Jenkins]

3370 Salgado, Germánico. Lo que fuimos y lo que somos (in Ecuador, hoy. Por Gerhard Drekonja et al. Apéndice documental, Gustavo Jarrín Ampudia. Bogotá: Siglo Veintiuno Editores, 1978, p. 19–58)

Good overview of economic change in Ecuador during the 20th century. Notes that lack of concern for the poor has been typical of most of the country's administrations.

Verduga, César and **Gustavo Cosse.** El Estado y el agro en el caso ecuatoriano: reflexiones sobre una investigación. See item **8282.**

VENEZUELA

JORGE SALAZAR-CARRILLO, *Chairman and Professor of Economics, Florida International University; Non-Resident Staff Member, Brookings Institution*

THIS IS THE FOURTH VOLUME of *HLAS* for which I review the economic literature on Venezuela. Even though progress has been noted before, first in quantity and then in quality, it is certainly only now, at the beginning of the 1980s, that it can be said that the publishing of economic research has come of age in Venezuela.

Three signs attest to the maturity of the discipline: quality, diversity, and the nationality of the authors. The quality of recent publications is exemplified by the fact that more than half of the items annotated below are of reasonable worth.

Diversity is evident from the unprecedented wide range of issues analyzed. And finally, only about 10 percent of the authors listed below are foreigners, the overwhelming majority being Venezuelans. Indeed, for the first time Venezuelan economists now figure prominently in the economic literature about Venezuela published abroad, proof of the international recognition accorded Venezuelan economists by their foreign peers.

Also worthy of mention in this year's section is the appearance of important studies dealing with Venezuela's main economic problems: development planning, monetary policy, industrial policy, fiscal policy, income distribution, agricultural policy, labor policy, and natural resource policy. Economics history is well-represented by solid pieces on public finance, the establishment of the Central Bank, and economic development during the last 35 years. This latter group of books are the latest examples of the Central Bank of Venezuela's continuing tradition of support for serious economic research.

There is no developing country that provides more enlightening information on the direct and indirect effects of the production, marketing, transportation and exploration of oil and its by-products than Venezuela. The literature on these topics, as well as on OPEC and Venezuela's position in it, is profuse, and may profitably be consulted by specialists from other developing countries.

A final trend that should be noted is the improvement in the publications of the Universidad Central de Venezuela. They have become more empirically and academically-oriented, as well as more diverse in their choice of topics.

In conclusion, I would like to thank Professor Mostaffa Hassan, of the Department of Economics of Florida International University, who has rendered invaluable assistance by annotating a number of items for this section and is identified by his initials. Annotations that appear without initials were written by this author.

3371 **Ablan de León, Evelyn** and **Mercedes M. da Costa F.** Demanda de dinero en Venezuela. Caracas: Banco Central de Venezuela, 1979? 47 p.; bibl.; graphs (Colección Premio Ernesto Peltzer; 4)

Consists of an empirical estimate of the demand for money in Venezuela which is applied to the country's monetary policy and planning. This very short essay merited the Peltzer Prize of the Central Bank of Venezuela.

3372 **Albornoz, Orlando.** Higher education and the politics of development in Venezuela (SAGE/JIAS, 19:3, Aug. 1977, p. 291–314, bibl., tables)

Article points out the contrast between Venezuela's modernization and recent development policies and its relatively antiquated system of higher education. Another paradox noted is that neither the presence nor the nationalization of oil resources has produced the improvement in human resources that development requires.

3373 **Armas D., Isbelia.** El seguro de crédito a la exportación en Venezuela (BCV/REL, 13:54, 1978, p. 277–297)

Describes Venezuela's system of credit insurance for export. Sec. 1 explains system's various aspects as established in a 1977 regulation; sec. 2 briefly compares credit insurance systems of Venezuela, Argentina, Colombia, and Mexico; sec. 3 evaluates system's effects on the promotion of exports. Author draws several conclusions in the final section. [MFH]

3374 **Ascanio, Alfredo.** Turismo y desarrollo de la comunidad: una experiencia venezolana (IEAS/R, 28:109, oct./dic. 1979, p. 53–69)

Article explaining a tourism program in the small rural community of El Cerrito in the state of Lara, Venezuela. After describing the community, author traces the program's development and analyzes its objectives. Stresses cooperative basis of program's administrative structure, concluding that this type of program benefits the community more than conventional ones. [MFH]

3375 Banco Central de Venezuela, *Caracas.* La economía venezolana e·n los últimos treinta y cinco años. Caracas: BCV, 1978. 331 p.; bibl.; graphs.

Important study of Venezuela's sectoral and overall economic and financial development (1940–75), presented through graphs and statistics. Part of series published every five years and aimed at the general public, this is the best compendium of its kind.

3376 Baptista, Asdrúbal. Gasto público, ingreso petrolero y distribución del ingreso (FCE/TE, 47[2]:186, abril/junio 1980, p. 431–464, tables)

Innovative attempt to analyze the use of petroleum-generated income in Venezuela within the framework of classical value and distribution theory. Author examines the system of using revenue generated by petroleum income for public expenditures, and analyzes the impact of this system upon income distribution in Venezuela in the post-World War II period. Concludes that the system favors the manufacturing capitalist class.

3377 Benko, François and Anne Benko de Rotaeche. La OPEP; presente y futuro (UCV/ECS, 17:1, junio/sept. 1978, p. 52–65)

Author describes the nature of OPEC, emphasizing the economic, political, social, and geographic dissimilarity of its member countries. Explains role of OPEC both within and outside of the petroleum-producing world, and makes recommendations to assure the organization's future success and the welfare of its members. [MFH]

3378 Bracho, Frank Enrique. El efecto demostración y su importancia como factor explicativo del subdesarrollo (BCV/REL, 12:47, 1977, p. 37–76, tables)

Incorporates the demonstration effect into a development theory after careful review of the concept. Venezuela is analyzed as specific case in point. [J. M. Hunter]

3379 Brito Figueroa, Federico. Historia económica y social de Venezuela: una estructura para su estudio. 3. ed. Caracas: Universidad Central de Venezuela, Ediciones

de la Biblioteca, 1979? 1 v.; bibl.; ill. (Colección Historia)

Historical analysis of the social and economic problems confronting Venezuela at the beginning of the 20th century, when oil companies began their activity. This development transformed Venezuela's backward agricultural economy into an oil-producing one. The substantial social, cultural, and demographic changes that resulted from the monopolistic exploitation of the country's natural resources were facilitated by the local oligarchy, led by Juan Vicente Gómez.

3380 Bueno, Gerardo M. Desarrollo y petróleo: la experiencia de los países exportadores (FCE/TE, 47[2]:186, abril/junio 1980, p. 283–301, tables)

Thoughtful review of the major economic changes produced in the OPEC countries by the sudden rise in oil prices. Author compares economic performance of these countries before and after the oil crisis. He is pessimistic about the use of oil revenues as a panacea for the significant socioeconomic problems of the oil-exporting countries, and urges their implementation of a more realistic economic policy.

3381 Bye, Vegard. Nationalization of oil in Venezuela: re-defined dependence and legitimization of imperialism (JPR, 16:1, 1979, p. 57–78, bibl.)

Analyzes principal effects of oil nationalization in Venezuela. Examines development of internal and external structures of dominance that led to the nationalization of oil, and predicts the long-term effects that nationalization will have on the structure of dominance of Venezuelan society.

3382 Calderón Berti, Humberto. Hacia una política petrolera integral: la responsabilidad nacional, el compromiso internacional. Caracas, Venezuela: Ministerio de Energía y Minas, 1979. 36 p.; ill. (La Alquitrana; 7)

Two speeches by the present Minister of Energy and Mines of Venezuela, one focusing on national policy; the other on the broader Latin American perspective. Also contains a joint statement issued by the Latin American energy ministers on the occasion of an extraordinary meeting of the Latin American Energy Organization (July 1979).

3383 CAP, cero en agricultura. José Luis Zapata et al; con prólogo de Luis Herrera Campins. Maracaibo: Fondo Editorial IRFES, 1977. 294 p. (Colección Crítica actual y alternativa; 78)

Collection of articles by a group of technicians and individuals familiar with Venezuelan agriculture, under the leadership of the current President of Venezuela, Luis Herrera Campins. Deals with the alleged collapse of the country's agriculture under the government of President Carlos Andrés Pérez. Weak in statistical analysis, the work reflects a political bias, since Herrera Campins was a member of the opposition during Pérez' presidency.

Castellanos, Diego Luis and **Guillermo D. Márquez.** La Ley de Comercio Exterior de los Estados Unidos: 1974. See item **2775.**

3384 Domínguez, Raúl. Apuntes sobre el desarrollo del capitalismo en el campo en la Venezuela contemporánea (UCV/ECS, 17:1, julio/sept. 1978, p. 66–90, tables)

This conference paper examines the spread of agribusiness, the impact of the oil boom, and the consequences of the agrarian reform in rural Venezuela. Also studies the existing social structure of agriculture and its relationship to the industrial process of import substitution that characterizes the urban economy.

3385 Edmonston, Barry and **Frank Wm. Oechsli.** Fertility decline and socioeconomic change in Venezuela (SAGE/JIAS, 19:3, Aug. 1977, p. 369–393, bibl., tables)

Authors examine the time trend of fertility for Venezuela and its component states, using data from the 1950, 1961, and 1971 censuses, and from vital statistics reports. Changes in fertility are analyzed in order to determine the relationship between fertility and an index of development and literacy for all Venezuelan states.

3386 Egaña, Manuel R. Documentos relacionados con la creación del Banco Central de Venezuela. Caracas: Banco Central de Venezuela, 1979/1980. 3 v.; bibl. (Colección histórico-económico venezolana; v. 15/17)

These three volumes, describing the historical, political, and economic factors that led to the establishment of the Central Bank of Venezuela, form part of a multi-volume work on Venezuelan economic history. They contain the principal documents related to the establishment of the Bank, including memoranda, technical papers, proposals, rationales, and drafts and final versions of the pertinent legislation. The introduction by Manuel Egaña provides a detailed account of the founding of the Bank.

3387 Egidi Belli, Raniero. Teoría y política monetarias. 2. ed. Caracas: Universidad Central de Venezuela, Facultad de Ciencias Económicas y Sociales, División de Publicaciones, 1977. 495 p.; bibl.; ill. (Colección Libros)

This work includes a wide variety of macroeconomic analyses. An introduction on the various aspects of money is followed by a discussion of monetary theory that is divided into two sections: one on the value of money and another on monetary standards. The book's last part, covering elements of monetary policy, is divided into three sections: on the banking system and other financial institutions; on business cycles; and on international monetary policy. [MFH]

3388 Flores D., Max. El capitalismo en la Venezuela actual (UCV/ECS, 18:1, enero/marzo 1979, p. 8–24)

Short essay examines the function of neo-capitalism in the Venezuelan economy. Author finds the state to be the essential component in the neo-capitalist structure of society.

3389 Fondo de Inversiones de Venezuela. Evolución de la deuda pública de Venezuela. Caracas: Fondo de Inversiones de Venezuela, 1979? 134, 2 p.; bibl.

Brief history of the Venezuelan public debt since the country's independence. This useful monograph relates government borrowing to various stages in the nation's economic history. Its purpose is to place the activities of the Venezuelan Investment Fund (Fondo de Inversiones de Venezuela) within the context of its financial evolution.

3390 Foro sobre Nacionalización Petrolera, *Universidad Central de Venezuela, 1978.* Resultados de la nacionalización petrolera. Caracas: Universidad Central de Venezuela, Facultad de Ciencias Económicas y Sociales, División de Publicaciones, 1979. 46 p. (Colección Esquema)

Proceedings of a forum organized by

the School of Economics at the Universidad Central of Venezuela. The topic, the effects of oil nationalization in Venezuela, is debated by that university's most distinguished professors of economics.

3391 Gutiérrez, Francisco J. Hacia el desarrollo integral de la Faja Petrolífera del Orinoco (Síntesis Geográfica [Universidad Central de Venezuela, Facultad de Humanidades, Escuela de Geografía, Caracas] 2:4, julio/dic. 1978, p. 3–8)

A summary of the Plan for the Development of the Orinoco River Petroleum Belt in Venezuela. Author considers the several factors that should be taken into account in such an expansion, particularly the increased environmental pollution it will bring about.

3392 Hernández D., Carlos and Oswaldo Rodríguez L. Las reservas internacionales en divisas del Banco Central de Venezuela. Caracas: El Banco, 1979. 53 p.; bibl. (Colección Premio Ernesto Peltzer; 2)

This essay, awarded the Ernesto Peltzer Prize of the Central Bank of Venezuela, indicates the increasing sophistication of Venezuelan economists. By applying an econometric model of the recursive kind, authors determine the optimal reserve holdings of the Venezuelan Central Bank (based on conditions existing in 1975).

3393 Historia de las finanzas públicas en Venezuela. v. 20, t. 9A, 1871–1874. Compilación, ordenación y análisis por Tomás Enrique Carrillo Batalla. Caracas: Banco Central de Venezuela, 1978. 375 p.; tables (Sección Doctrinal)

This volume compiles and organizes documents related to public finance in Venezuela for the period 1870–75. In his introduction, Carrillo Batalla outlines the important developments in public finance that took place during this period. The rest of the book consists of annual reports of persons and organizations involved in public finance, such as the Minister of Finance, Santiago Goiticoa (1871–72); Manuel M. Azpuruna on the protection of national industries (1871); Minister of Public Credit (1873); Minister of Development (1873); the Code of Finance; customs laws (1873); and the Treasury of Public Credit. [MFH]

3394 Khatkhate, Deena R.; Vicente G. Galbis; and Delano P. Villaneuva. A money multiplier model for a developing economy: the Venezuelan case (IMF/SP, 21:3, Nov. 1974, p. 740–757, bibl.)

Using Venezuela as an example, authors analyze determinants of the money multiplier process in a developing economy with a fixed exchange rate. Paper is divided into two sections: presentation and discussion of an annual money multiplier model, and an examination of the model's applicability to forecasting and policy stimulation.

3395 Kurze, Herbert. Ungleichmässigkeiten durch Diskriminierungen und Lücken in der Einkommensbesteuerung auf Barbados, Trinidad & Tobago und in Venezuela (DDW, 7:2, 1979, p. 159–172)

Author compares tax structures in Barbados, Trinidad, Tobago, and Venezuela, and comes to the conclusion that there are many loopholes in the general taxation systems of these countries that can be exploited by taxpayers. Considers the Venezuelan tax structure to be more equitable than the others. [R. V. Shaw]

3396 Latin American Institute for Economic and Social Planning. Universidad de los Andes de Venezuela: bases para una estrategia de su desarrollo. Prepared by J. Medina Echevarría et al. Santiago de Chile: El Instituto, 1976. 224 p. (Doctrina universitaria; 1)

Vol. 1 in a series projected by the University of Los Andes under the title *Doctrina Universitaria*. Series is designed to bring together essays of interest to both the academic and administrative units of the university. Volume opens with an introductory statement on higher education in socialist countries, and closes with a study prepared by ILPES on the development of the University.

3397 León de Labarca, Alba Ivonne. La integración económica y sus limitaciones en el ámbito de los países sub-desarrollados. Prólogo de Leontín Constantinesco. Maracaibo, Venezuela: Universidad del Zulia, Facultad de Derecho, 1979. 154 p.; 1 leaf of plates; bibl.; diagrs.; indexes.

Author uses the integrationist experience of the underdeveloped world in general, and of Latin America in particular, to criticize the neo-classical model of development and integration. Argues that the neo-classical model is based on socioeconomic and political structures that are not applicable to Latin America.

3398 López, Víctor Manuel. Venezuela hacia el año 2,000, éxito o fracaso? Caracas: Academia de Ciencias Físicas, Matemáticas y Naturales, 1977. 3 v.; bibl.; ill. (Biblioteca de la Academia de Ciencias Físicas, Matemáticas y Naturales; v. 17/19)

Vol. 1 is divided into two parts: one which analyzes the growth, distribution, educational levels, and standard of living of the Venezuelan population; and another which deals with the country's GNP, emphasizing the petroleum and public sectors. Vol. 2 describes three productive sectors of the Venezuelan economy: agriculture, manufacturing, and mining. Vol. 3 deals with the production, exploration, and reserves of petroleum in the various geographic regions of Venezuela. [MFH]

3399 Lovera, Aníbal. La nacionalización del petróleo en Venezuela: hechos y perspectivas. Caracas: Universidad Central de Venezuela, Facultad de Ciencias Económicas y Sociales, División de Publicaciones, 1980. 144 p.; bibl.; graph (Colección Libros—UCV, Facultad de Ciencias Económicas y Sociales)

Another book on a topic that holds continuing fascination for Venezuelan academicians, especially those at the Universidad Central of Venezuela. Although written in 1976, it contains policy recommendations for the public oil companies that are still relevant today.

Major companies of Brazil, Mexico and Venezuela 1979/1980. See *HLAS 42:151.*

3400 Martínez, Aníbal R. El camino de Petrolia. 2. ed. Caracas: Edreca, 1979. 156 p.; bibl.

Author traces the creation and development of Compañía Petrolia, Venezuela's first oil company. The short-lived company was formed in 1878 and operated in the oil field called "La Alquitrana." Charming and informative piece of research in economic history.

3401 Martz, John D. Policy-making and the quest for consensus: nationalizing Venezuelan petroleum (SAGE/JIAS, 19:4, Nov. 1977, p. 483–508, bibl.)

Historical review of the oil national-ization process in Venezuela that focuses on three issues: national values, policy objectives, and policy instruments. Lists the various persons involved in the nationalization process, and presents their different views. For political scientist's comment, see *HLAS 41:7625.*

3402 Mata Mollejas, Luis. Política económica para políticos. Caracas: Ministerio de Información y Turismo, 1980. 303 p.; bibl.; ill.

Textbook which applies macroeconomic theory and policy to advanced developing economies. Author, a professor at the Simón Bolívar University, uses Venezuelan economic policy to illustrate the application of macroeconomics to the theory and practice of economic planning. Valuable aid to understanding economics in Venezuela.

3403 Mayobre, José Antonio. Problemas de los países exportadores de petróleo (BCV/REL, 14:56, 1979, p. 37–49)

Conference papers by Venezuela's most distinguished economist, recently deceased. It deals with the problems facing petroleum-producing countries, particularly Venezuela, despite their rapid economic growth and increased buying power. Mayobre also considers inflationary tendencies largely caused by imported inflation. Finally, he discusses the future of the world oil market.

3404 Maza Zavala, D. F. Venezuela: coexistencia de la abundancia y la escasez, la difícil acumulación del excedente petrolero (UCV/ECS, 17:1, junio/sept. 1978, p. 7–27, bibl., tables)

Article highlights the paradox of the wide disparity that exists between rich and poor in Venezuela, a country blessed by an abundance of petro dollars. He concludes that the oil boom has increased the public's liquidity and enriched the state, but has had very little impact upon the true key variables of the economy.

3405 ———. Venezuela en los años treinta (*in* América Latina en los años treinta. Luis Antezana E. et al. Coordinador, Pablo González Casanova. México: Instituto de Investigaciones Sociales, Universidad Nacional Autónoma de México, 1977, p. 556–605, tables)

Historical analysis of economic development in Venezuela in the first four decades of the 20th century. Pt. 1 of article examines the pre-petroleum period (i.e., 1830–1916). It focuses on the dynamic nature of the economy (1916–30), the period during which Venezuela's economic base changed from agriculture to petroleum and analyzes government policy of 1930. Pt. 2 deals with various aspects of the Venezuelan economy in 1930 (e.g., foreign trade, investment, and infrastructure). Pts. 3/4 discuss the effects of the Great Depression on the economy and government policy. Last three sections deal with the dynamic economic policy of the periods 1929–35 and 1936–40, and contain a discussion of the economy in 1936. Article concludes with an analysis of factors affecting the power structure in Venezuela, and a comparison between the economic conditions of the 1930s and those of the present. [MFH]

3406 Mieres, Francisco. Nacionalización petrolera y dependencia tecnológica (UCV/ECS, 17:1, julio/sept. 1978, p. 28–51)

Study of the problems arising from the nationalization of oil in Venezuela. Author views the technical assistance and marketing contracts that Venezuela holds with the transnational oil companies previously operating in the country as a continuation of foreign dependence. Lists the most important projects proposed by the transnational companies, discussing some of them as evidence in support of his thesis.

3407 Núñez Tenorio, J. R. En defensa de la rebelión: contra la ideología del reformismo capitalista neocolonial. Caracas: Ediciones de la Biblioteca, Universidad Central de Venezuela, 1979. 295 p.; bibl. (His En defensa de la revolución; libro 4. Colección Avance; 47)

The last volume of a four-volume work by a revolutionary philosopher. Author justifies rebelling against the government and provides an objective which he defines in terms of national conscience, independence, and social justice. An examination of the meandering course of the national process, and of the ideals of the country's forebearers provides the framework for this defense.

3408 Palma C., Pedro A. Perspectivas de la economía venezolana para 1977–1979 (BCV/REL, 13:52, 1978, p. 129–152, tables)

Forecast for the Venezuelan economy during the 1977–79 period, based on an econometric model. Author also provides a description of the principal characteristics of the economy.

3409 Perdereau-Blanchet, Liliane. L'évolution des investissements français au Venezuela, 1830–1970 (UTIEH/C, 32, 1979, p. 107–128)

Historical analysis of French investment in Venezuela. Article's first part deals with French investment in Venezuelan mining, transportation, banking, finance, and other sectors of the economy up to the 1930s. Second part, covering the years since the 1930s, analyzes investment in such areas as banking, insurance, industry, mining and petroleum, and public works and equipment. [MFH]

3410 Pérez Sáinz, Juan Pablo and **Paul Zarembka.** Accumulation and the state in Venezuelan industrialization (LAP, 6[22]:3, Summer 1979, p. 5–29, bibl., tables)

Thorough Marxist analysis of the industrialization effort in Venezuela. Authors divide the growth of the industrial sector into different stages. An initial period dominated by the oil enclave gives way between 1958 and 1973 to a labor-absorptive phase conditioned by state intervention. The state dominates to an even greater extent in the most recent post-1973 period.

3411 Plaza, Salvador de la. La economía minera y petrolera de Venezuela. 2. ed. Caracas: Universidad Central de Venezuela, Facultad de Ciencias Económicas y Sociales, División de Publicaciones, 1980. 64 p.; bibl.; indexes (Colección Salvador de la Plaza)

A short history of the exploitation of oil and iron in Venezuela, written from a Marxist viewpoint. Reedited, after author's death, by the Faculty of Economics and Social Sciences of the Universidad Central of Venezuela.

3412 ———. El problema de la tierra. Caracas: Universidad Central de Venezuela, Facultad de Ciencias Económicas y Sociales, División de Publicaciones, 1980. Económicas y Sociales, División de Publicaciones, 1980. 2 v. (Colección Salvador de la Plaza)

In these two volumes this prolific author returns to subjects about which he has already published a great deal: Venezuela's agrarian reform and the organizational problems facing the country's agricultural system. Book makes ample use of de la Plaza's public addresses, which reflect his Marxist approach to these issues. Of particular interest are the chapters criticizing the substance and implementation of the Agrarian Reform Law, enacted in the early 1960s. Author argues that a new agrarian reform is fundamental to future national economic planning.

3413 Porra, Eloy. Semblanza biográfica de Juan Pablo Pérez Alfonzo: el hombre que sacudió al mundo. Caracas: Editorial Ateneo de Caracas, 1979. 204 p. (Colección Testimonios)

The biography of a distinguished Venezuelan, who, as the founder of OPEC (Organization of Petroleum Exporting Countries), was of central importance to the development of his own country and the rest of the world. Author analyzes the main events shaping Pérez Alfonzo's political and policy-making careers, as well as his role in OPEC.

3414 Quero Morales, Constantino. Imagen-objetivo de Venezuela: reformas fundamentales para su desarrollo. Caracas: Banco Central de Venezuela, 1978. 2 v. (1657 p., 3 fold. leaves of plates); ill. (Colección de estudios económicos; 6)

Extensive work by a former Venezuelan Minister involved in economics. After a relatively brief methodological and historical discussion, author addresses the reforms required to cure the economic ills of Venezuela. No topic is left untouched in these two volumes; careful reading is recommended. Of particular interest is vol. 2 in which Quero Morales considers the industrial and agricultural development of the 1960s and 1970s in the light of the debate on economic protection and government plans. The latter were designed to shape the country's economic growth.

3415 Quintero, Rodolfo. El petróleo y nuestra sociedad. Caracas: Universidad Central de Venezuela, Ediciones de la Biblioteca, 1970. 89 p.; bibl. (Nuevos planteamientos; 8)

Anthropological and cultural study of Venezuelan society in the early 20th century, when the expansion of the petroleum industry began. Author evaluates the impact of "oil colonialism" on the country's sociocultural patterns, calling for the Venezuelan people to free themselves of imported values and beliefs and return to their pristine roots.

3416 Rangel, Domingo Alberto. Capital y desarrollo. t. 2, El rey petróleo. 2. ed. Caracas: Universidad Central de Venezuela, Facultad de Ciencias Económicas y Sociales, División de Publicaciones, 1979? 1 v.; bibl. (Colección Libros)

The book consists of an introduction and five parts. Author's introduction gives a historical overview of the Venezuelan economy in the 19th century. Pt. 1 provides a history of the development of economic relations between the US and Europe on the one hand, and the US and Latin America on the other. It analyzes the capitalistic system, the petroleum market strategies of major countries and international companies, and international investment and trade in Latin America. Pt. 2 deals with the Venezuelan economy, describing the process of capital accumulation and the role of the petroleum industry. Pt. 3 outlines the industry's adverse effects on the country's agriculture. Pt. 4 discusses the effects of the petroleum industry on the role of government in the country's economy, and on the development of other industries. The final part analyzes three specific industries: electricity, beer, and cement. [MFH]

3417 Revel-Mouroz, Jean. Administration de l'espace et développement régional au Venezuela (UTIEH/C, 32, 1979, p. 129–147, maps, tables)

A discussion of regional planning, development, and administration in Venezuela. Pt. 1 covers in detail the organization of regional planning and administration in Venezuela. Pt. 2 deals with the Venezuelan Corporation in Guayana (Corporación Venezolana de Guayana). It analyzes its origins, current organization, and its ambiguous role, and explains the limits of rural space integration. [MFH]

3418 Rivero, Ramón. La OPEP y las nacionalizaciones: la renta absoluta. Caracas: Fondo Editorial Salvador de la Plaza, 1979. 385 p.; bibl. (El imperialismo petrolero y la revolución venezolana; t. 3)

The views of a well-known Venezuelan communist on the nationalization of oil and the role of OPEC. He reviews the creation of this organization, the effects of its oil policies, and the positions of various member countries. Criticizes the new form of oil imperialism, which is expressed as technological dependence. And, in deprecatory terms, describes oil service contracts as exemplifying this new type of domination.

3419 Rodríguez Trujillo, Manuel. La industria de bienes de capital en Venezuela (BCV/REL, 14:53, 1978, p. 35–108, tables)

Essay on the capital goods industry in Venezuela focuses on demand as well as production. Author demonstrates the extent of this industry's dependence on imports. Discusses labor force training, technology transfer, etc., as essential requirements for the development of capital goods production in Venezuela.

3420 Rubio Correa, Marcial. OPEP: imperialismo y Tercer Mundo. Lima: Centro de Estudios y Promoción del Desarrollo, 1976. 159 p.; bibl.

Book divided into five chapters: Chap. 1 deals with the development of the international petroleum industry up until the rapid oil price increases of the 1970s took place. It explains the early concessions to oil companies made in Venezuela and the Middle East. Chap. 2 outlines the factors that enabled the petroleum-exporting countries to achieve their current position of power. Chap. 3 analyzes the effect of the petroleum industry's situation since the early 1970s on the oil-exporting countries, the developed and underdeveloped oil-consuming countries, and the multinational oil corporations. Chap. 4 provides some perspective on the market strategy of OPEC and the oil-consuming countries. The final chapter considers the possibility of other developing countries imitating OPEC and the effects this revolutionary event would have on trade relations between the developing and underdeveloped countries. [MFH]

3421 Sequera de Segnini, Isbelia. Dinámica de la agricultura y su expresión en Venezuela. Caracas: Ariel-Seix Barral Venezolana, 1978. 331 p.; 2 leaves of plate; bibl.; ill.

Study of Venezuela's agricultural development. It is the magnitude of this sector rather than its rate of growth (which is far below that of industry) that represents its contribution to the economy. The resilience and dynamism of Venezuelan agriculture is dependent on successful collaboration between government and farmers; agricultural credit holds particular promise in this regard.

Unfortunately, the attraction of industry and oil profits conspire against the strength of the country's agriculture.

3422 Sierra, Enrique. Los compromisos de la planificación operativa en Venezuela (BCV/REL, 57/58, 1979, p. 63–152, tables)

Paper examines the major lessons to be drawn from Venezuela's economic planning experience, begun in 1958, one of the oldest in Latin America. Author applies these lessons to the Fifth National Plan, covering the period 1976–80. He describes the basic strategy of this plan, which avoids medium-term planning and planning-programming-budgeting, stressing operational planning instead.

3423 Silva, Carlos Rafael. Bosquejo histórico del desenvolvimento de la economía venezolana en el siglo XX (in Venezuela moderna, medio siglo de historia, 1926–1976. Ramón J. Velásquez et al. 2. ed. Caracas: Fundación Eugenio Mendoza; Editorial Ariel, 1979, p. 763–861, tables)

Outline of the economic development of Venezuela from 1936 to the late 1970s. Author is one of the country's leading economists, and ex-Minister of Education, and most recently, President of the Central Bank. One of the best available short introductions to the recent economic history of Venezuela.

3424 Sullivan, William M. El petróleo en Venezuela: una bibliografía. Winfield J. Burggraaff. Caracas: Ediciones Centauro, 1977. 229 p. (Colección Manuel Segundo Sánchez)

Comprehensive bibliography of materials on the petroleum industry in Venezuela. Contains listings of Masters' theses and PhD dissertations, periodicals publishing relevant articles, and US and Venezuelan government publications. The two largest sections are devoted to books and monographs, and periodical articles.

3425 Valente, Cecilia M. The political, economic, and labor climate in Venezuela. Philadelphia: Industrial Research Unit, Wharton School, University of Pennsylvania, 1979. 280 p.; bibl.; graphs; index (Latin American studies. Multinational industrial relations series; no. 4d)

One of a series of monographs prepared by the Industrial Research Unit of the Wharton School of Business, University of

Pennsylvania. Examines industrial relations and general economic and political conditions in Latin American countries. A little more than one third of this volume on Venezuela is devoted to a description of the country's politics and economics; the rest deals with labor law and practice and union structure.

3426 Venezuela. Banco Central. Los aspectos técnicos de la vinculación entre las políticas monetaria y fiscal en Venezuela (*in* Vinculación entre las políticas fiscal y monetaria: reuniones y seminarios, México, Centro de Estudios Monetarios Latioamericanos, 1979, p. 167–191, tables)

Analysis of the interrelation of fiscal policy and monetary policy in an economy, like Venezuela's, which is driven by tax revenues derived from petroleum. Studies the reaction of the monetary base, the money multiplier and monetary policies in Venezuela to the multiplying value of petroleum exports, and reviews the country's most important fiscal policy actions since the nationalization of the oil industry in 1973.

3427 ———. Ministerio de Energía y Minas. Dirección General Sectorial de Hidrocarburos. Dirección de Planificación y Economía de Hidrocarburos. Oficina de Información y Divulgación. Petróleo y otros datos estadísticos 1977. 20. ed. Caracas: 1977. 196 p.; maps; tables.

Yearly summary of developments in the Venezuelan oil industry. Contains statistics on production, exploration, reserves, consumption, and exports for natural gas as well as oil. Most of the volume is devoted to industry value figures: prices, costs and value added. A useful and reliable source.

3428 ———. Ministerio de Fomento. Dirección General de Estadística y Censos Nacionales. Encuesta de hogares por muestreo, resumen nacional: fuerza de trabajo. 1. semestre 1979– . Caracas.

Survey of Venezuela's labor force, corresponding to the first half of 1979. Data are summarized in 61 tables. Main variables considered are employment, occupation, earnings, age, education, sex, and labor force participation.

**3429 ———. ———.———. Indicadores socioeconómicos y de coyuntura. abril 1977– . Caracas.

Fourth publication in a series that presents current statistics on population, industry, foreign trade, financial and monetary matters in table form. Each section is preceded by a commentary.

3430 ———. Oficina Central de Coordinación y Planificación. El sistema de planificación en Venezuela. Caracas: La Oficina, 1973. 59 leaves; ill.

Describes the planning system of Venezuela and the coordinating role performed by the Planning Office, which holds ministerial rank. Of particular interest is the enumeration of the regional planning principles followed by CORDIPLAN.

3431 ———. ———. Unidad de Prospectiva. Venezuela: un estudio prospectivo, 1975–1990. Caracas: La Unidad, 1975. 96 leaves.

Contains predictions for the Venezuelan economy for the years 1975–90. Volume was produced by the Planning Agency (CORDIPLAN) to aid in the preparation of the Fifth National Plan.

3432 Vila, Marco Aurelio. Geoeconomía de Venezuela. Caracas: Corporación Venezolana de Fomento, Departamento Oficial de Información Pública, Sección de Publicaciones, between 1974 and 1977. 1 v.; bibl.; ill.

Historical analysis of Venezuela's economic and geographical development. Pt. 1 describes the country's basic economic resources concentrating on soil and water conditions as well as erosion. Pt. 2 examines the nation's economic-geographic evolution from the Spanish Conquest to the present, concentrating on the 1930s decade when substantial changes occurred in production, trade and social structure.

3433 Villalobos de Nucete, Mireya. Los principios contables y su vigencia en Venezuela. Caracas: Universidad Central de Venezuela, Facultad de Ciencias Económicas y Sociales, División de Publicaciones, 1978. 284 p.; bibl.; ill. (Colección Libros)

The book is divided into two parts. Pt. 1 treats the theory of accounting, and compares the systems used in various countries (e.g., US, Great Britain). After giving a historical overview of accounting in these countries, author explains the use of the principles of accounting at different administrative levels and the use of uniform accounting principles at the international level. Pt. 2 consists of a case study of accounting in Venezuela. It examines the tendency toward the presentation of financial statements, forms of auditing, the code of professional ethics, the law governing the practice of public accounting, the law of capital market, and the tendency toward a uniform system of accounting. [MFH]

3434 Viloria R., Oscar. Notas para un estudio sobre el desarrollo del capitalismo contemporáneo en Venezuela: génesis y proceso de la industrialización de los años sesenta (UCV/ECS, 17:1, julio/sept. 1978, p. 91–107, tables)

Short essay summarizing the industrialization process in Venezuela, with emphasis on the 1960s.

3435 World Conference on Agrarian Reform and Rural Development, *Rome, 1979.* Agrarian reform and rural development in Venezuela. Caracas: República de Venezuela, Ministerio de Agricultura y Cria, 1979. 52 leaves.

Study of Venezuela's agricultural development since 1960. This monograph was presented by the Ministry of Agriculture at the World Conference on Agrarian Reform and Rural Development which was organized by the Food and Agriculture Organization (FAO). Focuses on Venezuela's agrarian reform and recent agricultural policies. The Agrarian Reform Law sponsors rural development in Venezuela, and provides a link between the nation and the farmers' social, economic, political, and cultural life.

3436 Zanoni, José Rafael. La OPEP y los precios del petróleo. Diseño portada, Héctor Díaz. Caracas: Universidad Central de Venezuela, Facultad de Ciencias Económicas y Sociales, División de Publicaciones, 1979. 235 p.; ill. (Colección Libros)

This study of OPEC begins with a historical analysis of its formation, development, and organization. Chap. 2 gives the economic characteristics of OPEC members. Chap. 3 explains the system of determining petroleum prices and the distribution of petroleum revenues between government and petroleum companies, and analyzes the role of each of the petroleum companies, the governments of OPEC, and the consuming countries. Chap. 4 analyzes the economic consequences of the rapid increase in petroleum prices. Last chapter deals with the future of OPEC which will depend on the future of petroleum as a major source of energy. Study anticipated the continued dependence of major consumers of OPEC oil such as Europe and Japan but also notes OPEC problems which could generate friction in the future. Various measures are outlined to assure the future of OPEC.

CHILE AND PERU

MARKOS MAMALAKIS, *Professor of Economics, University of Wisconsin–Milwaukee*

CHILE: FREE MARKET ECONOMICS in the tradition of the Chicago School dominated by Friedrich von Hayek and Milton Friedman have provided the base for many strategies introduced in Chile during 1973–80. However, as late as 1981, major segments of the economy were still controlled by the State. Private enterprise, free markets, and minimum government intervention have been the pillars of economic policy during the Military Junta and the Presidency of Gen. Augusto Pinochet.

No systematic, comprehensive analysis of the economic events between 1973 and 1980 has appeared as yet. There exist, however, numerous solid studies on such orthodox topics as the demand for money, consumption functions, aggregate econometric models and cost-benefit analysis of various projects.

By early 1981, the rate of inflation in Chile had fallen below the two-digit level, the government budget was in surplus, and construction was booming. In spite of these notable achievements, discussion of an economic miracle seems to be fading since the rate of unemployment continues at the two-digit level for the seventh consecutive year, intolerable poverty still exists in major segments of the society, and income distribution is highly unequal. Other negative factors are falling rates of return for industrial firms in 1980, as compared to 1979, and relatively stagnant industrial, mining, and agricultural output during 1980–81.

Thus, while one set of studies on Chile is inspired by the prevailing winds of economic liberalism, another set deals in such important and unresolved economic issues as unemployment, income distribution, education, and rural and urban poverty. Finally, there is a third group of publications dealing with such neutral topics as public finance, manufacturing, demography, foreign trade, the Church, etc. The openly anti-Junta and anti-Allende articles form a distinct minority.

Among many excellent works annotated for this section, three stand out as major and lasting contributions to Chilean historiography: 1) the World Bank country study, *Chile: an economy in transition* published in 1980 (item **3454**) which contains the best available but nevertheless incomplete treatment of the post–1973 economic policies; 2) O'Brien's excellent article on the "Antofagasta Company" (item **3478**), a major contribution to the understanding of the 1880–1930 nitrate era; and 3) vol. 2 of *Historical statistics of Chile: demography and labor force* (item **3473**), which provides comprehensive statistical coverage and analysis sometimes as far back as the Conquest.

PERU: "An economy in crisis" is the consensus description of Peru made by Right, Left, and Center during the decade of the 1970s, and the economics of crisis is the most apt description of the subject matter of the books, articles, and other documents on Peru reviewed here. As expected, diagnoses of the crisis are as varied and contradictory as the recommended corrective strategies.

The "Peru in crisis" diagnosis and debate are neither new nor unique. What is new is the universal disillusionment with Velasco Alvarado's Peruvian revolutionary experiment. The pessimism pervading most publications is, however, both excessive and deceiving. Although the Peruvian revolutionary slogan of achieving development through "neither communism nor capitalism" has been proven an empty boast, one cannot justify the almost unanimous condemnation of Velasco's road to prosperity and posterity as being the shortest path to economic catastrophe. During the 1970s, Peru may have achieved the critical minimum level of irreversible institutional reform required for development. The current political rebirth and economic revival suggest that the crisis of that decade may have been the price paid for the pragmatism and, hopefully, the prosperity of the 1980s.

There is one study on Peru that is outstanding in terms of its originality, scholarship, and balance. It is Frits Wils' classic treatise on industrialization, industrialists, and the nation-state (item **3550**). Rural development, plural labor markets, export orientation, and the balance-of-payments are other favorite topics of research in the Peruvian literature reviewed.

Poverty, inequality, unemployment, and low productivity are still prevalent in both Peru and Chile. In both countries past economic strategies have had only limited success in insuring continued growth. For the elaboration of adequate development strategies more research is needed in identifying the morphology of production, distribution, and capital formation in each country, especially as it relates to exports. This difficult and elusive basic research is the goose that can lay the golden egg of development. Without this basic research which is yet to be done, communism, capitalism, or any other road to development are but mere labels, as the Chilean and Peruvian experiences have shown.

CHILE

3437 Acevedo, Julio and **Joaquín Vial.** Demanda por dinero y expectativas de inflación: Chile, 1976–1979 (UC/EE, 14:2, 1979, p. 133–169, bibl., tables)
Acevedo and Vial estimate the demand for money and inflationary expectations during 1976–79.

3438 Baltra Cortés, Alberto. Economía chilena y Unidad Popular (BCV/REL, 10:37, 1973, p. 101–150)
Critical examination of economic policy during the Allende presidency.

3439 El Banco Central de Chile: reseña de su historia, funciones y organización. Santiago: Banco Central de Chile, 1977. 71 p.; fold. table.
Reference document describing the history, structure, and functions of Chile's Central Bank.

3440 Barrera, Manuel. Estructura educativa de la fuerza de trabajo chilena (CPU/ES, 17:3, 1978, p. 125–144, tables)
Gives evidence in support of the hypothesis that the educational structure of Chile's economically active population is highly heterogeneous.

3441 Berger, Frederick E. Política cambiaria, el nivel de reservas y distorsión de expectativas. Santiago: Universidad Católica de Chile, Instituto de Economía, Oficina de Publicaciones, 1976. 87 p.; bibl.; graph (Documento de trabajo—Universidad Católica de Chile, Instituto de Economía; no. 52)
Comprehensive theoretical and empirical examination of the Chilean foreign exchange rate and regime, primarily between 1960 and 1976.

3442 Bitar, Sergio. La presencia de la empresa extranjera en la industria chilena (in Bitar, Sergio. Corporaciones multinacionales y autonomía nacional. Caracas, Venezuela: Monte Avila Editores, 1977, p. 87–123)
In this chapter, Bitar examines from a leftist perspective the role of foreign corporations in Chile's industrial sector. This material was originally published in article form in 1973.

3443 ———. Las relaciones económicas entre Chile y EE. UU. en el período 1971–1972 (in Bitar, Sergio. Corporaciones multinacionales y autonomía nacional. Caracas, Venezuela: Monte Avila Editores, 1977, p. 125–144)
Article, written before Allende's death, examines the economic links between Chile and the US during 1971–72.

Campero Q., Guillermo. Las nuevas condiciones en las relaciones del trabajo y la acción política en Chile. See item **6522.**

Cariola, Carmen and **Osvaldo Sunkel.** Chile. See *HLAS 42:3206.*

3444 Carkovic S., María Vicenta. La demanda por el dinero en Chile: su estabilidad en el período 1947–1970. Santiago, Chile: Pontificia Universidad Católica de Chile, Instituto de Economía, Oficina de Publicaciones, 1979. 185 p.; ill. (Documento de trabajo; no. 65)
Excellent study of the demand for money in Chile during the 1947–70 period.

Catalán, Oscar and **Jorge Arrate.** Chile: la política del régimen militar y las nuevas formas de desarrollo en América Latina. See item **6523.**

3445 Chaigneau, Sergio and **Raquel Szalachman.** Distribución de ingresos en el Gran Santiago: 1968–1969 (UC/EE, 12:2, 1978, p. 1–31, tables)
Important study of income distribution in greater Santiago during 1968–69. The very high degree of concentration is explained by the level of education and the occupational category of the family head.

3446 Chile. Oficina de Planificación Agrícola (ODEPA). Desarrollo rural integral II: estructura intermedia urbano rural, conceptualización. Santiago: Oficina de Planificación, Ministerio de Agricultura, 1977 or 1978. 97 p.; bibl.; ill.
Document presents a plan for integrated rural development in Chile.

3447 ———. ———. Directorio de productos exportables chilenos: agrícolas, pecuarios, forestales, del mar. v. 1. Santiago de Chile: ODEPA, 1976/1977 [i.e. 1977?]. 1 v.; graphs; tables.

Provides a detailed statistical picture of Chile's agricultural, livestock, and fishing exports during 1970–75.

3448 ———. ———. Directorio regional de productos exportables chilenos: agropecuarios forestales y del mar: temporada 1977–78. v. 1, I región a V región. v. 2, VI región a VIII región y área metropolitana. v. 3, IX región a XII región. Santiago: ODEPA, 1978. 3 v.

Three volumes provide a regional directory and a detailed regional statistical examination of Chile's agricultural, livestock, forestry, and fishing exports during the 1977–78 agricultural year.

3449 ———. **Oficina de Planificación Nacional** (ODEPLAN). Informe económico anual 1979. Santiago: ODEPLAN, 1980. 253 p.; tables.

Comprehensive examination of the Chilean economy during 1979, prepared by the Planning Office.

3450 ———. ———. Plan nacional indicativo de desarrollo, 1978–1983. Santiago: ODEPLAN, 1978. 137 p.

Describes the evolution of the Chilean economy between 1973–77 and presents government plans for the 1978–83 period.

3451 ———. ———. Posibles áreas de interés para inversiones extranjeras. v. 1, Descripción geo-económica de Chile. v. 2, Proyectos de inversión.

Since 1973 the Chilean government has followed a strategy of establishing a positive climate for private enterprise and of encouraging long-term, direct foreign investment. These two volumes describe Chile's foreign investment laws, the country's natural, human, and infrastructure resources, and gives a detailed list of possible areas of foreign investment.

3452 ———. ———. Comisión de Política Energética. Informe de la Comisión de Política Energética. Santiago: ODEPLAN, 1976. 194 leaves.

Comprehensive study of all aspects of energy supply and demand in Chile.

3453 ———. Universidad, Santiago. Departamento de Economía. Ocupación y desocupación, sectores urbanos de las regiones IV a X, excepto el Gran Santiago. Santiago: 1979. 1 v.

Contains employment and unemployment statistics for Sept. 1979, in urban centers of regions IV to V (except Gran Santiago).

3454 Chile, an economy in transition. Washington, D.C.: Latin America and the Caribbean Regional Office, World Bank, 1980. 584, 18 p.; 1 leaf of plates; bibl.; ill. (A World Bank country study)

World Bank country study constitutes the best survey available of the Chilean economy during the Military Junta (1973–77). In some areas it provides excellent analysis of economic events and policies under the Presidencies of Eduardo Frei and Salvador Allende. Extensive statistical appendix (270 p.).

3455 Corbo Lioi, Vittorio and **Patricio Meller.** Antecedentes empíricos de los sectores externo e industrial chilenos, 1950–1970. Santiago, Chile: Corporación de Investigaciones Económicos para Latinoamérica, 1978. 39, 2 leaves: bibl.; graphs (Apuntes CIEPLAN; no. 1)

Brief empirical examination of foreign trade regimes, the external sector, and Chile's industrial sector between 1950–70.

3456 ——— and ———. Estrategias de comercio exterior y su impacto sobre el empleo: Chile en la década del 60 (UC/EE, 13:1, 1979, p. 3–33, tables)

Attempt to measure the impact of Chile's trade structure upon employment during the decade of the 1960s.

3457 ——— and ———. Sustitución de importaciones, promoción de exportaciones y empleo: el caso chileno. Santiago, Chile: Corporación de Investigaciones Económicas para Latinoamérica, 1977. 48 p.; bibl. (Estudios CIEPLAN; 15)

Pamphlet examines the impact of import substitution and export promotion on employment in Chile.

3458 ——— and ———. La sustitución de trabajo, capital humano y capital físico en la industria manufacturera chilena (UC/EE, 14:2, 1979, p. 15–43, bibl., tables)

Corbo and Meller examine Chile's manufacturing sector, using translog production functions in 44 manufacturing subsectors at the ISIC four-digit level.

3459 Delavaud, Claude Collin. Panorama de l'économie chilienne en 1972 (IG, 37:2, mars/abril 1973, p. 61–73)

Objective statistical examination of Chile's economy during 1972.

3460 Diagnóstico y reestructuración del sector público chileno. Jefe del proyecto, Reymi Urrich G.; investigador revisor, Edmundo Borel Ch.; investigadores, Marianela Silva H. et al. Santiago: Departamento de Administración, Facultad de Ciencias Económicas y Administrativas, Universidad de Chile, 1974, 1976 printing. 319 p.; diagrs.

Excellent comprehensive and detailed description, critical examination and evaluation of the public sector of Chile. A major contribution to the description and diagnosis of the institutional edifice of Chile's complex public sector.

Duncan, Roland E. Chilean coal and British steamers: the origins of a South American industry. See *HLAS 42:3216.*

3461 Estimación de precios sociales de factores. Santiago: República de Chile, Presidencia de la República, Oficina de Planificación Nacional, 1976. 149 leaves; bibl.

Contains three superior studies on the shadow exchange rate (by Juan Coymans and Fernando Ossa), the rate of return on capital during 1960–74 (by Gert Wagner), and the social price of labor (by Osvaldo Schenone) in Chile.

3462 Foxley, Alejandro; Eduardo Aninat; and José Pablo Arellano. Efectos de la seguridad social sobre la distribución del ingreso. Santiago, Chile: Corporación de Investigaciones Económicas para Latinoamérica, 1977. 44 p. (Estudios CIEPLAN; 8)

Excellent study of the redistributive impact of Chile's social security system during 1969. Authors found that income was redistributed from the rich to the poor. They examine multiple dimensions of the social security system and make recommendations for reform.

3463 ———; ———; and ———. La política fiscal como instrumento redistributivo: la experiencia chilena (FCE/TE, 46[4]: 184, oct./dic. 1979, p. 831–866, tables)

In this fine study, Foxley, Aninat and Arellano analyze the degree of success of fiscal policy as an instrument for redistributing income in Chile during the 1965–73 period.

3464 Griffith-Jones, Stephany. A critical evaluation of Popular Unity's short-term and financial policy (WD, 6:7/8, July/Aug. 1978, p. 1019–1029)

Article provides a number of important insights into Allende's economic policies.

3465 Guardia B., Alexis. Clases sociales y subdesarrollo capitalista en Chile (UNAM/RMS, 41[41]:2, abril/junio 1979, p. 495–541, tables)

Article attempts to define and measure Chile's various social classes.

3466 Haynes, Robin M. El desarrollo socio-económico de las provincias chilenas: una clasificación basada en el análisis de componentes principales (UCC/NG, 5, 1976/1977, p. 65–75, bibl., ill., tables)

Using principal components analysis, Haynes identifies four major groups of provinces: 1) Santiago; 2) Valparaíso and Concepción; 3) the northern and extreme southern provinces; and 4) the rural provinces of central and southern Chile.

3467 Instituto de Capacitación e Investigación en Reforma Agraria. Análisis de la situación de los asignatarios de tierras a diciembre de 1976 (2. diagnóstico). Ministerio de Agricultura, Chile, Icira, Instituto de Capacitación e Investigación en Reforma Agraria; autores, Liliana Barría et al. Santiago de Chile: Programa de las Naciones Unidas para el Desarrollo, Organización de las Naciones Unidas para la Agricultura y la Alimentación, 1977. 177 p.; 1 leaf of plates; ill.

Very solid study of selected aspects of land reform, particularly, individual recipients of land in Chile in 1976.

3468 Kay, Cristóbal. Agrarian reform and the class struggle in Chile (LAP, 5[18]:3, Summer 1978, p. 117–137, bibl., tables)

Article examines selected aspects of agrarian reform in Chile between 1964–76.

3469 ———. El sistema señorial europeo y la hacienda latinoamericana. Traducción, Roberto Gómez Ciriza. México, D.F.: Ediciones Era, 1980. 140 p.; bibl. (Serie popular Era; 74)

Short economic history from a Marxist perspective focuses on agrarian institutions and reform in Chile.

3470 Letelier, Isabel and **Michael Moffitt.** Multinational banks in Chile (IRR/RC, 20:2, Autumn 1978, p. 111–128)

Openly anti-Junta article argues that "in order to establish its credit worthiness with foreign banks, the junta has sacrificed both the health of Chile's industrial structure and the welfare of the Chilean people." Authors fail to mention Junta's extremely restrictive policies with respect to short- and medium-term financial capital inflows.

3471 Macherone, Rafael. Estudio econométrico del consumo en Chile. Santiago, Chile: Pontificia Universidad Católica de Chile, Instituto de Economía, Oficina de Publicaciones, 1979. 113 p.; bibl. (Documento de trabajo—Instituto de Economía, Universidad Católica de Chile; no. 64)

Econometric study of consumption in Chile during 1950–76.

3472 Mamalakis, Markos J. The Allende experiment: chaos and destruction and idealism (Res Publica [Claremont Men's College, Claremont, Calif.] 2:3, Summer 1974, p. 42–49)

Article examines the various dimensions of Allende's income redistribution policies during 1970–73.

3473 ———. Historical statistics of Chile. v. 2, Demography & labor force. Westport, Conn.: Greenwood Press, 1980. 420 p.; bibl.

Vol. 2 consists of five parts and is a systematic, comprehensive, and up-to-date presentation of Chile's demographic and labor force statistics. Also describes and critically evaluates most of the statistics, and presents selected information on data, documents, and studies related to demography and the labor force. Pt. 1 contains five chapters dealing with population, natality and fertility, mortality, nuptiality, and age and sex composition. Pt. 2 consists of four chapters dealing with internal and international migration; projections of the population of Chile by age, sex, and regions; and educational attainment and institutions. Pt. 3 contains four chapters on labor force countrywide and in Santiago, unemployment and joblessness; and labor force participation

rates. Pt. 4 contains two chapters dealing with wages and salaries, and health and social security. The final part is composed of three chapters on population distribution by regions and provinces; urbanization; and size and growth of cities.

3474 ———. Monetary policy in a less developed country: the case of Chile, 1970–1973 (Scientific Yearbook of the School of Law and Economics [Aristotelian University of Salonica, Greece] 12, 1977 [i.e. 1980] p. 395–405)

Article describes in detail the use of monetary policy during Allende's presidency to establish socialism by changing the ownership of means of production in favor of the state and against the private sector.

Mayo, John. Before the nitrate era: British Commission Houses and the Chilean economy, 1851–80. See *HLAS 42:3238.*

3475 Meller, Patricio and **Manuel Marfán.** Pequeña y gran industria: generación de empleo y sectores claves. Santiago de Chile: Corporación de Investigaciones Económicas para Latinoamérica, 1977. 51 p.; bibl. (Estudios CIEPLAN; 20)

Study examines the impact upon employment of changes in goods produced and technology employed by industry.

3476 Monardes, Alfonso. Análisis de oferta y demanda de trabajo en la pequeña agricultura chilena (UCC/EE, 14:2, 1979, p. 45–74, bibl.)

Excellent statistical analysis of Chilean small-scale agriculture. Monardes finds that farmers are responsive to incentives and efficient, and emphasizes the need for better education and an integrated rural development strategy.

3477 Morandé, Felipe. Análisis de causalidad y pronóstico del precio del cobre: una aplicación de las técnicas de Box y Jenkins (UCC/CE, 16:47, abril 1979, p. 77–112, bibl., tables)

Article attempts to forecast the price of copper. Author finds that the only important determinant of the copper price is construction activity in the OECD countries.

3478 O'Brien, Thomas F. The Antofagasta Company: a case study of peripheral capitalism (HAHR, 60:1, Feb. 1980, p. 1–31, tables)

In this major contribution to Chilean historiography, O'Brien concludes that "the history of the Antofagasta Company suggests that the dysfunction of peripheral capitalism lay in the capability to promote growth while curbing those challenges to the traditional order that open the way to economic development." For historian's comment, see *HLAS 42:3245*.

————. Chilean elites and foreign investors: Chilean nitrate policy, 1880–1882. See *HLAS 42:3246*.

3479 Organización institucional para el control y manejo de la deuda externa: el caso chileno. Rodolfo Hoffman, consultor. Santiago: Comisión Económica para América Latina, 1979. 41 p.; tables (Cuadernos de la CEPAL; 28)

Study examines Chile's foreign debt during 1975–78 in great statistical, analytical, and institutional detail.

3480 Panayotou, Theodore. OPEC as a model for copper exporters: potential gains and cartel behavior (IDE/DE, 17:2, June 1979, p. 203–219, bibl., tables)

In this excellent article, Panayotou argues that a copper exporters' organization modeled after OPEC would have practically no chance for success.

3481 Programa Regional del Empleo para América Latina y el Caribe (PREALC). La ampliación de turnos en la industria chilena: la factibilidad de una política de empleo productivo. Santiago de Chile: Oficina Internacional del Trabajo, Programa Regional del Empleo para América Latina y el Caribe (PREALC), 1978. 53, 7 p. (Investigaciones sobre empleo; 8)

Careful and detailed study attempts to determine how employment *and* labor productivity can be increased through a strategy of multiple production shifts. Seeks to avoid a repetition of the Allende phenomenon of hidden underemployment (full employment but falling productivity) as well as the Military Junta's combination of rising labor productivity amidst widespread open unemployment.

3482 ————. Antecedentes para la planificación de los recursos humanos en Chile. Prepared by E. Schielfelbein et al. Organización Internacional del Trabajo, Programa Mundial del Empleo, Programa Re-

gional del Empleo para América Latina y el Caribe, PREALC. Santiago, Chile: PREALC, 1977. 215 p.: bibl.; ill. (Documento de trabajo—PREALC; 118)

Volume contains five background studies for human resources planning in Chile. They examine: 1) the relation between education and employment; 2) supply and demand of advanced education; 3) rate of growth of occupational categories requiring secondary and advanced education; 4) human resources in the "education" section; and 5) enrollment in the educational system in 1974.

3483 ————. La búsqueda de trabajo y los mecanismos de sobrevivencia de los desocupados en el gran Santiago, 1976. Prepared by V. Montecinos and S. Spessart. Organización Internacional del Trabajo, Programa Mundial del Empleo, Programa Regional del Empleo para América Latina y el Caribe, PREALC. Santiago, Chile: PREALC, 1977. 49, 38 p.; bibl. (Documento de trabajo—PREALC; 117)

Since 1973 open unemployment in Chile has reached levels close to those experienced during the Great Depression of the 1930s. This study examines how the unemployed have survived, how they participate in the labor market, and many other related issues.

3484 ————. Comercio informal en una comuna de Santiago. Edited by Alois Möller. Organización Internacional del Trabajo, OIT, Programa Mundial del Empleo, Programa Regional del Empleo para América Latina y el Caribe, PREALC. Santiago, Chile: PREALC, 1978. 96 p.; bibl. (Documento de trabajo—PREALC; 122)

Examination of informal trade in a community of Santiago.

3485 ————. Entrevistas en profundidad a empresas y trabajadores del sector informal en reparación de automóviles. Prepared by D. Benavente. Organización Internacional del Trabajo, Programa Mundial del Empleo, Programa Regional del Empleo para América Latina y el Caribe, PREALC. Santiago, Chile: PREALC, 1979. 227 p. (Documento de trabajo—PREALC; 175)

Scholars will find rich research materials in these interviews with firms and workers of the informal car repair sector.

3486 Provoste Fernández, Patricia. Antecedentes socioeconómicos para el desarrollo del sector de Isluga: proyecto de diagnóstico del altiplano, Convenio SERPLAC-U. del Norte. Iquique, Chile: Universidad del Norte, Dirección Académica, Centro Isluga de Investigaciones Andinas, 1977. 85 leaves, 3 fold. leaves of plates; bibl.; maps.

Excellent microstudy of the town of Isluga. Author describes its structure, its economic activities, and its problems.

Rector, John. Transformaciones comerciales producidas por la independencia de Chile: pts. 1/2. See *HLAS 42:3257.*

Richards, Alan R. The political economy of commercial estate labor systems: a comparative analysis of Prussia, Egypt, and Chile. See *HLAS 42:3260.*

Román, Charles G. Pregger. Economic interest groups within the Chilean government, 1851 to 1891: continuity and discontinuity in economic and political evolution. See *HLAS 42:3261.*

———. Role of the banking and insurance sector in the failure of the industrial revolution in nineteenth-century Chile. See *HLAS 42:3262.*

3487 Rosenn, Keith S. Adjusting taxation of business income for inflation: lessons from Brazil and Chile (Texas International Law Journal [University of Texas, School of Law, Austin] 13:2, Spring 1978, p. 165–197)

Article presents the pros and cons of tax indexation, based on the cases of Brazil and Chile. Author concludes that "the case for taxation of business entities on real rather than nominal income appears overwhelming."

3488 St. Flechsig. Einige Fragen der Entwicklung der verarbeitenden Industrie Chiles und ihrer Zweigstruktur—Hauptbestimmungsfaktoren (UR/L, 31:12, Herbstsemester 1978, p. 35–72, tables)

Detailed statistical analysis of Chile's manufacturing sector that provides many important insights. The study epitomizes Marxist-dependency interpretation of Chilean economic development. While Marxist and orthodox economists frequently agree on key features of underdevelopment (e.g., low capital formation, rural poverty, in-

adequate educational and health services), their diagnoses and development strategies differ diametrically.

3489 Sanfuentes V., Andrés. Perspectivas económicas de Chile (BCV/REL, 13:52, 1978, p. 193–214, tables)

Statistically based, careful, and objective treatment of the evolution of the Chilean economy between 1966–77. Sanfuentes argues that predictions about future economic development are very difficult to make because of many drastic changes in economic policies that have occurred during the decade of the 1970s.

Sater, William F. Chile and the world depression of the 1870s. See *HLAS 42:3263.*

3490 Sjaastad, Larry and **Hernán Cortés.** El enfoque monetario de la balanza de pagos y las tasas de interés real en Chile (UC/EE, 11:1, 1978, p. 3–68)

Consists of expert analysis of Chile's high real interest rates during 1973–77 in terms of monetary approach to the balance of payments.

3491 Sutulov, Alexander; Luis Blanco; and **Marcial Weisser.** Del cobre y nuestro desafío. Con la colaboración de Francisco Orrego, Juan Pallín e investigadores del CIMM. Santiago de Chile: Centro de Investigación Minera y Metalúrgica, 1978. 328 p.; bibl.; ill.

Five authors examine the role of copper in Chilean economic development.

3492 Tamblay, Jorge. El subsidio a la contratación adicional en mano de obra: el caso chileno (in Oficina Internacional del Trabajo. Programa Regional del Empleo para América Latina y el Caribe [PREALC]. Investigaciones sobre empleo. Santiago: Oficina Internacional del Trabajo, 1980, v. 19, p. 83–104, tables)

Extremely high rates of open unemployment in Chile since 1974 have prompted the government to introduce remedial strategies. Article examines the effectiveness of the program of subsidies for additional hiring of workers.

3493 Tokman, Victor E. Competition between the informal and formal sectors in retailing: the case of Santiago (WD, 6:9/10, Sept./Oct. 1978, p. 1187–1198)

In this well-written and well-researched article, Tokman argues that "informal" (i.e., small, retail) shops in Santiago are efficient and competitive. The usefulness of the term "informal" remains unclear, however.

3494 Vergara, Pilar. Necesidades básicas y políticas contra la pobreza: la experiencia de Chile. Santiago de Chile: Corporación de Investigaciones Económicas para Latinoamérica, 1978. 68 p.; bibl. (Estudios CIEPLAN; 27)

Vergara examines carefully rural and urban poverty in Chile. She also presents a set of strategies for removal of poverty and satisfaction of basic needs.

3495 Vergara Vergara, Sergio. Ahorro y bancos de desarrollo. Santiago de Chile: ALIDE, 1978. 132 p.; 4 leaves of plates; bibl.; ill.

Document traces in detail the relationship between saving, financial intermediation, and development banks.

3496 Viladrich Morera, Alberto. América Latina, la planificación hidráulica y los planificadores. Santiago de Chile: Editorial Universitaria, 1972. 98 p.; 2 fold. leaves of plates; bibl.; ill.

Study analyzes planning of water resources in Latin America.

Villela G., Hugo. Autoritarianismo y tenencia de la tierra: Chile, 1973–1976. See item **6591.**

3497 Yrarrázaval E., Rafael; Rodrigo Navarreta G.; and Víctor Valdivia P. Costos y beneficios sociales de los programas de mejoramiento varietal de trigo y maíz en Chile (UCC/CE, 16:49, dic. 1979, p. 283–302, bibl., tables)

Excellent cost-benefit analysis of programs undertaken in Chile to develop new varieties of wheat and corn between 1935 and 1978.

3498 Zemelman M., Hugo. El movimiento popular chileno y el sistema de alianzas en la década de los treinta (in América Latina en los años treinta. Luis Antezana E. et al. Coordinador, Pablo González Casanova. México: Instituto de Investigaciones Sociales, Universidad Nacional Autónoma de México, 1977, p. 378–450, bibl., map)

Openly Marxist interpretation of Chile's economic and political history during the decade of the 1930s that provides many novel insights.

PERU

3499 Agricultura en el Perú, s. XX [i.e. siglo veinte]: documentos. Pablo Macera. Lima: Universidad Nacional Mayor de San Marcos, Dirección Universitaria de Proyección Social, Seminario de Historia Rural Andina, 1977. 3 v. (524 p.)

Volume contains four historical microstudies of Peru's agricultural sector, three of them examining specific products during specific years, and one examining an *hacienda.*

3500 Amat y León Ch., Carlos. La economía de la crisis peruana. Lima, Perú: Fundación Friedrich Ebert, 1978. 116 p.; graphs; bibl. (Serie Materiales de trabajo—ILDIS; no. 16)

Multifaceted analysis of the Peruvian economy between 1968–77.

3501 ———— and Héctor León. Estructura y niveles de ingreso familiar en el Perú: cómo financian sus ingresos las familias en las diferentes áreas y regiones de residencia en el Perú? Lima: Universidad del Pacífico, Centro de Investigación, 1979. 199 p.; graphs (Serie Cuadernos—Universidad del Pacífico, Centro de Investigación. Trabajo de investigación—Universidad del Pacífico, Centro de Investigación; no. 10)

Extremely careful analysis of the structure and level of family income in Peru, based on a survey of family budgets between Aug. 1971–Aug. 1972.

3502 Arnold, Victor L. and John Hamilton. The Greene settlement: a study of the resolution of investment disputes in Peru (Texas International Law Journal [University of Texas, School of Law, Austin] 13:2, Spring 1978, p. 263–288, table)

Excellent description and analysis of the 1974 Greene settlement (Peru's lumpsum payment of expropriation compensation to the US). A study of major interest to scholars interested in Peru, nationalization, international law, and mineral resources.

3503 Bayer, David L. Reforma agraria peruana: descapitalización del minifundio y formación de la burguesía rural. La Molina,

Perú: Universidad Nacional Agraria, Centro de Investigaciones Socio-Económicas, 1975. 82 p.; bibl.; ill.

Monograph examines the formation of economic pluralism in rural Peru as a consequence of agrarian reform. Medium-sized farmers are portrayed as a group having increasing political clout.

3504 Bazán Gonzales, Mario. El sector externo de la economía peruana, 1950–1976. Lima?: Centro de Documentación y Estudios Sociales, between 1977 and 1979. 58 p.

Well-documented analysis of Peru's external sector between 1950–76.

3505 Benites M., Isidoro. Diagnóstico empresarial de la C.A.P. San Isidro Ltd. No. 176. Chiclayo, Peru: Area de Publicaciones CEAR, 1979. 130, 62 p.; bibl.; ill.

Microstudy of the Agrarian Production Cooperative (CAP) "San Isidro." Using a dependency framework, Benites M. provides a comprehensive, statistical analysis.

3506 Bernales B., Enrique. Expansión y redefinición del sistema universitario del Perú en un contexto de modernización. Lima: Pontificia Universidad Católica del Perú, Departamento de Ciencias Sociales, 1978. 126 p.; bibl.; graphs.

Study attempts to explain why the universities have been unable to respond to the challenge of and meet the needs of Peru's economic development.

Bonilla, Heraclio; Lía del Rió; and **Pilar Ortiz de Zevallas.** Comercio libre y crisis de la economía andina: el caso del Cuzco. See *HLAS 42:3061.*

3507 Bulavin, Vladimir. Peru: nueva política petrolera (URSS/AL, 1, 1977, p. 139–152)

In this well-written article, Bulavin, a Soviet scholar, reviews Peru's petroleum policy between 1969–77. Of special interest because it provides the Soviet perspective on this issue.

3508 Caballero, José María. Los eventuales en las cooperativas costeñas peruanas: un modelo analítico (PUCP/E, 1:2, agosto 1978, p. 57–80, tables)

Superb analysis of part-time labor in Peru's coastal cooperatives.

3509 Cao, Heip and **John Kuiper.** El uso de modelos econométricos y la planificación del desarrollo en el Perú (PUCP/E, 2:3, junio 1979, p. 85–115, tables)

Authors apply various econometric models to Peru. They question the usefulness of aggregate demand models in planning development of less advanced economies.

Caravedo, Baltazar. El problema del centralismo en el Perú republicano. See *HLAS 42:3062.*

3510 Caycho, Hernán. Las SAIS de la Sierra central. Lima: Escuela de Administración de Negocios para Graduados, Departamento de Investigación, 1977. 150 p.; bibl.; ill.

Excellent study examines carefully the Agricultural Societies of Social Interest (SAIS) in Peru's agrarian zone X (Sierra Central) during 1972–74.

3511 Cebrecos, Rufino. Construcción de vivienda y empleo (PUCP/E, 2:3, junio 1979, p. 49–84, tables)

Role of the construction sector in Peru's economic development between 1965–75 is carefully examined in this article. Cebrecos also makes some important recommendations for improving the performance of construction.

3512 CENCIRA. Dirección de Investigación. Los eventuales y los mercados de trabajo en la agricultura: valles Jequetepeque y Zaña. Lima: Centro Nacional de Capacitación e Investigación para la Reforma Agraria, 1976. 260 p.; bibl.; ill.

This book, which deals with the rural labor market in Peru, is divided into three parts. Pt. 1 treats theoretical demand and supply dimensions of the agrorural labor markets of non-permanent workers (*eventuales*). Pts. 2/3 measure and analyze the features and importance of non-permanent workers in the Zaña and Jequetepeque valleys. This excellent study, which confirms the existence of plural labor markets in Peru, finds extremely high levels of agrorural unemployment and underemployment, and presents a corrective strategy.

Chavarría, Jesús. The colonial heritage of national Peru: an overview. See *HLAS 42:3064.*

Claverías, Ricardo. El mercado interno y la espontaneidad de los movimientos campesinos: Puno, 1950–1968. See *HLAS 42:3067.*

3513 Cleaves, Peter S. and **Martin J. Scurrah.** Agriculture, bureaucracy, and military government in Peru. Ithaca, New York: Cornell University Press, 1980. 329 p.; bibl.; index.

Competent, detailed and innovative examination of agrarian reform, military rule, and bureaucracy in Peru. Authors conclude that neither the centralist, the liberal, nor the corporatist models of state-society relations and bureaucratic behavior are fully applicable to Peru.

3514 Collin-Delavaud, Claude. Le Pérou et ses frontières non consolidées: les difficultés de l'intégration économique (FDD/NED [Problèmes d'Amérique Latine, 53] 4533/4534, 31 oct. 1979, p. 99–107, maps)

Describes the difficulty of achieving economic integration within the Andean Pact and of establishing firm boundaries for Peru.

3515 Crónica de un colapso económico, Perú, 1974–1979. Guido Pennano A., editor; asistente, Juan Ramírez A. Lima: Universidad del Pacífico, Centro de Investigación; no. 6. Serie Cuadernos—Universidad del Pacífico, Centro de Investigación)

Two classic reference volumes on Peru's economic history between 1974 and 1979. They contain xerox copies of major documents published during that period.

3516 Cubas Alvariño, Ana M. Reforma agraria: bibliografía, catálogo colectivo, 1962–1972. La Molina, Perú: Taller de Estudios Andinos, Universidad Nacional Agraria, 1976? 67, 24 p.; bibl.; indexes.

Useful bibliography of publications between 1962–72 dealing with Peru's agrarian reform.

3517 Deal, J. Michael. El estado e inversión extranjera en el proceso de industrialización peruana. Lima: Universidad Nacional La Molina, 1976 or 1977. 101 p.; bibl.

Critical study with a generally negative perception of the role of foreign investment in Peru's industrialization process.

3518 Deere, Carmen Diana. The differentiation of the peasantry and family structure: a Peruvian case study (NCFR/JFH, 3:4, Winter 1978, p. 422–438, bibl.)

Provocative analysis of family structure during Peru's era of export orientation.

3519 Falaris, Evangelos M. The determinants of internal migration in Peru: an economic analysis (UC/EDCC, 27:2, Jan. 1979, p. 327–342)

Excellent analysis of migration in Peru concludes that internal migration has been motivated by economic opportunities.

3520 Ferro, Angelo and **Giovanni Scanagatta.** In tema di teoria della parità dei poteri d'acquisto: il tasso di cambio del sol peruviano nel periodi 1974–76 (IEI/EI, 32:4, nov. 1979, p. 414–435, bibl., ill., tables)

Authors examine the effective and theoretical foreign exchange rate in Peru during 1974–76.

3521 Figueroa, A. and others. La economía peruana en 1977 (PUCP/E, 1:2, agosto 1978, p. 171–225, tables)

Article examines the Peruvian economy between 1974–77.

3522 Fitzgerald, Edmund Valpy Knox. Capitalismo de estado no Peru (UFMA/DCP, 5, março 1979, p. 91–115, bibl., tables)

Discusses three sources of Peruvian capital or savings during 1967–74: state, national, and foreign.

————. The political economy of Peru, 1956–78: economic development and the restructuring of capital. See *HLAS 42:3075.*

3523 Flores Medina, Rosa and **Carmen Montero Checa.** Educación y empleo a nivel regional: informe. Lima: Instituto Nacional de Investigación y Desarrollo de la Educación "Augusto Salazar Bondy," Subdirección de Investigaciones Educacionales, Unidad de Análisis y Diseño, 1975. 319 p.

Study describes in detail the socioeconomic, educational, and occupational situation in Peru's regions between 1940–70.

3524 González Izquierdo, Jorge. Perú, una economía en crisis: interpretación y bases para un solución. Lima: Universidad del Pacífico, Centro de Investigación, 1978 or 1979. 190 p. (Trabajo de investigación—Universidad del Pacífico, Centro de Investigación; no. 9. Serie Cuadernos—Universidad del Pacífico, Centro de Investigación)

González diagnoses and interprets Peru's economic crisis during 1970–78 and suggests solutions.

3525 Gutiérrez Araya, Jorge; Delia Higa Tamashiro; and **Mercedes Bracco**

Dieckman. Los trabajadores eventuales en el cultivo del café: Chanchamayo y Satipo. s.l.: s.n., 1978? 103 p.; bibl.

Detailed examination of the market for seasonal workers in coffee cultivation in the Peruvian provinces of Chanchamayo and Satipo.

3526 Iguiñiz Echeverría, Javier. Ciclos en la economía peruana y crisis actual: avances de una investigación (PUCP/E, 1:2, agosto 1978, p. 81–135, tables)

Excellent secular and cyclical analysis of all major macro-variables affecting Peru's economic development between 1950 and 1976. It provides solid information on the determinants of Peru's gigantic economic crisis in the late 1970s.

3527 Instituto Nacional de Estadística (Peru). Dirección General de Censos, Encuestas y Demografía. II [i.e. Segundos] censos nacionales económicos, 1974. v. 1, Manufactura. v. 2, Construcción. v. 3, Minería e hidrocarburos. v. 4, Pesquería, pt. 1, Area de transformación. Lima: Presidencia de la República, Primer Ministro, Instituto Nacional de Estadísticas, Dirección General de Censos, Encuestas y Demografía, 1977. 3 v.

Peru's Second National Economic Census was undertaken between Sept. and Oct. 1974 and covered information pertaining to 1973. Present three volumes contain invaluable information on three sectors. Vol. 1 deals with the artisan sector (establishments employing one to four persons); vol. 2, pt. 3 with manufacturing (establishments employing five or more persons); and the rest of vol. 3 with the overall industrial sector (establishments employing one or more persons). These volumes on industry, the first to be published, will become classics in Latin America because they cover not only the manufacturing but also the artisan segment.

Kaerger, Karl. Condiciones agrarias de la Sierra Sur Peruana: 1899. See *HLAS 42:3086.*

3528 Kimmig, Karl-Heinz. Die Industriereform in Peru: sozio-ökonom. u. polit. Aspekte d. Strukturwandels im Industriesektor unter d. Militärregierung Velasco Alvarado. Meisenheim am Glan: Hain, 1978. 180 p.; bibl. (Transfines; Bd. 7)

Highly informative and innovative analysis and interpretation of industrial reform in Peru during the military dictatorship of Velasco Alvarado.

3529 León, Federico R. El rol de miembro del consejo de administración en las cooperativas agrarias de producción de la costa peruana. Lima: ESAN, Departamento de Investigación, 1977. 68 p.; bibl.; ill. (Documento de trabajo—ESAN, Departamento de Investigación; no. 15)

Major consequence of agrarian reform in Peru was establishment of the Agrarian Production Cooperatives (CAP). This study carefully analyzes the role of the director in the CAPs of Peru's coast.

3530 López Mas, Julio. La gran industria capitalista y el mercado interno (IPA/A, 12:13, 1979, p. 144–188, tables)

Article provides a statistical examination of manufacturing in Peru between 1918 and 1965.

Musgrove, Philip and **Robert Ferber.** Identifying the urban poor: characteristics of poverty households in Bogotá, Medellín and Lima. See item **2886.**

3531 Organization of American States. General Secretariat. Executive Secretariat for Economic and Social Affairs. Short-term economic reports. v. 7, Peru. Washington: 1979. 95 p.; tables (CIES. SG/Ser.G.41.10)

In 1978, Peru was facing a situation of economic decline, external disequilibrium, severe inflation, and soaring foreign debt payments. This report analyzes that situation and describes the effects of the corrective economic program for 1978–80 introduced by the government in cooperation with the IMP.

Pachas Castilla, Rolando. Economía y sociedad en el Valle de Chincha: 1860–1919. See *HLAS 42:3103.*

3532 Perú. Instituto Nacional de Planificación. Plan global de desarrollo para 1977 y 1978: aprobado por D.S. No. 008-77-PM del 28 de abril de 1977. Lima: El Instituto, 1977. 272 p.

Document contains the global plan for national development during 1977–78.

3533 ———. ———. Plan global de desarrollo para 1978 y 1979. Lima: El Instituto, 1978. 1 v. (Unpaged)

Provides quantitative goals of Peru's national plan for 1978–79.

3534 ———. **Ministerio de Economía y Finanzas.** Acción común y solidaria para salir de la crisis: producción, austeridad, responsabilidad, honestidad. Exposición del Ministerio de Economía y Finanzas, Javier Silva Ruete, transmitida al país por televisión y radio el 14 de junio de 1978. Lima: Ministerio de Economía y Finanzas, Oficina de Relaciones Públicas, 1978. 87 p.; graphs.

Address in which Javier Silva Ruete, Peru's Minister of Economics and Finance, presents a clear picture of the colossal economic crisis the nation faced in 1978.

3535 ————. ————. Principales aspectos del programa económico financiero 1978: Exposición del Ministro de Economía y Finanzas, General de División E.P., Alcibíades Sáenz Barsallo, transmitida al país por televisión el 13 de enero de 1978. Lima: Ministerio de Economía y Finanzas, Oficina de Relaciones Públicas, 1978. 215 p.; anexos.

General Alcibíades Sáenz Barsallo, Minister of Economics and Finance, describes in this address the fiscal, price, balance of payments, monetary, and credit policies required to solve Peru's enormous economic and financial crisis.

3536 Pillado Matheu, Armando. El capital hacía la crisis, Perú, 1965–78. Lima: Centro de Estudios y Promoción del Desarrollo, 1978. 96 p.; bibl.; ill.

Neo-Marxist analysis of Peru's economic crisis between 1965–78.

3537 Portocarrero, Felipe. El Estado y el capital internacional en el Perú (UNAM/RMS, 40[40]: 3, julio/sept. 1978, p. 977–990, tables)

Article examines the relationship between the state and foreign capital in Peru during 1968–76.

3538 Portocarrero, Gonzalo. Términos externos e internos del intercambio en la economía peruana, 1950–1973: informe preliminar. Lima: Pontificia Universidad Católica del Perú, Departamento de Ciencias Sociales, 1977. 119 p.; bibl.

Author carefully examines Peru's external and internal terms of trade during the 1950–73 period. The export sector is analyzed in detail.

3539 Programa Regional del Empleo para América Latina y el Caribe (PREALC). La comunidad laboral en Perú: participación, ingresos y empleo. Organización Internacional del Trabajo, Programa Mundial del Empleo Programa Regional del Empleo para América Latina y el Caribe PREALC. Santiago, Chile: Oficina Internacional del Trabajo, 1979. 102 p.; bibl. (Documento de trabajo, PREALC; 177)

Very careful examination of participation, income, and employment in the labor community of Peru during 1971–76.

3540 Proyecto plan de gobierno "Tupac Amaru:" período 1977–1980. Lima: s.n., 1977? 63 p.

Presents the global, economic, and social objectives and policy goals of the Peruvian government's Tupac Amaru Plan, for the 1977–80 period. For English translation of this work, see *Tupac Amaru Government Plan, 1977–80: the Peruvian Revolution* (Lima: National Information System, Information Service Enterprise, 1977, 70 p.)

3541 Quijano Obregón, Aníbal. El Perú en la crisis de los años treinta (*in* América Latina en los años treinta. Luis Antezana E. et al. Coordinador, Pablo González Casanova. México: Instituto de Investigaciones Sociales, Universidad Nacional Autónoma de México, 1977, p. 239–302)

Article provides numerous insights into Peru's economic history from the War of the Pacific to the late 1930s. For historian's comment, see *HLAS 42:3109.*

Reátegui Chávez, Wilson. Explotación agropecuaria y las movilizaciones campesinas en Lauramarca-Cusco. See *HLAS 42:3112.*

3542 Rénique, Gerardo. La agricultura del Valle del Mantaro: estadísticas socioeconómicas, 1950–1968. La Molina, Perú: Taller de Estudios Andinos, Departamento de Ciencias Humanas, Universidad Nacional Agraria, 1978. 180 p.; bibl.; diagrs. (Serie Andes centrales; no. 5. Informes de investigación—TEA, Universidad Nacional Agraria)

Statistical examination of agriculture during 1950–68 in the Mantaro Valley of Peru.

3543 Rivera Flores, Iván. La crisis económica peruana: génesis, evolución y perspectivas (PUCP/E, 2:3, junio 1979, p. 117–146, tables)

Careful statistical analysis of the causes of Peru's great economic crisis of the late 1970s.

3544 Roel Pineda, Virgilio. La República de las frustraciones: 1827–1878. Lima: Editorial Alfa, 1977. 32 p.; ill.

Fascinating description of Peru's economic, political, and social development before and during the age of guano (1827–78).

3545 Román de Silgado, Manuel. La dialéctica campo-ciudad y el desarrollo latinoamericano. Lima: Universidad del Pacífico, Centro de Investigación, 1978. 178 p. (Serie Ensayos—Universidad del Pacífico, Centro de Investigación; no. 14. Cuadernos—Universidad del Pacífico, Centro de Investigación)

Study focuses on the inadequate development of rural Peru. Economic stratifications and lack of education are singled out as factors responsible for rural backwardness.

3546 Roquez, Gladys. La agricultura peruana: estadísticas agrarias, 1950–1968. La Molina, Perú: Taller de Estudios Andinos, Departamento de Ciencias Humanas, Universidad Nacional Agraria, 1978. 145 p.; bibl.; tables (Serie Ensayos generales—TEA, Universidad Nacional Agraria; no. 1. Informes de investigación—TEA, Universidad Nacional Agraria)

Detailed statistical examination of Peru's agricultural sector between 1950–68 (some statistical time series begin as early as 1916).

3547 Saint Pol, Patrick. Sustitución de importaciones, producto potencial y crisis de coyuntura (PUCP/E, 1:2, agosto 1978, p. 137–167, tables)

Careful analysis of actual and potential product, foreign exchange constraint, terms of trade, and import substitution in Peru during 1950–74.

Samaniego L., Carlos and **Bryan Roberts.** El significado de la SAIS de la sierra central del Perú: el caso de la SAIS Cahuide. See *HLAS 42:3118.*

3548 Schydlowsky, Daniel M. and **Juan J. Wicht.** Anatomía de un fracaso económico: Perú, 1968–1978. Cubierta, Carlos Ausejo. 2. ed. Lima: Universidad del Pacífico, Centro de Investigación, 1979. 126 p.; bibl.

Authors examine causes and effects of Peru's worst economic crisis of the 20th century in this informative study. The "Peruvian experiment," or the ambiguous but promising revolution of 1968–78 is considered a complete failure and middle of the road corrective strategies are presented.

Smith, Gavin A. Socio-economic differentiation and relations of production among rural-based petty producers in central Peru: 1880 to 1970. See *HLAS 42:3122.*

3549 Universidad del Pacífico. Centro de Investigación. La economía peruana en 1978: análisis de coyuntura económica. Lima: Universidad del Pacífico, Centro de Investigación, 1979. 151 p.; graphs.

Very careful analysis of Peru's economy during 1978.

3550 Wils, Frits C.M. Industrialization, industrialists, and the nation-state in Peru: a comparative/sociological analysis. Berkeley: Institute of International Studies, University of California, 1979. 273 p.; bibl. (Research series—Institute of International Studies, University of California, Berkeley; no. 41)

One of the few original and objective treatises on the Peruvian economy to appear in the last decade. Although Frits Wils focuses primarily and brilliantly on Peru's industrialists and industrialization, his study is a major contribution to Latin American historiography as a whole. An extremely competent study.

BOLIVIA, PARAGUAY AND URUGUAY

MICHAEL L. COOK, *Associate Professor of Agricultural Economics, Texas A&M University*

THE ECONOMIC LITERATURE issuing from Bolivia, Paraguay and Uruguay continues to fluctuate in quality and quantity, and to range broadly in subject matter. Nevertheless, general trends noted in *HLAS 41*, continue in this volume, namely: 1) the non-controversial, market-oriented nature of the research; 2) the concentration of statistically-descriptive work; 3) publications that are scarce and mostly government sponsored; 4) in Bolivia: the marked preference to study human and natural resources rather than market imperfections; 5) in Paraguay: the qualitative improvement in the economic literature and its emphasis on international trade, monetary matters, and economic development; and 6) in Uruguay: the lack of studies of major structural and macroeconomic issues of the post-1973 period.

The one theme that underlies most of the heterogeneous 90 plus works reviewed in this section is an awareness of increasing international interdependence (see items **3568** and **3611**). Flecha's work on "el endeudamiento externo" (item **3593**) is a sensitive appreciation of this aspect of 20th-century economic history.

The most notable change in recent Bolivian economic literature is the decline in the number of mining and agriculture studies and the growing interest in economic development as a general phenomenon. A particularly valuable example of the latter tendency is Laba's article (item **3578**), an excellent examination of the cultural insensitivity of traditional economic planners. The second most striking feature of the more than 40 Bolivian works annotated here is a notable improvement in quality. Each one of these studies makes a real contribution towards understanding the complex and fragmented economy of Bolivia. Finally, one should note that the increasing number of works concerned with attacking Burke's study of Bolivia (item **3562**) represents a new trend in the literature.

With a few exceptions, the scientific level of Paraguayan economic research remains dismally low. The 20 pieces annotated below address issues in international trade, economic development, and agriculture. The two articles on balance-of-payments by Herken and Flecha (items **3593** and **3594**) are well-documented, thought-provoking overviews of the interdependency between the world economy and the economy of Paraguay, which has recently become export-oriented. Nickson's structural analysis of the important Paraguayan meat-packing industry (item **3596**) not only contributes to an understanding of the dynamic growth of the commercial agricultural sector, but also allows a glimpse into the legal and government policies that regulate Paraguayan industrial organization.

Themes that dominate economic publications in Uruguay are economic planning, economic history, and agriculture. The most notable work among those annotated here, is Melgar's study of the C.I.D.E. plan (item **3622**). Thoroughly-documented and well-organized, the latter essay has implications of relevance to all developing economies. Melgar concludes that no matter how rigorous, how well-conceptualized, or how detailed a national economic plan is, it will remain merely an academic exercise if it does not also take into account political realities. There is a surprising scarcity of material on the structural readjustment of the Uruguayan economy since 1973, and on the growing pains the country is undergoing. The quantity and quality of the literature devoted to economic history suggests that Uruguayan economists continue to be more fascinated with the past than with the future. Finally, the return of numerous foreign-trained agricultural economists to Uruguay is reflected in the high level of research on the agricultural sector.

In conclusion, a review of the economic literature issuing from Bolivia, Paraguay and Uruguay over the past few years suggests that their economists are making progress, particularly in the area of microeconomics. However, if the profession is to assist in improving the decision-making process that precedes the formulation of macroeconomic policies in all three countries, much remains to be accomplished by economists in areas such as coordination, funding and conceptual direction.

BOLIVIA

3551 Antezana E., Luis. Bolivia en las crisis de los años treinta (*in* América Latina en los años treinta. Luis Antezana E. et al. Coordinador, Pablo González Casanova. México: Instituto de Investigaciones Sociales, Universidad Nacional Autónoma de México, 1977, p. 193–213, bibl., tables)

Descriptive look at the crisis of the 1930s and its effects on the Revolution of 1952. Good article on political economy. For historian's comment, see *HLAS 42:3135.*

3552 Araníbar Quiroga, Ernesto. Problemas fundamentales de la teoría del desarrollo en Bolivia. La Paz?: Centro de Información y Documentación de Bolivia, 1979. 19 p. (Documentos socio-económicos: Serie S; no. 4)

Interesting essay on the unique problems faced by Bolivia in its attempt to develop its socioeconomic sectors.

3553 Arze Cuadros, Eduardo. La economía de Bolivia: ordenamiento territorial y dominación externa, 1492–1979. La Paz: Editorial Los Amigos del Libro, 1979. 578 p.; bibl.; maps.

This study is required reading for economists interested in Bolivia. Even though its methodological emphasis is on spatial and regional economics, historians also have much to gain from this well-documented piece. Based on author's French thesis (Paris, 1976).

3554 Asamblea Permanente de los Derechos Humanos de Bolivia. Encuesta sobre el aumento del costo de vida en el campo, 1972, 1974, 1978: conclusiones. La Paz: La Asamblea, 1979. 18 leaves.

Nonrigorous description of price changes for necessities in Bolivia from 1972–78.

3555 ———. Estudio sobre el valor adquisitivo del salario de los mineros. La Paz: Asamblea Permanente de los Derechos Humanos de Bolivia, 1978. 26, 41 p.; bibl.; graph.

Examines purchasing power of extraction industry's labor sector. Excellent data source for labor economists.

3556 Bedregal Gutiérrez, Guillermo. Bolivia: ¿crecimiento neocolonial o desarrollo liberador? La Paz: Editorial Los Amigos del Libro, 1979. 108 p. (Colección Texto y documento)

Well-articulated work by a Bolivian exile calling attention to the economically dependent position of Bolivia, and questioning the future direction of its socioeconomic development.

3557 Bellour, Jean Alain. La problemática agraria en el altiplano central. La Paz?: Centro de Información y Documentación de Bolivia, 1980. 147 p.; ill. (Documentos socio-económicos: Serie S; no. 5)

One of a series of works on Bolivian agricultural planning. Pt. 1 describes the problem statistically, and pt. 2 offers organizational and economic alternatives.

3558 Bolivia. Libro blanco de realizaciones del Gobierno de las Fuerzas Armadas: informe de las realizaciones del Gobierno de las Fuerzas Armadas, para el desarrollo económico y social. La Paz: s.n., 1978? 319 p., ill.

Pictorial review of the period 1971–78. Contains good illustrations and some interesting data, including project costs.

3559 ———. Banco Central de Bolivia [and] **Ministerio de Finanzas.** Aspectos generales de las políticas monetaria y fiscal de Bolivia (*in* Vinculación entre las políticas fiscal y monetaria; reuniones y seminarios. México: Centro de Estudios Monetarios Latinoamericanos, 1979, p. 69–77, tables)

Short but precise review of Bolivian monetary policies during the 1970s. Contains good aggregated tables.

3559a ———. Ministerio de Finanzas. Reforma fiscal en Bolivia, v. 1, El marco económico general. La Paz: El Ministerio, 1977 i.e. 1978. 1 v.; ill.

Excellent study by a distinguished group of international economists. It is divided into two sections: one on general Bolivian macroeconomic sector and another on Bolivian budget policy.

3560 ———. Ministerio de Planeamiento y Coordinación. Plan operativo 1978. t. 2, Plan social global. t. 3, Sectores agropecuario, alimentación y nutrición, desarrollo rural integrado. t. 5, Sectores hidrocarburos, energía, recursos hídricos. t. 8, Sectores construcciones, vivienda, urbanismo, saneamiento básico. La Paz: El Ministerio, n.d. 4 v.

The operating plan for the 1978 national economic plan. Includes income elasticities, which are estimated to be surprisingly low, particularly for food.

3561 ———. ———. Resumen. v. 1/11. La Paz: Ministerio de Planeamiento y Coordinación de la Presidencia de la República, 1978. 11 v.

Consists of 11 vols. of Bolivia's National Economic Plan of 1978. Vols. 1/2 consist of a summary, with vol. 1 containing good background material and a data base. The other volumes detail the particular sections such as rural, mining, industry, tourism, public health, etc.

Bolivian: Rückkehr zur bürgelichen Demokrarie?: Eine Pressedokumentation (Bolivia: ¿retorno a la democracia burguesa?: documentación de prensa). See item **6493.**

3562 Burke, Melvin. The stabilization programs of the International Monetary Fund: the case of Bolivia (RU/MP, 2:2, Summer 1979, p. 118–133, tables)

Scathing attack on the stabilization programs of the IMF. Author makes appropriate criticisms of IMF's inflexible solution to varying structural problems, using Bolivia as a case study.

Capriles Villazón, Orlando. Historia de la minería boliviana. See *HLAS 42:3143.*

3563 Cariaga, Juan L. and **Lane Vanderslice.** Introducción a los modelos macroeconómicos. La Paz, Bolivia: Academia Nacional de Ciencias de Bolivia, Editorial Los Amigos del Libro, 1979. 227 p.; bibl.; ill.

Intermediate-level macroeconomic theory text with emphasis on international factors. Contains good chapter on Bolivia's macro-economy which includes an aggregated model.

3564 Carranza Fernández, Gontrán. El proceso histórico de la planificación en Bolivia, 1928–1978. La Paz, Bolivia: Centro de Investigaciones Sociales, 1979. 143 leaves; bibl. (Serie Estudios de población y desarrollo; no. 19)

Detailed and relatively well-documented history of government planning in Bolivia.

3565 Corporación Minera de Bolivia. Corporación Minera de Bolivia, 1952–1975. La Paz: Departamento de Relaciones Públicas de COMIBOL, 1975? 104 p.; ill.; maps.

Non-rigorous description of the Bolivian mining sectors. Includes numerous photographs and maps.

3566 Documentos sobre política económica y social, 1975–1978. La Paz: Ministerio de Planeamiento y Coordinación de la Presidencia de la República, 1978 or 1979. 266 p.

Collection of 1975–78 government documents related to economic development planning. Contains some interesting background material.

3567 Eckstein, Susan. El capitalismo mundial y la revolución agraria en Bolivia (UNAM/RMS, 41[41]:2, abril/junio 1979, p. 457–480, bibl.)

Author utilizes different sociological and economic models to explain the land reform initiated in the post-1952 Revolution. Makes liberal use of Cuba as a comparative case study.

3568 Foro-Debate "Gas, Petróleo y Miseria," *Universidad Mayor de San Simón, 1978.* Gas, petróleo y miseria: un esclarecedor debate sobre los recursos naturales. Portada de Scorpio. Cochabamba, Bolivia: Federación Universitaria Local, Universidad Mayor de San Simón, 1979. 185 p. (Colección Recursos naturales)

Seven essays addressing the issue of the foreign exploitation of Bolivia's natural resources. All authors follow the dependency model to some degree; they agree that Bolivia needs to develop a more anti-interdependency attitude in its foreign economic relations.

3569 Gómez D'Angelo, Walter. La minería en el desarrollo económico de Bolivia, 1900–1970. La Paz: editorial Los Amigos del Libro, 1978. 249 p.; bibl.; ill.

Economic history of the role of mining in the economic development of Bolivia from 1900–70. Draws conclusions and offers alternative public policy strategies.

3570 González M., René. Informativo económico de Bolivia. 3. ed. La Paz: Editorial Los Amigos del Libro, 1979. 199 p.

Vertical subsector description of each of the major commodities produced in Bolivia, including linkage functions. Study is weak on the post-production levels.

3571 Hermosa Virreira, Wálter. Breve historia de la minería en Bolivia. La Paz:

Editorial Los Amigos de Libro, 1979. 218 p.; bibl.; ill. (Enciclopedia boliviana)

Descriptive economic history of Bolivia's mining industry devotes one third of the volume to pre-19th century (including precolumbian period); another third to the 19th century; and last third to the 20th century.

3572 Incógnita del petróleo boliviano.
Opinan, José Patiño Ayoroa et al. La Paz, Bolivia: s.n., 1979. 39 p. (Temas en la crisis; 6)

Elementary analysis of national petroleum policy in Bolivia which is too short to be useful. However, it provides insight into the diversity of opinions on this issue.

3573 Instituto Nacional de Estadística
(Bolivia). Resultados del Censo Nacional de Población y Vivienda, 1976. v. 1, Departamento de Chuquisaca. v. 2, Departamento de La Paz. v. 3, Departamento de Cochabamba. v. 4, Departamento de Oruro. v. 5, Departamento de Potosí. v. 6, Departamento de Tarija. v. 7, Departamento de Santa Cruz. v. 9, Departamento de Pando. República de Bolivia, Ministerio de Planeamiento y Coordinación, Instituto Nacional de Estadística. La Paz: El Instituto, 1978/ 1979. 12 v.; ill.

Consists of 12 vols. of the 1976 National Census. Vols. 1/9 present demographic data for each of the nine Bolivian departments; vols. 10/12 are data summaries.

3574 ———. Resultados provisionales: Censo Nacional de Población y Vivienda. v. 1, Departamento de Tarija. v. 2, Departamento de Chuquisaca. v. 3, Departamento de La Paz. v. 4, Departamento de Santa Cruz. v. 5, Departamento de Cochabamba. v. 6, Departamento de Potosí. v. 10, Total del país. República de Bolivia, Ministerio de Planeamiento y Coordinación, Instituto Nacional de Estadística. La Paz: El Instituto, 1977. 10 v.; ill.

Population of Bolivia by city, province, according to 1976 National Census.

3575 ———. **Departamento de Muestreo y Encuestas.** Resultados de la encuesta de empleo, ciudad de La Paz. República de Bolivia, Ministerio de Planeamiento y Coordinación, Instituto Nacional de Estadística, Departamento de Muestreo y Encuestas. La Paz: El Departamento, 1978. 72 p.

Employment Census of workers in La Paz, Bolivia. Data includes types of homes, demographic variables, education, salary and wage distributions, and type of work.

3576 ———. **División de Estadísticas Fiscales y Financieras.** Estadísticas fiscales y financieras, 1972–1976. República de Bolivia, Ministerio de Planeamiento y Coordinación, Instituto Nacional de Estadística, Departamento de Estadísticas Económicas, División de Estadísticas Fiscales y Financieras. La Paz: La División, 1978 or 1979. 29 p.; graphs; tables.

Bolivia fiscal and financial data for 1972–78.

3577 La Paz, *Bolivia.* **Dirección General de Desarrollo Urbano.** Modelo de crecimiento, Ciudad de La Paz. Jorge Saravia V., Jorge Otero R., Grover Villegas B. La Paz: Alcaldía Municipal, Dirección de Desarrollo Urbano, 1976. 148 leaves, 19 leaves of plates; bibl.; ill.

Meticulously presented urban planning model for the city of La Paz, Bolivia. Contains good demographic data.

3578 Laba, Román. Fish, peasants, and state bureaucracies: the development of Lake Titicaca (CPS, 12:3, Oct. 1979, p. 335–361, bibl., ill., table)

Article not only explores tentative explanations of the failure to develop a commercial fishing industry on Lake Titicaca, but also challenges the reasoning underlying the objections of the development project itself, now 45 years old. For political scientist's comment, see item **6459.**

3579 Medinacelli V., Juan and **Antonio Camberos B.** Algunos aspectos del enfoque monetario de la balanza de pagos: evidencia empírica para el caso boliviano (*in* El enfoque monetario de la balanza de pagos. México: Centro de Estudios Monetarios Latinoamericanos, 1980, p. 35–71, tables)

Empirical examination of the validity of monetary approach to macroeconomic policymaking for a small country. Authors' results are mixed.

Mitre, Antonio F. Estructura económica social de la minería boliviana de la plata en el siglo XIX. See *HLAS 42:3164.*

3580 Programa Regional del Empleo para América Latina y el Caribe. Archivo de datos sobre Bolivia. Prepared by O. Gout-man with the collaboration of A. Miranda. Organización Internacional del Trabajo, Programa Mundial del Empleo, Programa Regional del Empleo para América Latina y el Caribe, PREALC. Santiago, Chile: PREALC, 1979. 90 p.; bibl. (Documento de trabajo—PREALC; 169)

Descriptive analysis of the sources and quality of information and data on various economic sectors. Contains good general data on the level of socioeconomic development of Bolivia and excellent reference list of data sources.

3581 ———. Bolivia, informe sobre el uso de las estadísticas salariales para el estudio de la distribución del ingreso. Organización Internacional del Trabajo, Programa Mundial del Empleo, Programa Regional del Empleo para América Latina y el Caribe, PREALC. Santiago, Chile: PREALC, 1978. 37 p. (Documento de trabajo—PREALC; 149)

Methodological piece on use of data on salary relative to income distribution collected in a PREALC survey. Good for scholars concerned with economic performance definition in developing countries.

Revista de la Academia Boliviana de Ciencias Económicas. No. 1, enero 1980– . See *HLAS* 42:231.

3582 **Rivera Cusicanqui, Silvia.** La expansión del latifundio en el altiplano boliviano (IPA/A, 12:13, 1979, p. 189–218, tables)

Results of a 1979 empirical study of the structure of land holdings in Bolivia. Emphasizes the dynamics of growth of the *latifundio* and some institutional aspects of ownership.

3583 **Romero Loza, José.** El algodón en Bolivia. 2. ed. aumentada y rev. Cochabamba: Amigos del Libro, 1978. 142 p.; bibl.; ill.

Interesting description, rich in data, of the production and processing sectors of the Bolivian cotton industry.

3584 **Sanabria Fernández, Hernando.** Miguel Suárez Arana y la Empresa Nacional de Bolivia. Santa Cruz de la Sierra, Bolivia: s.n., 1977. 154 p.; port.

Biography of one of Bolivia's early en-

trepreneurs provides interesting economic history of the 1800s as a side benefit.

3585 **Vega López, Oscar.** Bolivia, causas de la crisis económica en el período 1971–1979: de la dictadura a la democracia: acto interpelatorio al Gabinete Ministerial de la Presidenta Sra. Lydia Gueiler, por las medidas económicas antipopulares del 30 de noviembre de 1979. La Paz, Bolivia: s.n., 1980. 108 p.; graphs.

Author combines political science and economics in a very insightful overview of modern Bolivia. Concentrates on the actions leading to the presidency of Lidia Gueiler.

3586 **Velagapudi, Gunvor.** La encuesta demográfica de Bolivia: algunas reflexiones sobre su contenido ocupacional. La Paz, Bolivia: Ministerio de Planeamiento y Coordinación de la Presidencia de la República, Instituto Nacional de Estadística, 1976. 14, 17 leaves; bibl. (Documento de trabajo—PREALC; 106)

Summary of a Bolivian demographic survey. Provides some interpretation and explanations of missing data and statistical outliers.

3587 **Zuvekas, Clarence.** Measuring rural underemployment in Bolivia: a critical review (IAMEA, 32:4, Spring 1979, p. 65–83)

Important methodological article because of its case study nature. Author examines various estimates of rural underemployment in Bolivia, shows why there are overestimations, and makes suggestions for improved research in the area.

PARAGUAY

3588 **Alvarez, Luis Alberto.** Prioridades nacionales en aspectos de producción y productividad del sector agropecuario y forestal del Paraguay. Asunción, Paraguay: Ministerio de Agricultura y Ganadería, Departamento de Divulgación, 1976. 142 leaves; bibl.; ill.

Description of domestic demand and supply of agricultural and livestock products. Also gives a good description of economic policymaking institutions.

3589 **Banco Central del Paraguay.** Cuentos nacionales del Paraguay, 1962/1975. Asunción: El Banco, 1976. 94 p.; tables (some

fold.) (División de Cuentas Nacionales; 12)
Macroeconomic data for 1962–75, includes population growth, GNP, prices, and price and quantity data for all economic sectors.

3590 ———. Memoria, 1976. Asunción: Banco Central del Paraguay, 1976? 223 p.; tables.
Annual Report of Central Bank of Paraguay contains particularly good data on the international monetary relations of Paraguay.

3591 Carbonell de Masy, Rafael. Hacia un desarrollo empresarial del cooperativismo Paraguayo (UCNSA/EP, 5:2, dic. 1977, p. 23–49, table)
Description of the ethnic and economic base of the 60 agricultural marketing cooperatives in Paraguay. In addition to Paraguayan groups, identifies Mennonites, Japanese, German Brazilians, and Germans as having a strong foreign influence on the development of these rural cooperatives.

3592 Enríquez Gamón, Efraím. Paraguay: economía y desarrollo, bosquejo para una política económica (UCNSA/EP, 6:2, dic. 1978, p. 45–118, bibl., tables)
Detailed description of the role played by government institutions and their policies in Paraguay's economic development. Contains little analysis and makes no recommendations.

3593 Flecha, Agustín Oscar. El sector y el endeudamiento externo (UCNSA/EP, 5:2, dic. 1977, p. 127–149, tables)
Author estimates simple domestic and foreign demand equations, and then analyzes the implications for the Paraguayan economy of increases in external debt. Makes several thought-provoking policy recommendations.

3594 Herken K., Juan Carlos. El sector externo en la economía paraguaya (UCNSA/EP, 6:1, sept. 1978, p. 87–112, tables)
Carefully formulated quantitative analysis of the changes in Paraguay's balance of payments. Includes data sets.

3595 Miranda T., Anibal. El comercio hispano-paraguayo (UCNSA/EP, 5:2, dic. 1977, p. 53–83, tables)
Detailed description of Paraguayan-Spanish trade. Presents data, describes financial arrangements, and documents foreign capital investment on a bilateral basis. Does not include rigorous trade analysis.

3596 Nickson, Andrés. Productividad y rentabilidad de las empaquetadoras de carne extranjeras en el Paraguay (UCNSA/EP, 5:2, dic. 1977, p. 87–126, tables)
Excellent statistical description of the market structure of the Paraguayan meat-packing industry. Estimates some performance measures. Excellent data source.

Oberbeck, Charles D. An annotated bibliography of income distribution in Paraguay. See *HLAS 42:57.*

3597 Paraguay. Cuenca del Plata: estudio para su planificación y desarrollo: República del Paraguay-Proyecto Aquidaban, desarrollo de la Región Nororiental. Realizado por la unidad técnica durante el período 1972–74, Gobierno del Paraguay y Departamento de Desarrollo Regional de la OEA. Washington: Secretaría General de la Organización de los Estados Americanos, 1975 i.e. 1976. 197 p.; ill.; maps (5 fold. in portfolio)
Well-documented examination of natural resource base and economic infrastructure by regions. Contains excellent tables and maps.

3598 ———. **Dirección General de Estadística y Censos.** Censo nacional de población y viviendas, 1972. Asunción: La Dirección, 1975. 561 p.; ill.; tables.
One-volume edition of the National Census of Population and Housing for 1972 that is very complete.

3599 ———. **Ministerio de Industria y Comercio.** Gabinete Técnico. Paraguayan investment panorama. Prepared by the Technical Department, Ministry of Industry and Commerce. Asunción: The Ministry, 1977. 35 leaves, 1 leaf of plates; ill.
Superficial treatment of Paraguay's economic structure, written by government officials.

3600 ———. **Secretaría Técnica de Planificación.** Plan Nacional de Desarrollo Económico y Social, 1977–1981: Paraguay. t. 1, Síntesis del diagnóstico socio-económico, 1970–1975. Asunción: La Secretaría, 1976. 1 v.; bibl.; ill.
Preliminary study for the development of the 1977–81 National Development Plan.

Of historical value in that a brief economic history of Paraguayan development from 1960–70 precedes a more detailed macroeconomic analysis of the 1970–75 period. Well-documented with good data.

3601 Paraguay, guía industrial: anexo exportadores, 1976–77. Asunción: Unión Industrial Paraguaya, 1977; 1 v.

A directory that lists Paraguayan exporters by product.

3602 Paraguay: oportunidad de inversión.

Documento elaborado en su esfuerzo coordinado del Ministerio de Industria y Comercio, Ministerio de Hacienda, Banco Nacional de Fomento, la Secretaría Técnica de Planificación y la Oficina Nacional de Proyectos. Asunción: s.n., 1974. 97 p., 3 leaves of plates (2 fold.); maps (some col.)

Well-documented but dated guide to business investment opportunities in Paraguay.

Pastore, Carlos. Introducción a una historia económica del Paraguay en el siglo XIX. See *HLAS 42:3463.*

3603 Prieto Yegros, Leandro. Estudio sobre la problemática poblacional en el Paraguay. Asunción, Paraguay: s.n., 1979. 50 leaves, 17 leaves of plates; bibl.; maps.

Analysis of the population problem. Author concludes that the state is not fulfilling its important leadership role by absence of population policy, which is especially important in a population-deficit country such as Paraguay.

3604 Registro General de Firmas. Guía del Paraguay: banca, industria, comercio 1978/79. Asunción, Paraguay: Editorial Tilcará, 1979. 1 v.; ill.

First general listing of Paraguay firms giving addresses, officers, and in some cases services or products. Provides no size criteria or relevant analytical data.

3605 Sosa, Horacio C. Stroessner en el desarrollo del Chaco: obras realizadas por el Gobierno nacional a partir de 1955, destinadas a crear las condiciones generales para el desarrollo de la región occidental del país. Asunción, Paraguay: Ministerio de Educación y Culto, 1978. 108 p.

Elementary description of development projects undertaken by Stroessner regime in the Chaco region. Of little research value.

Whigham, Thomas Lyle. The iron works of Ybycuí: Paraguayan industrial development in the mid-nineteenth century. See *HLAS 42:3473.*

3606 *Wirtschaftliche Entwicklung: Paraguay.* Bundesstelle für Aussenhandelsinformation. 1977– . Köln, Federal Republic of Germany.

Gives aggregated agricultural and industrial export/import data for 1972–77 period, and a listing of Paraguay's bilateral agreements as of 1977.

URUGUAY

3607 Cancela Vilanova, Walter. El Uruguay actual, un enfoque económico: tentativa de interpretación de sus variables básicas, primera aproximación. Montevideo: Fundación de Cultura Universitaria: Centro Latinoamericano de Economía Humana, 1979. 171 p.; bibl. (Economía y sociedad; 1)

Consists of first estimations of a macroeconomic model of the Uruguayan economy, yielding very modest results. Author gives detailed explanation of variable selection.

3608 Centro de Investigación y Experimentación Pedagógica. La demanda de capacitación técnica en el Uruguay. Montevideo: Centro de Investigación y Experimentación Pedagógica, 1977. 167 p.; bibl.; graphs (Investigaciones—CIEP; 2)

Complete study of the quality of labor and the technical school system in Uruguay. Makes the case for more vocational schools. Contains good set of data.

3609 Ciclo de conferencias sobre la empresa. Adolfo Gelsi Bidart et al. Montevideo: Asociación de Escribanos del Uruguay, Instituto de Investigación y Técnica Notarial, 1979. 133 p. (Conferencias y cursos; 7)

Consists of five essays on different aspects of business enterprises, two of which concern Uruguay: one on agribusiness by Bidart and another on business in regional integration groups by Vieira.

3610 Comcorde. Secretaría Técnica. El plan nacional de silos: descripción y características. Montevideo: La Secretaría, 1976. 60 p., 5 leaves of plates; ill.

Describes characteristics of the national grain and food elevator plan. Contains very good structural data but little on the risk management role played by reserve policies.

3611 ——. ——. Reflexiones sobre aspectos de la historia económicos del Uruguay, período 1900–1979. Prepared by W. Lusiardo Aznárez. Montevideo, Uruguay: COMCORDE, Secretaría Técnica, 1979. 99 p.

Analysis of the historic evolution of Uruguayan economy during the 20th century, divided into three periods: 1) growth period, 1900–30; 2) stagnation period, 1930–50; and 3) decline period, 1950–75.

Díaz, Nelson González. Los ferrocarriles ingleses en Uruguay desde sus orígenes hasta la crisis del noventa. See *HLAS 42:3486.*

3612 Diccionario de la producción y de la industria. 2. ed. Montevideo: Centro de Estudios y Publicaciones de la Industria y la Producción, 1977. 863 p.; ill.; index.

General index of all business, industry and service in Uruguay as of 1977.

3613 Echegaray, Alfredo. El convenio de cooperación económica entre Argentina y Uruguay (INTAL/IL, 1:6, sept. 1976, p. 20–29, table)

Detailed account of increased bilateral relations between two key River Plate nations. Excellent essay for students of the area and of the dynamics of integration.

Echenique, Carlos A. Junta Económico Administrativa de Cerro Largo 1852–1867: aspectos de suggestión como muestra de un proceso histórico, ensayos. See *HLAS 42:3487.*

Económico. Vol. 1, No. 1, nov. 1978– . See *HLAS 42:211.*

3614 Estrategias publicitarias y su evaluación. Héctor Bauza et al. Montevideo: Universidad de la República, Facultad de Ciencias Económicas y de Administración, Instituto de Administración, 1980. 185, 3 p., 4 leaves of plates; bibl.; ill.

Quasi-textbook on advertising in Uruguay. More conceptual than empirical in approach.

3615 Galmes, Miguel A. and **Chien-Pai Han.** Some aspects of the crop survey in Uruguay (IASI/E, 33:121, dic. 1979, p. 177–187, tables)

Good methodological study on probabilistic estimation of field crops. Particularly relevant because Uruguay has one of the highest coefficients of variations of crop production in the world. Paper discusses difficulties encountered and solutions adopted to overcome them.

3616 Ganón, Isaac. El Uruguay en los años treinta (*in* América Latina en los años treinta. Luis Antezana E. et al. Coordinador, Pablo González Casanova. México: Instituto de Investigaciones Sociales, Universidad Nacional Autónoma de México, 1977, p. 451–511, tables)

Even though primarily a sociopolitical history of Uruguay during the 1930s, this article contains much of value for the economic historian because the roots of many of the current economic problems were seeded during that time. A very well-written article that gives an interesting perspective on the subject.

3617 La Industrialización del Uruguay, 1870–1925 [i.e. mil ochocientos setenta mil novecientos veinticinco]: 5 perspectivas históricas. Alcides Beretta et al. Montevideo: Fundación de Cultura Universitaria, 1978. 224 p.; bibl. (Cuadernos de historia; 12)

Descriptive economic history of Uruguay's industrialization during the period preceding and during Batlle.

3618 Jacob, Raúl. El frigorífico nacional en el mercado de carnes: la crisis de 1929 en el Uruguay. Montevideo: Fundación de Cultura Universitaria, 1979. 162 p.; bibl. (Cuadernos de historia; 14)

Very detailed history of the important role played by the export-oriented meat packing industry during the world economic crisis of 1929. Well-documented work that contains some good data.

3619 Jacob, Raúl. El Uruguay en la crisis de 1929: algunos indicadores económicos. Montevideo: Fundación de Cultura Universitaria, 1977. 92 p.; tables.

Factual summary of important economic variables that explain the crisis of 1929.

3620 Lamboglia, Santiago and **Alba Ferme de Lamboglia.** Intercambio comercial: integración y desarrollo brasileño-uruguayo. Sant'Ana do Livramento, Brazil: Asociação Santanense pró Ensino Superior, 1977. 57

leaves (Cadernos de ASPES; no. 2: Economia)
Description of the objectives and format of bilateral economic agreements between Uruguay and Brazil. Important study for integration economists and specialists in geopolitics.

3621 Martorelli, Horacio. Minifundio rural y migración campo ciudad (CLAEH, 10, abril/junio 1979, p. 69–83, tables)
Well-documented essay on the rural and urban migration process related to changes in small-farm ownership.

3622 Melgar, Alicia. El Plan C.I.D.E.— Comisión de Inversiones y Desarrollo Económico: quince años después (CLAEH, 10, abril/junio 1979, p. 27–38)
Very interesting review of the outcome of the internationally acclaimed Plan CIDE—Uruguay's economic plan for the future, completed in 1965. Author concludes that no economic plan can be presented or implemented without serious study of its political impact. CIDE naively avoided these political implications, and therefore terminated as an academic exercise. Good article for macroeconomic planners.

3623 Mondino, Luis. Hacia un desarrollo agroindustrial en Uruguay (Geopolítica [Instituto Uruguayo de Estudios Geopolíticos, Montevideo] 3 : 6, dic. 1979, p. 16–21, tables)
Short essay on the differences between agribusiness and agricultural industries. Describes Uruguay's slow adoption of vertically integrated systems.

3624 Musso, Carlos. Acondicionamiento del espacio rural: la apertura de la economía y la dependencia externa, historia y caricatura. Montevideo: Centro Latinoamericano de Economía Humana, 1978. 102 p.; bibl.; ill.
Contains several articles on the interaction of human and natural resources. Major article addresses the misallocation of rural space in the interior of Uruguay.

3625 *Panorama Anual.* Bolsa de Valores, Asesoría Estadística. Vol. 24, 1977– . Montevideo.
Summary of the performance of both public and private equities in Uruguay during 1977.

3626 Presupuesto de gastos de fábrica en condiciones de inflación. Martha

Alonso et al.; coordinación, Instituto de Administración. Montevideo: Universidad de la República, Facultad de Ciencias Económicos y de Administración, 1980. 231 p.; bibl.; ill.
Gives standard treatment to firm budgeting models with and without inflation.

Revista Histórica. Año 70, Vol. 48, Nos. 142/144, dic. 1976 . See *HLAS 42:3502.*

Sierra, Gerónimo de. Consolidación y crisis del "capitalismo democrático" en Uruguay. See *HLAS 42:3504.*

3627 Torres, Generoso. Políticas antiinflacionarias en el Uruguay: 1955–1977. Montevideo, Uruguay: Centro Latinoamericano de Economía Humana, 1979. 75 p. (Serie Investigaciones—Centro Latinoamericano de Economía Humana; no. 7)
Brief but perceptive examination of Uruguay's inflation problem during the past 20 years. Presents both structuralist and monetarist analyses.

3628 Uruguay. Banco Comercial. Uruguay en cifras: 1979. Montevideo: 1979. 1 fold. brochure; tables.
General aggregated demographic and economic data for 1979.

3629 ———. Biblioteca del Poder Legislativo. Cooperativismo en el Uruguay. Montevideo: La Biblioteca, 1978. 231 p.; ill. (Serie de temas nacionales; 6)
Excellent description of the cooperative form of business in Uruguay. Detailed data on agricultural, consumer, credit, housing, and productive cooperatives. Also contains good legal section.

3630 ———. Dirección General de Comercio Exterior. Potencial de exportación. Ministerio de Economía y Finanzas, Dirección General de Comercio Exterior. Montevideo: La Dirección, 1977. 14 p.
Brief "how to" type publication concerning non-traditional export items, which gained in importance in Uruguay during the 1970s.

3631 ———. Dirección General de Estadística y Censos. V [i.e. Quinto] Censo general de población. Fasc. 1, Demografía. Fasc. 3, Características económicas. Presidencia de la República Oriental del Uruguay, Secretaría de Planeamiento. Coordinación y Difusión, Dirección General de Estadística y Censos. Montevideo: La Dirección, 1979/1980. 3 v.; tables.

Final population and housing results from the 1975 census, which is only the fifth census in Uruguay's history (1852, 1860, 1908, 1963, and 1975).

3632 ———. ———. V [i.e. Quinto] Censo general de población, III de viviendas, año 1975: datos preliminares. República Oriental del Uruguay, Ministerio de Economía y Finanzas, Dirección General de Estadística y Censos. 2. ed. Montevideo: La Dirección, 1976. 132 p.; maps.

Contains 1975 census results on population and housing at national and regional levels with demographic distributions, birth rates, literacy, and some employment data.

3633 ———. Dirección Nacional de Contralor de Semovientes, Frutos del País,

Marcas y Señales. Investigaciones sobre la problemática agropecuaria actual: apéndice, 1977. Ministerio de Agricultura y Pesca. Montevideo: Editorial Hemisferio Sur, 1977. 59 p.

Well-formulated analysis of the negative impact of indirect taxes on the livestock sector in Uruguay.

3634 Wonsewer, Israel. La apertura de la economía y la dependencia externa (CLAEH, dic. 1978, p. 41–54)

Pragmatic discourse on the costs and advantages of both a totally free market and a totally protected market. Author's policy suggestions represent a middle of the road position.

ARGENTINA

JAN PETER WOGART, Economist, The World Bank

IN CONTRAST TO THE STATE OF THE ECONOMY, Argentina's economic literature has flourished recently, in terms of both quantity and quality. Although financially hard pressed, most research institutions have been active in publishing studies on a large number of topics, ranging from comparative analysis of the prosperous second half of the 19th century to studies of the troublesome 1970s. New teams of researchers have challenged old theories and institutions, and the leading public research institutions have strengthened their staffs and increased their efforts to improve the quality of the basic economic information they provide.

After reexamining its national and international accounts, the Central Bank has published a set of revised data, some of which are rather drastic (item 3636). In addition to reducing the time lag between the collection and the publication of monetary statistics, the Central Bank's Center for Monetary Studies has issued an increasing number of technical studies, some of them with direct policy implications (items 3642–3643 and 3684). Several of these studies have been published— along with contributions to the Central Bank's annual conference—in the journal Ensayos Económicos. The Ministry of Economy managed both to upgrade and improve the National Statistical Institute (INDEC) and to publish weekly, monthly, and semi-annual reports dealing with new economic policy and legislation (items 3637 and 3638). Another agency within the Ministry, the Planning Institute, went beyond its original task of publishing the public investment program and conducted an interesting study of the development of labor productivity during the last decade (item 3639).

In the private sector, demand for economic information has grown rapidly, reflecting the increasing complexity of the economic environment during the last few years. Part of this demand was satisfied by domestic and foreign consultants and banks which provided interested customers with the sort of up-to-date economic information required for monitoring Argentina's rapidly changing situation.

Major research institutions, while increasingly involved in analyzing recent events, also found time to conduct historical research. The Di Tella Institute sponsored a seminar on the comparative development of Australia and Argentina from the 1850s to the 1970s (item **3640**), and Cortés Conde produced a thorough study on the rapid development of Argentina in the late 19th and early 20th centuries (item **3649**). There is also a useful study of the 20 years between the two World Wars, a period which proved to be crucial in setting the pattern for Argentina's unstable development after World War II (item **3697**). For the post-war period, Wynia's sociopolitical analysis attempts to explain the country's more recent economic problems in the light of a decision-making process which lacked the cooperation and participation of the Argentine people and their selected representatives (item **3699**).

Events leading to the implementation of Argentina's 1976–80 stabilization program continue to draw the attention of scholars. A variety of studies of these events exists, both in Spanish and other languages, some of which are in the process of being published. Among the latter, the most outstanding are by the researchers of CEMA, the Buenos Aires Center of Macroeconomic Studies; CEDES, the Center for Economic and Social Studies; IERRAL, the Fundación Mediterránea in Cordoba; FIEL, the Foundation for Latin American Studies; and IDES, the Institute for Economic and Social Studies (items **3641, 3645, 3659, 3662, 3665, 3681** and **3686–3688**).

Several scholars have addressed theoretical and empirical aspects of the monetary approach to stabilize the balance of payments (items **3667** and **3678**). Díaz-Alejandro's essay on the Southern Cone Stabilization Program offers a good introduction to the stabilization and trade liberalization programs that were implemented simultaneously in Argentina, Chile, and Uruguay (item **3651**). There have also been further attempts at testing the relationship between money and income (items **3658** and **3674**), and substantial microeconomic work on the banking sector, whose liberalization caused increasing problems for the productive sectors (items **3643** and **3656**). The analyses of industry and agriculture, the sectors most affected by the 1976–80 program, are of a more historical character (items **3671, 3689** and **3693**). Current research at the World Bank should provide some interesting information on the adjustment process taking place in these sectors in the late 1970s and early 1980s. Various studies have shed light on topics such as the functioning of this labor market, wages, and employment (items **3682–3683** and **3690**).

Looking ahead, one can expect that—in spite of the precarious financial situation of most research institutions and universities—economists inside and outside of Argentina will continue to generate important studies of the nation's economy. Although the possibility of these studies being translated into economic policy (as were some of those produced in the 1976–80 period) is less certain, the necessity for continued research of major issues confronting economic-policy makers is more urgent than ever.

3635 Allen, Julia Coan and **Frederick Stirton Weaver.** The fiscal crisis of the Argentine state (LAP, 6[22]: 3, Summer 1979, p. 30–45, bibl., tables)

After analyzing the early Perón administration with the help of a three-sector model developed by O'Connor, authors argue that the "fiscal crisis approach" is not only useful for relating the political-economic variables of the late 1940s and early 1950s, but can also be applied to later periods. The empirical evidence for such a bold statement is not entirely convincing.

3636 Argentina. Banco Central de la República Argentina. Gerencia de Investigaciones y Estadísticas Económicas. De-

partamento de Cuentas Nacionales. División de Actividad Industrial y de Actividad Agropecuaria. Estimaciones trimestrales y anuales de la oferta y demanda global de precios de 1970: metodología, fuentes de información y resultados. Buenos Aires: 1980. 168 p.; tables.

Recalculation and updating of national account statistics of the 1970s in 1970 prices, based on the results of more recent economic census (1974). New estimates lead to decreased growth calculations for GDP (annual average growth of GDP 2.5 percent instead of three percent between 1970–79), and substantial revisions of industrial sector accounts, with manufacturing activities now participating only 28 percent in GDP rather than the 36 percent estimated earlier (1960 prices).

3637 ———. **Ministerio de Economía.** Argentine economic development (L'évolution économique argentine). Buenos Aires: 1979? 1 v.

One of the surveys of recent economic development (in a bilingual English-French edition) first issued by the Economic Ministry in 1977 and updated semi-annually thereafter. Contains background information useful mainly to foreign investors and banks. In general, well-balanced description and analysis, which summarizes objectives and implementation of the 1976 economic program. Includes an increasingly specific public investment program and an analysis of most recent events.

3638 ———. ———. **Secretaría de Coordinación y Planeamiento.** Economic information on Argentina. Buenos Aires: 1980. 272 p.; tables.

Special English-language publication describes major economic developments in Argentina during 1976–80. Includes numerous statistics on and illustrations of the economy's productive and financial sectors during that period.

3639 ———. ———. **Secretaría de Estado de Programación y Coordenación Económica. Instituto Nacional de Planeamiento Económico** (INPE). Análisis de la productividad de la mano de obra. Buenos Aires: Minieconomía, 1980. 123 p.; bibl.; graphs; tables.

Study traces changes in labor productivity for the Argentine economy during

1971–79. While average annual gains of 1.8 percent were substantially below Argentina's previous record and also below the accomplishments of countries at a similar state of development during that decade, it is important to note that the 1976–79 period shows an annual gain of 3.8 percent, which was as good as any of the more rapidly expanding economies in the world. Authors attribute the change, on the one hand, to increased rationalization and capital intensification and on the other hand, its withdrawal of workers from the official labor market. Change was most pronounced in the manufacturing sector, which experienced annual productivity gains, averaging 7.5 percent during the 1976–79 period. This technical analysis is required reading for anyone interested in examining the effects of the 1976–80 program on structural change in the Argentine industrial sector and its labor force.

3640 **Argentina y Australia.** Edited by John Fogarty; Ezequiel Gallo; and Héctor Dieguez. Buenos Aires: Instituto Torcuato di Tella, 1979. 246 p.; tables.

Conference volume compares economic development and structural change in Australia and Argentina between 1850 and 1970. Various contributors point out: 1) the greater flexibility of Australia's external sector due to its large mining exports; and 2) the closer trade relations between Australia and the U.K., as compared to Argentina's efforts to be independent after the 1930s Great Depression. Essays go far beyond narrow economic comparisons, to considering variables such as ethnic differences and political power grouping. Also includes an essay on the methodology of country comparison and a comparative analysis of economic developments in Uruguay and New Zealand.

3641 **Arnaudo, Aldo** and **Roberto Domenech.** El déficit fiscal en los años 70 (IEERAL/E, 2:7, enero/feb. 1979, p. 13–36, tables)

Comprehensive study of Argentina's fiscal sector between 1970–78, providing estimates of the actual fiscal deficit by analyzing the sources of public sector financing. Results show that total deficit financing decreased substantially between 1975–76 and 1977–78 from over 10 percent to less than five percent of GDP, but remained above the 2.5 percent average financed during the early years of the 1970s.

Arnoux, Henri. Le role des Français dans la fondation de l'industrie argentine à la fin du XIXe et au début du XXe siècle. See *HLAS 42:3294.*

3642 Báez, Juan C. Estimación de componentes de la demanda de dinero (BCRA/EE, 12, dic. 1979, p. 35–67, tables)

Empirical analysis of the demand for money and its most important components between 1968–77 points out important role changing interest rates played in the distribution between demand and saving deposits.

Balán, Jorge and **Nancy G. López.** Burguesías y gobiernos provinciales en la Argentina: la política impositiva de Tucumán y Mendoza entre 1873 y 1914. See *HLAS 42:3299.*

3643 Balino, Tomás. Determinantes del diferencial entre las tasas activas y pasivas de los intermediarios financieros. Buenos Aires: Banco Central de la República, 1979. 27 p.; graphs (Serie de información pública; no. 8)

Study of the determinants of bank earnings derived from the difference between interest on deposits and loans. Author enumerates six major variables, of which reserve requirements and risk-taking are the most important.

3644 Buenos Aires (Province). **Secretaría de Planeamiento de Desarrollo.** Diagnóstico de la estructura económica de la Provincia de Buenos Aires. La Plata, Argentina: Gobernación de la Provincia de Buenos Aires, Secretaría de Planeamiento y Desarrollo, 1979. 154 p.; 29 leaves of plates; bibl.; ill.

Volume forms part of a large-scale planning effort which took place in the province of Buenos Aires in 1978/79. Provides background information on the major economic sectors in Argentina's most important province. Ample use of the detailed maps and graphs makes the study a regional planner's delight.

3645 Carnitrot, Adolfo. La disciplina como objectivo de la política económica: un ensayo sobre el programa económico del gobierno argentino desde 1976 (Estudios CEDES [Centro de Estudios de Estado y Sociedad, Buenos Aires] 2:6, 1979, p. 5–34)

Critical essay that examines the government's economic program for 1976–80, emphasizing its disciplinary and corrective characteristics. Author stresses growth as the major goal in all aspects of the program, which should continue to pursue price stabilization while stimulating investment in the private sector.

3646 Chudnovsky, Daniel. The challenge by domestic enterprises to the transnational corporations' domination: a case study of the Argentine pharmaceutical industry (WD, 7:1, Jan. 1979, p. 45–58, tables)

Interesting case study of the pharmaceutical industry, which traditionally has been dominated by multinationals in Latin America. In Argentina, however, domestic firms have challenged that pattern through product differentiation and an ingenious mixture of transfer-of-technology agreements, some reliance on unpatented sources, and some indigenous research and development.

3647 Colomé, Rinaldo Antonio. Excedente financiero del sector agropecuario argentino: reflexiones en torno de un trabajo anterior y nueva estimación (IDES/DE, 18:70, julio/sept. 1978, p. 275–282, tables)

Note on the agricultural sector surplus. Author's estimates are substantially lower than those presented in previous studies (see *HLAS 39:3547*). He demonstrates that for several years the surplus actually turned into a deficit.

3648 Conesa, Eduardo. Perspectivas de la economía argentina (BCV/REL, 13:52, 1978, p. 173–192)

Consists of a forecast of major development trends in the Argentine economy, undertaken in late 1977, intended to serve as a reference point for the desired direction of the economy in the 1980s.

3649 Cortés Conde, Roberto. El progreso argentino: 1880–1914. Buenos Aires: Editorial Sudamérica, 1979. 291 p.; tables.

Good quantitative analysis of the rapid development which took place in Argentina at the end of the 19th century. Author places major emphasis on the workings of and changes in the labor and land markets of the *pampa* region.

Cuccorese, Horacio José. Historia sobre el origen del Banco de la Nación Argentina: acción y reacción en Buenos Aires y Londres. See *HLAS 42:3324.*

———. La versión histórica argentina sobre la crisis de Baring Brothers & Co. en 1890. See *HLAS 42:3325.*

3650 Di Tella, Guido. Price oscillation, oligopolistic behaviour and inflation: the Argentine case (WD, 7:11/12, Nov./Dec. 1979, p. 1043–1052, bibl., table)

Interesting essay on the important role price variability plays in the inflationary process. Di Tella attributes the phenomenon to an underlying struggle of oligopolistic groups to increase their own income shares. While study uses empirical data for the 1973–76 period as an example, it is worth noting that the phenomenon of price variability continued to play a crucial role in the 1976–80 stabilization program.

3651 Díaz-Alejandro, Carlos. Southern Cone stabilization plans (*in* Economic stabilization in developing countries. Edited by William Cline and Sidney Weintraub. Washington, D.C.: The Brookings Institution, 1981, p. 119–1141)

Critical essay on the process of economic liberalization in three Southern Cone countries: Argentina, Chile, and Uruguay. While some important details get lost among sweeping generalizations, the article is useful in examining the problem of how to combine the fight against inflation with efforts to restructure the economy in Latin America.

3652 Diéguez, Héctor L. and Alberto Petracola. Distribución de ingreso en el Gran Buenos Aires. Buenos Aires: Instituto Torcuato Di Tella, 1979. 146 p.; tables.

Painstaking analysis of the 1970 family income distribution in Greater Buenos Aires includes an explanation of major variables contributing to inequality. Especially useful are the comparisons drawn between Buenos Aires and other metropolitan areas of the Third World, and the analysis of the importance of such factors as education, occupation, size of family, and age and experience of head of family in determining differences in income distribution.

3653 Dyster, Barrie. Argentine and Australian development compared (PP, 84, Aug. 1979, p. 91–110)

Historical comparison of the Argentine and Australian economies, with emphasis on developments in the 19th and early 20th centuries. Basic thesis is that the difference between the development paths followed by the two countries is closely linked to the way capital was "assembled" in each one. While the British were in control in Ar-

gentina, the Australians carried out most of the actual investing themselves, though financing may have been arranged through the U.K. For historian's comment, see *HLAS* 42:3336.

3654 Elías, Víctor Jorge. Dinero e ingreso nominal en la Argentina (BCRA/EE, 9, 1. parte, marzo 1979, p. 75–95, bibl., tables)

Another time-series analysis of major macro-variables to test the relationship between money and nominal income in Argentina. Uses data ranging as far back as 1902.

3655 ———. Productividad en el corto y largo plazo en la Argentina (IDES/DE, 18:70, julio/sept. 1978, p. 265–274, tables)

Author presents empirical estimates-based on thorough research of productivity changes in the Argentine economy between 1935–75. While total factor productivity nearly doubled, the fruits of these increases were unevenly distributed and changed frequently.

3656 Feldman, Ernesto. Costos bancarios: estimaciones mediante análisis de corte transversal y series de tiempo (UNLP/E, 24:1/3, enero/dic. 1978, p. 9–32, bibl., tables)

Interesting cross-section analysis of commercial banks' costs functions that detects a positive relation between lower average costs and specialization. The more traditional banks, which continued to have more diversified operations in 1977–80, had significantly higher operating costs. Some preliminary results of time-series data point to the existence of diseconomies of scale, contrary to the findings of the cross-section analysis. Clearly, further research is needed to throw more light on the problem of high banking costs during the 1976–80 period.

3657 Feltenstein, Andrew. A general equilibrium approach to the analysis of trade restrictions, with an application to Argentina (IMF/SP, 27:4, Dec. 1980, p. 749–784, tables)

With the help of a general equilibrium model, author attempts to simulate effects of tariff reductions on balance of payments and domestic economic variables. Estimates show that—after the initial shock—external balance should be reached within less than one year, especially if restrictive monetary policy and/or some compensatory devaluation are applied.

3658 Fernández, Roque Benjamín. Dinero y precios: su interrelación en el corto plazo (BCRA/EE, 12, dic. 1979, p. 5–33, tables)

Theoretical and empirical analysis of the relationship between money and prices, set within the framework of the monetary approach to the balance of payments. Author postulates that money is dependent on price developments, especially on the international level. He carefully qualifies his findings and suggests further research to clarify that relationship.

3659 ——. Hacia una reforma del sistema argentino de previsión social (IDES/DE, 19:76, enero/marzo 1980, p. 477–498, bibl., tables)

Critical analysis of Argentina's social security system. Author argues that the system is expensive, discriminatory, and contains an anti-investment bias. Essay concludes by outlining an alternative program.

3660 ——. Previsión social y crecimiento económico (UCC/CE, 17:50, abril 1980, p. 113–125, tables)

Comparison of two different ways of financing social security systems. Author favors a funded system over a "pay-as-you-go" system, because the latter tends to inhibit the process of capital formation and economic growth. Empirical analysis shows that the post-World War II Argentine social security system gave a subsidy to its contributors and thereby contributed to an increase in consumption rather than capital formation.

3661 Fernicci, Ricardo; Alberto Barbero; and **Mario Rapoport.** El sector industrial argentino: análisis estructural y situación actual. Buenos Aires: Fundación para el Estudio de los Problemas Argentinos, 1980. 35 p.; tables.

Three essays on Argentina's manufacturing sector, written by members of the research institute of the "desarrollista" school. Description of the major structural features of that sector during the 1976–79 period and a survey of private sector opinion on the program provide little information on the substantial changes which occurred during that period.

3662 Ferrer, Aldo. The Argentine economy, 1976–1979 (SAGE/JIAS, 22:2, May 1980, p. 131–162)

Critical essay on the 1976–79 stabilization and reconstruction program and on its impact on major economic variables. Author criticizes the program's strategy for inconsistency of goals (price stabilization vs. full employment) and specialization according to static rather than dynamic comparative advantage.

Fleming, William J. The cultural determinants of entrepreneurship and economic development: a case study of Mendoza Province, Argentina: 1861–1914. See *HLAS 42:3346.*

3663 Forni, Floreal and **María Isabel Tort.** La tecnología y el empleo en un nuevo enfoque del desarrollo agropecuario: el caso argentino (IDES/DE, 19:76, enero/marzo 1980, p. 499–538, tables)

Largely theoretical analysis of relation between technological development and agricultural employment, with some limited application to Argentina. Recommendations for new agricultural strategy are mostly general and of little practical value.

3664 Frigerio, Rogelio. Síntesis de la historia crítica de la economía argentina: desde la conquista hasta nuestros días. Ilus. interior, Hermenegildo Sabat. Buenos Aires: Hachette, 1979. 116 p.; 14 leaves of plates; bibl.; ill.

Sweeping summary of Argentina's economic history, from the conquest to present. The book is useful as an introduction to the thought of one of the most prominent representatives of the "developmentalist" school. However, the wide range of topics covered and the general treatment given them fail to do justice to Argentina's complex economic past.

3665 Fundación de Investigaciones Económicas Latinoamericanas. Apertura de la economía: el impacto de las modificaciones arancelarias, Argentina, 1979–1984. Buenos Aires: FIEL, 1981. 195 p.; tables.

Most comprehensive study on effective protection in Argentina discusses previous studies and then estimates protection for 1980–81; also makes projections based on gradual tariff declines until 1984. The investigation of the rate of protection is based on legal rates (e.g., official import tariffs, taxes, and other fees) rather than direct price comparisons. Nevertheless, study provides important insight into the structure and diversity of recent effective protection, which was estimated to have been—on the average—about 50 percent by early 1981, a rate which was below the estimated rate of overevaluation of the peso at the same time.

3666 Fundación para el Estudio de los Problemas Argentinos (F.E.P.A.), *Buenos Aires*. **Comité de Infraestructura Científica.** Constelación del poder real en Argentina: entidades agropecuarias. Buenos Aires: 1978? 14 p. (Documento de trabajo; 4)

Short but useful survey of Argentina's agricultural organizations and the role they play in the government's economic and political decision-making.

3667 García, Valeriano F. Ajuste del balance de pagos, política crediticia y control del endeudamiento externo (*in* La Política monetaria y el ajuste de la balanza de pagos: tres estudios. Edición de la Comisión Económica de América Latina. Santiago de Chile: Cuadernos de la CEPAL, 1979, p. 19–31)

Brief exposition of the model used for analyzing the monetary approach to the balance of payments, with application to Latin American countries. Author finds that small open economies have very little control over money supply, which is determined mainly by variable aggregate demand conditions. He concludes governments should concentrate on controlling net internal credit expansion and its relation to the changing demand for money.

3668 ——. El impuesto inflacionario y la distribución del ingreso en países menos desarrollados (UCC/CE, 45, 1978, p. 247–272)

Provides model of the impact of inflation on income distribution, with an empirical application to Argentina and Chile. Author maintains that the inflationary tax is non-neutral, since labor is believed to react more slowly in times of accelerating inflation, adjusting incomes with a lag and holding relatively more real cash balances than capital.

Girbal de Blacha, Noemí M. Comercio exterior y producción agrícola de la República Argentina: 1890–1900. See *HLAS 42:3355.*

3669 Gravil, Roger and **Timothy Rooth.** A time of acute dependence: Argentina in the 1930s (The Journal of European Eco-

nomic History [Banco de Roma] 7:2/3, Fall/Winter 1978, p. 337–378, tables)

Contrary to the notion that the World Depression was actually a blessing in disguise for the Latin American economies in general, and Argentina in particular, this essay maintains that the economic domination of the U.K. over Argentina increased significantly during those years. While author's thesis may well hold true for the 1930s, it can easily be argued that those years created the decisive climate for the autarchic economic policies pursued by the Perón regime. For historian's comment, see *HLAS 42:3356.*

Guy, Donna J. Argentine sugar politics: Tucumán and the generation of eighty. See *HLAS 42:3360.*

——. Carlos Pellegrini and the politics of early Argentine industrialization: 1873–1906. See *HLAS 42:3361.*

3670 Ikonicoff, Moisés. La industrialización y el modelo de desarrollo de la Argentina (FCE/TE, 47[1]:185, enero/marzo 1980, p. 159–192)

Wide-ranging narrative account of Argentina's general economic development and particularly of its industrialization during the post-World War II period. For French original, see *Notes et Etudes Documentaires: Problèmes d'Amérique Latine* (Paris, 50, 4499/4500, 29 déc. 1978, p. 65–92).

3671 Janvry, Alain de. Social structure and biased technical change in Argentine agriculture (*in* Binswanger, Hans P.; Vernon W. Ruttan; and Uri Ben Zion. Induced innovation: technology, institutions, and development [see item **2765**] p. 297–324, tables)

Uses a model of dialectic interaction between technical change and institutional organization to explain the failure of technical change as an important stimulus for the growth of Argentine agriculture. While the arguments are intriguing, no attempt is made to test the theory empirically; such a test would probably realize a recent surge in new technology in the agricultural sector. The impact of the latter is already evident in the output and productivity statistics of the late 1970s.

3672 Jones, Charles. Business imperialism and Argentina, 1875–1900: a theoretical note (JLAS, 12:2, Nov. 1980, p. 437–444)

Although author considers that conventional models of imperialism are irrelevant to Argentina's late 19th-century development, he enumerates different ways in which British capital undermined the authority of the Argentine state. These include its crucial possession of assets in the import-export business, local transportation and communication, and most importantly, finance.

3673 Llach, Juan José. La estructura occupacional argentina (CRIT, 50:1179/1780, 26 enero 1978, p. 10–17)

This brief survey of the occupational situation in Argentina maintains that the simple dualistic typification of Argentina's labor force has to be replaced by a multifaceted characterization.

3674 Machinea, José L. Los mecanismos de transmisión de la política monetaria en la Argentina: una síntesis de la evidencia empírica (BCRA/EE, 8:1, dic. 1978, p. 15–92, tables)

Detailed investigation into the various ways in which the implementation of monetary policy affects the real sectors of the economy. After comparing previous studies on the subject, author presents a synthesis which—although incomplete due to difficulties in analyzing fixed interest rates—emphasizes the significant impact which changes in money supply have on prices and price expectations.

3675 Marchionatti, Roberto; Perluigi Porta; and Pipo Ranci. La industria argentina: del proteccionismo a la economía abierta. Buenos Aires: Organización Techint, 1980. 117 p.; graphs; tables (Boletín informativo; no. 220)

Evaluation by three Italian economists of the change in Argentine industrial developments policy from import substitution to the rapid opening-up process of the late 1970s. While praising the objectives of the 1976–80 stabilization program, authors criticize the excessive reliance on economic theory in the application of the program. A very useful study because it places Argentine government policies within the context of current international events.

3676 Martel, Julian. Domination by debt: finance capital in Argentina (NACLA/LAER, 12:4, July/Aug. 1978, p. 20–38, ill., tables)

Discussion, from a Marxist perspective, of foreign capital's major objective: to gain control over the public sector. Although the management of Argentina's external debt constitutes a legitimate subject for critical evaluation—especially in light of the events of 1979–80—author's framework does not suffice to encompass the intricate relations between the country's public sector and international capital.

Martínez, Pedro Santos. Política y riqueza agropecuaria durante el peronismo, 1946–1955. See *HLAS 42:3387.*

3677 Martínez, Stella Maris. Sector energético: evolución reciente y Plan Energético Nacional. Buenos Aires: Fundación para el Estudio de los Problemas Argentinos, 1979. 33 p.; bibl.; tables (Documento de trabajo; 21)

Summary evaluation of Argentina's energy plan (1977–95). Author agrees with basic objectives and policies proposed, but warns that possible underestimation of financial requirements may lead to unforeseen bottlenecks in energy supply.

3678 Martirena-Martel, Ana María. Devaluación, restricción presupuestaria y el enfoque monetario neo-Keynesiano. Buenos Aires: Instituto Torcuato Di Tella, 1979. 70 p.; bibl.; graphs; tables.

Interesting contrast between the monetary approach to the balance-of-payments and an amplified neo-Keynesian system that includes price, income absorption, and monetary effects of a devaluation.

3679 ———. Minidevaluaciones y estabilidad macroeconómica: el caso argentino: 1971–1978. Buenos Aires: Instituto Torcuato Di Tella, 1980. 61 p.; tables.

Theoretical work on the "crawling peg" exchange rate policies, which became popular in Latin America during the late 1960s and early 1970s. Empirical application to Argentina between 1971–78 shows that the policies did not cause inflation, and that there was a considerable impact on international capital flows during periods when mini-devaluations lagged behind inflation.

Mason Lugones, Raúl. Argentina: el actual plan económico compromete el futuro del país, en particular la seguridad nacional. See item **6611.**

3680 Maxwell, Philip. Estrategia tecnológica óptima en un contexto económico difícil: la evolución de la planta siderúrgica de ACINDAR en Rosario, Argentina (FCE/TE, 45[4]: 180, oct./dic. 1978, p. 1033–1063)

Useful study of technology and its adaptation in Argentina's largest private steel company, ACINDAR. Author shows that the many difficulties that arose were overcome by management and workers in a relatively short period of time.

3681 Medina, Juan Jorge. Evaluación del Plan de Apertura de la Economía Argentina, 1979–84. Buenos Aires: CEMA, 1979. 45 p.; tables (Documento de trabajo; no. 15)

Evaluation of the tariff reduction program, which the Argentine authorities introduced in 1979 and modified in 1980. Designed to unify and lower protection in Argentina by the mid-1980s, the program was abandoned in 1981.

3682 Montuschi de Glew, Luisa. El poder económico de los sindicatos. Buenos Aires: Editorial Universitaria de Buenos Aires, 1979. 224 p.; bibl. (Temas)

Empirical analysis of the relationship between sociopolitical variables and wages, and strictly economic variables and wages. Author finds that the most important variable-determining wages in the period 1950–65 were cost-of-living increases, followed by productivity increases. Union power, regardless of how it is defined, did not play a significant role.

3683 ———. Tendencias del empleo y el cambio tecnológico en la Argentina 1950–1970 (BCV/REL, 14:56, 1979, p. 79–100, tables)

Empirical analysis of changes in output, employment, and productivity between 1950–65 shows that there was a significant relationship between technological change, increasing capitalization, and growth in Argentina's most important sub-sectors.

3684 Nogués, Julio J. Características factoriales asociadas a las exportaciones manufactureras: análisis del caso argentino (BCRA/EE, 11, sept. 1979, p. 47–98, bibl., tables)

Summary article of author's dissertation on the impact of Argentina's industrial exports on factor use. The analysis of com-

parative statistics cannot convey the dynamic benefits derived from these exports. Nevertheless, author concludes that major export drives in late 1960s and early 1970s continued to benefit capital intensive production, which was protected by high tariffs and negative interest rates. As a consequence, social benefits were substantially below private benefits.

Pablo, Juan Carlos de. Economía política del peronismo. See item **6623.**

3685 ———. Reflexiones sobre la cuestión arancelaria (BCRA/EE, 9:2, marzo 1979, p. 133–170, bibl., tables)

Lively contribution to the discussion on tariff reform. Proposes following the government's program with one important exception: adopting unified external tariff structure by the end of the transition period. Authorities later followed this suggestion.

3686 Petrei, Humberto and **Domingo Carvallo.** Las relaciones comerciales argentino-brasileñas (IEERAL/E, 3:4, abril/junio 1980, p. 68–113, tables)

Detailed review of Argentine-Brazilian trade relations, which received an important impetus with the consecutive meetings of the presidents of Brazil and Argentina in 1980. Brazil's exports to Argentina are more diversified and contain a relatively high proportion of manufactured consumer and capital goods.

3687 ———; Héctor Nazareno; and **Roberto Domenech.** Relaciones fiscales nación-provincias: los recursos (IEERAL/E, 3:13, enero/marzo 1980, p. 3–34, tables)

Analysis of the tax-sharing system in Argentina. After discussing major shortcomings of the present system and comparing it to foreign revenue sharing systems, authors propose several alternatives and innovations that would eliminate current shortcomings.

El petróleo nacional. See *HLAS 42:3403.*

3688 Pou, Pedro. Variabilidad de la tasa de inflación, riesgo y la demanda por dinero (BCRA/EE, 9, 2. parte, marzo 1979, p. 101–132, tables)

Interesting contribution to much-needed money studies, incorporating risk and the variability of inflation in the analysis. Model is tested with data from 1936–78.

Reber, Vera Blinn. British mercantile houses in Buenos Aires, 1810–1880. See *HLAS* 42:3411.

3689 Reca, Lucio. Argentina: country case study of agricultural prices and subsidies. Washington, D.C.: World Bank, 1980. 72 p.; graphs; tables (World Bank staffing papers; no. 386)

Study traces pricing policy for seven agricultural products during 1950–75. Improved growth record in the 1960s is linked to the period's lesser price and tax discrimination against the agricultural sector. Argentina's comparative advantage—here estimated by domestic resource costs—is evident in the case of coarse grains and wool but not for cattle and cotton.

3690 Sánchez, Carlos E.; Fernando Ferrero; and Walter E. Schulthess. Empleo, desempleo y tamañ de la fuerza laboral en el mercado de trabajo urbano de la Argentina (IDES/DE, 19:73, abril/junio 1979, p. 53–78, bibl., tables)

Significant investigation of Argentina's labor market between 1967–78, focusing on labor force participation changes and the impact of those changes on unemployment. Author argues that the major cause of the low and decreasing unemployment rate in 1976–78 and thereafter was the rather massive and mostly early retirement of persons 60 years old and older. See also the discussion of the reliability and significance of the data base employed by the authors in *Desarrollo Económico* (19:74, julio/sept. 1979).

3691 Sidicaro, Ricardo. Les grands propriétaires et les problèmes agraires en Argentina: 1973–78 (FDD/NED [Problèmes d'Amérique Latine, 50] 4499/4500, 29 déc. 1978, p. 44–64, tables)

Comparison of agricultural policies during the last 10 years. While author recognizes the progress made by 1976–78 policies, he maintains that the policies were not adequate to sustain prolonged rapid expansion of the primary sector.

3692 Sigaut, Lorenzo. Visión y retrospectiva y prospectiva (Carta Política [Buenos Aires] 67, junio 1979, p. 34–43, tables)

Review of economic development in Argentina between 1974–79 by the 1981 Minister of Finance and Economics. Author

agrees with the government's philosophy and policies of 1976–80 period.

Solberg, Carl E. Oil and nationalism in Argentina: a history. See *HLAS* 42:3425.

———. The origins of Yacimientos Petrolíferos Fiscales: prototype of state monopoly petroleum companies. See *HLAS* 42:3426.

3693 Sourrouille, Juan V. La presencia y el compartimiento de las empresas extranjeras en el sector industrial argentino (Estudios CEDES [Centro Estudios de Estado y Sociedad, Buenos Aires] 1:2, 1978, p. 1–73, graphs, tables)

Analysis of the impact which multinational investment in the manufacturing sector has on major economic variables, with special emphasis on the employment effect. Shows that both wages and employment patterns differed significantly between the international firms and their domestic competitors, specifically multinationals which generally pay higher wages and employ fewer people. Author examines data only up to the early 1970s, but it is interesting to note that the wage-employment pattern he discusses for the earlier period became more widespread in the late 1970s.

3694 Street, James H. Technological fusion and cultural interdependence: the Argentine case (*in* Technological progress in Latin America: the prospects for overcoming dependency [see item 2949] p. 227–245)

Institutionalist view of Argentina's failure to "take off" in the 20th century, stressing the unwillingness of Argentine society to adopt and adapt extensive technological change as well as to institute innovations in the country's education, administration, and policy making. While generally attractive, the framework used does not adequately explain the peculiar pattern that has characterized the Argentine economy since the early 1940s.

3695 Sturzenegger, Adolfo C. Multiplicidad tecnológica, intensidad en el uso de la tierra y política económica agropecuaria en el sector pampeano argentino (UNLP/E, 24:1/3, enero/dic. 1978, p. 87–121, bibl.; ill.)

Theoretical essay discusses the possibilities of improving agricultural production through a more rational pricing structure, leading to the adoption of new technologies and better use of land and capital. In addition, author advocates significant increases in the overall economic surplus.

3696 Teubal, Morris. Exportaciones de bienes primarios y desarrollo económico: el sector maquinaria. Buenos Aires: Instituto Torcuato Di Tella, 1980. 45 p.; graphs; tables.

Interesting three-sector model that analyzes the emergence of an industrial sector supplying sophisticated consumer goods in an economy that is a primary goods exporter and has already established a capital goods industry. Author's approach to formalizing the relationship between technical innovation and economic growth seems equally applicable to a number of semi-industrialized countries, especially in Latin America.

3697 Vázquez-Presedo, Vicente. Crisis y retraso: Argentina y la economía internacional entre las dos guerras. Buenos Aires: Editorial Universitaria de Buenos Aires, 1978. 301 p.; bibl.; graphs (Temas)

Careful empirical study of Argentina's economic development between the two World Wars. After a review of major economic and political events in the world economy (Europe and US), author concentrates on analyzing employment and finance. He also provides a sector analysis of agriculture and industry. Most interesting is the analysis of the structural changes taking place in these two major sectors, which set the pattern for the problems that arose in the post-World War II period.

3698 Vitelli, Guillermo. Estudios sobre ciencia y tecnología en la América Latina: cambio tecnológico, estructura de mercado y ocupación en la industria de la construcción argentina (FCE/TE, 45[5]: 180, oct./dic. 1978, p. 997–1031)

Case study of the technology, market structure, and employment pattern of Argentina's construction industry. Author demonstrates that the small gains in labor productivity between 1950–73 are reflected in the failure to introduce recent technology for construction as well as in the relatively low participation of international firms in Argentina's large construction projects.

Wainerman, Catalina H. Educación, familia y participación económica femenina en la Argentina. See item **4387.**

3699 Wynia, Gary W. Argentina in the postwar era: politics and economic policy making in a divided society. Albuquerque: University of New Mexico Press, 1978. 289 p.; bibl.; index.

Good exposition of the connection between post-World War II Argentine politics and economic policy making. Author argues persuasively that a crucial factor in Argentina's inability to follow an orderly development path was caused by the failure to incorporate citizen support in policy-making processes. For political scientist's comment, see *HLAS 41:7508.*

———. Illusion and reality in Argentina. See item **6640.**

BRAZIL

DAVID DENSLOW, *Associate Professor, University of Florida*
DENNIS J. MAHAR, *Economist, The World Bank*

SINCE THE PUBLICATION OF *HLAS* 41, the condition of the Brazilian economy has worsened appreciably. Various external and internal factors have contributed to this situation, the most important being further increases in petroleum prices, high international interest rates, recessions in the industrialized countries, poor domestic harvests owing to drought and frosts, public sector deficits and large pay hikes gained by certain occupational groups. The combined impact of the above has resulted in (slower growth −3.6% in 1981), widening balance-of-payments deficits, a resurgence of inflation to three-digit levels, growing urban unemployment, and a foreign debt of approximately $60 billion. Given this rather somber picture, it is understandable that much of the literature reviewed for this section is devoted to analyzing the causes of the present economic difficulties and possible means of alleviating them.

A general theme in the literature is the need for basic structural changes in the Brazilian economy that will enable it to adapt to an era of expensive energy and slower growth. Such adjustments would include, *inter alia*, trade liberalization, greater reliance on agriculture for export and energy, and a restructuring of industry, transforming the dependent, high-technology structure developed during the 1960s and 1970s into one dominated by labor-intensive activities producing goods for the mass market. The article by Malan (item **3756**) is most representative of this literature on the need for structural adjustment.

Another issue addressed in these works is the alleviation of poverty, both rural and urban. In the agricultural sector, some authors are disturbed by the rise of a rural proletariat, resulting from mechanization and labor laws that oblige landowners to abide by minimum wage and social security legislation. Others are concerned that policies intended to expand agricultural exports will result in decreased food production and a consequent decline in nutritional standards among the poor. In order to help alleviate rural poverty, some authors maintain that a comprehensive agrarian reform is necessary, while others argue for more realistic minimum crop prices, increased accessibility of rural credit to smallholders, and the implementation of "new style" integrated rural development projects.

The literature on urbanization and urban poverty is mainly concerned with the impact of intense in-migration on the adequacy of public services and on employment generation. In order to deal with these problems, the authors have recommended a strengthening of the urban planning apparatus, the spatial decentralization of economic activities, and the encouragement of labor-intensive industries. The article by Tolosa (item **3792**) on the causes of urban poverty in Brazil is a particularly insightful treatment of this topic.

Another notable trend in the economic literature is the large output of high-quality research on the problems of the Northeast. By and large this literature has been produced by Northeasterners associated with the post-graduate economic programs of the federal universities of Pernambuco (PIMES) and Ceará (CAEN), and with regional government agencies such as the Bank of the Northeast (BNB). The arguments of these authors are often reminiscent of those put forward by Furtado in the late 1950s and early 1960s (i.e., they consistently portray the Northeast as being dependent on the industrialized South). Most of the authors recommend greater economic independence for the region and expanded efforts by the government to reduce regional inequalities. Distinguished additions to the literature on Northeast development include an English-language translation of Andrade's *A terra e o homem no Nordeste* and a major survey of the Northeast economy carried out by Rebouças et al. (item **3703**) under the auspices of the BNB.

In summary, the economic literature on Brazil continues to be rich and diverse. In response to the present economic difficulties, discussions of short-term macroeconomic issues have increased in frequency. In subject areas of traditional concern, like income distribution and Northeast development, there has been a tendency to repeat old themes. Far from indicating a lack of imagination on the part of Brazilian economists, such repetition is a message to policy-makers that while they grapple with the new problems of inflation, foreign indebtedness, and the balance-of-payments, some important old problems remain unresolved.

3700 **Absorção e criação de tecnologia** na indústria de bens de capital. Fabio Stefano Erber, coordenador; José Tavares de Araújo Júnior et al. Rio de Janeiro: FINEP, 1974. 116 p.; bibl. (Série Pesquisas—FINEP, Grupo de Pesquisas; no. 2)

After giving a history of the capital-goods industry in Brazil, study describes the situation in the early 1970s, based on a survey of 35 factories. Closes with a summary and some recommendations.

3701 **Albuquerque W., María Beatriz de.** Incidencia del progreso tecnológico en el crecimiento económico: el caso brasileño (BCV/REL, 13:54, 1978, p. 181–207, tables)

Author discusses recent indications of possible changes in the scientific and technological policies of Brazil. She states that the success of a particular policy depends less on the adoption of partial means intended to correct isolated and circumstantial problems than on major changes in the style of development Brazil chooses in the future.

3702 **Almeida, Manoel Bosco de.** Estimativas da utilização de capital: Brasil, 1970 (BNB/REN, 11:1, jan./março 1980, p. 35–55, tables)

Capital in use, not capital installed, is the relevant factor in the analysis of productivity and rates of growth. Almeida has compared installed electric motor horsepower to the consumption of electricity in kilowatt hours in order to measure the effective utilization of capital. Study suggests that many electric motors are idle much of the time, which may indicate a misallocation of resources.

3703 **Andrade, Manuel Correia de Oliveira.** The land and people of Northeast Brazil. Translated by Dennis V. Johnson. Albuquerque: University of New Mexico Press, 1979. 1 v.; bibl.

Author argues that this transformation has primarily benefited the large landowner, while the standard of living of rural people in the Northeast has declined. He advocates rural unionization and agrarian reform as means to improve the socioeconomic position of the rural *nordestino*. Although these recommendations are not novel, the logic of Andrade's arguments is incontestable. First English translation of the classic book, *A terra e o homem no Nordeste*. Principal focus is on the changing man-land-labor relationships in the region, characterized by a decline in traditional paternalism and a concomitant rise of a rural proletariat.

3704 **Bacha, Edmar L.** and **Lance Taylor.** Brazilian income distribution in the 1960s: facts, model results and the controversy (JDS, 14:3, April 1978, p. 271–297, bibl., tables)

Critical review of a number of hypotheses used to explain the apparent worsening of income distribution in Brazil during the 1960s. Rejects contention that increased income concentration was more apparent than real, as well as hypothesis that increased inequity resulted from changes in composition of income-earning population. Based on an econometric model, authors conclude that major factor causing increased concentration was government policy of squeezing minimum-money wages.

3705 **Baer, Werner.** The Brazilian economy: its growth and development. Columbus, Ohio: Grid Inc., 1979. 239 p.; bibl.; index; map.

Interpretation of Brazilian economic history and current economic issues by a leading scholar. Accessible to undergraduates as well as graduate students and could be useful as a textbook. Chapters of particular current interest include those on the growth of the public sector, inflation and indexing, and regional imbalances.

3706 **Balanço de pagamentos** e divida externa (FGV/CE, 33:10, out. 1979, p. 53–65, tables)

Conjuntura Econômica warns its readers that it is dangerous to allow inflation and its attendant worries to obscure the problems associated with Brazil's balance of payments. To prevent this from happening, the journal invited three essayists to address these problems: 1) George Bezerra discusses the evolution of the balance of payments and the debt through 1979; 2) Claudio L. S. Haddad calls attention to the conflict between the rising price of petroleum and the loss of real income it represents for Brazil; and 3) Carlos Thadeu de Freitas Gomes examines the costs of financing the debt by means of borrowing as opposed to issuing securities with floating rates of interest.

3707 **Balassa, Bela.** Incentive policies in Brazil (WD, 7:11/12, Nov./Dec. 1979, p. 1023–1042, bibl., tables)

Article analyzes measures adopted by the government to deal with effects of the energy crisis on the balance of payments. Special emphasis is placed on the 1979 policy reforms. Author argues that the principal policy measures used for balance of payments purposes (i.e., import protection, export subsidization and encouragement of foreign capital inflows) have been reasonably successful. He recommends that the reduction of export subsidies enacted in 1979 should be accompanied by a reduction in import duties, greater automaticity in incentive policies, and improvements in public sector decision-making. An important article by a distinguished economist.

3708 Barat, Josef. Introdução aos problemas urbanos brasileiros: teoria, análise e formulação de política. Prefacio, Rubens Vaz da Costa. Rio de Janeiro: Editora Campus, 1979. 249 p.; 3 leaves of plates; bibl.; ill (Contribuições em desenvolvimento urbano; 1)

Study of the nature and problems of urban development by the former Secretary of Transportation of Rio de Janeiro. Using the latter as a case study, author emphasizes the diseconomies of uncontrolled urban growth, and makes a plea for more rational planning mechanisms. Highly recommended.

3709 Batista, Paulo Nogueira, Jr. Política tarifária britânica e evolução exportações brasileiras na primeira metade do século XIX (IBE/RBE, 34:2, abril/junio 1980, p. 203–239, bibl., tables)

British protectionism was one of the factors responsible for the relatively slow growth of Brazilian exports in the first half of the 19th century. Although British manufactured goods shipped to Brazil were taxed at only 15 percent, no commercial advantages were offered to Brazil in exchange: sugar was taxed at 122 percent in 1809 and up to 163 percent in 1830; coffee was taxed at 150 percent between 1820–44.

Beretta, Pier Luigi. Amazzonia Brasiliana: colonizzazione o popolamiento?: un contributo informativo e crítico. See item **5319.**

3710 Bernal, María Cleide Carlos. O modelo primário-exportador do Nordeste uma avaliação qualitativa (BNB/REN, 9:3, julho/set. 1978, p. 315–345, tables)

Study of the socioeconomic impact of export-oriented agriculture on the Northeast. Although government policies have favored export crops (mainly sugar), the effects of this official support have often been unfavorable. Among these unfavorable effects are an increased concentration of income and political power in the hands of large landowners and the proletarianization of the rural labor force. Calls for a reorientation of regional agricultural policy in favor of subsistence food crops.

3711 Bolaffi, Gabriel. A casa das ilusões perdidas: aspectos sócio-econômicos do Plano Nacional de Habitação. São Paulo: Editora Brasiliense, 1977. 64 p.; ill. (Caderno CEBRAP; 27)

Critical evaluation of Brazil's National Housing Plan, based on field studies carried out in 1971–72. Highlights deficiencies of the program, which have led to the abandonment of much public housing construction in poorer parts of the country. Blames unscrupulous contractors who produced poor quality housing and the impossibility for many prospective homeowners of meeting the financial terms established by the National Housing Bank (BNH).

3712 Braga, Helson C. and João L. Mascolo. A influência do tamanho sobre a rentabilidade na indústria brasileira (IBE/RBE, 34:2, abril/junho 1980, p. 251–278, bibl., tables)

Study of the relationship between size and profitability in Brazilian industry. Earlier studies on this subject yielded contradictory results. Using several econometric methods, authors conclude that there is a positive relationship between the two factors.

3713 Brazil. Superintendência do Desenvolvimento do Nordeste. Departamento de Indústria e Comércio. Divisão de Coordenação de Incentivos. Incentivos fiscais e financeiros para o Nordeste. Recife: A Divisão, 1978. 56 p. (Industrialização; 7)

A succinct guide to the fiscal and credit incentives available to corporations wishing to invest in the Northeast. Owing to the importance of these incentives to the recent industrialization of the region, an understanding of these mechanisms is essential to potential investors as well as to students of Northeast development.

3714 Brito, Ney O. and Luiz C. Kantz. Custo de capital e subsídios: o setor de energia elétrica no período 1972–1976 (IBE/RBE, 34:2, abril/junho 1980, p. 131–163, bibl., tables)

Work examines the cost of capital for the electric energy sector in the period 1972–76, and the sector's degree of dependence on subsidies. Results indicate that the cost of capital expressed as a real annual rate of interest rose from 13 percent in 1972 to 17 percent in 1976. Sector shows signs of decreasing returns to scale and an increasing dependence on subsidized capital.

3715 Buescu, Mircea. Brasil, disparidades de renda no passado: subsídios para o estudo dos problemas brasileiros. Rio de Janeiro: APEC, 1979. 136 p.; bibl.; ill.; tables.

Buescu, a prolific writer on Brazilian economic history, presents historical background information he hopes will help in solving the present problems of income disparities. He deals with international, regional, and personal disparities. Volume contains numerous tables and a bibliography.

3716 ———. O café na história do Brasil (IHGB/R, 321, out./dez. 1978, p. 235–236)

Short paper on the role of the coffee in light of economic development theory. Coffee served not only as a source of income but as a stimulus in the development of new industries and related activities (e.g., transport; banking and credit; exchange-rate policies; reinvestment in other industries; a higher level of technology; etc.).

3717 ———. Inegalités regionales au Brésil dans la seconde moitié du XIX siècle (IHGB/R, 321, out./dez. 1978, p. 222–223, tables)

Eminent economic historian's general conclusion is that the growth of the Brazilian economy always has created regional inequalities. Low revenue and less advantageous local conditions with respect to distances, cultural level, and economic structures all serve to hinder progress. He implies that regions with better soil, more favorable climate, and better transportation will inevitably capture a larger share of whatever progress is made in the nation.

3718 Campino, Antonio Carlos Coelho. Custos de programas de suplementação alimentar no meio urbano (BNB/REN, 11:2, abril/junho 1980, p. 269–291, bibl., tables)

Study of the costs and benefits of six different ways of providing nutrition supplements to urban pre-school children. Includes statistical tables that support the analysis.

3719 Cardoso, Eliana A. Incentivos as exportações de manufaturas: série histórica (IBE/RBE, 34:2, abril/junho 1980, p. 241–250, bibl., plates)

Brief historical appraisal of government subsidies and their effectiveness in promoting exports from Brazil during 1964–77. Contains summaries of some of the important fiscal incentives.

3720 Carone, Edgard. O Centro Industrial do Rio de Janeiro e sua importante participação na economia nacional: 1827–1977. Capa, Mário Salles Jr. Rio de Janeiro: O Centro, 1978. 196 p.; bibl.; ill. (Biblioteca do Centro Industrial do Rio de Janeiro; 1)

Written and published to commemorate the 150th anniversary of the Industrial Center of Rio de Janeiro, this book presents the history of the Center interwoven with a history of Brazilian economics. Contains biographies, bibliography, and photographs. For historian's comment, see *HLAS 42:3632.*

3721 Carvalho, José L. O Estado na economia: estudo de dois casos brasileiros. Prefacio Og Leme; capa, Orestes de Oliveira Filho. Rio de Janeiro: Expressão e Cultura, 1979. 116 [i.e. 123] p.; bibl.

Economist who earned his Ph.D. at the University of Chicago writes about government regulation of business in Brazil, citing the case of sugar production in Pernambuco and of banking concentration.

3722 Carvalho, Otamar de. Desenvolvimento rural integrado: nova estratégia para a redução da pobreza no campo (BNB/REN, 10:2, abril/junho 1979, p. 431–494, bibl., map, tables)

Essentially descriptive article focusing on new approaches to alleviate rural poverty in the Northeast. Emphasizes the POLONORDESTE program, established in 1974. Program's aim is to raise the socioeconomic well-being of smallholders in areas with agricultural potential by providing them with integrated packages of economic and social infrastructure and services. Gives little information on the actual effectiveness of this program in alleviating poverty.

3723 Castro, Ana Célia. As empresas estrangeiras no Brasil, 1860–1913. Capa de Eliane Stephan. Rio de Janeiro: Zahar Editores, 1979. 142 p.; bibl. (Biblioteca de ciências sociais: Economia)

History of the role played by foreign capital in Brazil during the years roughly between the American Civil War and World War I. Focuses on railroads, the rubber era, and power-and-light companies. Contains tables showing which countries invested the money and which industries absorbed it.

3724 Centro de Planejamento da Bahia. Economia baiana: subsídios para um plano de governo. t. 1, Diagnóstico institucional, setor público estadual. t. 2, Diagnóstico, da ação governamental. t. 3, Diagnóstico do setor agropecuário. t. 4, Diagnóstico do setor industrial. t. 5, Diagnóstico dos setores sociais. t. 6, Diagnóstico dos recursos naturais e da configuração espacial do Estado da Bahia.

In this six-volume set published by the state of Bahia, each volume is designed to serve as an aid to planning economic development. Vol. 1 covers public sector institutions at the state level; vol. 2, government actions at the state and federal levels; vol. 3, farming; vol. 4, industry; vol. 5, the social sector (human resources, housing, health, education); and vol. 6, natural resources and the utilization of space.

3725 Cew, Judson Marshal de, Jr.; Eduardo Dutra Aydos; and Luis Carlos Lucas. Déficit habitacional: quantificação da necessidade habitacional no Rio Grande do Sul, 1970/1973. Porto Alegre, Brasil: Pontifícia Universidade Católica do Rio Grande do Sul, Instituto de Estudos Sociais, Políticos e Econômicos (IESPE), 1975. 253 p.; bibl.; tables.

Quantitative part of a two-part study of housing in Rio Grande do Sul. The other part surveys the attitudes and needs of low-income families in the same state. The complete study is intended to supply a solid base for public policy planning in the housing sector. Includes numerous tables, by *municípios*, with data from 1970–83, including projections.

3726 Chaloult, Yves. Estado acumulação e colonialismo interno: contradições Nordeste/Sudeste, 1960–1977. Petrópolis: Editora Vozes, 1978. 150 p.; bibl.; tables.

Brazil's North and Northeast have been treated like colonies, their raw materials and human resources being siphoned off to contribute to the development of the Central-South and the Southeast. The private sector is to blame, but the government, by reinforcing the latter's activities, has also played a large role. However, author considers regional conflict a reflection of more universal conflicts existing in Brazilian society, such as the conflict between classes, and predicts that the study of internal colonialism will aid other societies that contain many classes. The solution to such conflicts lies in increased participation of the majority of the population in making important economic decisions.

3727 Comércio Externo do Brasil. Secretaria da Receita Federal, Centro de Informações Econômico-Fiscais. Ano 8, Vol. 2, 1979– . Rio de Janeiro.

Consists of approximately 800 p. of fine-print tables of Brazilian imports, organized by products and by countries of origin, and indicating quantities and values in both dollars and cruzeiros.

3728 Corrêa, José Rubem. Open-market— mercado aberto, conceitos e mecânica de funcionamento. Rio de Janeiro: Livraria Freitas Bastos, 1979. 301 p.; forms (Biblioteca Freitas Bastos)

Textbook-like study describes the operation of the Brazilian open market. Useful in that it deciphers complicated legislation, much of which is printed verbatim in the text.

3729 Costa, Fernando N. Os antigos bancos minerios (RBMC, 5:13, jan./abril 1979, p. 71–87, bibl.)

Brief historical essay recounting the birth, growth, and decline of banks in Minas Gerais from 1889–1964, which is a summary of author's Master's thesis (University of Campinas, 1979). Divides the history into four periods: 1) beginnings (1889–1920); 2) coffee and banks (1920s); 3) Vargas period (1930–45); and 4) SUMOC period (1945–64).

Cunningham, Susan M. Brazil: recent trends in industrial development. See item **5334.**

———. Multinational enterprises in Brazil: locational patterns and implications for regional developments. See item **5335.**

3730 Dantas, Antônio Luiz Abreu. Padrões estaduais de localização da atividade industrial do Nordeste: 1960/70 (BNB/REN, 8:3, julho/set. 1977, p. 425–444, bibl., tables)

Presents empirical results which, when complemented with other studies, may be quite useful to planners of state and regional development. On a sector basis, author used a quotient of localization, a coefficient of localization, and a coefficient of geographical association; on a regional basis, he used a coefficient of specialization.

Davidovich, Fany; Maria do Socorro Alves; and Marília Carneiro Natal. Funções urbanas no Nordeste. See item **5336.**

3731 Desenvolvimento do Nordeste: diagnóstico e sugestões de políticas; relatório síntese (BNB/REN, 10:2, abril/junho 1979, p. 189–430, tables)

Comprehensive socioeconomic survey of the Northeast in the post-World War II years. Argues that the income gap between the region and the rest of Brazil has widened, and that federal programs have done little to reverse this trend. Recommendations include a regionalization of the federal budget, the transfer of some government agencies to the Northeast, and strengthened fiscal incentives. A highly recommended work, containing a wealth of data.

3732 Diniz, Eli. Empresário, Estado, e capitalismo no Brasil, 1930–1945. Rio de Janeiro: Paz e Terra, 1978. 311 p.; bibl. (Coleção Estudos brasileiros; v. 27)

Describes the political role of the industrial bourgeoisie during title's 15-year period. Based on author's Ph.D. thesis (University of São Paulo, 1978).

3733 Doellinger, Carlos von. A inter-relação histórica entre investimento estrangeiro e comércio exterior nas relações econômicas Brasil/Alemanha Ocidental (RMBC, 5:13, jan./abril 1979, p. 29–44, bibl., tables)

Doellinger, an authority on Brazil's foreign trade, explores economic relations between Germany and Brazil from the perspective of Vernon's product cycle hypothesis. After the US, West Germany is Brazil's second most important economic partner as supplier, buyer, and investor.

3734 Durand, José Carlos Garcia. Pequena e média empresa no Brasil, 1963/1976. Henrique Rattner, coordenador; equipe responsável pela pesquisa, José Carlos Garcia Durand, Leôncio Martins Rodrigues, Sergio Miceli Pessôa de Barros, colaboradores, Ary R. de Carvalho et al. Capa, Moysés Baumstein e Alberto Baumstein. São Paulo: Edições Símbolo, 1979. 263, 1 p.; bibl. (Coleção Ensaio e memória; 15)

Presents some of the problems of small- and medium-sized businesses in a developing country. Compares results of surveys undertaken in 1963 and 1976, in São Paulo, Salvador, and Porto Alegre.

3735 Economia brasileira: uma visão histórica. Coordenador, Paulo Neuhaus. Rio de Janeiro: Editora Campus, 1980. 411 p.; 4 fold. leaf of plates; bibl.; graphs.

Collection of 10 essays on various aspects of Brazilian economic history. Some of the topics covered include: economic growth, 1900–76 (C. Haddad); demographic development (T. Merrick and D. Graham); economy of Rio in the 18th and 19th centuries (E. Lobo); foreign trade policy during World War II (M. Abreu); and public sector growth (W. Baer). Recommended for its consistently high quality.

3736 Economia Paraibana: Análisis Conjuntural. Fundação Instituto de Planejamento de Paraíbo (FIPLAN). No. 12, 1979–   . João Pessoa, Brazil.

Report on the performance of the economy in Paraíba during 1979. Several pages and abundant statistical tables give accounts each of the major sectors: agriculture, industry, and services.

3737 Eizirik, Nelson Laks. Auto-regulação: perspectivas após o "Caso Cepalma" (RBMC, 5:13, jan./abril 1979, p. 7–28, bibl.)

Attorney discusses the role to be played by self-regulation in the securities markets of Brazil, using the Cepalma Case that was heard by the Brazilian Supreme Court as a springboard for his discussion. Suggests some needed changes and clarifications in the rules.

Essays concerning the socioeconomic history of Brazil and Portuguese India. See *HLAS 42:3519.*

3738 Evans, Peter. Dependent development: the alliance of multinational, state, and local capital in Brazil. Princeton, N.J.: Princeton University Press, 1979. 362 p.; bibl.; index.

Impressively documented study of the role of international capital in the recent industrial development of Brazil. Argues that success of international capital in penetrating local markets is due in large part to the maintenance of an alliance between the multinationals, elite local capital and state capital through which all three benefit. The major disadvantage is that most of the Brazilian population is excluded from the economic rewards of this system. Author suggests that "dependent development" is inherently unstable and that the pressure of unsatisfied needs on the part of the masses will sooner or later lead to a redistribution of income and political power.

3739 Felix, Francisco Amadeu Pires. Aspectos institucionais do sistema monetário brasileiro (IBE/RBE, 34:2, abril/junho 1980, p. 279–292, bibl., tables)

Comments on the relationship between the monetary base and the supply of money in Brazil, with emphasis on the role of deposits in the Bank of Brazil.

3740 Fiorentino, Raul. Uma visão geral dos problemas de emprego e renda no setor rural do Nordeste brasileiro (BNB/REN, 8:3, julho/set. 1977, p. 381–412, bibl., tables)

Study describes labor conditions affecting rural workers in recent decades, and analyzes changes that have occurred in those conditions. It is apparent that changes in the mode of production not only have affected the level of work and income of rural laborers, but also have produced unstable conditions that foreshadow new and rapid changes in the next few years.

3741 Fontana, José Zeno. Variações sobre o papel do estado: uma interpretação político-econômica dos gastos públicos. São Paulo: Empresa Metropolitana de Planejamento de Grande São Paulo, 1979. 38, 42 p. (Serie monografias EMPLASA)

Monograph on patterns of public expenditures in the state of São Paulo. Author argues that functional allocation of expenditures needs to be more oriented toward services benefitting the poor. Recommends decentralization of spending powers to make government more responsive to community preferences.

3742 Fox, Roger. Preços mínimos garantidos e o setor agrícola no Nordeste do Brasil (BNB/REN, 10:2, abril/junho 1979, p. 551–604, bibl., tables)

Analyzes the minimum price program for agriculture in the Northeast. There is little evidence that minimum prices have achieved their principal objectives in the region (i.e., the expansion of production and the stabilization of prices and incomes). Author recommends, among other things, an increase in the minimum prices paid to Northeastern farmers and a reduction in the subsidy element of credit for crop storage.

3743 The Future of Brazil. Edited by William H. Overholt. Contributors, William L. Ascher et al. Boulder, Colo.: Westview Press, 1978. 289 p., bibl. (Westview special studies on Latin America)

Chapter titles and authors give an idea of the scope of this book: "The Future of Brazil: An Overview" by the editor, William H. Overholt (policy analyst at Hudson Institute and editor of *Global Political Assessment*); "Brazil's Future Foreign Relations" by William L. Ascher (professor of Latin American politics at Johns Hopkins University); "The Political Future of Brazil" by Riordan Roett (director of Latin American Studies at Johns Hopkins School of Advanced International Studies); "The Brazilian Economy: Structural Legacies and Future Prospects" by Douglas H. Graham (director of the Latin American Studies Program at Ohio State University); "The State and Brazilian Economic Development: The Contemporary Reality and Prospects for the Future" by Sylvia Ann Hewlett (professor of economics at Columbia University); "Brazil's Debt Burden," also by Overholt; and "Treatment of the Foreign Investor: The Brazilian Style" by Keith S. Rosenn (professor of law at Ohio State University and specialist on Brazilian law). See also item **7441.**

3744 Galey, John. Industrialist in the wilderness: Henry Ford's Amazon venture (SAGE/JIAS, 21:2, May 1979, p. 261–290, bibl.)

Short history of the Ford Corporation's ill-fated attempts to develop plantation rubber in the state of Pará during the period 1927–45. Reasons given for the failure include misunderstandings between Ford and the Brazilian government, labor shortages, and ecological constraints. Author concludes with a plea for greater international cooperation in the development of Amazonia. A good introduction to the topic, although the definitive work has yet to be written. For geographer's comment, see item **5349**, and for historian's, *HLAS 42:3660*.

3745 Galvão, Olímpio de Arroxelas. Integração econômica e desenvolvimento regional: Pernambuco no contexto nordestino e nacional (IPE/EE, 8:2, maio/agosto 1978, p. 129–189, bibl., tables)

Article explores the impact of "national integration" (essentially, the development of roads between regions) on the Northeast economy. Improved access to Northeastern markets on the part of economic interests in the Center-South has been prejudicial to Northeastern industry and agriculture. Author concludes that government policies to compensate for these negative effects have been insufficient and, in some cases, misdirected, in that they (especially fiscal incentives) have acted to reduce labor absorption rather than increase it.

3746 Gomes, Gustavo Maia. Perspectivas e realizações da irrigação do Nordeste: resenha de cinco estudos (BNB/REN, 11:1, jan./março 1980, p. 153–170, bibl.)

Substantial reviews of five papers dealing with irrigation in the Northeast. The papers reviewed are by GEIDA, 1971; Cline, 1972; Frederick, 1975; Hall, 1978; and PIMES, 1978.

Greenfield, Gerald Michael. Dependency and the urban experience: São Paulo's public service sector, 1885–1913. See *HLAS 42:3664*.

————. Lighting the city: a case study of public service problems in São Paulo, 1885–1913. See *HLAS 42:3665*.

3747 Guimarães, Alberto Passos. A crise agrária. Capa, Mario Roberto Corrêa da Silva. Rio de Janeiro: Paz e Terra, 1978. 362 p.; bibl.; index (Coleção O Mundo hoje; v. 29)

Although ostensibly a work of sociology and history, this book contains chapters on the following topics: the agricultural revolution; the industrialization of agriculture; the agribusiness complex; the limitations of agricultural growth; the scarcity of foodstuffs and agricultural power; the human factor in agriculture; and an essay on the future of Brazilian agriculture. Author believes the latter is in a state of crisis and proposes some

drastic changes (book is vol. 29 in monographic series *O Mundo Hoje*).

Hahner, June E. Women and work in Brazil, 1850–1920: a preliminary investigation. See *HLAS 42:3670*.

3748 Holanda, Antônio Nílson C. Desenvolvimento recente e perspectivas da economia brasileira. Fortaleza: Banco do Nordeste do Brasil, 1978. 35 p.; graphs.

Economist serving as president of a development bank in Brazil's Northeast describes the economic situation since 1964, and cautiously predicts that it will improve.

3749 Instituto de Desenvolvimento Econômico-Social do Pará. Diagnóstico do município de Itaituba. Belém: IDESP, Coordenadoria de Documentação e Informação-CDI, 1977. 224 p.; ill.; maps (2 fold. in pocket) (Série Relatórios de pesquisa; 9)

This late volume of a monographic series of eight devoted to the cities of the state of Pará, concerns the city of Itaituba. About four hours by air from Belém, Pará's state capital and major port of entry in northern Brazil, Itaituba had a population of 5,885 in 1975, expected to reach 15,000 by 1995. The volume includes descriptions and tables of water and telephone systems, bus service, literacy, marital status, and much more, as well as photocopies of two maps. A valuable source of information for planners charged with allocating economic resources for Brazilian development.

3750 La Palombara, Joseph G. and Stephen Blank. Multinational corporations and developing countries. New York, N.Y.: Conference Board, 1979. 215 p.; bibl.; ill. (Report—The Conference Board; no. 767)

Based on extensive interviews with elite in Nigeria, Malaysia, and Brazil. Deal more with "bread-and-butter" issues than with ideological ones. The "Brazil model" receives attention in the conclusion. [J. M. Hunter]

Leacock, Ruth. JFK, business, and Brazil. See *HLAS 42:3683*.

3751 Lemgruber, Antonio Carlos. Uma análise quantitativa do sistema financeiro no Brasil. Capa, ilustrações e diagramação, Departamento Editorial, Seção de Arte e Criação, IBMEC. Rio de Janeiro: Instituto

Brasileiro de Mercado de Capitais, 1978. 258 p.; bibl.; ill.

Presents a 27-equation model of the financial sector of Brazil, estimated from 1967–76 data. Author, who earned his Ph.D. in economics at the University of Virginia, is professor of economics at the Getúlia Vargas Foundation in Rio. Volume also contains statistical tables and a bibliography.

Levy, Maria Bárbara. História da Bolsa de Valores do Rio de Janeiro. See *HLAS 42:3529.*

3752 Lima, Antônio Aquilino de Macedo. Nordeste: aspectos macroeconômicos das cidades de porte médio. Fortaleza: Banco do Nordeste do Brasil, Departamento de Estudos Econômicos do Nordeste, Grupo de Estudos de Demografia e Urbanização, 1978. 132 p.; bibl.

A book for urban planners, published in Fortaleza by the Bank of Northeast Brazil. Covers 33 cities in the nine Northeastern states, excluding major metropolitan centers like Salvador, Fortaleza, Recife, and Belém, pointing out which of the medium-sized cities are gaining and which are losing relative importance in the Northeast. Numerous tables provide data on the economic activity of the cities, and show the 20-year growth or decline in absolute numbers and relative to the rest of the state and the region. Most of the data appears to have been taken from the 1950 and 1970 censuses.

3753 Lima, Heitor Ferreira. História do pensamento econômico no Brasil. São Paulo: Companhia Editora Nacional 1976. 198 p.; bibl. (Brasiliana; v. 360)

Traces evolution of economic thought in Brazil from colonial times to the post-World War II years. Issues discussed include paper vs. metal currency, free trade vs. protectionism, state planning vs. free market, and monetarism vs. structuralism. Also discusses roles and viewpoints of Brazil's many finance ministers. A well-documented and useful work.

Lobo, Eulalia Maria Lahmeyer. História do Rio de Janeiro: do capital comercial ao capital industrial e financeiro. See *HLAS 42:3530.*

3754 Longo, Carlos A. Considerações sobre a autonomia dos municípios (BNB/REN, 11:2, abril/junho 1980, p. 253–267, table)

Author favors taxes on real estate as a way to help *municípios* overcome their financial difficulties. His plan would require a change in the national tax laws.

3755 Magalhães, Antônio. Comércio e desenvolvimento: observações sobre as relações triangulares no comércio da região Nordeste (BNB/REN, 10:4, out./dez. 1979, p. 841–867, tables)

Brazil's Northeast made profits by supplying the south with raw materials for manufacture and other exports intended for southern consumption. However, author suggests that it might have been better for the Northeast to export directly abroad rather than to southern Brazil. He describes a "triangle of trade" involving the Northeast, the south, and the rest of the world.

Magalhães, Beatriz Ricardina de. Investimentos ingleses no Brasil e o Banco Londrino e Brasileiro. See *HLAS 42:3703.*

Maimon, Dália; Pedro Pinchas Geiger; and **Werner Baer.** O impacto regional das políticas econômicas no Brasil. See item **5371.**

Major companies of Brazil, Mexico and Venezuela 1979/1980. See *HLAS 42:151.*

3756 Malan, Pedro Sampaio. The Brazilian economy: options for the eighties (CEPAL/R, 8, Aug. 1979, p. 91–102)

Brief review of the causes and effects of the economic "miracle" of 1968–73, followed by policy recommendations for the 1980s. Argues that economic events of the past decade have been profoundly influenced by external factors. These have increased the vulnerability of the economy and created a capital intensive productive structure geared to the needs of a small elite. The government's preoccupation with technical solutions to short-term balance-of-payments and inflation problems has caused it to postpone its efforts to alleviate poverty and satisfy basic needs. Author recommends a restructuring of aggregate demand and supply so as to encourage labor-intensive industries that produce goods important to low-income groups. An important statement by one of Brazil's top young economists.

3757 Malloy, James M. The politics of social security in Brazil. Pittsburgh: University of Pittsburgh Press, 1979. 200 p.; bibl.; index (Pitt Latin American series)

Political history of Brazil's social security system. Author shows that the first social insurance law, passed in 1923, was a reformist elite's response to the "social question." Subsequently, the social security system became a means for the state to co-opt the urban working class and prevent it from challenging the political and economic status quo. Although the post-1964 military regime reformed the social security system, author suggests that it remains internally stratified and may worsen the distribution of income. An important contribution to the analysis of Brazilian public policies.

Marini, Mauro. Las razones del neodesarrollismo: respuesta a F. H. Cardosa y J. Serra. See item **8382.**

Mattoso, Katia M. de Queiros. Bahia: a cidade do Salvador e seu mercado no século XIX. See *HLAS 42:3713.*

3758 Melo, Fernando B. A agricultura de exportação e o problema da produção de alimentos (IPE/EE, 9:3, set./dez. 1979, p. 101–122, bibl., tables)
The alleged export-nutrition trade-off remains a controversial policy issue in Brazil. Melo contends that expansion of agricultural exports may have a detrimental effect on the nutritional standards of the poor. As evidence of this, he provides data showing that production of crops important in the diets of poverty groups has stagnated in recent years, causing prices to rise. Recommends some form of food subsidy.

3759 Merrick, Thomas William and **Douglas H. Graham.** Population and economic development in Brazil, 1800 to the present. Baltimore: Johns Hopkins University Press, 1979. 385 p.; bibl.; ill.; index.
Solid, scholarly work on the population of Brazil discusses such subjects as long-term trends in population growth, slavery, immigration, regional economic growth, the labor force, internal migration, urban poverty, fertility, mortality, and economic planning. A useful first chapter provides basic geographic and historical information. Authors conclude that "the prospects for Brazilian population growth in the next several decades are for continued growth, but at a decreasing rate." Contains an index and a bibliography of about 600 entries. For historian's comment, see *HLAS 42:3716.*

3760 Ness, Walter L., Jr. and **Rosanne H. Rebelo da Silva.** Análise conjuntural financeira das companhias abertas: pts. 1/2 (RBMC, 5:14, maio/agôsto 1979, p. 3–85, tables; 5:15, set./dez. 1979, p. 3–79, tables)
Two-part analysis. Pt. 1 examines 50 financial institutions and compares their performance in the first half of 1979 and first half of 1978. Companies with different fiscal years are also included so that the study actually encompasses 95 percent of the Brazilian securities business. Pt. 2 analyzes publicly-owned companies and compares performances of 213 enterprises registered with the National Securities Exchange Commission for the period May/Oct. 1979 and May/Oct. 1978. Both parts contain many tables and statistical data.

3761 Neuhaus, Paulo. Princípios para a reformulação da política comercial brasileira (IBE/RBE, 33:3, julho/set. 1979, p. 399–412, bibl., tables)
Author hypothesizes that, in the absence of tariff reductions, the gradual elimination of export subsidies announced in 1979 will produce an undesirable bias against exports. Recommends a new foreign trade policy that would equalize inter-industry effective rates or protection and eliminate non-tariff barriers to imports. Presents simulations showing rates of nominal protection required to achieve this objective.

3762 Neves, Renato Baumann. Os ciclos na indústria de transformação: um estudo da utilização da capacidade—Brasil, 1955/1975. Rio de Janeiro: Banco Nacional do Desenvolvimento Econômico, 1978. 137 p.; graphs.
Award-winning Master's thesis written for the University of Brasília that describes the sectoral impacts of fluctuations in industrial activity from 1955–75. Contains numerous tables and graphs.

3763 Newfarmer, Richard S. Transnational conglomerates and the economics of dependent development: a case study of the international electrical oligopoly and Brazil's electrical industry. Greenwich, Conn.: JAI Press, 1980. 442 p.; bibl.; index (Contemporary studies in economic and financial analysis; v. 23)
Implicit in Newfarmer's study is the belief that the role of the transnational conglomerates in developing countries forms

part of the struggle between the "haves" and the "have nots." His introduction states: "Posed in its starkest terms, at issue is whether transnational conglomerates promote development of poor countries and people, or whether they reinforce the pattern of uneven international and domestic development . . . This book addresses these questions through a case study of the international electrical industry and its growth in Brazil." Study implies that in today's political climate, any government that opposes the transnational conglomerates is not likely to succeed in development, and those governments that do cooperate with conglomerates may achieve development but not a drastic redistribution of wealth. To quote the author: "The structure of the modern international industry is highly concentrated. A relative handful of firms together produce the bulk of sales and control the industry's most advanced technology through the non-Socialist world. The leading firms are linked to each other through a complex web of cross-equity holdings, joint ventures, licenses, and other arrangements. Although they must contend with a strong fringe of competitive firms in some of their several markets, the TNCs tower above their less diversified rivals and are visible to each other across the world market. Taken together, they form what can loosely be called the "international electrical oligopoly."

3764 Nicholls, William Hord and **Ruy Miller Paiva.** Mudanças na estrutura e produtividade da agricultura brasileira, 1963/73: noventa e nove fazendas revisitadas. t. 1, O Brasil Sul de Sudeste. Rio de Janeiro: IPEA/INPES, 1979. 1 v. (Relatório de pesquisa—IPEA/INPES; no. 45)

Volume contains the partial findings of a 15-year collaborative effort between Ruy Miller Paiva, the doyen of Brazilian agricultural economics, and the late William Nicholls of Vanderbilt University. Study's innovative approach involves comparing the performance of selected farms in the South and Southeast over the period 1963–73 with respect to changes in land use, investment, employment, income, etc. Findings at the farm level are then put into the context of postwar national agricultural policies. The reader can only lament that, with the death of Professor Nicholls, this pioneering work may never be completed.

3765 Osório, Carlos. A pobreza e a riqueza das regiões (BNB/REN, 10:3, julho/set. 1979, p. 657–712, tables)

Article shows in quantitative terms the extent of interregional and intraregional inequalities in income and wealth. As expected, the study reveals the Northeast to be the poorest region. Contains little new analysis and most of the data are from the early 1970s.

Overholt, William H. The future of Brazil: an overview. See item **7441.**

3766 Paes, Renato Correia. Um estudo econômico do Brasil. Rio de Janeiro: Guavira Editores, 1978. 144 p.; bibl.; graphs.

Brief overview of the Brazilian economy, including balance-of-payments projections to 1975. Analyses presented are too superficial to be of much interest to economists. In addition, the projections, even for 1981, are very unrealistic largely owing to the author's gross underestimation of oil prices and international interest rates.

3767 Painel sobre o Desenvolvimento Sócio-Econômico de Centro-Oeste, *Goiânia, Brazil, 1978.* Painel sobre o Desenvolvimento Sócio-Econômico do Centro-Oeste. Rio de Janeiro: Confederação Nacional do Comércio, Departamento Técnico e de Operações, Serviço de Documentação e Informação, 1979. 175 p.; ill.

Proceedings of a two-day seminar on the development potential of the Center-West held in 1978. Themes discussed include: mining and energy, transport, education, and regional development priorities.

3768 Pinto, Agerson Tabosa. O Banco do Nordeste e a modernização regional. Fortaleza: Banco do Nordeste do Brasil, 1977. 157 p.; bibl.

Book contains information and statistical tables of value to those studying the Banco do Nordeste through 1973.

3769 A Problemática da localização industrial na Grande São Paulo. Bona de Villa et al. São Paulo: Universidade de São Paulo, Faculdade de Arquitetura e Urbanismo, 1975. 144 p.; bibl.

Seven short studies examine problems of locating industries, especially in Greater São Paulo. Authors are members of the School of Architecture and Urban Studies at the University of São Paulo.

3770 A Produção capitalista da casa (e da cidade) no Brasil industrial. Ermínia Maricato, organizadora; prefacio, Francisco de Oliveira; capa, Vera Altemberg. São Paulo: Editora Alfa-Omega, 1979. 166 p.; bibl.; ill. (Biblioteca Alfa-Omega de ciências sociais; Série l.a, Urbanismo; v. 1)

One economist and five architects contributed to this social essay about the slums surrounding the large cities of Brazil, particularly in São Paulo. Study focuses on the small dwellings people have constructed for themselves. Contains tables, graphs, and photographs.

3771 Queiroz, Carlos Alberto Reiz. A política monetária num contexto de indexação: o caso brasileiro (IBE/RBE, 34:2, abril/junho 1980, p. 165–202, bibl., tables)

In order to test Friedman's hypothesis that the short-term conflict between inflation and unemployment is reduced in an economic system with indexation, Queiroz studied Brazilian monetary policy in two different periods: 1957–64, when there was inflation but no indexation, and 1965–76, when most contracts contained monetary correction clauses. While the study appears to confirm Friedman, Queiroz refused to conclude that the effects of Brazilian monetary policy were completely neutral in the short-run for the indexed period.

3772 A questão agrária no Brasil. Carlos Marighella et al.; capa, Ary Normanha. São Paulo: Brasil Debates, 1980. 127 p.; bibl.

Collection of seven essays and one document concerning the nature of the agricultural sector during the 1960s. Emphasizes the skewed distribution of farmland and the need for a radical agrarian reform. General theme is that post-1964 government has not carried forward agrarian reform, but has instead favored the modernization of *latifundia*.

Ramos, Dulce Helena Alvares Pessôa. Un ejemplo de pesquisa bibliográfica como elemento da pesquisa pública: as teses americanas sobre o Brasil, 1960–1970. See *HLAS 42:160.*

3773 Rangel, Inácio. A inflação brasileira. Prefacio de Luiz Carlos Bresser Pereira. 3. ed. São Paulo: Editora Brasiliense, 1978. 150 p.; bibl.

Rangel's book, first published in 1963, is regarded as a "classic" by Luiz Carlos Bresser Pereira, who appears to have been instrumental in bringing out this third edition "without adaptations or alterations because they are not necessary."

Ravagni, Leda Almada Cruz de. Les investissements français au Brésil, 1890–1930. See *HLAS 42:3738.*

3774 Rebouças, Osmundo Evangelista. Análise social de projetos no planejamento econômico do Nordeste (BNB/REN, 11:2, abril/junho 1980, p. 205–216, tables)

Based on the accumulated experience of more than two decades of economic planning in the Northeast, author suggests six changes in the way projects are analyzed and evaluated.

3775 ———. Crescimento do Nordeste no contexto nacional: fatores condicionantes (BNB/REN, 9:4, out./dez. 1978, p. 453–467, tables)

Paper analyzes the postwar economic growth of the Northeast in relation to that of the rest of Brazil. Points to a decrease in regional income disparities during the 1950s, followed by an increase during the 1960s and 1970s. Author concludes that government programs have not contributed, in aggregate terms, to a reduction in regional disparities. A provocative article on an important topic.

3776 Reflexões sobre a agricultura brasileira. Maria de Nazareth Baudel Wanderly et al; coordenador, Braz José de Araújo; capa, Mario Roberto Corrêa da Silva. Rio de Janeiro: Paz e Terra, 1979. 180 p.; bibl. (Coleção Estudos brasileiros; v. 37)

Collection of four papers originally presented at the 30th annual meeting of the Brazilian Society for the Progress of Science (vol. 37 of the monographic series *Brazilian Studies*, published 1978). The following topics are covered: 1) capital and rural property in Brazilian agriculture; 2) the intensification of agri-business in the Federal District; 3) the Rural Labor Syndicate from 1964–76; and 4) agrarian reform: union and schism in the agroindustrial block.

3777 Resenhas de economia brasileira. Organizador, João Sayad; autores, Francisco Lafaiete Lopes et al. São Paulo, SP: Edição Saraiva, 1979. 291 p.; bibl.; graphs (Série ANPEC de leituras de economia)

Collected by the National Association of Graduate Schools of Economics, the four papers included in this volume comprise a Brazilian reader for Master's degree candidates: 1) a study of agricultural development by Fernando Homem de Melo; 2) a discussion of regional development by Jorge Jatobá; 3) a review of the literature of inflation by Francisco Lopes; and 4) a review of the literature on scientific and technological policy by Fábrio Stefano Erber.

3778 Rolfo, Jacques. Optimal hedging under price and quantity uncertainty: the case of a cocoa producer (JPE, 88:1, Feb. 1980, p. 100–116, bibl., tables)

Paper derives the optimal hedge for a producer who is subject to both price and quantity uncertainties. Major result of the analysis, established explicitly for the case of a risk-averse cocoa producer, is that a minimal usage of a future market (or none at all) may be superior to a full short hedge. Study is important to the developing countries of Ghana, Nigeria, Brazil, the Ivory Coast, and Cameroon, which together produce about 80 percent of the world's cocoa. Rolfo finds that the correlation of production uncertainties between Africa and Brazil is positive but low.

3779 Saffioti, Heleieth Iara Bongiovani. Emprego doméstico e capitalismo. Petrópolis: Editora Vozes, 1978. 197 p.; bibl. (Coleção Sociologia brasileira; v. 9)

Using data from interviews with 1,097 women in the city of Araraquara, in the interior of the state of São Paulo, author concludes that the continuing practice of employing female domestic servants in many Brazilian households is evidence of social discrimination against women.

3780 Saint, William S. and William W. Goldsmith. Cropping systems, structural change and rural-urban migration in Brazil (WD, 8:3, March 1980, p. 259–272, ill., tables)

Authors examine population dynamics in Bahia in terms of crop-production systems and social structure; migration and production systems; stagnation, enclosure and expulsion; and "pull" explanations of out-migration.

3781 Sanders, John H. and Vernon W. Ruttan. Biased choice of technology in Brazilian agriculture (*in* Binswanger, Hans P.;

Vernon W. Ruttan and Uri Ben-Zion. Induced innovation: technology, institutions, and development [see item **2765**] p. 276–296, tables)

Authors conclude that mechanized farming is more helpful on difficult soils than on good soils, and that government policies that in effect subsidize the purchase of tractors help large-farm owners more than small-farm owners.

3782 Santos, João Regis Ricardo dos. Mercado de ações: uma análise sobre o sistema de informações. Equipe técnico que participou deste trabalho, Jorge Thadeu Chaia de Sampaio et al. Rio de Janeiro: Instituto Brasileiro de Mercado de Capitais, 1978. 147 p.; bibl. (Série Estudos especiais—Instituto Brasileiros de Mercado de Capitais; 6)

Concerned about the role of the capital markets in the economic development process of Brazil, Dos Santos describes the capital market information system in Brazil. He devotes many more pages, however, to descriptions of the information system in the US.

3783 Sautchuk, Jaime; Horacio Martins de Carvalho; and Sergio Buarque de Gusmão. Projeto Jari; a invasão americana. Capa, Ary Normanha, Jaime Leão. São Paulo: Editora Brasil Debates, 1979. 110 p.; 1 leaf of plates; ill. (Brasil hoje; no. 1)

As its title indicates, work is another contribution to the large body of literature on supposed *cobiça internacional* ("international greed") in the Brazilian Amazon region. Subject is multimillionaire D. K. Ludwig's grandiose Jari project. Criticism of project focuses on the alleged collusion between 1 and 3.7 million hectares, depending on the source of information, and the misery of the workers. Technological advances introduced in Jari are likewise viewed in a negative light. Although authors offer few recommendations on what should be done with or for Jari, this is a useful work for readers interested in the opposition's view of foreign capital in Amazonia.

3784 Sáyad, João and Sebastião Jorge Jatobá. Efeitos espaciais da política monetária e financiera (BNB/REN, 11:1, jan./março 1980, p. 7–33, tables)

Brazilian development is taking a new turn that differs from the familiar patterns of the 19th century. In recent years growth has become more dependent on the financial system than on exchange rate policy, and the government is using credit as an instrument of planning equal in importance to the political bill of exchange in the earlier period. Authors did not find that bankers have delayed development in the Northeast because of their supposed aversion to risk.

Serra, José and **Fernando H. Cardoso.** Las desventuras de la dialéctica de la dependencia. See item **8395.**

3785 Silva, Janice Theodoro da. Raízes da ideologia do planejamento, Nordeste (1889–1930). São Paulo: Livraria Editora Ciências Humanas, 1978. 120 p.; bibl. (Brasil ontem e hoje; 7)

Study of the political and economic problems of Rio Grande do Norte during the First Republic. Author analyzes the "política dos governadores" through which the southern states gained hegemony over the Northeast. Author argues that ensuing political tensions gave rise to the concept of planning as a neutral way of dealing with Northeastern problems.

3786 Silva, Sergio. Expansão cafeeira e origens da indústria no Brasil. Capa, Agune, Falanqui & Tedeschi. São Paulo: Editora Alfa Omega, 1976. 120 p.; bibl. (Biblioteca Alfa-Omega de ciências sociais; Série 1, Economia; v. 1)

Silva, an economist who earned his Ph.D. at the university of Paris, lectured in 1973 at the Getulio Vargas Foundation, and since 1974 has been with the State University of Campinas. He presents a history of the Brazilian coffee economy, in particular as it relates to early industrialization. Contains a bibliography and tables.

3787 Simonsen, Marío Henrique. Palestras e conferências. v. 1, 1974. v. 2, 1. semestre de 1975. Rio de Janeiro: República Federativa do Brasil, Ministério da Fazenda, Gabinete do Ministro, 1974 [i.e. 1976]. 2 v.

Six speeches by the former Secretary of the Treasury, gathered together in one small volume. Topics include methods used to counter inflation and the legal environment of the stock market.

Soares, Sebastião Ferreira. Notas estatísticas sobre a produção ao agrícola e carestia dos

gêneros alimentícios no Imperio do Brasil. See *HLAS 42:3753.*

Sorj, Bernardo. Agrarian structure and politics in present day Brazil. See item **6755.**

3788 Souza Filho, Rui Guilherme and **Dulce Leoncy Souza.** Incentivos fiscais estaduais: a experiência do Pará. Belém: Governo do Estado do Pará, Instituto do Desenvolvimento Econômico-Social do Pará, 1975. 97 p.; bibl. (Série Monografias—Instituto do Desenvolvimento Econômico-Social do Pará; 16)

Publication of the Institute of Economic and Social Development of the State of Pará, Brazil. Contains summaries of the laws granting financial subsidies for industrial development within the state and summaries of subsidy use through 1972.

3789 The Structure of Brazilian development. Edited by Neuma Aguiar. New Brunswick, N.J.: Transaction Books, 1979. 258 p.; bibl.; index.

Collection of seven essays on the social structure and development of Brazilian society. Authors are young Brazilian social scientists, primarily concerned with the causes and effects of authoritarianism. Topics include: frontier development (O. Velho); rural conflicts in the Northeast (M. Palmeira); authoritarianism and populism (A. Camargo); social behavior of poverty groups in São Paulo (M. Berlinck and D. Hogan); and others. Also contains useful bibliography of Brazilian works on the social sciences published between 1960–77.

3790 Superintendência do Desenvolvimento da Região Sul. Agregados econômicos regionais: renda interna. Ministério do Interior, Superintendência do Desenvolvimento da Região Sul e Fundação Getúlio Vargas, Instituto Brasileiro de Economia. Porto Alegre: SUDESUL, 1977. 73 p.; 3 leaves of plates; maps (Série Região Sul em números; 1)

Book on the southern region of Brazil (the states of Paraná, Santa Catarina, and Rio Grande do Sul), contains statistical tables and introductory material showing income for agriculture, industry, and services for 1959–75. Data are aggregated by states and region, and one table gives figures for Brazil as a whole, for comparison. Also provides summaries of the data by microregions.

3791 Taylor, Kit Sims. Sugar and the under-development of northeastern Brazil, 1500–1970. Gainesville: University Presses of Florida, 1978. 167 p.; bibl.; ill. (University of Florida monographs; Social sciences; no. 63)

Historical interpretation of land-labor relationships in sugar-producing areas of the Northeast. Argues that the evolution of land-labor relationships has been primarily determined by the economic interests of the land-owning class, not feudal or traditional attitudes. More specifically, the monopoly of a few over landownership and political power has been used to impede the development of small-scale, food-producing agriculture and to maintain a labor supply willing to work at subsistence wages. Author is pessimistic about the willingness of government to change the status-quo. A provocative study which could be profitably updated to take into account the effects of PROALCOOL and the 1979 labor strikes in the sugar-producing areas.

3792 Tolosa, Hamilton C. Causes of urban poverty in Brazil (WD, 6:9/10, Sept./Oct. 1978, p. 1087–1101)

Paper measures poverty in 95 cities with populations exceeding 50,000, and attempts to explain its causes. Four major determinants of urban poverty are identified: 1) internal productive structure of the city; 2) functional position of the city in relation to the urban system; 3) demographic pressure mainly due to in-migration; and 4) impact of government social programs. Tolosa develops an index of urban poverty, and ranks the sample cities according to this index. Recommends policies to promote a spatial redistribution of urban population and the development of more labor intensive economic activities. A creative and highly useful work.

Topik, Steven. The evolution of the economic role of the Brazilian state, 1889–1930. See *HLAS* 42:3765.

3793 Tyler, William G. Technical efficiency and ownership characteristics of manufacturing firms in a developing country: a Brazilian case study (CAUK/WA, 114:2, 1978, p. 360–379, tables)

Tyler predicts that foreign firms will continue to increase their participation in Brazil's industrial economy. Examining data for 1971, he finds that foreign and govern-ment firms in Brazil tend to be more capital-intensive than privately-owned industrial enterprises. Disproves contention that foreign firms possess greater levels of technical efficiency than domestic firms, but does find evidence that foreign firms possess greater returns to scale and greater elasticities of substitution. This in turn suggests that foreign firms have a relative advantage in growing and coping with a changing economic environment.

3794 United States. Industry and Trade Administration. Brazil, a survey of U.S. export opportunities. Washington: The Administration: for sale by the Sup. of Docs., U.S. GPO, 1979. 277 p.: ill.

Survey of 20 economic sectors, ranging from road transport to publishing, written for the US businessman. Besides assessing the future growth prospects of these sectors, work also describes the "investment climate" for foreign firms in Brazil. Concludes that export opportunities are best in electric power, mining, metallurgy, chemicals, machinery, telecommunications, and electronics. A useful handbook subject to becoming rapidly outdated.

3795 Velloso, João Paulo dos Reis. Balanço preliminar do II [i.e. segundo] PND: exposição perante o Conselho de Desenvolvimento Econômico, CDE, em 20 de dezembro de 1978. Rio de Janeiro: IBGE, 1978. 28 p.

Official interim assessment of the 2nd National Development Plan, 1975–79. Socio-economic indicators for 1973 are compared to those of 1978 in order to measure progress. General conclusion is that the Plan achieved its objectives, even though some of the data seem to contradict this assertion.

3796 Versiani, Flávio Rabelo. Industrialização a experiência brasileira antes de 1914 (IBE/RBE, 34:1, jan./março 1980, p. 3–40, bibl., tables)

Versiani shows that in pre-1914 Brazil the manufacturing of cotton textiles developed in response to an increasingly protective tariff system and exchange-rate instability. The tariff enabled manufacturing undertakings to survive and grow in spite of adverse exchange-rate conditions. Furthermore, the capital for developing the textile industry came mostly from the re-investment of profits rather than from the coffee sector, as some have suggested. Author also finds that the expansion of industrial productive capacity was a more gradual process than commonly has been believed.

3797 Viana, M. Osório de Lima. Efeitos do mercado sobre a agricultura regional (BNB/REN, 11:1, jan./março 1980, p. 81–103, tables)

Attempt to give some idea of the reaction of agriculture in the Northeast to the general development of the economy. In particular, author addresses the questions of agriculture's response to the price mechanism of the market, the effect of prices on quantities offered and on the composition of areas cultivated. Apparently, most farmers live poorly, have little bargaining power, and experience relatively small portions of any price increases. Since they have little choice about what to produce or how much land to cultivate, their farming practices are not responsive to changing market prices. The tendency to continue the same practices year after year is stronger than the tendency to change crops to fit price fluctuations.

3798 Vianna, Pedro Jorge Ramos. Análise do balanço de pagamentos do Brasil: 1961–1976 (BNB/REN, 10:4, out./dez. 1979, p. 869–903, tables)

Author advocates long-term policies to diminish dependence to levels compatible with the economic development of the country. He estimates Brazil's foreign debt will be $40 billion (an overestimate, as proven by later events) by the end of 1980, and some $10.5 billion will be sent abroad to service the debt. However, author is not pessimistic, and recommends a series of policies intended to reduce Brazil's dependence on foreign capital.

3799 ———. A transferência de recursos nordestinos via comércio triangular: algunos comentários (BNB/REN, 11:2, abril/junho 1980, p. 231–251, bibl., tables)

Vianna pursues the subject discussed by Antonio Rocha Magalhães in *Revista Econômica do Nordeste* (10:4, out./dez. 1979). He proposes a new methodology and calculates the Northeast's annual loss at CR$4 billion per year (at 1979 prices) for 1954–75.

3800 Vieira, Dorival Teixeira. Especialização em comércio exterior: uma experiência interdisciplinar (*in* Encontro Interregional de Cientistas Sociais do Brail, 2d,

Garanhuns, Brazil, 1974. Anais do II [i.e. Segundo] Encontro Inter-regional de Cientistas Sociais do Brasil: reuniões realizadas de 21 a 25 de janeiro de 1973 em Garanhuns-PE. Recife: Ministério da Educação e Cultura, Instituto Joaquim Nabuco de Pesquisas Sociais, 1977, p. 120–135)

Vieira discusses a worldwide problem that is arising earlier than expected: the scarcity of agricultural projects. He maintains that Brazil needs to abandon its single-minded concentration on increasing its exports, and start paying attention to the relationship between exports and the internal market.

3801 Wanderley, Maria de Nazareth. Capital e propriedade fundiária: suas articulações na economia açucareira de Pernambuco. Rio de Janeiro: Paz e Terra, 1978. 145 p.; bibl.; ill. (Série Estudos sobre o Nordeste; v. 3)

Revision of author's doctoral dissertation, first published in French in 1975. Daughter of a sugar worker, she spent her childhood years on a sugar plantation, and later had contact with the rural syndicates of Recife. Explores relationships among diverse social agents in the sugar industry in Pernambuco. Statistical tables and a bibliography of nearly 300 entries add value to the work.

3802 Weisskoff, Richard. Orto y ocaso de la sustitución de importaciones en el Brasil: nueva evaluación (FCE/TE, 47[2]:186, abril/junio 1980, p. 377–430, tables)

In the first phases of import substitution the economic growth of Brazil was stimulated by the deliberate promotion of modern industry, a policy requiring a continually rising level of imports. More recently, the duality between agriculture and "modernized" industry, on the one hand, and subsistence agriculture and obsolete plantations, on the other, has sharpened regional and social tensions. The demand of the urban populace for higher salaries and greater health and education services created a need for structural reform from within, but increased the public indebtedness from without. According to Weisskoff, the solution to this problem has been to seek refuge in a greater integration with the international economy and its attendant crises, instead of beginning a new round of import substitution and the development of new patterns of consumption.

3803 Wright, Charles. Income inequality and economic growth: examining the evidence (JDA, 13:1, Oct. 1978, p. 49–66, tables)

Wright examines the following two hypotheses about income distribution: 1) the divergence-convergence hypothesis that relative income inequality increases during the early stages of economic growth before ultimately decreasing in the latter periods of growth; and 2) the institutional hypothesis that institutional structures and governmental policies are the chief determinants of relative inequality. He characterizes the Brazilian experience as conforming to the latter hypothesis.

JOURNAL ABBREVIATIONS
ECONOMICS

AAA/AE American Ethnologist. American Anthropological Association. Washington.

AEA/AER American Economic Review. Journal of the American Economic Association. Evanston, Ill.

AGRO Agrociencia. Secretaría de Agricultura y Recursos Hidráulicos, Colegio de Postgraduados de la Escuela Nacional de Agricultura. Chapingo, Mexico.

AI/I Interciencia. Asociación Interciencia. Caracas.

AJES The American Journal of Economics and Sociology. Francis Neilson Fund and Robert Schalkenbach Foundation. New York.

ANCE/A Anales de la Academia Nacional de Ciencias Económicas. Buenos Aires.

ARIAI/JRI The Journal of Risk and Insurance. American Risk and Insurance Association. Bloomington, Ill.

BCRA/EE Ensayos Económicos. Banco Central de la República Argentina. Buenos Aires.

BCV/REL Revista de Economía Latinoamericana. Banco Central de Venezuela. Caracas.

BID/INTAL Revista de Integración. Banco Interamericano de Desarrollo. Washington.

BNB/REN Revista Econômica do Nordeste. Banco do Nordeste do Brasil, Depto. de Estudos Econômicos do Nordeste. Fortaleza.

BNCE/CE Comercio Exterior. Banco Nacional de Comercio Exterior. México.

CAPR/RCA Revista de Colegio de Abogados. Colegio de Abogados de Puerto Rico. San Juan?

CAUK/WA Weltwirtschaftliches Archiv. Zeitschrift des Instituts für Weltwirtschaft an der Christians-Albrechts-Univ. Kiel. Kiel, FRG.

CCH/TTM The Tax Magazine. Commerce Clearing House. Chicago, Ill.

CEDE/DS Desarrollo y Sociedad. Univ. de los Andes, Facultad de Economía, Centro de Estudios sobre el Desarrollo Económico. Bogotá.

CEMLA/M Monetaria. Centro de Estudios Monetarios Latinoamericanos. México.

CEPAL/R CEPAL Review/Revista de la CEPAL. Naciones Unidas, Comisión Económica para América Latina. Santiago.

CLAEH Centro Latinoamericano de Economía Humana. Montevideo.

CM/DE Demografía y Economía. El Colego de México. México.

CM/FI Foro Internacional. El Colegio de México. México.

CPS Comparative Political Studies. Northwestern Univ., Evanston, Ill., and Sage Publications, Beverly Hills, Calif.

CPU/ES Estudios Sociales. Corporación de Promoción Universitaria. Santiago.

CRIT Criterio. Editorial Criterio. Buenos Aires.

CSUCA/ESC Estudios Sociales Centroamericanos. Consejo Superior de Universidades Centroamericanas, Confederación Universitaria Centroamericana, Programa Centroamericano de Ciencias Sociales. San José.

CUNY/CP Comparative Politics. The City Univ. of New York, Political Science Program. New York.

DDW Die Dritte Welt. Verlag Anton Hain. Meisenheim, FRG.

EHA/J Journal of Economic History. New York Univ., Graduate School of Business Administration *for* The Economic History Association. Rensselaer.

FBA/FBJ Federal Bar Journal. Federal Bar Association. Washington.

FCE/TE El Trimestre Económico. Fondo de Cultura Económica. México.

FDD/NED Notes et Études Documentaires. Direction de la Documentation. Paris.

FGV/CE Conjuntura Econômica. Fundação Getúlio Vargas, Instituto Brasileiro de Economia. Rio de Janeiro.

GDB/BR Business Review. Government Development Bank. San Juan?

HAHR Hispanic American Historical Review. Duke Univ. Press *for the* Conference on Latin American History of the American Historical Association. Durham, N.C.

HU/RES Review of Economics and Statistics. Harvard Univ. Cambridge, Mass.

IAA Ibero-Amerikanisches Archiv. Ibero-Amerikanisches Institut. Berlin, FRG.

IAMEA Inter-American Economic Affairs. Washington.

IASI/E Estadística. Journal of the Inter American Statistical Institute. Washington.

IAUPR/RI Revista Interamericana. Interamerican Univ. of Puerto Rico. Río Piedras?

IBE/RBE Revista Brasileira de Economia. Fundação Getúlio Vargas, Instituto Brasileiro de Economia. Rio de Janeiro.

IDE/DE The Developing Economies. The Journal of the Institute of Developing Economies. Tokyo.

IDES/DE Desarrollo Económico. Instituto de Desarrollo Económico y Social. Buenos Aires.

IEAS/R Revista de Estudios Agro-Sociales. Instituto de Estudios Agro-Sociales. Madrid.

IEERAL/E Estudios. Instituto de Estudios Económicos sobre la Realidad Argentina y Latinoamericana. Córdoba.

IEI/EI Economia Internazionale. Rivista dell'Istituto di Economia Internazionale. Genova, Italy.

IFH/C Conjonction. Institut Français d'Haïti. Port-au-Prince.

IG Information Geographique. Paris.

IHGB/R Revista do Instituto Histórico e Geográfico Brasileiro. Rio de Janeiro.

IIDC/C Civilisations. International Institute of Differing Civilizations. Bruxelles.

IMF/SP Staff Papers. International Monetary Fund. Washington.

INTAL/IL Integración Latinoamericana. Instituto para la Integración de América Latina. Buenos Aires.

IPA/A Allpanchis. Instituto de Pastoral Andina. Cuzco, Perú.

IPE/EE Estudos Econômicos. Univ. de São Paulo, Instituto de Pesquisas Econômicas. São Paulo.

IRR/RC Race & Class. A journal for black and Third World liberation. Institute of Race Relations and The Transnational Institute. London.

ISTMO Istmo. Revista del pensamiento actual. México.

JDA The Journal of Developing Areas. Western Illinois Univ. Press. Macomb.

JDE Journal of Development Economics. North Holland Publishing Co. Amsterdam.

JDS The Journal of Development Studies. A quarterly journal devoted to economics, politics and social development. London.

JLAS Journal of Latin American Studies. Centers or institutes of Latin American Studies at the universities of Cambridge, Glasgow, Liverpool, London and Oxford. Cambridge Univ. Press. London.

JPE Journal of Political Economy. Univ. of Chicago. Chicago, Ill.

JPR Journal of Peace Research. Edited at the International Peace Research Institute. Universitetforlaget. Oslo.

JT The Journal of Taxation. Journal of Taxation, Inc. New York.

LAP Latin American Perspectives. Univ. of California. Riverside.

LARR Latin American Research Review. Univ. of North Carolina Press *for the* Latin American Studies Association. Chapel Hill.

NACLA NACLA: Report on the Americas. North American Congress on Latin America. New York.

NACLA/LAER NACLAS's Latin America & Empire Report. North American Congress on Latin America. New York. *See also* NACLA.

NCFR/JFH Journal of Family History. Studies in family, kinship and demography. National Council on Family Relations. Minneapolis, Minn.

NSO Nueva Sociedad. Revista política y cultural. San José.

OAS/CI Ciencia Interamericana. Organization of American States, Dept. of Scientific Affairs. Washington.

OUP/OEP Oxford Economic Papers. Oxford Univ. Press. London.

PAN/ES Estudios Latinoamericanos Polska Akademia Nauk [Academia de Ciencias de Polonia], Instytut Historii [Instituto de Historia]. Warszawa.

PCE/TE *See* FCE/TE.

PP Past and Present. London.

PRNB/BGA Boletín de Gerencia Administrativa. Negociado de Presupuesto. San Juan?

PUCIS/WP World Politics. A quarterly journal of international relations. Princeton Univ., Center of International Studies. Princeton, N.J.

PUCP/E Economía. Pontificia Univ. Católica del Perú, Depto. de Economía. Lima.

PUJ/U Universitas. Ciencias jurídicas y socioeconómicas. Pontificia Univ. Javeriana, Facultad de Derecho y Ciencias Socioeconómicas. Bogotá.

RBMC Revista Brasileira de Mercado de Capitais. Instituto Brasileiro de Mercado de Capitais. Rio de Janeiro.

RES/EJ Economic Journal. Quarterly journal of the Royal Economic Society. London.

RU/MP Marxist Perspectives. Transaction Periodicals Consortium. Rutgers Univ. New Brunswick, N.J.

RU/SCID Studies in Comparative International Development. Rutgers Univ. New Brunswick, N.J.

SAGE/JIAS Journal of Inter-American Studies and World Affairs. Sage Publications for the Center for Advanced International Studies, Univ. of Miami. Coral Gables, Fla.

SS Science and Society. New York.

UC/EDCC Economic Development and Cultural Change. Univ. of Chicago, Research Center in Economic Development and Cultural Change. Chicago, Ill.

UC/EE Estudios de Economía. Univ. de Chile, Facultad de Ciencias Económicas y Administrativas, Depto. de Economía. Santiago.

UCC/CE Cuadernos de Economía. Univ. Católica de Chile. Santiago.

UCC/NG Norte Grande. Revista de estudios integrados referentes a comunidades humanas del Norte Grande de Chile, en una perspectiva geográfica e histórico-cultural. Univ. Católica de Chile, Instituto de Geografía, Depto. de Geografía de Chile, Taller Norte Grande. Santiago.

UCNSA/EP Estudios Paraguayos. Univ. Católica Nuestra Señora de la Asunción. Asunción.

UCV/ECS Economía y Ciencias Sociales. Univ. Central de Venezuela, Facultad de Economía. Caracas.

UFMG/DCP Cadernos DCP. Univ. Federal de Minas Gerais, Faculdade de Filosofia e Ciências Humanas, Depto. de Ciência Política. Belo Horizonte, Brasil.

UH/ED Economía y Desarrollo. Univ. de La Habana, Instituto de Economía. La Habana.

UJSC/ECA Estudios Centro-Americanos. Revista de extensión cultural. Univ. José Simeón Cañas. San Salvador.

UM/JIAS *See* SAGE/JIAS.

UNAH/RCE Revista Centroamericana de Economía. Univ. Nacional Autónoma de Honduras, Programa de Postgrado Centroamericano en Economía y Planificación. Tegucigalpa.

UNAM/RMS Revista Mexicana de Sociología. Univ. Nacional Autónoma de México, Instituto de Investigaciones Sociales. México.

UNESCO/CU Cultures. United Nations Educational, Scientific and Cultural Organization. Paris.

UNLP/E Económica. Univ. Nacional de La Plata, Facultad de Ciencias Económicas, Instituto de Investigaciones Económicas. La Plata, Argentina.

UP/CSEC Cuban Studies/Estudios Cubanos. Univ. of Pittsburgh, Univ. Center for International Studies, Center for Latin American Studies. Pittsburgh, Pa.

UP/TM Tiers Monde. Problèmes des pays sous-développés. Univ. de Paris, Institut d'Étude de Développement Économique et Social. Paris.

UPR/CS Caribbean Studies. Univ. of Puerto Rico, Instituto of Caribbean Studies. Río Piedras.

UPR/P Plerus. Planificación económica rural urbana y social. Univ. de Puerto Rico. Río Piedras.

UPR/R *See* UPR/P.

UPR/RAP Revista de Administración Pública. Univ. Puerto Rico. Río Piedras.

UPR/RCS Revista de Ciencias Sociales. Univ. de Puerto Rico, Colegio de Ciencias Sociales. Río Piedras.

UR/L Lateinamerika. Univ. Rostock. Rostock, GDR.

URSS/AL América Latina. Academia de Ciencias de la URSS (Unión de Repúblicas Soviéticas Socialistas). Moscú.

USC/SSR Sociology and Social Research. An international journal. Univ. of Southern California. University Park.

USDL/MLR Monthly Labor Review. United States Dept. of Labor. Washington.

UTIEH/C Caravelle. Cahiers du monde hispanique et luso-brésilien. Univ. de Toulouse, Institut d'Études Hispaniques, Hispano-Americaines et Luso-Brésiliennes. Toulouse, France.

UWI/CQ Caribbean Quarterly. Univ. of the West Indies. Mona, Jamaica.

UWI/SES Social and Economic Studies. Univ. of the West Indies, Institute of Social and Economic Research. Mona, Jamaica.

EDUCATION

LATIN AMERICA (except Brazil)

EVERETT EGGINTON, *Associate Professor, School of Education, University of Louisville*

PUBLICATIONS ON LATIN AMERICAN EDUCATION can be very diverse in scope, and the articles, books and documents reviewed hereafter bear this out. The remarks that follow are intended to provide a synthesis for the reader faced with this diversity.

Although the publications cover a wide range of subjects, there is heavy emphasis on certain topics. In an analysis of the characteristics of educational research in Latin America, García and Ochoa revealed that a disproportionate number of studies focus on higher education (item **4326**) and that insufficient attention is paid to primary education. Consistent with this finding, publications on higher education dominate the literature reviewed this year. In addition, qualitative advances in the literature are described by Schiefelbein (item **4352**) and by Kreimer (item **4333**) and are much in evidence in the literature reviewed below. In the same vein, Schiefelbein discusses the potential effect of educational research on national policy (item **4417**), and some major problems which still confront educational researchers are cited in essays prepared for the Centro de Investigaciones Educativas in Buenos Aires (item **4376**) and by Larralde *et al.* (item **4502**).

Closely related to the conduct of educational research is its dissemination. Annotated bibliographies certainly expedite dissemination, and a number of these which have been published recently are reviewed. Among the best of these of a general nature is the collection of *Resúmenes Analíticos en Educación* (item **4350**); among the best of a topical nature is the regular feature of the quarterly UDUAL journal which lists publications on higher education in Latin America (item **4365**). The single best annotated bibliography of those reviewed is Londoño Benveniste's on Colombian education (item **4435**).

In this year's university-related literature, the history of the Latin American university predominates. Its treatment ranges from a general history of the earliest Latin American universities (item **4359**), to specific historical analyses of higher education in Bolivia (item **4391**), Colombia (items **4437–4438**), Cuba (item **4451**) and Peru (item **4534**), and university-specific historical accounts (items **4379, 4411, 4469–4470, 4488, 4498** and **4571**). Several books of essays covering a range of topics related to higher education also were reviewed. As a rule, these compilations contain one or more essays on the history of the Latin American university and such topics as university autonomy, the role and mission of the university, and the role of the university in development. Tünnerman's collections of essays (items **4360** and **4404**) are the best, while lack of focus detracts only slightly from the essays compiled by the Corporación de Promoción Universitaria (item **4364**).

The issue of university autonomy is again popular among researchers. Garibay's essay (item **4328**) compares the Latin American view of university autonomy with the US and European views. Levy's outstanding analyses on university autonomy in Mexican universities (items **4507, 4509–4510**) conclude that the Mexican university in general and the National Autonomous University (UNAM) in particular still enjoy considerable self-rule despite strong government control and in contrast to the loss of autonomy among universities in most Latin American countries. Good companion pieces include items **4303, 4327** and **4361**.

There are those who argue that the mission of the university should go beyond teaching and research, and that it should be more assertive in promoting social change and contributing to development. Osorio Paz (item **4472**), with specific reference to the University of San Carlos in Guatemala, notes the paradox of the university that both contributes to society's development and criticizes society's injustices. Similarly, Santos asserts that the National Autonomous University of Honduras ought to both plan the country's future and represent its conscience (item **4484**). Other publications that argue for a more assertive university role in development and social change include items **4334, 4340, 4396** and **4441**.

The literature on Latin America's underdevelopment in science and technology is more extensive than usual. The university is explicitly criticized for contributing to this relative state of underdevelopment (items **4342, 4366** and **4368**). It is also singled out as the ultimate solution to the problem, at least among Convenio Andrés Bello member universities. Lópes' analysis of Latin America's economic and political dependence on developed countries as the principal factor behind its underdevelopment in these areas is compelling (item **4337**), as is Sagasti's claim that Latin America's hostile political history is the principal factor (item **4351**).

Criticism of traditional education has been somewhat muted; only one critic, other than Illich (item **4331**), calls for the total elimination of traditional schools, at least in their present "capitalist" context (item **4320**). More typical of the criticism is Salamanca Trujillo's assertion (item **4394**) that schools deserve the ridicule and criticism they receive, but that they should be reformed rather than abolished. Moreover, he argues that societal change must precede effective school reform. He is joined in this argument by Pereira and Jara (item **4345**), who claim that traditional educational systems are not equal to demands for social change, calling for nonformal alternatives. Other alternatives, such as radio, TV, and other forms of educational technology are discussed in items **4305, 4354, 4380, 4425** and **4501**.

Literacy and vocational education continue to receive attention. Díaz Araújo's article (item **4318**) attempts to discredit Freire's philosophy on literacy. Illiteracy remains a pressing concern all over the continent, a fact well documented by items **4341** and **4344**. White's intriguing essay (item **4316**) suggests that an alternative in traditional power structures is a necessary condition for effective literacy training, an assertion substantially consistent with Freire's philosophy. Vocational and technical education programs in Latin America are well established; thus, with one exception, the literature is directed either toward describing them (items **4310** and **4372**) or assessing their effectiveness (items **4432, 4439–4440** and **4530**). The most recent vocational and technical education program is Peru's Basic Manual Education (EBL) program, promulgated by law in 1972, and designed to provide unschooled adults with general and job-related technical education (items **4538** and **4546**).

The issue of educational equity has received considerable attention in the literature. Schiefelbein and Farrell (item **4420**), in their study of equal educational opportunity in Chile, address the issue from the perspectives of access, survival, output and outcome. This study provides an excellent theoretical framework for other works reviewed. Whenever differences in access, survival, output and outcome are explained by ethnicity, residence, sex, socioeconomic status or other like factors, inequities exist. It is heartening to see the literature address these inequities.

The complexity of the issue of equal educational opportunity is addressed in several works. For example, Piñera (item **4414**) correctly asserts that educational policy objectives of equal educational opportunity and economic growth are frequently in conflict. Moreover, he and Selowsky (item **4346**) argue that if educational resources are distributed on any basis other than ability, misallocation is the consequence. Schiefelbein, on the other hand, argues that there is a need to distribute educational resources more equitably (item **4353**), and Fuentes Molinar asserts that expansion of educational opportunities has not benefitted those most in need (item **4494**). The debate heats up; we will await additional literature on the subject.

The literature on education and development is, as expected, fairly extensive. The role of education in development is the focus of the essays presented at the International Congress of Education in Mexico City (item **4322**), the United Nations CINDA project's final report (item **4312**), and the Economic Commission for the Latin America's document (item **4362**). The relationship between formal education and economic growth in the Commonwealth Caribbean and in Haiti is the focus of item **4398** and the relationship between nonformal education and economic productivity in Guatemala is the focus of item **4473**. Comparative studies on education and development are presented by items **4374** and **4445**.

Publications on educational planning (items **4338** and **4466**), on financing education (item **4357**), and on educational reforms (items **4493, 4495, 4499** and **4503**) appear, but not in the numbers anticipated. The article by McGinn, Schiefelbein, and Warwick (item **4338**), in which they assert that a rationalist approach to educational planning is doomed to failure, might explain this dearth. Guzmán's argument (item **4499**) that previous educational reforms in Mexico have been totally ineffective suggests a possible reason for the lack of attention to educational reforms.

Finally, there is the literature which does not lend itself to simple classification. Publications on timely topics such as working women (item **4387**), special education (item **4306**), and sex education (items **4301, 4317** and **4427**) are beginning to appear. Issues surrounding bilingualism are beginning to receive considerable attention (items **4357, 4539, 4544** and **4548**). The account by Larson, Davis and Ballena (item **4539**) of an extensive bilingual education experiment in the Amazon region of Peru is first rate, as is Riedmiller's participant observation study (item **4544**) of linguistic conditions in a Quechuan-speaking area of Peru.

The literature on education in Latin America continues to be abundant; what is especially heartening is the improvement in quality. Convincing empirical and logical arguments are much in evidence; data are vast and analysis is improving. Especially encouraging is that dissemination has improved considerably over the last decade. Unsubstantiated, opinionated, dogmatic "research" on Latin American education is finally on the decline.

LATIN AMERICA: GENERAL

4301 Actitudes y opiniones de alumnos y profesores frente a la sexualidad (Educación Hoy [Perspectivas Latinoamericanas, Bogotá] 8 : 47/48, sept./dic. 1978, p. 83–144, tables)

Assessment of students' and teachers' attitudes, opinions and values regarding human sexuality. Study focused on physiology and reproduction, sexual development, male-female roles, sex education and other areas. To begin to dispel sexual myths and prejudices, author recommends preschool and primary school sex education programs.

Asociación Panamericana de Instituciones de Crédito Educativo. Centro de Información y Documentación. Instituciones que ofrecen estudios de archivística y bibliotecología en Latinoamérica y el Caribe: directorio. See *HLAS 42: 119.*

4302 Barbin, Christina. Nuevas prioridades para la educación en América Latina (FH, 18:205, enero 1980, p. 45–48)

Report of UNESCO's Conference of Ministers of Education and of Economic Planning held in Mexico City in Dec. 1979. While recognizing significant growth in primary, secondary, and higher education in Latin America, especially during last two decades, conference delegates unanimous in pointing out what still is needed to be done. Illiteracy, repetition, desertion, and inequitable education opportunities are among the problem areas discussed.

4303 Berry, Albert G. Can autonomy be preserved?: governance and autonomy in institutions of higher education (*in* Development issues, Caribbean-American dialogue: proceedings and papers from the Caribbean-American exchange program conducted by the Phelps-Stokes Fund. New York: The Fund, 1980, p. 80–92, bibl., tables)

Essay addresses question of whether or not university autonomy can be maintained. Concludes that if one holds to the strict meaning of the term, university autonomy neither can be maintained nor should be maintained. Reports results of 1975–76 Tennessee study. Focus is not on the Latin American university; however, conclusions should be of interest to the Latin American university community.

4304 *Boletín Documental.* Universidad del Zulia, Facultad de Humanidades y Educación, Centro de Documentación e Investigación Pedagógica. No. 6, 1978–. Maracaibo, Venezuela.

Entries on a variety of educational issues compiled from Latin American and German-Spanish language journals and annotated by Dunia García de Rincón.

4305 Braun, Juan. Les écoles radiophoniques: une stratégie de développement latino-américaine. Port-au-Prince: Centre Education intégrée pour le développement rural, 1978. 33 p.; 1 leaf of plates: graph (Série Formation technique; no. 4)

This study explores the use of radio for education in some 16 countries of Latin America. Among the general conclusions drawn by Braun are that while radio is the principal means for transmitting information in this type of education, flyers, books, and mobile units are also used; that male and female students live primarily in rural areas, and range in age from 18 to 50; that funding can be from international foundations, the state, or self-generated, in that order; and that a wide variety of subjects is covered, with the duration of courses being from one to 10 months. [June Blanchard Brown]

4306 Bravo Valdivieso, Luis. El retardo mental en los países en desarrollo: problemas para el diagnóstico: trabajo presentado al IV Congreso Internacional de la Asociación para el Estudio Científico de la Deficiencia Mental, Washington, agosto 1976. Santiago: Universidad Católica de Chile, Escuela de Educación, 1976. 61 leaves; bibl.

Paper presented at 4th International Congress of the Association for the Scientific Study of Mental Deficiencies held in Washington, D.C., Aug. 1976. Author, a psychologist from the Catholic University of Chile, argues that intelligence tests used in developing societies are exported versions of instruments constructed in developed societies and that cultural differences render them invalid.

4307 Briones, Guillermo. Universidad y estructura social. Bogotá, Colombia: Ediciones Tercer Mundo, 1980. 116 p.: graph (Colección Ciencias sociales: Teorías y métodos)

Contains four sociological essays which focus on the university and social class in Latin America. Underlying theme is that the Latin American university, despite attempts at reform, remains what it has always been, an educational institution dedicated to teaching and research. First essay explores relationship between university education and occupational structure; the second looks at the university and social class structure; the third analyzes university reforms in light of science and technology; and the last looks at education's role in modernization and urbanization.

4308 Bueno, Gerardo. Ciencia y tecnología en el desarrollo económico de América Latina (NSO, 42, mayo/junio 1979, p. 61–69, plates)

Author explores stages of technological and scientific development in Latin America. Concludes that development in these areas is retarded because of region's economic development strategies and its long-standing humanist traditions. While recognizing renewed interest in science and technology, author regrets belated development.

4309 Castro, Claudio de Moura and **Jorge A. Sanguinetty.** Custos e determinantes da educação na América Latina. Rio de Janeiro: Instituto de Tecnologia Educacional, 1978. 94 p.; bibl.; tables (Estudos e pesquisas; 3)

Preliminary results of large-scale study involving 10 Latin American countries (Argentina, Bolivia, Brazil, Chile, Colombia, Ecuador, Mexico, Paraguay, Peru, Costa Rica) under coordination of Program ECIEL. Based on review of research literature related to determinants of educational performance and on costs and finance of education, project has incorporated adaptation of and administration of various measurement instruments to students, teachers, and school administrators. Promising example of cooperative research endeavor. [K.B. Fischer]

4310 ——; Darcy Costa; and Gaudêncio Frigotto. Financiamento da educação vocacional na América Latina (Forum Educacional [Fundação Getúlio Vargas, Instituto de Estudos Avançados em Educação, Rio de Janeiro] 1:2, abril/junio 1977, p. 33–70, tables)

Comparative study of national level vocational education programs in Latin America. Study focuses on a comparison of vocational education finance and administration among Latin American countries. Addresses also such disparate areas as students' social origins, desertion from vocational education programs, and cost/benefits.

4311 Centro Interamericano de Investigación y Documentación sobre Formación Profesional. Participación de las organizaciones de trabajadores en la formación profesional: proyecto 118. Montevideo: CINTERFOR, 1977. 217 p. (Informes CINTERFOR; no. 78)

Report on CINTERFOR's Project 118 meeting held in Mexico City in Aug. 1977. Project 118 of the Centro Interamericano de Investigación y Documentación sobre Formación Profesional (CINTERFOR), a division of la Organización de Trabajo (OIT), focuses on the role of workers' syndicates and unions regarding professional and technical training programs. Thirteen Latin American countries were represented by 46 delegates and seven observers. Report contains proceedings, daily meeting schedules, list of participants, session briefs, country reports, conference recommendations, and other relevant documents.

4312 Centro Interuniversitario de Desarrollo Andino. Universidad y sector productivo: políticas y mecanismos de vinculación: informe final. Santiago de Chile: Centro Interuniversitario de Desarrollo Andino, 1979. 351 p.; bibl. (Proyecto PNUD-UNESCO, CINDA)

Final report of the Centro Interuniversitario de Desarrollo Andino's (CINDA) project: Universidad Sector Productivo—Políticos y Mecanismos de Vinculación. Supported by the United Nations Development Program and by UNESCO, this project focused on the role of the university in the development and transfer of technology for social and economic development of the Andean region.

4313 Christiansen, Jens. Teaching on Latin America: the dependency perspective (PCCLAS/P, 5, 1976, p. 95–100)

Introduction to the literature on dependence and underdevelopment in Latin America. Written for teachers of Latin American courses.

4314 La Ciencia y la tecnología en América Latina (OAS/CI, 20:3/4, abril 1979, p. 29–41)

Report of OAS member nations' scientific and technological activities.

4315 La Ciencia y la tecnología en América Latina: esfuerzos nacionales en estos campos (OAS/CI, 20:1/2, enero 1979, p. 19–32)

A country-by-country list (OAS member countries) of programs and activities, and other general information of interest to the scientific and technological community. Conference proceedings, research reviews, legislative actions, future events are included.

Ciencia y Tecnología. Vol. 1, No. 1, 1977– See *HLAS* 42:209.

4316 Congreso Internacional de Educación, *Mexico, 1978.* Perspectivas de la educación en América Latina. México, D.F.: Centro de Estudios Educativos, 1979. 381 p.; bibl.; illus.

Selection of papers presented at the annual meeting of the Comparative and International Education Society, held in Mexico City in March 1978. Published by the Centro de Estudios Educativos, book includes selections based on interest of participants, on requests, and on unusual or unique approaches. In an interesting and well-developed paper on literacy and social development, Robert A. White argues that effective literacy will be achieved only after the traditional power structure of underdeveloped countries has been altered. While book has two specific sections (Educational Research Priorities and Indigenous and Rural Education), focus of papers is very diverse.

4317 Conocimientos en sexualidad humana de alumnos y profesores (Educación Hoy [Perspectivas Latinoamericanas, Bogotá] 8:48, sept./dic. 1978, p. 14–82, ill., tables)

Comprehensive assessment of knowledge about human sexuality. Students from pre-primary through university as well as teachers were included in the study which focused on three areas: anatomy and physiology of reproduction, sexual development, and sexual response. Author's major conclusion is that a child becomes increasingly illiterate with respect to human sexuality as he/she progresses through the formal education system.

4318 Díaz Araújo, Enrique. Paulo Freire: seudólogo de la pedagogía dialéctica (UNC/BCPS, 23, 1978, p. 45–89)

Attempt to discredit Paulo Freire. Extensive documentation of Freire's written and spoken inconsistencies, obscurities and contradictions. While documentation is in parts convincing, author's approach toward discrediting Freire is too personal.

4319 *La Educación.* Revista interamericana de desarrollo educativo. Organization of American States, Secretaría General, Departamento de Asuntos Educativos. Año 22, Nos. 78/80, 1978– . Washington.

Special issue devoted to the first 10 years of OAS's Regional Educational Development Program (Programa Regional de Desarrollo Educativo or PREDE). Fourteen articles describe PREDE's achievements in different regions and in different curricular areas.

4320 La Educación burguesa. Guillermo Labarca et al. México: Editorial Nueva Imagen, 1977. 341 p.; bibl. (Serie Educación)

Collection of essays which focuses on a Marxist interpretation of education and social class relationship. Among the dogma expounded are the following: schools are an instrument of the state; schools function only in the best interest of the ruling elite; schools are a capitalist tool; capitalist schools cannot be reformed, they must be destroyed.

4321 La Educación y desarrollo dependiente en América Latina. Compilador: Daniel A. Morales-Gómez. Autores: Iván Espinoza et al. México: Ediciones Gernika, 1979. 334 p.; bibl.; ill. (Colección Educación y sociología; 5)

Essays on a variety of educational topics loosely focusing on issue of development. Justice, editor argues, constitutes common focus of essays. This rather obscure focus, unfortunately, is lost on the reader; result is a disjointed collection of essays, some good, others not. Good discussion of education's limitation in effecting social and economic change contained in essay by Daniel A. Morales-Gómez.

4322 Educación y realidad socioeconómica. México, D.F.: Centro de Estudios Educativos, 1979. 562 p.; bibl.; ill.

Compilation of papers presented at the International Congress of Education held in Mexico City in March 1978. Written by scholars representing most Latin American countries, papers report on research conducted in areas of higher education, adult education, education and employment, and teaching materials and methodologies. Diverse in scope; unifying theme is the role of education in development.

4323 Elías, Víctor Jorge. El stock de educación en Latinoamérica (BCV/REL, 11:42, 1975, p. 135–163, bibl., tables)

Detailed explanation of two methods for estimating the return on investment in education: rate of return and cost/benefit. Author attempts to develop statistical models which could be applied to different Latin American countries.

4324 Fondo de las Naciones Unidas para la Infancia (UNICEF). Desarrollo y educación. Guatemala: Oficina de Area, 1979. 12 leaves; tables.

According to the UN's Declaration of the Rights of the Child, education is a basic right of all young children, and moreover, equal educational opportunity is a matter of justice. This essay, prepared by the Guatemalan Area Office of UNESCO, argues that Latin American countries have failed to meet the challenge of developing sufficient educational opportunities to begin to achieve these ends.

4325 Formación de la mujer en el mundo actual. Confederación Interamericana de Educación Católica (CIEC). Bogotá: Secretaría General de la CIEC, 1976. 124 p.; bibl.

Proceedings and conclusions of seminar on education and training for women organized by the Inter-American Federation of Catholic Education (CIEC). Traditional role of women contradicts Christian philosophy regarding personal dignity. Yet, Catholic education still trains women for traditional roles, and thus is inherently discriminatory. This argument was both raison d'être and focus of seminar. Report includes recommendations and essays.

4326 García Huidobro, J.E. and Jorge Ochoa. La investigación latinoamericana en educación y el sistema escolar (Educación Hoy [Perspectivas Latinoamericanas, Bogotá] 8:46, julio/agosto 1979, p. 35–48, tables)

Analysis of characteristics of 1000 research studies on Latin American education. Sample reveals that disproportionate number of studies focuses on higher education and that insufficient attention is paid to primary education.

4327 García Laguardia, Jorge Mario. La autonomía universitaria en América Latina: mito y realidad. México: Universidad Nacional Autónoma de México, 1977. 131 p.; bibl. (Comisión Técnica de Estudios y Proyectos Legislativos; 10)

Examination of legislation, regulations and decrees related to university autonomy in Latin America. Includes country-by-country analysis.

4328 Garibay, Luis. Autonomy and accountability in Latin America (in Higher education in the world community. Edited by Stephen Bailey. Washington: American Council on Education, 1977, p. 160–168)

Examines concept of university autonomy in Latin America. While recognizing country-by-country variations, author traces the development of Latin American university autonomy from the epoch of the "Salamancan influences" through the 1918 Córdoba Reform to the present. Compares Latin American notion of university autonomy to that of continental Europe, England and US. Argues that autonomy requires accountability and responsibility without undue external intervention.

4329 Hanke, Lewis. The early development of Latin American studies in the U.S.A. (in Studying Latin America: essays in honor of Preston E. James [see item **4358**] p. 103–120)

Delightful account of the development of Latin American studies in the US including a capsule history of the Handbook of Latin American Studies and the Hispanic Foundation of the Library of Congress. Originally published by the University of Texas Press in 1967, Hanke's focus is on developments during the 1930s, a period that he describes as "significant yet not well known."

4330 Herrera, Guillermina. La escuela como vehículo para el logro de un bilingüismo social estable (URL/ES, 14, oct. 1979, p. 27–39, bibl.)

Argument for bilingual schools in heterogeneous bilingual/multilingual societies. Reference is made to Guatemala as "typical" of many multilingual countries.

4331 Illich, Iván. Alternativas. Introduction by Erich Fromm. 2. ed. México: Editorial Joaquín Mortiz, 1977. 185 p.

Collection of Illich's deinstitutionalization essays which have been previously published. School, church, medicine, industry all subjects of deinstitutionalization theme.

4332 Kliksberg, Bernardo. Formación de administradores en América Latina: modelos metodológicos para la investigación. Caracas: Ediciones de la Biblioteca, Universidad Central de Venezuela, 1980. 138 p.; bibl. (Colección Temas; 78)

Author argues that public administration programs in Latin American universities fail to consider national needs. Curricula, programs, required readings, Kliksberg argues, are largely unrelated to complexities of governmental administration. Comprehensive planning model to improve universities' public administration programs included.

4333 Kreimer, Osvaldo. La investigación educativa en Latinoamérica y el PREDE: sumario y perspectivas (OAS/LE, 22:78/80, 1978, p. 155–190, bibl., tables)

Author cites the improvement in quantity and quality of educational research in Latin America during the past decade. Support given by international organizations (e.g., OAS, UNESCO) highlights the reasons behind this improvement. Discussion of the fundamental differences between basic and applied research is the high point of this unnecessarily long article.

4334 Latapí, Pablo. Universidad y cambio social: siete tesis reconstruccionistas (UUAL/U, 77, julio/sept. 1979, p. 696–709)

Argues for active and direct university role in social change without the university's jeopardizing its traditional intellectual functions.

4335 The Latin American university. Edited by Joseph Maier and Richard W. Weatherhead. Albuquerque: University of New Mexico Press, 1979. 237 p.; bibl.; index.

Series of essays by different scholars who look at the Latin American university from a variety of viewpoints. In the introductory chapter, editors provide an excellent overview of the Latin American university. Especially noteworthy is discussion of the unforeseen consequences of the 1918 Córdoba Reform. For historian's comment, see *HLAS 42:1794.*

Llinas Alvarez, Edgar. La educación y el proceso integrador de América Latina. See *HLAS 42:1793.*

4337 Lopes, J. Leite. Science and the making of society in Latin America (AI/I, 5:3, May/June 1980, p. 159–165, bibl.)

Arguing that economic and political dependence of Latin American countries precluded the growth of science, author proposes development of science and technology based on a consideration of social, economic and political consequences.

4338 McGinn, Noel; Ernesto Schiefelbein; and **Donald P. Warwick.** Educational planning as political process: two case studies from Latin America (CES/CER, 23:2, June 1979, p. 218–239)

International donor agencies, as a rule, require "plans" of grantees as a prerequisite to receiving assistance. Moreover, developing a plan requires a "rationalist approach" to problems of education and development, replete with copious data and free from emotional considerations. Citing instances in Chile and El Salvador, authors argue that this kind of rationalist approach to educational planning is doomed to failure.

Mesa-Lago, Carmelo. Latin American studies in Europe. See *HLAS 42:153.*

New directions in language and area studies: priorities for the 1980's. See *HLAS 42:189.*

4339 Nixon, Raymond B. La enseñanza del periodismo en América Latina (CYC, 2, jan. 1978, p. 197–212, bibl., table)

Describes the state of the art of teaching journalism and communication in Latin America and suggests recommendations for improvement. Highlights contribution of the Centro Internacional de Estudios Superiores de Periodismo para América Latina (CIESPAL), one of four UNESCO-sponsored regional journalism centers in the world, toward professionalizing journalism and communication. Calls for more cooperation among Latin American institutions in improving the quality of journalism and communication.

4340 Novoa Monreal, Eduardo. La universidad latinoamericana y el problema social. México: Universidad Nacional Autónoma de México, 1978. 92 p.; bibl.

Provocative argument on the critical need for the Latin American university to strengthen its traditional research and teaching functions and, in addition, to assume the role of society's conscience. This role, author argues, is particularly pressing in light of injustices and inequities engendered by social and economic crises which confront most Latin American countries.

4341 Organización de los Estados Americanos. Departamento de Asuntos Educativos. Unidad de Planeamiento. Los déficits educativos en América Latina. v. 1, Atlas del analfabetismo y población sin instrucción de los países de América Central, América del Sur y México. Washington: 1979. 191 p.; bibl.; maps; tables (Serie atlas; 1. Colección de Monografías y estudios de la educación)

Compilation of tables which summarizes illiteracy (children 10 years old and older) and school attendance rates (children five years old to 14 years old) for South and Central American countries (including Mexico). Prepared by the Regional Educational Development Program (PREDE) of the Organization of American States.

4342 ———. Secretaría General. Departamento de Asuntos Científicos. Programa Regional de Desarrollo Científico y Tecnológico. Aspectos organizacionales de la política científica y tecnológica en América Latina: situación y perspectivas del proyecto multinacional. Washington: 1979. 66 p.; table (Estudios sobre el desarrollo científico y tecnológico; 35)

Progress report on OAS's project sponsored by its Regional Scientific and Technological Development Program. The project—"Aspectos Organizacionales de la Política Científica y Tecnológica en América Latina"—stemmed from OAS's concern over relative underdevelopment in science and technology among Latin American countries.

4343 Organización Internacional del Trabajo. Programa Mundial del Empleo. Programa Regional del Empleo para América Latina y el Caribe (PREALC). Empleo, educación y estilos de desarrollo rural. Santiago: 1976. 16 p.; tables (PREALC/98)

Essay of Oficina Internacional de Trabajo (OIT) on education and rural development. Author concludes that in order for campesinos to contribute to rural development, heavy emphasis on technical assistance is required. Formal higher education (e.g., at agricultural universities) would be too costly in the short term.

4344 Padua, Jorge. El analfabetismo en América Latina: un estudio empírico con especial referencia a los casos de Perú, México y Argentina. México: El Colegio de México, 1979. 192 p.; bibl.; maps (Jornadas—El Colegio de México; 84)

After 150 years of political discourse on the subject and 100 years since most Latin American countries enacted compulsory schooling legislation, the rate of illiteracy in most Latin American countries still exceeds 30 percent of the population over 15 years of age. Padua analyzes illiteracy rates by country and by region, and examines factors behind these differences. Mexico, Argentina, and Peru are analyzed in depth. Excellent data-based study.

4345 Pereira López, Manuel and José Eduardo Jara Vigueras. Educación no formal y extrema pobreza (Pensamiento y Acción [Editora Lautaro, Santiago] 8:23, 1978, p. 73–100)

Asserts traditional educational systems unequal to the demands for economic, social, political and cultural change in Latin America. Suggests consideration of nonformal alternatives and use of communication technology by educational planners and policymakers. Planning process is described.

4346 Piñera, Sebastián and Marcelo Selowsky. El costo económico del desperdicio de cerebros (UCC/CE, 15:46, dic. 1978, p. 349–405, bibl., tables)

Explores relationship between preschool ability and education. Authors attempt to demonstrate that when factors other than ability enter into the education selection process, a misallocation of educational resources results. The consequence is "internal brain drain"—capable children receiving less than optimal education—a phenomenon detrimental to high labor productivity. Replete with complex mathematical models and statistical formulas.

4347 Posada R., Enrique. La docencia como aprendizaje e investigación (UPB, 35:124, julio 1979, p. 33–37, plates)

An attempt to assuage the feelings of inadequacy felt by many young faculty, and in this way to stem the tide of those who leave teaching for other professions. Analyzes reasons behind faculty feelings of inadequacy and suggests measures to overcome them.

4348 Programa Regional del Empleo para América Latina y el Caribe. Educación y empleo en América Latina. Santiago: Oficina Internacional del Trabajo, Programa Regional del Empleo para América Latina y el Caribe, 1978. 41 p. (Investigaciones sobre empleo; 10)

One of a series of essays on different aspects of work and employment in Latin America. Series is published by the Programa Regional del Empleo para América Latina de la Oficina Internacional de Trabajo. Schiefelbein's essay reviews research and literature on education and employment in Latin America. Moral issues and diversity of Latin American countries, according to author, confound the relationship.

4349 Puiggrós, Adriana. La fragmentación de la pedagogía y los problemas educativos latinoamericanos (Thesis [Nueva revista de filosofía y letras, Universidad Nacional Autónoma de México, México] 2 : 5, abril 1980, p. 29–41, plates)

Author examines manner in which teacher training institutions conceptualize educational issues. Concludes that the institutions unnecessarily fragment issues, and that distortions, misunderstandings, and knowledge gaps result.

4350 *Resúmenes Analíticos en Educación.* Centro de Investigación y Desarrollo de la Educación. No. 1, oct. 1972 [through] No. 1809, enero/junio 1980–. Santiago.

Publication of the Centro de Investigación y Desarrollo de la Educación (CIDE), located in Santiago, first published in 1972. Consists of abstracts of key research studies on Latin American and Caribbean education. Topics include: non-formal education; teacher training ; primary, adult and higher education; politics of education; educational innovations; etc. A cumulative index for entries No. 1 through No. 1364 (1972–79) is available.

4351 Sagasti, Francisco. Esbozo histórico de la ciencia y la tecnología en América Latina (Esboço histórico da ciência e da tecnologia na América Latina) (AI/I, 3 : 6, nov./dic. 1978, p. 351–359, bibl.)

A political history hostile to dynamic interaction between pure science and applied technology is the principal reason for Latin America's scientific and technological underdevelopment. Development of a scientific and technological capacity in certain areas is still possible if one understands and takes into consideration the historical factors which have impeded development.

4352 Schiefelbein, Ernesto. Educational research networks in Latin America (UNESCO/IRE, 24 : 4, 1978, p. 483–500, tables)

Reports on the growth of quality Latin American educational research over the last 10 years. Recognizes that while diffusion of research has improved, financial constraints and inadequate communication have been a hindrance. Suggestions for improvements are made.

4353 ———. Gasto público y políticas educacionales y de desarrollo cultural para los sectores más pobres (Pensamiento y Acción [Editora Lautaro, Santiago] 8 : 23, 1978, p. 35–54)

Suggests need to consider more equitable distribution of educational resources so as to benefit all sectors of Latin American society rather than the culturally elite exclusively. Moreover, insists on the need for recognition and acceptance of cultural norms other than those of country's dominant culture. Current inequitable educational expenditures and the reality of cultural pluralism are the reasons cited.

4354 Schmelkes, Silvia. Contribución de la investigación al desarrollo de los procesos de teleducación de adultos en América Latina (CEE/RL, 9 : 3, 1979, p. 150–157)

Author argues that despite the high penetration of radio as an educational medium in Latin America's rural areas, many questions remain regarding both its effectiveness and its efficiency. Notes the paucity of research by Latin Americans in this area, citing that 70 percent research articles are in English and are geared to foreign audiences.

4355 Schnelle, Kurt. Problemas ideológicos del movimiento universitario en América Latina (BRP, 9 : 2, 1970, p. 246–252)

Analysis of leftist thinkers' contributions to 20th-century university reform movement in Latin America. Concludes that this movement is difficult to characterize because of the multiplicity of influences which have been brought to bear on the university.

4356 Secretaría Ejecutiva Permanente del Convenio Andrés Bello. Manual de organización y administración universitaria en ciencia y tecnología en la región andina. Bogotá, Colombia: La Secretaría, 1980. 118 p. (Serie Ciencia y tecnología; no. 1)

Argument and rationale for emphasizing science and technology among Convenio Andrés Bello member universities; discussion of political, organizational and functional factors which affect member universities' development of science and technology; and flexible model requiring minimal investment for developing member universities' science and technology programs.

4357 Seminario sobre Financiamiento de la Educación en América Latina, *1st, Washingon, D.C., 1976.* Financiamiento de la educación en América Latina. Compiladores, Mario Brodersohn y María Ester Sanjurjo. México: Fondo de Cultura Económica, Banco Interamericano de Desarrollo, 1978. 654 p.; bibl.; ill.; index (Sección de obras de economía)

Complete report, including all papers and documents presented, of an Inter-American Development Bank-sponsored seminar on financing of education in Latin America. Seminar held in Washington, D.C., Nov. 1976. Specialists representing many Latin American countries, international monetary and assistance organizations, foundations and universities were represented.

4358 Studying Latin America: essays in honor of Preston E. James. Edited by David J. Robinson. Ann Arbor, Mich.: Published for Dept. of Geography, Syracuse University, by University Microfilms International, 1980. 273 p.: ill.; index (Dellplain Latin American studies; 4. Monograph publishing: Sponsor series)

It is undeniably true, as David J. Robinson writes in the first of a collection of essays, "On Preston E. James and Latin America: A Biographical Sketch," "James has been a master craftsman of his profession, and Latin Americanists will be hard pressed in the future to find an equal." Among the volume's contributors are three former students. Additional contributors include Lewis Hanke, the "dean of Latin American historians," (see item **4329**) and Harold A. Wood, President, Geography Commission, Pan American Institute of Geography.

Tomé, Martha. EL PREDE y las bibliotecas escolares y universitarias. See *HLAS 42:89.*

4359 Traboulay, David M. The Church and the university in colonial Latin America (ZMR, 63:4, Okt. 1979, p. 283–294)

Author argues that the missionary orders—Dominicans, Franciscans, Augustinians and Jesuits—were in forefront of struggle against colonial cruelty and avarice. Raison d'être for earliest Latin American universities was missionaries' conviction that higher education could redirect New World toward "greater humanity" and "Christian ideals." Describes history and curricula of these early Latin American universities. For historian's comment, see *HLAS 42:1884.*

4360 Tünnermann Bernheim, Carlos. De la universidad y su problemática: diez ensayos. México: Universidad Nacional Autónoma de México: Unión de Universidades de América Latina, 1980. 196 p.; bibl.

In 10 essays written over a 10-year period (1969–79) author examines the role, the mission, and the problems which confront the Latin American university. The focus of the essays ranges from a very general treatment of the subject to a much more concentrated analysis of a particular issue (e.g., the problem of educational planning at the Universidad Nacional Autónoma de México).

4361 ——. Sesenta años de la reforma universitaria de Córdoba, 1918–1978. Ciudad Universitaria Rodrigo Facio: Editorial Universitaria Centroamericana, 1978. 103 p.; bibl. (Colección Añil)

Comprehensive examination of the Córdoba Reform of 1918. While acknowledging that the Córdoba Reform represents the single most important event in the history of the Latin American university, author recognizes its limitations. Specifically, Tünnermann argues that the reform succeeded in totally restructuring the system of university governance thus democratizing it, but that it failed to engender substantive academic and curricular changes.

4362 United Nations. Economic Commission for Latin America. Structure and dynamics of development in Latin America and the Caribbean and their implications for education. New York: The Commission, 1979. 72 p.; bibl. (Document—United Nations Educational, Scientific and Cultural Organization; ED-79/MINEDLAC/REF.1. Document—United Nations; E/CEPAL/L.208)

Prepared by the United Nation's Economic Commission for Latin America for presentation to the Regional Conference of Ministers of Education and for Economic Planning held in Mexico City in Dec. 1979. Analyzes issues related to economic growth and social development from a variety of perspectives including rural development, urbanization, education and income distribution.

4363 ———. **Educational, Scientific and Cultural Organization. Oficina Regional de Educación para América Latina y el Caribe.** Evolución reciente de la educación en América Latina: un estudio de la Oficina Regional de Educación de la UNESCO para América Latina y el Caribe, publicado con autorización de la UNESCO, París. t. 3, Análisis regional: Argentina, Barbados, Bolivia, Brazil. México: Secretaría de Educación Pública, 1977. 1 v.; bibl. (SepSetentas; 232)

Compendium of educational information prepared by UNESCO's Regional Education Office for Latin America and the Caribbean. Vol. 3 consists of educational profiles for Argentina, Barbados, Bolivia and Brazil. Well-organized, useful source.

4364 La Universidad latinoamericana: visión de una década. Editores: Patricio Dooner, Iván Lavados. Santiago, Chile: Corporación de Promoción Universitaria, 1979. 666 p.; bibl.

Published by the Corporación de Promoción Universitaria (CPU), consists of a series of 28 previously published essays about the Latin American university. Far ranging and broad essays focus on the 10-year period 1969–79 and are organized in four parts: 1) essays on theoretical and methodological concerns (e.g., the typology of Latin American universities); 2) essays compare Latin American universities; 3) essays are case studies; and 4) essays address science and technology and the Latin American university.

4365 *Universidades.* Unión de Universidades de América Latina. Año 18, No. 73, Serie 2, julio/sept. 1978 [through] Año 19, No. 78, Serie 2, oct./dic. 1979–. México.

Quarterly journal of UDAL. Regular features of the journal include: summary of activities of UDAL and of its member universities; annotated list of recent publications on Latin American higher education; etc. Issue No. 73 (julio/sept. 1978), for example, features essay by Pablo Latapí "Algunas Tendencias de las Universidades Latinoamericanas" which analyzes issues of interest to UDAL: educational access and employment; scientific and teacher training. Issue No. 75 (enero/marzo 1979) features a provocative essay by Carlos Tünnermann Bernheim which argues that an increase in university enrollments implies neither democratization of higher education nor increased opportunities for the lower classes. Issue No. 78 (oct./dic. 1979) describes the first 30 years of UDAL.

4366 Vargas, José Israel. El desarrollo de la ciencia y de la tecnología (UAG/D, 6:6, nov./dic. 1978, p. 47–61)

Author explores relationship between science and technology vis-à-vis the university. Concludes that in order for universities to provide adequate training in technical fields, a closer relationship between universities and industry is needed and more resources are necessary.

4367 Verner, Joel G. Socioeconomic environment, political system, and educational policy outcomes: a comparative analysis of 102 countries (CUNY/CP, 11:2, Jan. 1979, p. 165–188, tables)

Reports on a 1964–65 study exploring relationship between politics and educational policy in 102 developing countries in Asia, Africa, Latin America, and the Middle East. Finds level of socioeconomic development to be more important than political system variables as determinant of educational policy.

4368 Witker V., Jorge. Universidad y dependencia científica y tecnológica en América Latina. México: Universidad Nacional Autónoma de México, 1976. 87 p.; bibl. (Comision Técnica de Estudios y Proyectos Legislativos; 5)

Author considers reasons for Latin American dependence on developed nations for science and technology. Argues that their growth has been retarded by inappropriate and unplanned training, explained in part by the universities' protected position in society. Suggests regional-level cooperation and integration for planning purposes among universities, industries, and governments as a means toward scientific and technological independence.

ARGENTINA

4369 Aguerrondo, Inés. El centralismo en la educación primaria argentina. Buenos Aires: Centro de Investigaciones Educativas, 1976. 64 p.; bibl. (Cuadernos Centro de Investigaciones Educativas; no. 15)

In-depth analysis of Argentine laws which centralize national system of education: Laws No. 1420 of 1883; No. 2737 of 1890; and No. 4874 of 1905.

4370 Argumedo, Manuel. Perfeccionamiento y sistema educativo en Argentina. Buenos Aires: Centro de Investigaciones Educativas, 1979. 43 p.; bibl. (Serie Artículos del Centro de Investigaciones Educativas; no. 6. Cuadernos—Centro de Investigaciones Educativas)

In a study which looks at all facets of in-service teacher training in Argentina from 1970 to 1974—programs, institutions, laws and regulations—author concludes that efforts are ad hoc, sporadic and unplanned. In-service teacher training, author continues, is not an important component of the teaching profession in Argentina.

4371 Blum, Sigwart. Ayax Barnes: audiovisual programmes for Argentina's primary and elementary schools (Graphis [International journal of graphic art and applied art. The Graphis Press, Zürich] 33:192, 1977/1978, p. 358–363, colored plates, plates)

Describes OMAVA (Organización de Medio Audiovisuales Aplicados), an organization based in Buenos Aires to develop audio-visual materials for primary schools and to promote their use. Well-known Argentine authors and artists produce materials. Illustrations.

4372 CINTERFOR-SENAI Proyecto 046: métodos de enseñanza en la formación profesional, Rio de Janeiro, 5–9 de junio de 1978. Montevideo: Oficina Internacional de Trabajo, Centro Interamericano de Investigación y Documentación sobre Formación Profesional, 1979. 2 v.: ill. (Informes—C.I.N.T.E.R.F.O.R.; no. 90)

Proceedings of conference on technical education held in Rio de Janeiro in June 1978. Conference sponsored by CINTERFOR (Uruguay) and by SENAI (Argentina). National technical training centers from the following countries and international organizations were represented: Argentina, Bolivia, Brazil, Colombia, Costa Rica, Chile, Guatemala, Mexico, Paraguay, Uruguay, Venezuela, Interamerican Development Bank (BID), Food and Agriculture Organization (FAO), Organization of American States (OAS, and the Organización Internacional de Trabajo (OIT). The papers on teaching methodologies prepared by the representatives are useful for both practitioners and planners.

4373 Córdoba, Argentine Republic. Universidad Nacional. La. U.N.C. en cifras. Córdoba, UNC, 1978. 34 p.: ill.

Statistical profile of the National University of Córdoba (UNC) during 1972–77.

4374 Galvani Foresi, Victoria. La crisis de la educación institucionalizada en las sociedades nacionales: los casos de España y Argentina (CH, 342, dic. 1978, p. 529–545)

From an Argentine and Spanish perspective, article discusses the dual role of educators in transmitting cultural norms and conducting manpower-training. Author argues that economic growth and industrialization since mid-century have created manpower demands which neither country's educational system has been able to meet.

4375 Guía de investigaciones en curso en la Universidad de Buenos Aires. Buenos Aires: Instituto Bibliotecológico, Registro de Investigaciones, 1976. 1 v.

Annotated entries which describe research in progress as of 1976 at the Universidad de Buenos Aires. Research listed by department and indexed by theme and by author.

4376 Jornadas de Investigación Educativa, 5th, 1979? V [i.e. Quinta] Jornadas de Investigaciones Educativas. Buenos Aires: Centro de Investigaciones Educativas, 1979. 130 p.; bibl. (Cuadernos—Centro de Investigaciones Educativas; no. 28)

Prepared for the Fifth Jornadas de Investigación Educativa of the Centro de Investigaciones Educativas, Buenos Aires. Contains three high-quality articles with responses addressing the role of applied educational research: 1) Petty examines role of educational research in development; 2) Rigal looks at problem of compartmentalizing educational research; and 3) Tasso assesses the state of research on educational achievement.

Little, Cynthia Jeffress. Education, philanthropy, and feminism: components of Argentine womanhood, 1860–1926. See *HLAS 42:3377.*

4377 Manganiello, Ethel M. Historia de la educación argentina: periodización general. Buenos Aires: Librería del Colegio, 1980. 223 p.; bibl.

Historical analysis of Argentine education by its historical periods or "generations." Author presents case for this epochal or generational approach to analyzing Argentine educational history and then applies this approach to the 19th and 20th centuries.

4378 Penchansky, Mónica and **Alejandra Eidelberg.** La expresión corporal en la escuela primaria; un recurso didáctico. Fotografías, Andy Goldstein. Buenos Aires: Editorial Plus Ultra, 1980. 94 p.; bibl.; ill. (Biblioteca pedagógica; 4)

Attempts to outline both theoretical principles for emphasizing body movement activities in elementary schools and practical suggestions on specific activities to include in the educational program. Well-organized, useful text for elementary school teachers.

4379 Pérez, Daniel E. La Universidad de Tandil: historia de un esfuerzo. Buenos Aires: Grafitan, 1976. 137 p.; ill.

History of the University of Tandil. An interesting account of a Pampean community supporting the establishment of a university, a dream officially realized on 5 June 1964, when classes commenced in a rented building.

Pyenson, Lewis. The incomplete transmission of a European image: physics at greater Buenos Aires and Montreal, 1890–1920. See *HLAS 42:3408.*

4380 La Radio y la televisión al servicio de la educación. Buenos Aires: Fundación E. Navarro Viola y María F. Ayarragaray de Navarro Viola, 1978. 306 p.; 4 leaves of plates: graphs.

Contains four 1977 prize-winning essays which address the topic "Radio and Television in Service to (Argentine) Education" selected by the Enrique Navarro Viola and María Francisca Ayarragaray de Navarro Viola Foundation, Buenos Aires. Consensus

among essayists was that a vast untapped potential exists for utilization of radio and TV for educational purposes.

Rosa Olmos, Ramón. José Angelini Carafa: un educador olvidado. See *HLAS 42:3416.*

4381 Rotblat de Schapira, Martha B. Situaciones negativas en escuelas primarias: lo que dicen docentes argentinos (OAS/LE, 23:81, 1979, p. 115–133, tables)

Examining factors which contribute to school desertion, author concludes that lack of family interest is single most important cause. Factors external to the school clearly outweigh internal factors in contributing to desertion. Well-designed, well-controlled study gives added credence to results. Well-worth reading.

4382 Sábato, Jorge A. Ensayos en campera. Buenos Aires: Juárez, 1979. 175 p.

Collection of magazine articles and conference papers by a well-known Argentine physicist written during the 1970s. He emphasizes the need for more public sector support for basic research in countries like Argentina in order to reduce dependence on imported technology. [G. Wynia]

4383 Salonia, Antonio; Ricardo Guardo; Ricardo P. Bruera; and Carlos Burundarena. La educación en la República Argentina (IAEERI/E, 60, sept./dic. 1979, p. 47–104)

Verbatim account of round table discussion which focused on contemporary Argentine education. Organized by the Argentine Institute for Strategic Studies and International Relations. Panelists included leading Argentine educators as well as the National Minister of Culture and Education. Function of education, brain drain, and education and nationalism were among the questions addressed.

4384 Sánchez Guerra, José. Radiografía de una experiencia educativa. Buenos Aires: Centro de Investigaciones Educativas, between 1972 and 1977. 66 p.

Examination of Presidential and Ministerial Decree No. 4043/60 of April 1960, which authorized academic secondary schools to emphasize arts and sciences (Bacherillato en Ciencias y Letras). Pointing out that not one public school had been created under this decree, author concludes that such schools are not economical and are elitist.

4385 **Tedesco, Juan Carlos.** La crisis de la hegemonía oligárquica y el sistema educativo argentino, 1930–1945 (UPN/RCE, 4, 1979, p. 53–84, tables)

The hegemony of the agrarian oligarchy in Argentina was broken by the massive economic dislocations of the 1930s. Article discusses the consequences on Argentine education of the oligarchy's demise and of a totally restructured economic and political system, to wit: the imposition of dogma in religious and moral areas in lieu of strict ideological neutrality.

4386 **Velloso, Jacques R.** Antecedentes socio-económicos y rendimientos escolar en Argentina (CEE/Rl, 9:2, 1979, p. 39–76, bibl., tables)

Explores relationship between reading and math achievement and demographic variables among public and private primary and secondary students in Buenos Aires. Socioeconomic class of students is only variable which demonstrated consistent and significant effect upon achievement for all grades and subjects. Questions efficacy of schools as socioeconomic equalizer.

4387 **Wainerman, Catalina H.** Educación, familia y participación económica femenina en la Argentina (IDES/DE, 18:72, enero/mazo 1979, p. 511–537, bibl., tables)

Using 1979 census data, author studied characteristics of working women in Argentina. Results show that working women are more likely to be better educated, to be single, and to have fewer children than non-working women. Suggests that Argentine society would benefit by encouraging married women, with or without children, to enter work force.

BELIZE

4388 **Bennett, Joseph A.** Goals, priorities, and the decolonization of education in Belize (BISRA/BS, 7:5, Sept. 1979, p. 18–23)

Article (first given as a talk to a group of US students) discusses decolonization of education in Belize. While recognizing the strength of the legacy of colonial educational policy on the current education system and the positive aspects of this policy, author underscores needs of Belizeans to make their own educational plans and to set their own goals and priorities.

4389 **Giles, T.E.** and **T.J. Palacio.** Problems in teacher education in Belize (UPR/CS, 16:3/4, Oct. 1976/Jan. 1977, p. 207–216)

Report on a study to identify teacher education problems in Belize and to suggest strategies to deal with those problems. Study was based largely on questionnaire responses from Belize Teachers College faculty, staff and students.

BOLIVIA

4390 **Antología pedagógica de Bolivia.** Selección de Mariano Baptista Gumucio. La Paz, Bolivia: Editorial Los Amigos del Libro, 1979. 277 p. (Enciclopedia boliviana)

Collection of articles by a variety of authors including Simon Bolívar's tutor, Simón Rodríguez (1771 to 1854); Ivan Illich, who in a speech before the Congreso Pedagógico Nacional, La Paz, Bolivia, 1970, took his deschooling theme to Bolivian teachers; and the volume's editor, Mariano Baptista Gumucio, formerly Bolivia's Minister of Education. Common theme of diverse topics is critical posture toward all levels of education.

4391 **Bonifaz Ponce, Miguel.** La universidad en Bolivia: estudio crítico. La Paz: s.n., 1975. 57 p.; bibl.

In two parts: 1) traces history of the Bolivian university from its colonial beginnings (la Universidad de Real Audiencia de Charcas, 1694) to present; and 2) analyzes the contemporary Bolivian university. Author argues that the Bolivian university must both guide and contribute to the country's development.

4392 **Guzmán de Rojas, Iván.** El niño vs. [i.e. versus] el número. La Paz, Bolivia: Biblioteca Popular Boliviana de Ultima Hora, 1979. 158 p.: ill.

In 12 essays, author calls for total reform of mathematics curricula and teaching methodologies in primary schools. Written in recognition of the United Nations' International Year of the Child. Guzmán de Rojas calls traditional methods totally inappropriate because they emphasize obsolete topics and the "new mathematics," a recognized curricular failure.

4393 **Pilone, Jorge** and **Wilson Blacutt.** La situación educativa en Bolivia a través de la información censal de 1976. La Paz: República de Bolivia, Ministerio de Planeamiento y Coordinación, Instituto Nacional de Estadística, Departamento de Estadísticas Sociales, 1979. 31 p.: graphs.

Prepared by Bolivia's Instituto Nacional de Estadística and based on 1950 and 1976 census data. Consists of detailed data on education at all levels. Specific focus is on growth from 1950 to 1976. Good analysis.

4394 Salamanca Trujillo, Daniel. Liberación nacional y escuela Boliviana. La Paz, Bolivia: Empresa Gráfica Visión, 1979. 246 p.; bibl.; ill.

Wide-ranging exposition of author's views on schooling. Critical in tone, (indeed, author describes in detail deschooling philosophy of Illich, Reimer, et al., in the context of Bolivian education), he nonetheless rejects abolition of schools in favor of school reform. Schools reflect society, he argues; thus, societal change must precede school reform.

4395 Seminario de Planeamiento de la Educación Formal de la Iglesia en Bolivia, *Coroico, Bolivia, 1976.* Informe final. La Paz: Asociación Boliviana de Educación Católica: Secretariado Nacional de la Comisión Episcopal de Educación, 1977. 62 p.

Proceedings of the Seminario de Planeamiento de la Educación Formal de la Iglesia en Bolivia held in Coroico, Bolivia, Sept. 1976. Precipitated by the crisis of priests and nuns forsaking their educational mission, the seminar addressed such vital issues as the Church's educational mission, its educational objectives and priorities, and Church school finance.

4396 *Temas en la Crisis.* Año 1, No. 3, julio 1978– . La Paz.

New Bolivian serial. This issue contains a summary of eight responses by either professional or student, currently or at one time actively involved in Bolivian university affairs, to five questions on the role of the university in Bolivian society. Role of university in Bolivian development and proliferation of Bolivian universities among areas discussed. University rectors, professionals, students among those surveyed.

THE CARIBBEAN and THE GUIANAS: GENERAL

4397 Alleyne, Michael H. The PREDE in the English-speaking Caribbean (OAS/LE, 22:78/80, 1978, p. 33–44, tables)

Article addresses the special educational needs of Caribbean English-speaking nations in the Organization of American States. Describes modest but significant grant from OAS's Regional Educational Development Program (PREDE) to Trinidad-Tobago for in-service training of unqualified school teachers. Author contends if PREDE is to develop into a truly effective regional program, it must address the special educational needs of the recently admitted English-speaking Caribbean nations.

4398 Jones-Hendrickson, S.B. The role of education in the economic transformation of the state of St. Kitts-Nevis-Anguilla, 1950–1969 (UPR/CS, 14:4, Jan. 1975, p. 89–107, tables)

Explores, both theoretically and empirically, relationship between education and economic growth in the State of St. Kitts-Nevis-Anguilla (SKNA), Commonwealth Caribbean, from 1950 to 1969. While recognizing serious data limitations and allowing that the study is only exploratory, statistical relationship between education and economic growth confirmed only beyond the primary school years.

4399 Keller, Carol. Educational perspectives in the Caribbean (OAS/LE, 23:81, 1979, p. 103–114, bibl.)

Considers three issues as they related to education in the Caribbean countries: education and development, education and work, and international organizations and Caribbean education. Vague, disjointed arguments detract from author's well-meaning attempts to improve teacher training and educational research in the Caribbean.

4400 Organización de los Estados Americanos. Departamento de Asuntos Educativos. Unidad de Planeamiento.
Investigación y Estudios de la Educación. Los deficits educativos en el Caribe: atlas del analfabetismo y de la población sin instrucción de los países del Caribe. Washington: 1979. 128 p.; maps; tables.

Report on study carried out by Dept.

of Educational Affairs of the OAS. Data are broken down by OAS Caribbean members country (plus Guyana which has the status of observer) and consist of two categories: illiteracy rate among population aged 10 and over and population aged 5 to 24 out of school. Includes maps, charts, graphs.

4401 Select bibliography of education in the Commonwealth Caribbean, 1940–1975. Compiled by Amy Robertson, Hazel Bennett, Janette White. Mona, Jamaica: Documentation Centre, School of Education, University of the West Indies, 1976. 196 p.; index.

Bibliographic entries of reports and documents which describe educational systems of Commonwealth Caribbean or which relate to educational topics relevant to these countries. Majority of entries are unpublished or otherwise scarce reports, and access information is included. Major detraction from otherwise useful source is lack of annotations.

4402 Shorey, Leonard L. Problems and issues in Caribbean education (*in* Development issues, Caribbean-American dialogue: proceedings and papers from the Caribbean-American exchange program conducted by the Phelps-Stokes Fund. New York: The Fund, 1980, p. 67–72)

Very general discussion of major problems which confront primary, secondary, and university level education in the English-speaking islands, Belize, and Guyana.

CENTRAL AMERICA

4403 Hernández F. de Jaén, Mireya. Formación profesional de los catedráticos de historia y de geografía (SGHG/A, 47:1/, enero/dic. 1974, p. 131–140, bibl., tables)

Presented at the Congreso Centroamericano de Historia y de Geografía. Author examines obstacles to effective university level teaching and points out the need for well-defined policy for training professors of geography and history.

4404 Pensamiento universitario centroamericano. Carlos Tünnermann B., editor. Ciudad Universitaria Rodrigo Facio, Costa Rica: Editorial Universitaria Centroamericana, 1980. 521 p.; bibl. (Colección Aula)

Comprehensive collection of essays about contemporary higher education in Central America. In eight sections: 1) history of Central American higher education; 2) relationship between the university and society; 3) philosophical essays on the ends of higher education; 4) university autonomy in general, and more specifically, the Confederación Universitaria Centroamericana (CSUCA); 5) university reform; 6) teaching and research; 7) university integration; and 8) student movements. This book, which is dedicated to the Universidad de San Carlos, Guatemala, the oldest university in Central America, is a must for scholars interested in Latin American higher education.

4405 Seminario Latinoamericano sobre Nuevas Interrelaciones Educativas, *Santa Bárbara, Costa Rica, 1975.* Nuevas experiencias pedagógicas en América Central. Francisco Gutiérrez et al. San José, Costa Rica: CEDAL, 1975. 104 p.; bibl.; ill. (Colección Seminarios y documentos; 24)

Summary of the proceedings and five of the best papers prepared for UNESCO's "Seminario Latinoamericano sobre Nuevas Interrelaciones Educativas" held in Santa Barbara, Costa Rica, 1975. Hugo Assmann's essays "Hombre Abstracto y Hombre Concreto," which attempts to distinguish between communication for oppression and communication for liberation, is somewhat alarmist but worthwhile reading.

CHILE

4406 Bravo Valdivieso, Luis and **Hernán Montenegro Arriagada.** Educación, niñez y pobreza: dos estrategias para el desarrollo de niños de extrema pobreza. Santiago: Ediciones Nueva Universidad, Pontificia Universidad Católica de Chile, Vicerrectoría de Comunicaciones, 1977. 83 p.; bibl.

In pt. 1, Bravo Valdivieso argues that an effective education for children of extreme poverty—the disadvantaged—will allow them to develop intellectually and creatively, and will engender in them a desire to grow and to love. He concludes that to provide an effective education requires a thorough understanding of their psychological and social fabric (i.e., language, motivation patterns, abilities, deficiencies). In pt. 2, Montenegro

Arriagada, a child psychiatrist, argues that education for disadvantaged children must begin at birth.

4407 Cabezón Contreras, Eduardo. Fundamentos filosóficos de la política educacional chilena (EC/M, 26, 1978, p. 87–97, bibl.)

At outset, author points out that essay is nothing more than a "reflection" about education and educational policies in Chile. While author does not go beyond the objective, this conceptual analysis of fundamental educational concepts is clear and thought-provoking.

4408 Chile. Universidad, *Santiago.* **Servicio de Selección y Registro de Estudiantes. División Estudios.** Duración de los estudios de los titulados en la Universidad de Chile, 1957–1971. Presentado por Graciela Donoso Retamales and Gilberto Salinas Galdames. Santiago: Universidad de Chile, Vicerrectoría de Asuntos Académicos, Servicio de Selección y Registro de Estudiantes, División Estudios, 1977. 38 p.; bibl.; 16 leaves; tables (Monografías—Universidad de Chile, Servicio de Selección y Registro de Estudiantes, División Estudios; 1)

Requirements for different degrees at the Universidad de Chile with special emphasis on average, minimum, and maximum time required for completion.

4409 Clavel, Carlos and Ernesto Schielfelbein. Factores que inciden en la demanda por educación (UC/EE, 13, 1979, p. 85–123, bibl., tables)

Examines reasons behind the disparity in, and the factors which generate, demand for education in Chile. Source of data was a national survey of households conducted in 1968–69; results of survey were summarized using multivariate procedures. Study accounted for approximately one-half of the variance in demand for education, prompting author's suggestions for additional research.

4410 Fischer, Kathleen B. Political ideology and educational reform in Chile, 1964–1976. Los Angeles: UCLA Latin American Center, University of California, 1979. 174 p.; bibl.; index (Studies on social processes and change. UCLA Latin American studies; v. 46)

Study explores relationship between political ideology and educational reforms in

Chile. Argues that education reforms are sensitive to political ideologies; yet, interest groups and other intervening factors frequently affect reforms in unanticipated ways. For political scientist's comment, see item 6534.

4411 Imágenes de la Universidad de Chile. Santiago: Universidad de Chile, 1977. 253 p.: ill.

Beautiful portfolio depicting the chronological and juridical history of the University of Chile, and describing the University as it is today.

4412 Menanteau-Horta, Dario. El sistema educativo y su incidencia en la estratificación social en Chile (CPU/ES, 19, 1979, p. 113–124, tables)

Integrates results of Chilean studies that analyze occupational prestige and vocational aspirations. Concludes that while expansion of educational system holds promise for lower classes, prevailing occupational stratification reaffirms and maintains socioeconomic status quo.

4413 Navarro Abarzua, Iván. Función de la educación de adultos en las sociedades latinoamericanas (CPU/ES, 16, 1978, p. 45–77, tables)

Examination of adult education in Latin America in theory and in practice, with specific reference to Chile. While recognizing that adult education does serve a variety of purposes, author concludes that it tends to reinforce the class structure of Latin American society and provides few opportunities for socioeconomic mobility.

4414 Piñera Echenique, Sebastián. Orientaciones para una reforma al sector educacional chileno (UCC/CE, 17:50, abril 1980, p. 61–90, tables)

Identifies and analyzes economic factors which influence public educational policy in Chile. Educational policy objectives of equal educational opportunity (equity) and of economic growth (efficiency) are frequently in conflict, and educational policy decisions require severe trade-offs. Author recommends higher investment in preschool and primary education, and a more equitable distribution of public funds among the other levels.

4415 *Revista Universitaria.* Ediciones Nueva Universidad Pontificia Uni-

versidad Católica de Chile. No. 1, junio
1978– . Santiago.

New serial represents a rebirth of an
earlier Catholic University journal of the
same name which ceased in 1968 after 53
years of publication. This first issue includes
articles on: Abdón Cifuentes Espinosa,
founder of the Catholic University of Chile;
Carlos Casanueva Opazo, its Rector for 33
years; and the university's 90-year history.

4416 Riveros, Luis. Rentabilidad de la educación formal: una estimación de sus
fluctuaciones en el caso chileno (UC/EE, 13,
1979, p. 35–82, bibl., tables)

Cost-benefit analysis of Chilean public
and private formal educational systems.
Questionable assumptions regarding alternative costs to educational investments and
other measurement difficulties weaken author's finding that investment in education
provides a higher rate of return.

4417 Schiefelbein, Ernesto. Impacto de la
investigación educacional en Chile
(Educación Hoy [Perspectivas Latinoamericanas, Bogotá] 8:46, julio/agosto 1979, p.
21–34, tables)

Analyzes potential impact of educational research on educational policy in
Chile. Concludes that a variety of factors determine impact, and suggests a closer examination of some of these. For example,
studies which have been requested by policy-
makers, which involve policymakers, or
whose results are consistent with the philosophy of policymakers appear to have had
substantial influence.

4418 ——— and A.M. de Andraca. Características del alumnado y del proceso
de enseñanza universitaria en 1973 (CPU/ES,
15, 1978, p. 125–147, tables)

Reports results of longitudinal study of
Chilean university students surveyed during
their fourth year of secondary school and at
conclusion of their first year of university.
Relationship between full-time university
studies and the education and income level
of the family is affirmed.

4419 ——— and Carlos Clavel. Gastos en
educación y redistribución del ingreso
en Chile. Santiago: Organización Internacional del Trabajo, Programa Mundial del Empleo, Programa Regional del Empleo para
América Latina y el Caribe (PREALC), 1976.
7 leaves; tables.

An essay of la Organización Internacional de Trabajo (OIT) which examines income distribution and government investment in education in Chile for 1970. Looks
at differential effects of investment by social
class and by level of education.

4420 ——— and Joseph P. Farrell. Selectivity and survival in the schools of
Chile (CES/CER, 22:2, June 1978, p. 326–
341, tables)

Article focuses on equality of educational opportunity in Chile from 1970 to
1974. Equal educational opportunity, as authors point out, may be viewed from four
perspectives: access, survival, output, and
outcome. Current study addresses equality in
terms of survival and output at primary
level, and survival at secondary level. With
the caveat that progress has been made, authors conclude that educational inequality
persists.

**4421 Vaccaro, Liliana; Ernesto Schiefelbein;
and Cecilia Yáñez.** La escuela y la
comunidad: evaluación de una experiencia de
participación de padres de familia en una escuela básica que atiende alumnos de escasos
recursos económicos en Santiago (Educación
Hoy [Perspectivas Latinoamericanas, Bogotá]
9:49, enero/feb. 1979, p. 3–72, table)

Three-year study (1973–75) of parent
involvement in school policy and goverance
in Santiago. Authors assume that parental involvement in school affairs is worthwhile
goal and that by using appropriate strategies,
parents, especially those with limited economic resources, can be made to participate
actively. Authors conclude that schools' administration must welcome, and that faculty
must be prepared for, parental involvement.

4422 Valenzuela, Alvaro. El clima escolar y
el contexto organizacional de la escuela como objetos de innovación: análisis
de algunas variables mediadoras en el proceso de transferencia educativa (CPU/ES, 19,
1979, p. 125–144, bibl., table)

Reviews significant US-based research
on the effects of general ambience or "social
ecology" of educational institutions on students. Reviews are followed by comparison
between two innovative "child-centered"
schools: an American high school organized
around a "modular scheduling plan," and a
Chilean "open school." Author describes
problems related to transfer of education

innovations and suggests areas of needed research.

Yaeger, Gertrude Matyoka. Barros Arana, Vicuña Mackenna, Amunátegui: the historian as national educator. See *HLAS 42: 3280.*

COLOMBIA

4423 Alvarez L., Roberto and **Antonio José Giraldo.** Informe estadístico de la evolución de egresados y matriculados en la Facultad de Educación de la Universidad de Antioquia desde 1954 hasta 1973. Medellín: Universidad de Antioquia, Facultad de Educación, Centro de Invesitgaciones Educativas, 1974. 81, 28 leaves: ill.

Comprehensive statistical profile of graduates from the School of Education of the University of Antioquia from 1954 to 1974.

4424 Bases para un modelo pedagógico: USEMI, una experiencia indígena de educación. Beatriz Toro et al. Bogotá, Colombia: Librería y Editorial América Latina, 1979. 92 p.; bibl.; ill.

Recognizing the irrelevance of the Colombian Ministry of Education's conventional curricula among the country's various indigenous groups, authors present a model for an educational program which respects native cultures and prepares students to address local indigenous needs. Prepared in collaboration with the Colombian Ministry of Education, focus of model was an indigenous community in the Sierra Nevada region of Colombia.

4425 Bernal Alarcón, Hernando. Educación fundamental integral: teoría y aplicación en el caso de ACPO. Bogotá: Acción Cultural Popular, 1978. 285 p.; bibl.; ill. (Serie Educación fundamental integral; 2)

In two parts: 1) reviews Colombia's well-known radio education experiment ACCION CULTURAL POPULAR (ACPO); 2) is a lengthy philsophical discussion of fundamental integral education.

4426 Campo V., Rafael and **Elsa de Alvarez.** Innovaciones educativas en colegios de Bogotá D.E., 1973, 1974, 1975: primer informe. Bogotá: Pontificia Universidad Javeriana, Facultad de Estudios Interdisciplina-

rios, 1978. 106 p.; bibl.; ill. (Serie de investigaciones—Pontificia Universidad Javeriana, Facultad de Estudios Interdisciplinarios; no. 4)

Well-designed statistical study on utilization of educational technology in Bogotá schools. Correlational analysis revealed schools most likely to employ innovative techniques and practices were Catholic schools, schools of middle size, schools located in the south of Bogotá and primary schools.

4427 Capacidad de los profesores para responder a las demandas de información de los alumnos (Educación Hoy [Perspectivas Latinoamericanas, Bogotá] 8 : 47/48, sept./dic. 1978, p. 151–162, tables)

Article reports on a part of a Colombian questionnaire study of human sexuality. Sample from second-year primary through sixth-year secondary (bachillerato) students. This portion of the study evaluated teachers as a source of information. Principal conclusion drawn is that teachers are not adequately prepared to answer questions on human sexuality. This applies to cognitive, affective, and practical areas.

4428 Fuentes de información de los estudiantes en el campo de sexualidad humana (Educación Hoy [Perspectivas Latinoamericanas, Bogotá] 8 : 47/48, sept./dic. 1978, p. 163–174, tables)

Article reports on part of a Colombian questionnaire study on human sexuality. Sample included students from second-year primary through sixth-year secondary (bachillerato). This portion of study analyzed the different sources of information. Principal conclusion drawn is that sources of human sexuality knowledge depend largely on the age of the students. Summary tables included.

4429 Giraldo Gómez, Antonio José and **Jorge Eliécer Ruiz Gallego.** Escala de actitudes hacia el magisterio como profesión. Tesis dirigida por Julio Puig Farras. Medellín, Colombia: CIED y sus autores, 1971. 154, 7 p.; bibl.

After reviewing the literature on attitudinal measures, authors develop their own scale to assess attitudes toward the profession of education. Prepared in partial fulfillment of the requirements for the Masters degree at the University of Antioquia, rigorously developed scale certainly warrants testing.

4430 González, Fernán E. Educación y estado en la historia de Colombia. Bogotá: Centro de Investigación y Educación Popular, 1979. 154, 6 p.; bibl. (Serie Controversia; nos. 77/78)

Excellent historical analysis of the relationship between political ideologies and educational trends in Colombia. Author asserts that imprimatur of politics is indelibly etched on public education in Colombia, primary, secondary and university. Dependence on private education at all levels reflects Colombians' concern over their country's turbulent political history and the sensitivity of public education to divergent political ideologies.

4431 Hacia una sistema de educación post-secundaria para Colombia: comentarios del Consejo Directivo, Universidad del Valle (UPN/RCE, 4, 1979, p. 143–147)

Reports on the observations and criticisms of the Consejo Directivo de la Universidad del Valle (Cali, Colombia) toward a major study prepared principally by its faculty. The study, "Hacia una Sistema de Educación Post-Secundaria para Colombia," was prepared as part of a major effort at planning for post-secondary educational reform in Colombia. Principal observation advanced was that the study failed to address such vital issues as finance, access and coexistence of public and private universities.

4432 Instituto Colombiano para el Fomento de la Educación Superior. División de Educación Tecnológica y Ocupacional. Sección Programación. Informe de la encuesta para determinar perfiles profesionales de los egresados de la educación tecnológica. Bogotá: Ministerio de Educación Nacional, Instituto Colombiano para el Fomento de la Educación Superior, División de Documentación y Fomento Bibliotecario, 1978. 71 leaves (Serie documentos de divulgación; no. 37)

Report of an ICFES study of Colombian technical schools and their graduates. Purpose of study was to develop personnel profiles of technical school graduates, presumably to determine if their training focused on their employers' needs. Data are abundant, analysis is scant.

4433 Jaramillo, Carlos Eduardo. Stratégie pour l'introduction en Colombie de la tecnologie éducative (UP/TM, 20:29, juillet/sept. 1979, p. 479–486)

Author traces gradual introduction of educational technology in Colombia, from the late 1940s when radios and portable printing presses first appeared in rural areas, through recent attempts at using television and satellite transmission. Cites middle-class conservatism and clashes between students and professors as among reasons why progress in this area has been slow. [June Blanchard Brown]

4434 Le Bot, Ivon. Educación e ideología en Colombia. Carátula, diseño de Hugo Zapata. Bogotá: La Carreta, 1979. 345 p.; bibl.

Three previously published essays on Colombian education. First essay describes three periods of growth and change: 1886–1930; 1930–45; and 1945–70. Growth of student movement during the National Front are analyzed in the second essay. Third essay focuses on unforeseen consequences of dramatic educational growth. Among conclusions of this last essay is that education legitimizes social class while not providing avenues for social mobility. Useful appendix on governance and Colombian education.

4435 Londoño Benveniste, Felipe and **Hernando Ochoa Núñez.** Bibliografía de la educación en Colombia. Bogotá: Instituto Caro y Cuervo, 1976. 678 p.; index (Publicaciones del Instituto Caro y Cuervo: Serie bibliográfica; 12)

Annotated and comprehensive bibliography on all facets of education in Colombia. Annotations are clear, concise, and entries are exhaustive. Outstanding resource.

4436 Necesidades de información de los alumnos en el campo de sexualidad humana (Educación Hoy [Perspectivas Latinoamericanas, Bogotá] 8:47/48, sept./dic. 1978, p. 145–150, tables)

Article reports on part of a Colombian questionnaire study of human sexuality. Sample included students from second-year primary through sixth-year secondary (bachillerato). This portion of study addressed students' need for information on human sexuality. Principal conclusion drawn is that students at all levels have been left to their own devices to find information.

4437 Ocampo T., José Fernando. Reforma universitaria, 1960–1980. Bogotá: Centro de Investigación y Educación Popular, 1979. 102, 3 p.; bibl. (Serie Controversia; no. 79)

Short history of the Colombian university since the National Front. Examines university reforms based on analysis of conference proceedings, planning documents, and recommendations of international organizations. Culmination of 20-year history is the 1979 university reform which is based on three policy documents, and which, the author argues, is discriminating, antidemocratic, and, antinational. One-sided, but well worth reading.

4438 Parra Sandoval, Rodrigo and **María Elvira Carvajal.** La universidad colombiana: de la filosofía a la tecnocracia estratificada (UPN/RCE, 4, 1979, p. 131–141, tables)

Historical and contemporary examination of the evolution of the university in Colombia. Examines consequences of growth of universities, especially during last 50 years. Development of "elitist" universities and emphasis on technical training are two such consequences which suggest a need for a government-level systematic study of the Colombian university.

4439 Purrear, Jeffrey M. Vocational training and earnings in Colombia: does a SENA effect exist? (CES/CER, 23:2, June 1979, p. 283–292, tables)

Study of earnings effect of Colombia's National Apprenticeship Service (SENA). While positive effect on earnings is noted, author concludes that value of skills acquired explains only a portion of the earnings increment.

Repression in Colombia: political persecution in Colombian universities. See item **6363.**

4440 Reyes Posada, Alvaro and **Martha Isabel de Gomez.** El papel y las posibilidades de la educación técnica: el caso de Colombia. Bogotá: Corporación Centro Regional de Población, Area Socioeconómica, 1979. 67 p.; bibl.; graphs (Monografías de la Corporación Centro Regional de Población; v. 12)

Monograph prepared by the Corporación Centro Regional de Población (CCRP)

and financially supported by the Programa de Estudios Conjuntos sobre Integración Económica para América Latina (ECIEL). Presented at the Seminario sobre Educación y Mercado de Trabajo held in Paipa, Colombia, May 1979; authors conclude that technical education integrated into the traditional school curricula fails to train students adequately for technical positions.

4441 Rodríguez, Edmundo. Esquema para el análisis de las políticas de la educación superior en Colombia. Bogotá: Ministerio de Educación Nacional, Instituto Colombiano para el Fomento de la Educación Superior, 1978. 67 p.: ill. (Serie Documentos de divulgación—ICFES; no. 34)

Author attempts to develop both an evaluation plan to assess the effect of the Colombian universities on the political and socioeconomic development of the country and a model against which achievements in these areas can be measured.

4442 Rodríguez F., Jaime. Las transformaciones del sistema educativo y su repercusión sobre la universidad de la década del 80 en Colombia. Bogotá: Ministerio de Educación Nacional, Instituto Colombiano para el Fomento de la Educación Superior, División de Documentación y Fomento Bibliotecario, Biblioteca, 1975. 58, 28 p.; bibl.; ill. (Serie Documentos de divulgación. Instituto Colombiano para el Fomento de la Educación Superior, Biblioteca; no. 24)

Writing in 1975, author carefully forecasts primary, secondary, and university enrollments to 1980. Takes into consideration enrollment data from 1960 to 1974, the 1964 census data, and official government education policies.

4443 Schultz, P. Rentabilidad de la educación en Bogotá (UPN/RCE, 4, 1979, p. 85–128, tables)

Translated version of articles published by the Rand Corporation in 1968. This cost-benefit analysis of education in Bogotá, by the economist credited with first applying cost-benefit analysis to human capital, is considered landmark. Includes mathematical models, statistical formulas, and tables.

4444 Silva, Renán. Imagen de la mujer en los textos escolares: contribución a un análisis (UPN/RCE, 4, 1979, p. 9–52, bibl., table)

Examines textbooks used in primary schools in Colombia for evidence of sexual stereotyping. While allowing that the study represents only an initial attempt, author concludes that the textbook stereotype of women mirrors the perception of Colombian society at large, that is women are regarded as second-class citizens and are subjects of discrimination and segregation.

4445 Simmons, John. Education for development, reconsidered (WD, 7:11/12, Nov./Dec. 1979, p. 1005–1016, tables)

Relationship between education and development goals in lesser developed countries is explored. Data indicate formal education fails to promote development and exacerbates socioeconomic inequality. Suggests consideration of nonformal and informal education as alternatives. Cites specific examples in Pakistan, Colombia, China, and Sri Lanka.

COSTA RICA

4446 González, Luis Felipe. Historia del desarrollo de la instrucción pública en Costa Rica. Evolución de la instrucción pública en Costa Rica. pt. 1, La colonia; pt. 2, 1821–1884. San José, Costa Rica: Editorial Costa Rica, 1978. 519 p.; bibl. (Biblioteca Patria; 9)

Exceedingly comprehensive and well-documented history of Costa Rican education from 1522 to 1884. In two parts, 44 chapters. Pt. 1 looks at the history of education during the colonial period, and pt. 2 at the period from 1821 to 1884. Author describes in detail the events, the people, the church and all other factors which shaped Costa Rican educational history. A labor of love to write and to read.

4447 El Maestro de cambio y la permanencia en la escuela dinámica: informe de un seminario celebrado en San José, Costa Rica, entre el 14 y el 7 de mayo de 1975. Auspiciado por la Confederación Mundial de Organizaciones de Profesionales de la Enseñanza y la Asociación de Educadores de Costa Rica. Morges, Switzerland: Confederación Mundial de Organizaciones de Profesionales de la Enseñanza, 1975. 102 p.

Collection of papers and essays and proceedings of a seminar entitled "El

Maestro de Cambio y la Permanencia en la Escuela Dinámica" held in San José, Costa Rica, May 1975. The seminar, sponsored by the Confederación Mundial de Organizaciones de Profesionales de la Enseñanza and the Asociación de Educadores de Costa Rica, was attended by representatives of teacher organizations from Costa Rica, El Salvador, Honduras, Panama and Venezuela.

4448 Molina Chocano, Guillermo. The training process and research in Central America (UN/ISSJ, 31:1, 1979, p. 70–78)

Citing the experience of the Central American School of Sociology at the University of Costa Rica between 1973 and 1977, author describes a revisionist approach to teaching social sciences. Among suggestions discussed in this very good essay is making research the focus of social science training rather than a supplementary requirement. Author bemoans inappropriate theoretical and methodological training in the social sciences as antithetical to an effective commitment to political action.

4449 Monge Alfaro, Carlos and **Francisco Rivas Ríos.** La educación, fragua de nuestra democracia. San José: Editorial Universidad de Costa Rica, 1978. 202 p.; bibl.

Analysis, primarily historical, of education in Costa Rica. Despite the premium Costa Rica has placed on education throughout its history, a fact well documented throughout the book, author contends education is still in crisis. Economic and social crises have placed new demands on country's educational system, and it remains to be seen how the government will respond.

CUBA

4450 Calzadilla Núñez, Julia. Los poemas cantarines. Ilustraciones de Manuel Bu. Diseño y portada de Darío Mora. La Habana: Unión de Escritores y Artistas, 1974. 66 p.; col. ill.

Children's reader which expounds Cuban way of life as opposed to those countries not yet "liberated;" to wit: "Cuando yo sea grande y valiente seré, serás y seremos todos como el Che."

4451 Cuetos, Eustaquio Remedios de los and **Eddy Trimiño Vergara.** Algunas

consideraciones acerca de las tradiciones revolucionarias y nuestras tareas en la educación comunista (UCLV/I, 58, 1978, p. 3—21)

Historical analysis of the relationship
between the university and revolutionary
ideology in Cuba. Author examines the revo-
tionary traditions of the Cuban university
since the University of Havana student revolts of 1871. Cuban universities are currently serving the Revolution by instilling in
their students a commitment to serve others
and to engage in meaningful and productive
work. This ideology, the authors point out, is
consistent with the revolutionary tradition of
the Cuban university.

4452 Dabaguián, Emil. Los investigadores
soviéticos sobre la Isla de la Libertad
(URSS/AL, 1, 1979, p. 195—206)

Traces the development of Soviet research on Cuba since the Cuban Revolution
from its unsophisticated descriptive beginnings immediately after the Revolution to its
present sophisticated and scientific level. No
attempt to present a critical analysis of the
research is made.

4453 Fund Riverón, Thalía. Social sciences
in higher education: the case of Cuba
(UN/ISSJ, 31:1, 1979, p. 21—27)

Author argues that universities should
require all students to study social sciences
relevant to a country's needs along with the
study of technical subjects. For example,
cites need for technical graduates to understand economic and social problems, problems of scientific and technical policy, and
problems of an ethical or philosophical nature. Points out that in Castro's Cuba, greater
importance is placed on the teaching of social sciences in all high-level technical training programs.

**4454 García del Portal, Jesús; José Luis Al-
muiñas Rivero; and Benito Romero
Sotolongo.** Problemas de la organización del
ingreso en los Centros de Enseñanza Superior
(La Educación Superior Contemporánea [Re-
vista internacional de países socialistas, La
Habana] 4:16, 1976, p. 167—177, bibl., tables)

Examination of complex problems of
university admissions and manpower planning in Cuba since 1969—70, the year of
the initial attempt to document imbalance
between supply and demand for trained
manpower.

**4455 García Fernández, Oscar and Luis
Montero Cabrera.** Algunas cuestiones
fundamentales sobre la educación superior
en Cuba (UNAM/RMCPS, 23:90, oct./dic.
1977, p. 49—73, tables)

Following brief history of pre-revolutionary higher education in Cuba, author examines developments in postsecondary education since 1962, starting with La Reforma
de la Enseñanza Superior. Excellent treatment of the reorganization and growth of
higher education and their likely long-term
effects on Cuban society.

4456 Gillette, Arthur. Cuba: au-dela de
l'éducation rurale integrée (UNESCO/
IRE, 24:2, 1978, p. 187—196, bibl.)

Author discusses goal of integrated
rural education and its chances of success,
based on experiences of developing countries.
In Cuba, for example, goal has been to
change orientation of entire educational system to offer rural population improved living
conditions. Learning provided for workers
and peasants has been largely unified in content and organization, with emphasis on solution of practical problems. [June Blanchard
Brown]

4457 Leiner, Marvin. Los cambios principales en la educación (in Cuba: camino
abierto [see item **8189**] p. 224—273)

Observations on Cuban education by
North American who studied there on two
different occasions (1968—69 and 1971). Such
areas as quantitative growth, the "escuela en
el campo" concept, and teacher preparation
are among the 10 topics described. While
laudatory of changes in Cuban education
since the revolution, author recognizes its
limitations. Objective, nonpolemical treatment of the subject.

4458 López Palacio, Juan V. El perfeccionamiento del sistema nacional de educación y el sub-sistema de formación de
personal docente (UCLV/I, 55/56, sept.
1976/abril 1977, p. 213—220)

Review of teacher training effects in
Cuba since the Revolution. Polemical statements directed both at the pre-Revolution
Cuban government and at nonsocialist societies in general detract from an otherwise
interesting, albeit one-sided, account of educational reforms in Cuba since 1959.

4459 Memoria anuario: curso 1975–1976. La Habana: Universidad de La Habana, Secretaría General, 1977. 401 p.; plates, tables.

Catalogue of the University of Havana for 1975–76. Comprehensive and complete.

4460 Vicioso, Abelardo. La educación en Cuba (UASD/U, 7, 1978, p. 55–80)

Marxist interpretation of changes in Cuban education since the Revolution. Very polemical description of developments in primary, secondary, university, vocational, adult, and nonformal education in addition to changes in teacher training programs, curriculum and finance. Lack of any critical analysis of contemporary Cuban education depicted by author leads one to suspect considerable distortion.

4461 Werthein, Jorge. La economía política y la educación para adultos en Cuba (CEE/RL, 9:3, 1979, p. 89–122, tables)

Analysis of Cuban post-revolution educational reforms. Points out that resouces have been directed principally to primary, secondary and adult education with the goals of achieving positive revolutionary attitudes among the masses and increased worker productivity. Concludes that a basic policy of Cuban Revolution is education for all Cubans.

DOMINICAN REPUBLIC

4462 Batista del Villar, Guarocuya. Anteproyecto de enfoque metodológico para una UASD crítica. Santo Domingo: Departamento de Publicaciones, Universidad Autónoma de Santo Domingo, 1976. 20 p.; graph (Colección UASD crítica; no. 3. Publicaciones de la UASD; v. 208)

Author, Rector of the Universidad Autónoma de Santo Domingo (UASD), argues that UASD must recognize the Dominican Republic's dependent status and, moreover, must accept responsibility for the country's transformation from dependent to independent status. Describes necessary steps to which UASD must dedicate itself to achieve "national liberation goals."

4463 ———. La UASD, un centro educativo indispensable para el desarrollo autónomo del país. Santo Domingo: Departamento de Publicaciones, Universidad

Autónoma de Santo Domingo, 1977. 30 p.; ill. (Colección UASD crítica; no. 13. Publicaciones de la UASD; v. 229)

Reflections of the Rector of la Universidad Autónoma de Santo Domingo (UASD). Directed specifically at the President of the Republic, at other government officials, and especially at those who charge that UASD is communist. Rector reviews remarkable achievements of this 438-year-old university, and argues that it has been and always will be indispensable to the country.

4464 Encuentro Nacional sobre las Ciencias Políticas en la República Dominicana, *Santo Domingo, 1977.* Las ciencias políticas en la República Dominicana: una evaluación. Santo Domingo: Asociación para el Desarrollo, 1977. 85 p.; bibl.

Five Dominican political scientists evaluate the present state of the discipline in their country. [A. Suárez]

4465 Experiencias didácticas. Yolanda Fernández de Perdomo et al. Santo Domingo: Editora de la Universidad Autónoma de Santo Domingo, 1977. 530 p.; bibl.; ill.; index (Colección Educación y sociedad; no. 3. Publicaciones de la Universidad Autónoma de Santo Domingo; v. 235)

Handbook for the Dominican in-service and preservice Spanish language teacher. Prompted by a UNESCO/Dominican Government-inspired interuniversity agreement among the Dominican Republic's three principal universities, handbook consists of comprehensive units on language and communication theory, teaching guides, inquiry teaching and team teaching.

4466 Fernández, Jorge Max. El desarrollo del sector educativo dominicano: elementos de una estrategia (UUAL/U, 20:79, enero/marzo 1980, p. 47–87, bibl.)

General guidelines for educational planning in the Dominican Republic. Education, author argues, neither mirrors nor molds society; true role is somewhere between these extremes. Effective educational planning requires a recognition of historical forces and socioeconomic realities as well as a high level of participation from all sectors of society.

4467 Iglesias, Salvador. Educación pre-escolar (UNPHU/A, 22/23, julio/dic. 1977, p. 9–16)

Describes rationale for the educational objectives of two levels of preschool education in the Dominican Republic; maternal preschool—two to four years of age, and kindergarten—four and five years of age. Implores families to make financial sacrifices, if necessary, to enroll their children in legitimate preschool programs rather than leave them with uninformed and uneducated baby sitters.

4468 Latorre, Eduardo. La educación superior dominicana (UUAL/U, 20:79, enero/marzo 1980, p. 33–46)

Transcript of a speech by the Rector of the Instituto Tecnológico de Santo Domingo, Dominican Republic, given at La Quinta Semana Duartiana in Ponce, Puerto Rico. Describes six basic functions of the university, and then traces the development of the university in the Dominican Republic.

EL SALVADOR

4469 Durán, Miguel Angel. Historia de la Universidad de El Salvador, 1841–1930. 2. ed. San Salvador, El Salvador: Editorial Universitaria, 1975. 237 p.; port. (Colección Tlatoli)

Slow-moving historical account of the University of El Salvador from 1841 to 1930. Not for the historian interested in locating original documents and other sources since it lacks bibliography and notes. Useful merely because of scarcity of information on the subject.

GUATEMALA

4470 Guatemala (City). **Universidad de San Carlos.** Publicación conmemorativa, tricentenario, Universidad de San Carlos de Guatemala, 1676–1976. Guatemala: La Universidad, 1976. 341 p.; ill.

Beautifully designed commemorative publication in celebration of the 300th anniversary of the University of San Carlos of Guatemala (1676–1976). Includes copies of key historical documents and is replete with striking photographs throughout. Complete history and full description of present-day university also included.

4471 Kagan, Jerome; Robert E. Klein; Gordon E. Finley; and Barbara Rogoff. A study in cognitive development (NYAS/A, 284, March 18, 1977, p. 374–388, tables)

Focuses on differential growth of selected cognitive processes—recall and conservation—from age six through 13 in cultural settings differing in isolation, modernization, and child-rearing practices. Children from two neighboring villages in northwest Guatemala—one in process of modernization and one traditional—and children from the Boston area were selected. The two competencies tested were recall and conservation. Principal findings were most isolated children of all ages less adept at recall, and Boston children most sensitive to conservation concerns.

4472 Osorio Paz, Saúl. Educación y empleo (UUAL/U, 77, julio/sept. 1979, p. 678–695, tables)

Intriguing essay on paradoxical role of the university in a developing society, with specific reference to the Universidad de San Carlos, Guatemala. Author argues that to both contribute to a country's development and be critical of its injustices—important university functions—places many university graduates in a difficult position.

4473 O'Sullivan Ryan, Jeremiah. La educación y el agricultor de subsistencia: el caso del altiplano de Guatemala (URL/ES, 13, julio 1979, p. 43–62, bibl., tables)

Article reports results of study of the relationship between nonformal education and economic productivity in the Guatemalan highlands. Responses from a sample of peasant recipients of technical assistance and supervised credit were compared with those of a control group of nonrecipients. Results demonstrate nonformal education fails to generate greater productivity. Author concludes that without economic advancement and social mobility opportunities, both formal and nonformal education for rural populations is doomed to failure.

4474 Poitevin Dardón, René Eduardo. Quiénes somos?: la Universidad de San Carlos y las clases sociales. Guatemala: Universidad de San Carlos de Guatemala, Instituto de Investigaciones y Mejoramiento Educativo, 1977. 59 p.; bibl. (Criterios universitarios; no. 1)

First of a series of occasional papers published by the Instituto de Investigaciones y Mejoramiento Educativo of the University of San Carlos, Guatemala. Reports on questionnaire study of students' social class and attitudes toward society, self, and change. Study is replete with methodological problems, and the inferences have little to do with the data.

HAITI

4475 Brutus, Edner. Instruction publique en Haïti, 1492–1945. Port-au-Prince, Haïti: Editions Panorama, 1979. 2 v. (viii, 533 p.); bibl.

Vol. 1 of history of education (first published 1948) begins with a discussion of the educational system under the Spanish—the Catholic Church in particular—followed by the French takeover. The 270-p. volume traces education's development through the republic of Pétion and the work of such pioneers in the field as Honoré Frey, Jean-Baptiste Francisque, Jean Simon, and Elie Dubois. Concludes with a discussion of the parliamentary council which met in 1878 to debate the controversial issue of the shortage of teachers and schools in the rural areas. [June Blanchard Brown]

4476 Carrizo, Luis María. Eléments pour l'étude statistique du système scolaire et techniques de projection des effectifs scolaires: document préparé pour le séminaire de formation de techniciens pour la planification et l'administration de l'éducation. Port-au-Prince: Département de l'éducation nationale, Unité de planification et de programmation, 1978 or 1979. 41 leaves; bibl.; ill. (Document—Département de l'education nationale, Unité de planification et de programmation: no. 2. Projet Haiti/PNUD/UNESCO/77/006, Education pour le développement)

Defines scholarly ratios as relations between educated and the educable population. These ratios indicate both educational level attained by a country and the degree to which the system is responding to society's demands in the area of education. Study specifically examines Haiti. [June Blanchard Brown]

4477 Cauvin, Marcel; Joseph Herns Henry; and Luis María Carrizo. Distribution par âge et par année d'études des effectifs des écoles publiques en milieu rural: résultats de lénquête de mars 1976. Port-au-Prince: Département de l'éducation nationale, Unité de planification et de programmation, Section de statistiques, 1979. 14, 10 leaves; tables (Project Haiti/PNUD/UNESCO, Education pour le développement)

Tables provide a profile of the public school population of Haiti for 1976, by age, sex, school year and region of the country. Almost 50 percent of the students in rural areas are at primary level; their average age, both male and female, is 10.7 years; and 83.8 percent of students nationwide are behind their grade level because of late initial enrollment in school, poor organization of classes, lack of teachers, and frequent repetition of grades. [June Blanchard Brown]

Clément, Job B. History of education in Haiti: pt. 1, 1804–1915. See *HLAS 42:2559.*

4478 Cours international d'été d'Haïti, *Port-au-Prince, Haïti, 1979.* Education et développement: document de synthèse. Port-au-Prince: Centre haitien d'investigation en sciences sociales, 1979. 224 p. (Coleccion CHISS)

These proceedings of Haiti's 1979 International Summer Course on education and development include presentations on education and the economy, special education, racial problems, the mass media, Creole vs. French as the language of education, and vocational vs. classical instruction. Mona Chery Williams, coordinator of the course, notes in the introduction to the proceedings that students participated as actively as educators in the conference, whose goal every year is to promote the integration of the youth of Haiti with the essential values of their culture. [June Blanchard Brown]

4479 Haiti (Republic). **Département de l'éducation nationale. Section de statistiques.** Evolution des effectifs dans l'enseignement primaire en milieu urbain et rural: taux de scolarisation. Prepared by Marcel Cauvin; Joseph Herns Henry; Luis María Carrizo. Port-au-Prince, Haiti: La Section, 1979. 21 leaves; graphs (Etude—Département de l'éducation nationale, Section de statistique; no. 1. Project Haiti/PNUD/UNESCO. Education pour le développement)

Study uses tables to show relation of those receiving an education in the elementary schools to population as a whole, according to grade and age of students. It points to large educational disparity between urban and rural areas. [June Blanchard Brown]

4480 Mathelier, Georges. Histoire critique de l'enseignement haitien de 1844 à 1967 (ASHSH/B, 5, 1977, p. 29–51)

Reviews history of education in Haiti (1844–1967) including political upheavals and introduction of technical, community, and special education to formal educational program. Author's conclusion awaits examination of educational reforms undertaken in 1972–73. Also notes that problem of language with respect to education in Haiti deserves further examination. [June Blanchard Brown]

4481 Ortiz, Eduardo. Etude sur les conditions de service du personnel enseignant en Haiti et projet de statut du corps enseignant public primaire, secondaire, et professionnel et technique. Port-au-Prince, Haiti: Département de l'éducation nationale, 1979. 115 leaves (Project d'éducation no. 1—Haiti/BIRD)

Describes conditions of service of teachers in Haiti at primary and secondary levels in all types of schools, including compensation and incentives for professional development, and makes recommendations for improvement. Also proposes law to raise teaching profession to career level; and describes financial and institutional aspects of implementing such a law. [June Blanchard Brown]

4482 ———. Rapport sur l'administration de l'éducation en Haiti. Port-au-Prince: Département de l'éducation national, 1979. 144 leaves; ill. (Project d'éducation no. 1—Haiti/BIRD)

Study by UNESCO expert considers principal aspects of educational administration, including objectives, legal aspects, structure, function, planning, personnel, budget and equipment. Concludes with a detailed discussion of recommendations for improving Haiti National Education Dept. cautioning that change must take place gradually and only through necessary structures once they are in place. Among the recom-

mendations are the regrouping of homogeneous functions such as culture and research, and the strengthening of weak functions and the introduction of new functions which would favorably affect the others. [June Blanchard Brown]

HONDURAS

4483 Honduras. Universidad Nacional Autónoma, *Tegucigalpa*. Presupuesto por programas. Tegucigalpa: UNAH, 1979. 2 v.

In two volumes, 1979 budget of the National Autonomous University of Honduras in Tegucigalpa.

4484 Santos, Manuel Antonio. La universidad como factor de transformación social. Honduras: Centro Universitario de Estudios Generales, Universidad Nacional Autónoma de Honduras, 1977. 54 p.

After describing basic functions of the National Autonomous University of Honduras, author makes case for more direct university role in guiding Honduran society. Impotence of university to effectively deal with societal dislocations created by Hurricane Fifi suggests need for a more assertive role. Specifically, author concludes, university needs to be society's conscience and to direct societal change.

JAMAICA

4485 Gordon, Hopeton. Building Jamaica by educating adults (UWI/CQ, 23:4, Dec. 1977, p. 122–132)

Traces recent developments in formal and nonformal adult education in Jamaica. Author argues that while there is a growing awareness of the need for educating and training adults and that there are governmental and nongovernmental programs evolving that address this need, efforts are disparate and fragmented. Suggests development of a coordinating mechanism to serve clearinghouse and facilitator role.

4486 Haughton, John. A common sense look at education in Jamaica today. s.l.: National Union of Democratic Teachers, 1979. 20 p. (An NUDT booklet)

Author is a self-professed Jamaican community, secondary school teacher, and founder of the first Jamaican Teachers' Union. In the booklet he examines Jamaican public education and concludes that injustice and inequity are rampant at all levels. Argues that only by dismantling the country's economic and social system can people's living standards, including education, be improved.

4487 Keith, Sherry. An historical overview of the state and educational policy in Jamaica (LAP, 5[17]:2, Spring 1978, p. 37–52, bibl., tables)

Marxist interpretation of the relationship between educational development/reforms and development of capitalism in Jamaica through 1974. Author argues that major educational reforms merely create the illusion of democratization of educational opportunity when in fact reforms advance the interests of the privileged classes.

MEXICO

4488 Aldana Rendón, Mario A. Breve historia de la Universidad de Guadalajara. Guadalajara, Jalisco, México: Universidad de Guadalajara, Instituto de Estudios Sociales, 1979. 31 p.; bibl. (Temas de Formación Política. Colección Cuadernos universitarios; 12)

No. 12 of "Cuadernos Universitarios," an occasional publication of the University of Guadalajara, consists of a brief history of this university from its colonial beginnings (Charles IV of Spain granted the license on 18 Nov. 1791) to the present. The university enrolls more than 90,000 students in its diverse undergraduate, graduate and technical programs, and has more than 400 full-time and 3300 part-time faculty. Historical treatment is conventional but well worth reading given the importance of this university within Mexico's university system.

4489 ———. Política educativa del Gobierno Mexicano, 1867–1940. Guadalajara, Jalisco, México: Instituto de Estudios Sociales, Universidad de Guadalajara, Departamento Editorial, 1977. 51 p.; bibl. (Temas de formación política. Serie Cuadernos universitarios; no. 7)

Essay on the development of educational policy and the evolution of educational philosophy in Mexico. Three watershed years—1857, 1917 and 1934—are highlighted, 1857 for unifying the national conscience, 1917 for unifying the government and the people, and 1934 for addressing social and economic justice.

4490 Avances en la enseñanza y la investigación: 1977–1978. Chapingo, México: Colegio de Postgraduados, 1978. 384 p.; ill.; plates; tables.

Periodic publication of the Colegio de Postgraduados in Chapingo, Mexico. Abstracts of significant agricultural research in Mexico, including methodology and results, from February 1977 through Jan. 1978. Researchers, their educational backgrounds, and their current affiliations included in a separate section.

4491 Blanco, José Joaquín. El proyecto educativo de José Vasconcelos como programa político (in Seminario de Historia de la Cultura Nacional, Instituto Nacional de Antropología e Historia, 1976. En torno a la cultura nacional. Héctor Aguilar Camín et al. México: Instituto Nacional Indigenista, Secretaría de Educación Pública, 1976, p. 85–94 [Colección SEP-INI, 51])

Essay describing educational goals and philosophy of José Vasconcelos during his tenure as Mexico's Secretary of Public Education (1920–24). Emphasizes the participation of all classes in and on "mestizaje" as integral to Mexican education.

4492 Bolaño, Sara. Comprensión de lectura y clase social (Boletín de Antropología Americana [Instituto Panamericano de Geografía e Historia, México] 1, junio 1980, p. 106–116, bibl., ill., tables)

A well-designed correlation study of reading comprehension and socioeconomic class among upper-level primary students. Purpose is to analyze the consequences of Mexican policy of using a single textbook for all children at the same grade level regardless of geographic region or social class. Author finds that middle- and upper-class students read with greater comprehension than lower-class students.

Britton, John A. Teacher unionization and the corporate state in Mexico, 1931–1945. See *HLAS 42:2273.*

4493 Díaz de Cossío, Roger. Sobre la educación y la cultura: alternativas de cambio. México: Editorial Trillas, 1978. 119 p.; bibl.

Twelve articles by well-known Mexican sociologists which focus on education and society. Among recurring themes are educational change, life-long education and multiple solutions to educational problems. Author concludes implementation of educational reform is aggravated by failure to plan adequately.

4494 Fuentes Molinar, Olac. Educación pública y sociedad (in México, hoy. Por José Ayala et al. Coordinadores: Pablo González and Enrique Florescano. México: Siglo Veintiuno Editores, 1979, p. 230–265)

Comprehensive description of the growth of public education in Mexico since 1920. Written from a Marxist point of view, author argues that growth has not benefitted those in need and that education continues to reaffirm status rather than providing for social mobility. Particularly critical of the administration of López Portillo, author labels his National Education Plan of 1977 unrealistic and responsible for raising false hopes.

4495 ———. Enseñanza media básica en México: 1970–1976 (CP, 15, enero/marzo 1978, p. 90–104, tables)

Analyzes effects of secondary education reform in Mexico under President Echeverría from 1970–76. Reform was intended to render more systematic provisions of secondary education. Author analyzes results of reform in terms of the following goals: expansion of educational opportunities, increased emphasis on vocational training, and modernization of both curriculum and teaching methods.

4496 ———. Los maestros y el proceso político de la Universidad Pedagógica Nacional (CP, 21, julio/sept. 1979, p. 91–103)

On 15 March 1979, la Universidad Pedagógica Nacional de México (UPN) was officially inaugurated by President López Portillo. Describes planning for and analyzes significance of UPN on the Mexican educational, social and cultural scene.

4497 Glazman, Raquel. Trece principios que deben considerarse en el cambio de la educación superior (UUAL/U, 77, julio/sept. 1979, p. 710–728)

Author outlines 13 principles which need to be encompassed by universities dedicated to fulfilling their mission. While these principles were originally developed as the basis for restructuring the curriculum of the "Facultad de Medicina Veterinaria y Zootécnica, UNAM" (Mexico), author points out they should be applied to higher education in Mexico and elsewhere in Latin America.

4498 González Oropeza, Manuel. El régimen patrimonial de la Universidad Nacional Autónoma de México. México: Universidad Nacional Autónoma de México, 1977. 324 p.; bibl. (Comisión Técnica de Estudios y Proyectos Legislativos; 12)

Juridical history of the National Autonomous University of Mexico (UNAM). Extensive documentation appended.

4499 Guzmán, José Teódulo. Alternativas para la educación en México. México:Ediciones Gernika, 1978, 1979 printing. 310 p.; ill. (Colección Educación y sociología; 4)

Author argues that previous educational reforms in Mexico have been totally ineffective in that they have produced no substantive changes in the social structure. Illiteracy, unemployment, poverty are still rampant. To be effective, educational reform must be accompanied by modifications in the political and economic spheres. Model for effective educational reform included.

4500 *Indice de Artículos sobre Capacitación y Adiestramiento.* Servicio Nacional de Adiestramiento Rápido de la Mano de Obra en la Industria (ARMO). Vol. 8, No. 1, 1980– . México.

Useful index, with abstracts, of articles on teacher training, adult education, and human resources, published three times per year. Special emphasis on Mexican journals. Abstracts of English language journals are translated into Spanish.

4501 Klees, Steven J. Television as an educational medium: the case of Mexican secondary education (CES/CER, 23:1, Feb. 1979, p. 82–100, tables)

Evaluates Mexico's Telesecundaria system; specifically, the effects of Telesecundaria on language and mathematical achievement. Using multivariate analysis, research indicates Telesecundaria students achieve more in language and mathematics than traditional education students despite coming from more disadvantaged homes and school environments. Lack of random sampling and post-hoc controls weaken study's credibility.

4502 Larralde, Carlos et al. Sobre la práctica: la ciencia aplicada (Nexos [Sociedad, ciencia, literatura. Centro de Investigación Cultural y Científica, México] 2, feb. 1978, p. 7)

Wide-ranging analysis of problems which confront applied researchers and research institutions in Mexico. Author points out that recent efforts to promote applied research have been largely unsuccessful due to obstacles at every stage in the research process.

4503 Latapí, Pablo. Análisis de un sexenio de educación en México, 1970–1976. Portada, Alberto Diez. México: Editorial Nuevo Imagen, 1980. 256 p.; bibl.; graphs (Serie Educación)

Examines educational policy during the turbulent administration of Luis Echeverría, 1970–76. Includes very useful analytic model to systematically assess educational policy in light of actual social change, and breaks down educational process into manageable categories for analysis. Considers future direction of education in formal, nonformal, and informal sense.

4504 ———. Política educativa y valores nacionales. Prólogo de Julio Scherer García. Portada, Alberto Diez. México: Editorial Nueva Imagen, 1979. 235 p. (Serie Educación)

Collection of 73 articles published in *Excelsior* (Mexico) between 1974 and 1976. Articles critically examine questions of educational policy, educational reforms (1970–76), equal educational opportunity, and "Third World" education.

4505 Lee, James H. Clerical education in nineteenth-century Mexico: the conciliar seminaries of Mexico City and Guadalajara, 1821–1910 (AAFH/TAM, 36:4, April 1980, p. 456–477)

Triumph of secular liberalism in Mexico in 1857 created a political and intellectual environment hostile to the Church in general and to clerical teachers in particular. Conciliar seminaries in Mexico survived this transition but had to adjust to a society whose ruling elite no longer valued their services. Author explores role conciliar seminaries played both early in the century and then after 1857, focusing on those seminaries in Mexico City and Guadalajara. For more on this subject, see also *HLAS 42:2213*.

4506 Leff, Enrique. Dependencia científico-tecnológica y desarrollo económico (in México, hoy. Por José Ayala et al. Coordinado por Pablo González Casanova y Enrique Florescano. México: Siglo Veintiuno Editores, 1979, p. 266–285)

Arguing that Latin America's scientific and technological dependence on developed areas constitutes the principle obstacle to economic development, Leff calls on the working classes to organize and to establish their political base. Only in this way, author concludes, is scientific and technological self-determination possible. Specific references are made to Mexico.

4507 Levy, Daniel C. El gobierno de las universidades en Mexico desde una perspectiva internacional (CM/FI, 14:4, abril/junio 1979, p. 576–599, tables)

Brief history of the Mexican university and description of contemporary higher education (academic, technical and normal) in Mexico is followed by analysis of the effects of different organizational structures on the Mexican university. Levy's analysis of the effects of different organizational patterns on matters of university autonomy, academic freedom, curriculum and personnel is both intriguing and compelling.

4508 ———. Pugna política sobre quien paga la educación superior en México (CEE/RL, 9:2, 1979, p. 1–38, bibl., tables)

Author analyzes who pays for education—citizen or government. Systematic evaluation of both sides of argument is presented.

4509 ———. University and government in Mexico: autonomy in an authoritarian system. New York: Praeger, 1980. 173 p.; bibl.; ill.; index (The Praeger special studies series in comparative education)

Excellent and important study on the politics of higher education in Mexico. Unlike universities in most Latin American countries, Levy concludes Mexican universities have managed to retain a high level of institutional autonomy despite strong regime control and despite the fact that public universities receive approximately 90 percent of their funds from the government. Author calls for future research by comparative education scholars and political scientists on appointive, academic, and financial autonomy.

4510 ———. University autonomy in Mexico: implications of regime authoritarianism (LARR, 14:3, 1979, p. 129–152, tables)

Examining university autonomy from the perspective of personnel selection and finance, Levy convincingly argues that UNAM has remained substantially autonomous. Moreover, he asserts, that UNAM still enjoys considerable self-rule is particularly noteworthy in light of the tragic fate of university autonomy over the last decade in Cuba, Brazil, Peru, Uruguay, and Argentina.

4511 Mérida, Mexico. Universidad de Yucatán. Comisión de Planeación y Fomento de Actividades Académicas.
Alumnos: ciclos escolares 1960/61 a 1977/79. Mérida: Ediciones de la Universidad de Yucatán, 1978. 89 leaves (2 fold.): graphs; tables (Compendio estádistico—Universidad de Yucatán, Comisión de Planeación y Fomento de Actividades Académicas; no. 2)

Statistical profiles by concentration areas, by school or department, and by year, from 1960/61 to 1977/78 for the University of Yucatán.

4512 ———. ———. **Rectoría.** Monografía de la Universidad de Yucatán. Elaborada por Margarita P. de Hernández. Mérida: Universidad de Yucatán, 1977. 160 p.; ill.

Complete history of the University of the Yucatán, Mérida, Mexico. Last half of monograph describes the University of the Yucatán as it is today, with a separate chapter devoted to each of its schools.

Mexico. Secretaría de Educación Pública. Dirección General de Publicaciones y Bibliotecas. Directorio de bibliotecas de la República Mexicana. See *HLAS 42:155.*

4513 ———. **Universidad Nacional. Centro de Información Científica y Humanística.** Información y desarrollo. México: Asociación de Bibliotecarios de Instituciones de Enseñanza Superior e Investigación, 1976. 25 leaves of various foliations; bibl. (Cuadernos de ABIESI; no. 3)

Current issue consists of four studies selected from 25 prepared for the 38th Congreso Mundial de la Federación Internacional de Documentación held in Mexico City, Oct. 1976. Studies examine issue of information dissemination and development, and address the need for more effective coordination among those who catalogue, store, and disseminate information.

4514 Mora, Gabriel de la. Al encuentro de los jóvenes: las reformas educativas en México. México: B. Costa-Amic. Editor, 1976. 185 p.: ill.

Review and analysis of the watershed educational reform movements in Mexico. Writing from a philosophical rather than from a historical perspective, de la Mora argues that the next educational reform must emphasize agricultural training to alleviate hunger and, moreover, must bring youth together in a common cause.

4515 El Movimiento estudiantil mexicano en la prensa francesa. Introducción, compilación y traducción de Carlos Arriola. México: El Colegio de México, 1979. 191 p. (Jornadas—El Colegio de México; 88)

Concerns 1968 student riots in Mexico as reported in major French newspapers and wire services, *Le Figaro, L'Humanité, Le Monde.* Classic example of well-executed study based on documentary analysis. Reports in the French press tended to support the stereotype of the violent Mexican.

4516 Muñoz Izquierdo, Carlos; Pedro Gerardo Rodríguez; Patricia Restrepo de Cepeda; and **Carlos Borrani.** El síndrome del atraso escolar y el abandono del sistema educativo (CEE/RL, 9:3, 1979, p. 1–60, tables)

Questionnaire study of school desertion in Mexico involving a total of 1840 school-age children, 50 percent repeaters or drop-outs and 50 percent promoted from 23 different schools in three distinct regions. Multivariate analysis used to summarize 64 independent, control and dependent variables. Principal finding is school desertion generally occurs after several school-related failures. Implications for policy-makers are described.

4517 Nadal Egea, Alejandro. Instrumentos de política científica y tecnológica en México. México: Colegio de México, 1977. 309 p.; bibl. (Colección—Centro de Estudios Económicos y Demográficos; 5)

Report on Mexican portion of multinational study on science and technology policy and its relationship to development goals. Other Latin American countries included in the study directed by the International Development Research Center of Canada (Centro Internacional de Investigaciones sobre el Desarrollo) are Brazil, Colombia, Peru and Venezuela. One of the study's major conclusions is that a well-conceived plan to carry out development goals requiring science and technology input is necessary.

4518 Rangel Guerra, Alfonso. La educación superior en México. México: El Colegio de México, 1979. 146 p.; bibl. (Jornadas— El Colegio de México; 86)

Brief, carefully organized, description of higher education in Mexico, accomplished by author through a prudent selection of topics. After historical overview and analysis of the autonomy concept, remainder of book is organized in three parts: 1) general description, growth, organization; 2) administration, planning, integration, and coordination; and 3) effectiveness, capacity for change. Part of a 12-nation study of higher education sponsored by the International Council for Educational Development.

4519 Rodríguez Sala de Gómezgil, María Luisa. El científico en México: su imagen entre los estudiantes de enseñanza media. México: Universidad Nacional Autónoma de México, Instituto de Investigaciones Sociales, 1977. 228 p.; bibl.

Complete and comprehensive report on questionnaire survey of Mexican secondary school students' attitudes toward science and scientists. Portions of study, begun in 1966 and completed in 1974, have been published elsewhere. Major finding is that the Mexican secondary student has minimal contact with scientists, and thus is in no position to accurately perceive scientists' role in society.

4520 Samuels, Shimon. A research note on Jewish education in Mexico (WJC/JJS, 20:2, Dec. 1978, p. 143–148)

Reports results of a 1976–77 survey of Jewish university teachers, researchers, and professional university graduates in Mexico. Paucity of information on number of Jewish professionals and their sense of Jewish identity promoted the study. That Jewish identity among Jews is more likely to have Zionist base rather than religious base was the most significant result reported.

4521 Sierra, Justo. La educación nacional: artículos, actuaciones y documentos. Edición ordenada y anotada, Agustín Yáñez. México: Universidad Nacional Autónoma de México, 1977. 518 p.; bibl.; indexes; port. (His Obras completas; 8. Nueva biblioteca mexicana; 56)

Collection of selected works on education by Justo Sierra. Known in Mexico simply as "Maestro," Sierra was the son of a former Mexican president, was himself a former Minister of Public Education, a philosopher, a writer, and the "founder of modern Mexican education." This collection of works, in four parts, includes newspaper and magazine articles, legislative documents, personal memoranda and correspondence, and essays.

4522 Sotelo Marbán, Andrés. La enseñanza media en México: 1977–1978 (CEE/RL, 9:3, 1979, p. 181–201, tables)

Statistical compilation of Mexican secondary education enrollments for 1977–78, broken down by regions and by categories such as technical/general, public/private, and first three years/last two years.

Vaughan, Mary K. Women, class and education in Mexico, 1880–1928. See *HLAS* 42:2363.

4523 Villaseñor, Guillermo. Estado e Iglesia: el caso de la educación. México: Editorial Edicol, 1978. 198 p; bibl. (Sociología investigaciones)

Extensive examination of the issue of Church-state sovereignty in Mexico since independence. Battle over sovereignty in the political and economic sphere and in education has been long and intense. In this excellent historical analysis of the issue, author focuses on the battle in the field of education.

NICARAGUA

4524 Jacob, Esther. Un pueblo unido, jamás será vencido: lo que pasó en Nicaragua no es un cuento. México: Editorial Nueva Imagen, 1980. 48 p.

Book for children and youth, in large print, with illustrations on every page, written from the perspective of the Frente Sandinista de Liberación Nacional. Author describes alleged abuses and inequities under Somoza followed by the victory of the Sandinistas. Polemical treatment of the subject, but given the intended audience, very convincing.

4525 Nicaragua. Junta de Gobierno de Reconstrucción Nacional. Programa de gobierno de reconstrucción nacional. Managua: Ministerio de Educación, 1979. 32 p.

New revolutionary government's statement of its reconstruction plan for Nicaragua. Plan addresses four areas: political, economic, social, and institutional. Among its plans for education are the following: comprehensive educational reform at all levels, free and obligatory secondary education, price controls on textbooks and school uniforms, regulation of private schools, and a pledge to maintain the autonomy of the National Autonomous University of Nicaragua.

PANAMA

4526 Bloise, Blas and Abraham Bell E. Examen del movimiento estudiantil panameño. Panamá: Centro de Estudios Latinoamericanos Justo Arosemena, 1979. 24 p.; ill. (Cuadernos populares; 5)

History of student movement in Panama with a focus on activities during the 1950s. Includes a disjointed discussion of Panamanian social structure and its relationship to the student movement.

4527 León P., Raquel María de. La geografía y la historia en la escuela primaria panameña (SGHG/A, 47:1/4, enero/dic. 1974, p. 156–160)

Addresses need for social studies component in Panamanian primary school curriculum. Includes brief sections which define "social studies" and describe social studies objectives, curricular organization and texts, and other teaching material.

4528 ———. Los problemas básicos de la geografía en la educación primaria, secundaria y superior de América Central (SGHG/A, 47:1/4, enero/dic. 1974, p. 179–188, bibl.)

After describing geographical features of Central America and presenting arguments for the inclusion of a geography component in primary, secondary and university programs, author analyzes curricula, materials, methods and training relative to the teaching of geography. Cites teaching of geography in Panama as a positive example.

4529 Méndez Pereira, Octavio. La universidad autónoma y la universidad cultural: discursos académicos. Panamá: Editorial Universitaria, 1973. 236 p.; bibl.

Compilation of speeches by the Universidad Nacional de Panama's first Rector, Octavio Méndez Pereira, attest to his influence on both the creation and development of this university.

PARAGUAY

Clemente Filho, Antonio dos Santos. Participação da comunidade na integração do deficiente mental. See item **4592.**

4530 Corvalán, Grazziella. Educación técnica de nivel medio y mercado de trabajo: documento de trabajo presentado en la reunión de ECIEL sobre educación técnica, Rio de Janeiro, marzo de 1979. Asunción: Centro Paraguayo de Estudios Sociológicos, 1979. 225 p.; bibl.; graphs (Investigaciones—Centro Paraguayo de Estudios Sociológicos)

Questionnaire study on the effect of secondary technical education on occupational level. Using matched pair sampling (technical school graduates and nontechnical school graduates matched by sex and age), study revealed significant differences on levels of occupational and educational aspirations and on level of responsibility within occupations, but no significant differences with respect to salary and occupational choice.

4531 Ferraro, Oscar Humberto. Estudios y datos sobre educación técnica y agropecuaria en el Paraguay. Asunción: Centro Paraguayo de Estudios Sociológicos, 1978. 46 p.; indexes (Serie bibliográfica—Centro Paraguayo de Estudios Sociológicos)

Annotated list of publications on agricultural and technical education in Paraguay since 1970. Cross-referenced by topic, by author, and by institution.

Penna, Carlos Víctor. Estudio preliminar para la organización de un Servicio Nacional de Información Educativa en el Paraguay. See *HLAS 42:84.*

4532 Rivarola, Domingo M.; Grazziella Corvalán; and Luis Zúñiga. Determinantes del rendimiento educativo en el Paraguay. Asunción: Centro Paraguayo de Estudios Sociológicos, 1978. 213 p.; bibl. (Serie Educación)

Questionnaire study of determinants of educational achievements in Paraguay. Well-designed, well-executed study. Concludes that socioeconomic status is the single most important variable in predicting educational achievement.

Soler, Carlos A. Andrés Barbero: su vida y su obra. See *HLAS 42:3469*.

Speratti, Juan. Historia de la educación pública en el Paraguay, 1812–1932: origen y evolución histórica de la Escuela España de San Lorenzo, 1869–1975. See *HLAS 42:3470*.

4533 Winkler, Donald R. The distribution of educational resources in Paraguay: implications for equality of opportunity (CES/CER, 24:1, Feb. 1980, p. 73–86, tables)

Questionnaire study of Paraguayan school administrators which compared educational opportunities in urban and rural areas and in public and private institutions. Results of study confirm there is inequality in the distribution of educational resources in Paraguay: children in urban areas are advantaged relative to children in rural areas and children in private schools are better off than those in public schools.

PERU

4534 Bernales B., Enrique. Origen y evolución de la unniversidad [sic] en el Perú. Lima: Pontificia Universidad Católica del Péru, Departamento de Ciencias Sociales, 1978. 75 p.

History of the Peruvian university in two parts. First part traces history of the university from its colonial beginnings through the 19th century. Second part analyzes effects of the four 20th-century university reform movements: 1919, 1930–31, 1946 and 1960. Final section describes loss of autonomy under military government since 1968.

4535 ———. Reportaje a San Marcos (DESCO/Q, 1, 1979?, p. 86–119, tables)

Discussion of inability of the University of San Marcos, and by implication its graduates, to address pressing Peruvian social issues (e.g., poverty, misery, exploitation, domination). The University, which suffers from inadequate financing, poor organization, lack of space and overcrowding, is not up to the challenge of preparing its graduates to address these issues. Most of the article is verbatim account of interview with University's Rector, Gastón Pons Musso.

4536 Chong, Juan. Aspectos metodológicos del modelo de simulación EDUPERU, aplicado en la reforma de la educación peruana (OAS/LE, 23:81, 73–102, tables)

Description of mathematical model which was used to forecast consequences of implementing the Peruvian Educational Reform Law of 1972 and which will be used for other educational planning purposes by the Ministry of Education.

4537 Documento uno: una selección de prensa sobre la problemática universitaria. Lima: Centro de Información, Documentación y Publicaciones—CONUP, 1977. 260 p.; ill.

Selection of approximately 300 newspaper articles published in 1976, documenting the university crisis in Peru.

4538 Educación básica laboral: proceso a un proceso. Eduardo Ballón Echegaray et al. Lima: DESCO, 1978. 142 p.; bibl. (Praxis—Desco; no. 9)

Report describes purposes of the Basic Manual Education (Educación Básica Laboral) legislation in Peru and analyzes its possibilities. Promulgated by the Peruvian General Law of Education No. 19326 of 1972, EBL is designed to provide unschooled adults both general and job-related technical education.

4539 Educación bilingüe: una experiencia en la Amazonía Peruana: antología. Recopilación y revisión, Mildred L. Larson, Patricia M. Davis, Marlene Ballena Dávila. Lima: I. Prado Pastor, 1979. 520 p.; bibl.; ill.; index.

Complete and fascinating case study of an extensive bilingual education experiment among linguistically and culturally diverse ethnic groups residing in the Amazon region of Peru. At the request of the Peruvian Ministry of Education, and with the complete endorsement and full cooperation of the

Peruvian government, for 25 years beginning in 1948, the Summer Institute of Linguistic developed and implemented a bilingual education program among very diverse ethnic groups in the Amazon based on absolute respect for their language, values, cultural norms and integrity. This is the complete account.

4540 Escobar, Alberto. El problema universitario o el vacío ideológico (*in* Perú, hoy. Por Fernando Fuenzalida Vollmar et al. 3. ed. México: Siglo Veintiuno Editores, 1975, p. 260–304)

University Reform Law No. DL-13417, enacted by the military government not only contradicts certain constitutional guarantees but, according to the author, threatens academic freedom as well. For author's first article on this law, see *HLAS 33:4691.*

4541 Palomino I., Luis and Carlos Reyes M. La evaluación de las operaciones intelectuales en educandos de 5 a 8 años en Lima Metropolitana: informe final. Lima: Instituto Nacional de Investigación y Desarrollo de la Educación Augusto Salazar Bondy, Unidad de Investigación Curricular, Subdirección de Investigaciones Educacionales, 1976. 232 p.; bibl.

Description of the development and standardization of ability tests for five-to-eight years old in Lima, Peru. Using final instruments, authors test for significant differences by children's age, type of school (reform or traditional), sex and residence.

4542 Pezo del Pino, César; Eduardo Ballón Echegaray; and Luis Peirano Falconi. El magisterio y sus luchas, 1885–1978. Lima: DESCO, 1978. 276 p.; bibl.

History of teachers' syndicates in Peru. First part of book traces development of Peruvian educational policy as it has affected teachers; second part examines development and current status of teachers' unions.

4543 I [i.e. Primer] Conversatorio sobre los Objetivos de las Profesiones que Ofrece la Universidad Peruana, 21 y 22 de enero de 1974. Lima: Consejo Nacional de la Universidad Peruana, Dirección de Evaluación de Universidades, Oficina de Evaluación, 1974? 10, 21 leaves.

In two parts: 1) describes steps for university curricular planning: community needs assessment, development of educa-

tional objectives and content, curricular sequence, and teaching methodology and evaluation; and 2) consists of an annotated list of laws, decrees and regulations which govern university admissions in Peru.

4544 Riedmiller, Sibylle. Observaciones técnico-pedagógicas en las escuelas rurales en el área quechua del altiplano peruano (III/AI, 39[49]:4, oct./dic. 1979, p. 831–862, tables)

Participant observation study of linguistic conditions in rural schools in the Dept. of Puno, a largely Quechua-speaking area. Study addresses effectiveness of bilingual education and application of new participatory teaching methodology required by the Educational Reform of 1972. Concludes that while majority of teachers are bilingual, Quechua is not properly used in the classroom, and that teachers do not understand and thus cannot implement teaching methodology requirements of the new law.

Rubén González visto por varios autores. See *HLAS 42:3041.*

4545 Seminário sobre Maestrías y Doctorado, 1st, Universidad Nacional Mayor de San Marcos, 1975. Primer Seminário sobre Maestrías y Doctorado. Organizado por la Dirección de los Programas Académicos de Perfeccionamiento; auspiciado por el Consejo Nacional de la Universidad Peruana. Lima, Perú: Universidad Nacional Mayor de San Marcos, Dirección Universitaria de Biblioteca y Publicaciones, 1977. 113 p.; ill.

Proceedings of the Primer Seminario sobre Maestrías y Doctorado held in Lima, Peru, Oct. 1975. Organized and sponsored by la Universidad Nacional Mayor de San Marcos for university, government, and private sector representatives, seminar's primary purpose was to develop a strategy for initiating master's and doctoral level programs in Peru.

4546 Uzátegui Irigoyen, Luis and Luis Muelle López. Estudios sobre costos educacionales. Lima: Ministerio de Educación, Instituto Nacional de Investigación y Desarrollo de la Educación Augusto Salazar Bondy, Subdirección de Investigaciones Educacionales, Unidad de Análisis y Diseño, 1974. 143 p.; bibl.; graphs.

Pt. 1 of a study in process on the cost

of the government of implementing the Educación Básica Laboral (EBL) program. Contains theoretical and methodological sections.

4547 Vargas Vega, Raúl. Educación e identidad nacional (*in* Perú, identidad nacional. César Arróspide de la Flor et al. Lima: Centro de Estudios para el Desarrollo y la Participación, 1979, p. 365–377)

Discussion of the failure of the Peruvian educational system to recognize the native cultural roots of the people. Peru, author contends, is torn between two ideologies, the first imposed by the ruling elite and the second by the indigenous origins of the people. Because historically the Peruvian educational system has only recognized the first of these ideologies, author contends Peru has been denied a national identity.

PUERTO RICO

4548 Arnold, Marjorie R.; John W. Rosado, Jr.; and Douglas A. Penfield. Language choice by bilingual Puerto Rican children on a picture labeling task (MLTA/MLJ, 63:7, Nov. 1979, p. 349–354, bibl., tables)

Factors which affect language choice of bilingual Puerto Rican elementary school children are focus of this study. Specifically, the effects of the language of instruction (English, Spanish) and of the domain (home, church, school) are analyzed. In responding to school tasks, preference is English. When addressed in Spanish and when referring to home and church issues, preference is Spanish. Implications for bilingual education are discussed.

4549 Carreras, Francisco J. Educación universitaria: lo que va de ayer a hoy (UPR/RO, 2:2, junio 1978, p. 130–134)

Reflective essay on factors affecting higher education in Puerto Rico since 1962. Author, currently President of Catholic University of Puerto Rico, was a professor at the Colegio Regional de Humacao on its founding in 1962. Latter experience constitutes starting point of essay. Major factors noted were growth in enrollment, university's role as society's conscience, and student participation in university governance.

4550 Morales Carrión, Arturo. Testimonios de una gestión universitaria. Cari-

caturas, Miche Medina y Filardi. Rio Piedras: Editorial Universidad de Puerto Rico, 1978. 329 p.; ill.

Fascinating collection of speeches, essays and lectures by Arturo Morales Carrión, President of the University of Puerto Rico. First part includes works in Spanish; second part, those in English. Includes strong statement made before US Senate Committee on Foreign Relations on Latin America and the US. His reflections on being Hispanic and American are particularly moving.

4551 Quintero, Ana Helvia. Diferencias entre grupos socio-económicos en el aprendizaje de las matemáticas (UPR/RCS, 20:2, sept. 1978, p. 165–194, bibl., tables)

Examining relationship between socioeconomic class and mathematics achievement among Puerto Rican elementary school children, author finds that middle-class students learn concepts faster than lower-class students. While consistent with findings of North American studies cited in this article, important differences are noted.

4552 Vásquez Figueroa, Onel. Exito y aspiraciones en la socialización formal del estudiante puertorriqueña (UPR/RCS, 20:3/4, dic. 1978, p. 307–346, bibl., tables)

In a questionnaire study of 401 Puerto Rican senior high school students, author concludes that educational expectations and occupational aspirations are conditioned by social class. Moreover, a comparison of these attitudes by sex and by residence (rural, suburban and urban) revealed significant differences.

URUGUAY

4553 Centro de Investigación y Experimentación Pedagógica. Elementos para un diagnóstico del sistema educativo. Director del proyecto, Héctor Apezechea; responsable de los capítulos II y III, Aníbal Cagnoni, responsable del capítulo VIII, Myrian Varela; asistentes, Helios Segovia et al.; consultores, Beatriz Tavares de Garmendia et al.; edición a cargo de Alberto Gálvez. Montevideo: Centro de Investigación y Experimentación Pedagógica, 1977. 401, 7 p.; bibl.

Ambitious attempt to compile in one source all available relevant information on Uruguayan education. Prepared by Uruguay's

Centro de Investigación y Experimentación Pedagógica (CIEP). Book contains separate chapters for such topics as methodology and antecedents for present study; history; organization and administration; primary, secondary and technical education. Well documented. Vital source for students of Uruguayan education.

Clemente Filho, Antonio dos Santos. Participação da comunidade na integração do deficiente mental. See item **4592.**

4554 Meerhoff, Ricardo. La educación y el futuro. Montevideo: Universidad de la República, Facultad de Humanidades y Ciencias, Dirección General de Extensión Universitaria, División de Publicaciones y Ediciones, 1979. 7 p. (Estudios en teoría y filosofía de la ciencia)

Author argues that to plan for future of education in Uruguay, policy makers need not look to models outside of the country. Education sensitive to Uruguay's needs can be planned only by "looking inward." Argument is unconvincing.

Zubillaga, Carlos. Ciencias sociales en el Uruguay: historia. See *HLAS 42:3507.*

VENEZUELA

4555 Abreu, José Vicente. Rómulo Gallegos: ideas educativas en La Alborada. Caracas: Ediciones Centauro, 1977 [i.e. 1978]. 276 p. (Serie azul; no. 4)

Life and philosophy of Rómulo Gallegos, interpreted largely through his own writings in the popular journal *La Alborada.* Contains many fascinating insights into Venezuela's most influential educator. As early as 1909, for example, Gallegos likened schools to jails, a very early use of what has become a popular analogy among critics. Interesting reading.

4556 Albornoz, Orlando. Teoría y praxis de la educación superior venezolana. Caracas: Facultad de Humanidades y Educación, Escuela de Educación, UCV, 1979. 172 p.; bibl.

Seven essays which focus on higher education in Venezuela since 1958. Growth in primary and secondary education has been extraordinary. Essays look at consequences and implications of this growth on higher ed-

ucation. Addresses role of universities and professionals in national policy determination, in maintaining social and political stability, and in development.

4557 Aray, Julio. Sadismo en la enseñanza. Con la colaboración muy especial de Tomás Eloy Martínez y de las siguientes personas, José Ricardo Eliaschev et al.; portada, Juan Fresán. Caracas, Venezuela: Monte Avila Editores, 1979. 364 p.; bibl. (Colección Estudios)

In a series of essays, authors examine the destructive effects, i.e., sadismo, of television and newspaper, and schools, colleges and universities. In addition, Julio Aray, principal author and volume's editor, analyzes school attendance in Latin America and concludes that educational opportunities are not only unequal but, in fact, largely nonexistent.

4558 Beltrán Prieto, Luis. Un maestro especial (*in* Segal, Alicia Frelich de. Entrevistados en carne y hueso. Fotos de Jorge Pineda. Caracas: Librería Suma, 1976 or 1977, p. 279–290)

Verbatim interview with Luis Beltrán Prieto, one of Venezuela's best-known educators. Beltrán was founder and first president of the Venezuelan Teachers Federation (FVM) and Minister of Education 1947–48. In 1967, he founded the political party Movimiento Electoral del Pueblo (MEP), and is currently Senator from the state of Zulia. Among Beltrán's key points is his assertion that even the worst of Venezuela's public schools is superior to the best of its private schools.

4559 Cortés, Luis. Política de investigación en la Universidad Simón Rodríguez. Caracas: Universidad Nacional Experimental Simón Rodríguez, 1976. 18 p.; bibl.

Essay describes research policy of la Universidad Nacional Experimental Simón Rodríguez, Caracas. Consistent with its "experimental" mission, the following are among the components of the University's research policy: research must focus on science and technology and must be "applied" and "interdisciplinary." University is organized by research areas, and in this respect is truly experimental.

4560 Furter, Pierre. De la lucha contra el analfabetismo al desarrollo cultural. Traducido integramente del francés por Carmen Margarita Nonés de Guillet. Caracas: Fondo Editorial Común, 1978. 259 p.; bibl.; ill.

Against background of relatively high illiteracy rates in Latin America and the cultural domination and political oppression which are its consequences, author argues for a total revision of the "educational system" concept. Essential for cultural development is a policy of permanent, lifelong education encompassing all teaching directed at different groups in different situations at different times in their lives. Examples in Brazil and Venezuela are cited.

González, César. Rubén González, una vida al servicio de Venezuela. See *HLAS 42:3023.*

4561 Lerner de Almea, Ruth. Experiencias educativas. Caracas: Ministerio de Educación, Oficina Ministerial de Información y Relaciones, Departamento de Imprenta, 1977. 318 p.; 2 leaves of plates; bibl.; ill.

Collection of previously published essays and articles by well-known Venezuelan educator. The purpose of education, women in education and science, teacher training, and educational planning are among diverse topics included. Scope of book is testimony to the extraordinary range of experiences of this remarkable educator.

4562 Mancilla, Ramón. Professional manpower needs in Venezuela (*in* Higher education in the world community. Edited by Stephen K. Bailey. Washington: American Council on Education, 1977, p. 105–111)

Formal education in Venezuela has not met the challenges created by the radical change from an agricultural to an oil economy. While Venezuela now has the organizational structure to initiate development projects and to institute national income distribution programs, the author argues, its educational system has been largely unaffected by economic growth, and furthermore, has not contributed to it. Consideration of nontraditional means of meeting Venezuela's technical and social requirements is suggested.

4563 Maza Zavala, Domingo Felipe. Universidad, ciencia y tecnología. Carátula, Annelly Márquez. Caracas: Ediciones de la Biblioteca, Universidad Central de Venezuela, 1979. 336 p.; bibl. (Colección Temas; 80)

Collection of essays, articles previously published in Caracas' daily newspaper *El Nacional*, and speeches which loosely focus on university-related issues. Lack of focus detracts only slightly from Maza Zavala's thought-provoking and far-ranging essays.

4564 Prieto Figueroa, Luis Beltrán. El concepto del líder, el maestro como líder. Portada, Juan Fresán. 5. ed. Caracas, Venezuela: Monte Avila Editores, 1979. 217 p.; bibl. (Colección Estudios)

Fifth edition of same book with only minor modifications from earlier versions. Analyzes concept of "Líder," from the English word "leader," and argues that there is no Spanish word which means the same thing. Those who obey a leader do so voluntarily; not so those who obey a *caudillo, jefe, adalid, guía, conductor, director.* Applies concept to various settings, including education.

Rey Fajardo, José del. Los jesuitas en la historia de la educación en Coro. See *HLAS 42:2752.*

4565 Ribeiro, Darcy. Propuestas: acerca de la renovación. Caracas: Universidad Central de Venezuela, Comisión de Autoestudio y Planeamiento, 1970. 205 p.; bibl.; ill. (Ediciones del Rectorado)

Planning document for a proposed reorganization of la Universidad Central de Venezuela prepared at the request of its rector, Jesús M. Bianco. Intended as a discussion document; contains specific proposals for organizational changes in 12 areas.

4566 Roche, Marcel. Descubriendo a Prometeo: ensayos sobre ciencia y tecnología en Venezuela y Latinoamérica. Caracas: Monte Avila Editores, 1975. 218 p.; bibl. (Colección Estudios)

A collection of essays which explore relative underdevelopment of Latin American countries, especially Venezuela, in science and technology. Written by Marcel Roche while President of Venezuela's National Council of Scientific and Technological Research, essays focus on historical, psychological, social, and political explanations.

4567 ———. La investigación científica y tecnológica en Venezuela en los últimos cincuenta años (*in* Venezuela moderna, medio siglo de historia, 1926–1976. Ramón J. Velásquez et al. 2. ed. Caracas: Fundación Eugenio Mendoza: Editorial Ariel, 1979, p. 965–1004, bibl.)

Review of development of scientific and technological research in Venezuela. Author divides development into three periods which he labels: 1) individualistic—to 1954; 2) institutional—to 1969; and 3) planned—to present. Despite recent emphasis on planned scientific and technological research, author argues that in Venezuela the development of science in general has been ad-hoc.

4568 Rosenblat, Angel. La educación en Venezuela: voz de alerta. 2. ed. corr. y aumentada. Caracas: Monte Avila Editores, 1978. 221 p. (Colección Estudios)

In a series of essays on a variety of educational topics which range from primary schools through universities, from preschool to adult education, from humanities to social sciences, author argues that Venezuelan education is failing. Bemoans defeatist attitude of many who accept notion that education merely mirrors society's institutions, and because these are failing, so is education. Education, he argues, must be a force for positive societal change. First edition published in 1964.

4569 Seminario sobre Curriculum, Caracas, *1975.* Del diálogo a la acción: informe. Caracas: República de Venezuela, Ministerio de Educación, 1976. 2 v.; bibl.; ill.

Vol. 1 of final report of the Multinational Seminar on Curriculum held in Caracas, April 1975 and sponsored by Venezuela's Ministry of Education and by the OAS. Consists of three parts: 1) introduction which describes planning process for seminar including its history, program, and participants; 2) section on curriculum theory; and 3) abstracts of presentations.

4570 Seminario sobre la Problemática de la Educación Superior en Venezuela, *1st, Mérida, Venezuela, 1978.* El modelo tecnocrático y la educación superior en Venezuela. María del Pilar Quintero et al. Caracas, Venezuela,: Editorial La Enseñanza Viva, 1980. 208 p.; bibl. (Colección de bolsillo)

Generalizing from observations of the University of the Andes (Mérida), authors find that students do not think critically, have little or no sense of history, are incapable of analysis, and are not prepared to conduct research. These problems, authors continue, reflect educational deficiencies at all levels, primary through university. Major portion of book consists of eight appendices designed to address these deficiencies.

4571 Universidad Simón Rodríguez. Filosofía y estructura de la Universidad Símon Rodríguez: informe presentado al Consejo Nacional de Universidades, Barinas, mayo 1976. Caracas: La Universidad, 1976. 39 p.

Booklet describes present status and accomplishments to date of the Universidad Experimental Simón Rodríguez, created by Venezuelan Presidential Decree No. 1582 on 24 Jan. 1974

4572 ———. Informe sobre la creación de la Universidad Simón Rodríguez. Caracas: La Universidad, 1977. 91 p.; ill. (Documentos—Universidad Nacional Experimental Simón Rodríguez; 1)

Nov. 1973 report to the Venezuelan National Council of Universities prepared by the Organizing Committee of the Universidad Simón Rodríguez which was established by Decree No. 777 of 20 Oct. 1971. Commission recommended the creation of the Universidad Simón Rodríguez as an "experimental university."

4573 Venezuela. Consejo Nacional de Universidades. Oficina de Planificación del Sector Universitario. Matrícula estudiantil personal docente y de investigación y egresados del sector universitario. Caracas: La Oficina, 1975. 233 p.; graphs; tables (Boletín estadístico—Oficina de Planifación del Sector Universitario; no. 2)

Large volume of data well presented in tables, charts, maps, and graphs which summarizes a wealth of information on the Venezuelan university for 1970–76. No analysis.

4574 ———. Ministerio de Educación. Oficina Sectorial de Planificación y Presupuesto. Centro de Documentación. La revolución educativa. Caracas: Ministerio de Educación, Dirección de Apoyo Docente, Departamento de Publicaciones, 1976. 217 p.; ill.

In two parts: 1) consists of the entire report of the Venezuelan Minister of Education to the National Congress on Venezuelan educational programs during 1976–77; 2) consists of a statistical summary of all levels of Venezuelan education (primary, secondary, higher, technical, and adult).

4575 Yepes Boscán, Guillermo. Marco global de una política de educación superior. Caracas: Cidal, between 1973 and 1976. 24 p.; bibl. (Documentos—Centro de Información y Documentación para América Latina; entrega no. 31)

Exposition of author's views on philosophical, political and socioeconomic mission of higher education in Venezuela. Specific references are made to the mission of the university in the Venezuelan state of Zulia.

BRAZIL

KATHLEEN B. FISCHER, *Assistant Director, Latin American Center, University of California, Los Angeles*

SEVERAL TRENDS DOMINATE RECENT RESEARCH and writing about Brazilian education. First, the political *abertura*[1], or opening, is well in evidence. An outpouring of historical, philosophical, and sociological analyses challenge traditional interpretations of the role and function of education in Brazilian society. That many of these critiques adopt a "dependency" framework is not surprising in view of censorship restrictions removed only recently. A number of works are notable: Berger's *Educação e dependência* (item **4580**), the earliest (1976) and most global in scope; Freitag's *Escola, estado, e sociedade* (item **4605**), with an emphasis on developments since the military takeover of 1964; and the recently-initiated journal *Educação e Sociedade* (item **4596**), a triannual publication of the São Paulo-based Centro de Estudos Educação e Sociedade. Berger and Freitag, both German-educated, have strongly influenced various subsequent works. Cortez Editora, in fact, has established an entire publication series of high-quality master's theses and doctoral dissertations, all couched in "dependency" analyses (see items **4627, 4640** and **4645**).

Other recent social critiques are less strident in adopting models of conflict and control. For students and scholars of political socialization, Maria de Lourdes Chagas Deiró Nosella presents, in *As belas mentiras* (item **4626**) a fascinating look at underlying ideological messages in primary-level textbooks. Conflict stems, not merely from the ubiquitous stereotyping of individuals and social institutions, but from unrealistic impressions of the liberating potential of the school system.

The second perceptible trend in research and writing about Brazilian education relates to national policy emphasis on development of autonomous technology and scientific capability. Since articulation of the first Basic Plan of Scientific and Technological Development (PBDCT) for 1973–74, increasing attention has been focused on the directive to higher education to increase not only output of skilled graduates, but the research productivity of faculty and associated organizations. For a sense of the scope and commitment to this policy initiative, it is essential to review subsequent PBDCT's (items **4585** and **4586**). The history of national scientific development efforts in Brazil is nicely summarized by Richard Ferreira (item **4601**), and several works aim at assessment of higher education's response to post–1964 policy in this area. Ana Maria Fernandes Skeff (item **4641**) examines the productivity of the University of Brasília in terms of faculty research, publications, and innovation. Other publications explore the same theme with a particular focus on graduate-level studies in education (items **4584** and **4589**).

The political *abertura* has prompted critical analyses of the direction of scientific and technological development policy as well. Two significant works (items **4616** and **4624**) decry the evolution and orientation of nuclear policy in Brazil, arguing that technology transfer and expansion of productive capabilities have only modified the form and nature of technological dependency. Antônio de Souza Teixeira Júnior (item **4644**) calls for more restrictive policy measures to break the cycle.

With the emphasis on scientific development, and again in the spirit of the *abertura*,[1] several important works have proceeded to critically inquire into the Brazilian experience in higher education. Notable in this regard are Maria de Lourdes de Albuquerque Fávero's *A Universidade brasileira em busca de sua identidade* (1977, item **4598**) and Edson Machado de Sousa's cogent analysis (item **4617**) of the experience of the *vestibulares*, or university entrance examinations.

Attention to scientific development has necessitated the evolution of a technological infrastructure in the educational arena. A number of recent planning and evaluation studies accordingly reflect this pattern (items **4309** and **4590**). As a model of research and evaluation methodology, Goldberg and Franco's *Inovação educacional* (1980) is impressive in its comprehensive approach, and Eclea Guazzelli's study (item **4611**) of socioeconomic marginality and cognitive development among seven-year olds in Porto Alegre reflects the increasing application of research and evaluation strategies to educational problems of the disadvantaged. Nonetheless, there is still a relative paucity of literature related to education of Brazil's indigenous populations. A notable exception is Bartolomé Melía's anthropologically-based study of indigenous education and literacy (item **4622**).

Paulo Freire continues to inspire considerable research and inquiry (item **4613**). Silvia Maria Manfredi's *Política: educação popular* (1978, item **4618**) examines facets of the Freire experience in Brazil in the early 1960s, and Freire's own *Cartas a Guinea-Bissau* (1977, item **4602**) provides thoughtful reflection (in Spanish) on the 1975–76 literacy campaign there. The Freire influence is also evident in various works focusing on non-formal, or out-of-school, education (item **4607**).

Sweeping legislative reforms have marked the Brazilian educational experience since 1964. The *Lei de Diretrizes e Bases* (LDB) of 1971 has been analyzed from a variety of perspectives. Both Danilo Lima and Ester Buffa explore the influence and interests of the Catholic Church in the LDB promulgation in their respective studies (items **4587** and **4615**). Carlos Roberto Jamil Cury provides historical scope to the Church's involvement in Brazilian education in his study of ideological interest groups in conflict during the important 1930–34 period (item **4595**).

For those seeking a sound, English language introduction to Brazilian education, Haussman and Haar's *Education in Brazil* (1978) is a welcome addition to the literature. With the resurgence of liberal inquiry and advancements in educational technology in Brazil, a reference volume like that of Haussman and Haar is particularly useful for its overview and thoughtful perspective on the complexities and extraordinary dynamics of Brazilian education.

I am grateful for the assistance of Ana María Morales and the helpful suggestions of Mabel Oliveira and Candido Gomes in the preparation of this section.

1 For more on the *abertura*, see the GOVERNMENT AND POLITICS: BRAZIL section, p. 622–636.

4576 **Albuquerque, Lynaldo Cavalcante de.** Universidade e realidade brasileira. João Pessoa: Editora Universitária/UFPb, 1979. 187 p.

Volume of essays on various themes, the intent of which is to consider the current reality of Brazilian higher education, especially in the Northeast. Organized in three parts: 1) general commentaries based on author's experiences as professor and administrator; 2) policy pronouncements and speeches delivered 1976–79 during author's tenure as Rector of Federal University of Paraíba; and 3) work conducted for Council of Brazilian University Rectors, 1977–79. Considers such themes as technology transfer, scientific policy for the Northeast, the university and business, and education and industrial development.

4577 *Analysis & Documentary Information.* Ministry of Education and Culture (MEC), Brazilian Literacy Movement Foundation (MOBRAL), Center for Training, Research and Documentation (CETEP), Documentation Sector (SEDOC). Vol. 3, No. 2, abril/dez. 1977– . Rio de Janeiro.

In addition to lead articles dealing with adult education and community development themes, this English-language journal abstracts research and publications related to MOBRAL, on such topics as the regression phenomenon in former MOBRAL literacy students, elements for evaluation of functional literacy programs, MOBRAL clients and their characteristics, and the adult education teacher. Important source of documentation in English on MOBRAL.

4578 **Andrade, António Alberto Banha de.** A reforma pombalina dos estudos secundários no Brasil. São Paulo: Edição Saraiva, 1978. 226 p.; bibl.

Detailed historical study of Pombal reforms (1759), with specific reference to secondary level and to implementation of reforms in various parts of Brazil. Documentary appendix provides fascinating look at curricular changes.

4579 **Azevedo, Neíza Dias da Cruz.** Produtividade na escola: as contribuições da administração. Rio de Janeiro: Editora Rio, 1977. 439 p.; bibl.

Developed in conjunction with project to increase effectiveness (productivity) of military education. Stresses contribution of administrators in specifying objectives, norms, activities, curriculum and evaluation. Other chapters describe legislative requirements, university administration. Concludes with working plan for educational administration. Neglects external factors in pressing for technical solutions. [A.M. Morales]

4580 **Berger, Manfredo.** Educação e dependência. São Paulo: DIFEL [and] Universidade Federal do Rio Grande do Sul, Porto Alegre, 1976. 354 p.; bibl.

Originally presented as doctoral thesis in social sciences, Federal University of Bielefeld, Federal Republic of Germany. Analysis of Brazilian educational system with particular reference to its place in the global context of transnational dependency. Reviews perspectives of Ribeiro, Pereira and Cardoso as explanatory models for historical development of Brazilian education. Explores future prospects for overcoming dependency. Influential volume.

4581 **Biaggio, Angela Maria Brasil.** Achievement motivation of Brazilian students (International Journal of Intercultural Relations [Society for Intercultural Education, Training, and Research, Purdue, Ind.] 2:2, Summer 1978, p. 186–196, bibl., tables)

Two-stage study of achievement motivation among high-school students in state of Guanabara. In first stage, survey of 455 students revealed higher achievement motivation among females. In second stage, training program succeeded in raising scores on motivation scales of both males and females. Based on previous work of McClelland, Angelini, Kolb.

4582 **Boaventura, Edivaldo M.** Extensão universitária e formação continuada (UFP/EB, 3:4, 1977, p. 299–314, tables)

Draws upon international experiences in US and France to illustrate potential benefits of university extension as continuing education for adults. Reviews historical background of university extension in Brazil as well as implications of university reform legislation for extension education.

4583 ———; **José Silvério Baia Horta;** and **Paulo da Silveira Rosas.** Relatório-síntese dos trabalhos do seminário sobre o estudo da educação extra-escolar no Brasil (Forum Educacional [Fundação Getúlio Vargas, Instituto de Estudos Avançados em

Educação, Rio de Janeiro] 1:2, abril/junho 1977, p. 17–32)

Reports on main aspects of seminar on non-formal, or out-of-school, education held in 1976 under auspices of MEC/DAU/CAPES. Emphasis of seminar was on identification of theoretical and methodological frameworks for studying non-formal education.

Summarizes presentations of Pierre Furter and Claudio de Moura Castro, as well as presentations of case studies of non-formal education programs in Brazil. Valuable analysis and discussion of difficulties inherent in evaluation of non-formal education.

4584 Brazil. Ministério da Educação e Cultura. Departamento de Documentação e Divulgação. Seminario sobre a produção científica nos programas de pos-graduação em educação. Brasília: 1979. 93 p.

Proceedings of CAPES seminar held in May 1978. Focuses on directions of educational research, dissertations, and theses in graduate education and "scientific production." Presentations by Luiz Antonio Cunha, Claudio de Moura Castro, Jacques Velloso. Important as a form of self-assessment of policy implementation in graduate-level training in education.

4585 ————. Presidência da República. II [i.e. Segundo] Plano Básico de Desenvolvimento Científico e Tecnológico 1977–79. Brasília: 1977. 217 p.; charts; graphs; tables.

Details national policy for scientific and technological development, component of II Plano Nacional de Desenvolvimento 1975–79. Includes statements and program descriptions devoted to industrial, energy, agricultural policy, as well as to development of new technologies, strengthening of national industry, development of infrastructure (energy, transportation, communications). Additional sections on scientific development and training of human resources for research, institutional organization and support. Tables, graphs illustrate breakdown of resources, finances for 1975–77 period.

4586 ————. ————. Secretaria de Planejamento. III [i.e. Terceiro] Plano Básico de Desenvolvimento Científico e Tecnológico 1980–85. Brasília: 1980. 77 p.; charts; graphs; tables.

Statement of national policy directions in scientific and technological development for 1980–85 period. Building on earlier plans (1973–74 and 1975–79), adopts long-range perspective for realizing objective of growing scientific capability and increased technological autonomy through strengthening of Sistema Nacional de Desenvolvimento Científico y Tecnológico (SNDCT).

4587 Buffa, Ester. Ideologias em conflito: escola pública e escola privada. Capa de Guilherme Valpéteris. São Paulo: Cortez & Moraes, 1979. 130 p.; bibl. (Coleção Educação universitária)

Analysis of ideological interests of groups involved in struggle between public and private educational systems during formulation of LDB. Extensive bibliography.

Carvalho, Afrânio de. Raul Soares, um líder da República Velha. See *HLAS 42:3634.*

4588 Carvalho, Laerte Ramos de. As reformas pombalinas da instrução pública. São Paulo: Edição Saraiva, 1978. 241 p.; bibl.

Reedition of classic study by distinguished professor of philosophy and history. Interprets Pombal reforms in context of 18th-century Portugal, devoting special consideration to the illuminist movement, the contributions of Verney, the nature of Jesuit education, the role of the bourgeoisie. Appendix includes documents pertaining to Pernambuco educators of the period.

4589 Castro, Celia Lucia Monteiro de. Eficácia, eficiência e efetividade dos cursos de mestrado em educação no país (Forum Educacional [Fundação Getúlio Vargas, Instituto de Estudos Avançados em Educação, Rio de Janeiro] 1[1]:3/4, jan./março 1977, p. 111–142)

Analysis and assessment of development of Master's-level training in education points to certain continuing deficiencies: failure to fully respond to national needs; lack of adequate counseling in research orientations (for thesis); lack of adequate research sources. Based on 1975–76 study of institutional output, curricular selection, etc. of Master's training programs in education. Important topical work.

4590 Castro, Cláudio de Moura. O "management" da pesquisa (*in* Encontro Inter-regional de Cientistas Sociais do Brasil, 2d, Garanhuns, Brazil, 1974. Anais do II [i.e. Segundo] Encontro Inter-regional Cientistas

Sociais do Brasil: reuniões realizadas de 21 a 26 de janeiro de 1974 em Garanhuns-PE. Recife: Ministério da Educação e Cultura, Instituto Joaquim Nabuco de Pesquisas Sociais, 1977, p. 136–164)

Outlines views on research management with respect to such topics as criteria for selection and promotion of personnel, interdisciplinary and multi-institutional research, utilization of outside and foreign consultants and experts, and appropriateness of various methodological tools. Valuable as an early (1974) statement of perspective of later CAPES director.

————— and **Jorge A. Sanguinetty.** Custos e determinantes da educação na América Latina. See item **4309.**

4591 Ciclo de Estudos sobre as Grandes Diretrizes da Universidade Brasileira, *Belo Horizonte, Brazil, 1977.* As grandes diretrizes da universidade brasileira. Lynaldo Cavalcanti de Albuquerque et al. Belo Horizonte: Universidade Federal de Minas Gerais, 1977. 82 p. (Edições do cinqüentenário da UFMG; 2. Publicação—Universidade Federal de Minas Gerais; no. 659)

Presentations given at seminar commemorating 50th anniversary of Federal University of Minas Gerais. Several university rectors and government officials give views on role of higher education in contemporary Brazilian society.

4592 Clemente Filho, Antonio dos Santos. Participação da comunidade na integração do deficiente mental. Brasília: Departamento de Documentação e Divulgação, 1977. 60 p.; bibl.

Short monograph discussing role of the community in integration of the handicapped. Part of special multinational education project by Brazil, Uruguay, Paraguay. Chapters on lifelong programs for handicapped, role of the family and the community, rights and legislation, voluntary organizations, other resources for handicapped. Advocates holistic approach to the full integration of handicapped in all phases of life and work. Considerable portion of material adapted from material presented at Latin American conference in 1972.

4593 Costa, Diva de Moura Diniz. A CEAE e a formação de recursos humanos para a educação (INEP/RBEP, 142, maio/agôsto 1978, p. 119–125)

Brief report of objectives and activities of the Comissão de Ensino da Area da Educação (CEAE), a national-level planning and evaluation board linked to MEC's Dept. of University Affairs. Includes background rationale for formation and details of CEAE composition.

4594 Cunha, Luis Antônio. Educação e desenvolvimento social no Brasil. 2. ed. Rio de Janeiro: F. Alves, 1977. 291 p.; bibl.; tables.

Re-publication of highly influential critique of Brazilian education in context of development. Material reorganized into self-contained essays on: education and construction of open society; education and income distribution; inequality of schooling; unequal performance; educational policy: *contenção e liberação.* Final essay explores thesis that national educational policy has simultaneously pursued approaches that foster social class conflict and approaches that foster liberation.

4595 Cury, Carlos Roberto Jamil. Ideologia e educação brasileira: católicos e liberais. São Paulo: Cortez & Moraes, 1978. 201 p.; appendices; bibl. (Coleção Educação universitária)

Well-researched analysis of the ideological confrontation over education between the Catholic Church and the pioneers of the New School movement in Brazil in the critical 1930–34 period. Author contends that failure to seek compromise has had far-reaching consequences to the present day.

Díaz Araújo, Enrique. Paulo Freire: seudólogo de la pedagogía dialéctica. See item **4318.**

4596 *Educação e Sociedade.* Revista quadrimestral de ciencias da educação. Centro de Estudos Educação e Sociedade. No. 1, set. 1978 [through] No. 3, maio 1979– . São Paulo.

First three issues of new scholarly journal devoted to "critical analysis of education and society in Brazil" and to "assumptions about the struggle against colonial education:" No. 1 (set. 1978) includes articles by P. Freire (adult literacy), M. Gadotti (pedagogy of conflict), E.A. Vieira (power and education); No. 2 (jan. 1979) carries theme of "Administration, Power and Labor" with contributions by M.G. Arroyo (educational administration, power and participation), E.S.

de Sa Barreto (technological tradition and the instructional system), P.L. Goergen (university structure and function); and No. 3 (maio 1979) titled "Pedagogy of the Oppressed and Education of the Colonizer" contains several articles based on Campinas round-table on same theme held Nov. 1978 (V. Paiva, C. Brandão, P. de Tarso Santos, etc.) Published by Cortez e Moraes, São Paulo.

4597 Encontro universidade-indústria, setor tecnologia industrial. São Paulo: Instituto Roberto Simonsen, 1977. 95 p.

Proceedings of conference held April 1977, sponsored by Instituto Roberto Simonsen, a federation of Paulista industries. Purpose of Institute and conference: to gather suggestions, share information about teaching, research, and training related to improvement of industrial technology. Presentations on engineering programs, including discussion of *cursos integrados,* specialization studies, and the post-graduate system.

4598 Fávero, Maria de Lourdes de Albuquerque. A universidade brasileira em busca de sua identidade. Petrópolis, Brasil: Editora Vozes, 1977. 102 p.; bibl. (Coleção Educação e tempo presente; 13)

Analysis of function and objectives of the university in Brazil, from its inception through the 1968 reform. Useful bibliography of sources and legislation.

4599 Fávero, Osmar and **Victor Valla.** Educação extra-escolar no Brasil: revisão de conceitos básicos (Forum Educacional [Fundação Getúlio Vargas, Instituto de Estudos Avançados em Educação (IESAE), Rio de Janeiro] 1:3/4, jan./março, 1977, p. 53–62)

Reviews various theoretical models of non-formal education from international perspective; offers critique related to differences between developing and post-industrial societies. While acknowledging virtues of non-formal education, insists on need for thorough examination of underlying assumptions about Brazilian development and cautions against adoption of foreign models without independent examination of Brazil's unique reality.

4600 Ferraz, Ester de Figueiredo. Alternativas da educação. Rio de Janeiro: José Olympio Editora, 1976. 185 p.; tables.

Discusses possibilities of alternative education within context of Brazilian educational legislation. Misleading title to traditionalist and somewhat elitist view of educational options. Includes useful statistics. [A.M. Morales]

4601 Ferreira, Ricardo. Origens da atividade científica no Brasil (SBPC/CC, 30:11, nov. 1978, p. 1301–1307)

Historical overview of scientific development in Brazil. Highlights significance of national efforts. Good background piece.

4602 Freire, Paulo. Cartas á Guinéa-Bissau: registros de uma experiência em processo. Rio de Janeiro: Paz e Terra, 1977. 173 v.; bibl.; ill. (Coleção O Mundo, hoje; v. 22)

Freire reflects on process of educational transformation in Guinea-Bissau during 1975–76 period. Lucid, provocative account of mounting of adult literacy campaign. Title in Portuguese, text in Spanish.

4603 ———. Conciencia e historia: la praxis educativa de Paulo Freire. Antología. Selección, estudio preliminar y notas a cargo de Carlos Alberto Torres Novoa. México: Ediciones Gernika, 1978. 172 p.; bibl.; ill. (Colección Educación y sociología)

Anthology in Spanish of selected Freire excerpts as well as introductory section synthesizing Freire thought vis-à-vis "consciousness, history, and liberation." Particularly useful conceptual chapter on the research dimension of Freire's psycho-social literacy method.

4604 Freire, Sônia and **José Renato Monteiro.** Os "meios pobres" do audiovisual e a escola brasileira (INEP/RBEP, 63:144, maio/agôsto 1979, p. 43–52)

Argues for development of methodology and expanded use of A-V materials as a means to individualize instruction; suggests demystication of mass media from pilot project, Audiovisual na Educação (Aveduc), financed by INEP.

4605 Freitag, Barbara. Escola, estado e sociedade. São Paulo: São Paulo Livraria Editora Ltda., 1978. 135 p.

Examines history of educational development in Brazil, focusing particular attention on post–1964 period. Borrowing from Durkheim, Althusser, Schultz, and others, the author attempts to reconcile theoretical differences in illustrating the inherent instability of Brazil's approach to education as both a means to democratization and a form of investment in human capital production. Important and influential work.

Furter, Pierre. De la lucha contra el analfabetismo al desarrollo cultural. See item **4560**.

4607 ———. Os paradoxos da educação extra-escolar ou a gênese está no fim: comentários à guisa de conclusão para o Seminário sobre o Estudo da Educação Extra-Escolar no Brasil (Forum Educacional [Fundação Getúlio Vargas, Instituto de Estudos Avançados em Educação, Rio de Janeiro] 1:2, abril/junho 1977, p. 3–16)

Highlights various issues raised during seminar on non-formal, or out-of-school, education, sponsored by Instituto Superior de Estudos Avançados em Educação (IESAE) in 1976. Emphasizes importance of research and inquiry into relationship between formal and non-formal educational phenomena from variety of perspectives—anthropological, historical, political, and economic. Also raises pertinent questions about nature and role of researcher and nature of conceptual models adopted for conducting research and evaluation of non-formal education.

4608 Gama, Elizabeth M.P. and Paul Pedersen. Readjustment problems of Brazilian returnees from graduate studies in the United States (International Journal of Intercultural Relations [Society for Intercultural Education, Training and Research, Purdue, Indiana] 1:4, Winter 1977, p. 46–59)

Pilot study of 31 LASPAU scholars interviewed after return to Brazil. Taped interviews coded over 16-month period explored personal and professional problems. Professional adjustment problems included lack of facilities, intellectual stimulation, opportunity, and research time. In general, however, returnees coped adequately. Useful for research on transnational education programs, foreign students.

4609 Goldberg, Maria Amélia de Azevêdo and Maria Laura P.B. Franco. Inovação educacional: um projecto controlado por avaliação e pesquisa. Com a colaboração de Ana Maria Saul, Andiara A.A. de O. Balletta and Regina Helena Zerbini Denigres. São Paulo: Cortez & Moraes [and] Fundação Carlos Chaga, 1980. 434 p.; bibl.; ill.; tables.

Elaborately-documented study of re-

search and evaluation conducted in conjunction with development of scientific problem-solving instructional program for primary school. Valuable on several levels: as model of research and evaluation methods and procedures; as case study of problem-solving curricular program; as example of current state-of-the-art in Brazilian educational technology.

4610 ——— **and Clarilza Prado de Souza.** A prática da avaliação. Capa de Guilherme Valpéteris. São Paulo: Cortez & Moraes, 1979. 168 p.; bibl.; ill. (Coleção Educação universitária)

Practical guide to educational evaluation with attention to such areas as planning, methodology, and training. Examples of project evaluation included. Useful for university classes in education, as well as for curriculum supervisors, educational psychologists, and policy analysts.

4611 Guazzelli, Ecléa. A criança marginalizada e o atendimento pré-escolar. Porto Alegre: Editora Globo, 1979. 141 p.; bibl.; ill.

Exemplary study exploring relationship between socioeconomic marginality, pre-school education, and psychological development. Sample of 128 children from middle and low class in Porto Alegre. Opening chapters detail scope of problem with particular reference to Rio Grande do Sul where, in 1975, only 68.4 percent of seven-year olds attended school. Highly significant study of problem that stands at forefront of Brazilian education today.

4612 Haussman, Fay and Jerry Haar. Education in Brazil. Hamden, Conn.: Archon Books, 1978. 169 p.; bibl.; ill.; index (World education series)

Important reference volume examining structure and function of Brazil's public and private educational systems. Begins with general contextual introduction to Brazilian geography, culture, social class structure, and politics. Subsequent chapters treat Brazilian educational history, finance, legislation, administration, educational reform, and national policy. "First attempt to give a comprehensive overview of Brazilian education after 1971." Authors argue in foreword that Brazilian education has "gyrated between massive, but still inadequate, numerical expansions, and technical, but socially irrelevant, pedagogic reformulations."

4613 Jorge, J. Simões. A ideologia de Paulo Freire. São Paulo: Edições Loyola, 1979. 87 p.; bibl. (Coleção Paulo Freire)

Objective of this short monograph is to make better known fundamental points of Freire with respect to "education as a practice of freedom" and "conscientização." Includes biography of Freire, glossary of terms generated by Freire, and bibliography of works by and about Freire. One of seven monographs in Freire series by publisher.

4614 Liberdade acadêmica e opção totalitária: um debate memorável. Introdução e compilação de Antônio Ferreira Paim. São Paulo: Artenova, 1979. 172 p.

Compilation of letters, newspaper editorials, and other exchanges related to 1979 "crisis" at Rio de Janeiro's Catholic University (PUC-RJ) over alleged censorship of curriculum materials by administration and ensuing accusations of Marxist totalitarianism at PUC. Interesting for diverse views of academic freedom presented by some of Brazil's leading scholars of history and philosophy.

4615 Lima, Danilo. Educação, Igreja e ideologia: uma análise sociológica da elaboração da Lei de Diretrizes e Bases. Rio de Janeiro: Francisco Alves, 1978. 139 p.; bibl. (Série Educação em questão)

Explores role of Catholic Church in antecedents to and evolution of 1971 educational reform legislation (LDB). Couched in sociological framework of global totality and educational (*qua* political) ideology. Analysis focuses on issues of decentralization, private schooling, and radical Catholic doctrine as significant to Church's involvement.

Lima, Hermes. Anísio Teixeira: estadista da educação. See *HLAS 42:3690.*

4616 Lopes, J. Leite. Transferência de tecnologia e dependência (SBPC/CC, 31:1, jan. 1979, p. 3–8, bibl.)

Articulate statement by former member of Atomic Energy Committee of the Brazilian National Research Council. Argues that efforts at technology transfer typically provide few benefits to host nation (other than "learning to press a few necessary buttons"). Points blame at multinationals and local elites and gives, as example, case of nuclear energy development in Brazil.

4617 Machado de Sousa, Edson. Concurso vestibular: análisis de la experiencia brasileña (UAG/D, 6:6, nov./dic. 1978, p. 21–45, bibl., tables)

Examines historical background and current status of the "vestibulares," or university entrance examinations in Brazil. Argues that, although their utilization is understandable in view of the dramatic rise in demand for higher education and the concomitant need for a selection process, greater attention should be focused on research and methods in evaluation, in order to devise a more multi-faceted assessment sytem that takes into account such factors as motivation as well as ability. Recent modifications in the examination system make this study particularly compelling.

4618 Manfredi, Sílvia Maria. Política, educação popular. São Paulo: Edições Símbolo, 1978. 168 p.; bibl.; ill. (Coleção Ensaio e memória; 6)

Sociological study of Freire literacy training experience. Attempts to account for Freire method as response to historical, socioeconomic, and political forces. Includes details of four literacy training programs conducted in different regions of Brazil in early 1960s.

4619 Mattar, Maria Olga. Aspirações dos estudantes do curso de pedagogia referentes à sua profissionalização (UFP/EB, 1:2, 1976, p. 213–230, tables)

Survey of 371 education students in four institutions in Curitiba in 1975. Provides general profile of the predominantly female respondents and their attitudes toward their chosen profession. Reveals that most have realistic view of demands of teaching and of relatively poor extrinsic rewards. Also summarizes students' views of areas of teacher training most in need of revision: curriculum (need for greater relevance, clearer objectives) and methodology (need for greater emphasis on practice and on technological innovation).

4620 Medeiros, Marilu Fontoura de. Educação não formal e desenvolvimento: na perspectiva da educação de adultos; necessidade ou opção (SBPC/CC, 30:7, julho 1978, p. 799–804, bibl., tables) reviews basic arguments in support of non-formal education and basic characteristics of adult and non-formal education (self-help, cooperative orientation). Argues that convergence of concepts, characteristics between developmental needs and non-formal education make it a strongly-compelling policy approach for adult education.

4621 ———**; Lucila Maria Costi Santarosa; and Zaida Grinberg Lewin.** O papel do rádio no treinamento de professores (Educação e Realidade [Universidade Federal do Rio Grande do Sul, Faculdade de Educação, Porto Alegre, Brazil] 4 : 1, jan./junho 1979, p. 7–34, bibl., tables)

Study of 278 adult education (*ensino supletivo*) teachers receiving varying training treatment to test effectiveness of radio and self-instructional materials in educational psychology. Both experimental groups superior to control; experimental group receiving full treatment (radio plus materials) superior to group with partial treatment (radio only).

4622 Melía, Bartolomé. Educação indígena e alfabetização. Capa de Nelson de Moura. São Paulo: Edições Loyola, 1979. 91 p.; bibl.; ill. (Coleção Missão aberta; 2)

Provocative monograph examining issues of literacy education among indigenous Brazilian populations. Based on course for literacy workers given in 1978. Argues for consideration of distinct Indian reality and of strong indigenous traditions.

4623 Mello e Souza, Alberto de. Financiamento da educação e acesso à escola no Brasil. Rio de Janeiro: Instituto de Planejamento Económico e Social, Instituto de Pesquisas, 1979. 200 p.; bibl.; tables (Relatório de pesquisa no. 42)

Examines private and social costs and returns to education in Brazil. (Costs of higher education over 40 times greater per pupil than primary education.) Rising demand has led to soaring costs; teachers' salaries suffer, as does quality of teaching profession and education in general. Argues for redistribution of costs (including increased taxation of higher education graduates) and for increased scholarships for needy, beginning at primary level, in order to realize simultaneous goals of quality *and* increased access. Useful appendix of statistical tables. [A.M. Morales]

4624 Morel, Regina Lúcia de Moraes. Ciência e estado: a política científica no Brasil. São Paulo: T.A. Queiroz, 1979. 161 p.; bibl.; index (Biblioteca básica de ciências sociais: Série 1a. Estudos brasileiros; v. 4)

Based on ministerial documents, governmental and presidential pronouncements, author attempts to elaborate ideological tenets of Brazil's scientific development policy since the 1950s. Argues that, in the era of "big science," scientific development is not neutral but carries ideological premises related to societal conditions in which policy evolves (e.g., expansion of productive capability is regarded as criterion of policy effectiveness rather than as a self-legitimizing process of society's dominant forces). Rather than eliminate dependency on technologically-advanced nations, Brazil's policy of scientific development has merely shifted form and nature of dependency. Case study of nuclear policy in Brazil.

4625 Niskier, Arnaldo. Educação, para quê? Capa e programação visual, Maria Cambraia Fernandes. Rio de Janeiro: Bloch Educação, 1980. 208 p.; ill.

Collection of commentaries by the well-known Brazilian educator and journalist. Written over a two-year period, the short, crisp pieces treat subjects as diverse as university reform, sex education, compensatory education, and educational technology. Valuable as social chronicle of contemporary Brazilian education.

4626 Nosella, Maria de Lourdes Chagas Deiró. As belas mentiras: a ideologia subjacente aos textos didáticos. Capa de Guilherme Valpéteris. São Paulo: Cortez & Moraes, 1979. 237 p.; bibl.; ill. (Coleção Educação universitária)

Author reviewed over 20,000 p. of primary-level textbooks for this analysis of underlying ideological biases and stereotypes. Discussion organized thematically around themes such as: the family; the school; religion; nation; the environment; work; rich and poor; virtues; the Indian; etc. Important study of political socialization in curriculum.

4627 Oliveira, Betty Antunes de. O Estado autoritario brasileiro e o ensino superior. São Paulo: Cortez Editora, 1980. 111 p.

Examines legislation and other documents related to preparation of teachers for higher education. Finds contradictions in the system and in national policy.

4628 Park, Wook. Modernity and views of education: a comparative study of three countries (CES/CER, 24:1, Feb. 1980, p. 35–47, tables)

Examines assumption of linear relationship between investment view of education and level of modernization in Brazil, Ghana and India. On the basis of secondary analysis of interview data obtained from a University of Illinois project in 1972–73, author concludes, contrary to what was expected, that the more modern a person becomes, the more likely he is to value education not in an investment sense but rather in the consumption sense of learning for learning's sake. [E. Egginton]

4629 Paro, Vitor Henrique. Escola e formação profissional: um estudo sobre o sistema regular de ensino e a formação de recursos humanos no Brasil. São Paulo: Editora Cultrix, 1979. 95 p.; bibl.

Study examining Brazil's need for skilled manpower and capacity of regular educational system to meet such needs. Explores options outside regular schools and provides recommendations for professionalization activities at all educational levels, with stress on secondary.

4630 Paupério, Artur Machado. Fundamentos, diretrizes e imperativos da educação moral e cívica. Rio de Janeiro: Editora Rio, 1973. 133 p.; bibl.

Collection of four essays, nationally approved as curricular material for the teaching of moral and civic education in Brazil, by member of national commission. Includes appendices of pertinent legislation, other documents. Of particular interest for research in political socialization.

4631 Pereira, Mauro Nunes. O papel da universidade diante da dependência do Brasil no plano da tecnologia social de administração (Horizonte [Universidade Federal de Paraíba, João Pessoa, Brazil] 3:7, abril/junho 1978, p. 162–176)

Discusses failure of higher education to respond to changing socioeconomic climate in Brazil or to critically examine its dependence on foreign models and systems. Calls for new social technology in administration of higher education and greater linkages with management systems in both public and private sectors.

4632 Poerner, Arthur José. O poder jovem: história da participação política dos estudantes brasileiros. Prefácio do Pery Constant Beviláqua; apresentação Antônio Houaiss; capa, Dounê. 2. ed. ilustrada, rev. e ampliada. Rio de Janeiro: Civilização Brasileira, 1979. 381 p.; bibl.; 4 leaves of plates: ill.; index (Coleção Retratos do Brasil; v. 68)

Revised and updated edition of 1968 publication. Important historical work tracing roots of national student movements and political activities from colonial period to 1970s. Documentary appendix.

4633 Projeto educação: conferências, pronunciamentos e depoimentos. Brasília: Senado Federal, Comissão de Educação e Cultura, 1978– . 4 v.: diagrs.

Multi-volume collection of essays, speeches. Conference proceedings, letters, and other documents pertaining to the work of the Committee on Education and Culture of the Federal Senate. First two volumes provide documentary history of committee's work in 1977. Final two volumes consist of 19 essays by leading Brazilian educators on specialized themes such as graduate-level education (Newton Sucupira), *ensino supletivo* (Maria do Socorro J. Emerenciano), educational technology (A. Niskier). Important resource.

4634 Renan, Iale and **Ricamor P. de Brito Fernandes.** Sistema educacional brasileiro: legislação e estrutura. Rio de Janeiro: Editora Rio, 1977. 112 p.; appendices.

Study of legislation governing instruction. Authors support direction of educational reform from humanistic formation to more technical emphasis at secondary level. Provide useful recommendations for compliance with legislation related to *habilitação* (professional or technical training). Valuable for legislative research. [A.M. Morales]

4635 Ribeiro, Maria Luisa Santos. Historia da educação brasileira: a organização escolar. São Paulo: Cortez & Moraes, 1978. 139 p.; bibl.; tables.

Interesting presentation of Brazilian educational history utilizing a dependency framework and focusing on educational responses to broader sociopolitical and economic phenomena. Extended application of dialectic method introduced in earlier work. Useful statistics.

4636 ————. Introdução a historia da educação brasileira. São Paulo: Cortez e Moraes, 1978. 143 p.; bibl. (Coleção Educação universitaria)

Useful effort to develop and apply a dialectic method to the analysis of Brazilian educational history. Extensive bibliography.

4637 Romanelli, Otaíza de Oliveira. História da educação no Brasil: 1930–1973. Prefácio do Francisco Iglésias. Petrópolis, Brasil: Editora Vozes, 1978. 267 p.; bibl.; ill.

Sometimes breezy account of educational developments in Brazil, 1930–73. Adopts dependency framework. Designed for graduate students of education.

4638 Rossi, Wagner Gonçalves. Capitalismo e educação: contribuição ao estudo crítico da economia da educação capitalista. São Paulo: Cortez & Moraes, 1978. 160 p.; bibl. (Coleção Educação universitaria)

Radical analysis that views institutionalized education as reproducer of status quo/class relations. Attempts to "demystify" meritocratic ideology of capitalist education.

4639 Sander, Benno. Educação brasileira: valores formais e valores reais. São Paulo: Pioneira, Fundação Biblioteca Patricia Bildner [and] Fundação Nacional de Materia Escolar, Rio de Janeiro, 1977. 289 p.; bibl.; appendices.

Examines discrepancies (o formalismo) between promulgated legislation and actual implementation, providing both theoretical framework and case study of implementation of LDB middle school reform in Rio Grande do Sul. Argues that "formalism" not exclusive phenomenon in educational sector; rather, endemic to societies "in transition." Interesting thesis, but fails to critically analyze context of educational reform and diverts attention from more fundamental socioeconomic and political obstacles. Appendices of major national education legislation (1961, 1968, 1971). [A.M. Morales]

4640 Saviani, Dermeval. Educação: do senso común a consciência filosôfica. São Paulo: Cortez Editora, 1980. 1 v.

Series of author's essays dealing with role and nature of philosophy in education. Some general essays; others focus on Brazil and give critical analysis of effects of educational reforms of 1968 and 1971.

Schwartzman, Simon. Formação da comunidade científica no Brasil. See *HLAS 42:3554.*

4641 Skeff, Ana Maria Fernandes.
Qualificação dos docentes e produção científica: Universidade de Brasília (UMG/RBEP, 48, jan. 1979, p. 219–241, tables)

Analysis of scientific production (publications, research, innovation) as a function of institutional characteristics in 23 departments within the University of Brasília. Considers such characteristics as size, degree of centralization, autonomy, qualifications, and budget. Author posits that level of productivity is as important a measure of university effectiveness as is output of graduates, especially in view of traditional role of Latin American countries as importers of technological and scientific know-how and in view of specific Brazilian efforts to establish national infrastructure for technological development. Most significant factors seem to be faculty qualifications and department size.

4642 Souza, Albenides Ramos de. Estudo locacional para a implantação de escolas profissionalizantes de 2.°grau no Município de Nova Iguaçu, Rio de Janeiro (IBGE/R, 40:3/4, julho/dec. 1978, p. 131–232, bibl., maps, tables)

Elaborate study examining comparative feasibility of two models of scale for the location of professional high schools in the municipality of Nova Iguaçu, Rio de Janeiro. Utilizes data on demographic density, demand for schooling, and accessibility of proposed sites. Methodology of particular interest to educational planners.

4643 Souza, Heitor Gurgulino de. Formação de tecnólogos (SBPC/CC, 30:8, agosto 1978, p. 928–939, bibl., map, tables)

Emphasizes potential of short-term professional/technical courses for training of highly needed middle-level technologists. Traces historical/legislative antecedents in this area, arguing that idea is not so new.

4644 Teixeira Júnior, Antônio de Souza. Tecnologia importada e ensino

(SBPC/CC, 31:8, agôsto 1979, p. 837–850, tables)

Based on comparative indices of research and development in various countries, author argues for protective tariffs and carefully-planned augmentation of nationally-focused research and development activities as strategy for breaking cycle of Brazil's scientific and technological dependency.

Toledo, Caio Navarro de. ISEB: fábrica de ideologias. See *HLAS 42:3764.*

4645 Xavier, Maria Elizabete Sampaio Prado. Poder político e educação de elite. São Paulo: Cortez Editora: Autores Associados, 1980. 144 p.; bibl. (Coleção Educação contemporânea)

Historical analysis, beginning in post-Independence period, that seeks to account for failure of Brazilian educational system to meet popular needs. Contends that illusion of pedagogical "autonomy" primarily fostered by and benefitted internally-dominant social classes. Emphasis of most dependency theorists somewhat misplaced, according to the author: greater attention should be directed to role of internal elites. Traces social, political, and economic roots of various educational approaches and policy orientations, including importation of educational ideas and practices. Radical and provocative treatise.

JOURNAL ABBREVIATIONS EDUCATION

AAFH/TAM The Americas. A quarterly publication of inter-American cultural history. Academy of American Franciscan History. Washington.

AI/I Interciencia. Asociación Interciencia. Caracas.

ASHSH/B Bulletin de l'Académie des Sciences Humaines et Sociales d'Haiti. Port-au-Prince.

BCV/REL Revista de Economía Latinoamericana. Banco Central de Venezuela. Caracas.

BISRA/BS Belizean Studies. Belizean Institute of Social Research and Action [and] St. John's College. Belize City.

BRP Beiträge zur Romanischen Philologie. Rütten & Loening. Berlin.

CEE/RL Revista Latinoamericana de Estudios Educativos. Centro de Estudios Educativos. México.

CES/CER Comparative Education Review. Comparative Education Society. New York.

CH Cuadernos Hispanoamericanos. Instituto de Cultura Hispánica. Madrid.

CM/FI Foro Internacional. El Colegio de México. México.

CP Cuadernos Políticos. Revista trimestral. Ediciones Era. México.

CPU/ES Estudios Sociales. Corporación de Promoción Universitaria. Santiago.

CUNY/CP Comparative Politics. The City Univ. of New York, Political Science Program. New Xork.

CYC Comunicación y Cultura. La comunicación masiva en el proceso político latinoamericano. Editorial Galerna. Buenos Aires y Santiago.

DESCO/Q Quehacer. Realidad nacional: problemas y alternativas. Revista del Centro de Estudios y Promoción del Desarrollo (DESCO). Lima.

EC/M Mapocho. Biblioteca Nacional, Extensión Cultural. Santiago.

FH Folia Humanística. Ciencias, artes, letras. Editorial Glarma. Barcelona.

IAEERI/E Estrategia. Instituto Argentino de Estudios Estratégicos y de las Relaciones Internacionales. Buenos Aires.

IBGE/R Revista Brasileiro de Geografia. Conselho Nacional de Geografia, Instituto Brasileiro de Geografia e Estatística. Rio de Janeiro.

IDES/DE Desarrollo Económico. Instituto de Desarrollo Económico y Social. Buenos Aires.

III/AI América Indígena. Instituto Indigenista Interamericano. México.

INEP/RBEP Revista Brasileira de Estudos Pedagógicos. Instituto Nacional de Estudos Pedagógicos, Centro Brasileiro de Pesquisas Educacionais. Rio de Janeiro.

LAP Latin American Perspectives. Univ. of California. Riverside.

LARR Latin American Research Review. Univ. of North Carolina Press *for the* Latin

American Studies Association. Chapel Hill.

MLTA/MLJ Modern Language Journal. The National Federation of Modern Language Teachers Associations. Univ. of Pittsburgh. Pittsburgh, Pa.

NSO Nueva Sociedad. Revista política y cultural. San José.

NYAS/A Annals of the New York Academy of Sciences. New York.

OAS/CI Ciencia Interamericana. Organization of American States, Dept. of Scientific Affairs. Washington.

OAS/LE La Educación. Organization of American States, Dept. of Educational Affairs. Washington.

PCCLAS/P Proceedings of the Pacific Coast Council on Latin American Studies. Univ. of California. Los Angeles.

SBPC/CC Ciência e Cultura. Sociedade Brasileira para o Progresso da Ciência. São Paulo.

SGHG/A Anales de la Sociedad de Geografía e Historia de Guatemala. Guatemala.

UAG/D Docencia. Univ. Autónoma de Guadalajara. México.

UASD/U Revista Dominicana de Antropología e Historia. Univ. Autónoma de Santo Domingo, Facultad de Humanidades, Depto. de Historia y Antropología, Instituto de Investigaciones Antropológicas. Santo Domingo.

UC/EE Estudios de Economía. Univ. de Chile, Facultad de Ciencias Económicas y Administrativas, Depto. de Economía. Santiago.

UCC/CE Cuadernos de Economía. Univ. Católica de Chile. Santiago.

UCLV/I Islas. Univ. Central de las Villas. Santa Clara, Cuba.

UFP/EB Estudos Baianos. Univ. Federal da Bahia, Centro Editorial e Didático, Núcleo de Publicações. Bahia, Brazil.

UMG/RBEP Revista Brasileira de Estudos Políticos. Univ. de Minas Gerais. Belo Horizonte, Brazil.

UN/ISSJ International Social Science Journal. United Nations Educational, Scientific, and Cultural Organization. Paris.

UNAM/RMCPS Revista Mexicana de Ciencias Políticas y Sociales. Univ. Nacional Autónoma de México, Facultad de Ciencias Políticas y Sociales. México.

UNC/BVPS Boletín de Ciencias Políticas y Sociales. Univ. Nacional de Cuyo, Facultad de Ciencias Políticas y Sociales. Mendoza, Argentina.

UNESCO/IRE International Review of Education. United Nations Educational, Scientific and Cultural Organization, Institute for Education. Hamburg, FRG.

UNPHU/A Aula. Univ. Nacional Pedro Henríquez Ureña. Santo Domingo.

UP/TM Tiers Monde. Problèmes des pays sous-développés. Univ. de Paris, Institut d'Étude du Développement Économique et Social. Paris.

UPB Universidad Pontificia Bolivariana. Medellín, Colombia.

UPN/RCE Revista Colombiana de Educación. Univ. Pedagógica Nacional, Centro de Investigaciones. Bogotá.

UPR/CS Caribbean Studies. Univ. of Puerto Rico, Institute of Caribbean Studies. Río Piedras.

UPR/RCS Revista be Ciencias Sociales. Univ. de Puerto Rico, Colegio de Ciencias Sociales. Río Piedras.

UPR/RO Revista de Oriente. Univ. de Puerto Rico, Colegio Universitario de Humacao. Humacao.

URL/ES Estudios Sociales. Univ. Rafael Landívar, Instituto de Ciencias Políticas y Sociales. Guatemala.

URSS/AL América Latina. Academia de Ciencias de la URSS [Unión de Repúblicas Soviéticas Socialistas]. Moscú.

UUAL/U Universidades. Unión de Universidades de América Latina. Buenos Aires.

UWI/CQ Caribbean Quarterly. Univ. of the West Indies. Mona, Jamaica.

WJC/JJS The Jewish Journal of Sociology. The World Jewish Community. London.

WD World Development. Pergamon Press. Oxford, United Kingdom.

ZMR Zeitschrift für Missionswissenschaft und Religionswissenschaft. Lucerne, Switzerland.

GEOGRAPHY

GENERAL

CLINTON R. EDWARDS, *Professor of Geography, University of Wisconsin-Milwaukee*

GIVEN THE CHARACTER OF SEVERAL IMPORTANT ITEMS reviewed this *HLAS*, the past two years might be called the biennium of stock-taking and *festschriften*. Coincidentally, three major figures in Latin American geography are represented in this section: Carl Sauer, Robert West, and Preston James. Furthermore, the Conference of Latin Americanist Geographers celebrated its tenth anniversary in 1980.

Robert West continues his long and effective service to geographic research in Latin America by presenting two informative, balanced, yet affectionate essays on the career of Carl Sauer as it pertained to Latin America. Both essays emphasize Sauer's role as teacher, the one (item **5034**) describing his great skill in translating field observations to the classroom and publication; the other (item **5033**) ranging beyond Sauer's teaching and example to give an over-all perspective of his and his students' contributions to the development of Latin American geography.

West himself receives well-deserved recognition in a volume of essays on the historical geography of Latin America (item **5016**). The individual articles in the volume are reviewed in appropriate sections of this *HLAS*. They are preceded by a biographical essay written by Davidson and Parsons, which includes a résumé of West's foreign field research and a list of his publications to 1978.

Another *festschrift* is devoted to Preston James, with biographical material supplied by Robinson (item **5025**) and Wood (item **5035**). The latter emphasizes James' considerable contribution as a link between academic geography and public affairs in the context of Latin American studies.

In April 1980, the Conference of Latin Americanist Geographers celebrated its tenth anniversary at Ball State University, Muncie, Indiana, where it all began in April 1970. Publication of the proceedings is forthcoming, but was not available for review in this volume. A comparison of the general subject headings of sessions listed in the pre-conference collection of papers for 1980 with those of 1970, reveals that several themes have persisted, while others are new to the later collection. Ecology, population and settlement, and geographical methodology pertaining to Latin American studies are represented in both; new themes are general economic geography and instructional strategies. Physical and social geography, designated "neglected fields" in 1970, are represented without such designation in 1980. The proceedings of the 1980 Conference will be the eighth in a series that has emphasized the role of geographers in development, a theme which has, however, not dominated to the exclusion of other aspects of geographical research.

Environmental problems continue to be well-presented in geographic literature originating in Latin America. The growing importance of this concern is highlighted by the *Directorio del Medio Ambiente* (item **5019**), which lists and describes an impressively large number of agencies and academic units devoted to questions of adverse human effects on environments. The closely related field of resource development is also represented strongly, with urban studies and urban-rural relationships receiving continued attention.

Interest in historical aspects of Latin American geography is reflected in the current examples of the perennial interest in Humboldt, historical cartography, and Columbus (item **5026**). Anyone who has consulted the *Diccionario geográfico-histórico de las Indias Occidentales*, first published in 1786, will be interested in the biographical material on its author and on the background of this great work's composition provided by Durán Pombo (item **5011**).

5001 Acosta-Solís, Misael. El avance de la desertización: grave problema para la humanidad (IGME/RG, 11, 1979, p. 73–98, maps)

Defines and discusses distribution of the world's arid zones, with résumé of declarations and plans of the International Union of Conservation of Nature and Natural Resources, and the United Nations conference of 1977 in Madrid.

5002 Agua, desarrollo y medio ambiente en América Latina: informe. Santiago de Chile: Naciones Unidas, Comisión Económica para América Latina, Programa de las Naciones Unidas para el Medio Ambiente, 1980. 443 p.; ill.

Extensive, detailed treatment, including case studies of hydroelectric, irrigation, and other projects in Mexico, Venezuela, Colombia, Peru, Chile and Brazil.

5003 América Latina. Dirección de Carlos Gispert. Barcelona: Danae, D.L., 1978. 2 v.; ill. (Gran colección geográfica Danae)

Profusely illustrated lexicon of geography, culture, history, architecture, art, and other features of Latin American lands and peoples.

5004 Boadas, Antonio R. Las tierras nuevas tropicales americanas: criterios y lineamientos para su aprovechamiento. Caracas: Universidad Central de Venezuela, Facultad de Ciencias Económicas y Sociales, División de Publicaciones, 1979. 117 p.; bibl.; maps (Colección Libros)

The "new lands" are mostly in the lowland, humid tropics, and are characterized by insufficient knowledge of their natural resources, inhabitants living at "low levels" of subsistence, means of investigation and adequate technology. Various physical and cultural characteristics of these lands are shown in maps and tables. Recommendations include maintenance of ecological integrity, directed rather than spontaneous pioneer settlement, maintenance of the social, economic, and cultural organization and values of native peoples, and the assurance that development will benefit the countries concerned rather than convert them into international enclaves or "national colonies."

5005 Cohen, Marjorie Adoff. The budget traveler's Latin America. Council on International Educational Exchange, in cooperation with the Australian Union of Students. Edited by Margaret E. Sherman. 2. ed. New York: E.P. Dutton, 1979. xxxiv, 251 p.; bibl.; maps.

Second edition, with change of title, of the *Student guide to Latin America*. A straightforward and useful guide, necessarily selective.

5006 Crespi, M.B.A. La energía nuclear en América Latina: necesidades y posibilidades (AI/I, 4:1, enero/feb. 1979, p. 22–31, tables)

By conservative projection, in a century the only feasible means of providing sufficient power in Latin America will be from nuclear or solar sources. Describes current progress, types of reactors, and regional resources in Latin America for development of nuclear power. Advocates development of other sources, education in nuclear technology, investigation of smaller plants, use of thorium, and keeping abreast of progress in fusion technology.

5007 Davidson, W.V. and **J.J. Parsons.** Robert C. West, geographer (*in* Historical geography of Latin America: papers in honor of Robert C. West [see item **5016**] p. 1–8)

An academic biography of one of the foremost fieldworkers and scholars of Latin

American geography. Includes a detailed list of 51 of West's field trips (1936–78), and a list of his publications to 1978.

5008 Denevan, William M. La geografía cultural aborigen de los Llanos de Mojos. Versión castellana de Josep M. Barnadas. La Paz: Librería Editorial Juventud, 1980. 172 p.; bibl.

Revision and translation of the author's *The aboriginal cultural geography of the Llanos de Mojos of Bolivia* (Berkeley: University of California Press, 1966). Contains some new material on raised fields and demography, and an updated bibliography.

5009 Documentos: tendencias demográficas y opciones para políticas de población en América Latina (BCV/REL, 10:37, 1973, p. 213–299)

A general review of demographic trends, with commentary on relationships between population increase and economic, social, and political development.

5010 Drewes, Wolfram. Geography in the development of Latin America as a part of the Third World (*in* Studying Latin America: essays in honor of Preston E. James [see item **4358**] p. 245–267, ill., table)

The general trends of applied geography have changed over the past three decades, with more attention now given to projects that respond directly to specific problems. Resource evaluation agencies that work with national planning boards of ministries, focusing on the application of technology to development have increased in number, and analytical techniques, especially remote-sensing and computerization of data, have been improved. The predicted "data glut" will force development geographers to become "computer oriented."

5011 Durán Pombo, Jaime. Los Alcedos (ACH/BHA, 64:719, oct./dic. 1977, p. 561–585, bibl.)

Biographies of Dionisio de Alcedo y Herrera, who held several high offices in 18th-century Viceroyalty of Peru, and of his son, Antonio. The father's *Aviso histórico-político-geográfico . . . Perú, Tierra Firme, Chile, y Nuevo Reino de Granada* (1740) was expanded greatly by Antonio, and became the *Diccionario geográfico histórico de las Indias Occidentales . . .* (1786), a valuable

source for historical geography of Latin America.

5012 Feder, Ernest. La irracional competencia entre el hombre y el animal por los recursos agrícolas de los países subdesarrollados (FCE/TE, 47[1]:185, enero/marzo 1970, p. 49–84, tables)

Detailed economic and social critique of the wholesale conversion of agricultural land to pasture, with emphasis on Latin America and specific examples from Mexico.

5013 García M., Luis E. Alcance del Seminario "Utilización de la Percepción Remota en la Evaluación y Manejo de los Recursos Naturales para el Desarrollo en un Area Piloto" (PAIGH/RC, 33, junio 1978, p. 117–120)

Report on a seminar sponsored by the Pan American Institute of Geography and History. Describes a remote sensing project and its application in Guatemala, using the María Linda Valley as pilot area.

5014 Giacottino, Jean-Claude. La ville tropicale et ses problèmes d'environnement (SGB/COM, 32:125, jan./mars 1979, p. 22–38, bibl.)

Some urban problems are peculiar to settlements in the tropics, especially those related to water supply, sanitation, and transportation. These problems often occur in the context of spontaneous slums, and administrations in underdeveloped countries are often ill-equipped to cope with them.

5015 Gokhman, V.M. and **G.V. Sdasyuk.** Socio-economic geography in the West at a turning point (AGS/SG, 21:5, May 1980, p. 284–293, bibl.)

Article does not focus specifically on Latin America, but is relevant to Western geographers in Marxist theory and its application to socioeconomic and geographical questions in Latin America.

5016 Historical geography of Latin America: papers in honor of Robert C. West. Editors, William V. Davidson and James J. Parsons. Baton Rouge: School of Geoscience, Louisiana State University, 1980. 163 p.; bibl.; ill. (Geoscience and man; v. 21)

Collection of studies by students and colleagues of Robert C. West. Individual articles are annotated in this volume and entered under author's name.

5017 Jones, David M. The green revolution in Latin America: success or failure (*in* International aspects of development in Latin America: geographical perspectives. Edited by Gary S. Elbow. Muncie, Ind.: Ball State University, Department of Geography and Geology, Conference on Latin Americanist Geographers [CLAG], 1976, p. 55–63, bibl., map)

Traces development and dispersal of high-yielding varieties of grain from Mexico, assesses their importance in Latin America, and comments on differential acceptance by farmers. The impact of the "green revolution has been greater in other parts of the world than in Latin America," where progress has been relatively slow due to lack of follow-up data on plantings, lack of government support, and the failure yet to achieve a breakthrough in maize breeding equivalent to that in wheat.

5018 Konecny, Gottfried. Métodos para la obtención de información para establecer un sistema de registro de tierras con propósito múltiple en zonas urbanas y rurales con especial énfasis en la fotogrametría (PAIGH/RC, 29, junio 1975, p. 11–22)

Using tables, author describes the types of maps most helpful in various phases of economic development. Advocates the establishment of an information system for monitoring environmental change, and provides technical and cost information on the making of special maps. Describes new methods of photogrammetry applicable to developing areas.

5019 Latin American Centre for Economic and Social Documentation. Directorio del medio ambiente en América Latina y el Caribe, 1977: Cladir II, versión definitiva. Santiago de Chile: Naciones Unidas, CEPAL/CLADES, 1977 or 1978. iv, 576 p.; indexes.

Consists of an annotated listing of governmental and private agencies, and departments and other university units involved in environmental investigations and planning. Covers all Latin American and Caribbean countries, and includes entries for international organizations. Contains subject and alphabetical indexes.

5020 Lavrov, S.B.; V.S. Preobrazhenskiy; and G.V. Sdasyuk. *Radical geography*: its roots, history and position (AGS/SG, 21:5, May 1980, p. 308–321, bibl.)

Soviet assessment of radical geography as presented in the book edited by Richard Peet, *Radical geography* (Chicago: Maaroufa Press, 1977). Reviewer notes that although the book is not based on Marxist-Leninist theory and contains almost no reference to Soviet works on planning and regional policy, Soviet geographers will be interested in its presentation of a "serious new trend." The work expresses some "anarchist" and "ultraleft" views, and is "prone to excesses in its outright rejection of quantitative techniques and of behavioral geography." Does not focus specifically on Latin America, but is of interest for the application of Marxist theory to Latin American questions.

5021 McGee, Terence G. Western geography and the Third World (ABS, 22:1, Sept./Oct. 1978, p. 93–114)

The relationship indicated by the title has undergone three phases since 1945: western domination, western concern, and challenge by the Third World. Liberal geographers now demand relevance, radicals reject the "development paradigm," and criticism from within the Third World is increasing.

Melo Gallegos, Carlos. El paisaje geomorfológico mexicano en el atractivo natural de los parques nacionales; Desarrollo de los parques nacionales mexicanos; Balance analítico de la operación del sistema mexicano de parques nacionales: tres estudios sobre el mismo tema. See item **5125.**

5022 Palacio, Francisco J. Marine science in Latin America (OCEANUS, 23:2, Summer 1980, p. 39–49, plates, tables)

Interesting historical review of contributions to marine science by Latin Americans. Today, marine science is underdeveloped and only weakly supported in almost all Latin American countries. Greatest recent growth has taken place in biology, but much of its support comes from international agencies. Contains outline of a marine resource development program.

5023 Pan American Institute of Geography and History. Cartografía temática: símbolos y criterios normativos. Buenos Aires: El Instituto, 1976 [c1975]. 2 v.; bibl.; ill. (Publicación—Instituto Panamericano de Geografía e Historia; no. 362)

Illustrated manual of symbols, colors, and styles for thematic mapping.

5024 Revelle, Roger. Flying beans, botanical whales, Jack's beanstalk, and other marvels (AI/I, 4:2, March/April 1979, p. 92–103, bibl., plates, tables)

A non-technical review of plant species which have the potential to increase the agricultural productivity of the humid and arid tropics. [G.S. Elbow]

5025 Robinson, David J. On Preston E. James and Latin America: a biographical sketch (*in* Studying Latin America: essays in honor of Preston E. James [see item 4358] p. 1–101, facsimiles, maps, plates, tables)

Outlines James' academic career, accomplishments, and contributions to Latin American and general geography. Includes excerpts from accounts, notebooks, and other records of his work, as well as interesting quotations from his letters.

5026 Sanz López, Carlos. Descubrimientos geográficos. Madrid: Edic. Cultura Hispánica del Centro Iberoamericano de Cooperación, 1979. 542 p.; bibl.; 4 leaves.

Memorial selection of works by Carlos Sanz López, the distinguished Spanish historian. His most notable contributions were to the history of cartography, Columbus studies, and Hispanic American historical bibliography.

5027 Simposio Interdisciplinario sobre Paleogeografía Mesoamericana, *México, 1973.* Conexiones terrestres entre Norte y Sudamérica. Ismael Ferrusquía-Villafranca, editor. México: Universidad Nacional Autónoma de México, Instituto de Geología, 1977, cover 1978. 329 p.; bibl.; 17 fold. leaves of plates; ill. (Boletín—Universidad Nacional Autónoma de México, Instituto de Geología; 101)

Includes papers on geology, geophysics, plate tectonics, paleontology, flora and fauna, and distributions and migrations.

5028 Solntsev, N.A. Physical geographic regionalization of the world ocean (AGS/SG, 203, March 1979, p. 154–159, bibl.)

Recommends that the character of the seabed be used in categorizing sectors of the world ocean. Contains no direct reference to Latin America, but is relevant to preparation in the Soviet Union of a multi-volume regional geography of the world ocean.

5029 Spurgeon, David. Agroforestry: a promising system of improved land management for Latin America (AI/I, 5:3, May/June 1980, p. 176–178, bibl.)

"Agroforestry" is land use of trees, food or forage crops, and livestock raising, occurring simultaneously or sequentially in a single farming system. The system enhances nutrient cycles and makes maximum use of available good soil. Author considers agroforestry an acceptable ecological alternative to shifting field agriculture in the humid tropics.

5030 Tafur Hernández, Isaac A. Polución ambiental y su clasificación (SGL/B, 94, enero/junio 1975, p. 24–37, bibl., tables)

Classifies pollution as atmospheric, terrestrial, or aquatic, and categorizes general location of each. Pollutants are natural or artificial, with sub-categories according to type and location. Contains synopses of urban pollution problems in Chile, Peru, Colombia, Venezuela, Paraguay, Brazil, Panama, Costa Rica and Mexico.

5031 Tellería V., Rodolfo. Perspectivas de la hidroelectricidad en el Continente Americano (BCV/REL, 11:41, 1975, p. 63–84, bibl., tables)

Traces development and use of hydroelectric power during the last 20 years, and projects future needs. Advocates further development in Latin America as a substitute for fossil fuels.

5032 Vargas, José A. and **James F. Page.** Progress of the Harbor Survey Assistance Program (PAIGH/RC, 33, junio 1978, p. 71–94, maps, tables)

Program provides technical and material aid for developing hydrographic charting capabilities in 14 Latin American countries.

5033 West, Robert Cooper. Berkeley perspective on the study of Latin American geography in the United States and Canada (*in* Studying Latin America: essays in honor of Preston E. James [see item 4358] p. 135–175, tables)

In addition to the Berkeley orientation, contains much interesting general information on trends in Latin American geographical study in the US and Canada. Gives data on dissertations and regional emphases in various university geography departments. Carl Sauer's role in developing Latin American geography, his own field work, and the "post-Sauer" period are described. A survey of the contributions of "Berkeley satellites" and other departments completes the perspective. Since World War II, funding of geographical field work in Latin America has diminished. However, renewed possibilities exist for funding development studies, urbanization, and environmental problems.

5034 ———. Carl Sauer's fieldwork in Latin America. Ann Arbor, Mich.: *Published for* Department of Geography, Syracuse University *by* University Microfilms International, 1979. xviii, 165 p.; bibl.; index (Dellplain Latin American studies; 3. Monography publishing: sponsor series)

Traces routes and areas covered in Sauer's fieldwork, discusses his methods, interests, funding, and the relationship be-

tween his fieldwork and classroom presentations. Each trip is described in detail, giving anecdotes and impressions of participants, extensive quotations from Sauer's notes, letters and other writings, and photographs and route maps. West's treatment is straightforward and non-eulogizing, allowing the narrative to speak for itself. A first-rate example of how the inquiring mind and observant eye can bring natural and cultural phenomena and their explanations to the printed page and classroom.

5035 Wood, Harold A. Preston James and the Pan American Institute of Geography and History (*in* Studying Latin America: essays in honor of Preston E. James [see item 4358] p. 121–134)

James' most significant role was the development and guidance of the Geography Commission of PAIGH. Wood considers James an ideal link between government and academe, exemplifying the public-spirited professor.

MIDDLE AMERICA
(Caribbean Islands, Central America and Mexico)

TOM L. MARTINSON, *Professor of Geography, Ball State University*
GARY S. ELBOW, *Associate Professor of Geography, Texas Tech University*

THE CONTRIBUTIONS ON MEXICAN GEOGRAPHY included in this volume are dominated by the output of the Puebla-Tlaxcala Project, a joint German-Mexican research program funded by the Deutsche Forschungsgemeinschaft. The history of this project is summarized in a report by Lauer (item **5119**). The project has produced papers that range across physical and cultural geography, covering such topics as soils, ecosystems, groundwater, agricultural systems, periodic markets, urban change, and vernacular mapping. The success of the Puebla-Tlaxcala Project demonstrates the value of long-term funding and close international cooperation in regionally-based research.

Agriculture, as usual, is the object of several studies in this section. Papers by Clawson (item **5103**) and Clawson and Hoy (item **5104**) examine why peasant farmers failed to adopt agricultural innovations. Williams, in a Spanish translation of her doctoral dissertation, reports on the persistence of traditional agricultural landscapes despite a shift in the employment base from agricultural to non-agricultural activities in a village on the edge of the Mexico City conurbation (item **5152**). Agricultural colonization, long a popular theme of geographical research, is analyzed in papers by Fuentes Aguilar and Siemans, both of which are critical of government-sponsored settlement projects (items **5110** and **5141**).

Concern among Mexicans for their country's rapid population growth is reflected in two books on population, one by Francisco Alba-Hernández (item **5102**), and another consisting of the *Memorias de la I Reunión Nacional sobre la Investigación Demográfica (item* **5136***).*

To judge by the literature reviewed for this bibliography, Mexico's rise to prominence as a producer of petroleum and natural gas has gone largely unnoticed by geographers. Only one paper by Pierre George (item **5112**), deals directly with this matter, and it is largely a status report on production, distribution, and refining capabilities in the country. Given the importance of petroleum to Mexico's future, as well as the possible development of other energy sources, such as nuclear power (item **5124**), one hopes that more research by geographers on energy in Mexico will be forthcoming.

Insofar as publications on the Caribbean and Central America are concerned, geographers paid more attention to technical aspects of area development than to population and agriculture, still both prominent themes. Pollard and Eastwood discuss agricultural change in dairying (item **5068**); and Miller observes it in beef cattle production (item **5071**). Nuñes offers an account of stresses generated by agricultural change in Belize (item **5078**).

The most important development in population study this year is the CICRED series. Examples of the series pertaining to Costa Rica, Trinidad and Tobago, Panama, and Cuba are included in this section. In addition there is a welcome new demographic atlas from Cuba (item **5040**).

Work on natural resource inventory is still necessary in Middle America, and volumes such as the PAIGH Salvador guide (item **5088**) provide important basic information in this area. How geographers and others use this information is shown in a report on an integrated development project in the Darién (item **5101**). A promising new technique that deserves wider application is remote sensing, as illustrated in Elizondo Solís' article on Costa Rica (item **5080**). An older technique, in-depth fieldwork coupled with perceptive reporting, is still alive and well, as can be seen in Nietschmann's *Caribbean edge* (item **5096**).

CARIBBEAN
GENERAL

5036 Adams, John E. From landsmen to seamen: the making of a West Indian fishing community (PAIGH/G, 88, dic. 1978, p. 151–166, bibl., maps)
Records the environmental, cultural and historical factors responsible for the growth and importance of fishing in Bequia.

5037 Dale, Edmund H. Spotlight on the Caribbean, a microcosm of the Third World. Regina: Department of Geography, University of Regina, 1977. 95 p.; bibl.; ill.; maps (Regina geographical studies; no. 2)
Political geography explores strengths and weaknesses of small and middle-sized Caribbean states, with emphasis on Jamaica.

5038 Eyre, Alan. A new geography of the Caribbean. 5. ed. London: G. Philip, c1979. v, 161 p.; bibl.; ill.; index.

General survey of Caribbean geography oriented to the British middle-school pupil, concentrates on Commonwealth territories.

5039 Stuart, K.L. Science for development: agriculture and food sufficiency in the Caribbean (UWI/CQ, 23:4, Dec. 1977, p. 106–115)
Survey of needs for improving agriculture calls for more research on water and chemicals.

CUBA

Atlas demográfico de Cuba. See item **5437**.

5040 Cuba. Comité Estatal de Estadísticas. Atlas demográfico de Cuba. La Habana: Instituto Cubano de Geodesia y Cartografía, 1979. 98 p.; colored maps.
Choropleth maps predominate in this beautifully-illustrated but thin volume.

5041 Díaz-Briquets, Sergio and **Lisandro Pérez.** Cuba: the demography of Revolution. Washington: Population Reference Bureau, 1981. 43 p.; bibl.; map; plates; tables (Population bulletin; 36:1)

Masterly survey of Cuban population issues, including demographic changes resulting from social, political, and economic conditions of post-revolutionary Cuba and their implications for US immigration policy.

5042 Hardoy, Jorge E. Estructura espacial y propiedad (*in* Cuba: camino abierto [see item **8189**] p. 274–311, tables)

Cuba's experimental rural towns do not permit the variety of activities, richness of interactions, and economy of scale that would justify their existence.

5043 Havana. Universidad. Centro de Estudios Demográficos. La población de Cuba. Edición, Ernesto Chávez Alvarez. La Habana: Editorial de Ciencias Sociales, Instituto Cubano del Libro, 1976. 236 p.; 2 leaves of plates; bibl.; ill. (Committee for International Coordination of National Research in Demography. C.I.C.R.E.D. series)

Instituto Cubano de Geodesia y Cartografía. Atlas de Cuba: aniversario de la Revolución Cubana. See item **5439**.

5044 Pérez-López, Jorge F. The Cuban nuclear power program (UP/SCEC, 9:1, Jan. 1979, p. 1–42)

Cuba's projected nuclear power plant will be a large facility, useful for military purposes, but lacking important safeguards.

DOMINICAN REPUBLIC

5045 Augelli, John P. Nationalization of Dominican borderlands (AGS/GR, 70:1, Jan. 1980, p. 20–35, maps, plates)

Border friction may be eased by cooperative ventures between these national governments.

5046 Franjul, Marcos Peña. Las lagunas como recursos naturales: Lagunas Saladilla y Salada (UNPHU/A, 22/23, julio/dic. 1977, p. 17–38)

Arguments in favor of the establishment of a national park to include Lagunas Saladilla and Salada. Appendixes include lists of bird and plant species observed near the lakes.

5047 García Tatis, Ezequiel. La administración de la planificación urbana en la R.D. (UNPHU/A, 6:27, oct./dic. 1978, p. 17–46, tables)

Reviews laws governing and financial support sources for urban planning in the Dominican Republic.

5048 Nicholls, David. Prosperous state of unrest: Dominican Republic under pressure (GM, 51:8, May 1979, p. 555–559, map, plates)

Considerable poverty still exists in the Dominican Republic, but economic conditions are gradually improving.

5049 Rodríguez, Cayetano Armando. Geografía de la Isla de Santo Domingo y reseña de las demás Antillas. 2. ed. Santo Domingo: Sociedad Dominicana de Geografía, 1976. 504 p.; ill. (Biblioteca dominicana de geografía y viajes; v. 11)

Reprint of 1915 edition valuable primarily for its toponomy and photographs.

HAITI

5050 Houry, Jean Michel. Analyse du réseau de transport public sur Port-au-Prince (IFH/C, 119, fév./mars 1973, p. 37–40)

Compares the costs of different types of transport to the capital.

Rodríguez, Cayentano Armando. Geografía de la Isla de Santo Domingo y reseña de las demás Antillas. See item **5049**.

5051 Ronceray, Hubert de. Enquête empirique au Bel-Air (IFH/C, 119, fév./mars. 1973, p. 19–29)

Review of the growth, prospects, and problems of a Port-au-Prince neighborhood.

JAMAICA

5052 Baxter, Ann. The diffusion of innovations; soil conservation techniques in the Yallahs Valley, Jamaica (IJ/JJ, 9:4, 1975, p. 51–56, ill.)

Case study of diffusion indicates that soil conservation techniques in Jamaica spread similarly to other techniques in "developed" areas.

5053 Day, Michael J. The hydrology of polygonal karst depressions in Northern Jamaica (ZG, 32, April 1979, p. 25–34, map, tables)

Slow, diffuse, vertical water percolation is dominant in the creation of Jamaican "cockpits."

5054 Eyre, L. Alan. Quasi-urban melange settlement: cases from St. Catherine and St. James, Jamaica (AGS/GR, 69:1, Jan. 1979, p. 95–100)

A sense of community is missing, and private and narrow interests prevail, as settlement explodes near major urban centers in Jamaica.

5055 Nkemdirim, Lawrence C. Spatial and seasonal distribution of rainfall and runoff in Jamaica (AGS/GR, 69:3, July 1979, p. 288–318, maps, tables)

Runoff can be predicted from rainfall on the island, providing information necessary for water management in this developing nation.

5056 Wood, P.A. Suspended sediment in a tropical environment of seasonal flow and large floods: Hope River, Jamaica (USM/JTG, 45, Dec. 1977, p. 65–69, bibl., maps, tables)

First study of its kind in the Caribbean indicates that sediment concentration is related to stream discharge.

LESSER ANTILLES

5057 Bird, J. Brian; A. Richards; and P.P. Wong. Coastal subsystems of Western Barbados, West Indies (SSAG/GA, 61A:3/4, 1979, p. 221–236, bibl., maps, tables)

The west coast beaches, now deteriorating, result from sea-level fluctuations and extensions of coral terraces in the Quaternary.

5058 Doran, Michael F. and Renée A. Landis. Origin and persistence of an inner-city slum in Nassau (AGS/GR, 70:2, April 1980, p. 182–193, maps, table)

Originally designed as a slum, Over-the-Hill retains this character despite growth occurring elsewhere in the city.

5059 Smith, S. Ivan. Sugar production potential in Barbados (USM/JTG, 42, June 1976, p. 59–77, bibl., maps, tables)

Sugar production fluctuates annually not only in response to environmental factors, but also because of inefficient production and processing methods.

PUERTO RICO

5060 Auty, Richard M. Technological change in plantation transport systems: a Caribbean example 1930–1970 (USM/JTG, 41, Dec. 1975, p. 1–8, bibl., ill., maps, tables)

Small sugar mills have survived because of low transport costs resulting from the introduction of truck transportation of cane.

5061 Boswell, Thomas D. Inferences concerning intermunicipio migrations in Puerto Rico: 1955–1960 (USM/JTG, 45, Dec. 1977, p. 1–11, bibl., maps, tables)

Most migration among *municipios* resulted from economic forces, but personal factors and counter-stream movements may also be strong influences.

5062 Geovisión de Puerto Rico: aportaciones recientes al estudio de la geografía. María Teresa B. de Galiñanes, editora. Río Piedras: Editorial Universitaria, Universidad de Puerto Rico, 1977. 413 p.; bibl.; ill.

One geographer participated in this review, which contains chapters on the geomorphology, climate, soils, population, industrial geography, and minerals of Puerto Rico. Social geography sections stress a political approach to problem-solving.

5063 Monk, Janice J. and Charles S. Alexander. Modernization and rural population movements: western Puerto Rico (SAGE/JIAS, 21:4, Nov. 1979, p. 523–550, maps, tables)

Considers the effects of urbanization on change in traditional rural areas, concluding that while changes in settlement patterns and access to services have occurred, strong rural values persist.

5064 Oxford, P. Ireland. Geomorphological variations of "case-hardening" in Puerto Rico (ZG, 32, April 1979, p. 9–20, maps, plates, tables)

Case-hardened limestone beds in north-central Puerto Rico are uniform in thickness and not dominant in *mogote* formation.

5065 Tata, Robert J. Puerto Rican economic growth: estimation of a time series model in the presence of multicollinearity (USM/JTG, 45, Dec. 1977, p. 58–64, bibl., tables)

Considerable increases in wealth and well-being have resulted from Puerto Rico's Operation Bootstrap.

5066 ———. Statistical explanation of the regional variation in growth of median family income in Puerto Rico (PAIGH/G, 88, dic. 1978, p. 79–88, bibl., maps, table)

Most of the growth in median family income is explained by changes in median number of school years completed, non-worker/worker ratio, absolute population, population density, population urbanized, and percentage of employees in manufacturing.

TRINIDAD AND TOBAGO

5067 Harewood, Jack. The population of Trinidad and Tobago. Paris: s.n., 1975. xvii, 237 p.; bibl.; ill. (Committee for International Coordination of National Research in Demography. C.I.C.R.E.D. series)

5068 Pollard, H.J. and **D.A. Eastwood.** Dairying and development at Wallerfield, Trinidad (TESG, 67:5, 1976, p. 289–299, bibl., map, tables)

Highly motivated and trained farmers are more important than a sound economic framework for producing economic efficiency in an agricultural development project.

CENTRAL AMERICA
GENERAL

5069 Bovallius, Carl Erik Alexander. Resa i Central-Amerika, 1881–1883. Traducido del sueco por Camilo Vijil Tardón. Managua: Fondo de Promoción Cultural, Banco de América, 1977. 316 p.; ill.; indexes (Serie Viajeros; no. 1. Colección Cultural Banco de América)

Reprint of 1887 edition concentrates on Nicaragua's flora, fauna, and archaeological treasures.

5070 Maldonado-Koerdell, M. Bibliografía geológica y paleontológica de América

Central (BNBD, 27, enero/feb. 1979, p. 119–129)

Brief introduction to the area's geology is a good guide for beginning students, but is not comprehensive.

5071 Miller, Elbert E. The raising and marketing of beef in Central America and Panama (USM/JTG, 41, Dec. 1975, p. 59–69, bibl., maps, tables)

Reviews ecological and economic conditions that explain the distribution and export of beef cattle in Central America.

5072 Vieillard Baron, Alain. América Central, introducción al estudio de los países de la región. Caracas: Centro de Información, Documentación y Análisis Latinoamericano, between 1975 and 1978. 56 p.; 1 leaf of plates; bibl.; maps (Documentos—Centro de Información, Documentación y Análisis Latinoamericano; entrega no. 70/71)

Brief, general introduction to Central America concentrates on economic integration.

5073 Weyl, Richard. Geschichte und Stand: Geowisenschaftlicher forschung in Zentralamerika (IAA, 4:4, 1978, p. 307–322, bibl., ill., maps, plates, tables)

Review article lists geological research agencies in Central America.

BELIZE

Commonwealth Institute, *London.* Guyana and Belize: a teacher's guide to study resources. See item **5256.**

5074 Demyk, Michel. Belize: enjeu territorial et enjeu pétrolier (CDAL, 18, 2. semestre, 1978, p. 93–105, maps)

Long-standing social and economic differences between Guatemala and Belize may be exacerbated by oil discoveries in disputed territory.

5075 Furley, Peter A. and **Alexander John Crosbie.** Geography of Belize. London: Collins, 1974. 48 p.; charts; ill.; index; maps.

Good introductory geography text for beginning students.

5076 McDonald, Roy Charles. Tower karst geomorphology in Belize (ZG, 32, April 1979, p. 35–45, ill.; maps)

Karst tower landforms result from direct rainfall and overland runoff, as well as subsurface runoff.

5077 Menon, P.K. The Anglo-Guatemalan territorial dispute over the colony of Belize (British Honduras) (JLAS, 11:2, Nov. 1979, p. 343–371)

A careful and complete analysis of a long-standing, unresolved Central American political conflict.

5078 Nunes, Frederick E. Administration and culture: subsistence and modernization in Crique Sarco, Belize (UWI/CQ, 23:4, Dec. 1977, p. 17–46, bibl., map)

Failure of this agricultural modernization project is the result of a large social gap between policy makers and beneficiaries.

COSTA RICA

5079 Casey Gaspar, Jeffrey. El ferrocarril al Atlántico en Costa Rica: 1871–1874 (UCR/AEC, 1976, p. 291–344, tables)

Recounts the construction of the railroad with emphasis on costs and crews.

5080 Elizondo Solís, Carlos L. Uso de sensores remotos en la evaluación de los recursos naturales de Costa Rica (PAIGH/RC, 33, junio 1978, p. 121–128, maps, tables)

Earth satellite imagery permits the classification of land use in Costa Rica.

5081 Fernández Arias, Mario E.; Annabelle Schmidt de Rojas; and Víctor Basauri. La población de Costa Rica. Ciudad Universitaria Rodrigo Facio: Universidad de Costa Rica, Instituto de Investigaciones Sociales, 1976. 199 p.; bibl.; ill. (Committee for International Coordination of National Research in Demography. C.I.C.R.E.D. series)

Useful handbook contains data and text on practically every aspect of population in Costa Rica, although many of its maps are illegible. Part of a series for the *World Population Year* (1974) by the Comité Internacional de Investigaciones Nacionales en Demografía (CICRED). Other entries in this series are on Panama (Vilma N. Medica); Cuba (La Habana: Universidad, Centro de Estudios Demográficos); and Trinidad and Tobago (Jack Harewood).

5082 Madrigal G., Rodolfo. Evidencias geomórficas de movimientos tectónicos recientes en el Valle de El General (UCR/CT, 1:1, junio 1977, p. 97–108, bibl., maps, tables)

Tectonic movements in the Pleistocene produced most geomorphological features in this Costa Rican valley.

5083 Meléndez Chaverri, Carlos. El medio geográfico (*in* Costa Rica contemporánea. Prólogo y dirección, Chester Zelaya. Colaboradores, Carlos Meléndez Chaverri and others. San José: Editorial Costa Rica, 1979, t. 1, p. 39–74, map)

General survey of the geographical base of the country, including physical geography and planning regions.

Molina de Lines, María; Josefina Piana de Cuestas; and Ana I. Fuentes de May. El escenario geográfico de Costa Rica en el siglo XVI según los informes de Gonzalo Fernández de Oviedo en la *Historia general y natural de las Indias*. See HLAS 41:2411.

5084 Ortega G., Antonio. Situación demográfica actual de Costa Rica y perspectivas futuras (*in* Seminario Nacional de Demografía, 6th, Heredia, C.R., 1976. Informe. San José: Universidad Nacional de Costa Rica, 1976, v. 1, p. 19–70, tables)

Excellent brief survey of Costa Rica's population, including population growth, migration, urbanization, and predicting future trends.

5085 Ratcliffe, Jane E. La base funcional de ciudades pequeñas: ejemplo costarricense (UCR/AEC, 1976, p. 345–368, bibl., maps, tables)

Central place theory is useful in understanding the functional bases of small Costa Rican cities.

5086 Salar Ulate, Walter E.; Manuel Villa Issa; and Luis E. Chalita Tovar. Rentabilidad económica nacional proyecto de riego en la cuenca del Río Itiquis, Alejuela, Costa Rica (AGRO, 30, 1977, p. 3–18, bibl.)

Socioeconomic survey based on present net worth, cost-benefit relations, and internal rate of return indicates this irrigation project should be completed.

5087 Schmidt-Effing, Reinhard. Alter und Genese des Nicoya-Komplexes, einer ozeanischen Paläokruste (Oberjura bis Eozän) im südlichen Zentralamerika (GV/GR, 68:2, 1979, p. 457–494, bibl., ill., maps)

The first attempt to regionally differentiate the basaltic Nicoya Complex reveals that this structure developed over long periods of geological time.

EL SALVADOR

5088 El Salvador. Ministerio de Obras Públicas. Instituto Geográfico Nacional Ingeniero Pablo Arnoldo Guzmán. Guía para investigadores: República de El Salvador. México: Instituto Panamericano de Geografía e Historia (IPGH), 1977. 81 p.; maps.

Another addition to an excellent series of resource books that contain indexes to map series necessary for planning, sponsored by the Pan American Institute of Geography and History.

GUATEMALA

5089 Deevey, E.S. and others. Mayan urbanism: impact on a tropical karst environment (AAAS/S, 206:4416, 19 Oct. 1979, p. 298–306, bibl., maps, tables)

Limnological data from the Petén indicate serious nutrient depletion in agricultural soils due to erosion and slopewash associated with Classic Mayan urbanism. Population growth was not affected until Late Classic time at the earliest.

Giessen. Universität. Tropenistitut. Agrarwissenschaftliche Forschung in den humiden Tropen. See item **5238.**

5090 Guatemala. Instituto Geográfico Nacional. Guía geográfica de Guatemala, para investigadores = Research guide of Guatemala. Preparado e impreso en el Instituto Geográfico Nacional para el Instituto Panamericano de Geografía e Historia. Guatemala: 1978. 157 p.; bibl.; maps (Publicación IPGH; no. 319)

A detailed listing of maps, aerial imagery, and published data sources on the Republic of Guatemala that appears to be complete through 1976. Emphasizes the physical environment, but also contains information on urban and rural land use, cadastral, and other map series for cultural features. Bilingual text (Spanish and English).

5091 Mulvihill, James L. A locational study of primary health services in Guate-

mala City (AAG/PG, 31:3, Aug. 1979, p. 299–305, bibl., maps)

Analysis of locational efficiency of primary health centers in Guatemala City utilizing a location-allocation model. Suggests modifications in location of health centers.

5092 Ordóñez Morales, César Eduardo; Antonio Martín del Campo; and **Ramón Fernández Fernández.** Estructura agraria en el altiplano occidental de la República de Guatemala, un caso: el altiplano del Departamento de Quezaltenango (AGRO, 29, 1977, p. 3–16)

Three forms of agricultural production are identified: 1) capitalist; 2) simple mercantile; and 3) semi-proletariat. The capitalist form is dominant among these three highly articulated systems.

HONDURAS

5093 Flores Andino, Francisco A. Toponimias indígenas de los departamentos de Gracias a Dios, Olancho, El Paraíso y Choluteca (AHGH/R, 63:23/24, enero/junio 1979, p. 66–70, bibl., map)

Gathering Indian names is the first step in studying the historical geography of this frontier zone.

NICARAGUA

Bovallius, Carl Erik Alexander. Resa i Central-Amerika, 1881–1883. See item **5069.**

5094 Incer, Jaime. Comentarios a la obra de Pablo Levy (BNBD, 25, sept./oct. 1978, p. 64–72, plate)

Levy, an engineer, was a student of Nicaraguan environment and culture 100 years ago. For new edition of Levy's work, see item **5095.**

5095 Lévy, Pablo. Notas geográficas y económicas sobre la República de Nicaragua. Introducción y notas, Jaime Incer Barquero. Managua: Fondo de Promoción Cultural, Banco de América, 1976. 548 p.; bibl.; index; map (fold. col. in pocket) (Serie Geografía y naturaleza; no. 1. Colección cultural Banco de América)

This reprint, annotated by Incer, of Levy's 1837 work, reveals the insights of one of the first students of Nicaraguan physical and cultural geography.

5096 Nietschmann, Bernard. Caribbean edge: the coming of modern times to isolated people and wildlife. Indianapolis: Bobbs-Merrill, c1979. 280 p.; ill.; index.

Entertaining account of field work in Nicaragua should be required reading for cultural geographers.

5097 ———. Ecological change, inflation, and migration in the far western Caribbean (AGS/GR, 69:1, Jan. 1979, p. 1–24, maps, plates, tables)

The Miskito are becoming economically dependent on endangered species and declining resources, thereby diminishing their ability to adjust to the demands of a modern world.

5098 Salvatierra, Sofonías. Los ferrocarriles de Nicaragua (BNBD, 27, enero/feb. 1979, p. 106–114)

Historical evolution of the Nicaraguan rail system, part of a special study in this issue of the *Boletín*.

PANAMA

5099 Lamarre, Denis. Notion d'année et des mois pluviometriques caracteristiques: exemple de l'Isthme de Panama (Characteristic pluviometrical year and month in the Panama Isthmus) (AGF/B, 55:456/457, nov./déc. 1978, p. 315–320, map, tables)

The year 1949 is typical for rainfall, and can therefore be used for comparison with other years.

5100 Médica, Vilma N. La población de Panamá. Panamá: DEC, Contraloría General, 1974. 147 p.; bibl.; ill. (Committee for International Coordination of National Research in Demography. C.I.C.R.E.D. series).

5101 Proyecto de desarrollo integrado de la región oriental de Panamá-Darién. Estudio realizado por la Unidad Técnica del Proyecto Panamá-Darién durante el período 1975–1978, Gobierno de la República de Panamá, Programa de Desarrollo Regional. Washington: Secretaría General de la Organización de los Estados Americanos, 1978. 308 p.; ill.; portfolio (5 fold. maps)

Study designed to show how the Darién region's physical, human, and financial resources can be developed in conjunction with the construction of the last section of the Pan American Highway. Accompanying map packet contains valuable aerial data.

MEXICO

5102 Alba-Hernández, Francisco. La población de México. México: Centro de Estudios Económicos y Demográficos, El Colegio de México, c1976. xiv, 122 p.; bibl.; ill. (Committee for International Coordination of National Research in Demography. C.I.C.R.E.D series)

An analysis of Mexican demography with chapters on components of population growth, social characteristics, distribution (with migration), employment, and future growth. Most data are aggregated at the national level and current through the 1970 census. For sociologist's comment, see item **8074.**

Bunster, Enrique. Crónicas del Pacífico. See item **5156.**

5103 Clawson, David L. Intravillage wealth and peasant agricultural innovation (JDA, 12:3, April 1978, p. 323–336, map, tables)

Author presents a case study from the Mexican community of Nealtican that tests the relationship of peasant wealth to the propensity to innovate.

5104 ——— and **D.R. Hoy.** Nealtican, Mexico: a peasant community that rejected the 'Green Revolution' (AJES, 38:4, Oct. 1979, p. 371–388, map)

Lack of consideration of the specific village physical and cultural setting is the primary cause of rejection of a family garden program that was part of Plan Puebla. From the villager's perspective, failure to adopt Green Revolution innovations is a rational decision. The authors suggest more study of local environmental diversity, including social factors, and the use of an ecological systems approach to help make Green Revolution products compatible with the peasant's world.

5105 Coll de Hurtado, Atlántida. Aspects de la géographie économique du Mexique

(SG/AG, 89:494, juillet/aôut 1980, p. 424–453, maps, tables)

A general overview of the economic geography of present-day Mexico that includes sections on environment, demography, agriculture, industry, transportation, and development of tertiary economic activities.

5106 ———. El suroeste de Campeche y sus recursos naturales. México: Universidad Nacional Autónoma de México, Instituto de Geografía, 1975. 84 p.; bibl.; ill. (Serie Cuadernos—Instituto de Geografía)

Description of the physical environment and resource base of the area surrounding Laguna de Términos in southwestern Campeche state.

5107 Desarrollo de la cuenca Grijalva Usumacinta: décima novena serie de mesas redondas realizadas en el Anfiteatro del IMSS, Villahermosa Tabasco del 17 al 21 de mayo de 1976 bajo el patrocinio de la Secretaría de Recursos Hidráulicos, Comisión del Río Grijalva. México: Instituto Mexicano de Recursos Naturales Renovables, 1976, 1977. 275 p.; graphs.

Published results of a series of roundtable discussions held in 1976 under the sponsorship of the Río Grijalva Commission. Emphasizes the physical resource base, with sections on agricultural and forest resources, fisheries, freshwater resources, hydrocarbons, and the accomplishments and plans of the Río Grijalva Commission.

5108 Doolittle, William E. Aboriginal agricultural development in the valley of Sonora, Mexico (AGS/GR, 70:3, July 1980, p. 328–342, map, photos, tables)

Research in northern Mexico supports the hypothesis that prehispanic agriculturalists developed optimal land (land requiring least work) first, and only expanded to marginal land as demand for agricultural products increased.

5109 Ferras, Robert. Ciudad Nezahualcóyotl, un barrio en vías de absorción por la ciudad de México. Traducción del francés de María Dolores de la Peña. México: Centro de Estudios Sociológicos, El Colegio de México, 1977. 37 p.; bibl.; ill. (Cuadernos del CES; no. 20)

A short monograph analyzing the development of Ciudad Nezahualtóyotl. Land uses are well established, but development of public services lags behind. Useful data on urban physical development and population characteristics in Mexico's largest marginal settlement.

Ferrocarriles de México: reseña histórico-reglamentos: siglo XIX. See *HLAS 42:2193.*

5110 Fuentes Aguilar, Luis. El estado como organizador del espacio: el plan Chontalpa, un ejemplo (Boletín del Instituto de Geografía [UNAM, México] 8, 1978, p. 67–82, bibl., maps, tables)

The author outlines the short history of an agricultural development project in the tropical lowlands of Tabasco. The paper contains data of interest to those concerned with agricultural development in the tropics. Conclusion is mildly critical of the development plan.

5111 García Palomares, Fernando I. El uso de la Carta Predial Rural con fines de Catastro Fiscal, un ejemplo: Municipio de Corregidora, Oro, México (PAIGH/RC, 33, junio 1978, p. 47–58, bibl., table)

Describes test of a plan to estimate land value for cadastral purposes utilizing the DETENAL 1:50,000 scale map series. Values are based on accessibility, proximity, geology, land use, agricultural land capability, erosion, rockiness and topography, among other factors.

5112 George, Pierre. La relève mexicaine (SG/AG, 88:486, mars/abril 1979, p. 225–238, maps, tables)

Author summarizes the location of Mexican petroleum-production facilities and discusses the benefits and potential problems associated with expansion of production.

5113 Gormsen, Erdmann. La zonificación socio-económica de la ciudad de Puebla: cambios por efecto de la metropolización (FAIC/CPPT, 15, 1978, p. 7–20, bibl., maps)

Paper focuses on changes in the central sector of Puebla over the past century, with emphasis on current developments and ensuing problems. Four areas of conflict in future development are identified: 1) economic demands for high-rise buildings in the central business district where land values are highest; 2) a growing historical preservation movement to save downtown buildings and areas of historical importance; 3) flight of well-to-do families to the suburbs and their replacement by poorer families, accompanied by conversion of old single-family housing to multi-family; and 4) traffic congestion in the central city, producing noise and air pollution. Author offers no solutions to these problems.

Guillén, Clemente. Clemente Guillén, explorer of the South: diaries of the overland expeditions to Bahía Magdalena and La Paz, 1719, 1720–1721. See *HLAS 42:2129.*

5114 Heine, Klaus. Blockgletscher- und Blockzungen-Generationen am Nevado de Toluca, Mexiko (GEB/E, 107:4, Jan. 1976, p. 330–352)
The first study of rock glaciers and icecored moraines in Mexico.

5115 ———. Mensch und geomorphodynamische Prozesse in Raum und Zeit im randtropischen Hochbecken von Puebla/Tlaxcala, Mexiko (Deutscher Geographentag [Franz Steiner Verlag, Wiesbaden, FRG] 41, 1978, p. 390–406, bibl., maps, tables)
An examination of the role of human activities and natural processes in shaping the landscape of a portion of the Mexican highlands near Puebla. This article contains several excellent maps.

5116 Iltis, Hugh H.; John F. Doebley; Rafael Guzmán M.; and Batia Pazy. *Zea diploperennis* (Gramineae): a new teosinte from Mexico (AAAS/S, 203:4376, 12 Jan. 1979, p. 186–187, photos)
A brief technical report describing a perennial teosinte formerly believed to be extinct.

5117 Knoblich, Klaus. La cuenca de El Seco/Oriental: una reserva de agua subterránea natural para el futuro (FAIC/CPPT, 15, 1978, p. 231–234, bibl., maps)
Estimate of amount and quality analysis of replenishable groundwater reserves in a highland Mexican basin.

5118 Lauer, Wilhelm. Ökologische Klimatypen am Ostabfall der mexikanischen Meseta (Ecological-climatic types on the eastern slopes of the Mexican meseta) (UGBI/E, 32:2, Juni 1978, p. 101–110, bibl., tables)
Classification and mapping of local climates on a 1:500,000 scale permits identification of climate/vegetation associations and development of a general model.

5119 ———. Puebla-Tlaxcala: a German-Mexican research project (GeoJournal [Akademische Verlagsgesellschaft, Wiesbaden, FRG] 3:1, 1979, p. 97–105, bibl., map)
A complete review of the activities of the joint West German-Mexican Puebla-Tlaxcala Project, sponsored by the Deutsche Forshungsgemeinschaft. The bibliography lists 130 publications by individuals affiliated with the project at various times throughout its 17-year existence.

5120 ———. Tipos ecológicos del clima en la vertiente oriental de la meseta mexicana: comentario para una carta climática, 1:500,000; apéndice (FAIC/CPPT, 15, 1978, p. 235–248, bibl., tables)
Text to accompany a new Mexican climate map explains organization of the data, and relates climate characteristics to vegetation. A slightly modified version of the author's article in German (see item **5118**).

5121 Lentnek, Barry; Mark Charnews; and John V. Cotter. Commercial factors in the development of regional urban systems: a Mexican case study (CU/EG, 54:4, Oct. 1978, p. 291–308)
Authors utilize data from Aguascalientes, Mexico, to test hypotheses regarding the development of regional primacy. Study concludes that local primacy develops as a result of consumer behavior determined by per capita income.

5122 Macazaga Ordoño, César. Nombres geográficos de México. Edición, introducción, topónimos e iconografía por César Macazaga Ordoño. Con un suplemento facsimilar de los nombres de lugar, escrito en 1885 por Antonio Peñafiel. México: Editorial Innovación, 1978. 94, 260 p.; bibl.; ill.
A two-part reference work on Mexican place names. Pt. 1 is a simplified and expanded version of a study of 462 Nahuatl topographic name glyphs, written by Antonio Peñafiel in 1885; pt. 2 is a reproduction of the original work.

5123 McGoodwin, James Russell. The decline of Mexico's pacific inshore fisheries (OCEANUS, 22:2, Summer 1979, p. 51–59, bibl., maps, plates, tables)
Describes a combination of factors that have affected the productivity of fisheries: development of export markets, improved fishing technology, increasing local

population, and occasional environmental disaster. Based on a case study, south Sinaloa state, article concludes with suggested government policy changes in fishery management (e.g., reduction of exports, reorientation to domestic markets, and local subsistence production).

5124 Martínez Gómez, Lorenzo. La alternativa nuclear en México (CP, 16, abril/junio 1978, p. 5–15)

An analysis of Mexican nuclear energy potential which concludes with a critique of Mexico's nuclear energy development plan.

5125 Melo Gallegos, Carlos. El paisaje geomorfológico mexicano en el atractivo natural de los parques nacionales; Desarrollo de los parques nacionales mexicanos; Balance analítico de la operación del sistema mexicano de parques nacionales: tres estudios sobre el mismo tema. México: Instituto de Geografía, UNAM, 1977. 232 p.; bibl.; ill. (Série varia—Instituto de Geografía, UNAM; 1:3)

Consists of three essays: a landscape evaluation, critique, and plan for future development of the Mexican national park system. A careful and complete analysis of value to those interested in recreation and/or environmental preservation in Mexico, applicable to other parts of Latin America as well.

5126 Mexico. Dirección General de Oceanografía y Señalamiento Marítimo. Estudio geográfico de la región de Mazatlán, Sin. Estados Unidos Mexicanos, Secretaría de Marina, Dirección General de Oceanografía y Señalamiento Marítimo. México: La Dirección, 1974. 353 p.; 1 leaf of plates; ill.

A detailed and complete regional description of Mazatlán and the surrounding area. Includes much tabular data on Mazatlán and the State of Sinaloa, as well as many maps and photographs. A useful reference tool for scholars planning to work in this part of Mexico.

Mexico. Secretaría de Fomento, Colonización, Industria y Comercio. Caminos de la República a la época de la Reforma, años de 1856–1857. See *HLAS 42:2221.*

5127 Miranda Villaseñor, Luis E. Los censos nacionales y el municipio (PAIGH/RC, 33, junio 1978, p. 41–46)

For the 1980–81 census period Mexico

has implemented a system of Basic Geo-Statistical Areas that will establish permanent boundaries among urban and rural sectors. The system will reduce confusion that results from combining data from urban and rural areas within the political boundaries of *municipios.*

5128 Mumme, Stephen P. U.S.-Mexican groundwater problems: bilateral prospects and implications (SAGE/JIAS, 22:1, Feb. 1980, p. 31–55, bibl.)

A largely political analysis of past and potential conflicts over groundwater development along an international boundary. Differing objectives and approaches to groundwater development create problems that will be exacerbated by continuing exploitation of a limited resource.

5129 Muría, José María. La jurisdicción de Zapotlán el grande del siglo XVI al XIX (INAH/A, 6:54, 1976, 7. época, p. 23–42, maps, tables)

Description of boundary changes in a *municipio* in the state of Jalisco. Zapotlan's modern name is Ciudad Guzmán.

5130 Nolan, Mary Lee. Impact of Parícutin on five communities (*in* Volcanic activity and human ecology. Edited by Payson D. Sheets and Donald K. Grayson. New York: Academic Press, 1979, p. 293–338, bibl., maps, plates, tables)

Discussion of the human response to the Parícutin eruption. Author concludes that the community response to the eruption tended to be of two types: 1) a fatalistic attitude causing community members to react to change only when forced by uncontrolled events, or 2) an organized attempt by community members to anticipate the natural event and plan a course of action. Author does not explain why some communities were better equipped to deal with disaster than others.

5131 Ohngemach, Dieter and **Herbert Straka.** La historia de la vegetación en la región Puebla-Tlaxcala durante el cuaternario tardío (FAIC/CPPT, 15, 1978, p. 189–204, bibl., map, tables)

Presentation of results of pollen analysis on samples taken from five profiles in the vicinity of Mt. Orizaba.

5132 Patiño, Emilio Alanís. Megalópolis mexicana: la impotencia de las medidas para disminuir el ritmo del crecimiento metropolitano (AGRO, 32, 1978, p. 101–124, ill., tables)

Comparison of rates of population growth, population density, and other factors among selected Mexican cities and between Mexico City and other major urban centers. Contains many tables with estimated population data for Mexican cities through 1976.

5133 Popp, Kilian. El cambio del paisaje cultural en el Valle de Atlixco (FAIC/CPPT, 15, 1978, p. 73–82, maps)

Notes landscape changes in a valley dominated by *latifundia* until 1930, when some properties were expropriated. Concludes with observations on the nature of adoption and diffusion of innovations among the region's farmers. This summary of the author's thesis (in German) contains several interesting maps.

5134 Recursos naturales renovables de México: situación, problemas, perspectivas: ciclo de conferencias sustentadas en el auditorio del IMERNAR del 17 al 28 de octubre de 1977 para conmemorar el XXV aniversario del Instituto Mexicano de Recursos Naturales Renovables. México: Instituto Mexicano de Recursos Naturales Renovables, 1979. 267 p.; bibl.; ill.

A collection of nine papers on the current status of Mexican renewable natural resources and efforts toward their study and preservation over the past 25 years. Individual papers deal with soils, forest resources, grazing lands, terrestrial fauna, fisheries, the physical environment, population, environmental education, and conservation legislation. The quality of papers varies; some present useful summaries of accomplishments and current status with detailed bibliographies.

5135 Rees, John D. Effects of eruptions on Parícutin Volcano on landforms, vegetation, and human occupancy (*in* Volcanic activity and human ecology. Edited by Payson D. Sheets and Donald K. Grayson. New York: Academic Press, 1979, p. 249–292, bibl., maps, plates, tables)

Account of the effect of the Parícutin eruption on surrounding areas includes discussion of impact on resource base and its recovery between the initial eruption in 1943 and 1978.

5136 Reunión Nacional sobre la Investigación Demográfica en México, *1st*, *México, 1977.* Memorias de la I Reunión Nacional sobre la Investigación Demográfica en México, realizada en México, D.F., del 14 al 18 de Junio de 1977. México: Programa Nacional Indicativo de Investigación Demográfica, Consejo Nacional de Ciencia y Tecnología, 1978. 485 p.; bibl.; graphs.

Proceedings of a meeting held in 1977 contains 30 papers, of which over half present the results of population research in Mexico. Individual papers deal with such topics as impact of family planning programs, life expectancy and socioeconomic indicators, underreporting of infant mortality, internal and international migration, employment and the work force, and population distribution. Also contains general papers dealing with research methods and demographic theory, historical demography, and data sources.

5137 Revel-Mouroz, Jean. Economie frontalière et organisation de l'espace: réflexions à partir de l'exemple de la frontière Mexique-Etats Unis (CDAL, 18, 2. semestre, 1978, p. 7–16, map)

The economies of the frontier zone are highly articulated, but the financial and administrative power of US interests make it, in reality, an extension of that country's economic space. Mexican attempts to modify the situation (PRONAF, Border Industrialization Program) have only consolidated the border zone's dependency.

5138 Sander, Hans-Joerg. Análisis de la estructura socio-económica en unos pueblos de la región del Proyecto Puebla-Tlaxcala (FAIC/CPPT, 15, 1978, p. 67–72, tables)

A comparison of economic base of families in two Tlaxcala towns, according to a model developed by the author.

5139 Schneider, Hans. La agricultura en Valsequillo: aspectos del desarrollo de la estructura agraria en el área de riego Atoyatempan-Tecamachalco (FAIC/CPPT, 15, 1978, p. 61–66, bibl., table)

Examination of the changes in agrarian structure that occurred following the construction of an irrigation project in the late 1940s. Some middle-sized operators have taken advantage of the benefits of irrigation and have installed capital-intensive operations, while others have resisted such changes since the adoption of irrigation. Although most operators of small farms have failed to adopt the benefits of irrigation, a small number have increased production. The result of these conditions is a polarization of agriculture such that larger properties serve urban markets while small farms absorb surplus labor.

5140 Sevilla Hernández, María Luisa. Desarrollo pesquero en México (IPN/EP, 13:2/3, 1976, p. 23–30)

Analysis of the Mexican fishing industry. Contains data through 1972 (some to 1974), and offers general suggestions for future development of the industry.

5141 Siemens, Alfred H. A decade of 'colonization' along a tropical lowland river in Mexico (GeoJournal [Akademische Verlagsgesellschaft, Wiesbaden, FRG], 3:1, 1979, p. 41–51, bibl., ill.)

The planned agricultural scheme on the Río Candelaria in Campeche state provides a test for cost-benefit analysis of government planned and initiated colonization in tropical regions. Investment in the Candelaria project is high relative to benefits, and the settlement has not fulfilled expectations. The conclusion is that *ejido*-type settlements may not be suited to tropical frontier conditions. As an alternative, author suggests promoting spontaneous colonization through establishment of rudimentary infrastructure.

5142 Silva Martínez, Daniel and **Luis E. Chalita Tovar.** La situación económica de las hortalizas en el sistema de Riego Culiacan, estado de Sinaloa (AGRO, 29, 1977, p. 29–44, bibl.)

A linear programming model is utilized to determine the most efficient use of land resources for two crop years. The results suggest that sugar cane, historically the region's primary cash-crop, is not cost-efficient, and that various horticultural crops will yield more income.

5143 Simposio sobre Relaciones Campo-Ciudad, *Mexico, 1978.* Simposio sobre Relaciones Campo-Ciudad: Instituto de Geografía, UNAM, 4–8 septiembre, 1978. México: El Instituto, 1978 or 1979. 263 p.; bibl.; ill.

A collection of 22 papers on rural-urban relations in Mexico. Authors represent most social science disciplines, and topics range from studies of infrastructure and long-term development programs to reports on migration, population growth, and economic and social activities.

5144 Sprague, Milton A. and others. Alternatives to monoculture of henequen in Yucatan, pt. 1: the agriculture, climate soil, and weed control; pt. 2, studies with maize, sorghum and sesame; pt. 3: performance for forage crops and livestock (AI/I, 3:5, Sept./Oct. 1978, p. 285–290, map, plates, tables; 4:2, March/April 1979, p. 84–91, bibl., plate, tables; 4:3, May/June 1979, p. 157–163, plates, tables)

Three-part article. Pt. 1 describes environmental conditions that require special cultural management techniques. Pt. 2 reports on the results of experiments with selected varieties of maize, sorghum, sesame, soybeans and possible cash crops in Yucatan. Pt. 3 presents the results of experiments with selected grasses and other forage crops and livestock (i.e., cattle, swine, sheep).

5145 Tyrakowski, Konrad. Cartografía lugareña: un ejemplo contemporáneo del pueblo de San Juan Cuautinchán, Pue. (FAIC/CPPT, 15, 1978, p. 143–150, bibl., tables)

Description of four maps drawn by a local resident of the pueblo of San Juan Cuautinchán. Such maps are valuable as historical records of the *municipio*, and reveal the perceptions of local residents of their habitat. Author also notes certain artistic elements that appear to be of precolumbian origin.

5146 ———. El tianguis central de Tepeaca: función e importancia de un mercado complejo (FAIC/CPPT, 15, 1978, p. 47–60, bibl., maps, tables)

The market of Tepeaca has expanded greatly over the years as a result of the town's growth, and as lack of employment forces greater number of people to seek income as merchants. Several suggestions are made for improvement of the market and alleviation of problems, especially traffic congestion.

5147 **Van Young, Eric.** Urban market and hinterland: Guadalajara and its region in the eighteenth century (HAHR, 59:3, Nov. 1979, p. 593–635, maps, tables)

Historical geographical sketch of the Guadalajara market and its area of supply in the late colonial period (1760–1820). Author concludes that rural-urban integration in colonial Latin America was better developed and more typical than previously thought.

5148 **Vanneph, Alain.** Pole petrolier et frontière: Reynosa, Mexique (CDAL, 18, 2. semestre, 1978, p. 17–23, map)

The traditional border function of Reynosa has been supplemented by installation of a petrochemical complex, giving the city a dual functional base. The result is a city that is neither a characteristic border town nor a typical petrochemical center, but a unique product of the interplay of the two functions.

5149 **Villasana, J. Alberto** and **R.B. Southard.** Cartographic cooperation along the United States-Mexico international border (PAIGH/RC, 32, dic. 1977, p. 13–24, map, table)

Describes cooperative activities and agencies involved in mapping along the frontier. Includes a map showing boundary mapping in progress.

5150 **Werner, Gerd.** Génesis, distribución y destrucción de los suelos del sur del estado de Tlaxcala (FAIC/CPPT, 15, 1978, p. 225–229, bibl.)

A summary of the soils work carried out as part of the Puebla-Tlaxcala Project. Contains a useful bibliography.

5151 ———. Los suelos y las sociedades de suelos de Puebla-Tlaxcala (FAIC/CPPT, 15, 1978, p. 205–224, bibl., maps, table)

Description of the soils found in the area covered by the joint German-Mexican Puebla-Tlaxcala Project that is intended to accompany a 1:100,000 scale soil map published separately.

5152 **Williams, Bárbara J.** Paisaje de atraso: aprovechamiento traditional de la tierra y economía moderna en Huizquilucan, estado de México (Boletín del Instituto de Geografía [UNAM, México] 8, 1978, p. 123–188, bibl., maps, tables)

In certain communities subsistence agricultural land-use patterns persist after the employment structure shifts to non-farm activities. Develops a model for analyzing the relationship between land-use and employment structure.

SOUTH AMERICA (except Brazil)

ROBERT C. EIDT, *Professor of Geography, University of Wisconsin-Milwaukee*

IN THE ARTICLES, BOOKS, AND MAPS REVIEWED for this *Handbook*, there is a general emphasis on regional-planning studies in all countries (36 percent of total items). Two other major groups of articles appear in this section, one dealing with various aspects of settlement analysis (25 percent of total), and the other with physical geography-geology (15 percent of total). More reports directly related to economic geography might have been expected, but these amounted to only about 10 percent of the total. Of note is a larger-than-usual general section (15 percent of total), in which the major topics are regional-planning, physical geography-geology, and biographical works. Representing the latter are a long-awaited new text on South America by Morris (item **5159**) and biographical reports on scientific travellers of the last century by Krämer.

The IPGH continues to perform valuable tasks and has announced its usual series of important conferences on cartography, history, geodesy, remote-sensing, and applied geography. Commendation is due to the organization for its efforts to establish a special commission on anthropology. The spread of urbanism and of modern agricultural land reclamation over areas of great archaeological value, as well as the effects of these phenomena on indigenous populations, led to the establishment in 1977 of a committee that is considering all aspects of these problems. Simultaneously, a proposal for an Andean Institute of Anthropology was made by the Bolivian Ministry of Education and Culture. These proposals should greatly interest geographers and other social scientists who deal with land-use planning in its various forms.

The growing relevance of archaeological matters to an increasing number of disciplines is exemplified by a contract established between the University of Wisconsin-Milwaukee State Soils Laboratory (Department of Geography) and the Colombian National Institute of Archaeology (Museo del Oro) for research on raised field anthrosols in the San Jorge River Valley of that country. Here, one of the largest, if not the largest, regions of precolumbian raised fields in America (estimated to be 200,000 km²) may be lost in a large-scale land reclamation scheme, a review of which will appear in the next *HLAS*.

It is hoped that full-scale investigations will be carried out prior to the destruction of these and other relics of great earth-moving societies that vanished before the arrival of the Spanish. Already, invaluable precolumbian settlements and raised fields have been lost recently on the Sabana de Bogotá, Colombia, and in other smaller level Andean areas. Having sounded the alarm, we will follow closely the reports of the IPGH and others concerning this issue in future volumes of *HLAS*.

GENERAL

5153 Arbuet Vignali, Heber; Roberto Pucero Ripoll; and Belter Garré Copello. Antártida: continente de los más para los menos. Montevideo, Uruguay: Fundación de Cultura Universitaria, 1979. 122 p.; fold. leaves of plates; bibl.; maps.

Analysis of the physical geography of Antarctica includes chapters on development of international law in the region, activities of various nationalities in the zone, the Conference in Washington in 1959, and cooperative investigations.

5154 Bonaparte, José F. El Mesozoico de América del Sur y sus tetrápodos. Tucumán, República Argentina: Ministerio de Cultura y Educación, Fundación Miguel Lillo, 1978. 596 p.; bibl.; ill.; index (Opera Lilloana; 26)

The first half of this volume, devoted to general geology of South America, will be useful to those needing an overview of the continent. The latter half focuses specifically on tetrapods from Triassic, Jurassic, and Cretaceous formations.

5155 Bruggmann, Maximilien. Die Anden: von der Karibik zum Kap Hoorn. Textbeiträge von Hugo Loetscher, Jean-Christian Spahni und Herbert Wilhelmy. Photographien von . . . Luzern, Switzerland: Verlag

C.J. Bucher, 1977. 204 p.; facs.; fold. maps, ill.; plates; table.

Superbly informative and well-written material on physical and cultural geography of the Andean countries. Historical, economic, political and literary peaks are discussed and analyzed with clarity.

5156 Bunster, Enrique. Crónicas del Pacífico. Santiago: Editorial Andrés Bello, 1977. 202 p.; bibl.; ill.

An attempt to explain the spread of knowledge and settlement of land masses in the Pacific Ocean. Such topics as the galleon trade between Manila and Acapulco are treated in an interesting manner and copiously illustrated.

5157 Graham, Robert Bontine Cunninghame. The South American sketches of R.B. Cunninghame Graham. Selected and edited, with an introduction, notes, glossary, and bibliography, by John Walker. Norman: University of Oklahoma Press, 1978. 292 p.; bibl.

Selected writings of the Englishman who became "more gaucho than poet," after years of living in Argentina. His "Cruz Alta," "La Pampa," "Los llanos del Apure" and other prose pieces are masterful descriptions of different areas of South America that should be read by every serious student of the region.

5158 Instituto Antártico Chilena. INACH Serie científica. Vol. 2, No. 1, 1971– Santiago.

This journal is divided into two sections: Earth Sciences and Biological Sciences. The first part, of special interest to geographers, deals with the evolution of Decepción Island, a volcanic eruption of 1970, and the vegetation of islands in Antartica.

5159 Morris, Arthur Stephen. South America. New York: Barnes & Noble Books, 1979. 271 p.; bibl.; ill.; index.

This text on South America is a welcome edition to the field which has been largely neglected since the last revision of Preston James' *Geography of Latin America*. Pt. 1 presents a systematic geography of the continent; pt. 2 describes the regional geography of individual countries in great detail, thus avoiding repetition; and pt. 3 focuses on economic development and international relations. Includes simplified, original illustrations. Recommended for introductory college and university courses.

5160 Pöppig, Eduard Friedrich. Selbstanzeige der Reisebeschreibung. In der Nähe des ewigen Schnees: e. Anden-Reise im 19. Jh. Hrsg. u. mit e. Nachw. vers. von Dieter Kühn. Frankfurt am Main: Insel-Verlag, 1975. 190 p.; numerous ill. (Insel Taschenbuch; 166)

Eduard Pöppig, physician and botanist, published two volumes about his South American trip in 1835–36. This small volume summarizes Pöppig's observations and comments on the contribution of this well-traveled scientist.

5161 Quintanilla, Víctor G. Diccionario de biogeografía para América Latina. Valparaíso: Ediciones Universitarias de Valparaíso, Universidad Católica de Valparaíso, 1977. 249 p.; 19 leaves of plates; bibl.; ill.

A dictionary of biogeography more useful to students of South America than of Latin America. Drawings and maps of distributional phenomena are well done and frequently illustrate changes over time, such as those undergone by the *caatinga* of Brazil.

5162 *Revista Cartográfica.* Instituto Panamericano de Geografía e Historia (PAIGH). Comisión de Cartografía. Año 21, no. 23, dic. 1972– . México.

Two articles in this issue should be of interest to geoscientists dealing with South America. The first establishes the reasons for selection of the South American datum of 1969 for use as a control for mapping. The second describes the Omega system of global navigation, in which Argentina is a major participant.

5163 ———. ———. ———. Nos. 24/25, enero/dic. 1973– . México.

Issue contains studies of remote-sensing of forest damages, computer uses in aerial triangulation adjustment errors, bathimetric photogrametry, and notes on the use of maps for integral studies of hydraulic resources.

5164 Rodríguez Zía, Jorge L. El poder del pan: misión universal de los países de la Cuenca del Plata. Buenos Aires: Editorial Moharra, 1977. 216 p.; bibl. (Colección Meridiano argentino)

A geopolitical study of food production contends that the Cuenca del Plata must become one of the world's major food suppliers by the year 2000, and suggests cooperation among Bolivia, Paraguay, Uruguay, and Argentina. Author is pessimistic about the role of the US and Brazil.

5165 Scurla, Herbert, *comp.* Im Banne der Anden: Reisen dt. Forscher d. 19. Jh. Thaddaeus Haenke et al. Hrsg. von Herbert Scurla. Einf., Walter Krämer. Ill., Manfred Butzmann. 3., überarb. Aufl. Berlin: Verlag der Nation, 1979. 591 p.; ill.; maps.

Fascinating accounts of the lives of Thaddaeus Haenke, A. von Humboldt, Eduard Poeppig, Rudolph Philippi, Herman Burmeister, Alphons Stübel, and Wilhelm Reiss, and of their activities in South American Andean areas.

5166 Tanner, Hans. Südamerika. Bd. 1 Andenstaaten. Braunschweig: Westermann, 1978– . 1 v.; ill. (some col.); index.

Volume one of a series on South America intended for the general public. Deals with the Andean countries in a relatively detailed and up-to-date fashion. Useful introduction to the geography, history, and economy of the region.

5167 Weizmann, H.G. Rural growth poles and land settlement: a multiple case experience in Latin America (*in* Physical planning. Tel Aviv, Israel: Association of Engineers and Architects in Israel, International Technical Cooperation Center, The Engineer's Institute, 1973?, p. 306–330, maps, plates, tables)

Land, leadership, and institutional programs are discussed in example pioneer settlements in South America. Claims that economically aggressive foreigners produced growth poles whose influence is extending outward from key centers.

ARGENTINA

5168 Alvarez, Antonio. Crónica de la Patagonia y tierras australes desde el descubrimiento hasta la colonización. Buenos Aires: Talleros Gráficos Editorial Lito, 1978. 189 p.

Good summary of the Spanish settlement of Patagonia from its discovery by Magellan to its colonization. Includes discovery history and settlement phenomena relating to the Falklands, Georgias, Sandwich Islands, Orkney Islands, and Antarctica.

5169 Argentina. Instituto Nacional de Tecnología. Centro de Investigaciones de Recursos Naturales. Difusión geográfica de cultivos: índices en la provincia de Santiago del Estero y sus causas. Buenos Aires: 1974. 85 p.; bibl.; maps (Suelos. Publicación; 146)

One of a series of original works depicting agroclimatic districts within an Argentine province. Since the introduction of this now well-known method of mapping crop zones, 271 have been identified in the country. The studies are used in agricultural planning.

5170 ———. Ministerio de Guerra y Marina. Campaña de los Andes al sur de la Patagonia, año 1883: partes detalladas y diario de la expedición, Ministerio de Guerra y Marina. Submitted by Joaquin Viejobueno. 2. ed. Buenos Aires: Editorial Universitaria de Buenos Aires, 1978. 438 p.; map (1 fold. col. in pocket) (Lucha de fronteras con el indio)

Scientific and historical notes made by military commanders occupying the area of Nahuel-Huapi, Argentina during the late 1880s. For historian's comment, see *HLAS* 42:3293.

5171 Arias, Raúl J. and **Diógenes R. Ocampo.** Argentina. Buenos Aires: Artes Gráficas Planeta, 1975? 112 p.; plates.

Land, people, and tourism are briefly discussed and illustrated with exceptionally beautiful photography. Text in Spanish, German, and English.

5172 Basualdo, Mario Angel and **Félix Argentino Escurra.** Fundamentos geográficos: introducción al estudio de la geografía histórica de Santiago del Estero. Santiago del Estero [Argentina]: Librería Técnica Científica, 1976. 73 p.; bibl.; ill.; tables.

This volume explains the major tectonic formations in the Province of Santiago del Estero, Argentina. Two major formations are related to all other phenomena: the *nesocratones*, or lesser shield areas with substable traits, and the *valles pericratónicas*, located along the western border of the former. Both of these entities control sedimentation and tectonic processes that contributed to the formation of the present landscape.

5173 Belza, Juan E. Romancero del topónimo fueguino: discusión histórica de su origen y fortuna. Buenos Aires: Instituto de Investigaciones Históricas Tierra del Fuego, 1978. 239 p., 8 leaves of plates; ill.; index.

Historical citations on place names in Tierra del Fuego.

5174 Berthelemy, Carlos Jorge. La sombra del condor: autobiografía. Buenos Aires: Editorial Stilcograf, 1976. 246 p.

Autobiography of a life in rural Argentina from the 1920s to modern times. Gives a nostalgic picture of difficult and good times.

Bosch Vinelli, Julia Beatriz. Notas sobre navegación fluvial: 1843–1853. See *HLAS* 42:3309.

5175 Buenos Aires (Province). **Secretaría de Planeamiento y Desarrollo.** Estrategias para el desarrollo y modernización del eje metropolitano. La Plata: Gobernación de la Provincia de Buenos Aires, Secretaría de Planeamiento y Desarrollo, 1978 [i.e. 1979]. 120 p.; bibl.; maps.

The metropolitan axis of Buenos Aires is defined as an area including 51 *partidos* of the Province of Buenos Aires and the Federal Capital. It occupies 13 percent of the region's area and has a density of 172 people per km². Explains the processes of populating the axis and gives recommendations for restructuring planning operations to include scientific soil study, building restoration, etc.

5176 Canoba, Carlos. Utilización en geología de las imágenes landsat. Rosario, Argentina: Universidad Nacional de Rosario, Facultad de Ciencias Exactas e Ingeniería, Instituto de Fisiografía y Geología Dr. Alfredo Castellanos, 1977. 18 p.; 5 leaves of plates; ill. (Publicaciones—Universidad Nacional de Rosario, Facultad de Ciencias Exactas e Ingeniería, Instituto de Fisiografía y Geología Dr. Alfredo Castellanos; 61)

Application of landsat images in geology, with emphasis on surveying and mapping, and references to a mountainous area, a semiarid one, and a subhumid plain in Argentina. Also discusses the limitations of the method.

Capdevila, Pedro V. La estancia argentina. See *HLAS 42:3314.*

5177 Corrientes (Province), *Argentina.* **Subsecretaría de Coordinación y Programación Económica.** Corrientes. Corrientes, Argentina: 1977. 113 leaves; bibl.; maps; tables.

General biography of the Province of Corrientes, Argentina. Contains useful statistics and maps, some depicting crop production areas.

5178 *Cuadrante.* Revista del Centro de Estudios Regionales. No. 1, n.d. Buenos Aires?

First issue of new journal published by the Center for Regional Studies, founded to promote scientific investigation in northeast Argentina. Articles deal with the concept of regionalism.

5179 Cúneo, Carlos; Gianni Ciardini; and **Ginés Gomariz.** Mendoza. Fotografías, Josifoch et al. Traducción, Patricio Duggan. Buenos Aires: Editorial Turismo, 1978. 96 p.; ill. (some col.).

A well-illustrated Spanish-and-English description of modern landscape features of the Province of Mendoza, Argentina.

5180 Dorsch, Víctor. Los días que se fueron. Santa Fe, Argentina: Librería y Editorial Colmegna, 1978. 193 p.

Nostalgic, detailed account of a Lutheran pastor's life in colony of Volga Germans near Santa Rosa, in the Province of La Pampa, Argentina, during the 1950s. Well

written descriptions of transition to modernization and mechanization of more traditional settlement and agricultural systems.

5181 Fontana, Luis Jorge. El gran Chaco. Estudio preliminar de Ernesto J.A. Maeder. Buenos Aires: Ediciones Solar/Hachette, 1977. 200 p.; ill.; plates (Biblioteca dimensión argentina)

Reproduces observations of Luis Jorge Fontana on geology, hydrography, meteorology, ethnology, zoology, and botany of the Chaco, as preserved in his diary of 1881.

5182 Gaea, Sociedad Argentina de Estudios Geográficos. Geografía de Catamarca: contribuciones presentadas en la XXXV Semana de Geografía. Por Oscar Albert et al. (Serie especial—Gaea, Sociedad Argentina de Estudios Geográficos; no. 5)

A publication resulting from the 25th Semana de la Geografía held in Argentina. Topics covered are climate, water problems, vegetation, agricultural economy (including farming systems), mining, and land use.

5183 ———. Geografía del Chubut: contribuciones presentadas en la XXXVI semana de geografía. Por Héctor C. Alvarez et al. Buenos Aires: Gaea, Sociedad Argentina de Estudios Geográficos, 1978. 209 p.; bibl.; ill. (Serie especial—Gaea, Sociedad Argentina de Estudios Geográficos; no. 6)

A contribution of the well-organized Semanas de Geografía in Argentina, focusing on the physical and human geography of the Province of Chubut. Regionalization, population distributional phenomena, and resources are main topics covered.

5184 Gioja, Rolando I. Entre ejército y montañas: aproximación al desarrollo cumunitario. Buenos Aires: Centro Militar, 1970. 221 p.

Describes army life and methods of army participation in rural development programs in Argentina.

5185 Gramajo de Martínez Moreno, Amalia. Consideraciones histórico-geográficas de la ciudad de Frías. Santiago del Estero, Rep. Argentina: s.n., 1977. 82 p.; 18 leaves of plates; bibl.; ill. (Serie Historia de los pueblos de Santiago del Estero)

Interesting documentation of the birth and growth of Frías, one of Argentina's less well-known cities. Includes photographs of the city's earlier days and of gracious changes introduced since, through the centenary year of 1975.

5186 Great Britain. Foreign and Commonwealth Office. Falkland Islands and dependencies: report for the years 1972 and 1973. London: Her Majesty's Stationery Office, 1976. 70 p.; bibl.; fold. maps; plates; tables (Biennial reports series).

Increased economic activity due to the demand for wool has resulted in improvements on the islands. Since an 800 meter-long airport was finished in 1972, weekly service from the mainland is possible.

5187 Guía paleontológica argentina. Buenos Aires: Consejo Nacional de Investigaciones Científicas y Técnicas, 1979. v. 1; ill.

Carboniferous and Permian fossil identification and correlation from a narrow band starting in La Rioja and ending in Chubut, Argentina.

5188 Guzmán, Yuyú. Estancias de Azul y pobladores franceses en la zona rural de Azul. La Plata, Argentina: Instituto San Vicente de Paul, 1978. 222 p.; bibl.; map.

Detailed history of settlement by families in a part of the Province of Buenos Aires.

5189 Inter-American Development Bank (IDB), *Buenos Aires*. **Instituto para la Integración de América Latina** (INTAL). **Sector Proyectos de Cooperación Técnica.** Inventario de proyectos de integración física en la Cuenca del Plata. . . . : mapas. Buenos Aires: Ministerio de Relaciones Exteriores y Culto de la República [and] INTAL, 1977? 77 leaves; fold. tables, inserted maps, maps, tables.

Continuation of a series started in 1972, dealing with integration of programs for development of the Cuenca del Plata. Discussion of projects and location maps show great scope of planning.

Karukinka. No. 5, julio 1973 [through] No. 13, junio 1975– . See *HLAS 42:3370.*

5190 Larra, Raúl. La conquista aérea del desierto. Tapa de Bartolomé Mirabelli. Buenos Aires: Ediciones Anfora, 1979. 142 p.; 4 leaves of plates; ill.

Fascinating history of aviation in Argentina from the first flights in 1914 to the first crossing of Antarctica by an Argentine C-130 in 1973.

López, Norberto Aurelio. El pleito de la patria. See *HLAS 42:3378.*

5191 Marateo, Mario Miguel. El aficionado a los pájaros. Fotografías, Ernesto C. Gorgoglione. Dibujos, Ernesto C. Gorgoglione y Mario M. Marateo. Buenos Aires: Offset Grama, 1978. 278 p.; 10 leaves of plates; bibl.; ill. (some col.).

Drawings, photographs, and descriptions of birds of Argentina. Useful as a field guide.

Martínez Ruiz, Bernabé. La colonización galesa en el Valle del Chubut. See *HLAS 42:3388.*

5192 Martínez Sierra, Ramiro. El mapa de Las Pampas: primer premio en el género ensayo del Certamen Literario del Sesquicentenario del Congreso de Tucumán y de la Declaración de la Independencia: 1966. t. 1/2. Buenos Aires: Dirección Nacional del Registro Oficial, 1975. 2 v. (287, 261 p.); facsim.; fold. maps; maps.

Historical analysis of maps of South America, with emphasis on Argentine pampas. Facsimile reproductions of earliest maps will be appreciated by geographers and historians.

Martinic Beros, Mateo. Historia del Estrecho de Magallanes. See item **5226.**

5193 Matijevic, Nicolás and **Olga H. de Matijevic.** Bibliografía patagónica y de las tierras australes. v. 2, Geografía. Bahía Blanca, Argentina: Centro de Documentación Patagónica, Universidad Nacional del Sur Dr. Miguel López Francés, 1978. 383 p.; bibl.; index.

Vol. 2 consists of a bibliographical listing of items on physical geography, human geography, transportation, and the Antarctic. Most titles included are modern, but some date from the last century. For bibliographer's comment, see *HLAS 42:53.*

5194 Meyer-Clason, Curt. Erstens die Freiheit: Tagebuch e. Reise durch Argentinien u. Brasilien. Wuppertal: Hammer, 1978. 128 p.

Reflections on social problems in several South American cities. Discusses the lack of freedom and the problems of intellectuals in Argentina, and gives a colorful description of economic functions of interior landscapes.

5195 Miranda, Guido A. and **Juan Carlos Vidarte.** El rostro cambiante del Chaco cultural nordeste. Resistencia, Argentina: s.n., 1973. 40 p.; ill.

Brief history of pioneer settlement of the Chaco since formation of the Government of Chaco in 1872.

Moncaut, Carlos Antonio. Estancias bonaerenses: con la menuda historia de algunos establecimientos, entre otros, de los partidos de Chascomús, Ranchos, Magdalena, General Lavalle y Luján: historia y tradición. See *HLAS 42:3392.*

5196 La pesca comercial en Argentina: ciclo de exposiciones realizadas durante el seminario organizado por la Fundación Argentina de Estudios Marítimos entre el 10 de octubre y el 21 de noviembre de 1972, bajo la dirección del doctor Antonio E. Malaret. Buenos Aires: Fundación Argentina de Estudios Marítimos, 1973. 190 p.; maps; plates; tables.

A panoramic study of world fishing followed by detailed summary of fishing resources in the Argentine Sea and a discussion of the economics of fishing. Of much interest are seasonal maps of the distribution of fish by types off the Argentine coast.

5197 Pesce, Hugo. Misiones: un testimonio en imágenes. Fotografías, Hugo Pesce; textos, Ricardo Freire y Horacio Mac Dougall. s.l.: Edición del Superior Gobierno de la Provincia de Misiones, 197-? 100 p.; chiefly ill. (some col.).

Photographic record of modern economic functions in Misiones Province, Argentina.

5198 Pugliese, José. La Boca del Riachuelo: sus calles, plazas y puentes: origen, evolución y significado de sus nombres. Buenos Aires: Edición de la Agrupación de Gente de Arte y Letras Impulso, 1978. 143 p.; bibl.; map.

A historical view of the district known as La Boca in Buenos Aires.

5199 Raone, Juan Mario. Los indios de la Provincia del Neuquén. Neuquén, Argentina: Siringa Libros, 1978. 55 p.; 1 leaf of plates; ill. (His Neuquén, la provincia de los grandes lagos; 2)

Rare description of Indian tribes by resident of Neuquén, Argentina, based on personal experience. Includes historical data and photographs but no bibliography.

Revista Cartográfica. Año 21, no. 23, dic. 1972– . See item **5162.**

5200 Wilkie, Richard W. Migration and population imbalance in the settlement hierarchy of Argentina (*in* Environment, society, and rural change in Latin America. Edited by David A. Preston. Chichester, New York: J. Wiley, 1980, p. unavailable)

Since the 1950s nearly half the population of Argentina resides in the five largest cities: Buenos Aires, Rosario, Córdoba, La Plata, and Mendoza. Article examines urban-rural trends, internal migration, and local-level changes in population, with case example.

5201 ———. The rual population of Argentina to 1970 (*in* Statistical abstract of Latin America. James W. Wilkie and Peter Reich, editors. Los Angeles: UCLA, Latin American Center, 1980, p. 562–580)

Statistical summary and introductory discussion of the decline of Argentina's rural population to 18 percent, the lowest level for any Latin American country.

5202 ——— and **Jane Riblett Wilkie.** Environmental perception and migration behavior: a case study in rural Argentina (*in* Internal migration systems in the developing world: with special reference to Latin America. Robert N. Thomas and John M. Hunter, editors. Cambridge, Mass.: Schenkman Publishing Co., 1980, p. 135–151)

A discussion of environmental and spatial attitudes as they contribute to migration factors.

5203 ——— and ———. Migration and Argentine rural community in transition. Amherst: University of Massachusetts, International Area Studies Programs, 1980. 32 p.; ill. (Program in Latin American Studies occasional papers series; 12)

Account of rural change in Aldea San Francisco, a Volga-Deutsch village settlement founded in 1878 in Argentina.

Williams, Glyn. Welsh settlers and native Americans in Patagonia. See *HLAS 42:3443.*

BOLIVIA

5204 Alvarado, José María. Jaime Mendoza: el macizo andino. Prólogo de Eduardo

Ocampo Moscoso. La Paz: Editorial El Siglo, 1977. 306 p.; bibl.; facs.; plates.

Geo-history of the influence of a Bolivian intellectual whose keen attention to the natural and human landscapes have made a significant contribution to knowledge of his country.

5205 Ayala Z., Alfredo. Geografía general de Bolivia: estudios físico, político y económico de Bolivia. La Paz: s.n., 1978. 485 p.; 15 leaves of plates; bibl.; ill.; maps (1 fold. in pocket)

Physical, political, and economic study of Bolivia with useful historical information. A good reference tool on modern Bolivia for geographers and others.

5206 Boero Rojo, Hugo. La Paz y alrededores. Artículos especializados, Osvaldo Rivera Sundt et al. La Paz: Editorial Los Amigos del Libro, 1978. 263 p.; 1 leaf of plates; ill. (Colección Bolivia mágica)

Consists of description of the *altiplano* which surrounds La Paz, Bolivia, and of the city itself, addressed to the general public. Contains modern, color illustrations.

5207 Carvalho Urey, Antonio. Visión del Beni. Trinidad, Bolivia: s.n., 1978. 140 p.; 7 leaves of plates; ill.

Landscape description of the Beni, northeast Bolivia, includes aspects of settlement, economy, and history. Places some emphasis on oral tradition.

5208 Christiansen, Holger. Berge, Bauern, Bananeros: Reisenotizen aus Chile, Peru, Ekuador und Panama. Leipzig: F.A. Brockhaus, 1977. 270 p.; 28 leaves of plates; ill. (some col.)

Somewhat outdated travel notes on Chile, Peru, Ecuador, and Panama made by a traveler from the German Democratic Republic, addressed to the general public.

5209 Ergueta Arana, Armando. La riqueza minera en Bolivia. La Paz: n.p., 1976. 117 p.; bibl.; fold. table; tables.

Lists major metals and their uses with some historical background and statements about occurrence in Bolivia.

5210 Guzmán, Augusto. Geografía de Cochabamba. La Paz: Librería Editorial Juventud, 1978. 103, 6 p.; ill.

Geographically-oriented survey of the Department of Cochabamba, Bolivia, with map of the city of Cochabamba. Intended for tourism, the work contains no bibliography.

5211 Homenaje al profesor Arturo Posnansky en el centenario de su nacimiento. Ed. especial. La Paz: Comité Conmemorativo del Centenario del Nacimiento de Arturo Posnansky, 1974, cover 1975. 109 p.; 3 leaves of plates; bibl.; ports.

In 1973 the Bolivian government recognized the centenary of A. Posnansky with a week of events honoring the well known Austro-Bolivian scientist. This publication lists his bibliography, including theoretical works, and other accomplishments.

5212 Monje Roca, Raúl. El Río Mamoré. Ilus., Ignacio Gonzáles Y. La Paz: Instituto Boliviano de Cultura, 1977. 167 p.; ill. (some col.)

One of Bolivia's educators has assembled a useful "guide" for the Mamore River region, which includes detailed physical and human geographical data of interest to all social scientists. Includes drawings, photographs, and explanations of plant and animal life, and data concerning settlements.

5213 El País erial: la crísis ecológica boliviana. Mariano Baptista Gumucio, editor. La Paz: Ediciones Los Amigos del Libro, 1977. 136 p. (Minicolección "Un siglo y medio")

One of a growing number of books dedicated to the problem of conservation in South America. This work on Bolivia contains studies on natural resources, contamination of the atmosphere, devastation of soils, and discusses pioneers in the field of resource evaluation.

5214 Pers García, Walter. Límites de Bolivia. La Paz: Ediciones Carmarlinghi, 1977. 204 p.; 2 leaves of plates; ill.

Detailed historical treatment of negotiations with surrounding countries concerning the establishment of Bolivian national borders.

5215 Pinto Parada, Rodolfo. Rumbo al Beni. Trinidad, Bolivia: s.n., 1878 [i.e. 1978]. 245 p.

Narration and historical documents on the opening of the Beni region of Bolivia by means of road building.

5216 **Schoop, Wolfgang.** Die bolivianischen Departementszentren im Verstädterungsprozess des Landes. Wiesbaden: Steiner, 1980. 319 p.; ill. (Acta Humboldtiana. Series geographica et ethnographica; Nr. 7)

Describes urban evolution in Bolivia in the area between Andes, Amazonia, and La Plata Basin, analyzing its colonial beginnings, expansion during the mining boom, and modern growth problems.

5217 ———. Vergleichende Untersuchungen zur Agrarkolonisation der Hochlandindianer am Andenabfall und im Tiefland Ostboliviens. Wiesbaden, FRG: Aachener Geographische Arbeiten, 1970. 298 p.; fold. maps; plates (Heft 4)

This report studies three types of colonies formed with Indian settlers and discusses the future of settlement in the eastern Bolivian lowland.

5218 **Serrate Paz, José Mario.** Cochabamba, sede del Gobierno Nacional: imperativo de un traslado (estudio sobre la necesidad del traslado de la sede de Gobierno a los volles [i.e. valles] de Cochabamba). Cochabamba: Editorial Canelas, 1975. 63 p.

Exposition of reasons for transfer of the capital of Bolivia to Cochabamba.

5219 **Somoza, Jorge L.** Encuesta demográfica nacional de Bolivia: informe sobre aspectos demográficos. La Paz: Presidencia de la República, Ministerio de Planeamiento y Coordinación, Instituto Nacional de Estadística, Centro Latinoamericano de Demografía, 1976. 53 p.; bibl.; tables.

Examines birth rates, mortality, and natural growth rates for Bolivia, based on 1975 statistics. Migration from the country is estimated at 5,000 persons per year.

5220 **Yacimientos Petrolíferos Fiscales Bolivianos. Servicio Geológico de Bolivia.** Mapa geológico de Bolivia: memoria explicativa. Por Jorge Pareja L. et al. La Paz: YPFD, 1978. 27 p.; bibl.; 6 maps (4 fold. col. in pocket)

Consists of text and four colored maps encompassing the geology of the entire country. The two main subdivisions depicted are: 1) Cordillera Oriental y Altiplano, and 2) Región Faja Subandina.

CHILE

5221 **Bähr, Jürgen.** Chile. Stuttgart: Klett, 1979. 204 p.; bibl.; ill.; col. map (in pocket) (Länderprofile, geographische Strukturen, Daten, Entwicklungen)

This geographically-organized profile of Chile addressed to the general public touches on basic physical features, population dynamics, urbanization, agricultural and industrial rivalries, and general economic problems.

5222 **Bahre, Conrad J.** Destruction of the natural vegetation of north-central Chile. Berkeley: University of California Press, 1979. x, 117 p.; 3 leaves of plates; bibl.; ill.; index (University of California publications in geography; v. 23)

Documentation of the destruction of the wild lands of Coquimbo Province, Chile, by land use methods developed in the 16th century and perpetuated to the present by conservative *campesinos*.

Bermúdez Miral, Oscar. Estudios de Antonio O'Brien. See *HLAS 42:3197.*

Cárdenas Tabies, Antonio. Usos y costumbres de Chiloé. See *HLAS 42:1198.*

5223 **Caviedes L., César.** The politics of Chile: a sociogeographical assessment. Boulder, Colo.: Westview Press, 1979. xii, 357 p.; bibl.; ill.; index (Westview special studies in Latin America)

The politics of Chile are examined from the point of view of a geographer trained in three continents. Five chapters discuss the following topics: 1) socioeconomic landscapes; 2) the various classes of Chileans; 3) their voting habits; 4) assessment of the nation's democracy; and 5) regionalization of politics. Excellent reading for the serious student of Chilean social and political development. For political scientist's comment, see item **6525.**

Chile: the land and the people. See *HLAS 42:3210.*

5224 **Expedición a Chile.** v. 1/2. Santiago: Editora Nacional Gabriela Mistral, 1975? 2 v. (244, 244 p.) facs.; fold. maps (inserted in pockets); ill.; maps; plates; tables.

Nicely-illustrated tour through Chile, intended for the general public. Acquaints readers with salient features of the natural and human landscapes of the country.

5225 Llanquihue, 1852–1977: aspectos de una colonización. Eduardo Tampe Maldonado et al. Presentación, Max Müller Vega. Introducción, Marcos Gerding Gilchrist. s.l.: Liga Chileno Alemana, 1977. 148 p.; ill.

Detailed history of German colonization in southern Chile, with bibliographical sketches of major individuals involved. Although the text is marred by poor printing and repetition of pages, it is one of the few sources dealing with this phase of Chilean colonization.

5226 Martinic Beros, Mateo. Historia del Estrecho de Magallanes. Santiago: Editorial Andrés Bello, 1977. 261 p.; 1 leaf of plates; bibl.; ill.; index.

The first part of this book is a summary of major geological events associated with formation of the Strait of Magellan and its physical geography. The second part surveys the discovery and exploration of the Strait, and the remaining sections discuss the population and navigation of the Strait, and development of the related boundary dispute between Argentina and Chile from the Chilean point of view.

5227 Norte Grande. Revista de estudios integrados referentes a comunidades humanas del Norte Grande de Chile, en una perspectiva geográfica e histórico-cultural. Universidad Católica de Chile, Instituto de Geografía, Departamento de Geografía de Chile, Taller Norte Grande. Vol. 1, No. 2, dic. 1974– . Santiago.

The second issue of a journal founded in 1974 to promote regional investigation of an interdisciplinary nature focuses on physical and human geographical aspects of various northern Chilean pampas.

Ondarza O., Antonio. Grandeza y ruina de Cobija. See *HLAS 42:3247.*

Philippi, Federico. Viaje de Don Federico Philippi por el desierto de Atacama en 1885. See *HLAS 42:3250.*

Pinochet de la Barra, Oscar. La Antártica chilena. See *HLAS 42:3252.*

5228 Symposium Internacional sobre el Desarrollo de la Antártica, *Punta Arenas, Chile, 1977.* Desarrollo de la Antár-

tica. Obra editada bajo la dirección de Francisco Orrego Vicuña y Augusto Salinas Araya. Santiago de Chile: Editorial Universitaria, 1977. 374 p.; bibl.; ill. (Estudios internacionales)

Consists of 22 articles and commentaries on scientific and economic events in the Antarctic. Some items are in English, including one on the International Southern Ocean Studies mission funded by the US and Argentina. The concluding section deals with international cooperation in the Antarctic.

5229 Villalobos R., Sergio. La aventura chilena de Darwin. Santiago: Editorial Andrés Bello, 1974 or 1975. 103 p.; 2 leaves of plates; ill.

This small volume merits attention for its useful presentation of the various historical incidents and factors that combined to influence Darwin and his trip to America.

5230 Walters, Rudy Schmidt and **Patrio Valdes Sagrista.** Atlas: Chile y sus nuevas provincias. Santiago?: Dirección de Fronteras y Límites del Estado, 1976. 32 p.; bibl. (on back cover of book); maps.

Atlas of Chile, designed for non-scientific audiences, gives brief general description of each of 12 regions.

COLOMBIA

5231 Boletín de la Sociedad Geográfica de Colombia. Sociedad Geográfica de Colombia. Vol. 31, No. 111, 1977 [through] Vol. 31, No. 112, 1978– . Bogotá.

Issue No. 111 contains an account of a Polish expedition to the Colombian departments of Huila and Santander, comments on Humboldt's use of Caldas' invention for determining altitude by boiling pure water, notes on the Valle de las Papas and on the Colombian habitat, and other items of interest to social scientists. Issue No. 112 is devoted to general aspects and problems of planning on a regional basis, as seen from the Colombian viewpoint.

5232 Castro Caycedo, Germán. Perdido en el Amazonas. Bogotá: C. Valencia Editores, 1978. 290 p.; ill.

Account of a sailor who was lost in the Amazon Valley (Colombia), based on interviews with him and related field work.

Contains useful photographs of Indian settlement.

5233 Colombia. Instituto Geográfico Agustín Codazzi. Monografía del Departamento del Atlántico. Bogotá: 1973. 126 p.; bibl.; fold. map; map; plates; tables.

Part of the monograph series dealing with departments in Colombia. Topics treated include agrarian reform efforts, banking, mining, public transport, soils, climate, vegetation, etc.

5234 ⸺. ⸺. Subdirección Agrológica. Estudio general de suelos de los Municipios de Carmen de Bolívar, San Jacinto, San Juan Nepomuceno, Zambrano, El Guamo y Córdoba (Departamento de Bolívar). Por: Cruz Molina Hurtado et al. Bogotá: 1975. 274 p.; bibl.; fold. maps in pocket; ill. (Boletín; v. 11, no. 3)

Colombia has adopted the US Soil Taxonomy derived from the 7th Approximation for this series on soil classification and description of Departmental *municipios*.

5235 Díaz Galindo, Félix. Monografía del Archipiélago de San Andrés. Bogotá: Ediciones Medio Pliego, 1978. 117 p.; 2 leaves of plates (1 fold.); bibl.; 2 maps.

Historical survey of San Andres places it in the cross currents of contending political powers from its discovery to the present. [T.L. Martinson]

Echavaría M., Guillermo. Camilo C. Restrepo. See *HLAS 42:2978.*

5236 Estrada Ortiz, Gonzalo; Romualdo de Palma; and Marceliano E. Canyes. Geografía de la Comisaría Especial del Amazonas y notas históricas. Leticia, Colombia: Prefectura Apostólica de Leticia, 1973. 70 p.; fold. maps; plates.

Photographic résumé of life in the Comisaría of Leticia, Colombia.

5237 García Barriga, Hernando. Flora medicinal de Colombia: botánica médica. t. 2. Bogotá: Universidad Nacional, Instituto de Ciencias Naturales, 1975. 538 p.; ill.; plates; tables.

This is a welcome addition to the botanical works on medicinal plants in Colombia. Organized by orders and families, the book identifies plants by description and drawing, but is not as practical a field manual as others which employ common names.

5238 Giessen. Universität. Tropeninstitut. Agrarwissenschaftliche Forschung in den humiden Tropen. Mit Beiträgen von J. Alkämper et al. Hrsg. von Klaus Grenzebach. Giessen: Tropeninstitut, 1977. 145 p.; bibl.; ill.; maps (Giessener Beiträge zur Entwicklungsforschung: Reihe 1, Symposien; Bd. 3)

Although this volume deals primarily with tropical agriculture in Asia and Africa, two articles will be of direct interest to Latin Americanists. One analyzes the production of ornamental plants in Guatemala, and the other explains the importance of the C/P ratio in tropical soils with regard to phosphate efficiency, using an example from Colombia.

5239 Gómez Picón, Rafael. Orinoco, río de libertad: biografía, aspectos geográficos, históricos, socioeconómicos. 2. ed., rev. y corr. por el autor. Bogotá: Banco de la República, 1978. 501 p.; 16 leaves of plates; bibl.; ill.

Detailed commentary on human and physical conditions along the length of the Orinoco River, including useful information on Indian veneration of certain trees, etc.

5240 Londoño Bolívar, William. Panorama socio-económico del Departamento de Risaralda. Bogotá: Talleres Editoriales de la Librería Stella, 1972. 477 p.; maps; tables.

Statistical and encyclopaedic socioeconomic treatment of the Department of Risaralda, Colombia, created in 1966.

5241 López Hoyos, Alonso and **Abdón Cortés Lombana.** Los suelos orgánicos de Colombia: su origen, constitución y clasificación. Bogotá: Instituto Geográfico Agustín Codazzi, Subdirección Agrológica, Ministerio de Hacienda y Crédito Público, 1978. 190 p.; ill.

Organic soils exist in important quantities in the *altiplanos* of Colombia's Cordillera Oriental and on the coastal plains. Text discusses chemical and physical characteristics of Histosols and methods of laboratory analysis.

Loy, Jane M. Rebellion in the Colombian Llanos: the Arauca affair of 1917. See *HLAS 42:2985.*

5242 Medellín, 1675–1975. Bogotá: Ediciones Sol y Luna [and] Celanese Colombiana, 1975. 118 p.; ill.; plates.

Summary of important historical factors in the evolution of the city of Medellín and its satellite pueblos.

5243 Molano Campuzano, Joaquín. Geografía de la pesca y caza: deportivas en Colombia. Bogotá: Universidad de Bogotá Jorge Tadeo Lozano, n.d. 64 p.; bibl.; map; plates; tables.

Analyzes the geography of sport fishing according to national development of resource use, fish stocks, and distribution of fishing areas. Contains a useful lexicon of Colombian fish types with their English names.

5244 Palacios, Marco. Coffee in Colombia, 1850–1970: an economic, social, and political history. Cambridge; New York: Cambridge University Press, 1980, 338 p.; bibl.; ill.; index (Cambridge Latin American studies; 36)

This scholarly work presents new evidence regarding the emergence of 19th-century Colombia as a coffee-exporting country and effects on contemporary Colombia of entry into the world market system. Geographers and others will appreciate the careful examination of unusual sources of information and refreshing mistrust of conventional statistical publications. The adaptation and assimilation of external trade activities produced regional idiosyncrasies in Colombia even without the early or continued presence of a centralized government. A major reason for this stems from the stability of an established hacienda society—a feature which prompted the author to devote the first 120 p. to a fascinating analysis of the hacienda in Colombia. The birth of the Colombian small landowner system becomes clear with use of case examples, as do the relationships among latifundium, parvifundium, and minifundium. The latter part of the book stresses expansion of coffee, private appropriation of public land in western Colombia, and the international cycle with its effects on modernized coffee cultivation. Good maps and clear analysis characterize the materials presented in this book. For historian's comment on "the most outstanding study of coffee written to date," see HLAS 42:2989. For sociologist's comment, see item 8276.

5245 Parsons, James J. Uraba, salida de Antioquia al mar: geografía e historia de la colonización. Bogotá?: Instituto de Integración Cultural [and] Banco de la República [and] Corporación Regional de Desarrollo de Urabá (CORPOURABA), n.d. 164 p.; bibl.; maps; plates; tables.

Translation of the English version of Parson's book.

5246 Programa Orinoquia-Amazonia. Comisión Bibliográfica. Orinoquia-Amazonia, reseñas analíticas. Bogotá: Comisión Bibliográfica, Programa Orinoquia-Amazonia, Universidad Nacional de Colombia, 1977. 107 p. (Serie Bibliografía y documentación; v. 2)

Contains summaries of published research works on the Orinoco-Amazon region.

5247 Rieger, Walter. Vegatationskundliche Untersuchungen auf der Guajira-Halbinsel (Nordost-Kilumbien). Giessen, FRG: Geographisches Institut, 1976. 142 p.; plates.

Author distinguishes vegetation groupings on different soil types, with exception of some red soils of possible fossil origin. Surprising richness of vegetation, including arboreal types, characterizes the Guajira Peninsula.

Villamarín, Juan A. and **Judith E. Villamarín.** Chibcha settlement under Spanish rule, 1537–1810. See HLAS 42:2784.

ECUADOR

Bromley, Rosemary D.F. Disasters and population change in central highland Ecuador, 1778–1825. See HLAS 42:2786.

———. Urban-rural demographic contrasts in highland Ecuador: town recession in a period of catastrophe, 1778–1841. See HLAS 42:2632.

5248 Bustamante Yepez, Marco A. Ecuador país tropoandino. Quito: Editorial Casa de la Cultura Ecuatoriana, 1976. 19 p.; tables (Cartillas de divulgación ecuatoriana; 9)

One of a series of pamphlets explaining geographical phenomena in Ecuador. Defines climatic terms as they related to Ecuador and its ecological altitude zones.

5249 ———. La línea equinoccial en el territorio de la República del Ecuador. Quito: Editorial Casa de la Cultura Ecuatoriana, 1977. 22 p.; ill.; map (Cartillas de divulgación ecuatoriana, 14)

Historical-geographical note on the determination of the position of the equator in Ecuador.

5250 Ecuador. Comandancia General de Marina. Departamento de Relaciones Públicas. Armada del Ecuador. La aventura del mar. Quito: 1976. 104 p.; ill.; maps; plates; tables.

Physical geography and economic analysis of the "fifth province of Ecuador," the sea coast. Includes good introductory marine biology and color photographs.

5251 Gallegos Marchena, Carlos. Monografía de Ecuador. Realizado por: Raúl Iglesias Lanatta and José Jorquiera Naranjo. Lima: Ministerio de Integración (MINT), Dirección General de Asuntos Especiales y de Investigación, Dirección de Investigación, 1976. 84 leaves; tables.

National statistical summary based on data from the 1970s. Gives limited information on population, manufacturing, transportation, and finance.

5252 Investigación y Promoción de la Amazonía (Project). Estudio socio-económico de los ríos Amazonas y Napo. v. 1, Visión de los caseríos muestra y aspectos demográficos y migratorios de los dos ríos. v. 2, El trabajo, el comercio y la agricultura en los ríos Amazonas y Napo. s.l.: Publicaciones CETA, [between 1972 and 1979]. 2 v.; maps.

This first investigation by IPA (Investigación y Promoción de la Amazonía) consists of two volumes: vol. 1 gives a brief description of foundation, economic development, and political situation in *caseríos* along the Peruvian Amazon and Napo Rivers, and vol. 2 deals with labor, commerce and agriculture in the region.

5253 Sampedro V., Francisco. El problema geográfico-geomorfológico del CENEPA: estudio estrictamente geográfico, sin ninguna relación con la posición oficial de la cancillería ecuatoriana. Quito: Editorial Casa de la Cultura Ecuatoriana, 1979. 21 p.; maps (Cartillas de divulgación ecuatoriana; 19)

Discussion of problems involved in Ecuador's eastern border demarcation since discovery of the Río Cenepa in 1947.

5254 White, Alan. Hierbas del Ecuador: plantas medicinales (Herbs of Ecuador: medicinal plants). Dibujos: Gerald Strasser. Introduction by Plutarco Naranjo. Quito?: ZIKR Publications, 1976. 315 p.; bibl.; ill.; tables.

Discusses therapeutical herbs, their uses, and local medicinal preparations, with drawings of plants and a glossary of their common names.

FRENCH GUIANA

5255 Brasseur, Gérard. La Guyane Française: un bilan de trente années. Paris: Sécretariat Général du Gouvernement Direction de la Documentation Française, 1978. 184 p., bibl., maps, tables (Notes et études documentaires, 4497/4498)

Excellent general work on French Guiana. Includes much data on the country's physical and human geography and many good maps. Special sections are devoted to: 1) government, political administration and public finances (p. 43–80); 2) to economic activities (p. 81–136); and 3) to social development (housing, employment, health, education, leisure, etc.) including many helpful tables (p. 137–176). Also includes several useful appendixes: a political and administrative chronology, tables on the municipal elections of 1977, list of government officials, a good bibliography and many tables. Given the scarcity of literature on the Guianas (Surinam, Guyana, and French Guiana), this is a most welcome addition. For bibliographer's comment, see *HLAS 41:149*. [Ed.]

5256 Dubois, Pierre; Elaine Dubois; and Régis P. Nogara. Guyane. Paris: Delroisse, 1979? 175 p.; col. ill.

Well-illustrated book that contains general historical, settlement, and economic phenomena on Guyane (French Guiana) in four languages.

GUYANA

5257 Commonwealth Institute, *London.* Guyana and Belize: a teacher's guide to study resources. London: 1976. 12 p.; col. map.

Partial bibliography of materials available for purchase or reference at the Commonwealth Institute Services Library and Resource Center in London.

5258 Guyana. Information Services. A portrait of Guyana. Design and layout by Designs & Graphics. Foreword by Linden Forbes Sampson Burham. Georgetown: 1976? 128 p.; map; plates; tables.

Modern photographs of Guyana with little text.

5259 ———. Ministry of National Development and Agriculture. Lands and Survey Department. Cartographic Division. Gazetteer of Guyana. Preface by J.A. Sweetnam. Georgetown: 1974. 181 p.; map; tables.

A compilation of physical and cultural place names (including those of villages), from records of the Lands and Surveys Department.

Strum, Fred and **Robert J. Goodland.** The ecology of Guyana: a bibliography of environmental resources. See *HLAS 42:65.*

PERU

5260 *Boletín Informativo.* Centro de Estudios de Población y Desarrollo. Año 6, Nos. 25/26, nov. 1972– . Lima

Contains articles on population characteristics of Peru, including "geo-economic regionalization," health problems, census data from 1972, etc.

5261 Documental del Perú: Segunda serie, El Reto geográfico y el hombre peruano. Pedro Felipe Cortázar, director. Lima: Ioppe: Distribuidora Inca, 1972. 160 p.; maps; plates.

Physical and economic geography of the Amazon portion of Peru, with special reference to Basin lakes and rivers, mining, fishing, farming, and tourism. Contains outstanding color photographs.

Heras D., P. Julian. Los franciscanos en el Pongoa, Tambo y Alto Ucayali a fines del siglo XVII. See *HLAS 42:2701.*

5262 Informe del Perú. v. 2, Junín, incluye: guía turística, guía bibliográfica, guía del comprador. Edición internacional por el sesquicentenario de la Batalla de Junín. Lima: Promotora Editorial Latinoamericano, 1974? 152 p.; bibl.; ill.; maps; plates; tables.

Statistical guide for the general public

contains information on physical geography and economic life in the Department of Junín, Peru.

5263 ———. v. 4, Piura, incluye: guía turística, guía bibliográfica, guía del comprador. Lima: Promotora Editorial Latinoamericano, 1975. 160 p.; bibl.; ill.; maps; plates; tables.

Tourist guide with brief bibliography. Includes census data from 1972.

5264 ———. v. 5, Cuzco, incluye: guía turística, guía bibliográfica, guía del comprador. Lima: Promotora Editorial Latinoamericano, 1975. 192 p.; bibl.; ill.; maps; plates.

A statistical summary on the Department of Cuzco is part of a series on Peruvian departmental geography and history aimed at the general public.

Investigación y Promoción de la Amazonía (Project). Estudio socio-económico de los ríos Amazonas y Napo. See item **5252.**

5265 Middendorf, Ernest W. Perú observaciones y estudios del país y sus habitantes durante una permanencia de 25 años. Traducción, Ernesto More. t. 2, La Costa. t. 3, La sierra. 1. Versión española. Lima: Universidad Nacional Mayor de San Marcos, n.d. 2 v.; bibl.; ill.; index.

Three-volume translation of a well-known work first printed in German in 1894. Contains detailed description and analysis of physical and human phenomena in the various regions of Peru. Text is balanced with excellent photographs and maps.

5266 Ponce, Fernando. La ciudad en el Perú. Lima: Retablo de Papal Ediciones, 1975. 186 p.; bibl.; ill.; maps; plates; tables (21).

Since 1965 the urban sector has made up more than half the total population in Peru. This book, a dissertation from the University of Texas, analyzes the various social and historical factors responsible for that urban growth.

5267 Ráez, Nemesio A. Monografía de Huancayo y otros estudios. Huancayo: Universidad Nacional del Centro del Perú, Departamento de Publicaciones, 1978? 116 p. (Estudios andinos del centro; 1. Cuadernos universitarios)

Mimeographed publication contains

geographic studies on the Province of Huancayo, Peru.

5268 Recursos naturales del Perú: antología. Compilación, Plácido Díaz Suárez. Lima: Retablo de Papel, Ediciones, 1978. 2 v.; bibl.; ill. (Retablo de Papel, Ediciones; 28–29)

Selected papers mainly by Peruvian authors on climatic, hydrographic, edaphic, and forest resources in Peru.

5269 Rivera Palomino, Jaime. Geografía de la población de Ayacucho. Ayacucho, Perú: Universidad Nacional de San Cristóbal de Huamanga, 1977. 175 p.; bibl.; map; tables (Serie Tricentenario, 1677–1977)

Useful summary of statistical and other information about the Department of Ayacucho. Contains data on population, with 1972 census material, fairly detailed soils analysis, and climatic averages. Settlements are listed by districts and rural agglomerations by size.

Slater, David. El capitalismo subdesarrollado y la organización del espacio, Perú, 1920–1940. See *HLAS 42:3121.*

5270 Sueldo Nava, Pedro. Guía completa de Machupicchu. Cusco: Editorial de Cultura Andina, 1976. 49 p.; 1 fold. leaf of plates; ill.

Useful guide book with drawings and maps depicting important aspects of Machupicchu. Includes brief biography of Hiram Bingham and map of ruins.

SURINAM

5271 Lindblad, Jan. Stenålder och vita indianer. Stockholm: Bonnier, 1977. 188 p; ill.

The author, a Swedish zoologist, has made several films for Swedish television describing the life of Waiana, Trio, and Akurio Indians who live in the almost impenetrable jungles of Surinam, formerly Dutch Guayana. The Akurios are white skinned and live a stone age life. They were discovered in 1968. The author sees the medical, educational and religious services provided to these Indian tribes by missionaries as mainly beneficial. He wants to alert his readers to the dangers of hunting too many jungle animals and to the destruction of nature which will follow with the opening of these areas to the modern world. Outstanding color photograph illustrations. Attractive format. [R.V. Shaw]

URUGUAY

5272 Castellanos, Alfredo Raúl. Nomenclatura de Montevideo. Montevideo: Intendencia Municipal de Montevideo, 1977. 547 p.; 16 leaves of plates; ill.

An encyclopaedic presentation of place names, individuals, and nations having to do with Montevideo in particular and Uruguay in general.

5273 Centro Latinoamericano de Economía Humana. Regionalización: un aporte al estudio del caso uruguayo. Montevideo: 1977. 78 p.; bibl.; maps; tables.

One of the most outstanding works in geography to come from Uruguay, this small volume presents themes of regionalization according to Friedman's growth pole notions, political considerations, administrative organization, historical influences, and a specific regional development project.

5274 Gaudiano, María Josefina and others. Uruguay, datos básicos: salud, educación, población, población activa, vivienda. Montevideo: Fundación de Cultura Universitaria (FCU), 1976. 213 p.; fold. tables; maps; tables.

Analysis of population statistics, housing, education and health. Reports the 1975 population at 2,764,000 inhabitants.

González Díaz, Nelson. Los ferrocarriles ingleses en Uruguay desde sus orígenes hasta la crisis del noventa. See *HLAS 42:3486.*

5275 Medina, Omar. Santa Clara del Olimar Grande, 1878–1978. Montevideo: Tall. Graf. de Sheraá, 1978. 410 p.; bibl.

Description of the origin and development of settlement in Santa Clara del Olimar Grande, in the Cuchilla Grande area of Uruguay. This account of rural events and progress in a remote part of the country contains much geography and history from the period of founding in 1878 to 1978.

5276 Proceso de asentamientos urbanos en el Uruguay: siglos XVIII y XIX. Angel Mario Cocchi et al. Montevideo: Centro de Informaciones y Estudios del Uruguay (CIESU), 1977. 35 p.; maps (mimeo)

Brief analysis of economic, political, and demographical evolution of urbanism in Uruguay, with emphasis on the 18th and 19th centuries. Initial part of a larger study (see item **5275**) resulting from seminar held in Asunción in 1977 on population and territorial occupation. Study suggests that Uruguay would be a good place for Christaller central place research.

5277 Una red urbana ordenadora de un espacio vacío: el caso uruguayo. Angel Mario Cocchio et al. Montevideo: Centro de Informaciones y Estudios del Uruguay (CIESU), 1977. 172 p.; ill. (mimeo)

Gives a detailed summary analysis of the growth of urban centers in Uruguay from the colonial period, when political considerations account for settlement location to the rise of a cattle "monoregional economy" and emergence of new centers accommodating movement of beef.

5278 Uruguay. Ministerio de Economía y Finanzas. Dirección General de Estadística y Censos. Datos preliminares: V [i.e. Quinto] censo general de población, III de viviendas, año 1975. 2. ed. Prefacio de Horacio H. Parodi. Montevideo: 1976. 1 v. (Unpaged); maps; tables.

Compilation of essential statistics by departments, using 1975 census data. Includes maps of departments and useful information about settlements.

VENEZUELA

5279 Aguilera, Jesús Antonio. La población de Venezuela: dinámica histórica, socio-económica y geográfica. Caracas: Universidad Central de Venezuela, Facultad de Ciencias Económicas y Sociales, División de Publicaciones, 1975. 85 p.; bibl.; tables.

Discusses population growth traits, distribution, and movements, focusing on problems of sanitation, education, and the need for planning. Author suggests moving the Federal District of Venezuela to the state of Bolívar.

5280 Anduze, Pablo J. Bajo el signo del Mawari. Introducción de Martín Vegas. Caracas: Imprenta Nacional, 1973? 415 p.; facsims.; maps; plates.

Consists of ethnological, zoological,

botanical and other observations made during a 1958 journey through remote parts of Amazonia in Venezuela.

5281 Azpúrua G., Pedro Pablo. 25 [i.e. Veinticinco] de 35. Caracas: Editorial Latina, 1975. 408 p.; bibl.; maps; tables.

Author expresses opinions on various aspects of Venezuelan life, with some emphasis on urbanism and planning. Detailed descriptions of sections of cities such as Maracaibo may be useful to urban specialists.

5282 Chen, Chi-yi. Desarrollo regional-urbano y ordenamiento del territorio: mito y realidad. Con la colaboración de María C. Múgica de Fawler and others. Caracas: Universidad Católica Andrés Bello, 1978. 319 p.; bibl.; maps; tables (Colección Manoa; 13)

Enlightening analysis of the hierarchy of cities in Venezuela whose general theme is that there are no underdeveloped regions, only underdeveloped human capacities. Makes good use of statistical formulas and interpretation of results.

5283 Chocrón, Isaac E. Maracaibo 180° [i.e. ciento ochenta grados]. Fotografías, Emmanuel Quintero. Maracaibo: Ediciones Centro de Bellas Artes, 1978. ca. 150 p.; ill.

Humorous look at the city of Maracaibo with color illustrations of some merit.

5284 Conferencia Geológica Inter-Guayanas, *9th, Guyana, Venezuela. 1972.* Memoria. Caracas: Ministerio de Minas e Hidrocarburos, Dirección de Geología [and] Editorial Sucre, 1979? 692 p.; bibls.; fold. maps; ill.; maps; tables (Boletín de Geología. Publicación especial; 6)

This volume, containing the results of the 9th Inter-Guayana conference on geology, appears to have been printed in 1979. Consists of articles in English or Spanish, with English abstracts, from the various commissions (on general geology, geomorphology, regional geology, stratigraphy, mineralogy, mineral resources, geophysics, and remote sensing.

5285 Corporación de Turismo de Venezuela. Comarca al mar. Textos, Gabriel Rodríguez. Caracas: Ministerio de Información y Turismo, Corporación de Turismo de Venezuela, 1978. 147 p.; ill.

Photographic description of the central coastal region of Venezuela.

5286 **Drenikoff, Iván.** Impresos y mapas antiguos de Venezuela. Caracas: Ediciones del Congreso de la República, 1975. 189 p.; maps; tables.

Identification of 359 maps of Venezuela published between 1808–21.

5287 **Ecología y conservación.** Valencia, Venezuela: Universidad de Carabobo, Departamento de Extensión Científica, 1976. 124 p.; ill. (Ediciones de la Dirección de Cultura—Universidad de Carabobo)

Series of articles on animal population and limiting factors of physical and biological types, conservation of Amazon forests, contamination of waters in Lake Valencia (Venezuela), problems in mangrove swamps, and global considerations based on contemporary knowledge of ecology and conservation. ·

5288 **Fundación para el Desarrollo de la Región Centro Occidental de Venezuela** (FUDECO). Mejoramiento del cultivo del café en la región a nivel de asentamientos campesinos. Barquisimeto, Venezuela: FUDECO, 1975. 69 leaves; bibl.; map; tables.

Venezuelan coffee production does not meet the quota allowed by international convention of coffee growers. This study analyzes in detail labor, transportation, and planting requirements for several rural settlements in the coffee region.

5289 **García Méndez, Guillermo.** Maracaibo, retrato de la ciudad generosa. Fotografía, J.J. Castro, J.B. Staley y colaboración de las fototecas de Graziano Gasparini et al. Dibujos, Reiner Vetter. Caracas: Banco Central de Venezuela, 1970. 172 p.; chiefly ill.

Description of the modern city of Maracaibo with well-chosen photographs.

5290 **González Cerruti, Ramón** and **Snehendu B. Kar.** Venezuela. New York: Consejo de Población, 1975. 27 p.; map (Perfiles de países)

In the 50 years following 1920, Venezuela's population changed from primarily rural to primarily urban. Authors discuss problems of economy, health, etc., stemming from over-population and explain government family planning program initiated in 1974. This series entitled, *Country profiles*, appears in English and Spanish and is pro-

duced by the Population Council of New York.

5291 **Méndez Baamonde, José.** Archipiélago Los Roques/Islas de Aves. Caracas?: Departamento de Relaciones Públicas de Lagoven, 1978. 48 p.; col. ill. (Cuadernos Lagoven)

One of the only descriptions available of the Archipiélago Los Roques off the northern coast of Venezuela. Coral reefs are still being formed in the archipiélago.

5292 **Misle, Carlos Eduardo.** Plaza Mayor—Plaza Bolívar: corazón pulso y huella de Caracas. Caracas: Talleres Gráficos de Mersifrica, 1964. 118 p.; ill.; plates (Materiales para el estudio de la historia de Caracas; 3)

Traces the 400-year development of the central plaza area of Caracas (1567–1964). Contains brief descriptions from documented sources.

5293 **L'Orénoque aux deux visages.** Par Jean Chaffanjon et Jules Verne; présenté par Arnaud Chaffanjon. Paris: D. Pierron, 1978. 573 p.; 16 p. of plates; maps.

Consists of the travel journals (1886–87) of the French expeditions to the Orinoco led by J. Chaffanjon and Jules Vernes.

5294 **Salazar-Quijada, Adolfo.** La toponimia en Venezuela. Caracas: s.n., 1975. 313 leaves; bibl.; ill.

Analyzes native, African, Hispanic, and other names and presents maps of movement of these peoples in Venezuela. Reviews and illustrates some theory and methodology in the analysis of names. No foreign bibliographical items are cited, in spite of the detailed work on this subject which exists in German.

5295 **Schnee, Ludwig.** Plantas comunes de Venezuela. 2. ed. Maracay: Universidad de Venezuela, Facultad de Agronomía, Instituto de Botánica Agrícola, 1973. 806 p.; plates.

Useful handbook of plants in Venezuela. Plants are listed alphabetically by common names and described in some detail. Color photographs augment text.

5296 **Sequera de Segnini, Isbelia.** Estudio geo-económico de la región de Barlovento. Caracas: Edición Patrocinada por la

Gobernación del Estado Miranda, 1976. 149 p.; ill.

Regional analysis of a subregion of the Valle del Tuy, Venezuela, consisting of five chapters that define physical landscape, traits, demography, economy and conclusions. Low elevation, high precipitation and a variety of products characterize the zone. Along with another subregion, Ocumare del Tuy, this area is becoming an important center of agriculture and tourism.

5297 Tovar, Ramón A. Perspectiva geográfica de Venezuela: para una compreensión realista del espacio geográfico de Venezuela. Valencia, Venezuela: Vadell Hnos., 1978. 151 p.; bibl.; ill.

A geography, aimed largely at the general public, that divides Venezuela into spatial realms (e.g., the agricultural Caribbean and Orinoco tributary regions, and the zone dominated by petroleum exploitation).

5298 Valery S., Rafael. Los caminos de Venezuela. Caracas?: Departamento de Relaciones Públicas de Lagoven, 1978. 48 p.; bibl.; ill. (El Hombre y su ambiente. Cuadernos Lagoven)

Brief description of development of roads in Venezuela, especially during the present century. Includes maps illustrating changes.

5299 Venezuela. Ministerio de Fomento. Dirección General de Estadística y Censos Nacionales (DGE/CN). IV [i.e. Cuarto] censo agropecuario. t. 1, Estado de Aragua. Caracas: 1973. 188 p.; tables.

Statistical presentation based on 1971 census data of land-tenure facts, crop type, production, and holding sizes for the state of Aragua, Venezuela.

5300 ———. **Ministerio de Obras Públicas. Dirección de Cartografía Nacional. División de Cartas. Sección de Nombres Geográficos.** Gacetilla de nombres geográficos. Caracas: 1974. 248 p.; fold. map (Edición provisional; 4)

List of place names with coded information about local geography, earth coordinates, and map sources.

5301 Venezuela y su mar. Caracas: Instituto Nacional de Canalizaciones, 1973. 99 p.; bibl.; ill.; plates.

Information concerning marine life in coastal Venezuela aimed primarily at the general public. Contains diagrams and pictures.

5302 Vila, Marco-Aurelio. Diccionario de tierras y aguas de Venezuela. Presentación de Adolfo Salazar Quijada. Caracas: Ministerio de Obras Públicas, Dirección de Cartografía Nacional, 1976. 290 p.; plates.

An alphabetical listing and brief description of place names of both important and obscure physical features in Venezuela.

5303 ———. La geoeconomía de la Venezuela del siglo XVI: notas. Caracas: Ediciones de la Facultad de Humanidades y Educación, Escuela de Historia, Universidad Central de Venezuela, 1978. 174 p.; 1 leaf of plates; bibl.; maps (Serie Varia—Escuela de Historia, Universidad Central de Venezuela; v. 17)

Presents historical data on introduction of cattle, production of crops and trade items such as pearls, and on administrative problems of the settlement of Venezuela in the 16th century beginning with the Maracaibo region and extending eastward along the coast and to the interior.

BRAZIL

MÁRIO HIRAOKA, *Associate Professor of Geography, Millersville State College*

THE LITERATURE ON BRAZIL OF INTEREST to geographers continues to multiply at an unprecedented rate. As a result, both the search for and the selection of newly published materials is becoming ever more difficult. Undoubtedly, a large body of important works—particularly those printed in non-Western countries— never comes to the attention of the reviewer. Such limitations on comprehensiveness should be kept in mind when perusing the present section.

A survey of items by region reveals a preponderance of scholarly interest in two areas: Amazonia and the Northeast. In the former region, the topics that continue to interest specialists are farming and its environmental and socioeconomic implications. The number and quality of these studies has risen rapidly from their humble beginnings only a decade ago. At that time, most of the reports were based on sketchy information and short field investigations; the most recent ones are characterized by greater accuracy and conceptual sophistication, reflecting increased data availability.

The Instituto Nacional de Pesquisas da Amazônia (INPA), which has attracted a considerable number of researchers, and older, respected centers like the Museu Paraense Emílio Goeldi, have contributed greatly to the collection and dissemination of important findings on the North (items 5333 and 5393). Among the topics reviewed in this issue, multinationals (items 5342, 5349 and 5378); agricultural colonization and traditional farming (items 5317, 5348, 5380, 5405 and 5411); evaluation of environmental bases (items 5333, 5379 and 5416); and monocultural crop production (item 5341) are worthy of note. Although dissimilar in focus and methodology, most of these works share one overriding concern: alarm at the deterioration of the human and physical ecological bases in Brazil. The concern of researchers has in turn heightened public interest and influenced governmental policies in this area, as is reflected in the proceedings of recent international meetings and in President Figueiredo's proclamation of 1979 as the International Year of the Amazon.

Poverty in the Northeast—the result of socioeconomic inequalities, population problems, and ineffective regional development programs—continues to command the attention of Brazilian specialists. A number of studies included in this section treat the physical difficulties of life in the rural sector, with its increasing social and economic disparities created by the land tenure system and changing land uses (items 5315, 5324, 5332 and 5419). Other studies deal with the processes and patterns of an ongoing phenomenon that still involves a sizeable segment of the Northeastern population: the exodus from traditional farming areas to new ones, as well as to coastal cities (items 5365, 5384 and 5402). Therefore, considerable energy is expended in explaining the processes and patterns of this phenomenon. Other themes discussed in the literature are changes in urban hierarchies and the regional economy (items 5336, 5359 and 5412). Several institutions in the region are publishing high-caliber works on subjects of interest to geographers, such as migration, regional development, and urbanization. There are the Banco de Nordeste do Brasil's Departamento de Estudos Econômicos do Nordeste (ETENE), and the Instituto Joaquim Nabuco de Pesquisas Sociais (IJNPS). The *Série Estudos e Pesquisas*, published by the latter organization, is particularly relevant for geographers.

Of the remaining regions of Brazil, the most studied is the Central West (i.e., the "last frontier"). The *cerrados*, which began to assume importance beginning in the 1960s and increasingly in the 1970s, have now become one of the principal areas of commercial agricultural development in the country. Nevertheless, scientific knowledge about what constitutes a rational man-environment system in this region or in the rest of Brazil has lagged far behind development. However, some items reviewed in this section indicate there is a concerned effort to fill this lacuna (items 5338, 5352, 5385, 5414 and 5423). In contrast to the Northeast, scholars interested in the South and Southeast focus primarily on two subjects: the causes and effects of continued urbanization and industrialization, and problems of uncontrolled growth.

Brazilians view the production of alternate and inexpensive sources of energy as the nation's most urgent task, an indispensable requirement for improving the sluggish Brazilian economy. The abundance of materials published on this topic underscores the magnitude of the problem. Investigation of nonconventional sources of power such as nuclear, solar, alcohol, and wind-energy is underway and each one of them is at a different stage of research and/or production. Concurrently, there is a debate concerning attempts to solve Brazil's energy problem on a regional basis (see items 5321–5322, 5327 and 5351).

The topic of environmental protection continues to be in vogue among a growing number of Brazilian geographers. Their studies have not only contributed significantly towards a better understanding of environmental problems but have improved noticeably in quality as well. Analytical works now prevail over the more descriptive studies of earlier years.

The proliferation of historical accounts, especially of urban areas, has facilitated historical reconstruction of man-land relationships in Brazil. The *Coleção Paulística*, published by the State of São Paulo, and the *Série Reconquista do Brasil*, by the University of São Paulo (items 5310, 5350 and 5389) deserve special mention here.

5304 **Abreu, Adilson Avansi de.** Geografia e planejamento: estudo de um caso. São Paulo: Instituto de Geografia, Universidade de São Paulo, 1977. 15 p.; bibl.; maps (Geografia e planejamento; 29)

An attempt to demonstrate the relevance of geomorphological studies to regional planning. To illustrate the point, author surveys the morphogenetic, geologic, and related physical aspects of an island off the coast of São Paulo, and suggests which sectors of the island are ecologically suitable for recreational development purposes.

5305 ———. Relevos cuestiformes do leste paulista: o exemplo do Alto Vale do Ribeirão dos Porcos (AGB/BPG, 51, junho 1976, p. 47–56, bibl., ill., map, plates)

Morphogenesis of a small area within the Jaguarí-Mirim drainage basin in the state of São Paulo.

5306 **Ab'Sáber, Azis Nacib.** Diretrizes para uma política de preservação de reservas naturais no Estado de São Paulo. São Paulo: Instituto de Geografia, Universidade de São Paulo, 1977. 27 p. (Geografia e planejamento; 30)

A review of environmental deterioration in Brazil by regions leads author to conclude that current ecological problems are the outcome of incipient and uncoordinated attempts at environmental management. Proposes as solutions a novel spatial organization scheme and an integrated environmental planning agency.

5307 ———. Potencialidades paisagísticas brasileiras. São Paulo: Instituto de Geografia, Universidade de São Paulo, 1977. 27 p.; bibl.; map (Geomorfologia; 55)

Divides the Brazilian landscape into six major physiographic-ecologic regions, reviewing the extent of human intervention and changes in each. Author concludes that the greatest degradations have taken place in the tropical portions.

5308 ———. Problemática da desertificação e da savanização no Brasil intertropical. São Paulo: Universidade de São Paulo, Instituto de Geografia, 1977. 19 p. (Geomorfologia; 53)

Description of processes and patterns of desertification and savannization in the intertropical parts of Brazil. Direct or indirect anthropic actions, in combination with geoecologic conditions, seem to be the major agents responsible for the degradational processes.

5309 **Aguiar, Durval Vieira de.** Descrições práticas da Província da Bahia: com declaração de todas as distâncias intermediárias das cidades, vilas e povoações. Pref.de Fernando Sales. Capa, Luís Carlos Dias. 2. ed. Rio de Janeiro: Livraria Editora Cátedra *em convênio com* o Instituto Nacional do Livro, Ministério da Educação e Cultura, 1979. 320 p.

First published in 1888, this compendium of towns in 19th-century rural Bahia contains valuable information on population, settlement size, location, functions, and a variety of socioeconomic data.

5310 Alincourt, Luiz d'. Memória sobre a viagem do porto de Santos à cidade de Cuiabá. Pref. de. Mário Guimarães Ferri. São Paulo: Editora da Universidade de São Paulo, 1975. 207 p.; 5 leaves of plates; ill. (Reconquista do Brasil; v. 25)

Alincourt's descriptions of man and environment are comparable to those produced by such perceptive travellers and scientists as Aires de Casal, Saint-Hilaire, D'Orbigny, and Gardner. Written in the closing years of the colony, this chorography of a transect between the coast of São Paulo and Mato Grosso increases understanding of the early 19th-century Paulista frontier.

Apesteguy, Christine. L'intervention fédérale en Amazonie: éléments pour une définition de l'état militaire au Brésil. See item **6724**.

5311 —— and **Hervé Thery.** Les frontières du Nord-Brésil: de l'indépendance au Pacte Amazonien (CDAL, 18, 2. semestre, 1978, p. 69–76)

A synopsis of boundary changes in Amazônia between Brazil and its neighboring countries since the colonial period. Political and economic rivalries led to largely unsuccessful boundary adjustments. The Amazonian Cooperation Treaty, the most recent attempt to reduce tensions in the basin, is viewed as another imperialist attempt by Brazil to expand its influence in the interior of South America.

5312 ——; **Guy Martiniere**; and **Hervé Thery.** Frontières en Amazonie: la politique du Brésil et l'integration de l'Amérique du Sud (FDD/NED [Problèmes d'Amérique Latine, 53] 4533/4534, 31 oct. 1979, p. 76–98, maps, tables)

A study of changing spatial relations and human activities in Amazônia. Focuses mainly on Brazil's role in fashioning these mutations. The success of current highway and development projects and of the Amazonian Cooperation Treaty in fostering fraternity with neighboring countries is also explored.

5313 Araújo Filho, J.R. de. O café em São Paulo (AGB/BPG, 50, março 1976, p. 57–81, bibl., map, tables)

A summary of the evolution of coffee cultivation in the state of São Paulo, with emphasis on recent problems and trends.

5314 Augel, Johannes. Der Stausee von Sobradinho/Bahia, Brasilien: Wirtschaftliche und soziale Implikationen eines Entwicklungsprojekts = The reservoir of Sobradinho/Bahia, Brazil: economic and social implications of a development project (PGM, 123:2, 1979, p. 109–117, map, tables)

Assesses the socioeconomic and ecological implications of the Sobradinho dam and reservoir, located upstream from Juazeiro, Bahia state.

5315 Augel, Moema Parente. Ludwig Riedel, viajante alemão no Brasil. Capa, Roberto Romero. Salvador: Fundação Cultural do Estado da Bahia, 1979. 90 p.; 9 leaves of plates; bibl.; ill. (Coleção Frei Vicente do Salvador; v. 2)

An introduction to the writings of Ludwig Riedel which interprets the German botanist's diaries and observations resulting from his early 19th-century travels in east and west-central Brazil.

5316 Barro, Máximo. Nossa Senhora do Ó. São Paulo: Departamento do Patrimônio Histórico, Divisão do Arquivo Histórico, 1977 or 1978. 140 p.; 11 leaves of plates; bibl.; ill. (Histórica dos bairros de São Paulo; v. 13)

Brief history of a *bairro* of São Paulo covering such topics as demography, spatial, economic, religious, and educational changes. The appended maps, although poorly reproduced, serve as aids in tracing the evolution of the city.

5317 Becker, Bertha K. Uma hipótese sobre a origem do fenômeno urbano numa fronteira de recursos do Brasil (IBGE/R, 40:1, jan./março 1978, p. 111–122, map, tables)

An attempt to explain the numerous villages that appear along settlement frontiers as gathering points of surplus population and products. They disappear or are incorporated into an urban hierarchy as soon as the influences from the center become manifest.

5318 ———. Política regional e mobilidade populacional numa fronteira de recursos do Brasil (IBGE/R, 41:4, out./dez. 1979, p. 146–168, bibl., maps, tables)

Review of regional development policies of sparsely occupied regions and their effects on the migrants' horizontal and vertical mobilities. Field data from recently occupied northern and central Goiás state suggest that present government schemes of colonization, fiscal incentives, and road building provide limited opportunities to the landless and family farmers.

5319 Beretta, Pier Luigi. Amazzonia Brasiliana: colonizzazione o popolamiento?: un contributo informativo e critico (IAA, 4:4, 1978, p. 289–306, bibl.)

Accounts of colonization activities in Amazonia since 1970. Author contends that structural, environmental, technical, and social inadequacies have served to attract settlers only marginally suited for pioneering activities. Consequently, the government has had to adopt traditional solutions for developing the region (i.e., attracting farmers from the south who have proven agricultural expertise).

5320 ———. Contribuição para uma bibliografia geográfica do Rio Grande do Sul, Brasil. Tradução: Elisabeth de Castro Borges (DRG/BG, 21:19, jan./dez. 1976, p. 28–50)

A well-documented list of geographical literature of the 19th and 20th centuries. The 437 entries covering a wide range of topics should be of special interest to those interested in the foreign colonization areas of Rio Grande do Sul.

5321 Berutti, Paulo Azevedo. Contribuição energética das florestas brasileiras (SBPC/CC, 29:3, mar 1977, p. 274–283, bibl., tables)

About 30 percent of total energy consumed in Brazil is contributed by the forests. The tropical location of the country, combined with the renewable nature of forests, suggest that forests can be a sustained energy source. Production potential can be increased by improved management and application of new technology.

5322 Beyna, Jean-Michel. Crise de l'énergie et développement régional au Brésil (FDD/NED [Problèmes d'Amérique Latine, 48] 4474, 13 juillet 1978, p. 123–136)

Analyzes problems and prospects of traditional and new sources of energy, and explains changes in patterns of regional energy consumption.

5323 Boneff, Alfredo. Elementos de demografia e algumas características demográficas, econômicas sociais do Brasil. Belém: Universidade Federal do Pará, Sub-Reitoria de Pesquisa, Planejamento e Desenvolvimento, 1977. 317 p.; bibl.; ill. (Série Pesquisa—Universidade Federal do Pará, Sub-Reitoria de Pesquisa, Planejamento e Desenvolvimento; no. 5)

Pt. 1 of this study presents general demographic concepts and techniques; pt. 2 contains an overview of Brazilian population characteristics. The last four chapters give detailed information on the inhabitants of Pará, and may therefore be of value to those interested in that state.

5324 Brito, Sebastiana Rodrigues de and **Luiz Sérgio Pires Guimarães.** Conseqüências sociais da seca no Nordeste: pt. 4 (IBGE/R, 41:4, out./dez. 1979, p. 90–99, bibl., tables)

Describes the socioeconomic effects of government programs designed to cushion the 1979 drought in the Northeast. Authors contend that official relief efforts assisted only the larger landholders, and that what the Northeast needs is a coherent and continuous assistance plan intended for the masses.

5325 Bunker, Stephen G. Forces of destruction in Amazonia (Environment [The Committee for Environmental Information, St. Louis, Mo.] 22:7, 1980, p. 14–43)

Critical review of agricultural developments conducted in Amazônia; describes the boom-and-bust stages of exploitation, and discusses their effects on human and natural environments.

Bunse, Heinrich A.W. Dialetos italianos no Rio Grande do Sul. See *HLAS 42:4627.*

5326 Capacidade de uso da terra das microregiões do nordeste paraense. Zebino Pacheco do Amaral Filho et al. Belém: Governo do Estado do Pará, Instituto de Desenvolvimento Econômico-Social do Pará, 1975. 189 p.; 2 fold. leaves of plates; bibl.; ill. (Série Monografias—Instituto do Desenvolvimento Econômico-Social do Pará; 17)

Attempts to provide specific data for

agricultural land use in northeast Pará state. Following a review of the literature, the 1:250,000 radar images were used to delimit the physiographic units in order to draft soil and land use capability maps. The Bennema, Beek, and Camargo system was employed to evaluate land-use capabilities in the region.

5327 Carvalho, Arnaldo Vieira de, Jr.; Alcir de Faro Orlando; and Dino Magnoli. Solar energy for steam generation in Brasil (AI/I, 4:3, May/June 1979, p. 140–148, map, tables)

A greater emphasis should be placed on converting solar energy to steam generation. Although technology to produce ethanol as a substitute for gasoline has received much attention, research on direct conversion of solar radiation into heat generation within the 100° and 125°C range has been limited. The potential contribution of this form of energy is enormous, since the technology is simple, the location of the country is favorable, and approximately 10 percent of the national primary energy is channeled into steam generation.

5328 Carvalho, José Cândido de Mello. Considerações sobre o uso da terra na Amazônia brasileira. Rio de Janeiro: Fundação Brasileira para a Conservação da Natureza, 1979. 79 p.; 2 leaves of plates; bibl.; ill. (Série Divulgação—Fundação Brasileira para a Conservação da Natureza; no. 10)

A bureaucrat's view of conservation in Amazônia which offers a generalized description of practices exploitive of the environment and presents a list of conservationist measures adopted by the government.

5329 Carvalho, Lívio de. Uma nota sôbre a ocupação em areas de fronteira: o caso de Rondônia (IBE/RBE, 34:2, 1980, p. 293–306)

Study consists of labor absorption patterns in the Federal Territory of Rondônia projected from migration and occupational experiences in the 1970s. If present economic trends continue, and if the government does not alter land distribution mechanisms that favor large landowners, the region should continue to absorb the increased population resulting from natural growth and migrations.

5330 Coelho, Correia. Crato em diagnóstico: 1975 (ICC/I, 19, 1975, p. 61–80, tables)

Listing of some socioeconomic data of a rapidly changing município in southern Ceará state, followed by a short interpretation.

5331 Costa Ferreira, João da. A Cidade do Rio de Janeiro e seu termo. Rio de Janeiro: Prefeitura da Cidade do Rio de Janeiro, 1978? 379 p. (Coleção Memória do Rio; 1)

A portrayal of some of the physical characteristics of Rio de Janeiro between the 16th and 18th centuries, based on two codices from the Municipal Archives of Rio de Janeiro and secondary sources.

5332 Critchfield, Richard. Small is beautiful (if enormously problematical) in northeast Brazil. Hanover, N.H.: American Universities Field Staff, 1976. 24 p.; bibl.; ill. (East Coast South America series; v. 20, no. 1. Fieldstaff reports)

Description of life in a small village in the Recôncavo of Bahia. A case study that points out the difficulties of rural development and the need for new approaches for promoting change, similar to those proposed by E.F. Schumacher.

5333 Cunha, Osvaldo Rodrigues da and Therezinha Xavier Bastos. A contribuição do Museu Paraense Emílio Goeldi à meteorologia da Amazônia. Belém, Brazil: Conselho Nacional de Pesquisas, Instituto Nacional de Pesquisas da Amazônia, Museu Paraense Emílio Goeldi, 1973. 42 p.; bibl.; tables (Publicações avulsas; 23)

Study compares two different periods of meteorological data gathered at the Museu Paraense Emílio Goeldi: 1895–1922 and 1933–60. Results indicate that no major climatic changes have occurred in the region since the late 19th century.

5334 Cunningham, Susan M. Brazil: recent trends in industrial development (Bank of London and South America Review [London] 13:4, 1979, p. 212–220)

Review of Brazilian industrial programs within the last 20 years. Explains the changing relationships between the three major sets of industrial interests (i.e., the public sector, multinational companies, and private domestic firms). Author emphasizes that industrialization in Brazil in the late 1970s was characterized by an increasing proportion of technical assistance programs instead of direct investments by joint ventures, and the expanding role of private industries.

5335 ———. Multinational enterprises in Brazil: locational patterns and implications for regional developments (AAG/PG, 33:1, 1971, p. 48–62)

Comparison of locational patterns of multinational and domestic enterprises to assess their effects on regional developments. In contrast to national concerns, multinationals show a propensity for spatial concentration, especially in metropolitan areas.

5336 **Davidovich, Fany; Mario do Socorro Alves; and Marília Carneiro Natal.** Funções urbanas no Nordeste. Fortaleza: Banco do Nordeste do Brasil, Departamento de Estudos Econômicos do Nordeste, 1977. 88 p.; 6 leaves of plates; bibl.; ill.

Inquiries into the structure of regional urban systems in Northeast Brazil for socio-economic planning purposes, using Robert H.T. Smith's method of functional town classification.

5337 **Delson, Roberta Marx.** New towns for colonial Brazil: spatial and social planning of the eighteenth century. Ann Arbor, Mich.: *Published for* Department of Geography, Syracuse University, *by* University Microfilms International, 1979. 212 p.; bibl.; ill.; index (Dellplain Latin America studies; 2. Monograph publishing; Sponsor series)

Refutes the view that town planning in colonial Brazil did not exist. Provides evidence to demonstrate that, beginning in the 18th century, new towns were built as part of Portugal's colonial administration.

5338 **Dupon, Jean-François and André Vant.** Contrastes et changements dans l'agriculture du Goiás central (SBG/COM, 23: 127, juillet/sept. 1979, p. 217–252, maps, tables)

Planned development of Amazônia and the Center-West begun in the 1960s received added impetus from the Second National Development Program (1975–79). A comparative assessment of farming in central and southern Goiás reveals considerable regional differences. In the south, mechanized commercial farming and cattle ranching are creating a large class of landless people, while in the north, the scarcity of labor is responsible for the development of extensive cattle rearing.

5339 **Empresa Metropolitana de Planejamento da Grande São Paulo.** O desafio metropolitano. Secretaria de Estado dos Negócios Metropolitanos, EMPLASA, Empresa Metropolitana de Planejamento da Grande São Paulo. São Paulo: EMPLASA, 1976. 214 p.; 16 fold. leaves of plates; bibl.; ill. (Série Documentos—EMPLASA; 1)

The volume, written by a multi-disciplinary team, attempts to give a global view of Greater São Paulo and the problems associated with metropolitan planning. Treats such topics as mass transportation, urban structure, protection and provision of water resources.

5340 **Faissol, Sperdião.** Geography and spatial planning in Brazil (*in* Studying Latin America: essays in honor of Preston E. James [see item **4358**] p. 194–213)

An explanation of the importance of geography in national regional planning. After briefly describing the French and American influences on Brazilian geographical thoughts, author discusses the changing roles of the National Council of Geography in influencing spatial policy decisions.

5341 **Fearnside, Philip M.** Cattle yield prediction for the Transamazon Highway of Brazil (AI/I, 4:4, julio/agosto 1979, p. 220–226, bibl.)

Argues that the high cattle-yield figures often presented by researchers and government agencies are misleading. The author claims that a more realistic figure for sustainable carrying capacity of pastures along the Transamazonian highway should take into account variables like rates of soil changes under pasture, soil nutrient levels and pasture growth, proportion of weeds, and conversion of grasses to pasture grass dry weight.

5342 ——— and **Judy M. Rankin.** Jari and development in the Brazilian Amazon (AI/I, 5:3, May/June 1980, p. 146–156, bibl., col. plates)

An overview of the Jarí Project and evaluation of the forestry activities being carried out in monocultural fashion. The authors conclude that ". . . the appropriateness of the Jarí Project as a model for development is far from being demonstrated and needs much more study before it can be recommended for other parts of the Amazon." (p. 155).

5343 **Federici, Hilton.** História de Cruzeiro. v. 1, Das origens remotas até a instalação do município. v. 2, Da instalação do município (1873) até a transferência da sua sede. Campinas, Brazil: Academia Campinense de Letras, 1974. 2 v.; bibl.; ill.; maps (some fold.) (Publicações da Academia Campinense de Letras; no. 28)

Chronological account of the evolution of a *município* along the Paraíba do Sul Valley in the state of São Paulo. The socioeconomic and demographic data can be useful for understanding the changing land uses that occurred in the valley following the arrival of coffee boom in early 19th century.

5344 **Figueroa, Manuel.** O problema agrario no Nordeste do Brasil. São Paulo: HUCITEC, 1977. 272 p.

A general treatment of contemporary farming characteristics and problems. Since author does not treat the problems regionally, the work is of limited value.

5345 **Fortes, Amyr Borges.** Compêndio de geografia geral do Rio Grande do Sul. 6. ed. rev. e ampliada. Porto Alegre: Sulina, 1979. 97 p.; 13 fold. leaves of plates; ill.

Although this regional textbook on Rio Grande do Sul is fairly elementary it does provide a useful general background on the state.

5346 **Fundação Centro Tecnológico de Minas Gerais** (CETEC). Situação ambiental da região noroeste de Minas Gerais (IBGE/R, 41:4, out./dez. 1979, p. 127–145, maps, table)

Preliminary survey of environmental elements of a 117,000 km² area in northwest Minas Gerais. This multidisciplinary study of a newly occupied region was designed to provide a general background on its physical elements and socioeconomic characteristics, as well as data for formulating environmentally compatible development guidelines.

5347 **Fundação de Desenvolvimento da Região Metropolitana do Recife.** Região Metropolitana do Recife: plano de desenvolvimento integrado. Governo do Estado de Pernambuco, Secretaria de Planejamento, Fundação de Desenvolvimento da Região Metropolitana do Recife-FIDEM. Recife: A Fundação, 1976. 274 p.; 23 fold. leaves of plates; ill.

Although intended as an urban planning manual, the book provides comprehensive coverage of most urban functions, infrastructures, and physical environmental aspects of Recife. The detailed statistics and maps of the metropolitan area are a major asset for those interested in urban research.

5348 **Furtado, Lourdes Gonçalves.** Aspectos históricos e econômicos de Marapanim-nordeste Paraense. Belém, Brazil: Instituto Nacional de Pesquisas da Amazônia, Conselho Nacional de Desenvolvimento Científico e Tecnológico, 1978. 32 p.; bibl.; maps; plates (Boletim do Museu Paraense Emílio Goeldi. Nova série. Antropologia; 67)

A study of man-environment relations in two distinctive ecological zones of the *municípios* of Marapanim, Northeast Pará. Increasing penetration of capitalism in the area has led to the progressive marginalization of the population. Programs suited to local ecological and cultural conditions are needed to solve the present problems.

5349 **Galey, John.** Industrialist in the wilderness: Henry Ford's Amazon venture (SAGE/JIAS, 21:2, May 1979, p. 261–290, bibl.)

The difficulties of opening and establishing large scale monocultures in the Amazon basin is illustrated by Henry Ford's attempts to cultivate rubber trees at Fordlândia and Belterra. The experiment seems to illustrate that environmentally incompatible agricultural systems have limited possibilities for success. Ford's experience also illustrates the difficulties encountered by foreign enterprises in sparsely occupied areas like the Amazon, where every activity is under the scrutiny of the host country.

Gall, Norman. Letter from Rondônia. See item 6737.

5350 **Godoy, Joaquim Floriano de.** A Província de S. Paulo: trabalho, estatístico, histórico e noticioso. Introdução e notas de Brasil Bandecchi. 2. ed., facsimilada. São Paulo: Governo do Estado de São Paulo, 1978. 157 p.; 1 fold. leaf of plates; map (Coleção Paulística; v. 12)

An encyclopedic description of the Province of São Paulo in the 1870s. The socioeconomic and biophysical information, especially the statistical data are invaluable for the understanding of late 19th-century men and society in São Paulo.

5351 Goldemberg, José. Energia nuclear no Brasil: as origens das decisões. São Paulo: Editora, 1978. 90 p. (Coleção Estudos brasileiros; 11)

An anthology of genesis of nuclear energy development and policies in Brazil.

5352 Goodland, Robert J.A. and Mário G. Ferri. Ecologia do cerrado. Tradução, Eugenio Amado; capa, Cláudio Martins. Belo Horizonte: Livraria Itatiaia Editora, 1979. 193 p.; 7 leaves of plates; bibl.; ill. (Coleção Reconquista do Brasil; v. 52)

This valuable contribution to the study of *cerrados* was translated from an English version originally written in 1969. A synthesis of the ecology of the *cerrado*, the present work is of major value to students of the Brazilian Central West. Includes a comprehensive, annotated bibliography, updated through 1977.

5353 Graham, Douglas H. Interstate migration and the industrial labor force in Center-South Brazil (JDA, 12:1, Oct. 1977, p. 31–48)

Investigates the role of interstate migration in the development of industrial labor force in central and southern Brazil, using the 1970 population census and the National Manpower Department's published data.

5354 Grewe, Klaus. Future aspects of new vehicle distribution from VW of Brazil (Geojournal [Akademische Verlagsgesellschaft, Wiesbaden, FRG] 3:1, 1979, p. 27–34)

Plan of future of Brazilian railroad network based on cost-benefit analysis of new vehicle distribution. In order to lessen oil consumption, urban congestion and noise, and excessive transport cost, the government relied on Volkswagen do Brasil to draft an optimal spatial pattern for transportation of manufactured goods from the manufacturing core of the country. The planned network consists of five rail routes with a focus on São Paulo.

5355 Guimarães, Lais de Barros Monteiro. Luz. São Paulo: Prefeitura do Município de São Paulo, Secretaria Municipal de Cultura, Departamento do Patrimônio Histórico, Divisão do Arquivo Histórico, 1977. 118 p.; bibl.; ill. (part fold.) (História dos bairros de São Paulo; v. 12)

History of one of the oldest *bairros* of São Paulo. The focal point of the city during the railroad age, the Bairro da Luz served to channel immigrants to the interior and coffee to the port of Santos. Contains useful information for urban geographers. For art historian's comment, see *HLAS 42:481.*

5356 Hohé, Margreet. Brazilië.ś-Gravenhage: Staatsdrukkerij, 1979. 85 p.; bibl.; fold. map; ill. (Landendocumentatie; 1978, nr. 4)

A profusely-illustrated synthesis of Brazilian geography. Clear and concise tables, current data, and informative maps and photographs offer a sound introduction to the country.

5357 Ilg, Karl. Das Deutschtum in Brasilien. Wien: Schutzverein Osterr. Landsmannschaft, 1978. 103 p.; maps (Eckartschriften; Heft 68)

A concise history of German settlement in Brazil.

5358 Joffily, Geraldo Irenêo. Brasília e sua ideologia. Fotografias, Franklin Vergara. Brasília: Thesaurus, 1977. 138 p.; bibl. (Série Cadernos de história; 2)

Descriptive synopsis of the evolution of Brasília from idea to reality.

5359 Johnson, Dennis. Sorgo granífero no Nordeste do Brasil (BNB/REN, 9:4, out./dez. 1978, p. 483–500, bibl., tables)

Discusses the potential value of grain sorghum as a substitute for corn in the semiarid Northeast. Experimental plantings of the cereal in a colonization project in Rio Grande do Norte demonstrates its environmental adaptability.

5360 Klein, Peter. Die deutschbrasilianische Nuklear-kooperation (BESPL, 1:6, Juli/August 1976, p. 3–12)

Interesting article on German-Brazilian cooperation in the field of nuclear energy. The author maintains that Brazil is the logical country for developing nuclear capability. [G.M. Dorn]

5361 Knight, Patrick. Lobster exports in the Northeast (Brazilian Business [National Association of American Chambers of Commerce in Brazil, Rio de Janeiro] 59:4, April 1979, p. 63–65, plates, table)

Short essay on lobster fishing and export from Northeast Brazil, especially Ceará.

5362 Lapa-PR, 205 anos de fundação, 1769–1974: album histórico. Organizado por Heitor Cardoso. Curitiba, Brasil: Editora Lítero-Técnica, 1974 or 1975. 52 p.; ill.; ports.

History of the agricultural *município* of Lapa, located southwest of Curitiba in Paraná state.

5363 Le Doare, Hélène. Le Brésil et la Cône Sud: les conflits frontaliers (CDAL, 18, 2. semestre, 1978, p. 215–225)

An annotated bibliography on border problems between Brazil and the southern cone countries. Citations are limited to those that treat the frontier concepts and national security within a geographical context. Among the subjects covered are the Itaipú dam, exploitation of Mutun iron ore deposits, and the maritime aspirations of Bolivia.

5364 Lemps, Alain Huets de. La canne a sucre au Brésil: types d'agriculture commerciale (Travaux et Documents de Géographie Tropicale [Centre Nacional de la Recherche Scientifique, Centre d'Études de Géographie Tropicale, Bordeaux, France] 29, juin 1977, n.p.)

A comprehensive geographical study of sugarcane in Brazil. The detailed coverage of all aspects of sugarcane cultivation, processing, and marketing provides not only an excellent background of the social, economical, and political institutions associated with the crop, but also important understanding of the future of the plant.

5365 Levy, Henrique. Posse da terra e migrações em Pernambuco. Recife, Brazil: Instituto Joaquim Nabuco de Pesquisas Sociais, 1977. 56 p. (Série monografias; 8)

Discusses the causes of urbanward migrations in the Northeast, as well as the changing land uses in the *caatinga*.

5366 Linhares, Temístocles. Estado do Paraná. Fotos, Manchete. Rio de Janeiro: Bloch Educação, 1976. 63 p.; bibl.; ill. (Coleção Nosso Brasil)

A work useful for its concise background notes on the state.

5367 Lins, Rachel Caldas. A bovinocultura no Nordeste. Recife, Brazil: Ministerio de Educação e Cultura, Instituto Joaquim Nabuco de Pesquisas Sociais, 1976. 1 v. (Série monografias, 6)

Treats selected aspects of cattle ranching in Northeast Brazil in a sketchy manner. No original findings are reported.

5368 Loureiro, Arthur A.; Marlene F. da Silva; and Jurandyr da Cruz Alencar. Essências madeireiras da Amazônia. Manaus, Amazonas: Conselho Nacional de Desenvolvimento Científico e Tecnológico, Instituto Nacional de Pesquisas da Amazônia, 1979. 1 v.; bibl.; ill.; index.

Morphologic and anatomic descriptions of 105 Amazonian plant species having economic value. Includes information about physical and mechanical properties, common habitats, uses, some silvicultural processes, and local names. Accompanying illustrations facilitate the identification of each species.

5369 McIntyre, Loren. Jarí: a billion dollar gamble in Brazil (NGS/NGM, 157:5, May 1980, p. 686–711, plates)

An informative report on Daniel K. Ludwig's Jarí project near the mouth of the Amazon River. Provides a balanced, general background of the controversial and expensive agroindustrial undertaking.

5370 Magalháes, José Cezar de. A energia eléctrica no Estado do Rio de Janeiro (AGB/BCG, 24, 1973/1975, p. 33–62, maps, tables)

Synopsis of energy generation, distribution, and consumption in the State of Rio de Janeiro.

5371 Maimon, Dália; Pedro Pinchas Geiger; and Werner Baer. O impacto regional das políticas econômicas do Brasil (IBGE/R, 39:3, julho/set. 1977, p. 3–53, tables)

Brief outline of national development plans and their regional influences. Analyzes the characteristics of individual development programs, and discusses their relevance to the improvement of spatial inequalities.

5372 Mamigonian, Armen. Notas sobre os frigoríficos do Brasil central pecuário (AGB/BPG, 51, junho 1976, p. 7–14, maps)

Discusses the changing distribution and ownership patterns, and size of packing plants in Central and Southeast Brazil. The packing plants have become increasingly dispersed, nationally owned, more specialized in handling the animals, and smaller in size.

5373 Margolis, Maxine. Seduced and abandoned: agricultural frontiers in Brazil and the United States (*in* Brazil, anthropological perspectives: essays in honor of Charles Wagley. [see item **1081**] p. 160–179)

Compares two frontier plantation agricultural regions, one in southern Brazil (coffee), and another in southern US (cotton), in order to demonstrate that under similar ecological and economic conditions the inhabitants have similar responses toward land and land use.

5374 Martinière, Guy. Les stratégies frontalières du Brésil colonial et l'Amérique Espagnole (CDAL, 18, 2. semestre, 1978, p. 45–68, maps)

An examination of the temporal and spatial changes in Brazilian borders during the colonial period. Identifies chronologically activities responsible for the territorial expansion beyond the limits established by the Tordesillas Treaty.

5375 Meira Mattos, Carlos de. Una geopolítica para la Panamazónica (IAEERI/E, 54, sept./oct. 1978, p. 33–41, bibl., map, table)

Proposals for a regional integration scheme among countries sharing the Amazon basin. Proposes the ecological similarities as the principal basis for a cooperative undertaking. Development should begin with establishment of international growth poles around existing urban places.

5376 Mello Júnior, Donato. O capitão, engenheiro João André Schwebel, documentarista da Amazônia: seus mapas, plantas e panoramas urbanos (CFC/RBC, 19, jan./março 1974, p. 147–165)

Explanation of maps, urban places, the settlement sketches of Northern Amazônia drafted between 1753 and 1758 by João André Schwebel, a member of the boundary demarcation mission organized by Portugal following the 1750 Treaty of Madrid.

5377 Mesquita, Olindina Vianna; Rivaldo Pinto de Gusmão; and Solange Tietzmann Silva. Proposição metodológica para estudo de desenvolvimento rural no Brasil (IBGE/R, 38:3, julho/set. 1976, p. 93–115, bibl.)

Presents a methodology that includes sectorial, regional, and structural components for studying rural developments.

5378 Molano Campuzano, Joaquín. Las transnacionales en la Amazonia (NSO, 37, julio/agosto 1978, p. 31–40, bibl., ill., table)

Reflections on current developments in Brazilian Amazônia lead the writer to surmise that the expansionism of that country toward the tropical Andean nations is inevitable.

5379 Momsen, Richard P., Jr. Projeto Radam: a better look at the Brazilian tropics (Geojournal [Akademische Verlagsgesellschaft, Wiesbaden, FRG] 3:1, 1979, p. 3–14)

The Radam Project conducted between 1971–75 eventually covered 54 percent of the national territory. The radar images thus obtained can be a major tool for interpreting a number of hitherto unknown cultural and physical phenomena (e.g., vegetation, relief, land use, drainage conditions). The major barrier to a comprehensive interpretation has been the difficulty in obtaining these remotely-sensed data from the government.

5380 Moran, Emilio F. The Trans-Amazonica: coping with a new environment (*in* Brazil, anthropological persectives: essays in honor of Charles Wagley. [see item **1081**] p. 133–159, map, tables)

A study of adaptive strategies of family farmers along the Transamazon highway, based on a sample of settlers around Altamira, author concludes that individuals with previous management skills or horticultural holdings are likely to succeed economically, and favors *caboclos* because of their ability to adapt to changing conditions.

5381 Moreira, Carlos de Sá. Brésil. Papeete: Editions du Pacifique, 1978. 151 p.; col. ill.

Pictorial travel guide of the major geographic regions of Brazil, especially the Northeast, Southeast, and North.

5382 Moreira Pinto, Alfredo. A cidade de São Paulo em 1900. Prefácio e notas de Byron Gaspar. 2. ed. facsimilada. São Paulo: Governo do Estado de São Paulo, 1979. 279, 57 p. (Coleção Paulística; v. 14)

Description of urban features of São Paulo at the turn of the century. Detailed study of churches, public structures, recreational areas, industrial establishment, and their distribution, provides an added dimension to knowledge of the city's physical structure.

5383 Morrill, Richard L. and **Juan J. Angulo.** Spatial aspects of a smallpox epidemic in a small Brazilian city (AGS/GR, 69:3, July 1979, p. 319–330, tables)

A methodological study of spatial-temporal spread of *variola minor*, a mild form of smallpox, at Bragança Paulista, São Paulo state.

5384 Moura, Hélio Augusto de. O balanço migratório do Nordeste no período 1950/70 (BNB/REN, 10:1, jan./março 1979, p. 47–86, map, tables)

Presents net migration variations in the Northeast between 1950–70. Author finds that: 1) migrations are increasingly of short distance; 2) growth of urban population is accelerating, due to past migrations; 3) largest demographic gains have occurred in the metropolitan centers; and 4) colonization areas in Maranhão have reached their maximum absorption capacity.

5385 Muller, Paul. Campo Cerrado: forest or savanna? (Geojournal [Akademische Verlagsgesellschaft, Wiesbaden, FRG] 3:1, 1979, p. 15–25)

The origins of extensive tropical savannas of Central Brazil have long been the topic of heated arguments. Based on evidence provided by plant species, fauna, soil chemistry, and areal distribution of flora and fauna, this study contends that *campos cerrados* are primeval, natural flora, and not the by-product of human interferences.

Muricy, José Candido da Silva. Viagem ao país dos jesuítas. See *HLAS 42:3724.*

5386 Myers, Norman. What future for Amazonia? (OAS/AM, 32:10, Oct. 1980, p. 18–25, map, plates)

Review of current developments in Amazônia. The author shows considerable optimism concerning the future of the region, based on recent reassessments made by Brazil and neighboring countries.

5387 Nimer, Edmon. Um modelo metodológico de classificação de climas (IBGE/R, 41:4, out./dez. 1979, p. 59–89, bibl.)

Proposes a new climatic model for Brazil which combines traditional and dynamic elements for classifying climates (e.g., patterns of atmospheric circulation, temperature, and precipitation).

5388 Nixdorf, Oswald. Pionier im brasilianischen Urwald: d. abenteuerl. Geschichte d. dt. Siedlung Rolandia. Tübingen, Basel: Erdmann, 1979. 319 p.; ill.

Account of German pioneering activities in the Colony of Rolândia in Northern Paraná. The detailed descriptions of settlement activities spanning a period of 50 years provide valuable information on the evolution of an immigrant-influenced cultural landscape.

5389 Nóbrega, Humberto Mello. História do Rio Tietê. Ilustrações de J. Wasth Rodrigues. Introdução de Leonardo Arroyo. 2. ed. São Paulo: Governo do Estado de São Paulo, 1978. 219 p.; 1 leaf of plates; bibl.; ill. (Coleção Paulística; v. 8)

Focuses on Rio Tietê, the most important waterway for inland incursions and transportation for residents of São Paulo during the 18th century. In its second edition, this well-documented book continues to provide useful information about the river and the activities that took place along it, although additional archival material has been uncovered in recent years.

5390 Oliveira, Acary de Passos. Roncador-Xingú: roteiro de uma expedição, Barra do Rio das Garças-Rio das Mortes, Aragarças, Xavantina, 1943–1944. Goiânia: Oficinas Gráficas da Universidade Federal de Goiás, 1976? 181 p.; bibl.; ill.

Accounts of a journey between Aragarças on the shores of Rio Araguaia and Chavantina, along the margins of Rio das Mortes. The book provides only limited geographic information.

5391 Oliveira, Jane Maria Pereira Souto de. Condições de vida da população de baixa renda nas áreas metropolitanas do Rio de Janeiro e Porto Alegre (IBGE/R, 41:4, out./dez. 1979, p. 3–58, tables)

Describes the main characteristics of low-income groups in the metropolitan areas of Rio de Janeiro and Porto Alegre. Includes detailed discussions of indices of food, dwelling, means of transportation, educational levels, and health conditions.

5392 Organization of American States. Department of Regional Development. Marajó: um estudo para o seu desenvolvimento. Prefácio de Kirk P. Rodgers. Washington: OAS, General Secretariat, 1974. 124 p.; maps; tables.

A survey of environmental and agropastoral characteristics of Marajó island.

5393 Pahlen, Alejo von der; Warwick Estevam Kerr; Hiroshi Noda; and Waldelice Oliveira de Paiva. Melhoramento de hortaliças na Amazônia (SBPC/CC, 31:1, jan. 1979, p. 17–24, bibl., tables)

Progress report of attempts to stabilize vegetable supply in the markets of Manáus. Discusses the difficulties of cultivating traditional horticulture items in the interior of Amazônia and the efforts of INPA to correct the situation.

5394 Pandolfo, Clara Martins. Seminário sobre a realidade amazônica, para professores da disciplina "Estudos de Problemas Basileiros." Belém, Brazil: Ministério do Interior, Superintendência do Desenvolvimento da Amazônia (SUDAM), 1973. 43 p.; maps.

Description of basic biophysical resources and studies currently undertaken for evaluating them in Amazonia.

5395 Passos, Claribalte. Ecologia: o homem no rumo da sobrevivência. Recife: Universidade Federal de Pernambuco, 1979. 84 p.

Poorly organized, alarmist collection of vignettes about environmental deterioration, written by a journalist. Topics covered range from deforestation to water quality, but the work offers no new insights.

5396 Pebayle, Raymond. Frontières et espaces frontaliers du Brésil meridional (CDAL, 18, 2. semestre, 1978, p. 33–44)

A description of the characteristics of open borders based on three representative areas: Northwest Rio Grande do Sul, Western Paraná, and the area south of Rio Jacuí.

5397 Pereira, Armand F. and Seymour Warkov. Energy for development in semiarid areas of Northeastern Brazil (AI/I, 4:5, Sept./Oct. 1979, p. 272–281, ill., tables)

A progress report of alternative energy sources for the Northeast. Discusses the development of non-conventional energy sources, such as solar, eolian, and biomass, and their possible socioeconomic impact on the region.

5398 Pinheiro, Neusa Catarina. Bibliografia sobre espécies florestais nativas. Orientadores, José Flavio Candido, Maria das Graças M. Ferreira. Compilada pelos engos. florestais, Neusa Catarina Pinheiro e Sebastião Machado Fonseca. Viçosa, Brasil: Universidade Federal de Viçosa, Biblioteca Central, Seção de Bibliografia e Documentação, 1975. 153 p.; index (Série Bibliografias especializadas—Universidade Federal de Viçosa, Biblioteca Central; 14)

Compilation of published materials about native flora available at the Federal University of Viçosa, Minas Gerais. Contains useful information on economically valuable flora.

5399 Pinto-Coelho, Aristides. Antarctic influence on Brazil's environment (SBPC/CC, 29:1, jan. 1977, p. 33–35)

Ice accumulations and their influence on atmospheric conditions in the Antarctic area are believed to be the main elements conditioning southern Brazilian weather. Author presents meteorological data from southern Brazil and Antarctica between 1973–75 that seems to support this assumption.

5400 Potencialidade e utilização da água subterrânea na bacia do Rio São José dos Dourados, sp. Sérgio Mezzalira et al. São Paulo: Governo do Estado de São Paulo, Secretaria da Agricultura, Coordenadoria da Pesquisa de Recursos Naturais, Instituto Geológico, 1979. 67 p.; 10 leaves of plates; ill. (Boletim—Governo do Estado de São Paulo, Instituto Geológico; no. 3)

An investigation of possible ground water use in the São José dos Dourados basin. The watershed, located in the northwest of São Paulo state, is a marginal area for agriculture without irrigation, especially during the long dry season. Study analyzes yield and quality of water in the Bauru formation aquifer in an effort to promote agroindustrial development in the region.

5401 Regionalização e urbanização. Organizadores, Jacob Binsztok e Roberto Levy Benathar. Capa, Eugênio Hirsch. Rio de Janeiro: Editora Civilização Brasileira, 1979. 172 p.; bibl. (Coleção Retratos do Brasil; v. 132)

A collection of seven articles focused on urbanization and regionalization. However, the diversity of the topics covered ranging from methodological tendencies in urban geography to decentralization of education, limits the usefulness of the volume.

5402 Riedel, Olvaldo Hugo Montenegro.
Nordeste: níveis e evolução recente da fecundidade feminina. Recife: Banco do Brasil, Departamento de Estudos Económicos do Nordeste, Gedur, 1977. 1 v.
Study of fertility in Northeast Brazil, based on the 1970 census. Regional vital statistics show that crude birth rates have increased in the last decade, and population growth continues to be high in both rural and urban areas.

5403 Rivière d'Arc, Hélène. La formation du lieu amazonie au XIXe siècle (CDAL, 18, 2. semestre, 1978, p. 183–213, bibl., maps)
Article demonstrates how and why Amazônia was integrated to Brazil despite the existence of centrifugal and separatist forces during the 19th century. Also discusses the principle of *uti possidetis*, as well as the shrewd diplomatic negotiations that were successfully carried out.

5404 Rizzini, Carlos Toledo. Tratado de fitogeografia do Brasil. v. 1, Aspectos ecológicos. v. 2, Aspectos sociológicos e florísticos. São Paulo: Editora de Humanismo, Ciência e Tecnologia *com a colaboração da* Universidade de São Paulo, 1976. 2 v.; bibl.; ill.; index.
Classification and description of Brazilian vegetation complexes divides them into 10 major phytogeographic regions.

5405 Ross, Eric B. The evolution of Amazon peasantry (JLAS, 10:2, 1980, p. 193–218)
The colonialist economy in Amazônia, based on the exploitation of natural resources, has led to the emergence of a production unit based on relatively isolated nuclear families that rely primarily on manioc as a source of subsistence.

5406 Saad, Edla Pacheco. Itapirapuã, a sesmaria e a cidade. Goiânia: Instituto Goiano do Livro, 1978. 163 p.; ill.
Historical sketches of a *município* of Goiás. Although poorly organized, the book provides data on the economy, politics, and society of small communities in Central Brazil.

5407 Salvia, Flávia La and Elisabeth Fichtner Marodin. Evolução municipal: uma análise geográfica (DRG/BG, 21:19, jan./dez. 1976, p. 3–16, bibl., maps, tables)

Synopsis of *município* evolution in Rio Grande do Sul. The number and aerial extent of *municípios* show major differences between the pastoral south and the agricultural north and Northeast.

Sampaio, Theodoro Fernandes. São Paulo no século XIX [i.e. dezenove] e outros ciclos históricos. See *HLAS 42:3552.*

5408 Santos, Carlos Nelson F. dos and Paulo Fernando Cavallieri. Como vai a pesquisa urbana brasileira? (Revista de Administração Municipal [Instituto Brasileiro de Administração Municipal, Rio de Janeiro] 27:154, jan./março 1980, p. 6–34, tables)
Summary of a report on urban research activities in Brazil. The report, based on investigations conducted by the Centro de Pesquisas Urbanas, Instituto Brasileiro de Administração Municipal, details the nature, relevance, and limitations of urban studies in 24 institutions, including government agencies and universities.

5409 São Paulo, Brazil (City). São Paulo, 1975–1979: a cidade, o habitante, a administração. São Paulo: Prefeitura do Município de São Paulo, 1979. 171 p.; bibl.; ill.; index.
Although published as a report of activities by a mayor of São Paulo, this profusely-illustrated book offers valuable basic information on the metropolis' contemporary characteristics.

5410 ——— (State). Secretaria de Economia e Planejamento. O programa nacional do álcool e a política de desenvolvimento urbano e regional. Governo do Estado de São Paulo, Secretaria de Economia e Planejamento. São Paulo: A Secretaria, 1976. 44 leaves; 3 fold. leaves of plates; maps (Série Documentos—Governo do Estado de São Paulo, Secretaria de Economia e Planejamento; 3)
Describes plan to decentralize the population growth and manufacturing capacity of Greater São Paulo. Its two objectives are: 1) to promote the growth of medium and small cities in the interior, and 2) to revitalize the agricultural sector, especially the cultivation of sugar cane and manioc to contribute to the National Alcohol Program.

5411 Sawyer, Donald R. Colonização da Amazônia: migração de nordestinos para uma frente agrícola no Pará (BNB/REN,

10:3, julho/set. 1979, p. 773–812, maps)

The colonization experience at Capitão Poço in northeast Pará state suggests that new land opening by small farmers can be successful if access to land, transportation, and markets are provided at the outset. Assistance in the form of special incentives, technical aid, and social infrastructures are not necessarily prerequisites in the early stages of settlement.

5412 Scaico, Marcos A. A baleia no Nordeste brasileiro (Horizonte [Universidade Federal de Paraíba, João Pessoa, Brazil] 3:7, abril/junho 1978, p. 177–187, bibl., tables)

Summary of whaling activities in Brazil and its effects on the whale population. The total catch monitored by the International Whaling Commission is not large, but it benefits a relatively large segment of low-income groups in the Northeast, where whale meat is consumed as *charque* and beef substitute.

5413 Seelenberger, Sérgio. Planejamento dos transportes urbanos (Revista de Administração Municipal [Instituto Brasileiro de Administração Municipal, Rio de Janeiro] 27:154, jan./março 1980, p. 36–41)

Consists of short and long-range proposals for urban transportation planning in the decade of 1980–90. In view of increasing cost of fossil fuel, priority should be given to developing integrated metropolitan mass transport systems, at the expense of automobiles. A number of novel ideas are proposed (e.g., land use and transport coordination, coordination by federal authorities, and integrated long-range development programs).

5414 Simpósio sôbre o Cerrado, 4th, Brasília, 1976. IV Simpósio sôbre o Cerrado: bases para utilização agropecuária. Coordenador: Mário G. Ferri. Apresentação de José Dion de Melo Teles. Nota de Wenceslau J. Goedert. São Paulo: Editora da Universidade de São Paulo [and] Livraria Itatiaia Editora, 1977. 405 p.; bibls.; maps; plates; tables (Coleção Reconquista do Brasil; 38)

Reflecting the increasing interest in, as well as exploitation of the *cerrado*, a number of symposia have been organized by the University of São Paulo. The present volume, composed of 23 articles, includes a state-of-the-art description of *cerrado* studies, as well as fundamental environmental information on crop and livestock raising.

5415 Simpósio sobre Política Urbana, 1st, Brasília, 1975. O homem e a cidade: simpósio sobre política urbana. v. 1/2. Coordenador-geral: Ney Lopes. Secretária-geral: Stella Prata da Silva Lopes. Brasília: Fundação Milton Campos, 1975. 2 v. (191, 599 p.)

Transcripts of urban symposium held in Brasília in Nov. 1975. The participants, legislators and social scientists, explore subjects such as the causes and processes of accelerated and uncoordinated urbanization, political and legal barriers to planned growth of cities, and possible solutions, to these problems.

5416 Smith, Nigel J.H. Anthrosols and human carrying capacity in Amazônia (AAG/A, 70:4, 1980, p. 553–556)

A review of theories and analysis of physical and chemical properties of black soil sites in Amazônia lead the author to conclude that their origins are anthropogenic. The black earth patches, termed *terra preta do indio*, indicate dense aboriginal population in the precolumbian period.

5417 Smith, Robert J. The ethnic Japanese in Brazil (The Journal of Japanese Studies [The Society for Japanese Studies, University of Washington, Seattle] 5:1, Winter 1979, p. 53–70, bibl.)

A well-balanced study of the Japanese and their descendants in Brazil. The article is useful as an introduction to the subject of Japanese immigration.

Stiel, Waldemar Corréa. História dos transportes coletivos em São Paulo. See *HLAS* 42:3757.

5418 Strang, Harold Edgard. Conservação do meio ambiente. Rio de Janeiro: Superintendência de Recursos Naturais e Meio Ambiente, 1977. 63 p.; ill. (Série Paulo de Assis Ribeiro; 3)

This short volume treats three topics: conservation of natural environment, ecology and conservation in the state of Guanabara, and world environmental conservation. The section on Guanabara offers some idea of environmental policies emerging in Brazil.

5419 Suarez, Maria Teresa S. de Melo. Cassacos e corumbas. São Paulo: Editora

Atica, 1977. 144 p.; bibl.; forms (Ensaios; 33)

A study of the *município* of Ribeirão in the Zona da Mata of Pernambuco as an example of an area where proletarization of rural workers is taking place. Provides interesting insights on the effects of economic and social structures in a sugarcane-growing area on regional migration patterns.

5420 Súarez-Villa, Luís. Distribuição ordem-tamanho, hierarquias de cidade pelo tamanho e o modelo de Beckmann: alguns resultados empíricos (IBGE/R, 41:4, out./dez. 1979, p. 117–216, bibl., maps, tables)

Empirical evaluation of hierarchy and order-size distribution of urban places according to Martin Beckman's model. By applying the model to Southeast Brazil, the author concludes that there is a mathematical relationship between the two functions.

5421 Tase, Norio and Masami Ichikawa. Salinization of surface water in Northeast Brazil (Annual Report of the Institute of Geoscience [University of Tsukuba, Japan] 6, 15 Oct. 1980, p. 41–43)

Brief analysis of fresh water quality in the semi-arid portions of Pernambuco, Paraíba, and Ceará.

Teles, José Mendonça. Vida e obra de Silva e Souza. See *HLAS 42:3557.*

5422 Thomas, Carmen. Conquista e povoamento do Rio Grande do Sul (DRG/BG, 21:19, jan./dez. 1976, p. 17–27, bibl., maps)

Informative summary of the settlement history of Rio Grande do Sul that distinguishes between the early Portuguese settlement sites and those of later European colonization. Well-illustrated with maps.

5423 Une, Mitiko Yanaga. Fatores climáticos influenciando a agricultura em Campo Grande (IBGE/R, 41:1/2, jan./junho 1979, p. 3–31, bibl., tables)

The scrubby savannas covering about one-third of the national territory, offer the most potential for agricultural expansion. Article analyzes climatic data from Campina Grande in order to determine the agricultural potential and limitations of *cerrados*. Although output of crops like sugarcane, manioc, maize, and beans show close correlations with rainfall, additional variables like soil chemistry, relief and water balance need to

be known so as to determine the region's potential.

5424 Valverde, Orlando. Recursos naturais e o equilíbrio das estruturas regionais. Rio de Janeiro: Superintendência de Recursos Naturais do Meio Ambiente, 1977. 38 p.; bibl.; ill. (Série Paulo de Assis Ribeiro; 7)

The oft-cited socioeconomic disparities between regions are influenced to a considerable extent by the ecological disequilibrium caused by humans. Using Minas Gerais as an example, Valverde reviews rural activities and their results, explaining the likely outcome of the rapid environmental deterioration taking place in various parts of Brazil.

5425 Vergara Filho, Otto. Investimento em rodovias e suas implicações no desenvolvimento: um estudo de caso da rodovia Rio-Bahia trecho Leopoldina-MG—Feira de Santana-BA (IBGE/RBE, 30:4, out./dez. 1976, p. 501–533, bibl., tables)

Analyzes the economic effects of a new highway construction project on the regional economy. Although the agricultural and processing sectors received the greatest impetus, economic effect tended to fluctuate with distance to major markets and access to highways.

5426 Vetter, David Michael; Rosa Maria Ramalho Massena; and Elza Freire Rodrigues. Espaço, valor da terra e eqüidade dos investimentos em infra-estrutura do município do Rio de Janeiro (IBGE/R, 41:1/2, jan./junho 1979, p. 32–71, bibl., tables)

A study in economic geography, attempting to demonstrate the influence of public, urban, infrastructural investments on the level and interpersonal distribution of income. Water and sewer investments in Rio de Janeiro between 1975–77 indicate that: 1) high-income areas were the major beneficiaries; 2) infrastructural improvements increased the value of properties; and 3) such valorization excluded the poor.

5427 Victor, Mauro. Raízes históricas do movimento conservacionista brasileiro (SBPC/CC, 31:6, junho 1979, p. 644–651)

Author traces the origins of Brazilian conservation movement to the indiscriminate and large-scale deforestation that began in the mid-19th century with the establishment of coffee plantations and railroad construction in the State of São Paulo.

5428 Webb, Kempton E. Developments in Brazilian geography during the twentieth century (*in* Studying Latin America: essays in honor of Preston E. James [see item **4358**] p. 177–194)

A tribute to Preston E. James by one of his best-known students. After briefly describing the development of geography in Brazil, Webb discusses James' activities and influence on Latin American geography, especially that of Brazil. The volume also provides concise information on trends in the field.

5429 Wesche, Rolf. A moderna ocupação agrícola em Rondônia (IBGE/R, 40:3/4, julho/dez. 1978, p. 233–247, ill., maps, table)

An insightful synthesis of recent colonization activities in the federal territory of Rondônia. After commenting briefly on land allocation techniques, author points out the main problems associated with land use (e.g., lack of locally-adapted agricultural system, difficulty of access to credits, and the absence of well-integrated conservation measures).

CARTOGRAPHY

ANDREW M. MODELSKI, *Bibliographer, Geography and Map Division, Library of Congress*

ALTHOUGH THE TOTAL NUMBER OF ENTRIES appearing in this volume of *HLAS* is comparable to that of the previous one the number of Latin American maps and atlases acquired by the Library of Congress declined sharply in this reporting period. Regrettably, the sharpest decrease occurred in accessions from Chile, previously one of the leading publishers of excellent cartographic works. However, high-quality publications continue to appear in most Latin American countries (e.g., Argentina, Brazil, Colombia, Ecuador, Mexico, Panama, and Venezuela). A welcome change in this volume is the increasing number of technical thematic cartography covering all aspects of the physical and socioeconomic landscape. Noteworthy examples are the following atlases: *Atlas Regional del Caribe* (item **5430**); *Atlas de Cuba* (item **5439**) and *Atlas Demográfico de Cuba* (item **5437**); *Atlas Geográfico del Ecuador* (item **5616**); *Atlas de El Salvador* (item **5477**); *Mapas y Planos de Santo Domingo* (item **5442**).

In the spirit of hemispheric cooperation and with a desire to assist in the economic and social development of the region, the member states of the Pan American Institute of Geography and History (PAIGH), Commission on Cartography is sponsoring the production and publication of a unified hemispheric map series at the scale 1 : 250,000. The series is scheduled for completion within an eight-year time period.

This project is of great significance to the development of the hemisphere, in that these maps produced will provide a unified topographic base on which development projects can be planned and natural resource and environmental information can be plotted. The program will contribute to future hemispheric development projects by providing a common topographic base of reference, which can be utilized by the organizations responsible for the execution or approval of such projects. The 1 : 250,000 scale is in accord with the depth of information available from earth resource satellites and the scale needed to study national and transnational development projects and problems.

The undertaking is a major effort of the PAIGH Commission on Cartography and the participating nations to contribute to the development of the hemisphere. The nations are contributing their resources towards the production of these maps, asking only that the subscriber cover the cost of printing and mailing.

THE CARIBBEAN
GENERAL

5430 Atlas regional del Caribe. Realizado por el Departamento de Geografía Económica del Instituto de Geografía de la Academia de Ciencias de Cuba. s.l.: Editorial Academia; La Habana; Editorial Científico-Técnica, 1979. 69 p.; maps; 33 x 54 cm.

Good thematic atlas defining the Caribbean region and displaying socioeconomic conditions.

5431 Hurricane tracking map, 1979 hurricane season: Caribbean region. s.l.: s.n., 1979. 1 map; 26 x 31 cm. Scale ca. 1 : 16,000,000.

Includes text and advertisements.

5432 Société nouvelle pétrole et affrètements. Caribbean area. Paris: Société nouvelle pétrole et affrètements, 1979. 1 map; 61 x 68 cm.

Legend in English and French. Shows petroleum shipping terminals and capacities of terminals. Includes distance lists and inset of Maracaibo Lake.

5433 Vega, Bernardo. Los cacicazgos de la Hispaniola. Edición al cuidado de José Chez Checo; portada de Nicolás Pichardo. Santo Domingo: Museo del Hombre Dominicano, 1980. 88 p.; 2 folded leaves of plates; maps (some col.); 19 x 22 cm. (Investigaciones antropológicas; no. 13)

Non-traditional explanation of the native chiefdoms of Hispaniola, through selected early maps.

THE BAHAMAS

5434 Great Britain. Directorate of Overseas Surveys. The Commonwealth of the Bahamas. Recompiled by the British Government's Ministry of Overseas Development, Directorate of Overseas Surveys from the *Atlas of the Commonwealth of the Bahamas*, and information supplied by the Department of Lands and Surveys, 1977. Nassau: Department of Lands and Surveys, 1978. 1 map: col.; 35 x 38 cm. Scale 1 : 2,300,000.

General map of the islands with depths shown by gradient tints. "Previously D.O.S. 954." Includes location map and inset of "New Providence Island."

5435 William G. Browning, Weaver, Inc., *Atlanta, Georgia*. Bahamas air navigation chart. Nassau: Bahamas Tourist Office, 1978. 1 map: col.; on sheet 76 x 86 cm. fold. to 25 x 18 cm. Scale ca. 1 : 1,000,000.

Data on this chart was obtained from the Department of Lands and Surveys and the Department of Civil Aviation and is current as of June 15, 1978. Includes text. Map of Bahamas with list of accommodations, text, directory of Bahamas Tourist Office, and col. ill. on verso.

CAYMAN ISLANDS

5436 Great Britain. Directorate of Overseas Surveys. Cayman Islands, visitors map. Prepared by D.O.S., 1978. Tolworth, Eng: Directorate of Overseas Surveys; Grand Cayman: Department of Tourism, 1979. 3 maps: col.; on sheet 79 x 99 cm. (Series D.O.S.; 428P) Scale 1 : 50,000.

Constructed from air photography flown for Cayman Islands Government by Meridian Airmaps Ltd., Oct. 1977. Includes text, maps of "George Town" and "Air communications," and location map.

CUBA

5437 Atlas demográfico de Cuba. República de Cuba, Comité Estatal de Estadísticas. La Habana: Instituto Cubano de Geodesia y Cartografía, 1979. 99 p.; col. ill.; maps; 33 cm.

Excellent population study of Cuba.

5438 Defense Mapping Agency. Aerospace Center. Cuba JPC-12. Prepared by DMAAC. St. Louis, Mo.: DMAAC, 1980. 1 map; col.; on sheet 44 x 56 cm. Scale 1 : 3,568,451.

Air navigation plotting chart.

5439 Instituto Cubano de Geodesia y Cartografía. Atlas de Cuba: XX aniversario del triunfo de la revolución cubana. La Habana: Instituto Cubano de Geodesia y Cartografía, 1978. 143, 25 p.; col. ill.; col. maps; 26 x 36 cm. Index.

Contents: Introducción; Mapas de la naturaleza y recursos; Mapas de la economía; Mapas de la población y cultura; Mapas de la historia; Mapa geográfico general.

5440 Petroconsultants. Cuba: synopsis 1978. Geneva, Switzerland: Petroconsultants, 1979. 1 map: 55 x 125 cm. Scale 1:1,000,000.

Map showing oil and gas leases with depths shown by contours. Includes statistical data and location map.

DOMINICA

5441 Great Britain. Directorate of Overseas Surveys. Dominica, Lesser Antilles. Prepared by the Government of the United Kingdom, Directorate of Overseas Surveys for the Government of Dominica. Tolworth, Eng.: The Directorate, 1979. 1 map: 101 x 56 cm. (Its D.O.S.; 2910) Scale 1:50,000.

Relief shown by contours, spot heights, and land form drawings. Includes indexed parish boundaries.

DOMINICAN REPUBLIC

5442 Mapas y planos de Santo Domingo. Emilio Rodríguez Demorizi, compilador; estudio preliminar y adiciones del Lic. Pedro J. Santiago. Santo Domingo: Editora Taller, 1979. xxiv, 371 p.; maps, plans; 36 cm. (Publicaciones—Fundación Rodríguez Demorizi; v. 13)

Reproductions of maps and plans from various sources, produced from 1493 to the 20th century. Bibliography: p. xxiii–xxiv. Includes indexes.

5443 Museo de las Casas Reales. Plano monumental de Santo Domingo: publicación del Museo de las Casas Reales, 1978. Santo Domingo: El Museo, 1978. 1 map: col.; 34 x 36 cm.

Monuments shown pictorially. Includes descriptive index to monuments. His-

torical text, descriptive list of monuments, and col. ill. on verso.

5444 República Dominicana, desarrollo regional de la línea noroeste. Santo Domingo: 1978. 4 maps; 48 x 59 cm. Scale 1:250,000.

Two maps show soils, forests, administrative and political boundaries.

5445 Santo Domingo. Universidad Autónoma. Instituto Geográfico Universitario. Duvergé, planos de ciudades, República Dominicana. Control por el IGU y el Inter American Geodetic Survey. Santo Domingo: 1978. 1 map: col.; 47 x 59 cm. Scale 1:5,000.

Topographic map of the city of Duvergé.

5446 ——. ——. ——. Plano de la ciudad de Santo Domingo: vias troncales, 1978. Santo Domingo: El Instituto, 1978. 1 map: col.; 40 x 49 cm. Scale 1:50,000.

Street guide to the metropolitan area.

5447 Turismap (firm). Puerto Plata: plano ciudad, guías turística (Tourist guide). Santo Domingo: Turismap, 1978? 1 map: col.; 34 x 45 cm.

Selected points of interest shown pictorially. Includes index to points of interest, indexed inset showing northern coast of Dominican Republic, and advertisements. Text, directories, distance list, and advertisements on verso.

5448 Vimenca Tours (firm). Metropolitan Santo Domingo. Santo Domingo: Vimenca, 1979? 1 map; 27 x 41 cm.

Includes indexed inset of "Old Santo Domingo" and indexes to points of interest, distance chart, and directory of Vimenca on verso.

GRENADA

5449 Great Britain. Directorate of Overseas Surveys. Grenada, island of spice. Ed. 3-D.O.S. 1979. St. George's, Grenada: Lands and Surveys Department, Office of the Prime Minister, 1979. 1 map: col.; on sheet 70 x 80 cm. (Its Seires; E703) (D.O.S.; 442) Scale 1:50,000.

Detailed topographic map with relief

shown by contours, shading, gradient tints, and spot heights. Includes text, indexed insets of "Southwest peninsula" and St. George's, inset of parish boundaries, location map.

HAITI

5450 Haiti. Institut haïtien de statistique. Section de cartographie. Departement de l'Ouest, Arrond. Arcahaie, Commune Duvalier-ville, Sect. rur. le boucassin. Port-au-Prince: Institut haïtien de statistique, 1978. 1 map; on sheet 46 x 58 cm. Scale 1 : 25,000.
Village location map for Le Boucassin.

5451 Imprimerie Henri Deschamps. République d'Haïti. Carte de la République d'Haïti realisée par les serves techniques de l'Imprimerie Henri Deschamps, d'après les données recueilliés d'organismes nationaux et internationaux. Port-au-Prince: l'Imprimerie, 1978. 1 map: col.; 49 x 67 cm. Scale 1 : 500,000.
General reference map of Haiti.

5452 Publicités Rossard. Haïti, plan-guide: carte d'Haïti, plan de Port-au-Prince et de Pétion-ville, historique et renseignments divers. Port-au-Prince: Rossard, 1980. 1 map: col.; 35 x 45 cm. Scale ca. 1 : 700,000.
Relief shown by hachures and spot heights. Includes indexed map of Pétionville, advertisements, and col. ill. Tourist information in French and English, indexed map of Port-au-Prince, and advertisements on verso.

5453 Rand McNally and Company. Haïti. Ed. du 1979. Chicago: Rand McNally; Port-au-Prince: Texaco, 1979. 1 map: col.; 44 x 61 cm. Scale ca. 1 : 700,000.
Road transportation map with relief shown by hachures and spot heights. French. Includes text and inset of "West Indies," in English, indexes, distance chart, and illustrations. Indexed map of "Port-au-Prince" and "Cap-Haïtien" on verso.

5454 Wah, M. Port-au-Prince City and Pétion-Ville guide map. Port-au-Prince: Nader's Art Gallery, 1978. 1 map; 40 x 27 cm.
Selected points of interest shown pictorially. Includes list of "Distances from a few places to Nader Art Galleries," index to points of interest.

JAMAICA

5455 General Drafting Company, Inc. Jamaica. Convent Station, N.J.: General Drafting Co.; Kingston, Jamaica: Esso Standard Oil, 1979. 1 map: col.; 45 x 72 cm. 11 cm. Scale 1 : 356,000.
Folded title: Discover Jamaica, road map. Relief shown by spot heights. Includes location map, distance chart, index, descriptive index to points of interest, and insets of "Ocho Rios and vicinity" and "Port Antonio." Maps of "Montego Bay," "Mandeville and vicinity," and "Spanish Town" and indexed map of "Kingston and Lower St. Andrew" on verso.

PUERTO RICO

5456 Editorial Cordillera. Mapa físico de Puerto Rico: Isla de Puerto Rico. Ed., Héctor E. Serrano. s.l.: 1980. 1 map: col.; 92 x 122 cm. Scale ca. 1 : 150,000.
Physical and reference map. Relief shown by gradient tints and spot heights. Depths shown by gradient tints. Includes four island insets. On verso: Mapa Político; Las Américas; América Central y el Caribe; Puerto Rico y los Países Vecinos.

5457 Goushá (H.M.) Company. Puerto Rico. Preparado en cooperación con la Administración Federal de Carreteras, Departamento de Transportación Federal. 1979 ed. San Jose, Calif.: H.M. Goushá Co., 1979. 1 map: col.; 56 x 95 cm. Scale ca. 1 : 300,000.
Official transportation map. Includes text, island inset, distance chart, and maps of Arecibo, Mayagüez, Ponce, Caguas, Carolina, and "Ruta de Lanchas." Map of San Juan with index to bus lines on verso.

5458 United States. Geological Survey. Hydrologic-data stations and hydrologic investigations in Puerto Rico and the U.S. Virgin Islands, as of June 1978. Department of the Interior, United States Geological Survey, in cooperation with the Commonwealth of Puerto Rico, Government of the U.S. Virgin Islands, and federal agencies. Reston, Va.: The Survey, 1979. 1 map: col.; 54 x 61 cm. Scale ca. 1 : 625,000.
Includes text, statistical data, island inset, and maps of Puerto Rico showing "Average annual precipitation" and "Average

annual runoff." Text and maps of Puerto Rico showing "Drainage areas developed for public water use," "Availability of ground water," and "Representative chemical analyses of surface water" on verso.

TRINIDAD AND TOBAGO

5459 Petroconsultants. Synopsis 1978 including current activity, Trinidad offshore. Geneva, Switzerland: Petroconsultants, 1979. 1 map; 55 x 83 cm. Scale 1: 500,000.

Map showing oil and gas leases covers Trinidad and Tobago. Includes "Summary of activity during 1978," "List of rightholders," statistical data, and index map.

VIRGIN ISLANDS

5460 Great Britain. Directorate of Overseas Surveys. Saint Christopher and Nevis, Lesser Antilles. Tolworth, Eng.: Directorate of Overseas Surveys; Basseterre, St. Kitts: Survey Division, Central Housing Authority, 1979. 1 map; col.; 79 x 78 cm. (Its Series; E703) (D.O.S.; 443) Scale 1: 50,000.

Detailed topographic map with relief shown by contours, shading, spot heights, and land form drawings. Includes indexed insets of "Parish boundaries" and "Brimstone Hill Fortress, St. Christopher," insets on Basseterre and Charlestown, text, and location map.

5461 Stephens, Ford. Chartsman's guide to the Virgin Islands. Tortola, British Virgin Islands: 1979. 1 map; col.; 64 x 97 cm. Scale 1: 100,000.

Sailing chart. Includes notes, descriptive index to points of interest, abbreviations, and four insets. Relief shown by contours and spot heights. Soundings in fathoms. "This chart has been photographically reproduced (and enlarged) from the NOS chart #25641, corrected to May 1978."

5462 United States. National Park Service. Virgin Islands. U.S. Department of the Interior. Washington: The Service, 1979. 1 map; col.; on sheet 33 x 36 cm. Scale ca. 1: 100,000.

National park guide with relief shown by spot heights. Includes text, descriptive points of interest, inset of Cruz Bay Village.

5463 Virgin Islands of the United States. Division of Tourism. St. Thomas/St. John. Charlotte Amalie: The Division, 1978. 4 maps: col.; on sheet 46 x 60 cm.

Tourist map.

CENTRAL AMERICA
BELIZE

5464 Great Britain. Army. 42d Survey Engineer Regiment. Stann Creek, Belize town plans. Produced by 42d Survey Engineer in 1978 from rectified air photography dated 1977. London: Director of Military Survey, Ministry of Defense, United Kingdom, 1979. 1 map: col.; 66 x 38 cm. (Its Series; E953) Scale ca. 1:5,000.

Photomap.

5465 ———. Directorate of Military Survey. Corozal, Belize town plans. Produced under the direction of the Director of Military Survey, Ministry of Defense, United Kingdom 1979; produced by 42d Survey Engineer Regiment in 1978 from rectified air photography dated 1977. London: HSMC, 1979. 1 map: col.; 58 x 78 cm. (Its Series; E953) Scale ca. 1:5,000.

Photomap. Indexed for points of interest.

5466 Petroconsultants S.A. Belize, synopsis 1979, including current activity. Geneva, Switzerland: Petroconsultants, 1979. 1 map: 63 x 67 cm.

Map showing oil and gas leases, depths shown by contours. At head of title: Foreign Scouting Service, April 1979. Includes "Geological sketch map of Belize," "List of rightholders," statistical data, and location map.

COSTA RICA

5467 Bergoeing G., Jean Pierre. Geomorfología, área del Cantón de Buenos Aires, Provincia de Puntarenas, Costa Rica. Dibujado y litografiado por el Instituto Geográfico Nacional, Ministerio de Obras Públicas y Transportes. San José: El Instituto, 1978. 1 map: col.; 31 x 24 cm. Scale 1: 200,000.

Geomorphology map of Buenos Aires Canton, Costa Rica.

5468 ———. Geomorfología de la cuenca media e interior del Río Tempisque, Provincia de Guanacaste, Costa Rica. Dibujado y litografiado por el Instituto Geográfico Nacional, Ministerio de Obras Públicas y Transportes. San José: El Instituto, 1978. 1 map: col.; 42 x 41 cm. Scale 1 : 200,000.

Geomorphology map of the Tempisque River watershed.

5469 Costa Rica. Dirección General de Aduanas. Costa Rica, mapa de zonas, jurisdicción aduanera. Ministerio de Hacienda. San José: La Dirección, 1979. 1 map: col.; 37 x 40 cm. Scale 1 : 1,000,000.

Customs administration map with relief shown by spot heights. Includes index to customs districts and inset of "Isla del Coco."

5470 ———. **Instituto Geográfico Nacional.** Ciudad de Golfito, Costa Rica. Preparado por el Instituto Geográfico Nacional, Ministerio de Obras Públicas y Transportes; colaboro el Servicio Geodésico Interamericano. San José: El Instituto, 1979. 1 map: col.; 48 x 60 cm. (Its Series; E961) Scale 1 : 10,000.

Detailed city plan with relief shown by contours and spot heights. Depths shown by contours and soundings. Includes index to points of interest and location map.

5471 ———. **Oficina del Café.** Café de Costa Rica, el mejor del mundo: mapa ilustrado de Costa Rica. Editado por Oficina del Café. San José: La Oficina, 1979. 1 map: col.; 61 x 76 cm.

Pictorial map. Includes statistical data, relief profile, inset of "Isla del Coco," and inset showing trade routes from Costa Rica.

5472 Ferrocarriles de Costa Rica. Ferrocarril interoceánico y ramales: Costa Rica. San José: Los Ferrocarriles, 1978. 1 map; 45 x 97 cm. Scale 1 : 250,000.

Railroad map, and profile of the main line.

5473 Instituto Costarricense de Turismo. Mapa turístico de Costa Rica. Dib., H. Cantillano A., A. Arguedas A. San José: Publicitaria Turística de C.A., 1978. 1 map: col.; 43 x 55 cm. Scale 1 : 800,000.

Relief shown by spot heights. Spanish and English. Includes three insets, col. ill., and advertisements. Descriptive index to points of interest, map of "Ciudad de San José" with descriptive index to points of interest, and keyed advertisements on verso.

5474 Pérez R., Samuel. Asociación de subgrupos de suelos de Costa Rica: mapa preliminar. San José: Oficina de Planificación, Sectorial Agropecuaria, 1978. 9 maps: col.; 49 x 71 cm. Scale 1 : 200,000.

Soil map with relief shown by contours and spot heights. Depths shown by contours. Includes boundary map and index map. Some sheets include compilation diagrams and insets.

5475 ———. Capacidad de uso del suelo: Costa Rica. San José: Oficina de Planificación, Sectorial Agropecuaria, 1978. 9 maps: col.; 49 x 71 cm. and 54 x 71 cm. Scale 1 : 200,000.

Soil use map with relief shown by contours and spot heights. Depths shown by contours. Includes boundary map and index map. Some sheets include compilation diagrams and insets.

5476 Petroconsultants S.A. Costa Rica, synopsis 1978. Geneva, Switzerland: Petroconsultants, 1979. 1 map; 54 x 61 cm.

Map showing oil and gas leases, depths shown by contours. At head of title: Foreign Scouting Service, April 1979. Includes table of "Costa Rica tests," statistical data, and location map.

EL SALVADOR

5477 Atlas de El Salvador. Ministerio de Obras Públicas, Instituto Geográfico Nacional Ing. Pablo Arnoldo Guzmán. San Salvador: El Instituto, 1979. 87 p.; 1 p. of plates; ill.; maps (some col.); 38 x 55 cm.

Good general atlas with physical, geological, mineral, hydrologic, climatic, ecological, and economic maps.

5478 El Salvador. Instituto Geográfico Nacional. Clases de tierras de acuerdo a su capacidad de uso, Departamento de La Paz, mapa básico. San Salvador, Ministerio de Agricultura y Ganadería, Dirección General de Recursos Naturales Renovables, Programa Determinación del Uso Potencial del Suelo, 1978. 1 map: col.; 50 x 49 cm. Scale 1 : 100,000.

Detailed soil map of the Department of La Paz.

5479 Holdridge, Leslie R. Mapa ecológico de El Salvador. Sistema de zona de vida del Dr. L.R. Holdridge; elaboraron, Joseph Tosi, Jr., Gary Hartshorn. San Salvador: Ministerio de Agricultura y Ganadería, Dirección General de Recursos Naturales Renovables, Programa Determinación del Uso Potencial del Suelo, 1978. 1 map: col.; 53 x 97 cm. Scale 1:300,000.

A detailed ecological map. Published jointly with Centro Agronómico Tropical de Investigación y Enseñanza, Subprograma Suelos Análogos de Centroamerica. Includes "Diagrama para la clasificación de zonas de vida."

5480 Instituto Geográfico Nacional Ingeniero Pablo Arnoldo Guzmán. Carta aeronáutica, República de El Salvador. En colaboración con la Dirección de Aeronáutica Civil de El Salvador y con el Servicio Geodésico Interamericano de los E.U.A. San Salvador: El Instituto, 1978. 1 map: col.; 34 x 58 cm. Scale 1:500,000.

Detailed air navigation chart. Relief shown by contours, gradient tints, shading, and spot heights.

5481 ———. Mapa oficial de la República de El Salvador. San Salvador: El Instituto, 1978. 1 map: col.; 79 x 145 cm. Scale 1:200,000.

General map with relief shown by shading and spot heights. Includes list of administrative divisions.

5482 ———. San Salvador y alrededores. Ministerio de Obras Públicas. 4. ed. San Salvador: El Instituto, 1979. 1 map: col.; 99 x 151 cm. Scale 1:15,000.

General reference map.

5483 Petroconsultants S.A. El Salvador, synopsis 1978. Geneva, Switzerland: Petroconsultants, 1979. 1 map: photocopy; 60 x 81 cm. Depths shown by contours.

Map showing oil and gas leases. Includes text, statistical data, "Designation of blocks and sub-blocks," and location map.

5484 United States. Central Intelligence Agency. El Salvador. Washington: The Agency, 1980. 1 map: col.; 27 x 44 cm.

General location map.

GUATEMALA

5485 Guatemala. Instituto Geográfico Nacional. Ciudad de Guatemala. Ministerio de Comunicaciones y Obras Públicas. Guatemala: El Instituto, 1979. 1 map: col.; 61 x 51 cm. Scale 1:25,000.

Detailed city plan of the metropolitan area.

5486 ———. ———. Mapa de cuencas de la República de Guatemala: identificación de cuencas principales y localización de estaciones hidrológicas y meteorológicas hasta diciembre 1973. Ministerio de Comunicaciones y Obras Públicas. Guatemala: El Instituto, 1978. 1 map: col.; 111 x 109 cm. on 4 sheets 58 x 58 cm. Scale 1:500,000.

Map showing watersheds, hydrological and meteorological stations.

5487 ———. ———. Mapa de la República de Guatemala. Guatemala: El Instituto, 1979. 1 map: col.; 57 x 56 cm. Scale 1:1,000,000.

General reference map.

5488 ———. ———. Mapa escolar de la República de Guatemala. Ministerio de Comunicaciones y Obras Públicas. Guatemala: El Instituto, 1978. 1 map: col.; 111 x 109 cm. on 4 sheets 58 x 58 cm. Scale 1:500,000.

Detailed reference map with relief shown by shading. Includes table of "Municipios de la República de Guatemala" and "Símbolos patrios," inset of "Ejemplos de accidentes geográficos en perspectiva," and relief profile of "Principales volcanes de Guatemala."

5489 ———. ———. Mapa hipsométrico de la República de Guatemala. Ministerio de Comunicaciones y Obras Públicas. 7. ed. Guatemala: El Instituto, 1979. 1 map on 4 sheets: col.; 111 x 108 cm., sheets 58 x 58 cm.

Good physical map.

5490 Rand McNally and Company. Guatemala. Chicago: Rand McNally; Guatemala: Texaco, 1979. 1 map: col.; 63 x 46 cm. fold. to 23 x 11 cm. Scale ca. 1:1,200,000.

Road map.

HONDURAS

5491 Instituto Geográfico Nacional. Mapa general, República de Honduras. Ministerio de Comunicaciones, Obras Públicas y Transporte. 8. ed. Tegucigalpa: El Instituto, 1980. 1 map: col.; 45 x 71 cm. Scale 1:1,000,000.
Detailed reference map.

5492 ———. Tegucigalpa: Ciudad Tegucigalpa. Tegucigalpa: El Instituto, 1978. 1 map: col.; 63 x 60 cm. Scale 1:12,500.
Detailed city plan.

5493 Instituto Hondureño de Turismo. San Pedro Sula. Cortesia del Instituto Hondureño de Turismo. Tegucigalpa: Secretaria de Cultura y Turismo, 1978? 1 map: col.; 37 x 31 cm.
Includes inset of central city. Text in Spanish and English and indexes on verso.

5494 Petroconsultants. Honduras: synopsis 1978. Geneva, Switzerland: Petroconsultants, 1979. 1 map; 62 x 125 cm. Scale 1:1,000,000.
Map showing oil and gas leases.

5495 Rand McNally and Company. Honduras. Chicago: Rand McNally; San Pedro Sula, Honduras: Texaco, 1979. 1 map: col.; 44 x 61 cm. Scale ca. 1:1,150,000.
Relief shown by shading and spot heights. Includes text, index, distance chart, and col. ill. Insets: Tegucigalpa-Comayagüela; San Pedro Sula; La Ceiba; Isla Santanilla o de el Cisne. Indexed map of "Central America" with legend and text in Spanish and English, and distance chart on verso.

NICARAGUA

5496 Instituto Geográfico Nacional. San Juan del Sur, pictomapa de ciudad. Preparado por IGN y el Inter American Geodetic Survey; compilación 1977. Managua: IGN, 1979. 1 map: col.; 48 x 70 cm. (Its Serie; EO51) Scale 1:5,000.
Topographic reference map of the city.

5497 Nicaragua. Dirección General de Caminos. Red vial de Nicaragua. Ministerio de Obras Públicas. Managua: La Dirección, 1978. 1 map; 44 x 50 cm. Scale ca. 1:1,100,000.
General road map.

5498 ———. Plan Regulador de Managua. Plano básico regional de Managua. Oficina Nacional de Urbanismo, Ministerio de Obras Públicas y Ministerio del Distrito Nacional. Dibujo, G.J. Castillo. Managua: El Plan, 1978. 1 map; on sheet 65 x 107 cm. Scale 1:27,500.
General reference map.

5499 Petroconsultants S.A. Synopsis 1978, including current activity, Nicaragua. Geneva, Switzerland: Petroconsultants, 1979. 1 map; 53 x 97 cm.
Depths shown by contours. Map showing oil and gas leases. Includes "List of rightholders," table of "Summary of activity during 1978," statistical data, and location map.

5500 United States. Central Intelligence Agency. Nicaragua. Washington: The Agency, 1979. 1 map: col.; 39 x 42 cm. Scale 1:1,500,000.
Reference map showing relief by shading and spot heights. Includes location map, comparative area map, graph of "Ethnic composition," and maps of "Population," "Economic activity," and "Land utilization and vegetation."

PANAMA

5501 Instituto Geográfico Nacional Tommy Guardia. Mapa oficial de la República de Panamá, división político-administrativa. Panamá: El Instituto, 1979. 1 map: col.; 36 x 66 cm. Scale 1:1,000,000.
Administrative and general reference map.

5502 ———. República de Panamá. Ministerio de Obras Públicas. Ed. 6. Panamá: El Instituto, 1980. 1 map: col.; 26 x 56 cm. Scale ca. 1:1,170,000.
General reference map. Map of "Ciudad de Panamá," map of Panama showing population data, distance diagr., and tables of statistical data on verso.

5503 Petroconsultants S.A. Panama, synopsis 1979, including activity. Geneva, Switzerland: Petroconsultants, 1980. 1 map; 54 x 82 cm.
Map showing oil and gas leases. Includes "Geological sketch map of Panama," "List of rightholders," table of "Summary of

activity during 1979," "Key to wildcats," statistical data, and location map.

MEXICO

5504 Asociación Nacional Automovilística. Carta geográfica de México. 10. ed. México: ANA, 1980. 1 map: col.; 84 x 116 cm. Scale ca. 1 : 2,550,000.

Popular road and reference map. Includes inset of Mexico City region. Distance chart in accompanying index. Accompanied by: Carta geográfica de México: índice general de poblaciones y pueblos.

5505 Atlas geográfico del Estado de Michoacán. México: EDDISA, 1979. General reference atlas of the state.

5506 Automobile Club of Southern California. Baja California. Los Angeles: The Club, 1979. 1 map: col.; on sheet 108 x 45 cm. Scale ca. 1 : 800,000.

Relief shown by shading and spot heights. Includes text, distance chart, and index. Insets: Tijuana; Ensenada; Mexicali; La Paz.

5507 Cámara Nacional de Comercio de Monterrey. Monterrey. Monterrey, México: La Camara, 1980. 1 map: col.; on sheet 22 x 33 cm.

Tourist guide map.

5508 La Ciudad de México 1520. México: Mapoteca Manuel Orozco Y Berra, Dirección General del Servicio Meteorológico Nacional, 1978. 1 map; on sheet 41 x 56 cm.

Reproduction of the famous rare original. "La impresión original de este mapa se encuentra en la Mapoteca 'Manuel Orozco y Berra' de la Dirección General del Servicio Meteorológico Nacional. La investigación bibliográfica estuvo a cargo de Cristina Treviño Urquijo de Soto." Outline map redrawn on verso for locating placenames.

5509 Editorial Cartográfica Flecha. Plano de la ciudad de México. México: Librería Patria, 1980. 1 map: col.; 93 x 64 cm. Scale ca. 1 : 32,500.

Tourist guide map of the metropolitan area.

5510 Esparza Torres, Héctor F. Chiapas. México: Librería Patria, 1979? 1 map: col.; 47 x 67 cm. (Serie Patria; 7) Scale 1 : 900,000.

Includes text, index, tourist information, distance chart, maps of "Extraordinaries [sic] places, beauty's [sic] Chiapas State" and "'Palenque' and vicinity," and indexed maps of "Palenque archaeological city."

5511 ———. Chihuahua. México: Librería Patria, 1979? 1 map: col.; 67 x 46 cm. (Serie Patria; 8) Scale 1 : 300,000.

Includes text, index, distance lists, tourist information, distance chart, indexed maps of Chihuahua City, Ciudad Juárez, and "Municipalities border at Chihuahua City" on verso.

5512 ———. Colima. México: Librería Patria, 1979? 1 map: col.; 46 x 67 cm. (Serie Patria; 6)

Includes text, index, tourist information, distance chart, map of "Bahia de Manzanillo," and indexed map of Colima City, central Colima, and Manzanillo on verso.

5513 ———. Quintana Roo. México: Librería Patria, 1979. 1 map: col.; 67 x 46 cm. (Seria Patria; 22)

Includes text, index, distance lists, tourist information, distance chart, and indexed maps of Cancún, central Cancún, Cozumel, central Cozumel, Chetumal, central Chetumal, Mujeres Island, and Isla Mujeres City on verso.

5514 ———. República Mexicana, mapa general de carreteras. México: Librería Patria, 1979? 1 map: col.; 54 x 75 cm. fold to 24 x 12 cm. (Serie Patria) Scale 1 : 4,000,000.

Includes index, equivalency chart, distance chart, and col. ill. of road signs. Indexed maps of Mexico City region and Mexico City metropolitan area and maps of Guadalajara, Oaxaca, and Mérida on verso.

5515 ———. Veracruz. México: Librería Patria, 1979. 1 map: col.; 83 x 54 cm. (Serie Patria; 29) Scale 1 : 1,000,000.

Includes text, index, inset of Veracruz City region, tourist information, distance chart, indexed maps of Jalapa, Veracruz City, and Orizaba region.

5516 Gastil, R. Gordon and Daniel Krummenacher. A reconnaissance geologic map of the west-central part of the state of Nayarit, Mexico. Boulder, Colo.: Geological Society of America, 1978. 1 map: col.; 52 x 41 cm. Scale 1 : 200,000.

Detailed surface geology map and profiles.

5517 **Gómez Leal, Arturo.** Plano de la
     ciudad de Monterrey, México. 2o. ed.
Monterrey: 1980. 1 map: col.; 45 x 68 cm.
Scale: 1:38,500.
     General reference and guide map.

5518 **Goushá (H.M.) Company.** Mexico.
     Compliments of Seguros La Provin-
cial, S.A. San Jose, Calif.: 1980. 1 map: col.;
39 x 67 cm. Scale ca. 1:5,448,960.
     General road map. On verso with in-
dexes: Central Mexico City; Metropolitan
Mexico City; Guadalajara; Downtown Guadalajara; Monterrey; Downtown Monterrey;
Cuernavaca; Downtown Cuernavaca.

5519 ———. Northwestern Mexico. Com-
     pliments of Sanborn's. San Jose, Calif.:
H.M. Gousha Co., 1979. 1 map: col.; 26 x 20
cm. Scale ca. 1:5,448,960.
     Road map locating "Sanborn's" author
insurance offices.

5520 **Guía Roji, S.A.** Ciudad de México.
     México: Guía Roji, 1980. 1 map: col.;
118 x 83 cm. Scale 1:32,500.
     Postal zone and guide map.

5521 ———. Estado de Jalisco. México:
     Guía Roji, 1980. 1 map: col.; 56 x 56
cm. Scale 1:800,000.
     General reference and guide map.

5522 ———. México. México: Guía Roji,
     1980. 1 map: col.; 53 x 64 cm. Scale
1:400,000.
     General reference and guide map.

5523 ———. Monterrey. México: Guía Roji,
     1980. 1 map: col.; 62 x 86 cm. Scale
1:32,500.
     Guide map of metropolitan Monterrey.

5524 ———. Yucatan. México: Guía Roji,
     1980. 1 map: col.; 50 x 70 cm. Scale
1:600,000.
     General reference and guide map.

5525 **México. Comisión Nacional de los Sa-
     larios Mínimos.** Estados Unidos Mexi-
canos, zonas económicas para la fijación de
los salarios mínimos 1977: división municipal por zonas económicas actualizado a
diciembre de 1977. México: La Comisión, 1978. 1 map; 55 x 88 cm. Scale ca.
1:4,000,000.
     Map showing distribution of income.

5526 ———. Dirección General de Análise
     de Inversiones. Mapa turístico de ca-

rreteras: México (Tourist road map). Secretaría de Asentamientos Humanos y Obras
Públicas. México: La Secretaria, 1979. 1 map:
col.; 68 x 94 cm.
     Includes inset of Mexico City region,
diagr. of "Approximate driving time," distance chart, and index. Tourist information
on verso.

5527 ———. Dirección General de Estudios
     del Territorio Nacional. Carta topo-
gráfica: Estados Unidos Mexicanos. México:
Secretaría de Programación y Presupuesto,
Coordinación General del Sistema Nacional
de Información, 1978. 4 maps: col.; 111 x 132
cm. Scale 1:1,000,000.
     Excellent topographical map. "Proyec-
ción cónica conforme de Lambert." Relief
shown by contours and spot heights. North
sheet includes compilation diagram and index map.

5528 ———. Dirección General de Minas.
     Plantas de beneficio instaladas en la
República Mexicana. Secretaría de Patrimonio y Fomento Industrial, Subsecretaría
de Minas y Energía. Ed. sept. de 1978. México: La Dirección, 1979. 1 map: col.; 31 x 44
cm.
     Shows location of minerals and capac-
ity of mines. List of concessions on verso.
Accompanied by list of concessions.

5529 ———. Principales centros mineros
     productores de oro, plata, plomo, cobre
y zinc, con datos de producción de 1978:
México. Secretaría de Patrimonio y Fomento
Industrial, Subsecretaría de Minas y Energía.
México: La Direccioín, 1979. 1 map: col.; 31
x 45 cm.
     Mines and mineral resources. Statis-
tical data of "Producción por municipios
durante los años 1977–1978" on verso. Accompanied by: "Producción por municipios
durante los años 1977–1978.

5530 **Mirafuentes Galván, José Luis** and **Ar-
     turo Soberón Mora.** Mapas y planos
antiguos de Colima y del occidente de México, 1521–1904. Peña Colorado: Consorcio
Minero Benito Juárez, 1978. 239 p.; maps; 32
x 45 cm. (Colección Peña Colorada)
     Facsimile maps with historical text.

5531 **Nuevo León, México. Dirección Esta-
     tal y Delegación Federal de Turismo.**
Inventario turístico del Estado de Nuevo
León. Monterrey: 1980. 1 map; 27 x 21 cm.

Shows major roads. Includes location map. Tourist information on verso.

5532 Petróleo Internacional. Mapa petrolero de México, 1980. Compilado y editado por Petróleo Internacional y *Oil & Gas Journal.* Tulsa, Okla.: Petroleum Pub. Co., 1979. 1 map: col.; on sheet 56 x 59 cm.

Includes two insets of Tabasco region, inset of Baja California.

5533 Petroleum Publishing Co. Mexican oil and gas at a glance. Compiled and edited by *Oil & Gas Journal.* Tulsa, Okla.: Petroleum Pub. Co., 1979. 1 map: col.; on sheet 56 x 58 cm.

Originally published by the author in *Oil & Gas Journal* (77 : 34, 1979).

5534 United States. Central Intelligence Agency. Mexico, consular districts, January 1, 1979. Washington: Central Intelligence Agency, 1979. 1 map: col.; 17 x 24 cm. Scale ca. 1 : 12,500,000.

SOUTH AMERICA
GENERAL

5535 Bartholomew (John) and Son, Ltd. South America. Edinburgh: Bartholomew, 1978. 1 map: col.; 86 x 61 cm. (Bartholomew world travel series) Scale 1 : 10,000,000.

Cover title: World travel map, America, South. Lambert azimuthal equal area projection. Relief shown by gradient tints and spot heights. Depths shown by gradient tints. Inset; Galapagos Islands. List of points of interest in cover.

5536 Commission for the Geological Map of the World. Tectonic map of South America. Produced by Ministry of Mines and Energy, National Department of Mineral Production (Brazil); with the collaboration of UNESCO; coordinator general, Fernando Flávio Marques de Almeida. Aerofotogramétricos Cruzeiro do Sul S.A. Brasília: The Department, 1978. 1 map: col.; 152 x 114 cm. on 2 sheet 83 x 118 cm. Scale 1 : 5,000,000.

Compilation and interpretation (1974) based on documents presented and discussed at several international meetings, with the participation of delegates from geological services of South American countries. Biopolar oblique conformal conic projection. Relief

shown by spot heights. Depths shown by contours and soundings. Geographic basis: Map of South America, scale 1 : 5,000,000 of the American Geographical Society of New York (1955), simplified. Accompanied by text in English, Spanish, Portuguese, and French: Tectonic map of South America, explanatory note.

5537 Cook, Hammond & Kell Ltd. The Oilman: South American oil and gas map, 1979. London: Maclean-Hunter, 1979. 1 map: col.; 87 x 118 cm. Scale ca. 1 : 8,000,000.

Map showing oil and gas leases, pipelines, and refineries. Includes six insets and advertisements.

5538 Geographic International Inc. South America. Montreal: Geographic International, 1980. 1 map: col.; 95 x 67 cm. Scale 1 : 9,000,000.

A good general map on Lambert's azimuthal equal area projection. Relief shown by spot heights. Insets: Galapagos Islands (Archipiélago de Colón); Central America and the Caribbean; Panama Canal.

5539 Kümmerly and Frey, *Bern.* Südamerika. Bern, Switzerland: 1980. 1 map: col.; 114 x 76 cm. fold in cover 24 x 14 cm. Scale 1 : 8,000,000.

General map with cover title: Südamerika, Kontinentkarte mit Länderlexikon. Relief shown by shading and spot heights. Legend in six languages. "No. 4251." Includes two insets.

5540 National Geographic Society. Cartographic Division. South America. Richard J. Darley, chief cartographer. Washington, D.C.: The Society, 1980. 1 map: col.; 145 x 108 cm. Scale 1 : 5,540,000.

General reference map with relief shown by shading and spot heights. Depths shown by bathymetric tints and soundings. Includes lists of geographical equivalents and abbreviations.

5541 Philip (George) and Son, Ltd. South America. London: London Geographical Institute, 1978. 1 map: col.; 174 x 114 cm. on 2 sheets 95 x 117 cm. (Philips' series of physical large school maps) Scale 1 : 6,000,000.

Projection: Lambert's equidistant azimuthal. Relief shown by gradient tints, shading, and spot heights. Depths shown by gradient tints. Inset shows political map of South America.

5542 Touring y Automóvil Club del Perú. Departamento de Cartografía. Ruta Panamericana, Caracas-Lima-Buenos Aires. Lima: El Club, 1979. 1 map: col.; 56 x 22 cm. Scale ca. 1:10,000,000.

Route map of the Panamerican highway. Relief shown by spot heights. Text and table of time and distance on verso.

ARGENTINA

5543 Argentina. Subsecretaría de Turismo. Argentina: todos los climas y bellezas del mundo. Secretaría de Estado de Deportes y Turismo, Subsecretaría de Turismo. Buenos Aires: La Subsecretaría, 1978. 1 map: col.; 46 x 31 cm. Scale 1:8,500,000.

Informative tourist map with relief shown by gradient tints and spot heights. Depths shown by gradient tints. Spanish and English. Includes inset of "Territorio Nacional de la Tierra del Fuego, Antártida e Islas del Atlántico sur," list of "Distance and air timetables," index to points of interest, col. ill.; and location map.

5544 Auto Mapa (firm). Buenos Aires. Buenos Aires: Auto Mapa, 1979. 1 map: col.; on sheet 38 x 54 cm. fold. to 10 x 14 cm. Scale 1:50,000.

Detailed city map. Folded title: Capital Federal, plano guía: guía de calles, transportes. Includes tables of "Líneas de colectivos." Map of "Subterráneos" and index on verso.

5545 ————. Provincia de Buenos Aires. Buenos Aires: Editorial Automapa, 1979. 1 map: col.; on sheet 80 x 58 cm. Scale 1:1,100,000.

Road map with inset of "La Plata" and location map. Maps of "Accesos," "Bahía Blanca" "Zona Atlántica, San Clemente del Tuyú-Necochea," and "Zona Atlántica, Necochea-Bahía Blanca" and indexed map of the "Mar del Plata" on verso.

5546 ————. Rutas de la República Argentina. Dirección, Mario Borio. Buenos Aires: Editorial Automapa, 1979. 1 map: col.; on 2 sheets 58 x 80 cm. Scale 1:2,000,000.

Detailed road map printed on both sides of sheet. Relief shown by spot heights.

Includes text, index map, inset, and maps of "Accesos," "Islas Malvinas," and "Argentina (con proyección hasta el Polo)."

5547 Automóvil Club Argentino. Area de Cartografía Vial y Turística. Mendoza, Argentina. Dibujó Juan C. Corso. Buenos Aires: El Club, 1979. 1 map: col.; 69 x 48 cm. (Publicación; 691) Scale ca. 1:1,000,000.

Relief shown by shading and spot heights. Includes index, distance chart, distance list, location map, and col. ill. Text, maps of Mendoza and San Rafael with indexes to points of interest on verso.

5548 ————. ————. Provincia de Catamarca. Buenos Aires: El Club, 1979. 1 map: col.; 50 x 43 cm.

Relief shown by shading and spot heights. Includes inset of Catamarca city region, location map. Text, index, distance map, map of "San Fdo. del Ve. de Catamarca" with index to points of interest, and color illustration on verso.

5549 ————. ————. Provincia de La Pampa. Buenos Aires: El Club, 1979. 1 map: col.; 45 x 43 cm. (Publicación; 696) Scale ca. 1:1,100,000.

General map with relief shown by shading and spot heights. Includes distance chart, location map, and color illustration. Text, maps of Santa Rosa and General Pico with indexes to points of interest on verso.

5550 ————. División Cartografía Vial y Turística. República Argentina, red caminera principal. Dibujó, Juan C. Corso. Buenos Aires: El Club, 1980. 1 map: col.; 98 x 59 cm. (Publicación; 710) Scale 1:4,000,000.

Relief shown by shading. Depths shown by gradient tints. Includes three insets. Text, index, map of "Esquema de distancias," map showing distances from Buenos Aires, and directories of Automovil Club Argentino's lodgings, recreational facilities, and automobile service station on verso.

5551 Borrello, Angel V. Mapa geotectónico de la República Argentina. Buenos Aires: Servicio Geológico Nacional, 1978. 1 map: col.; 163 x 84 cm. on 2 sheets 89 x 114 cm. and 87 x 114 cm. Scale 1:2,500,000.

Geological map showing relief by spot heights. Inset: Territorio Nacional de la Tierra del Fuego, Antártida e Islas del Atlántico Sur.

5552 Buenos Aires (province), *Argentina*. **Dirección de Geodesia. División Cartografía.** Provincia de Buenos Aires, referencias cartográficas de la Conquista del Desierto. Buenos Aires: La Dirección, 1979. 1 map: col.; 101 x 72 cm. Scale 1 : 1,000,000.

Historical map with relief shown by shading. "Las referencias históricas han sido volcadas sobre un mapa con el actual estado físico, cultural y político, por considerar instructivo el conocimiento de los parajes en que se desarrollaron las acciones de la conquista del desierto, en relación a los lugares del presente acontecer." Includes location map and list of partidos.

5553 Córdoba (province), *Argentina*. **Secretaría de Estado de Minería y Recursos Naturales no Renovables.** Córdoba, mapa orohidrográfico y político. Córdoba: La Secretaría, 1979. 1 map; 129 x 79 cm. Scale 1 : 500,000.

General map showing drainage system for the province of Córdoba.

5554 Ediciones Cartográficas Pedersen. República Argentina, red caminera principal. Guía de rutas-mapas. Buenos Aires: Pedersen, 1979. 1 map: col.; 106 x 70 cm. Scale ca. 1 : 3,700,000.

Detailed route map with a distance list and seven insets. Includes 35 route maps on verso.

5555 Ediciones Cicerone. Plano general de la Ciudad de La Plata: zonas adyacentes Ensenada, Berisso, Villa Elisa, Ringuelet, Melchor Romero. Buenos Aires: Cicerone, 1979? 1 map; 63 x 50 cm.

General city map of the metropolitan area of La Plata.

5556 Ildefonso V. Torres (firm). Nuevo plano general de la zona de Pilar. Buenos Aires: Ildefonso V. Torres, 1979. 1 map; 85 x 138 cm. Scale 1 : 5,000.

Real property map.

5557 ———. Nuevo plano general de la zona Vicente López, San Isidro, San Fernando. Buenos Aires: Ildefonso V. Torres, 1979. 1 map; 96 x 150 cm. Scale 1 : 10,000.

Map of Buenos Aires, its suburbs and environs. Includes cadastral information.

5558 Mapa de ferrocarriles en Argentina. Buenos Aires: s.n., 1979. 1 map; 99 x 67 cm.

Railroad map with insets of Rosario y alrededores; Southern Argentina; Buenos Aires y alrededores.

5559 Mario Menconi, E. Mapa físico político, Provincia de Buenos Aires. 13. ed. Buenos Aires: Editorial Mapa, 1979. 1 map: col.; 98 x 64 cm. Scale 1 : 1,000,000.

Administrative map with relief shown by shading and spot heights. Includes inset of "Alrededores de Buenos Aires," location map, and distance list. Accompanied by index: Plano de Buenos Aires, guía suplementaria, información general (7 p.).

5560 Peuser (Jacobo) Ltda., S.A. *Buenos Aires.* Guía Peuser, para el turista: Buenos Aires. Nueva ed. Buenos Aires: Editorial Circulación Latinoamericana, 1979. 1 map: col.; 44 x 52 cm. Scale 1 : 40,000.

Includes text, inset, index of transit routes, maps of "Buses in the city" and "No cars," and advertisements. Map of "Guía Peuser, combinaciones de subterráneos y colectivos" and advertisements on verso. Map of "Red de subterráneos" on cover. Accompanied by indexes: "Guía Peuser de la Capital Federal y alrededores, año 93 no. 809 marzo–abril: colectivos y calles actualizadas con la guía de subtes."

5561 Santa Fe (city), *Argentina*. **Dirección de Planeamiento Urbano y Proyectos.** Santa Fe, Argentina. Santa Fe: La Dirección, 1979? 1 map; on sheet 76 x 68 cm. Scale 1 : 20,000.

Detailed city map with relief shown by contours.

5562 Sediment isopach map, Argentine continental margin, Argentine shelf, Argentine Basin, Falkland Plateau. W.J. Ludwig et al. Illustrator, Virginia Rippon. Tulsa, Okla.: American Association of Petroleum Geologists, 1978. 1 map: col.; 85 x 116 cm.

Technical map showing marine sediments. Depths shown by contours. Includes text and bibliography.

BOLIVIA

5563 Bolivia. Programa del Satélite Tecnológico de Recursos Naturales. Fajas mineralizadas de los Andes bolivianos. ERTS—COMIBOL—Observatorio San Calixto; Dirección, Carlos Brockmann H. y

Ramón Cabré S.J.; preparado por, Hernán Claure V., Estela Minaya R.; control cartográfico y dirección separación a colores, Oscar Torrez W.; grabado y separación a colores, Eduardo Pacheco A. La Paz: El Programa, 1979. 1 map: col.; 102 x 72 cm. Scale 1 : 1,000,000.

Detailed map showing mines and mineral resources of the Bolivian Andes compiled from LANDSAT photography.

5564 ———. ———. Lineamientos y cuerpos intrusivos de los Andes bolivianos. Organizado, ejecutado y preparado por el Programa ERTS—GEOBOL en colaboración con COMIBOL y el Observatorio San Calixto; dirección, Carlos Brockmann H. y Ramón Cabré S.J.; preparado por Hernán Claure V., Estela Minaya R.; control cartográfico y dirección separación a colores, Oscar Torrez W.; grabado y separación a colores, Eduardo Pacheco A. La Paz: El Programa, 1979. 1 map: col.; 102 x 72 cm. Scale 1 : 1,000,000.

Detailed structural geology of the Bolivian Andes compiled from LANDSAT photography.

5565 ———. ———. Mapa de cobertura y uso actual de la tierra, Bolivia. ERTS-Bolivia, Programa del Satélite Tecnológico de Recursos Naturales. Dirección, Carlos E. Brockmann H.; preparado por Rubén Zeraín P., Reinaldo Oroz E., Jorge Córdova G. La Paz: El Programa, 1978. 1 map: col.; 168 x 142 cm on 4 sheets 106 x 77 cm. Scale 1 : 1,000,000.

Detailed land-use map compiled from LANDSAT photography.

5566 ———. ———. Mapa de complejos de tierra: estudio integrado de recursos naturales del Oriente Boliviaro. Autores, Carlos E. Brockmann H., director Programa ERTS et al.; cartografía y separación a colores, Oscar Torrez W.; dirección, Estela Pinto M.; operación, Eduardo Pacheco A., colaboración. La Paz: Programa ERTS, 1979. 1 map: col.; 168 x 143 cm on 4 sheets 91 x 77 cm. (Serie; 7331) Scale 1 : 1,000,000.

Detailed soil map compiled from LANDSAT photography.

5567 ———. ———. Metalogénesis de los Andes bolivianos, relación con la placa de Nazca. Organizado y preparado por el Programa ERTS-GEOBOL en colaboración de COMIBOL y el Observatorio San Calixto. Dirección, Carlos E. Brockmann H. y Ramón Cabré S.J.; preparado por Hernán Claure V. y Estela Minaya R.; dirección cartografía y separación a colores, Oscar Torrez W.; grabado y operación separación a colores, Eduardo Pacheco A. La Paz: El Programa, 1979. 1 map: col.; 102 x 72 cm. Scale 1 : 1,000,000.

Detailed map showing ore deposits in the Bolivian Andes compiled from LANDSAT photography.

5568 Comisión Mixta Peruana Boliviana. Lago Titicaca. Servicio de Hidrografía Naval, Bolivia, Dirección de Hidrografía y Navegación de la Marina, Armada Peruana. Lima: 1979. 1 map: col.; 73 x 77 cm. (Its Carta; no. 3,000) Scale 1 : 250,000.

Hydrographic chart with relief shown by form lines and spot heights. Depths shown by contours, gradient tints, and soundings.

5569 Corporación Regional de Desarrollo de Cochabamba. Mapa del Departamento de Cochabamba, guía-política, vial e hidrográfico. Dirigido por Fructuoso Orellana; dibujado por Alfredo García P. Cochabamba, Bolivia: La Corporación, 1979. 1 map; 166 x 130 cm. on 2 sheets 102 x 141 cm. Scale 1 : 250,000.

General map including table of administrative divisions.

5570 Guarachi Roca, Mario. Guía Gráfica de la ciudad de La Paz, Bolivia. s.l.: The Author, 1980. 1 map: col.; 56 x 91 cm.

Indexed city map with relief shown by hachures.

5571 ———. Guía gráfica de turismo: Titikaka, La Paz, Yungas, República de Bolivia. La Paz, Bolivia: IBT, 1979. 1 map: col.; 49 x 70 cm. Scale 1 : 500,000.

Lake Titicaca region of Peru and Bolivia. Relief shown pictorially and by gradient tints, shading, and spot heights. Includes notes, distance list, indexed "Plano turístico de la ciudad de La Paz."

5572 Martínez, C. Carte structurale des Andes septentrionales de Bolivia. Dressée en 1976 par C. Martínez et P. Tomasi; Service Cartographique de l'O.R.S.T.O.M., M. Danard, 1978. Paris: Office de la recherche scientifique et technique outre-mer, 1978. 1 map: col.; 72 x 91 cm. fold. in cover 24 x 16 cm. (Notice explicative; no. 77) Scale 1 : 1,000,000.

Geological map published jointly with Servicio Geológico de Bolivia and Programa ERTS Bolivia. Includes four cross sections and location map. Accompanied by text (14 p.)

5573 Pareja L., Jorge. Mapa geológico de Bolivia. Compilación geológica, Jorge Pareja L., Raúl Ballón A.; comite del mapa geológico, Ramiro Suárez S. et al.; dirección del mapa geológico, Jaime Oblitas G., Carlos Brockmann H.; dib. R. Carrasco C. y M. Morales Ch. La Paz?: Yacimientos Petrolíferos Fiscales Bolivianos, 1978. 1 map: col.; 168 x 141 cm. on 4 sheets 89 x 76 cm. Scale 1: 1,000,000.

"Este mapa es un compilación de los principales trabajos geológicos publicados, informes inéditos, o en elaboración de Yacimientos Petrolíferos Fiscales Bolivianos y del Servicio Geológico de Bolivia; complementada e integrada con interpretación sobre imagenes LANDSAT y fotografías aéreas."

5574 Sheriff, Fernando. Carte climatique de la région andine bolivienne (Carta climática de la región Andina boliviana). Compilation des données calculs statistiques et préparation de la carte, Fernando Sheriff; dessin, Isabelle Díaz; supervision, André Hufty et Jean Raveneau; collaboration, Marius Thériault. Québec: Laboratoires de climatologie et de cartographie, Departement de géographie, Université Laval, 1979. 2 maps: col.; each 62 x 35 cm. Scale ca. 1: 1,500,000.

Climatic map of the Bolivian Andes.

5575 Zeballos Miranda, Luis. Mapa artesanal de Bolivia. Ilustraciones de Ignacio González Yampa. La Paz: Instituto Boliviana de Cultura, Instituto Nacional de Antropología, División de Investigación y Catalogación Artesanal, 1978. 1 map: col.; 37 x 33 cm.

Ethnographic map showing Indians of Bolivia, their folk art and industries.

BRAZIL

5576 Brazil. Departamento Nacional de Estradas de Rodagem. Grupo de Projetos Cartográficos. Mapa rodoviário, Distrito Federal. Mapa elaborado na Directoria de Planejamento, Divisão de Planos e Programas, Grupo de Projetos Cartográficos; planejamento, preparo para impressão e impresso

por Aerofoto Cruzeiro S.A., Rio de Janeiro. Brasília: Ministerio dos Transportes, Departamento Nacional de Estradas de Rodagem, 1980. 1 map: col.; 66 x 96 cm.

Example of a series of excellent road and general maps covering all of Brazil's states and territories at scales varying from 1:400,000 to 1:2,200,000.

5577 ———. Ministério do Interior. Ministério do Interior, programas de desenvolvimento regional 1974/79: República Federativo do Brasil. São Paulo: Editora Monumento, 1979. 1 map: col.; on sheet 96 x 72 cm. Scale 1:6,650,000.

A good regional planning map.

5578 Centro de Planejamento da Bahia. Coordenação de Recursos Naturais. Setor de Cartografia. Estado da Bahia, mapa político. Secretaria do Planejamento, Ciência e Tecnologia. Cartografia por Geocarta S.A. Salvador: O Centro, 1978. 1 map: col.; 113 x 104 cm. Scale 1:1,000,000.

General map with relief shown by spot heights. Depths shown by contours. Also shows high-tension power lines.

5579 Companhia do Metropolitano do Rio de Janeiro. Diretoria de Planejamento. Plano metroviário do Rio de Janeiro. Planejamento cartográfico e preparo para impressão por Aerofoto Cruzeiro S.A. Rio de Janeiro: A Companhia, 1979. 1 map: col.; 40 x 59 cm. Scale 1:100,000.

Subway map of Rio de Janeiro.

5580 Costa, Manoel Teixeira da. Estado de Minas Gerais, mapa tectônico. Cartografia por Geocarta S.A. Belo Horizonte, Brasil: Instituto de Geociências Aplicadas, Secretaria de Estado de Ciência e Tecnologia, 1978. 1 map: col.; 67 x 81 cm. Scale 1: 1,500,000.

Structural geology map.

5581 Editora Cartomapas. Carta de Brasília: edição comemorativa do 18. aniversario, governo do Distrito Federal. Editado por Editora Cartomapas Ltda. Brasília: 1978. 1 map: col.; 82 x 101 cm.

Good tourist map of Brasília.

5582 Editora Monumento S.A. Mapa do Estado de Mato Grosso. Publicação da Editora Monumento S.A. São Paulo: 1979. 1 map: col.; 48 x 67 cm. Scale 1:2,500,000.

Detailed general map of the state.

5583 **Empresa de Portos do Brasil, S.A.** (Portabrás). Rede hidroviaria brasileira— 1978. Ministério dos Transportes. Brasília: A Empresa, 1978. 1 map: col.; 97 x 107 cm. Scale 1:5,000,000.
Inland navigation map. Includes inset of "Canalização do sistema Tietê-Paraná" with profile.

5584 **Fundação Instituto Brasileiro de Geografia e Estatística** (IBGE), *Rio de Janeiro*. **Superintendência de Cartografia.** República Federativa do Brasil. Secretaria de Planejamento da Presidência da República, Fundação Instituto Brasileiro de Geografia e Estatística, Directoria de Geodésia e Cartografia. Brasília: A Superintendência, 1979. 1 map: col.; 32 x 36 cm. Scale ca. 1: 17,500,000.
Good general map.

5585 **Goiás** (state), *Brazil*. **Secretaria do Planejamento e Coordenação. Fundação Instituto de Desenvolvimento Urbano de Regional. Coordenação de Desenvolvimento Institucional.** Atlas geográfico do Estado de Goiás. Goiania: 1979. 21 leaves; col. maps; 68 cm.
Excellent thematic atlas of the state including geology, soils, ecology, hydrography mines. Physical and socioeconomic conditions.

5586 **Instituto Brasileiro de Geografia e Estatística.** República Federativa do Brasil. Secretaria de Planejamento da Presidência da República, IBGE. 13. ed. Rio de Janeiro: IBGE, 1980. 1 map: col.; 95 x 114 cm.
Good general map showing state boundaries and the drainage and transportation networks.

5587 **Instituto de Geo-Ciências Aplicadas. Diretorias de Geologia e Cartografia.** Estado de Minas Gerais, mapa de ocorrências de calcário. Preparo para impressão, Geocarta S.A. Belo Horizonte: O Instituto, 1978. 1 map: col.; 67 x 81 cm. Scale 1:1,500,000.
Map showing dolomite and limestone deposits.

5588 **Instituto de Terras e Cartografia** (Paraná). Estado do Paraná. Vinculado a Secretaria da Agricultura, Governo do Paraná. Curitiba: O Instituto, 1979. 1 map; 30 x 42 cm. Scale ca. 1:1,650,000.
Administrative map of the state.

5589 **Martines, Luis Emilio V.** Carta geomorfológica do vale do Rio de Peixe em Marília. Composto no Instituto de Geografia, Universidade de São Paulo. Levantamento de campo em 1972, A. Carvalho, em 1976, J.P. Coutard; elaboração da maquete, A. Scatolini Watanabe. São Paulo: O Instituto, 1978. 1 map: col.; 36 x 26 cm. on sheet 46 x 52 cm. Scale 1:100,000.
Detailed geomorphology map with relief shown by contours and spot heights. Legend in Portuguese and French.

5590 **Polimapas Editora.** Mapa polivisual de Santa Catarina, político, turístico, didático, regional, rodoferroviário. Desenhado por José Nönoya Filho. 3 ed. São Paulo: Polimapas Editora, 1979/1980. 1 map: col.; 80 x 109 cm. Scale 1:500,000.
Detailed road map. Includes indexes and insets of "Planta da cidade de Florianópolis" and "Ilha de Santa Catarina."

5591 ———. Planta polivisual de Cidade de Manaus. São Paulo: Polimapas Editora, 1979. 1 map: col.; 84 x 110 cm. Scale 1: 13,000.
Detailed city plan of Manaus.

5592 **Rabinowitz, Philip D.** and **James R. Cochran.** Free-air gravity anomalies of the continental margin of Brazil. Drafted by Virginia Rippon. Tulsa, Okla: American Association of Petroleum Geologists, 1978. 1 map: col.; 117 x 77 cm.
Atlantic coast of Brazil with depths shown by contours. "Gravity contour interval 25 mgal." Includes text, location map of gravity and topographic profiles, and eight diagrams of gravity and topographic profiles. Bibliography.

5593 **Rio de Janeiro** (state), *Brazil*. **Departamento de Recursos Minerais.** Mapa de situação de depósitos e ocorrências minerais: Estado do Rio de Janeiro. Secretaria de Indústria, Comercio e Turismo. Rio de Janeiro: O Departamento, 1978. 1 map: col.; 76 x 110 cm. Scale 1:400,000.
Detailed map showing mines and mineral resources.

5594 **Salvia, Flávia la.** Mapas temáticos do Rio Grande do Sul: divisão municipal, 1965. Cartografia, Miron Zaions. Porto Alegre: Governo do Estado do Rio Grande do Sul, Secretaria da Agricultura, Supervisão de

Comandos Mecanizados, Unidade de Geografia e Cartografia, 1979. 1 map; 44 x 60 cm. Scale 1 : 1,800,000.

Administrative and political divisions. Includes three insets showing municipal divisions of 1809, 1841, and 1954.

5595 São Paulo (state), *Brazil*. **Secretaria de Economia e Planejamento. Coordenadoria de Ação Regional.** Atlas regional do Estado de São Paulo. São Paulo: 1978. 11 v.

Excellent, detailed series of loose leaf thematic atlases covering each of the 11 territories of the state of São Paulo. Major aspects of physical and socioeconomic geography are covered.

5596 ———. **Secretaria da Educação. Assessoria Técnica de Planejanento e Controle Educacional. Equipe de Caracterização Sócio-Econômica dos Municipios.** Cartogramas básicos para planejamento educacional. São Paulo: O Equipe, 1978. 18 leaves: col. maps; 46 x 89 cm.

Excellent atlas for study and teaching. Contains socioeconomic data.

5597 Schaeffer, Juan E. Rio, Cidade do Rio de Janeiro, Estado do Rio de Janeiro. 9. ed. Rio de Janeiro: Editora Presidente, 1979. 1 map: col.; 79 x 113 cm. (Guia Schaeffer do bolso; 325) Scale 1 : 27,000.

Detailed street map with index on verso.

5598 Sociedade Comercial e Representações Gráficas. Brasil: 1979/80. Curitiba, Paraná: A Sociedade; Rio de Janeiro: Editora Geográfica Paulina, 1979. 1 map: col.; 103 x 97 cm. Scale 1 : 4,500,000.

Relief shown by spot heights. Depths shown by contours and gradient tints. Insets: Distrito Federal de Brasília; Capital Federal de Brasília; Ilha da Trinidade; Território de Fernando de Noronha; Penedos S. Pedro e S. Paulo; Ilhas Martin Vaz.

CHILE

5599 DICARTEC. Diseño Cartográfico y Turístico. Mapa de Chile, físico-turístico. s.l.: DICARTEC, 1980. 3 maps: col.; on sheet 109 x 55 cm.

General tourist and highway map showing relief by shading. Also shows locations of Shell service stations. "Base cartográfica: Instituto Geográfico Militar."

5600 General Drafting Company, Inc. Chile, guía turística y plano de Santiago. Convent Station, N.J.: General Drafting Co.; Santiago de Chile: Esso Chile S.A. Petrolera, 1978. 3 maps: col.; on sheet 85 x 62 cm.

Tourist guide map with relief shown by spot heights. Includes index, 4 insets, distance chart, list of "Regiones de Chile," and "Mapa panorámico de Chile." Street plan of Santiago on verso.

COLOMBIA

5601 Colombia. División de Conservación de Carreteras. Red de carreteras nacionales en conservación: Colombia. Ministerio de Obras Públicas y Transporte, Dirección General Operativa. Bogotá: La División, 1978. 1 map; 91 x 127 cm. Scale 1 : 1,500,000.

Map showing the road network. Insets: Situación de los territorios insulares de Colombia; San Andrés; Providencia y Santa Catalina; Malpelo.

5602 ———. **Instituto Geográfico Agustín Codazzi.** Departamento del Atlántico. Bogotá: Instituto Geográfico Agustín Codazzi, Subdirección Cartográfica, 1978. 1 map. col.; 107 x 75 cm. Scale 1 : 100,000.

Relief shown by contours, gradient tints, and spot heights. Includes table of "Coordenadas y altitud en metros de puntos geodésicos," "Indice de planchas a escala 1 : 100,000 que cubren el mapa," and location map.

5603 ———. ———. Mapa de la Sabana de Bogotá, Departamento de Cundinamarca, República de Colombia. Ministerio de Hacienda y Crédito Público. 2. ed. Bogotá: 1978. 1 map: col.; 60 x 99 cm. Scale 1 : 50,000.

5604 ———. ———. Mapa en relieve de la República de Colombia. Elaborado por el Instituto Geográfico de Colombia "Agustín Codazzi; dib. lit. en el IGAC. 3. ed. Bogotá: El Instituto, 1978. 1 relief model: col., plastic; 132 x 94 cm. Scale 1 : 1,500,000.

Relief shown by contours, gradient tints, and spot heights. Depths shown by contours and gradient tints. Includes list of administrative divisions, statistical data, and location map. Insets: Map Pelo; San Andrés;

Providencia y Sta. Catalina; Situación de los territorios insulares de Colombia.

5605 ———. ———. Plano de la Ciudad de Bogotá. Bogotá: Instituto Geográfico Agustín Codazzi, Subdirección Cartográfica, 1979. 1 map: col.; 69 x 99 cm. Scale 1: 25,000.

City plan. Text, indexes, and maps of "Bogotá y sus alrededores: and "Ciudad de Bogotá, zona del centro" on verso.

5606 ———. ———. Región del Darién, República de Colombia. Preparado por el Instituto Geográfico Agustín Codazzi para la unidad técnica del Proyecto Darién. Medellín: El Proyecto, 1978. 7 maps; 100 x 80 cm. Scale 1:250,000.

Maps indicate geology, minerals, soils, geomorphology, forests, and ecological zones. Includes location map, indexed inset of "Croquis de ubicación," and inset of "Indice de seguridad." Accompanied by: Proyecto Darién: estudio para la orientación del desarrollo integral de la región del Darién colombiano. (158 p.)

5607 Corporación Nacional de Turismo de Colombia. Parque Nacional de Puracé. Ministerio de Desarrollo Económico. Bogotá: Fundación Parques Nacionales, 1978. 1 map: col.; on sheet 25 x 69 cm. Scale ca. 1:100,000.

National park recreational map with relief shown by gradient tints. Includes location map. Text and color illustration on verso.

5608 Kassem Bustamante, Taissir. Mapa geológico del Departamento de Antioquia. Elaboración cartográfico y edición, Ingeominas. Bogotá: República de Colombia, Ministerio de Minas y Energia, Instituto Nacional de Investigaciones Geológico-Mineras, 1979. 1 map: col.; 97 x 75 cm. Scale 1: 500,000.

Geological map with relief shown by contours.

5609 República de Colombia, localización de oleoductos, refinerías y campos en explotación. Bogotá: s.n., 1978? 1 map; 51 x 39 cm. Scale 1:4,000,000.

Oil and gas map indicating pipelines, oil and gas fields, and refineries.

ECUADOR

5610 Centro Panamericano de Estudios de Investigaciones Geográficas. Ecuador: división política-territorial del Ecuador. s.l.; El Centro, 1980. 1 map; 33 x 55 cm. Scale 1:3,000,000.

"División política-territorial, según el Instituto Nacional de Estadística y Censos 1979." Includes index and inset of "Archipiélago de Colón (Provincia de Galápagos)."

5611 Ecuador. Instituto Geográfico Militar. Mapa didáctico de la República del Ecuador. Quito: El Instituto, 1980. 1 map on 2 sheets: col.; 62 x 159 cm., sheets 89 x 97 cm. and 89 x 94 cm.

Good descriptive general map.

5612 ———. ———. Plano de la Ciudad de Guayaquil. Guayaquil: Almacenes Editorial Colón, 1979. 1 map: col.; 182 x 122 cm. on 2 sheets. Scale 1:10,000.

Detailed city plan with relief shown by contours and spot heights. Includes indexes, hymn, indexed inset of "Diagrama de parroquias urbanas."

5613 ———. ———. República del Ecuador, mapa físico. Quito: El Instituto, 1979. 1 map: col.; 43 x 56 cm. Scale 1:2,000,000.

Relief shown by shading, gradient tints, and spot heights. Depths shown by gradient tints. Includes inset of "Provincia de Galapagos, Archipiélago de Colón (territorio insular)," location map, and relief profiles.

5614 ———. ———. República del Ecuador, mapa geográfico. Quito: El Instituto, 1978. 1 map on 4 sheets: col.; 166 x 219 cm., sheets 96 x 122 cm.

Detailed general map with relief shown by contours, shading hypsometric tints, and spot heights. Depths shown by contours and bathymetric tints. Includes compilation diagram, location map, two relief profiles, and color illustrations. Insets: situación del Archipiélago de Galapagos con relación al territorio continental; Provincia de Galápagos, Archipiélago de Colón (territorio insular).

5615 Petroconsultants S.A. Ecuador, synopsis 1978. Geneva, Switzerland: Petroconsultants, 1979. 1 map: 92 x 79 cm.

Depths shown by contours. Map showing oil and gas leases. Includes graph of

"Crude oil production, 1977–78," list of "Wildcat wells in Sta. Elena area," table of "Summary of activity during 1978," "List of rightholders," statistical data, and location map.

5616 Sampedro V., Francisco. Atlas geográfico del Ecuador "SAM": con las básicas nociones históricos de la nacionalidad. Editor, Vicente Wilfrido Maldonado Polo. Revisado y aprobado por el Instituto Geográfico Militar y por el Ministerio de Relaciones Exteriores. Quito, Ecuador: Librería Cuna, 1979/1980. 87 p.; ill. (some col.); maps; 22 x 32 cm.

General reference atlas.

5617 Tufiño P., Carlos A. República del Ecuador, mapa de las principales carreteras. s.l.: s.n., 1979. 1 map: col.; 44 x 62 cm. fold. to 23 x 11 cm. Scale 1 : 2,000,000.

Folded title: "Mapa turístico de las principales carreteras del Ecuador: conozca el Ecuador. Includes descriptive list of provinces, inset of "Archipiélago de Colón, Provincia de Galápagos, territorio insular," relief profile of principal volcanoes, location map.

GUYANA

5618 Guyana. Geological Surveys and Mines Department. Drawing Office. Provisional map of Guyana showing drainage pattern. Compiled in the Geological Surveys & Miners Drawing Office; I.V. Lowe, cartographic supervisor. Georgetown: 1978. 1 map 87 x 59 cm. Scale 1 : 1,000,000.

5619 ——. Road Division. Map of Guyana showing communication system— 1978. Ministry of Works and Transport (Works), Roads Division; done by Patrick A. Ramgolam. Georgetown: The Division, 1978. 1 map; 95 x 52 cm. Scale 1 : 1,000,000.

Transportation map of Guyana.

PARAGUAY

5620 Asunción. Universidad Nacional. Departamento de Producción Animal. Región oriental del Paraguay, mapa de grandes tipos de vegetación. Realizado por Universidad Nacional de Asunción, Facultad de Ingeniería Agronómica, Departamento de

Producción Animal, Contapar S.R.L., consultores agropecuarios y forestales. Asunción: La Facultad, 1978. 1 map: col.; 125 x 94 cm. Scale 1 : 500,000.

Detailed vegetation map.

5621 Paraguay. Asunción: s.n., 1978. 4 maps: col.; on 2 sheets 34 x 27 cm. Scale ca. 1 : 3,800,000 and ca. 1 : 5,000,000. Printed on both sides of sheets.

Maps showing transportation, industries, agriculture, and forests. Sheet of "Vias de Comunicación" includes inset.

5622 Paraguay. Instituto Geográfico Militar. Caacupé, mapa de ciudades del Paraguay. Controlado por Instituto Geográfico Militar; preparado e impreso, IGM, año 1979. Asunción: El Instituto, 1979. 1 map: col.; 48 x 55 cm. (Its Serie; H941) Scale 1 : 10,000.

Topographic city plan.

5623 ——. ——. Gran Asunción, carta nacional, Paraguay. Control por Instituto Geográfico Militar; preparado e impreso, I.G.M. 1978. Asunción: El Instituto, 1978. 4 maps: col.; 48 x 68 cm or smaller (Its Serie; H741) Scale 1 : 25,000.

Topographic city plan.

5624 ——. ——. Puerto Presidente Stroessner, mapa de ciudades del Paraguay. Controlado por Instituto Geográfico Militar; preparado e impreso, IGM, año 1978. Asunción: El Instituto, 1978. 1 map: col.; 49 x 56 cm. (Its Serie; H941) Scale 1 : 10,000.

Topographic city plan.

5625 Proyecto Catastral. Departamento Alto Paraná, división política, compañías lugares, límites distritales. Asunción: El Proyecto, 1979? 1 map; on sheet 101 x 64 cm. Scale 1 : 100,000.

Administrative boundaries of the department have been added by hand.

5626 ——. Sección Preparación. Departamento de Caazapá. Trabajo realizado por la Sección Preparación; delineado por Reina Leiva G., Tito L. Segovia M., Carlos Barressi Ch.; supervisión, Oscar A. Boltes M. Asunción: Proyecto Catastral DII, 1979. 1 map; on sheet 69 x 87 cm.

Administrative boundaries of the department have been added by hand.

5627 ——. ——. Departamento de Paraguarí, división política, compañías lugares, límites departamentales y distritales.

Trabajo realizado por la Sección Preparación; delineado por Tito Livio Segovia et al.; supervisión, Oscar A. Boltes. Asunción: Proyecto Catastral DII, 1979? 1 map; 43 x 33 cm. Scale 1 : 200,000.

Administrative boundaries of the department have been added by hand.

5628 ———. ———. Departamento Guairá, división política, compañías lugares, límites distritales. Trabajo realizado por la Sección Preparación; delineado por Tito Segovia, Reina Leiva G., Carlos Barressi; supervisión, Oscar A. Boltes. Asunción: Proyecto Catastral DII, 1978. 1 map; 37 x 51 cm. Scale 1 : 200,000.

Administrative boundaries of the department have been added by hand.

PERU

Comisión Mixta Peruana Boliviana. Lago Titicaca. See item **5568.**

5629 Editorial Navarrete. Mapa política del Perú. Lima: Navarrete, 1980. 1 map: col.; 86 x 61 cm. Scale 1 : 2,400,000.

Administrative map. Includes location map, statistical tables, distance chart.

5630 Góngora Perea, Amadeo. Plano de la Ciudad de Lima metropolitana. Lima: Cartográfica Nacional, 1979. 1 map: col.; 61 x 88 cm. Scale ca. 1 : 25,000.

Street plan of Lima with street index.

5631 Peru. División de Estudios de Tráfico. Mapa del Perú, volumen de tránsito: índice medio diario, año 1978. Ministerio de Transportes y Comunicaciones, Dirección General de Transporte Terrestre, Dirección de Ingeniería. Dibujo, R.C. Rodríguez. Lima: La División, 1979. 1 map; 113 x 78 cm. Scale ca. 1 : 2,000,000.

Traffic flow map.

5632 ———. **Fondo de Promoción Turística. Dirección Regional en Tacna.** Tacna. Secretaría de Estado de Turismo. Lima: La Dirección, 1979. 1 map; 21 x 28 cm.

Reference and tourist guide.

5633 ———. ———. **Dirección Regional VIII, Huancayo.** Map of Huancayo, Peru. Secretaría de Estado de Turismo. Lima: La Dirección, 1979. 1 map; 21 x 28 cm.

Includes index to points of interest, text, and tourist information.

5634 ———. **Instituto Geográfico Militar.** Departamento de Pasco, mapa físico, político. Compilado por el Instituto Geográfico Militar. Lima: El Instituto, 1979. 1 map: col.; 56 x 78 cm. Scale 1 : 375,000.

Good example of a detailed series of general reference maps for each department of Peru. Relief shown by gradient tints and spot heights. Includes table of statistical data and location map.

5635 ———. ———. Lima y alrededores. Lima: El Instituto, 1979. 63 maps; 60 x 60 cm. Scale 1 : 5,000.

Excellent detailed maps of Lima and its metropolitan area. Relief shown by contours and spot heights on some sheets. Shows wards, house numbering system, and major buildings. Geographic coverage complete in 63 sheets. Includes index map and index to adjoining sheets.

5636 ———. ———. Mapa de carreteras del Perú. Lima: El Instituto, 1979. 1 map: col.; 96 x 67 cm. Scale 1 : 2,200,000.

Relief shown by spot heights. Includes location map, inset of "Esquema vial," and distance chart. Indexed maps of "Lima metropolitana y alrededores" and "Centro de Lima," 22 local route maps.

5637 ———. **Oficina Sectorial de Planificación Agraria.** Perú mapa distritos forestales. Ministerio de Agricultura y Alimentación, Oficina General de Catastro Rural. Lima: La Oficina, 1979. 1 map: col.; 42 x 31 cm. Scale 1 : 5,000,000.

Shows forests and forestry areas.

5638 ———. ———. Perú, mapa físico. Ministerio de Agricultura y Alimentación, Oficina General de Catastro Rural. Lima: La Oficina, 1978. 1 map: col.; 42 x 31 cm. Scale 1 : 5,000,000.

Physical map with relief and depths shown by contours.

5639 Petroconsultants. Peru: synopsis first half 1979. Geneva, Switzerland: Petroconsultants, 1979. 1 map: 111 x 83 cm. Scale 1 : 2,000,000.

Map showing gas leases, depths shown by contours. Includes statistical data, "List of rightholders," and location map.

5640 Touring y Automóvil Club del Perú. Departamento de Cartografía. Mapa vial del Perú. Dibujos, G. Paucarcaja B., C. Rincón P., A Cano S. Lima: 1979. 1 map: col.; 69 x 49 cm. Scale ca. 1 : 3,500,000.

Detailed road map.

5641 ——. ——. Zonas turísticas y Cuzco. Lima: El Club, 1979. 1 map: col.; 70 x 47 cm. Scale 1 : 363,000.

Reference and guide map. Includes index and color illustrations. "Plano de Machu Picchu," map of "Parque Arqueológico Nacional de Machupicchu," and indexed map of Cuzco on verso.

5642 Vallenas Santos, César; Oscar Villegas Gonzales; and Luis Urday Revilla. Plano básico de Arequipa. Arequipa, Perú: Empresa de Saneamiento de Arequipa, 1979. 1 map; on sheet 142.x 102 cm. Scale 1 : 10,000.

City plan.

SURINAM

5643 Dahlberg, H.N. Kaart van Suriname (Map of Surinam) (Mapa del Surinam). Vervaardigd door Djambatan, 's-Gravenhage. Paramaribo: C. Kersten, 1978? 1 map: col.; 72 x 55 cm. Scale 1 : 1,000,000.

General reference map with relief shown by shading, gradient tints, and spot heights. Includes location map and explanatory notes.

5644 Stichting ter Bevordering van het Toerisme. Paramaribo. Uitg. door de Stichting ter Bevordering van het Toerisme. Paramaribo, Suriname: De Stichting, 1978. 1 map: col.; 46 x 44 cm. fold in cover 24 x 11 cm.

Tourist guide and reference map.

5645 Teunissen, P.A. Cverzichtskaart, Surinaamse laagland ecosystemen (kustvlakte en savannegordel) (Reconnaissance map, Suriname lowland ecosystems, coastal plain and savanna belt). Paramaribo: Stichting Natuurbehoud Suriname (STINASU), 1978. 1 map: col.; 80 x 200 cm. on 8 sheets 46 x 56 cm. Scale 1 : 200,000.

Coastal ecology. "Map based on aerial photographs (Central Bureau for Aerial Survey, Paramaribo, 1970–1973), field reconnaissance (1974–1977) and reconnaissance soil maps (Department of Soil Survey, Paramaribo, 1978)."

URUGUAY

5646 Carta geológica del terciario del Uruguay. Montevideo?: s.n., 1979? 1 map: col.; 36 x 30 cm.

Geological sketch map. "Carta autorizada por el Servicio Geográfico Militar Según Decreto 974/973."

5647 Guía y Planos Eureka. Mapa "Eureka" de Montevideo. Montevideo: Eureka, 1979. 1 map: col.; 54 x 79 cm.

General reference and guide map. Relief shown by contours and spot heights. Depths shown by contours and soundings. Includes three town maps. Maps of "Montevideo histórico," "Principales vias de comunicación," and "República Oriental del Uruguay," telephone directories, and index on verso.

5648 Uruguay. Administración de Ferrocarriles del Estado. AFE, República Oriental del Uruguay, red ferroviaria. Montevideo: AFE, 1978. 1 map: col.; 39 x 30 cm. Scale ca. 1 : 2,000,000.

Good railroad map. Includes inset of Montevideo and statistical data.

5649 ——. Instituto Geográfico Militar. Uruguay. Montevideo: El Instituto: Shell, 1978. 1 map: col.; 87 x 61 cm. Scale ca. 1 : 1,000,000.

General road and reference map.

VENEZUELA

5650 Venezuela. Dirección de Aeronáutica Civil. Carta de radionavegación: AIP Venezuela: servicio de tránsito aéreo, espacio aéreo inferior, rutas ATS—sectores y áreas de control terminal (Radionavigation chart: AIS Venezuela: air traffic services, lower airspace, ATS routes-sectors and terminal control areas). Ministerio de Transporte y Comunicaciones, Dirección General de Transporte y Tránsito Aéreo. Caracas: Dirección de Aeronáutica Civil, 1978. 3 maps: col.; 66 x 63 cm. Scale ca. 1 : 1,437,500.

Official aeronautical charts. Geographic coverage complete in three sheets.

Includes index map, "Communications information," and cruising level diagrams.

5651 ———. **Dirección General de Vialidad Terrestre.** Estado Nueva Esparta: Venezuela. Caracas: 1979. 1 map; 75 x 98 cm. Scale ca. 1 : 100,000.
Road transportation map. Includes 11 insets of "Región insular."

5652 ———. ———. Región centro occidental: Venezuela. Caracas: Dirección General de Vialidad Terrestre, 1979. 1 map: 98 x 75 cm. Scale 1 : 500,000.
Road transportation map. Covers Falcon, Lara, Portuguesa, and Yaracuy. Insets: Parcelamiento Las Majaguas; Parcelamiento Turen; Guanare y vecindad.

5653 ———. ———. Región nor-oriental: Venezuela. Caracas: 1979. 1 map. 76 x 98 cm. Scale 1 : 500,000.
Road transportation map. Covers Sucre, Anzoategui, and Monagas.

5654 ———. ———. Región Zuliana: Venezuela. Caracas: 1979. 1 map; 98 x 74 cm. Scale 1 : 500,000.
Road transportation map.

5655 ———. **Oficina Ministerial del Transporte.** Metro de Caracas: sistema Metro, 1990. Ministerio de Obras Públicas. Caracas: La Oficina, 1979. 1 map; 37 x 52 cm.
Subway map of metropolitan Caracas.

JOURNAL ABBREVIATIONS
GEOGRAPHY

AAAS/S Science. American Association for the Advancement of Science. Washington.

AAG/A Annals of the Association of American Geographers. Lawrence, Kan.

AAG/PG Professional Geographer. Journal of The Association of American Geographers. Washington.

ACH/BHA Boletín de Historia y Antigüedades. Academia Colombiana de Historia. Bogotá.

AGB/BCG Boletim Carioca de Geografia. Associação dos Geógrafos Brasileiros, Secção Regional do Rio de Janeiro. Rio de Janeiro.

AGB/BPG Boletim Paulista de Geografia. Associação dos Geógrafos Brasileiros, Secção Regional de São Paulo. São Paulo.

AGF/B Bulletin de l'Association de Géographes Français. Paris.

AGRO Agrociencia. Secretaría de Agricultura y Recursos Hidráulicos, Colegio de Postgraduados de la Escuela Nacional de Agricultura. Chapingo, México.

AGS/GR The Geographical Review. American Geographical Society. New York.

AGS/SG Soviet Geography: Review and Translation. American Geographical Society. New York.

AHGH/R Revista de la Academia Hondureña de Geografía e Historia. Tegucigalpa.

AI/I Interciencia. Asociación Interciencia. Caracas.

AJES The American Journal of Economics and Sociology. Francis Neilson Fund and Robert Schalkenbach Foundation. New York.

BCV/REL Revista de Economía Latinoamericana. Banco Central de Venezuela. Caracas.

BESPL Berichte zur Entwicklung in Spanien, Portugal, Lateinamerika. München, FRG.

BNB/REN Revista Econômica do Nordeste. Banco do Nordeste do Brasil, Depto. de Estudos Econômicos do Nordeste. Fortaleza.

BNBD Boletín Nicaragüense de Bibliografía y Documentación. Banco Central de Nicaragua, Biblioteca. Managua.

CDAL Cahiers des Amériques Latines. Paris.

CFC/RBC Revista Brasileira de Cultura. Ministério da Educação e Cultura, Conselho Federal de Cultura. Rio de Janeiro.

CP Cuadernos Políticos. Revista trimestral. Ediciones Era. México.

CU/EG Economic Geography. Clark Univ. Worcester, Mass.

DRG/BG Boletim Geográfico do Estado do Rio Grande do Sul. Diretório Regional de Geografia e da Secção de Geografia. Porto Alegre, Brazil.

FAIC/CPPT Comunicaciones Proyecto Puebla-Tlaxcala. Fundación Alemana para la Investigación Científica. Puebla, México.

FCE/TE El Trimestre Económico. Fondo de Cultura Económica. México.

FDD/NED Notes et Études Documentaires. France, Direction de la Documentation. Paris.

GEB/E Die Erde. Zeitschrift der Gesellschaft für Erdkunde zur Berlin. Walter de Gruyter & Co. Berlin.

GM The Geographical Magazine. London.

GV/GR Geologische Rundschau. Internationale Zeitschrift für Geologie. Geologische Vereinigung. Ferdinand Enke Verlag. Stuttgart, Germany.

HAHR Hispanic American Historical Review. Duke Univ. Press *for the* Conference on Latin American History of the American Historical Association. Durham, N.C.

IAA Ibero-Amerikanisches Archiv. Ibero-Amerikanisches Institut. Berlin, FRG.

IAEERI/E Estrategia. Instituto Argentino de Estudios Estratégicos y de las Relaciones Internacionales. Buenos Aires.

IBE/RBE Revista Brasileira de Economia. Fundação Getúlio Vargas, Instituto Brasileiro de Economia. Rio de Janeiro.

IBGE/R Revista Brasileiro de Geografia. Conselho Nacional de Geografia, Instituto Brasileiro de Geografia e Estatística. Rio de Janeiro.

ICC/I Itaytera. Instituto Cultural do Cariri. Crato, Brazil.

IFH/C Conjonction. Institut Français d'Haïti. Port-au-Prince.

IGME/RG Revista Geográfica. Instituto Geográfico Militar del Ecuador, Depto. Geográfico. Quito.

IJ/JJ Jamaica Journal. Institute of Jamaica. Kingston.

INAH/A Anales del Instituto Nacional de Antropología e Historia. Secretaría de Educación Pública. México.

IPN/EP Economía Política. Instituto Politécnico Nacional, Escuela Superior de Economía. México.

JDA The Journal of Developing Areas. Western Illinois Univ. Press. Macomb.

JLAS Journal of Latin American Studies. Centers of institutes of Latin American studies at the universities of Cambridge, Glasgow, Liverpool, London and Oxford. Cambridge Univ. Press. London.

NGS/NGM National Geographic Magazine. National Geographic Society. Washington.

NSO Nueva Sociedad. Revista política y cultural. San José.

OAS/AM Américas. Organization of American States. Washington.

OCEANUS Oceanus. Oceanographic Institution. Woods Hole, Mass.

PAIGH/G Revista Geográfica. Instituto Panamericano de Geografía e Historia, Comisión de Geografía. México.

PAIGH/RC Revista Cartográfica. Instituto Panamericano de Geografía e Historia, Comisión de Cartografía. México.

PGM Petermanns Geographische Mitteilungen. Geographische-Kartographische Anstalt. Gotha, Germany.

SAGE/JIAS Journal of Inter-American Studies and World Affairs. Sage Publication *for the* Center for Advanced International Studies, Univ. of Miami. Coral Gables, Fla.

SBPC/CC Ciência e Cultura. Sociedade Brasileira para o Progresso da Ciência. São Paulo.

SG/AG Annales de Géographie. Société de Géographie. Paris.

SGB/COM Les Cahiers d'Outre-Mer. Publiée par l'Institut de Géographie de la Faculté des Lettres de Bordeaux, par l'Institut de la France d'Outre-Mer, par la Société de Géographie de Bordeaux *avec le concours* de Centre National de la Recherche Scientifique et de la VI. section de l'École Pratique des Hautes Études. Bordeaux.

SGL/B Boletín de la Sociedad Geográfica de Lima. Lima.

SSAG/GA Geografiska Annaler. Svenska Sällskapet för Antropologi och Geografi. Stockholm.

TESG Tijdschrift voor Economische en Sociale Geographie. Netherlands Journal of Economic and Social Geography. Rotterdam, The Netherlands.

UCR/AEC Anuario de Estudios Centroamericanos. Univ. de Costa Rica. Ciudad Universitaria "Rodrigo Facio." San José.

UCR/CT Ciencia y Tecnología. Revista semestral de la Univ. de Costa Rica. San José.

UNPHU/A Aula. Univ. Nacional Pedro Henríquez Ureña. Santo Domingo.

UP/CSEC Cuban Studies/Estudios Cubanos. Univ. of Pittsburgh, Univ. Center for International Studies, Center for Latin American Studies. Pittsburgh, Pa.

USM/JTG The Journal of Tropical Geography. Univ. of Singapore and Univ. of Malaya, Depts. of Geography. Singapore.

UWI/CQ Caribbean Quarterly. Univ. of the West Indies. Mona, Jamaica.

ZG Zeitschrift für Geomorphologie. Gebrüder Borntraeger. Berlin.

GOVERNMENT AND POLITICS

GENERAL

6001 Adams, Richard Newbold. The structure of participation: a commentary (*in* Political participation in Latin America. Edited by John A. Booth and Mitchell A. Seligson. v. 2, Politics and the poor. New York: Holmes & Meier, 1978, p. 9–17)

A summary and critique of the concept of participation as used by political scientists in a conference on the Faces of Participation in Latin America. Author turns participation "upside down" by indicating that governments in Latin America (and elsewhere) often do things to influence (positively and/or negatively) the masses rather than the other way around. A valuable commentary for those interested in the concept of power. [D.W. Dent]

6002 Aguilar García, Francisco Javier. El sindicalismo del sector automotriz: 1960–1976 (CP, 16, abril/junio 1978, p. 44–64, tables)

Organized in four parts: 1) the trade union experience in the car industry; 2) political trends in the labor movement; 3) ways of labor organization peculiar to the industry; and 4) a description of the different labor movements. [A. Suárez]

6003 Alexander, Robert J. Latin America: continuing struggle, some gains (Freedom at Issue [Freedom House, New York] 49, Jan./Feb. 1979, p. 27–29)

A short report. The purpose is mainly informative. [A. Suárez]

6004 ———. Latin America: freedom gains (Freedom at Issue [Freedom House Pub., New York] 54, Jan./Feb. 1980, p. 27–30)

A brief review of political events in 1979 reveals that Latin America has experienced a shift toward freedom and democratic government in Bolivia, Ecuador, Peru, Brazil,

and Nicaragua. No explanation is offered for this shift but the author is cautious about the end to military dictatorships in the region. [D.W. Dent]

6005 América Latina en los años treinta. Luis Antezana E. et al.; coordinador, Pablo González Casanova. México: Instituto de Investigaciones Sociales, Universidad Nacional Autónoma de México, 1977. 605 p.; bibl.

The relationship between the economic crisis of 1929–32 and social and political relations in Latin America is examined in considerable detail by 14 social scientists. While some countries are left out—Cuba, Colombia, Guatemala, Costa Rica, and Panama—the events related to the collapse of capitalism are treated with considerable sophistication. [D.W. Dent]

6006 Bayart, Jean-François. L'analyse des situations autoritaires: étude bibliographique (FNSP/RFSP, 26:3, juin 1976, p. 483–520)

A review-article. Attached is a bibliography with 133 titles covering Europe, Asia, Africa, the Arab countries, and Latin America. Three general orientations are found in the literature under review: developmentalism, Marxism, and a variety of "heterodox" positions. With a few exceptions, the Latin American titles were published before 1972. This means that seminal works by Guillermo A. O'Donnell and other recent ones are missing. [A. Suárez]

6007 Baylis, Thomas A. The facts of participation: a comparative perspective (*in* Political participation in Latin America. Edited by John A. Booth and Mitchell A. Seligson. v. 1, Citizen and state. New York: Holmes & Meier, 1978, p. 34–42)

A comparison of political participation

in authoritarian, communist, Third World, and Western capitalist settings. Author finds that participation is multifunctional and may serve different purposes for governing elites and for regular citizens. Somewhat general and in need of a chart comparing systems and functions but still important for understanding different types of participation. [D.W. Dent]

6008 Booth, John A. Political participation in Latin America: levels, structure, context, concentration and rationality (LARR, 14:3, 1979, p. 29–60, bibl.)

The leaders of the Third World have discovered that mobilizing the masses under strict control can become a significant political resource. The difference between mass mobilization and political participation (when individuals have choices) is not emphasized by this author. He defines political participation as "behavior influencing or attempting to influence the distribution of public goods," and regime stability as one of these "public goods." Thus, supportive behavior, like orchestrated mass demonstration, becomes political participation. Article includes a good discussion of the literature, but most of the data is drawn from 25 items all of them previously published in a reader edited by the author and M.A. Seligson. [A. Suárez]

6009 ―――― and **Mitchell A. Seligson.** Images of political participation in Latin America (*in* Political participation in Latin America. Edited by John A. Booth and Mitchell A. Seligson. v. 1, Citizen and state. New York: Holmes & Meier, 1978, p. 3–33)

Five conflicting images of political participation are critically evaluated in order to reach a theory of Latin American political participation integrating both systemic and individual perspectives. The major findings stress that Latin American political participation is not characteristically violent, passive, irrational, severely limited by state actions, or monopolized by upper-class elements. A highly competent review and assessment of the current scholarly literature and the empirical validity of the conventional wisdom. [D.W. Dent]

6010 Busey, James L. Latin American political guide. 17. ed. Manitou Spring, Colo.: Juniper Editions, 1980. 52 p.; maps.

A brief summary of 21 political systems of Latin America with less emphasis than in past editions on the achievement or non-achievement of constitutional democracy. However, the key to Latin American stability and democratic rule rests with socioeconomic systems based on widely distributed individual proprietorship, literacy, and civic-minded leadership. One wonders why more emphasis is not placed on political factors as independent variables. [D.W. Dent]

6011 Calvo, Roberto. The Church and the doctrine of national security (SAGE/JIAS, 21:1, Feb. 1979, p. 69–88, bibl.)

Summarizes the doctrine of national security as it has been stated by some Latin American military theoreticians (Meira, Villegas, do Couto e Silva, etc.) and confronts it with documented criticisms made by the Catholic Church. A fair treatment, though the suggestion that military anticommunism in Latin America reflects the influence of the US Army seems far-fetched. [A. Suárez]

6012 Cardoso, Fernando Henrique. Capitalist development and the state: bases and alternatives (UC/I, 7:2/8:1, 1978, p. 7–19)

Dependent development continues its ties to the entrepreneurial state, multinational corporations, and the internationalized sector of the bourgeoisie. By growing to significant proportions, the state has expressed a relationship of class domination and policies detrimental to the interests of the nation. All this tends to block a proletarian route to socialism. The alternatives, however, are not clearly stated. [D.W. Dent]

6013 Carranza, Mario Esteban. Fuerzas armadas y estado de excepción en América Latina. México: Siglo Veintiuno Editores, 1978. 269 p. (Sociología y política)

The author develops a provocative analysis of the military authoritarian regime of the post-1964 period. Drawing primarily on Marxist theories of the state, he reviews critically the academic literature on the subject and offers interpretations of his own of the relationship between the capitalist state and military rule. The reader will find a useful review and comparison of diverse literature on the subject as well as some challenging arguments. [G. Wynia]

6014 Centro de Estudios para el Desarrollo e Integración de América Latina. Complemento a la bibliografía. pt. 1, Desarrollo y revolución. pt. 2, Iglesia y liberación. Bogotá: CEDIAL, 1974. 2 v.

Bibliography consisting of 800 items on the Church and liberation theology covering the last 10 years; however, many of the sources would be difficult to obtain. [D.W. Dent]

6015 Centro Latinoamericano de Economía Humana. Desarrollo y democracia. Montevideo: C.L.A.E.H., 1978. 76 p. (Serie Estudios; no. 9)

This volume is composed of three papers on Latin American economic and social thought and practice: one on economic planning by Raúl Prebisch; one on democracy and authoritarianism by Gino Germani; and a third on education by Germán Rama. All present ideas of the authors seen in print previously. [G. Wynia]

6016 Chaffee, Wilber A. Let Jorge do it: a rational choice model of political participation (*in* Political participation in Latin America. Edited by John A. Booth and Mitchell A. Seligson. v. 2, Politics and the poor. New York: Holmes & Meier, 1978, p. 18–34)

Study designed to examine the micro political-economic choices of people engaged in making political demands. By investigating individual and collective decisions to participate in politics, author presents several valuable hypotheses tied to the calculus of costs and benefits. An important contribution to understanding the basis of collective action and political demand making. [D.W. Dent]

6017 Chalbaud Zerpa, Reinaldo. Estado y política. Mérida, Venezuela: Universidad de los Andes, Consejo de Publicaciones, Facultad de Derecho, Centro de Investigaciones Jurídicas, 1978. 422 p.; bibl.

Comparative institutional analysis including the provisions of the US Constitution and the constitutional history of Cuba including the design of the new socialist state. Emphasis is placed on the theory of the state, the organization of power, nationalism, and representation. [D.W. Dent]

6018 Chaney, Elsa. Supermadre: women in politics in Latin America. Austin: Published for Institute of Latin American Studies by University of Texas Press, 1979. 210 p.; bibl.; index (Latin American monographs; no. 50)

In this scholarly work the author examines the role of women in Latin American politics in search for explanations of their subordinate position. After reviewing cultural, social and other explanations, she examines women in Peru and Chile using the results of interviews and case studies to demonstrate how women's attitudes about themselves restrain their political activism. [G. Wynia]

6019 Child, John. Geopolitical thinking in Latin America (LARR, 14:2, 1979, p. 89–112, maps, plate)

The concept of geopolitics is alive and well among Latin America's military minds. A valuable study (and concept) for "understanding and explaining the self-perceptions held by national leaders, and their concern with international development and external projection of influence and power." Most of the recent literature is from Brazil (ESG), Argentina (INSAR), Chile, and Bolivia. [D.W. Dent]

6020 Churches and politics in Latin America. Edited by Daniel H. Levine. Preface by John P. Harrison. Beverly Hills: Sage Publications, 1980. 288 p.; bibl. (Sage focus editions; 14)

An examination of the relationship between religion and the state in Latin America based on 11 essays by scholars from both North and South America. The essays focus on the new social role of religion and the conflicts it has brought with governments more interested in national security doctrines than in human rights and redistributive policies that affect the poor. A valuable work for understanding the 10 years of change in the Catholic Church from Medellín to Puebla. [D.W. Dent]

6021 Ciria, Alberto. Ideologies: alive and well in Latin America (UCSD/NS, 7:1/2, 1978 [i.e. 1979] p. 283–290)

In reviewing two recent collections of readings on ideology and politics, author finds several gaps in the analysis but offers some valuable suggestions for future research. While old "ideologies" may still linger, newer ones are alive and well and open new paths for political inquiry. [D.W. Dent]

526 / Handbook of Latin American Studies

6022 Collier, David. Industrial modernization and political change: Latin American perspective (PUCIS/WP, 30:4, July 1978, p. 593–614, tables)

An attempt to build on O'Donnell's analysis of modernization and political change by presenting a revised and unified model of national political change emphasizing such variables as economic resources, strength of the popular sector, and the perception of threat to the existing economic and political order. In exploring ways to resolve the problems posed in O'Donnell's analysis, author suggests that "A principal challenge to students of political change is to understand not only the conditions that lead to the collapse of democratic regimes, but also the conditions that lead to the collapse of authoritarian regimes." [D.W. Dent]

6023 Comblin, Joseph. The Church and the national security state. Maryknoll, N.Y.: Orbis Books, 1979. 236 p.; bibl.

Belgian theologian applies the Pope's statement about "false ideologies" to the doctrine of national security that military-authoritarian governments have used to legitimize their repressive rule. Given the evils of a national security ideology, it is perfectly legitimate for the Catholic Church to oppose military geopolitical doctrines and advocate theology of liberation principles that publicly champion the rights of human beings. A useful polemic against military rule from a member of the Catholic left. [D.W. Dent]

6024 Comisión Evangélica Latinoamericana de Educación Cristiana. Notas acerca de las dictaduras en América Latina. Lima: Caledec, 1979 or 1980. 47 p.; bibl.; ill. (Cuadernos de estudio—CELADEC; 6)

In this brief work the authors describe the repression found in contemporary military regimes and trace their rise to the region's penetration by multinational corporations. Though informative on some issues, it is largely a superficial characterization rather than a useful analysis of major issues. [G. Wynia]

6025 Comunicación social e Iglesia: documentos latinoamericanos, 1959–1976. Benito D. Spoletini, compilador. Bogotá: Ediciones Paulinas, 1977. 271 p.; bibl.; index (Colección Comunicación; 1)

Series of 27 documents on the role of the Catholic press (written and broadcast) and film in social and religious communication. Documents begin with the First Congress of the Catholic Press in 1959 and end with the Second Meeting on Radio and Television Liturgy in 1976. [D.W. Dent]

6026 Conferencia General del Episcopado Latinoamericano, 3d, Puebla, Mexico, 1979. Evangelization at present and in the future of Latin America: conclusions. Washington, D.C.: National Conference of Catholic Bishops, Secretariat, Committee for the Church in Latin America, 1979. 220 p.; index.

English translation of *Evangelización en el presente y el futuro de América Latina,* the Official Conclusions of the Conference of Latin American Bishops which met at Puebla, Mexico in Jan. 1979. The conclusions cover five parts: 1) Pastoral Overview of the Reality that is Latin America; 2) God's Saving Plan for Latin America; 3) Evangelization in the Latin American Church: Communion and Participation; 4) A Missionary Church Serving Evangelization in Latin America; and 5) Under the Dynamism of the Spirit: Pastoral Options. The comments on political power are most suggestive: "Political power is divinized when in practice it is regarded as absolute. Hence the totalitarian use of power is a form of idolatry; and as such, the Church completely rejects it. We grieve to note the presence of many authoritarian and even oppressive regimes on our continent . . . There is an urgent need to liberate our peoples from the idol of absolutized power so that they may live together in a society based on justice and freedom." [D.W. Dent]

Conflict, order and peace in the Americas. See *HLAS 42:1925.*

6027 Congreso Latinoamericano de Derecho Constitucional, 1st, México, 1975. El predominio del poder ejecutivo en Latinoamérica. Manuel Barquín Alvarez et al. México: UNAM, Instituto de Investigaciones Jurídicas, 1977. 450 p.; bibl. (Serie B, Estudios comparativos—UNAM, Instituto de Investigaciones Jurídicas: d. Derecho latinoamericano; no. 13)

This collection of articles on the political executive in Latin America joins very formalistic essays that focus almost entirely on constitutions used in the region during the past 160 years. [G. Wynia]

6028 The Continuing struggle for democracy in Latin America. Edited by Howard J. Wiarda; coauthored by Lee C. Fennell et al. Boulder, Colo.: Westview Press, 1980. 313 p.; bibl.; ill.; index (Westview special studies on Latin America and the Caribbean)

Series of 14 essays in honor of Harry Kantor on the quest for democracy in Latin America and the Caribbean. The major themes include the viability and appropriateness of democracy in Latin America and the special meaning the term carries south of the border. A serious effort to avoid the ethnocentrism of many North American scholars and to offer a "new formulation based on indigenous, Latin American institutions and understandings." According to Wiarda's "yardstick," Costa Rica, Venezuela, Colombia, and the Dominican Republic are the most democratic although they are "quite distinct from the Anglo-American variety." Democracy is by no means dead as a formulation for rule in Latin America despite the rash of military coups and widespread violations of human rights. [D.W. Dent]

6029 Cueva, Agustín. Teoría social y procesos políticos en América Latina. México: Edicol, 1979. 195 p.; bibl. (Línea crítica)

Ecuadorian sociologist attempts a dialectical analysis of the process of political change in Latin America over the past 15 years in order to demonstrate the rise of the fascist state. The critique of dependency models has more value than the conceptual treatment of fascism. [D.W. Dent]

6030 Debray, Régis. The revolution on trial. Translated by Rosemary Sheed. Harmondsworth, Eng.: Penguin Books, 1978. 364 p.; bibl. (His A critique of arms; v. 2. Peregrine books)

Further thoughts on the theory of guerrilla warfare by the leading international exponent of Guevarism. Three cases—Venezuela, Guatemala and Uruguay (Tupamaros)—are studied for what the revolutionary struggle tells us about the strategy, tactics, and goals of the key participants in their efforts to seize power and overthrow the bourgeois state. The general "lesson" from the Venezuelan story is that "revolutionary violence cannot win against a broadly liberal republic in which universal suffrage and a

normal political life serve to canalize and deflect the energy of the masses." The Guatemalan revolution is plagued by the difficulty of integrating the Indians into the planning, execution, and leadership of the guerrilla struggle. The effort to write revolutionary theory is not matched by the author's impassioned plea for the necessity of profiting from past mistakes. Original French title *Epreuves du feu*. [D.W. Dent]

6031 Desco. Area de Estudios Políticos. Genocidio económico en el Cono Sur: derechos humanos y gran capital. Lima: Desco, 1978. 115 p.; bibl.; graph (Praxis-Desco; no. 13)

Written by the staff of the Center for the Study and Promotion of Development in Lima, Peru, this study examines the human rights and economic consequences of the military authoritarian regime. It draws its evidence primarily from Argentina, Brazil and Chile and is more concerned with the description of conditions than theoretical development. [G. Wynia]

6032 Dias David, Mauricio. El estado en América Latina y los militares en la política latinoamericana (UC/I, 7:2/8:1, 1978, p. 133–160)

The topics of these two select bibliographies are the state in Latin America (193 items) and the role of the military over the past 15 years (301 items). Major focus is on Argentina, Brazil, Chile, Peru, and Mexico. Conspicuously absent is material from Cuba and Ecuador. [D.W. Dent]

Dix, Robert H. Non-urban oppositions in Latin America. See *HLAS 42:1927.*

6033 Dodson, Michael. The Christian left in Latin American politics (SAGE/JIAS, 21:1, Feb. 1979, p. 45–68, bibl.)

A critical examination of the developmental role of the Christian left in Argentina (Movement of Priests for the Third World) and Chile (Christians for Socialism). The developmentalist literature offers little for explaining the strategy and tactics of radicals seeking social change within the Church. An important corrective for the developmental paradigm using the two cases of Argentina and Chile. [D.W. Dent]

6034 ———. Liberation theology and Christian radicalism in contemporary Latin America (JLAS, 2:1, May 1979, p. 203–222)

Using the Argentine Movement of Priests for the Third World as a case study, author examines the politics of liberation theology focusing on their theories of underdevelopment, justification for political action, and attempts to achieve religious and secular goals. Valuable in its discussion of the genesis of Christian radicalism. However, the connection between dependency and oppression is not well established but some of the pitfalls in liberation theology's simple dependency model are well taken. [D.W. Dent]

6035 Encuentro Latinoamericano de Científicos Sociales y Teólogos, *San José, Costa Rica, 1978.* Capitalismo, violencia y anti-vida: la opresión de las mayorías y la domesticación de los dioses: ponencias del Encuentro Latinoamericano de Científicos Sociales y Teólogos, auspiciado por el CSUSA, San José, 21–25 de febrero de 1978. Elsa Tamez y Saúl Trinidad, eds.; portada, Hugo Díaz. Ciudad Universitaria Rodrigo Facio, Costa Rica: Editorial Universitaria Centroamericana, 1978. 2 v.; bibl. (Colección DEI)

Contributions by Christians in search of a revolutionary theory. More relevant for theologians than political scientists. [A. Suárez]

6036 Escovar Salom, Ramón. El presidencialismo en América Latina (ACPS/B, 38:75/76, oct. 1978/marzo 1979, p. 119–134)

The Latin American president is an outgrowth of the caudillo-military tradition with emphasis on a strong and personalistic ruler. Author sees the paternalistic and authoritarian nature of the presidential office as a consequence of the poorly integrated and weakly institutionalized societies of Latin America. This Weberian analysis places considerable emphasis on legitimizing authority as the key to democratic rule in Latin America. A brief but thoughtful analysis. [D.W. Dent]

6037 Francis, Michael J. Studying Latin American politics: methods or fads? (UND/RP, 42:1, Jan. 1980, p. 35–55)

A review of the major intellectual currents in the study of Latin American politics reveals a tendency towards fadishness exemplified by approaches with labels such as bureaucratic-authoritarianism, corporatism, clientelism, dependency, and functionalism.

Author calls for a more comparative and theoretically balanced approach to the study of Latin America by political scientists on both sides of the Rio Grande river. Brief, but a rather convincing critique. [D.W. Dent]

6038 Galeano, Eduardo. Open veins of Latin America: seven years after (MR, 30:7, 1978, p. 12–35)

This journalist, who wrote a popular book criticizing the exploitation of the Latin American masses by their leaders and foreigners, reviews conditions in the region seven years after the book was published. He concludes that the plight of the masses is even more desperate than before. [G. Wynia]

6039 García, Pío et al. La cuestión del fascismo en América Latina (CP, 18, oct./dic. 1978, p. 13–33)

The problem of the meaning and significance of fascism is considered through an assessment of dependency theorists such as Marini (fascismo militar) and dos Santos and Cueva (fascismo dependiente). Latin American fascism is understood to mean a form of bourgeois counterrevolution rooted in the contradictions and inequalities found in the capitalist-imperialist system. Socialist-imperialism and fascism do not seem to be analytic categories in the estimation of the author. [D.W. Dent]

6040 Gastil, Raymond D. The comparative survey of freedom IX (Freedom at Issue [Freedom House, New York] 49, Jan./Feb. 1979, p. 3–14, tables)

With freedom defined in terms of political rights and civil liberties, gains and losses for 1978 are measured in 211 independent nations and territories. Some of the progress—Dominican Republic (registered "the greatest advance in Latin America"), Panama, Brazil, Ecuador, Peru—is attributed to the Carter Administration. A somewhat ethnocentric index with considerable emphasis on pluralist democracies. Interestingly, Iran experienced a slight "improvement in freedom" in 1978. [D.W. Dent]

6041 Gooch, Herbert E. The military and politics in Latin America. Los Angeles: Latin American Studies Center, California State University, 1979. 76 p. (Latin America bibliography series; no. 7)

Excellent bibliography on the political activity of the Latin American armed forces.

Works of a general nature are included with studies of individual countries. The subdivisions of the first section are quite valuable since they distinguish between studies that focus on the military and its changing structure and role, intervention and rule, and theoretical studies of civil-military relations in general. The next step should be a bibliography of biographies of Latin American military leaders. [D.W. Dent]

6041a Grabendorff, Wolf. Militärherrschaft in Lateinamerika (BESPL, 1:5, Mai/Jun. 1976, p. 23–38)

Succinct analysis of the phenomenon of burgeoning military-authoritarian regimes in Latin America, denoting weak and underdeveloped political and social institutions in Latin America, a trend that seems will continue in the foreseeable future. [G.M. Dorn]

6042 Graham, Lawrence S. Democracy and the bureaucratic state in Latin America (*in* The Continuing struggle for democracy in Latin America [see item **6028**] p. 255–271)

Examines post-1964 South America in which bureaucratic states encompassing military and civilian elements have emerged seeking to achieve economic growth, political order, and regulated social change. Two themes are stressed. First, that the bureaucratic state is only one alternative to perpetual political conflict (Argentina) or fundamental social revolution based on Marxist-Leninist ideology (Cuba). Second, that the institutionalization of a democratic order in Venezuela is a product of "how political leaders in the major parties (AD, URD, and COPEI) responded to . . . various crises" rather than in the availability of extensive oil revenues. Author sees the forces supporting democracy on the upswing. [D.W. Dent]

6043 ———. Latin America, illusion or reality?: a case for a new analytic framework for the region (*in* Politics and social change in Latin America: the distinct tradition. Edited by Howard J. Wiarda. Amherst: University of Massachusetts Press, 1974, p. 231–248 [The University of Texas at Austin, Institute of Latin American Studies. Offprint series; 176])

Critical analysis of the "cultural unity thesis" indicating the need for a broader concept of "cultural area" to include some parts

of Latin America with Mediterranean Europe. An important step toward middle-level theory-building with important policy implications. [D.W. Dent]

6044 Hay que reinventar la democracia. Luis Herrera Campins et al. Maracaibo: Fondo Editorial Irfes, 1976. 364 p.; bibl.; ill. (Colección El Hombre y el Estado)

Latin American Christian Democratic leaders meet to discuss participatory democracy. There is more rhetoric than data in the outcome. The title of the book should be understood as a goal. It is doubtful that here they have made any progress. [A. Suárez]

6045 Hill, Kim Qualle and **Patricia A. Hurley.** Freedom of the press in Latin America: a thirty-year survey (LARR, 15:2, 1980, p. 212–218, table)

A very brief research note that presents an index of press freedom in Latin America and then applies it to all countries for the 1945–75 period. Designed to illustrate the utility of the index for measuring the phenomenon. [G. Wynia]

6046 Hopkins, Jack W. Democracy and elites in Latin America (*in* The Continuing struggle for democracy in Latin America [see item **6028**] p. 147–163)

The rapid decrease in both substantive and procedural democratic values in the Latin American political process is examined by author in the light of elite theory. An excellent survey of the literature is followed by a general critique of potentially relevant theory. Author examines elites in Peru, Mexico, Bolivia, and Cuba and concludes that in all four instances elites have sacrificed economic and political participation when they perceived that their respective political structures were threatened. The discussion is presented within the framework of Wiarda's conceptualization of corporatism. (For a complimentary argument, see Stepan's study of Peru, item **6480**.) Hopkins' excellent study will stimulate discussion of the credibility of elites in revolutionary societies such as the four studied here. A thoroughly provocative piece of research and writing. [W.R. Garner]

Huizer, Gerrit. Ciencia social aplicada y acción política: notas sobre nuevos enfoques. See item **8026**.

6047 La Iglesia y América Latina: aportes pastorales desde el CELAM, conclusiones de los principales encuentros organizados por el CELAM en los diez últimos años. Bogotá: Consejo Episcopal Latinoamericano, Secretariado General de CELAM, 1978. 1 v. (Auxiliar para la III Conferencia General del Episcopado Latinoamericano; 2)

Conclusions from 20 meetings organized by the Council of Latin American Bishops, 1968–78. Emphasis in vol. 2 is placed on the family and pastoral problems. [D.W. Dent]

6048 Inter-American Commission on Human Rights. Annual report of the Inter-American Commission on Human Rights to the General Assembly. Washington: General Secretariat, Organization of American States. 1 v. (OEA/ser.L/V/II)

This is the annual report of one of the primary investigators of human rights violations in the hemisphere. It is informative on the types of violations common to the region, offering descriptions of particular complaints that have been filed, though no data on the number of cases that exist in each country. Also offers some insight into what the Commission can and cannot do to reduce violations. [G. Wynia]

6049 Jackson, Steven; Bruce Russett; Duncan Snidal; and David Sylvan. An assessment of empirical research on *dependencia* (LARR, 14:3, 1979, p. 7–28, bibl., ill.)

A three-part essay designed to take stock of dependency theory after roughly 10 years of empirical research. The basic tenets of the pioneering works in dependency theory are examined, distinct methodologies designed to test the theory are scrutinized, and recent attempts to assess the utility and validity in the US and Europe are discussed. Their major conclusion is "that there is a need for a closer examination of the particular mechanisms of *dependencia* and for testing on both a cross-national and longitudinal basis." [D.W. Dent]

Johnson, Kenneth and **Miles W. Williams.** Democracy, power and intervention in Latin American political life: a study of scholarly images. See *HLAS 42:1931.*

6050 Kanyó, András. Latin-Amerika jövöje. Budapest: Ságvári Endre Könyvszerkesztöség, 1979. 184 p.

Hungarian analysis of contemporary Latin American politics which focuses on

the progress of revolutionary movements. Deals with the impact of the Russian Revolution and Marxism-Leninism, the Popular Front governments, and the Cuban Revolution. Emphasizes the role of multinational corporations and how they affect internal and external politics in the hemisphere. [G.M. Dorn]

6050a Kaplan, Marcos. Der Faschismus in Lateinamerika (BESPL, 1:6, Jul./Aug. 1976, p. 23–32)

Brief analysis of fascism as a phenomenon in Latin American politics in the last four decades, pointing out the ebb and flow of this tendency. Whenever there is a strong urge toward law and order, fascistic trends make their appearance. [G.M. Dorn]

6051 Kelly, Philip L. Abraham Guillén and the strategy of the urban guerrilla: a model for Latin American revolution (*in* Rocky Mountain Council on Latin American Studies, XXV, Tucson, Ariz., 1977. Proceedings. Lincoln: University of Nebraska, 1977, p. 93–99)

A description and evaluation of the major elements of Guillén's strategies for revolution in Latin America with emphasis on: 1) the conditions for Latin American revolution; 2) continental revolutionary strategies; 3) urban guerrilla tactics; and 4) an assessment of his theories. Guillén is an important theorist who deserves more research attention than he has received given the rising urban unrest in the Third World. [D.W. Dent]

6052 Kryzanek, Michael J. Political parties, opposition politics, and democracy in Latin America (*in* The Continuing struggle for democracy in Latin America [see item 6028] p. 127–145)

The future of Latin American democracy and the potential role of political parties. Present parties are categorized in four groups: survivors, compromisers, outlaws, and victors. The author perceives some recent developments in the area opening a more favorable period for oposition parties. [A. Suárez]

6053 *Latin America 1978.* Facts on File, Inc. 1978– . New York.

As with other volumes in this annual series, it offers lists of the major events in each Latin American country during 1978. It is a useful reference work. [G. Wynia]

6054 Latin American politics & development. Edited by Howard J. Wiarda & Harvey F. Kline. Boston: Houghton Mifflin, 1979. 525 p.; bibl.; ill.; index.

Introductory textbook with a country-by-country approach designed to incorporate the bulk of the recent literature on Latin American politics and development: dependency, corporatism, state capitalism, and military authoritarianism. Both similar and differential aspects of the Latin American political tradition are examined through its Catholic-Latin heritage and efforts to gradually absorb new groups "into the political process without the old ones being destroyed or the basic hierarchical structure of society upset." The country studies are a bit uneven but the book manages to capture both the common patterns and the nuances of modern American politics. Authors detect many changes on the horizon with both a decline in US domination and a developmental path for Latin America that "may not be in conformity with historic U.S. and West European experiences." [D.W. Dent]

6055 Lechner, Norbert. La crisis del Estado en América Latina. Diseño tapa, Luis Marsón. Caracas: El Cid Editor, 1977. 160 p.; bibl. (Colección Estudios interdisciplinarios; 6)

From the standpoint of international law and political philosophy, author examines the present functions of the state as: 1) nation-state; 2) government; 3) a system for socialist development; or 4) for dependency and domination. Writing from his experiences as participant in the Allende administration and his perceptions of the present Pinochet regime, author presents various definitions of the state as options. This is a significant departure from the usual leftist perspective of the "state" as a negative or policy-oriented concept. A thoughtful essay in political philosophy by a Marxist. [W.R. Garner]

6056 Lernoux, Penny. Cry of the people: United States involvement in the rise of fascism, torture, and murder and the persecution of the Catholic Church in Latin America. Garden City, N.Y.: Doubleday, 1980. 535 p.; index.

A vivid account of the Catholic Church's struggle against military dictatorships in Latin America. Author depicts a reign of terror unequalled in the history of Latin America where dictatorial regimes, supported by the Central Intelligence Agency, the Defense Department, and multinational corporations, have openly attacked the Church as subversive due to its evangelizing activities since 1968. Appendices include a "Martyr Survey" and a Pentagon course for Latin American military officers on "Utilization and Containment of Rumors" to combat subversion. [D.W. Dent]

6057 ———. The Latin American Church (LARR, 15:2, 1980, p. 201–211, bibl.)

A examination of the literature available on recent developments in the Latin American Catholic Church, especially magazines and newspapers. [A. Suárez]

6058 Levine, Daniel H. Authority in church and society: Latin American models (CSSH, 20:4, 1978, p. 517–544)

An examination of the changing relationship between religion and contemporary Latin American society and politics. Methodological issues and conceptual difficulties are debated while the author argues for a more phenomenological approach to understanding contemporary religious behavior. The changing concepts of authority are examined through several case studies of individual attitudes (bishops), structures (national Catholic organizations and local dioceses) and national contexts (Venezuela and Colombia). Theoretically interesting and empirically valuable comparative analysis. Author's conclusions indicate a "trend toward action, participation, testimony, and witness as basis for authority, and the development of a framework of collective responsibility as their expression." [D.W. Dent]

6059 Lewis, Paul H. Development strategies and the decline of the democratic left in Latin America (in The Continuing struggle for democracy in Latin America [see item 6028] p. 185–199)

An examination of the rise of dictatorships in Latin America (1961–76) with an emphasis on economic causes as central to the breakdown of democratic regimes. After reviewing three strategies—monetarism, moderate structuralism, and radical structuralism—author concludes that "democracy is unlikely to flourish in Latin America for some time." [D.W. Dent]

6060 Linz Storch de Gracia, Juan José. The breakdown of democratic regimes: crisis, breakdown, and reequilibration. Baltimore: Johns Hopkins University Press, 1978. 130 p.; bibl.; index (A Johns Hopkins paperback)

Excellent theoretical discussion of the breakdown of democracies with considerable emphasis on the interplay of leadership effectiveness and regime legitimacy. Author concludes with a perceptive dilemma for political elites: "The vain hope of making democracies more democratic by undemocratic means has all too often contributed to regime crisis and ultimately paved the way to autocratic rule." Essential reading for understanding one of Latin America's core political problems: the establishment of legitimate authority. For historian's comment, see *HLAS 42:1920*. [D.W. Dent]

6060a Merin, Boris M. Revoliutsiia i kontrrevoliutsiia v Latinskoi Amerike [Revolution and counter-revolution in Latin America]. Moscow: Izdatel'stvo Politichesko literatury, 1977. 77 p.

A political analysis of the "revolutionary process in Latin America" which emphasizes the role of the "heroic working class"—its basic motive force. [R.V. Allen]

6060b Mexiko, Brasilien, Argentinien: Aspekte eines Vergleichs (UB/GG, 2:2, 1976, p. 234–240)

In comparing the revolutions of Mexico, Brazil and Argentina, the article points out that the post-revolutionary development of Mexico and Brazil has been more favorable economically than that of Argentina, because the earlier revolutions gave the countries enough time to pull their resources together and reorganize their countries. [R.V. Shaw]

6061 Movimientos revolucionarios en América Latina: documentación propia. t. 1, Guatemala, Colombia, Venezuela. 2. ed. Caracas: Información Documental de América Latina, 1972. 1 v.; bibl.; indexes (Dossier—Información Documental de América Latina; no. 1)

Selection of original documents from 10 revolutionary groups in Guatemala (2), Colombia (6), and Venezuela (2). Ideology, strategy, tactics, and goals are emphasized in

what have to be rather rare documents. An interesting annex contains the translated Guide for Counterinsurgency Planning from the US Army Warfare School, Fort Bragg, North Carolina. [D.W. Dent]

6061a Nekotorye problemy natsional'noosvoboditel'noi bor'by v Latinskoi Amerika [Some problems of the national liberation struggle in Latin America]. Prague: Mezhdunarodnoe izdatel'stov "Mira i sotsializm," 1977. 208 p.

Part of this volume consists of articles from the journal *Problemy Mira i Sotsializma* (*Problems of Peace and Socialism*) and the other of papers from a symposium held in Havana on "Protection of natural resources as a weapon in the struggle for the freedom of Latin America." Participants in this all seem to be Latin Americans. [R.V. Allen]

6062 The New authoritarianism in Latin America. David Collier, editor; contributors, Fernando Henrique Cardoso et al.; sponsored by the Joint Committee on Latin American Studies of the Social Science Research Council and the American Council of Learned Societies. Princeton, N.J.: Princeton University Press, 1979. 456 p.; bibl.; ill.; index.

This work is a major addition to the study of military authoritarianism in the region. It is composed of original articles by the leading scholars in the field that respond to and extend the analysis of Guillermo O'Donnell and other pathfinders of the early 1970s. It raises many theoretical issues and offers a variety of solutions for them. [G. Wynia]

6063 Nichols, Glenn A. Further misadventures in the study of Latin American politics: pluralism, Marxism, corporatism and an alternative (*in* Rocky Mountain Council on Latin American Studies, XXV, Tucson, Ariz., 1977. Proceedings. Lincoln: University of Nebraska, 1977, p. 111–119)

A study of the Brazilian National Democratic Union (1945–60) suggests to the author an alternative theory for the explanation of Latin American politics called social fragmentation. Closed, non-competitive decision-making regimes in the region, reflect social fragmentation and its outcome, lack of consensus. The new approach seems to be a reformulation of some thoughts offered by Charles W. Anderson years ago. [A. Suárez]

6064 Nixon, Raymond B. La enseñanza del periodismo en América Latina (CYC, 2, jan. 1978, p. 197–212, bibl., tables)

What kind of training does the professional journalist receive in Latin America? The teaching of professional journalists has made great strides in the creation of centers of journalistic studies (e.g., CIESPAL—International Center for Advanced Studies of Journalism for Latin America) through local and international efforts. Yet journalists still must face political systems that produce a general frustration after learning the craft. Useful assessment of the journalism profession as of 1970. [D.W. Dent]

6065 Nunn, Frederick M. Latin American militarylore: an introduction and a case study (AAFH/TAM, 35:4, April 1979, p. 429–474)

"Militarylore" is largely the *civilian perception* of the strength, expertise, education, and other qualities of a nation's armed forces as well as their value as "symbol" (a subjective or psychological factor). If the perception of the general population is negative, then the military must create images that preserve their symbolic/subjective as well as objective capabilities as an internal national force. Author uses the Chilean military as the case study for the application of these hypotheses. Formerly perceived as professionals in the European sense, Chile's armed forces by 1970 experienced both a sense of loss of civilian respect and much of its positive self-image. As a result, the military became highly reactive, hyper-sensitive, apprehensive, and defensive. Most officers were "convinced that civilians held them in low regard." This problem of morale was "solved" by the conflict between the Allende administration and of right-wing groups committed to its overthrow. Thus, the conflict bolstered the military's perception of themselves and allowed a non-political, professional group to engage in activity which would have normally been beneath them—the 11 Sept. 1973 coup which toppled the Allende government—and placed them squarely in the seat of Chilean political power. This, according to the author, represented the rebirth of "unchanging military ideals." For historian's comment, see *HLAS 42:3244.* [W.R. Garner]

6066 Pearson, Neale J. Peasant and worker *sindicatos* and democracy in Latin America (*in* The Continuing struggle for democracy in Latin America [see item **6028**] p. 79–106, tables)

This study of rural and urban worker political participation begins with development of a typology of union or syndicate organizational forms. Some of the organizations are *organic* in the sense that they are controlled from above (usually by government), others are sub-system dominant and are organized/controlled from the bottom. The major question asked by the author concerns the degree of system-dominance exhibited in each classification. Pearson concludes that a marked increase in organizational skills and political creativity will be necessary before organized labor can be assured independence in the face of constant threats on the part of government and informal elites. [W.R. Garner]

6067 Peña, Alfredo. Democracia y golpe militar. Diálogos de Rafael Caldera et al.; diseño portada, Jorge Pizzani. Caracas: Editorial Ateneo de Caracas, 1979. 292 p. (Colección Actualidad política. Grandes reportajes de Alfredo Peña)

Written by a journalist interested in the views of Latin American presidents who have been deposed by their countries' military, the book includes the texts of interviews with six presidents, two of whom were deposed by officers in the 1960s: Arturo Illia of Argentina and Fernando Belaunde Terry of Peru. Interesting reading, if only to acquaint one with the thoughts of a few Latin American leaders. [G. Wynia]

6068 Petras, James F. The Latin American agrotransformation from above and outside and its social and political implications (Journal of the Hellenic Diaspora [Pella Publishing Company, New York] 4:4, Winter 1978, p. 28–48, tables)

Challenging the stereotype of the inefficiently run *latifundista* agricultural enterprise, Petras asserts that agribusiness, in its "most capital-intensive" and efficient forms, is now the norm in Latin American rural areas. Still, this does not meet the needs of rural labor displaced or otherwise dispossessed of their small land holdings by an agricultural phenomenon now a firm part of the contemporary internal and international industrial-commercial spheres. Petras argues persuasively that exploitation of rural labor is the key to an understanding of agricultural export expansion in recent years which, in turn, is "part of the larger problems of a capitalist society." As corollaries to the above generalizations, author suggests that changes in the organization of latifundia, the emergence of a "new class" of landowners (hacendados), and the novel form of problems now faced by rural populations is the result of government action (usually of the "dictatorial" or single-party type) which provides the major impetus for corporate growth of a "capitalist agriculture" and a new "agroimperialism." Although the thesis is not entirely new or entirely Marxist, the analysis is strong and the article includes much hard data (note the exhaustive tables at the end of the piece). [W.R. Garner]

6069 ———. Social democracy in Latin America (NACLA, 14:1, Jan./Feb. 1980, p. 36–39)

In raising questions about recent conceptualizations of military rule, the author Author sees an increasing intervention of European social democracy in Latin America due to the convergence of military-authoritarianism and the expansion of European trade and investment in the area. These efforts to extend social democracy can be seen in efforts to win over major elements within the Sandinista Movement, the Brazilian Labor Party, the New Jewel Movement in Grenada and the People's National Party in Jamaica. Social democracy is portrayed as a failure due to its disinterest or inability to "alter the fundamental property, class and state relations that perpetuate inequalities." [D.W. Dent]

6070 Philip, George. The military institution revisted: some notes on corporatism and military rule in Latin America (JLAS, 12:2, Nov. 1980, p. 421–436)

In raising questions about recent conceptualizations of military rule, the author contrasts the studies of the 1960s (Huntington, et al.) with those of the 1970s (Schmitter, Stepan, et al.). He stresses importance of not losing sight of traits of the military itself (e.g., ideology, subjective outlook, institutional behavior) as well as specific coup-provoking crises in understanding the rise and institutional weaknesses of contemporary military rule. A welcome reflection on the state of knowledge. [G. Wynia]

6071 Poblete, Renato. From Medellín to Puebla (SAGE/JIAS, 21:1, Feb. 1979, p. 31–44)

Author reflects on the maturation process of the Latin American Church from Medellín (1968) to Puebla (1978) with special reference to its evangelizing mission. Medellín set the tone for the necessity of awakening the masses to consciousness so that they could become true agents of their own liberation from oppressiveness—economic, political, and cultural. In the Pre-Document of Puebla both individualistic and collectivistic ideologies are criticized as materialistic and atheistic. A thoughtful piece from a Chilean Jesuit priest. [D.W. Dent]

6072 The Politics of terrorism. Edited by Michael Stohl. New York: M. Dekker, 1979. 419 p.; bibl.; index (Political science; 9)

Twelve essays on the theory and practice of political terrorism. The major theories, concepts, strategies, ideologies, practices, and implications are explored to assist in the understanding of terrorism in a cross-national context. Stohl's analysis of "enforcement" terror and "agitational" terror in the Southern Cone nations highlights the fact that "the greater resources of the Latin American governments allow them to engage in levels of enforcement terror that have so far overwhelmed the practitioners of agitational terrorism." An important book for all those who want to understand unconventional political behavior by the right and left. Recommended reading for the Reagan foreign policy team. [D.W. Dent]

6072a Politisches Lexikon Lateinamerika. Hrsg. von Peter Waldmann unter Mitarbeit von Ulrich Zelinsky. München, FRG.: Verlag C.H. Beck, 1980. 421 p.; maps (Beck'sche Schwarze Reihe; Bd. 221)

Thorough and detailed political dictionary which provides basic historical, economic, demographic, political, and other pertinent information on each Latin American and Caribbean country and territory. Each country entry is followed by a brief bibliography. A special section is devoted to inter-American and regional economic organizations (e.g., Andean Pact, Inter-American Development Bank, etc.). A total of 25 West German scholars contributed to this valuable and up-to-date reference work. German, US, and Latin American primary and secondary sources were used to compile this dictionary. [G.M. Dorn]

6073 Posadas, J. El desarrollo económico, la democracia y la lucha por el socialismo en América Latina. México, D.F.: Costa-Amic, 1979. 157 p. (Colección Ciencia, cultura y política)

Collection of Marxist articles on such subjects as the lack of uniformity in present political structures for functional conflict in Latin American anti-imperialist wars. Author stresses the breakdown of capitalism, the present state of Latin American development, and the need for unity in the present situation of exploitation. Peruvian, Bolivian, and Chilean case studies are presented in an effort to demonstrate the necessity of a Muscovite-Marxist solution. Interesting polemic. [W.R. Garner]

Rachum, Ilan. The Latin American revolutions of 1930: a non-economic interpretation. See *HLAS 42:1941.*

6074 Ranis, Peter. Latin American chronicle: the worker and the state in Latin America; patterns of domination and subordination (IIDC/C, 29:1/2, 1979, p. 157–174)

How has the Latin American industrial laborer been treated by the state? Using the four cases of Chile and Argentina (repressive state system), Mexico (cooptative state system), and Puerto Rico (circumscriptive state system), author examines the plight of the working classes under government policies of import-substitution industrialization. The conclusions indicate that urban labor has retrogressed in terms of civil liberties and economic power, and one is left with the gnawing question of how long these negative patterns can continue. [D.W. Dent]

6075 Revel, Jean-François. The trouble with Latin America (FIU/CR, 8:3, Summer 1979, p. 13–17, ill.)

The backwardness of Latin America is attributed to indigenous political causes rather than colonialism, imperialism, scarcity of natural resources, or overpopulation. An interesting and valuable comparative assessment of the use of language in explaining Latin America's development problems. The trouble with Latin America is "the underdevelopment of political intelligence." [D.W. Dent]

6076 Reynaga Burgoa, Ramiro. Ideología y raza em América Latina. La Paz?: Ediciones Futuro Bolivia, 1972. 205 p.; bibl.

Radical assessment of the Indian problem which author sees as stemming from the deliberate exclusion of all indigenous peoples from modern structures and practices of Latin American political life. Author indicts abuse and exclusion (the "two Americas" concept) and calls for mobilization ("concientización") of Indian populations in recognition of the fact that their race is stronger than that of whites and mestizos. Author demands that Indians be included in "anti-imperialist wars," guerrilla movements and, in general, Latin American policies for an "Indianization of Marxism." Latin American history must be rewritten and indigenous groups must be formed into syndicates and political parties with all efforts leading to total war against both internal and international forms of discrimination. This broadside attack on virtually all non-Indian groups is one of the angriest volumes to be published in recent years and reflects the author's indiscriminate acceptance of a genetic/Marxist determinism. [W.R. Garner]

Reynal, Susana Mallo. Bibliografía sobre movimiento obrero latinoamericano. See *HLAS 42:61.*

6077 Rosa M., Martín de la. La Iglesia Católica en México: del Vaticano II a la CELAM III, 1965–1979 (CP, 19, enero/marzo 1979, p. 88–104)

The Catholic Church in Mexico is in a state of crisis due to a mixture of views on goals and tactics for bringing about social change within the leftist elements of the Church. The details of the cases of Lemercier and Ilich provide interesting examples of the four periods that are investigated, 1965–79. [D.W. Dent]

6078 Rosenberg, Mark B. and **James M. Malloy.** Indirect participation versus social equity in the evolution of Latin American social security policy (*in* Political participation in Latin America. Edited by John A. Booth and Mitchell A. Seligson. v. 1, Citizen and state. New York: Holmes & Meier, 1978, p. 157–171)

What is the relationship between indirect citizen participation and social security policy development in Latin America? The cases that are examined reveal that a negative relationship exists and the more successful efforts to broaden social equity have come about through authoritarian regimes where political competition is held at bay. [D.W. Dent]

6079 Scaff, Lawrence A. and **Edward J. Williams.** Participation and the primacy of politics in developmental theory (*in* Political participation in Latin America. Edited by John A. Booth and Mitchell A. Seligson. v. 1, Citizen and state. New York: Holmes & Meier, 1978, p. 43–58)

A restatement and defense of political participation and the "primacy of politics" in the contemporary developmental process, based on the need for organization, communication, legitimacy, consultation, accountability, justice, political education, and efficacy. The anti-authoritarian critique is quite commendable but the pluralist democratic bias is also evident. [D.W. Dent]

6079a Schöpfer, Hans. Zum Status quaestionis der lateinamerikanischen Befreiungstheologie (ZMR, 1:62, jan. 1978, p. 46–51)

This article is followed by an English summary: "In this article, which is part of a report on a 3 months journey through several Latin-American countries, the author starts off with the explanation of the manifold uses of the term 'liberation', the content (and meaning) of which depends very much on the political situation in the various countries, and on the individuality of the various theologians themselves. He goes on to point out the growing discussion on hermeneutics within the dialogue with European theologians. He proposes the term 'social engagement' as a new common working tool for the socio-theological field. The author then talks of the development in the ecumenic field where we can discern a certain convergence of the various dominations through their common social engagement. Finally, he refers to the tensions within the Church and to the internationalisation of matters which are the special concern of the political theology." [R.V. Shaw]

6080 Seligson, Mitchell A. Unconventional political participation: cynicism, powerlessness, and the Latin American peasant (*in* Political participation in Latin America. Edited by John A. Booth and Mitchell A. Seligson. v. 2, Politics and the poor. New York: Holmes & Meier, 1978, p. 134–146, tables)

A cross-cultural survey of attitudes of Costa Rican peasants (small holders, squatters, landless) toward land invasions (squatting) reveals some interesting parallels with unconventional participation in the US. Author finds small-holders to be both trusting and efficacious while the landless peasants feel politically powerless and cynical. Squatters, however, were found to have higher levels of both cynicism and efficacy than the other two types. An important empirical study with powerful policy implications. [D.W. Dent]

6081 —— and **John A. Booth.** Development, political participation, and the poor in Latin America (*in* Political participation in Latin America. Edited by John A. Booth and Mitchell A. Seligson. v. 2, Politics and the poor. New York: Holmes & Meier, 1978, p. 3–8)

An assessment of the Huntington thesis in which the authors argue that some forms of participation are not inherently destabilizing and capable of exacerbating socioeconomic inequality. Their findings, however, pose an interesting paradox: "Communal participation, by helping alleviate some of the more acute manifestations of poverty for individuals and increasing economic development independently of the state, may by these very acts help perpetuate regimes responsible for the gross inequities between rich and poor in Latin America." Valuable normative analysis of the costs of non-revolution. [D.W. Dent]

6082 Sheahan, John. Market-oriented economic policies and political repression in Latin America (UC/EDCC, 28:2, Jan. 1980, p. 267–291, tables)

The military regimes that arose in Latin America after 1964 usually were repressive and often pursued market-oriented economic policies. In this article, the author explores this relationship and finds that although repression is increasingly believed necessary to pursue economic development, development can be promoted in Latin America without it. He suggests ways of increasing economic efficiency while reducing repression. A thoughtful essay on a very important relationship in need of much greater analysis. [G. Wynia]

6083 Shepherd, George W. Liberation theology and class struggle in Southern Africa and Latin America (NEA/RBPE, 9:2, Winter 1979, p. 159–173)

The theology of liberation concept is viewed as a version of the class struggle carried out in the confrontation between the First and Third Worlds of development. Parallels are drawn between liberation theology in Africa and Latin America with emphasis on goals, strategies, and stages of development. [D.W. Dent]

6084 Smith, Brian H. Churches and human rights in Latin America: recent trends in the subcontinent (SAGE/JIAS, 21:1, Feb. 1979, p. 89–128, bibl.)

Covers Chile, Brazil, Paraguay, Bolivia, and Argentina since the early 1970s. Analyzes programs, range of activities, and impact of both on the political system and the Church itself. At least, the Church is blunting the impact of the repression applied by military regimes. [A. Suárez]

6085 Los Textos de Medellín y el proceso de cambio en América Latina. San Salvador: Universidad Centroamericana José Simeón Cañas, UCA Editores, 1977. 157 p. (Colección La Iglesia en América Latina; 1)

Full text of the 1968 meeting of the Latin American episcopate in Medellín, Colombia, where three fundamental topics were discussed: human promotion by the reaffirmation of peace and justice, evangelization, and reflection on the visible Church and its structure. Contains a useful index for locating major themes in the documents. [D.W. Dent]

6086 Therborn, Göran. Las tribulaciones de la democracia en América Latina (Estudios Contemporáneos [Universidad Autónoma de Puebla, México] 1:1, enero/marzo 1980, p. 67–97, tables)

Historical analysis of the tribulations of bourgeois democracy in Latin American development with an emphasis on electoral fraud, inter-party conflict resolution, the role of the lower classes, and social inequalities. The classification scheme is interesting but not very helpful in understanding democratic reform governments. [D.W. Dent]

6087 Tobón, Nydia. Carlos, ¿terrorista o guerrillero?: mis vivencias. Barcelona: Ediciones Grijalbo, 1978. 217 p. (Colección Nuevo norte; 24)

"Carlos" is the nom-de-guerre of the international terrorist born in Venezuela, Ilich Ramírez Sánchez. A semi-fictional account of the semi-romantic involvement between the author, a Colombian ex-communist and Ilich. A combination soap-opera/thriller. [A. Suárez]

6088 Trías, Vivian. Getulio Vargas, Juan Domingo Perón y Batlle Berres-Herrera: tres rostros del populismo (NSO, 34, enreo/feb. 1978, p. 28–39, ill.)

Superficial comparison of three Latin American populist leaders that attempts to distinguish the political movements they generated from those associated with bourgeois revolutions in 19th-century Europe. [G. Wynia]

6088a Uschner, Manfred. Neue revolutionäre Erschütterungen in Lateinamerika (IIB/DA, 24:12, Dez. 1979, p. 42–55)

East German author summarizes recent revolts and riots in several Central American and South American countries. He deplores the actions of the Social Democrats who are proselytizing in South America and also gaining ground there. His article is the usual diatribe against US imperialism in South America. He predicts the continuation of class warfare in the South American countries. [R.V. Shaw]

6088b ———. Zu den gegenwärtigen Entwicklungstendenzen in Lateinamerika (IIB/DA, 22:6, 1977, p. 57–67)

The author describes the political atmosphere of different Latin American countries from a thoroughly Marxist viewpoint. Although he anticipates the victory of counter-revolutionary forces in 1977, he points to Cuba as the beacon of hope for the years to come. [R.V. Shaw]

6089 Varela, Roberto. The limits of Latin American political participation: a critique of the revisionist literature (in Political participation in Latin America. Edited by John A. Booth and Mitchell A. Seligson. v. 2, Politics and the poor. New York: Holmes & Meier, 1978, p. 147–152)

A critical examination of descriptive and theoretical material on the political participation of the Latin American peasantry. Valuable comments from an anthropologist who feels that complex quantitative methodologies are not entirely suitable for understanding Latin American peasant societies. What is apparently missing is an emphasis on power structures as important elements of a theory of political participation. [D.W. Dent]

6090 Vekemans, Roger. Teología de la liberación y cristianos por el socialismo. Bogotá: CEDIAL, 1976. 592 p.; bibl.

Two-part study of the theology of liberation in Latin America and the Christians for socialism in Chile. [D.W. Dent]

6091 Verner, Joel G. Socioeconomic environment, political system, and educational policy outcomes: a comparative analysis of 102 countries (CUNY/CP, 11:2, Jan. 1979, p. 165–188, tables)

Using an Eastonian systems conceptualization of politics, author attempts to locate the independent variables associated with educational policy outcomes. Are political variables or environmental factors the key determinants of educational outcomes? Multivariate analysis shows that socioeconomic environmental variables are more important in determining educational outcomes. [D.W. Dent]

6092 Villegas, Abelardo. Cultura y política en América Latina. México: Extemporáneos, 1978. 157 p.; bibl. (Colección Latinoamericana: Serie Ensayo; 5)

Papers written by a student of Latin American philosophy and previously published. The title reflects more intention than performance. [A. Suárez]

6092a Wagner de Reyna, Alberto. Lateinamerika zwischen Okzident und Dritter Welt (IA/ZK, 26:1, 1976, p. 52–58)

The author discusses the position of Latin America between the West and the Third World. He deplores the quantitative measurements employed by the West to measure the progress of man and maintains that the spiritual values of Latin America have been ignored by the developed nations. This may alienate Latin America from the Western powers. [R.V. Shaw]

Wiarda, Howard J. Corporatist theory and ideology: a Latin American development paradigm. See *HLAS 42:1824.*

———. Critical elections and critical coups: state, society and the military in the process of Latin American development. See *HLAS 42:1952.*

6093 ———. Critical elections and critical groups: the processes of sociopolitical realignment in Latin American development (*in* The Continuing struggle for democracy in Latin America [see item **6028**] p. 27–69)

Realignment as a concept is expanded to include "critical coups" in Latin America which are hypothesized to serve as functional equivalents of elections as they exist in the Anglo-American tradition. Some preliminary ideas for testing empirically the "critical coup" and additional areas of study are suggested. The key to this study "is the idea that in Latin America what has been termed 'critical realignments' can be either by elections *or* by coups, or some combination of the two, depending on the country, the time period, and the circumstances." A serious effort to use a comparative approach to expand theoretical knowledge and understanding of Latin America on its own terms. [D.W. Dent]

6094 Wilde, Alexander. Ten years of change in the Church: Puebla and the future (SAGE/JIAS, 21:3, Aug. 1979, p. 299–312, bibl.)

An account of the theological directions forged by the texts of Medellín in 1968, the rise of military-authoritarian governments, and the evolution of a more socially committed and political aware church leadership. Author argues that the future cannot be extrapolated from the changes of the past 10 years but the "political context of particular national churches and the degree to which unity and momentum can be maintained around the central purposes of evangelization" will help to shape the role of the Latin American church in the years to come. [D.W. Dent]

6095 Würtele, Werner. La FITIM y las corporaciones multinacionales (NSO, sept./oct. 1978, p. 67–93, tables)

Concentrating on metal and automobile industries (world-wide and particularly within Latin America), author offers the interesting hypothesis that the growth of international unionism—coinciding with the increase of multinational corporate influence in Latin America—has resulted in a confrontation of labor and management in which unions are relatively weaker. The comparative disadvantage of union organizations is heightened by "dependency" economics. The present system is aided by internal/national Latin American elites and, particularly, national military governments thereby sapping the potential strength of increasingly sophisticated union organizations. A novel, important contribution. [W.R. Garner]

6096 Zegeye, Befekadu. On the nature of "leftist juntas" (MR, 31:3, July/Aug. 1979, p. 51–61)

Author, an Ethiopian Marxist, explores the nature of military "fascisms"

claiming socialist/revolutionary goals. The present power of military regimes in the Third World is seen as a result of deliberate sabotage of civilian political processes "in the last stages of colonialism." Military groups, now aligned with national civilian bourgeois groups demand a quality of "order" for their own particular internal exploitation and, toward this end, have formed "corporatist" political structures. Control of the society's productive enterprise is achieved through nationalization in the name of socialist "revolution" with the national bourgeois ruling class serving as manager. Thus, the marriage of military with bourgeois management through government bureaucracy assures control of economic power in the furtherance of the armed forces' interests. [W.R. Garner]

MEXICO, CENTRAL AMERICA, THE CARIBBEAN AND THE GUIANAS

ANDRES SUAREZ, *Professor of Political Science, Center for Latin American Studies, University of Florida*

THE PRESENT CENTRAL AMERICAN CRISIS, precipitated by the increasing military power of the Nicaraguan Sandinistas, is beginning to generate a body of literature that attempts to articulate the leadership's new revolutionary policy. Several items reviewed for this section offer glimpses into the origins and elaboration of this policy, referred to in the literature as a "politico-military strategy." A good example is the tract issued by the FSLN (item **6222**). Published eight months before the Sandinista victory, it contains no intimation that the authors, members of a political trend within the leadership known as the Proletarian Tendency, felt any need to alter their standard mode of operation. The authors strongly criticize both the old Communists and the "bourgeois voluntarism" represented by members of the second trend or the Guerra Popular Tendency, but strikingly enough, they make no reference to the third trend, the "Terceristas." Such an omission suggests that even in the last stages of the struggle the one trend that was to prevail over all others had not yet coalesced, or, at least, was not perceived as the embodiment of a new revolutionary strategy. In any case the contributions of Humberto Ortega (items **6231–6232**), particularly his interview with Marta Hanecker reproduced by *Nicarahuác*, provide the most informative statements on the nature of the new strategy, even if Ortega fails to clarify how the strategy originated. Also noteworthy are the observations of Régis Debray, an old friend of the Sandinistas, published after his visit to Nicaragua (item **6217**). Unfortunately, this knowledgeable and authoritative source fails to provide any information on either the new strategy or the real political orientations within the Sandinista leadership, now firmly in command, except to observe that "the rest is nothing else but a simple question of government."

Another item in the Central American section that deserves attention, for very different reasons, is R.W. Shaw's essay on integration (item **6162**). Using the approach suggested by recent studies of foreign policies in Third World countries, Shaw focuses on the main purpose of domestic elites (i.e., to obtain external resources). He explains the frustrations of the integrative process in a way that is both original and insightful.

The Caribbean section contains some remarkable contributions. Piero Gleijeses has written a very competent and impartial study of the 1965 Dominican crisis (item **6292**), particularly valuable for the impressive amount of information collected on the activities of the extreme left during the period. S. Sariola (item **6325**) contributes a thorough and impartial discussion of the very complex problem of Puerto Rico's political situation. Winston Mahabir's witty piece (item **6329**) belongs to a genre that unfortunately is neglected by scholars working on this area: an insider's revelations of the way in which ministerial business is transacted on a daily basis in Trinidad and Tobago. Finally, there is the massive book on Cuba by Jorge Domínguez (item **6265**). Some readers may find Domínguez's style too dry and his use of political science jargon disconcerning, and the book suffers from the lack of a concluding chapter which might have summarized the author's interpretation of the Cuban revolutionary phenomenon. However, the standard of scholarship in the book is consistently high, and some chapters, such as the one on agrarian question, are excellent. Although not a definitive work, the book represents a lasting and significant contribution to the study of Cuba.

The section on Mexico reflects an increasing interest in the role of the working class. Among the valuable studies on this topic are those by Aguilar García (item **6002**); Reyna (item **6148**); Loyo and Pozas (item **6133**); and Rosborough and Zapata (item **6150**). An important paper by John and Susan Kaufman Purcell questions the institutionalization of the Mexican regime. In so doing, they join the increasing number of analysts who reject the characterization of Mexico as an authoritarian state in the same category as Brazil, Argentina, Chile, and Uruguay.

MEXICO

6097 Abascal, Salvador. La revolución anti-mexicana. México: Editorial Tradición, 1978, 302 p.

Articles published in *La Hoja de Combate* during the last 10 years by Catholic polemicist. Designed to prepare Christian fighters against the Revolution. A sample of medieval debate.

6099 Bailey, John J. Presidency, bureaucracy, and administrative reform in Mexico: the Secretariat of Programming and Budget (IAMEA, 34:1, Summer 1980, p. 27–59, tables)

A good discussion based on research done in Mexico, despite the use of the term "corporatism," introduced without definition.

6100 Bennett, Douglas and **Kenneth Sharpe.** The state as banker and entrepreneur: the last-resort character of the Mexican state's economic intervention, 1917–76 (CUNY/CP, 12:2, Jan. 1980, p. 165–189)

A valuable effort to improve Alexander Gerschenkron's suggestion concerning the role of the state in development. Instead of perceiving class or group interests as variables that explain state action, authors' historical research indicates that state power and orientations explain the increasing role of the Mexican state after the Revolution. A suggestive paper.

6102 Cabrera, Luis. Obras completas. t. 3/4, Obra política. México: Ediciones Oasis, 1972/75. 2 v.; bibl.; port.

A participant, Cabrera was also one of the most lucid observers and analysts of the Mexican Revolution. The Mexican historian Eugenia Mejer has performed an invaluable service for scholars by editing these two volumes of Cabrera's political works, particularly vol. 3 which includes his most enduring contributions (the other volumes are: t. 1, *Obra jurídica*, and t. 2, *Obra literaria*). Vol. 3 is organized in three parts introduced by the editor who used original manuscripts whenever possible.

6103 _amp, Roderic Ai. The elitelore of Mexico's revolutionary family (UCLA/JLAL, 4:2, Winter, 1978, p. 149–181, table)

Based on interviews with members of the political elite between 1946–70. A brief appendix explains how the sample was chosen. "Elitelore" refers to beliefs and values as well as rationale offered for them. Includes information not easily available in other sources but there is much that remains questionable in the author's approach.

6104 ——. Mexico's leaders: their education and recruitment. Tucson: University of Arizona Press, 1979. 1 v.; bibl.; index.

Using his own excellent data bank of Mexican political biographies, the author discloses, among other significant findings, the paramount role played by UNAM, the National University, in the recruitment process. The book is a mine of information and offers insightful observations on the regime. But it does not go beyond the parameters of such research, never trying to link background variables to policies.

6105 ——. Quiénes alcansan la cumbre: la élite política mexicana (CM/FI, 19:1, julio/sept. 1978, p. 24–61, tables)

Another contribution by the author specialized in the study of the Mexican political elite. Uses a sample of 900 top positions in government, political parties, and trade unions. Independent variables are place of birth, social background and career patterns.

6106 ——. Women and political leadership in Mexico: a comparative study of female and male political elites (SPSA/JP, 41, 1979, p. 417–441)

Examination of the literature on Mexican women, and comparison between female and male political elites using background data collected by the author.

6107 Castillo, Herberto. La matanza fue preparada por Luis Echeverría (Puntos de Vista [Centro de Estudios Económicos y Sociales, San Luis Potosí] 5:18, oct./dic. 1978, p. 57–78, table)

Extremely revealing on some aspects of Mexican politics usually not available in the specialized literature: the author recounts a conversation with Alfonso Martínez Domínguez where the latter directly indicts President Echeverría as having ordered the students' massacre of June 1971. Martínez Domínguez, a top official at the time, resigned, an action regarded as an admission of responsibility for the crime.

Castillo V., Gustavo del. Crisis y transformación de una sociedad tradicional. See item **8082**.

6108 Congreso Obrero, *1st, Motul, México, 1918.* Tierra y libertad: Primer Congreso Obrero Socialista celebrado en Motul, Estado de Yucatán: bases que se discutieron y aprobaron. 2. ed. México: Centro de Estudios Históricos del Movimiento Obrero Mexicano, 1977. 117 p. (Cuadernos obreros; 11)

Minutes of the First Labor Congress held in 1918 and summoned by Felipe Carrillo Puerto as Chairman of the Partido del Sureste. No notes or introduction.

6109 Corbett, John G. Role conflict as a local-level constraint on decision-making in Mexico (PCCLAS/P, 5, 1976, p. 77–85)

In small and medium-size Mexican communities there are often conflicts between the perception local authorities have of their roles and the expectations of the local community. This study concentrates on how this conflict, a consequence of social change, has generated strains in these communities. Report of research in progress which does not include supportive data.

6110 Córdova, Arnaldo. La política de masas y el futuro de la izquierda (*in* México, hoy. Por José Ayala and others. Coordinado por Pablo González Casanova y Enrique Florescano. México: Siglo Veintiuno Editores, 1979, p. 385–404)

By "mass politics" the author understands trade-union politics. "There is no future for the left outside of the trade union organization." Although most of the criticism of the Mexican left is probably right, it is formulated from a strategic viewpoint without a discussion of tactics.

6111 Craig, Richard. Operation Condor: Mexico's antidrug campaign enters a new era (SAGE/JIAS, 22 : 3, Aug. 1980, p. 345–363, bibl.)

Since 1975 the Mexican government has been involved in an anti-marihuana campaign using defoliants which growers have resisted. According to this report about 100 federal police and soldiers have been killed. Author speculates on government's motivations for launching such an unprecedented campaign. Informative and striking article.

6112 Las Crisis en el sistema político mexicano, 1928–1977. México: Colegio de México, Centro de Estudios Internacionales, Colegio de México, 1977. 217 p.; bibl.; ill. (Colección Centro de Estudios Internacionales; 19)

A collection of excellent papers. The contribution by Meyer, although hardly original, constitutes a good summary of this crucial period. Loaeza compares the role of rumor and gossip during the last months of the Díaz Ordaz' and Echeverría's periods. Drawing on Gramsci and comparative politics, Camacho offers an original perspective of "nudos históricos" or problems faced by the regime today. On this basis, the analyst makes predictions on the future behavior of the system. For historian's comment, see *HLAS 42:2287.*

6113 Fernández, Nuria. La reforma política: orígenes y limitaciones (CP, 16, abril/junio 1978, p. 16–30)

The Mexican political reform as a "bourgeois alternative." A Marxist critique discussing the process of the reform since 1971.

6114 Fernández Christlieb, Fátima. El derecho a la información y las medios de difusión masiva (*in* México, hoy. Por José Ayala et al. Coordinado por Pablo González Casanova y Enrique Florescano. México: Siglo Veintiuno Editores, 1979, p. 329–347)

Discusses recent projects concerning freedom of the press and worries over policies of "international monopolistic capital."

6115 Flores, Heriberto. L'évolution du régime mexicain: de l'ouverture démocratique à la réforme politique (FDD/NED [Problèmes d'Amérique Latine, 57] 4579/4580, 28 juillet 1980, p. 47–72, table)

Description of the Mexican parliamentary elections of July 1979, after the political reform, designed for the layman, informative, balanced, well written.

6116 Las Fronteras del control del estado mexicano. México: Colegio de México, Centro de Estudios Internacionales, 1976. 175 p.; bibl. (Colección Centro de Estudios Internacionales; 16)

Competent contributions by well-known Mexican social scientists (e.g., Rafael Segovia "Tendencias Políticas en México;" Miguel Angel Granados Chapa "Nayarit: Consolidación del Mono-Partido;" Carlos Arriola "Los Grupos Empresariales frente al Estado: 1973–1975;" Manuel Camacho "Control sobre el Movimiento Obrero en México;" and Samuel I. de Villar "Depresión en la Industria Azucarera Mexicana."

6117 Gilly, Adolfo. La revolución de la madrugada. México: Ediciones Transición, 1977. 154 p.; ill. (Socialismo; no. 2)

A short and not very insightful discussion of contemporary Mexican politics followed by 11 theses on "national identity, proletarian hegemony, socialist revolution." The approach is Trotskyite.

6118 Gómez A., Pablo. Democracia y crisis política en México. México: Ediciones de Cultura Popular, 1976. 119 p.; bibl. (Biblioteca del militante; 15)

A contribution by a leader of the Mexican Community Party to internal discussions preceding changes in the program adopted in 1974. Naturally, the author's approach is Soviet-Leninist. Sample comment: that the present Mexican political crisis is not revolutionary.

6119 Gomezjara, Francisco A. El proceso político de Jenaro Vázquez hacia la guerrilla campesina (UNAM/RMCPS, 23 : 88, nueva época, abril/junio 1977, p. 87–126)

Consists of a political biography of the guerrilla leader prior to beginning the armed struggle. Informative on politics in the state of Guerrero.

6120 González Casanova, Pablo. Las alternativas de la democracia (*in* México, hoy. Por José Ayala et al. Coordinador por Pablo González Casanova y Enrique Florescano. México: Siglo Veintiuno Editores, 1979, p. 363–371)

A veteran of the Mexican political jungle performs one more balancing act: on the one hand, he advised leftist parties to behave after the recent political reform; and on the other, he condemns the repressive policies of fascists and neo-fascistas such as the International Monetary Fund and "Hirschman" (does the author mean Albert O. Hirschman, the prestigious professor at Yale?).

6121 ———. México: el desarrollo más probable (in México, hoy. Por José Ayala et al. Coordinado por Pablo González Casanova y Enrique Florescano. México: Siglo Veintiuno Editores, 1979, p. 405–419)

Another discussion on the impact of the political reform. The most probable future: "monopolistic capitalism, monopolistic liberalism (!) and unequal development."

6122 González-Polo, Ignacio F. Bibliografía general de las agrupaciones y partidos políticos mexicanos, 1910–1970. México: Reforma Política, 1978. 317 p.; index (Reforma política. Serie Bibliografías; 4)

Consists of more than 1800 items, most of them briefly described in the annotations. A competent work whose usefulness is enhanced by an analytical index.

6123 Gordillo, Gustavo. Estado y sistema ejidal (CP, 21, julio/sept. 1979, p. 7–24)

A summary report of research in progress regarding the ejido sector, state policies concerning it and the evaluation of such policies. It is difficult to formulate a judgment from this abridged report much of it written in jargon.

6124 Grayson, George W. Oil and politics in Mexico (CUH, 78:454, Feb. 1980, p. 53–56, 83)

A factual and very informative report on Mexican politics in 1979, including the first electoral results after the "Political Reform."

6125 Handelman, Howard. Unionization, ideology and political participation within the Mexican working class (in Political participation in Latin America. Edited by John A. Booth and Mitchell A. Seligson. v. 2,

Politics and the poor. New York: Holmes & Meier, 1978, p. 154–168, tables)

As other contributions to this reader, this article is less a real contribution to the political understanding of the topic than a display of statistical manipulation of shaky data, different sources and years (1960–73). Recommended only as an academic exercise.

Hellman, Judith Adler. Mexico in crisis. See HLAS 42:2314.

6126 Hirales Morán, Gustavo A. La Liga Comunista 23 [i.e. Veintitres] de Septiembre: orígenes y naufragio. Portada, Carlos Palleiro. México: Ediciones de Cultura Popular, 1977, 1978 printing. 112 p.

A member of a schismatic faction of the Mexican Communist League September 23, writes a post-mortem from jail, noting that the League is "now extinct." Quotes Lenin repeatedly and is ostensibly deferential towards the Mexican Communist Party.

6127 Historia de la acción pública: Adolfo López Mateos 1958–1964. v. 1, Las ideas. Lourdes Celis et al.; presentación de Fernando Zertuche Muñoz. México: Fondo para la Historia de las Ideas Revolucionarias en México, 1978. 1 v.; bibl.; ill.

Consists of speeches, interviews, political messages and reports by this Mexican President. The introduction provides a biographical sketch of López Mateos. An undistinguished, ordinary edition.

6128 Johnson, Kenneth F. Mexican democracy: a critical view. New York: Praeger, 1978. 267 p.; bibl.; index.

Author believes the independent variable is "the Mexican psyche," which can be traced all the way back to a pre-Cortesian past and which has been described by exceptional Mexican writers such as Octavio Paz and Carlos Fuentes. Includes good section on "camarillas," although most of the information is drawn from unidentified confidential sources. Outside the mainstream of current Mexican political analysis, the book is definitely not for beginners.

6129 Junquera, Rafael. La reforma política. Lomas del Estadio, Xalapa, México: Biblioteca de Humanidades, Universidad Veracruzana, 1979. 207 p. (Serie Política, economía y administración)

The book's value lies chiefly in its including the whole text of the Federal Law for

Political Organizations and Electoral Processes (i.e., the so-called "Political Reform" enacted by the Mexican government in 1978).

6130 Kaufman Purcell, Susan and **John F.H. Purcell.** Estado y sociedad en México: debe un sistema político estable, institucionalizarse? (CM/FI, 20:3, enero/marzo 1980, p. 427–462)

Unlike other modern states, the Mexican one is weak in the institutional sense, being based on "a constantly renewed political bargain among ruling groups with different political interests." Authors drive one more nail into the coffin of the corporatist model and recognize Douglas Chalmers' insights of years ago. Article reflects the usual high standards of these two very competent Mexican specialists (for English version, see *World Politics*, 32:2, Jan. 1980, p. 194–227).

6131 Landsberger, Henry A. and **Bobby M. Gierisch.** Political and economic activism: peasant participation in the *ejidos* of the Comarca Lagunera of Mexico (*in* Political participation in Latin America. Edited by Mitchell A. Seligson and John A. Booth. v. 2, Politics and the poor. New York: Holmes & Meier, 1978, p. 76–96, tables)

Describes peasant participation in the *ejido*, the credit society, and voting. Draws survey data from a sample of 350 peasants. Findings tend to confirm the model of political rationality outlined by J.A. Booth in another contribution to the same reader.

6132 Lerner de Sheinbaum, Berta. México: una burocracia gobernante (UNAM/RMS, 41[41]:2, abril/junio 1979, p. 573–595)

Tries to determine what is the right conceptualization for Mexico's ruling group, one which does not fit the concepts of oligarchy, social class, political class, estate, governing group, or elite, but which is a bureaucracy.

6133 Loyo, Aurora and **Ricardo Pozas H.** La crisis política de 1958: notas en torno a los mecanismos de control ejercidos por el estado mexicano sobre la clase obrera organizada (UNAM/RMCPS, 23:89, julio/sept. 1977, p. 77–118)

A searching study of labor strikes in 1958 (telegraph operators, railroad and oil workers, teachers). Authors emphasize the control mechanisms of the state while recog-

nizing the "admirable flexibility" of the political elite, the principal determinant of its longevity.

6134 Mancke, Richard B. Mexico's petroleum resources (CUH, 76:44, Feb. 1979, p. 74–77)

Serves as an introduction to the topic.

6135 Martínez Verdugo, Arnoldo. Partido Comunista Mexicano, trayectoria y perspectivas. México: Ediciones de Cultura Popular, 1971, 1977 printing. 116 p. (Biblioteca del militante; 22)

Mexican communists face the same old problem: how to have a "free" discussion inside the Party that will lead to the adoption of preestablished Leninist resolutions. Pt. 1 of this book entitled "Some Features of the Communist Party's Historical Experience" distorts past events and presents the usual slanderous accusations against Trotskyites.

6136 ———. El Partido Comunista Mexicano y la reforma política. Diseñó la portada, Carlos Palleiro. México: Ediciones de Cultura Popular, 1977. 156 p. (Biblioteca del militante; 23. El Libro popular)

A report by the Secretary General of the Mexican Communist Party followed by other documents on political reform.

6137 Medina, Luis. Evolución electoral en el México contemporáneo. México: Reforma Política, 1978. 49 p.; bibl. (Serie Ensayos; 5)

An overview of Mexican electoral legislation up to 1977. Descriptive.

6138 Mexico. Comisión Federal Electoral. Reforma política: gaceta informativa de la Comisión Federal Electoral. v. 1, Audiencias públicas. v. 2, Comentarios. v. 3, Reformas a la constitución. México: La Comisión, 1977. 3 v.; bibl.; indexes.

Consists of three volumes: vol. 1 covers reports and statements submitted to the Federal Electoral Commission by political parties, political organizations, representatives of academic institutions, and individuals; vol. 2 reproduces editorials and articles from national journals and newspapers (April/Aug. 1977); and vol. 3 fully transcribes the minutes of a public session held in order to discuss the Mexican political reform. A valuable source.

México: Artículos Clasificados. Vol. 2, Nos. 5/6, nov./dic. 1979– . See *HLAS 42:156.*

6139 México, realidad política de sus partidos: una investigación psicosocial acerca de los partidos políticos mexicanos. Director de la investigación, Antonio Delhumeau Arrecillas; investigadores, Bertha Lerner Sigal et al. 2. ed., corr. y aumentada. México: Instituto Mexicano de Estudios Políticos, 1977. 341 p.; bibl.

First published in 1970, the book only covers the following parties: PRI, PAN, PPS and PARM. It applies a framework denominated "psycho-social" and described in the initial chapter.

6140 Molina A., Daniel. La caravana del hambre. México: Ediciones el Caballito, 1978. 117 p.; bibl. (Colección Fragua mexicana; 30)

Describes the coal-miners' strike in the state of Cohauila (1950–51) and the subsequent "hunger march." Uses incriminating terms to denounce the Mexican bourgeoisie and the "charro" labor leaders.

Montaño, Jorge. Los pobres de la ciudad en los asentamientos espontáneos: poder y política. See item **8114.**

El Movimiento estudiantil mexicano en la prensa francesa. See item **4515.**

6141 Muñoz Ledo, Porfirio. El sistema político mexicano (*in* Simposio sobre México hoy, 1978. Visión del México contemporáneo. México: El Colegio de México, 1979, p. 21–32)

A short address by a member of Mexico's governmental elite delivered before an audience of American laymen. Provides more rationalization than explanation.

6142 Oaxaca una lucha reciente: 1960–1978. Bustamante et al. México: Ediciones Nueva Sociología, 1978. 236 p.; 4 leaves of plates; ill.

Includes contributions by six different authors, all of them committed to revolution, and offers information on the activities of several radical leftist groups during the period. The final contribution summarizes the lesson drawn from experience: neither elections nor guerrillas.

6143 Ovalle Favela, José. Algunas consideraciones sobre el municipio mexicano (UNAM/RFD, 28:111, sept./dic. 1978, p. 779–815)

A legalistic examination of the evolution of Mexican local government from precolumbian times. Also includes a more in-depth discussion of the municipio of Netzahualcóyotl, in the state of Mexico.

6144 Paoli Bolio, Francisco J. El cambio de presidente: elecciones mexicanas de 1976 (UNAM/RMS, 41[41]:1, enero/marzo 1979, p. 325–352)

Unexciting and trite discussion of "tapadismo" and "destapamiento." Extensive use of Mexican news.

6145 El Partido Comunista Mexicano en el campaña electoral: textos de una polémica. Pablo Gómez et al.; diseñó la portada, Carlos Palleiro. México: Ediciones de Cultura Popular, 1977. 137 p. (Biblioteca del militante; 21. El Libro popular)

Leaders of the Mexican Communist Party examine several contemporary issues with their characteristic lack of originality or imagination.

6146 Paz, Octavio. El ogro filantrópico: historia y política, 1971–1978. 2. ed. México: J. Mortiz, 1979. 348 p.; index (Confrontaciones: Los críticos)

The "philantropic ogre" of the title is the contemporary Mexican state. With remarkable courage and in superb Spanish, one of the most lucid Latin American intellectuals exposes the country's bureaucracy and corruption as well as the intellectual intoxication caused by the adoption of "simplistic and simplifying ideologies." Strongly recommended.

6147 Reyes Heroles, Jesús. México: historia y política. Madrid: Editorial Tecnos, 1978. 320 p.; bibl. (Serie de ciencia política. Semilla y surco)

Written between 1952–75, this collection is designed to introduce Reyes Heroles to the Spanish public. It is organized in three parts: 1) History; 2) Politics; and 3) Essays. Most of the papers in the history section are on Mexican Liberalism and "the Reform," topics which the author has addressed with persistence.

6148 Reyna, José Luis. El movimiento obrero en una situación de crisis: México 1976–1978 (CM/FI, 19:3, enero/marzo 1979, p. 390–401)

Discusses the impact of devaluation (1976) on the living standard of the Mexican working class and notes how the reduction in real income has affected the political behavior of Mexican workers.

6149 Rodríguez Araujo, Octavio. La reforma política y los partidos en México. México: Siglo Veintiuno Editores, 1979. 267 p.; bibl.

Pt. 1 applies a neo-Marxist approach to a discussion of the project of political reform suggested by López Portillo in 1977. Pt. 2 synthesizes information on 12 Mexican political parties, especially their proposals concerning the reform and the positions they adopted regarding the State, imperialism, etc.

6150 Roxborough, Ian and **Francisco Zapata.** Algunos mitos sobre el sindicalismo en México (CM/D, 14:6[84], nov./dic. 1978, p. 24–26)

The myths are: identifying Mexico's labor movement with the CTM; assuming that organized trade unions are weak and lacking in internal democratic practices as well as that official trade unions are less effective than independent ones; and finally, misunderstanding the true nature of labor movements in industrialized countries. One should not underestimate the significance of this short paper.

6151 Santa Gertrudis, testimonios de una lucha campesina. Lorena Paz Paredes, Julio Moguel, compiladores. México: Ediciones Era, 1979. 106 p. (Serie popular Era; 69)

Consists of interviews with participants of peasant resistance movements recorded for a documentary film. The editors' literary style attempts to preserve peasant language.

6152 Segovia, Rafael. Las elecciones federales de 1979 (CM/FI, 20:3, enero/marzo 1980, p. 397–410, tables)

Consists of data on: abstentions; PRI's decreasing majorities; PAN's and the Communists' increasing electoral support; urban voting patterns; etc.

Smith, Peter H. The Mexican Revolution and the transformation of political elites. See *HLAS 42:2359.*

6153 ——. Wounds of history (WQ, 3:3, Summer 1979, p. 130–141)

An introduction for non-specialists, written by a historian who has made significant contributions to the study of the Mexican elites.

6154 Spalding, Rose J. Welfare policymaking: theoretical implications of a Mexican case study (CUNY/CP, 12:4, July 1980, p. 419–438)

After discussing the most relevant literature on welfare policy, author analyzes Mexican social security programs. She finds that diffusion processes, patterns of socioeconomic change, and a corporatist state, all play equally decisive roles in directing such programs. Although the operationalization of some of the independent variables is extremely crude, the exercise is interesting.

6155 Suárez, Luis. Echeverría rompe el silencio: vendaval del sistema. 4. ed. México: Editorial Grijalbo, c1979. 243 p.; ill.

President Echeverría answers questions on his presidential period, including a frustrated coup by unidentified persons in Nov. 1976.

6155a Tobler, Hans-Werner. Die Mexikanische Revolution zwischen Beharrung und Veränderung (UB/GG, 2:2, 1976, p. 188–216)

Examines the Mexican Revolution from the vantage point of the 1970s, pointing out that the land-owning upper class is now supplanted by a rising class of business entrepreneurs who form the powerful elite. Great strides in economic development are being wiped out by the ever-increasing population and chronic unemployment among the marginated classes. A well-researched and thoughtful article which will be of interest to the student of 20th-century Mexico. [G.M. Dorn]

6156 Vellinga, Menno. Industrialización, burguesía y clase obrera en México: el caso de Monterrey. Traducción de José Sernaudi. México: Siglo Veintiuno Editores, 1979. 275 p.; bibl.; tables (Sociología y política)

An interesting contribution. Uses a modified version of the Marxist class model and interviews with workers, labor leaders, employers and executives. An appendix elaborates on different aspects of the research.

6157 Villoro, Luis. La reforma política y las perspectivas de democracia (*in* México, hoy. Por José Ayala and others. Coordinado por Pablo González Casanova y Enrique Florescano. México: Siglo Veintiuno Editores, 1979, p. 348–362)

Comments on the recent political reform from a point of view referred to as "the Democratic Left."

CENTRAL AMERICA
GENERAL

6158 Gandásegui, Marco A. Liberación nacional y los nuevos órdenes sociales (RCPC, 159, abril/junio 1978, p. 22–31)

Touches on very different topics and lacks a central theme. More relevant for Central American readers than for the general public.

6159 Grieb, Kenneth J. The myths of a Central American Dictators' League (JLAS, 10:2, Nov. 1978, p. 329–345)

Describes squabbles and quarrels among Central American "strongmen" in the 1930s and 1940s, using as main sources Guatemalan Foreign Ministry Archives and US State Department papers.

6160 Hándal, Schafik Jorge. América Central: crisis de las dictaduras militares (URSS/AL, 1, 1980, p. 23–41)

The Secretary General of the Salvadorian Communist Party repeats the standard analysis of Latin American politics formulated, at least a decade ago, by Communist parties. Hardly original.

6161 Instituto Centroamericano de Administración Pública. Entidades públicas descentralizadas del Istmo Centroamericano. San José, Costa Rica: Editorial ICAP, 1979. 198 p.; bibl.

A very useful tool which provides a general discussion of the region by several Central American specialists, followed by country-by-country descriptions. Includes Panama.

6162 Shaw, Royce Q. Central America: regional integration and national political development. Boulder, Colo.: Westview Press, 1978. 242 p.; bibl. (A Westview replica edition)

The failure of CACM cannot be attributed either to the impact of external actors nor to the theory of regional integration. Author's third approach focuses on domestic politics and the role of political leadership. National leaders perceived CACM as a mechanism for obtaining more foreign resources and postponed or avoided internal reforms. Suggestive and well argued.

COSTA RICA

6163 Aguilar Bulgarelli, Oscar R. Democracia y partidos políticos de Costa Rica, 1950–1962. San José, Costa Rica: s.n., 1977. 175 p.; bibl.

Consists of a descriptive introduction to the history of Costa Rican political parties based on interviews with leaders and documents from the archives of Jorge Rossi. Appendixes include interviews and documents.

6164 Ameringer, Charles D. Don Pepe: a political biography of José Figueres of Costa Rica. Albuquerque: University of New Mexico Press, 1978. 324 p.; bibl.; index; map.

Author had access to Figueres' private archive and other unpublished sources. Extensive use of newspapers and complementary bibliography. More a chronicle than a "political biography," the book devotes equal attention to small incidents and significant events and fails to yield a clear picture of either the leader's personality or of his impact. Provides interesting account of contemporary cabals and machinations in the region. For historian's comment, see *HLAS 42:2426.*

6165 Arrieta Quesada, Santiago. El pensamiento político-social de Monseñor Sanabria. Ciudad Universitaria Rodrigo Facio, Costa Rica: Editorial Universitaria Centroamericana, 1977. 334 p.; bibl. (Colección Aula)

Archbishop Sanabria played a crucial role in Costa Rican politics and social policies from 1940–50. This book studies his ideas and their influence. Includes appendix of documents discussed in the text.

6166 Backer, James. La Iglesia y el sindicalismo en Costa Rica. 2. ed. San José: Editorial Costa Rica, 1975. 335 p.; bibl.

Another study of Archbishop Sanabria's period (1940–52) but one which lives up to academic standards by providing a good bibliography and supportive evidence in the form of numerous interviews with Church and trade union leaders. In general, author regards the Costa Rican Church as a hindrance to socioeconomic development and of little help in improving the lot of the poor.

6167 Booth, John A. Are Latin Americans politically rational?: citizen participation and democracy in Costa Rica (*in* Political participation in Latin America. Edited by John A. Booth and Mitchell A. Seligson. New York: Holmes & Meier, 1978, p. 98–113)

Criticizes the narrow concept of political rationality adopted by democratic elitists, and offers a new concept in which the relevance of institutions is related to the achievement of personal goals. Uses a 1973 national probability sample of heads of family in order to measure levels of popular involvement at the national, local, and community level.

6168 ———. Organizational processes in the growing community: strategies for development. Austin: Institute of Latin American Studies, The University of Texas, n.d. 25 p.; bibl.; tables (Offprint series; 167)

Applies a model relating community organizational processes to community growth in Costa Rica.

6169 ¿Democracia en Costa Rica?: cinco opiniones polémicas. Chester Zelaya et al. San José, Costa Rica: Editorial Universidad Estatal e Distancia, 1978. 248 p.; graphs (Serie Estudios sociopoliticos; no. 1)

Consists of the following "polemical opinions" by five qualified Costa Rican scholars who, from different perspectives, examine the roots, weaknesses and strengths of that rare achievement of the region, Costa Rican democracy: Chester Zelaya "Apuntes Historiográficos sobre la Democracia en Costa Rica;" Oscar Aguilar Bulgarelli "Costa Rica: Evolución Histórica de una Democracia;" Daniel Camacho "¿Por Qué Persiste el Juego Democrático en Costa Rica?: Algunas Hipótesis;" Rodolfo Cerdas "Costa Rica: Problemas Actuales de una Revolución Democrática;" and Jacobo Schifter S. "La Democracia en Costa Rica como Producto de la Neutralización de Clases."

6170 Jiménez Castro, Wilburg. Las elecciones (*in* Costa Rica contemporánea. Prólogo y dirección, Chester Zelaya. Colaboradores, Carlos Meléndez Chaverri et al. San José: Editorial Costa Rica, 1979, t. 1, p. 135–158)

An overview which includes legislation and electoral behavior.

6171 Prieto Jiménez, Marcelo. Militarismo y democracia en Costa Rica (NSO, 42, mayo/junio 1979, p. 119–130, bibl., ill., plate, table)

Author believes the National Liberation Party will grow obsolete unless it radicalizes its program. Otherwise, new external and domestic conditions may lead to the establishment of an authoritarian state, portents of which the author perceives in the increasing militarization of President Carrazo's administration. The argument fails to persuade and the data is scant.

6172 Rosenberg, Mark B. Social security policy-making in Costa Rica: a research report (LARR, 14:1, 1979, p. 116–133, bibl.)

Uses four case studies to examine decision-making concerning social security between 1924–75. Finds that paternalistic elitism rather than pressure groups played the decisive role in the creation of social insurance programs. In later years, however, other factors such as progressive leadership, the bureaucracy, and ILO's influence determined the evolution of Costa Rica's social security policy.

6173 Schifter, Jacobo. La fase oculta de la guerra civil en Costa Rica. Ciudad Universitaria Rodrigo Facio, Costa Rica: Editorial Universitaria Centroamericana, 1979. 158 p.; bibl.; ill. (Colección Seis)

This heterodox interpretation of the Costa Rican Revolution presents Figueres and his followers as authoritarians who failed to institutionalize a corporative state because of their inability to modify the existing social alignments of the early 1940s. The Costa Rican author is a competent political scientist, but his argument is not persuasive.

6174 ———. Los partidos políticos (*in* Costa Rica contemporánea. Prólogo y dirección, Chester Zelaya. Colaboradores, Carlos Meléndez Chaverri et al. San José: Editorial Costa Rica, 1979, t. 1, p. 75–134, bibl., tables)

Descriptive account which includes a good bibliography.

6175 Seligson, Mitchell A. Development and participation in Costa Rica: the impact of context (*in* Political participation in Latin America. Edited by John A. Booth and Mitchell A. Seligson. New York: Holmes & Meier, 1978, p. 145–153)

Contradicts the hypothesis that countries with higher economic development have higher rates of political participation. Economic development is measured by "industrialization" (workers in industry) and "infrastructure" (quality of sanitary facilities plus number of high-school students). Identifies four modes of political participation, including voting, and uses sample of 531 male peasants. The analysis shows that "peasants living in the least developed areas exhibit the highest levels of participation."

6176 ——— and **John A. Booth.** Structure and levels of political participation in Costa Rica: comparing peasants with city dwellers (*in* Political participation in Latin America. Edited by John A. Booth and Mitchell A. Seligson. v. 2, Politics and the poor. New York: Holmes & Meier, 1978, p. 62–75, tables)

Not only is the notion of the passive peasant a myth but in some modes of political participation peasants are more active than urbanites. Includes survey data.

6177 **Vega Carballo, José Luis.** Democracia y dominación en Costa Rica (CM/FI, 20:4, abril/junio 1980, p. 646–672)

Author identifies the following four trends that have favored democratization in the historical evolution of Costa Rica: 1) basic egalitarianism; 2) state institutionalization; 3) indirect domination; and 4) abstract domination. This is a well argued and valuable contribution.

6178 ———. Elecciones en Costa Rica: ¿opción por un nuevo modelo de desarrollo? (NSO, 34, enero/feb. 1978, p. 82–87)

Author tries to create a new model defined as "social-capitalismo benefactor" or the intermediate stage between present and future social-democratic society.

EL SALVADOR

6179 **Armstrong, Robert** and **Janet Shenk.** El Salvador: why revolution? (NACLA, 19:2, March/April 1980, p. 3–35, plates, tables)

A quotation on the initial page notes that since the 1932 massacre "all [Salvado-

rians] were born half-dead" and survivors are "half-alive." A portent of authors' unintended purpose: to emphasize the tragic aspects of contemporary Salvadorian politics to such an extent that only the most calloused readers will finish the article.

6180 **Bourdillat, Nicole.** Dictature et opposition au Salvador: 25 janvier 1961–15 octobre 1979 (FDD/NED [Problèmes d'Amérique Latine, 57] 4579/4580, 28 juillet 1980, p. 7–27, bibl., maps, table)

This introductory description includes little that is original and was probably written before the coup of 15 Oct. 1979, as it mentions it only in a footnote.

6181 **Dalton, Roque.** El Salvador: monografía. Ciudad Universitaria, El Salvador: Editorial Universitaria, 1979. 224 p.

The author, a poet and member of the Salvadorian Communist Party, was assasinated by a rival guerrilla group, a few years after writing this handbook. Without footnotes or bibliography, the book consists of an interpretative historical essay which includes lengthy transcriptions of Communist Party documents and similar materials.

6182 **El Salvador under General Romero:** an analysis of the first nine months of the regime of President Romero. London: Latin America Bureau, 1979. 254 p.; bibl.

More than analysis, this work constitutes a denunciation of civil rights' violations and is based on an exhaustive use of press sources. Originally published in Spanish, it was written by social scientists from the area.

6183 **Flores Pinel, Fernando.** El estado de seguridad nacional en El Salvador: un fenómeno de crisis hegemónica (CM/FI, 20:4, abril/junio 1980, p. 575–600)

Military authoritarianism in El Salvador is not the consequence of the verticalization of the economy or its penetration by multinationals. Rather, it is the outcome of an hegemonic crisis generated by the loss of power of the traditional oligarchy, the frustrations of industrialization, the concomitant failure of the Central American Common Market, and the Salvadorian military's accommodation to the US doctrine of national security.

6184 **Hernández, Francisco Javier.** Estado y sociedad: crisis hegemónica y lucha ideológica en el coyuntura de la transformación agraria en El Salvador, 1975–1976 (UNAM/RMS, 41[41]:1, enero/marzo 1979, p. 279–295)

On June 1975 the government enacted a Law of Agrarian Transformation. The purpose of this paper is to use Gramscian framework in order to analyze the crisis that followed the law's implementation. But unfortunately, the author's convoluted language and his tiresome use of undefined class-concepts frustrate his good intentions.

6185 Iglesia de los pobres y organizaciones populares. Oscar A. Romero et al. San Salvador, El Salvador: UCA Editores, Universidad Centroamericana José Simeón Cañas, 1979. 249 p.; bibl. (Colección La Iglesia en América Latina; v. 4)

This pastoral letter No. 3 on the Church and popular organizations was signed on 6 Aug. 1978 by Archbishop Oscar A. Romero who was later assasinated, and by Bishop Arturo Rivera Damas. The text is followed by an appendix consisting of comments and theological reflections on the Church of the Poor. Highly significant publication for those interested in the study of contemporary Salvadorian politics.

6186 Inter-American Commission on Human Rights. Report on the situation of human rights in El Salvador. Washington: General Secretariat, OAS, 1978. 188 p. (OEA/Ser. L; V/II.46, doc. 23 rev. 1)

Report issued by the OAS Commission after visiting the country (3 Oct. to 12 Nov. 1977) at the invitation of the Salvadorian government.

6187 Makofsky, Abraham. Voluntary association in a climate of repression: union activities in El Salvador (SAA/HO, 37:1, Spring 1978, p. 57–63)

A descriptive study based on observation and interviews with labor leaders. In plain English and without jargon or statistics, author communicates the feeling that he knows what he is talking about, the first requirement of good research.

6188 News from Latin America (BNCE/CE, 26:3, March 1980, p. 89–94)

A short, informative summary on political events in El Salvador as of March 1980.

6189 Pronunciamiento de la UCA ante la nueva situación del país: febrero/80 (UJSC/ECA, 35:375/376, enero/feb. 1980, p. 5–18)

An important source for the study of the current tragic political process in El Salvador: a document issued by the Consejo Superior of the Universidad Centroamericana analyzing the situation as of Feb. 1980.

6190 Sucesos nacionales (UCA/E, 14, julio/dic. 1978, p. 3–29)

Another very helpful summary of national events which are published periodically in *Encuentro*. This one covers period from mid-1978 to initial months of 1979.

6191 Webre, Stephen. José Napoleón Duarte and the Christian Democratic Party in San Salvadoran politics, 1960–1972. Baton Rouge: Louisiana State University Press, 1979. 233 p.; bibl.; index.

Neutral and undistinguished political history. Epilogue summarizes events of 1972–77. Main sources: the Salvadorian daily press and a few interviews not conducted by the author. The book offers no indication as to whether or not he visited El Salvador.

6192 Wickham, Woodward A. Letter from El Salvador (RF Illustrated [The Rockefeller Foundation, New York] 4:3, Sept. 1979, p. 14–15, ill.)

Describes a visit to an agrarian cooperative whose real name cannot be disclosed for fear of retaliations against its members. Another example of the pathological conditions endured by the unfortunate Salvadorian people.

GUATEMALA

6193 Aguilera P., Gabriel. The massacre at Panzos and capitalist development in Guatemala (MR, 31:7, Dec. 1979, p. 13–23, map)

Guatemalan political scientist examines the development of the so-called "Northern Transverse strip," covering an area of 8,016.41 square kilometers. Describes the exploitation therein of agriculture, nickel, oil, copper, etc., as well as the bloody clashes with local peasants.

6194 ———. La tragicomedia electoral de la burguesía: un análisis sociológico del proceso electoral del 5 de marzo de 1978 (USCG/PS, 2:5, enero/junio 1978, p. 159–171)

This informative and insightful analysis is hampered by the author's identifying of political parties with social classes without providing any supportive evidence to that effect.

6195 Booth, John A. A Guatemalan nightmare: levels of politial violence, 1966–1972 (SAGE/JIAS, 22:2, May 1980, p. 195–225, tables)

This sophisticated exercise, worthy of careful reading, attempts to correlate levels of violence to the strength of contending parties and rapid social change. Author is explicit about the limitations of his data.

6196 CIDAMO (Center for Information, Documentation and Analysis of the Latin American Workers' Movement). The workers movement in Guatemala (NACLA, 14:1, Jan./Feb. 1980, p. 28–35, plate, table)

A short history of the Guatemalan labor movement uses the standard New Left interpretation, which in this case is almost identical to the Soviet version. Interestingly, there is no mention whatever in this article of the important role played by the pro-Soviet Communist Party of Guatemala in the country's labor movement.

6197 Fuentes Mohr, Alberto. Situación y perspectivas políticas en Guatemala (NSO, 34, enero/feb. 1978, p. 82–87)

The recently assassinated Guatemalan leader describes the political situation before the elections of 1978.

6198 Grieb, Kenneth J. Guatemalan caudillo, the regime of Jorge Ubico: Guatemala, 1931–1944. Athens: Ohio University Press, 1979. 384 p.; bibl.; index; maps.

Modern politics began in Central America and the Caribbean with confrontations against dictators such as Ubico, Carías, Trujillo, etc. Understandably, those who deposed the dictator presented a bleak picture of their mortal enemies. Grieb's book is a revision of one of these stereotypes based on archival sources and interviews with Ubico's collaborators. The study, however, is not a definitive biography of the Guatemalan dictator, largely because the author is not familiar with the sociological and political work being done on Latin American authoritarianism. Still, the book constitutes an important step in the right direction.

Irías de River, María Amalia and **Irma Violeta Alfaro de Carpio.** Guatemalan working women in the labor movement. See *HLAS 42:2460.*

6199 Riding, Alan. Guatemala: state of siege (The New York Times Magazine [New York] 24 Aug. 1980, p. 16–29, 66–67, map, plates)

Political violence has been part of Guatemalan life, at least, since the conquest, not since "1954 when the C.I.A. organized an invasion." Certainly "fierce anti-communism" was not born "at that time." The name of the "guerrilla-hunter," as the author refers to ex-President Arana is not Araña (spider). No doubt, assassinations and terrorism are now daily events in Guatemala. Unfortunately, the mistakes in this article prevent one from telling what is the real evidence found by the author from his own misconceptions and misperceptions that turn his account into a piece of sensationalist journalism.

6200 Salvadó C., Luis Raúl. Crónica de una huelga (USCG/PS, 2:5, enero/junio 1978, p. 173–191)

Much more than a "crónica," this description of the strike is followed by considerations of the socioeconomic transformation underway in the Verapaz region of Guatemala and the new role of the state. Author is a Guatemalan sociologist. His quotations from Marx and Lenin are not intrusive in this serious attempt to understand social change.

6201 Solórzano Martínez, Mario. La constitución de un nuevo bloque histórico en Guatemala (USCG/PS, 2:5, enero/junio 1978, p. 67–127, table)

The Church, political parties, the bureaucracy, and American policies are the forces under scrutiny in this attempt to apply Gramsci's concepts to Guatemalan politics.

6202 ———. Guatemala "democracia" con fraude y represión (NSO, 42, mayo/junio 1979, p. 103–118, ill.)

One more sociopolitical study of contemporary Guatemala applies Poutlanzas' framework and makes usual reference to Marx. Lacks anything original.

6203 Torres-Rivas, Edelberto. Crisis y coyuntura crítica: la caída de Arbenz y los contratiempos de la revolución burguesa (UNAM/RMS, 41[41]:1, enero/marzo 1979, p. 297–324)

A reexamination of Guatemalan events (1944–55) which the author, a well known Guatemalan sociologist, regards as "a bourgeois revolution." Criticizes the Left noting it never understood that in an underdeveloped country, a successful bourgeois revolution requires non-bourgeois actors and methods. Fails to identify what actors and methods he means. Lacks any new sources.

6204 ———. Guatemala: crisis and political violence (NACLA, 14:1, Jan./Feb. 1980, p. 16–27, plates)

A shortened version of a paper presented at the Latin American Sociology Conference, Nov. 1979. Author defines the present regime as a militarized state or one in which all functions are performed by the military, except for the judiciary. Since 1979 the Army Chief of Staff decides all bureaucratic appointments and functions as if he were a sort of Super-Minister.

6205 ———. Vida y muerte en Guatemala: reflexiones sobre la crisis y la violencia política (CM/FI, 20:4, arbril/junio 1980, p. 549–574, tables)

Offers an explanation of contemporary politics in Guatemala based on class-analysis with frustrating results.

6206 Villagrán Kramer, Francisco. Estudios de ciencia política y otros ensayos. Guatemala: Serviprensa Centroamericana, 1979. 280 p.; bibl.

Collection of papers, written by the Guatemalan Vice-President who went into exile, covers such topics as: Guatemalan constitutions, Central American integration, and the Latin American right. The result is a rather legalistic study seasoned with bits of history and sociology.

HONDURAS

6207 Aguilar B., Gustavo Adolfo. Honduras: situación actual y perspectivas políticas (CM/FI, 20:4, abril/junio 1980, p. 601–611)

The title is misleading. The article consists of a trite manifesto denouncing "imperialist strategy" in the country and offers no data.

6208 Leiva Vivas, Rafael. Honduras: Fuerzas Armadas, dependencia o desarrollo. n.p.: n.p., 1973. 163 p.; tables.

This moderate, unsystematic treatment of Honduras socioeconomic problems makes no attempt to offer a program. It is clear, however, that the author assigns a critical role in the development process to the country's Armed Forces.

6209 Morris, James A. Political modernization in Honduras: the evolution of campesino organizations (in Rocky Mountain Council on Latin American Studies, XXV, Tucson, Ariz., 1977. Proceedings. Lincoln: University of Nebraska, 1977, p. 100–110)

A well-balanced and well-researched paper which delivers much more than the title suggests. Author analyzes the increasing role of the peasantry in the political system and with much perception discusses several patterns of future evolution.

6210 Padilla, Rigoberto. Entrevista al Vice-Secretario General del Partido Comunista de Honduras (URSS/AL, 4:20, 1978, p. 71–87)

Interview published in the Soviet journal *América Latina* offers some information on the process leading to the organization of the Honduran Communist Party. With regard to current political events, the Party is critical of the "adventurist left."

NICARAGUA

Amnesty International, *New York.* Reporte sobre la República de Nicaragua incluyendo los resultados de una misión, 10–15 de mayo de 1976. See *HLAS* 42:2427.

6211 Arce, Bayardo. El difícil terreno de la lucha: el ideológico (NMC/N, 1, mayo/junio 1980, p. 152–157)

A top FSLN leader explains government policies with regard to culture.

6212 Borge Martínez, Tomás. Carlos, el amanecer ya no es una tentación (CDLA, 19:114, mayo/junio 1979, p. 104–119)

Borge, the only survivor among the founders of the FSLAN, offers some fascinating biographical data in this article. Also includes information on: Carlos Fonseca Amador; the evolution of the FSLN; guerrilla activity; the unfailing support extended by Cuba; cooperation with other guerrilla groups such as the Guatemalan and Palestinian; etc. Although Borge is evidently a better guerrilla than writer, this piece is an indispensable source.

6213 Bourdillat, Nicole. Nicaragua, la Dynastie Somoza (FDD/NED [Problèmes d'Amérique Latine, 51] 4517/4518, 22 juin 1979, p. 95–124)

Written in April 1979, the article covers events until Dec. 1978. Perceives Nicaragua as a case of "continuismo" and fulfills its informative purpose. Observes that "the hesitations of American policy and the conflicts inside the opposition prevent predictions on the nature of the regime to succeed [Somoza]."

6214 Burbach, Roger and Tim Draimin. Revolution in the making (NACLA, 14:3, May/June 1980, p. 2–35, plates, table)

A friendly report on the first year of the Nicaraguan revolutionary government. The real nature of this government is candidly stated: "Standing behind the five-member Junta is the nine-member National Directorate of the FSLN, which sets the political direction for the government and controls the Sandinista Popular Army." It is also interesting to learn from this source that multinationals were not important in Nicaragua. Total foreign investment was only $180 million.

6215 Castillo, Donald. Perspectivas en la situación sociopolítica de Nicaragua (NSO, 42, mayo/junio 1979, p. 87–102, ill., plate)

Writing before the Sandinista victory and well acquainted with Nicaraguan politics, the author seriously doubted that the FSLN would become "an effective political instrument." Despite the wrong prediction, this is a sober analysis.

6216 Chamorro Cardenal, Pedro Joaquín. Estirpe sangrienta: los Somoza. Prefacio de Gregorio Selser. México: Editorial Diógenes, 1979. 283 p.

Autobiographical account by the Edi-

tor of *La Prensa* of the frightful experience he endured in 1954 when he was jailed and tortured by the National Guard. The personal intervention of "Tachito" led to the arrest and charge that Chamorro had assassinated "Tacho."

6217 Debray, Régis. Nicaragua año cero (CDLA, 20:117, nov./dic. 1979, p. 79–90)

A partisan account by the author of *Revolution within the Revolution?* (see HLAS 29:6646). He believes that "the main problem, the problem of state power has been solved" as, in his view, power belongs to the army and the army is under the tight control of the FSLN. Not all observers are that perceptive.

6218 Epica Task Force. Nicaragua, a people's revolution. Washington, D.C.: The Force, 1980. 103 p.; ill.

The publication is dedicated to "los muchachos" of Washington, D.C., "a veritable international brigade." As customary with "los muchachos" (prior to July 1979), this tract serves to reflect the interest and thought of the FSLN. After the latter's victory, however, its critics were labeled according to three categories: 1) Ultra-Left Reaction; 2) Ultra-Right Reaction; and 3) Middle-Class Opportunism. Only the FSLN is right.

6219 Eugarrios, Manuel. Dos . . . uno . . . Cero, comandante. 3. ed. San José, Costa Rica: Lehmann, 1979. 128 p.; ill.

A journalist and accidental witness tells the story of the assault of the Nicaraguan Presidential Palace on 22 Aug. 1978, when members of the Sandinista Front, disguised as soldiers of the National Guard, occupied the Palace.

6220 Faillos Navarro, Francisco. Los partidos políticos y la coyuntura de 1978 (UCA/E, 14, julio/dic. 1978, p. 37–41)

A well articulated, sober, non-Marxist analysis. Written in 1978, the article underestimated the resources and recklessness of the FSLN but was very perceptive as to the limited options available to the US.

6221 Frente Amplio Opositor, *Managua.* Exposición del Frente Amplio Opositor (FAO) de Nicaragua a los gobiernos de los países miembros de la Organización de Estados Americanos (RCPC, 33:160, julio/ sept. 1978, p. 93–100)

This document, signed 24 Nov. 1978, constitutes an important source for this crucial period of Nicaraguan history. It requests that Somoza be tried and sentenced.

6222 Frente Sandinista de Liberación Nacional. FSLN proletario. s.l.: FSLN, 1978. 118 p. (Documentos básicos—FSLN; 1)

An invaluable source for the study of the FSLN. Eight months before the final victory of July 1979, *FSLN Proletario* denounced "the failure of messianic voluntarism brought to the FSLN by the hegemonic petite-bourgeoisie," and publicized a project for a program and byrules. While both the old communist PSN and the Guerra Popular Prolongada tendencies are explicitly criticized, there is no mention of the Tercera Posición, suggesting the latter had not yet coalesced. Both the program and bylaws reflect a heavy influence of Soviet Marxism.

6223 García Márquez, Gabriel. Nicaragua: el asalto a la casa de los chanchos (OCLAE, 13:2, 1979, p. 28–36, plates)

Journalistic account of the Sandinista commando operation to seize the National Palace in which the novelist's imagination has somewhat embellished the facts.

6224 Gutiérrez Mayorga, Gustavo. El reformismo artesanal en el movimiento obrero nicaragüense: 1931–1960 (RCPC, 159, abril/junio 1978, p. 2–21)

Includes some interesting data on the Nicaraguan labor movement and on the 1944 foundation of the country's communist Party.

6225 Herrera Zúñiga, René. Nicaragua: el desarrollo capitalista dependiente y la crisis de la dominación burguesa; 1950–1980 (CM/FI, 20:4, abril/junio 1980, p. 612–645, tables)

Uses a dependentista approach in terms of classes and economic groups within the bourgeoisie. Includes very little on the revolutionary movement or on the future of the revolutionary government. Describes sectors of the bourgeoisie which are members of the governmental coalition and how American pressures are applied through area nations (e.g., Mexico, Venezuela, Costa Rica, Panama).

6226 Inter-American Commission on Human Rights. Informe sobre la situación de los derechos humanos en Nicaragua: resultado de la observación "in loco" practicada del 2 al 12 de octubre de 1978. Aprobado por la Comisión Interamericana de Derechos Humanos en su sesión no. 604 del 45° período de sesiones celebrada el 16 de noviembre de 1978. Washington: CIDH, 1978. 81 p.; bibl. (OEA/ser. L/V/II, 45, doc. 16, rev. 1, 17 noviembre 1978, original: español)

6227 López, Armando and **Juan B. Arrién.** El papel de la Iglesia en la coyuntura nacional 1978 (UCA/E, 14, julio/dic. 1978, p. 85–138)

Useful collection of documents issued by the Nicaraguan Church (1974–78) followed by an analysis of the texts.

6228 Mendieta Alfaro, Róger. El último Marine: 1979, año de la liberación. Managua, Nicaragua: Editorial Unión Cardoza, 1979. 314 p.; ill.

The final struggle for Managua as perceived by an eyewitness who is both a conservative and opponent of Somoza. This impressionist document stresses street fights, the perverse madness of the Somocistas and unmatched heroism of the Sandinistas.

Nicaragua. Junta de Gobierno de Reconstrucción Nacional. Programa de gobierno de reconstrucción nacional. See item **4525.**

6229 Nicaragua: la lucha popular contra la dictadura (CP, 20, abril/junio 1979, p. 104–115)

Document signed by three factions of the Frente Sandinista on March 1979 consists not of a program but of an analysis of the situation. It denounces US attempts at mediation, asks for international solidarity, and reaffirms the strategy of popular insurrection. Important source.

6230 The Nicaraguan revolution. Edited, with an introduction by Pedro Camejo and Fred Murphy. New York: Pathfinder Press, 1979. 79 p.; ill.

Consists of contributions by Jaime Wheelock and Daniel Ortega (leaders of the FSLN) and by Fidel Castro. Also includes the Statute on the Rights of Nicaraguans enacted by the new Revolutionary Government.

6231 Ortega Saavedra, Humberto. Cincuenta años de lucha sandinista. Portada de Efraín Herrera. México: Editorial Diógenes, 1979. 139 p.; 8 leaves of plates: bibl.; ill.

Written in 1976 by a member of the National Directorate of the FSLN. The 50-year period (1929–79?) is presented as a single, continuing process of revolutionary war, with ups and downs, advances and retreats. Attempts to draw from the Nicaraguan experience general principles for a contemporary successful politico-military strategy.

6232 ———. La insurección nacional victoriosa (NMC/N, 1, mayo/junio 1980, p. 26–57, map, plates)

The commander in Chief of the Nicaraguan Army today and one of the main leaders of the Sandinista Front answers questions concerning the organization and different stages of the insurrection. A valuable source.

6233 Quijano, Carlos. Nicaragua, un pueblo, una revolución: ensayo sobre el imperialismo de los Estados Unidos. Palabras preliminares por Pablo González Casanova. México: Editorial Pueblo Nuevo, 1978. 141 p.

The ex-editor of the Uruguayan weekly *Marcha*, exiled now in Mexico and an "old hand" in the anti-imperialist struggle, is the author of this strong, and not very novel, denunciation of American domination of Nicaragua (1912–27).

6234 Ramírez M., Sergio. Breve historia contemporánea de Nicaragua (CDLA, 20:117, nov./dic. 1979, p. 17–39)

Written by a member of the present Nicaraguan revolutionary government, this article exemplifies the sort of nationalistic history that is unconcerned with the reliability of sources. The central figure, of course, is Sandino. Since Ramírez' essay was written sometime ago, the editors tacked on additional pages covering recent events written by a different author.

6235 ———. Los intelectuales en el futuro revolucionario (NMC/N, 1, mayo/junio 1980, p. 158–162)

Intellectuals are not only writers and artists but also "promoters of culture," (i.e., teachers, journalists, etc.). A leader of the Nicaraguan government elaborates on the revolutionary role of "intellectuals," as defined in the new Nicaragua. He also discusses the concept of "revolutionary culture."

6236 Ruiz, Henry. La montaña era como un crisol donde se forjaban los mejores cuadros (NMC/N, 1, mayo/junio 1980, p. 8–24, map, plates)

A fascinating interview with the leader of the Guerra Prolongada tendency within the Sandinista Front. Indispensable reading for those interested in guerrillas and revolutionary strategy.

6237 Testimonios (CDLA, 20:117, nov./dic. 1979, p. 159–178)

Consists of the following accounts: the unfinished diary of Sandinista Commander Germán Ordóñez Pomares; the uprising at Monimbó by Juanita, an eyewitness; and the garrison attack by Alejandro Guevara, one of the participants; sources for the study of the Nicaraguan struggle.

6238 Trabajar, avanzar, combatir, vencer. La Habana: Frente Sandinista de Liberación Nacional en Cuba, Comisión de Información, n.d. 40 p.

A propaganda tract issued by Sandinista representatives in Cuba. Includes some unreliable information such as a battle front dispatch stating that Sandinistas were fighting against Guatemalan and Salvadorian "troops."

6239 Urcuyo Maliaño, Francisco. Solos: las últimas 43 horas en el bunker de Somoza. Guatemala: Editorial Académica Centroamericana, 1979. 209 p.; ill.

The last gasps of Somocismo according to Somoza's successor as President for 43 hours. Strongly critical of the Carter administration, the book offers interesting glimpses of Ambassador Pezullo's arm-twisting as well as of quarrels between the State Dept. and the Pentagon.

6240 Walker, Thomas W. The Sandinist victory in Nicaragua (CUH, 78:454, Feb. 1980, p. 57–61, 84)

Describes the Sandinista victory and the initial steps taken by the new government. Author's detachment borders on insipidity. Compare to Debray's article (item **6217**).

PANAMA

6241 Manduley, Julio. El proceso panameño (CP, 15, enero/marzo 1978, p. 62–74)
A study in dependent capitalism in which socioeconomic factors are so important that the author performs his analysis with only one mention of Gen. Omar Torrijos.

6242 Navas, Luis. El movimiento obrero en Panama, 1880–1914. Ciudad Universitaria Rodrigo Facio, Costa Rica: Editorial Universitaria Centroamericana, 1979. 176 p.; bibl. (Colección Seis. Colección Rueda del tiempo)
Recognizes the role of migration from the Caribbean and Europe in the development of the country's labor movement. Author openly identifies with Marxism-Leninism and makes no pretense at objectivity. Nevertheless, he does include data not easily available elsewhere.

6243 Souza, Rubén Darío. Panamá: nueva etapa (URSS/AL, 1, 1980, p. 42–52)
Secretary General of the Panama People's Party (Communist), the author elaborates on the party's position after the treaties signed by President Carter and Gen. Torrijos, one that is supportive of the latter.

THE CARIBBEAN
GENERAL

6244 Lewis, Gordon K. The claim for Caribbean identity (in Cultural traditions and Caribbean identity: the question of patrimony. Edited by S. Jeffrey K. Wilkerson. Gainesville: University of Florida, Center for Latin American Studies, 1980, p. 375–436)
Once more the author displays his mastery of Caribbean history and literature, particularly concerning the British Caribbean, as well as his unorthodox ideas. In the final analysis, Caribbean identity withstands the siege of one of its most persistent and qualified students.

6245 Maingot, Anthony P. Ideological dependency and the origins of socialism in the Caribbean (in The Continuing struggle for democracy in Latin America [see item 6028] p. 217–299, tables)

"Dependency is not only an economic condition: it is also political and intellectual . . ." Author draws comparison, in the context of ideological dependence, of socialist ideas in Cuba, Trinidad and Tobago, and Jamaica. This article offers short but incisive criticism of the strong bias of most dependency literature.

6246 ———. The role of the opposition in the Caribbean: parliamentary politics in the West Indies (FIU/CR, 7:4, oct./dec. 1978, p. 22–26, ill., plate)
Consists of the introduction to an issue of *Caribbean Review* devoted to political opposition in the Caribbean. The author is very familiar with the area, even if his remarks here are particularly novel.

6247 Mass media in/on Cuba and the Caribbean area: the role of the television, radio, and the free press. Edited by Jan Herd. Erie: Northwestern Pennsylvania Institute for Latin American Studies; Mercyhurst College, 1979. 79 leaves (Latin American monograph series; no. 10)
Consists of original and interesting contributions on a topic that has been seriously underestimated in the literature: John A. Lent "Recent Political Economic Aspects of Mass Media in Trinidad, Barbados, Jamaica and Guyana; Judy Oliver Milner "Fidel Castro and the Cuban Media;" Jon D. Cozean "Profile of U.S. Press Coverage on Cuba: Was Bay of Pigs Necessary?;" and Marvin Alisky "Governmental Mechanisms of Mass Media Control in Mexico." For bibliographer's comment, see *HLAS 42:186.*

SECOLAS Annals. Vol. 11, March 1980– .
See *HLAS 42:193.*

6248 Williams, Linda Faye. Development and dependence in the process of Caribbean urbanization (in Development issues, Caribbean-American dialogue: proceedings and papers from the Caribbean-American exchange program conducted by the Phelps-Stokes Fund. New York: The Fund, 1980, p. 31–54; tables)
Criticizes what is called: the modernization perspective (urbanization as the chief consequence of industrialization). Although article pays some attention to demographic factors, a dependentist approach prevails. Includes data on the British and Spanish Caribbean and provides a good introduction.

CUBA

6249 Así se derrotó al imperialismo. v. 1, Preparando la defensa. v. 2, El combate y la victoria. México: Siglo Veintiuno, 1978. 2 v.; ill. (Colección América nuestra; 19–20: Caminos de liberación)

Vol. 1 consists mainly of speeches by Castro; and vol. 2 of a narrative written by a war pilot, interviews with Bay of Pigs prisoners by Cuban journalists, and another Castro speech. Volumes lack introduction, notes, or any reference to the sources from which these materials were drawn. All of which leads one to conclude that the work is merely another propaganda item.

6250 Azicri, Max. The institutionalization of the Cuban state: a political perspective (SAGE/JIAS, 22:3, Aug. 1980, p. 315–344, bibl.)

In convoluted language, this article attempts to prove that the Cuban regime can institutionalize itself while Castro remains at the helm, as always. The elaborated and strenuous argument chiefly supported by references to recent legislation starting with the 1976 Cuban Constitution, makes for frustrating reading.

6251 Bondarchuk, Vladimir. El tránsito al socialismo: algunos aspectos socioeconómicos de la experiencia cubana (URSS/AL, 1, 1979, p. 25–40)

Capitalistic relations of production prevailed in the Cuban countryside before 1959. Peasants were only 10.7 percent of the working force. Thus the Cuban Revolution was not a peasant revolution. The high levels of capitalism achieved by Cuba before 1959 helped to shorten the period of transition to socialism.

6252 Bonich Fernández, Georgina. Ernesto (Che) Guevara, estudio bibliográfico. Bajo la dirección de Georgina Bonich Fernández; compilado por Hilda Maidique Patricio. La Habana; Centro de Información Científica y Técnica, Universidad de La Habana, 1975? 37 p.

Consists merely of a list of titles, most of them published in Cuba, organized in alphabetical order.

6253 Brandão, Ignácio de Loyola. Cuba de Fidel: viagem à ilha proibida. São Paulo: Livraria Cultura Editora, 1978. 120 p.

A Brazilian journalist invited by Casa de las Américas tells the story of his visit: hotels, theaters, the cinema, restaurants, and other tourist attractions in Cuba.

6254 Castillo Bernal, Andrés. Algunas consideraciones acerca de la guerra de guerrillas (Santiago [Universidad de Oriente, La Habana] 30, junio 1978, p. 173–196)

Marxist-Leninist study of the topic, based almost entirely on Guevara's works and the Cuban experience, starts with the government's offensive of May 1958. Regular rather than guerrilla war is the right label for these military operations.

6255 Castro, Fidel. Discursos. La Habana: Editorial de Ciencias Sociales, Instituto Cubano del Libro, 1975. 1 v.

Consists of seven speeches delivered 1961–72, without introduction, notes, or indication of selection criteria used.

6256 ———. La estrategia del Moncada (CDLA, 29:109, julio/agosto 1978, p. 3–31)

Castro offers information on his childhood, youth, and the planning and execution of the Moncada attack in this previously published interview with Swedish journalists (Cuba Internacional, Jan. 1978).

6257 ———. Fidel Castro's address to the National People's Government Assembly (APS/WA, 143:1, Summer 1980, p. 20–64)

Although never published in the Cuban press, the authenticity of this speech was never denied by the Cuban government. It seems that the regime regarded its message as too damaging: "we are sailing in a sea of difficulties," Castro frankly recognizes and, for once, offers no solution.

6258 ———. La Revolución Cubana. Selección y notas de Adolfo Sánchez Rebolledo. 3. ed. México: Ediciones Era, 1976. 636 p. (Colección El Hombre y su tiempo)

Vol. 1 covers from Moncada to the October Crisis and is organized in the following six sections: 1) "Against the Dictatorship;" 2) "A Democratic Revolution;" 3) "Towards Socialism" 4) "The Socialist and Democratic Revolution;" 5) "Cuban Socialism;" and 6) "The October Crisis." Consists of speeches, writings, and documents, some of which are signed by the Council of Ministers or the Cuban Communist Party but not all of which are reproduced in full. The introduction notes that additional volumes are planned.

6259 Cuba. Comités de Defensa de la Revolución (CDR). Testimonios. La Habana: Editorial Orbe, 1977. 136 p.; plates.

Members of the CDR answer two questions: "What is their evaluation of the organization?" and "What influence did the organization have on their formation and revolutionary development?" The answers are very positive.

6260 Cuba, dictatorship or democracy? Edition includes account of national experience of People's Power. Edited, and with an introduction by Marta Harnecker. Translation into English by Patrick Greanville. 5th ed., rev. and expanded. Westport, Conn.: L. Hill, 1980. 239 p.; bibl.

An updated edition of the Spanish original published in 1975 (see *HLAS* 41:7201).

6261 Darusenkov, O. Cuba strides into socialism (IA, 8, August 1978, p. 31–38) The author is the Chief of the Cuban Department of the Central Committee of the Communist Party of the USSR. Offers the standard Soviet interpretation of the Cuban Revolution and emphasizes "fraternal" relations between both countries.

6262 Del Mar, Marcia. A Cuban story. Winston-Salem, N.C.: J.F. Blair, 1979. 170 p.

This attempt to present the personal story of a Cuban middle-class woman (13 years old when she left Havana for exile in the US) is marred by numerous errors (e.g., names of persons, places, wrong descriptions of events, localities, uses, etc.) all of which make one question the memoir's authenticity.

6263 Dessau, Alberto. Los estudios latinoamericanos en la República Democrática Alemana y la Revolución Cubana (CDLA, 19:112, enero/feb. 1979, p. 69–72)

Consists of a short report on research underway on the subject of Cuba in the German Democratic Republic.

6264 Díaz, Carmen Guerra. Del pensamiento de Carlos Baliño (UCLV/I, 60, mayo/agosto 1978, p. 29–48)

Short selection of texts from Baliño

who, according to Cuban Marxists, constitutes the link between the struggle for national independence and the attainment of contemporary socialism.

6265 Domínguez, Jorge I. Cuba: order and revolution. Cambridge, Mass.: Belknap Press of Harvard University Press, 1978. 683 p.; bibl.; index.

Consists of 511 p. of regular text, 90 p. of notes, 36 p. of bibliography, 90 tables and six appendixes (including one on "Change in the Heights of Cubans"). A book for specialists divided into three parts: 1) Pre-Revolutionary Cuba since 1902; 2) Revolutionary Cuba: Government through Centralization; and 3) Political Processes and Change. See the introduction to the present section for comments.

6266 Eckstein, Susan. Capitalist constraints on Cuban socialist development (CUNY/CP, 12:3, April 1980, p. 253–274)

"Cubans currently are guaranteed employment, housing costing no more than 10 percent of family income, free medical care, extensive public education, and equitable rationing of basic goods." It is amazing how such statements, contradicted recently by the testimonies of more than 100,000 "boat people" and even by the Cuban daily press, continue to appear in scholarly journals. One possible explanation might be that there was not a single Cuban specialist among the readers (listed in a footnote) who evaluated a previous version of this paper.

6267 Fernandes, Florestan. Da guerrilha ao socialismo: a Revolução Cubana. Capa, Depto. de Arte da TAQ e Sérgio de Bonis. São Paulo: TAQ, 1979. 231 p.; 3 leaves of plates; graphs (Biblioteca de estudos latino-americanos; v. 1)

Based on a course taught in Brazil, the book consists of an introduction and body organized in four parts: 1) The Colonial and Neocolonial Past; 2) The Guerrillas and the Conquest of Power; 3) Economy and Society under Socialism; and 4) The Revolutionary State and Popular Power. Author acknowledges he is not a Cuban specialist but notes "socialist interpretation" of the Revolution, which one is not certain.

6267a Goetze, Dieter. Charisma, Innovation und Traditionalismus: der Fall Kuba (DDW, 2:3, 1973, p. 297–319)

The author discusses three features of the Cuban revolution: land reform, educational reform, and political reeducation. He wants to show the traditional charismatic leadership figure as continued in the macho role of Castro which is partially based on the Martí-cult embraced by the majority of the Cuban population. [R.V. Shaw]

Guerra Díaz, Carmen; Liana Bosch Rodríguez; and Juan A. Sánchez Bermúdez. Mella en la historia. See *HLAS 42:2605.*

6268 Jacqueney, Theodore. Face to face with Huber Matos: an interview (Worldview [Council on Religion and International Affairs, New York] 23:4, April 1980, p. 4–7, plates)

After 20 years in jail, this well-known Commander of the Rebel Army, once a close associate of Castro's, answers questions on his experience as a Cuban political prisoner under Castro.

6269 Klein, L.B. The Socialist Constitution of Cuba: 1976 (Colombia Journal of Transnational Law [Columbia University, School of Law, Columbia Journal of Transnational Law Association, New York] 17:3, 1978, p. 451–515)

A perceptive analysis of the Cuban Constitution in light of the nation's constitutional history and of contemporary socialist models, particularly the Soviet Constitution of 1936. Reading this astute piece, it is difficult to understand why the author concludes that such Constitution is a "significant gain for the Cuban citizen."

6270 Kuzin, Alexandr. Cuestiones de la defensa armada de la Revolución Cubana (URSS/AL, 1, 1979, p. 17–24)

Short description of the evolution of the Cuban Armed Forces which is based mostly on speeches by Fidel and Raúl Castro.

6271 LeoGrande, William M. The Communist party of Cuba since the First Congress (JLAS, 12:2, Nov. 1980, p. 397–419, tables)

Half the paper is devoted to the First Congress. Main data sources are the Cuban press and the *Directory of Cuban Officials* published by the CIA. As in other works by this author he tends to agree with Cuban interpretations. Moreover, he fails to provide footnotes for the new data he includes (e.g., What is the source for the statement that

Vilma Salinas "was added to the Central Committee as an Alternate Member" since 1978?).

6272 ———. Mass political participation in socialist Cuba (*in* Political participation in Latin America. v. 1, Citizen and state. Edited by John A. Booth and Mitchell A. Seligson. New York: Holmes & Meier, 1978, p. 114–128, table)

After rejecting the standard concept of political participation as too ethnocentric, author expands it to include supportive behavior ("voluntary" work, community projects, work as socialist emulation), and communal activity such as non-electoral behavior to influence local policy). Using exclusively Cuban official sources, he constructs a table that shows high levels of political participation, as defined, by socialist Cuba. If adopted by American political scientists, this table might serve to assuage anxieties in this country about current low levels of political participation.

6273 ———. Party development in revolutionary Cuba (SAGE/JIAS, 21:4, Nov. 1979, p. 457–480, table)

The author's principal assumption that the Cuban Communist Party "has emerged from the 1970s as the central political institution" is probably wrong. With that caveat in mind, the paper can be read chiefly as a friendly interpretation based almost entirely on official Cuban sources, especially the weekly *Granma*, and the very small literature available on the topic.

6274 Le Riverend, Julio. Etapas del proceso revolucionario (URSS/AL, 1, 1979, p. 9–16, plate)

Article does not constitute a serious attempt at presenting a historical periodization of the Revolution but rather a retelling of the main events since Moncada.

Mencía, Mario. Fidel Castro en el bogotazo. See item **6355.**

6275 Milkowski, Tadeusz. La problemática de la Revolución Cubana en la prensa polaca: 1953–1961 (PAN/ES, 3, 1976, p. 179–193)

It was only after the Bay of Pigs invasion (1961) and the October Crisis (1962), that the Polish press began to report on the Cuban Revolution with regularity and competence. Before, both Cuba and Castro were *terra incognita.*

Pérez, Louis A., Jr. "La Chambelona;" political protest, sugar, and social banditry in Cuba, 1914–1917. See *HLAS 42:2614.*

6276 ———. In the service of the Revolution: two decades of Cuban historiography, 1951–1979 (HAHR, 60:1, Feb. 1980, p. 79–89)

The article is not an analysis of "two decades of Cuban histography" but rather a description of how the present Cuban regime uses history as "a deliberate device for garnering loyalty and sacrifice." For historian's comment, see *HLAS 42:2615.*

6277 ———. Intervention, revolution, and politics in Cuba, 1913–1921. Pittsburgh: University of Pittsburgh Press, 1978. 198 p.; bibl.; index (Pitt Latin American series)

A version based almost exclusively on research conducted in American archives. The final chapter includes an interesting discussion of the political and diplomatic aspects of US-Cuban relations. Now we need a Cuban version based on an equally exhaustive search of Cuban archives. For historian's comment, see *HLAS 42:2616.*

Pierre-Charles, Gérard. Génesis de la Revolución Cubana. See *HLAS 42:2617.*

Pino Santos, Oscar. La oligarquía y yanqui en Cuba. See *HLAS 42:2618.*

6278 Prendes, Alvaro. En el punto rojo de mi kolimador. La Habana: Editorial de Arte y Literature, Instituto Cubano del Libro, 1974. 328 p.; 14 leaves of plates: ill.

A Cuban air-pilot and fighter in the Bay of Pigs invasion tells the story of his fight against the invaders. More of a source for personal experiences than a study of the invasion itself.

6279 Ripoll, Carlos. Dissent in Cuba (The New York Times Book Review [New York] 11 Nov. 1979, p. 11, 30)

Describes Cuban intellectual dissenters (writers, artists, etc.) and provides enough data to demonstrate that the intelligentsia's support of the regime has almost vanished.

Rodríguez-Loeches, Enrique. Bajando del Escambray. See *HLAS 42:2623.*

6280 Rous de Manitzas, Nita. Clase social y nación: nuevas orientaciones (*in* Cuba: camino abierto [see item **8189**] p. 60–97)

Published in 1972, this piece was written when Cuban political leaders proclaimed the country's arrival to communism and before planned military adventures with the Soviets were given priority in the policy agenda, a development which coincided with the official promotion of inequality. This contribution should serve as a warning never to base research entirely on statements by political leaders.

6281 ———. El marco de la Revolución (*in* Cuba: camino abierto [see item **8189**] p. 13–59)

Very similar to Robin Blackburn's interpretation of more than a decade ago which, although not entirely original, was a definite improvement over the very shallow Marxist interpretation of the socioeconomic background of revolutionary Cuba prevalent at the time. Still, this article includes at least one major error: Castro did not enter Cuban politics "for the first time" at the beginnings of 1952, but several years before when he became involved in gangsterlike revolutionary activities.

6282 Santamaría, Haydée. Moncada, memories of the attack that launched the Cuban Revolution. Translation and introduction by Robert Taber; afterword by Roberto Fernández Retamar. Secaucus, N.J.: L. Stuart, 1980. 118 p.

Remembrances not only of Moncada but of the struggle against Batista, by one who was very close to Fidel Castro, until she committed suicide in 1980 in Havana. This is a conversation with her recorded in 1967 when it was still possible for a leader to say: "We did not go to Moncada to make a socialist revolution."

6283 Serviat, Pedro. Carlos Baliño: sus actividades en el movimiento socialista hasta la formación del Partido Comunista de Cuba (UCLV/I, 60, mayo/agosto 1978, p. 15–28)

Repeats the standard interpretation of Baliño as the "direct linkage" between Martí and the first Cuban Communist Party.

6284 United States. Central Intelligence Agency. National Foreign Assessment

Center. Cuban chronology: a reference aid. Washington: 1978. 94 p.

Describes only foreign events involving Cuba for 1975–77 and mentions no sources. Organized by countries in alphabetical order. Although useful, one expects something better from the CIA.

6285 ——. ——. ——. Directory of officials of the Republic of Cuba. Washington: The Center; Springfield, Va.: may be purchased from National Technical Information Service, 1979. 298 p.; 1 fold. leaf of plates; index; map (A Reference aid—National Foreign Assessment Center. CR 79-15444)

Consists of a list of official positions, names, and dates (earliest and latest) of information. A "reference aid" of very limited use.

6286 Volsky, George. Cuba twenty years later (CUH, 76:44, Feb. 1979, p. 54–57)

A journalistic account by an observer who visited Havana recently and who has nothing that is strikingly new to report.

6287 Zuikov, Guennadi. Política social del poder popular (URSS/AL, 1, 1979, p. 41–55, table)

An unimaginative repetition of the achievements of the Cuban regime (e.g., health, education, social legislation) based exclusively on official sources. Apparently the author is ignorant of the fact that most labor benefits guaranteed by the Constitution of 1976 were already guaranteed by the previous Constitution of 1940.

DOMINICAN REPUBLIC

6288 Balaguer, Joaquín. La palabra encadenada. Santo Domingo: s.n., 1975. 312 p.; 37 leaves of plates; ill. (His Discursos; t. 4)

A book about Trujillo by a scholar and politician who was Trujillo's protégé since the 1930s. Balaguer is very well qualified to write about the Dictator's life. Pt. 1 consists of Balaguer's speeches delivered when he was Trujillo's sycophant. Pt. 2 constitutes the initial installment of another book to be published 20 years after Balaguer's death. The contrast between the two parts should not prevent one from paying close attention to

this attempt at understanding the many complexities of the Dictator's character.

6289 Bosch, Juan. Breve historia de la oligarquía y Tres conferencias sobre el fuedalismo. Cubierta, Amaury Villalba. 2. ed. Santo Domingo: Editora Alfa y Omega, 1977. 223, 5 p.; bibl.

Political frustrations have yielded Juan Bosch the free time necessary for making forays into the field of social history. Here, he first outlines the evolution of the concept of "oligarchy" from the Greeks to contemporary Latin America and then, discusses the concept of "feudalism," referring chiefly to Soviet historians and Marx.

6290 Caamaño Deñó, Francisco Alberto. A golpes de heroísmo: discursos pronunciados durante su mandato constitucional. Santo Domingo: Editorial MIROX, 1978. 36 p.; port. (Colección Pueblo y conciencia)

Highly rhetorical speeches by the "Constitutional President" of the Dominican Republic, (1965), later a frustrated guerrilla.

6291 Cuello H., José Israel and Julio F. Peynado. La Gulf and Western en el reformismo. Santo Domingo: Taller, 1974. 69 p. (Colección Debate; 4)

Reproduces the debate between Communist leader and Gulf's Dominican lawyer concerning the fairness of the contracts signed between the Dominican government and the American corporation in the 1970s.

6292 Gleijeses, Pedro. The Dominican crisis: the 1965 Constitutionalist revolt and the American intervention. Translated by Lawrence Lipson. Baltimore: Johns Hopkins University Press, 1978. 460 p.; bibl.; index.

The book is a mine of information, particularly concerning the Radical Left during the period (1961–66). Author's main thesis is that the coup presented a unique opportunity for setting up a democratic experiment which owed nothing to Cuba, an opportunity missed chiefly because American decision-makers and officials in the field "wanted anti-Communist stability more than democracy." The introduction to the main event announced in the title runs 158 p. and is followed by a detailed historical narrative ending with the elections of June 1966. Includes appendixes, 96 p. of footnotes, plus a bibliographical essay. Original title in French: *La crise dominicaine: 1965.*

6293 Moreno, José Antonio. The Dominican revolution revisited. Erie: Northwestern Pennsylvania Institute for Latin American Studies, 1978. 32 leaves; bibl. (Latin American monograph series; monograph no. 7)

The "aborted" Dominican revolution of 1965 is reexamined by a sociologist who published a book on the topic in 1975. No new sources or interpretations.

6294 Peña, Angela. Partidos políticos y presidentes dominicanos. Prólogo de Juan Bosch. Santo Domingo: s.n., 1978 or 1979. 132 p.; bibl.; ill.

A collection of journalistic pieces on traits peculiar to "underdevelopment politics" (e.g., cockfights and politics), customs usually dismissed by political scientists as unworthy of study.

6295 Peña Durán, Eliseo de. Actual realidad política en República Dominicana (NSO, 34, enero/feb. 1978, p. 88–96, ill.)

The political situation before the general elections of 1978.

Peña Rivera, Víctor A. Trujillo: la herencia del caudillo. See *HLAS 42:2613.*

6296 Urbano Gilbert, Gregorio. Mi lucha contra el invasor yanqui de 1916. Santo Domingo: Editora de la Universidad Autónoma de Santo Domingo, 1975. 289 p. (Colección Historia y sociedad; no. 19. Publicaciones de la Universidad Autónoma de Santo Domingo; v. 187)

Memoirs of a Dominican who, barely 17 years old, killed a US Marine officer when the Americans landed in 1917. Information on the *gavilleros* (fighters against the invaders), Dominican resistance, and the unruly behavior of American troops in the island.

6297 Vilas, Carlos María. Desarrollo capitalista periférico y las transformaciones políticas en la República Dominicana (UPR/RSS, 20:3/4, dic. 1978, p. 349–377, bibl., plates, tables)

An insightful analysis of changing socioeconomic and political conditions under Balaguer. The author's terminology is heavily influenced by Poutlanzas but his approach is creative and leads to plausible analysis.

HAITI

6298 Eugène, Grégoire. Plaidoyer en faveur des partis politiques. s.l.: s.n., 1979. 18 p.

Author advocates a dialogue among the Haitian elites and the establishment of political parties.

JAMAICA

6299 Bell, Wendell and **David L. Stevenson.** Attitudes toward social equality in independent Jamaica: twelve years after nationhood (CPS, 11:4, Jan. 1979, p. 499–523)

A replication, in 1974, of one study made by Moskos in 1962, using survey data. While some Jamaican leaders were more egalitarians in their attitudes in 1974 than in 1962, the role of the state in the economy constituted the principal contention between the two parties in 1974.

6300 Cumper, George Edward. The political economy of information: or, who runs Jamaica? s.l.: Cumper, 1979. 30 p.

Author draws a parallel between control of land and capital and control of information and perceives both types of control as generating class relations. Jamaica is ruled by an elite whose power base is information. This elite, however, cannot fulfill its function because the capitalist class has failed to develop the necessary material foundation. Book lacks both data and bibliography.

6301 Democratic socialism: the Jamaican model. Kingston?: People's National Party, 1976. 52 p.; ill.

A booklet for political education which consists only of general principles and statements condemning capitalism yet extolling private enterprise. The cover's motto is revealing: "Socialism is love."

6302 Gannon, John C. The racial ideology in Jamaican politics: the People's Political Party in the parliamentary elections of 1962 (UPR/CS, 16:3/4, Oct. 1976/Jan. 1977, p. 85–108)

An article of doubtful significance studies a political party (founded in 1961) which got only 2.24 percent of the vote in the general election of 1962.

6303 Hillman, Richard S. Jamaica's political leaders: Michael Manley and Edward Seaga (FIU/CR, 8:3, Summer 1979, p. 28–31, plates)

Both leaders answer questions on the 1976 elections and the ideologies and parties headed by them.

6304 ———. Legitimacy and change in Jamaica (JDA, 13:4, July 1979, p. 395–414, tables)

Based on 61 formal and informal interviews conducted from Jan. to May 1978. Disenchantment with Manley's government is not tantamount to questioning the legitimacy of the regime.

6305 Johnson, Caswell J. Political unionism and autonomy in economies of British colonial origin: the cases of Jamaica and Trinidad (AJES, 39:3, July 1980, p. 237–248)

A short and rather unconvincing attempt to compare the impact of political unionism on economic development both during the process of independence and after.

6306 Landau, Saúl. Jamaica's hot politics (Mother Jones [Foundation for National Progress, San Francisco, California] 5:8, Sept./Oct. 1980, p. 18–24, 63–65, plates)

In this article, published before the elections that defeated Manley and his party (PNP), the author himself recognizes that his view is "partisan," strongly sympathetic to Manley and written with little effort and even less imagination.

Post, Kenneth William John. Arise ye starvelings: the Jamaican labour rebellion of 1938 and its aftermath. See *HLAS 42:2619.*

6307 Seaga, Edward. The role of the opposition in Jamaica (FIU/CR, 7:4, Oct./Dec. 1978, p. 27–30, plate)

The leader of the winning party in the recent elections suggests steps to improve the role of the opposition before the elections were announced. He also answers questions on the present and future of Jamaican politics.

6308 Shearer, Hugh Lawson. Alexander Bustamante: portrait of a hero: based on a tribute. Kingston: Published for the Bustamante Industrial Trade Union by Kingston Publishers, 1978. 126 p.; 1 leaf of plates; chiefly ill.

Excellent pictures but laudatory texts.

LESSER ANTILLES

6309 DaBreo, D. Sinclair. The prostitution of a democracy: the agony of Grenada. St. George's, Grenada, West Indies: DaBreo, 1974? 62 p.; ill.

Condemns the unlawful behavior of Eric Gairy, the recently deposed Prime Minister of Grenada. Gairy believed in UFOs and in "cosmic connections."

6310 Emmanuel, Patrick. Crown Colony politics in Grenada, 1917–1951. Cave Hill, Barbados: Institute of Social and Economic Research (Eastern Caribbean), University of the West Indies, 1978. 198 p.; bibl. (Occasional paper—Institute of Social and Economic Research-Eastern Caribbean-University of the West Indies; no. 7)

Offers a political history based mainly on government sources. The last chapter covers the emergence of labor politics and Eric Gairy.

6311 Mark, Francis. The history of the Barbados Workers' Union. Bridgetown? Barbados: The Union, 1966? 168 p.

This history, commissioned by the Union, does not disclose sources used nor does it provide information on membership, internal organization, etc.

6312 Searle, Chris. Grenada's revolution: an interview with Bernard Coard (IRR/RC, 21:2, Autumn 1979, p. 171–188)

A member of Grenada's revolutionary government relates the history of the New Jewel Movement, and elaborates on future policies.

6313 Walker, Annette. The New Jewel: revolution in Grenada (NACLA, 14:1, Jan./Feb. 1980, p. 40–43, map, plate)

A brief and sympathetic account.

PUERTO RICO

6314 Berrios M., Rubén. Puerto Rico: ¿cómo salvar nuestra nacionalidad? (UNAM/PDD, 9:35, agosto/oct. 1978, p. 50–63, ill., plate)

The President of the Independentist Party applies a new label ("new working middle class") to employees and bureaucrats, and attempts to prove against most evidence, that eventually such strata will understand that there is no other alternative but independence.

6315 Galvin, Miles E. The organized labor movement in Puerto Rico. London; Granbury, N.J.: Associated University Press, 1979. 241 p.; bibl.; ill.; index.

Well-researched and competent study which the author himself modestly designates as "a chronicle of institutional development and labor leadership." More than that, the book is the first comprehensive treatment of the topic known to this reviewer.

6316 Matthews, Thomas. PDP + NPP = A*pa*thy: the end of the Popular Party (FIU/CR, 9:3, Summer 1980, p. 9–11, plate)

Although strongly biased against the PPD (later elections have shown the party alive and well) this short article contains some bits of interesting information about Muñoz Marín and other party leaders.

6317 Ojeda Reyes, Félix. Vito Marcantonio y Puerto Rico: por los trabajadores y por la nación. Traducción documentos Marcantonio, Carmen Rivera Izcoa. Diseño portada, Antonio Martorell. Río Piedras, P.R.: Ediciones Huracán, 1978. 154 p.; bibl.; ill.

Consists of speeches delivered by the American politician in the US House of Representatives. A long preliminary study introduces the reader to Marcantonio's ties to the US Communist Party, as well as to the valuable services which American communists performed on behalf of Puertorican independence in the 1930s.

6318 Olivieri Cano, Héctor. Puerto Rico: liberación nacional y socialismo (EDTM, 2:2, junio 1979, p. 317–364)

Author gets so involved in discussing world Marxist thinkers, including several pages on Stalin (!), international revolutionary movements, liberation struggles, etc., that he runs short of space to say very much about Puerto Rico.

6319 Puerto Rico y la ONU. Compilación de Carmen Gautier Mayoral and María del Pilar Argüelles. Río Piedras: Editorial Edil, 1978. 250 p.; bibl.; index.

Useful collection. Some documents are extracts or partial quotations and the last one is dated Aug. 1977. Introduction favors independence.

6320 Quintero-Rivera, A.G. Notes on Puerto Rican national development: class & nation in a colonial context (RU/MP, 9, Spring 1980, p. 10–30)

Author of several significant contributions to the understanding of Puerto Rican politics and history. Uses class analysis in an independent and original way.

6321 Romero-Barceló, Carlos. Statehood is for the poor. San Juan, P.R.: Romero-Barceló, 1978. 106 p.; 2 leaves of plates; ill.

The present Governor of Puerto Rico explains in very plain language to his fellow Puerto Ricans the "blessings of bringing Statehood to the Island:" the "fat cats" will pay more taxes and the poor will get more aid from the Federal Government. The Spanish original, published in 1973, was entitled: *La estadidad es para los pobres.*

6322 Samoiloff, Louise Cripps. Puerto Rico: the case for independence. With foreword by Gordon K. Lewis. Cambridge, Mass.: Schenkman Pub. Co., 1974. 169 p.; bibl.; map.

A strong plea for independence and socialism. Written when the island's ecology appeared threatened by a project to build a petrochemical complex. More heat than light.

6323 Sánchez Tarniella, Andrés. Contradicciones en las distintas alternativas políticas de Puerto Rico y Los costos de la estadidad. Río Piedras, P.R.: Ediciones Bayoán, 1979. 133 p.; bibl.

Pt. 1 concludes that all the varieties of "electoralism" are so wrong as the representatives of the "pseudo-left." Pt. 2 shows a striking ignorance of the American federal system.

6324 ———. La política puertorriqueña y la crisis de la identidad: con notas sobre los costos de la estadidad para Puerto Rico. Hato Rey, P.R.: Ramallo Bros., 1977. 156 p.; bibl.

A diagnostic of the present Puerto Rican "massive and almost compulsive flight from identity." Very critical of "estadidad." Although there is a short discussion on the economic costs of statehood, history and literature prevail.

6325 Sariola, Sakari. The Puerto Rican dilemma. Port Washington, N.Y.: Kennikat Press, 1979. 200 p.; bibl.; index (National university publications)

"Political leaders must take Puerto Rico's structural dependency for granted; this dependency can no longer be undone, it only can be replaced by a new dependency relationship." It is not clear what kind of dependency the author has in mind, since the one he favors should be "willed by the Puerto Ricans themselves." Some scattered insightful remarks on the Puerto Rican working class. Author is a sociologist, but the approach is historical, and the book begins with "the colonial foundation." Historians will probably raise objections.

6326 Silvestrini de Pacheco, Blanca. Los trabajadores puertorriqueños y el Partido Socialista (1932–1940). Río Piedras: Editorial Universitaria, 1979. 196 p.; bibl.

It was during this period that the Socialist Party formed a coalition with the Republican Union, the status issue prevailing over labor demands. However, increasing workers' dissatisfaction led to the final collapse of the party. Originally a dissertation, the book fulfills its academic requirements, but misses out on the significance of these events in Puerto Rican history. Original English title: *Puerto Rican workers and the Socialist Party, 1932–1940*.

TRINIDAD AND TOBAGO

6327 Brassington, F.E. The politics of opposition. Diego Martin, Trinidad: West Indian Sun Pub. Cl., 1976? 189 p.; 1 leaf of plates; ill. (A West Indian book)

Describes maneuvering, rivalries and squabbles within the Democratic Labour Party, the main opposition party in Trinidad and Tobago, founded in 1957. The author was Honorary Secretary of the party (1958–60)

6328 Crisis. Edited and with a foreword by Owen Baptiste. St. James, Trinidad: Inprint Caribbean, 1976. 417 p.; ill.

The editor, also editor of *Caribbean Contact*, presents a collection of reports, interviews, photos and documents concerning labor demonstrations in Trinidad (Feb.–March 1975).

6329 Mahabir, Winston. In and out of politics: tales of the government of Dr.

Eric Williams, from the notebooks of a former minister. Port of Spain, Trinidad: Inprint Caribbean, 1978. 220 p.; 6 leaves of plates; ill.

This delightful account is, according to the publisher's note: "the first PNM politician, outside of Dr. Williams, to write about his experiences in office." The chapters on Eric Williams—unfortunately too short—are gems. After a long immersion in the kind of stuff generated by "a rat-dominated set of experimental social scientists"—author's words—this reviewer is deeply appreciative of Mahabir's writing.

6330 Panday, Basdeo. The role of the opposition in Trinidad & Tobago (FIU/CR, 7:4, Oct./Dec. 1978, p. 31–36, plate)

A judicious discussion of contemporary Trinidad and Tobago politics by the leader of the parliamentary opposition: the racial problem, oil, the limits of the Westminster system, etc.

THE GUIANAS: Guyana

6331 Burnham, Forbes. Economic liberation through socialism. Address by . . . at the Second Biennial Congress of the People's National Congress, Sophia, August 12–20, 1977. Georgetown: Office of the Prime Minister, 1977? 32 p.

Burnham adds nothing to the clarification of his variety of socialism. He relinquishes his duties as rapporteur of the Congress in a perfunctory way.

6332 Harry, Carlyle. Hubert Nathaniel Critchlow, his main tasks & achievements. Georgetown: Guyana National Service Pub. Centre, 1977. 50 p.; ill.

A profile of the founder of Guyana's organized labor movement, written by a fellow trade-unionist.

6333 Jagan, Cheddi. The role of the opposition in Guyana (FIU/CR, 7:4, Oct./Dec. 1978, p. 37–41, plate)

In this "dialectical" exercise, the PPP's leader asks socialist countries (including Cuba, of course) "to exert as much pressure as they can," in order to convince Burnham of the convenience to get Jagan into the government.

6334 ———. The West on trial: the fight for Guyana's freedom. Berlin: Seven Seas Publ., 1975. 435 p.; index; map (Seven Seas books; 7)

Chapters in the original British edition (reproduced by International Publishers in 1967) have disappeared and new sections have been added to this edition. However, it continues to provide Jagan's version of what was originally "my fight" and is now "the fight against imperialism and for Guyana's freedom."

Lewis, Gordon K. "Gather with the saints at the river:" the Jonestown Guyana holocaust of 1978: a description and interpretative essay on its ultimate meaning from a Caribbean viewpoint. See HLAS 42:2609.

6335 Manley, Robert H. Guyana emergent: the post-independence struggle for nondependent development. Boston: G.K. Hall, 1979. 158 p.; bibl.; index.

A short chapter serves as introduction to this political history of Guyana (1966–76) which consists chiefly of an endless stream of "ideological" pronouncements by Guyanese leaders. Author makes no attempt to assess how changing socioeconomic conditions are related to the verbalizations drawn from his main sources: the Guyanese press and party documents. Includes a helpful bibliography.

6336 People's Progressive Party. Central Committee. For a National Front government. Georgetown, Guyana: People's Progressive Party, 1977. 31, 8 p.

Analyzes the Guyanese situation in order to justify the slogan: "For a National Front government." An appendix consisting of texts by Georgi Dimitrov, V. Afanasyev, and K. Brutents is designed to strengthen the image of the PPP as a pro-Soviet party.

SURINAM

6337 Dew, Edward. The difficult flowering of Surinam: ethnicity and politics in a plural society. The Hague: Martinus Nijhoff, 1978. 234 p.; bibl.; index.

One of the very few available books on Surinamese politics for the English-speaking reader. A short background introduction leads to a detailed political history beginning with the emergence of political parties (1942–48). Author's research was conducted in Surinam and The Netherlands. In his search for an explanation of how politics works in this plural society, author uses the "consociational" democracy model in his conclusion. For anthropologist's comment, see item 975.

SOUTH AMERICA: Colombia, Venezuela and Ecuador

DAVID W. DENT, *Associate Professor of Political Science, Co-Director, Latin American Studies Program, Towson State University*

IN THIS BIENNIUM ON THE THREE DEMOCRACIES of northern South America there is a slight increase in the literature as a result of presidential elections, the changing role of the Church, and the growing opposition from political forces on the left. Most of the literature is traditional in approach but several works reveal sophisticated comparative methods, statistical techniques, and valuable case studies. While both Venezuela and Ecuador are members of OPEC, the politics of energy has not received the attention it deserves in the literature. As with past volumes of the *Handbook*, conflicting ideological perspectives continue to affect the type of research and the conclusions that are researched.

The literature on Ecuador is sparse as usual but several works by national and foreign writers deserve mention. A useful series of essays on political economy can be found in Drekonja (item **6421**). Jácome's (item **6427**) comparative treatment of

11 political parties is a valuable reference for understanding the array of political parties and their governmental programs. Foreign writers such as Martz (items 6429–6431) and Handelman (item 6424) provide important insights into recent trends in party politics, civil-military relations, regime legitimacy, and populism. A partial gap in our understanding of the politics of the news media is filled by Albuja Galindo (item 6420) who discusses media ownership and how information is controlled and disseminated.

The literature on Colombia continues to focus on the National Front and its aftermath but much of what has been written since *HLAS 41* is useful and reflective of the growing number of national and foreign scholars. What impressed this reviewer are the recent efforts to understand Colombian democracy and its survivability. The edited work by Berry, Hellman, and Solaún (item 6362) provides 14 excellent essays on consociational democracy and its inner-workings by some of the most knowledgeable students of Colombian political affairs. This exhaustive work is complimented by Dix (item 6343) who compares the National Union coalition with the National Front and Wilde (item 6372) who argues that the breakdown of Colombian democracy in 1949 occurred because the political process was too informal, narrowly based, and personalistic. The recent elections, abstentionism, and the strength of the party system have led scholars to again examine the possibility of regime breakdown. Ruhl (item 6366) argues that predictions of traditional political party collapse are premature and unfounded. Wilde's assessment (item 6373) detects a growing weakness and illegitimacy of democratic political institutions but does not foresee a coup by the military. Serious efforts to understand the party system and electoral behavior can be found in Hoskin (item 6352), Ungar (item 6370) and Losada and Liebig (item 6344). Unfortunately, there seems to be very little agreement among scholars on the causes and consequences of electoral abstention.

The literature on Venezuela tends to shift back and forth between those on the fringes of the political system who continue to denounce Venezuelan democracy and those in the middle who often engage in breast-beating over the accomplishments of democratic reformism. In between these perspectives one finds some useful and provocative research. At the forefront of research on Venezuelan electoral behavior is Baloyra and Martz (items 6381 and 6383) whose empirical and theoretical work breaks new ground for understanding electoral behavior and Venezuelan democracy. In Baloyra and Martz (item 6382) democratic political participation is found to be closely tied to attitudes toward the regime rather than socioeconomic status. Efforts to understand the consolidation of democracy can be found in numerous works by national and foreign scholars. A valuable historico-institutional analysis of the Venezuelan state can be found in Brewer-Carías (item 6390). The significance of "loyal" opposition viewpoints is analyzed in conference papers by intellectuals and politicians (item 6401). The process of regime legitimization since 1958 is analyzed in a perceptive historical-structural work by Silva Michelena (item 6413).

The party system is examined in two useful works by foreign scholars: Herman (item 6399) stresses the importance of AD-COPEI opposition and cooperation as key factors in the survival of Venezuelan democracy; Myers (item 6404) presents a valuable account of how Venezuela's traditional communist party has been replaced by the Movement Toward Socialism. The relationship between petroleum revenues and democratic rule is something that few scholars seem to be able to agree upon. Blank (item 6388) sees an end to the populist brokerage style of democracy when petroleum income begins to evaporate. Levin (item **6402**) places less emphasis on oil wealth than the emergence of prudent leadership, party organization, and social learning. In a personal account of the history of oil and democratic politics, former president Betancourt (item **6386**) puts primary emphasis on the judicious leadership of the founders of Acción Democrática.

What research needs to be done? The quality of the debate over what makes and sustains democracy in Venezuela, Colombia, and Ecuador has improved in a number of areas but considerably more work needs to be done on theory-building and comparative cross-national designs. More needs to be said about the politics of trade unionism than is noted in the few leftist-oriented histories (items **6351** and **6405**) that have been published recently. We know very little about the impact of drugs (marihuana and cocaine) and the news media on national-level politics in Colombia. Little has been done on the question of power and who's running Colombia. In all three cases we are in desperate need of political biographies that highlight the role of leadership in democratic reform governments in South America. To compliment the excellent theoretical discussion of the breakdown of democracies by Linz (see *HLAS 42:1920*) we need a comparable work on the breakdown of authoritarian regimes. Perhaps those interested in the military-authoritarian regimes of the Southern Cone can begin to fill this void when the time comes?

COLOMBIA

6338 Abella, Arturo. Así fue el 13 [i.e. trece] de junio. Bogotá: Ediciones Aquí Bogotá, 1973. 80 p.; ill. (Aquí Bogotá; no. 2)

Descriptive chronicle of the coup d'état of 13 June 1953 that removed President Gómez and ushered in Gen. Rojas Pinilla. Useful documentary materials for the events that preceded and precipitated the intervention in Colombian politics by the military.

6339 Administración López Michelsen, 74–78 [i.e. setenta y cuatro-setenta y ocho]: una gestión con proyecciones hacia el año dos mil. s.l.: A. Castellanos, 1978 or 1979. 135 p.; ill.

Pictoral and written account of public expenditures and infrastructure development during the four years of Liberal President López Michelsen. A highly favorable account by the top ministers of the president's "team."

6340 Avila, Abel. Abstencionismo y anticarisma en Colombia. Bogotá: Ediciones Universidades Simón Bolívar, Libre de Pereira y Medellín, 1980. 233 p.; bibl. (Colección Universidad y pueblo)

Barranquillero Liberal offers some clues for understanding voting abstention in Atlántico and Colombia. Through an analysis of class domination, author suggests that

the electoral system is a farce and therefore democracy is a myth. The explanation is carried into an analysis of voting patterns in Barranquilla and 20 small towns in the Department of Atlántico. Useful for understanding the politics of the north coast.

6341 Booth, John A. Comparing political violence in Colombia and Guatemala (*in* Political participation in Latin America. Edited by John A. Booth and Mitchell A. Seligson. v. 2, Politics and the poor. New York: Holmes & Meier, 1978, p. 97–115, table)

The sources of violent political participation are sought through an examination of both context (socioeconomic conditions) and political structures (strength of partisan loyalties, regime coerciveness, legitimacy) in two of Latin America's most violent polities. The propositions, drawn from relative deprivation theory, seem rather obvious and inadequately tested. The "single most powerful" determinant of political violence turned out to be the parity of electoral support between Liberals and Conservatives and between reformists and counter-revolutionary groups. In the end, the legacy of violence becomes a key variable by itself.

6342 Corporación Pro-Régimen Federal. Comisión de Abogados Constitucionalistas. Federalismo moderno: un proyecto de constitución para Colombia.

Medellín: Corporación Pro-Regimen Federal, 1979. 143 p.

Various members of Medellin's elite present a strong case for a federal regime instead of the present unitary system. An answer to the frequent complaint made by many regional elites of the unequal and detrimental consequences of *centralismo*.

6343 Dix, Robert H. Consociational democracy: the case of Colombia (CUNY/ CP, 12:3, April 1980, p. 303–321)

Elite accommodation as part of the theory of consociational democracy is examined for its applicability to the Colombian case. Why did conflict regulation fail in the National Union coalition of 1945–49 but succeed with the National Front arrangement of 1958–74? Author attempts to isolate alternative sets of factors that were present in one case but absent in the other. The findings suggest that most of Lijphart's conditions of consociational democracy apply "but poorly to the Colombian case" because they are "essentially static over time." The key to explaining behavioral change in the Colombian case is the shift in incentives to accommodate during 1948–58.

Echavarría M., Guillermo. Camilo C. Restrepo. See *HLAS 42:2978.*

6344 Las Elecciones de 1978 en Colombia. Contribuciones por Luis Carlos Galán et al.; editores, Rodrigo Losada Lora, Georg Liebig. Bogotá: Fundación Friedrich Naumann, 1979. 174 p.; bibl.; graphs.

Excellent analysis of the 1978 congressional and presidential elections by six participants in a seminar on Colombian electoral politics in 1978. Most of the analysis focuses on the rate of abstention, the openness of the party system, the role and strength of opposition parties, and the future of Colombian democracy. The interpretations of electoral abstention are by no means uniform.

6345 Espriella, Ramiro de la. Conciencia subversiva: ejército y pueblo. Bogotá: s.n., 1976. 129 p.

Series of four essays by a journalist who would like to see the emergence of a military government that would reject civilian "immorality" for a more assertive nationalism and legitimate government.

6346 Fernández, Raúl A. Imperialist capitalism in the Third World: theory and evidence from Colombia (LAP, 6[20]:1, Winter 1978, p. 38–64, bibl., tables)

Using Lenin's theory of imperialism, author attempts to adduce the consequences of capitalism on Colombian economic development. Colombia is portrayed as a neo-colony of US imperialism. The assertion that Colombian workers would be better off if capitalist industrialization had not occurred is rather equivocal and not well substantiated. However, the critiques of aid programs such as the Integrated Rural Development strategy of the World Bank are quite valuable.

6347 Gallón Giraldo, Gustavo. Quince años de estado de sitio en Colombia, 1958–1978. Bogotá: Librería y Editorial América Latina, 1979. 195 p.; bibl.

An examination of the functions and consequences of the state of siege as a component of the Colombian political process. The impact of lower classes, the rise of the military, the erosion of civil rights, and the diminution of political legitimacy is evident and serves to highlight the precariousness of the political apparatus and liberal democratic ideology. What started out as a temporary means of reducing conflict has turned into a permanent form of elite domination.

García, Antonio. Colombia: medio siglo de historia contemporánea. See *HLAS 42:2980.*

6348 García Márquez, Gabriel. Periodismo militante. Ilustraciones de C. María Casablanca. Bogotá: Máquina Editores, 1978. 250 p.; ill.

Chronicles, articles and newspaper reports by Colombia's most famous socialist writer. A wide variety of political topics are covered to highlight this writer's service to the Latin American revolution. The interviews with Régis Debray, Gen. Omar Torrijos, and Felipe González are interesting while "Gabo's" ideology comes through loud and clear.

6349 Gilhodes, Pierre. Les élections colombiennes de 1978 (FDD/NED [Problèmes d'Amérique Latine, 52] 4523/4524, 20 juillet 1979, p. 64–88, map, tables)

Sound and useful report on both 1978 congressional elections: one held in Feb. and Presidential one in June. Electoral participation in the former was 32.5 percent increasing to 40 percent in June. Includes some pages discussing the phenomenon of electoral abstention. [A. Suárez]

————. La violence en Colombie, banditisme et guerre sociale. See *HLAS 42:2980.*

6350 Gómez Buendía, Hernando. Alfonso López Michelsen, un examen crítico de su pensamiento y de su obra de gobierno. Bogotá: Tercer Mundo, 1978. 367 p.; bibl. (Colección Tribuna libre)

A critical examination of the political thought and works of President López Michelsen. López is criticized for his presidential style, the state of siege, economic policy, the lack of interest in agrarian reform. Promises to "close the gap" have not been fulfilled according to this author.

6351 González, Fernán E. Pasado y presente del sindicalismo colombiano. Bogotá: Centro de Investigación y Acción Social: distribuidor, Librería América Latina, 1975. 216, 1 p.; bibl.

Leftist-oriented history of 20th-century trade unionism during 1920–74. The weakness of labor unions is linked to the elitist nature of party politics, socioeconomic inequalities, and the rather conservative role of the Catholic Church.

Guillén Martínez, Fernando. El poder político en Colombia. See item **8268.**

6352 Hoskin, Gary. Belief systems of Colombian political party activists (SAGE/JIAS, 21:4, Nov. 1979, p. 481–504, tables)

Interviews with 412 party leaders (Liberal, Union Conservative, Independent Conservative, and ANAPO) in Bogotá establish the data base for measuring six political belief dimensions: religiosity, pro-communism, political efficacy, class conflict, partisanship, and anti-system orientation. Party affiliation is the most powerful predictor of belief systems although level in the party hierarchy is also important. The importance of political party socialization is underscored as well. Findings suggest a number of factors in the survivability of the Colombian political system.

6353 López Michelsen, Alfonso. El gobierno del mandato. t. 1, 7 de agosto de 1974, 6 de febrero de 1975. t. 2, 7 de febrero de 1975, 7 de agosto de 1975. t. 3, 7 de agosto de

1975, 6 de febrero de 1976. t. 4, 7 de febrero a 6 de agosto de 1976. t. 5, 7 de agosto de 1976 a 3 de febrero de 1977. Bogotá: Talleres Editoriales de la Imprenta Nacional de Colombia, 1975/1978. 5 v.: ill.; indexes.

Consists of addresses, essays and lectures on a wide diversity of subjects during the political transition from the National Front to a more competitive political system. President López Michelsen's speeches stress democratic reform rhetoric within the context of the "clear mandate" theme.

6354 López Pumarejo, Alfonso. Obras selectas. Presentación y compilación de Jorge Mario Eastman. Bogotá: Cámara de Representantes, 1979. 1 v. (Colección Pensadores políticos colombianos; v. 10)

Consists of the first articles and political statements of López during his first presidential campaign and messages during the first four years (1934–38) of his presidency. Liberal ideology and the Good Neighbor Policy are important subjects in this work.

Lynch, Dennis O. Lawyers in Colombia: perspectives on the organization and allocation of legal services. See item **8270.**

6355 Mencía, Mario. Fidel Castro en el bogotazo (OCLAE, 10, 1978, p. 4–31, plates)

Fidel Castro's early university experience and his participation in the *bogotazo* are examined in an effort to explain his role in the Cuban Revolution. The lessons that are learned from the *bogotazo* will be applied to Cuba in the years to come. The death of Gaitán and the failure of revolution in Colombia taught Fidel the need for developing an organizational base, the value of charismatic leadership, and the inherent weaknesses of capitalist societies. Author also maintains that Fidel did not murder Manolo Castro.

6356 La Miseria de los partidos. Bogotá: Centro de Investigación y Educación Popular, 1980. 100 p.; bibl. (Controversia; no. 84)

The continual decline in turnout for congressional elections (25 percent in 1980) is examined for causes and consequences. Authors find that the concentration of economic and political power, the rigidity of the party system, and the fragmentation of the left are prime causes of abstention. Unfortunately, the descriptive material is better than the explanation for turnout decline.

6357 Molina, Gerardo. Las ideas liberales en Colombia. t. 1, 1849–1914. t. 2, 1915–1934. t. 3, De 1935 a la iniciación del Frente Nacional. Bogotá: Ediciones Tercer Mundo, 1970/1977. 3 v. (Colección Manuales universitarios tercer mundo; 3, 9, 11)

A social history of Liberal thought from 1849 to 1958. Each volume covers a distinct period of Colombian political and social history. A valuable leftist account of ideological transformation and adaptation. For historian's comment, see *HLAS 38:3336.*

6358 Morales, Alberto. Colombia: elecciones y crisis política (NSO, 34, enero/feb. 1978, p. 56–72, tables)

Further efforts to understand why the electoral abstention and political conflict in Colombian presidential politics does not produce a breakdown in the democratic system and the intrusion of military power. Some clues are offered but the analysis is rather superficial.

Ortiz Márquez, Julio. El hombre que fue un pueblo. See *HLAS 42:2988.*

Palacios, Marco. Coffee in Colombia, 1850–1970: an economic, social, and political history. See *HLAS 42:2989.*

6359 Partido Comunista de Colombia. Los principios orgánicos comunistas. Por Juan Viana. Tercera edición del manual de organización del Partido Comunista de Colombia . . . ampliado y corregido. Bogotá: Ediciones Suramérica, 1977. 166 p.; bibl.

Most recent edition of the Colombian Communist Party's manual of organization. Emphasis is placed on the theory and practice of mass-based revolutionary change.

6360 Pécaut, Daniel. La Colombie de 1974 a 1979: du *Mandat Clair* a la *Crise Morale* (FDD/NED [Problèmes d'Amérique Latine, 52] 4523/4524, 20 juillet 1979, p. 10–61, tables)

An excellent analysis of Colombian politics during the period which draws together domestic economic, social, and political factors in a manner that allows the author to indicate some general trends in Colombian society. The feat is performed without a conceptual framework, merely by a mastering of information which reveals the author's thorough familiarity with the country. [A. Suárez]

6361 Pérez González-Rubio, Jesús. Reformar las instituciones. Bogotá: Secretaría de Información de la Presidencia de la República, 1979. 101 p.; bibl.

A proposal for congressional reform that would strengthen the powers of Congress while at the same time help to solve the problems connected with administrative and fiscal centralization in Bogotá that deprives the departments and municipalities of political power.

6362 Politics of compromise: coalition government in Colombia. Edited by R. Albert Berry, Ronald G. Hellman, Mauricio Solaún. New Brunswick, N.J.: Transaction Books, 1979. 1 v.

A series of 14 essays on the Colombian National Front as a coalition political system with emphasis on its origins, characteristics, and consequences for social, political, and economic development. The interplay between periods of major political violence, the unusually minor role of the military, the changes in the Catholic Church, and the salience of two major political parties has created the incentives for political coalition. The success of political institution-building combined with economic development does not mean that problems of political legitimacy, socioeconomic inequalities, and political violence have been solved. Rather, questions of power and legitimacy still persist within a framework of elite-dominated, bipartisan "hegemonic" politics. An excellent treatment of consociational democracy and its inner-workings by some of the most knowledgeable students of Colombian political affairs. A valuable work for its treatment of regime transformation, civil-military relations, and democratic reformism.

6363 Repression in Colombia: political persecution in Colombian universities (IRR/RC, 20:2, Autumn 1978, p. 189–191)

The increase in political persecution and military repression of university students is attributed to US domination of the economy and efforts to make the Colombian educational system conform to the needs of multinational investors. Dubious and unsupported analysis.

6364 Rezazadeh, Reza and **Joseph Mac-Kenzie.** Political parties in Colombia: continuity in political style. Ann Arbor, Mich.: Published for University of Wisconsin-Platteville by University Microfilm International, 1978. 89 p.; bibl.; graphs (Monograph publishing on demand: Sponsor series)

An analytically weak treatment of political party style, partisanship and voter turnout during the National Front coalition period. Authors argue that Colombian desire leaders who can be characterized as "mystic caudillos" who "will neither have connections with economic establishments nor will compromise with them." Such moral-ethical leadership will evidently not emerge in Colombia given the present system of political party recruitment.

Rodríguez Garavito, Agustín. Jorge Eliécer Gaitán: biografía de una sombra: oligarquía, burguesía, democracia, oclocracia en Colombia. See *HLAS 42:2991.*

6365 Rojas H., Fernando. El Estado en los ochenta, un régimen policivo? Bogotá: Centro de Investigación y Educación Popular, 1980. 187 p. (Serie Controversia; no. 82–83)

Marxist critique of Colombian democracy with dismal predictions for the 1980s: more militarism, less democracy, and more administrative chaos.

6366 Ruhl, J. Mark. Party system in crisis?: an analysis of Colombia's 1978 elections (IAMEA, 32:3, Winter 1978, p. 29–45, tables)

An analysis of Colombia's 1978 elections reveals that, despite a turnout of 41 percent, predictions of traditional political party collapse and the rise of class politics are premature and unfounded. "The Colombian public has demonstrated that it will vote in large numbers when attractive candidates and clear policy choices are offered." The weakness of the Colombian left is an important part of the strength of the traditional parties but no explanations for this are offered.

6367 Sanín Echeverri, Jaime. Ospina supo esperar. Bogotá: Editorial Andes, 1978. 267 p.; 2 leaves of plates; ports.

Favorable biography of one of Colombia's most notable Conservative presidents and families.

6368 Taussig, Michael. Black religion & resistance in Colombia: three centuries of social struggle in the Cauca Valley (RU/MP, 2:2, Summer 1979, p. 84–117)

The association of black religion to social and political struggles is presented in a detailed historical analysis of south-west Colombia. Valuable for its treatment of black identification with Liberal ideology based on its position on abolition, Catholicism, free trade, and land reform. A fascinating account of class, party, and religion in one region of of class, party, and religion in one region of Colombia with emphasis on the 19th century.

Tirado Mejía, Alvaro. Las guerras civiles en Colombia. See *HLAS 42:2995.*

6369 Turbay Ayala, Julio César. Pensamiento democrático de Julio César Turbay Ayala. Presentación de Hernán Echavarría Olózaga, Jaime Michelsen Uribe, Hernando Morales Molina; prólogo de César Castro Perdomo. Bogotá: Talleres Ediciones Paulinas, 1978. 504 p.

President Turbay's political ideas and programs are captured in 35 essays and lectures. The political rhetoric is quite heavy while the coverage of Liberal democratic thought is rather light.

6370 Ungar Bleier, Elizabeth and **Angela Gómez de Martínez.** Aspectos de la campaña presidencial de 1974: estrategias y resultados. Bogotá: ANIF, 1977. 302 p.; bibl.

Political Science thesis on the 1974 presidential election campaign. A valuable theoretical and empirical treatment of elections, political parties, the press, electoral behavior, and the candidates during the National Front period.

Urrutia, Miguel. El sindicalismo durante el siglo XIX. See *HLAS 42:2997.*

6371 Vázquez Carrizosa, Alfredo. El poder presidencial en Colombia: la crisis permanente del derecho constitucional. Bogotá: E. Dobry, Editor, 1979. 437 p.; bibl. (Colección Ciencia política)

Excellent constitutional history of executive power from the "imperial presidency" of Simón Bolívar to the "constitutional presidency" of Alfonso López Michelsen by one of Colombia's best-known lawyers and journalists. A well-documented study of the growing tendency to concentrate economic and political power in the hands of a few and its impact on future efforts to solve the problem of legitimate authority. Author considers the permanence of the state of siege as a constitutional crisis.

6372 Wilde, Alexander W. Conversations among gentlemen: oligarchical democracy in Colombia (in The Breakdown of democratic regimes: Latin America [see *HLAS 42:1920*] p. 28–81, ill.)

The breakdown of Colombian democracy in 1949 is attributed to changes in political institutions (primarily the party system) and rules (attitudes toward competition and consent) as perceived by major political actors in the political system. "Democracy broke down in Colombia in 1949 because the mechanisms upon which it rested were too informal, personalistic, and narrowly based." The reincarnation of oligarchical democracy occurred because of the *violencia*, the Rojas dictatorship, and prudent leadership. Study confirms the weakness of class and ideology as explanatory variables in the breakdown of Colombian democracy.

6373 ———. Is Colombia on the brink of anything? (Worldview [Council on Religion and International Affairs, New York] 23:6, June 1980, p. 15–16)

Using the diplomatic hostage-taking by M-19 revolutionaries as a point of departure, Colombia's political malaise is scrutinized to assess the growing importance of the military as a power contender in the *país político*. Author believes that while a coup is not in the cards, the growing weakness and illegitimacy of Colombia's political institutions does not augur well for democratic politics.

6374 Zelinsky, Ulrich. Kontinuität und Wandel im politischen Kräftefeld Kolumbiens (BESPL, 3:15, Januar/Februar 1978, p. 2–13)

The numerous reform movements during the last 15 years in Colombia are described by the author who ends the article on a very pessimistic note. He predicts that a military regime with a puppet president seems to be the only type of government that could save the country from total chaos. [R.V. Shaw]

6375 Zuleta Ferrer, Juan. La historia contra la pared: selección de ensayos y editoriales, *El Colombiano*, 1930–1973. Medellín: Biblioteca Pública Piloto, 1978. 403 p. (Colección Biblioteca Pública Piloto; v. 1)

Selection of editorials and essays by the editor of The Medellín newspaper *El Colombiano* and one of Antioquia's influential voices of Conservative thought. Editorials cover 1930–78 and contain some valuable observations on political and economic events during that period of time.

VENEZUELA

6376 Acción Democrática y la cultura. Caracas: Ediciones Centauro, 1977. 1 v.; ports.

Brief political biography on six prominent intellectual leaders of the Acción Democrática party including their contributions to the development of the AD party and the richness of the national culture.

6377 Albornoz, Orlando and **Ariel Dorfman.** El intelectual y el estado: Venezuela-Chile. Saúl Sosnowski, editor. College Park: University of Maryland, Department of Spanish and Portuguese, 1980. 69 p. (Occasional papers in Latin American studies)

Two essays on the distinct role of the intellectuals in the politics of Chile and Venezuela. Patterns of cooperation and conflict prevail but the Venezuelan case demonstrates that intellectuals and university professors have fared rather well as a result of the semi-pluralist democratic principles and upward social mobility. Author argues that in terms of privilege, university professors and the military rank among the highest in the nation. Obviously, this has not been the case in Chile.

6378 Ameringer, Charles D. Leonardo Ruiz Pineda: leader of the Venezuelan resistance, 1949–1952 (SAGE/JIAS, 21:2, May 1979, p. 209–232, bibl.)

An historical account of AD resistance to military rule by one of its founders and democratic revolutionaries until his death in 1952. Although Pérez Jiménez continued to rule for five years after Ruiz Pineda's death, his struggle provided a powerful legacy for the eventual restoration of Venezuelan democracy after 1958. For historian's comment, see *HLAS 42:3003*.

6379 Aquí hace falta una oposición revolucionaria. Diseño de la portada, Elides J. Rojas. Caracas: El Pueblo Avanza, 1979. 134 p.; bibl.; ill.

Why did the Venezuelan left fail in its efforts to win the 1978 elections? The answer lies in the failure of socialism to adjust to the needs of the masses and the distortions in a monopolistic and dependent capitalist state. An interesting critique of the left, right, and center by a group (EPA) advocating a revolutionary alternative to democratic reformism.

6380 Asociación Pro-Venezuela. Nueva concepción del Estado. Caracas: La Asociación, 1979. 86 p.; index.

The problem of excessive politico-administrative centralization is addressed with suggestions for reform that would seriously alter the flow of power both politically and economically. Valuable suggestions for those interested in a more authentic federalism for Venezuela.

6381 Baloyra, Enrique A. Criticism, cynicism, and political evaluation: a Venezuelan example (APSA/R, 73:4, Dec. 1979, p. 987–1002, bibl., tables)

Case study based on a national sample survey designed to clarify the analytical distinction between political cynicism and political criticism. Path analyses show that criticism is tied to predominantly political orientations while political cynicism arises from a rigidified form of criticism rooted in the social circumstances of individuals. An important contribution to the literature on the interaction between citizen and government in democratic institutions in addition to an understanding of the high levels of public criticism found in Venezuela. The key point seems to fit the maxim that: "all cynics are critical but not all critics are cynical."

6382 ———— and John D. Martz. Dimensions of campaign participation: Venezuela, 1973 (*in* Political participation in Latin America. Edited by John A. Booth and Mitchell A. Seligson. New York: Holmes & Meier, 1978, p. 61–84)

What happens to the determinants of political participation—social status, political efficacy, partisan attachments—when there is compulsory voting as in the case of

Venezuela? Using a data base of 1,521 interviews with a stratified random sample of eligible Venezuelan voters, authors find that by separating three aspects of the campaign, activism can be predicated with relative certainty. The findings support the significance of attitudes toward the regime over socioeconomic status for predicting levels of campaign involvement. A valuable theoretical and empirical contribution to participatory behavior in democratic regimes.

6383 ———— and ————. Political attitudes in Venezuela: societal cleavages and political opinion. Austin: University of Texas Press, 1979. 300 p.; bibl.; ill. (The Texas Pan American series)

A highly competent study of voter attitudes and preferences that contributes to our understanding of Venezuelan democracy and adds new insights for survey research methodology in Latin America. With an analytical focus on the relationship between major societal cleavages—class, status, community context, religion, ideology, and partisanship—and political opinion and behavior, authors find that the Venezuelan electorate is not so easy to define. Their feelings suggest "that Venezuelan political opinion responds primarily to the individual's overall orientation to politics" and that political-apolitical status is more relevant than whether the voter is "on the left or right, *adeco* or *copeyano*, male or female, young or old, urban or rural, and poor or middle class."

6384 Betancourt, Rómulo. América Latina, democracia e integración. Barcelona: Seiz Barral, 1978. 235 p. (His Obras selectas; 2)

Betancourt's personal views on the Latin American economy, economic integration, the OAS, coups, democracy, and despots.

6385 ————. El 18 [i.e. dieciocho] de octubre de 1945: génesis y realizaciones de una revolución democrática. Introducción de Simón Alberto Consalvi; prólogo y notas de Diógenes de La Rosa. 2. ed. Barcelona: Seix Barral, 1979. 412 p.; 6 leaves of plates; ill. (His Obras selectas; 4)

Series of documents that capture the role of Rómulo Betancourt in the revolution of Oct. 1945 that overthrew the *neogomecista* government of President Medina Angarita. A useful account of the beginnings of

Venezuelan democracy and the creation of a constitutional regime.

6386 ———. Venezuela, oil and politics. Translated by Everett Bauman; foreword by Arthur M. Schlesinger, Jr.; introduction by Franklin Tugwell. Boston: Houghton Mifflin, 1979. 418 p.; bibl.; index.

Venezuela's former democratic reform president gives his personal explanation and justification of his country's political history from the end of the 19th century through 1956. Primary emphasis is placed on leadership support for a democratic system, the gradual nationalization of foreign oil companies, and the formation of OPEC. Valuable source for understanding how Venezuelan leaders have become committed to a democratic form of government. One of the best chapters is on the Pérez Jiménez dictatorship. For historian's comment, see *HLAS 42:3009*. Original Spanish title: *Venezuela, política y petróleo*.

6387 Bigler, Gene E. Congress, parties, and regimes in Venezuelan budgetary politics. n.p.: n.p., n.d. 28 p.; tables.

A mostly descriptive essay on the political elements of the budgetary decision-making process with an emphasis on three factors: 1) regime type (military autocratic vs. democratic reformist); 2) congressional involvement; and 3) the role of political parties. Some of the generalizations are suggestive but nevertheless rather weak. Presentation delivered at the Conference on National Styles of Policy Making held at the Instituto de Estudios Superiores de Administración (IESA), Caracas, March 1976.

6388 Blank, David Eugene. Oil and democracy in Venezuela (CUH, 78:454, Feb. 1980, p. 71–75, 84–85)

The difficulties of managing the new-found abundance of oil with a democratic reform government are examined in terms of the emergence of new groups, stability, leadership style, and economic development. Author sees an end to the populist brokerage style of democratic reform politics because of a decline in national income. A major test looms on the horizon when the government asks the people to make sacrifices for the collective good.

6389 Bravo, Argelia. La crisis y las definiciones. Carátula, Andrés Salazar. Caracas,

Venezuela: Editorial Ruptura, 1976. 227 p.

Wife of former guerrilla Douglas Bravo describes the revolutionary struggle in Venezuela starting with the resistance to the Pérez Jiménez dictatorship. The goals of nationalism, socialism, and anti-imperialism are interwoven with reflections on strategy, tactics and the role of revolutionary women.

6390 Brewer-Carías, Allan R. 50 [i.e. Cincuenta] años en la evolución institucional de Venezuela, 1926–1976 (*in* Venezuela moderna, medio siglo de historia, 1926–1976. Ramón J. Velásquez et al. 2. ed. Caracas: Fundación Eugenio Mendoza; Editorial Ariel, 1979, p. 533–764, tables)

The subtle and dramatic transformation of the role of the Venezuelan state is analyzed in terms of its causes and consequences over the past 50 years. Several core political problems are covered such as the organization and distribution of power, the establishment of legitimate authority and the role of the state in economic development. The resolution of these core problems is closely tied to the influence of petroleum coupled with capitalist and pluralist attitudes among the Venezuelan elite. A valuable historico-institutional analysis of federalism, decentralization, regionalization, representation, presidentialism, public administration, law and interest groups. The changes are portrayed as a virtual "revolution" with the diminution of regionalism and provincialism producing a more viable and integrated polity.

Brito Figueroa, Federico. Las repercusiones de la Revolución Socialista de Octubre de 1917 en Venezuela: conferencia sustentada el 11 de noviembre de 1977, con ocasión del 60° aniversario de la Revolución Socialista de Octubre, Caracas, Venezuela. See *HLAS 42:3014*.

6391 Bye, Vegard. Nationalization of oil in Venezuela: re-defined dependence and legitimization of imperialism (JPR, 16:1, 1979, p. 57–78, bibl.)

Despite the nationalization of oil on 1 Jan. 1976, author argues that external dominance (economic penetration, technological penetration, and trade dependency) will increase unless there is a fundamental alteration in the structure of power/class within Venezuela. Nationalization has had little influence on foreign trade dependence, mono-production, and the internal structure of dominance. Speculative but applicable to other mono-production economies in the Third World dominated by multinational corporations. For economist's comment, see item **3381**.

Caballero, Manuel. Rómulo Betancourt. See *HLAS 42:3015.*

6392 Castellanos V., Rafael Ramón. El presidente Carlos Andrés Pérez: bibliografía. Caracas: Oficina de Coordinación General de Publicaciones de la Presidencia de la República, 1978. 38 leaves.

An extensive bibliography (222 items) composed of speeches and statements made by President Pérez (1974–78). All items are located in the Central Information Office, Caracas.

6393 La Constitución de 1961 [i.e. mil novecientos sesenta y uno] y la evolución de Venezuela. Elaboración: J.M. Casal Montburn y Alfredo Arismendi A. t. 1, v. 1/2, Actas de la Comisión Redactora del Proyecto. t. 2, v. 1/2, Forma del Estado: el órgano deliberante regional. Caracas: Ediciones del Congreso de la República, 1971/1972. 2 v. in 4 pts.

Useful study of the basic design and historical evolution of constitutionalism in Venezuela with emphasis on federalism, national legislative and executive powers, and municipal government.

6394 Dáger, Jorge. Testigo de excepción: en la trincheras de la Resistencia, 1948–1955. Carátula, digujo de fondo por Dario Lancini. Caracas: Ediciones Centauro, 1979. 366 p.

One of the early founders of Acción Democrática relives the years of resistance to miitary rule and the triumph of democracy in 1958. However, the reasons for his eventual break with AD are not discussed.

Ellner, Steven. The Venezuelan left in the era of the Popular Front: 1936–45. See *HLAS 42:3018.*

6395 Ewell, Judith. Administrative corruption as a political issue in Venezuela (*in* Rocky Mountain Council on Latin American Studies, XXV, Tucson, Ariz., 1977. Proceedings. Lincoln: University of Nebraska, 1977, p. 85–92)

Four types of political corruption:

1) campaign spending; 2) land speculation; 3) bribery; and 4) mixed enterprises are examined as part of a shifting concern among political parties of the left over the past 25 years. The early banner against administrative corruption by AD has been replaced by the socialists and communists who blame corruption on "rapid economic development within the context of democratic politics." Author correctly observes the fallacious arguments on both sides.

6396 Febrer, Françoise. Le quinquennat de Carlos Andrés Pérez au Venezuela: 1974–1979 (FDD/NED [Problèmes d'Amérique Latine, 51] 4517/4518, 22 juin 1979, p. 9–77, tables)

Informative discussion of economic policies, foreign policy and political parties which includes a 20-page chronology of events 1974–78. The significance of the "quinquennat" for Venezuelan politics, however, is beyond the scope of this purely descriptive paper. [A. Suárez]

6397 Fejes, Fred. Public policy in the Venezuelan broadcasting industry (IAMEA, 32:4, Spring 1979, p. 3–32)

A brief history of the broadcasting industry (1930–70) with an emphasis on public-private sector relations internally. However, some interesting financial ties to North American networks such as NBC, CBS, and ABC are also discussed. As the present system has grown, and Venezuela has emerged into a middle-level economic power, a public policy to guide this activity has become an issue. A component of Venezuelan politics that needs further investigation.

6398 Gilhodes, Pierre. Les élections vénézuéliennes de 1978 (FDD/NED [Problèmes d'Amérique Latine, 51] 4517/4518, 22 juin 1979, p. 78–94, bibl., maps, tables)

This description of the electoral system and the electoral campaign, includes a good analysis of electoral results. Instead of polarization, the elections indicated the emergence of three blocs: AD, COPEI and the Left. [A. Suárez]

———. Venezuela: genèse de son système de partis. See *HLAS 42:3022.*

González Herrera, Luis. Rómulo en Berna: un documento para la historia de Acción Democrática. See *HLAS 42:3024.*

6399 Herman, Donald L. Christian Democracy in Venezuela. Chapel Hill: University of North Carolina Press, 1980. 1 v.; bibl.; index.

An analysis of the history, ideology, and internal structure of the Christian Democratic Party (COPEI) and the policy performance of Rafael Caldera's COPEI government. The importance of AD-COPEI opposition and cooperation as key factors in Venezuelan democracy is supported with many interviews in Venezuela and a substantial amount of primary and secondary materials. Author is optimistic about the future of democracy in Venezuela: "it may well be that twenty-two years of effective cooperation between the leaders of AD and COPEI have provided a sufficient basis for stable democracy in Venezuela."

6400 Herrera Campins, Luis. Palenque, retrospectiva de un compromiso con Venezuela. Compilación e introducción de Guillermo Yepes Boscán; portada, Eloy Martínez. Maracaibo, Venezuela: Fondo Editorial Irfes, 1979. 2 v. (883 p.) (Colección El Hombre y el Estado)

A series of articles from the newspaper *Panorama* (1955–74) by Venezuela's current president and most influential *copeyano* leader. A useful series from which to glean political history and Social Christian ideology. Author discusses such topics as education, social welfare, political economy, public administration, democracy, national politics, foreign policy, and the significance of various world leaders from J.F. Kennedy to Fidel Castro.

Un hombre llamado Rómulo Betancourt: apreciaciones críticas sobre su vida y su obra. See *HLAS 42:3026.*

Howard, Harrison Sabin. Rómulo Gallegos y la revolución burguesa de Venezuela. See *HLAS 42:3027.*

6401 Jornadas sobre la Democracia en Venezuela, *Caracas, 1978.* Sobre la democracia: ciclo de conferencias sobre la democracia en Venezuela, realizadas en junio y julio de 1978, bajo el auspicio del Ateneo de Caracas y la Escuela de Estudios Políticos y Administrativos de la U.C.V. Rafael Caldera et al.; prólogo, Hans Leu; diseño portada, Jorge Pizzani. Caracas, Venezuela: Editorial

Ateno de Caracas, 1979. 336 p. (Colección Teoría política)

Venezuela politicians and intellectuals analyze the foundations and institutions of Venezuelan democracy over the past 20 years in a series of conference papers covering: the roots of contemporary democracy, government reforms, socialism, trade unionism, education, human rights, and the crisis of dependent capitalism. The growth and strength of the democratic rules of the game coupled with a significant tolerance of opposition viewpoints receive considerable attention.

6402 Levine, Daniel H. Venezuela since 1958: the consolidation of democratic politics (*in* The Breakdown of democratic regimes: Latin America [see *HLAS 42:1920*] p. 82–109, tables)

By comparing structural and behavioral dimensions of the *trienio* with post-1958 political development, author makes a convincing case for prudent leadership, party organization, and social learning as key factors in the consolidation of the democratic regime. The situation where opposition and conflict are tolerated and built into the system is a remarkable feat of political institution-building. A balanced analysis with important correctives to those who argue that oil wealth has made the consolidation of democratic politics possible.

6403 Liscano Velutini, Juan and **Carlos Gottenberg.** Multimagen de Rómulo: vida y acción de Rómulo Betancourt en gráficas. Foto de la portada, Francisco Barrenechea. 5. ed. Caracas, Venezuela: Orbeca, 1978. 550 p.; chiefly ill.

A pictorial and written account of the life and accomplishments of Rómulo Betancourt. The brief biographical account is helpful while the reasons for the survival of democracy in Venezuela are not.

Liss, Sheldon B. Diplomacy & dependency: Venezuela, the United States, and the Americas. See *HLAS 42:3029.*

Maza Zavala, D.F. Historia de medio siglo en Venezuela, 1926–1975. See *HLAS 42:3031.*

Mesa, Salom. Por un caballo y una mujer: relato autobiográfico. See *HLAS 42:3032.*

Moron, Guillermo. Historia política contemporánea de Venezuela, 1936–1976. See *HLAS 42:3033.*

6404 Myers, David J. Venezuela's MAS (USIA/PC, 39:5, Sept./Oct. 1980, p. 16–27, plates, tables)

Venezuela's Movement Toward Socialism (MAS) is assessed in terms of: 1) how and why it has been able to establish itself as a significant force on the left replacing the traditional Communist Party, and 2) the changes of MAS's success within Venezuela's democratic system. The MAS experience is considered to have important consequences for independent communist movements in the Third World where independence from Moscow, Havana, and Peking are of increasing concern.

6405 Nehru Tennassee, Paul. Venezuela, los obreros petroleros y la lucha por la democracia. Madrid: E.F.I.P.-Editorial Popular, 1979. 351 p.

Leftist political history of Venezuelan petroleum workers. While the petroleum workers have not fared well under what the author considers a neocolonial capitalist system, they are given some credit for the eventual nationalization of the industry. A well-documented history of a key component of the Venezuelan labor movement.

6406 Núñez Tenorio, J.R. La izquierda y la lucha por el poder en Venezuela: 1958–1978. Diseño portada, Jorge Pizzani. Caracas: Editorial Ateneo de Caracas, 1979. 281 p. (Colección Actualidad política)

Based on a series of four conferences in which six leftist political parties discuss past political mistakes (23 Jan. 1958; the strategy of armed resistance during the 1960s) and offer an assessment of the current situation with suggestions on how to unify and obtain power. The self-criticism is interesting but the struggle for power is unlikely to attract large numbers of followers.

6407 Peña, Alfredo. Conversaciones con Américo Martín. Caracas: Editorial Ateneo de Caracas, 1978. 225 p. (Colección Actualidad política. Grandes reportajes de Alfredo Peña)

Interview with the leader of the Movement of the Revolutionary Left (MIR) and unsuccessful candidate for the presidency in the 1978 elections. The Venezuelan socialist leader tries to address the complexities of various political ideologies and how they apply to the nation in the 1970s.

6408 ———. Conversaciones con José Vicente Rangel. Caracas; editorial Ateneo de Caracas, 1978. 200 p. (Colección Actualidad política. Grandes reportajes de Alfredo Peña)

Series of conversations on contemporary Venezuelan politics by the 1978 presidential candidate for MAS who obtained five percent of the votes in the election. The major theme is socialist ideology and its application to Venezuelan development.

6409 ———. Conversaciones con Luis Beltrán Prieto. Diseño portada, Jorge Pizzani; foto, José Sardá. 3. ed. Caracas: Editorial Ateneo de Caracas, 1978 [i.e. 1979]. 196 p. (His Grandes reportajes de Alfredo Peña. Colección Actualidad política)

Series of interviews on Venezuelan politics by one of the founders of Acción Democrática who later split to form the People's Electoral Movement (MEP), a social democratic party, in 1967. Some interesting perspectives on different models of political development.

6410 Pérez, Carlos Andrés. Manos a la obra: textos de mensajes, discursos y declaraciones del presidente de la República. v. 1, pts. 1/2. v. 2, pt. 1. Caracas, Venezuela: Ediciones de la Presidencia de la República, 1977/1979. 2 v.

Text of the speeches, messages, and declarations of President Carlos Andrés Pérez from March 1975 to March 1978. Unlike other documents of this nature, these are indexed by names, places, institutions, and themes for quick reference.

6411 Rangel, Carlos. Latinoamérica en el diván (in Segal, Alicia Freilich de. Entrevistados en carne y hueso. Fotos, Jorge Pineda. Caracas: Librería Suma, 1976 or 1977, p. 189–203)

The author of *Del buen salvaje al buen revolucionario* (see *HLAS 41:7065* and *HLAS 42:1809*) is interviewed with many questions dealing with the Latin American reaction to his book's controversial themes: mestizaje, Latin American underdevelopment, imperialism, Catholicism, revolution, etc. He communicates and defends his thoughtful and conservative views drawing interesting contrasts with the US.

6412 Rangel, Domingo Alberto. Los mercaderes del voto. Valencia, Venezuela:

Vadell Hermanos Editores, 1978. 164 p.; bibl.
Caustic analysis of the 1978 presidential elections. Author argues that Venezuela has evolved into an AD-COPEI system of party domination that tends to obscure the lack of representative democracy in the nation. With the flaws in the internal dynamics of the political process and the dependency on a declining commodity (petroleum), a fascist system may be on the horizon. The forecast may be as flawed as the analysis.

6413 Silva Michelena, José Augustín and **Heinz Rudolf Sonntag.** El proceso electoral 1978 [i.e. mil novecientos setenta y ocho]: su perspectiva histórico-estructural. Equipo de investigación, José A. Silva Michelena et al. Caracas: Editorial Ateneo, 1979. 173, 12 p.; bibl.; diagrs. (Colección Teoría política)
Part of a larger study of the structure and processes of Venezuelan electoral politics since 1958 with emphasis on the legitimization of peripheral capitalist societies, the role of elections in legitimizing the political system, the role of the party system in the transition from military rule, the role of the Supreme Electoral Council, the vicissitudes of the 1978 electoral campaign in political recruitment, and an interpretative overview of 20 years of representative democracy in Venezuela. A valuable work for those interested in electoral politics and regime legitimization.

6414 Sociedad comunitaria y participación. Luis Herrera Campins et al.; prólogo, Abdón Vivas Terán. Caracas: Editorial Ateneo de Caracas, 1979. 252 p.; bibl. (Colección Teoría política)
Series of 10 essays-lectures by nine Christian Democrats on the concept of a communitarian society whereby the ultimate goal is pluralism, solidarity, and participation. Much of Herrera Campins' Social Christian ideology can be found in these essays.

6415 Steiner, Stan. In search of the jaguar. New York: Times Books, 1979. 187 p.
Can Venezuela move from the Third to the First World of technological independence without succumbing to the problems of a modern industrial society and losing its national identity? Author attempts to answer this question by searching for the real Venezuelan in the "Arabia of the Americas." The

dialogues with Venezuelan characters are fascinating but little effort is made to put the humanistic perspectives on development in a broader comparative perspective.

6416 Venezuela. Presidencia. Venezuela; mensaje del Presidente de la República . . . al Congreso Nacional. No. 4, 1978–   . Caracas.
President Carlos Andrés Pérez's Message to Congress in 1978 includes references to economic and social conditions, foreign policy, regional policy, and the armed forces.

Venezuela bajo el signo del terror: libro negro 1952. See *HLAS 42:3045.*

6417 Vigencia y proyección de Rómulo: 50 años de liderazgo político. Caracas: Partido Acción Democrática, 1978. 247 p.; ill.
Lectures, essays, and letters commemorating 50 years of political leadership by the founder of Venezuelan democracy. Letters from such important figures as David Rockefeller can be found along with those from Michael Manley and Leopold Senghor.

Wright, Winthrop R. Race, nationality, and immigration in Venezuelan thought, 1890 to 1937. See *HLAS 42:3046.*

6418 Zago, Angela. Entre ayer y hoy (*in* Segal, Alicia Freilich de. Entrevistados en carne y hueso. Caracas: Librería Suma, 1976 or 1977, p. 291–311)
Interview with ex-guerrilla, Angela Zago, on such subjects as machismo, women's liberation, party politics, Communist youth, guerrilla recruitment, Venezuelan democracy, and Cuban Socialism.

6419 Ziems, Angel. El gomecismo y la formación del Ejército Nacional. Prólogo, Ramón J. Velázquez; diseño portada, Jorge Pizzani. Caracas, Venezuela: Editorial Ateneo de Caracas, 1979. 277 p.; bibl.; ill. (Colección Historia)
Fascinating historical account of the formation and evolution of the armed forces under Juan Vicente Gómez. Author argues, in a well-documented study, that the armed forces were a key element in the centralization of power, the creation of a national identity, and the formation of a modern capitalist economy. Excellent military history for the period 1909–1935 but few clues are offered for the depoliticization of the military after 1958.

ECUADOR

6420 Albuja Galindo, Alfredo. El periodismo en la dialéctica política ecuatoriana. Quito, Ecuador: Talleres Gráficos Minerva, 1979. 392 p.; bibl.

History of print and broadcast journalism with emphasis on the interconnection between politics and the news media. The ebb and flow of a variety of political systems—military-authoritarian, populist, traditional, democratic reform—coincide with various forms of criticism, support, and manipulation. The discussion of who owns the media and how information is controlled by the government fills an important gap in our understanding of Ecuadorian politics.

Blanco, Guillermo. Los incidentes de Riobamba y Pudahuel en tres diarios chilenos. See item **6519.**

Drekonja Kornat, Gerhard. Ecuador: ensayo bibliográfico. See *HLAS 42:180.*

6421 Ecuador hoy. Por Gerhard Drekonja et al.; apéndice documental, Gustavo Jarrín Ampudia. Bogotá: Siglo Veintiuno Editores, 1978. 381 p.; bibl. (Historia inmediata)

Useful series of essays on political economy in contemporary Ecuador. While examining major themes—petroleum policy, industrialization, dependency, agricultural development, populism, civil-military relations—authors attempt to refute some of the persistent myths about *el país bananero* and point up the multifaceted reality of Ecuadorian politics and its economic development. For comments on individual articles, see items **6422–6423** and **6425.**

6422 Egas, José María. La correlación de fuerzas en la escena política ecuatoriana, 1972–77 (*in* Ecuador, hoy [see item **6421**] p. 238–265)

An examination of the correlation of forces—landowners, entrepreneurs, transnational organizations—that participated in the efforts to thwart the "nationalist" and "revolutionary" government of Gen. Guillermo Rodríguez Lara. A leftist account of how the populist military government gave in to the forces of international capitalism.

6423 Galarza Zavala, Jaime. Ecuador, el oro y la pobreza (*in* Ecuador, hoy [see item **6421**] p. 9–18)

A revision of von Humboldt's vision of the contrasts between Ecuador's mineral and agricultural wealth and its social misery. A significant assessment of the economic and political consequences of the petroleum bonanza for overall development with an emphasis on dependency themes.

6424 Handelman, Howard. Ecuador, a new political direction? Hanover, NH: AUFS, 1979. 24 p.; bibl.; ill. (Reports—American Universities Field Staff; 1979, no. 47, South American 0161-0624)

Excellent study of recent trends in Ecuadorian national politics emphasizing the transformation of leadership, political parties and elections, and civil-military relations. Author concludes that long-term political development will depend on the dwindling of personalism, continued civilian rule, and the concerted efforts to foster the legitimacy of the new constitutional order.

6425 Hurtado, Osvaldo. El proceso político (*in* Ecuador, hoy [see item **6421**] p. 166–197)

An examination of the transformation of the hacienda system into a capitalist system driven by the quest for petroleum revenues. The effects of these changes are examined through the economy, elite-mass relations, government policies, ideologies, regional conflicts, the party system, and military reformism. An important article on how the political participants and rules of the political game have changed over the past several decades.

6426 Iglesias, Angel María. El diálogo con los comunistas y otros temas. Cuenca, Ecuador: Editorial Amazonas, 1976. 59 p.

Catholic priest from Cuenca presents a series of arguments against the compatibility of communism and Christianity. Suggests that true Christians should avoid identification with ideologies of the left or right.

6427 Jácome, Nicanor and **Patricio Moncayo.** Partidos políticos y programas de gobierno del Ecuador. Quito?: Cesla, 1979. 104 p.

Comparative analysis of 11 political parties stressing their origins, tactics, ideology, and programs. A valuable reference for understanding Ecuadorian political parties and their governmental programs.

6428 Maldonado Lince, Guillermo. La reforma agraria en el Ecuador (UTIEH/C, 34, 1980, p. 33–56)

Former Minister of Agriculture criticizes the opposition to the recent military government's agrarian reform efforts. The context, and consequences of the 1973 Agrarian Reform are discussed with considerable objectivity. Author calls for more concern for the Agrarian Reform law and the agricultural sector and less emphasis on import-substitution-industrialization policies.

6429 Martz, John D. Marxism in Ecuador (IAMEA, 33:1, Summer 1979, p. 3–28)

The marginality of Marxism as a political movement is examined for its causes and consequences. Author predicts that Ecuadorian Marxism will become more active in the 1980s as a result of civilian rule but the forces on the left can hardly expect to determine public policy given the dominant political and economic forces.

6430 ———. The quest for popular democracy in Ecuador (CUH, 78:454, Feb. 1980, p. 66–70, 84)

An assessment of the difficulties of returning to civilian rule and governing democratically after nine years of military rule. Social and economic problems—foreign debt, inflation, inequalities in economic development, unrealized goals from the oil bonanza—are the major hurdles for an elected government whose strength lies in popular support. A clear reaffirmation of the difficulties of governing Ecuador regardless of the type of regime.

6431 ———. The regionalist expression of populism: Guayaquil and the CFP 1948–1960 (SAGE/JIAS, 22:3, Aug. 1980, p. 289–314, bibl., table)

The populism of Guayaquil's CFP (Concentración de Fuerzas Populares) is examined in terms of sources of support, lead-ership style and organization, political doctrine, and regionalism. With populistic appeals and personal authoritarian guidance, the CFP emerges as a distinct example of regional populism reflecting the demographic and socioeconomic realities of Ecuador in the 1950s.

6432 Moore, Richard J. The urban poor in Guayaquil, Ecuador: modes correlates, and context of political participation (*in* Political participation in Latin America. Edited by John A. Booth and Mitchell A. Seligson. v. 2, Politics and the poor. New York: Holmes & Meier, 1978, p. 198–219, bibl., tables)

Study of political participation in six squatter settlements in which author finds "little confirmation for the radical marginal argument." Yet participation does take place depending on perceptions, previous experience, and attitudes of the squatter. An important study for its findings that land invasion and political radicalism are not connected.

6433 Ramírez Alvarez, Jorge. El derecho a la huelga en la legislación ecuatoriana (ACPS/B, 28:75/76, oct. 1978/marzo 1979, p. 157–168)

Legal study of Ecuadorian law concerning the concept of the strike (labor, student or functional groups). Stress is on *types* of worker stoppage and how the law applies to each classification. Author notes gaps in the law which neglect certain strike situations and lead to inequities. [W.R. Garner]

6434 Velasco, Fernando. Reforma agraria y movimiento campesino indígena de la Sierra: hipótesis para una investigación. Quito, Ecuador: Editorial El Conejo, 1979. 167, 6 p.; 5 leaves of plates; bibl.; ill.

Leftist analysis of land reform and indigenous peasant movements in highland Ecuador. Author finds profound and inevitable contradictions between capitalist development and government land reform efforts.

Peru, Bolivia and Chile

WILLIAM R. GARNER, *Director of Graduate Studies and Associate Professor of Political Science, Latin American Studies Advisory Committee, Southern Illinois University-Carbondale.*

CHILEAN MATERIALS—especially those coming from the center and center-left—are pessimistic in tone and, at best, express anger and frustration with present political realities. This negativism, resulting from a perceived lack of alternatives, succeeds the serious post-mortem analyses of the Allende period noted in *HLAS 41*.

Since the publication of *HLAS 41*, however, a number of important contributions to the literature on Chile have appeared. Robert Alexander's *The tragedy of Chile* (item **6514**) is a major study of the evolution of Chilean politics from the first Alessandri administration through that of the present Junta, and is crucial to an understanding of both the Allende period *and* the Pinochet regime. Gil, Lagos, and Landsberger have published *Chile at the turning point* (item **6527**), an excellent collection of papers on the Unidad Popular period. Arturo Valenzuela's study (item **6589**) of the UP crisis is probably the best single analysis to date of Allende's failure.

In the area of political thought, major contributions have been made by Pedro Vuskovic Bravo (item **6594**) and Catalán, the latter focusing on the "new intellectuals . . . who co-govern with Pinochet" (item **6523**). Rodríguez (item **6578**) and Silva Bascuñán (item **6579**) test the legality of the institutional Acts under which the military government functions. Two studies that support the military regime are *Jornadas sobre la nueva institucionalidad y nueva democracia* (item **6547**), which probes the issue of novel forms of "authentic social participation," and Julio Muhlenbrock's interpretation of the Junta's major goal of bringing about the end to Chile's "Marxist illusion" (item **6564**).

Among the works presenting a specific assessment of the military government and by far the most provocative is Frederick Nunn's (item **6568**), which deals with current misconceptions of Chilean reality propagated by the world press. In the same vein, Gen. Leigh (item **6553**) published an impressive rationale for the military takeover. *Negative* critiques of the Junta are found in Almeyda M. (item **6516**), who treats the manipulation of nationalist symbols, and Angell (item **6517**), on internal military fragmentation and the power of the Church as the only possible means for bringing about a return to democracy. Catalán and Arrate (item **6523**) deal with the public administration costs of the government's program; Bravo Lira (item **6520**) denounces the Junta on legal grounds; and Marcella (item **6558**) addresses the public relations efforts of the military. There are also valuable studies on the still unresolved Letelier assassination by Solar (item **6583**) and Varas (item **6590**); a copy of the legal documents of indictment in the case is found in item **6546**.

Criticism of various facets of the Allende period continues to appear. Bitar (item **6518**) and Palacios (item **6571**), both write from the perspective of the Socialist Party left in the Allende coalition. Garretón and Moulian (item **6538**) believe the UP was doomed from the beginning because of the pre-existing economic crisis and political fragmentation. Garretón Merino (item **6537**), Hellinger (item **6543**), Valenzuela (item **6589**), and Teitelboim (item **6586**) attribute the UP's failure to class and/or party polarization, coalition squabbles, and the ensuing loss of the moderating "center." Smirnow (item 6582) and Sparagna (item 6581) fault US imperialism and leftist fragmentation, Sparagna stressing the impact of the Chilean failure on Euro-Communist theory and practice.

Interesting analyses of efforts on the part of the Chilean Church to pressure or "bait" the military may be seen in *Catholic Church . . .* (item 6524), *Simposium internacional* (item 6580), and Villela G. (item 6592). Blanco's study (item 6519) of the "Riobamba Case" (Ecuador military harrassment and final deportation of Chilean and other Latin American bishops on charges of "subversion") is of considerable value. The pro-MAPU/Christians for Socialism (anti-Silva Henríquez) study by López Fernández (item 6555) should be read along with that of Tagle Martínez (item 6585), in which the author affirms that Friedman's economic policies are in perfect accord with the social doctrine of the Church. Gilfeather (item 6540) presents an interesting discussion of the new roles and challenges faced by nuns associated with Chile's numerous "Basic Communities." Villela G. (item 6592) notes that the Chilean Church—in contrast to other Latin American churches—no longer acts as the traditional "legitimizer of domination."

Statements on US-Chilean relations are found in Greenfield's study of *The Los Angeles Times* (item 6541) and that of Letelier and Moffitt (item 6554), examining the increment of financial assistance to Chile from private US banks in the wake of faultering interest on the part of international lending agencies. Loveman's history of Chile (item 6556) fills a long existing gap in the literature, although the volume is far too brief, especially with regard to its treatment of the Frei, Allende, and Pinochet periods.

The labor movement is the subject of an excellent article by Alexander (item 6515), as well as the contributions of Campero Q. (item 6522), Chonchol (item 6529), Collins (item 6530), and Zapata (item 6596). Lovemen (item 6557) and Muhlenbrock (item 6564) focus attention on labor's political participation.

Important research on the subject of female political participation has been long in coming; we now have the valuable studies of Kyle and Francis (item 6549), and Neuse (item 6566). Fischer's work (item 6534) on Chilean educational policy is a major, original contribution to the field, as is the essay in political psychology by Huneeus (item 6545). Finally, Oppenheimer (item 6569) has prepared a thorough and comprehensive bibliography in monograph form that covers Chile's entire national history.

PERU: Alfred C. Stepan's *The state and society: Peru in comparative perspective* (item 6480) fills a need for renewed theorizing on the organic view of state and society. The author's major contribution in this vein is his differentiation between organic-statism and the term "corporatism." Also significant is the application of the theory to Peru. This study is one of the most impressive works to be produced in several years, and, a welcomed addition to the literature on comparative politics and political philosophy. Two other authors make substantial theoretical contributions: Althaus (item 6435), by differentiating between "nation" and "nation-state" (something rarely done in the literature), Bravo Bresani (item 6443), by distinguishing between "dependency" and "domination." Palmer's (item 6468) short but thorough study on authoritarianism traces this ancient strain in Peruvian politics from the period of the Incas through the Velasco/Morales Bermúdez "leftist revolution." Two publications by Julio Cotler (items 6446 and 6447) address the "costs and risks" of hyper-participation in economically insecure democracies, a thesis reinforced by Pease García (item **6472**). Frederick Nunn's insightful article (item **6467**) on militarism and the 1968 coup should be complemented by a reading of José García's critique of it and Nunn's rejoinder (item **6456**). More general criticisms of the military *decenio* can be found in Aníbal Quijano's sophisticated treatment (item **6474**).

In the area of urban studies, scholars have focused attention on the dynamics of city squatter settlements, as can be seen in three studies by Dietz (items **6450–6452**), on *poblador* political participation. Fishel (item **6455**), Matos Mar (item **6463**), and Sánchez León (item **6478**) have also produced excellent studies of the slum-dweller phenomenon. Among works dealing with political participation in general Sandra Woy's article on SINAMOS (item **6485**) is a particularly valuable contribution.

Marxist/leftist analysis takes the forms of heated debate over the respective roles of Haya de la Torre and Mariátegui. This is evidenced by the statements of Barba (item **6438**), the Partido Comunista Peruano (item **6469**), and Partido Comunista Revolucionario (item **6470**). The Urviola study (item **6481**) of "treasonous revisionism" by a splinter group—the Partido Comunista Peruano-UNIDAD—also illustrates the significant problem of leftist fragmentation.

APRA and Haya de la Torre are subjects of much more research than in the past, due most probably to APRA's majority vote in the Constituent Assembly elections of 1978, as well as to Haya's presidential candidacy on the Aprista ticket in 1979 and his death later that year. One should note also important studies by Balbi (item **6437**), Collin-Delavaud (item **6445**), Bernales B. (item **6441**), Chirinos Soto (item **6444**), Barba Caballero (item **6438**), and Sánchez (item **6477**). Belaúnde Terry's essay (item **6440**) is interesting in view of his second presidential term. The first Belaúnde administration is the subject of a critique by Lizarzaburu T. (item **6460**). Reactions of the Peruvian Church to the current situation are described in Mooney and Suderland's (item **6465**) intriguing comparative analysis of priests' perception of their role in the "Peruvian revolution." An ambitious study by the inter-American organization, Justicia y Paz written with a Peruvian public in mind, gives a fairly detailed country-by-country assessment of human rights in Latin America.

BOLIVIA: The literature on Bolivia reviewed for this volume is of higher quality than that found in *HLAS* 39 and 41. Several important theoretical studies warrant attention. Almaraz Paz's thoughtful and well written essay (item **6487**) reflects his pro-MNR sentiments after "converting" from the Bolivian Communist Party in 1950. Mayorga's study, "Dictadura Militar y Crisis del Estado: el Caso Boliviano, 1971–1977" (item **6504**), is interesting but flawed, owing to its definition of the state solely in terms of policy implementation and substance. Although the author's criticism of the MNR victory and its aftermath (1952–75) is provocative, it is hampered by the careless application of concepts, particularly "fascism." Guillermo Lora's *¿Qué es el trotskysmo?* (item **6502**) is a valuable contribution to political theory in general and to the literature on his Partido Obrero Revolucionario (POR) in particular.

Predictably, most of the studies in this section deal with the aftermath of the Banzer period. Araníbar Quiroga has published a sophisticated Gramsci attack on the military regime (item **6490**), probably the best of the negative treatments reviewed. Studies by Bedregal Gutiérrez (item **6492**) and Bedregal Gutiérrez et al. (item **6507**) are also worthy of mention. Other notable contributions are a German "photodocumentation," *Bolivien . . .* (item **6493**), Lavaud's "Le gouvernement

Banzer" (item **6500**), and Toranzo Roca's study (item **6512**). Vargas Valenzuela's work (item **6513**), a *pro*-Banzer/military piece, should be consulted as well. Prognostications concerning the trend of the Banzer regime—and its successors— towards alliance with Southern Cone states such as Argentina and Brazil and, consequently, its movement away from the Andean Pact states are contained in *Bolivien* (item **6493**) and Córdova-Claure (item **6495**).

Mayorga, in his *National-popular State* . . . (item **6505**), examines thoroughly the continuing intra-MNR conflict and the formation of right- and left-wing coalitions. Andrade (item **6488**) and Ramos Sánchez (item **6509**) present the right-wing perspective, while the left MNR-1 coalition is supported in studies by Antezana (item **6489**), Bedregal Gutiérrez (item **6492**), and Córdova-Claure (item **6495**). Fairly neutral positions urging reconciliation are represented by Salamanca Trujillo (item **6510**), Lavaud (item **6500**), and *El sistema político boliviano* (item **6511**).

PERU

Alisky, Marvin. Historical dictionary of Peru. See *HLAS 42:3053.*

6435 Althaus, Miguel de. Identidad nacional y Estado en el Perú (*in* Perú, identidad nacional. César Arróspide de la Flor et al. Lima: Centro de Estudios para el Desarrollo y la Participación, 1979, p. 209–234, bibl.)

Author observes correctly that the "nation" exists as a *separate entity* from the "state." The "nation-state" exists, however, only if the state utilizes its power to erase traditional inequities and societal divisions stemming from the Colonial and capitalist periods of development. A novel Marxist study.

Aranda, Arturo and **María Escalante.** Lucha de clases en el movimiento sindical cusqueño, 1927–1965. See *HLAS 42:3054.*

Baella Tuesta, Alfonso. El miserable. See *HLAS 42:3055.*

6436 ———. Secuestro. Lima: Ediciones El Tiempo, 1978. 448 p.; ill.

Case study written by Lima editor of *El Tiempo* whose paper was closed various times after its initial appearance in Oct. 1975. Paper was closed in May 1978 and Baella Tuesta was deported to Buenos Aires where he remained for five months until he was allowed to return to Peru. The thrust of this volume is the dissemination of a general view of the Morales Bermúdez administration in the months just before the calling of the Constituent Assembly. Author believes Morales' admission of a political error after Baella's return in Oct. 1978, influenced vot-

ing patterns in the Assembly, apparent in the surge of votes for traditional center-liberal, center-left parties. An interesting if overly emotional rightist political testimony directed against *both* First and Second (Velasco and Morales Bermúdez) phases of the Peruvian "revolution." It includes negative predictions concerning the future of Peruvian politics under "leftist" (Belaúnde Terry's Acción Popular) control!

6437 Balbi, Carmen Rosa and **Laura Madalengoitia.** Parlamento y lucha política: Perú, 1932. Lima: Centro de Estudios y Promoción del Desarrollo, 1980. 199 p.

Analysis of factors in the 1931 Constitutional Convention and the 1933 Constitution which gave rise to APRA and Haya de la Torre, two watershed phenomena in Peruvian politics.

6438 Barba Caballero, José and **César Lévano.** La polémica Haya de la Torre-Mariátegui. Editor, José Luis Delgado Nuñez del Arco; portada y diseño, Simeón Bastidas; fotografía, Juan Carlos Calderón. s.l.: s.n., 1979. 88 p.; bibl.; ill.

Published debate between Aprista spokesman, Barba, and César Lévano, representative of the Peruvian Communist Party. Compares the ideological positions of Victor Raúl Haya de la Torre, founder of APRA, with those of José Mariátegui, the supposed founder of Peru's CP. Barba's position, that Mariátegui was *not* the CP's founder sets the tone of the debate.

6439 Barcelli S., Agustín. Crónicas de las luchas obreras en el Perú. t. 1, Historia sindical internacional. 2. ed. corr. y actualizada. Lima, Perú: s.n., 1979. 1 v.; ill. (Cuadernos sindicales)

Leftist account of the world-wide evolution of worker syndicalism that devotes much space to Western European Marxist theoreticians (Marx, Engels, Trotsky, and Bakunin), and includes a description of union development in the US. After a general focus on union organization in Latin America as a whole, author ends study with a tracing of events in the development of Peruvian syndicalism between 1911–13.

Basadre, Jorge. Leyes electorales peruanas, 1890–1917: teoría y realidad. See *HLAS* 42:3057.

6440 Belaúnde Terry, Fernando. Pensamiento política de Fernando Belaúnde Terry. Lima: Populista, 1979. 279 p. (El Populista; 1)

Collected writings of Belaúnde Terry reflecting the political thought of former President reelected in 1980. Of interest to students of Acción Popular and Belaúnde, especially in his second presidential period.

Berg, Ronald H. and **Frederick Stirton Weaver.** Toward a reinterpretation of political change in Peru during the first century of independence. See *HLAS* 42:3058.

6441 Bernales B., Enrique. Perú: el retorno a la práctica electoral (UNAM/PDD, 9:35, agosto/oct. 1978, p. 97–114, tables)

Analysis of voting behavior in the June 1978 elections for the Constituent Assembly. Extensive quantification including relevant tables and tight data analysis make this an important key to understanding the realignment of political forces at the end of the Velasco-Morales Bermúdez *docenio*.

6442 Bourque, Susan C. and **Kay B. Warren.** Female participation, perception, and power: an examination of two Andean communities (*in* Political participation in Latin America. Edited by John A. Booth and Mitchell A. Seligson. v. 2., Politics and the poor. New York: Holmes & Meier, 1978, p. 116–133)

A discussion of the relevant literature on the topic based on data collected during 1974 and 1975. Authors conclude that prevalent assumptions concerning power accumulation and political participation did not apply to women in the two communities. Rather, the sociopolitical organization of both towns excluded women from the political and most of the economic decision-making processes. The lower socioeconomic status of women together with restrictive policies applied to them prevented their effective participation in the power base for the communities and allowed them fewer socioeconomic options than were open to men. Any apparent improvement in women's position or participation in traditionally weak political structures remains insignificant due to other discriminatory social values. An important study.

6443 Bravo Bresani, Jorge. Dinámica y estructura del poder: reflexiones preliminares (*in* Perú, hoy. Por Fernando Fuenzalida Vollmar et al. 3. ed. México: Siglo Veintiuno Editores, 1975, p. 175–259, ill.)

Author bases study on the IPC expropriation and derives five propositions from the data: 1) expropriation and expulsion of US technicians left Peruvian nationals incapable of running the corporate complex; 2) the oligarchy tended to place their trust in persons incapable of running the elite's sugar properties efficiently; 3) regardless of their status under national law, the real power of multinational corporations lies in their economic *domination* (*not* dependency); 4) groups capable of resisting the domination of multinationals did not do so; and 5) the Armed Forces are the only institution capable of charting the future of a "dominated" economy and defending its course. Bravo then argues that the moderate Belaúnde programs, Velasco's radical actions and, in general, all Marxist plans for economic equity and development cannot meet the challenge. He calls for a slow, educated approach to freeing Peru (and other nations in like circumstances) from corporate domination. A detailed analysis well researched and clearly written. Gives little insight, however, into the solution he prescribes or into the special talents he perceives both in the Peruvian military and in the Church.

Caravedo, Baltazar. El problema del centralismo en el Perú republicano. See *HLAS* 42:3062.

Chavarría, Jesús. José Carlos Mariátegui and the rise of modern Peru, 1890–1930. See *HLAS* 42:3065.

6444 Chirinos Soto, Enrique. Pido la palabra ante la Segunda Fase. Lima; Editorial Andina, 1978. 159 p.; ports.

This is one of the better statements on the development of the Aprista movement, interestingly dedicated to French President Giscard d'Estaing. The volume includes a section on d'Estaing's philosophical position as well as lengthy editorial opinions on such themes as APRA's ideology, the application of Aprismo to petroleum development, human rights, inflation, and Belaúnde's Acción Popular presidency (1963–68). Much of what the author says appears to be unrelated to the basic thrust of the book. For example, one section excoriates contemporary Peruvian novelist Vargas Llosa while another glorifies General Juan Velasco Alvarado (President during the First Phase of the Peruvian military "revolution"). The volume is valuable, however, for its commentary on a wide variety of topics germane to 20th-century Peruvian politics and public policy, especially APRA.

6445 Collin-Delavaud, Claude. Pérou: vers un régime civil (FDD/NED [Problèmes d'Amérique Latine, 54] 4545/4546, 18 déc. 1979, p. 62–88, tables)

Historical account of events leading to the calling of Constituent Assembly in 1978. Author gives extensive quantitative data on the Peruvian party system and the nation's economy for the period immediately before the return to representative institutions. A dysfunctional relationship between Peru's economic characteristics and its fragmented party system leads to a negative prognosis.

6446 Cotler, Julio. Crisis política y populismo militar (in Perú, hoy. Por Fernando Fuenzalida Vollmar et al. 3. ed. México: Siglo Veintiuno Editores, 1975, p. 87–174 [El Mundo del hombre: sociología y política])

Cotler's general theme is that democratic sytems lack the capability to cope with novel and increasingly complex political pressures. He believes that military intervention or "corporatist" structures are necessary to control democratic-participatory pressures until a government is ready to respond to them. Little is said concerning the qualities of such prescribed corporatist institutions. Author's premise is that the "costs and risks" of truly open democratic political participa-

tion may be too high for a nation such as Peru, an idea reminiscent of Robert Dahl's "economics of political participation."

————. Perú: estado oligárquico y reformismo militar. See *HLAS 42:3069.*

6447 ————. A structural-historical approach to the breakdown of democratic institutions: Peru (in The Breakdown of democratic regimes: Latin America. Edited by Juan J. Linz and Alfred Stepan. Baltimore: Johns Hopkins University, 1978, p. 178–206)

The weakness of Peru's democratic institutions—the result of "dependency" on the industrialized nations—plus the absence of a bourgeoisie capable of meeting the requirements of democracy, work against the development of moderate institutions sensitive enough to meet the increasingly complex system of demands emanating from the lower classes. The Belaúnde regime failed owing to such weakness and ushered in the Velasco and Morales Bermúdez periods (the *decenio* of military "revolution"). Cotler's prognosis for the political system is not optimistic. An interesting contribution of considerable merit. For historian's comment, see *HLAS 42:3070.*

6448 De Morococha a Talara: Perú, 1930–1931. Rubén Durand P. et al. Lima: Taller de Estudios Políticos, Programa Académico de CCSS, Universidad Católica del Perú, 1979. 37 p.; bibl.

Analysis of the worker movement and development of the Peruvian Communist Party in the crucial 1930–31 period when the Constituent Assembly for the 1933 Constitution was convoked. Authors conclude that conditions for a revolutionary movement did not exist during that period of economic crisis. The fragmentation of the worker movement and the Communist Party rendered the PCP's tactics ineffective in bringing about Leftist revolution. Interesting self-criticism 50 years after the fact.

6449 Déniz, José. La revolución por la fuerza armada: Perú, 1968–1977. Salamanca: Ediciones Sígueme, 1978. 206 p.; bibl. (Tierra dos tercios; 8)

An anti-Velasco/Morales Bermúdez tract denounces military "syndicalism," the "new role of the State," educational reforms, press censorship and most other changes brought about by the military. The author criticizes Velasco's new capitalism and both phases of the military "revolution." Nevertheless, the criticism is more balanced than others of this period and an important contribution to current and future assessments of the military experiment.

6450 Dietz, Henry A. Poverty and problem-solving under military rule: the urban poor in Lima, Peru. Austin: University of Texas Press, 1980. 286 p.; ill. (Latin American monographs; no. 51)

An excellent contribution by Dietz. Given the coexistence of military government and massive urban migration into the Peruvian cities (especially Lima), author examines (through 1975) the factors of poverty, urban slum conditions, and the termination of electoral politics as an *input potential* for Lima's urban poor. The failure of SINAMOS as the political mobilization apparatus of the "leftist revolution" is compensated for by local community organizations resulting from the grass-roots planning of *pobladores* living within the squatter settlements (*not* through governmentally constituted/controlled machinery). Worthy of careful perusal by all political scientists, especially those concerned with the Velasco and Morales-Bermúdez administrations.

6451 ———— and **David Scott Palmer.** Citizen participation under innovative military corporatism in Peru (*in* Political participation in Latin America. Edited by John A. Booth and Mitchell A. Seligson. v. 1, Citizen and state. New York: Holmes & Meier, 1978, p. 172–188)

After stating the currently accepted argument that military regimes and civilian participation are incompatible, authors suggest that one must differentiate among military regimes through careful case study. Uses the case of Peru to arrive at several generalizations: 1) the military has been essentially reform-oriented and ideologically committed to high levels of participation; 2) the regime's concern for national security has hampered full participation; and 3) the consequent suppression of political party and union organization has restricted the desired amount of participation. Dietz further observes that popular organizations created by the government generally were not repressive (compare with Stepan, item **6480**) and attributes this to the role of the Church and CAEM (Peru's

prestigious military training center). While political structures have been less effective in increasing participation, the government's most important goal *was* national security. The conflict between encouraging citizen participation and insuring national security was solved by: 1) equating national security with national development; 2) the government's unwillingness to be repressive; and 3) the ability of the mass-base to function *without* officially sanctioned institutions. A provocative, novel analysis.

6452 ———— and **Richard J. Moore.** Political participation in a non-electoral setting: the urban poor in Lima, Peru. Athens: Ohio University, Center for International Studies, 1979. 102 p.; bibl. (Papers in international studies: Latin America series; no. 6)

Study of the post–1968 *pueblos jóvenes* or "new towns," the numerous squatter settlements which ring the city of Lima. Writer suggests that in spite of the prevalent assumptions about political participation in non-participatory authoritarian regimes, the peripheral slum populations have developed novel forms of participation, demand inputs, successful techniques for receiving necessary goods and services and effective methods for getting the attention and response of the military government. A conceptually tight and theoretically important contribution to the literature on political participation in urban Peru.

6453 Espinoza M., Gustavo and **Andrés Peredes L.** La clase obrera y el proceso revolucionario peruano (URSS/AL, 3, 1975, p. 34–47, plate)

An emotional application of ideology to and an expression of Party sympathy for the Peruvian "proletariat" rather than any meaningful attempt at Marxist analysis. The article is significant for its demonstration that the Peruvian Communist Party gives no serious consideration to Peru and its concrete problems. Apparently intended for Soviet consumption, this polemic is an example of support for the Muscovite PCP and is of value for this reason.

6454 Fernández Salvatteci, José Antonio. Yo acuso: la Revolución Peruana. Tacna, Perú: Editorial El Siglo, 1978. 266 p.

Fernández, a higher echelon army officer active in Velasco's First Phase of the Peruvian "revolution," sees the Morales Bermúdez Administration as "treasonous" to the original goals of the military government. This emotional outpouring is revealing of the differences perceived by many between the First and Second (consolidating) Phase of the "revolution," a consolidation which made a socialist Peru impossible. Author accuses Morales of selling out to the US, the CIA, international imperialism, an "opportunistic" APRA and to most other top-level military officials.

6455 Fishel, John T. Political participation in a Peruvian highland district (*in* Political participation in Latin America. Edited by John A. Booth and Mitchell A. Seligson. v. 2, Politics and the poor. New York: Holmes & Meier, 1978, p. 51–61, tables)

Fischel focuses on the Mancos district, an area generally neglected by the military government and, in general, far poorer in public services than Peru's central cities. He presents two models of participation: the "relevancy" and "irrelevancy" frameworks. Political participation in Mancos is characterized as "relevent" due to the high level of voluntary, self-help activity, and the many projects begun and finished by the local citizenry. At best, only one-third of these projects involving education, irrigation, roads, and other public works, have been financed even partially by the national government. The study concludes that such citizen activity cannot be considered as "pastime" or "symbolic," but rather as intense political participation within a parochial context. Partisan mobilization was found to be a major catalyst in addition to more informal client-patron relationships. An important case study; many more of this type are required to assess accurately the national characteristics of rural and urban political behavior in comparative perspective. A solid contribution.

Flores Marín, José and **Rolando Pachas Castilla.** Luchas campesinas en el Perú. See *HLAS 42:3078.*

6456 García, José Z. Critique of Frederick M. Nunn's "Professional militarism in twentieth century Peru: historical and theoretical background to the golpe de estado of 1968." Reply by Frederick M. Nunn (HAHR, 60:2, May 1980, p. 303–312)

García's response to the Nunn study (see item **6467**) is made within the context of research published in 1969 by Víctor Villa-

nueva and Luigi Einaudi. Cautious in describing the Peruvian military's "revolution" as leftist, both authors were later vindicated when the government turned right after Velasco's ouster in 1975. García agrees with the Nunn thesis that Peru's military training under the French in the latter part of the 19th century provides evidence that actions of the military in 1968 followed a "long intellectual gestational period" linked to the French experience. However, García disagrees with Nunn's proposition that the Peruvian military's First Phase was not "leftist" at all but reformist. Author holds that the Peruvian military was and is not ideologically monolithic and that while some have used the rhetoric of structural reform cynically, many were sincere in their commitment to it. The failure to recognize military factionalism is seen by García as the major weakness in the study. In his reply to García, Nunn concurs with the latter's reference to Einaudi and Villanueva on the need for a more cautious use of the term "leftist" and for "more fruitful explanation . . . of what [García] sees as 'contradictions of the regime'."

Giesecke Sara-Lafosse, Margarita. Masas urbanas y rebelión en la historia: golpe de estado, Lima. 1872. See *HLAS 42:3080.*

González Prada, Manuel. Sobre el militarismo, antología: *Bajo el oprobio.* See *HLAS 42:3081.*

Gorman, Stephen M. The state, elite, and export in nineteenth century Peru: toward an alternative reinterpretation of political change. See *HLAS 42:3082.*

6457 Guerra García, Francisco. Política e identidad nacional (*in* Perú, identidad nacional. César Arróspide de la Flor et al. Lima: Centro de Estudios para el Desarrollo y la Participación, 1979, p. 305–364)

Traces the historical evolution of present Peruvian military "revolution" through 1975 (Velasco's First Phase) and perceives the period as a culmination of the Marxist thinking begun by Mariátegui, Victor Raúl Haya de la Torre, and Jorge Basadre. Mariátegui and Haya de la Torre also forged the development of worker consciousness and the concomitant entrenchment of the oligarchy under Belaúnde Terry. Author praises the First Phase/Velasco regime, but treats that of the Morales Bermúdez Second Phase with considerable scorn, calling Morales the "Avila Camacho of the Peruvian Revolution." (Avila Camacho, former President of Mexico, is generally regarded as having begun the consolidation or "bourgeoisization" stage of Mexico's revolution.) A provocative, angry statement from the Peruvian left.

6458 Haya de la Torre, Víctor Raúl. El libro rojo de Haya de la Torre: Haya de la Torre y el cambio social en América Latina. Selección y notas por Rolando Pereda Torres. Lima: Instituto de Estudios Antimperialistas, 1979. 360 p.; bibl.; ill. (Publicaciones del Instituto de Estudios Antimperialistas; no. 3)

Published in the year of Haya de la Torre's death, this volume is a sympathetic collection of Haya's ideological tenets. Presented as a memorial to the founder of Peruvian Aprismo, it includes selections from Haya's writings and speeches spanning a period of more than 50 years. Compare with Luís Alberto Sánchez, *Haya de la Torre o el político* (see item **6477**).

6459 Kaba, Román. Fish, peasants, and state bureaucracies: the development of Lake Titicaca (CPS, 12:3, Oct. 1979, p. 335–361, bibl., ill., table)

Author attributes the decline of local fishing activity and the closing of commercial fishery at Lake Titicaca to a three-country effort by US, Bolivia, and Peru begun in 1935. Although the fishery closed in 1968, continued flow of investment and the growth of administrative structures in the tri-partite development scheme damaged the Titicaca ecological balance and subsistence fishing industry of the indigenous populations. The failure was double: a *technical* and a *normative* one with regard to the original goals of the project. This study touches three important areas: 1) the lake's ecosystem; 2) the Indian's ancient socioeconomic system; and 3) the adverse effects of a thoughtless bureaucracy on the first two. This is an intriguing case study of the "first international cooperative venture in Latin America." It raises important questions regarding some basic assumptions of developmentalism and the effects of an inept, dysfunctional administration.

Kapsoli E., Wilfredo. Las luchas obreras en el Perú, 1900–1919: por las ocho horas de trabajo. See *HLAS 42:3087*.

———. Los movimientos campensinos en el Perú, 1879–1965: ensayos. See *HLAS 42:3088*.

Klaiber, Jeffrey L. Religión y revolución en los Andes en el siglo XIX. See *HLAS 42:3092*.

6460 Lizarzaburu T., Pedro. La caída del régimen belaundista: un análisis político: o, La tragicomedia de los hombres de la renovación. Lima: Pontificia Universidad Católica del Perú, Departamento de Ciencias Sociales, Area de Sociología, 1976. 59 p.; bibl. (Serie Publicaciones previas—Centro de Investigaciones Sociales, Económicas, Políticas y Anthropológicas; no. 16. Publicaciones CISEPA)

Monograph describes the "sociology of political change" and the manner in which that change interacted with social class structure between 1960–74. Author offers the following conclusions: 1) Belaúnde's period was noted for its protection of middle-sector interests; 2) the middle sectors themselves were too fragmented to coalesce for their own protection; 3) Belaúnde's Acción Popular (AP) heightened the factionalism of these groups; and 4) the AP collapse in 1968 was the result of such middle-sector weakness—seen especially in AP's "Carlist" right-wing.

6461 Las Luchas campesinas en Piura. s.l.: Ediciones Labor, 1977. 100 p.; ill.

Study traces peasant conflict through colonial period to the Velasco administration (characterized by its "bureaucratic-authoritarianism") and ends with a denunciation of the Morales Bermúdez regime's persecution of the peasant cooperative movement. A broadside attack on the landed *hacendado* class, the US, imperialism in general, the Prado and Odría administrations, the Belaúnde years and the decade of the Velasco/Morales Bermúdez "revolution." Of interest to those who would use the Peruvian Piura region as a geographic focus for Marxist analysis.

Luna Vegas, Ricardo. Mariátegui, Haya de la Torre y la verdad histórica. See *HLAS 42:3093*.

6462 Luna-Victoria, Romeo. Por una democracia socialista en le Perú. Diseño de carátula, Alfredo Berríos Reiterer. Lima: Ediciones Agape, 1978. 188 p.

Written at the end of the Morales Bermúdez period, author asks for a return to democratic forms that are neither capitalist nor communist, but "semi-socialist." This study is alternatively naive and smug, as well as badly written. The discussion is limited by its use of irrelevant and archaic Catholic sources. An interesting addition to the literature on the Church in that it points up major deficiencies in some Catholic intellectual circles.

Masterson, Daniel M. Soldiers, sailors, and apristas: conspiracy and power politics in Peru, 1932–1948. See *HLAS 42:3097.*

6463 Matos Mar, José. La coyuntura del Perú de hoy (*in* Perú, hoy. Por Fernando Fuenzalida Vollmar et al. 3. ed. México: Siglo Veintiuno Editores, 1975, p. 338–366)

Article stresses Lima's importance in the Peruvian socioeconomic and political system. Likens this "center-periphery" relationship *within* Peru to the colonial era during which Spain was the "center" and perceives present system (as of 1975) to be little changed. "Internal colonialism," a term utilized extensively by Mexican economist Rudolfo Stavenhagen, would have been applicable here but is not utilized. Matos apparently expected a change in center-peripheral relationships in the last months of the Velasco period which was not realized during the Second Phase under Morales Bermúdez.

Melgar, Jorge. A Belaúnde lo que es de Belaúnde. See *HLAS 42:3098.*

6464 Montoya, Rodrigo. Changes in rural class structure under the Peruvian agrarian reform (LAP, 5[4]:19, Fall 1978, p. 113–136, plate)

Study compliments government action in the peripheral areas of the country during the First Phase of the Peruvian agrarian reform under Velasco Alvarado. During this period, the federal oligarchy was broken through government expropriation projects and the neutralization of international and internal Peruvian capitalist enclaves. There remained, however, areas of the country controlled by small "petty patrones" and "local despots" where the potential for effective governmental action was low. Immigrants flooded from these areas into cities and mining towns and, as of 1975, posed the greatest challenge to the success of the agrarian re-

form. Author is not optimistic about the potential for effective government policy in these areas. An important critique.

6465 Mooney, Mary H. and **Walter C. Soderland.** Clerical attitudes toward political development in Peru (JDA, 12:1, Oct. 1977, p. 17–30, tables)

This 1975 study suggests that the largely foreign-born clergy working in Peru are non-committal about social change under the military government. The sample of priests from the US, Peru, and Spain surveyed in the study supported social equality and Church doctrine as a foundation for the building of Peruvian socialism in theory, but were not responsive to questioning about changes in Church structure necessary to bring about those goals. The study indicates that the clergy most willing to cooperate in supporting change are from the US and the least willing from Spain. Native Peruvian clergy strongly supported the concept of *comunidades de base* (self-sufficient Catholic communities at the grass roots level) and greater political activity among the clergy. Interesting article, well-written and researched.

6466 Morales Bermúdez C., Francisco. La Revolución Peruana. Lima: Oficina Central de Información, 1977. 1 v.

Speeches by President Morales Bermúdez (Aug. 1976) referring to the military's policy on certain public works for the cities of Arequipa and Tacna and pledging that "the revolution will never lose its course."

Moya Obeso, Alberto. Sindicalismo aprista y sindicalismo clasista en el Perú, 1920–1956. See *HLAS 42:3100.*

6467 Nunn, Frederick M. Professional militarism in twentieth-century Peru: historical and theoretical background of the golpe de estado of 1968 (HAHR, 59:3, Aug. 1979, p. 391–417)

Rather than emphasizing the immediate causes of Velasco's 1968 coup, author stresses the long-range historical and cultural conditions which brought about the leftist military "revolution." Primary importance is given to the following factors: 1) the long-standing hostility to civilian rule which emerged, for example, in the APRA-military conflict at the end of the Belaúnde administration; 2) the historic Peruvian economic nationalism and drive for development; 3) a preexisting demand by Peru's professional groups for comprehensive modernization; 4) the traditional ideological orientation of the military and the sophistication of the military's prize academic center (CAEM). An important contribution to the literature on the 1968–1980 *docenio* in Peru. Compare with García's critique of this study and Nunn's reply (item **6456**).

6468 Palmer, David Scott. Peru: the authoritarian tradition. New York: Praeger Publishers, 1980. 134 p.; bibl.; index.

Study interprets Peruvian authoritarian tradition in historical terms, from the theocratic Incan period through the centralized Conquest and 19th-century independent creole government. The 1870–1930 period is seen as an interregnum of laissez faire liberalism abruptly ended by the Great Depression. The cooperative efforts of Peru and the US during WW II and the threat of international Communism in the 1950s prepared the country for the production of military regimes concerned with the politics of national security. Palmer considers the military interventionism now chronic in the Peruvian political process to be part of an ancient pattern. Discussion of Haya de la Torre and APRA in chapters 5 and 6 are of special importance. An impressive, thoroughly documented study of Peruvian political trends through 1975.

6469 Partido Comunista Peruano: documentos para su historia, 1931–1934. Wilfredo Kápsoli Escudero, compilador; ed. al cuidado de Miguel Angel Rodríguez Rea. Lima: Ediciones Documentos, 1978. 122 p.; bibl.

Compilation of early documents from the 1931–34 period which seeks to prove active participation of Mariátegui in the original formation of the PCP. Compare with items **6438** and **6470**.

6470 Partido Comunista Revolucionario (Peru). **Conferencia Nacional,** 2d, 1977. Línea básica de la Revolución Peruana. Lima: Partido Comunista Revolucionario: Distribuidora y Editora Peruana, 1979. 318 p.

Collection of reports from the Second National Conference of a splinter group organized in 1974 as the "true party of Mariátegui." This Maoist organization seeks a "return of the Communist movement to the principles of Mariátegui" (and presumably

away from the revisionism of the Peruvian Communist Party). Compare with items **6438** and **6469**.

6471 Pásara, Luis. Reforma agraria, derecho y conflicto. Lima: Instituto de Estudios Peruanos, 1978. 184 p. (Estudios de la sociedad rural; 6)

Critique of the 1969 Agrarian Reform program instituted by President Velasco. The volume relates then existing property law to the vagaries of public policy governing the peasant sector. Pásara treats legal theory in general and evaluates the legal basis for state protection or appropriation of property. He concludes that the Agrarian Reform instituted early in Phase One of the "revolution" contravened traditional Peruvian and Latin American legal norms. An important philosophical discussion—from the Peruvian right—of the law in relation to both society and state. Of interest to scholars of comparative law.

Pease García, Henry. Los caminos del poder: tres años de crisis en la escena política. See *HLAS 42:3106.*

6472 ——. Perú actual: crisis política tras una década militar (CP, 19, enero/marzo 1979, p. 68–87)

In this analysis of the Second Phase of the Peruvian "revolution" (1975–78), author contrasts the deterioration of the Belaúnde administration, a sell-out to the oligarchy, with the reconsolidation of economic power by the state during the Velasco period (First Phase). The most significant portion of this analysis is Pease García's appreciation of the difference between "revolution" and "reform," and his denial that the Armed Forces government was, in fact, revolutionary. The author sees the authoritarian and corporatist tendencies of the Velasco period continuing in the Second Phase under Morales Bermúdez, a thoroughly "rightist" repressive regime which has only a symbolic allegiance to the original promises of Oct. 1968. A Third-Phase scenario is presented based on the high percentage of votes APRA (Haya de la Torre) won in the 1978 Constituent Assembly elections. Author envisions an Aprista government in possible alliance with the Acción Popular of Belaúnde and/or with the "bourgeois" Popular Christian Party (PPC). Despite its somewhat dubious predictions, this is an interesting and provocative study.

6473 Proyecto plan de gobierno "Tupac Amaru:" período 1977–1980. Lima: s.n., 1977? 67 p.

Complete text of President Morales Bermúdez plan "Tupac Amaru" designed to serve as basis for Peruvian economics during the Second (or consolidation) Phase of the "revolution." The goal of the program is presented as a "Communist State" or, failing this, a governmental structure superior to capitalism. Interesting statement on the Morales administration's final major policy thrust.

6474 Quijano, Aníbal. La lucha de clases en el Perú actual (CP, 15, enero/marzo 1978, p. 44–61)

Quijano asserts that as of 1976, the so-called Second Phase set the stage for the final conflict between the Peruvian proletariat and bourgeoisie. Author predicts the period beginning 1978 will become known as that of the "bankruptcy" of reformism under such bourgeois democratic movements as APRA and Acción Popular (AP). After a long period of conflict between the traditional bourgeois parties and those groups representing the true interests of Peru's working class, revolutionary socialism will emerge under the leadership of the Peruvian Communist Party. As a sober, non-quixotic analysis from the Marxist (Muscovite) left, this study merits the attention of students of Peruvian and Latin American Marxism. See also *HLAS 42:3108.*

————. El Perú en las crisis de los años 30. See *HLAS 42:3109.*

Ramos Alva, Alfonso. Siete tesis equivocadas del marxismo-leninismo sobre Indoamérica. See *HLAS 42:3110.*

6475 El Reformiso burgués (1968–1976).
Mirko Lauer, moderador; Félix Arias Schreiber et al. Lima: Mosca Azul Editores, 1978. 253 p. (Debate socialista; 2)

Leaders of the Peruvian Communist Party and other leftist groups criticize the Velasco regime's dealings with the Peruvian oligarchy. The left here dispassionately criticizes its own fragmentation, which prevented it from steering the Velasco government closer to its objectives. This study is a sophisticated debate on the weakness of the left during the First Phase (Velasco) of the Peruvian military "revolution."

Rénique, José Luis. Los descentralistas arequipeños en la crisis del 30. See *HLAS 42:3115.*

6476 Ruiz Bendezú, Miró. Cultura cívica: conocimientos fundamentales de, 1. Capitalismo, imperialismo económico, marxismo leninismo. Lima?: s.n., between 1972 and 1978. 125 p.; ill.

A civics textbook that defines and discusses a variety of political systems. The author's leftist assumptions become clear in his discussion of Peruvian civil culture which includes scathing denunciation of the Peruvian Catholic Church and Catholicism in general. An interesting but intensely biased political "catechism."

6477 Sánchez, Luis Alberto. Víctor Raúl Haya de la Torre o el político: crónica de una vida sin tregua. 3. ed. Lima, Perú: E. Delgado Valenzuela, 1979. 241 p.

Published shortly before Haya de la Torre's death at age 84, this is a revision of the original 1936 biography written by one of his early followers. Stresses Haya's early life.

6478 Sánchez León, Abelardo and **Julio Calderón Cockburn.** El laberinto de la ciudad: políticas urbanas del estado, 1950–1979. Lima: DESCO, Centro de Estudios y Promoción del Desarrollo, 1980. 168 p.

A sophisticated study of the squatter-settlement phenomenon in and around Lima. The volume addresses state response to massive internal migration, the resulting reorganization of metropolitan Lima and the forms of political participation engaged in by the *pobladores.* The section on governmental response is particularly noteworthy, but probably gives the military government too much credit for solving the problems of the *pueblos jóvenes.* Compare with the two Dietz studies (items **6451** and **6452**). A first-rate contribution to the literature on Latin American urbanization.

6479 Shulgovski, Anatoli. Aspectos ideológicos y teóricos del proceso revolucionario peruano (URSS/AL, 1975, p. 7–33, plate)

Analysis by a Soviet Latin Americanist of the first six years of the Peruvian "revolution." Author criticizes the Velasco period for not being sufficiently concerned with Third

World problems of "dependency." Shulgovski praises SINAMOS as a means for mobilizing the masses against the Peruvian oligarchy and for transferring political power to the people; attacks APRA as "fascist" for attempting to block Velasco's internal policies; blames Quijano, Cotler, and Villanueva for their misperceptions of Peruvian reality; and lauds the Peruvian Communist Party (PCP) as the leader of Peru's transformation. Author considers that the fragmentation of the left has prevented any united resistance to the military of the Morales Bermúdez period, and affirms the possibility of cooperation among all sympathetic revolutionary forces. A predictable Moscovite assessment of the Peruvian situation with its generalized support for the PCP.

Skinner, Geraldine. José Carlos Mariátegui and the emergence of the Peruvian socialist movement. See *HLAS 42:3120.*

6480 Stepan, Alfred C. The state and society: Peru in comparative perspective. Princeton, N.J.: Princeton University Press, 1978. 348 p.; bibl.; ill.; index.

This ambitious and important study applies what the author terms the "organic-statist" model of society in Latin Europe to Latin America and Peru (see chapters 1, 2, 3, and 8). Specific attention is paid to the Velasco period since 1968. Stepan provides an incisive analysis of Liberal-Pluralist, Classical Marxist, and "Corporatist" models and a provocative description of the contemporary literature on Latin American corporatism. He firmly distinguishes between the latter's "exclusionary" and "inclusionary" types and applies five preditive hypotheses to four major case studies. The author then defines the Peruvian experiment of 1968–75 as a benign inclusionary manifestation of organic statism and describes the factors that made it possible. Stepan concludes, however, that the lack of governmental organizations capable of enlisting the loyalty of the many diverse grass-roots groups prevented the institutionalization of the revolution. This is a provocative, well documented, and well written contribution both to political theory and Peruvian politics from a comparative perspective.

6481 Urviola, Ezequiel and Eduardo Quispe. Las tesis agrarias del P.C. Unidad: una crítica al revisionismo. Lima: Ediciones Populares César Benavides, 1979. 18 p.

Peruvian Communist Party tract characterizes splinter group (PCP-UNIDAD) treasonous for not denouncing the cooptation of PCP's peasant leagues by the Velasco, Morales Bermúdez, and Belaúnde Terry governments. The PCP accuses the PCP-U of betraying its Marxist-Leninist principles when it opposed National Agrarian Conference's pressure for devoting more governmental attention to peasant needs. Interesting intra-left squabble over what is termed "flagrant revisionism."

6482 van Eeuwen, Daniel. Le projet théorique de la "Revolution Peruvienne" (UCL/CD, 11:4, 1979, p. 527–550)

A simplistic, flamboyant description of the Velasco military solution for Peru written in a somewhat condescending vein by a representative of the European left as a eulogy for the deceased President. Author criticizes APRA for abandoning Velasco and the "revolution."

Vassallo, Manuel. Rumi Maqui y la nacionalidad quechua. See *HLAS 42:3128.*

6483 Vorozhéikina, Tatiana. Los militares en el poder: experiencia peruana (URSS/AL, 4[20], 1978, p. 53–70)

Somewhat naive Soviet analysis of the weakness of the revolutionary system in Peru notes that the military government failed to relinquish power once it had implemented its goals. Author also stresses the fragmentation within the Peruvian left and the military government itself. The results of elections for the Constituent Assembly indicate a growing polarization of social classes which will destroy whatever unity the military has achieved. The revolution will be further jeopardized by the world capitalist economy, the state's protection of small and medium-sized property holdings, and "inevitable corruption" during "these prerevolutionary circumstances." In short, even if the military remains united it has much to accomplish.

6484 Werlich, David P. Peru: the lame-duck revolution (CUH, 76:44, Feb. 1979, p. 62–65)

Author analyzes the failures of Peru's military experiment in the period immediately before the return of Morales Bermúdez to military life and the end of the *decenio* of "leftist military revolution." He attributes those failures to economic problems caused by "combination of bad luck and mismanagement." Morales, committed to the correction of Velasco's errors led Peru into the Second Phase of the "revolution," which had as its major objective the "consolidation of gains." Peru's economic problems, the fragmentation of the military, the deliberate dismantling of structures from the Velasco period, the failure of Plan Túpac Amaru, and a drastic reduction in industrial worker participation—all these led to the calling of elections for the Constituent Assembly to consider fresh alternatives to ancient Peruvian social problems. A good, succinct analysis.

6485 Woy, Sandra L. Infrastructure of participation in Peru: SINAMOS (National System for the Support of Social Mobilization) (*in* Political participation in Latin America. Edited by John A. Booth and Mitchell A. Seligson. v. 1, Citizen and state. New York: Holmes & Meier, 1978, p. 189–208)

This study focuses on two types of democratic behavior—"plebiscitary" and "participatory"—and argues that SINAMOS is participatory in nature. Author finds that participation in SINAMOS was voluntary and that SINAMOS generally provided aid to voluntary groups that requested it. Woy presents case study of TUP, a voluntary organization of university students, showing that its leaders and policies were chosen democratically. On the other hand, SINAMOS retained the prerogative of accepting or rejecting offers of participation on ideological grounds. Woy's general conclusion is that organizations like SINAMOS often cannot deal effectively with too much pressure for participation. However, if the government does not accommodate demands for participation it may be faced with the significant problem of alienation. Only within these limits can organizations like SINAMOS be considered truly "participatory." A superior contribution to the literature on Peru and SINAMOS.

Zitor (pseudonym). Historia de la principales huelgas y paros obreros habidos en el Perú, 1896–1946. See *HLAS 42:3133*.

BOLIVIA

6486 Alcoreza, Carmen and **Javier Albó.** 1978 [i.e. Mil novecientos setenta y ocho], el nuevo campesinado ante el fraude. Colaboración de Isabel Arauco et al. La Paz: Centro de Investigación y Promoción del Campesinado, 1979. 176 p.; bibl.; ill. (Cuaderno de investigación—CIPCA; 18)

Study of the fraud involved in the controversial elections of July 1978 results of which were annulled by President Hugo-Bánzer Suárez' military regime. Author describes the techniques often associated with Latin American electoral fraud and the coup led by Bánzer's heir apparent, Gen. Juan Pereda Asbún, but focuses primarily on the extent of peasant support for representatives of pro-democratic (particularly MNR) groups. A well-documented, intriguing case study.

6487 Almaraz Paz, Sergio. Para abrir el diálogo: ensayos, 1961–1967. La Paz, Bolivia: Ediciones Los Amgios del Libro, 1979. 203 p.; bibl.; port. (Colección Pensadores bolivianos contemporáneos)

A memorial volume of essays by the Under-Secretary of Labor of the MNR. Almaraz' view of Bolivian politics is based on his own "conversion" from the Communist Party to the MNR in 1950. This collection of his writings offer a provocative philosophical reflection on the Bolivian polity.

Alvarez España, Waldo. Los gráficos en Bolivia de la organización y luchas de los trabajadores de este sector social. See *HLAS 42:3134*.

6488 Andrade, Víctor. La revolución boliviana y los Estados Unidos, 1944–1962. 2. ed. aumentada y corr. La Paz, Bolivia: Gisbert, 1979. 341 p.; 4 leaves of plates; ports.

Memoirs of Andrade, one of the principal leaders of the MNR (1943–62). Focuses on his role as Bolivian/MNR Ambassador to the US, describing his activities in Washington, at the Mexico City Conference on the Problems of War and Peace (1945), and at the San Francisco Conference in the same year. Andrade also recounts his experiences as Visiting Professor at the New School for Social Research in New York. His generally agreeable diplomatic and party relations ended when schisms in the MNR forced his resignation in 1962. Original English title: *My missions for revolutionary Bolivia, 1944–1962.*

6489 Antezana E., Luis. Hernán Siles Zuazo, el estratega y la contrarrevolución. La Paz, Bolivia: Editorial Luz, 1979. 187 p.; bibl.; ill.

Important work about one of the first leaders of the MNR and President of the Republic (1956–60). Siles accuses right-wing elements of "infiltrating" the MNR, causing the present division of the movement into the conservative (Paz Estenssoro's MNR-Histórico) and liberal (Siles' own MNR-Izquierda) coalitions. The volume also covers important aspects of Siles' tenure as President.

6490 Araníbar Quiroga, Ernesto. Crecimiento económico y procesos políticos. La Paz, Bolivia: Distribuidores, Amigos del Libro, 1978. 140 p.; bibl.

An economist trained at the Universities of Cochabamba and Louvain, author comments on the fall of the MNR and its replacement by regimes like Banzer's that allowed "bourgeois capital accumulation." A "Gramsci" study on the economic results of "fascism." A major weakness of this study, as in much of the leftist literature on Bolivian/ militarism, lies in its failure to define what is meant by "fascism."

6491 Arguedas, Alcides. Cartas a los presidentes de Bolivia. Selección, prólogo, y notas de Mariano Baptista Gumucio. La Paz, Bolivia: Ultima Hora, 1979. 223 p.; ill. (Biblioteca popular boliviana de Ultima Hora)

Memorial collection of letters to seven Bolivian Presidents commemorates the 100th anniversary of the birth of Arguedas, former Chaco War hero. The volume provides interesting views on the state of Bolivian politics in the post-Chaco War period.

Barrero, Francisco. Radepa y la Revolución Nacional. See *HLAS 42:3139.*

6492 Bedregal Gutiérrez, Guillermo. Bolivia: la apertura democrática y las tareas de los partidos políticos (NSO, 34, enero/feb. 1978, p. 115–122, ill.)

Leftist analysis of military authoritarianism during the seven-year Bánzer regime. Includes a discussion of the concept of "apartheid" as it relates to the Bolivian indigenous population and rural peasantry. Author

also criticizes the following governmental policies: 1) the fragmentation of urban and rural labor organizations; 2) the destruction of Bolivian political parties; 3) socioeconomic polarization; 4) the inducement of conformism; and 5) the paternalistic limitations imposed on democratic grass roots political participation. Author supports the MNR-Izquierda under Hernán Siles Zuazo and other aligned leftists groups, but doubts that any partisan movement will reinstitute party politics and democratic institutions in Bolivia.

6493 Bolivien: Rückkehr zur bürgerlichen Demokrarie?: Eine Pressedokumentation (Bolivia: ¿retorno a la democracia burguesa?: documentación de prensa). Edited and compiled by Heiner Jörg Hermes. Hamburg, FRG: Institut für Iberoamerika-Kunde, Dokumentations Leitstelle Lateinamerika, 1979. 90 p.; facsims.; maps (Aktueller Informationsdienst Lateinamerika; 11/12)

Consists of a bilingual (German-Spanish) compilation of newspaper articles on the subject of a possible return to democratic institutions in Bolivia. Articles explore impact of the Bánzer regime on the foreign debt, the mining industry, petroleum production, education, health and nutrition, agrarian reform, and living conditions of the rural peasantry. The MNR is still seen as the transcendent political symbol for the country. Also surveys the role of the military and US in Bolivia, and the important issue of the country's international trade patterns and its economic position as a "satellite" of Brazil and Argentina. This well documented compilation is a major contribution to the current literature on Bolivia.

6494 Los Campesinos en el proceso político boliviano: documentos de la C.N.T.C.B. Recopilación histórica y presentación de Daniel Salamanca Trujillo. La Paz: s.n., 1978. 280 p.; 12 leaves of plates; bibl.; ill.

A former Under-Secretary for Peasant Affairs in the Bánzer regime writes an interesting essay in support of the Bolivian military which he dedicates to Bánzer and Natusch. Author believes the Bánzer regime was especially effective in promoting the political participation of Bolivian peasants.

6495 Córdova-Claure, Ted. Siles Suazo: las banderas de Abril del 52 (NSO, 41, marzo/abril 1979, p. 124–128, plate)

Interview with early MNR leader and former President of the Republic (1956–60). Siles now leads the Popular Democratic Union (UDP) coalition that won the 1978 elections subsequently nullified by Bánzer. Siles weighs the relative effectiveness of both left-center and leftist groups in relation to the current military situation and suggests that a coalition between the UDP and the Bolivian Communist Party (PCB) would be the most effective alternative. He also discusses the growing economic cooperation of Bolivia with Brazil and Argentina, as a substitute for Bolivia's continued participation in the Andean Pact. An important contribution to the literature on Bolivia.

Dómich Ruiz, Marcos. Ideología y mito: los orígenes del fascismo boliviano. See *HLAS 42:3150.*

6496 El Fraude electoral: un atentado contra la voluntad popular: elecciones nacionales del 9 de julio de 1978. La Paz: Asamblea Permanente de Derechos Humanos de Bolivia, 1979. 199 p.; 5 leaves of plates; bibl.; ill.

Study by the Permanent Assembly on Human Rights in Bolivia which describes and analyzes the fraud connected with the July 1978 elections that were annulled by the Bánzer government. Author views the ineptitude and corruption of the Bánzer administration and pressures from the US as forcing the elections to be called, paving the way for the Pereda Asbún coup and the UNP coalition. Includes a daily chronology of events of the period, major governmental decrees on the conduct of the voting, and the testimony of international observers, mainly representatives of various Latin American Catholic organizations. An anti-US and anti-Bánzer military statement.

6497 Greaves, Thomas and **Javier Albó.** An anatomy of dependency: a Bolivian tin-miners' strike (*in* Political participation in Latin America. Edited by John A. Booth and Mitchell A. Seligson. v. 2, Politics and the poor. New York: Holmes & Meier, 1978, p. 169–182)

A dependency-theory and corporatist analysis of the failure of the tin miners' strike at Bocaza in 1976. Authors attribute the strike failure to governmental control. The study's most notable contribution consists of the authors' description of their experience as residents of the mining camp while conducting research.

6498 Huelga de hambre. La Paz: Asamblea Permanente de los Derechos Humanos en Bolivia, 1978 or 1979. 285, 33 p.; 10 leaves of plates; ill.

Description of the hunger strike against the Bánzer government which began in Dec. 1977, on a very small scale, and grew to include more than two million Bolivians. This somewhat flamboyant volume includes valuable statements by the government, the Church, the media and general public. Appendix includes a good chronology and a series of statements concerning official negotiations to end the strike.

Kohl, James V. Peasant and revolution in Bolivia: April 9, 1952–August 2, 1953. See *HLAS 42:3158.*

6499 Kolle Cueto, Jorge. Conversación con el Primer Secretario del Comité Central del Partido Comunista de Bolivia (URSS/AL, 2, 1977, p. 117–134)

Interesting Soviet analysis of an interview with Kolle Cueto of Bolivia's CP, on the origins of the Bánzer regime. Mentions such factors as the intervention of MNR in the leftist military experiment of Torres, the importation of "European fascism," and general tendencies of the Bolivian military establishment. Kolle envisions a coalition of Siles' MNR-I, the Socialist Party, and Juan Lechín's Revolutionary Party of the Nationalist Left as the only solution for Bolivian political life.

6500 Lavaud, Jean-Pierre. Le gouvernement Bánzer de 1971 à 1976 (FDD/NED [Problèmes d'Amérique Latine, 54] 4545/4546, 18 déc. 1979, p. 11–62, tables)

Author examines the democratic pressures brought to bear on the Bánzer regime by the Carter administration, the Bolivian Church, the labor unions, and political parties. He also discusses the negative effects caused by the regime's own internal fragmentation, the failure to regain access to the Pacific and the ensuing break in relations with Pinochet's Chile. The annullment of the 1978 elections and the subsequent Pereda Asbún coup are considered as typical military responses to pressure from groups on the extreme left. And although the 1979 elections signaled a return to democratic institutions, the percentage of votes received by Bánzer's Acción Democrática Nacional led to an invalidation of the outcome which in turn ushered in the Guevara-Arze "interim Presidency," the Natusch coup and thus a return to militarism. Lavaud believes Bolivia's problems stem from the MNR's failure to reconcile the Siles Zuazo and Paz Estenssoro factions as well as from the weakness of Bolivian rural and urban labor groups. Study includes a series of political biographies and a good chronology of events.

6501 Lora, Guillermo. Contribución a la historia política de Bolivia. La Paz: Ediciones ISLA, 1978. 383 p.; bibl. (Colección Historia y documentos-ISLA; 1)
Leader of the orthodox faction of the Bolivian Revolutionary Workers' Party (POR) presents history of this Trotskyite organization and its role in the evolution of the country's politics.

———. A history of the Bolivian labour movement, 1848–1971. See *HLAS 42:3162.*

6502 ———. ¿Qué es el trotskysmo? y Bolivia y la revolución permanente. La Paz: Ediciones El Amauta, 1978. 285 p.
A discussion of the relevance of Marxist ideology and POR party structure to contemporary political problems by the leader of the Trotskyite Bolivian Revolutionary Workers' Party (POR). The second portion of the volume is dedicated to an extensive discussion of Trotskyism. This is an important contribution to the literature on the radical left.

6503 La Masacre del Valle, Cochabamba, enero 1974. 2. ed. La Paz: Cuadernos Justicia y Paz, 1975. 77 p.; map (Cuadernos Justicia y paz; 2)
Consists of a description by the Inter-American Human Rights Organization Justice and Peace of the Cochabamba massacre of June 1974 when more than 100 peasants seeking land reform were murdered. This report should be read in conjunction with one submitted by LADOC (Latin American Documentation, see *HLAS 39:7397).*

6504 Mayorga, René Antonio. Dictadura militar y crisis del Estado: el caso boliviano, 1971–1977 (CP, 20, abril/junio 1979, p. 64–88)
Author ascribes current problems in Bolivia to the "bourgeois," "authoritarian,"

"oligarchic," and "populist" policies implemented by Bánzer's "dictatorial state." The weakness of this analysis, as in much of the so-called legal writing on the concept of the state in Latin America, lies in its criticism and rejection of policies (e.g., "reformist nationalism," "proimperialist liberalism," etc.) as legitimate ones for adoption by a government. Compare this piece with Lechner's in item **6055.**

6505 ———. National-popular state, state capitalism and military dictatorship in Bolivia: 1952–1975 (LAP, 4[17]: 2, Spring 1978, p. 89–119, bibl.)
Mayorga assesses "bourgeois" revolution that followed the 1952 MNR victory, and that eventually displaced both urban and rural labor, setting the stage for continuous military intervention in the political process. The author equates such interventionism with "fascism," redefined in Marxist terms as: 1) domination by imperialist monopoly capital "in alliance with the internal bourgeoisie"; 2) use of terror to prevent urban and rural labor revolt; and 3) superimposition of military apparatus on all socioeconomic and political activities (see item **6504).** According to Mayorga, the New Order established by Bánzer in 1974 is "fascist" because of its "stabilization of order by means of a personal concentration of rule" and the "depoliticization" of labor. A sloppy application of Marxist polemics to explain the Bolivian situation. For historian's comment, see *HLAS 42:3163.*

Ocampo Moscoso, Eduardo. Historia del periodismo boliviano. See *HLAS 42:3169.*

6506 Partido Obrero Revolucionario (Trotskista-posadista). Continuar la revolución boliviana!: documento político de la conferencia nacional extraordinaria de mayo, 1975. Programa para sacar a Bolivia del atraso: aprobado en la XXII Conferencia Nacional del P.O.R. t-p, IV International, 29–30, diciembre, 1977. La Paz, Bolivia: El Partido, 1979. 80 p.; bibl.
Consists of the program of the Bolivian Workers' Party, resulting from two planning conferences convened during the 1970s, and designed to promote Trotskyite activity among urban and rural labor.

6507 La política nacional: democracia, continuismo, golpe de estado. Opinan

Guillermo Bedregal Gutiérrez et al. La Paz: 1978. 24 p. (Temas en la crisis; 2)

Statements by leaders of leftist political groups on such topics as the significance of the Bánzer period, the fragmentation of leftist parties and the use of existing political structures to solve Bolivia's problems. Generally negative viewpoints on the current state of party organization and the continued intervention of the armed forces. An important compilation of political thought by some of Bolivia's most powerful party leaders.

6508 Queiser Morales, Waltraud. Bolivia moves toward democracy (CUH, 78:454, Feb. 1980, p. 76–79, 86–88)

Author discusses the numerous coups since the 1964 fall of the MNR, points out the polarization of Bolivia's remaining political parties and coalitions, and regards the "dependence" of the country on multinational corporations as symptoms of illness in any would-be democratic polity. Author believes "generational" conflict within the military, among other forms of military factionalism, increases the confusion in the present political system. Nevertheless, the author is extremely optimistic about Bolivia's new "odyssey" toward democracy.

6509 Ramos Sánchez, Pablo. La democracia boliviana, sus defensores y sus enemigos. La Paz, Bolivia: Librería Editorial Juventud, 1979. 98 p.; bibl.

A sympathetic discussion of Guevara Arze's Authentic Revolutionary Party (PRA), a splinter group of the MNR formed in 1960. The study was written after Guevara, Interim-President during Aug. 1978, had returned to the older conservative faction of the MNR, led by Paz Estenssoro. Ramos attacks the Bolivian armed forces as well as the US State Department and CIA. A valuable statement of PRA's ideological position after the defection of its founder.

6510 Salamanca Trujillo, Daniel. Colapso político en Bolivia. Diseño de la carátula por el autor y Emilio Colodro. Oruro, Bolivia: Editora Quelco, 1978. 505 p.; bibl.; facsims.

Former Minister of Education and private secretary to President René Barrientos (1966–69), author also served as Director of the National Confederation of Rural Workers. His study covers all recent political parties and movements in Bolivia's problems to the dissolution of political consensus and the military's continuous interruption of partisan politics. The failure of MNR experiment and the death of Barrientos led to a steady weakening of democratic organization. A major contribution to the literature on Bolivian political groups through 1978.

6511 El Sistema político boliviano. Jorge Agreda V. et al. Bogotá: Publicaciones Codex, 1974 [i.e. 1976]. 60 p.

The most important findings of this seminar held at the Catholic University in Bogotá (Nov. 1974) are that: 1) the Bolivian party system exists in a state of "permanent crisis" due to the country's "enclave economy;" 2) the crisis is intensified by the party leaders' inability to produce a platform attractive to all classes and social groups; 3) the continued domination of party politics by military cliques has escalated economic and political conflict; and 4) the growth of these conflicts during the first half of this century led to the 1952 MNR victory. The presence of multinational corporations, the legacy of the Chaco War, and anti-latifundia prejudice, the fragmentation of labor, and the proliferation of political ideologies are all perceived as negative results of the MNR's toppling by the Falange Nacional, an event from which the nation never recovered. Bolivia's present crisis is due to the nation's inability to incorporate the MNR and other parties into an authoritarian military regime of national unity. Interesting analysis by pro-MNR participants.

6512 Toranzo Roca, Carlos. La lucha política en Bolivia (CP, 16, abril/junio 1978, p. 90–113)

Leftist analysis of seven years of "Banzerism." Most interesting is the author's critique of the Carter policy toward Latin American dictatorships in general and Bánzer's in particular. Toranzo suggests that Carter's insistence on democratic regimes of a "populist" type intensified governmental attempts to control all segments of Bolivian life through corporatist-syndicalist structures. Author concludes that majority rule will not in itself guarantee an equitable "social democracy" for Bolivia's urban and rural working classes. A provocative assessment and prognosis from the left.

6513 Vargas Valenzuela, José. Nacionalismo con desarrollo y seguridad: con reflexiones sobre algunos temas de análisis en la Escuela de Altos Estudios Militares. La Paz: Editorial Los Amigos del Libro, 1977. 265 p.

This volume is a memorial to former Presidents Busch, Villarroel and Barrientos. Vargas, who is Director of the Center for Naval Studies, dedicates this study to the Bolivian Armed Forces, "untiring pioneers, protagonists, and martyrs for the noble cause of prosperity and greatness in Bolivia." An interesting philosophical analysis of nationalism, the state, and national priorities by a member of the armed forces elite who, although not closely aligned with recent military regimes, espouses their ideological position (i.e., that the Bolivian state must be an "integral," "ordered," "unified," and "progressive" entity). Although smug and stiffly written, the work is an interesting reflection of the military's perceptions of the political process.

CHILE

Albornoz, Orlando and **Ariel Dorfman.** El intelectual y el estado: Venezuela-Chile. See item **6377.**

Alexander, Robert Jackson. Arturo Alessandri: a biography. See *HLAS 42:3189.*

6514 ——. The tragedy of Chile. Westport, Conn.: Greenwood Press, 1978. 509 p.; bibl.; index (Contributions in political science; no. 8)

Penetrating study of 20th-century Chilean political and economic evolution that includes a thorough discussion of the Allende years (1970–73) and the Pinochet regime, written by a student of Chilean politics for over three decades. This well researched study is highly recommended for its balanced, comprehensive treatment of the policies of both Allende and Pinochet.

6515 ——. Turning back the clock on Chilean labor (Freedom at Issue [Freedom House Pub., New York] 53, Nov./Dec. 1979, p. 11–13)

Author, a long-time student of Latin American contemporary labor organization, criticizes the following aspects of Pinochet's labor policy: 1) government dissolution of most union organizations; 2) abolition of the union shop; 3) establishment of regulations preventing the organization of peasant or small urban labor groups; and 4) labor leadership regulations that favor pro-Junta personnel. Alexander deplores the loss of most of the gains achieved by organized labor since the passage of the Alessandri Labor Code of 1924.

6516 Almeyda M., Clodomiro. El nacionalismo latinoamericano y el fascismo de Pinochet (UNAM/PDD, 9:35, agosto/oct. 1978, p. 19–34, ill., tables)

Long-time member of the Socialist Party and Foreign Minister under Allende, who now teaches at Mexico's UNAM, author distinguishes among various types of Latin American "nationalisms." He states that nationalism in Chile today is a "cynical fabrication" based on the manipulation of traditional national symbols, and equates Pinochet's "fascism" with corporatist/military authoritarianism.

Alvear Godoy, Aníbal. Por los caminos de Chile: ayer y hoy, hechos históricos y anécdotas, 1810–1976. See *HLAS 42:3190.*

6517 Angell, Alan. Chile after five years of military rule (CUH, 76:44, Feb. 1979, p. 58–61)

Author notes the disparity between Pinochet's apparent optimism concerning the Chilean economy and the uncertainty he conveyed to the European press in interviews in late 1978. Among the problems facing Pinochet, Angell emphasizes military stability, political repression, the response of the Chilean Catholic hierarchy to the continued violation of human rights in the country, widespread antagonism caused by the application of Milton Friedman's economic theory, and the as yet unsolved Letelier assassination. In the concluding section of this article, Angell criticizes Pinochet's ideas on economic progress. A valuable negative assessment of the Junta from the British left.

Biblioteca Nazionale Centrale di Firenze, *Italy.* Un popolo unito, Cile: 1970–1974; dal governo di Unitá Popolare alla giunta di Pinochet, bibliografia ragionata. See *HLAS 42:3199.*

6518 Bitar, Sergio. Transición, socialismo y democracia: la experiencia chilena. México: Siglo Veintiuno Editores, 1979. 380 p.; bibl.; diagrs. (Sociología y política)

Author, an economist and representative of the Christian left, analyzes the dysfunctional results of economic change during the Allende period. Bitar's position as former Minister of Mining in the UP government (1973) allowed him to witness the weakening of the Allende coalition from within, making his relatively sympathetic analysis all the more credible. While he is not totally in agreement with Allende's policies, the author presents one of the most intriguing and sophisticated statements of avant-garde socialism to come out of the 1970–73 period.

6519 Blanco, Guillermo. Los incidentes de Riobamba y Pudahuel en tres diarios chilenos. Santiago: Instituto Chileno de Estudios Humanísticos, 1977. 174 p.

Reactions by a professor of Journalism at the Catholic University of Chile to the Ecuadorian government's harrassment and expulsion of 17 bishops of the Latin American Church attending a conference at Riobamba, Ecuador. This study—which the author claims was heavily censored—bases its analysis of the "Riobamba Case" on information drawn from three major Chilean newspapers, *El Mercurio, El Cronista*, and *La Segunda*. Also included is a statement from the Chilean hierarchy bitterly attacking the Ecuadorian actions. The major focus of this interesting discussion of the Ecuadorian military's inept search for Church subversives is its concern about the lack of press freedom in Chile under the Pinochet regime.

6520 Bravo Lira, Bernardino. Régimen de gobierno y partidos políticos en Chile, 1924–1973. Santiago de Chile: Editorial Jurídica de Chile, 1978. 320 p.; bibl.; graphs.

Legal expert traces the constitutional and statutory position of Chilean political parties (1924–73). Bravo dispassionately discusses the position of the Chilean Court and Legislative systems as "satellites" of the President's Office, and concludes that present military realities will not allow continuation of the partisan, judicial, and democratic legislative practices traditional in Chile and which ended sometime before the final months of the Allende government.

6521 Briones, Alvaro. Ideología del fascismo dependiente: estado y seguridad nacional. Consejo editorial, Enrique D. Dussel, Fernando Danel, Francisco Blanco; diseño de la portada, Arturo Silva. México: Editorial

Edicol, 1978. 206 p. (Colección Filosofía y liberación latinoamericana; 19: Temas)

Focusing primarily on Chile (and to a lesser extent Argentina), the author seeks to demonstrate that the indigenous and foreign capitalist class created the present military regime in order to consolidate its own interests. More effective in describing the current Chilean regime than in defining its causes. [G. Wynia]

6522 Campero Q., Guillermo. Las nuevas condiciones en las relaciones del trabajo y la acción política en Chile (UNAM/RMS, 41[51:2], abril/junio 1979, p. 484–494, tables)

Campero describes evolution of the Chilean economy, the gains of labor up to the period of the UP—when "unions acquired more than anything the role of principal mediators of conflict and decision-makers."—and labor's many losses under the military regime. Interestingly, his discussion of the "divorce" of labor from the formal institutions of Chilean government appears to be · calling for quasi-corporatist structures of labor assistance (and control). A provocative analysis.

6523 Catalán, Oscar and Jorge Arrate. Chile: la política del régimen militar y las nuevas formas de desarrollo en América Latina (CEDLA/B, 25, dic. 1978, p. 51–71, tables)

Trenchant indictment of Pinochet's economic policy. Authors claim that the policy is actually counterproductive as it requires such a costly reordering of priorities in those groups that stand to benefit from it. These high public-administration costs have inflicted unconscionable economic suffering on the vast majority of Chileans. Furthermore, the repressive nature of the regime's implementation of its economic policy is foreign to democratically-oriented groups. Chile's economic programs are now being co-directed by followers of Milton Friedman's monetarist economic theory and the armed forces. The latter govern the country in a totally capricious manner, their actions not subject to judicial review. An excellent politico-economic analysis from the moderate left.

6524 Catholic Church. Comisión Pontificia Justitia et Pax. La Iglesia y los derechos del hombre. Santiago de Chile?: Instituto Chileno de Estudios Humanísticos, 1976. 85 p.; bibl.

Chilean publication of document produced by the Vatican Commission on Justice and Peace that gives the Church's position on the question of human rights. An important contribution in light of Carter's Latin America policy and the growth of militancy within the Latin American Church.

6525 Caviedes L., César. The politics of Chile: a sociogeographical assessment. Boulder, Colo.: Westview Press, 1979. 357 p.; bibl.; ill.; index (Westview special studies in Latin America)

A geographer applies novel, methodological tools to the study of voting and other political behavior. This quantitative and "sociogeographical" analysis constitutes a stimulating attempt to explain Chilean politics over the past two decades. The book is likely to generate important case studies of political participation in diverse ideological settings. A major contribution to the literature on Chilean politics of the past two decades. For geographer's comment, see item **5223**.

6526 Chile at the turning point: lessons of the socialist years, 1970–1973. Edited by Federico G. Gil, Ricardo Lagos E., Henry A. Landsberger; translated by John S. Gitlitz. Philadelphia: Institute for the Study of Human Issues, 1979. 480 p.; bibl.; index.

Collection of 20 papers presented at a University of North Carolina seminar on the Allende period which addresses the following issues: 1) a description of Allende's policy; 2) analysis of Unidad Popular's failure; 3) the nature of the Pinochet military government which toppled the UP; and 4) the international repercussions of the UP and the authoritarian regime that replaced it. Contributors include former representatives of the Allende government, opposition leaders, and Latin Americanists interested in the period. This volume is a major contribution.

6527 Chile, ayer, hoy. Santiago: Editora Nacional Gabriela Mistral, 1975. 102 p.; chiefly ill.

This trilingual pictoral essay, published under the military-controlled press, depicts Chile as finally having arrived at sociopolitical maturity after 50 years of political "decay" and "loss of moral principles" in democracy. Intriguing attempt at establishing international legitimacy for the present regime.

6528 Chile, una esperanza aplastada. Estella: Editorial Verbo Divino, 1975. 420 p. (Tercer mundo; 3)

A chronicle of specific acts of violence committed by the military government during the six months following the 1973 coup. Also discusses the reaction to the atrocities of some Christian and international organizations. While many of the incidents included are unverifiable, the account corroborates other testimony about this period. [Ann Hagerman-Johnson]

6529 Chonchol, Jacques. El sistema burocrático: instrumento y obstáculo en el proceso de reforma agraria chilena (C/I, 7:2/8:1, 1978, p. 55–67)

Former MAPU leader and Minister of Agriculture in the UP government criticizes agrarian policy during the UP period for its decentralization and lack of coordination, especially as regards the *tomas*—land seizures by the rural peasantry. A study of interest to those in the areas of public administration and/or implementation of socialist policies.

6530 Collins, Joseph. Agrarian reform and counter-reform in Chile (MR, 31:6, Nov. 1979, p. 28–42)

Undocumented polemic against the Chilean Junta's agrarian policy. An example of careless popular writing that should be contrasted with other more careful analyses that document similar criticisms. Interesting because of the fact that *Monthly Review* accepted the article for publication.

6531 Cox Balmaceda, Ricardo. La crisis democrática. Santiago, Chile: Editorial Andrés Bello, 1978. 389 p.

Cox treats Chile as a microcosmic example of the conflict between Anglo/Northern European and Marxist "democracy." Christian Democracy under Eduardo Frei sought to insure northern European democratic political structures, but the Tomic candidacy splintered the political consensus achieved by Frei's "center," thereby aiding its fall. The Allende victory and the actions of right-wing Church factions initiated the destruction of Chile's democratic traditions which Pinochet continues. An interesting essay.

6532 Cumplido, Francisco and **Ignacio Balmontin.** Proyectos de cambio e institucionalidad jurídico-política: Chile 1964–1973 (CPU/ES, 17:3, 1978, p. 57–95, tables)

Authors' discussion of major changes in the law during the 1964–73 period reaches the following conclusions: 1) Chile was legally constituted as a democracy; 2) this fact prevented the profound socioeconomic and political changes now being made by the military; 3) the requirements of the legal order meant that change could only be effected by a great amount of pressure and a universal consensus among pressure groups; 4) the accumulation of projects for legal and political change awaiting formal action was paralleled by an increase in the number of illegal political actions. The court system was incapable of dealing with the overload of demands, thereby contributing to the crisis in democratic institutions. This is a debatable but interesting thesis since one might argue that the court system was capable of handling the "overload" but that it was simply circumvented.

Drake, Paul W. Socialism and populism in Chile, 1932–52. See *HLAS 42:3215.*

Elgueta, Belarmino and **Alejandro Chelén R.** Breve historia de medio siglo en Chile. See *HLAS 42:3218.*

6533 Filippi, Emilio. Libertad de pensar, libertad de decir. Santiago de Chile: CISEC, 1979. 130 p. (Monografía sobre la nueva institucionalidad en Chile. Por el camino de la paz)

Passionate statement against the Military Junta's repression by a Jesuit priest who stresses the absence of freedom of speech and press in the post-1973 period.

6534 Fischer, Kathleen B. Political ideology and educational reform in Chile, 1964–1976. Los Angeles: UCLA Latin American Center, University of California, 1979. 174 p.; bibl.; index (Studies on social processes and change. UCLA Latin American studies; v. 46)

This novel study analyzes the relation between ideological change and educational policy in Chile. Author compares three periods: 1) the Frei administration (1964–70); 2) the Unidad Popular/Allende government (1970–73); and 3) the first three years of the Pinochet regime (1973–76). Author finds

that Frei's educational program, based on the French Maritain model, was aimed at social mobilization, while Allende's sought total resocialization of the nation, stressing social cohesion and thorough Marxist principles. The goal of Pinochet's "fascist" and "corporatist" administration is the dismantling of the previous two governments' policies and structures. This is a fine introduction to the subject, but it lacks a much-needed detailed treatment of concepts and ideological positions. For education specialist's comment, see item **4410.**

6535 Frei Montalvo, Eduardo. Latin America, the hopeful option. Translated by John Drury. Maryknoll, N.Y.: Orbis Books, 1978. 271 p.; bibl.

English translation of *América Latina: opción y esperanza* (1977, see *HLAS 41:7402*).

6536 Gallo Madariaga, Arturo. Nacionalismo—sentimiento o doctrina? Santiago de Chile: Gallo Madariaga, 1977. 165 p.; bibl.

Written by a former press officer under Eduardo Frei, this essay consists of a defense of pre-Allende Chilean life and an apologia for the military government's action following the 1970–73 period.

6537 Garretón Merino, Manuel Antonio. De la seguridad nacional a la nueva institucionalidad (CM/FI, 19:1, julio/sept. 1978, p. 103–127)

After announcing that the article's purpose is to examine "ideological aspects of the new authoritarian regimes," author merely discusses Chile under Pinochet. Furthermore, in the specific case of Chile, he ignores the challenge which provoked the authoritarian response and also fails to look for authoritarian precedents in Chile's own history (e.g., Portales). Concludes by attributing authoritarian ideology to "foreign socialization," US influence and the needs of the military. [A. Suárez]

6538 ——— ** and **Tomás Moulian. Análisis coyuntural y proceso político: las fases del conflicto en Chile, 1970–1973. Ciudad Universitaria Rodrigo Facio, San José, Costa Rica: Editorial Universitaria Centroamericana, 1978. 113 p. (Colección Ciencias sociales)

Garretón's discussion of Chilean political conflict during the Allende period emphasizes the vacillation of the Christian Democrats, polarization of left and right, the loss of a "center," and the further fragmentation of the Unidad Popular coalition. A short, solid analysis.

6539 —— and ——. Procesos y bloques políticos en la crisis chilena: 1970–1973 (UNAM/RMS, 41[41]:1, enero/marzo 1979, p. 150–204)

Authors suggest that the 1970 elections took place during the time of "partial" political and economic crisis. The existing capitalist system was characterized by dependency development and incapable of insuring constant growth and an equitable distribution of economic returns. The UP compromised its economic aims and thus brought on the political crisis. Highly recommended.

6540 Gilfeather, Katherine Anne. Women religious, the poor and the institutional Church in Chile (SAGE/JIAS, 21:1, Feb. 1979, p. 129–155, bibl.)

Author, a Maryknoll nun, discusses the new role of nuns and women lay workers who function in marginal areas of Chilean life. These women experience extreme poverty, great loneliness, and the historic discrimination against female leadership in the Church. The Latin American and Chilean *comunidades de base* (self-sustaining Christian communities) can provide an outlet for the tensions of female religious. However, this solution has been frustrated in part by lack of support from the male-dominated hierarchy. Women working in these communities are deprived of regularized group prayer and meditation, new techniques of deepening their spiritual life, regular spiritual direction by priests, and strengthening of their religious vows and commitments to the poor. In response to these problems, they have evolved a "new spirituality." A provocative analysis of "liberationist" theological practice with important political and socio-economic ramifications for the Chilean Church and people.

Godoy Urzúa, Hernán. El carácter chileno: estudio preliminar y selección de ensayos. See *HLAS 42:3223.*

6541 Greenfield, Michael Gerald. Creating a climate of opinion? the *Los Angeles Times* and Salvador Allende (PCCLAS/P, 5, 1976, p. 57–68)

A valuable case study of how the press molds public opinion. Author contends that the function of the *Los Angeles Times* was to generate support in southern California for the Christian Democratic opposition to Allende's candidacy. The paper opposed Allende, the UP candidates and all those to the left of Tomic (PCD candidate after the Frei Presidency, 1964–70) including centrists. An interesting example of the sort of non-governmental "destabilization" attempt which can be undertaken by the media.

6542 Gruber, Hans. Achtung des chilenischen Faschismus durch die XXXI: UNO-Vollversammlung (IIB/DA, 22:3, März 1977, p. 79–89)

East German author discusses the United Nations General Assembly of 16 Dec. 1976 which condemned the Pinochet government in Chile for its violations against human rights. [R.V. Shaw]

6543 Hellinger, Daniel. Electoral change in the Chilean countryside: the presidential elections of 1958 and 1970 (UU/WPQ, 31:2, June 1978, p. 253–274, tables)

Quantitative study compares voting patterns in the elections of 1958 and 1970. Author considers the 1970 elections a classic example of class polarization within the Chilean electorate, a conclusion that substantiates the general reaction of most political observers. Of interest to the student of political behavior and voting analysis both for the methodology utilized and the conclusion drawn.

6544 Hudson, Rexford A. The role of the constitutional conflict over nationalization in the downfall of Salvador Allende (IAMEA, 31:4, Spring 1978, p. 62–79)

Author suggests that Allende's attempt to nationalize economic enterprise in Chile ran afoul of the existing constitutional system. This conflict began the steady decline of the Unidad Popular regime. Allende's way of dealing with a recalcitrant Congress and Supreme Court, as well as the crucial Comptroller General's Office, was to demand that issues be resolved by national plebiscite rather than by constitutional means. In light of this, author maintains that Allende's "road to socialism" was illegal and unconstitutional.

6545 Huneeus, Pablo. Cambios estructurales en la mentalidad chilena (UCC/RU, 1, junio 1978, p. 75–86)

In view of the existing tension between individuals and government in Chile, author suggests that the stability of future Chilean regimes will result more from economic equity than from political and social order or constitutional norms. A stimulating, if questionable viewpoint for those interested in the Chilean system and the future of all forms of political organization.

6546 Indictment for conspiracy to murder Orlando Letelier (IRR/RC, 20:2, Autumn 1978, p. 184–189)

Publication of the original Grand Jury Brief charging Chilean government officials with conspiracy in the Letelier and Moffitt murders. Also contains a chronology of events in the alleged conspiracy.

6547 Jornadas Sobre la Nueva Institucionalidad y Nueva Democracia, *Universidad de Chile, 1978.* Jornadas Sobre la Nueva Institucionalidad y Nueva Democracia, enero de 1979. Santiago: Facultad de Derecho, Universidad de Chile, 1978. 251 p.

A collection of papers given by faculty members of the National University after its reorganization. Most of the presentations deal with the comparative advantage of "new" democratic systems over previous ones, which allowed the country to be overwhelmed by Marxism. The problems facing the country today are the remnants of Marxism and its continued attempts to return to "demagogic politics" and outdated judicial practices. The solution to these problems will be provided by a novel Chilean democracy which is "authoritarian, protective, technically competent and based on authentic social participation."

6548 Korolev, Iurii N. Chili: revoliutsiia i kontr-revoliutsiia [Chile: revolution and counter-revolution]. Moscow: Izdatel'stov 'Mezhdunarodnye otnoscheniia,' 1976. 173 p.

Soviet work on Chilean politics. While the publisher's blurb notes this is to be based on "new documentary material," there is no bibliography that would establish just what this material might be, and one has to examine the somewhat scanty footnotes to determine what sources there might be and, of course, it would take an expert's knowledge

to pick out the new items. It begins with a quotation from some French journalist named Niederang [!!] and ends with one from Brezhnev. [R.V. Allen]

6549 Kyle, Patricia and **Michael Francis.** Women at the polls: the case of Chile, 1970–1971 (CPS, 11:3, Oct. 1978, p. 291–310)

Study of female voting patterns in two elections during the first year of the Allende administration, that makes available significant data on women's voting patterns. Authors conclude that urban women tended to vote "left" more frequently than did their rural counterparts and, interestingly, that female votes for the left correlated positively with the voters higher literacy rates and standards of living. Authors note that the higher percentage of women voters in the 1971 elections is a phenomenon that remains to be analyzed. Interesting study of voting behavior.

6550 Labarca Goddard, Eduardo. Vida y lucha de Luis Corvalán. Entrevistas compiladas por Eduardo Labarca Goddard. México: Ediciones de Cultura Popular, 1976. 153 p. (Democracia y socialismo)

Collection of interviews with Corvalán, Secretary-General of the Chilean Communist Party from 1957 until his imprisonment by the Pinochet government. It includes interesting comments on Chilean poet, Pablo Neruda's political life in the Chilean CP. A flattering political biography.

6551 Labbé, Octavio and **Zbigniew Marcin Kowalweski.** La discusión sobre el proletariado en Chile (PAN/ES, 3, 1976, p. 217–230)

An exchange in the form of "correspondence" concerning change in Chilean class-consciousness which centers on the relevance of contemporary Marxist literature and on the problem of the proletariat's *aburguesamiento* (their becoming increasingly more bourgeois). Labbé attributes this change in Chilean working-class attitudes to the shift from traditional forms of industrialization to more sophisticated ones. An interesting debate between two Marxist ideologues.

6552 Lavretski, I.R. Salvador Allende: Ministro del Frente Popular (UCP/IAP, 10, 1976, p. 137–156)

Short personal and political biography

of Allende by Soviet writer provides background for Chilean political history. Of value for its biographical data and pro-Moscow ideological perspective.

6553 Leigh, Gustavo. La Junta de Gobierno frente a la juridicidad y los derechos humanos: discurso pronunciado por el general Leigh el 29 de abril de 1974 en la Universidad Católica de Chile. Santiago: Editora Nacional Gabriela Mistral, between 1974 and 1977. 29 p.; port.

Leigh's address to faculty and students of Santiago's Catholic University seeks to correct various misconceptions about Pinochet's government. Topics include the legitimacy of the military regime, the military's respect for the judiciary and the Comptroller General's office, administration of justice during the state of siege, the function of law during a period of civil war, and the general theme of human rights. Leigh blames "demagogic intellectuals," Marxists "masquerading as Christians," and "visionless" party officials for distorting public opinion about the military government.

6554 Letelier, Isabel and Michael Moffitt. Multinational banks in Chile (IRR/RC, 20:2, Autumn 1978, p. 111–128)

Authors contrast the increasing economic support given the Junta government by private banks with the declining support of international lending agencies. The US and Britain are seen as the most prolific lenders in the post-1976 period when international political pressures discontinued governmental assistance. This is a provocative piece written by the widow and widower, respectively, of the former Chilean (UP) Minister of Foreign Affairs and Ambassador to the US and his aide, both of whom were assassinated in Washington (1976) allegedly by agents of the Pinochet regime. The Carter administration is severely criticized for the post-1977 increase in private economic assistance to Chile on the part of US banks.

6555 López Fernández, Francisco. Lutte pour l'hégémonie et production de sens dans l'Eglise Catholique chilienne: 1970–1973 (FERES/SC, 26:2/3, 1979, p. 285–308)

A study derived from the author's doctoral dissertation on religious conflict among the Church hierarchy, the Christian Democratic Party, and the Christians for Socialism

(MAPU) movement. The following conclusions are drawn: 1) that the chief concern of Chile's "state ecclesiastical institution" under Cardinal Silva Henríquez is the strengthening of the world capitalist economic order; 2) that during the Allende period, the Church and the Christian Democrats acted as agents for capitalist development, to the detriment of the UP program; and 3) that this description of the role of the Church in Chile is also applicable to the rest of Latin America. The leftist MAPU received no support from the Chilean hierarchy because it did not support its above-mentioned "capitalist goals." Provocative, leftist sociological analysis of political conflict within the Chilean Church.

6556 Loveman, Brian. Chile: the legacy of Hispanic capitalism. New York: Oxford University Press, 1979. 429 p.; bibl.; index; maps (Latin American histories)

A new history of Chile written from a leftist perspective of neo-colonialism and dependency. Loveman's original and concise work treats not only Chile's geographic and ethnic background, but also the effects on the country of what he terms "Hispanic capitalism," the continued economic exploitation of Chile from the colonial period through the present. One weakness of the work is its meagre treatment of political issues—less than one-tenth of the volume is devoted to the political economy of the UP and an exceptionally short "Epilogue" describes the military government which replaced the UP. However, Loveman includes a 50-page bibliographic essay useful for anyone seeking additional materials. A good introductory history. For historian's comment, see *HLAS 42:3233.*

6557 ———. Political participation and rural labor in Chile (*in* Political participation in Latin America. Edited by John A. Booth and Mitchell A. Seligson. v. 2, Politics and the poor. New York: Holmes & Meier, 1978, p. 183–197, tables)

Study of rural labor behavior patterns in the 1932–73 period of "formal democracy" in Chile. The Christian Democrats are credited with aiding rural labor in the 1964–70 period despite "ritual appeals" to the PDC to halt worker strikes and *tomas* (illegal land seizures). The rapid increase of these activities in the 1970–73 period radicalized the landholding class and made the military coup virtually inevitable. As a result, both the politicization of rural labor and the level of governmental repression remain high. Loveman's discussion of what "political behavior" means in countries other than Chile is fascinating. This well-written analysis is important for anyone seeking to understand rural labor movements in general and post-UP Chilean workers in particular.

6558 Marcella, Gabriel. The Chilean military government and the prospects for transition to democracy (IAMEA, 33:2, Autumn 1979, p. 3–19)

Author maintains that in spite of the Junta's gestures toward more open political processes (e.g., the ouster of Gen. Gustavo Leigh from the Junta for "moral" and "patriotic" reasons), the military's sole purpose remains permanent "guardianship" of all Chilean economic and political activities through a neo-corporatist guided democracy. The 4 Jan. 1978 referendum and Pinochet's rebuke of the UN's 1977 resolution condemning human rights violations in the country support the hypothesis. Author hopes that the three stages of "recovery," "transition," and "consolidation" will be implemented by the end of the century, but doubts that the various military factions will be able to effect the necessary compromise.

6559 Mattelart, Michèle and Mabel Piccini. La televisión y los sectores populares (CYC, 2, enero 1978, p. 3–76)

Leftist assessment of the positive and negative roles of television during the Allende years, including case studies of three working-class districts in Santiago. Authors assert that the most important function of the media in general, and of television in particular, was to reorient and consolidate the UP program and to raise the consciousness of the public.

6560 Merino Medina, Antonio. Reflexiones sobre la cultura política chilena. Santiago: Universidad Católica de Chile, 1978. 42 leaves; bibl. (Cuadernos del Instituto de Ciencia Política; no. 27)

This essay offers a sophisticated and competent treatment of political culture, an important topic in contemporary Anglo-US comparative politics. Political culture requires the ability to moderate and compromise on issues and ideology, and where such abilities are lacking, the author's implication

being that this is true of contemporary Chile, political culture cannot exist and military intervention is inevitable. An important analysis of Chilean political dynamics, well documented with references to Parsons, Pye, Almond, Verba, Coleman and others.

Monteón, Michael. The *enganche* in the Chilean nitrate sector, 1880–1930. See *HLAS 42:3242.*

6561 Moulian, Tomás. Religion and authoritarianism (FERES/SC, 26:2/3, 1979, p. 331–344)

After an introduction to the topic of legitimization of authoritarian regimes through religious symbols and concepts, author explores the role of religion under the Chilean military regime. Concludes that religion in Chile performs the following functions: 1) resolution of conflict between "the public [i.e., citizens] at large" and the "private [elite] in power;" 2) production of national unity in face of factionalism and class polarization; and 3) reconstruction of a destroyed nation. Moulian believes that all these provide a license for repression in the name of a Christian world-view. Excellent philosophical analysis of political religion using the Chilean situation as focus for theoretical observations. Highly recommended.

6562 Muhlenbrock, Gisela von. La participación política: aproximación a sus motivaciones y causas. Santiago: Instituto de Ciencia Política, Universidad Católica de Chile, 1978. 28 leaves; bibl. (Cuadernos del Instituto de Ciencia Política; no. 25)

A comprehensively-researched bibliographical analysis of political participation. The author does not reflect on contemporary Chilean politics specifically except possibly in her comment that "regardless of the form of political structures, the psychological and social bases of political participation must be viewed as normal" in any political system. A well-integrated and thoughtful work, whose inter-disciplinary approach includes the field of psychology.

6563 ———. La política laboral en Chile en 1977. Santiago: Instituto de Ciencia Política, Universidad Católica de Chile, 1978. 91 leaves (Cuadernos del Instituto de Ciencia Política; no. 21)

A respected professor-researcher at Santiago's Catholic University assesses the new institutionalization of Chilean labor under the Military Junta. The year in question (1977) is characterized by the many "[demand] inputs" of labor groups. All such labor activity must be carried out within the limits of "patriotism, love of country, loyalty to those in power." In addition, all political participation by groups such as labor must be in harmony with the interests of the entire social system. The corporate/authoritarian nature of the Chilean system is clearly conveyed by the author.

6564 Muhlenbrock, Julio von. La concepción de una nueva democracia para Chile. Santiago: Instituto de Ciencia Política, Universidad Católica de Chile, 1976. 35 leaves (Cuadernos del Instituto de Ciencia Política; no. 11)

Muhlenbrock describes the 1973 coup by Pinochet as the "end of the great illusion of Marxism." He then cautiously calls for the Constitution promised by the military regime, remarking that the "capability" of the country is jeopardized with it. However, he affirms that the military has a responsibility to continue its strict supervision of political party activity until the "New Institutionality" is established.

6565 Nef, Jorge. Chile: a post-mortem (UCSD/NS, 7:1/2, 1978 [i.e. 1979] p. 271–282)

Important review essay of two books: De Vylder's *Allende's Chile* (see *HLAS 39:7511*) and Carlos Altamirano's *Dialéctica de una derrota* (see *HLAS 41:7376*), by a scholar who shares the ideology of both authors and offers an interesting analysis of the UP period as a Chilean political watershed.

6566 Neuse, Steven M. Voting in Chile: the feminine response (*in* Political participation in Latin America. Edited by John A. Booth and Mitchell A. Seligson. New York: Holmes & Meier, 1979, p. 129–144)

Study of female voting patterns in Chile (1932–73). Up until the elections of 1970, women voters exhibited traits of passivity and apathy and the tendency to follow the male vote. However, in the elections for Allende greater politicization and a higher participation rate of women were observed. Neuse concludes that women voters for Allende felt they would have a more active role in the UP regime, and therefore placed more importance on voting, a finding that is substantiated by other studies of female voting in 1970. The study contributes new views on the effective voter mobilization techniques used by both the left and right.

6567 Novoa Monreal, Eduardo. ¿Vía legal hacia el socialismo?: el caso de Chile, 1970–1973. Caracas: Editorial Jurídica Venezolana, 1978. 136 p.; bibl. (Colección Monografías políticas; no. 1)

Novoa, who served as economist and legal counsel in the Allende administration, contends that the idea of a democratic route to socialism was fundamentally flawed given the inability of the UP to develop mass support for the creation of new political and economic structures.

6568 Nunn, Frederick M. El Chile antiguo y el nuevo: la política de transición, 1973–79. Santiago: Pontificia Universidad Católica de Chile, Instituto de Ciencia Política, 1979. 48 leaves (Cuadernos del Instituto de Ciencia Política; no. 28)

Written after the author's visit to Chile in 1978, this work attempts to correct misperceptions about the Pinochet regime propagated by the world press. Nunn asserts the following: 1) there had not been a stable democratic system in Chile for at least 50 years prior to Allende's election; 2) the Chilean government has always been rife with demagoguery and as incapable as its Latin American neighbors in developing viable democratic institutions; 3) Allende did not come to power in a "normal" fashion since he received only a plurality of the votes; 4) the majority of Allende's electoral support came from lower-class individuals who did not realize the extent of his commitment to Marxism; 5) Allende's "peaceful road" to socialism was doomed from the start by the lack of national consensus evident in the 1970 elections; 6) Allende had no mandate to form a Marxist society because the majority of the 1970 vote was anti-Marxist; and 7) media control and military infiltration demonstrated the anti-democratic nature of the UP. In contrast to the Allende government, the Junta has both a "center" and a "true mass base" ("probably 60 percent of the population" supports it), and can therefore avoid the polarization of the Allende period. Author praises the Junta's economic policies, noting that Chile's "GNP is second only to Paraguay's real growth."

What unemployment and economic hardship do exist presently are only the result of the Junta's elimination of wasteful practices. Chile is now on the way to "full recovery" and a higher level of economic health and political freedom than ever before. This has been achieved in spite of the following obstacles: 1) US intervention in the death of Orlando Letelier in Washington in 1976; 2) world press denunciation of the Jan. 1978 plebiscite that indicated 75 percent for the Junta; 3) the external campaign of international communism; 4) UP's legacy of rampant inflation; and 5) the Carter administration's intervention in Chilean affairs, under the guise of human rights advocacy. This novel treatment of the military's response to 20th-century Chile and the Allende period in particular is an important contribution to the current debate on Chile. It should be read by all Chileanists.

———. Latin American militarylore: an introduction and a case study. See item **6065.**

6569 Oppenheimer, Robert. Chile. Los Angeles: Latin American Studies Center, California State University, 1977? 91 p., 1 leaf of plates; ill. (Latin America bibliography series; 6)
    This comprehensive bibliography includes the most important works dealing with Chilean national history. The volume is divided among general works, those dealing with the period from independence through 1920, and those covering the 50 years up to Allende's election in 1970. The entire last half of the bibliography covers the period of the Unidad Popular and Pinochet regimes. An outstanding contribution.

6570 Orrego Vicuña, Claudio. Tres ensayos acerca del futuro. Santiago: Ediciones Aconcagua, 1978. 147 p. (Colección Lautaro)
    Collection of three philosophical essays written within the framework of Pope Paul VI's "social doctrine of the Church." Includes a favorable view of the Frei faction of Christian Democracy. The writer, who appears to have undergone a philosophical/theological conversion (compared with *HLAS 39:7483*), now favors Church action within the ideological bounds established by the Medellín Conference of Latin American Bishops, Brazil's Dom Helder Cámara, and the UN.

6571 Palacios, Jorge. Chile: an attempt at "historic compromise:" the real story of the Allende years. Chicago: Banner Press, 1979. 519 p.; bibl.; index.
    Palacio, former Chairman of the Dept. of Philosophy at the National University of Chile and founder of the Revolutionary Communist Party of Chile, discusses the limits the Allende government imposed on itself by taking the "peaceful road to socialism." He blames Allende for succumbing to US-USSR rivalry over "the global offensive of imperialism" in his compromise with the right-wing faction of the Christian Democratic Party. Author also deals at length with attempts by the US State Department and CIA to "destabilize" the Allende government. An angry, intensely radical statement from a man now living in exile in France and originally published in Spanish as *Chile: un ensayo de compromiso histórico* (Barcelona: Editorial 7 1/2, 1978, 272 p.).

6572 Petras, James F. and **Morris Morley.** The United States and Chile: imperialism and the overthrow of the Allende government. New York: Month Review Press, 1975. 217 p.; bibl.
    One of the more sophisticated attempts at a Marxist analysis of the role of the US in the overthrow of the Allende government. Includes complete documentation from US Senate Committee hearings on US actions against Allende. The volume treats US-Chilean relations during the Frei administration, the attempt of the US to prevent Allende's election, Washington policy toward Chile within the context of US policy toward Brazil and Peru, and its support of the Pinochet government in the aftermath of the Sept. 1973 coup. The volume is of importance for all interested in the Chilean system and especially the Allende period.

6573 Pizarro C., Cristóstomo. Rol de los sindicatos en Chile. Santiago de Chile: Corporación de Investigaciones Económicas para Latinoamérica, 1978. 41 p.; bibl. (Estudios CIEPLAN; 22)
    Short monograph focusing on the evolution of the Chilean labor movement and its prospects for reorganization once democracy is reestablished in Chile.

6574 Pollack, Benny and **Hernan Rosenkranz.** Una ideología latinoamericanista: apuntes sobre el Partido Socialista chileno (NSO, 37, julio/agosto 1978, p. 95–108)

Authors assess the Chilean Socialist Party's performance immediately before and during the Allende period. Especially significant are their remarks on the party's behavior within the context of Sino-Soviet conflict, its "radicalization" along Cuban lines, and the ensuing fragmentation that contributes to the weakness of the UP and the intervention of the armed forces. Interesting apologia by two sophisticated thinkers of the Marxist left.

6575 Prensa y lucha ideológica en los cordones industriales de Santiago: testimonios (CYC, 2, jan. 1978, p. 77–108)

Interviews with workers employed in industrial cordons during the last year of the UP. Sheds light on the political perceptions of workers employed in industries that were nationalized as "social property" during the last months of the Allende regime.

Puente, Mario. Chile, enseñanzas y balance de un proceso revolucionario. See *HLAS 42:3255.*

6576 Quijada Cerda, Aníbal. Cerco de púas. La Habana: Casa de las Américas, 1977. 170 p.

Written in form of a novella and published in Cuba, this small volume describes the author's three months in a Junta concentration camp. Quijada was a long-term career bureaucrat in the Chilean Society Security Administration and also served as a functionary in the Chilean Communist Party. A first-hand account (possibly overly dramatized) of repressive Junta policy in the months after Allende's overthrow.

6577 Reiman Weigert, Elisabeth and **Fernando Rivas Sánchez.** Chile, antecedentes para un análisis. La Habana: Editorial de Ciencias Sociales, 1977. 453 p.; ill. (Ediciones políticas)

Both authors, a former Marxist editor of *Puro Chile* and a columnist for *Clarín*, blame Allende's fall on the Christian Democrats, the Roman Catholic Church (particularly Santiago's Cardinal Archbishop Raúl Silva Henríquez), and Chile's armed forces. Now in exile after a long association with Chilean media, the authors have written a long, angry tirade against the enemies of the Allende administration.

6578 Rodríguez, Pedro Jesús. Limitaciones al poder constituyente de la junta de gobierno (CPU/ES, 15:1, 1978, p. 25–36)

Former professor of Civil Law at Santiago's Catholic University examines the Constitutional Acts that form the basis of the Pinochet government in light of the precedents established by the 1925 Constitution and concludes that they grant the government excessive power. Articulate and dispassionate criticism of the Junta.

Román, Charles G. Pregger. Economic interest groups within the Chilean government, 1851 to 1891: continuity and discontinuity in economic and political evolution. See *HLAS 42:3261.*

Shazo, Peter de. The Valparaíso maritime strike of 1930 and the development of a revolutionary labor movement in Chile. See *HLAS 42:3266.*

6579 Silva Bascuñán, Alejandro. La experiencia chilena sobre referendum y su valoración. Santiago: Instituto de Ciencia Política, Universidad Católica de Chile, 1977. 29 leaves (Cuadernos del Instituto de Ciencia Política; no. 19)

A discussion of the law governing the approval of new constitutional documents. This is a good reference work written with the Pinochet regime's promised Fundamental Charter in mind.

6580 Simposium Internacional sobre Derechos Humanos, *Santiago de Chile, 1978.* Simposium internacional: experiencia y compromiso compartidos. Santiago de Chile: Arzobispado de Santiago, Vicaría de la Solidaridad, 1979. 181 p.; ill.

The proceedings of a symposium on human rights organized by Chilean Cardinal Archbishop Raúl Silva Henríquez to celebrate the UN's Year of Human Rights (1978). The volume, published by the Archdiocese of Santiago, consists of a photographic essay and statements by participants from Europe, North America, and other Latin American countries, among them Brazilian Cardinal Paulo Arns and the Argentinian theologian Dr. José Míguez Bonino. Included are a "Latin American Declaration" and the "Letter from Santiago de Chile," both condemning the violation of human rights throughout the world and specifically in Chile under the Pinochet government. A bold and significant statement by the Chilean hierarchy.

6581 La Sinistra cilena di fronte alla crisi: marzo-settembre 1973. A cura di Vincenzo Sparagna. Palermo; Roma: Praxis, 1974. 221 p. (Documenti)

Italian Communist's analysis of the role of the US in the overthrow of Allende, placing particular emphasis on the period March–Sept. 1973. Criticizes the Christian Democrats and factionalism within the UP as well as the Chilean military. Of particular interest is author's discussion of UP's influence on European Communist organizations and his intention that the Chilean experience, critical for the rest of Latin America and the Third World, is as relevant for the parties of Western Europe.

6582 Smirnow, Gabriel. The revolution disarmed, Chile, 1970–1973. New York: Monthly Review Press, 1979. 170 p.; bibl.

Smirnow, one of the founders of the Movement of the Revolutionary Left (MIR) and the Secretary of Quimantú (the Allende regime's official publishing house), argues that the failure of the UP was due to "imperialist" influences, the CIA, multinational corporations (mainly US), and internal "deviationism." Smirnow left the MIR to join the Socialist Party of Allende in 1970, and his analysis provides a classic example of Socialist Party criticism of the 1970–73 period. Originally published in Spanish as *Revolución desarmada: Chile, 1970–1973*.

6583 Solar, Edmundo del. Orlando Letelier: biographical notes and comments. Translated into English from Spanish by Caridad Inda and María del Solar. New York: Vantage Press, 1978. 90 p.

A selection of reminiscences by Orlando Letelier's uncle of the period before and after the assassination of one of Allende's last Cabinet appointees.

6584 Spence, Jack. Search for justice: neighborhood courts in Allende's Chile. Boulder, Colo.: Westview Press, 1979. 206 p.; bibl. (A Westview replica edition)

Comparative legal study of UP's experimentation with neighborhood courts and "Audiencias Populares" in the context of Allende period politics. The work's major contribution is the distinction it draws between the two "decentralized" juridical experiments. An intriguing study but its analysis of the political/partisan environment is not as strong as one might wish.

Super, Richard R. The Seguro Obrero massacre. See *HLAS 42:3271.*

6585 Tagle Martínez, Hugo. Visión de la doctrina económica de la Iglesia Católica. Santiago, Chile: Instituto de Estudios Generales, 1978. 76 p.; bibl.

Interesting essay on the economic doctrine of the Church by Chilean spokesman for the right. Author attempts to fuse Milton Friedman's economic policy as applied to Chile at Pinochet's invitation with the official position of the Vatican on economic matters. A valuable philosophical/theological reflection on economic systems.

6586 Teitelboim, Volodia. La lucha continúa: pólvora del exilio. Cuidó la ed., Electa Haro. México: Ediciones de Cultura Popular, 1976. 137 p.

Consists of collected essays by former Chilean Communist Party leader and member of the Central Committee of the Chilean party, written in Moscow where the author resided when the Sept. 1973 coup occurred. These short pieces cover the period from mid-Sept. 1973 through the end of 1974 and contain interesting observations from one of the major critics of the most extreme-left factions in Allende's coalition.

6587 Todo hombre tiene derecho a ser persona: concursos, afiches-literario-pintura infantil. Santiago de Chile: Arzobispado de Santiago, Vicaría de la Solidaridad, 1978. 172 p.; col. ill.

This volume, published by the Archdiocese of Santiago, was generated by the Chilean Conference on Human Rights summoned by Cardinal Archbishop Raúl Silva Henríquez. It includes case studies, art work, posters, poetry and a strong statement decrying the violation of human rights. Interesting exception to the censorship that has been imposed on the Chilean publishing industry.

6588 Urzúa Valenzuela, Germán. Diccionario político institucional de Chile. Santiago: Editorial Ariete, 1979. 242 p. (Colección Ensayos; no. 1)

A dictionary of Chilean politics, presumably acceptable to the present government. Focuses on institutions, ideology, and politics under the Pinochet regime. Its treatment of political parties is notable for its emphasis on their "historical legacy." A fairly inocuous but characteristic product of the time.

6589 Valenzuela, Arturo. The breakdown of democratic regimes, Chile. Baltimore: Johns Hopkins University Press, 1978. 140 p.; bibl.; ill.; index.

This small volume is extracted from the larger work by Linz and Stepan *The breakdown of democratic regimes* (see *HLAS 42:1920*). This study of Valenzuela's is one of the most important works on Chilean politics produced during the 1970s. Contains an examination of factors leading to the "political crisis" of the Frei administration, an excellent socioeconomic analysis of the Allende coalition that led to political polarization and loss of a moderating "center," as well as a study of the nature of the Chilean military throughout the 20th century, particularly in the period immediately preceding the coup against Allende. This thorough, balanced, and well written study of Chile's "institutional breakdown" is highly recommended.

6590 Varas, Florencia and Claudio Orrego. El caso Letelier. Santiago de Chile: Ediciones Aconcagua, 1979. 160 p.; ill. (Colección Lautaro)

Investigation by Chilean reporters into the 1976 assassination of Orlando Letelier and Ronni Moffitt in Washington. Includes interviews and research conducted by the authors. They conclude that a CIA agent with no Chilean government connections was responsible for the murders.

6591 Villela G., Hugo. Autoritarianismo y tenencia de la tierra: Chile, 1973–1976 (UNAM/RMS, 41[41]:1, enero/marzo 1979, p. 205–241, tables)

Study describes changes in land tenure patterns from the time of the 1973 coup through 1976. Author attributes the 1975–76 fall in agrarian production to: a) the concentration of land ownership that occurred in 1973–76 when the Junta repossessed lands obtained in *tomas* (land seizures that occurred during the Christian Democratic and UP periods); and b) to the new capitalist farmers who were given the lands taken by peasants in the 1964–73 period. Also studies the Junta's new rules for the redistribution of land that represent an attempt to "re-order" the agrarian sector of the economy. Finally, the author places this re-ordering of the agrarian sector through land tenure policy in the context of the military's general national security concerns.

6592 ———. The Church and the process of democratization in Latin America (FERES/SC, 26:2/3, 1979, p. 261–284)

Author uses the Chilean example to illustrate the relationship between the Church and the democratization process. He makes the following observations: 1) authoritarian politics challenge the Latin American Church hierarchy to abandon its traditional role as an arm of the state (e.g., the Chilean Church no longer serves as the "legitimizer of domination"); 2) the "Social Christian" movement is increasingly aware of its role as "center of cohesion for civil society" and protector of societal pluralism and now recognizes the "reality and legitimacy of social conflict"; and 3) the social-Christian "utopia" is a society based on the achievement of "justice in liberty." Author observes that the Church in Chile, as in many other Latin American countries, is attempting to instill spiritual values in the capitalist order and is thereby strengthening its position in society. A controversial, important contribution to the literature on the subject.

6593 Vives Solar, Fernando. El humanismo de Fernando Vives. Francisco Javier Cid, editor. Santiago de Chile: Instituto Chileno de Estudios Humanísticos, 1976. 132 p.

This small volume studies the 1930s writing of the Christian humanist Vives, showing that he anticipated many of the Church's current social doctrines and their implications for Chilean society. Interesting example of the long heritage of ideological ferment within the Chilean hierarchy.

6594 Vuskovic Bravo, Pedro. Una sola lucha: el desafío político de Chile. México: Editorial Nuestro Tiempo, 1978. 264 p.; bibl. (Colección Latinoamérica ayer y hoy)

Former Socialist Party leader Vuskovic, who serves as Allende's Economics Minister and advisor during the entire UP period, mounts a massive attack on the Chilean military as well as on the problem of factionalism within the UP. This collection of essays was published after author's 1973 exile to Mexico.

6595 Witker Velásquez, Alejandro. El compañero Tohá: esbozo biográfico, testimonios, documentos. México: Casa de Chile en México, 1977. 124 p.

Writer describes the role of José Tohá

in the UP government as Interior Minister and, later, Minister of Defense (until July 1973). Tohá died "a suicide" in a Chilean concentration camp after seven months imprisonment. Funeral mass was celebrated by Cardinal Archbishop Silva Henríquez.

Yeager, Gertrude Matyoka. The Club de la Unión and kinship: social aspects of political obstructionism in the Chilean Senate, 1920–1924. See *HLAS 42:3281.*

6596 Zapata, Francisco. Las relaciones entre la Junta Militar y los trabajadores chilenos: 1973–1978 (CM/FI, 20:2, oct./dic. 1979, p. 191–219, bibl., tables)
    Article treats the generally deteriorating conditions suffered by Chilean workers under the Junta: repression, inflation combined with falling wages, a decline in overall industrial production since the coup, and the unemployment resulting from all of these. Author blames Chile's underproductivity and worker malaise on the Junta's Institutional Acts but is optimistic about the effectiveness of boycott techniques and deliberate work slow-downs developed in the final months of 1978 even if he doubts that the labor organization is possible under the current regime.

6597 Zemelman, Hugo. Los regímenes militares en América Latina: ¿problema coyuntural? notas para una discusión sobre la hegemonía burguesa (UNAM/RMS, 40[40]: 3, julio/sept. 1978, p. 831–850)
    Are military regimes an expression of the political history of Latin America or part of the symptoms of the breakdown of capitalism? Marxist analysis places emphasis on the latter revealing a continuation of class dominance despite civil-military alterations. Chile is used as a case study. [D.W. Dent]

Argentina, Paraguay and Uruguay

GARY W. WYNIA, *Professor of Political Science, University of Minnesota*

THIS HAS NOT BEEN A TIME CONDUCIVE TO POLITICAL research in the River Plate region. Many scholars have been forced to leave their countries and no longer enjoy the time or resources necessary for investigation. Moreover, those who remain have been discouraged by censorship and a publishing industry suffering from financial troubles. Foreign scholars, though more productive in terms of volume, have not entirely made up for this loss. The reduced demand for Latin America specialists in the academic marketplace, as well as restricted access to officials and public records in authoritarian regimes has meant fewer doctoral dissertations and less field research than in the late 1960s and early 1970s.

As in the past, Paraguay received the least attention during the biennium. However, at long last we do have a survey of the country's politics, written by Paul Lewis (item **6644**). This fundamental study of political control facilitates an understanding of the Stroessner regime and its longevity.

Uruguay continues to be studied by only a few scholars. Among these Finch (item **6648**), Biles (item **6647**), and Lerin (item **6651**) have added to our understanding of the collapse of democratic rule in the early 1970s, and Debray has written a lengthy case study of the guerrilla strategy employed by the Tupamaros (item **6030**). In addition, there are a few works (items **6652** and **6655**) that express the views of the combatants in the country's internal war.

As in the past, Argentina has been the object of much study, though even in this case, the volume has decreased. Leading the list are works aimed at explaining the rise of the military authoritarian regime in the 1960s and 1970s. O'Donnell's essay (item **6620**) links political alliances to economic cycles; Kvaternik (item **6606**) offers a constructive critique of the "impossible game" concept previously used by O'Donnell, suggesting that party fragmentation is largely responsible for persistent government instability during the past three decades. Of more narrow scope is an article by Landi (item **6607**) that examines the resurgence of the populist coalition in 1973, and a book by de Pablo (item **6623**) presenting a very useful analysis of the economic policies employed by Peronists in the mid-1970s.

The labor movement continues to attract inquiry. Montuschi de Glew (item **6614**) examines union power between 1950 and 1964; Cavarozzi (item **6601**) has written a detailed study of government-union relations in the late 1950s, and Senan González (item **6632**) looks at union behavior under the recent Peronist administration. There have also been some interesting exercises in quantitative analysis: Wellhoffer (item **6638**) examines the bases of Socialist party support and the Peronist vote, and Schoultz (item **8331**) uses survey data to determine the sources of anti-Americanism among Argentines. Last but not least is Potash's excellent history of military politics during the 1945–62 period (item **6625**), which can be added to his previously published work on the 1930s and early 1940s.

Conspicuously absent from recently published works are serious studies of the military authoritarian regime and its politics, either as a general phenomenon or in its specific manifestation. Clearly, the secretive and elitist nature of military regimes does not lend itself to academic research but far more work is needed on the characteristics of these institutions in Argentina and Uruguay if we are to understand how military regimes operate as well as how they go about reconstructing political processes.

ARGENTINA

6598 Aguado, Jorge R. Cuatro años de acción gremial. Buenos Aires: CARBAP, 1977. 378 p.

This is a documentary history of the positions taken by one of Argentina's most influential farmer and cattlemen's associations during the mid-1970s. These speeches and position papers offer insights into the association's defense of its interests against the Peronist regime.

Alvarado, Ricardo. L'évolution historique du syndicalisme argentin entre 1955 et 1973. See *HLAS 42:3287.*

6599 Arias Pelerano, Francisco. Argentina, los grandes desafíos. Buenos Aires: Editorial F.E.P.A., 1979. 180 p. (Colección los desafíos argentinos)

An essay by the Director of Political Science at the Catholic University of Buenos Aires, this work examines the failure of the Argentine constitutional system. He emphasizes the failure to create legitimate leadership capable of offering logical justifications for its rule. More of an exercise in political theory than analysis.

6600 Botana, Natalio; Mario Fernández; and Carlos Huneeus. Los caminos a la de-

mocracia: los casos de Argentina, España, Grecia y Portugal. Introducción de Claudio Orrego Vicuña. Santiago: Ediciones Aconcagua, 1978. 198 p.; bibl. (Colección Lautaro)

A very brief case study (20 p.) in a volume of cases dealing with the problem of political order and legitimate authority. It consists of a broad review of the past 30 years and the repeated legitimacy crises. Unfortunately, the editor makes no effort to compare the Argentine experience with those of Spain, Greece, and Portugal.

Briones, Alvaro. Ideología del fascismo dependiente: estado y seguridad nacional. See item **6521**.

6601 Cavarozzi, Marcelo. Sindicatos y políticas en Argentina, 1955–1958. Buenos Aires, Argentina: Centro de Estudios de Estado y Sociedad, 1979. 87 p. (Estudios CEDES; v. 2, no. 1)

This study of labor-government relations during the period of reconstruction that followed the overthrow of Perón in 1955 argues that the nation's political process was substantially changed during these years. It is a thoughtful and detailed analysis of how labor and government struggled to define the country's new political rules at this critical time. It is another of the excellent studies sponsored by the Centro de Estudios de Estado y Sociedad.

Controversia: Para el Exámen de la Realidad Argentina. See *HLAS 42:210.*

D'Amico, David F. Religious liberty in Argentina during the first Perón regime, 1943–1955. See *HLAS 42:3326.*

Domínguez, Nelson. Conversaciones con Juan José Taccone sobre sindicalismo y política. See *HLAS 42:3334.*

Doyon, Louise M. Conflictos obreros durante el régimen peronista: 1946? See *HLAS 42: 3335.*

6602 Estep, Raymond. The Argentine Armed Forces and Government. Maxwell Air Force Base, Ala.: Documentary Research Division, Aerospace Studies Institute, 1970. 116 p.; bibl.; col. map (Air University documentary research study AU—207—69—ASI)

This old (published 1970) Air University survey of Argentine political history since 1930 is quite conventional but does offer useful information on military behavior and education.

Falcoff, Mark. Was war der Peronismus von 1946 bis 1955? See *HLAS 42:3342.*

6603 Fennell, Lee C. Leadership and the failure of democracy (*in* The Continuing struggle for democracy in Latin America [see item **6028**] p. 201–214)

The article is part of a volume devoted to explanations of the performance of democratic government in Latin America. Citing evidence from the case of two-time Argentine President Hipólito Irigoyen during the 1920s along with other cases, author argues that leader attitudes toward political opposition frequently undermine democratic authority. Specifically, narrow partisanship is seen as the culprit.

6604 Futuro político de la Argentina. V.R. Beltrán, comp.; N. Botana et al. Buenos Aires, Argentina: Editorial del Instituto, Instituto Torcuato Di Tella, 1978. 227 p. (Serie Verde: Jornadas)

This volume published by the Di Tella Institute is composed of articles and commentaries by some of the country's leading historians, sociologists and political analysts. The topics treated—political culture, foreign affairs, the party system, and future institutions—are important but the work is disappointing due to the general and speculative character of the articles.

6605 Ghioldi, Rodolfo. Escritos. Selección realizada por M. Moscovici. Buenos Aires: Editorial Anteo, 1975–1977. 4 v.; bibl.

In this four volume collection of the writings of Argentine Communist Party leader Rodolfo Ghioldi the reader is given a tour of the past 50 years of Argentine political history by a Marxist-Leninist guide. It will be useful for students of the country's politics as well as those with narrow interests in communist movements in the region.

Guy, Donna J. Argentine sugar politics: Tucumán and the generation of eighty. See *HLAS 42:3360.*

Heaps-Nelson, George. Emilio Civit and the politics of Mendoza. See *HLAS 42:3363.*

Jordan, David C. Argentina's military commonwealth. See item **7402**.

6606 Kvaternik, Eugenio. Sobre partidos y democracia en la Argentina entre 1955 y 1966 (IDES/DE, 18:71, oct./dic. 1978, p. 409–431, table)

Skillfully presented critique of Guillermo O'Donnell's thesis about the "impossible game" that characterized Argentine politics before 1966. Author offers an alternative explanation of the fragmentation of Argentine parties which generated electoral coalitions unable to execute policies acceptable to coalition members after they had taken office. A stimulating piece of work.

6607 Landi, Oscar. Argentina, 1973–76: la génesis de una nueva crisis política (UNAM/RMS, 41[41]:1, enero/marzo 1979, p. 89–127)

This penetrating analysis of the resurgence of a populist coalition in the 1973 election and its performance thereafter suggests that the ill-conceived political strategies of anti-Peronists facilitated the Peronist's victory. However, contradictions within the latter's economic program divided and undermined its own coalition and government.

———. La tercera presidencia de Perón: gobierno de emergencia y crisis política. See *HLAS 42:3372.*

6608 Leonard, Virginia W. Education and the Church-state clash in Argentina: 1954–1955 (ACHA/CHR, 46:1, Jan. 1980, p. 34–52)

This historical study of Church-state relations under Perón's first government argues that Peron's "totalitarian" intentions rather than political opportunism led to his attack on the Church in the early 1950s. This controversial thesis places undue emphasis on Perón's vague philosophy as the source of his actions.

Little, Cynthia Jeffress. Education, philanthropy, and feminism: components of Argentine womanhood, 1860–1926. See *HLAS* 42:3377.

6609 Little, Walter. La organización obrera y el estado peronista: 1943–1955 (IDES/DE, 19:75, oct./dec. 1979, p. 331–376, tables)

The author provides a detailed study of the capture of organized labor by Juan Perón and identifies the effort's three distinct phases: 1) capture (1943–46); 2) expansion and consolidation (1946–51); and 3) monolithic control (1951–55). Though the study offers few new insights, it provides useful details on the General Labor Confederation and its internal politics.

6610 Más allá de Videla (Carta Política [Persona e Persona, Buenos Aires] 76, abril 1980, p. 30–39, ill., plate)

Given the paucity of studies of the Videla administration (1976–81), this is a welcome summary of its political program, the transition to a new president, and its problems in building a new political consensus. Offers interesting speculation about the future.

6611 Mason Lugones, Raúl. Argentina: el actual plan económico compromete el futuro del país, en particular la seguridad nacional (IAEERI/E, 61/62, nov. 1979/feb. 1980, p. 64–75)

Reviewing the performance of the Videla government, a retired naval officer resurrects the argument that, like so many of its predecessors, the current government is perpetuating the nation's development problems by favoring the Buenos Aires area over the rest of the country.

6612 Massera, Emilio E. El camino a la democracia. Caracas: El Cid Editor;

Buenos Aires: distribución en Argentina, Librería del Colegio, 1979. 151 p.

The most interesting aspect of this book is the author: a member of the junta that governed Argentina between (1976–78). Primarily a collection of speeches, it offers a view of the modes of self-justification employed by junta members in their formal dialogues with fellow officers and members of business and agriculture associations.

6613 Milenky, Edward S. Arms production and national security in Argentina (SAGE/JIAS, 22:3, Aug. 1980, p. 267–288, bibl., table)

A brief survey of the development of the Argentine arms industry and its strategic justifications. It concentrates on describing weapons production rather than supplying data on the volume and its relative size within the Argentine arsenal.

6614 Montuschi de Glew, Luisa. El poder económico de los sindicatos. Buenos Aires: Editorial Universitaria de Buenos Aires, 1979. 224 p.

Author seeks to study union power theoretically, historically and empirically during the 1950–65 period. The study moves beyond familiar assertions about union power and analyzes determinants of wage rates using available data and regression techniques. Good example of data analysis possibilities in the area of Argentine labor relations.

6615 Moreno, Oscar. Acerca del peronismo (NSO, 36, mayo/junio 1978, p. 105–116)

Author gives an analysis of the peronism since the mid-1960s with most space devoted to its tactics under the Onganía regime (1966–70). It emphasizes conflicts and contradictions within the movement.

6616 Most, Benjamin A. Authoritarianism and the growth of the state in Latin America: an assessment of their impacts on Argentine public policy, 1930–1970 (CPS, 13:2, July 1980, p. 173–203, bibl., table)

In this empirical study of the relationship between the emergence of ruling coalitions and public policy change, the author seeks to disaggregate the linkages found in structuralist analyses of O'Donnell et al. He argues that the relationship is conditioned by the presence of four constraints: 1) unionized public sector; 2) cabinet instability; 3) resource limitations; and 4) authority crises. Quantitative indicators are examined and the degree of policy change estimated to test constraint hypotheses. A creative approach whose findings seldom disconfirm general knowledge.

6617 Muñoz Grande, Juan Ramón. Argentina: objetivo orgánico del ejército para el largo plazo (IAEERI/E, 60, sept./oct. 1979, p. 37–43)

This brief statement of the goals of Argentine military during the 1970s, written by one of its supporters, exemplifies the logic used by the armed forces to justify its dominant role in the nation's politics.

6618 Naipaul, V.S. Argentine terror: a memoir (The New York Review of Books [New York] 26:15, 11 Oct. 1979, p. 13–16, ill.)

A fascinating, grim interpretation of Argentine terror by the celebrated Trinidadian novelist who notes that "torture is not new in Argentina" and quotes from the right and the left to the effect that "there is good torture and bad torture." Fundamentally, Naipaul implies, the tragedy of Argentina, is the deep-seated conviction among both right and left that the solution to political problems of the country can only be achieved by "killing the right people" (by terror on the left, by murder on the right). The conviction is, in turn, the result of a general assumption that the country's political problems are always due to outside forces (the imperialists and capitalists for the left; the communist conspiracy for the right) and that the fault never lies with the Argentines themselves and their abysmal incapacity to govern. [Ed.]

6619 Nota de tapa: los puntos sobre las íes (Carta Política [Personal e Persona, Buenos Aires] 61, dic. 1978, p. 32–37)

An informative point-by-point description of the political objectives of the Argentine military government launched in 1976. Authors raise provocative questions about contradictions inherent in the military's political strategy.

Odena, Isidro J. Libertadores y desarrollistas, 1955–1962. See *HLAS 42:3395.*

6620 O'Donnell, Guillermo A. Estado y alianzas en la Argentina, 1956–1976. Buenos Aires: Centro de Estudios de Estado y Sociedad, 1976. 40 p., 7 leaves of plates; bibl.; graphs (Documento CEDES/G.E. CLASCO; no. 5)

Another of the very creative and systematic analyses of Argentine politics written by O'Donnell. In it he identifies sectoral and class interests and links them to cycles of economic performance in order to demonstrate how insecure and shifting political alliances have repeatedly weakened the Argentine state. It should be read carefully by students of Argentine politics. An English translation of this monograph appeared as an article: "State and Alliances in Argentina: 1956–1976" in *Journal of Development Studies* (15:1, Oct. 1978, p. 3–33)

6621 ———. Notas para el estudio de procesos de democratización política a partir del estado burocrático-autoritario: documento de trabajo (Estudios CEDES [Centro de Estudios de Estado y Sociedad, Buenos Aires] 2:5, 1979, p. 3–27)

A few reflections by the author on the transition from a bureaucratic authoritarian regime to a democratic one. It focuses on the political process, emphasizing the role of a moderate opposition and some of the conditions for a successful transition. The vagueness of the article reflects the difficulty of conceptualizing a political process which is not as easily conveyed by structural analysis as is the rise of a bureaucratic authoritarian regime.

6622 ———. Permanent crisis and the failure to create a democratic regime: Argentina, 1955–1966 (*in* The Breakdown of democratic regimes: Latin America [see *HLAS 42:1920*] p. 138–177, ill.)

This is a reprint of a chapter in O'Donnells' 1973 book: *Modernization and bureaucratic authoritarianism in South American politics* (see *HLAS 37:4740*). It deals with economic and political conflict leading to the 1966 coup.

6623 Pablo, Juan Carlos de. Economía política del peronismo. Buenos Aires: El Cid Editor, 1980. 1 v.

A well written and organized description of the economic policies followed by the peronist government between 1973 and 1976. Author, a well known Argentine economist, sifts through this confusing period and finds the essential features of government policy by looking at the objectives of each Economics Minister, the methods he used, and the consequences of his effort. An essential work for anyone seeking to understand this episode in Argentine public life.

Pavón Pereyra, Enrique. Conversaciones con Juan Domingo Perón. See *HLAS 42:3399.*

6624 Políticos y militares: la di-con-vergencia (Carta Política [Persona e Persona, Buenos Aires] 74, feb. 1980, p. 26–33)

A general historical overview that traces civil-military relations since 1890. It offers insight into the variety of coalitions that have characterized this relationship as well as their impact on the political process.

6625 Potash, Robert A. The army & politics in Argentina. v. 2, 1928–1945, Yrigoyen to Peron. Stanford, Calif.: Stanford University Press, 1980? 1 v.; bibl.; facsim.; plan; ports.

This book is author's long awaited sequel to his study of the Argentine military during the 1930s (see *HLAS 32:2599a* and *HLAS 34:2783*). It is a narrative history of high quality, prodigiously researched and filled with details gleaned from interviews with military officers as well as personal diaries, newspapers and public documents. It offers insights into personal relations within the military and between military and political leaders under the peronist regime (1946–53) and the two administrations that succeeded it (1955–62).

Prieto, Ramón. Treinta años de vida argentina, 1945–1975. See *HLAS 42:3407.*

6626 Ranis, Peter. Early peronism and the post-liberal Argentine state (SAGE/JIAS, 21:3, Aug. 1979, p. 313–338, bibl.)

Author discusses the rise of Juan Perón in the early 1940s by examining his political writings and reactions to the political setting of the period. Article provides more detail than insight into Perón's behavior.

6627 La Represión en Argentina, 1973–1974: documentos. México: Universidad Nacional Autónoma de México, 1978. 227 (Serie Estudios—Facultad de Ciencias Políticas y Sociales; 55)

Sponsored by LASA (Latin American Studies Association), this study was researched and written by anonymous Argentine social scientists. It systematically describes repression under the peronist regime

in 1973–74 and emphasizes the fate of the political left, Peronist Youth, labor dissidents, and university students. It should be read by anyone studying this period.

6628 Riquet, Michel. L'Argentine entre la dictature militaire et l'Eglise (NRDM, 9, sept. 1978, p. 526–537)

A brief essay by a French Jesuit who examines the Argentine military regime in light of current theological debates among Latin American clergy.

6629 Rock, David. Repression and revolt in Argentina (UCSD/NS, 7:1/2, 1978 [i.e. 1979] p. 105–120)

An informative and well organized essay that describes the Argentine guerrilla movements and their strategies during the 1970s and how political authorities dealt with them. Though brief, this is a useful summary.

Rodríguez, Celso. Lencinas y Cantoni: el populismo cuyano en tiempos de Yrigoyen. See *HLAS 42:3415.*

6630 Rouquié, Alain. L'Argentine du Général Videla: deux ans de réorganisation national, 1976–1978 (FDD/NED [Problèmes d'Amérique Latine, 50] 4499/4500, 29 déc. 1978, p. 10–43)

The author presents a review of politics in Argentina (1976–78) concentrating on guerrilla movements and strategies, the organization of the military regime, and its economic policies.

6631 ———. Les éternels retours à la légalité constitutionnelle (FDD/NED [Problèmes d'Amérique Latine, 54] 4545/4546, 18 déc. 1978, p. 110–129)

Straightforward reportage on military-civilian relations in Argentina during the 1970s that describes the policies of the Videla regime.

Schoultz, Lars. The nature of anti-U.S. sentiment in Latin America: a preliminary analysis with Argentine data. See item **7410.**

6632 Senén González, Santiago. El poder sindical. Buenos Aires: Plus Ultra, 1978. 138 p.; bibl. (Colección Esquemas políticas; 6)

An interesting history of union politics under the peronist regime (1973–76). Though lacking in analysis and interpretation, it provides much needed information about conflicts between the General Confederation of Labor and the government, after Perón's death.

6633 Smith, Peter H. Argentina: the uncertain warriors (CUH, 78:454, Feb. 1980, p. 62–65, 85–86)

Excellent summary and analysis of Argentine events during 1979. It stresses divisions within the Videla government, reviews economic performance and human rights problems and suggests alternative political scenarios for the immediate future.

6634 ———. The breakdown of democracy in Argentina: 1916–30 (in The Breakdown of democratic regimes: Latin America [see item *HLAS 42:1920*] p. 3–27, tables)

For this brief synthesis of author's published research on pre-Depression Argentine politics, he argues that political rather than economic factors explain the 1930 coup. A crisis of legitimacy was caused by Radical leaders breaking political rules set down by the Conservatives. For historian's comment, see *HLAS 42:3423*.

6635 Snow, Peter G. Political forces in Argentina. New York: Praeger, 1979. 166 p.; bibl.; index.

Updated edition of one of the few texts on Argentine politics written expressly for undergraduates. Like the first edition, it offers clear and concise descriptions of the principal actors in the political process and is based on recent academic literature as well as on author's excellent studies of post-World War II party behavior in the country.

Solberg, Carl E. Oil and nationalism in Argentina: a history. See *HLAS 42:3425*.

6636 Timerman, Jacobo. Reflections: no name, no number (The New Yorker [New York] 20 April 1981, p. 45–130)

The product of deep reflection and literary skill, this article is Jacobo Timerman's story of victimization by the military rulers who seized control of Argentina's government in 1976. In a lengthy and engrossing narrative Timerman, founder and editor of the once prominent Argentine daily *La Opinion*, tells of solitary confinement and torture, the cruel and self-serving judgments of his captors, and the authoritarian mentality obsessed by fears of Zionism and Communism. At the same time, Timerman, the

hardnosed Argentine journalist shares his insights into Argentine life, its frustrations and immense capacity for self-defeat. In sum, a sensitive and rewarding piece of work. The article is an abridged version of the book *Prisoner without a name, cell without a number* (New York: Knopf/Random House, 1981, 164 p.) which appeared at press time and will be annotated in *HLAS 45*.

Vuotto, Pascual. Vida de un proletario: el proceso de Bragado. See *HLAS 42:3435*.

6637 Waldmann, Peter. Terrororganizationen in Argentinien (BESPL, 2:10, März/April 1977, p. 10–22)

The author describes the two important guerrilla bands: the Montoneros and the Marxist ERP and their terror deeds in Argentina. With the rise of the opposing extreme right guerrilleros, the country is caught in a situation very closely resembling a Civil War! [R.V. Shaw]

6638 Wellhofer, E. Spencer. Peronism in Argentina: the social base of the first regime; 1946–1955 (JDA, 11:3, April 1977, p. 335–356, tables)

Using voting data at the district level from the 1946 and 1954 elections, the study focuses on the social base of the peronist vote. Concludes that the base spread across social classes more broadly than is often assumed. For historian's comment, see *HLAS 42:3442*.

6639 ———. Strategies for party organization and voter mobilization: Britain, Norway, and Argentina (CPS, 12:2, July 1979, p. 169–204, bibl., tables)

The study uses data on the Argentine Socialist Party after the turn of the century as part of a cross-national study of hypotheses regarding party responses to the extension of suffrage. It represents a sophisticated statistical analysis of theories of organizational behavior.

6640 Wynia, Gary W. Illusion and reality in Argentina (CUH, 80:463, Feb. 1981, p. 62–65, 84–85)

Summary and analysis of the performance of the Argentine government and its economic policies during 1980. It focuses on contradictions in the military's political strategy as well as the limited success of its economic reconstruction program.

PARAGUAY

6641 Bareiro Saguier, Rubén. Los intelectuales frente a la dictadura: la represión cultural en Paraguay (NSO, 35, marzo/abril 1978)

A brief article that examines political repression in Paraguay, concentrating on its effects on the Guaraní culture and its popular theater.

6642 Bridges, Sydney. Politician and farm hand: a tale of two Paraguayan prisoners (Worldview [Council on Religion and International Affairs, New York] 22:7/8, July/Aug. 1979, p. 35–39, plates)

Using the experiences of two former Paraguayan political prisoners as case studies, author draws on their words to present insights into the repression endured by those who live under the country's authoritarian regime.

6643 Kroer, Hubert. Tapferes Paraguay. 3. überarbeitete Auflag. Würzburg, FRG: Marienburg-Verlag, 1979. 129 p.; bibl.

A balanced, succinct introduction to contemporary Paraguay, now in a third and enlarged edition, which emphasizes the country's political structure. Also provides information on economic conditions and cultural life within the historical context of Paraguay's past. An important contribution, which is well written and thoughtful. [G.M. Dorn]

6644 Lewis, Paul H. Paraguay under Stroessner. Chapel Hill: University of North Carolina Press, 1980. 1 v.: bibl.; index.

At last we have a major work on the Stroessner regime in Paraguay. Beginning with the origins of the current regime, author systematically examines the means it has employed to retain control over the country, including the development of a mass party organization along with patronage, repression and other conventional instruments. This study is recommended to anyone interested in authoritarianism as well as those who want to know how its country is ruled and what will remain when Stroessner is no longer there to hold it together.

6645 Stroessner, Alfredo. Mensajes y discursos del Excelentísimo Señor Presidente de la República del Paraguay General del Ejército Don Alfredo Stroessner. t. 1, Mayo de 1954–diciembre de 1959; t. 2, Febrero de 1960–diciembre de 1964; t. 3, Marzo de 1965–diciembre de 1972; t. 4, Enero de 1973–mayo de 1979. Asunción: Presidencia de la República, Subsecretaría de Información y Cultura, 1979. 4 v. (759, 789, 1037, 935 p.); plates; tables.

This four-volume collection of speeches by autocrat Alfredo Stroessner (1954–79) will be of interest to students of Paraguay and/or authoritarianism. Provides good examples of the autocrat's rhetoric and insights into his self-image.

Warren, Harris Gaylord and **Katherine F. Warren.** Paraguay and the Triple Alliance: the postwar decade, 1869–1878. See *HLAS 42:3472.*

White, Richard Alan. Paraguay's autonomous revolution, 1810–1840. See *HLAS 42:3475.*

URUGUAY

6646 Amaro, Sixto. Por un Uruguay sin presos sindicales y políticos (NSO, 42, mayo/junio 1979, p. 131–144, ill., plates)

In this interview, an Uruguayan labor leader expresses his views on the current military regime and its repression of organized labor.

6647 Biles, Robert E. Political participation in urban Uruguay: mixing public and private ends (*in* Political participation in Latin America. Edited by John A. Booth and Mitchell A. Seligson. New York: Holmes & Meier, 1978, p. 85–97)

Using survey data collected in 1970 in Uruguay, author demonstrates the profound effect of patronage in shaping political participation in the country. A well executed empirical study.

6648 Finch, M.H.J. La crisis uruguaya: tres perspectivas y una posdata (NSO, 10, enero/feb. 1974, p. 38–57)

An English social scientist, writing seven years ago, seeks an explanation for the country's unprecedented crisis in the early 1970s. He presents a clear summary of the economic problems that arose in the 1960s and undermined a political system held together by the ability of the government to extract enough of a surplus to pacify its working and middle-class constituents.

6649 Guerrero Martín, José. Los Tupamaros, segundo poder de Uruguay. Barcelona: Ediciones Clío, 1972. 95 p.; bibl. (Clío actualidad; 11)

Written when the Tupamaros seemed so successful (1971–72) they were referred to as Uruguay's "second power." This book consists of a summary of the few Uruguayan sources available at the time. [A. Suárez]

Hierro, Luis Antonio. Batlle: democracia y reforma del estado. See *HLAS 42:3490*.

6650 Kaufman, Edy. Uruguay in transition: from civilian to military rule. New Brunswick, N.J.: Transaction Books, 1979. 126 p.; bibl.; index.

Analysis of the major variables that have affected the political development of Uruguay from a state with a reputation as a democratic island in Latin America to a state controlled by the military. The author, admittedly biased, bases much of his work on research he undertook for Amnesty International. [C.N. Ronning]

6651 Lerin, François and Cristina Torres. Les transformations institutionnelles de l'Uruguay: 1973–1977 (FDD/NED [Problèmes d'Amérique Latine, 49] 4485/4486, 6 nov. 1978, p. 9–59, map)

Authors present a useful summary in a few pages of the transformation of the nation's government from a constitutional democracy to military authoritarianism in the mid-1970s.

6652 Michelini, Zelmar. Uruguay vencerá: discursos, entrevistas y artículos. Selección y prólogo de Mario Jaunarena. Barcelona: Laia, 1978. 315 p. (Laia paperback; 39)

Consists of a collection of articles written by the late Zelmar Michelini, a former Blanco Party leader who was assassinated while in exile in Argentina in 1976. Written during the early 1970s, they present Michelini's views on human rights and military repression at the time of the Uruguayan

military's seizure of control of the country's government. It should be read by anyone seeking to understand the views of participants in the nation's crisis.

Montevideo. Intendencia Municipal. Gobernantes municipales de Montevideo: datos biográficos-fotografías. See *HLAS 42:3497*.

6653 Rocha Imaz, Ricardo. Los blancos: breviario de hombres y hechos del Partido Nacional, 1836–1966. Montevideo?: Cerno Editorial, 1978. 86 p.

A very brief history (86 p.) of the Partido Nacional or Blanco Party that describes its leaders and major turning points since 1836.

6654 Seguí González, Luis. Ley de Migración: instrumento para el desarrollo y la seguridad (Geopolítica [Instituto Uruguayo de Estudios Geopolíticos, Montevideo] 3:6, dic. 1978, p. 29–37)

A legalistic discussion of Uruguayan immigration law and an argument for a new law built on a rational strategy of national development.

6655 Uruguay. Junta de Comandantes en Jefe. Las Fuerzas Armadas al pueblo oriental. t. 1, La subversión. 2. ed. Montevideo: República Oriental del Uruguay, Junta de Comandantes en Jefe, 1977. 1 v.; ill.

In this volume the Uruguayan Junta offers documents and commentaries aimed at justifying its charges of subversion of the country by Marxist movements in the early 1970s. It is an example of military investigation and documentation resembling those issued by juntas in neighboring countries.

6656 Uruguay: balance de 20 años de lucha en la universidad (OCLAE, 10, 1978, p. 32–42, plates)

A brief history of university-government relations in Uruguay that seeks to defend recent student movements against charges of subversion made by the country's current military leaders.

Brazil

MARGARET DALY HAYES, *Committee on Foreign Relations, United States Senate*

IN THE LAST FEW YEARS, Brazilian political scientists, essayists and historians have been prolific in producing a literature of high caliber. This development can be attributed, on the one hand, to the *abertura*—the "political opening," and evolution of a freer political climate that includes, among other manifestations, the relaxation of censorship and the granting of political amnesty—which has permitted the publication of works on a number of themes that could not have appeared before. And on the other hand, scholarship in Brazilian universities, particularly by young professors and their graduate students, has generated a body of political science literature of excellent quality and scope. It is encouraging that many of the more ambitious research projects in Brazil are being organized as collaborative efforts among scholars at a number of institutions. Many of the professors and scholars active in this research completed their graduate work in North American and European universities in the 1960s and have now returned to Brazil to set up their own graduate programs.

Brazil's political opening has made possible the publication of a number of enlightening essays, memoirs and testimonials by members of the left, participants in the urban guerrilla movement of the late 1960s and others who experienced long imprisonment and torture at the hands of the political police. Salles (item **6622**) and Perrin (item **6621**) give grim and detailed accounts of life in a political prison and of their efforts to plead their cases through the legal system. Gabeira (item **6717**) is the author's memoirs as a participant in the guerrilla movement and helps in understanding the nature of Brazil's radical left. However, the most important contributions to the study of this period are Jordão's story of the Herzog Case (item **6719**) involving the murder of a journalist in political prison, and Bicudo's personal memoir (item **6713**) of his efforts to reveal civil and military involvement in the São Paulo Death Squad. Both provide unique, in-depth accounts of how the Brazilian system of repression and justice operated at the time.

Brazilian political figures have also been writing memoirs that shed valuable light on political processes of the 20th century, especially the period 1930–64. Not only are such memoirs crucial for reconstructing the political past, but they are also useful in anticipating the future, especially the direction in which Brazil's more open political system may evolve in this decade. The best of this genre to appear in the last two years are the two-volumes of Brazilian Communist party leader, Gregorio Bezerra (item **6683**). This fascinating book is full of new information about the party's activities from the late 1920s to Bezerra's release from prison and exile in 1979. Juscelino Kubitschek's three-volume memoirs (item **6687**) gives a similarly detailed account of legalized political activity in the local, state, and national levels in pre-revolution Brazil. It provides particularly good insight into the politics of Minas Gerais. The political diaries of participants in the post-1964 military governments are likewise beginning to emerge. Portella de Mello (item **6689**) and Abreu (item **6682**), who headed the military "household" under Costa e Silva and Geisel, respectively, both document the politics and intrigue of those governments. Their accounts are of value because of the privileged vantage point—unusually close to the seat of power—they reflect.

The handful of studies that have appeared on voting behaviors reflect the increasing sophistication of Brazilian scholarship in political science. Of these, Reis (item 6674), reflecting collaborative research conducted by Brazilian social scientists in several important universities, is particularly useful and detailed.

Considerably more attention is being focused on the history of ideas in Brazil, especially to Brazilian adaptations of European and North American political thought. If journalistic accounts and autobiographies are providing the richest raw material for the study of recent Brazilian politics, the field of history of ideas and political movements is stimulating some of the best scholarly research. Trindade's study (item 6712) of the integralist movement is clearly the outstanding work of Brazilian political science reviewed in this *HLAS* volume. The author's use of survey, voting and interview data, as well as his analysis of documents, makes this a near-definitive study. Other good analyses of individual political philosophers that have appeared are Frei Caneca (item 6706), Alberto Torres (item 6705), and Octavio de Faria (item 6709). All of them are examples of a high quality of scholarship carried out by Brazilian graduate students.

In contrast to the great volume of significant materials coming from Brazil, North American scholarship on Brazil has slowed to a trickle in the last few years. Nevertheless, two books by North American authors are worthy of special mention. Malloy's examination (item 6745) of social security policy from the 1920s to 1970 is a thorough and detailed contribution to an understanding of the policy process, and Parker's study (item 6749) makes a unique contribution to the study of the 1964 revolution because of her examination of documents in presidential archives.

In this volume, *HLAS 43*, this section will be subdivided into the following subsections: 1) General Essays; 2) Biography and Memoirs; 3) Parliamentary and Presidential Speeches; 4) Political Philosophy; 5) Terrorism and Torture; and 6) Miscellaneous.

GENERAL ESSAYS

6657 Antunes, Ricardo L.C. O que é o sindicalismo. Coordenação, Vanya Sant'Anna; capa, Mário Camerini, caricatura, Emílio Damiani. São Paulo: Editora Brasiliense, 1980. 95 p.; ill. (Coleção primeiros passos)

One of a series of pamphlets intended for young readers. Explains the difference between syndicates and trade unions, and the differences between anarchist, Christian, corporatist and communist syndicates. Pt. 2 provides an excellent summary of syndicate organization in Brazil, including discussion of resurgence of activity after 1978.

6658 Arrães, Miguel. Conversações com Arraes. Por Cristina Tavares, Fernando Mendonça; capa, Branca de Castro. Belo Horizonte, Brasil: Editora Vega, 1979. 131 p.; 3 leaves of plates: ill.

Consists of a long interview with Mi-

guel Arraes, taped in the first half of 1980. Questions cover diversity of topics (e.g., revolution of 1964, Brazil's emerging international role, the state of the economy, interest and pressure groups in Brazil, current events such as the Brazil-West Germany nuclear agreement, political amnesty). Interviewers are former associates of Arraes in the state government of Pernambuco.

6659 Bardawil, José Carlos. Os sobreviventes. Brasília: Senado Federal, Centro Gráfico, 1977. 142 p. (Coleção Machado de Assis; v. 7)

Collection of articles by author culled from Brazilian newsmagazines or newspapers consist chiefly of profiles or interviews with prominent political figures from the present and past (e.g., Plinio Salgado). Additional chapters reflect on the Janio Quadros resignation, the Kubitschek government, peasant life in the mid-1970s. Good for "local color."

6660 Bittencourt, Getúlio. A quinta estrela: como se tenta fazer um presidente no Brasil. São Paulo: Livraria Editora Ciências Humanas, 1978. 204 p. (Temas atuais; 1)

Collection of author's articles from *Folha de São Paulo* which comments on the 1977–78 period of the presidential succession campaign. Includes interviews with several of the principal figures in the campaign, and a heretofore unpublished written interview with Luis Carlos Prestes. Good background material for the study of recent politics.

6661 Camargo, Aspásia Alcántara de. Authoritarianism and populism: bipolarity in the Brazilian political system (*in* The Structure of Brazilian development [see item **3789**] p. 99–126, bibl.)

Good overview of Brazilian political history from Empire to date.

Canêdo, Letícia Bicalho. O sindicalismo bancário em São Paulo no período de 1923–1944: seu significado político. See *HLAS 42:3630.*

6662 Castello Branco, Carlos. Os militares no poder. v. 1, Castelo Branco. v. 2, O ato 5 [i.e. cinco]. v. 3, O baile das solteironas. Rio de Janeiro: Editora Nova Fronteira, 1976/1977. 3 v. (Coleção Brasil século 20)

For the annotation of vol. 1, *Castelo Branco*, see *HLAS 41:7524.* Vol. 2, *O ato 5,* covers the period 1967–68 or from the inauguration of Costa e Silva to the promulgation of Institutional Act No. 5. This detailed *crônica* offers a day-by-day play of events in Brazilian politics as reported by one of the country's foremost political observers in his column in *Jornal do Brasil.* Vol. 3, *O baile das solteironas,* provides more day-by-day accounts of political developments within Brazil's military government, for the period 1969–70. At that time, however, strict censorship forced the columnist "to alter the style of his reporting." Although the texts lack the benefit of hindsight and analysis, they are important sources because of the function served by the column (i.e., to communicate information on behind-the-scenes political developments to the Brazilian public).

6663 Chacon, Vamireh. O dilema político brasileiro. São Paulo: Editora Convívio, 1978. 108 p.

Articles published in various newspapers (1976–77) examine why political processes, since the 1964 revolution, have evolved as they have in Brazil. Author speculates as to what might be the nature of Brazilian democracy.

6664 Cintra, Antônio Otávio. Traditional Brazilian politics: an interpretation of relations between center and periphery (*in* The Structure of Brazilian development [see item **3789**] p. 127–166, bibl.)

Bibliographic review of center-periphery relations as applied to Brazil in analyses from Empire to date.

6665 As Eleições no Rio Grande do Sul. Capa, Fernando Sgrillo. Porto Alegre: Editora Síntese, 1978 or 1979. 369 p.

Consists of raw data without analysis, chiefly total votes and percentage for municipal elections of 1976 and state and federal elections of 1945–78.

6666 Encontro Nacional pela Democracia, *Rio de Janeiro, 1978.* Painéis da crise brasileira: anais do Encontro Nacional pela Democracia. t. 1, Sessão de abertura e Painel I: Balanço eleitoral. t. 2, Painel II: Perspectivas do quadro econômico e social e Painel III: A crise constitucional. t. 3, Painel IV: A evolução do quadro político e Painel V: A articulação da sociedade brasileira. Promovido pelo Centro Brasil Democrático; capa, Eugênio Hirsch. Rio de Janeiro: Editora Avenir, 1979. 3 v.; ill.

Essentially unedited statements made by panelists at 1978 convention in which political leaders, labor leaders, academics and others discussed the direction the political system would take under the new president to be installed in March 1979. Useful commentary by Brazilians on their political system, most spokesmen represent opposition viewpoints.

6667 Ferreira Filho, Manoel Gonçalves. A reconstrução da democracia: ensaio sobre a institucionalização da democracia no mundo contemporâneo, e em especial no Brasil. São Paulo: Edição Saraiva, 1979. 230 p.; bibl.

A straightforward analysis of the evolution of democratic institutions, their role and functioning which also examines the "fit" between political process and institutions in Brazil as compared to the ideal model. The discussion of the Brazilian political process is particularly clear.

6668 Fleischer, David V. Renovação política-Brasil 1978: eleições parlamentares sob a égide do "Pacote de abril." Brasília: Fundação Universidade de Brasília, 1980. 41 leaves (Série Sociologia; 24. Trabalhos em ciências sociais)

Quantitative analysis of political career, occupation and educational background of deputies elected to the Federal Chamber in 1978.

6669 Gall, Norman. In the name of democracy: Brazil's Presidential succession. Hanover, NH: American Universities Field Staff, 1978. 12 p.; bibl.; ill. (Reports—American Universities Field Staff; 1978, no. 3, South America 0161-0724)

In the tradition of the *American Universities Field Staff Reports*, this is an excellent background article on the subject of the nomination of Gen. João Baptista Figueiredo to succeed Gen. Ernesto Geisel as President of Brazil in 1979. Provides information on Figueiredo himself and on changing policies under the Geisel government, especially its growing commitment to political openness and respect for human rights.

6670 Garcia, Alexandre. João presidente. Rio de Janeiro: Editora Artenova, 1978? 127 p.; port.

Consists of quotable quotes, often humorous, by Gen. João Baptista de Figueiredo to reporters during the presidential campaign of 1978.

6671 Grabendorff, Wolf and Manfred Nitsch. Brasilien: Entwicklungsmodell und Aussenpolitik. München, FRG: Wilhelm Verlag, 1977. 303 p.; bibl.; tables (Beiträge zur Soziologie und Sozialkunde Lateinamerikas; Bd. 15)

Nitsch analyzes the Brazilian government's efforts at legitimization and institutionalization since 1964. He also examines the country's economic growth and trade policies, based on a thorough examination of government documents and official statistics. Grabendorff looks at Brazil's relations with its neighbors and focuses on specific economic and geopolitical interests, especially Brazil's ties with the US, Portugal, and Africa. This is a thoughtful and scholarly study of Brazilian politics in the 1960s and 1970s. [G.M. Dorn]

6672 Guimarães, J.C. de Macedo Soares. Para onde vamos? Rio de Janeiro: Editora Record, 1977. 173 p.

Political commentary—generally sympathetic criticism—on a broad variety of themes in *Jornal do Brasil* and *Estado de São Paulo* (Sept. 10, 1976—Sept. 16, 1977).

Lamounier, Bolivar and **Maria D'Alva Gil Kinzo.** Partidos políticos, representação e processo eleitoral no Brasil, 1945—1978. See *HLAS 42:48.*

Lima Júnior, Olavo Brasil de. Evolução e crise do sistema partidário brasileiro: as eleições legislativas estaduais de 1947 a 1962. See *HLAS 42:3692.*

Mallon, Florencia E. Peasants and rural laborers in Pernambuco: 1955—1964. See *HLAS 42:3704.*

6673 Moura, Clóvis. Sacco e Vanzetti: o protesto brasileiro. Capa, Ary Normanha. São Paulo: Brasil Debates, 1979. 79 p.; ill. (Brasil memoria; 1)

Provides history and documentation on how the Brazilian press and incipient labor movement reacted to the case and trial of Sacco and Vanzetti. Most of the articles were culled from leftist and anarchist newspapers of the period. Author argues that the case's impact in Brazil was such that it sowed the seeds of proletarian revolution, a process truncated by the *tenente* rebellion of 1930.

Nichols, Glenn A. Further misadventures in the study of Latin American politics: pluralism, Marxism, corporatism and an alternative. See item **6063.**

6674 Os Partidos e o regime: a lógica do processo eleitoral brasileiro. Fábio Wanderly Reis, organizador; Bolivar Lamounier et al. São Paulo: Edições Símbolo, 1978. 315 p.; bibl.; ill.

In this excellent study of the 1976 municipal elections in four cities, authors review the campaign process and voting data in order to draw conclusions about public opinion trends concerning political and other important issues. A valuable work for anyone studying the current political system and prospects for a political opening and democracy in Brazil.

6675 Pereira, Astrojildo. Ensaios históricos e políticos. Apresentação, Heitor Ferreira Lima; capa, Adrian B. Cooper. São

Paulo: Editora Alfa-Omega, 1979. 240 p.; bibl. (Biblioteca Alfa-Omega de ciências sociais: Série la., Política; v. 9)

Consists of essays, the most important of which is "Formation of the Brazilian Communist Party," by one of the PCB's founders. Other essays comment on Brazilian political events 1930–33.

6676 Santos, Wanderley Guilherme dos.
Poder e política: crónica do autoritarismo brasileiro. Rio de Janeiro: Forense-Universitária, 1978. 211 p.; bibl.

This thoughtful analysis, principally of political processes during the 1970s, devotes attention to the impact of authoritarianism on the efficient functioning of the policy machinery. Analysis of voting data for 1974–76 is useful and timely.

6677 ——— and Olavo Brasil de Lima Júnior. Public policy analysis in Brazil (in The Structure of Brazilian development [see item **3789**] p. 203–222, bibl.)

Review of the literature on the analysis of Brazilian public policy is generally inconclusive.

6678 Souza Júnior, Cezar Saldanha. A crise da democracia no Brasil: aspectos políticos. Rio de Janeiro: Forense, 1978. 208 p.; bibl.

Somewhat oversimplified analysis of why the present Brazilian system of government does not function as a democracy should.

6679 Stumpf, André Gustavo and Merval Pereira Filho. A segunda guerra: sucessão de Geisel. Prefácio de Mino Carta. São Paulo: Editora Brasiliense, 1979. 138 p.

Journalistic but detailed and useful account of the rise and fall of political fortunes associated with the presidential succession of Gen. João Baptista Figueiredo. Authors were based in Brasília and closely followed events of the period 1976–77. Lacks documentation but provides good coverage of Risk Contract decision, the April political reforms, and US-Brazil relations over the nuclear accord.

Toledo, Caio Navarro de. ISEB: fábrica de ideologias. See *HLAS 42:3764.*

6680 Troyano, Annez Andraus. Estado e sindicalismo. São Paulo: Edições Símbolo, 1978. 184 p.; bibl.; ill. (Coleção Ensaio e memória; 12)

Consists of author's thesis (University of São Paulo) describing the evolution of syndicate (i.e., union) organization and political activity from the early 1930s (Vargas "social pact") through the early 1970s. The Chemical and Pharmaceutical Workers Syndicate of São Paulo is used as case study. Author argues that the increasing diversity of the industrial base made possible the growing political and economic activity of independent syndicates, and shows how this occurred in the 1950s and early 1960s until the 1964 revolution superimposed anew the state-oriented leadership of the Estado Novo period. Author, a sociologist with the Inter-Syndical Department for Statistics and Socioeconomic Studies, a syndicate-sponsored research institute, concludes by stating the need for a new labor code. Book provides good background on Brazil's syndicate movement.

6681 Uricoechea, Fernando. The patrimonial foundations of the Brazilian bureaucratic state. Berkeley: University of California Press, 1980. 1 v.; bibl.; index.

Bureaucratic authoritarianism is generally hypothesized to be a phenomenon of later stages of political-economic development. This author traces the origins of the bureaucratic state in Brazil to the patrimonial bureaucracy of Portugal, and argues that centralization under a patrimonial bureaucracy in Brazil was only possible because of several chance historical events.

BIOGRAPHY AND MEMOIRS

6682 Abreu, Hugo. Tempo de crise. Capa, Vitor Burton. Rio de Janeiro: Editora Nova Fronteira, 1980. 295 p. (Coleção Brasil século 20)

Vol. 2 consists of a political testimonial by the Chief of the Military Household under President Ernesto Geisel in which Abreu explains his divergences with the course of the "revolution" and his reasons for resigning his office when Geisel's successor, was named. Bulk of text deals with the internal jockeying for the nomination as successor and ultimate election in 1978. This is a valuable source for understanding the politics of the military establishment.

6683 Bezerra, Gregório. Memórias. pt. 1, 1900–1945. pt. 2, 1946–1969. Capa,

Eugênio Hirsch. Rio de Janeiro: Civilização Brasileira, 1979. 2 v.; ill. (Coleção Retratos do Brasil; v. 127)

Excellent, exceptionally detailed memoirs of a principal member of the Brazilian Communist Party. In pt. 1, author details his party recruitment in 1930, his participation in the 1935 communist uprising, and his imprisonment in 1935–45 under Vargas. Pt. 2 details reorganization efforts after 1946 and attempts to organize labor and peasants in the Northeast with Miguel Arraes and Julião, among others. Memoirs end with the 1969 exchange of the author and other political prisoners for US Ambassador Burke Elbrick. Provides extensive coverage of more than 50 years of political activity making it a unique contribution to Brazilian contemporary history. Provides useful new information about activities and organization of the Brazilian Communist Party.

6684 Cavalcanti, Paulo. O caso eu conto, como o caso foi (da Coluna Prestes à queda de Arraes): memórias. São Paulo: Editora Alfa-Omega, 1978. 409 p.; 6 leaves of plates: ill. (Biblioteca Alpha-Omega de cultura universal: Série 1a., Coleção Esta América; v. 6)

Political memoirs of a Pernambucan politican of leftist-nationalist leanings. Author covers period from 1930 to date, but his own political activities began with his graduation from Law School during the Estado Novo. Good discussion of Recife politics in 1950s and 1960s deals with Miguel Arraes, Gregório Bezerra (see item **6683**) and others of the Northeastern left.

6685 Goldman, Alberto. Caminhos de luta: peripécias de um político na democracia relativa. São Paulo: Núcleo de Divulgação Editorial, 1978. 242 p.; 1 leaf of plates; ports.

This political diary by a São Paulo State Deputy, member of the opposition party MDB, covers 1970–77. Includes tracts of author's speeches before the Senate Assembly. Replete with details on São Paulo state politics for the period, this book is well recommended as background to the political process of the 1970s. Detailed coverage of the campaign and election of 1974 in which MDB made significant gains.

6686 Jurema, Abelardo de Araujo. Juscelino & Jango: PSD & PTB. Rio de Janeiro: Editora Artenova, 1979. 268 p.

Reflections on personalities and events of the period 1956–64 by the man who was leader of the Chamber's government coalition under Juscelino Kubitschek, and Minister of Justice under João Goulart. Brief essays are mostly personal and of more human than political interest. Still, they are useful as the annals of a politician's "first hand" experiences.

6687 Kubitschek, Juscelino. Meu caminho para Brasília: memórias. Rio de Janeiro: Bloch Editores, 1974. 3 v.; ports.

Memoirs consist of three volumes: Vol. 1 deals with Kubitschek's life prior to his election as Mayor of Belo Horizonte in 1940; Vol. 2 covers his public life up to his election as President; and Vol. 3 describes the years of the presidency, 1956–60. Invaluable reading for understanding people and political process of pre-1964 Brazil.

6688 Lins, Etelvino. Um depoimento político: episódios e observações. Prefácio de Carlos Castello Branco. Rio de Janeiro: Livraria J. Olympio Editora, 1977. 163 p.; 4 leaves of plates; ill.

Political memoirs of former Interventor and Governor of the State of Pernambuco, Federal Senator and Deputy and candidate for the presidency in 1955. For historian's comment, see *HLAS 42:3694*.

6689 Mello, Jayme Portella de. A revolução e o Governo Costa e Silva. Rio de Janeiro: Guavira Editores, 1979. 1032 p.; 24 leaves of plates; ill.

Very detailed, but unedited, history of the Costa e Silva government by Costa e Silva's Chief of Military Household. An obviously important, sympathetic contribution to the history of contemporary Brazil.

Morão Filho, Olympio. Memórias: a verdade de um revolucionário. See *HLAS 42:3722*.

Tavares, Aurélio de Lyra. O Brasil de minha geração. See *HLAS 42:3760*.

PARLIAMENTARY AND PRESIDENTIAL SPEECHES

6690 Badaró, Murilo. Memorial político. Brasília: s.n., 1976. 178 p.

Selected articles and speeches (1961–75) by Badaró delivered in the Legislative Assembly of Minas Gerais, and in the Federal Chamber. Of limited interest.

6691 Campos, Francisco. Francisco Campos; discursos parlamentares. Seleção e introdução, Paulo Bonavides. Brasília: Câmara dos Deputados, 1979. 153 p.; indexes (Perfis parlamentares; 6)

Early, "antiliberal" parliamentary speeches by future author of the corporatist constitution of 1937.

6692 Cardoso, Fernando Henrique. Democracia para mudar: Fernando Henrique Cardoso em 30 horas de entrevistas. Rio de Janeiro: Paz e Terra, 1978. 108 p. (Coleção Documentos da democracia brasileira; v. 4)

Author's speeches delivered during his 1978 campaign for State Senator of São Paulo, reveal much that is useful about the posture of the intellectual opposition on issues such as the political opening and the future of the political system.

6693 Geisel, Ernesto. Discursos. Brasília: Assessoria de Imprensa e Relações Públicas da Presidência da República, 1975/1976. 2 v.

Two of five volumes of speeches by President Ernesto Geisel during his tenure, 1974–79. Vol. 5 covers the final year of Geisel's presidency and includes topics such as travel in Mexico, West Germany, Uruguay, Paraguay (Itaipú), and throughout Brazil; the question of political transition; and the economic difficulties facing the country. Vol. 2 covers visits to Uruguay and Paraguay; the creation of PORTOBRAS and IMBEL (the Brazilian War Materials Industry); Message to Congress; and more on the country's economic situation in 1975.

6694 ———. Um homem chamado Geisel: história do Brasil; fatos, mensagens, discursos, política interna, forças armadas. Levy Cury; capa, Cláudio Bravo Cepeda. Brasília: Horizonte Editora, 1978. 253 p. (Movimento cultural brasileiro)

Provides a brief biography of President Ernesto Geisel as well as selected speeches delivered while in office. Same material is available elsewhere in collections of presidential speeches published by the government (e.g., see item 6693).

6695 O Homem e a liberdade: MDB, 1°. simpósio nacional, Florianópolis, 17 e 18 de junho de 1976. Brasília: Instituto de

Estudos Políticos Pedroso Horta, 1976. 200 p.

These seven speeches by prominent MDB politicians and writers delivered at the first symposium of Instituto Pedroso Horta, the MDB's "think tank," represent an effort to develop a party platform.

6696 Mangabeira, Octavio. Discursos parlamentares. Seleção e introdução de Josaphat Marinho. Brasília: Câmara dos Deputados, 1978. 557 p.; bibl.; indexes (Perfis parlamentares; 10)

Parliamentary speeches by a Brazilian politician and statesman whose career covers 1912–60. Of particular interest are his speeches on the political situation in 1946 and 1955–60, and the wise perspective provided by his analysis of increasing tensions among political parties.

6697 Neves, João. João Neves da Fontoura, discursos parlamentares. Seleção e introdução de Hélgio Trindade. Brasília: Câmara dos Deputados, 1978. 722 p.; bibl.; ill.; indexes (Perfis parlamentares; 8)

Speeches delivered by the representative of Rio Grande do Sul during the period of support for the Liberal Alliance (1929–30); the constitutionalist revolt in São Paulo; and 1935–37, after João Neves returned from exile to speak out in public and in the Chamber against Getúlio Vargas' intentions. A useful brief introduction provides historical background to the speeches. Volume is No. 8 of a monographic series published by the Chamber of Deputies and entitled "Perfis Parlamentares" (see *HLAS 42:3732*).

6698 Ottoni, Theóphilo Benedicto. Discursos parlamentares. Seleção e introdução, Paulo Pinheiro Chagas. Brasília: Câmara dos Deputados, 1979. 1151 p. (Perfis parlamentares; 12)

Parliamentary speeches of Liberal politican during the Empire (1840–69). Topics cover a variety of interesting themes such as the slavery question and the Paraguayan War. Includes excellent introduction by Chagas, Ottoni's biographer. No. 12 of a monographic series published by the Chamber of Deputies and entitled "Perfis Parlamentares" (see *HLAS 42:3732*).

6699 Reis, Antônio Carlos Konder. Encurtando distâncias. Florianópolis, Brazil: Gabinete do Governador, Casa Civil, 1976/1980. 4 v.

Collection of speeches by the Governor of Santa Catarina in four volumes cover period 1975–Feb. 1979, when his term ended. Good source for the history of Santa Catarina.

6700 Saraiva, José Antônio. José Antônio Saraiva (conselheiro Saraiva), discursos parlamentares. Seleção e introdução, Alvaro Valle. Brasília: Câmara dos Deputados, 1978. 661 p.; index; port. (Perfis parlamentares; 4)

Parliamentary speeches by a prominent politician of the Empire (1852–90) covering issues such as the Paraguayan War, slavery and abolition, electoral reforms, and the Republic.

6701 Tavares Bastos, Aureliano Cândido. Discursos parlamentares. Brasília: Senado Federal, 1977. 612 p.

Parliamentary speeches by Representative from Alagoas, delivered during three legislative terms (1861–68). Topics include problems of the armed forces, especially the Navy; coastal and river navigation; and the Paraguayan War. This edition lacks the very useful biographic essays included in volumes of the monographic series "Perfis Parlamentares" (see items 6696–6698 and 6700).

6702 Vilela, Teotônio Brandão. A pregação de liberdade: andanças de um liberal. Prefácio de Carlos Chagas. Porto Alegre: L&PM Editores, 1977. 335 p.

Consists of political speeches and interviews (1974–77) by Senator from Alagoas and liberal member of the government's political party.

POLITICAL PHILOSOPHY

6703 As Idéias políticas no Brasil. Coordenador, Adolpho Crippa; colaboradores, João Alfredo de Souza Montenegro et al.; capa, Francisco Amêndola. São Paulo: Editora Convívio, 1979. 1 v.; bibl.

Good collection of scholarly essays on the history of political thought in Brazil which emphasizes the evolution of liberalism. Coverage ranges from Portuguese absolutism, radical liberalism of the Empire, Rui Barbosa's liberalism and advent of positivism. Also includes author's essay on Brazilian political culture.

Ideologia autoritário no Brasil, 1930–1945. See *HLAS 42:3174.*

6704 Konder, Leandro. A democracia e os comunsitas no Brasil. Capa, Sônia Maria Goulart. Rio de Janeiro: Graal, 1980. 156 p.; index (Biblioteca de ciências sociais. Série Política; v. no. 15)

A sympathetic history of the Communist Party of Brazil from origins to present, and of its adaptations to the circumstances created by the evolution of Brazilian democratic processes. A good, brief review.

6705 Marson, Adalberto. A ideologia nacionalista em Alberto Torres. São Paulo: Livraria Duas Cidades, 1979. 210 p. (Coleção Historia e sociedade)

Author's doctoral dissertation analyzes in great detail the political writings of one of the principal spokesmen of Brazilian statist-nationalism as practiced in the pre-Estado Novo of the 1930s and in the 1950s. The review of literary primary sources is more thorough than the analysis.

Mercadante, Paulo. Militares & civis: a ética e o compromisso. See *HLAS 42:3536.*

6706 Montenegro, João Alfredo de Sousa. O liberalismo radical de Frei Caneca. Rio de Janeiro: Tempo Brasileiro, 1978. 216 p.; bibl. (Coleção Caminhos brasileiros; 4)

In this important contribution to the history of ideas in Brazil, author examines in detail the European philosophical currents that influenced Frei Caneca. His adaptation of European ideas to the Brazilian context led to the development of his own nationalist and radical liberal philosophical works published in Brazil at the turn of the 18th century (see also *HLAS 42:7643*).

6707 Romero, Sylvio. Parlamentarismo e presidencialismo. Introdução de Pedro Calmon; capa, Gaetano Ré/Cícero. Brasília: Senado Federal, 1979. 66 p. (Coleção Bernardo Pereira de Vasconcelos; v. no. 14: Série Estudos políticos)

Reedition of "pioneer" statement on the merits of parliamentarism for Brazil, written in 1890(?) in the form of letters to Rui Barbosa. Will be useful to those interested in the origins of the parliamentary school of thought in Brazil.

6708 ———. Realidades e ilusões no Brasil: Parlamentarismo e presidencialismo e outros ensaios. Seleção e coordenação de Hildon Rocha. Petrópolis, Brasil: Editora Vozes, 1979. 324 p. (Coleção Dimensões do Brasil; 14)

This reedition of essays by an important political thinker of turn-of-the-century Brazil praises the parliamentary system as the most appropriate republican form for Brazil. Author also comments on the mixing of nationalities in Brazil, emphasizes concern for the concentration of German immigrants in the south, and advocates the expansion of Portuguese immigration as the most compatible nationality for Brazil. Other essays comment on the appropriateness of socialism in the Brazilian context, and on the development of political parties in the early years of the Republic. Good collection by important author.

6709 Sadek, Maria Tereza Aina. Machiavel, machiavéis: a tragédia octaviana: estudo sobre o pensamento político de Octávio de Faria. São Paulo: Edições Símbolo, 1978. 205 p.; bibl. (Coleção Ensaio e memória; 10)

In this excellent contribution to the history of political thought in Brazil, author examines the ideological context of the first third of the century when Octavio de Faria wrote. She distinguishes the latter's political theses from those advocated by integralism, a school traditionally associated with Octavio de Faria. For literary critic's comment, see *HLAS 42:6477.*

6710 Saldanha, Nelson Nogueira. O pensamento político no Brasil. Rio de Janeiro: Forense, 1979. 159 p.; bibl.; indexes.

A good review of themes in Brazilian political thought from the colonial, monarchical and republican periods, with emphasis on the latter. Coverage stops at the Estado Novo. Useful reference for history of ideas.

6711 Spindel, Arnaldo. O que é o comunismo. Coordenação, Vanya Sant'-Anna; capa, Mário Camerini; caricatura, Emílio Damiani. São Paulo: Editora Brasilunse, 1980. 86 p.; ill. (Coleção Primeiros passos)

Introduction to communism for young people and part of a collection by the publisher on various political ideologies and trends. Author bases his essay on his thesis, published by the same house: *O Partido Comunista na génese do populismo.*

6712 Trindade, Hélgio Henrique. Integralismo: o fascismo brasileiro na década de 30. São Paulo: DIFEL (Difusão Européia do Livro); Porto Alegre, Brazil: Univer-

sidade Federal do Rio Grande do Sul, 1974. 379 p.; bibl.; facsims.; indexes; plates; tables (Corpo e alma do Brasil; 40)

Based on extensive documentation, this is the most thorough (and one of the few) studies of Brazilian fascism. Author explores the relation between Brazilian integralism and Catholicism, the military, and Italian and German fascisms. He then examines the social cultural and intellectual background of Integralist leader Plinio Salgado, the historical conditions in which Integralism emerged in Brazil in the 1930s and finally, the ideological content of Brazilian Integralism. In this latter section, author presents data from interviews with former members of the National Directorate of the Integralist Party. A translation of author's thesis *L'action intégraliste brésilienne* (Univ. de Paris I, 1971), this is an extremely important book for its insight into ideology of the Estado Novo and subsequent politics of the right in Brazil.

TERRORISM AND TORTURE

6713 Bicudo, Hélio Pereira. Meu depoimento sobre o esquadrão da morte. 6. ed., rev. e aumentada. São Paulo: Pontifícia Comissão de Justiça e Paz e São Paulo, 1977. 307 p.

Consists of story of author's efforts to identify and bring to justice members of São Paulo's infamous Death Squadron. Author was State's Attorney who dared to make an issue of police involvement in the Death Squadron activities. Argues that officers involved in crimes and corruption infiltrated the political police, their activities becoming matters of national security. The courts and legal system were cowardly in their pursuit of justice. Concludes on a pessimistic note about the ultimate success of the battle against the Death Squadron noting that the identities of the Squadron's "intellectual" leaders have not been revealed to the public. A fascinating report.

6714 Boal, Augusto. Milagre no Brasil. Capa, Eduardo. Rio de Janeiro: Civilização Brasileira, 1979. 291 p. (Coleção Perspectivas no homem; v. 126)

Memoirs of a Brazilian playwright of São Paulo's modernist Teatro de Arena who spent time in prison in 1971. Author's vocation leads to the dramatization of his experience. Principally of literary interest.

Brandão, Octávio. Combates e batalhas: memórias. See *HLAS 42:3628.*

6715 Christo, Carlos Alberto Libanio. Das catacumbas: cartas da prisão, 1969–1971. Frei Betto [i.e. Carlos Alberto Libanio Christo]. Rio de Janeiro: Civilização Brasileira, 1978. 183 p.

Prison letters to family and friends over a two-year period, detail the minutiae of life in jail and slow process of bringing the case before the military courts. Not an angry statement but more of literary than political interest.

6716 Gabeira, Fernando. Carta sobre a anistia; a entrevista do Pasquim; conversação sobre 1968. Rio de Janeiro: CODECRI, 1979. 79 p.; ill. (Coleção Edições do Pasquim; v. 48)

One of the principal figures in the urban guerrilla movement of 1968 discusses: 1) causes of the movement; 2) reasons why he became a guerrilla; 3) the repressive apparatus; and 4) the meaning of amnesty for those in exile. Book provides good insight into the thinking of the Brazilian radical left of 1968.

6717 Gabeira, Fernando. O que é isso, companheiro?: depoimento. Capa, Rafael Siqueira. Rio de Janeiro: Editora CODECRI, 1979. 190 p. (Coleção Edições do Pasquim; v. 66)

Personal memoirs of participant in Brazil's urban guerrilla describes his early political contacts, recruitment into the movement, the kidnapping of US Ambassador Burke Elbrick, time spent in hiding and in prison. Very well written account includes initial sections which are very useful for understanding the origins and organization of the left in Brazil.

6718 A Guerrilha do Araguaia. Palmério Dória et al.; capa, Paulo Orlando Láfer de Jesus; arte, Paulo Orlando Láfer de Jesus et al.; revisão, Júlio Cezar Garcia, Benjamin Sérgio Gonçalves; ilustração, Jaime Leão; fotos, Hélio Campos Mello et al. São Paulo: Alfa-Omega: distribuida pela Abril 1978. 78 p.; ill. (História imediata; 1)

Report of "secret" war in Araguaia Valley, Brazil's northern interior. Prior press censorship kept all news of this guerrilla war

from public attention. Reports include tales of problems with land title, repression by army and military police. Guerrilla had the evident support and participation of members of the Communist Party of Brazil (P.C. do B). Interesting as documentary material.

6719 Jordão, Fernando. Dossiê Herzog: prisão, tortura e morte no Brasil. Capa, Jaime Leão. São Paulo: Global Editora, 1979. 223 p.; bibl.; ill. (Passado & presente; 1)

Provides details on the journalists' campaign to publicize the murder of their fellow journalist Vladimir Herzog by São Paulo's military police. The Herzog Case was crucial in mobilizing public opinion against regime brutality and ultimately in setting the stage for the political opening of 1978–79.

6720 Lago, Mário. Reminiscências do sol quadrado. Rio de Janeiro: Avenir Editores, 1979. 97 p. (Coleção Depoimentos; 9)

Personal memoirs, of more literary than political value, of the two months (April–May 1964) author spent in jail as a political prisoner of the 1964 revolution.

6721 Perrin, Dimas. Depoimento de um torturado. Prefácio, Edgar da Mata-Machado. Rio de Janeiro: Novacultura Editora, 1979. 192 p.; ill.

Accused of aiding in the reorganization of the Communist Party of Brazil, the author of these memoirs describes his time in prison, his torture, and efforts to defend himself through the military court system. An excellent chronicle of the difficulties involved in processing the case of a political prisoner through Brazil's military court system.

6722 Salles, Antônio Pinheiro. Confesso que peguei em armas. Capa, Branca de Castro. Belo Horizonte, MG: Editora Vega, 1979. 118 p.

Well written and grim history of author's nine years in prison for armed opposition to the post-1964 regime. With cold detachment, he describes his recruitment by the militant left and his tortures in prison.

MISCELLANEOUS

6723 Alvaro Moisés, José and **Verena Stolcke.** Urban transport and popular violence: the case of Brazil (PP, 86, Feb. 1980, p. 174–192)

Riots on suburban trains that bring workers from the outskirts to their places of employment are attributed to rapidly declining quality of service as well as to the danger involved in riding neglected commuter trains, rather than to fare increases that diminished worker's salary purchasing power, though the two are linked. Authors argue that the state's failure to remedy a miserable and long deteriorating service sparked the riots.

6724 Apesteguy, Christine. L'intervention fédérale en Amazonie: éléments pour une définition de l'état militaire au Brésil (CDAL, 19, 1979, p. 89–100)

Author reviews federal programs for developing the Amazon since 1965 and anticipates that the state's role will evolve from one of federal (military) leadership in defining development goals to one of federal manipulation by private monopolies.

6725 Bacha, Edmar Lisboa and Roberto Mangabeira Unger. Participação, salário e voto: um projeto de democracia para o Brasil. Rio de Janeiro: Paz e Terra, 1978. 75 p. (Coleção Estudos brasileiros; v. 24)

A proposal for restructuring Brazil's political economy by providing for redistribution of income and political participation, beginning with redistribution of income to eliminate misery. Authors argue that democracy in Brazil will only be possible with such reforms. The authors, two distinguished young economists foresee the discussion of many of the policy initiatives of the administration that took office in 1979. Their discussion of tensions between interest groups and economic classes is excellent and perceptive.

6726 Blay, Eva Alterman. The political participation of women in Brazil: female mayors (UC/S, 5:1, Autumn 1979, p. 42–59, tables)

Excellent data-based analysis finds that women were elected as mayors only in the poorest communities. Author partly attributes this development to the fact that in early 1970 Brazil's national political party showed no interest in municipal level politics.

6727 Brasileiro, Ana Maria. A fusão: análise de uma política pública. Maria Thereza L. de Souza Lobo, colaboradora. Brasília:

Instituto de Planejamento Econômico e Social, Instituto de Planejamento, IPLAN, 1979. 364 p.; bibl.; maps (Série Estudos para o planejamento; no. 21)

Detailed study by expert in public administration of the union of Guanabara state (former Federal District) with Rio de Janeiro state, and the creation of Rio de Janeiro municipality in 1974–77.

6728 Burgess, Mike and Daniel Wolf. Brasil: el concepto de poder en la Escuela Superior de Guerra (CP, 20, abril/junio 1979, p. 89–103)

Analysis of definition of power and other political concepts based on a reading of the Escola Superior da Guerra *Basic Manual* for 1974 and other publications of the ESG.

6729 Cammack, Paul. O"cornelismo" e o "compromisso coronelista:" uma crítica (UFMA/DCP, 5, março 1979, p. 1–20)

In this useful critical review essay, author concludes with 12 points on which he disagrees with Nunes Leal's analysis and conclusions.

6730 Cardoso, Fernando Henrique. Les impasses du régime autoritaire: le cas brésilien (FDD/NED [Problèmes d'Amérique Latine, 54] 4545/4546, 18 déc. 1979, p. 89–108)

A prominent political sociologist discusses the future of Brazil's authoritarian regime through an analysis of how the government negotiated the process which led to the *abertura* or political opening.

6731 Carvalho, Ferdinando de. O arraial: se a revolução de 1964 não tivesse vencido. Rio de Janeiro: Guavira Editores, 1978. 170 p.

Political fiction by former instructor of the Superior War College (ESG) and official in charge of parliamentary inquiry into the activity of Brazil's Communist Party. Author speculates on what might have happened had the 1964 revolution failed and Goulart imposed a socialist government in Brazil voting that resistance would have emerged. Book provides interesting insight into the political thinking of Brazil's military.

6732 Cehelsky, Marta. Land reform in Brazil: the management of social change. Boulder, Colo.: Westview Press, 1979. 261 p.; bibl.; ill.; index (A Westview replica edition)

Author's dissertation studies the politics of land reform in Brazil, during the João Goulart and Castello Branco governments (1961–69). Offers important insights into the perceptions of different sectors of the need for land reform as well as into the latter's political and economic impacts. Extensive interviews and content analysis of the congressional debate over the land reform bill support the work.

6733 Chacon, Vamireh. Capitalismo de estado e burocracia no Brasil (UMG / RBEP, 48, jan. 1979, p. 101–120)

Good overview of the literature on the themes of "state capitalism" and "bureaucratic statism" in Brazilian politics from colonial period to date.

Conniff, Michael L. The *tenentes* in power: a new perspective on the Brazilian revolution of 1930. See *HLAS 42:3642.*

Dutra, Eliana Regina de Freitas. A Igreja e as classes populares em Minas na década de vinte. See *HLAS 42:3650.*

6734 Dye, David R. and **Carlos Eduardo de Souza e Silva.** A perspective on the Brazilian state (LARR, 14:1, 1979, p. 81–98, bibl.)

Useful critique of Philippe Schmitter's 1973 description of bonapartism as applied to Brazil.

6735 Forman, Shepard. The significance of participation: peasants in the politics of Brazil (*in* Political participation in Latin America. Edited by John A. Booth and Mitchell A. Seligson. v. 2, Politics and the poor. New York: Holmes & Meier, 1978, p. 36–50)

Peasants participate in the political process in Brazil because it serves their interests in the dependency relationship they have with government, landowner, etc. Analysis based on review of theoretical and secondary literature.

6736 ——— and **Joyce F. Riegelhaupt.** The political economy of patron-clientship: Brazil and Portugal compared (*in* Brazil, anthropological perspectives: essays in honor of Charles Wagley [see item **1081**] p. 379–400)

Authors dispute the hypothesis that peasant politics in Brazil or Portugal follow the pattern of patron-clientism. A review of peasant participation in Brazilian politics since independence shows that peasants

have been in step with national political processes.

6737 Gall, Norman. Letter from Rondônia. Hanover, NH: American Universities Field Staff, 1978. 1 v.: bibl. (American Universities Field Staff reports; 1978, no. 10, South America 0161-0724)

Monograph consisting of five-part article discusses the opening and settlement of a new frontier. Author reviews the history of frontier expansion in Rondônia, and describes life therein. Despite author's tendency to stress the violent and dangerous aspects of settlement, this is an excellent journalistic report.

6738 Green, Jim. Liberalization on trial: the workers' movement (NACLA, 13:3, May/June 1979, p. 14–25, map, plates)

Review of recent mobilization of worker movements in Brazil. Author documents the fact that liberalization efforts by the military will have to take worker demands into account.

Greenfield, Gerald Michael. Lighting the city: a case study of public service problems in São Paulo, 1885–1913. See *HLAS 42: 3665.*

6739 Greves operárias: 1968–1978. Conselho editorial, Guido Mantega et al.; ilustrações e fotos, Haroldo Rodrigues et al. Belo Horizonte: Editora Aparte, 1978. 96 p.; ill. (Cadernos de presente; 2)

Provides background reading for understanding recent activities within the Brazilian labor movement. The wave of strikes which began in São Paulo in 1978 provide rationale to look back at the 1968 strikes in Osasco, São Paulo, and Contagem, Minas Gerais. Collection contains interviews and journalistic analysis of the 1968 cases.

Indice de Ciências Sociais. Ano 1, No. 1, julho 1979– . See *HLAS 42:221.*

6740 Krischke, Paulo José. A Igreja e as crisis políticas no Brasil. Petrópolis, Brasil: Vozes, 1979. 170 p. (Publicações CID: História; 7)

Collection of articles, most of them previously published in English, on role of the Church in Brazil. Author's perspective is that of the post-Medellín Church, and to him the Brazilian Church is less motivated by social ideology than other Latin American churches. In fact, the Brazilian Church's cooperation in the political compromise of the Estado Novo explains the absence of an active Christian Democracy in the country. A good collection of articles on a subject that has been neglected.

6741 Levine, Robert M. Perspectives on the mid-Vargas years, 1934–1937 (SAGE/JIAS, 22:1, Feb. 1980, p. 57–80, bibl.)

Review of new archival material available since the declassification of British and American materials of the Vargas period. Suggests that British and American authorities were well informed about political currents in Brazil. Useful new information by authority on the period.

6742 Lewin, Linda. Some historical implications of kinship organization for family-based politics in the Brazilian Northeast (CSSH, 21:2, April 1979, p. 262–292, tables)

Excellent review of kinship relations and their implications for politics. Based on a review of literature. For historian's comment, see *HLAS 42:3689.*

Linhares, Maria Yedda. As listas eleitorais do Rio de Janeiro no século XIX. See *HLAS 42:3693.*

6743 McCann, Frank D., Jr. Origins of the "new professionalism" of the Brazilian military (SAGE/JIAS, 21:4, Nov. 1979, p. 505–522, table)

In this critical review of Stepan's concept of the "new professionalism" of internal security, the author reviews the history of the Brazilian military, finds that the inward-looking perspective has dominated its history, and concludes that there is nothing "new" of the definition of professional roles by the contemporary Brazilian military. Excellent review.

6744 Madeira, João Lyra. Elementos de análise dos processos demográficos do Nordeste (*in* Encontro Interregional de Cientistas Sociais do Brasil, 2d, Garanhuns, Brazil, 1974. Anais do II [i.e. Segundo] Encontro Interregional de Cientistas Sociais do Brasil: reuniões realizadas de 21 de janeiro de 1974 em Garanhuns-PE. Recife: Ministério da Educação e Cultura, Instituto Joaquim Nabuco de Pesquisas Sociais, 1977, p. 165–185, tables)

Straightforward demographic analysis of rural-urban and north-south migration in Northeast Brazil.

6745 Malloy, James M. The politics of social security in Brazil. Pittsburgh: University of Pittsburgh Press, 1979. 200 p.; bibl.; index (Pitt Latin American series)

A thorough study of social security policy from inception in the early 20th century, elaboration under the 1930s Vargas governments, the post-1946 struggle for reform and depolitization, through the final reform under the post-1964 military government. Author argues that social insurance policy is a classic example of public policy-making under corporativist regime in delayed, dependent, capitalist development economic systems. Concludes that the political paralysis that resulted from civilian competition to control the machinery of this particularly distributive policy generated the technocratic support for the authoritarian military government that emerged in 1964. For historian's comment, see *HLAS 42:3705.*

6746 Mikkelsen, Vagn. State and military: some considerations on Latin America and the Brazilian case (UC/I, 7:2/8:1, 1978, p. 77–88)

Military ideology cannot explain the policies of Brazil's military governments. Opportunities presented by both socioeconomic development and environment as well as cooperation between bureaucracies explain it better. Interesting analysis from a perspective that is often ignored.

Moisés, José Alvaro. Greve de massa e crise política: estudo da greve dos 300 mil em São Paulo, 1953/54. See *HLAS 42:3718.*

6747 Nichols, Glenn. Venturas e desventuras no estudo da política na América Latina (UMG/RBEP, 48, jan. 1979, p. 47–84, tables)

Interesting study of the organizational difficulties of the UDN political party. Author concludes UDN failed because of the impossibility of maintaining party unity in a chaotic electoral atmosphere.

Oliveira, Lucia Lippi. Revolução de 1930: uma bibliografia comentada. See *HLAS 42:58.*

6748 Olson, Richard Stuart. Expropriation and economic coercion in world politics: a retrospective look at Brazil in the 1960s (JDA, 13:3, April 1979, p. 247–262, tables)

Brazilian dependency permitted the

application of limited, unofficial and subtle economic coersion by the US to weaken some groups and strengthen others, in the latter case, especially the dominant economic elite which included US and other multinationals.

Pang, Eul-Soo. Bahia in the First Brazilian Republic: coronelismo and oligarchies, 1889–1934. See *HLAS 42:3727.*

6749 Parker, Phyllis R. Brazil and the quiet intervention, 1964. Austin: University of Texas Press, 1979. 147 p.; bibl.; index (Texas Pan American series)

An important contribution to the history of the Brazilian "revolution" of 1964. Based on detailed interview material and documents from the Lyndon B. Johnson Presidential Archives, the text develops a detailed account of US perceptions of crisis in the J. Goulart government and of the nature of US "collaboration" in the military coup of 31 March. Also provides exceptionally good, new coverage of the crucial days March 31 to April 3–4.

Resende, Maria Efigênia Lage de. Manifestações oligárquicas na política mineira: 1892–1897. See *HLAS 42:3741.*

6750 Roett, Riordan. The political future of Brazil (*in* The Future of Brazil. Edited by William H. Overholt. Contributors, William L. Ascher et al. Boulder, Colo.: Westview Press, 1978, p. 71–102)

A current assessment of changes in political institutions, social and economic conditions, and foreign relations ca. 1979 by an expert Brazilianist. Useful encapsulation of facts.

6751 Romano, Robert. Brasil, Igreja contra Estado: crítica ao populismo católico. São Paulo: Kairós Livraria e Editora, 1979. 270 p. (Coleção Primas; 1)

Detailed, and very well documented and footnoted work examines the evolution of the "progressive sociology" of the Brazilian Catholic Church. Describes the role of Church and state, and the history of antagonisms between them from the colonial period to the present, with extensive reference to ecclesiastical writings. Also places the Brazilian case within the larger context of the universal debate as to what are the roles of Church and state. Book is based on au-

thor's dissertation at the Paris École des Hautes Études en Sciences Sociales.

6752 Sá, Maria Auxiliadora Ferraz de. Dos velhos aos novos coronéis: um estudo das redefinições do coronelismo. Por M. Auxiliadora Ferraz de Sá. Recife: Universidade Federal de Pernambuco, PIMES, 1974. 137 p.; bibl.

Book is author's Master's thesis, a case study of municipal politics in the Pernambucan sertão that finds "coronelism" as described by V. Nunes Leal (see *HLAS 41:7554*) to continue to be the dominant political pattern in the Northeast interior, in spite of the substantial change in politics that has occurred at other levels of government.

6753 Schneider, José Odelso; Matias Martinho Lenz; and Almiro Petry. Realidade brasileira: estudo de problemas brasileiros. 5. ed. Porto Alegre: Editora Sulina, 1979. 426 p.; bibl.; graphs (Coleção universitária)

This textbook was sponsored by the Ministry of Education, for a university level civics course entitled "Study of Brazilian Problems" required by a 1969 law which dictated the teaching of moral and civic education in all schools. Text covers political-social-economic history and current situation in Brazil, examines social religious and population problems and proposes solutions. Includes substantial facts and details but "official" (i.e. government-line) solutions are emphasized.

6754 Soares, Glaucio Ary Dillon. Después del milagro (UNAM/RMS, 41[14]:2, abril/junio 1979, p. 429–456, tables)

Author, a recognized scholar who specializes in Brazilian politics, offers an unoriginal analysis: argues that the military regime based its claim to legitimacy on its ability to achieve high levels of growth of GDP but that when growth slowed or ceased the regime went into crisis. Author speculates that a change process must entail reduction of state intervention, development of alternative representational systems, and finally, a change in the political power structure.

6755 Sorj, Bernardo. Agrarian structure and politics in present day Brazil (LAP, 7[1]:24, Winter 1980, p. 23–34, tables)

Capitalization of agriculture in Brazil

is creating a "reserve army" of peasants who are not employable either in food production or in the industrial sector. Author emphasizes the importance of maintaining small-scale farming in societies with large peasant populations and archaic agrarian structures. Based on large-scale research project.

6756 Stepan, Alfred. Political leadership and regime breakdown: Brazil (*in* The Breakdown of democratic regimes: Latin America [see *HLAS 42:1920*] p. 110–137)

Summary of the causes of regime failure in 1964 by an authority on the period.

Topik, Steven. The evolution of the economic role of the Brazilian state, 1889–1930. See *HLAS 42:3765.*

———. Middle-class Brazilian nationalism, 1889–1930: from radicalism to reaction. See *HLAS 42:3766.*

Vianna, Luiz Werneck. Estudos sobre sindicalismo e movimento operário: resenha de algumas tendências. See *HLAS 42:71.*

Vieira, Evantina Pereira. Dinâmica das transformações eleitorais em Minas Imperial. See *HLAS 42:3775.*

6757 Wallerstein, Michael. The collapse of democracy in Brazil: its economic determinants (LARR, 15:3, 1980, p. 3–45, tables)

Economic decline resulted in a crisis of confidence in the political coalition that governed Brazil in the 1950s and 1960s and set social classes against each other. The loss of middle class support brought about the collapse of the regime. Author's analysis of economic determinants of the collapse of democracy are not new but he proposes unique economic solutions that might have saved the system.

JOURNAL ABBREVIATIONS
GOVERNMENT AND POLITICS

AAFH/TAM The Americas. A quarterly publication of inter-American cultural history. Academy of American Franciscan History. Washington.

ACHA/CHR Catholic Historical Review. American Catholic Historical Association. The Catholic Univ. of America Press. Washington.

ACPS/B Boletín de la Academia de Ciencias Políticas y Sociales. Caracas.

AJES The American Journal of Economics and Sociology. Francis Neilson Fund and Robert Schalkenbach Foundation. New York.

APS/WA World Affairs. The American Peace Society. Washington.

APSA/R American Political Science Review. American Political Science Association. Columbus, Ohio.

BESPL Berichte zur Entwicklung in Spanien, Portugal, Lateinamerika. München, FRG.

BNCE/CE Comercio Exterior. Banco Nacional de Comercio Exterior. México.

C/I *See* UC/I.

CDAL Cahiers des Amériques Latines. Paris.

CDLA Cada de las Américas. Instituto Cubano del Libro. La Habana.

CEDLA

CM/D Diálogos. Artes/Letras/Ciencias Humanas. El Colegio de México. México.

CM/FI Foro Internacional. El Colegio de México. México.

CP Cuadernos Políticos. Revista trimestral. Ediciones Era. México.

CPS Comparative Political Studies. Northwestern Univ., Evanston, Ill., and Sage Publications, Beverly Hills, Calif.

CPU/ES Estudios Sociales. Corporación de Promoción Universitaria. Santiago.

CSSH Comparative Studies in Society and History. An international quarterly. Society for the Comparative Study of Society and History. The Hague.

CUH Current History. A monthly magazine of world affairs. Philadelphia.

CUNY/CP Comparative Politics. The City Univ. of New York, Political Science Program. New York.

CYC Comunicación y Cultura. La comunicación masiva en el proceso político latinoamericano. Editorial Galerna. Buenos Aires y Santiago.

DDW Die Dritte Welt. Verlag Anton Hain. Meisenheim, FRG.

EDTM Estudios del Tercer Mundo. Centro de Estudios Económicos y Sociales del Tercer Mundo. México.

FDD/NED Notes et Études Documentaires. France, Direction de la Documentation. Paris.

FERES/SC Social Compass. International review of socio-religious studies (Revue internationale des études socio-religieuses). International Federation of Institutes for Social and Socio-Religious Research (Fédération Internationale des Institutes des Recherches Sociales et Socio-Religieuses [FERES]). The Hague.

FIU/CR Caribbean Review. Florida International Univ., Office of Academic Affairs. Miami.

FNSP/RFSP Revue Française de Science Politique. Fondation Nationale des Sciences Politiques, l'Association Française de Science Politique *avec le concours du* Centre National de la Recherche Scientifique. Paris.

HAHR Hispanic American Historical Review. Duke Univ. Press *for the* Conference on Latin American History of the American Historical Association. Durham, N.C.

IA International Affairs. A monthly journal of political analysis. Moskova.

IA/ZK Zeitschrift für Kulturaustausch. Institut für Auslandsbeziehungen. Stuttgart, FRG.

IAEERI/E Estrategia. Instituto Argentino de Estudios Estratégicos y de las Relaciones Internacionales. Buenos Aires.

IAMEA Inter-American Economic Affairs. Washington.

IDES/DE Desarrollo Económico. Instituto de Desarrollo Económico y Social. Buenos Aires.

IIB/DA Deutsche Aussenpolitik. Institut für Internationale Beziehungen. Berlin, GDR.

IIDC/C Civilisations. International Institute of Differing Civilizations. Bruxelles.

IRR/RC Race & Class. A journal for black and Third World liberation. Institute of Race Relations and The Transnational Institute. London.

JDA The Journal of Developing Areas. Western Illinois Univ. Press. Macomb.

JLAS Journal of Latin American Studies. Centers or institutes of Latin American studies at the universities of Cambridge, Glasgow, Liverpool, London and Oxford. Cambridge Univ. Press. London.

JPR Journal of Peace Research. Edited at the International Peace Research Institute. Universitetforlaget. Oslo.

LAP Latin American Perspectives. Univ. of California. Riverside.

LARR Latin American Research Review. Univ. of North Carolina Press *for the* Latin American Studies Association. Chapel Hill.

MR Monthly Review. An independent Socialist magazine. New York.

NACLA NACLA's Latin America & Empire Report. North American Congress on Latin America. New York.

NEA/RBPE The Review of Black Political Economy. National Economic Association and Atlanta Univ. Center. Atlanta, Ga.

NMC/N Nicaráuac. Revista bimestral del Ministerio de Cultura. Managua.

NRDM La Nouvelle Revuew des Deux Mondes. Paris.

NSO Nueva Sociedad. Revista política y cultural. San José.

OCLAE OCLAE. Revista mensual de la Organización Continental Latinoamericana de Estudiantes. La Habana.

PAN/ES Estudios Latinoamericanos. Polska Akademia Nauk (Academia de Ciencias de Polonia), Instytut Historii (Instituto de Historia). Warszawa.

PCCLAS/P Proceedings of the Pacific Coast Council on Latin American Studies. Univ. of California. Los Angeles.

PP Past and Present. London.

PUCIS/WP World Politics. A quarterly journal of international relations. Princeton Univ., Center of International Studies. Princeton, N.J.

RCPC Revista del Pensamiento Centroamericano. Centro de Investigaciones y Actividades Culturales. Managua.

RU/MP Marxist Perspectives. Transaction Periodicals Consortium. Rutgers Univ. New Brunswick, N.J.

SAA/HO Human Organization. Society for Applied Anthropology. New York.

SAGE/JIAS Journal of Inter-American Studies and World Affairs. Sage Publication *for the* Center for Advanced International Studies, Univ. of Miami. Coral Gables, Fla.

SPSA/JP The Journal of Politics. The Southern Political Science Association *in cooperation with the* Univ. of Florida. Gainesville.

UB/GG Geschichte und Gesellschaft. Univ. Bielefeld. Bielefeld, FRG.

UC/EDCC Economic Development and Cultural Change. Univ. of Chicago, Research Center in Economic Development and Cultural Change. Chicago.

UC/I Ibero-Americana. Univ. of California Press. Berkeley.

UC/S Signs. Journal of women in culture and society. The Univ. of Chicago Press. Chicago.

UCA/E Encuentro. Revista de la Univ. Centroamericana, Instituto Histórico. Managua.

UCC/RU Revista Universitaria. Anales de la Academia Chilena de Ciencias Naturales. Univ. Católica de Chile. Santiago.

UCL/CD Cultures et Développement. Revue internationale des sciences du développement. Univ. Catholique de Louvain *avec le concours de la* Fondation Universitaire de Belgique. Louvain, Belgium.

UCLA/JLAL Journal of Latin American Lore. Univ. of California, Latin American Center. Los Angeles.

UCLV/I Islas. Univ. Central de las Villas. Santa Clara, Cuba.

UCP/IAP Ibero-Americana Pragensia. Univ. Carolina de Praga, Centro de Estudios Ibero-Americanos. Prague.

UCSD/NS The New Scholar. Univ. of California, Center for Iberian and Latin American Studies and Institute of Chicano Urban Affairs. San Diego, Calif.

UFMG/DCP Cadernos DCP. Univ. Federal de Minas Gerais, Faculdade de Filosofia e Ciências Humanas, Depto. de Ciência Política. Belo Horizonte, Brazil.

UJSC/ECA Estudios Centro-Americanos. Revista de extensión cultural. Univ. José Simeón Cañas. San Salvador.

UM/JIAS *See* SAGE/JIAS.

UMG/RBEP Revista Brasileira de Estudos Políticos. Univ. de Minas Gerais. Belo Horizonte, Brazil.

UNAM/PDD Problemas del Desarrollo. Univ. Nacional Autónoma de México, Instituto de Investigaciones Económicas. México.

UNAM/RFD Revista de la Facultad de Derecho. Univ. Nacional Autónoma de México. México.

UNAM/RMCPS Revista Mexicana de Ciencias Políticas y Sociales. Univ. Nacional Autónoma de México, Facultad de Ciencias Políticas y Sociales. México.

UNAM/RMS Revista Mexicana de Sociología. Univ. Nacional Autónoma de México, Instituto de Investigaciones Sociales. México.

UND/RP The Review of Politics. Univ. of Notre Dame. Notre Dame, Ind.

UPR/CS Caribbean Studies. Univ. of Puerto Rico, Institute of Caribbean Studies. Río Piedras.

UPR/RCS Revista de Ciencias Sociales. Univ. de Puerto Rico, Colegio de Ciencias Sociales. Río Piedras.

URSS/AL América Latina. Academia de Ciencias de la URSS (Unión de Repúblicas Soviéticas Socialistas). Moscú.

USCG/PS Política y Sociedad. Univ. de San Carlos de Guatemala, Facultad de Ciencias Jurídicas y Sociales, Escuela de Ciencia Política, Instituto de Investigaciones Políticas y Sociales. Guatemala.

USIA/PC Problems of Communism. United States Information Agency. Washington.

UTIEH/C Caravelle. Cahiers du monde hispanique et luso-brésilien. Univ. de Toulouse, Institut d'Études Hispaniques, Hispano-Americaines et Luso-Brésiliennes. Toulouse, France.

UU/WPQ   Western Political Quarterly. Univ. of Utah, Institute of Government *for the* Western Political Science Association; Pacific Northwest Political Science Association; and Southern California Political Science Association. Salt Lake City.

WQ   The Wilson Quarterly. Woodrow Wilson International Center for Scholars. Washington.

ZMR   Zeitschrift für Missionswissenschaft und Religionswissenschaft. Lucerne, Switzerland.

INTERNATIONAL RELATIONS

YALE H. FERGUSON, *Professor of Political Science, Rutgers University—Newark*
C. NEALE RONNING, *Professor of Political Science, New School for Social Research*

REVIEWING THE LITERATURE PUBLISHED OVER THE PAST two years, we are struck by two major trends. The first is the re-emergence in the US of writings that adopt a distinctly right-wing ideological perspective, the likes of which has not been seen (outside of the John Birch-style "underground" press) since the 1950s. A second trend is a large increase in the volume of literature on Mexico, Central America, and the Caribbean islands, coupled with some decrease in materials focusing on South America. This shift is obviously a function of Mexico's growing importance as a supplier of energy and immigrants; its cooperation and rivalry with Venezuela; the Nicaraguan revolution; violence in El Salvador and related political tensions throughout Central America; the Panama Canal treaties; Cuba's continued involvement in Africa and alleged meddling in Central America; mounting interest in the future status of Puerto Rico; Jamaica's change in leadership from Michael Manley to Edward Seaga; and in general, the increasingly prominent international role being played by the English-speaking Caribbean states. At the same time, Brazil's stature as an emergent middle power on the world scene has been somewhat diminished by the country's dependence on foreign oil, a slowdown in the "economic miracle," and the political strains of *abertura*.

The new generation of right-wing literature primarily concerns US policies toward Latin America, and it clearly represents part of the "conservative" and "neoconservative" (or more accurately, "reactionary") tide that almost defeated the Panama Canal treaties (e.g., item **7236**) and subsequently swept the new administration into office. With few exceptions, writings from this quarter contain neither scholarship nor analysis, but rather propaganda of a strident sort resembling nothing so much as the "capitalist dog" school of Communist broadsides which even the Kremlin eschews today. Most of these essays would be downright silly if their authors were not so close to the center of power, a fact which forces us to take such works seriously and, indeed, lends them a certain sinister quality. Consistently the worst are the publications from the Washington-based Council for Inter-American Security (CIAS), embodying a curious mixture of old-fashioned geopolitical determinism, apocalyptic visions of Communist plans for world domination, and a fervent devotion to private enterprise. Convinced of the supreme righteousness of their own cause, the authors of these essays are the foreign policy equivalent of the Moral Majority.

A cut above the products of institutions such as CIAS are the writings of Jeane Kirkpatrick (items **7058** and **7059**) and Roger Fontaine (item **7306**, co-authored with DiGiovanni and Kruger). Both authors are ideological, and thus their policy prescriptions are quite predictable. Neither is above using an occasional rhetorical flourish or innuendo in support of a line of argument. Their policy positions are quite predictable. Fontaine (through the Committee of Santa Fé) has been closely linked to the CIAS (item **7091**). However, since Kirkpatrick and Fontaine at least make an attempt to rationalize their prescriptions, their works offer a genuine intellectual framework and policy alternative.

Nevertheless, as we have suggested, neither the assumptions behind the policies nor the policies themselves are really new; rather they are simply warmed-over versions of those prevailing prior to the Kennedy Alliance for Progress. The right-wing critique admires JFK's anti-Communism, overlooks his interest in further-ing democracy in Latin America, and condemns the Alliance as a foolish effort of fuzzy-minded "social reformers." In this view, the Alliance was a watershed com-parable to FDR's New Deal, a period when "liberals" began to get the upper hand and US policy toward Latin America started to go astray. President Johnson, iron-ically, gets higher marks than Nixon-Ford-Kissinger, who did well in Allende's Chile but committed the unpardonable sin of advancing the transfer of the Panama Canal to (in Kirkpatrick's words) "a swaggering Latin dictator of a Castroist bent."

Although President Carter is blamed for negotiating the final terms of the Canal transfer, it is his administration's human rights policy that draws the most fire. The central assumptions of the right wing regarding Latin America are that the Castroist (Soviet) threat is immediate and serious, and that rapid social change in the region may be inimical to US interests, insofar as it is likely to bring the "ex-treme left" to the fore. The right alleges that, in places like Nicaragua and El Salva-dor, the Carter policy undermined "moderate autocrats" friendly to the US and paved the way for the radicals. Adding insult to injury, Carter was unduly toler-ant—in the name of "ideological pluralism," "diversity," and/or respect for national sovereignty—of human rights violations in Communist countries.

Former Assistant Secretary of State for Inter-American Affairs Viron P. Vaky writes (item **7153**): "The Reagan Administration is likely to have a good apprecia-tion of power, but it may also underestimate the importance of 'abstractions' such as human rights." Tom Farer, (item **7032**) addressing Kirkpatrick, maintains that a human rights policy can be applied to Latin American corporatist regimes (e.g., Argentina) without the risk of creating social chaos, and that the long-range pros-pect for democracy appears bright in many countries.

It is too soon to expect any more definitive critiques of Reagan administration policies. The challenge for analysts when tackling this task will be to avoid reply-ing to ideology with ideology. For example, Kirkpatrick, *et al.*, do have a point when they insist that, as concerns human rights, the Carter administration was not as hard on some US "enemies" as on some US "friends," whether in order to avoid a "Cold War" posture, to preserve East-West negotiations on arms control and other matters, or for whatever reason. Moreover, some scholarly commentators have preferred to ignore or downplay grave human rights abuses under "progressive" authoritarian regimes while decrying the excesses of rightist military governments.

Urgently needed, then, are self-consciously "objective" (or as nearly "objective" as possible) answers to such basic and interrelated questions as the following: How actively are the Soviet Union and Cuba currently engaged in fostering "revolution" in Central America and elsewhere in Latin America? Would the existence of more radical-left regimes in Central America or the Caribbean actually be a serious threat to US security? Is the US more or less likely to shape favorable political outcomes by adopting a strict non-interventionist stance or by supporting the sta-tus quo, reformist forces, or even (if they are likely to win anyway) the radical left? Must the foregoing question be answered only on a country-by-country basis? If "support" is required, what form should it take? Given US domestic political con-straints, is it realistic to expect that the US can either long remain aloof from, or risk creating instability in, any situation where radicalism is a possible outcome?

Are any "human rights" universal, or are all culture-bound? In either case, is a human rights policy a moral imperative, or is there a higher morality in not trying to impose one country's values on another? To what extent is the US conception of human rights already shared by Latin American cultures? Is an inconsistently applied human rights policy inherently suspect and therefore likely to lose most of its force? Or is consistency an unattainable and unnecessary goal? Do selective applications leading to occasional gains in specific countries constitute a "policy"? Can adequate stability and/or socioeconomic change be achieved in Latin America without repression? Are tensions between security and human rights, and between political rights and socioeconomic rights, inevitably so severe as to foredoom even a flexible policy?

Anyone seeking answers to these questions will find useful some of the materials under review concerning human rights and the Carter policies. John D. Martz (in item **7067**) and C. Neale Ronning (item **7118**) point out contrasts between North and Spanish American views of democracy. Richard L. Clinton and R. Kenneth Godwin (in item **7067**) deal with traditional US neglect of the economic and social dimensions of human rights. Lars Schoultz stresses the menace posed by human rights policy to "the existing structure of privilege" (item **7128**), demonstrates that a disproportionate amount of US aid in the mid-1970s went to repressive governments (item **7129**), and examines the major policy shift during the early years of the Carter administration (in item **7067**). Howard Warshawsky (item **7158**) presents a case study of the organization and functioning of the Human Rights Bureau within the "pragmatic" Department of State; G. D. Loescher and Joseph Eldridge explore the interaction over human rights between the Executive Branch and Congress (items **7031** and **7075**); and Lewis H. Diuguid discusses the activities of human rights lobbies in Washington (item **7028**). Also interesting, especially in light of the ideological right's denunciation of the Carter human rights policy as "soft" on leftist regimes and undermining friendly authoritarian governments, is the conviction of leftist observers that the human rights policy was nothing but a shrewd capitalist ploy. James Petras (item **7108**), the Soviet analyst, Atroshenko (item **7008**), and leading Marxist dependency theorist, Theotonio dos Santos (item **7123**)—all charge, essentially, that the Carter policy was merely a cosmetic attempt (required after Vietnam, Watergate, the Allende murder, etc.) to bolster the US's sagging image in the world and to disguise continued US intervention and imperialism.

The Reagan administration's revival of geopolitics and its sending of military advisers to El Salvador lends heightened relevance to several items on inter-American military relations. John Child (items **7017** and **7018**) traces US strategic conceptions of Latin America and institutional links with the Latin American military from the end of World War I to the present. Harvey G. Sherzer et al. (item **7134**) examine the policies, laws, and bureaucratic procedures relating to US foreign military sales. John Samuel Fitch and Claude Heller (items **7034** and **7045**) wrestle with the perennial question of the local political impact of US military assistance.

Additional materials reviewed offer historical perspective on US-Latin American relations and case studies of some relatively recent events. Charles Henry Brown (item **7229**) narrates the exploits of the Manifest Destiny filibusterers. Thomas David Schoonover (item **7209**) documents the ideological convergence (1861–67) between Mexico's Liberals and the new Republican Party in the US, asserting that it had long-range economic consequences. Allan Peskin (item **7106**) upgrades Garfield's contribution to a renewed US interest in Latin America in the late 19th century. Lester D. Langley (item **7327**) gives us a straightforward diplomatic history of 20th century US relations with the Caribbean countries. Irwin F. Gellman's book on the Good Neighbor Policy (item **7040**) supplements the many other works on this era by emphasizing the personalities and roles of key policy-makers. Peter Wyden's account of the Bay of Pigs (item **7359**), based on interviews with participants and newly de-classified materials, is the most complete to appear to date. Piero Gleijeses (item **7310**) adds to our understanding of the 1965 Dominican intervention by presenting information on the maneuvering of various groups and personalities, and Howard J. Wiarda (item **7357**), reviewing Gleijeses' book and others, points out several important aspects of the Dominican case that still need clarification. John Dinges and Saul Landau (item **7454**) examine in excruciating detail the 1976 murder of Orlando Letelier and Ronni Moffitt, the plot that led up to it, and the aftermath.

The literature on Mexico has been growing in direct proportion to the energy-rich country's international status. An outstanding collection of essays edited by Susan Kaufman Purcell (item **7193**) covers the full gamut of Mexico's current relations with the US. Another similar collection, edited by Robert J. McBride (item **7192**), is also worthy of special note, as are two from the Colegio de México, on contemporary Mexico and Mexican foreign policy (items **7189** and **7211**).

Readers interested in the domestic and international politics of Mexican energy should not overlook the most recent books and articles by two prominent North American students of the subject, George W. Grayson (item **7043**) and Edward J. Williams (item **7223**); a Rand study done for the US Department of Energy (item **7206**); and a major essay by Richard R. Fagen and Henry R. Nau (in item **7016**) on US-Mexican negotiations over natural gas. Not surprisingly, Mexican and other Latin American scholars, e.g., Olga Pellicer (item **7199**), emphasize the need for Mexico to proceed with due caution and careful planning, so that its new wealth will be channeled into genuine national development and not result in an even more complex pattern of dependency on the US.

Most analysts, regardless of nationality, stress the fact that energy development in Mexico is inextricably linked to a host of other issues, most of which also involve the US. A subliterature of sorts is building up on frontier problems: Migration of workers is treated in two essays by Wayne A. Cornelius (in items **7192** and **7193**); Jean Revel-Mouroz writes on border industries (item **7204**); Stephen Mumme and C. Richard Bath deal with groundwater (item **5128** and in item **7193**); and Bath and Alberto Székely discuss coastal waters (item **7214**). On yet another important issue, Mexico's treatment of foreign capital, see especially Douglas C. Bennett's and Kenneth E. Sharpe's excellent case study of transnational automobile corporations (item **7168**), and essays by Richard A. Weinert (in item **7193**) and Robert S. Tancer (item **7217**).

On Mexico's relations with countries other than the US, three documentary anthologies should be highlighted. Two were published by the Secretariat of Foreign Relations, one on Mexico and Japan in the 19th century (item **7195**) and the other on Mexican-Russian relations from 1789–1927 (item **7172**). A third collection deals with Mexico and Spain from 1821 to 1977 (item **7203**).

The literature on Cuban foreign policy has also been growing rapidly, reflecting Castro's greater activism in recent years. General reference works include a calendar and analysis of Cuban bilateral agreements from 1959–76 (items **7339** and **7341**), a CIA chronology of Cuba's bilateral relationships 1975–77 (item **7349**), and a survey of Soviet writings on the Cuban Revolution from 1959–77 (item **7331**).

Few military campaigns of non-major powers in history have received as much consideration in print as Cuba's campaign in Africa. Two first-rate symposia on this subject have appeared in the journal *Cuban Studies* (Jan. and July 1980 issues). Among the most thoughtful and comprehensive analyses are those by Jorge I. Domínguez, William J. LeoGrande, and Wolf Grabendorff (items **7300, 7312** and **7329–7330**). Virtually all observers conclude, with Cole Blasier (item **7289**), that Cuba is acting as a "partner" rather than a "pawn, surrogate, or proxy" of the USSR.

Another substantial body of writings reviewed concerns the 1979 meeting of the Nonaligned Movement in Havana. Most of the material comes from Cuban and Soviet sources, which naturally overlook or underplay the schism at the meeting between those countries that did and those that did not regard Cuba's close association with the Soviets as compromising its nonalignment. Dietrich Schlegel, a German journalist, provides a more balanced assessment of the meeting (item **7126**). For a good general background, see also Robert A. Mortimer's volume on the Third World coalition (item **7087**).

The impact of Cuba's ties with the Soviet Union on the Western Hemisphere was the concern of extensive hearings in mid-1980 before the House Subcommittee on Inter-American Affairs (item **7350**). *The Restless Caribbean*, an anthology edited by Richard Millet and W. Marvin Will (item **7343**), deals with Cuba and a wide range of other regional issues. Another collection edited by Basil A. Ince (item **7295**) addresses principally, but not exclusively, the international relations of the English-speaking Caribbean. W. Andrew Axline's book-length study of Caribbean integration (item **7283**) is both useful for its information and interesting from a theoretical standpoint.

Puerto Rico, too, has received more attention, as Cuba and other Latin American states have begun to take positions on the question of its status. Particularly recommended are articles by José Cabranes, Alfred Stepan, and pro-statehood Governor Carlos Romero Barceló (items **7141, 7286** and **7291**).

Overviews of the continuing political turmoil in Central America and US policies toward the subregion can be gleaned from several items, written from a wide variety of perspectives. Mexican scholar Luis Maira contributes an unusually perceptive article on the evolution of Carter administration policies (item **7255**). In additional House Subcommitttee on Inter-American Affairs hearings in mid-1980, officials of the American Chamber of Commerce express their alarm about the political inroads of the left in several countries (item **7274**). Richard Millett and Thomas W. Walker (items **7260** and **7276**) advance their own policy prescriptions for the US; respectively, they are to involve other Latin American and Western alliance countries in the search for a solution, and to adopt a less negative attitude toward insurgency and "distributive justice."

Little of substance has yet been written about the foreign policy and international relations of the revolutionary government of Nicaragua. What has appeared would seem to bolster, perhaps misleadingly, the view that the government is inexorably moving to the left; they range from enthusiastic praise by Fidel (item **7261**) and other Marxist observers, to fiery speeches by Nicaraguan leaders like Daniel Ortega (item **7262**) and dire warnings from conservative congressmen and business spokesmen in the US (item **7275**).

The literature analyzing the political crisis in El Salvador is by no means complete either. However, as the 1969 conflict passes into history, we have at least two good studies of El Salvador's "Soccer War" with Honduras: one by Mary Jeanne Reid Martz (item **7258**) which emphasizes OAS peacekeeping; and another by William H. Durham (item **7239**) blaming the war on landholding patterns in both countries rather than population pressures *per se*. As for the current turmoil, there is some useful material—especially several articles that appear together in the

Summer 1981 issue of *Foreign Policy* (items **7244, 7249, 7265** and **7271**)—but readers may be bewildered by wildly varying assessments of how genuinely reform-minded the Duarte regime is, the extent to which the left is dominated by extremists, and what US policy toward the country should be.

Olga Pellicer de Brody terms Reagan administration policies in El Salvador "disconcerting, even stupefying to Mexico" (item **7265**). Central America itself also can be described as stupefying, not only because the political situation in much of the subregion is so fluid, but also, frankly, because that this is a part of the world that even most Latin American specialists know precious little about. In El Salvador, as in Iran, the US is paying a price for its longstanding neglect of area studies! Guatemala, as Marlise Simons reminds us (item **7268**), may well become the next hot spot where ideology will have to fill the vacuum of ignorance when it comes to policy-making.

Moving beyond the traditional boundaries of Central America, we come to Panama and the central issue of the new Canal treaties. As noted above, prior to the ratification of the new agreements, a strong current of opinion in the US held that they were unduly prejudicial to US interests. Conservatives protested what they regarded as a "surrender" of US "sovereignty" over the Canal (item **7236**), and even some less ideologically-inclined observers found certain ambiguities in the treaties that could cause future problems for the US (item **7269**). Now that the treaties are being implemented, it is intriguing and perhaps a bit ominous that much of the Latin American commentary criticize the agreements for not going far enough in advancing Panama's exclusive control over the Canal and ending the US hegemonic role.

Lastly, a few items of importance that do not fit neatly into any of our other categories should be mentioned: Howard J. Wiarda's challenging attempt to draw parallels between Latin American corporatism and corporatist trends in the US (item **7160**); Tony Smith's provocative critique of dependency theory (item **7139**); a careful analysis of Europe's past, present, and probable future orientation toward the developing South, by one of the best dependency theorists, Constantine V. Vaitsos (item **7152**); a collection edited by Richard R. Fagen on *Capitalism and the state in Latin America* (item **7016**); and article by a leading student of the multinationals, Raymond Vernon, making a case for divorcing the multinationals entirely from the protection or control of their home governments (item **7156**); an in-depth study by Edy Kaufman *et al.* of Israel's relations with Latin America (item **7055**); J.C.M. Oglesby's review of a decade (1968–78) of Canadian overtures to Latin America under Prime Minister Trudeau (item **7098**); a documentary anthology of the declarations of Latin American bishops' meetings over the same decade (item **7095**); and a valuable reference directory of inter-American and Latin American international organizations (item **7101**).

The literature of South America, as noted above, has declined in number over the past two years. Moreover, most of what we have continues along familiar lines. The same old boundary disputes are discussed with little new information and even less objectivity. The same may be said concerning works on the Law of the Sea. Geopolitics has been "rediscovered" by many writers, but elaborate and competent reviews of the subject by the established theorists, such as MacKinder and Haushofer, are seldom related or applied to the reality on which they are supposed to shed light, one exception being Lewis Tambs' "The Changing" (item **7391**). Sometimes the "geopolitical theme" is also a convenient vehicle to focus on an old grievance as in Baptista Gumucio's "Antología Geopolítica" (item **7416**).

Brazil's foreign policy continues to interest its neighbors. Argentines usually demonstrate varying degrees of concern, but at least one Peruvian, Edgardo Mercado Jarrin (item **7380**), has found reason for optimism. Brazilian nuclear policy receives a substantial amount of critical attention, and has been the subject of at least one full length monograph by Kurt Mirow (item **7439**).

A number of solid studies of Venezuelan diplomatic history and foreign policy stand in refreshing contrast to the many tired trends still being debated on the continent. The studies by Sheldon Liss and Aristides Calvani (items **7474** and **7477**) are two interesting and useful examples.

Also notable are the worthwhile attempts to reassess Argentine policy during World War II. This reassessment is overdue, and should lead to further interesting work.

General

7001 Ad Hoc Working Group on Latin America. The southern connection: recommendations for a new approach to inter-American relations. Washington: Transnational Institute, 1977. 22 leaves.

Report presenting the views on US policy toward Latin America of an ad hoc group of North American specialists on inter-American affairs that was brought together in 1976 under the auspices of the Institute for Policy Studies in Washington, D.C. Those endorsing the final draft were Guy F. Erb, Richard R. Fagen, Michael Locker, Abraham F. Lowenthal, Riordan Roett, and Roberta Salper. Robert Pastor, Carter's National Security Council adviser on Latin America, was a member of the group but had to bow out before the report was in final form. The report foreshadowed several aspects of the Carter policies, including human rights, "ideological pluralism," and a Panama Canal settlement. Conservative critics of Carter (see item **7306**) subsequently made much of the fact that the report was published by the IPS Transnational Institute, headed (until his murder) by former Allende official, Orlando Letelier. [F.]

7002 Aguilar M., Alonso. La crisis del capitalismo y el Nuevo Orden Económico Internacional (Economía Política [Universidad Nacional Autónoma de Honduras, Instituto de Investigaciones Económicas y Sociales, Tegucigalpa] 16, julio 1978/marzo 1979, p. 81–144)

Aguilar applauds the post-energy-crunch "decline" of capitalism, which he regards as a crisis of "over-production," but he warns that the battle for socialism is by no means over. An alliance of repressive state-capitalist regimes and imperialism, including the multinationals, is continuing to repress the masses in Latin America. In his view, the reforms of the New International Economic Order are not likely to be achieved until socialism has triumphed. [F.]

7003 Alexander, Robert F. Diminishing U.S. aid in Latin America (CUH, 77:448, July/Aug. 1979, p. 18–21, 26)

Outline of some of the major patterns in US economic aid to Latin America since the Franklin D. Roosevelt administration founded the Export-Import Bank. Notes the impact of decisions in the 1970s to assist bilaterally only the poor majority of developing countries, to focus on projects supposedly reaching the poor majority of persons within those countries, to link aid more directly to human rights, and to urge other countries to bear a greater share of multilateral aid. [F.]

7004 Amadeo, Mario. Manual de política internacional: los principios y los hechos. 2. ed., corr. y actualizada. Buenos Aires: Abeledo-Perrot, 1978, 691 p.; bibl.; index.

This should be a valuable college level textbook for international politics. The standard topics are covered in addition to chapters on colonialism, development and underdevelopment, new problems in international relations, and "Ibero-American regionalism." [R.]

American Jewish Committee. South America Office. Comunidades judías en Latinoamérica: 1973–1975. See item **8003**.

7005 Antecedentes, balance y perspectivas del sistema interamericano. Obra editada bajo la dirección de Rodrigo Díaz Albonico. Santiago de Chile: Editorial Universitaria, 1977. 243 p.; bibl. (Estudios internacionales)

A group of academicians from the University of Chile discuss and analyze a wide range of activities within the inter-American system—collective security, pacific settlement of disputes, commercial relations, transfer of technology and institutional relations between the OAS and the UN are among the most prominent. The treatment is both analytical and critical. [R.]

Arbitration treaties among the American nations, to the close of the year 1910. See *HLAS 42:1764.*

7006 Arnold, Hans. Kulturelle Zusammenarbeit mit Lateinamerika (AZIF, 25:1, 1974, p. 73–79)

A high official in the Foreign Office of the German Federal Republic outlines the aims and priorities of Germany's cultural exchange programs with Latin America, while also describing briefly the mechanisms to carry out these goals. Reflects the heightened interest of the Federal Republic in Luso-Hispanic America. [G.M. Dorn]

7007 Artemiyev, P. and **A. Klimov.** The Havana Summit in retrospect (IA, 12, Dec. 1979, p. 27–32)

Speaking for the "world progressive public" and the "Soviet people," these two Soviet authors proclaim the 1979 Nonaligned Conference in Havana to have been a truly smashing success! [F.]

7008 Atroskenko, A. The USA's Latin American doctrines (IA, 12, Dec. 1979, p. 52–59)

"The 'human rights' doctrine was conceived as the ideological basis for the crusade against socialism and democracy and as a means for improving the USA's image abroad, which was tarnished by the dirty war in Indochina and the Watergate scandal . . . [and] to dissociate [the US], if only as a token gesture, from reactionary military, fascist or semi-fascist regimes in Latin America." [F.]

7009 The Automotive industry in Latin America. Edited by Jan Herd. Erie, Pa.: The Northwestern Pennsylvania Institute for Latin American Studies, Mercyhurst College, 1980. 178 p. (Latin American monograph series; no. 12)

Contains three interesting and data-rich essays: Charles A. Ford, "Past Developments and Future Trends in Mexican Automotive Policy: Implications for United States-Mexican Trade;" George H. Westacott, "The Brazilian Automobile Industry: Development and Outlook;" and John H. Hoagland "Some Possible Trends in Latin America: Passenger Car Production 1980–1985." Significant reading for students of the countries involved, trade, industrial development policy, and the multinationals. [F.]

Baecker, Thomas. Deutschland im karibischen Raum im Spiegel amerikanischer Akten: 1898–1941. See *HLAS 42:2592.*

7010 Bajitov, Rustem. Pekín y su política en América Latina (URSS/AL, 4, 1979, p. 35–51)

According to this Soviet analyst, who carefully details the People's Republic of China's relations with Latin America during the 1970s, the Chinese are up to no good (as usual) in the region. They are seeking to maximize their own selfish interests, including continuing contacts with reactionary forces and governments, and most recently have even been drawing closer to the US. Moreover, their development model is absolutely unsuited to Latin America. [F.]

7011 Barraclough, Geoffrey. La pugna por el Tercer Mundo (RO, 1, abril/junio 1980, p. 25–42)

Abbreviated version, published in a Spanish journal, of an article that appeared previously in *The New York Review of Books.* It is a general look at economic multipolarity in the North, different forms and degrees of underdevelopment among the countries of the South, and the proposed New International Economic Order. Finding a way to meet some or all of the NIEO demands, Barraclough believes, is one of the great challenges facing the contemporary world. [F.]

Boletín de Ciencias Económicas y Sociales. Año 2, No. 11, abril 1979–   . See *HLAS 42:198.*

Boletín Informativo Trotskysta. No. 1, abril 1979– . See *HLAS* 42:202.

Britain and Latin America. See *HLAS* 42:203.

7012 Bruce, David C. The impact of the United Nations Economic Commission for Latin America: technocrats as channels of influence (IAMEA, 33:4, Spring 1980, p. 3–28, tables)

Interesting attempt to assess the influence of ECLA by looking at 1) the extent to which ECLA training shaped technocrats' thinking (questionnaire); and 2) the career patterns of *ex-cepalinos*, by way of determining whether they were in a position to affect government policies. Among Bruce's findings is that more ECLA-trained technocrats remained in government circles in high-growth countries like Brazil. [F.]

7013 Bull, Hedley. The Third World and international society (LIWA/YWA, 1979, p. 15–31).

Bull addresses several related issues: the extent to which a "Third World" actually exists and is united in its policies, the degree to which the demands of Third World spokesmen are truly "revolutionary," and the consensus or lack thereof on the rules or norms that should govern the contemporary international system. He leans heavily on the work of Ada Bozeman. [F.]

7014 Cabello Sarubbi, Oscar J. La participación de los Estados in litoral en la Tercera Conferencia de las Nacionas Unidas sobre el Derecho del Mar (UCNSA/EP, 6:1, sept. 1978, p. 63–84)

States without a seacoast and geographically disadvantaged states, acting in their own self interest have been the principal defenders of the "common patrimony" doctrine with regard to oceans and ocean resources. Nevertheless, it would be very difficult to measure their influence and what effect it might have on other states. [R.]

7015 Cannabrava F., Paulo. Carter y la Trilateral (UNAM/PDD, 9:35, agosto/oct. 1978, p. 73–83, ill.)

This article is illustrated with drawings of rather obscene skulls and skeletons, depicting—in the author's subtle manner—the "imperialist alliance" of the Trilateral Commission. Presumably it will get you if you don't watch out! [F.]

7016 Capitalism and the State in U.S.-Latin American relations. Edited by Richard R. Fagen; contributors, Cynthia Arnson et al. Stanford, Calif.: Stanford University Press, 1979. 446 p.; bibl.; index.

Collection of essays which, the editor states, "continues the work begun earlier under the auspices of the SSRC-ACLS and reported in Julio Cotler and Richard R. Fagen eds., *Latin America and the United States: the changing political realities* (1974, see *HLAS* 37:8716). Definitely an important book, well worth reading; however, it is not as satisfying as its predecessor, mainly because of its rather pronounced ideological bias critical both to US policy and international capitalism. In short, there has been little or no attempt to make this a "balanced" collection. This said, particularly some of the case studies in pt. 2 are excellent. This reviewer especially admired: Barbara Stallings' "Peru and the U.S. Banks: Privitization of Financial Relations;" Peter Evans' "Shoes, OPIC, and the Unquestioning Persuasion: Multinational Corporations and US-Brazilian Relations;" and Richard R. Fagen's and Henry R. Nau's "Mexican Gas: the Northern Connection." Also thought-provoking is Fagen's Introduction, in which he observes: "In sum, we are still a long way from having generated the frameworks necessary for analyzing the new political economy of U.S. foreign policy—frameworks that would take full cognizance of contemporary capitalism, on the one hand, and link the insight gained there to detailed understandings of the contemporary state, on the other." [F.]

Catholic Church. Comisión Pontificia Justitia et Pax. La Iglesia y los derechos del hombre. See item **6524.**

Chester, Edward. The United States and six Atlantic outposts: the military and economic considerations. See *HLAS* 42:2596.

7017 Child, John. From "color" to "rainbow:" U.S. strategic planning for Latin America, 1919–1945 (SAGE/JIAS, 21:2, May 1979, p. 233–260, bibl., maps, table)

Interesting and important article by a leading student of US military relations with Latin America. Child's archival research documents US military planners' "unilateral interventionist strategic approach embodied in the concept of the 'American Lake'; the slow abandonment of the 'American Lake' concept in the face of the multilateral Good Neighbor Policy; and the adoption of a bilateral World War II approach best described as special bilateral relationships with key countries in the Quarter Sphere." He notes that "the U.S. military departments were prepared to return to unilateral approaches, and planned for them, if the bilateral approach should fail to obtain U.S. objectives in the key nations in the Quarter Sphere—most importantly Brazil and Mexico." For historian's comment, see *HLAS 42:1924.* [F.]

————. Geopolitical thinking in Latin America. See item **6019**.

7018 ————. Unequal alliance: the inter-American military system, 1938–1979. Boulder, Colo.: Westview Press, 1980. 253 p.; bibl.; map (A Westview replica edition)

Pioneering, unusually well-researched and documented study of US-Latin American military relations over a 30-year span since the eve of World War II. Doctoral dissertation written by a US Army Lt. Colonel and faculty member at the Inter-American Defense College. Despite current "fragmentation" in the inter-American system, Child argues, the US has benefitted and continues to benefit from the channels of influence its institutional links to the Latin American military provide. Author perhaps accepts a little too uncritically the notion that all the results of the system, even for the US, have been good: Others would argue, for example, that the hard-line anti-Communist doctrine transmitted to the Latin American military has frustrated not only radical revolution but also needed reform. [F.]

7019 Cobo, Juan. El foro de los No Alineados (URSS/AL, 1, 1980, p. 4–22)

Writing in a Soviet journal, Cobo praises the accomplishments of the 1979 Nonaligned Meeting in Havana, which he interprets as a major step forward for the Third World and a severe blow to the forces of Western imperialism. No mention is made of the split at the gathering over the problem of Soviet "hegemony," highlighted by the fact that the delegates were hosted by a government rather clearly aligned with the USSR. [F.]

7020 Communist relations with Latin America in 1977 (IAMEA, 32:4, Spring 1979, p. 85–94)

Material taken from CIA research paper, "Communist Aid to Less-Developed Countries of the Free World, 1977." [F.]

Conflict, order and peace in the Americas. See *HLAS 42:1925.*

7021 Connell-Smith, Gordon. Latin American relations with the world, 1826–1976. London: Hispanic and Luso Brazilian Council: Distributed by Grant and Cutler, 1976. 20 p.; bibl. (Annual lecture—Canning House; 21. Diamante; 26)

Address given by British historian of the inter-American system at Canning House in London, on the occasion of the 150th anniversary of Bolívar's Panama Congress. He observes that since that time: "Latin America's relations with the world have changed, but the world has changed more than has Latin America." [F.]

7022 Conta, Manfred von. Lateinamerika und die USA am Ende der Äre Kissinger (BESPL, 2:9, Januar/Februar 1977, p. 24–29)

Author summarizes Carter's Latin American policy for German readers. Points out that it is no longer based on the idea of "national security" but on the following goals: an end to intervention and paternalism in Latin American affairs; 2) "economic security" as a goal; 3) refusal to deal with repressive regimes; 4) the establishment of special relationship with each individual country; and 5) a realization that not all desirable goals can be achieved. [R.V. Shaw]

7023 Cooperación internacional y desarrollo. Iván Lavados Montes, editor; Enrique Iglesias et al. Santiago de Chile: Corporación de Promoción Universitaria, 1978. 303 p.

These highly informative, critical essays cover a wide range of topics relating to international cooperation and development—the impact of (and upon) universities, political consequences, problems of public information and regional cooperation in Latin America. Content of articles is both general and oriented to Latin America. [R.]

Costello, Gerald M. Mission to Latin America: the successes and failures of a twentieth century crusade. See *HLAS 42:1926.*

7024 A Crise da ordem mundial. Organizador, Henrique Rattner; editor, Moysés Baumstein; illustração de Moysés Baumstein. São Paulo: Edições Símbolo, 1978. 243 p.

A collection of papers delivered by an international group of scholars at a conference in São Paulo. Most of the works have a global orientation but Helio Jaguaribe's paper on "Latin America and the World System" and Celso Lafer's contribution on the Latin American Alliance will be of particular interest to Latin Americanists. Jaguaribe considers the larger options now opening to Latin America. [R.]

7025 Crowe, Brian G. International public lending and American policy (*in* Debt and the less developed countries. Edited by Jonathan David Aronson. Boulder, Colo.: Westview Press, 1979, p. 27–55, tables)

Excellent discussion of US and international lending practices and the problem of debt-servicing. Crowe concludes that, despite significant policy differences between lenders and borrowers: "If a reasonably healthy international economy can be maintained, serious debt-servicing problems should continue to be confined to the relatively few countries where they can be handled effectively in a manner similar to the approach used in the past." This, however, will not help the situation of the poorer developing countries, who urgently need increased concessionary lending. [F.]

Cummins, Light T. John Quincy Adams and Latin American nationalism. See *HLAS 42:1903*.

7026 Danilo, Héctor. La CIA, Washington y las transnacionales. La Habana: Editorial de Ciencias Sociales, 1977. 45 p.

Bits and pieces of information on the CIA, the military-industrial complex, and the United Brands scandal from such sources as *Fortune* magazine. [F.]

Dependency unbends: case studies in inter-American relations. See *HLAS 42:1172*.

7027 Los Derechos humanos hoy en Latinoamérica: las declaraciones y documentos de las iglesias latinoamericanas, de la Iglesia Universal y de las Naciones Unidas. Selección de textos y documentos, Alberto Rodríguez, Jesús Valverde y Eduardo Bastos. Lima: Centro de Proyección Cristiana, 1977. 168 p.; index (Cuadernos de teología actual, ciencias sociales y realidad nacional; no. 2)

Regional publication of the inter-American "Justice and Peace" organization on the general topic of human rights in Latin America. References are made to pertinent discussions in Canon Law, international and inter-American legal concepts and the general position of the Roman Catholic hierarchy. Comments on the status of human rights in various Latin American states. The ambitious scope of this work results in a rather thin coverage of each broad topic or national system. Nevertheless, an important contribution for the reader wishing an introduction to ecclesiastical and legal bases for this important group's concern with human rights violations by both rightist and leftist authoritarian regimes in contemporary Latin America. [W.R. Garner]

7028 Diuguid, Lewis H. Lobbying for human rights (Worldview [Council on Religion and International Affairs, New York] 21:9, Sept. 1978, p. 9–12, plates)

An Assistant Foreign Editor of the *Washington Post* examines human rights lobbyists in Washington, primarily the Washington Office on Latin America (WOLA) and the Council on Hemispheric Affairs (COHA). He quotes Patricia Derian, head of the Rights Bureau at the State Department, to the effect that these lobbyists approach the Jewish community in their effectiveness. [F.]

7029 Documentos: declaración conjunta de los presidentes de los Estados Unidos Mexicanos y de la República de Venezuela (BCV/REL, 10:40, 151–168)

Text of the 1974 joint declaration between presidents Luis Echeverría Alvarez of Mexico and Carlos Andrés Pérez de Venezuela that looked toward the establishment of SELA. [F.]

7030 Documentos básicos del Nuevo Orden Económico Internacional, 1974–1977. Lima: Junta del Acuerdo de Cartagena, Biblioteca, 1978. 247 p.; index.

These early documents relevant to the so-called New International Economic Order are important to any understanding of the Third World and are conveniently available here. The collection begins with the UN General Assembly declaration on the establishment of a new International Economic Order "1974" and concludes with the report of the so-called North-South Conference of

1977. Hopefully, later documents will appear in a similar collection. [R.]

7031 Eldridge, Joseph T. Política de los derechos humanos para Latinoamérica: papel del Congreso (EEUU/PL, 4, 2. semestre, 1978, p. 275–284)

The Director of the Washington Office on Latin America (WOLA) discusses Congress' role with regard to human rights, both immediately prior and in response to the Carter administration's policy on this issue. [F.]

7032 Farer, Tom J. Reagan's Latin America (NYRB, 28:4, March 19, 1981, p. 10–15, ill., plate)

A critique of Jeane Kirkpatrick's controversial article on "Dictatorships and Double Standards" (see item **7058**) by the Carter administration's delegate to the OAS Inter-American Commission on Human Rights. Farer accuses Kirkpatrick of developing a position that "rests on an almost demented parody of Latin American political realities as well as on a grave misperception of Carter's policies and achievements." According to Farer, she seems to focus on the old-style caudillo, while ignoring the human rights problem and stability (hardly likely to fall overnight into US-security-threatening social chaos) of the institutionalized corporatist regimes in places like Argentina. More important, she ignores the fact that close to half of the members of the OAS "are recognizable democracies," as well as the view of many scholarly students of Latin America that the prospect for future advances of democracy in the region are reasonably bright. Farer calls upon "responsible Republicans" to "urge [President Reagan] to reject association of American power with conservatism that relies on vicious repression. They should act because it is the right thing to do; and because it is in the national interest that Latin America succeed in establishing capitalism with a human face." [F.]

7033 Ferguson, Yale H. Latin America (in Comparative regional systems: West and East Europe, North America, the Middle East, and developing countries. Edited by Werner J. Feld and Gavin Boyd. New York: Pergamon Press, 1980, p. 300–354)

Ferguson's chapter is the most concise, authoritative and useful recent short reference on Latin America. It contains basic economic, social, and political information and cites dozens of the leading sources on the region. The concluding section discusses foreign policies and international relations as well as most of the new regional and subregional organizations concerned with integration. [Cole Blasier]

7034 Fitch, John Samuel. Consecuencias políticas de la ayuda militar estadounidense a América Latina (EEUU/PL, 4, 2. semestre 1978, p. 167–193)

Fitch's study is based primarily, although not exclusively, on US military assistance to Ecuador. His evidence suggests that the effect of this assistance has not been so much to serve as an instrument of US "control" of the Latin American military. Rather, US assistance has tended to make the military more professional, which, in turn, has encouraged them to intervene more often in politics through the *golpe* mechanism; and repeated *golpes*, finally, have been a major impediment to both political and socioeconomic development. [F.]

7035 Fogel, Walter. United States immigration policy and unsanctioned migrants. Comment by Michael J. Piore (CU/ILRR, 33:3, April 1980, p. 295–314)

Fogel disputes the notion, common to some of proponents of a liberal US immigration policy, that immigrants tend to take mainly jobs that US labor disdains. He believes that reducing the numbers of legal and illegal immigrants would have the effect of raising the wages of low-skilled US workers, and he recommends such a policy, as well as the levying of penalties on employers who hire illegal aliens. [F.]

7036 Friedler, Egon. Historias más o menos circuncisas. Montevideo?: Editorial Lapid, 1978. 145 p.

A collection of brief articles from a number of Latin American periodicals which, in the author's words, has a Jewish focus and treats "with an acceptable amount of good humor, the consistent bad humor with which Jews were treated throughout history." [R.]

7037 Furlong, William L. Democratic political development and the Alliance for Progress (in The Continuing struggle for democracy in Latin America [see item **6028**] p. 167–184)

Rather superficial discussion of the Alliance's failure to promote the development of democracy in Latin America, including some of the cultural patterns which inhibit democracy. [F.]

7038 Gannon, Francis X. Far beyond the Good Neighbor Policy (Worldview [Council on Religion and International Affairs, New York] 22:4, April 1979, p. 17–22, ill.)

An advisor to the OAS Secretary General, formerly aide to Senator Hubert Humphrey, looks back at the accomplishments of the inter-American organization over the years and argues that it can and should be revitalized. The main barrier to revitalization, he feels, is the pervasive self-confirming notion that the OAS is largely dead. Moreover, in his view, Latin Americans would not be averse to US leadership on this score. [F.]

7039 Garbuny, Siegfried. Neue Beziehungen: USA and Lateinamerika (AZIF, 29:2, 1978, p. 145–158)

The author summarizes the new relations between the United States and Latin America during the administration of President Carter. He points out that the Latin American countries have started to follow their own different paths of development expecting always US aid but not wanting to accept US ideas on human rights. [R.V. Shaw]

7040 Gellman, Irwin F. Good Neighbor diplomacy: United States policies in Latin America, 1933–1945. Baltimore: Johns Hopkins University Press, 1979. 296 p.; bibl.; index (The Johns Hopkins University studies in historical and political science; 97th ser., 2)

Good study based mainly on archival sources that supplements, rather than supplants, previous works on this era by Bryce Wood and others. Gellman believes that he is the first to have had access to FBI files on Sumner Wells, and Nelson Rockefeller also granted him both extensive interviews and privileged access to his oral history at Columbia University. A strength of this book is its insights into the personalities and roles of the policy-makers involved. Welles receives the credit for being the principal architect of the Good Neighbor Policy; and the Depression, for providing a unique opportunity for new US initiatives in the hemisphere. [F.]

7041 Gochman, Charles S. and **James Lee Ray.** Structural disparities in Latin America and Eastern Europe, 1950–1970 (JPR, 16:3, 1979, p. 231–254, bibl., tables)

This is an interesting empirical study of major powers and their subordinates. It focuses on three dimensions—capabilities, diplomacy, and trade—in relations between the US and Latin America and the Soviet Union and Eastern Europe. Authors conclude that along these three dimensions the similarities between the two systems are greater than their differences. Although study oversimplifies relations for the sake of measurement, it does raise some interesting issues regarding basic power relations in regional politics. [G. Wynia]

7042 González Casanova, Pablo. Imperialismo y liberación en América Latina: una introducción a la historia contemporánea. México: Siglo Veintiuno Editores, 1978. 297 p.; bibl. (Historia)

Short history, written from a Marxist perspective, of "the people's" struggle—era-by-era and country-by-country—against US imperialism. [F.]

Gonzalo, Marisol de. Relaciones entre Estados Unidos y América Latina a comienzos de la primera guerra mundial: formulación de una política comercial. See HLAS 42:1929.

7043 Grayson, George W. The United States and Latin America: the challenge of human rights (CUH, 76:44, Feb. 1979, p. 49–53)

A useful review of the Carter Latin American policy with emphasis on his commitment to human rights. The obstacles the policy encountered are given considerable attention. With few exceptions, Carter's human rights policy is given high marks in the positive impact that it has had in Latin America. [D.W. Dent]

7044 Guardia, Ernesto de la. Tercera Conferencia de las Naciones Unidas sobre el Derecho del Mar: realidades y perspectivas (IAEERI/E, 54, sept./oct. 1978, p. 59–71, maps)

Review of the evolution of the International Law of the Sea, including unresolved issues, to 1978. [F.]

7045 Heller, Claude. La asistencia militar norteamericana a América Latina: una perspectiva política (EEUU/PL, 4, 2. semestre 1978, p. 137–166, tables)

Unusually balanced assessment of the impact of US military aid on Latin American politics. Heller acknowledges that US aid has strengthened military establishments, been a conduit for an ideology of anti-communism, and so on; also, that the US has customarily found right-wing military regimes in Latin America to be favorable to its interests. On the other hand, Heller emphasizes, the military would have been a prominent factor in contemporary Latin American politics regardless; some military regimes (e.g., Peru 1968) have clashed directly with Washington; others (like Brazil) have been highly nationalistic and have sought to prove their "independence" in foreign-policy matters; and several right-wing regimes found themselves the target of President Carter's human rights campaign. In short, it is very hard to generalize. [F.]

7046 Hodara, Joseph. El orden latinoamericano: cinco escenarios (LARR, 14:2, 1979, p. 180–197)

Hodara sketches five possible future structures of international relations for Latin America: 1) a general Latin American "community;" 2) on alliance of the great with the weak; 3) the individual ascension of the great coupled with the compartmentalized segregation of the others; 4) spheres of influence in which the weak depend on the strong; and 5) the capitalist ascendancy of the great and the developmental socialism of the weak. [F.]

7047 Hollander, Paul. Reflections on anti-Americanism in our times (Worldview [Council on Religion and International Affairs, New York] 21:6, June 1978, p. 46–51, ill.)

Hollander maintains that Americans are, to a large extent, responsible for "anti-American" sentiments in the world because they themselves (at least intellectuals and many other opinion leaders) are currently "down" on their country. He exhorts us, essentially, to start feeling good about ourselves again—thus perhaps anticipating one of the messages of the Reagan movement. [F.]

7048 Hollist, W. Ladd and **Thomas H. Johnson.** Political consequences of international economic relations: alternative explanations of United States/Latin American noncooperation (SPSA/JP, 41:4, Nov. 1979, p. 1125–1155, tables)

Integration theorists maintain that,

generally, economic intercourse between states augurs well for political cooperation. Dependency theorists, on the other hand, stress that economic intercourse between unequal parties make for political conflict. Who is correct? This is the question the authors of this article set out to answer empirically, focusing on US relations with Mexico and Brazil. The results are somewhat inconclusive but tend to give greater support to the dependency perspective. [F.]

7049 Inter-American Commission on Human Rights. Informe anual de la Comisión Interamericana de Derechos Humanos a la Asamblea General: 1977. Washington, Secretaría General de la Organización de los Estados Americanos, 1978. 91 p. (Documentos oficiales—Organización de los Estados Americanos, OEA/ser.L/V/II.43)

The annual report for 1977 of the Inter-American Commission on Human Rights. Focuses on the powers of the Commission, progress made in several countries enhancing human rights, and continued problems in Chile (in-depth review). [F.]

7050 ———. Informe sobre la labor desarrollada por la Comisión Interamericana de Derechos Humanos: en su trigésimosegundo período de sesiones, 8 al 18 de abril de 1974. Washington: OAS, Secretaría General, 1975. 74 p. (OEA/Ser.L/V/11.32, doc. 31, rev. 1, 20 febrero 1975)

Series of communications to the Inter-American Commission on Human Rights of the OAS concerning cases of possible violations of human rights in the Americas from 14 countries including the US. The frustration of this work is clear throughout the document. [D.W. Dent]

7051 Inter-American Juridical Committee. Work accomplished by the Inter-American Juridical Committee during its regular meeting held from Jan. 15 to Feb. 9, 1979. Washington: General Secretariat of the Organization of American States, 1979. 249 p. (OEA/Ser.Q/IV.19. CJI-39)

At this meeting the IAJC passed resolutions on several rather controversial matters, including the Belize case, "torture as an international crime," and the transfer of technology. [F.]

7052 Intergovernmental Conference on Cultural Policies in Latin America and the

Caribbean, *Bogotá, 1978*. Final report. Paris: Unesco, 1978. 114 p.; index.

Report of a UNESCO meeting held in Bogotá in Jan. 1978. Very bland document. [F.]

7053 Joes, Anthony James. The fascist century (Worldview [Council on Religion and International Affairs, New York] 21:5, May 1978, p. 19–23, ill.)

What many analysts call "corporatism" in the developing world, Joes prefers to call "fascism." Pejorative, surely, but there is at least some truth in the label. Nevertheless, one will wish to question Joes' knowledge of some of the historical examples he uses. For example, his comment that the Peruvian military took power in 1968 "for largely selfish and limited reasons but soon found itself driven step by step to enunciating and achieving goals that any Fascist of the 1920's would have understood and approved." That is hardly a good characterization of the Velasco experience. [F.]

7054 Johnson, John J. Latin America in caricature. Austin: University of Texas Press, 1980. 330 p.; bibl.; ill.; index (The Texas Pan American series)

"Fun," but in its way a revealing and sad collection of US newspaper cartoons concerning Latin America from the 19th century to the recent past. One cannot help being at least mildly shocked by some of the stereotypes. [F.]

7055 Kaufman, Edy; Yoram Shapira; and Joel Barromi. Israeli-Latin American relations. New Brunswick, N.J.: Transaction Books, 1979. 256 p.; bibl.; ill.; index.

The definitive work to date on this subject, including bilateral relations but also such matters as "Latin American Decision-Makers and Their Psychological Environment" and Latin American voting on UN resolutions of concern to Israel. This volume is further evidence of the sophisticated work now being done by Israeli scholars on Latin America. [F.]

Kelly, Philip L. Abraham Guillén and the strategy of the urban guerrilla: a model for Latin American revolution. See item **6051**.

7056 Khachaturov, Karen A. Ideologicheskaia ekspansiia SSha v Latinskoi Amerike [The ideological expansion of the USA in Latin America]. Moscow: Izdatel'stov

"Mezhdunarodnye otnoscheniia," 1978. 26 p.

A Soviet study of American "psychological warfare" in Latin America, and how it overthrows "lawful" governments and replaces them with "pro-imperialist regimes." The mass media are particularly important weapons in this process, with even "Sesame Street" carrying a camouflaged pro-imperialist message. A few notes but no bibliography. [R. Allen]

7057 ———. Maoism in Latin America (IA, 3, March 1979, p. 55–63)

Khachaturov accuses the Chinese of contributing to US imperialism's propaganda in Latin America, earlier (for example) by providing an embarrassing split in the world socialist movement and, more recently, by normalizing relations with the US and drifting away from socialism. [F.]

7058 Kirkpatrick, Jeane. Dictatorships and double standards (Commentary [American Jewish Committee, New York] Nov. 1979, p. 34–45)

A very controversial article that, reportedly, brought its author to the attention of the Reagan administration and, ultimately, to the post of US Ambassador to the UN. It begins with a cheap shot: "The failure of the Carter administration's foreign policy is now clear to everyone except it architects, and even they must entertain private doubts, from time to time, about a policy whose crowning achievement has been to lay the groundwork for a transfer of the Panama Canal from the United States to a swaggering Latin dictator of a Castroist bent." Then Kirkpatrick turns to two cases, Iran and Nicaragua, where, she says, "the Carter administration not only failed to prevent the undesired outcome, it actively collaborated in the replacement of moderate autocrats friendly to American interests with less friendly autocrats of extremist persuasion." (This article coined the term "moderate autocrat.") Kirkpatrick complains: "We seem to accept the status quo in Communist nations (in the name of 'diversity' and national autonomy), but not in nations ruled by 'right-wing' dictators or white oligarchies." Query: would she accept a human rights policy applied to both, without a "double standard," or is she recommending a double standard tilted in favor of the latter? In her view: "Groups which define themselves as enemies should be treated as enemies." With perhaps more persuasiveness, she concludes: "The United States is not in fact a racist, colonial power, it does not practice genocide, it does not threaten world peace with expansionist activities . . . For these reasons and more, a posture of continuous self-abasement and apology vis-à-vis the Third World is neither morally necessary nor politically appropriate." For author's reply to critics of this article (e.g., item **7032**) and for a more detailed elaboration of her positions, see item **7059**. [F.]

7059 ———. U.S. security and Latin America (Commentary [American Jewish Committee, New York] 71:1, Jan. 1981, p. 29–40)

Essentially an elaboration of some of the themes of Kirkpatrick's earlier article, "Dictatorships and Double Standards," (item **7058**) and a reply to critics of same. Whether one agrees with her or not (this reviewer largely does not), this is obviously a much better article than its predecessor—more reasoned, in-depth discussion of examples, and less overtly propagandistic. Kirkpatrick sets forth her statement of the presumed assumptions of the Carter policies, which she finds articulated in Brzezinski's *Between two ages*, the Linowitz Commission report, and the report of the Institute for Policy Studies Ad Hoc Working Group (see item **7001**). Her particular target, again, is Carter's human rights policy, which she argues was not applied to "activities of terrorists and guerrillas," the Castro regime, or Torrijos. Moreover, she maintains that the threat from Cuba is real, both in Africa and in Central America, and that shifts to the radical left in places like Nicaragua and El Salvador distinctly menace US national security. She also criticizes US efforts to engineer free elections in Bolivia that might have brought Hernán Siles to power. She writes: "Because it failed to take account of basic characteristics of Latin political systems, the Carter administration underestimated the fragility of order in these societies and overestimated the ease with which authority, once undermined, can be restored. Because it regarded revolutionaries as beneficent agents of change, it mistook their goals and motives and could not grasp the problem of government which become the object of revolutionary violence. Because it misunderstood the relations between eco-

nomics and politics, it wrongly assumed (as in El Salvador) that economic reforms would necessarily and promptly produce positive political results. Because it misunderstood the relations between 'social justice' and authority, it assumed that only 'just' governments can survive. Finally, because it misunderstood the relations between justice and violence, the Carter administration fell (and pushed its allies) into an effort to fight howitzers with land reform and urban guerrillas with improved fertilizers." [F.]

7060 Klare, Michael T. and **Nancy Stein.** Armas y poder en América Latina. Traducción, Isabel Vericat. México: Ediciones Era, 1978. 251 p.; bibl. (Serie popular Era; 61)

Somewhat sensationalized account of the involvement of the Pentagon in repression in Latin America, written by two authors associated with NACLA (the North American Congress on Latin America). Not one of NACLA's better products; in fact, the whole thing has a sort of sophomoric quality. [F.]

7061 Klimov, A. On the Havana Conference (IA, 9, Sept. 1979, p. unavailable)

Soviet author charges that since 1976 "the West has been attempting to minimize the antiimperialist essence of the nonaligned movement and to undermine relations between the nonaligned and socialist countries." China has been cooperating in this strategy by attempting to have such countries as Cuba, Vietnam, Afghanistan, and the People's Republic of Kapuchea excluded from the movement. [F.]

7062 Klochkovsky, L. The struggle for economic emancipation in Latin America (IA, 4, April 1979, p. 39–47)

According to this Soviet analyst, Latin American countries have shown increasing signs—both in terms of their domestic economic policies (like nationalizations of foreign enterprises) and cooperation with one another (e.g., SELA)—of rejecting the perpetuation of "dependent development." By making some trade concessions, supporting the concept of a code of conduct for multinational corporations, increasing technology transfer, and so on, the Carter administration is trying to demonstrate its "good intentions." However, such belated US attempts to counter Latin America's "struggle for economic emancipation" will not succeed. [F.]

7063 Knothe, Tomasz. Los estados de América Latina en la Conferencia de Paris de 1919 (PAN/ES, 3, 1976, p. 111–128)

Knothe reviews the participation of some Latin American countries at the 1919 Paris Peace Conference, which he says was not very significant because the conference was clearly dominated by the great powers. Latin American neutral states were not represented, and the League Covenant specifically mentioned the Monroe Doctrine in favorable terms as a "regional understanding." [F.]

7064 Kosobchuk, S. Latin America: against economic diktat (IA, 10, Oct. 1978, p. 71–76)

Soviet writer discusses monetary and credit problems faced by Latin American countries and some of the efforts made to deal with them. Concludes that US and "other" capitalist countries have adopted measures to strengthen their own financial positions at the expense of Latin American and developing countries. [R.]

7065 Kowalewski, Zbigniew Marcin and Henryk Szlaifer. Las corporaciones internacionales y las burguesías nacionales de Latinoamérica (PAN/ES, 3, 1976, p. 231–249)

Nothing much new in this Polish analysis: the multinational corporations and Latin American national bourgeoisie are cooperating in the monopolization of international and domestic markets, creating a distorted pattern of development in which they—rather than the masses—benefit. [F.]

7066 Lateinamerika im antiimperialistischen Kampf; Probleme eines Kontinents. Autorenkollektiv unter Leitung Adalbert Dessau. Berlin: Akademie-Verlag, 1978. 591 p.; bibl. (Studien über Asien, Afrika un Lateinamerika; Bd. 25)

A group of East German scholars analyze the different "struggles for liberation" and revolutionary movements in Latin America in the 20th century. The sources used are Communist Party documents and some writings by social scientists. The Mexican, Bolivian, and Cuban revolutions are examined within the context of contemporary politics. [G.M. Dorn]

7067 Latin America, the United States, and the inter-American system. Edited by John D. Martz and Lars Schoultz. Boulder, Colo.: Westview Press, 1980. 271 p.; bibl.; index.

High-quality collection of essays by former students and colleagues of Federico Gil of the University of North Carolina at Chapel Hill. The essays are grouped around three central themes: 1) Theoretical Perspectives, 2) General US Policies, and 3) US Human Rights Policies. In pt. 1, Steven W. Hughes and Kenneth J. Mijeski examine "contemporary paradigms," finding most to some extent useful; John S. Gitlitz and Henry A. Landsberger point to the weaknesses and some strengths of dependency theory; and Gustavo Lagos and Alberto Van Klaveren examine alternative conceptions of international structure into which Latin America might be fitted. Pt. 2 includes an essay by Kenneth M. Coleman on the "political mythology" of the Monroe Doctrine; one by Enrique A. Baloyra on US-Cuban relations in the 1970s, when both countries grew somewhat closer without ever completing normalization; and yet another by John D. Martz that stresses the ethnocentrism of US efforts to foster democracy in Latin America, while at the same time noting that there is a pro-democracy ideology in the region that competes with an authoritarian tradition. In pt. 3, Lars Schoultz looks at the Carter administration's initial record on human rights, concluding that US policies did change importantly in 1977; Joseph S. Tulchin focuses specifically on the evolution of human rights problems and US policies in Argentina; and Richard L. Clinton and R. Kenneth Godwin emphasize that US human rights policies have traditionally paid inadequate attention to the economic and social dimension. [F.]

7068 Latin America and the New International Economic Order. Edited by Jorge Lozoya, Jaime Estévez. New York: Published for UNITAR and the Center for Economic and Social Studies of the Third World (CEESTEM) by Pergamon Press, 1980. 93 p.; bibl.; index. (Pergamon policy studies on the new international economic power)

Collection of six NIEO-related essays published in a series sponsored in part by UNITAR. Most interesting to this reviewer is one by Armando Arancibia and Marc Rimez on "Latin American Foreign Trade and the

New International Economic Order"—a neat summary of NIEO trade demands, the rationale for them, and the status of North-South negotiations on this subject through the 1970s. [F.]

Latin American politics & development. See item **6054**.

7069 Laviña, Felix and **Horacio Baldomir.** El proceso histórico de la diplomacia interamericana y la vigencia de sus principios. Montevideo: Fundación de Cultura Universitaria, 1978. 261 p.; 3 leaves of plates; maps.

A rather rare publication these days, at least coming from a Latin American source: a detailed history of the inter-American system, including the contemporary framework of the Organization of American States. That this volume comes from Uruguay makes it perhaps less surprising; however, the concluding chapter concerns the international protection of human rights. [F.]

7070 Leff, Nathaniel H. Technology transfer and U.S. foreign policy: the developing countries (FPRI/O, 23:1, Spring 1979, p. 145–165)

According to Leff, both Third World leaders and US policy-makers—hard pressed to find common ground on many "New International Economic Order" questions—are now tending to focus their efforts on the technology transfer issue. He discusses some of the barriers to the flow of technology to the developing countries and offers a "modest" list of measures that might increase that flow. [F.]

7071 Leiken, Robert S. Eastern winds in Latin America (FP, 42, Spring 1981, p. 94–113)

Leiken surveys the increasing Soviet presence in Latin America—ships and submarines, trade, economic assistance, and diplomatic contacts. The reader should not overlook the exchange in the "letters" column of *Foreign Policy* (No. 43, Summer 1981), between Leiken and Cole Blasier. As Blasier stresses, Leiken perhaps draws too ominous an interpretation from his facts: Soviet trade (though apparently increasing) is still relatively small in volume, Soviet participation in many economic development projects is only fractional, and so on. [F.]

7072 Lelong Fleury, Rose Marie. El movimiento de los países no alineados: de Bandung, 1955, a Cuba, 1979 (UNAM/RI, 2:1, marzo 1979, p. 155–176, tables)

The author looks back over the long history of conferences and participants in the Nonaligned Movement, culminating in the 1979 Sixth Conference in Havana. She is struck by the definitional problem posed by Cuba's prominence, which translated into political tensions at the Havana meeting. How can Cuba be considered nonaligned? [F.]

Lernoux, Penny. Cry of the people: United States involvement in the rise of fascism, torture, and murder and the persecution of the Catholic Church in Latin America. See item **6056**.

7073 Levy, Nelson. A crise do imperialismo e a revolução análise crítica da teoria dos três mundos. Capa, Ary Normanha. Pinheiros, São Paulo: Brasil Debates, 1980. 167 p.; bibl. (Coleção Alicerces; no. 1)

A Brazilian in exile has presented a rather standard critique of the crisis of capitalism but argues that "the two superpowers, by the necessarily offensive character of their strategies, are equally agents of a possible Third World conflict and (are also) centers of international reaction." [R.]

7074 Lewis, Robert P. Sovereign immunity and international organizations: Broadbent v. OAS (GWU/JILE, 13:3, 1979, p. 675–693)

Lewis takes issues with a US court verdict, Broadbent vs. OAS (1978), that the 1976 Foreign Sovereign Immunities Act bestowed immunity to the OAS equivalent to the immunity granted sovereign states. The case involved several OAS employees suing to overturn a verdict of an OAS administrative tribunal regarding their dismissal by the Secretary-General in a reduction in force. [F.]

7075 Loescher, G.D. Human rights and American foreign policy executive-legislative interaction (Jahrbuch des öffentlichen Rechts der Gegenwart [J.C.B. Mohr—Paul Siebeck—Tübingen] 28, 1979, p. 559–587)

Good study of human rights theme in US foreign policy, stressing the interaction between Congress and the Executive Branch (including the rather different policy perspectives of particular bureaucracies). The article does not focus primarily on Latin America but does provide the larger context in which policies toward the region emerged and evolved. However, the pro-democracy postures of the Wilson and Kennedy administrations, which had human rights dimensions, receive inadequate consideration. [F.]

7076 Lofredo, Gino. La cumbre de La Habana y la política exterior norteamericana (AR, 6:21, 1979, p. 5–9, plates)

The gist of this short article is that all is well with the Nonaligned Movement, which at its 1979 Havana meeting repeatedly expressed itself in opposition to US policies regarding such matters as the Palestinian issue. However, the author carefully omits any discussion of the schism that was clearly in evidence at the meeting between those countries who did and did not regard Cuba's close association with the Soviets as compromising its nonalignment. [F.]

7077 López Martín, Alfonso. La Comunidad Iberoamericana de Naciones. San José: Instituto Costarricense de Cultura Hispánica, 1978. 105 p.; bibl.

Writings on the contemporary spirit of *Hispanidad* by a former Spaniard now residing in Costa Rica. [F.]

7078 Lowenthal, Abraham F. and **Gregory Traverton.** La formulación de políticas norteamericanas hacia América Latina: algunas proposiciones especulativas (CM/FI, 14:4, abril/junio 1979, p. 600–617)

Some sage observations and other more "speculative" propositions about the making of US policies toward Latin America—the fact that many policies affecting Latin America are not made with Latin America primarily in mind, the relatively rare involvement of the President, and so on. Well worth reading, although some of the generalizations may be a little too sweeping; several would bear being treated as hypotheses for further investigations through case studies. [F.]

7079 Lunin, V. and **P. Yakovlev.** Washington's Latin America policy (IA, 3, 1980, p. 20–27)

Soviet article that is more worth reading than most. Reviewing the Carter policies, authors find virtually all of them to constitute desperate and unsuccessful attempts to react to growing independence on the part of leading Latin American states, concern in the region over the US-based multinational

enterprises, energy scarcity, and other woes (from Washington's standpoint). In their view, the US approach under Carter was "not aimed at a drastic structural change in inter-American relations, but merely at modifying them in its own interests, in order to slow down the erosion of US positions in the region . . . Washington is engaging in active manoeuvres to camouflage its true intentions and the imperialist essence of its policy." [F.]

7080 Magdoff, Harry. Imperialism: from the colonial age to the present: essays. New York: Monthly Review Press, 1978. 279 p.

Essays grouped under three headings: 1) History; 2) Theory and the Third World; and 3) Reply to Critics. Pt. 1, the historical section, provides a general overview of the stages in the rise of the modern imperialism, including the historiography. Pt. 2 deals with theoretical questions and, in the author's view, "bourgeois academic failings in the study of the latter as well as with issues such as multinational corporations and the state in the Third World, militarism, US policy, and the transfer of technology problem. Pt. 3 contains replies to critics of all of these essays, all of which have appeared elsewhere. [V.C. Peloso]

7081 Maríategui, Juan. Comentarios sobre el Tercer Mundo. Lima: Editorial Minerva, 1978. 277 p.; bibl.; map.

Short essays on Third World themes written by a Peruvian journalist from 1975–77. [F.]

7082 Mezhgosudarstvennye otnosheniia v Latinskoi Amerike [Inter-state relations in Latin America]. Moscow: Izdatel'stvo 'Nauka,' 1977. 332 p.; bibl.

Sponsored by Institut Latinskoi Ameriki of the Academy of Sciences of the USSR. Survey, in historical perspective, of intergovernmental cooperation of Latin American states, both against international monopolies and for joint economic and political development. [R.V. Allen]

7083 Miller, Linda B. Morality in foreign policy: a faimed consensus? (AAAS/D, Summer 1980, p. 143–158, bibl.)

Miller writes: "Wary of the elaborations of American-style realism in the Nixon era and idealism in the Carter years, the attentive public awaits a more serious statement of purpose." If there is to be a new "consensus"—and Miller is by no means certain that one can be arrived at—it must find some way of reconciling the pursuit of America's "best" values with security and other US "interests." But, this reviewer would query, wasn't this balancing of competing priorities not only what the Carter administration had to do, and did, but also even what the administration clearly *said* it was doing? Isn't labeling the Carter policy "idealism" in the absolute sense simply, inaccurately and unfairly, setting up a straw man? [F.]

7084 Minello, Nelson. Las relaciones militares entre los Estados Unidos y América Latina: un intento de análisis (EEUU/PL, 4, 2. semestre, 1978, p. 195–226, tables)
Survey of US military assistance programs from about 1938 to the Carter administration, with little in the way of a real thesis or conclusion. [F.]

7085 Moreno Pino, Ismael. Orígenes y evolución del sistema interamericano. Tlatelolco, México: Secretaría de Relaciones Exteriores, 1977. 431 p.; anexos; map (Colección del archivo histórico diplomático mexicano; 3. epoca: Obras monográficas; 9)
Relatively detailed history of the evolution of the inter-American system from a Mexican perspective. Published under the auspices of Mexico's Secretariat of Foreign Relations. [F.]

7086 Morgan, Iwan. French policy in Spanish America: 1830–48 (JLAS, 10:2, Nov. 1978, p. 309–328)
The French policy in Spanish America was based on erroneous conceptions of French interests (surplus population, immigration, trade) and a faulty (haphazard, ethnocentric) policy making process. Author makes a convincing argument based on archival material from the French Ministry of Foreign Affairs. For historian's comment, see *HLAS 42:1911.* [D.W. Dent]

7087 Mortimer, Robert A. The Third World coalition in international politics. New York: Praeger, 1980. 147 p.; bibl.
A scholarly survey of the progress (and lack thereof) of the Third World movement from the 1955 Bandung Conference through 1979. Chapters are organized chronologically. This would make a useful text for courses in world politics or international relations were it available in a paperback edition and kept updated. [F.]

Movimiento de países no alienados: bibliografía. See *HLAS 42:55.*

Movimientos revolucionarios en América Latina: documentación propia. See item **6061**.

7088 Mullick, M.A. Hussein. Überlegungen zum sozialen Rahmen von Entwicklung in der Dritten Welt (DDW, 1:4, 1972, p. 469–478)
The author discussed India, Pakistan and Latin America as three parts of the 3rd world where economic reforms are badly needed. He maintains that the World Bank and other international organizations tend to maintain the power of the existing ruling classes without strengthening the economic life of the have-nots. He sees this dilemma as an explosive problem that must be solved. [R.V. Shaw]

7089 Murphy, Ewell E., Jr. Decision 24, Mexicanization, and the New International Economic Order: the anatomy of disincentive (Texas International Law Journal [University of Texas, School of Law, Austin] 13:2, Spring 1978, p. 289–308)
Article with literary and philosophical overtones of the sort more often encountered in Latin American, rather than North American, writings—although the conclusions are not typically Latin! Murphy maintains that Latin American economic nationalism is setting the two Americas on divergent paths, at a time when Latin America could learn from many of North America's mistakes in overemphasizing industrial development and when a post-industrial North America urgently needs some of Latin America's humanism. He regrets not so much what he sees as likely less foreign investment, etc., in Latin America in future years, but the loss of a cultural "dialogue" that accompanies economic relations. [F.]

7090 Naudón de la Sotta, Carlos. El nuevo escenario latinoamericano: un enfoque global. Santiago: Instituto de Ciencia Política, 1978. 49 leaves; bibl. (Cuadernos del Instituto de Ciencia Política; no. 26)
Relations among Latin American nations have changed radically and so have relations between this area and the rest of the world. The OAS is no longer the old "Latin American Club" that it once was but more of a mini-UN with all the difficulties and problems which that implies. [R.]

7091 A new Inter-American policy for the eighties. Foreword by Ronald E. Docksai. Washington: The Committee of Santa Fé *for the* Council for Inter-American Security, 1980. 53 leaves.

One might easily take this document for a John Birch Society tract, but it is actually a position paper for the Reagan Administration, produced by members of the Reagan "team" on the Committee of Santa Fé of the Council for Inter-American Security (L. Francis Bouchey, Roger W. Fontaine, David C. Jordan, Gordon Sumner, and Lewis Tambs). Samples: "During the last several years," the US has pursued a policy of "'anxious accommodation,' as if we would prevent the political coloration of Latin America to red crimson by an American-prescribed tint of pale pink" (from the Foreword by Council President Ronald F. Docksai). "The Americas are under attack. Latin America, . . . is being penetrated by Soviet power. The Caribbean rim and basin are spotted with Soviet surrogates and ringed with socialist states." "The United States must reject the mistaken assumption that one can easily locate and impose U.S. style democratic alternatives to authoritarian governments and the equally pervasive belief that change *per se* in such situations is inevitable, desirable, and in the American interest." "The United States should promote a policy conducive to private capitalism, free trade and direct local and foreign investment in productive enterprises in Latin America." [F.]

7092 Nitoburg, E.L. From the "big stick" to the Good Neighbor Policy (*in* Soviet historians on Latin America: recent scholarly contributions [see *HLAS 42:1817*] p. 273–298, table)

Soviet historian looks at the Roosevelt Good Neighbor Policy from a Marxist perspective, that is, he regards it as basically a response to workers' pressures in the US and to restive countries attempting to cast off the yoke of neocolonialism in Latin America. [F.]

7093 Norton, Augustus R. and **Martin H. Greenberg.** International terrorism: an annotated bibliography and research guide. Boulder, Colo.: Westview Press, 1980. 218 p.; index (Westview special studies in national and international terrorism)

Section L contains a list of 56 books and articles on terrorism in Latin America. [F.]

7094 Nuevas perspectivas de la integración latinoamericana. Santiago de Chile: Editorial Universitaria, 1977. 1 v. (Estudios internacionales)

This collection of essays might be said to focus on one theme in particular: why the process of economic integration has not made a large contribution to the development of Latin America. Emphasis is on economic factors but political factors are not ignored. [R.]

7095 Los Obispos latinoamericanos entre Medellín y Puebla: documentos episcopales 1968–1978. San Salvador: UCA Editores, 1978. 261 p. (Colección La iglesia en América Latina; v. 3)

Important collection of texts of declarations adopted by Latin American bishops in meetings held during the critical decade (1968–78) when the Church in Latin America took an increasingly bold stand in opposition to political repression and in favor of socioeconomic change. [F.]

7096 O'Brien, William Vincent. U.S. military intervention: law and morality. Preface by David M. Abshire; Center for Strategic and International Studies, Georgetown University. Beverly Hills: Sage Publications, 1979. 86 p. (Washington papers; v. 7, 68. Sage policy papers)

Legalistic attempt to apply the "Just War" concept to an analysis of the 1965 Dominican Republic intervention and Vietnam. O'Brien insists that it is "permissible" to defend against *prior* intervention by outside Communist powers, but not (as he believes was the case in the Dominican example) to put down a domestic rebellion, whatever its political character or international implications. [F.]

7097 La OEA como organismo catalizador (OAS/AM, 30:11/12, nov./dic. 1978, p. 21–44)

A popular account and description of a variety of economic, technical and cultural activities carried out by the OAS in member countries. [R.]

7098 Oglesby, J.C.M. A Trudeau decade: Canadian-Latin American relations, 1968–1978 (SAGE/JIAS, 21:2, May 1979, p. 187–208, bibl., table)

Significant article, none the least because so little information is available on this subject. Oglesby states: "The Trudeau decade—a decade 60% of which fell in the most prosperous years Canada has experienced, indeed it may have been the apogee of Canada's standard of living—has seen the most active Canadian effort toward Latin America since the decade of 1895–1905." Tracing the Trudeau initiatives, Oglesby concludes that there were signs by the end of the 1970s that the "Canadian thrust was about over;" nevertheless, Canadian-Latin American relations had by then achieved their own momentum, with the Latin Americans perhaps to play a more leading role in the years ahead. For historian's comment, see *HLAS 42:1935*. [F.]

7099 Oliveira Campos, Roberto de. The New International Economic Order: aspirations and realities (*in* World change and world security. Edited by Norman C. Dahl and Jerome B. Wiesner. Cambridge, Mass.: MIT Press, 1978, p. 73–87)

An intellectually honest appraisal of the developing New International Economic Order. Treats both industrialized and developing countries fairly and unobjectively. Concludes that developing countries must drop their penchant for "escapism" and "demonology;" and industrialized countries must in turn abandon their "hypocritical stance" on the New International Economic Order. [R.]

7100 Olson, Richard Stuart. Economic coercion in world politics: with a focus on North-South relations (PUCIS/WP, 31:4, July 1979, p. 471–494, tables)

Intriguing theoretical essay which attempts to "build bridges between various islands of literature" with relevance to the North's use of economic sanctions against the South. Among other things, Olson cites approvingly James Caporaso's distinction between the concepts of "dependence" and "dependency." Olson concludes: ". . . First World sanctions work through the structure of dependency of a target-LCD to interact with both the target's international economic position *and* domestic political economy. The study of economic coercion in world politics requires a careful combination of insights from the study of international and transnational relations, comparative politics, foreign policy, and economics." [F.]

7101 Organismos interamericanos. Madrid: Ediciones Cultura Hispánica del Centro Iberoamericano de Cooperación, 1978. 520 p.; index.

Up-to-date (to 1978) directory, published in Spain, of 108 inter-American and Latin American international organizations. Includes brief histories of the organizations and lists of their members, purposes, activities, institutions, publications, etc. Invaluable reference work, especially as regards some of the more obscure organizations. [F.]

7102 Organization of American States. Comisión Interamericana de Derechos Humanos (CIDH—Interamerican Commission on Human Rights). Manual de normas vigentes en materia de derechos humanos; actualizado a julio de 1980. Washington: General Secretariat, Organization of American States, 1980. 153 p.; facs. (OEA/Ser. L/V/II.50; doc. 6)

Useful document collection published by the Inter-American Commission on Human Rights. Includes the American Declaration of the Rights and Duties of Man, the American Convention on Human Rights (with instruments of ratification), the Statute of the Commission, the Statute of the Inter-American Court of Human Rights, and the blank form utilized by the Commission for reports of violations of human rights. [F.]

7103 ——. General Secretariat. Inter-American Treaties and Conventions: signatures, ratifications, and deposits with explanatory notes. Rev. ed. Washington: Organization of American States, General Secretariat, 1980. 306 p.; tables (Treaty series; 9)

This volume, which was also published in Spanish in 1976, contains complete information on each inter-American convention or treaty relating to the place and date of subscription, the signatory countries, and the date of deposit of the instrument of ratification. Additional information is also included for each treaty on the countries that have made reservations thereto, and on the depositories of the original texts and of the instruments of ratification; the instruments that have replaced former ones on the same subject matter during the course of time are also included. [R.]

Parkinson, F. Latin America, the Cold War, and the world powers, 1945–73. See *HLAS 42:1936*.

7104 Parrilla-Bonilla, Antulio. La Iglesia y los derechos humanos (NSO, 36, mayo/junio 1978, p. 45–52)

Review of Catholic doctrine, mainly

papal pronouncements, on the subject of human rights. [F.]

7105 Perroux, François. Las firmas transnacionales y la América Latina (UNAM/RFD, 28:111, sept./dic. 1978, p. 817–833)

Unexceptional article by a French professor discussing the challenge posed by the multinational corporation to the nation-state in Latin America and expressing the hope that a meaningful code of conduct for such enterprises may yet be formulated by the UN. He is not optimistic about multinationals being banished from the world scene, as urged by Marxists, nor about the potential for regulation of foreign capital by subregional integration schemes like ANCOM. [F.]

7106 Peskin, Allan. Blaine, Garfield and Latin America: a new look (AAFH/TAM, 36:1, July 1979, p. 79–89)

Intriguing revisionist essay downgrading Blaine's and upgrading Garfield's contribution to an increased US interest in Latin America during the early 1880s. Peskin argues: "As a congressman [Garfield] anticipated many of the new foreign policy directions which would later be associated with his administration . . . In the day-to-day operations of the [State] Department the President may have allowed Blaine a free hand, but the broad policy decisions all bore Garfield's unmistakable stamp. The foreign policy of the Garfield administration was Garfield's foreign policy." For historian's comment, see *HLAS 42:1912.* [F.]

Petras, James F. Imagen y realidades de la violencia: los Estados Unidos y América Latina. See item **8051.**

7107 ———. La nueva moralidad del presidente Carter y la lógica del imperialismo (Docet [CELADEC, Centro de Documentación y Editorial, Lima] Serie D:4, s.n., p. 9–14, ill.)

According to Petras, Carter's "new morality" is little more than a domestic attempt to bolster the US's sagging image in the world after Watergate, the Allende murder, and other excesses of the Nixon era. Imperialists, by definition, cannot be altruistic. [F.]

7108 ———. U.S. foreign policy: the revival of interventionism (MR, 31:9, Feb. 1980, p. 15–27)

In Petras's view, Carter's human rights policy was essentially a "transnational" policy, designed to overcome post-Vietnam and Watergate cynicism about the US and its role in the world—and thus lay the foundation for a new era of US interventionism. [F.]

7109 Petrov, M. The Soviet Union and the denuclearized zone in Latin America (IA, 12, Dec. 1979, p. 95–99)

Like so many other things, we are told, the Soviet Union invented the concept of nuclear-free zones. Hence it is not surprising that it has consistently backed the Treaty of Tlatelolco, which was an attempt to achieve such a zone in Latin America. [F.]

7110 Piacentini, Horacio J. Las reservas en el derecho internacional y sus efectos en el Tratado de Tlatelolco (IAEERI/E, 58, mayo/junio 1979, p. 71–79)

Piacentini examines the formal reservations various states have attached to their signature and/or ratification of the Treaty of Tlatelolco (banning nuclear weapons in Latin America). He concludes that some of these reservations are dangerously ambiguous and may even be inconsistent with the essentials of the Treaty, and he suggests means of dealing with this problem. None of these means—Mexico (the initiator of the Treaty) attempting to pass on certain reservations, an international conference, etc.—seems likely to be successful. Isn't the central problem the fact that some Latin American states are still unwilling to rule out the nuclear option, rather than that no one has noticed the full implications of the reservations they have attached? [F.]

7111 Pino Santos, Oscar. Problemas económicos del Tercer Mundo y estrategia de los países no alineados. México: Editorial Nuestro Tiempo, 1976. 100 p.; bibl. (Colección Temas de actualidad)

Discussion of the 1976 Colombo conference of the Nonaligned countries and some of the Third World economic problems that the conference highlighted. [F.]

7112 Plaza Lasso, Galo. Siete años de evolución, 1968–1975. Washington: Organización de los Estados Americanos, 1975. 139 p.; ill.

Report of OAS Secretary-General Galo Plaza on the activities of the organization during his tenure. Appendixes include a chronology of meetings and other events of significance, and charts of technical assistance and other direct services provided to member states. [F.]

7113 Poitras, Guy. Latin America and the changing global system (IAA, 4:3, 1978, p. 171–183, bibl.)

Short essay tracing recent developments in the Third World movement and within Latin America. Poitras observes: ". . . it is more appropriate to discuss Latin American nations and their involvement in Third World affairs rather than to imply that Latin America *as a region* is moving toward greater interdependence with other Third World nations." [F.]

The Politics of terrorism. See item 6072.

7114 Quagliotti de Bellis, Bernardo. Nacionalismo e integración. Montevideo: Geosur, 1979. 23 p.

Author argues for a new or modern concept of Nationalism—one that accepts and even depends on the necessity of economic integration. The New International Economic Order also implies the renovation of such concepts as Nationalism, sovereignty and independence. [R.]

7115 ¿Qué democracia? (Carta Política [Persona e Persona, Buenos Aires] 72, nov. 1979, p. 30–35)

Protests the fact that Uruguay, Chile and Paraguay should have been condemned by the OAS for Human Rights violations while nothing is said about Cuba and countries such as Nicaragua, El Salvador, Peru, Haiti and Mexico sit as accusers. [R.]

7116 Raymont, Henry. "Mainstreaming" the New World (The Washington Quarterly [A review of strategic and international issues, Georgetown University, Center for Strategic and International Studies, Washington] 3:4, Autumn 1980, p. 40–53)

Article by former *New York Times* correspondent, currently chairman of the People-to-People Task Force of the OAS. He decries what he terms "an unceremonious burial of the idea of Pan-Americanism," and he asks: "Could it be, . . . that what passes for a case against regional multilateralism is more likely an implicit admission of our frustration over the region's idiosyncracies and political instability, a rationalization of the low priority Latin America continues to represent in the mind of U.S. policy-makers,

and a convenient evasion of choice?" He believes (doubtful, in this reviewer's opinion) that the OAS could be revivified, in part, by having it address "such common concerns as the ecological, social, and cultural factors in development" to which "nobody has yet found wholly adequate answers." [F.]

7117 Revel-Mouroz, Jean. Coopération et conflits dans les zones frontalières en Amérique Latine: le point de la situation (FDD/NED [Problèmes d'Amérique Latine, 53] 4533/4534, 31 oct. 1979, p. 31–44, map)

Revel-Mouroz surveys the principal boundary conflicts in contemporary Latin America, as well as institutions of multilateral and bilateral cooperation in the region. In this definition, the latter include mechanisms for the coexistence of twin border communities like El Paso-Juárez. [F.]

7118 Ronning, C. Neale. National priorities and political rights in Spanish America (*in* Human rights: cultural and ideological perspectives. Edited by Adamantia Pollis and Peter Schwab. New York: Praeger, 1979, p. 101–114)

Ronning writes: "The fact of the matter is that the 'essential rights of man' stated or implied in the right of elections have been, and are, rejected by an important current of thought in Spanish America." He examines this "current" in three periods: 1) immediate post-independence; 2) the late 19th century; and 3) post-World War II. All critics of elections, he finds: "from Bolívar and Portales through the científicos and down to the contemporary Cubans and Chileans, have firmly believed that elections would have to wait for the achievement of a very fundamental national goal—*the creation of a new kind of citizen*. . . . The Cubans alone have emphasized an equitable *distribution* of wealth . . . " [F.]

7119 Ruilova, Leonardo. China Popular en América Latina. Quito: Instituto Latinoamericano de Investigaciones Sociales, 1978. 302 p.; bibl.; graphs.

Study done by an Ecuadorian scholar under the auspices of an Institute supported by the Friedrich Foundation of the Federal Republic of Germany. Ruilova examines Chinese ideology and relations with Latin America, with particular attention to the years 1970–78, an eight-year period which is the focus of a chronology of events in the appendixes. [F.]

7120 Samponaro, Frank N. The Committee for Political Defense and Hemispheric Security (The Social Science Journal [Colorado State University, Western Social Science Association, Fort Collins] 16 : 1, Jan. 1979, p. 29–42)

Reviewing the activities of the World War II Emergency Advisory Committee for Political Defense, Samponaro observes: "The most remarkable aspect of the history of the CPD is . . . that the overwhelming majority of Latin American governments, either tacitly or through their active cooperation, allowed the Committee to serve as a thinly veiled instrument of the United States to pressure three other Latin American governments to realign their policies in accordance with the wishes of the State Department." [F.]

7121 Sanjuan, Pedro. Why we don't have a Latin American policy (The Washington Quarterly [A review of strategic and international issues, Georgetown University, Center for Strategic and International Studies, Washington] 3 : 4, Autumn 1980, p. 28–39)

Truly "off-the-wall" critique of the Carter policies by an individual who, incredibly, is reportedly part of the inner circle of Latin American advisors in the Reagan administration. This is a pure sample of propaganda the likes of which one rarely encounters apart from the mills of Havana. Example: "When Carter became president, the reactionary liberals and the rural mystics joined hands in a new crusade that was a mawkish caricature of the flawed crusade of the sixties." [F.]

7122 Santos, Theotonio dos. La crisis imperialista y la política norteamericana: cómo entender a Jimmy Carter. Diseñó la portada, Carlos Palleiro. México: Ediciones de Cultura Popular, 1977. 95 p. (El Libro popular)

In a series of articles published in *El Sol de México* (Dec. 1976–Feb. 1977), a leading Marxist dependency theorist takes potshots at the Carter administration policies. They may *look* progressive in some respects (e.g., human rights) but they have had little effect on the fundamental imperialist orientation of the US toward Latin America. [F.]

7123 ———. Dependence relations and political development in Latin America: some considerations (NOSALF/IA, 7 : 1, 1977, p. 11–20)

Familiar analysis of the evolution of capitalism and dependency in Latin America, with some comparisons with patterns in Europe since the article is intended primarily for that audience. [F.]

7124 Schaposnik, Eduardo Carlos. Las relaciones económicas internacionales y América Latina. Caracas: Universidad Central de Venezuela, Facultad de Ciencias Jurídicas y Políticas, Instituto de Derecho Público, Sección Integración, 1978. 678 p.; bibl.; graphs.

Lengthy, ideologically moderate overview of major patterns and issues of international economic relations, including Latin American positions on these issues and the roles of pan-Latin American institutions like ANCOM and OLADE. [F.]

7125 Schiff, Warren. German-Latin American relations: the first half of the twentieth century (SAGE/JIAS, 22 : 1, Feb. 1980, p. 109–117)

In this review essay Schiff discusses some of the recent literature in German on Germany's relationship with Latin America. He concludes that 20th century relations have been dominated by economic considerations. [R.]

7126 Schlegel, Dietrich. The non-aligned states in and after Havana (AZIF, 30: 4, 1979, p. 453–461)

Schlegel, a German journalist, offers a balanced view of the maneuverings at the 1979 Nonaligned Meeting in Havana. He notes that Tito and Nyerere led a group of states that succeeded in inserting a preamble to the final document drafted by Cuba, which insertion condemned all forms of "hegemony" and violence (whether from West or East). This step forestalled an open split in the movement. However, Schlegel observes, if the "classical non-aligned countries" wish to avoid the movement's drifting toward the Eastern bloc, they will have to remain "vigilant" until the seventh summit in Baghdad in 1982. [F.]

7127 Schori, Pierre. Social democracia y América Latina: un punto de vista sueco (UNAM/PDD, 9 : 35, aogosto/oct. 1978, p. 115–124)

Short article by the Swedish International Secretary of the Social Democratic movement, listing the political parties of this persuasion in Latin America and detailing some of the contacts between them and the Socialist International. There is also some mention of Sweden's foreign policy in this context. Author feels that Sweden, and social democracy generally, should continue to seek closer relations with Latin American democratic governments and parties, but at the same time not shun a reasonable level of dialogue with Cuba. [F.]

7128 Schoultz, Lars. Human rights and United States policy toward Latin America (UCSD/NS, 7:1/2, 1978 [i.e. 1979] p. 87–104)

Schoultz points out that a human rights policy must, if it is to be successful, "threaten the existing structure of privilege" in Latin America and therefore groups to which the US is "linked by long and extremely cordial international relationships." Thus those who seek to gain support for such a policy must argue "that dramatic changes in the structure of Latin American privilege will enhance rather than damage the long-term interests of the United States," which Schoultz, in fact, believes is true. However, he is not optimistic either that critics of a human rights policy will be convinced or even that human rights advocates fully appreciate all the ramifications of their position. [F.]

———. The nature of anti-U.S. sentiment in Latin America: a preliminary analysis with Argentine data. See item **7410.**

7129 ———. US foreign policy and human rights violations in Latin America (CUNY/CP, 13:2, Jan. 1971, p. 149–170)

Using quantitative data, Schoultz demonstrates that "during the mid-1970s United States aid was clearly distributed disproportionately to countries with repressive governments, that this distribution represented a *pattern* and not merely one or a few isolated cases, and that human needs was not responsible for the positive correlations between aid and human rights violations." He acknowledges that he does not explore the second question, why aid was so distributed—the economic fitness of certain regimes, their anti-communism, etc. [F.]

7130 Schröder, Hans-Jürgen. Grenzen der Good Neighbor Policy (JGSWGL, 14, 1977, p. 378–385)

Schröder discusses the role of the Export-Import Bank in the Roosevelt administration's Good Neighbor posture toward Latin America. Most officials, he maintains, thought of US policy strictly in political terms and were indifferent to what was going to become a key economic dimension. [F.]

7131 Seminario sobre el Nuevo Orden Internacional, *Bogotá, 1977.* Hacia un nuevo orden internacional: este libro reúne las conferencias dictadas en el Seminario sobre el Nuevo Orden Internacional organizado por la Asociación Nacional de Instituciones Financieras, ANIF, con el auspicio de la Comisión Nacional para la UNESCO. Indalecio Liévano Aguirre et al. Bogotá: ANIF, 1978. 140 p.; bibl. (Biblioteca ANIF de economía; 12)

Proceedings of a 1977 seminar on the NIEO organized by the Colombian National Association of Financial Institutions (ANIF). [F.]

7132 Seminario sobre la Enseñanza del Derecho Internacional, *2d, Bogotá, 1979.* Exposiciones, Segundo Seminario sobre la Enseñanza del Derecho Internacional, 24–28 septiembre 1979, Bogotá, Colombia. Washington, D.C.: Secretaría General, Organización de los Estados Americanos, 1980. 523 p.

These important seminars are making an unusual contribution to the understanding of new directions in the development of international law. Studies of particular interest in this volume include expropriation, human rights and multi-national corporations as well as general studies on "new directions in international law" and proposals relating to the New International Economic Order. [R.]

7133 Shaw, Timothy M. The semiperiphery in Africa and Latin America: subimperialism and semiindustrialism (NEA/RBPE, 9:4, Summer 1979, p. 341–358)

Shaw identifies several so-called subimperial states in Latin America—"Brazil, Argentina, and Mexico, with Cuba poised to play such a role within the socialist system"—and compares these to a longer list of supposedly similar states in Africa. Should Argentina be so ranked any longer? [F.]

7134 Sherzer, Harvey G.; Michael T. Janik; and Allen B. Green. Foreign military sales: a guide to the United States bureaucracy (GWU/JILE, 13:3, 1979, p. 545–599)

Interesting, detailed review of the policies, laws, and bureaucratic procedures involved in US military sales abroad. Authors note that the law reflects the conflicting policy considerations at work, the desire to curb somewhat the US customary role as the world's largest supplier of weapons versus the influence and economic benefits supposedly gained by such sales. They observe: ". . . reality suggests and existing United States law makes certain that there will be no real curtailment of America's weapons business in the near future." [F.]

7135 Shulgovski, Anatoli. Revolución y contrarrevolución en América Latina a la luz de la experiencia de la Gran Revolución Socialista de Octubre (URSS/AL, 4, 1977, p. 33–52)

Soviet author warns Latin American revolutionaries that the glorious revolution in his own country suffered from the assaults of reactionary forces and they cannot expect any better. [F.]

7136 ———. The social and political development in Latin America (IA, 11, Nov. 1979, p. 52–61)

The invariable Soviet optimistic assessment of social forces favoring socialism in the area. Author draws most of his data from speeches made by Latin American Communist leaders. [A. Suárez]

7137 Sizonenko, Alexandr. Cómo tergiversan en Occidente las relaciones soviético-latinoamericanas (URSS/AL, 2, 1979, p. 78–94)

A rare item: A Soviet reviewer looks at various books and articles written by Westerners on the subject of Soviet relations with Latin America. He observes that the flood of material does suggest that the Soviet-Latin American partnership is moving ahead, but otherwise (not surprisingly) he is not much impressed with the quality of the works under review. Among other things, they persist in attributing evil intentions to the USSR's desire for friendship and commerce with all nations. [F.]

7138 Sklar, Richard L. Postimperialism: a class analysis of multinational corporate expansion (CUNY/CP, 9:1, Oct. 1976, p. 75–92, table)

Sklar's essay "draws attention to the coalescent relationship between two dominant classes—the managerial bourgeoisie [in newly developing countries] and the corporate international bourgeoisie. In doing so, it seeks to make the hypothesis of transnational class formation credible." [F.]

Smith, Brian H. Churches and human rights in Latin America: recent trends in the subcontinent. See item **6084.**

Smith, Joseph. Illusions of conflict: Anglo-American diplomacy toward Latin America, 1865–1896. See *HLAS 42:1915.*

———. New World diplomacy: a reappraisal of British policy toward Latin America, 1823–1850. See *HLAS 42:1916.*

7139 Smith, Tony. The underdevelopment of development literature: the case of dependency theory (PUCIS/WP, 31:2, Jan. 1979, p. 247–288)

Monograph-length article consists of a critique of dependency literature dealing with Latin America and other areas as well. The critique is profound, a real intellectual tour de force. Smith's arguments are far too complex to summarize, but (among other things) he maintains that dependency theorists have given inadequate attention to the nature of the state in the "South," that there were hardly any alternatives (except continued backwardness) to the South's developing the way it did, that the allegation that developing areas are being "decapitalized" is false, and that the public and private sectors of developing countries appear to be gaining increasing control over the multinationals. Smith has certainly thrown down the gauntlet, and whether or not he has made his case, it will be hard to discuss dependency hereafter without some reference to his work. [F.]

7140 La Social Democracia Internacional y América Latina (URSS/AL, 4[20], 1978, p. 88–138)

A roundtable of Soviet historians comment on social democratic movements in Latin America. Generally, they find social democracy to spring from genuine desires for socioeconomic change and anti-imperialism, which aims are often frustrated by reactionary forces at home and abroad. Latin America needs true revolutionary socialism rather than "reform," although reformist forces can on occasion be supported and may help pave the way for socialism over the longer haul. [F.]

7141 Stepan, Alfred. United States-Latin American relations (CFR/FA, 58:3, [special issue] 1980, p. 659–692)

Excellent review of the Carter policies toward the end of his administration. Especially good on Mexico, Central America, and Puerto Rico. Stepan outlines the case against utilizing a plebiscite to decide on Puerto Rico's future. [F.]

7142 Sterling, Claire. Qaddafi spells chaos (The New Republic [Washington] 18:10, 7 March 1981, p. 15–20)

Some discussion in this article about Qaddafi's sponsoring the 1979 Benghazi Conference. Sterling comments: "He might have been taking over from Fidel Castro . . . judging from his guest list: Sandinistas from Nicaragua, exiled Tupamaros from Uruguay, wandering Montoneros from Argentina, Marxist guerrilla bands from Chile, Costa Rica, Bolivia, Mexico, Brazil. His practical purpose at the meeting was to revive Castro's sagging Latin American Junta for Revolutionary Coordination and its European brigade." [F.]

7143 ———. The strange case of Henri Curiel (The Washington Post Magazine [Washington] March 15, 1981, p. 26–30, 38–39, plate)

The article, written in a journalistic style bordering on the sensational, is well-titled: The case of this French Communist and financial supporter of Third World liberation movements is indeed a strange one! Sterling details his alleged activities, including ties to the KGB and the notorious Venezuelan terrorist, Ilich Ramírez Sánchez ("Carlos, the Jackal"), as well as efforts to create a "Europe Brigade" made up of recruits from various Latin American revolutionary groups. Curiel was assassinated in Paris in 1978. [F.]

7144 Sucre, José Francisco. Cuál civilización, cuál ideología? Portada, Juan Fresán. Caracas: Monte Avila Editores, 1979. 181 p. (Colección Documentos)

A Venezuelan journalist offers a collection of brief commentaries on a wide range of issues in contemporary international affairs. There is little on Latin America but it

provides an example of the analyses of a "Third World" journalist. [R.]

Supplement to a bibliography of United States-Latin American relations since 1810. See *HLAS 42:67.*

7145 Terrorism: documents of international and local control. Compiled by Robert A. Friedlander. Dobbs Ferry, N.Y.: Oceana Publications, 1979. 1 v.; bibl.; ill.

Massive collection of documents of international legal materials regarding the control of terrorism. Section H includes the American Convention on Human Rights (1969) and various OAS resolutions and draft conventions (1969–73). [F.]

7146 Timmler, Markus. Manila: an opportunity missed (AZIF, 30:4, 1979, p. 462–494)

German writer reviews the negotiations, which led mainly to deadlocks, at UNCTAD V held in Manila in 1979. Despite frustrations and recriminations, he believes, some progress was made in that "a handful of people" seem to be beginning to recognize that the North-South debate is continuing in an atmosphere of greater interdependence. [F.]

7147 Torshin, Mijaíl. Relaciones internacionales de los trabajadores de la URSS y de América Latina (URSS/AL, 4[20], 1978, p. 138–149)

A Soviet historian outlines the activities of the Organización Internacional de Ayuda a los Revolucionarios in the 1920s and 1930s with particular reference to Latin America. [H.A. Spalding, Jr.]

7148 Trías, Vivian. La crisis del imperio. Buenos Aires: Editorial Cimarrón, 1974. 310 p.; bibl.

"In order to analyse the present situation of capitalism and the perspective of popular liberation struggles—the central topic of this work—it would be necessary to update Lenin's classic and notable book on the phenomenon of imperialism . . . To arrive at this conclusion and point out that it is out of our reach presents no difficulty . . . thus, the reader should expect to find only . . . a consideration of the transcendental questions of our time and of our suffering and oppressed Latin America." [R.]

7149 ———. Iberoamérica: "balkanización," "integración dependiente" e "integración liberadora" (NSO, 37, julio/agosto 1978, p. 41–53, ill.)

The author (an Uruguayan historian, writer, and politician) traces three concepts in the history of Latin America; 1) "Balkanization" prior to the post-World War II emergence of various integration schemes; 2) "dependent development" despite such experiments as LAFTA and CACM (that fit into the US "Grand Design" for the region); and 3) "liberating integration" which he believes is only now beginning to get underway with the creation of SELA (even recognizing the shortcomings of that organization). [F.]

7150 United States. Congress. House. Special Study Mission to Venezuela, Barbados, Brazil, and Costa Rica. Assessment of trends and conditions in the Inter-American region: report of a Special Study Mission to Venezuela, Barbados, Brazil, and Costa Rica, January 13–20, 1980, to the Committee on Foreign Affairs, U.S. House of Representatives. Washington: GPO, 1980. 33 p.

Report of an early 1980 study mission to Venezuela, Barbados, Brazil, and Costa Rica undertaken by Rep. Gus Yatron, Chairman of the Subcommittee on Inter-American Affairs of the House Committee on Foreign Affairs, and several other congressmen. There are a few modest recommendations, probably the most significant of which is for a reexamination of US policy restraining arms shipments, but most of this document is in the familiar "and then the Treasury minister said" style that has contributed to the bad reputation of congressional junkets. [F.]

7151 Urquidi, Víctor L. Población y Nuevo Orden Internacional: ¿falta un eslabón? (CM/FI, 19:3, enero/marzo 1979, p. 377–389)

Looking at the results of the 1974 Bucharest World Population Conference, Urquidi maintains that neither population specialists nor proponents of the New International Economic Order have taken adequate account of the relationship between population (growth and migration) and development. [F.]

7152 Vaitsos, Constantine V. De un pasado colonialista a una interdependencia asimétrica: el papel de Europa en las relaciones Norte-Sur (FCE/TE, 46[3]: 183, julio/sept. 1979, p. 591–637, tables)

Thoughtful and complex analysis by one of Latin America's ablest economists and dependency theorists of Europe's past, present, and possible future orientation toward the needs and demands of the underdeveloped South. In his view, whatever the ideology of governing political parties in the European countries, Europe's contribution to the South will be seriously constrained by certain economic realities. [F.]

7153 Vaky, Viron P. Hemispheric relations: everything is part of everything else (CFR/FA, 59:3, special issue, 1971, p. 616–647)

Article by long-time foreign service officer and Assistant Secretary of State for Inter-American Affairs (1978–80), obviously addressed in part to the incoming Reagan administration. Surveys Mexico, Cuba, human rights, and other matters of significance to the Carter years. Vaky writes: "The Reagan administration is likely to have a good appreciation of power, but . . . it may also underestimate the importance of 'abstractions' such as human rights. Indeed, one has an uneasy feeling of *déjà vu* when one reads currently the same kinds of concepts and arguments as those that marked U.S. policy in the 1950s." [F.]

Vargas Hidalgo, Rafael. Africa en las miras de América Latina. See *HLAS 42:1951.*

7154 Vargas Silva, Jorge A. Terminología sobre derecho del mar. México: Centro de Estudios Económicos y Sociales del Tercer Mundo, 1979. 344 p.; bibl.; ill.; index.

This will be an essential handbook for any student of the law of the sea. There are 268 p. of definitions of terms that have been invented or revised by conferences, jurists or geologists. They are more than definitions, however; each is a brief scholarly treatment of these often confusing terms. There is also an interesting and useful chronology of events relating to the law of the sea, and of particular interests to Latin America, from 1492 to 1979. [R.]

7155 Vasilyev, M. Pan-Americanism today: rhetoric and politics (IA, 2, Feb. 1980, p. 28–37)

Soviet analyst accuses the US of reviving Pan Americanism as a concept in hopes of keeping disputes in the OAS rather than the UN, countering nationalist impulses in the region, and curbing revolution against the likes of Somoza. Interestingly enough, contrary to some of Carter's conservative critics in the US, Vasilyev maintains that the the "emphasis on 'human rights' is directed against the socialist countries and against the Communist ideology." [F.]

7156 Vernon, Raymond. The multinationals: no strings attached (FP, 33, Winter, p. 121–134)

Important article by a leading student of the multinationals. Vernon argues that an international agreement should be negotiated whereby governments renounce any claims to a right to protest and/or control the activities of multinationals in foreign countries. He would also like to see an international code or codes of conduct for the multinationals that could be enforced by governments solely upon those multinationals within their own jurisdiction. [F.]

7157 Vishnia, Grigorii Fedotovich. SSha— Latinskaia Amerika; vneshnepoliticheskie otnosheniia v sovremennykh usloviiakh: 1968–1976 (USA—Latin America; foreign relations in contemporary conditions: 1968–1976). Moscow: Izdatel'stov 'Nauka,' 1978. 143 p.

Sponsored by the Institute of World Economics and International Relations. Not a work of original scholarly research, but it comes from a high-level 'think-tank' and is probably a rather thoughtful analysis, within the bounds of the system. The frame of reference is an official one. [R.V. Allen]

7158 Warshawsky, Howard. The Department of State and human rights policy: a case study of the Human Rights Bureau (APS/WA, 142:3, Winter 1980, p. 188–215)

Good case study of the organization and functioning of the Human Rights Bureau in a rather hostile environment, the "pragmatically"-inclined Department of State. Based on interviews conducted during the summer of 1978. Bureaucratic politics dimension of the study is more interesting than the conclusions, which merely summarize some of the familiar pros and cons of a foreign policy emphasis on human rights. [F.]

7159 *West Watch.* A report on the Americas and the World. Council for Inter-American Security. Vol. 4, No. 10, Dec. 1980– . Washington.

An issue in the monthly journal published by the ultra-conservative Council on Inter-American Security. All you ever wanted to know, and more, about the insidious advances of the Soviet menace in the Western Hemisphere. [F.]

7160 Wiarda, Howard J. The Latin americanization of the United States (UCSD/NS, 7:1/2, 1978 [i.e. 1979] p. 51–86)

Brilliant comparison of corporatism in the Iberic-Latin American tradition with "the emergence of bigness, impersonalism, large-scale organization, and . . . a technocratic state apparatus that in considerable measure runs contrary to the whole liberal-democratic tradition" in the US. Excellent reading assignment for courses in Latin American politics, US politics, or comparative politics. [F.]

7161 Wolff, Thomas. In pursuit of tuna: the expansion of a fishing industry and its international ramifications: the end of an era, 1890–1976. Tempe: Center for Latin American Studies, Arizona State University, 1979. 1 v.; bibl. (Special study—Arizona State University, Center for Latin American Studies; no. 19)

A study of the growth and development of southern California tuna industry and its implications for Latin American and international affairs. [R.]

7162 Wolpin, Miles D. Military technology transfers and Third World Development strategies (UWI/CQ, 23:4, Dec. 1977, p. 47–70, tables)

This article is less about military technology transfers than about the developmental record of military regimes in the Third World. Wolpin notes that most radical military regimes have been "subverted" by right-wing military factions or have themselves to some extent abandoned their commitment to change. He comments: ". . . it is worth pondering that only Marxist-inspired mobilizational systems in the underdeveloped areas seem to be closing the gap with the advanced capitalist societies—and even so they are developing at a rather moderate pace for the most part. Perhaps Marxist ideology and concomitant civilian cadre party supremacy are the vital requisites for both stability and all-round development which even the more radical military regimes lack." Hence, according to Wolpin, one might recommend diversifaction of transfers of military technology "only among various Communist donors until such a time as a Marxist-inspired *de classe* military faction opted to arm civilian revolutionaries dedicated to a syncretic restructuring of society from the bottom up . . ." [F.]

7163 Wood, Bryce. The Organisation of American States (LIWA/YWA, 1979, p. 148–167)

Wood briefly surveys the origins, evolution, and functions of the OAS. Concludes that, although the organization has slipped from its former "lofty perch" at the "apex of the inter-American system," it is likely to continue to survive because most of its members still find it to some extent useful. For Latin Americans it remains a means of access to the US, an occasional mediator in regional conflicts, and the performer of various helpful non-political functions like disaster relief. [F.]

7164 World Council of Peace. World Peace Council and Latin America: documents on Latin America. Helsinki: Information Centre for the World Peace Council, 1973. 31 p.

Texts of the Council's declarations in support of Panama's sovereignty over the Ca-nal, Allende's government in Chile, and other radical causes. [F.]

7165 Zemskov, Valeri. Sobre las relaciones histórico-culturales de América Latina y el Occidente: el conflicto de Calibán y Próspero (URSS/AL, 2, 1979, p. 95–116)

First part of an essay by a Soviet writer suggesting that Rodó and others have failed to adopt the correct analogies from *The tempest* for the historical-cultural contrast between the West and Latin America. Latin America is Calibán (a "noble savage"); and the West, Próspero (the dominant colonizer). Sort of fun. [F.]

7166 Zyblikiewicz, Lubomir. La política latinoamericana de Wilson, 1913–1921: ensayo de interpretación (PAN/ES, 3, 1976, p. 69–89)

The thesis of this article is that, although President Woodrow Wilson's public posture was one of high principles, he was in fact responsible for a considerable advance of US imperialism in Latin America. The author offers as evidence not only US military interventions in Mexico and the Caribbean but also the Wilson administration's abortive proposal for a Pan American Pact, foreshadowing to some extent later inter-American association. [F.]

Mexico

The Automotive industry in Latin America. See item **7009**.

7167 Bender, Lynn Darrell. Mexico and its oil: still far from heaven and close to the United States (RRI, 9:1, Spring 1979, p. 1–4)

Author applauds Mexico's stated intention to develop its oil reserves at a moderate pace, consistent with "sound economic management," but he expresses some skepticism that this will be possible—given the lure of fast wealth, the US' urgent need for new sources of supply, and Mexico's essential dependency on the US.

Benjamin, Thomas. Recent historiography of the origins of the Mexican War. See *HLAS* 42:2173.

7168 Bennett, Douglas C. and **Kenneth E. Sharpe.** Agenda setting and bargaining power: the Mexican state versus transnational automobile corporations (PUCIS/WP, 32:1, Oct. 1979, p. 57–89, table)

Splendid case study of negotiations between the Mexican state and transnational automobile firms between 1960–64. Bennett and Sharpe conclude that in high-technology, consumer-goods manufacturing (contrasting with natural resource industries): "Access to the domestic market is the state's principal basis of bargaining power, and can be used most effectively at the point of initial investment." However: "whether a [bargaining] resource can serve as a source of potential power depends on the context—particularly on the structure of domestic and international relationships in which each actor is enmeshed . . . It was, for example, the relationship between the Mexican state and certain domestic classes that established Mexico's 'need' for a domestic automobile industry and thus allowed the TNCs' control of automobile technology to serve as their power resource."

7169 Berbusse, Edward J. General Rosecrans' forthright diplomacy with Juárez's Mexico: 1868–1869 (AAFH/TAM, 36:4, April 1980, p. 499–514)

Berbusse is not an admirer of Benito Juárez nor of his successor, Sebastián Lerdo de Tejada, mainly because of their anti-Church policies; in fact, he goes so far as to praise Porfirio Díaz for subsequently establishing what he regards as a much more tolerant Liberal dictatorship. In this context, Berbusse praises the diplomacy of Brevet Major Gen. William S. Rosecrans, railroad entrepreneur and Envoy Extraordinary / Minister Plenipotentiary of the US during one year (1968–69) of the Juárez administration. Rosecrans' "forthright" dispatches bluntly criticized the "intolerances, lack of business sense and anti-foreign prejudices" he found in Mexico.

Boletín Informativo para Asuntos Migratorios y Fronterizos. See *HLAS 42:201.*

7170 Bustamante, Jorge A. El estudio de la zona fronteriza México-Estados Unidos (CM/FI, 19:3, enero/marzo 1979, p. 471–516)

Short essay on the literature concerning the US-Mexico frontier, followed by an extensive bibliography.

———. Facts and perceptions of undocumented migration from Mexico. See item **8079**.

7171 Capetillo, Ileana Cid. Apuntes para el análisis de un proceso internacional: la crisis del petróleo y el caso de México (UNAM/RI, 6:21, abril/junio 1978, p. 71–94, bibl.)

Analysis of the international energy crisis and Mexico's role as a producer and consumer of energy, from a "dialectical materialism" perspective. It is interesting, however, that this avowedly Marxist essay comes to essentially the same conclusions as the López Portillo administration: Mexico needs a comprehensive energy plan, should attempt to diversify trading partners, needs to explore other energy sources than oil and gas for domestic use, and so forth.

7172 Cárdenas, Héctor. Las relaciones mexicano-soviéticas: antecedentes y primeros contactos diplomáticos, 1789–1927. Prólogo, Roque González Salazar. México: Secretaría Relaciones Exteriores, 1974. 93 p.; bibl.; ill.; index (Colección del archivo histórico diplomático mexicano; 3. época: Serie Divulgación; 2)

Another publication derived from Mexico's diplomatic archives, this is an account of that country's relations with Russia and the USSR from the 18th century through the first decade of the Soviet Revolution. Narrative is generously laced with quotations from diplomatic dispatches and other official documents.

7173 Cárdenas N., Joaquín. Vasconcelos visto por la Casa Blanca: según los Archivos de Washington, D.C. Selección, traducción y comentarios de Joaquín Cárdenas N.; como prólogo, carta inédita de José Vasconcelos. México: s.n., 1978. 278 p.; 20 leaves of plates; bibl.; ill

Study of the political campaign of José Vasconcelos (1928–29) written by a participant observer and friend of Vasconcelos. Drawing on US State Department archives, author demonstrates that Washington took a keen interest in the events following Obregón's assassination and may have been influential in Vasconcelos' defeat. This defeat, he believes, was a key factor in the emergence of what he terms a one-party "dictatorship" in Mexico.

Clements, Kendrick A. Emissary from a Revolution: Luis Cabrera and Woodrow Wilson. See *HLAS 42:2282.*

7174 Colina, Rafael de la. El protocolo de reformas al Tratado Interamericano de Asistencia Recíproca: participación de México. Tlatelolco, México: Secretaría de Relaciones Exteriores, 1977. 238 p.; 5 leaves of plates; bibl.; index; maps (Cuestiones internacionales contemporáneas; 9)

Analysis of Mexico's 1975 proposals for change in the Rio Treaty. The proposals aimed at enhancing "ideological pluralism," eliminating ambiguities that could serve as an excuse for unilateral or collective "intervention," and more clearly subordinating the inter-American system to the UN.

7175 Czerny, Miroslawa. Las políticas del desarrollo regional del Caribe: México y Venezuela (PAN/ES, 4, 1978, p. 205–218, bibl.)

This article by a Polish author is misleadingly titled. It is almost exclusively about Mexico and Venezuela (rather than the Caribbean) and focuses almost entirely on government institutions in the two countries that are engaged in planning and implementing plans for regional development (not the "politics" involved).

Davids, Jules. American political and economic penetration of Mexico, 1877–1920. See *HLAS 42:2187.*

Ehrlich, Paul R.; Loy Bilderback; and Anne H. Ehrlich. The golden door: international migration, Mexico and the United States. See item **8088**.

La expropriacíon petrolera. See *HLAS 42:2291.*

7176 Fagen, Richard R. An inescapable relationship (WQ, 3:3, Summer 1979, p. 142–150)

Short piece, obviously intended for general public, summarizing a few matters at issue in US-Mexican relations.

Fernández, Raúl A. The United States-Mexico border: a politico-economic profile. See *HLAS 42:2294.*

Fitchen, Edward D. Self-determination or self-preservation: the relations of independent Yucatán with the Republic of Texas and the United States, 1847–1849. See *HLAS 42:2195.*

7177 Franco, José Luciano. Armonía y contradicciones cubano-mexicanas: 1554-1830. La Habana: Casa de las Américas, 1975. 102 p.; bibl. (Estudios monográficos—Casa de las Américas; 9)

Monograph by a Cuban scholar that compares and contrasts the historical evolution of Cuba and Mexico from the Spanish Conquest through the early 19th century.

7178 Galán, Israel. Energéticos, desarrollo económico y emigración: el caso de México y los Estados Unidos (UNAM/RI, 6:21, abril/junio 1978, p. 95–114, tables)

Overview of economic patterns on both sides of the US-Mexico border which impact on the two issues of energy and immigration. Most of the detail is devoted to the first few years of energy negotiations under Carter.

7179 García, Juan Ramón. Operation Wetback: the mass deporation of Mexican undocumented workers in 1954. Westport, Conn.: Greenwood Press, 1980. 1 v.; bibl.; index (Contributions in ethnic studies; no. 2)

As the title suggests, a study of the first big "flap" over the illegal alien issues in US-Mexican relations—a mass deporation of Mexican workers in 1954. García makes the case study more meaningful by preceding it with an analysis of the evolution of the bracero program.

7180 García Robles, Alfonso. 338 [i.e. Trescientos treinta y ocho] días de Tlatelolco. México: Fondo de Cultura Económica, 1977. 284 p. (Sección de obras de política y derecho)

Speeches, press bulletins and conferences, and international agreements negotiated by former Mexican Foreign Minister Alfonso García Robles. The period covered in this volume is 11 months in 1976.

7181 Gira de trabajo del presidente Luis Echeverría Alvarez a catorce países de América, Africa y Asia, 8 de julio a 22 de agosto de 1975. A cargo de Manuel Tello. Tlatelolco, México: Secretaría de Relaciones Exteriores, 1975. 267 p. (Colección del archivo histórico diplomático mexicano; 3. época: Serie de Obras especiales; 1)

Collection of President Luis Echeverría's principal speeches and texts of joint communiqués and protocols concluded during his trips to some 14 Latin American, African, and Asian countries, 8 June–22 August 1975. Ironic in the light of later events is his warm speech and toast in the presence of the Shah of Iran.

González, Heliodoro. The ultimate cosmetic touch for US-Mexican relations. See *HLAS 42:2302.*

7182 González-Souza, Luis F. Bracerismo vs. derechos humanos: un complejo natural de contradicciones necesariamente reflejado en la política exterior de los Estados Unidos (UNAM/RI, 6:20, enero/marzo 1978, p. 61–70)

González-Souza critica Carter's abortive plan for dealing with undocumented aliens as inconsistent with his administration's supposed emphasis on human rights.

Graebner, Norman A. Lessons of the Mexican War. See *HLAS 42:2200.*

7183 **Grayson, George W.** Oil and U.S.-Mexican relations (SAGE/JIAS, 21:4, Nov. 1979, p. 427–456)

Excellent analysis of bilateral energy politics to 1978, emphasizing the various actors and patterns of policy-making on both sides of the border. Grayson comments: "Newspaper, magazine, and television commentaries have paid inordinate attention to prickly toasts, artless references to 'Montezuma's revenge,' and recriminations over the natural gas negotiations. Largely ignored has been the remarkable degree of cooperation in energy matters between Mexico and private and public groups in the United States." For historian's comment, see *HLAS 42:2305.*

7184 ———. The politics of Mexican oil. Pittsburgh, Pa.: University of Pittsburgh Press, 1981. 336 p.; bibl.; map; tables.

One of the best, and certainly the most up-to-date, general book on the title subject. Covers the period 1901 to the present, with emphasis on the decade of the 1970s. Deals with politics in Pemex and Oil Workers Union, as well as the impact of oil on Mexico's relations with the US and other countries. Might be read in conjunction with Williams, *The rebirth of the Mexican petroleum industry* (see item **7223**).

7185 **Guimarães, Irineu.** Puebla, O Papa no continente dos índios. Prefácio, Antônio Carlos Vilaça; capa, Augusto Siqueira. Rio de Janeiro: Expressão e Cultura, 1979. 141 p.; ill. (Coleção A História e sua hora)

An account of Pope John Paul II's visit in Jan. 1979 to Mexico and the Latin American Bishops conference at Puebla. The visit was significant, in part, because the Pope cautioned against carrying "liberation" theology too far. Texts of major speeches included, as well as excerpts from others. See also item **7201**.

Harper, James W. The El Paso-Juárez Conference of 1916. See *HLAS 42:2308.*

———. Hugh Lenox Scott y la diplomacia de los Estados Unidos hacia la Revolución Mexicana. See *HLAS 42:2309.*

Harris, Charles H., III and **Louis R. Sadler.** The Plan of San Diego and the Mexican-United States war crisis of 1916: a re-examination. See *HLAS 42:2310.*

Harrison, Benjamin T. Chandler Anderson and business interests in Mexico, 1913–1920: when economic interests failed to alter U.S. foreign policy. See *HLAS 42:2311.*

Heller, Claude. Las condiciones internacionales del cambio social y participación política en México. See item **8098**.

Horn, James J. Mexican oil diplomacy and the legacy of Teapot Dome. See *HLAS 42: 2318.*

Indocumentados: mitos y realidades. See item **8099**.

7186 **International issues:** Mexico and the United States. April 9–11, 1980. Conference sponsored by The Stanley Foundation. Muscatine, Iowa: The Stanley Foundation, 1980? 18 p.

Report prepared by the rapporteur following the conference, which gathered together a number of US and Mexican government representatives, officials of international organizations, and others. They discussed trade, energy, border areas and migration, science and technology transfer, development, and disarmament.

7187 **Jiménez González, Eduardo.** Embajador por 700 [i.e. setecientos] días: misión confidencial. México: J. Pablos Editor, 1979. 106 p.; 8 leaves of plates; ill.

Brief memoirs of a Mexican diplomat, mainly concerning his service from 1975–78, including posts in West Germany and Norway. The volume is dedicated to "my friend" Willy Brandt.

7188 **Kraft, Joseph.** A reporter at-large: the Mexican oil puzzle (The New Yorker [New York] Oct. 15, 1979, p. 152–181, ill.)

Gunther-like article by a prominent journalist, complete with interviews with López Portillo and Pemex chief Díaz Serrano, tours of the oil fields and *gasoducto*, and other local color. Good of this type.

7189 **Lecturas de política exterior mexicana.** México: Centro de Estudios Internacionales, El Colegio de México, 1970. 452 p.; bibl.; map.

Excellent anthology of essays on Mexico's foreign relations produced by scholars connected with the Colegio de México. Most, not surprisingly, are concerned with relations with the United States; however, others focus on Mexico's policies toward the Third World, Allende's Chile, the Soviet Union and China, and Spain. Includes an essay by Jorge Castañeda, Mexico's Foreign Minister under López Portillo.

7190 Loehr, William. Population, migration and income distribution: a proposed analytic framework (*in* U.S.-Mexico economic relations [see item **3040**] p. 215–232, tables)

Loehr examines "the relationship between income distribution and two independent variables, population growth and rural-to-urban migration in developing countries, with some specific reference to Mexico." He proposes a model for research that, he maintains, would separate the influence of demographic factors from other forces influencing income distribution.

7191 Lutzker, Michael A. Can the peace movement prevent war?: the U.S.-Mexican crisis of April 1914 (*in* Doves and diplomats: foreign offices and peace movements in Europe and America in the twentieth century. Edited by Solomon Wank. Westport, Conn.: Greenwood Press, 1978, p. 127–153 [Contributions in political science; 4]

Lutzker examines the reaction of various self-styled "peace groups" in the US to President Wilson's landing of marines at Veracruz in the 1914 crisis with Mexico. Concludes: "It remains a disturbing fact that had Wilson determined war was necessary, he could have found support for it in the statements of a number of peace groups . . . they spoke with a divided voice, or spoke not at all. For many it was enough that Wilson's heart was pure. They would have followed him, misgivings and all, to war."

Mexico. Secretaría de Relaciones Exteriores. Representantes diplomáticos en México en Washington, 1822–1973. See *HLAS 42:2222.*

7192 Mexico and the United States: energy, trade, investment, immigration, tourism; the American Assembly. Edited by Robert J. McBride. Englewood Cliffs, N.J.: Prentice-Hall, 1981. 197 p.

Eight good essays on the US-Mexico relationship, three of which focus on the immigration question. Emanating from a 1980 conference sponsored by Columbia's American Assembly.

7193 Mexico-United States relations. Edited by Susan Kaufman Purcell. New York: Academy of Political Science, 1971. 213 p.; bibl.; index (Proceedings of the Academy of Political Science, 0065–0684; v. 23, no. 1)

Exceptionally good collection of essays on the bilateral relationship, including contributions by many leading scholars north and south of the border. Most highly recommended of all such collections now in print, and definitely required reading for the specialist.

7194 México, URSS, Bulgaria. México: Dirección General de Información y Relaciones Pública de la Presidencia de la República, 1978. 188 p.; 8 leaves of plates: ill.

Texts of speeches, correspondence, and other documents—also pictures—relating to President López Portillo's official visits to the USSR and Bulgaria in May 1978.

7195 México y Japón en el siglo XIX: la política exterior de México y la consolidación de la soberanía japonesa. Introducción, selección y notas de María Elena Ota Mishima. Tlatelolco, México: Secretaría de Relaciones Exteriores, 1976. 149 p.; 2 leaves of plates; bibl. (Colección del archivo histórico diplomático mexicano; 3. época: Serie documental; 14)

Documents from the Mexican diplomatic archives concerning Mexico's relations with the "emerging" country of Japan in the nineteenth century. Invaluable reference work for anyone interested in that bilateral connection, with more material than might have been expected.

7196 Michels, Elizabeth F. Standard Oil of New Jersey fights Mexican expropriation, 1938–1942. Washington: Georgetown University, Latin American Studies Program, 1980. 17 p. (Occasional paper no. 2)

Paper developed from a term paper written in a graduate course at Georgetown. Intelligent summary of events drawn mainly from secondary sources.

7197 Millor Mauri, Manuel. Un enfoque interno de la problemática de los trabajadores migratorios mexicanos (UNAM/RI, 6:20, enero/marzo 1978, p. 37–60)

Sophisticated analysis of the domestic economic, social, and political factors in both Mexico and the United States that are shaping the migratory worker issue.

Mumme, Stephen P. The Battle of Naco: factionalism and conflict in Sonoro, 1914–15. See *HLAS 42:2338.*

————. U.S.-Mexican groundwater problems: bilateral prospects and implications. See item **5128.**

7198 **Paz, Octavio.** Mexico and the United States (The New Yorker [New York] 17 Sept. 1979, p. 137–153, ill.)
One of Mexico's leading poets and thinkers reflects on the cultural differences that complicate relations between the United States and Mexico. Nothing very surprising here for the specialist, but, needless to say, well-written.

Pellicer de Brody, Olga. El Salvador: the current danger; Mexico's position. See item **7265.**

7199 ————. Relaciones exteriores: interdependencia con Estados Unidos o proyecto nacional (*in* México, hoy. Por José Ayala et al. Coordinado por Pablo González Casanova y Enrique Florescano. México: Siglo Veintiuno Editores, 1979, p. 372–384)
This eminent Colegio de México professor warns that Mexico's new petroleum wealth could lead to greater integration with the US economy, without the genuine national development that only policies aimed at the internal integration of Mexico's *marginados* could achieve.

7200 **Peña Guerrero, Roberto.** Crisis: readjuste, hegemonía y dependencia (UNAM/RI, 6:21, abril/junio 1978, p. 17–70, tables)
Long article that actually says little more than: 1) the energy and monetary crisis posed a serious threat to world capitalism, from which the capitalist countries—especially the US—have recovered reasonably well; and 2) Mexico's oil is a part of the US grand design for solving its future energy needs; and 3) the Mexican government had best formulate its own national energy plans carefully or risk being drawn even further into a relationship of dependency.

7201 **Perea, Francisco J.** El Papa en México: presencia y mensaje de Juan Pablo II. México: Editorial Diana, 1979. 302 p.; ill.
Another account (see item **7185**) of Pope John Paul II's visit to Mexico and the Puebla conference of Latin American bishops

in 1979. Numerous pictures and an appendix of some of the Pope's poems and short excerpts from his speeches in Mexico.

Portes, Alejandro. Illegal immigration and the International System: lessons from recent legal Mexican immigrants to the United States. See item **8122**.

7203 **Relaciones diplomáticas** México-España: 1821–1977. Compilación de Luis Miguel Díaz y Jaime G. Martini. México: Editorial Porrúa, 1977. 508 p.
Extensive collection of documents concerning Mexico's relations with Spain, although there are only a few on the years after the Spanish Civil War. A treasure trove for those persons interested in this subject from a historical perspective.

Revel-Mouroz, Jean. Economie frontalière et organisation de l'espace: réflexiones à partir de l'exemple de la frontière Mexique-Etats Unis. See item **5137**.

7204 ————. Mobilité du travail ou mobilité du capital?: accords et conflits à la frontière Mexique-Etats Unis (FDD/NED [Problèmes d'Amérique Latine, 53] 4533/4534, 31 oct. 1979, p. 45–75, map, tables)
Sophisticated and well-documented analysis of two central problems in US-Mexico relations: migration (legal and illegal) and border industries. There are other studies of these issues, but this one is particularly significant as an indication of the progress of French scholarship on inter-American relations.

7205 **Romo, Rosa María** and **María de Lourdes Urbina.** La política exterior de México y los Estados Unidos frente al problema de los trabajadores migratorios (UNAM/RI, 6:20, enero/marzo 1978, p. 13–35)
Survey of the history of migration of persons in both directions across the US-Mexican border since the colonial era, culminating in the current undocumented alien problem. Authors maintain that the only permanent solution to conflicts over migration today is more economic development in Mexico coupled with more effective Mexican diplomacy in support of the cause of the migrant worker.

7206 **Ronfeldt, David; Richard Nehring; and Arturo Gándara.** México's petroleum and U.S. policy: implications for the 1980s. Prepared for the U.S. Department of Energy. Santa Monica, Calif.: The Rand Corporation, 1980. 97 p.; maps; tables (Department of Energy contract no. R-2510-DOE)

Detailed study of Mexican energy resources, with a concluding section exploring some of the implications for U.S.-Mexican relations. Author's estimate of probable reserves is well below some such estimates; for example, they believe there is only a 10 percent probability that Mexico will eventually produce more than 120 billion barrels. They also stress the obvious, but nonetheless important, fact that energy is only one of several issues making Mexico a key country for the US; at the same time, there is certain to be some spillover from energy to other matters.

7207 Ross, Stanley R. México y los Estados Unidos patrocinan un programa de estudio de su problemas fronterizos (UNAM/RI, 6:20, enero/marzo 1978, p. 71–75)

Ross discusses the origin and initial plans of The Mexico-United States Program of Frontier Studies, created in 1976 as an institution to encourage cooperation in investigating frontier problems among scholars and government officials on both sides of the border.

7208 Saxe-Fernández, John. Petróleo y estrategia: México y Estados Unidos en el contexto de la política global. Portada de Anhelo Hernández. México: Siglo Veintiuno Editores, 1980. 177 p.; ill.

Saxe-Fernández warns that the new oil wealth of Mexico could prove to be a liability insofar as it prompts the US to devise additional means of drawing Mexico into a relationship of dependency (like a proposed scheme for a North American Common Market).

7209 Schoonover, Thomas David. Dollars over dominion: the triumph of liberalism in Mexican-United States relations, 1861–1867. Baton Rouge: Louisiana State University Press, 1978. 316 p.; bibl.; index.

Noteworthy study of US-Mexican relations during a critical period. Schoonover stresses that the Liberals in Mexico and the reigning Republican party in the US shared much the same ideology of laissez-faire liberalism, which facilitated cooperation in the struggle against the conservative French-Maximilian intervention. He agrees with William H. Seward, who "clearly and emphatically interpreted the Civil War-French intervention era as the turning point in the clash between the New World republican "system" and the Old World, "conservative," monarchical and aristocratic "system." After the crisis had passed, the same ideological affinity led the Mexicans to welcome US economic penetration. For historian's comment, see *HLAS 42:2239.*

7210 Sierra, Justo. El exterior: revistas políticas y literarias. Ed., notas e índices, José Luis Martínez. México: Universidad Nacional Autónoma de México, 1977. 426 p.; 1 leaf of plates; ill.; indexes (His Obras completas; 7. Nueva biblioteca mexicana; 55)

One volume in the series of the "complete works" of Justo Sierra, including writings of this famous Mexican statesman on his country's foreign policy and international affairs generally.

7211 Simposio sobre México hoy, 1978. Visión del México contemporáneo. México: Colegio de México, 1979. 148 p.

Another good collection of essays emanating from the Colegio de México, this one concerning both domestic and international matters. Pt. 1 focuses on "Mexico and the World;" pt. 5 on Mexico's relations with the US.

7212 Sloan, John W. United States policy responses to the Mexican Revolution: a partial application of the bureaucratic politics model (JLAS, 10:2, Nov. 1978, p. 283–308)

Ambitious and not entirely successful attempt to explain US-Mexican relations over an extended period (1911–41) by applying the bureaucratic-political model and using dependency theory. Based on secondary sources. For historian's comment, see *HLAS 42:2358.* [A. Suárez]

7213 Smith, Peter H. Mexico, the quest for a U.S. policy. Editor, Wallace Irwin, Jr. New York, N.Y.: Foreign Policy Association, 1980? 32 p.; bibl.; ill.

Excellent review of the major issues in US-Mexican relations as of 1980. Written for the Foreign Policy Association with the intelligent lay reader obviously in mind, but the specialist will also find it useful. Smith stresses the linkages among issues.

7214 Székely, Alberto. The exclusive economic zone: a carefully legislated development of great significance for Mexico's future (*in* The future of Mexico. Edited by Lawrence E. Koslow. Tempe: Center for Latin American Studies, Arizona State University, 1977, p. 223–241)

Examines the economic potential of Mexico's coastal waters and the evolution in international and Mexican law of the concept of the Exclusive Economic Zone (EEZ). Useful background for an understanding of recent disputes between the US and Mexico over fishing and other marine resources.

7215 Tamayo Rodríguez, Jaime E. Los principios de la política internacional de México. Guadalajara, México: Instituto de Estudios Sociales, Universidad de Guadalajara, 1978. 90 p. (Ensayos y monografías—Instituto de Estudios Sociales, Universidad de Guadalajara)

Very forgettable summary of some of the principles like self-determination that Mexican foreign policy has supported over the years. Almost a third of this short volume is devoted to reprinting the "Organic Law of the Mexican Foreign Service."

7216 Tambs, Lewis A. and Thomas Aranda, Jr. Cooperation or confrontation?: a view from the border (*in* Mexico 2000: a look at the problems of modern Mexico. Washington: Council for Inter-American Security, 1980, p. 55–65, ill.)

General discussion of the problem of illegal immigration and various options for dealing with it—none specifically endorsed—in light of Mexico's new energy resources.

7217 Tancer, Robert S. Regulating foreign investment in the seventies: the Mexican approach (*in* The future of Mexico. Edited by Lawrence E. Koslov. Tempe: Center for Latin American Studies, Arizona State University, 1977, p. 191–222, table)

Careful analysis of Mexican laws relating to foreign investment and technology transfer going back to the 1917 Constitution, but with emphasis on the changes introduced by the Echeverría administration.

Tenenbaum, Barbara A. Merchants, money, and mischief: the British in Mexico, 1821–1862. See *HLAS 42:2249.*

7218 Torres Bodet, Jaime. Memorias. v. 5, Equinoccio. México: Editorial Porrúa, 1974. 1 v.

Another volume in the memoirs of this prominent Mexican statesman and diplomat, covering the years 1931–43.

7219 Update: United States-Canadian/ Mexican relations; hearings before the Subcommittee on Inter-American Affairs of the Committee on Foreign Affairs, House of Representatives, Ninety-Sixth Congress, Second Session, June 17 and 26, 1980. Washington: GPO, 1980. 71 p.

General dialogue between the Subcommittee and Carter Administration spokesmen regarding the current status of issues affecting US bilateral relations with Canada and Mexico.

7220 Urbina, María de Lourdes and Javier Rodríguez Piña. La migración de trabajadores mexicanos a Estados Unidos: referencia bibliográfica (UNAM/RI, 6:20, enero/marzo 1978, p. 77–81)

Short bibliographical essay on works, both Mexican and US, dealing with the migration issue.

7221 U.S. policies toward Mexico: perceptions and perspectives. Edited by Richard D. Erb and Stanley R. Ross. Washington: American Enterprise Institute for Public Policy Research, 1979. 1 v.; bibl. (AEI symposia; 79H)

Volume consists essentially of the proceedings of a conference sponsored by the American Enterprise Institute in Houston, Texas, 5 Feb. 1979. All of the essays are very brief and general, even superficial. There must have been better conferences. Foreword by George Bush.

Villasana, J. Alberto and R. B. Southard. Cartographic cooperation along the United States-Mexico international border. See item **5149.**

Vollard, Klaus. Das Dritte Reich und Mexiko. See *HLAS 42:2366.*

Walker, William O., III. Control across the border: the United States, Mexico, and narcotics policy, 1936–1940. See *HLAS 42:2367.*

7222 Williams, Edward J. Mexican hydrocarbon export policy: ambition and reality (*in* International energy policy. Edited by Robert M. Lawrence and Martin O. Heisler. Lexington, Mass.: Lexington Books, 1980, p. 65–79 [Policy Studies Organization series])

Williams explains how Mexican decision-makers, after their country's new oil wealth began to be apparent, "were playing export policy by ear, informed by a combination of ideological prejudices, unanticipated economic imperatives, and changing reserve and production scenarios." Now that the policy-making scene has somewhat stabilized, he argues, one can expect "the maintenance of high prices, a rather clear commitment to expanded quantities of foreign sales, large exports to the United States, and ongoing attempts to diversify markets."

7223 ———. The rebirth of the Mexican petroleum industry: developmental directions and policy implications. Lexington, Mass.: Lexington Books, 1979. 218 p.; bibl.; ill.; index.

Excellent study focusing mainly on the period since Mexico discovered substantial new energy resources, mid-1970s through 1979. Might be read in conjunction with Grayson, *The politics of Mexican oil* (see item **7184**).

7224 **Zea Prado, Irene.** Introducción al problema de los indocumentados (UNAM/RI, 6:20, enero/marzo 1978, p. 7–12)

This "introduction" says little more than the problem of undocumented aliens in US-Mexican relations is hard to solve because it relates to the problem of poverty in Mexico.

Central America

7225 **Argüello, Alvaro.** Incidencias del imperialismo en el proceso político de Nicaragua (RCPC, 159, abril/junio 1978, p. 32–37)

Term-paper-like survey of the events surrounding the US military intervention in Nicaragua from 1909 through the late 1920s.

7226 **Arismendi, Rodney.** Primavera popular en Nicaragua (URSS/AL, 26:2, 1980, p. 10–40)

The author is the First Secretary of the Communist Party of Uruguay. He rejoices that the Nicaraguan revolution against Somoza succeeded, despite all the efforts of imperialists, the multinationals, Henry Kissinger, the CIA, President Carter (and all the rest of the reactionary camp) to defeat it. It is part of an inevitable wave of popular revolutions that began with the one in Cuba. Now the revolution must be consolidated, as Fidel put it, not into "another Cuba" but into a "New Nicaragua."

7227 **Bernal, Miguel Antonio.** Panamá: el nuevo Tratado del Canal; planteamiento histórico general (UNAM/RI, 5:18, julio/sept. 1977, p. 7–13)

A Panamanian lawyer and professor at UNAM in Mexico condemns the new Canal treaties as a Panamanian sell-out to the US.

7228 **Berner, M.F.C.** The Panama Canal and future United States hemispheric policy (LIWA/YWA, 34, 1980, p. 205–219)

Berner examines the final stages of negotiations over the new Panama Canal treaty, both in terms of the bilateral relationship between US and Panama, and domestic politics in the two countries. Applauding the settlement, he is nevertheless doubtful whether it will greatly improve hemispheric relations generally, which depends to a large extent on resolution of fundamental North-South economic issues.

7229 **Brown, Charles Henry.** Agents of Manifest Destiny: the lives and times of the filibusters. Chapel Hill: University of North Carolina Press, 1980. 525 p.; 8 leaves of plates; bibl.; ill.; index.

Enjoyable, well-documented narrative of the exploits of William Walker and other US adventurers during the Manifest Destiny era.

7230 **Burbach, Roger.** Nicaragua: the course of the revolution (MR, 31:9, Feb. 1980, p. 28–39)

Burback asserts: "while the ultimate destiny of the revolution has not been decided, developments in Nicaragua demonstrate that the bourgeois reformists are not in control of the government and that the Sandinista Front and the popular sectors are leading the country forward on a revolutionary socialist trajectory."

7231 Campo, Andrés Ventosa de. El enclave económico de los Estados Unidos sobre Panamá (UNAM/RI, 5:18, julio/sept. 1977, p. 39–54)

Campo insists that the new Panama Canal treaties have not gone far enough in respecting Panamanian sovereignty and eliminating the US' economic and military enclave in Panama.

7232 El Canal de Panamá: origen, trauma nacional y destino. Muñoz Pinzón et al.; recopilación, prólogo y notas de Enrique Jaramillo Levi. México: Editorial Grijalbo, 1976. 163 p.; bibl. (Colección 70 [i.e. Setenta]; 3. ser., 146)

Collection of articles on the Panama Canal issue written not long before the conclusion of the new treaty.

7233 Castillero Calvo, Alfredo. La historia del enclave panameño frente al Tratado Torrijos-Carter. Panamá: Universidad de Panamá, Facultad de Filosofía, Letras y Educación, 1977. 35 p. (Ediciones nueva universidad; no. 5)

Short favorable commentary on the new Panamanian Canal Treaty, with some historical background on the old regime governing the Canal.

7234 Castro Herrera, Guillermo. Panamá ante la década de 1980 (CM/FI, 20:4, abril/junio 1970, p. 673–695)

The author regards the new Panama Canal Treaties as merely ushering in a "second phase" of "neocolonialism" in his country. He quotes Che Guevara approvingly, to the effect that the Panamanian people will one day throw off the yoke of imperialism entirely.

7235 ———. Panamá 1977: apuntes para un análisis (UNAM/RI, 5:18, julio/sept. 1977, p. 15–37, table)

From the perspective of this Marxist writer, the Carter-Torrijos treaties regarding the Panama Canal simply do not go far enough in favor of Panama—something that might have been expected, given the non-socialist character of the Panamanian government. Never fear, however, because the Panamanian "working class" is obviously on

the march, and they will shape matters up in due course.

7236 Crane, Philip M. Surrender in Panama: the case against the treaty. Introduction by Ronald Reagan. New York: Dale Books, 1978. 258 p.; bibl.

Written by a prominent conservative congressman—on the eve of the ratification of the new treaty—, with an introduction by none other than Ronald Reagan. Useful as a summary of right-wing arguments opposed to the "surrender" of the Panama Canal—the alleged US "sovereignty" over the Canal, unpredictability of the Torrijos government, Communist designs, and so on. Reagan endorsed continued negotiations with Panama but insisted that "the United States must retain practical control over the canal for the security of the entire hemisphere."

7237 Crosby, Elisha Oscar. Guatemala en la diplomacia de la Guerra Civil norteamericana (IAHG/AHG, 2:1, 1979, p. 223–250)

Excerpt from the memoirs of Elisha Oscar Crosby, with an introduction by a Guatemalan historian Francis Polo Sifontes. Crosby was a US emissary to Guatemala and other Central American governments during Abraham Lincoln's administration. His mission was to explore the possibility of establishing a colony of free blacks in Central America and otherwise to win the support of Central American governments to the cause of the Union in the Civil War.

Demyk, Michel. Belize: enjeu territorial et enjeu pétrolier. See item **5074.**

7238 Díaz Castillo, Roberto. Panamá: Torrijos y el proceso transformador (USCG/PS, 2:5, enero/junio 1978, p. 215–226)

Paean of praise to the Torrijos "revolution" in Panama, expressing the hope that it might turn out to be a "socialist" transformation, while acknowledging that the decision in this respect must remain up to the Panamanian people.

7239 Durham, William H. Scarcity and survival in Central America: ecological origins of the Soccer War. Stanford, Calif.: Stanford University Press, 1979. 209 p.; bibl.; maps; plates; tables.

Interesting and important analysis of the "demographic" Soccer War in 1969 between El Salvador and Honduras. Durham maintains that the *basic* cause of the war was not the emigration of Salvadoran citizens to Honduras in response to population pressures, *per se*, but the scarcity of land because of *latifundio* holdings in both countries that made the peasants a threat to the established order.

7240 Facio, Gonzalo J. Política exterior (*in* Costa Rica contemporánea. Prólogo y dirección, Chester Zelaya. Colaboradores, Carlos Meléndez Chaverri et al. San José: Editorial Costa Rica, 1979, t. 1, p. 159–188, bibl.)

Essay summarizing the assumptions underlying Costa Rica's post-World War II foreign policy by a man who played a leading role in shaping and implementing that policy as Ambassador to the US and the OAS, and his country's Foreign Minister (1970–78). Among the assumptions: 1) that "Marxist determinism" has been refuted by history; 2) that "democracy is not synonymous with either capitalism or socialism;" 3) that the greatest threat to peace is not nuclear weapons but world poverty; and 4) that Costa Rica "cannot be neutral in the struggle for democracy."

Faillos Navarro, Francisco. Los partidos políticos y la coyuntura de 1978. See item **6220**.

7241 Fallas, Carlos Luis. Un mes en la China Roja. Compilación y ed. por Eduardo Saxe Fernández, con la colaboración de Zahyra A. de Fallas. Ciudad Universitaria Rodrigo Facio, San José: Editorial Universidad de Costa Rica, 1977. 123 p.

Collection of short essays previously published in *Adelante*, a Costa Rican weekly. Consists of a Costa Rican journalist's reflection on his short visit to the People's Republic of China in 1956 in which he expresses his admiration for the people of China and the spirit of Mao's Revolution.

Fielding, John. La diplomacia norteamericana y la reincorporación de la Mosquitia. See *HLAS 42:2445*.

7242 Fonseca, Cristina da. ¿Quién le tiene miedo a Belice libre? (UNAM/PDD, 9:35, agosto/octo. 1978, p. 64–72, map)

Passionate defense of the concept of Belize's independence, coupled with criticism of Guatemala, the British, the US—all of whom at one time or another have opposed or delayed independence.

7243 Fonseca Amador, Carlos. Un nicaragüense en Mòscú. Managua: Secretaría Nacional Propaganda y Educación Política, F.S.L.N., 1980. 78 p.; port.

Book written by one of the founders of the Sandinista Front (FSLN) in Nicaragua and published posthumously by the FSLN's National Secretary of Propaganda and Education. Fonseca Amador was killed in combat in 1976. The volume is essentially the journal he kept during his visit to Moscow in 1957. Obviously, he had a good time and was impressed by the accomplishments of the Soviet revolution.

7244 Gómez, Leonel and **Bruce Cameron.** El Salvador: the current danger; American myths (FP, 43, Summer 1981, p. 71–78)

Article coauthored by former chief advisor to the assassinated President of the Salvadorian Land Reform Agency, which addresses alleged "myths" in US understanding of the situation in El Salvador and makes some policy recommendations. Argues that the land reform has been at least partially successful, that neither the old oligarchs nor civilians have great influence in the present military dictatorship, that the FDR's power over the FSLN guerrilla organization is easily overestimated, and that the Salvadorian guerrillas do have an extreme left (and for this reason are not comparable to the more moderate Sandinistas of Nicaragua). According to the authors, the Reagan administration's plan for eventual stabilization and elections will fail unless extraordinary measures are taken to break the pattern of military control, repression, and corruption. They suggest the creation of an electoral commission, the establishment of a 2,000-man international peace-keeping force, and the removal and exile of many high-ranking officers.

7245 Gonionskii, Semen A. Panama i Panamskii kanal [Panama and the Panama Canal]. Moscow: s.n., 1976. 58 p.; plate.

Author is identified in the publisher's blurb as a Soviet diplomat and historian who has studied Panama for many years. The pamphlet is described as covering the basic stages of the Panamanian struggle for national liberation and the history of the clash with American imperialism for sovereignty over the Canal Zone. Within the bounds of Soviet outlook on such things, this appears a useful, popular summary of the situation. [R.V. Allen]

7246 Gorostiaga, Xavier. Los acomodos del Imperio: el caso panameño, 1968–1978 (UNAH/RCE, 1:1, sept. 1979, p. 32–53, bibl.)

Gorostiaga maintains that the new treaties governing the Canal represent merely an effort by the US, in league with Panama's bourgeoisie, to perpetuate imperialism (protect Panama as a banking service center for multinational corporations, and so on).

7247 Goytía, Víctor Florencio. Cómo negocia Panamá su canal. San José, Costa Rica: Impr. y Litografía Lehmann, 1974. 270 p.; maps.

One of the many books published prior to the new treaty, tracing the history of the Canal and negotiations over particular issues between Panama and the US. Includes numerous documents.

7248 Guatemala. Ministerio de Relaciones Exteriores. Dirección de Asuntos Centroamericanos. Memoria. Memoria de las labores desarrolladas por la Dirección de Asuntos Centroamericanos durante el período comprendido entre el 1° de julio de 1977 al 30 de junio de 1978. Guatemala: 1978. 346 p.

Consists of various reports issued by the Guatemalan Ministry of Foreign Relations, Office of Central American Affairs, for the period mid-1977 through mid-1978. Includes a summary of activities regarding the Belize controversy with related documents (p. 49–68); a detailed survey of intra-Central American relations involving Guatemala during this period such as ODECA meetings and a ministerial conference (p. 69–102); and a summary of the enrollment and activities of a Central American School of International Relations (p. 341–346).

Guerra, Sergio and **Rosa Pulpeiro.** Política demográfica de la United Fruit. See *HLAS* 42:2604.

7249 Hehir, J. Bryan. El Salvador: the current danger; a view from the Church (FP, 43, Summer 1981, p. 83–88)

The Director of the US Catholic Conference's Office of Foreign Affairs maintains that the Catholic Church's opposition to US policy in El Salvador should not be seen as an isolated effort, rather as part of the Church's worldwide alliance with the poor. According to Hehir, the Church opposes US military aid to El Salvador and the internationalization of the conflict there, and strongly favors a locally negotiated political solution.

7250 Herrera Cáceres, H. Roberto. El diferendo hondureño-salvadoreño; su evolución y perspectivas. Tegucigalpa: Universidad Nacional Autónoma de Honduras, Facultad de Ciencias Jurídicas y Sociales, 1976 [i.e. 1977]. 215 p.; annexes; bibl. (Colección Investigaciones jurídicas)

Relatively objective survey by a Honduran professor, with documents, of the Honduras-El Salvador negotiations 1973–76.

Herrera Zúñiga, René. Nicaragua: el desarrollo capitalista dependiente y la crisis de la dominación burguesa; 1950–1980. See item 6225.

7251 Horowitz, Paul. United States: big business vs. the "Big Stick" (NACLA, 13:5, Sept./Oct. 1979, p. 3–11, plates)

Horowitz notes that the US private business community was overwhelmingly in support of the new Panama Canal treaties, and he argues that this was because they recognized that their interests—rather than Panama's "fundamental aspirations"—were being served. In this context, Horowitz regards it as both rather ironic and significant that the themes sounded by US ultra-conservatives in opposition to the treaties "were themes that had been advanced by America's corporate elite when they were useful and even necessary to generate popular acceptance of an earlier, more brazenly colonialist policy in Panama."

7252 Instituto Mexicano Matías Romero de Estudios Diplomáticos. La frontera Sur de México: breve ensayo bibliográfico. Por María Carmen Pérez-Anta et al. México: Secretaría de Relaciones Exteriores, Instituto Mexicano "Matías Romero" de Estudios Diplomáticos, 1976. 34 leaves.

Bibliography of works concerning the southern frontier of Mexico, including the Belize controversy. Compiled by the Mexican Secretariat of Foreign Relations, and helpful for anyone interested in Mexican boundary problems.

7253 López Portillo y Pacheco, José. En la ONU, Washington y Panamá. México: Secretaría de Programación y Presupuesto, Dirección General de Documentación y Análisis, 1979. 123 p.; index (Cuadernos de filosofía política; no. 25)

Rather pretentious collection of documents, speeches, etc., concerning the role of Mexico's President López Portillo in the ceremonies inaugurating the new treaties governing the Panama Canal.

7254 Madalengoitia, Laura. La victoria sandinista: repercusiones en América Latina (DESCO/Q, 2, nov./dic. 1979, p. 50–57, map)

According to the author, the Nicaraguan revolution was the most serious blow the Colossus of the North suffered since Fidel liberated Cuba and is a clear indication that the "Latin American popular movement"—frustrated in Chile—has gathered real momentum in Central America.

7255 Maira, Luis. Fracaso y reacomodo de la política de Estados Unidos hacia Centroamérica (CM/FI, 20:4, abril/junio 1980, p. 696–724)

Maira, one of the most insightful and objective Latin American analysts of US foreign policy, discusses the evolution of US policies toward Central America under Carter—the early context and assumptions, unforeseen developments, and the US response to changing circumstances.

7256 Marcoleta, José de. Documentos diplomáticos de José de Marcoleta, ministro de Nicaragua en los Estados Unidos, 1854. Managua: Fondo de Promoción Cultural, Banco de América, 1976. 84 p. (Serie Fuentes históricas; no. 3. Colección cultural Banco de América)

Collection of the diplomatic correspondence of José de Marcoleta, Nicaragua's Minister to the US in 1854. Publication supported by the Nicaraguan branch of the Bank of America in the days before the deluge.

7257 Marthoz, Jean Paul. Panama: la malédiction du canal. Bruxelles: La Relève, 1979. 183 p; bibl. (Collection Dossiers-reportages)

Book published in Belgium by a European journalist who has written extensively in French, Belgian, and Latin American newspapers and was a professor at the University of San José, Costa Rica (1974–75). General discussion of the controversy over the Panama Canal and an examination of the principal terms of the new treaties, which Marthoz regards as still prejudicial to Panamanian interests.

7258 Martz, Mary Jeanne Reid. The Central American Soccer War: historical patterns and internal dynamics of OAS settlement procedures. Athens: Ohio University, Center for International Studies, 1978. 113 p.; bibl. (Papers in international studies: Latin America series; no. 4).

One of the very few careful, "objective" studies of the 1969 Soccer War between El Salvador and Honduras and the OAS attempt to settle the conflict. Martz surveys prior OAS experience with peaceful settlement, pointing out that the 1969 war was to some extent "different" because it involved both demographic pressures and issues arising out of regional economic integration. She decries the fact that the OAS has done little to refine its peaceful settlement procedures, especially since (in her view) "the conditions for dramatic conflictual confrontations are proliferating and becoming more complex."

7259 Medrano Castañeda, Lianella. El agente diplomático hondureño: tesis. Tegucigalpa: Universidad Nacional Autónoma de Honduras, Facultad de Ciencias Jurídicas y Sociales, 1978. 117 leaves.

Thesis submitted at the Universidad Nacional Autónoma de Honduras examining the organization and functioning of the Honduran diplomatic corps in the context of general international law. Not a study that will be of much help to students of comparative foreign policy.

Menon, P.K. The Anglo-Guatemalan territorial dispute over the colony of Belize (British Honduras). See item **5077**.

7260 Millett, Richard. Central American paralysis (FP, 39, Summer 1980, p. 99–117)

Good survey of Central American developments as of early 1980. With some foresight, Millett wrote that "current international domestic political trends may tip the balance toward [US military] intervention." In his view, "one possible avenue of escape" from this might be actively to seek "major involvement by others, such as Venezuela, Mexico, Western Europe, and even Japan, in efforts to stabilize and develop Central America." How Western Europe and

Japan are to be lured in in "major" ways is not made clear. Otherwise, Millett appears to be laying his main stress on the US role, stating: "What has been lacking is a definite commitment by the United States to support political and financial alternatives to the violent revolutions of the far left or the brutal repression by the entrenched right." The past and probable future unwillingness of the US to make such a commitment is what he means by "paralysis."

7261 Nicaragua se va a convertir en una nueva Nicaragua (OCLAE, 2/3, 1980, p. 18–31, plates)

Address by Fidel on 26 July 1979, dealing mainly with the new regime in Nicaragua. He says: "The Sandinistas are revolutionaries, . . . but they are not extremists, rather realists. And the stuff of realists makes the best revolutions (APPLAUSE), the best and the more profound revolutions."

7262 Ortega, Daniel. Comandante Daniel Ortega ante el Plenario de la VI Cumbre (AR, 6:21, 1979, p. 10–14, plates)

Fire-breathing speech, invoking the shade of Sandino, delivered to the Non-aligned Meeting in Havana by a prominent member of the Governing Junta of Nicaragua's National Government of Reconstruction.

7263 Panama. Treaties, etc. Tratados sobre el Canal de Panamá suscritos entre la República de Panamá y los Estados Unidos de América (Treaties on the Panama Canal signed between the United States of America and the Republic of Panama). Washington, D.C.: Secretaría General, Organización de los Estados Americanos, 1979. 2 v.; ill. (Serie sobre tratados; 57–57A. OEA Documentos oficiales; OEA/Ser.A/34)

The official texts of the new Panama Canal Treaties and instruments of ratification, published by the OAS.

7264 The Panama Canal treaties: the final chapter (IAMEA, 33:2, Autumn 1979, p. 87–91)

Text of speech by Congressman Murphy of New York on 30 July 1979, and other comments from the *Congressional Record* grumbling about the White House's out-maneuvering of Murphy-introduced H.R. 111—legislation he claims "very clearly laid out a regime to protect America's interest in

the Panama Canal Zone area for the next 20 years." The Editor of *Inter-American Economic Affairs* reprints this material, agreeing with Murphy that the "final chapter" was one of "disgraceful circumstances" and adding (just for good measure) that it was "as disgraceful as the circumstances that marked the original 'success'" of the Carter administration in getting the Panama Canal treaties passed.

7265 Pellicer de Brody, Olga. El Salvador: the current danger; Mexico's position (FP, 43, Summer 1971, p. 88–92)

Prominent Mexican analyst of her country's foreign policy states: "The new U.S. policy toward El Salvador appears disconcerting, even stupefying, to Mexico . . . The tendency to simply Third World affairs into nothing but negotiating items for the superpowers and the arrogant exercise of hegemonic power over zones of influence are intolerable . . ."

7265a Pérez Venero, Mirna. La novela *canalera* de Panamá: antecedentes literarios y sociales (LNB/L, 264/265, feb./marzo 1978, p. 28–53)

As the title suggests, a survey of Panamanian novels and other fiction literature relating to the Panama Canal. There has obviously been quite a lot of such literature.

7266 Salisbury, Richard V. Costa Rica y la crisis hondureña de 1924 (UNCR/R, 3:6, enero/junio 1978, p. 43–68)

Well-documented, detailed account of the involvement of Costa Rican representatives in helping to resolve a controversy over presidential succession in Honduras in 1924—a conflict that threatened the precarious peace of the subregion achieved under the Washington treaties.

7267 Selser, Gregorio. Centroamérica: entre la atrocidad y la esperanza (CM/FI, 20:4, abril/junio 1980, p. 527–548)

Not-especially-enlightening survey of conditions of unrest in much of Central America. Much breast-beating about violence and brutality, corrupt oligarchies, and the US role in the region—offset with an expression of confidence that "the people" are slowly winning their long struggle for socio-economic justice.

7268 Simons, Marlise. Guatemala: the coming danger (FP, 43, Summer 1981, p. 93–103)

Simons argues that the "real test of the Reagan administration's Central American policy will come in Guatemala, not El Salvador." The reason, in her view, is that the Reagan administration can disguise its "raw anticommunism" in El Salvador by pointing to the ruling junta's at least nominal commitment to democracy and social reform. The government in Guatemala makes no such pretense and is openly allied with right-wing "death squads." Little middle ground seems to exist in a looming civil war.

7269 Smit, Hans. The proposed Panama Canal treaties: a triple failure (Columbia Journal of Transnational Law [Columbia University, School of Law, New York] 17 : 1, 1978, p. 1–32)

International lawyer attacks, not the basic notion that the US should relinquish the old regime governing the canal, but the precise terms of the new treaties. On the whole, a rational critique that highlights some of the ambiguities in the new agreements.

7270 Tambs, Lewis A. Estratégia, poder naval e sobrevivência: argumentos para manter o Canal do Panamá (ADN, 66:682, março/abril 1979, p. 101–117, maps)

Tambs insists that the Panama Canal is too important geopolitically not to have it remain in US hands, although he reviews other options (to reject them). The Brazilian military was apparently so impressed with Tamb's logic that they reprinted his article even after the new treaties were ratified.

7271 Thompson, W. Scott. El Salvador: the current danger; choosing to win (FP, 43, Summer 1981, p. 78–83)

Thompson (consultant to the Reagan administration) recognizes that the Duarte regime in El Salvador has some "defects," but he argues that it could be worse, especially since Duarte himself won "truly free elections" and "is a reformer." According to the author: "The Reagan administration's commitment to reform enormously strengthens Duarte's hands against primitives of the far right. This happens as Nicaragua bends toward the totalitarian model of its communist benefactors . . ."

7272 Torrijos Herrera, Omar. La quinta frontera: partes de la batalla diplomática sobre el Canal de Panamá. Ciudad Universitaria Rodrigo Facio, Costa Rica: Editorial Universitaria Centroamericana, 1978. 101 p.; ill. (Colección Seis)

Collection of speeches, documents, and miscellaneous writings relating to the new Panama Canal treaties and the "diplomatic battle" surrounding them, edited by deceased Gen. Omar Torrijos. The "Fifth Frontier" is a phrase from Graham Greene, whose short essay concludes the volume.

7273 Tulchin, Joseph S. Por qué los Estados Unidos ratificaron los nuevos tratados sobre el Canal de Panamá (IAEERI/E, 57, marzo/abril 1979, p. 45–54)

Discussion by a North American analyst for a Latin American audience of the new Panama Canal treaties and the politics of ratification in the US, as well as a little background on the history of the Canal. Tulchin thinks the history is relevant, that some Americans were a bit ashamed of the circumstances surrounding the US' initial acquisition of the Canal and the extent of US control. This reviewer does not think such altruism had much to do with US acquiescence in a new arrangement.

7274 United States. Congress. House. Committee on Foreign Affairs. Subcommittee on Inter-American Affairs. Assessment of conditions in Central America. Hearings before . . . Ninety-sixth Congress, Second Session, on April 29 and May 20, 1980. Washington: GPO, 1980. 137 p.

Hearings in which various officials of the American Chamber of Commerce give their assessments of conditions in each of the major countries of Central America, followed by the assessments of Carter Administration officials (Assistant Secretary of State for Inter-American Affairs William G. Bowdler and US Ambassador to Nicaragua Lawrence Pezzullo). Not surprisingly, the business perspective evidences less concern for the shortcomings of right-wing regimes and more concern about leftist currents in the subregion.

7275 ———. ———. ———. ———.

———. Review of the presidential certification of Nicaragua's connection to terrorism: hearing before the Subcommittee on Inter-American Affairs of the Committee on Foreign Affairs, House of Representatives, Ninety-sixth Congress, September 30, 1980. Washington: GPO, 1980. 50 p.

Hearing held at request of conservative Congressmen after President Carter had certified that the revolutionary government in Nicaragua was not supporting international terrorism, which certification was a prerequisite for freeing US assistance funds to that country. Testimonies of Congressmen Bauman and Young, as well as a letter submitted by the Regional Vice President for Central America of the Association of American Chambers of Commerce in Latin America (R. Bruce Cuthbertson), attack the policies of the Nicaraguan government.

7276 Walker, Thomas W. The US and Central America: the growing crisis and American interests (FIU/CR, 8:3, Summer 1979, p. 18–23, map)
Walker charges: "At present US goals in the third world in general and in Central America in particular are short-termed, reactive, and excessively concerned with stability and, hence, the maintenance of an elite-dominated status quo. These policies pose a grave threat to long-range US interests by contributing to the continuation of socially-unjust systems and thereby increasing the probability of civil and regional conflict and stimulating an ever-growing feeling of anti-Americanism among the peoples of the region." He argues that the US commit itself to support "distributive justice" in the region, reduce or terminate military assistance programs, adopt a much more flexible attitude toward insurgency, and normalize relations with Cuba.

7277 Zammit, J. Ann. The Belize issue. London: Latin America Bureau, 1978. 77 p.; bibl.; maps.
Very good short discussion of the background and current status (to 1978) of the controversy over Belize, including a chapter on "The Belizean Economy and People."

7278 Zorina, A.M. The Clayton-Bulwer Treaty of 1850 and Russian diplomacy (*in* Soviet historians on Latin America: recent scholarly contributions [see *HLAS* 42:1817] p. 209–220)
The author, a Soviet historian looking at the archival records in Russia regarding the 1850 Clayton-Bulwer Treaty, concludes: ". . . the prospect of constructing an interoceanic canal was not without interest for the ruling circles of the Russian state. The creation of a new maritime route would promote the development of Russian trade relations with the west coast of America and China, the growth of Russian-American Company commercial operations, and also the supply of Russian colonies in the American Northwest. Not until significantly later than the 1850s did tsarism take into account the great strategic significance of an interoceanic canal, which made possible the transfer of the U.S. navy from the Atlantic Ocean to the Pacific."

The Caribbean and the Guianas

7279 Abdi, Said Yusuf. Comment: one Somali perspective (UP/CSEC, 10:1, Jan. 1980, p. 85–89)
Abdi complains that Valdés' discussion of the Ethiopia-Somali conflict (see item 7353) gives insufficient weight to Somali's side of the case.

7280 Abel, Christopher A. A breach in the ramparts (Proceedings [United States Naval Institute, Annapolis, Md.] 106:7, July 1980, p. 47–50, plates)
Author, a Coast Guard officer, traces the step-by-step escalation of the USSR's naval presence in the Caribbean since 1969. The tone is concerned but not alarmist.

Pointing out that the Soviets have yielded somewhat in every instance that the US has officially complained about their increased presence, Abel urges Washington policymakers to be watchful and forthright on this score.

7281 Armas, Manuel de. Acciones de la CIA en América Latina para entorpecer las relaciones diplomáticas con Cuba. La Habana: Editorial de Ciencias Sociales, 1976. 43 p.; ill.
Text of Cuban National Television's program featuring the "revelations" of ex-CIA agent Manuel de Armas about the Agency's continuing "dirty tricks" aimed at the Castro regime.

7282 Arriola S., María del Carmen. La política internacional de la Revolución Cubana (EDTM, 2:2, junio 1979, p. 365–390)

After an overview of the Revolution and basic watersheds and themes in Cuba's foreign policy, author shifts to her main concern, Castro's involvement in Africa. In her view, Castro's African adventures, although backed by the Soviet, have evidenced a substantial measure of independence.

7283 Axline, W. Andrew. Caribbean integration: the politics of regionalism. London: Frances Pinter; New York: Nichols Pub. Co., 1979. 233 p.; bibl.; index.

The most thorough and sophisticated study of Caribbean integration to appear to date. Axline discusses the progress and problems experienced to date in the subregion, and he does this in the context of both general integration theory and the actual record of other integration schemes. He concludes that, although there have been significant institutional changes in the shift from CARIFTA to CARICOM, Caribbean integration is still a long way from an emphasis on coordinated production, rather than a "simple" freeing of trade—a "deepening" rather than or in addition to, a "widening" approach.

Baptiste, Fitzroy A. The anti-Vichyite movement in French Guiana, June to December 1940. See *HLAS 42:2593*.

7284 ——. The British grant of air and naval facilities to the United States in Trinidad, St. Lucia and Bermuda in 1939: June–December (UPR/CS, 16:2, July 1976, p. 5–37)

Examining the archives, Baptiste discovers that the UK actually concluded arrangements to lease Caribbean bases to the US in 1939, a year earlier than the well-known destroyer-bases agreement of 1940. For variety of reasons, which author explores, the US failed to make use of the leased facilities.

7285 Barbados. Ministry of External Affairs. Annual report: 1974. St. Michael: Barbados Government Printing Office, 1974? 45 p.; tables.

Summary of the international activities of Barbados during 1974, including participation in various international organizations, development assistance received, and official visits to the country.

7286 Barceló, Romero. Puerto Rico, USA: the case for statehood (CFR/FA, 59:1, Fall 1980, p. 60–81)

The Governor of Puerto Rico, a leader of the statehood movement, makes his case with an eye to building support for this position in the US. His essential argument is that the statehood alternative, contrary to the views of some of its critics, would actually be less expensive for the US—politically and economically—than independence.

7287 Bender, Gerald. Comment: past, present, and future perspectives of Cuba in Africa (UP/CSEC, 10:2, July 1980, p. 44–54, table)

Bender maintains that, given the importance which successive US administrations have attached to Cuba's role in Africa for determining US bilateral relations with Cuba (as well as the USSR, Angola, Ethiopia, and Mozambique), "one would hope that there would be a better appreciation for the realities—i.e., the limitations—of Cuban influence over the foreign and domestic policies of countries she assists in Africa."

7288 Bender, Lynn Darrell. Cuba and the hemisphere: present and future (RRI, 8:2, Summer 1978, p. 289–296)

Reviewing the current status of the Cuban Revolution and the issue of accommodation with the US, Bender concludes that the outlook for Cuba's "return" to the Americas is still "somewhat less than sanguine."

7289 Blasier, Cole. Comment: the consequences of military initiatives (UP/CSEC, 10:1, Jan. 1980, p. 37–42)

Blaiser maintains that: 1) the economic burden to Cuba of Castro's African initiatives have usually been underestimated; 2) Castro's Cuba is more accurately to be regarded as a "partner" rather than a "pawn, surrogate, or proxy" of the USSR; and 3) the US initial response to crisis in Angola and Ethiopia was "particularly ill-conceived because truly vital U.S. interests were not at stake."

7290 Boersner, Demetrio. Una estrategia "tercermundista" para el Caribe (NSO, 37, julio/agosto 1978, p. 54–63, ill.)

The author, a Venezuelan, sets forth various factors making the notion of a *tercermundista* international posture appealing in the Caribbean (broadly conceived) and offers a list of rather predictable policy recommendations—sovereignty over national resources, integration, etc.

7291 Cabranes, José A. Puerto Rico: out of the colonial closet (FP, 33, Winter 1978/79, p. 66–91)

Surveying increasing concern at the UN and elsewhere over the issue of Puerto Rico's status, as well as the declining economy and strong statehood movement on the island, Cabranes convincingly concludes: "The days when Washington could treat Puerto Rico with benign neglect are over."

Calder, Bruce J. *Caudillos* and *gavilleros* versus the United States Marines: guerrilla insurgency during the Dominican intervention, 1916–1924. See *HLAS 42:2595*.

7292 El Caribe, un mar entre dos mundos. Ernesto Mayz Vallenilla et al. Caracas: Equinoccio, 1978. 297 p.

Proceedings of a conference held at Simón Bolívar University in Caracas, 12–15 May 1977, are actually just a series of two-page speeches on a variety of topics concerning the Caribbean.

7293 Carnegie, A.R. Commonwealth Caribbean regionalism: legal aspects (LIWA/YWA, 1979, p. 180–200)

Careful examination of the "legal aspects" of integration schemes in the Caribbean, unfortunately with little attention to the inter-relationship between the law and political realities in the region.

7294 Cockcroft, James D. Recent Caribbean developments and need for theoretical expansion (LAP, 5[17]:2, Spring 1978, p. 29–36)

Commenting on an article by Clive Y. Thomas, Cockcroft urges Marxian analysts to give greater attention to the concept of "non-capitalist" development as one path to socialism. The model involves at least an initial political framework of "national democracy" (as in Jamaica under Manley) but assumes neither the prior establishment of indigenous capitalism nor capitalism as an inevitable outcome. Cockcroft points out a number of pitfalls of utilizing this route to socialism, which he believes its proponents also generally recognize.

7295 Contemporary international relations of the Caribbean. Edited by Basil A.

Ince. St. Augustine, Trinidad/Tobago: Institute of International Relations, University of the West Indies, 1979. 367 p.; bibl.; graphs; indexes.

Good collection of essays on various aspects of the international relations of the Caribbean by scholars from the region.

Cortada, James W. Economic issues in Caribbean politics: rivalry between Spain and the United States in Cuba, 1848–1898. See *HLAS 42:2563*.

7296 Cuba: Declaration of the Cuban Government (Direct from Cuba [Prensa Latina, La Habana] 231, April 15, 1980, p. 1–8)

Cuban government statement regarding the Cuban refugees seeking asylum on the grounds of the Peruvian embassy in Havana—labeled here as "delinquents, *lumpens*, anti-socials, loafers and parasites in their vast majority." Peru is also criticized for its handling of the crisis, which allegedly was responsible for the loss of life of a Cuban soldier.

7297 Declaraciones de La Habana y Santiago. La Habana: Editorial de Ciencias Sociales, 1976. 70 p. (Ediciones políticas)

Collection of resolutions condemning Yankee imperialism and other evils, emanating from the General Assembly of the People of Cuba from 1960–64. There was some lead-time in getting resolutions published.

7298 Díaz Barreiro, Francisco. El Dr. Nicolás I. Vavílov y las primeras relaciones científicas soviéticas con Cuba. La Habana: Academia de Ciencias de Cuba, Museo Histórico de las Ciencias Carlos J. Finlay, 1977. 101 p.; bibl.; ill.

Cuban study of leading Soviet geneticist and botanist, Nikolai I. Vavilov, provides all details of his visit to Cuba in 1932 but fails to mention the controversy that made him famous: his stand against the politicization of science and on behalf of free inquiry, his subsequent replacement in 1940 as director of the Institute of Genetics with Stalin's candidate, Lysenko, and his deportation to a concentration camp in Siberia where he died in 1943.

7299 Dietz, James L. Imperialism and Puerto Rico (MR, 30:4, Sept. 1978, p. 18–28)

According to Dietz, statehood is no solution to Puerto Rico's "massive economic and social problems:" "Independence for Puerto Rico—and ultimately socialism—is the only permanent solution. The transformations which the Puerto Rican economy and people would be forced to go through as an independent nation are very real, but also very necessary if the deformities which have resulted from imperialist-dominated capitalist industrialization are to be overcome." In this struggle Puerto Rico can count on the aid of "progressive Third World nations and socialist nations, especially Cuba."

7300 Domínguez, Jorge I. Political and military limitations and consequences of Cuban policies in Africa (UP/CSEC, 10:2, July 1980, p. 1–35, tables)

According to Domínguez, Cuba has experienced significant costs in its African adventures—not only lives lost and higher military budgets, but also political costs such as finding Cuba's own military choices constrained by host governments. However, Cuba "has managed to remain an ascendant Lilliput far more effectively than other major powers that fought conventional wars far from their shores in recent decades." Neither the aforementioned costs nor pressures from other African states, the USSR, or the US are likely to have as great an influence on future Cuban actions as the specific opportunities (or lack thereof) inherent in certain African situations (Namibia, etc.).

7301 Durch, William J. The Cuban military in Africa and the Middle East: from Algeria to Angola (USC/SCC, 11:1/2, Spring/Summer 1978, p. 34–74, maps)

Overview of Soviet-Cuban relations over the years coupled with an excellent, detailed examination of the record of Cuba's involvement in Africa from the early 1960s. On the Angola case, Durch concludes: "Cuba had ample reason incentives to send its troops to Angola, apart from any reasons the Soviets may have had and independent of any Kremlin orders to do so. This is not to say that Cuba's behavior did not serve Soviet interests, but only to observe that Soviet behavior equally served Cuban interests—the two sets converged. A focus on Soviet interests alone leads to a characterization of Angola as a war by proxy—with patron and clients, chessmaster and pawns—when it perhaps ought to be characterized as a war

conducted by allies, which the Marxist allies won."

7302 Eckstein, Susan. Comment: the global political economy and Cuba's African involvement (UP/CSEC, 10:2, July 1980, p. 85–90)

Comment on an article by Sergio Roca (see item **7344**). Eckstein holds that Roca failed "to understand the economic dynamics that have induced the revolutionary regime to divert resources to Africa, while domestic needs go unfulfilled." In her view, Castro is looking for trade and other economic opportunities in Africa.

7303 Erisman, H. Michael. Conflicto sino-cubano: la lucha por influencia en el Tercer Mundo (AR, 5:19/20, número extraordinario, 1979, p. 12–19)

Erisman discusses long-standing frictions between China and Cuba as partly the result of their rival aspirations for leadership of the Third World. Although China is not a formal member of the Nonaligned Countries movement, its alternative to Soviet-Cuban influence was definitely a factor in controversies at the 1979 Nonaligned conference in Havana.

7304 ———. La normalización de relaciones entre Cuba y E.U.: el caso de Cuba en America (AR, 5:17, 1978, p. 20–25, bibl., ill., plates)

Article in Cuban periodical expresses the hope that the Carter administration will "see the light" and separate the issue of normalization of relations between the US and Cuba from the issue of Cuban troops in Africa.

7305 Fessehatzion, Tekie. Comment: one Eritrean View (UP/CSEC, 10:1, Jan. 1980, p. 80–85)

Author takes issue with Valdés' judgment (see item **7353**) that Cuba has not been involved "militarily" in the Eritrean conflict, and he insists that ultimately the "human factor" will prevail over "sophisticated weaponry."

7306 Fontaine, Roger; Cleto DiGiovanni, Jr.; and Alexander Kruger. Castro's specter (The Washington Quarterly [A review of strategic and international issues. Georgetown University, Center for Strategic and International Studies, Washington, D.C.] 3:4, Autumn 1980, p. 3–27)

Article written by Reagan's principal Latin American adviser (Fontaine), a former CIA officer (DiGiovanni), and a US-educated Venezuelan businessman (Kruger). According to the authors, until the Carter administration, US Latin American policy was generally "effective;" even the Kennedy-Johnson policy "under the rubric of an alliance for progress protected friendly regimes from attack by manifestly unfriendly forces sponsored for the most part by Castro." However, they take strong exception to what they see as the three basic tenets of Carter's posture: 1) "democracy and human rights are concepts that can be transferred with relative ease if the United States is prepared to make such a transfer a priority matter;" 2) "the United States is strong enough to avoid the taint of association with countries in security arrangements who are not democratic;" and 3) "social forces in the nonindustrialized world are no threat to us particularly if we avoid both force and fraud in our relations with them." The complaint is not only that these basic premises are flawed but also that Carter policymakers showed "a clear bias" favoring the "extreme left:" "the tendency to characterize [at least part of] the left as respectable while denoting the right as militant and irresponsible; downgrading the role of Cuban and Marxist influence in the turmoil; the inclination to disavow US intervention in the affairs of other nations—except when it would help the left; an erratic human rights policy that punished the right more than the left for human rights violations; and the tendency to provide more money for leftists [sic] regimes." The article identifies a number of highly respected scholars and policy-makers as having been associated with an Institute for Policy Studies Working Group on Latin America; then identifying former Allende official, Orlando Letelier, as the director of the Transnational Institute which published the Group's report (see item **7001**) and as a man with "Cuban contacts." Authors generously grant that there is no "proof or even indication" that the IPS or the Group knew of Letelier's Cuban associations, but they accuse "some" of the Group's members of being "strongly and actively committed to advancing leftist causes." Any knowledgeable observer would know that *very* few of the Group's members could be so described. Moreover, the article's

characterization of the "Kennedy-Johnson" policy is badly warped: There were fundamental differences between the Kennedy and Johnson approaches, none the least Kennedy's angering of rightist regimes by attempting to cultivate a democratic-left alternative to Castroist change in Latin America.

Franco, José Luciano. Armonía y contradicciones cubano-mexicanas: 1554–1830. See item **7177**.

7307 García, Ines and **Alberto Adrianzén.** VIa. [i.e. Sexta] Cumbre en La Habana y consolidación del Movimiento No-Alineado (DESCO/Q, 1, 1979?, p. 76–85)

Summary of the proceedings of the 1979 Nonaligned conference in Habana, with only a passing mention of a key issue at the meeting: Cuba's position that the USSR and the "socialist community" were "natural allies" of the Nonaligned.

García Godoy, Frederico. El derrumbe. See *HLAS 42:2602.*

7308 García Muñiz, Humberto. Puerto Rico in the United Nations, 1953: an appraisal (UPR/CS, 16:2, July 1976, p. 44–91)

García Muñiz discusses in great detail the maneuvering in the UN in 1953, when the General Assembly voted to recognize that Puerto Rico had achieved sufficient political autonomy to be exempted from consideration as a "non-self-governing territory."

7309 Gavrikov, Yuri. Las líneas fundamentales de la política exterior de Cuba (URSS/AL, 1, 1979, p. 87–99)

Soviet writer finds Cuban foreign policy supporting all the worthwhile things of this world—socialism, liberation, progress, development, Latin American economic integration, etc.—arm in arm with the Soviet Union.

Gilbert, Gregorio Urbano. Mi lucha contra el invasor yanqui de 1916. See *HLAS 42:2603.*

7310 Gleijeses, Piero. The Dominican crisis: the 1963 Constitutionalist revolt and American intervention. Translated by Lawrence Lipson. Baltimore: Johns Hopkins University Press, 1978. 460 p.; bibl.; index.

Useful addition to the literature on the 1965 Dominican crisis, which is especially good on maneuverings among Dominican political groups and personalities. Gleijeses is generally pro-Bosch and the rebel "constitutionalists," and bitterly critical of US policies. He sees little difference between the policies of the Kennedy and Johnson administrations. There is an interesting bibliographical essay, part of some 130 p. devoted to appendixes, footnotes, and index. Translation of French original *La crise dominicaine* (1965).

7311 González, Edward. Comment: operational goals of Cuban policy in Africa (UP/CSEC, 10:1, Jan. 1980, p. 43–48)

In González's view, Cuba's African policy has three main goals: 1) to broaden ties with "socialist-oriented" African regimes; 2) to promote Cuban leadership of Third World and nonaligned states; and 3) to lessen Cuba's one-way dependence upon the Soviets by becoming a more valued ally.

7312 Grabendorff, Wolf. Cuba's involvement in Africa; an interpretation of objectives, reactions, and limitations (SAGE/JIAS, 22:1, Feb. 1980, p. 3–29)

German political scientist compares and contrasts Cuban, Soviet, US, and African perspectives on Cuba's role in Africa. Concludes with a list of factors both encouraging and limiting Cuba in that role.

7313 Hart Dávalos, Armando. Intervención en la IX [i.e. novena] reunión de ministros de cultura de los países socialistas. Ciudad de La Habana: Editorial Letras Cubanas, 1978. 40 p.

Speech made by the Cuban Minister of Culture at the Ninth Meeting of Ministers of Culture of the Socialist Countries, in Moscow, 7 July 1978.

7314 Heine, Jorge. A people apart (WQ, 4:3, Spring 1980, p. 119–131, ill., plates, table)

Anticipating a small margin, perhaps 55 percent, for the statehood option in the next plebiscite regarding Puerto Rico's status, Heine asks: "Does 55 percent of the electorate have the right to impose on the other 45 percent something as definitive and permanent as full incorporation into another nation?" The question, of course, glosses over the point that the 45 percent remaining would probably not agree as to a different status; moreover, some would argue, rightly or wrongly, that Puerto Rico is not a "nation" even in the non-legal sense. In any event,

Heine opposes statehood on the grounds that it "would only exacerbate the deep structural imbalance in the Puerto Rican economy that led voters to endorse statehood in the first place."

7315 Hernández, Eugenio. Cuban-Soviet relations: divergence and convergence. Washington, D.C.: Georgetown University, Latin American Studies Program, 1980. 16 p. (Occasional paper no. 3)

Review-essay dealing with the convergence-divergence issue as treated in five books published in the 1970s by Domínguez, González, Levesque, Mesa-Lago, and Torres Ramírez. Hernández concludes that Cuba's involvement both in Africa and the Nonaligned Movement is evidence of substantial convergence with the USSR, although not Cuban subservience to Moscow.

7316 Hevia Cosculluela, Manuel. Pasaporte 11333: ocho años con la CIA. La Habana: Editorial de Ciencias Sociales, 1978. 287 p.; 20 leaves of plates; ill.

Memoirs of a Cuban agent who presumably penetrated the CIA operation in Uruguay.

7317 Hoskins, Linus A. The Caribbean and Africa: a geo-political analysis (*in* The Caribbean issue of emergence: socio-economic and political perspectives. Edited by Vincent R. McDonald. Washington: University Press of America, 1980, p. 147–169)

Analysis of the policies of Barbados, Guyana, Jamaica (under Manley), and Trinidad and Tobago toward Cuban involvement in Africa. All four governments are vocal proponents of the liberation of black peoples in Africa, and all but Barbados have taken a "radical, almost revolutionary, stance" in endorsing armed struggle. However, Jamaica alone went on record specifically supporting Cuban intervention.

7318 Ince, Basil A. The information gap and non-consultation: effects on foreign policy-making in Commonwealth Caribbean states (CIIA/IJ, 34:2, Spring 1979, p. 227–250)

Ince bemoans the fact that, like other new states, those of the Caribbean lack the intelligence services, libraries, staff experts, and other aids to effective information-gathering for the making of foreign policy; nor is the general public as informed as it often is with regard to some issues in the Western developed countries. What little information is available tends to be monopolized by governments, thus helping to exclude the opposition from any meaningful role in policy-making. Noteworthy article for those interested in comparative foreign policy.

7319 ———. The racial factor in the international relations of Trinidad and Tobago (UPR/CS, 16:3/4, Oct. 1976/Jan. 1977, p. 5–28)

Interesting article on a subject that rarely receives the sort of non-polemical treatment which it does here. Ince examines Trinidad and Tobago's positions on international issues like South Africa that concern race, and he delves further into the role of various ethnic groups in shaping the country's policies generally.

7320 **Jamison, Edward Alden.** Cuba and the inter-American system: exclusion of the Castro regime from the Organization of American States (AAFH/TAM, 36:3, Jan. 1980, p. 317–346)

The then-Alternate US Representative on the OAS Council and a participant at all the key OAS conferences recounts the events and diplomatic bargaining over several years that led up to the exclusion of Cuba at the Punta del Este meeting in 1962. Useful addition to the literature on a critical period.

7321 **Jiménes-Grullón, Juan Isidrol.** John Bartlow Martin, un procónsul del imperio yanqui: respuesta a su libro *El distino domincano*. Mérida, Venezuela: Universidad de los Andes, 1977. 590 p.; bibl.

Lengthy "analysis" of Dominican history and John Bartlow Martin's memoir, *Overtaken by events*, covering his experiences as US Ambassador under Kennedy to the Bosch government and President Johnson's special emissary during the 1965 Dominican crisis. As the subtitle suggests, the author's effort is to demonstrate that Martin acted as an agent of "Yankee imperialism."

7322 **Kikkert, O.H.** and **A.A.M. Bekman.** Drempelvrees: een boek over Curaçao aan de vooravond van de onafhankelijkheid. Assen: Van Gorcum, 1977. 143 p.; 4 leaves of plates; ill.

Written by an economist and a sociologist, this book examines why there exists a fear of independence in the Netherlands Antilles. Authors indicate ways to attain independence that are reasonable and feasible but offer no opinion as to whether Curaçao should become an independent entity by itself or part of a larger Caribbean Confederation. Pt. 1 describes physical aspects of Curaçao; pt. 2 describes essential features of this society and offers a personal view of contemporary problems; and pt. 3 speculates on the consequences of independence and the future of a sovereign Curaçao. [J. Darilek]

7323 **Kokrev, Vladimir.** La solidaridad de Cuba con Angola (URSS/AL, 1, 1979, p. 113–129, map, plate)

Relatively unpropagandistic account by a Soviet analyst of Cuba's role in the Angolan conflict, 1975–76 primarily.

7324 **Kula, Marcin.** Cuba en la conferencia de Montevideo (PAN/ES, 3, 1976, p. 91–110)

Author notes that the Grau San Martín government of Cuba was one of the leaders among the Latin American countries pressuring the US to subscribe to the principle of non-intervention at the 1933 Montevideo conference. The Cuban regime was fresh from a clash with Sumner Welles, which helps explain some of its enthusiasm for the principle. Unfortunately, author appears unaware of Bryce Wood's work on the Good Neighbor Policy, which reveals that the experience with Cuba in this period was also to affect the Roosevelt administration's attitude toward non-intervention—not only eschewing armed intervention but also attempting to minimize intervention in Latin American domestic politics.

7325 **Kuzin, Alexandr.** Cuestiones de la defensa armada de la Revolución Cubana (URSS/AL, 1, 1979, p. 17–24)

Soviet analyst holds that the Castro regime is a splendid example of Lenin's dictum that any revolution is only as good as its defense. Cuba's has been excellent, thanks both to its own army and the fraternal assistance of the USSR.

7326 **Landis, Joseph B.** Commitment to socialism and nonalignment among Guyanese and West Indian leaders (UPR/CS, 14:4, Jan. 1975, p. 109–126, tables)

Study, based on interview data, analyzes the attitudes and backgrounds of Guyanese and West Indian political leaders. The Guyanese were much more committed to socialism and nonalignment in their attitudes, as well as public actions. Landis attributes the contrast to the fact that "Guyanese leaders were younger and better educated . . . and that a much larger proportion of Guyanese leaders were drawn from the intelligentsia," a group he views as "substantially independent of the business class."

7327 Langley, Lester D. The United States and the Caribbean, 1900–1970. Athens: University of Georgia Press, 1980. 324 p.; bibl.; index; map (on lining papers)
Straightforward survey of 20th-century (to 1970) US relations with the Caribbean. Brief—for example, only 33 p. are devoted to "The Turbulent Sixties." Langley concludes: "By 1970 the Caribbean empire of the United States, created in the aftermath of the war with Spain, was already disintegrating, though the American people were scarcely aware of its demise." Useful bibliographical essay.

7328 LeoGrande, William M. Cuban dependency: a comparison of pre-revolutionary and post-revolutionary international economic relations (UP/CSEC, 9:2, July 1979, p. 1–28, tables)
LeoGrande looks at Cuban economic dependency before and after the Castro Revolution using such indicators as export concentration, monoculture, trade partner concentration, capital dependency, and external debt burden. Quoting from the summary: "The data show that on most indicators Cuba's dependency is lower in the post-revolutionary period than it was previously. However, the absolute levels of dependency remain fairly high, and the revolutionary government has had little success in reducing dependency during the post-revolutionary period itself."

7329 ———. Cuban-Soviet relations and Cuban policy in Africa (UP/CSEC, 10:1, Jan. 1980, p. 1–36)
Good survey of Cuba's past policies in Africa, as well as an analysis of the reasons behind them and of the likelihood of Cuba's involvement broadening. LeoGrande holds that Cuba has consistently sought both to support friendly governments and national liberation movements in the region, but has

only committed troops when there was direct foreign intervention against the former. In his view, Castro has decided to intervene independently of the Soviet Union; although there is considerable convergence of Cuban and Soviet policies, there are also some noteworthy differences. Because of costs to Cuba in the case of Ethiopia, any "future Cuban interventions are likely to be carefully calculated" and will depend "primarily upon the course of events in Africa." Southern Africa is probably the most probable arena for a new Cuban military intervention.

7330 ———. Cuba's policy in Africa, 1959–1980. Berkeley: Institute of International Studies, University of California, 1980. 82 p.; bibl. (Policy papers in international affairs; no. 13)
Short monograph examining Cuba's role in Africa over more than a two-decade time-span, by a scholar who has written extensively on this subject in article form.

7331 Lévesque, Jacques. The USSR and the Cuban revolution: Soviet ideological and strategical perspectives, 1959–77. Translated from the French by Deanna Drendel Leboeuf. New York: Praeger, 1979. 215 p.; bibl.
Translated from the French (*L'URSS et la Révolution Cubaine*). Careful analysis of a full-range of Soviet writings and pronouncements on the Cuban Revolution from its origin through 1977.

Lewis, Gordon K. "Gather with the saints at the river:" the Jonestown Guyana holocaust of 1978: a description and interpretative essay on its ultimate meaning from a Caribbean viewpoint. See *HLAS 42:2609.*

7332 McEachrane, Helen. Descolonización y nacionalismo en el Caribe: la ampliación del espacio geopolítico (UNAM/RI, 2:1, marzo 1979, p. 9–46, bibl., tables)
Overview of recent trends in the Caribbean, with emphasis on the sheer variety of countries and problems. Nationalism, McEachrane notes, has been perhaps the dominant movement in the subregion, but she believes more intra-regional cooperation is needed.
Her recommendation is the formation of a "political assembly" composed of all the states of the region, whatever their "political tendency," to further such ends as "represen-

tative democracy" and economic integration. Mexico is projected as a key source of energy for the region. Cuba is to be a member, although the author does not feel obliged to explain exactly how Castro is expected to contribute to the strengthening of representative democracy.

7333 M'Bow, Amadou-Mahtar. Latin America and the Caribbean: cultural dimension of the development (UNESCO/CU, 5 : 3, 1978, p. 11–17)

Excerpts from the address given by the Director-General of UNESCO in Bogotá, on the opening of the Intergovernmental Conference on Cultural Policies in Latin America and the Caribbean, 10 Jan. 1978. The thrust of his message: ". . . there are no powerful countries or deprived countries, no rich or poor community; all cultures deserve the same consideration. Their diversity can be a source of reciprocal fecundation if their contract . . . is based on open-mindedness, understanding and mutual tolerance."

7334 Mederos, Elena. Human rights and Cuban law (Worldview [Council on Religion and International Affairs, New York 22 : 11, Nov. 1979, p. 42–44)

Castro's first Minister of Social Welfare (now in exile) charges with a point by point comparison, that the Cuban Constitution and other Cuban law does not conform to the dictates of the Universal Declaration of Human Rights.

7335 Milkowski, Tadeusz. La problemática de la Revolución Cubana en la prensa polaca: 1953–1961 (PAN/ES, 3, 1976, p. 179–193)

Milkowski surveys virtually every item appearing in Polish publications from 1953–61 regarding Cuba and the Castro Revolution, concluding that it was not until later—when Cuba became increasingly important in the Communist world and more Polish observers had an opportunity to learn more about the country and to visit the island—that Cuban developments began to be reported in a "coherent manner."

Miller, Kethly. Les paysans haïtiens et l'occupation américaine d'Haïti, 1915–1930. See HLAS 42 : 2612.

7336 Moreira, Neiva and **Beatriz Bissio.** Os cubanos na Africa. São Paulo: Global, 1979. 110 p. (Coleção Passado & presente; no. 9)

Book provides a popularized account of Cuba's efforts to bring the blessings of liberation and economic and social justice to downtrodden Africans.

7337 *OCLAE*. Revista mensual. Organización Continental Latinoamericana de Estudiante. No. 12, 1979– . La Habana.

Compendium of speeches made by the Cuban delegation and Fidel Castro to the 1979 Nonaligned Conference in Havana.

7338 Papp, Daniel S. The Soviet Union and Cuba in Ethiopia (CUH, 76 : 445, March 1979, p. 110–114)

Papp examines Soviet and Cuban involvement in Ethiopia, with particular emphasis on the dilemmas for both countries posed by Ethiopia's conflict with the Eritrean rebels.

Pérez, Luis A., Jr. Intervention, revolution, and politics in Cuba, 1913–1921. See HLAS 42 : 2616.

7339 Pérez-López, Jorge F. A calendar of Cuban bilateral agreements, 1959–1976. Pittsburgh, Pa.: University of Pittsburgh, Center for International Studies, 1980. 99 p. (Latin American monograph & document series; 2)

Annotated chronological list of Cuban bilateral agreements from the onset of the Castro Revolution to 1976. Cross-referenced by partner country and subject matter of agreement. Very useful reference work, and it might be interesting to subject some of this data to quantitative analysis.

7340 ———. Comment: economic costs and benefits of African involvement (UP/CSEC, 10 : 2, July 1980, p. 80–85)

Comment on an article by Sergio Roca (see item **7344**). While agreeing that the economic costs of Cuba's African adventures probably outweigh the benefits, Pérez-López (with reference to fishing, construction, and foreign aid) emphasizes the fact that analysts lack sufficient hard data to know for sure.

7341 ——— and **René Pérez-López.** Cuban international relations: a bilateral agreements perspective. Erie, Pa.: The Northwestern Pennsylvania Institute for Latin American Studies, Mercyhurst College, 1979. 39 leaves; tables (Latin American monograph series; 8)

Monograph written in conjunction with another study by the authors, *A calen-*

dar of Cuban bilateral agreements: 1959–1976 (see item **7339**). After explaining the methodology used in Calender, they discuss Cuba's relations during the period with certain groups of countries (emphasizing frequency of agreement) and generally.

Pierre-Charles, Gérard. Génesis de la Revolución Cubana. See *HLAS 42:2617*.

Pino Santos, Oscar. La oligarquía yanqui en Cuba. See *HLAS 42:2618*.

Porter, David Dixon. Diario de una misión secreta a Santo Domingo, 1846. See *HLAS 42:2584*.

7342 **Proyección internacional** de la Revolución Cubana. Compiled by Juan J. Soto Valdespino. Habana: Editorial de Ciencias Sociales, Instituto Cubano del Libro, 1975. 432 p.

Collection of various speeches by Cuban leaders and declarations of such institutions as the National General Assembly of the People of Cuba regarding Cuban foreign policy. This book was issued in commemoration of the First Congress of the Communist Party of Cuba.

7343 **The Restless Caribbean:** changing patterns in international relations. Edited by Richard Millett and W. Marvin Will. New York: Praeger, 1979. 295 p.; bibl.; map; index.

Generally high-quality anthology of 21 essays covering almost every aspect of contemporary international relations in the Caribbean (to 1979). Pt. 1 deals with the history of the Caribbean and some of the internal and external constraints on the regional systems. Pt. 2 stresses such current issues as migration of peoples, multinational corporations, the Panama Canal, and Puerto Rico. Pt. 3 puts the emphasis on national policies, including those of the US and the Soviet Union. Pt. 4 examines Caribbean integration, as well as the role of Caribbean states in the UN, OAS, and Inter-American Development Bank.

7344 **Roca, Sergio.** Economic aspects of Cuban involvement in Africa (UP/CSEC, 10:2, July 1980, p. 55–80, tables)

A cost-benefit analysis of Cuba's involvement in Africa in the 1970s, especially in Angola and Ethiopia. Roca judges that the costs outweigh the benefits and that the greatest costs are lost "domestic opportunity" in the areas of fishing, transportation,

social services, construction, and "leadership commitment to economic tasks." Based on this situation, he predicts, future Cuban commitments abroad are likely to be of a civilian nature. Is there too little attention paid in this article to ideological and political benefits?

7345 **Rodríguez, Carlos Rafael.** Entrevista (AR, 6:21, 1979, p. 14–19, plates)

Lengthy interview with an elder statesman of the Castro regime, on the subject of Cuba's foreign policy.

7346 **Sariola, Sakari.** The Puerto Rican dilemma. Port Washington, N.Y.: Kennikat Press, 1979. 200 p.; bibl.; index (National university publications)

In this study of the "tension between the intentional-political and the spontaneous-popular reactive processes in Puerto Rico," author considers the reactive, willful, ideologically-determined action to be the key feature in social and political change. Starting with the 19th century, he traces the different schools of thought and movements concerned with the relationship of Puerto Rico and the US. Suggests that culture and social structure are not as important factors as the influence of the US over the island. The implication is that the Commonwealth status may be the best solution for Puerto Rico (as opposed to either a socialist-based independence or a capitalist integration into the American system), as long as Puerto Ricans control the basic means of production. This is a subtle defense of Puerto Rican national capitalism. [N. Valdés]

7347 **Schori, Pierre.** The Cuban Revolution in 1978: at home and in Africa (UC/I, 7:2/8:1, 1978, p. 118–132)

Rambling, adulatory analysis of Castro's 1977 "Christmas speech," conditions in Cuba, and Cuba's involvement in Africa. Interesting only because the article was written by a former member of the Board, Institute of Latin American Studies, Stockholm, and International Secretary, Social Democratic Party of Sweden. This article is also available in Spanish as "Cuba en Africa," *Nueva Sociedad* (San José, No. 36, mayo/junio 1978, p. 94–104).

7348 **Tambs, Lewis A.** Brazil and the Caribbean link: a geopolitical overview of World War III (*in* Free world security and the South Atlantic: Inter-American Symposium,

1979. Washington: Council for Inter-American Security [and] The Institute of American Relations, 1979, p. 59–65, map)

The Russians are coming! The Russians are coming! And, alas, only the Brazilians seem to recognize the dreadful danger. Will America awake in time?

7349 United States. Central Intelligence Agency. National Foreign Assessment Center. Cuban chronology. Washington: Central Intelligence Agency, National Foreign Assessment Center, 1978. 94 p. (A Reference aid)

Chronology of events in Cuba's bilateral relationships with most of the countries of the world, from 1975 through 1977. Events listed under country subheadings.

7350 Congress. House. Committee on Foreign Affairs. Subcommittee on Inter-American Affairs. Impact of Cuban-Soviet ties in the Western Hemisphere, Spring 1980. Hearings before . . . Ninety-sixth Congress, Second session, on March 26–27, April 16–17, May 14, 1980. Washington: GPO, 1980. 122 p.

Important hearings, despite numerous "security deletions," which give a good picture of Cuba's domestic conditions and international activities—including relations with both the USSR and US—at the close of the Carter Administration. The balanced statement of State Department spokesman Myles R.R. Frechette might be compared with some of the more alarmist assessments later emanating from the Reagan Administration.

7351 ——. ——. ——. Permanent Select Committee on Intelligence. Subcommittee on Oversight. The Cuban emigres: was there a U.S. intelligence failure?: Staff report. Washington: GPO, 1980. 5 p.

A staff report of the Oversight Subcommittee of the House Committee on Intelligence concludes that whatever "mismanagement" might have occurred in the US government's handling of the 1980 influx of Cuban refugees was not the fault of the US intelligence community, which had predicted a new mass exodus from Cuba.

7352 ——. ——. ——. Special Study Mission to Jamaica, Cuba, the Dominican Republic, and the Guantanamo Naval Base. Caribbean nations, assessments of conditions and U.S. influence: report of a Special

Study Mission to Jamaica, Cuba, the Dominican Republic, and the Guantanamo Naval Base, January 3–12, 1979 to the Committee on Foreign Affairs, U.S. House of Representatives. Washington: GPO, 1979. 48 p.

Short report submitted to the House Committee on Foreign Affairs by Representatives Jonathan B. Bingham, Benjamin A. Gilman, and Robert J. Lagomarsino on the early 1979 study mission they and several other congressmen and staff members undertook to Jamaica, Cuba, and the Dominican Republic. The report urges ratification of the International Sugar Agreement, support for Caribbean integration, greater acess to the US market for Caribbean rum, and other not-especially-startling steps—but the congressmen were divided on the key issue of ending the US embargo toward Cuba.

7353 Valdés, Nelson P. Cuba's involvement in the Horn of Africa: the Ethiopian-Somali War and the Eritrean Conflict (UP/CSEC, 10:1, Jan. 1980, p. 49–80)

Valdés believes that Cuba would like to find a political solution to conflicts involving Ethiopia but, meanwhile, will probably remain in Ethiopia militarily and help defend the country from any attack from abroad.

7354 Valenta, Jiri. Comment: the Soviet-Cuban alliance in Africa and future prospects in the Third World (UP/CSEC, 10:2, July 1980, p. 36–43)

The "comment" is really on an article by Jorge I. Domínguez (see item **7300**). Valenta stresses several of the factors making it difficult to predict Cuba's future role in Africa—and also the Caribbean.

7355 ——. The Soviet-Cuban intervention in Angola: 1975 (USC/SCC, 11:1/2, Spring/Summer 1978, p. 3–33)

Valenta's study focuses mainly on the motives for Soviet involvement in Angola but discusses Cuba's role enroute. He writes: "It may not be far-fetched to think of the involvement in Angola rather as the action of two allies than as that of Cubans subservient to Soviet politics. Cuba appears to have been more eager than the U.S.S.R. to get involved vigorously on behalf of the MPLA. Cuban willingness, perhaps even pressuring, to do the job provided an important input to Soviet decision-making."

7356 *The Washington Star:* "Cuba's 20 Years of Victory," Sunday, May 18, 1980 (APS/WA, 143:1, Summer 1980, p. 65–67)

Scathing editorial printed in *The Washington Star* that wouldn't be worth considering if *World Affairs* hadn't seen fit to reprint it. The editorialist mocks Castro's penchant for glossing over some of the shortcomings of life in Cuba and even "Newspeak"-like, turning them into advantages— unemployment is a "surplus of workers," and so on. He comments: "Yet the irony remains. However much trouble he may have at home, Fidel Castro is still doing fine in many Third World imaginations . . . The attractions of the Castro model are still strong. Except where it has been tried." Can we now, please, have an editorial explaining why the Cuban model is attractive to some and why, with all the problems, the Castro regime still remains secure at home?

7357 **Wiarda, Howard J.** The United States and the Dominican Republic: intervention, dependency, and tyrannicide (SAGE/JIAS, 22:2, May 1980, p. 247–260)

Thought-provoking essay-review on the 1965 Dominican intervention. While observing that one of the works reviewed offers new insights into the local Dominican politics side of the case, Wiarda suggests that several important matters still need clarifying. Among these are linkages between the US intervention and US domestic politics, as well as Vietnam; the "precise nature" of the Dominican revolution; and the involvement of US private business groups in the Trujillo assassination conspiracy that ushered in a new political era in the country.

7358 **Willers, David.** Cuba, Angola and the West (International Affairs Bulletin [The South African Institute of International Affairs, Johannesburg] 2:3, 1978, p. 24–33)

Brief, balanced discussion of the Angolan case to 1978 by a South African analyst (addressing the South African Institute of International Affairs). Willers stresses the point that Castro was apparently influential in saving Angola's President Neto from defeat by a pro-Soviet faction in the MPLA in 1977, and that Neto subsequently was actively considering entering the Western trading camp via adherence to the Lomé Convention.

7359 **Wyden, Peter.** Bay of Pigs: the untold story. New York: Simon and Schuster, 1979. 352 p.; 16 leaves of plates; bibl.; ill.; index.

The most definitive account of the Bay of Pigs operation that has appeared to date, and perhaps the most definitive ever likely to appear, since Wyden had the benefit of interviews with many of the leading participants (including six hours with Fidel). He also had access to classified documents that he was largely responsible for bringing to light under the "Freedom of Information" laws. The writing style is occasionally irritatingly "popular," but the book is definitely interesting and worthwhile reading for the specialist. Wyden, among other things, reveals that the US military role in the actual invasion was greater than has previously been believed. He essentially seconds the opinion of Professor Irving L. Janis that the US decision-makers involved were "victims of Groupthink."

South America

GENERAL

7360 **Argentina, Chile:** present situation on the border controversy in the southern region (Estado actual de los diferencias sobre límites en la Zona Austral). Washington: Embassy of the Argentine Republic, 1978. 24 p.; map.

English and Spanish texts of documents showing joint efforts to deal with the problem of the Beagle Channel after the Argentine government declared the Arbitral award null and void on 25 Jan. 1978.

7361 **Argentina en el Atlántico,** Chile en el Pacífico. Isaac F. Rojas, Arturo L. Medrano. Buenos Aires: Nemont Ediciones, 1978. 47 [i.e. 57] p.; maps.

Historical and legal arguments to show that Argentina has retreated for too long and given up too much territory. A firm stand against Chilean pretenses in the Beagle Channel is essential.

7362 Baily, Samuel L. The United States and the development of South America, 1945–1975. New York: New Viewpoints, 1976. 246 p.; bibl.; index; map.

This book is a reflection of the author's first-hand experience in South America. His main concern is how American policy toward the region seems to contribute to its problems. He suggests that many of the problems encountered are not the result of neglect but rather of misunderstanding.

Blakemore, Harold. Limitation of dependency: an historian's view and case study. See *HLAS 42:3201.*

7363 Bond, Robert D. Venezuela, Brazil and the Amazon Basin (FPRI/O, 22:3, Fall 1978, p. 635–650, map)

Discussion of historical and contemporary aspects of relations between Brazil and Venezuela. Emphasis is on the enhanced possibility of improvements in bilateral relations as a result of the Amazon Pact agreement. A thorough and realistic assessment of a complex situation.

7364 Botelho Gosálvez, Raúl. Proceso del subimperialismo brasilēno. 3. ed., rev. Nueva York: Maity Pub. Co., 1977. 211 p.; bibl.; index; 3 maps.

Bolivian diplomat raises a serious question and suggests an answer. Will Brazil continue its policy of expansion at the cost of its neighbors? Everything seems to indicate that in spite of its territorial expansion ever since the Treaty of Tordasillas, its geographic ambitions have not been satisfied.

Bratzel, John F. The Chaco dispute and the search for prestige. See *HLAS 42:3141.*

7365 Cavalla Rojas, Antonio. Notas sobre un posible conflicto en el Cono Sur: las hipótesis de guerra y la correlación de fuerzas militares en Argentina, Bolivia, Chile y Peru (EEUU/PL, 4, 2. semestre, 1978, p. 227–254, appendixes, tables)

Author estimates that in a war where Bolivia and Peru would be allied against Chile the former would have a slight advantage. A war between Chile and Peru would be inconclusive. Argentina would have distinct advantages in a war with Chile and it is not likely that Brazil would join Chile. Appen-

dixes contain much information on size and equipment of these countries' armed forces.

Cerda Catalán, Alfonso. La guerra entre España y las repúblicas del Pacífico, 1864–1866: pt. 1, Antecedentes diplomáticos, militares y económicos. See *HLAS 42:3063.*

7366 Congrains Martín, Eduardo. Guerra en el Cono Sur. Lima: Editorial Ecoma, 1979. 347 p.; facs.; maps; plates (Colección Centenario)

This work is billed as "political fiction." It concerns a hypothetical war in the Southern Cone projected from past and present developments and especially those growing out of the controversy over the Beagle Channel.

7367 El Control político en el Cono Sur: seminario de México, diciembre de 1976. Gérard Pierre-Charles et al. México: Siglo Veintiuno Editores, 1978. 302 p. (Sociología y política)

Series of articles concerned with the type of regimes that have emerged in the Southern Cone of South America as part of the phenomenon of dependent capitalism. Some of the articles would be much better had they not tried to equate these regimes with fascism. Papers were presented at a conference in Mexico in 1976 but are still relevant.

Di Ció, Miguel Angel. Chile contra Bolivia y Perú, 1879–1883: la guerra de los diez centavos. See *HLAS 42:3213.*

Etchepareborda, Roberto. La intervención argentina en el conflicto chileno-norteamericano de 1892: el caso del "Baltimore." See *HLAS 42:3340.*

Garbi Sánchez, José. Alzamientos, cárceles y experiencias: historia contemporánea. See *HLAS 42:3021.*

Geosur. Año 1, No. 2, sept. 1979– . See *HLAS 42:217.*

7368 Gorman, Stephen M. Present threats to peace in South America: the territorial dimensions of conflict (IAMEA, 33:1, Summer 1979, p. 51–72)

Discussion of the declining leadership of the US in resolving inter-American disputes and the increasing importance of territorial boundaries as a source of interstate tension. Author concludes that there is a need to encourage cooperative agreements between states, revitalize the OAS by increasing the use of the Inter-American Development Bank, and by recognizing Brazilian leadership in solving regional security problems. Interesting comments on the emerging "balance of power" in South America.

Guerrero, Julio C. 1879–1883 [i.e. Mil ochocientos setenta y nueve a mil ochocientes ochenta y tres]: la guerra de las ocasiones perdidas; con el texto de los Tratados de Ancón y de Arica. See *HLAS 42:3084.*

7369 Guglialmelli, Juan E. Corpus-Itaipú: tres batallas perdidas por la Argentina y, ahora peligrosas perspectivas: el papel de socio menor del Brasil (IAEERI/E, 61/62, nov. 1979/feb. 1980, p. 7–29)

Traces recent Argentine-Brazilian relations to show that Argentina has been losing ground. Now three prospects face Argentina: 1) becoming a junior partner of Brazil; 2) standing up to Brazil, even at the risk of armed conflict; or 3) forming an alliance of equals. Author is hopeful that the third prospect is possible.

7370 Hrubý, Zdeněk; Daniel Pátek and **Bohdan Koch.** Andská skupina. Bolívie-Ecuador. Praha: Institut zahraničního obchodu, 1977. 315 p.

Of interest chiefly because of its account of trade relations between the Andean countries (Colombia, Venezuela, Ecuador, Peru, Chile and Bolivia) and Czechoslovakia. [G.J. Kovtun]

7371 Infante C., María Teresa. La posición de Chile en los acuerdos del Pacífico Sur (UCC/RU, 3, abril 1980, p. 64–75, map, plate)

Article sheds some light on what might be called "an emerging community of the South Pacific."

7372 Inter-American Symposium, *Catholic University of America, 1979.* Free world security and the South Atlantic. Washington, D.C.: Council for Inter-American Security: Institute of American Relations, 1979. vi, 99 p.; maps.

The theme of this symposium publication is the one that could be expected, given the sponsorship of the ultra-conservative Council for Inter-American Security: the worldwide Soviet threat. The "South Atlantic" aspect of the title is, therefore, some-

what misleading, except as there is some stress on the matter of keeping the South Atlantic sea lanes open. In this context, various contributors decry US policies that allegedly "alienate" and/or "confuse" white-dominated and pro-West black regimes in Africa. [F.]

Klaiber, Jeffrey L. Los cholos y los rotos: actitudes raciales durante la Guerra del Pacífico. See *HLAS 42:3091.*

7373 Latin American Symposium, 2d, *Allegheny College, 1977.* New directions in inter-American relations: prospects for the Carter Administration. Presentation by Robert Kaufman, Gerald Canto, Austin Linsley. Edited by Giles Wayland-Smith. Meadville, Pa.: Allegheny College, 1977? 28 p.

Texts of the presentations at the "Latin American Symposium II" sponsored by the Northwestern Pennsylvania Institute for Latin American Studies in the spring of 1977. Robert Kaufman examines general issues in U.S.-Latin American relations facing the then-new Carter Administration; Gerald Canto, the cases of Argentina and Chile; and Austin Linsley, Venezuela's foreign policy. [F.]

7374 El Laudo arbitral del Canal Beagle. Selección y notas de Germán Carrasco. Santiago: Editorial Jurídica de Chile, 1978. 212 p.; 1 leaf of plates; map.

Pt. 1 includes major documents (1881–1977) related to the so-called "Beagle" Case, including arbitral judgment of 1977, the remainder of the book reproduces editorial opinion on the judgment from Chilean newspapers.

7375 Lefever, Ernest W. Nuclear arms in the Third World: U.S. policy dilemma. Washington: Brookings Institution, 1979. 154 p.; bibl.; index.

Consists of chap. 6 of a Brookings-sponsored study which focuses on Brazil and Argentina. Authors note that both countries are "keeping their nuclear arms options open;" however, the manuscript was apparently completed prior to the indications of recent years that, despite historical rivalries, Brazil and Argentina are interested in exploring the potential for cooperation in this field. [F.]

López Videla, Winsor. Documentos para la historia: sinopsis del Chaco Boreal, acciones del III Cuerpo de Ejército, calendario de las acciones de guerra, 1932–1935. See *HLAS* 42:3159.

Manrique, Nelson. Los movimientos campesinos en la Guerra del Pacífico. See *HLAS* 42:3096.

7376 Marín Madrid, Alberto. El Caso del Canal Beagle (SCHG/R, 145, 1977, p. 185–197)

The arbitral award of 1977 (the Beagle Channel Case) was clear and correct. There is now only one road to follow and that is observation of the award.

7377 Martínez, Eduardo N. Entrevistas presidenciales Ecuador-Colombia. Quito: Casa de la Cultura Ecuatoriana, 1978. 24 p.

Consists of the texts of brief speeches given by Colombian and Ecuadorian presidents on the occasion of five different border meetings between 1920 and 1977. They are interesting as a documentary of the evolution of international themes and rhetoric over a period of more than half a century.

7378 Matias de la Cruz, Eduardo. Límites entre Bolivia y Argentina (IAEERI/E, 54, sept./oct. 1978, p. 43–57)

Treats the long history of Argentine-Bolivian border negotiations which ended successfully in the Protocol of 1941. It was a case where the principle *Uti Possedatus* could not be applied. This is one of the very few discussions of these negotiations that has come to this reviewer's attention.

7379 Meneses Ciuffardi, Emilio. La organización del Tratado del Atlántico Sur: una visión crítica. Santiago: Instituto de Ciencia Política, Universidad Católica de Chile, 1977. 29 leaves; 7 leaves of plates; maps (Cuadernos del Instituto de Ciencia Política; no. 20)

Brief discussion of the activities, objectives, forces available and the geopolitical setting for the South Atlantic Treaty Organization.

7380 Mercado Jarrín, Edgardo. Pacto Amazónico: dominación o integración? (NSO, 37, julio/agosto 1978, p. 5–18, ill.)

Peruvian military officer and ex-Minister of Foreign Relations argues that the recent treaty for the integration of the Amazon (in which Brazil was the central party) holds out real prospects for beneficial cooperation, especially through the integration and "self-affirmation" of the entire area.

7381 Milenky, E.S. The Cartagena Agreement in transition (LIWA/YWA, 1979, p. 167–179)

Account of the development of the Andean Group with particular emphasis on the crisis of 1975–76. Author suggests that the group is best understood as an evolving response to the contradictory pressures of international interdependence and the desire for national autonomy.

7382 Moneta, Carlos Juan. Aspectos conflictivos de las relaciones afro-latinoamericanas: las vinculaciones políticas, económicas y militares de Sudáfrica con los países del Atlántico Sur latinoamericano (UNAM/RI, 6:22, julio/sept. 1978, p. 55–104, tables)

Emphasis is on the relations between South Africa on the one hand and Argentina and Brazil on the other, with some attention also to South Africa's relations with Chile, Paraguay, and Uruguay. Author argues that these relations have become more important in recent years and attempts to show why this has been the case.

7383 Montevideo. Biblioteca del Poder Legislativo. Departmento de Relaciones Públicas y Publicaciones. Visita del Presidente Argentino, Teniente General Jorge Rafael Videla. Idea, selección y textos, Wilfredo Pérez. Montevideo: La Biblioteca, 1977. 203 p.; bibl.; ill.

Contains the texts of several bilateral agreements between Argentina and Uruguay, the most important being Salto Grande.

Moscoso, Oscar. Recuerdos de la Guerra del Chaco. See *HLAS* 42:3166.

7384 Nekotorye problemy mezhlatino-amerikanskikh otnoshenii: materialy nauchnoi konferentsii (Some problems of inter-Latin American relations: materials of a scholarly conference). Moscow: Institut Latinskoi Amerikia Akademii nauk SSSR, 1976. 205 p.

Papers from a conference held 13 July 1975 dealing with a number of aspects of the interrelationships of the Latin American countries—including joint struggles against the banana monopoly, the River Plate countries vis-à-vis Brazil, and the question of "Pan Hispanicism." [R.V. Allen]

7385 Ovando Sanz, Jorge Alejandro. La invasión brasileña a Bolivia en 1825: una de las causas del Congreso de Panamá. La Paz, Bolivia: Ediciones Isla, 1977. 182 p.; bibl.; index.

"The theme of the Brazilian invasion of the (Bolivian) province of Chiquitos in 1825 has not, until now, been the subject of a sufficiently broad monograph in Bolivia . . . we believe this event has an extraordinary importance for the analysis of contemporary Brazilian diplomacy."

7386 Pacto andino: desarrollo nacional e integración andina. Ernesto Tironi, compilador. Lima: Instituto de Estudios Peruanos, 1978. 365 p.; bibl. (América problema; 10)

Each of the five excellent essays analyzes the significance of the Andean Pact and the problems encountered by the five members (Bolivia, Colombia, Ecuador, Peru, and Venezuela). It is clear that each country has different problems and that the pact has a different significance for each one.

7387 Perry, Richard O. Argentina and Chile: the struggle for Patagonia, 1843–1881 (AAFH/TAM, 36:3, Jan. 1980, p. 347–363)

Historical survey of the struggle between Argentina and Chile over Patagonia and the Straits of Magellan. Author suggests that there are weaknesses in the arguments of Chilean revisionist historians who have recently reintroduced more controversy into the affair by suggesting that traditional Chilean claims to Patagonia should be pursued anew.

7388 Quagliotti de Bellis, Bernardo. Constantes geopolíticas en Iberoamérica. Diseño de la tapa y mapas de Bernardo Quagliotti de Bellis. Montevideo: GEOSUR: distribuye Tarino Libros, 1979. 46 p.; bibl.; maps.

Briefly outlines a long tradition of South American geopolitical thought and offers a geopolitical "esquema" for the development of the continent: eight cohesive nuclei "united by socioeconomic axes to centers of development."

7389 ———. Geopolítica del Atlántico Sur. Cartografía por Alberto R. Goyeneche de Simone. Montevideo: Fundación de Cultura Universitaria, 1976. 73 p.; bibl.; maps.

Discusses briefly the interests and conflict of interest or objectives among the members of the South Atlantic Treaty Organization.

7390 Roca Castellanos, Manuel. Colombia y Venezuela integración. Bogotá; Colombia, Ediciones Tercer Mundo, 1979. 90 p.

Very interesting, though perhaps optimistic, discussion of the necessity and prospects for Colombian-Venezuelan integration includes especially interesting references to specific geographic areas for possible integration.

SELA en Acción. No. 5, feb. 1979– . See *HLAS 42:234.*

7391 Tambs, Lewis A. The changing geopolitical balance of South America (The Journal of Social and Political Studies [Council on American Affairs, Washington] 4:1, Spring 1979, p. 17–35)

In what is essentially an updated version of a 1965 article, Tambs argues, from the geopolitical perspective, that the Soviet danger to South America is stimulating the continent's Spanish and Portuguese nations into closer economic, political, and military cooperation. For historian's comment, see *HLAS 42:1947.*

7392 ———. Factores geopolíticos en América Latina. Montevideo: Asociación Sudamericana de Estudios Geopolíticos e Internacionales, 1979. 22 p. (Geosur)

Overview of recent and possible near-future geopolitical trends in Latin America, stressing the importance of the Southern Cone countries and the grave need to continue to curb Soviet penetration. [F.]

7393 Vargas-Hildago, Rafael. The crisis of the Andean Pact: lessons for integration among developing countries (JCMS, 17:3, March 1979, p. 213–226)

Argues that law has a major role to play in the functioning of economic integration systems. Particular attention is paid to the minimal level of community within the Andean Pact. Points to many of the problems facing the Andean Pact.

7394 Villalobos R., Sergio. El Beagle, historia de una controversia. Santiago, Chile: Editorial Andrés Bello, 1979. 133 p.; ill.

Noted Chilean historian presents a

brief and well documented historical defense of Chilean claims in the Beagle Channel.

Villegas, Osiris Guillermo. En conflicto con Chile en la región austral. See *HLAS 42: 3434.*

ARGENTINA

7395 Aguilar, Juan Carlos. Geopolítica nacional: Paraná medio, el Itaipú argentino (IAEERI/E, 61/62, nov. 1979/feb. 1980, p. 49–63, bibl., maps)

The great hydroelectric enterprise, Paraná Medio, now only under study, is seen as a means of regaining Argentine initiative in the Plata Basin.

Alén Lascano, Luis C. Yrigoyen y la guerra mundial. See *HLAS 42:3285.*

7396 La Argentina en el Beagle y Atlántico Sur. J.S. Campobassi et al.; coordinación, Isaac Francisco Rojas. Buenos Aires: Nemont Ediciones: distribución exclusiva, Editorial Diagraf, 1978. 1 v.; maps.

Consists of a collection of papers presented at a conference on the Beagle Channel and the South Atlantic. All papers present the Argentine case and most deal with historical and juridical matters already covered many times in the past. Most useful, perhaps, are several which present Argentina's case for not accepting the 1977 arbitral award.

Davis, Thomas B. A young Argentine in the United States: 1824. See *HLAS 42:3329.*

7397 Ferrari, Gustavo. La política exterior argentina a través de la bibliografía general (RIB, 30:2, 1980, p. 133–147)

This very useful bibliographic essay on basic sources for the study of Argentine foreign policy constitutes an ideal point of departure for anyone interested in the subject.

7398 Foulkes, Haroldo. Las Malvinas: una causa nacional. Buenos Aires: Ediciones Corregidor, 1978. 147 p. (Serie popular)

Useful only as an example of the kind of "appeals" or arguments used by some Argentine writers to bring other Argentines into their crusade for sovereignty over the Malvinas (Falkland Islands).

7399 Fraga, Jorge A. La Argentina y los principios de la geopolítica (AFS/JAF, 58,

mayo/junio 1979, p. 21–25)

Argentine naval officer argues that, geopolitically, Argentina is a great open space which will be filled in the 21st century: "if we don't do it, others will try."

7400 Gobbi, Hugo J. Argentina, legalismo, pragmatismo y error en su política internacional (IAEERI/E, 57, marzo/abril 1979, p. 34–44)

Argentine writer concludes that "it may be that an introverted country such as ours, with enormous internal problems and large areas of semivacant land can momentarily turn its attention from international affairs. But, although many of us remain indifferent, the new generation will be aware that the promiscuity of great words only serves to cover up great mistakes."

7401 Hernández, Pablo José and **Horacio Chitarroni.** Malvinas: clave geopolítica. Buenos Aires: Ediciones Castañeda, 1977. 126 p.; bibl. (Colección Perspectiva nacional; 3)

In addition to the usual arguments in support of Argentine claims to the Malvinas (Falkland Islands), author notes their importance to Argentina, especially with reference to petroleum and other strategic considerations.

7402 Jordan, David C. Argentina's military commonwealth (CUH, 76:44, Feb. 1979, p. 66–69)

This informative review of Argentine events during 1978 looks at the political consolidation of the military regime, its initial economic performance, and the country's foreign policies, focusing on the border conflict with Chile. [G. Wynia]

López, Norberto Aurelio. El pleito de la patria. See *HLAS 42:3378.*

7403 MacDonald, C.A. The politics of intervention: the United States and Argentina, 1941–1946 (JLAS, 12:2, Nov. 1980, p. 365–396)

Author clearly and correctly depicts US policy as one of considerable confusion largely due to a lack of understanding of what was happening in Argentina.

McLynn, F.J. The Argentine presidential election of 1868. See *HLAS 42:3384.*

Martinelli, Andrés Juan. La Argentina en el Océano Pacífico. See *HLAS 42:3386.*

7404 Matijevic, Nicolás. Bibliografía sobre el Canal de Beagle: primera contribución. Palabras liminares por Camilo H. Rodríguez Berrutti. Bahía Blanca, Argentina: Universidad Nacional del Sur, Departamento de Ciencias Sociales, Centro de Documentación Patagónica, 1978 or 1979. 26 leaves; index.

Contains few, if any, references published in Chile or anywhere except Argentina. Should be useful for anyone studying the Argentine arguments and case.

7405 Moneta, Carlos Juan. La política exterior del peronismo: 1973–1976 (CM/FI, 20:2, oct./dic. 1979, p. 220–276)

Author's review of the complex and numerous internal and external, economic and ideological factors of 1970s peronism leads him to conclude that Argentine foreign policy in the period 1973–76 was only another "turn of the screw" in the Argentine dependency syndrome of the previous decade.

7406 Rapoport, Mario. La política de Estados Unidos en Argentina en tiempos de la Segunda Guerra Mundial: 1943–1945 (FEPA/EI, 1:2, agosto 1979, p. 14–19)

Author's interesting and useful critique of the economic and ideological motives behind Hull's wartime policy in Argentina is based on carefully researched materials.

7407 ———. Las relaciones anglo-argentinas: aspectos políticos y económicos; la experiencia del gobierno militar, 1943–1945. Buenos Aires: Fundación para el Estudio de los Problemas Argentinos (FEPA), 1979. 32 p. (Documento de trabajo; 20)

Although emphasis is on Argentine-British relations, this very useful study includes much information and analysis of US-British relations and the impact of the latter on the subject of primary interest. There is also much on Argentine domestic politics.

7408 Rojas, Isaac Francisco. La ofensiva geopolítica brasileña en la Cuenca del Plata. Buenos Aires: Ediciones Nemont, 1979. 189 p.; ill.

Argues that Argentina faces a serious threat because of Brazilian imperialist "manifest destiny." The weakness of Argentine foreign policy stems from internal weaknesses, especially paternalistic statism. A series of case studies (Alto Paraná, Corpus,

Itaipú and others) are offered as examples of the Brazilian offensive and Argentine retreat.

7409 Salguero, Ramón. Todo sobre el Beagle. Buenos Aires: El Cid Editor, 1978. 82 p.; ill. (Colección Geopolítica; 7)

A standard appeal for Argentine sovereignty in the Beagle.

7410 Schoultz, Lars. The nature of anti-U.S. sentiment in Latin America: a preliminary analysis with Argentine data (CUNY/CP, 11:4, July 1979, p. 467–481, tables)

This creative research note empirically tests some notions about anti-Americanism in Latin America using survey data collected in Argentina in 1965. It finds less hostility than assumed and argues that it is sustained more by ideological than psychological factors. [G.W. Wynia]

Scroggins, Daniel C. Leopoldo Lugones' defense of the Monroe Doctrine in the *Revue Sud-Américaine*. See *HLAS 42:3420.*

7411 Serres Güiraldes, Alfredo Marcelo. De cómo la República Argentina perdió su salida al Océano Pacífico. Buenos Aires: Editorial Moharra, between 1969 and 1979. 31 p.; bibl.; maps.

Brief history of a lesser known territorial dispute between Argentina and Chile spells out the chronology of action and reaction (1881–93). With the final act (Protocol of 1893), Argentina gave up, *motu propio*, her exit to the Pacific.

7412 Stemplowski, Ryszard. Las potencias anglosajonas y el neutralismo argentino: 1939–1945 (PAN/ES, 3, 1976, p. 129–159)

British and US interests were frequently at odds during this period. The consistency of British policy stands in sharp contrast with that of the US as does the clarity with which British policy makers were able to conceptualize the idea of a national interest. For author's book on this subject, see item **7413.** For historian's comment, on this article, see *HLAS 42:3428.*

7413 ———. Zale żność i wyzwanie: Argentyna wobec rywalizacji mocarstw anglosaskich i III Rzeszy. Warszawa: Kaiąžka i Wiedza, 1975. 403 p.; bibl.; index.

A Polish historian who specializes in Latin America analyzes relations between Argentina and three of the contenders during

World War II: the US, Great Britain and Nazi Germany. Author believes Argentine neutrality during 1939–45 was chiefly the result of Argentine-US rivalry. In the British-US competition for South America, Argentina stood with Great Britain on economic issues while competing with the US for political influence in the southern hemisphere. Nazi Germany, in turn, strengthened its ties with Argentina and encouraged its anti-US policy. Book includes an extensive bibliography of secondary literature, mostly German and Polish titles, as well as primary sources drawn from Polish diplomatic archives, British Foreign Office records, and German and US diplomatic materials published by the US State Dept. [G.J. Kovtun]

7414 Tesler, Mario. Malvinas, cómo EE.UU. provocó la usurpación inglesa. Buenos Aires: Editorial Galerna, 1979. 158 p.; bibl.

Study of a little-known but important aspect of US-Argentine relations argues that conflicts between the US and Argentina in waters near the Malvinas (Falkland Islands) in the 1820s and 1830s contributed to the British occupation.

7415 Woods, Randall Bennett. The Roosevelt foreign-policy establishment and the Good Neighbor: the United States and Argentina, 1941–1945. Lawrence: Regents Press of Kansas, 1979. 277 p.; bibl.; index.

Argues that during World War II the US attempt at the "Good Neighbor Policy" was undermined by Argentina's refusal to make an all-out commitment to the war effort. Further, Washington's response to Argentina's neutrality was based more on bureaucratic infighting within the Roosevelt Administration than an external consideration.

BOLIVIA

Andrade, Víctor. La revolución boliviana y los Estados Unidos, 1944–1962. See item **6488.**

7416 Antología geopolítica de Bolivia. Bajo la dirección de Mariano Baptista Gumucio, Agustín Saavedra Weise. La Paz: Ediciones Los Amigos del Libro, 1978. 389 p.; bibl.; ill. (Enciclopedia boliviana)

This is more than a collection of articles on the geopolitics of Bolivia. It is rather a collection dealing with the geopolitics of the continent of which Bolivia has been and continues to be the victim. Includes an interesting and useful selection of writings by 19th-century and contemporary authors, Bolivian and foreign.

Bocchio Rejas, Luis Orlando. Los tacneños y el corredor para Bolivia. See *HLAS 42:3059.*

Botelho Gosálvez, Raúl. Breve historia del litoral boliviano: la misión Jaimes Freyre en Santiago. See *HLAS 42:3140.*

7417 Canelas L., René. El poder y la nación: tesis geopolítica, ensayos. La Paz, Bolivia: Edit. Letras, 1978. 175 p.; bibl.

Bolivian development requires the formation and participation of the nation but the latter also requires a process of development. These thoughtful essays center around a theme of "revolutionary nationalism" which will promote structural, economic and social changes that will integrate society and open new perspectives for human achievement.

7418 Canelas Orellana, Amado. Bolivia: mito y realidad de su enclaustramiento. Lima: Canales Orellana, 1977. 266 p.

In addition to a brief historical treatment of Bolivia's lost maritime territory, this work contains much information on Bolivia's domestic and international politics related to the problem.

7419 Castro Rodríguez, Carlos. La soberanía marítima de Bolivia (SGHS/B, 56:461/463, 1976/1978, p. 98–116, bibl.)

Contains a summary of the events leading up to Bolivia's loss of its maritime territory and the long history of efforts to regain it!

Córdova-Claure, Ted. Siles Suazo: las banderas de Abril de 52. See item **6495.**

7420 Documentos sobre la mediterraneidad boliviana. Agustín Saavedra Weise, compilador; prólogo del doctor Jorge R. Vanossi. Buenos Aires: Depalma, 1979. 167 p.; bibl.; map.

Contains the texts of treaties, declarations, diplomatic exchanges and memoranda (1866–78) relating to Bolivia's lost maritime territory. This is a useful collection that should be in every library of inter-American diplomatic history.

7421 Escobari Cusicanqui, Jorge. El derecho al mar. 2. ed. La Paz: s.n., 1979. 310, 18 p.; bibl.; ill.

Contains a solid historical treatment of the controversy over Bolivia's lost maritime territory and the usual legal arguments in support of Bolivia's case. More frequently heard contemporary arguments such as the importance of a just settlement in the light of continental harmony and regional integration are effectively treated.

El Fraude electoral: un atentado contra la voluntad popular: elecciones nacionales del 9 de julio de 1978. See item **6496.**

Greño Velasco, José Enrique. Bolivia y su retorno al mar. See *HLAS 42:3155.*

7422 Guevara Arze, Wálter. Radiografía de la negociación con Chile. Cochabamba, Bolivia: Editorial Universo, 1978. 235 p.; maps.

The author sets out to show that Bolivia's controversy concerning its lost maritime territory is not exclusively nor even principally a bilateral matter between Bolivia and Chile but that it concerns Peru as well, and interests other countries such as Brazil and Argentina. Book concentrates on recent diplomatic history and criticizes the policies of the Bolivian military.

7423 Jordán Sandoval, Santiago. Bolivia y el equilibrio del Cono Sudamericano. Cochabamba, Bolivia: Editorial Los Amigos del Libro, 1979. 270 p.; bibl.

Argues that Bolivia, because of its "axial geographic location," has a crucial position in the equilibrium of the South American Cone. This holds true especially in economic matters and the future of subcontinental integration.

Kolle Cueto, Jorge. Conversación con el Primer Secretario del Comité Central del Partido Comunista de Bolivia. See item **6499.**

Lavaud, Jean-Pierre. Le gouvernement Bánzer de 1971 à 1976. See item **6500.**

Lora, Guillermo. Estudios histórico-políticos sobre Bolivia. See *HLAS 42:3161.*

7424 Morzone, Luis Antonio, hijo. La mediterraneidad boliviana ante el derecho internacional: posición argentina. Buenos Aires: Depalma, 1979. 209 p.; bibl.

A good historical treatment, from an Argentine perspective, of the problem of Bolivia's lost maritime territory. Of particular interest are discussions of Bolivia's action in the League of Nations, the UN and the OAS. The summary presents Bolivia's case for rightful recovery of the territory.

Moya Quiroga, Víctor. Internacionalización de Arica: documentos para la historiografía de una salidad al mar. See *HLAS 42:3167.*

7425 Oblitas Fernández, Edgar. Bolivia y su derecho al Pacífico. La Paz: Ediciones Populares Ultima Hora, 1978. 93, 35 p.; 2 leaves of plates; bibl.; maps (Colección Litoral boliviano. Biblioteca popular boliviana de Ultima Hora)

Book is principally devoted to refuting the Chilean argument that Bolivia never had access to the sea. Includes a supposedly secret Chilean study of Bolivian geography, dated 1879, which proves the falsity of the Chilean argument.

Pers García, Walter. Límites de Bolivia. See item **5214.**

Ramos Sánchez, Pablo. La democracia boliviana, sus defensores y sus enemigos. See item **6509.**

7426 Saavedra Weise, Agustín. Bolivia: geopolítica y relaciones internacionales (IAEERI/E, 58, mayo/junio 1979, p 49–54)

Geopolitics must remain central in the definition and pursuit of Bolivia's national interest. This requires a realization of Bolivia's position on the continent and, above all, a policy of internal unity, including recovery of lost maritime territories.

7427 La Salida al Mar: una necesidad imperiosa. La Paz, Bolivia: Secretaría General de Informaciones de la Presidencia de la República, 1978. 97 p.

Consists of a collection of speeches by Bolivian Presidents and diplomats; joint declarations with other countries and declarations by foreign diplomats, all relating to Bolivia's need for and right to an access to the sea. Documents are dated 1974–78.

7428 *Temas en la Crisis.* Año 1, No. 4, oct. 1978– . La Paz.

A group of Bolivian jurists reply to a variety of questions concerning the possibilities of regaining their country's lost maritime territory and some of the policies that might contribute to that end. By and large, the replies are thoughtful and moderate. They are preceded by a list of military figures who did not reply to similar questions.

Vaughn, Courtney Ann. By hook or by crook: Alfalfa Bill Murray, colonizer in Bolivia. See *HLAS 42:3185.*

Zavaleta Mercado, René. Consideraciones generales sobre la historia de Bolivia, 1932–1971. See *HLAS 42:3188.*

BRAZIL

Apesteguy, Christine and **Hervé Thery.** Les frontières du Nord-Brésil: de l'independance au Pacte Amazonien. See item **5311.**

7429 Ashcer, William L. Brazil's future foreign relations (*in* The future of Brazil. Edited by William H. Overholt. Contributors, William L. Ashcer and others. Boulder, Colo.: Westview Press, 1978, p. 49–70 [Westview special studies on Latin America])

This somewhat optimistic survey of Brazil's foreign relations emphasizes the view that future international relations will depend heavily on the economic context in which they develop. Concludes that since Brazil's fate lies with the developed nations, so too do Brazil's international politics.

The Automotive industry in Latin America. See item **7009.**

Black, Jan Knippers. United States penetration of Brazil. See *HLAS 42:3626.*

Cintra, Antônio Otávio. Traditional Brazilian politics: an interpretation of relations between center and periphery. See item **6664.**

7430 Corrêa da Costa, Sérgio. A diplomacia no Marechal: intervenção estrangeira na revolta da Armada. 2. ed. Rio de Janeiro: Tempo Brasileiro, 1979. 303 p.; 6 leaves of plates; bibl.; ill.; index (Coleção Caminhos brasileiros; 5)

Pts. 1–2 of this history deal not only with diplomacy but with the domestic history of Brazil during the government of Floriano Peixoto as well as the contrast in personalities between the latter and Saldanha da Gama. Pts. 3–4 cover a wide range of diplomatic issues raised by the naval revolt of 1893.

7431 Evans, Peter. Shoes, OPIC, and the unquestioning persuasion: multinational corporations and U.S.-Brazilian relations (*in* Capitalism and the State in U.S.-Latin American relations. Edited by Richard R. Fagen. Contributors, Cynthia Arnson et al. Stanford, Calif.: Stanford University Press, 1979, p. 302–336)

This discussion of the ups and downs of US-Brazilian economic relations devotes particular attention to the changing role of the multinational corporation. Author analyzes what he calls the "triple alliance" (i.e., the multinational, the Brazilian state, and the elite local capital within Brazil) and concludes with an examination of the varieties of nationalistic reaction to the multinational in both Brazil and the US.

Galey, John. Industrialist in the wilderness: Henry Ford's Amazon venture. See item **3744.**

7432 Gambini, Roberto. O duplo jogo de Getúlio Vargas: influência americana e alemã no Estado Novo. Editor, Moysés Baumstein. São Paulo: Edições Símbolo, 1977. 175 p.; bibl. (Coleção Ensaio e memória; 4)

Important study of the evolution of Brazilian relations with the rest of the capitalist world between 1929 and World War II. Some of the important changes within Brazil include an increase in the economic activities of the state, definition of national goals, priority to industrialization and increased power of interest groups. They took place at a time when Brazil found new ways to pursue its national interests abroad.

7433 Grabendorff, Wolf. La política exterior del Brasil, entre el primer y tercer mundo (NSO, 41, marzo/abril 1979, p. 108–119)

Brazil has not yet found its position in the international system but there is a growing realization in the country that its present policy of "leaving its options open cannot continue much longer."

———— and **Manfred Nitsch.** Brasilien: Entwicklungsmodell und Aussenpolitik. See item **6671.**

7434 Hilton, Stanley E. Brazil and the post-Versailles world: elite images and foreign policy strategy; 1919–1929 (JLAS, 12:2, Nov. 1980, p. 341–364)

"Brazil's foreign policy strategy in the 1920s was generally well-advised but produced uneven results. The rebuff by European powers at Geneva in 1926 was certainly a major diplomatic defeat . . . Brazilian policy makers judged the alleged special relationship with the United States a useful deterrent . . . but subsequent history suggests that the relationship existed more in the minds of Brazilian leaders than in Washington's calculations."

7435 Kucinski, Bernardo. La Amazonia y la geopolítica del Brasil (NSO, 37, julio/agosto 1978, p. 26–30)

Brazil led in efforts to establish an Amazon development treaty with other states in the area. The objective was a desire to change its continental image and regain initiatives lost to Venezuela.

Le Doare, Hélène. Le Brésil et le Cône Sud: les conflits frontaliers. See item **5363**.

7436 Leacock, Ruth. JFK, business, and Brazil (HAHR, 59:4, Nov. 1979, p. 636–673)

Thorough and detailed analysis of the Kennedy Administration's relations with Brazil against the background of US business interests. Leacock argues that Kennedy made an effort to distance himself from the business community when he launched his Latin American policy but that this distance was maintained for only one year. What mattered most to Kennedy was winning the Cold War. He perceived Latin America as a developing area in the Cold War and came to believe that winning the war was easier with business cooperation. For historian comment, see *HLAS 42:3683*.

7437 Luddeman, Margarete K. Nuclear technology from West Germany: a case of disharmony in US-Brazilian relations. Washington: Latin American Studies Program, Georgetown University, 1978. 25 p. (Occasional paper; 1)

"Considering Brazil's nuclear ambition, energy problems, and worldview, the lack of success of US pressure could have been predicted. In fact the Brazilians were perhaps quite inadvertently reinforced in their position by the Russian demarche in Bonn, which was meant to demonstrate unity of cause with the US and to persuade the Germans to contemplate carefully the mutual worry over proliferation."

7438 Mar territorial. Brasília: Marinha do Brasil, 1971 or 1972. 3 v.

Three-volume collection of documents consists of articles and speeches rather than a systemic treatment of the subject. Vol. 1 includes brief introductory chapter with the remainder devoted to Brazilian legislation on the subject, the texts of a few foreign laws or decrees and UN and OAS treaties and declarations. Vol. 2 is principally a collection of reports and articles on the subject and speeches by Brazilian diplomats and congressional representatives. Vol. 3 reproduces nine papers presented by Brazilian academicians at a Porto Alegre conference in 1972 plus additional UN and OAS documents.

Meira Mattos, Carlos de. Una geopolítica para la Panamazónica. See item **5375**.

7439 Mirow, Kurt Rudolf. Loucura nuclear: os enganos do Acordo Brasil-Alemanha. Capa, Eugênio Hirsch. Rio de Janeiro: Civilização Brasileira, 1979. 299 p.; bibl. (Coleção Retratos do Brasil; v. 126)

Well documented study of every aspect of Brazilian nuclear policy. As the title suggests, author is extremely critical of the policy and argues that the recent agreement with West Germany was more in the latter's interest than Brazil's.

Molano Campuzano, Joaquín. Las transnacionales en la Amazonia. See item **5378**.

7440 Morris, Michael A. International politics and the sea, the case of Brazil. Boulder, Colo.: Westview Press, 1979. 291 p.; bibl. (A Westview replica edition)

This book surveys major aspects of Brazilian ocean policy and offers a thorough analysis of Brazil's emergence as a major ocean power. National policies are related to international politics and the final chapter compares Brazilian ocean policy to the ocean policies of both developed and developing states.

Namor, Paul. Un prolétariat en uniforme et une révolution "honnête:" quelques considérations sur la rébellion des équipages de la Flotte Brésilienne de Haute Mer, en novembre 1910. See *HLAS 42:3707*.

7441 Overholt, William H. The future of Brazil: an overview (*in* The future of Brazil. Edited by William H. Overholt. Boulder, Colo.: Westview Press, 1979, p. 1–48)

An optimistic yet balanced account of

the long-term problems Brazil faces. Though the emphasis of this essay is economic, the social and political consequences of Brazil's "economic miracle" are also dealt with. Author concludes that present trends justify much of the confidence Brazilians express as they confront their problems. Particularly good treatment of the balance of payments problem and Brazil's experiment in "indexing."

7442 Panorama do poder marítimo brasileiro. Coordenação da obra CMG Mario César Flores. Rio de Janeiro: Serviço do Documentação Geral da Marinha, 1972. 445 p.; plates (Biblioteca do Exército; 429. Coleção General Benício; 105)

Highly informative volume on Brazilian naval power. Includes data and discussion on construction, port facilities, merchant marine, geography and other related matters. The political, economic and security foundations of Brazil's policy on the Law of the Sea are also treated.

7443 Parker, Phyllis R. Brazil and the quiet intervention: 1964. Austin: University of Texas Press, 1979. 147 p.; bibl.; index (Texas Pan American series)

An account of Brazilian affairs in the early 1960s with special reference to the 1964 crisis. The emphasis is on US activities in Brazil during this important period. For historian's comment, see *HLAS 42:3730*.

Roett, Riordan. The political future of Brazil. See item **6750**.

7444 Schilling, Paulo R. El expansionismo brasileño. México: El Cid Editor, 1978. 314 p.; bibl.; maps (Coleccíon Geopolítica; 2)

In a collection of related essays rather than in a systematic treatment, author discusses Brazilian expansion in the Plata basin and Amazon area, at the expense of its neighbors. Describes how Uruguay became Brazil's satellite and its attempt to extend its influence in Africa and Portugal.

7445 Silva, Golbery do Couto e. Geopolítica del Brasil. Traducción y notas de Paulo R. Schilling. México: El Cid Editor, 1978. 311 p.; bibl.; ill. (Colección Geopolítica; 1)

Spanish translation of a book that was most influential in shaping the ideology of the Brazilian Escola Superior de Guerra and the military government of 1964. "Aggression" for Brazil was "indirect communist ag-

gression" utilizing local discontent, misery and hunger. Thus, there is urgent need for strong planning and strong government to insure the internal stability necessary to implement planning and development.

7446 Simpósio sobre os 70 [i.e. Setenta] Anos da Imigração Japonesa: simpósio realizado em 16 e 17 de maio de 1978, pela Comissão de Relações Exteriores, em comemoração aos 70 anos da imigração japonesa. Brasília: Câmara dos Deputados, 1978. 117 p.

Contains some brief but informative lectures, not only on Japanese immigration to Brazil but on Japanese cultural influence. Lectures by Hiroshi Saito and Kenzo Yoshida are of particular interest.

7447 Soares, Alvaro Teixeira. Importancia geopolítica de la Amazonia. Montevideo, Uruguay: Geosur, 1979. 24 p.; maps.

A too brief but useful historical description of Brazil's development of the Amazon region.

7448 Soares d'Araújo, Maria Celina and **Gerson Moura.** O Tratado Comercial Brasil-EUC de 1935 e os interesses industriais brasileiros (FGV/R, 21:1, enero/marzo 1978, p. 55–73, bibl.)

Excellent discussion of the play of forces for and against the Treaty of 1935 and the decisive influence of the US State Department and the Brazilian Executive in securing congressional approval in Brazil.

Souza, Carlos Alves de. Um embaixador em tempos de crise. See *HLAS 42:3756*.

Strauss, Norman T. Brazil after the Paraguayan War: six years of conflict, 1870–1876. See *HLAS 42:3758*.

Tambs, Lewis A. Brazil and the Caribbean link: a geopolitical overview of World War III. See item **7348**.

Valla, Victor V. A penetração norte-americana na economia brasileira, 1898–1928: sempre de acordo ou nobre emulação? See *HLAS 42:3768*.

7449 Viagem do Presidente Geisel ao México: registro histórico, repercussões. Brasília: Assessoria de Relações Públicas da Presidência da República, 1978. 40 p.; ill.

Consists of the usual "good will" speeches, some of which and especially the press interviews offer insights into Brazil's foreign policy and self-image in world affairs.

7450 Viktorova, I. and **N. Yakovlev.** Modern trends in Brazil's foreign policy (IA, 1, Jan. 1980, p. 57–64)

Soviet authors summarize their views about "certain changes" taking place in Brazilian foreign policy. Predictably, they note strains in Brazil's relations with the US and possibilities for closer relations with the USSR despite Brazil's capitalist economy.

CHILE

Bermúdez Miral, Oscar. Repercusiones en Cobija de la guerra con España. See *HLAS 42:3198.*

7451 Bitar, Sergio. Las relaciones económicas entre Chile y EE. UU. en el período 1971–1972 (*in* Bitar, Sergio. Corporaciones multinacionales y autonomía nacional. Caracas: Monte Avila Editores, 1977, p. 125–144)

Author argues that because international conditions in 1971–72 prevented the US from implementing a blockage or using open force against Chile, the US government found it necessary to resort to less visible means which he terms "economic asphixiation."

7452 Buzeta, Oscar. Chile geopolítico: presente y futuro. Santiago de Chile: CISEC, 1978. 348 p; bibl. (Estudios globales de la estructura chilena)

Chilean naval officer argues that the military government of Chile has made important advances but that new directions are now needed. Those who, with good intentions, think that they are protecting the democratic system by imposing restrictions are constructing a society that will be neither democratic nor social nor Christian.

7453 Cortes Rencoret, Gerardo. Introducción a la seguridad nacional. Santiago: Universidad Católica de Chile, Instituto de Ciencia Política, 1976. 26 leaves; bibl. (Cuadernos del Instituto de Ciencia Política; no. 2)

Citing only from US Army and Navy field manuals, the author discusses the quest for national security in face of the bipolar threat of nuclear war between US and the USSR. It is the fundamental right of all nations to protect their sovereignty; hence the need for a strong armed forces capable of

politicizing the population, collecting intelligence, planning for national security, coordinating all national security activities, and protecting the nation from internal subversion. Includes brief statement concerning the "mandate" extended to Pinochet's Junta by contemporary Chilean society. [W.R. Garner]

Cuccorese, Horacio Juan. La cuestión limítrofe con Chile: tiempo de agudización del conflicto, 1900–1901. See *HLAS 42:3323.*

7454 Dinges, John and **Saul Landau.** Assassination on Embassy Row. New York: Pantheon Books, 1980. 411 p.; 16 leaves of plates; ill.; index.

Account of the 1976 assassination of Orlando Letelier and Ronni Moffitt—the plot that preceded it and the legal maneuverings that were the aftermath. Written under the aegis of the Institute for Policy Studies, where Letelier and Moffitt's husband (Michael) were based, as part of the IPS's "investigation of the investigation." Despite the IPS connection and obvious sympathy for Letelier and Allende's Chile, the book is fact-filled and appears generally objective. Gripping, often appalling reading. [F.]

La Guerra con Chile en sus documentos. See *HLAS 42:3083.*

Inter-American Commission on Human Rights. Informe anual de la Comisión Interamericana de Derechos Humanos a la Asamblea General: 1977. See item **7049.**

7455 Naudón de la Sotta, Carlos. El proceso de distensión y América Latina. Santiago: Instituto de Ciencia Política, Universidad Católica de Chile, 1978. 58 leaves (Cuadernos del Instituto de Ciencia Política; no. 22)

Author asserts that given changes in the international order (e.g., the decline of Western Europe as a colonial power and the Cold War between the US and USSR) world politics must be viewed as a pragmatic, nationalist, decentralized "international ecology." In the face of chronic US intervention in western hemisphere affairs, Latin American nations—and implicitly, Chile—must overcome their "identity crisis" and stand aloof from the US and the "vacillating" policies of the Carter administration. An interesting essay published during the fifth year of the Pinochet regime. [W.R. Garner]

7456 Nogee, Joseph L. and John W. Sloan.
Allende's Chile and the Soviet Union: a policy lesson for Latin American nations seeking autonomy (SAGE/JIAS, 21 : 3, Aug. 1979, p. 339–368, bibl.)
Excellent account of the efforts of Allende's Chile to remain economically viable after its reform of the Chilean economy offers instructive conclusion. Latin American nations that aspire to achieve socialism and/or autonomy from the US cannot expect decisive help from the Soviet Union but must depend primarily on internal sources.

Petras, James F. and Morris Morley. The United States and Chile: imperialism and the overthrow of the Allende government. See item **6572**.

Pinochet de la Barra, Oscar. La Antártica chilena. See *HLAS 42:3252*.

7457 Pinochet Ugarte, Augusto. Geopolítica de Chile. México: El Cid Editor, 1978. 248 p.; bibl.; ill. (Colección Geopolítica; 4)
New edition of *HLAS 39:8877* includes a prologue which offers a "scientific" justification for Chilean territorial expansion.

Presa Casanueva, Rafael de la. Venida y aporte de los españoles a Chile independiente. See *HLAS 42:3254*.

Shurbutt, Ray T. The personnel approach to United States relations with Chile, 1823–1850. See *HLAS 42:3267*.

Simposium Internacional sobre Derechos Humanos, *Santiago de Chile, 1978.* Simposium internacional: experiencia y compromiso compartidos. See item **6580**.

La Sinistra cilena di fronte alla crisi: marzo-settembre 1973. See item **6581**.

COLOMBIA

7458 Dziubiński, Andrzej. Intentos de establecer relaciones diplomáticas entre Colombia y Marruecos en los años 1825–1827 (PAN/ES, 3, 1976, p. 51–68)
Polish author shows how early Latin American states became involved in international diplomacy and offers interesting information and insights into diplomatic methods and power politics of the early 19th century.

Loy, Jane M. Rebellion in the Colombian Llanos: the Arauca affair of 1917. See *HLAS 42:2985*.

7459 Politique etrangère et situation économique de la Colombie en 1978 (IRRI/SD, 32:4, 1979, p. 383–393)
Study of linkages between Colombia's domestic economy (trends and government policies) and what was happening elsewhere in 1978 in the UN, the Western Hemisphere, Europe, and Asia. [F.]

Randall, Stephen J. The diplomacy of modernization: Colombian-American relations, 1920–1940. See *HLAS 42:1942*.

ECUADOR

7460 Barberis Romero, Jaime O. Nociones generales de geopolítica. Quito: Editorial Instituto Geográfico Militar, 1979. 2 v.; bibl.; ill.
During the past decade Latin American writers, especially the military, have shown increasing interest in geopolitics. This two-volume work by an Ecuadorian military officer is an example. In the first volume and most of the second, classic works and theory of geopolitics are competently treated. The final 160 p. of vol. 2 apply these concepts to Ecuador. A useful work for anyone interested in Latin American diplomacy and inter-American relations.

7461 Borja O., Rafael A. El descalabro del 41: visión de un periodista. Quito: Casa de la Cultura Ecuatoriana, 1978. 254 p.
Ecuadorian journalist gives an "eye witness" account of the 1941 Peruvian invasion and occupation of territory claimed by Ecuador and the diplomatic controversies that followed.

Fitch, John Samuel. Consecuencias políticas de la ayuda militar estadounidense a América Latina. See item **7034**.

7462 Medina Castro, Manuel. La responsabilidad del Gobierno Norteamericano en el proceso de la multilación territorial del Ecuador. Guayaquil: Departamento de Publicaciones de la Universidad de Guayaquil, 1977. 215 p.; bibl.
Through research in diplomatic correspondence, "uninterrupted communist militancy" and "illuminated by the splendid

science of Marxism-Leninism," author concludes that since 1827 the US has been involved in the territorial mutilation of Ecuador.

7463 Pérez Concha, Jorge. El Protocolo de Río de Janeiro. Guayaquil: Departamento de Publicaciones de la Universidad de Guayaquil, 1977. 116, 5 p.; bibl.

Critical study of the agreement of 1942 by which Ecuador lost a large part of what it claimed as national territory. Antecedents to the Protocol are treated in great detail.

PARAGUAY

Chiavenatto, Julio José. Genocídio americano: a Guerra do Paraguai. See *HLAS 42: 3452.*

Salum-Flecha, Antonio. Historia diplomática del Paraguay de 1869 a 1938. See *HLAS 42:3468.*

Tate, E. Nicholas. Britain and Latin America in the nineteenth century: the case of Paraguay, 1811–1870. See *HLAS 42:3471.*

PERU

Bonilla, Heraclio. The War of the Pacific and the national and colonial problem in Peru. See *HLAS 42:3060.*

7464 Caballero Méndez, Asunción. La amistad peruano-soviética (URSS/AL, 3, 1975, p. 158–165)

Brief review of Peruvian-USSR cultural activities with emphasis on activities since 1971.

Cotler, Julio. Perú: estado oligárquico y reformismo militar. See *HLAS 42:3069.*

7465 Ferrero Costa, Eduardo. El nuevo Derecho del Mar: el Perú y las 200 millas. Lima: Pontificia Universidad Católica del Perú, 1979. 456 p.; fold. map; fold. table; tables.

Standard but solid treatment of the evolution of the Law of the Sea. Emphasis in some chapters is on Peruvian doctrine and practice.

7466 Matlina, Anna. El imperialismo y la revolución de los militares (URSS/AL, 2, 1979, p. 62–73)

Concludes that, in US-Peruvian relations, the US has adapted its methods to new situations but that the role of foreign influence continues to be extraordinarily strong in the Peruvian "military revolution."

7467 Muñiz, Carlos. Peru-URSS: 10 años por el camino de las buenas relaciones (URSS/AL, 4, 1979, p. 52–59)

Contains useful statistics and other information on Soviet economic and technical aid to Peru, 1969–79.

Normano, João Frederico and Antonello Gerbi. The Japanese in South America: an introductory survey with special reference to Peru. See *HLAS 42:3101.*

Quijano, Aníbal. Imperialismo, clases sociales y estado en el Peru: 1895–1930. See *HLAS 42:3108.*

Real de Azúa, Mario Federico. La misión diplomática del peruano Manuel Corpancho: 1862–1863. See *HLAS 42:3111.*

7468 Sanz de Santamaría, Carlos. Fin del asilo del Doctor Víctor Raúl Haya de la Torre: 1954. Bogotá: Fundación Centenario del Banco de Colombia, 1978. 205 p.

An excellent treatment of what was certainly the most notorious case of "diplomatic asylum" in the annals of Latin American diplomacy. The author feels that such a study is in order at this time inasmuch as a new generation may not know of the episode and should be aware of its importance.

Shulgovski, Anatoli. Apectos ideológicos y teoréticos del proceso revolucionario peruano. See item **6479.**

7469 Stallings, Barbara. Peru and the U.S. banks: privatization of financial relations (*in* Capitalism and the state in U.S.-Latin American relations. Edited by Richard R. Fagen. Contributors, Cynthia Arnson et al. Stanford, Calif.: Stanford University Press, 1979, p. 217–253)

Private bank funding, "privatization," has now become the dominant trend in US-Latin American financial relations. This article presents an excellent analysis of this trend and its problems as they developed in Peru. The conclusion is instructive. Banks have been the primary beneficiaries of "privatization." Fears that private bank loans would give Third World governments increased leverage in dealing with the banks because of the threat of default have proved groundless.

7470 Ugarteche, Pedro. Antología y bio-bibliografía. Lima: Biblioteca Nacional, 1979. 72 p.; 1 leaf of plates; port.

Contains what is apparently a complete bibliography of the works of the distinguished Peruvian diplomat and prolific writer (Pedro Ugarteche). Works on early diplomatic history as well as those on Peruvian diplomacy and foreign policy are especially noteworthy.

URUGUAY

Hevia Cosculluela, Manuel. Pasaporte 11333: ocho años con la CIA. See item **7316**.

Kaufman, Edy. Uruguay in transition. See item **6650**.

7471 Organization of American States. General Secretariat. La OEA en Uruguay. Montevideo: Oficina de la Secretaría General de la OEA en Uruguay, 1978. 76 p.; ill.

Popular but useful summary of OAS activities in Uruguay.

7472 Quagliotti de Bellis, Bernardo. Uruguay en el Cono Sur: destino geo-político. Prólogo del Rúben A. Bulla. Montevideo: Quagliotto de Bellis, 1974. 224 p.; 1 leaf of plates; bibl.; ill.

Discusses the possibilities of Uruguay in the La Plata Basin, its key position in this economic area as a natural outlet to the Atlantic and steps that should be taken, especially with regard to markets. Another interesting example of the influence of geo-political considerations on contemporary Latin American thought.

VENEZUELA

7473 Altuve Carrillo, Leonardo. Yo fui embajador de Pérez Jiménez. Caracas: distribuidor exclusivo: Libroven, 1973. 494 p.; bibl.; facsims.

It is difficult to determine what is the purpose of this book other than to present an apology for a number of people associated with Pérez Jiménez. It is autobiographical although the author claims it is not. It does, however provide considerable information on Venezuelan politics and foreign policy during the Pérez Jiménez years. Book's approach is anecdotal and its organization confused.

Betancourt, Rómulo. Venezuela: oil and politics. See *HLAS 42:3009*.

7474 Calvani, Arístides. La política internacional de Venezuela en el último medio siglo (*in* Venezuela moderna, medio siglo de historia, 1926–1976. Ramón J. Velásquez et al. 2. ed. Caracas: Fundación Eugenio Mendoza: Editorial Ariel, 1979, p. 435–531, tables [Horas de Venezuela, 3])

This thoughtful essay on Venezuelan foreign policy of the last half century makes a notable contribution in terms of providing factual and documentary material as well as interpretative analysis. Unfortunately the very brief "conclusion" is more an apology than a conclusion.

Czerny, Miroslawa. Las políticas del desarrollo regional del Caribe: México y Venezuela. See item **7175**.

7475 Gill, Henry S. Understanding Venezuela's foreign policy (UWI/SES, 27:3, Sept. 1978, p. 350–363, bibl.)

This review article summarizes briefly some of the works available on Venezuela's foreign policy both in English and Spanish. Though technically a review of Robert Bond's *Contemporary Venezuela and its role in international affairs*, it goes on to discuss some of the shortcomings in research on Venezuela's foreign policy.

7476 Humberto Quintero, José. El Convenio con la Santa Sede: cartas cruzadas entre S.E. Cardenal José Humberto Quintero y el Presidente Rómulo Betancourt. Caracas: Colegio de Ingenieros de Venezuela, 1977. 194 p.; col. ill.

Cardinal Quintero has been credited with playing a crucial role as "neutral moderator" or "honest broker" in Venezuela's political struggles. The letters published here provide important documentation relating to this matter.

7477 Liss, Sheldon B. Diplomacy & dependency: Venezuela, the United States, and the Americas. Salisbury, N.C.: Documentary Publications, 1978. 356 p.; bibl.; index; map.

History of Venezuelan foreign policy from the turn of the century to the present with emphasis on inter-American relations.

A thorough and detailed survey which concludes that though Venezuela was and is a sovereign state, its foreign policies were often influenced or determined by outsiders. For historian's comment, see *HLAS 42:3029.*

Rodríguez Leal, Edgard. Relaciones entre Francia y Venezuela, 1832–1918. See *HLAS 42:3039.*

7478 Rojas, Armando. Historia de las relaciones diplomáticas entre Venezuela y los Estados Unidos. v. 1, 1810–1899. Caracas: Ediciones de la Presidencia de la República, 1979. 1 v.; indexes; ports.

Using documents in the National Archives of both the US and Venezuela, author has written a systematic and highly readable history of Venezuela's relations with the US. In recent years Venezuelan scholars have produced a number of excellent works on diplomatic history to which this volume should be added.

Wright, Winthrop R. Race, nationality, and immigration in Venezuelan thought, 1890 to 1937. See *HLAS 42:3046.*

JOURNAL ABBREVIATIONS
INTERNATIONAL RELATIONS

AAAS/D Daedalus. Journal of the American Academy of Arts and Sciences. Harvard Univ. Cambridge, Mass.

AAFH/TAM The Americas. A quarterly publication of inter-American cultural history. Academy of American Franciscan History. Washington.

ADN A Defesa Nacional. Revista de assuntos militares e estudo de problemas brasileiros. Rio de Janeiro.

AFS/JAF Journal of American Folklore. American Folklore Society. Austin, Tex.

APS/WA World Affairs. The American Peace Society. Washington.

AR Areito. Areíto, Inc. New York.

AZIF Aussenpolitik. Zietschrift für Internationale Fragen. Deutsche Verlags-Austalt. Hamburg, FRG.

BCV/REL Revista de Economía Latinoamericana. Banco Central de Venezuela. Caracas.

BESPL Berichte zur Entwicklung in Spanien, Portugal, Lateinamerika. München, FRG.

CFR/FA Foreign Affairs. Council on Foreign Relations. New York.

CIIA/IJ International Journal. Canadian Institute of International Affairs. Toronto.

CM/FI Foro Internacional. El Colegio de México. México.

CU/ILRR Industrial and Labor Relations Review. A publication of the New York School of Industrial and Labor Relations, a Contract College of the State Univ., Cornell Univ. Ithaca.

CUH Current History. A monthly magazine of world affairs. Philadelphia, Pa.

CUNY/CP Comparative Politics. The City Univ. of New York Political Science Program. New York.

DDW Die Dritte Welt. Verlag Anton Hain. Meisenheim, FRG.

DESCO/Q Quehacer. Realidad nacional: problemas y alternativas. Revista del Centro de Estudios y Promoción del Desarrollo (DESCO). Lima.

EDTM Estudios del Tercer Mundo. Centro de Estudios Económicos y Sociales del Tercer Mundo. México.

EEUU/PL Estados Unidos: Perspectiva Latinoamericana. Cuadernos semestrales. Centro de Investigación y Docencia Económica (CIDE). México.

FCE/TE El Trimestre Económico. Fondo de Cultura Económica. México.

FDD/NED Notes et Études Documentaires. France, Direction de la Documentation. Paris.

FEPA/EI F.E.P.A. Estudios e Investigaciones. Fundación para el Estudio de los Problemas Argentinos. Buenos Aires.

FGV/R Revista de Ciência Política. Fundação Getúlio Vargas. Rio de Janeiro.

FIU/CR Caribbean Review. Florida International Univ., Office of Academic Affairs. Miami.

FP Foreign Policy. National Affairs, Inc. and Carnegie Endowment for International Peace. New York.

FPRI/O Orbis. A journal of world affairs. Foreign Policy Research Institute, Philadelphia, Pa. *in association with the* Fletcher School of Law and Diplomacy, Tufts Univ. Medford, Mass.

GWU/JILE Journal of International Law and Economics. George Washington Univ., The National Law Center. Washington.

HAHR Hispanic American Historical Review. Duke Univ. Press *for the* Conference on Latin American History of the American Historical Association. Durham, N.C.

IA International Affairs. A monthly journal of political analysis. Moskova.

IAA Ibero-Amerikanisches Archiv. Ibero-Amerikanisches Institut. Berlin, FRG.

IAEERI/E Estrategia. Instituto Argentino de Estudios Estratégicos y de las Relaciones Internacionales. Buenos Aires.

IAHG/AHG Antropología e Historia de Guatemala. Instituto de Antropología e Historia de Guatemala. Guatemala.

IAMEA Inter-American Economic Affairs. Washington.

IRRI/SD Studia Diplomatica. Chronique de politique etrangère. Institut Royal des Relations Internationales. Bruxelles.

JCMS Journal of Common Market Studies. Oxford, England.

JGSWGL Jahrbuch für Geschichte von Staat, Wirtschaft und Gesellschaft Lateinamerikas. Köln, FRG.

JLAS Journal of Latin American Studies. Centers or institutes of Latin American studies at the universities of Cambridge, Glasgow, Liverpool, London and Oxford. Cambridge Univ. Press. London.

JPR Journal of Peace Research. International Peace Research Institute, Universitetforlaget. Oslo.

LAP Latin American Perspectives. Univ. of California. Riverside.

LARR Latin American Research Review. Univ. of North Carolina Press *for the* Latin American Studies Association. Chapel Hill.

LIWA/YWA The Yearbook of World Affairs. London Institute of World Affairs. London.

LNB/L Lotería. Lotería Nacional de Beneficencia. Panamá.

MR Monthly Review. An independent Socialist magazine. New York.

NACLA NACLA: Report on the Americas. North American Congress on Latin America. New York.

NEA/RBPE The Review of Black Political Economy. National Economic Association and Atlanta Univ. Center. Atlanta, Ga.

NOSALF/IA Ibero Americana. Scandinavian Association for Research on Latin America (NOSALF). Stockholm.

NSO Nueva Sociedad. Revista política y cultural. San José.

NYRB The New York Review of Books. New York.

OAS/AM Américas. Organization of American States. Washington.

OCLAE OCLAE. Revista mensual de la Organización Continental Latinoamericana de Estudiantes. La Habana.

PAN/ES Estudios Latinoamericanos. Polska Akademia Nauk (Academia de Ciencias de Polonia), Instytut Historii (Instituto de Historia). Warszawa.

PUCIS/WP World Politics. A quarterly journal of international relations. Princeton Univ., Center of International Studies. Princeton, N.J.

RCPC Revista del Pensamiento Centroamericano. Centro de Investigaciones y Actividades Culturales. Managua.

RIB Revista Interamericana de Bibliografía (Inter-American Review of Bibliography). Organization of American States. Washington.

RO Revista de Occidente. Madrid.

RRI Revista/Review Interamericana. Univ. Interamericana. San Germán, Puerto Rico.

SAGE/JIAS Journal of Inter-American Studies and World Affairs. Sage Publication *for the* Center for Advanced International Studies, Univ. of Miami. Coral Gables, Fla.

SCHG/R Revista Chilena de Historia y Geografía. Sociedad Chilena de Historia y Geografía. Santiago.

SGHS/B Boletín de la Sociedad Geográfica e Histórica Sucre. Sucre, Bolivia.

SPSA/JP The Journal of Politics. The Southern Political Science Association *in cooperation with the* Univ. of Florida. Gainesville.

UC/I Ibero-Americana. Univ. of California Press. Berkeley.

UCC/RU Revista Universitaria. Anales de la Academia Chilena de Ciencias Naturales. Univ. Católica de Chile. Santiago.

UCNSA/EP Estudios Paraguayos. Univ. Católica Nuestra Señora de la Asunción. Asunción.

UCSD/NS The New Scholar. Univ. of California, Center for Iberian and Latin American Studies and Institute of Chicano Urban Affairs. San Diego.

UNAH/RCE Revista Centroamericana de Economía. Univ. Nacional Autónoma de Honduras, Programa de Postgrado Centroamericano en Economía y Planificación. Tegucigalpa.

UNAM/PD Problemas del Desarrollo. Univ. Nacional Autónoma de México, Instituto de Investigaciones Económicas. México.

UNAM/RFD Revista de la Facultad de Derecho. Univ. Nacional Autónoma de México. México.

UNAM/RI Relaciones Internacionales. Revista del Centro de Relaciones Internacionales. Univ. Nacional Autónoma de México, Facultad de Ciencias Políticas y Sociales. México.

UNCR/R Revista de Historia. Univ. Nacional de Costa Rica, Escuela de Historia. Heredia.

UNESCO/CU Cultures. United Nations Educational, Scientific and Cultural Organization. Paris.

UP/CSEC Cuban Studies/Estudios Cubanos. Univ. of Pittsburgh, Univ. Center for International Studies, Center for Latin American Studies. Pittsburgh, Pa.

UPR/CS Caribbean Studies. Univ. of Puerto Rico, Institute of Caribbean Studies. Río Piedras.

URSS/AL América Latina. Academia de Ciencias de la URSS (Unión de Repúblicas Soviéticas Socialistas). Moscú.

USC/SCC Studies in Comparative Communism. An international interdisciplinary journal. Univ. of Southern California, School of International Relations, Von Klein Smid Institute of International Affairs. Los Angeles.

USCG/PS Política y Sociedad. Univ. de San Carlos de Guatemala, Facultad de Ciencias Jurídicas y Sociales, Escuela de Ciencia Política, Instituto de Investigaciones Políticas y Sociales. Guatemala.

UWI/CQ Caribbean Quarterly. Univ. of the West Indies. Mona, Jamaica.

UWI/SES Social and Economic Studies. Univ. of the West Indies, Institute of Social and Economic Research. Mona, Jamaica.

WQ The Wilson Quarterly. Woodrow Wilson International Center for Scholars. Washington.

SOCIOLOGY

GENERAL

8002 Alberts, Joop. Migración hacia áreas metropolitanas de América Latina: un estudio comparativo. Santiago de Chile: Centro Latinoamericano de Demografía, 1977. 278 p.; bibl. (Serie E—Centro Latinoamericano de Demografía; no. 24)

Comparative analysis of rural-urban migration. Alberts synthesizes the results of studies carried out in several countries, and discusses attributes of the migratory process (volume, distance, stages); selectivity by sex, age, education, and occupation; migrants' motivations; the process of assimilation; and the direct and indirect demographic effects of mass migration. A very useful study. [C.H. Waisman]

8003 American Jewish Committee. South American Office. Comunidades judías de Latinoamérica, 1973–1975. Buenos Aires: Oficina Sudamericana del Comité Judío Americano, Instituto de Relaciones Humanas, 1977. 343 p.; bibl.; index.

Study of the major characteristics of Jewish communities in Latin America and the Caribbean in 1973–75. There is information on the size and composition of the communities; their religious, educational, and political life; relations with Israel; and the effects on them of the global society. The book also includes essays on different aspects of the Jewish population and community life, the most interesting being a careful study of U.O. Schmelz on the size of Argentine Jewry. [C.H. Waisman]

8004 Blejer, Juan. Clase y estratificación social. México: Editorial Edicol, 1977. 244 p.; bibl. (Sociológica, conceptos; 7)

Short introductory textbook on social stratification with chapters on the classic writers (Marx, Weber, Pareto, and Schumpeter), modes of stratification, social mobility, methodological problems of measurement. Contains selected readings by Weber, Davis and Moore with Tumin's critique, Stavenhagen, Lipset and Bendix. [A. Ugalde]

8005 Bojar, Jordi. Movimientos sociales urbanos. Buenos Aires: Ediciones Siap-Planteos, 1975. 122 p.

Study deals with rapid social change and the conflict it generates in urban situations. Theoretical in orientation, the book could be used in a university course on social movements. [Q. Jenkins]

Borón, Atilio A. El fascismo como categoría histórica: en torno al problema de las dictaduras en América Latina. See *HLAS 42: 1919*.

Briones, Guillermo. Universidad y estructura social. See item **4307**.

8006 Cabezas de Gonzales, Betty and **Edmur Fonseca.** Social marginality (*in* Congreso Interamericano de Planificación, VII, Lima, 1968. Latin America in the year 2000. Edited by Joseph S. Tulchin. Reading, Mass.: Addison-Wesley, 1975, p. 169–189)

Authors discuss origin and meaning of marginality as a scientific term, and show how sociohistoric factors have made Latin America a "middle class continent." Drastic changes in both "values and culture" are recommended in order to overcome marginality. [Q. Jenkins]

8007 Camacho García, Armando. Migraciones laborales e integración. Bogotá: Pontificia Universidad Javeriana, Facultad de Ciencias Jurídicas y Socioeconómicas, 1980. 223 p.

Commendable work on the increasingly important topic of international labor migration, and one of the best available treatments of labor migration between nations of the Andean Pact. The analysis is presented within a well-developed theoretical framework and is prefaced by a discussion, for comparative purposes, of similar migrations within the European community. [L. Pérez]

Cancian, Francesca M.; Louis Wolf Goodman; and Peter H. Smith. Capitalism, industrialization, and kinship in Latin America: major issues. See *HLAS 42:1922*.

8008 Chaney, Elsa. Supermadre: women in politics in Latin America. Austin: published for Institute of Latin American Studies by University of Texas Press, 1979. 210 p. (Latin American monographs; no. 50)

Chaney's remarkable analysis of the role of women in Third World development is a much needed contribution to the field of public administration. Author finds that although women in developing areas have attained some degree of emancipation, the highest positions they can expect to attain are in the lower echelons of bureaucracy. Furthermore, they must justify their activities outside of the home by assuming the role of "supremadre," providing what Verba has termed an affective/emotional leadership for a society that is still male dominated. This highly-recommended study includes extensive analysis of relevant literature. [W.R. Garner]

8009 The Child in Latin America and the Caribbean: report on the special meeting, Mexico, 16–18 May 1979. Santiago of Chile: United Nations Children's Fund, 1979. 123 p.

Collection of 11 conference papers that relate the general situation of children in Latin America since 1950 to social and economic problems resulting from demographic trends, employment and income patterns, and the relationship of nutrition, health, housing, and habitat. Contains suggested policies for dealing with these problems, and a declaration on attention to children in Latin America and the Caribbean (The Declaration of Mexico). [N. Valdés]

8010 Conferencia General del Episcopado Latinoamericano, 3d, Puebla, Mexico, 1979. Iglesia y América Latina: cifras. Bogotá: CELAM, 1978. vi, 138 p.; bibl.; ill. (Auxiliar para la III Conferencia General del Episcopado Latinoamericano; 1)

Provides statistical information on the Catholic Church and on social and economic life in Latin America. The section on the Church includes data on parishes, priests and seminaries, and baptisms and marriages for each country, but gives no information on church attendance. General section summarizes data on population, economic growth, income distribution, education, health, housing, and social security. Also contains a series of brief Church position papers on a variety of issues, ranging from the situation of youth to inflation. [C.H. Waisman]

Cueva, Agustín. Teoría social y procesos políticos en América Latina. See item **6029**.

Dealey, Glen C. The public man: an interpretation of Latin American and other Catholic countries. See *HLAS 42:1771*.

Dix, Robert H. Non-urban oppositions in Latin America. See *HLAS 42:1927*.

8012 Elkin, Judith Laikin. Jews of the Latin American republics. Chapel Hill: The University of North Carolina Press, 1980. 298 p.; bibl.; plates; tables.

Outstanding work on a neglected and formidable subject. Thoroughly documented (multilingual bibliography runs 22 p.), the book is that rare combination of careful scholarship and good reading. It traces the Jewish experience from the Iberian peninsula to the present. Author offers a penetrating analysis of the "diabolization" of Jews in Iberian culture and its various Latin American manifestations, down to present-day anti-Semitism (see item **6636**). The final chapter, which compares the Jewish experience in the US and Latin America, sheds much light on the nature of prejudice, alienation and assimilation in both regions. Includes numerous tables on demography, migration, labor patterns, etc. Highly recommended. [Ed.]

8013 Fals Borda, Orlando. The negation of sociology and its promise: perspectives of social science in Latin America today (LARR, 15:1, 1980, p. 161–166)

Articles that should be read by all sociologists, not just Latin Americanists. Fals Borda discusses four new developments in the social sciences in Latin America that he finds both interesting and productive: 1) modesty in research; 2) primacy of the qualitative; 3) autonomous development of theoretical models; 4) interdisciplinary research; and 5) broader acceptance of individual action and commitment as validating elements for research. [L. Pérez]

8014 Firebaugh, Glenn. Structural determinants of urbanization in Asia and Latin America: 1950–1970 (ASA/ASR, 44:2, April 1979, p. 199–215, bibl., tables)

Analysis of urbanization and development indicators from 27 Asian and Latin American countries suggests that urbanization is caused not only by economic growth, but also by adverse agrarian conditions. Two of these conditions, agricultural density and the existence of plantation agriculture, appear to be significant determinants of the degree of urbanization. [C.H. Waisman]

Fogel, Walter. United States immigration policy and unsanctioned migrants. See item **7035**.

Formación de la mujer en el mundo actual. See item **4325**.

8015 Fox, Robert W. Tendencias del crecimiento de la población urbana en América Latina. Washington: D.C. Inter-American Development Bank, 1975. 108 p.; tables.

Projection of the urban population of Argentina, Brazil, Chile, Mexico, Peru, and Venezuela up to the year 2000. Study includes a report on the findings, detailed case studies by country, a description of methodology used, and projections for all significant metropolitan areas. [C.H. Waisman]

8016 Fuerza de trabajo y movimientos laborales en América Latina. Rubén Kaztman y José Luis Reyna, compiladores. México: Colegio de México, 1979. 337 p.; bibl.

Collection of papers that evaluate the literature on the Latin American working class, focusing on three main questions: 1) the weak structural power of the labor force; 2) the dependent nature of the unions, vis-à-vis the state and/or the employers; and 3) the ambiguous nature of working-class ideologies. Four papers consider different aspects of the composition of the labor force and the urban labor markets: the volume of the labor supply (Muñoz and Oliveira); theories of employment (Singer); the dynamics of labor markets, especially in the "peripheral" sectors (Tokman); and the global issue of development and employment (Peattie). Labor movements are discussed in six papers: Sigal and Torre analyze the general problem of heteronomy and the crisis of the state; Blasco examines the mechanisms of collective bar-

gaining; Zapata discusses trade unions; Jelin focuses on working class orientations and ideologies; and Faletto analyzes the political behavior of the labor movement. In an appendix, Eckstein examines the functioning of the labor markets and the labor movement in Cuba. This collection represents the "state-of-the-art" in the study of the Latin American working class. [C.H. Waisman]

8020 Gilhodès, Pierre. Fuerzas e instituciones políticas en América Latina. Presentación, Oscar Arango Gaviria; carátula, Carlos Ruiz; fotografía carátula, Jorge Silva. Pereira, Colombia: Publicaciones Universidad Libre de Pereira, 1979. 252 p. (Publicaciones Universidad Libre de Pereira; 2)

Volume contains seven lectures delivered by French professor Gilhodès at the Universidad Libre in Bogotá. Topics covered include: dependence and foreign investments; social classes; pressure groups; political parties; electoral behavior; and the military. Intended for a broad, non-academic audience. [A. Ugalde]

8021 González Casanova, Pablo. Sistema y clase en los estudios de América Latina (UNAM/RMS, 40[40]:3, julio/sept. 1978, p. 867–880)

Systems analysis, whether functionalist, Marxist, or structuralist, is the approach that prevails in contemporary Latin American sociology. González Casanova contends that from this perspective groups and movements disappear as actors, and history becomes the analysis of the variations and mutations of the system. Another consequence of the approach is that empirical work becomes classificatory. Author calls for sociological research, which can only be "a concrete analysis of a concrete situation," to concentrate anew on classes, and their alliances and conflicts. [C.H. Waisman]

8023 Harris, Richard L. Marxism and the agrarian question in Latin America (LAP, 5[4]:19, Fall 1978, p. 2–26)

Overview of the key issues and problems found in the Marxist literature on agrarianism. Author is positive about the theoretical and practical significance of Marxism for understanding the transformation of rural Latin American societies. He emphasizes the need for recognizing the heterogeneous character of the rural population of Latin America in order to improve mobilization strategies. [D.W. Dent]

8024 Herrera Lane, Felipe. Las políticas culturales y la identidad latinoamericana. Santiago, Chile: Instituto de Ciencia Política, Universidad Católica de Chile, 1977. 40 leaves; bibl. (Cuadernos del Instituto de Ciencia Política; no. 15)

Leading Latin American international official discusses the need for systematic cultural policies in Latin America that would conserve and guarantee human freedom. Latin American nations are slowly becoming aware of their cultures, and are developing the organizational and financial mechanisms for the protection of their cultural heritage, and for cultural creativity. Herrera also analyzes different aspects of the Latin American cultural identity: the Hispanic dimension; the effect of the idea of progress; cultural conflict; alienation; and reactions to consumerism. [C.H. Waisman]

8025 Houtart, François. Religion et lutte des classes en Amérique Latine (FERES/SC, 26:2/3, 1979, p. 195–236)

Discussion of the historical role of the Latin American Catholic Church in social conflict. Author analyzes the function of the Church in the constitution of colonial society, the religious support for populist regimes, and Church opposition to the "national security" doctrine of contemporary authoritarian regimes. He argues that, even though the Church as an institution tends to identify itself with the powerholders, it also reflects the contradictions inherent in the society, by expressing the religious interests and aspirations of different social groups. [C.H. Waisman]

8026 Huizer, Gerrit. Ciencia social aplicada y acción política: notas sobre nuevos enfoques (UNAM/RMS, 41[41]:3, julio/sept. 1979, p. 1013–1040, bibl.)

Humanistic essay advocates the use of social science research for the betterment of mankind. Author draws on his extensive fieldwork experience in Latin America to argue that unless theory is followed by and grounded in applied research, grave errors will ensue. Thus, when innovations based on "sound western theory" are rejected by the peasantry, social scientists tend to attribute the peasants' behavior to primitive values. However, fieldwork would reveal that the rejection reflects the peasants' understanding of the existing power structure and their knowledge that the powerful eventually use innovations to exploit them further. [A. Ugalde]

8028 Ianni, Octávio. Escravidão e racismo. São Paulo: Editora HUCITEC, 1978. 142 p.; bibl. (Coleção Estudos brasileiros)

Collection of essays surveys relations among slavery, capitalism and racism in the Americas. Author, a social scientist, reviews recent scholarship, especially that of US historians. His principal thesis is that capitalism created and then destroyed slavery, but that it still incorporates racism. [S. Harkess]

8029 Kaplan, Marcos. Deficit de la izquierda y radicalización cristiana en América Latina (NSO, 36, mayo/junio 1978, p. 5–13)

Author argues that the emergence of mass Christian radicalism in Latin America is the result of the inefficiency of the traditional revolutionary left. The latter, as a consequence of its dogmatism and sectarianism, would have been unable to incorporate all the mobilized and radicalized forces. Kaplan concludes that the presence of the Christian left "ratifies the infinite wealth of the social-historical movement," in which the variety of tendencies of the left represent different aspects of the same revolutionary process. [C.H. Waisman]

8030 ———. El leviatán criollo: estatismo y sociedad en la América Latina contemporánea (UNAM/RMS, 40[40]:3, julio/sept. 1978, p. 795–830)

Discussion of the relative autonomy of the state in Latin America. Although the roots of statism and militarism developed in colonial times, these characteristics of the state became central starting in 1930. Author analyzes state intervention in the structuring and reproduction of society. He focuses on the state's instruments for performing the following five functions: 1) creation and preservation of the conditions of structuring and reproduction through collective organization and economic policy; 2) institutionalization and maintenance of consensus; 3) coercion; 4) education and propaganda; and 5) participation in international relations. [C.H. Waisman]

8031 Landsberger, Henry A. Continuity and change in Latin America's rural structure: changing perspectives in the study of rural Latin America (*in* The process of rural transformation: Eastern Europe, Latin America, and Australia. Edited by Ivan Volgyes, Richard E. Lonsdale, and William P. Avery. New York: Pergamon Press, 1979, p. 269–288)

In the decade of the 1970s, social scientists have increasingly advocated Marxist solutions to the problem of modernization of the Latin American peasantry. Author argues that there are no scientific grounds to support the belief that the implementation of leftist programs will improve the quality of life of the peasantry any more than earlier, unsuccessful capitalist efforts. A questionable apology for social science conservatism. [A. Ugalde]

8032 Latin American Centre for Economic and Social Documentation. Interpretaciones sociológicas sociopolíticas del desarrollo de América Latina: bibliografía de 25 años. Santiago de Chile: Naciones Unidas, CEPAL, 1975. 2 v. (658 p.); indexes.

This very useful ECLA publication is a bibliography of 1,500 works published 1950–75 on the economic, social, and political development of Latin America. Almost 85 percent of the works included were found in libraries in Santiago, Chile. Contains analytical and author indexes. [C.H. Waisman]

Levine, Daniel H. Authority in church and society: Latin American models. See item **6058.**

8033 Maduro, Otto. Avertissements épistémologico-politiques pour une sociologie latino-americaine des religions (FERES/SC, 26:2/3, 1979, p. 179–194)

The task of sociology of religion is to apprehend the multiple relationship between a society and the religious systems that operate in it. However, the author contends, since knowledge of that relationship is always partial, partisan, presumptive, and provincial, an "epistemologico-political reflection" is necessary. Maduro examines issues such as the meaning of the totality; the nature of reality and knowledge; values and interests; science and political action; religion as an object of knowledge; the degree of generalization in science; ethnocentrism and political constraints; and the language of sociology. His goal is to produce research that provides "a systematic re-elaboration of the experience

lived by the Latin American popular strata." [C.H. Waisman]

8035 Marini, Ruy Mauro. La crisis de la sociología política latinoamericana (*in* Problemas económicos y sociales de América Latina. Raúl Prebisch et al. Bogotá: Ediciones Universidades Simón Bolívar y Libre de Pereira, 1979, p. 161–166)

Relates the evolution of Latin American political sociology to the stages of economic and social development of Latin American societies. The current hegemonic crisis produces a parallel crisis in the paradigms of political sociology. [C.H. Waisman]

8036 Martins, José de Souza. Sobre o modo capitalista de pensar. São Paulo: HUCITEC, 1978. 82 p.; bibl. (Coleção Ciências sociais: Série Linha de frente)

Four brief, trenchant lectures and essays on capitalism's production of ideas—including common sense and scientific knowledge—necessary to its reproduction. For Martins sociology has the potential to support or transform capitalism. His specific concerns in this volume are fetishism, the university, and rural sociology. [S. Harkess]

El Medio ambiente en México y América Latina. See item **8111.**

8038 Meios de comunicação, realidade e mito. Jorge Werthein, organizador; pref. de Fernando Henrique Cardoso; tradução de Maria Cândida Diaz Bordenave, Sigrid Sarti, Teresinha J. Direne; capa, Haniel. São Paulo: Companhia Editora Nacional, 1979. 277 p.; bibl.; ill. (Biblioteca universitária: Série 2a., Ciências sociais; v. 55)

Collection of nine essays by European, Latin and North American sociologists, and others on the effects of international domination of mass communication. They treat the following topics: how external ideological domination maintains the status quo of dependent nations; foreign control of means of communication as a mechanism of domination (including extensive documentation by Nordenstreng and Varis); and internal inequalities in access; and communications and cultural dependency theories. One of two articles by Brazilians concerns national communications policy. [S. Harkess]

8040 La Mujer: explotación, lucha, liberación. Clara Eugenia Aranda et al. México: Editorial Nuestro Tiempo, 1976. 369 p.;

bibl.; index (Colección Temas de actualidad)

Eight essays written by five separate authors who offer a "planteamiento marxista" of the feminist question in Latin America and who are very critical of "reformist" positions. Margarita de Leonardo writes about women and social classes in Mexico, concentrating on industrial labor from 1930–74. Another essay by the same author treats education and women in Mexico, and includes an interesting discussion of the effect of gender on educational performance. Jorge Carrión in "La Mujer: Continente Oscuro" studies the dominant class ideology keeping women in subordinate positions. Teresa Arreola deals with birth-control programs, which she sees as a weapon of imperialism ("guerrillas are killed in the uterus" viewpoint). Clara Eugenia Aranda deals in very general terms with capitalism and women, offering no new material, merely a review of secondary sources. Elaine Levine and Clara Eugenia Aranda end the book by stating that socialism is the solution and men are not enemies. The contributors do not refer to works by other Marxists who have addressed the subject more specifically. [N. Valdés]

8041 Mujer y sociedad en América Latina. Selección y prólogo, Lucía Guerra-Cunningham. Irvine: Universidad de California; Santiago, Chile: Editorial del Pacífico, 1980. 261 p.; bibl.

Collection of 19 brief readings on a broad range of topics related to women, divided into two major themes: 1) change and marginality, and 2) Latin American women as depicted in the arts. [L. Pérez]

8042 Myers, George C. Fécondité et mobilité en Amérique Latine (Population [Institut National d'Etudes Démographiques, Paris] 35:6, nov./déc. 1980, p. 1041–1055, tables)

Surveys sponsored by the Centro Latinoamericano de Demografía in Buenos Aires, Río, Bogotá, San José, Mexico City, and Caracas provide the data for this study of the relationship between fertility and migration. Although female migrants to cities have higher fertility than female city-dwellers, the author maintains that migration itself is not responsible for higher fertility. [L. Pérez]

8043 Noggler, Othmar. Glaube und Sozialer Umbruch in Lateinamerika (ZMR,

57:4, Okt, 1973, p. 243–261)

Contains synopses of papers presented at a symposium on Religion and Social Change in Latin America, held at El Escorial in 1972. The following themes, among others, were addressed: Renato Poblete "The Question of Secularization in Latin America;" Enrique Dussel "The Impact of Christianity on Social Change within a Historical Context;" Miguel J. Bonino "Social Change in the Non-Catholic Denomination;" Juan Luis Segundo "The Elites;" Joseph Comblin "Social Movements in Latin America;" and Rolando Ames "Socio-Economic Factors in the Process of Liberation." This was a major meeting of students of liberation theology and social change and political activism in Latin America. [G.M. Dorn]

8045 Oszlak, Oscar. Critical approaches to the study of state bureaucracy: a Latin-American perspective (UN/ISSJ, 31:4, 1979, p. 661–681)

Author criticizes the literature on Latin American public bureaucracy for its misconceptions and intellectual clichés; its application of concepts derived from the study of private organizations to the study of the state; and its neglect of the social, cultural, and historical environment in which bureaucracies operate. Oszlak argues that in order to understand the social impact of public administration, it is necessary to analyze the internal differentiation of the bureaucracy and its relationship to the civil society. He emphasizes the intrinsically conflicting nature of the state bureaucracy's functions and the need to place analytical factors in their historical context by studying the development process of bureaucracies. [C.H. Waisman]

8046 ———. Notas críticas para una teoría de la burocracia estatal (IDES/DE, 19:74, julio/sept. 1979, p. 211–250, bibl.)

Author criticizes various approaches to the study of state bureaucracy: the historical-structural tradition; the administrative-organizational school; the models utilized by political scientists; and the paradigms implicit in administrative reform literature. Each of these approaches defines its unit of analysis differently, and is likely to generate different research questions. However, they all fail to establish a level of analysis that clarifies the inter-relationship between global social processes and the dynamics of the state bureaucracy, and in most cases they exhibit privatistic or ethnocentric biases. Oszlak emphasizes the specificity of the bureaucracy as well as the need to examine the historical and contextual determinants of bureaucratic behavior. Discussion includes Latin American evidence. [C.H. Waisman]

8047 Ozanam de Andrade, Raymundo.
Nuevas formas de hegemonía militar en América Latina (NS, 3:5/6, 1978, p. 44–52)

An analysis of the "new militarism" in Latin America. Since the 1960s, military dictatorships of a new type have been established in Brazil, Argentina, Peru, and other countries. Rather than acting as immediate representatives of various political forces, or seizing power in a situation of stalemate, the military have now developed their own conception of the national future, and consider their domination the means of realizing it. Author attributes this shift to the impossibility of bourgeois hegemony in "deformed" and dependent societies. The new militarism was produced by changes in the internal relations of forces and in the functioning of the world system. [C.H. Waisman]

8050 Petras, James F. Critical perspectives on imperialism and social class in the Third World. New York: Monthly Review Press, 1978. 314 p.; bibl.

Considerable coverage of Latin American Marxist analysis seeking principally to incorporate dependency notions with more traditional ideas of "class." [J.M. Hunter]

8051 ———. Imagen y realidades de la violencia: los Estados Unidos y América Latina (UNAM/RMS, 40:40[E], 1978, p. 195–231)

Comparative examination of the role of violence in the accumulation of capital in the US and Latin America, from colonial times to the present. Petras argues that large-scale violence has accompanied the process of colonization, economic expansion and political consolidation; and has been utilized as an instrument for social change both in the US and in Latin America. Violence has been not only the midwife of revolution, but also the midwife of accumulation. [C.H. Waisman]

———. The Latin American agrotransformation from above and outside its social and political implications. See item **6068**.

8052 La política de población en América Latina, 1974–1978. Santiago: Centro Latinoamericano de Demografía, 1979. 171 p.; graphs; tables (Cuadernos del CELADE; 1)

First issue of *Cuadernos del CELADE* contains eight separately-authored chapters by members of the CELADE staff. They deal with different aspects of population policies throughout Latin America: the demographic context, intergovernmental meetings on population, the institutional framework of population policies, population redistribution policies, fertility-related policies, international migration, statistical bases for policy-making, and the role of international financial assistance. [L. Pérez]

8054 Rivera, Julius. Latin America: a sociocultural interpretation. New York: Irvington Publishers: distributed by Halsted Press, 1978. 246 p.; 1 leaf of plates; bibl.; ill.

A reedition, with an added 34-p. postscript that contains helpful new data on population, trade areas, Latin American integration, and a useful overview of developments in the 1970s. [Q. Jenkins]

8055 Ruddle, Kenneth and **Ray Chesterfield.** Traditional skill training and labor in rural societies (JDA, 12:4, July 1978, p. 389–398, ill., tables)

Authors demonstrate the tremendous amount of concern and time devoted to teaching skills in rural societies. If the process they describe is pervasive, study raises some important questions regarding development. [Q. Jenkins]

8056 Safa, Helen Icken. The changing class composition of the female labor force in Latin America (LAP, 4:4[15], Fall 1977, p. 126–136, bibl.)

Examination of changes in female participation in the labor force. Increases in female employment tend to benefit women from the upper and middle classes more than those from the lower classes. Lower-class females are likely to remain locked in marginal jobs with little opportunity for upward mobility. The political consequences of this pattern are that women entering the white-collar world are mostly young and withdrawn after marriage; they are not, therefore, prone to express discontent. On the other hand, employment for working-class females is less likely to develop, due to the structural characteristics of Latin American industrialization. [C.H. Waisman]

8057 Silva Fuenzalida, Ismael. Sociedad, marginalidad y tecnología en América Latina (NSO, 42, mayo/junio 1979, p. 49–60, ill., plate)

Discusses functionalist and Marxist approaches to the analysis of social marginality in Latin America. In the first of these theories, marginality appears as a pathological and conjunctural problem, the lowest rank is a stratification continuum. On the other hand, in Marxist approaches, marginality is conceptualized as a consequence of Latin America's dependent role in the international economy, and thus becomes a "necessary" structural component. As an alternative, author examines a "structural-culturalist" hypothesis, according to which marginals are outside the class system, an "extra-systemic proletariat." [C.H. Waisman]

Sofer, Eugene F. and **Mark D. Szuchman.** City and society: their connection in Latin American historical research. See *HLAS 42:1816.*

8059 Stavenhagen, Rodolfo. El campesinado y las estrategias del desarrollo rural. México: Centro de Estudios Sociológicos, Colegio de México, 1977. 31 p. (Cuadernos del CES; 19)

Criticism of capitalist approaches to rural development which only produce increases in agricultural output. Author proposes integral strategies to improve the quality of life of the peasantry that could vary from region to region in response to historical, economic and cultural variations. [A. Ugalde]

8060 ———. La sociedad plural en América Latina (*in* Problemas económicos y sociales de América Latina. Raúl Prebisch et al. Bogotá: Ediciones Universidades Simón Bolivar y Libre de Pereira, 1979, p. 215–231 [Colección Universidad y pueblo; 381])

Excellent summary of reasons for and conditions of exploitation of Amerindian ethnic units by dominant national cultures. Offers a bleak prognosis of these ethnic groups' future predicting either continuing exploitation or ethnocide. [A. Ugalde]

8061 Symposium on Equality of Opportunity in Employment in the American Region, *Panama, 1973.* Equality of opportunity in employment in the American region: problems and policies: report and documents of a regional symposium (Panama, 1–12 October 1973). Geneva: International Labour Office, 1974. 133 p.; bibl.

Collection of Symposium papers on problems and policies relating to equality of opportunity and treatment in employment in the US, Canada, and several Latin American countries. Topics include: the existence of different ethnic and cultural groups; their place in the occupational and reward systems; the role of economic, legal, and cultural factors in the maintenance of discrimination; and methods for the promotion of equality of opportunity (educational and legislative action, economic and social policy, and action by employers' and workers' organizations). [C.H. Waisman]

8062 Tejeira, Otilia Arosemena de. La jaula invisible: la mujer en América Latina: ensayos. México: B. Costa-Amic, 1977. 142 p.; bibl. (Colección Escritores hispanoamericanos; 10)

Personal reflections by former president of the Inter-American Women's Commission written for the general public. Work contains platitudes and doubtful assertions that contradict social science data. [A. Ugalde]

8063 Thompson, William R. and **Jon A. Christopherson.** A multivariate analysis of the correlates of regime vulnerability and proneness of the military coup (NIU/JPMS, 7:2, Fall 1979, p. 283–289, bibl., tables)

Multivariate analysis of indicators of regime vulnerability of military coups in Latin America and sub-Saharan Africa. Indicators used are: economic development, social mobilization; trade dependency; government extractive capability; age of the political system; military strength; and coup experience. Regional aggregations produce stronger regression coefficients than a "world" equation, but these indicators still fail to account for most of the variance. [C.H. Waisman]

8064 Torres Novoa, Carlos Alberto. Sociología de la religión: religión y praxis social en América Latina (USB/F, 21:61, enero/abril 1979, p. 89–104)

General discussion of the ideological and political changes in the Catholic Church since the 1960s. Author examines the development of the "theology of liberation," the radicalization of a sector of the Church and of the Catholic lay organizations, the reconsideration, by some segments of the Church, of the Christian-Marxist opposition, and the emergence of activist Christian movements. He analyzes three different pastoral types: "traditionalist," "modernizing," and "popular;" and discusses the conflict among different factions of the Church, especially in authoritarian contexts. [C.H. Waisman]

8065 Torres Riva, Edelberto. La crisis de la dominación burguesa en América Latina (*in* Clases sociales y crisis política en América Latina: Seminario de Oaxaca [see *HLAS 41:9007*] p. 13–112)

Analysis of class relations and the political crisis after 1930 in the "lesser" Latin American countries. Political crisis is defined as the disadjustment accompanying modifications in a society's power structure due to a weakening of the traditional bases of power and the irruption of new social forces. Author discusses the economic and political consequences of the Depression, World War II, and the post-war period, focusing on the inability of the bourgeoisie to become hegemonic. [C.H. Waisman]

8066 Tyree, Andrea; Moshe Semyonov; and Robert W. Hodge. Gaps and glissandos: inequality, economic development and social mobility in 24 countries (ASA/ASR, 44:3, June 1979, p. 410–424, bibl., tables)

Examination of the relationship between level of economic development and inter-generational mobility in 24 countries, including five in Latin America. Concludes that the observed effect is spurious, and derives from the shape of the stratification system which is shaped by reward distributions and occupational distributions. Argues that mobility is a function of the existence of positions ordered in a continuum of incomes, and of the availability of many middle-status jobs. [C.H. Waisman]

Varese, Stefano. Una dialéctica negada: notas sobre la multietnicidad mexicana. See item **8133.**

8067 Velagapudi, Gunvor. La mujer y el empleo en América Latina. Santiago de Chile: Organización Internacional del Trabajo, Programa Regional del Empleo para América-Latina y el Caribe, 1976. 17, 16, 3 p.; bibl.; ill. (Documento de trabajo. PREALC; 99)

Review of literature on factors affecting supply and demand of female labor in Latin America. Also traces size and evolution of female labor force in urban and rural areas between 1960–70. Includes a good bibliography of official documents. [N. Valdés]

8068 Véliz, Claudio. The centralist tradition of Latin America. Princeton, N.J.: Princeton University Press, 1980. 355 p.; bibl.; index.

History of the Latin American state. Author contends that the present wave of authoritarianism is not an aberration, but rather the current form of a long-standing secular trend of bureaucratic rationalization and centralization. This trend is not, as in the "Northwest," a consequence of the reformation and industrial and democratic revolutions, since Latin America did not experience feudalism, and was bypassed by the religious, economic, and political transformations mentioned above. Centralism in Latin America derives from the institutions of the Castilian monarchy, and its social base is the large tertiary sector that evolved since colonial times. In Véliz's interpretation, this centralist tradition has shaped Latin American societies, and is a constitutive principle of their economy, their politics, and their culture. [C.H. Waisman]

8069 Vessuri, Hebe M.C. Technological change and the social organization of agricultural production (UC/CA, 21:3, June 1980, p. 315–327)

Discusses the structural framework of technological change in agriculture, concluding that, since agricultural techniques form part of technocultural complexes, prevailing social relations are the central factors in the explanation of the nature and direction of technological change. In capitalist social formations, system dynamics favors the conception and persistence of techniques that maintain continuity. Author examines the role of the state in generating and adopting technological innovations in underdeveloped countries. Includes extensive comments by other anthropologists and author's replies. [C.H. Waisman]

8071 Weaver, Jerry L. The politics of Latin American family-planning policy (JDA, 12:4, July 1978, p. 415–437, table)
In the late 1960s and early 1970s, there was a major shift in family planning policies in Latin America as most governments came to support, or at least tolerate family planning. The author analyzes this reorientation using a model of the policy formation process that is based on Warren and Ilchman. He concludes that, at the level of the "core combination," the shift was supported by technocrats, officeholders and the representatives of external assistance agencies, who were allied with middle class professionals, and was opposed by senior military officers allied with the Church and the "oligarchy." The media usually support family planning, while students, leftist intellectuals, and extreme leftists usually oppose it. [C.H. Waisman]

8072 Wiarda, Iêda Siqueira. Women, population policy, and democracy in Latin America (*in* The Continuing struggle for democracy in Latin America [see item **6028**] p. 107–126)
Good overview of systematic discrimination against women in Latin American political and legal systems. [M.D. Hayes]

Wilkie, James W. and Edna Monzón de Wilkie. Dimensions of elitelore: an oral history questionnaire. See *HLAS 42:1953.*

8073 Williamson, Robert C. Orientation to change in advanced and developing societies: a cross-national sample (NYAS/A, 284, March 18, 1977, p. 565–581, tables)
Cross-cultural study compares four examples of industrialized Western cultures, two from Latin American nations in different stages of development. The analysis gauges, from a functionalist point of view, the factors involved in the process of modernization. [Q. Jenkins]

Würtele, Werner. La FITIM y las corporaciones multinacionales. See item **6095.**

MEXICO AND CENTRAL AMERICA

ANTONIO UGALDE, *Associate Professor of Sociology, University of Texas, Austin*

POLITICAL EVENTS IN SOUTH and Central America have resulted in a continued high rate of migration of social scientists to Mexico and Costa Rica. This intellectual enrichment has promoted research of high quality in these two countries.

In the case of Mexico, important additional factors are the continuing expansion of its university system and the relatively free ideological environment in which sociologists work. It can be said without exaggeration that Mexican sociology is close to achieving a leading position in the world in terms of both its theoretical contributions to the field and its methodological sophistication. The trend is exemplified by the following books by: Gomez-Jara (item **8093**), Leñero Otero (item **8102**), and Paré (item **8120**), all of which are important theoretically; and those by Castillo (item **8082**) and Muñoz and Stern (item **8113**) which are methodologically elegant.

In Central America the work by Torres Rivas in Costa Rica (item **8160**) and the volume edited by Camacho (item **8151**) should be singled out for their contribution towards an understanding of class configuration and the nature of some of the region's basic social problems. It is not possible to review the most notable sociological contributions from this area without referring to the work edited by the late Archbishop of San Salvador (item **8152a**). Refreshing for its humanity and philosophical depth, this volume is of undeniable value to scholars and policymakers attempting to understand the nature of violence in that country.

Two broad areas dominate the sociological literature of this period: 1) political sociology, primarily concerned with rural development, class configuration and conflict, and the social problems created by foreign capital penetration; and 2) formal demography, with emphasis on internal and international migration, labor force and fertility.

Two major events of interest to sociologists took place in the region. The Latin American Sociological Association met in Panama City in Dec. 1979 under the able leadership of its president, Marco Gandásegui. A complete set of approximately 50 papers presented at the conference can be obtained by writing to CELA, Apartado 6-3093, El Dorado, Panama, Panama, at a cost of 60 US dollars. The 5th World Congress of Rural Sociology, held in Mexico City in Aug. 1980, attracted scholars from the five continents. In 1972 in preparation for the World Congress, Mexican sociologists organized the First Meeting of Students and Schools of Sociology in Guadalajara, and the First National Conference of Sociology and Rural Development in Chapingo. The Chapingo conference was held in conjunction with the National Peasants' Meeting, and it approved a resolution calling for a sociology dedicated to social change in the service of the poor (sociología comprometida).

MEXICO

8074 Alba-Hernández, Francisco. La población de México: evolución y dilemas. México: Centro de Estudios Económicos y Demográficos, Colegio de México, 1977. 189 p.; bibl.; graphs.

Useful pocket-book introduction to Mexico's demography. Short chapters are organized by traditional topics: population growth (with fertility, fecundity, and mortality by cause and by region); internal and international migration; civil status and age; and employment. Last four chapters contain projections to year 2000. These chapters insightfully relate demographic changes, social problems and policy issues. See also item **5102**.

8075 Alegría, Juana Armanda. Mujer, viento y ventura. México: Editorial Diana, 1977. 221 p.; bibl.; ill.

In first five chapters, psychologist Alegría presents her thoughts on female sexual liberation, abortion, mass media influence on sex-role stereotypes, and the potential of small cooperatives for women. Also includes brief and interesting personal diary of events of the 1975 Conference of the International Year of the Woman. Concludes with nine short papers on topics of varying quality by female Mexican professionals.

8076 Alzate Montoya, Rubelia. El desenvolvimento de la estructura del poder en una comunidad agraria (UNAM/RMCPS, 23:88, abril/junio 1977, p. 159-186, bibl.)

Essay views government from a Marxist perspective, as an instrument of the capitalist class. Well-documented examples of legal, political, economic, and social techniques for exploitation and destruction of the peasantry are drawn from fieldwork in a Toluca village.

8077 Arizpe, Lourdes. Mujeres migrantes y economía campesina: análisis de una cohorte migratoria a la ciudad de Mexico; 1940-1970 (III/AI, 38:2, abril/junio 1978, p. 303-326, bibl., tables)

Secondary analysis of a sample of 79 rural female migrants to Mexico City between 1940-70. Variables cross-tabulated are: family size of migrant by occupation of migrant's household head and by migrant's birth position, and age at migration by migration companions. Article also examines different occupational and social mobility by age cohorts.

Arnold, Linda. Social, economic, and political status in the Mexico City central bureaucracy: 1808-1822. See *HLAS 42:2008.*

Arrom, Silvia M. Marriage patterns in Mexico City: 1811. See *HLAS 42:2009.*

8078 Bartra, Roger. Modes of production and agrarian imbalances (UN/ISSJ, 31:2, 1979, p. 226-236)

Discourse on class systems and modes

of production using Mexico's agricultural evolution as the basis for the discussion. Author distinguishes three social classes in the countryside: agrarian bourgeoisie, rural proletariat and the peasantry.

8079 Bustamante, Jorge A. Facts and perceptions of undocumented migration from Mexico (*in* U.S.-Mexico Relations [see item 3040] p. 171–182)

Citing his own fieldwork and other studies, Bustamante argues that undocumented workers do not displace US workers and are not a burden to US tax payers. Migrants satisfy US demand for cheap labor and reduce unemployment in Mexico; as such it is an international issue and should not be resolved unilaterally by the US.

8080 Cardoso, Lawrence A. Protestant missionaries and the Mexican: an environmentalist image of cultural differences (UCSD/NS, 7:1/2, 1978 [i.e. 1979] p. 223–236)

Historical materials presented in this paper illustrate the increasing contact protestant missionaries had with Mexican people after the Juárez reforms. Author indicates that these contacts were instrumental in the clergy's understanding Mexican culture and in opposing Anglo racism. Yet North American missionaries could not overcome their ethnocentrism and contributed to the Mexican's acculturation and acceptance of Anglo values.

8081 Careaga, Gabriel. Biografía de un joven de la clase media. 2. ed. México Editorial J. Mortiz, 1978. 160 p. (Cuadernos de Joaquín Mortiz; 45/46)

This study portrays the life of a professional in Mexico City. Author's overemphasis on the protagonist's sexual life leaves the reader wondering whether the biography represents a deviant personality or the "average" middle-class Mexican. Author fails to explain the methodology followed in the selection and editing of data. Entertaining but of limited sociological value.

8082 Castillo V., Gustavo del. Crisis y transformación de una sociedad tradicional. Portada, Marcos Kurtycz, sobre una foto de G. del Castillo. México: Centro de Investigaciones Superiores del INAH, 1979. 177 p.; bibl.; ill. (Ediciones de la Casa Chata; 10)

This is a skillful investigation of the political history of the municipality of Arandas (Altos de Jalisco, Mexico), one of the many rural areas left untouched by the 1910 Revolution. Author makes a significant contribution to the study of the evolution of *caciquismo*, social class transformation and conflict in rural Mexico and the role of the PRI in incorporating the region to national politics.

8083 Clawson, D.L. and D.R. Hoy. Nealtican, Mexico: a peasant community that rejected the "Green Revolution" (AJES, 38:4, Oct. 1979, p. 371–388, map)

Nealtican is one of the villages included in the Plan Puebla of the International Maize and Wheat Improvement Center (CIMMYT) sponsored by the Rockefeller Foundation. Paper describes the peasants' logic for rejecting the project and attributes their refusal to accept it to the poverty of their village.

8084 Concheiro, Elvira; Antonio Gutiérrez; and Juan Manuel Fragosa. El poder de la gran burguesía. Diseñó la portada, Carlos Palleiro. México: Ediciones de Cultura Popular, 1979. 343 p.

This book is an important contribution to the political sociology of Mexico and consists of a scholarly study of the country's grand bourgeoisie. Authors divide the latter into three subtypes: 1) the Northern or "Monterrey Group," under the leadership of the Garza-Sada clan and including industrialists from Puebla and Jalisco as well as from the northeastern agrarian bourgeoisie, they consist of independent individuals who are antagonistic towards the government and very conservative in their political opinions; 2) the "Group of the Forties" refers to men who emerged after World War II, profiting from import-substitution policies, and who are closely intertwined with the upper echelons of Mexico's bureaucracy; and 3) the "Central Group" applies to individuals involved with financial capital, exemplified by firms such as BANCOMER, BANAMEX and CREMI, and a number of industrialists who occupy key posts in the government, men of moderate ideological views who represent the most powerful segment of all.

8085 Craig, Richard B. Human rights and Mexico's antidrug campaign (IDES/

DE, 19:74, julio/sept. 1979, p. 691–701, bibl.)

Well-written exposé on the use of dangerous herbicides and of how the police and army abuse their power in the countryside under the pretense of conducting antidrug campaigns. According to the author, the real objective of Mexico's campaign and its concomitant human rights violations is the wish to uproot rural guerrillas rather than marihuana plants or opium poppies.

8086 Davis, Charles L. The persistence of erosion of a legitimating revolutionary ideology among the lower class in Mexico City (NIU/JPMS, 7:1, Spring 1979, p. 35–52, bibl., tables)

Using a 1973 survey of 346 households, author explores reasons why Mexico City's lower classes support and believe the regime's rhetoric. Data were originally analyzed in a doctoral dissertation. Space limitations prohibit sufficient explanations of research procedures and statistical treatment.

8087 Deverre, Christian and Raúl Reissner. Les figures de l'Indien-problème: l'évolution de l'indigènisme méxican (FS/CIS, 68, 1980, p. 149–169, bibl., tables)

Well-documented history of Mexican public policies concerning Indians, from 1910 to present. Article emphasizes how contrasting views on development and modernization were held by both social scientists and members of the Instituto Nacional Indigenista where the divergence generated conflicts.

Díaz de Cossío, Roger. Sobre la educación y la cultura: alternativas de cambio. See item **4493.**

8088 Ehrlich, Paul R.; Loy Bilderback; and Anne H. Ehrlich. The golden door: international migration, Mexico, and the United States. New York: Ballantine Books, 1979. 402 p.; bibl.; index.

Lengthy background on Mexican history, development problems, US-Mexican relations, and US migration and population policies precede author's analysis of contemporary Mexican migration to the US. Although much of the information provided will be familiar to experts, the book includes some interesting sections on the US Immigration and Naturalization Service and its Border Patrol.

8089 Finkler, Kaja. From sharecroppers to entrepreneurs: peasant household production strategies under the *ejido* system of Mexico (UC/EDCC, 27:1, Oct. 1978, p. 103–120, tables)

Study of peasant village in the Mexquital Valley in Hidalgo reveals that sharecropping produces more economic benefits to sharecroppers than to landlords, increases economic differentiation among villagers and contradicts the egalitarian principles that supported the organization of *ejidos* after the Mexican Revolution. Author's hypotheses are based on 116 in-depth interviews with sharecroppers and observations conducted during an extended period of time.

8090 Gatti, Luis María and Graciela Alcalá. Los trabajadores asalariados de la zona citrícola de Nuevo León (CM/RE, 1:1, invierno 1980, p. 129–140, bibl.)

Vertically integrated citrus-fruit industry is the setting for the research on the relation between types of employment and class formation. Wage labor is predominant but not the only source of income for most workers. Variations in non-wage income and the workers' different relations to the means of production generate several class formations and lead to ideological fragmentation among laborers.

8091 Glantz, Susana. Manuel, una biografía política. Portada, Kurtycz. México: Centro de Investigaciones Superiores del Instituto Nacional de Antropolgía e Historia; México: Editorial Nueva Imagen, 1979. 226 p.

Drawing information from 80 hours of taped interviews, author compiles the life history of an *edijo* leader in Los Mochis (Michoacán). Interesting contribution to post-revolutionary agrarian politics. Author explains the methodology followed in the editing of tapes in the preface.

8092 Godwin, R. Kenneth. Mexican population policy: problems posed by participatory demography in a paternalistic political system (*in* The Future of Mexico. Edited by Lawrence E. Koslow. Tempe: Center for Latin American Studies, Arizona State University, 1977, p. 145–168)

The general principle that economic growth leads to a decline in population does not apply to Mexico where growth has not redistributed wealth or population-control programs changed cultural values that encourage large families. Given Mexican political realities, author doubts that collective incentives (i.e., public services to communities that reduce fertility rates) would improve wealth distribution or lead to a more successful strategy for population control.

8093 Gómez-Jara, Francisco A. Bonapartismo y lucha campesina en la Costa Grande de Guerrero. México: Editorial Posada, 1979. 321 p.; bibl.; ill. (Colección Ideas políticas)

Political history of the State of Guerrero from colonial days to the present provides a carefully documented exposé of the subjection of the peasantry to extreme political violence and exploitation by public officials and representatives of the national and international capitalist class. Author claims that the Mexican political system combines elements of the Asian mode of production, populism, Keynesian economics and Stalinism, which facilitates the bourgeoisie's exploitation of the working class. Acapulco's urbanization provides an excellent case for applying author's theoretical framework of agrarian politics to an urban setting.

8094 ———. 50 [i.e. Cincuenta] años de sociología rural en México (CNC/RMA, 13:1, enero/marzo 1980, p. 89–108, plate)

In this outstanding review of origins and contemporary ideological trends in Mexican rural sociology, author provides an important critical discussion of social scientists and research institutions, in terms of their theoretical perspectives, explains US influence in promoting functionalism, and analyzes liberal and neo-Marxist currents in the field.

8095 González de la Rocha, Mercedes and **Agustín Escobar Latapí.** Agricultura capitalista y procesos migratorios: un caso en el sur de Jalisco (CM/RE, 1:2, primavera 1980, p. 189–197)

According to article's thesis, internal and international migration in a small rural community of Jalisco are linked as follows: after returning from the US, migrants buy land from the poorer peasants with capital accumulated in the US whereupon the former owners or new landless peasants are forced to migrate to nearby towns and cities in search of work.

8096 Heer, David M. What is the annual net flow of undocumented Mexican immigrants to the United States? (PAA/D, 16:3, Aug. 1979, p. 417–424, bibl., table)

With figures from the Current Population Survey of the US Bureau of the Census, author gives seven estimates of netflow of Mexican undocumented workers to the US during the 1970–75 period. According to the calculations the yearly net migration flow falls between 82,300 and 232,400.

8097 Heilskov Rasmussen, Christian. Tamapatz, en landsby i Mexico. Redaktion, Bjørn Førde; fotos, Christian Heilskov Rasmussen, Bjørn Førde, Jens Lohmann, o.a. København: Mellemfolkeligt Samvirke, 1978. 40 p.; ill.; bibl.

Danish social scientist uses village of Tamapatz to show cycle of economic bondage (in this case, sugar and coffee cultivation) that enslaves the Mexican poor. Includes good photographs and numerous tables. [R.V. Shaw]

8098 Heller, Claude. Las condiciones internacionales del cambio social y participación política en México (CM/FI, 20:3, enero/marzo 1980, p. 411–426)

Interesting essay examines US responses to internal political crisis in Mexico. Author argues that a major concern of the US is for Latin American and Mexican "political" stability. He attributes the lack of US apprehension over the weakening legitimacy of Mexico's political system to the fragmentation of the Mexican left and the lack of an organized revolutionary movement.

8099 Indocumentados, mitos y realidades. México: Colegio de México, Centro de Estudios Internacionales, 1979. 238 p.; bibl.; graphs.

Consists of eight papers presented at a 1978 Colegio de Mexico symposium on illegal Mexican migration to the US. Also includes description and discussion of fieldwork findings and policy recommendations by Mexican and US experts. A significant work in which the often divergent views of Mexican and US scholars may be appreciated.

8100 Inmigrantes y refugiados españoles en México: siglo XX. Michael Kenny et al. México: Centro de Investigaciones Superiores del INAH, 1979. 369 p.; ill. (Ediciones de la Casa Chata; 8)

Excellent volume consists of five essays on 20th-century Spanish migration and settlement patterns in Puebla, Veracruz, Federal District, Tehuacan, Chihuahua and Torreón. Volume also explores differences between political refugees who arrived after the fall of the Republic and other migrants. Each essay discusses occupational status and mobility, social and economic organization of city migrants. The methodology is anthropological with in-depth interviews and relatively small samples.

8101 Kasschau, Patricia. Political alienation in a sample of young Mexican children (USC/SSR, 60:3, April 1976, p. 290–313, bibl., tables)

A 1971 Survey of 400 children (grades 2–9) following the conceptual approach of Greenstein and Hess. According to findings, a child's positive perception of the political system decreases with maturation and negative feelings towards the political system are more prevalent among upper and middle-class children than among lower-class children.

8102 Leñero Otero, Luis. Valores ideológicos y las políticas de población en México. Diseño de la portada, Jorge Silva R. México: Editorial Edicol, 1979. 236 p.; bibl. (Investigaciones, Sociología)

Mexico's official population policy changed radically in 1973 when, for the first time, the government (i.e., Echeverría's administration) endorsed population control programs. Leñero has written a brilliant study of this important change and of the policy formulation process that preceded it. The book examines how political compromises among various ideological groups were attained and the role of the bureaucracy in implementing birth-control programs. Author's study makes an important contribution to understanding the values of policy makers, bureaucrats and consumers as well as how the perception of these values by social classes determines the acceptance or rejection of population control programs. The research is based on in-depth interviews with policymakers, civil servants and practitioners of birth control programs.

8103 Lerner de Sheinbaum, Berta. México: una burocracia gobernante (UNAM/RMS, 41[41]:2, abril/junio 1979, p. 573–595) Theoretical discussion of the nature of

the political system in Mexico which, according to the author is best described as a "bureaucratic state." She does not believe that categories such as oligarchy, class and elites are meaningful in explaining the distribution of power in Mexico.

8104 Levenstein, Harvey. Sindicalismo norteamericano, braceros y "espaldas mojadas" (CH/HM, 28:2, oct./dic. 1978, p. 153–184, bibl.)

Article summarizes author's previously published research on the role of US and Mexican interest groups, particularly labor federations, in influencing US labor importation policies. Levenstein advocates a return to legalized labor imports.

8105 Logan, Kathleen. Migration, housing, and integration: the urban context of Guadalajara, Mexico (UA, 8:2, Summer 1979, p. 131–148, bibl.)

Explains Guadalajara's success in providing adequate housing and integration for rural migrants by examining available subdivisions developed by private interests. The subdivisions provide land and urban services at an affordable cost, and migrants build their own houses. Additional reasons for success are the special characteristics of migrants to Guadalajara, promotion of festivities by the Church and the progressiveness of some Church and city policies. Weak data and unconvincing explanations.

8106 Lomnitz, Larissa. Mechanisms of articulation between shantytown settlers and the urban system (UA, 7:2, Summer 1978, p. 185–205, bibl.)

After studying a poor neighborhood in Mexico City and observing two others, author develops a typology of asymmetric or patron-client relationships. Three main types of patrons are discussed: labor recruiters, political leaders, and brokers in the field of production.

8107 ——— and Marisol Pérez Lizaur. The history of a Mexican urban family (NCFR/JFH, 3:4, Winter 1978, p. 392–409, bibl., tables)

Data are gathered through unstructured interviews, participant observation and archival materials for a five-generation study of a prominent family. Scholarly research highlights relations between family networks and business activities and is based on Lévi-

Strauss' communication or exchange theory of messages, services, and women.

8108 Lustig, Nora and **Teresa Rendon.** Female employment, occupational status, and socioeconomic characteristics of the family in Mexico (UC/S, 5:1, Autumn 1979, p. 143–153, tables)

Statistical analysis of female participation in labor force based on a 1968 Family Income and Expenditures Survey by Banco de México. The study is limited by the exclusion of households headed by females. Two important findings are: rates of female employment increase with household income, and self-employed females tend to belong to low income groups.

8109 Lynn de Uriarte, Mercedes. Some perspectives in cross-cultural image manipulation (PCCLAS/P, 5, 1976, p. 25–44, plates)

Attempts to show that promotion of consumerism by US advertising firms in Mexico also promotes foreign values.

8110 McGoodwin, James Russell. Mexico's marginal inshore Pacific fishing cooperatives (CUA/AQ, 53:1, Jan. 1980, p. 39–47, bibl.)

Author attributes decline of inshore cooperatives in south Sinaloa to excessive federal controls, incompetent and corrupt government policies, natural catastrophes and counter-productive technological innovations. Also influential was the central government's policy of favoring the economically more profitable offshore shrimp cooperatives while ignoring the more marginal inshore ones.

8111 El Medio ambiente en México y América Latina. Edited by Francisco Szekely. México: Editorial Nueva Imagen, 1978. 159 p.

This excellent book, one of the first on the topic of the environment, properly studies it from an interdisciplinary perspective. Nine articles written by sociologists, environmental and sanitation engineers, demographers and economists treat five major themes: the ecosystem or general environment; water resources and contamination; environment and development; population; and human settlements. Five articles focus on Latin America in general and four on Mexico.

8112 Mendieta y Núñez, Lucio. Temas sociológicos de actualidad. México: Universidad Nacional Autónoma de México, 1978. 238 p.; bibl.

Author of this compilation is one of the founding fathers of Mexican sociology. His essays, written in a clear and jargon-free style, are addressed to the informed layman rather than to specialists. Half of them concern issues of crime and delinquency, the rest cover diverse topics such as population explosion, drugs, war, the younger generation, inflation and political sociology.

8113 Migración y desigualdad social en la ciudad de México: Humberto Muñoz, Orlandina de Oliveira, Claudio Stern, compiladores. México: Instituto de Investigaciones Sociales, Universidad Nacional Autónoma de México, 1977. 249 p.; bibl.; ill.

Articles in this volume report results of a carefully executed survey of 2,500 households in Mexico City (1970–71) jointly sponsored by the Universidad Nacional Autónoma de México and the Center for Economic and Demographic Studies of El Colegio de México. The first four articles describe the study's methodologial aspects and another 10 substantive articles are grouped in four sections according to the following topics: 1) socioeconomic and mobility differences between migrants and natives; 2) the ebb and flow of migration and ensuing demographic impact on Mexico City; 3) the city's capabilities for employing migrants; and 4) ideological differences among various occupational groups. Previously published in Mexican and Latin American journals, many of these essays are now conveniently available in one volume (see *HLAS 39:2999*).

8114 Montaño, Jorge. Los pobres de la ciudad en los asentamientos espontáneos: poder y política. Portada de Ricardo Harte. 2. ed. México: Siglo Veintiuno Editores, 1979. 224 p.; bibl. (Sociología y política)

In nine poor neighborhoods of Mexico City, Monterrey and Chihuahua, author examines issues of land tenure, neighborhood organization, leadership, political attitudes, behavior and attitudes towards the government. Chapter concerning government's policies and responses to demands of the urban poor is particularly enlightening. This is a landmark study in urban and political sociology and dispels the notion that political behavior is uniform throughout poor barrios.

8115 Moreno Toscano, Alejandra. La crisis en la ciudad (*in* México, hoy. Por José Ayala and others. Coordinado por Pablo González Casanova y Enrique Florescano. México: Siglo Veintiuno Editores, 1979, p. 152–176, bibl., table)

This is a penetrating analysis of the relationship between capitalist urban policies and the uncontrolled and phenomenal growth of Mexico City. But even more fascinating is author's explanation of how the same policies that generated political support for the PRI among slum dwellers facilitate the amassing of fortunes for land speculators and construction companies. Includes good documentation of bureaucratic chaos and infighting among several agencies responsible for urban policies.

8116 Novela, Victoria and **Augusto Urteaga.** La industria en los magueyales: trabajo y sindicatos en Ciudad Sahagún. Portada, Kurtycz. México: Centro de Investigaciones Superiores del Instituto Nacional de Antropología e Historia: Editorial Nueva Imagen, 1979. 229 p.; bibl.; ill.

Ciudad Sahagún (Hidalgo, Mexico) consists of a conglomerate of industrial state enterprises organized in the 1950s under growth pole theory. This book thoroughly documents the evolution of the city and the organizational and political aspects of labor unions and includes some especially interesting materials on how labor-conflicts are resolved in state enterprises. Using anthropological techniques of participant observation and in-depth interviewing, authors have written a significant monograph.

8117 Oswald, Ursula. Mecanismos de la implantación del capitalismo estatal y transformación de la estratificación social: desarrollo cooperativista (UNAM/RMCPS, 23:88, nuevo época, abril/junio 1977, p. 127–158)

Article provides additional information to the study by the author and Serrano (see item **8119**) but both articles present the same findings.

8118 ———. Penetración ideológica del campesinado a través de las estructuras productivas (Boletín de Antropología Americana [Instituto Panamericano de Geografía e Historia, México] 1, junio 1980, p. 117–123, ill., tables)

Examination of mechanisms of exploitation of *barbecho* pickers by Mexican government agencies and multinational pharmaceutical industries. Author attributes changes in traditional values and the practice of subsistence agriculture among the peasantry to the influence of government extension workers. Believes that the latter together with the introduction of consumerism has resulted in the peasants' dependence on outside political and economic forces and thus in the availability of their cheap labor.

8119 ——— and **Jorge Serrano.** El cooperativismo agrario en México: implantador del capitalismo estatal dependiente (UNAM/RMS, 40:40[E], 1978, p. 273–284)

Devastating evaluation of a rural development program funded by national banks and the World Bank in the *ejido* of Costa Chica in Guerrero. The sponsoring agencies imposed capital intensive technologies on the *ejido*, a shift from maize cultivation to livestock raising and the organization of a cooperative. Authors argue these changes led to the pauperization of *ejidatarios*. See also item **8117**.

8120 Paré, Luisa. El proletariado agrícola en México: campesinos sin tierra o proletarios agrícolas? México: Siglo Veintiuno Editores, 1977. 255 p.; bibl.; ill. (Sociología y política)

Important contribution to the study of class relations. Author details relations between rural proletarians (landless peasants) and semi-proletarians (seasonal salaried workers who are also *minifundistas*) and between these two classes and the rural bourgeoisie. Also describes labor organization and the trade union movement among the peasantry. Based on intensive fieldwork in Valle del Mesquital and the sugar-cane *ejido* of Atecingo.

8121 Petterson, John S. Fishing cooperatives and political power: a Mexican example (CUA/AQ, 53:1, Jan. 1980, p. 64–74, bibl.)

Author describes success of tuna cooperatives in Ensenada, Baja California, since their establishment in 1966. After examining their organization as well as the social, political, and economic benefits fishermen have gained from cooperativism, author suggests the Mexican example could be used for organizing US tuna cooperatives.

8122 Portes, Alejandro. Illegal immigration and the International System: lessons from recent legal Mexican immigrants to the United States (SSSP/SP, 26:4, April 1979, p. 425–438, tables)

Data drawn from a sample of undocumented workers suggest that large numbers of migrants do not originate in poor rural regions nor do they work in US agriculture but in urban services and industries. Author concludes migration will continue while wealth differentials between the two countries remain wide. US policy proposals dealing with illegal migration are also reviewed.

8123 Rendón G., Jorge Leopoldo. Participación de la mujer en la fuerza de trabajo, significado e implicaciones: el caso específico del Estado de México. México: Centro Nacional de Información y Estadísticas del Trabajo, 1977. 110 p.; bibl., graphs (Serie Avances de investigación; 1)

Secondary analysis of a 1973 household survey of I.D.R.H.E.M. Monograph provides frequencies and crosstabs of income, occupation, self-employment, unemployment by sex and age groups. Survey's sample size is not mentioned. Descriptive statistical analysis which could be useful for comparative purposes.

8124 Romero A., Lourdes and Ana María Quintanilla E. Prostitución y drogas: estudio psicológico de la prostitución en México y su relación con la farmacodependencia. México: Editorial Trillas, 1976 [i.e. 1977]. 192 p.; bibl.

Findings from 27 interviews with prostitutes in four Mexican cities are noted by generalizations unsupported by data. With the exception of alcohol no other drug appears to be related to prostitution. Monograph ends with sketches of five different "types" of prostitutes.

8125 Saldívar, Américo. Alianzas de clase y política del Estado mexicano (1970–1976). Puebla: Escuela de Filosofía y Letras, Universidad Autónoma de Puebla, 1977. 44 p.; bibl. (Serie Filosofía y letras; 6)

Consists of collection of hypotheses about class formation and alliances among dominant classes. Author criticizes role of Echeverría's administration in arbitrating class conflict but offers no empirical data to support his assertions.

8126 Schryer, Frans J. The rancheros of Pisaflores: the history of a peasant bourgeoisie in twentieth-century Mexico. Toronto; Buffalo: University of Toronto Press, 1980. xii, 210 p.; 2 leaves of plates; bibl.; ill.; index.

Political history of a rural municipality in the highlands of Hidalgo emphasizes class configuration and conflict from the Revolution to the present. Author suggests that government gained control of the peasantry by manipulating conflict among factions of the rural bourgeoisie. Solid fieldwork conducted under a Marxist theoretical perspective offers a refreshing and insightful view of rural politics in Mexico.

8127 Serrón, Luis A. Scarcity, exploitation, and poverty: Malthus and Marx in Mexico. With foreword by Irving M. Zeitlin. Norman: University of Oklahoma Press, 1980. 279 p.; bibl.; index.

Review of Mexico's literature on economic development and population growth leads author to conclude that poverty is not caused by population explosion but by a class system that exploits the peasantry and the working class.

8128 Singelmann, Peter. Rural collectivization and dependent capitalism: the Mexican collective ejido (LAP, 5[18]:3, Summer 1978, p. 38–61, bibl.)

Useful summary review of the fate of the collective *ejidos*, written from Guerrero, Bartra and Stavenhagen's imperialist/dependency perspective.

Smith, Peter H. The Mexican Revolution and the transformation of political elites. See *HLAS 42:2359.*

8129 Stavenhagen, Rodolfo. Capitalism and the peasantry in Mexico (LAP, 5[18]:3, Summer 1978, p. 27–37, bibl.)

Despite multiple mechanisms of exploitation by the capitalist sector, infrasubsistence agriculture has not been displaced by agribusinesses in Mexico. On the contrary, it is increasing and 84 percent of all farm units are classified under subsistence levels. According to the paper's thesis dependent capitalism requires maintenance of an impoverished peasant economy, which has been accomplished by agrarian reform, limited industrialization and population growth.

8130 Stern, Claudio and **Fernando Cortés.**
Hacia un modelo explicativo de las diferencias interregionales de los volúmenes de migración a la Ciudad de México, 1900–1970. México: Centro de Estudios Sociológicos, El Colegio de México, 1979. 54 p.; bibl. (Cuadernos del CES; no. 24)

Uses regression analysis in order to model migration flows and divides 20th-century migration to Mexico City into three age cohorts to test hypothesis that the migration behavior of each cohort responds to different factors. Authors use an interactive model to establish that rural and urban migration to Mexico City respond to different factors.

Taylor, William B. Drinking, homicide and rebellion in colonial Mexican villages. See *HLAS 42:2097.*

8131 Trejo Delarbre, Raúl. El movimiento obrero: situación y perspectivas (*in* México, hoy. Por José Ayala et al. Coordinado por Pablo González Casanova y Enrique Florescano. México: Siglo Veintiuno Editores, 1979, p. 121–151, tables)

Insightful review of various ideologies, leadership selection and labor tactics in Mexican trade unions. Useful and informative essay covers developments during the decade of the 1970s.

8132 Unikel, Luis. El desarrollo urbano en México (*in* Simposio sobre México hoy, 1978. Visión del México contemporáneo. México: El Colegio de México, 1979, p. 47–53)

A brief description of urban growth which includes evaluation of the 1970s public policies designed to achieve a geographical distribution of industries. Written for the layman.

8133 Varese, Stefano. Una dialéctica negada: notas sobre la multietnicidad mexicana (UNAM/RMCPS, 23:88, nuevo época, abril/junio 1977, p. 35–51)

Theoretical essay suggests that, in capitalist societies, policies designed to foster cultural homogeneity are actually new forms of ethnic exploitation in disguise while in socialist nations, they constitute a means to achieve centralization and control. Ethnicity precedes class formation and persists even after the disappearance of social classes in socialist countries. Author advocates the preservation of multiethnic societies in Mexico and Latin America and regards them as more dynamic than their homogeneous counterparts.

Vaughan, Mary E. Women, class, and education in Mexico, 1880–1928. See *HLAS 42: 2363.*

8134 Vizgunova, ÎULiiâ Ivanovna. La situación de la clase obrera en México. Tradujó, Rina Ortiz; recopilación de notas, Amanda Rosales Bada; diseño la portada, Carlos Palleiro. México: Ediciones de Cultura Popular, 1978. 202 p.; bibl.

Originally published in the Soviet Union in 1973, the statistical data in this book were outdated by the date of publication in Spanish. Writing from a Marxist-Leninist perspective, author illustrates capitalism's exploitation of the working class. The last section, which describes the organization of the labor movement and emphasizes the role of the Mexican Communist Party, is the most interesting.

8135 Warman, Arturo. Ensayos sobre el campesinado en México. Capa, Alberto Díez. México: Editorial Nueva Imagen, 1980. 216 p.; bibl. (Serie Sociedad, proceso, coyuntura)

Consists of 10 essays by one of Mexico's leading rural sociologists, all but two of which have been previously published. The last chapter "Rural Classes in Mexico" was especially written for this volume and synthesizes author's controversial and provocative views on social organization of the Mexican peasantry.

Wasserman, Mark. Foreign investment in Mexico, 1876–1910: a case study of the role of regional elites. See *HLAS 42:2258.*

8136 Zavala de Cosio, María Eugenia. Problèmes de population au Mexique (CDAL, 17, 1978, 89–111, bibl., tables)

After a brief historical presentation of the evolution of Mexico's population author reminds the nation's policymakers that population growth potential remains high and that economic development policies will not succeed unless demographic aspects are taken into account to insure employment for the entering labor force.

CENTRAL AMERICA

8137 Acuña B., Olda M. and **Carlos F. Denton L.** La familia en Costa Rica. San José: Ministerio de Cultura, Juventud y Deportes, 1979. 98 p.; ill.

Demographic study of household composition, fertility and birth control utilization, age at marriage and at divorce, and female employment. The monograph includes a few tables on female attitudes towards marriage. Data from a survey by UNCR and Cornell University.

Aguilera P., Gabriel. La tragicomedia electoral de la burguesía: un análisis sociológico del proceso electoral del 5 de marzo de 1978. See item **6194.**

8138 Arias Sánchez, Oscar. Desarrollo económico y social (in Costa Rica contemporánea. Prólogo y dirección, Chester Zelaya. Colaboradores, Carlos Meléndez Chaverri and others. San José: Editorial Costa Rica, 1979, t. 1, p. 189–209)

This prescription for the socioeconomic development of Costa Rica, within a capitalist system, proposes fostering internal capital accumulation and simultaneously reducing the dependence on foreign capital. Wealth distribution, a requirement for development, can be achieved by increasing the political participation of the masses. Failure to do so may provoke violence which has negative effects on the economic process and threatens political liberties.

8139 Asturias, Miguel Angel. Guatemalan sociology: the social problem of the Indian-Sociología guatemalteca: el problema social del Indio. The original Spanish text, followed by an English translation by Maureen Ahern; introduction by Richard J. Callan. Tempe, Ariz.: Arizona State University, Center for Latin American Studies, 1977.

A bilingual edition of Nobel Prize winner Miguel Angel Asturias' Masters thesis, submitted in 1923 to the Faculty of Law and Social Sciences, National University of Guatemala. As sociology it is outdated; and is an indication of the poor state of sociological knowledge at the time, and of the limitations that such lack of knowledge imposed on a progressive and humane writer like Asturias. The work will also interest sociologists of literature and others concerned with the literary creative process.

8140 Bermúdez M., Alicia and **Manuel Rincón M.** Costa Rica: migraciones interprovinciales, 1963–1973 (in Seminario Nacional de Demografía, 6th, Heredia, Costa Rica, 1976. Informe. San José: Universidad Nacional de Costa Rica, 1976, v. 2, p. 191–255, tables)

Formal demographic study of internal migration including net migration by provinces and rates of migration by sex and age groups. The 1963–73 within provincial and interprovincial migration flows are estimated from national census figures. The two main conclusions are: socioeconomic factors are the primary determinants of the direction and flow of geographical mobility in the country and these factors tend to explain sex and age variance in migration rates.

8141 Bertrand, Jane T.; Maria Antonieta Pineda; and **Fidel Enrique Soto.** Communicating family planning to rural Guatemala. Prepared by the Pro-Bienestar de la Familia Guatemala and Community and Family Study Center, the University of Chicago. Chicago: The Center, 1978. 103 p.; bibl.; ill. (Family planning monographs)

Authors draw from the statistical analysis of survey data (567 male and female respondents) in order to identify 10 sociopsychological factors which best explain attitudes toward the use of birth control. Research includes selection of most adequate means of dissemination of information about birth control after accounting for ethnic, language, and socioeconomic variables of target population.

8142 Bibliografía sobre el Mercado Común Centroamericano. Compiled by Eduardo Lizano Fait and Marizta Huertas (CSUCA/ESC, 24:8, sept./dic. 1979, p. 271–329)

About 500 entries classified alphabetically by author through 1977. Includes documents from international organizations and university dissertations.

8143 Caldera, Juan Rafael. Las fuerzas de la cuadrilla indígena (Alero [Universidad de San Carlos, Guatemala] 2, 4. época, julio/agosto 1979, p. 73–91, ill., map, plates)

Case study of migrant laborers in a Guatemalan sugar plantation. On the basis of fieldwork, author describes system of labor recruitment, living arrangements within the plantation, and work organization. All were primarily designed to maximize worker exploitation. Author also explores prospects for creating class consciousness and liberation of peasants.

8144 Cardona, Rokael. Descripción de la estructura social y económica en el agro guatemalteco, 1954–1975 (USCG/PS, 6, julio/dic. 1978, p. 5–43)

Excellent secondary analysis of effects of capital accumulation on land utilization. Data show that capital accumulation leads to latifundia formation and cash crops for exports. Establishes correlation between these effects and low agricultural productivity, rural unemployment, large seasonal rural migration, slow growth of national demand and foreign dependency. Based on 1964 Agricultural Census, 1975 Central American Statistical Abstract SIECA and an ILO unpublished report.

8145 Carter, William E. and William R. True. Family and kinship among the San José working class (*in* Family and kinship in Middle America and the Caribbean: proceedings of the 14th seminar of the Committee on Family Research of the International Sociological Association, Curaçao, September 1975. Arnaud F. Marks, René A. Römer, editors. Willemstad, Netherlands: Institute of Higher Studies in Curaçao, 1976?, p. 227–250, bibl., tables)

Descriptive information about family organization based on secondary analysis of 82 life histories originally gathered for study of cannabis users. Authors conclude that stable and tightly integrated traditional family structures imported to the city by rural migrants significantly contribute to overall well-being of new urbanites.

8146 Carvajal Herrera, Mario. Actitudes políticas del costarricense: análisis de opinión de dirigentes y partidarios. San José: Editorial Costa Rica, 1978. 320 p.; bibl.; ill.

Statistical exploration of the relations among democracy, stability and political change based on a 1971 sample of 305 persons and 100 leaders in three cantons. Analytical framework is grounded on functional structuralism. Study is limited by sample size and failure to account for sex of respondents.

8147 Chavarría de Ponce, Carmen Yolanda. Discriminación de la mujer guatemalteca. Guatemala: Ediciones Gamma, 1975. 1 v.

This review constitutes the first book on the subject of the social and legal status of Guatemalan women. Emphasizes health conditions, education, housing, employment and prostitution.

8148 Chinchilla, Norma S. Familia, economía y trabajo de la mujer en Guatemala (CM/DE, 12:1[34], 1978, p. 99–112)

Based on the 1973 *National Census* and the 1972 *Income and Expenditures Survey*, author presents tables on: urban and rural household composition; occupational status, according to sex, of the active labor force; household income differentials, according to sex of head of household; and family income, according to family size and occupation of head of household.

Dávila Bolaños, Alejandro. Calendarios indígenas de Nicaragua y sus relaciones con el santoral católico. See *HLAS 42:1523*.

Durham, William H. Scarcity and survival in Central America: ecological origins of the Soccer War. See item **7239**.

Figueroa Navarro, Alfredo. Aproximación a la sociología histórica del grupo dominante coclesano: 1821–1850. See *HLAS 42:2446*.

8149 Flores, Gilberto; Eugene Kaiser; Ignacio Pérez Salgado; and Kare Sørbø. Diagnóstico básico de la administración pública: un enfoque metodológico (IIAS/IRAS, 45:2, 1979, p. 103–109)

Identifies administrative constraints of program implementation in Honduras public sector and, on the basis of this experience, outlines a practical guide to determine implementation constraints. Unfortunately, authors offer no solutions for the latter.

8150 Fox, Robert W. and Jerrold W. Huguet. Tendencias demográficas y de urbanización en América Central y Panamá. Washington: Banco Interamericano de Desarrollo, 1978. 239 p.; bibl.; tables.

Demographic study includes rates of population growth, age and sex distribution, rural-urban fertility differences and estimates through the year 2000. A regional analysis (10 p.) is followed by country studies.

8151 El Fracaso social de la integración centroamericana: capital, tecnología, empleo. Daniel Camacho et al. Ciudad Universitaria Rodrigo Facio, Costa Rica: Editorial Universitaria Centroamericana, 1979. 373 p.; bibl. (Colección Seis)

The Center for Central American Studies of the Universidad de Costa Rica with the financial assistance of the German Foundation Friedrick Ebert undertook the research for this momentous book in which the region's massive unemployment and social problems are linked to the penetration of US capital and technology. Each chapter covers a Central American nation and is written by a prominent and nationally recognized social scientist. Book includes a 210-item bibliography on Central American employment, industrialization, Common Market and related topics.

8152 Herrera Morán, Aída and Francisco Altschul. Proyecto experimental rehabilitación del mesón el progreso (estudio monográfico). San Salvador, El Salvador: Fundación Salvadoreña de Desarrollo y Vivienda Mínima, 1979. 62, 22 p.

The Foundación Salvadoreña de Desarrollo y Vivienda Mínima undertook the reconstruction of a rundown housing project (*mesón*). This report beautifully details the successful planning and implementation of improvements by the community and the beneficial social side-effects. Authors clearly warn that the experience cannot be duplicated in *mesones* with higher density of dwellers which unfortunately constitute the majority in San Salvador.

8152a Iglesia de los pobres y organizaciones populares. Oscar A. Romero et al. San Salvador, El Salvador: UCA Editores, Universidad Centroamericana José Simeón Cañas, 1978. 249 p.; bibl. (Colección La Iglesia en América Latina; v. 4)

In 1978 the ideological cleavage among the Catholic bishops of El Salvador surfaced after the issuing of two contrasting documents, one by conservatives and the other by more reform-minded bishops. This volume collects the progressive pastoral letter by the late Archbishop of San Salvador, Oscar Romero, and his colleague Arturo Rivera plus articles by theologians reviewing the church's support of human rights, her doctrine on social and political violence, her sympathy and understanding for the plight of the poor, and the foundations of a theology of human liberation. Published a few months before the brutal assassination of Archbishop Romero by rightists, this timely and excellent volume provides an unusual insight of current violence in El Salvador and the Church's predicament in Latin America.

Irias de Rivera, María Amalia and Irma Violeta Alfaro de Carpio. Guatemalan working women in the labor movement. See *HLAS 42:2460.*

8153 Jacob, Jeffrey C. Urban poverty, children, and the consumption of popular culture: a perspective on marginality theses from a Latin American squatter settlement (SAA/HO, 39:3, Fall 1980, p. 233–241, bibl.)

Article describes entertainment of children and youth in a poor neighborhood in Guatemala City where soccer, movies, wrestling, television programs (e.g., soap opera, westerns, sports) and comic-book magazines lead as forms of recreation. Through these media, the slum's youth is integrated into the nation and frequently the international world.

8154 Montes, Segundo. La estratificación social: "¿funcional" para qué tipo de sociedad? (UJSC/ECA, 35:376/376, enero/feb. 1980, p. 55–27, plates, tables)

Author rejects functionalism theory as a justification for social stratification on the basis of data gathered while examining the relation between salary differentials and training requirements for different occupations in El Salvador. Author concludes that the disproportionately large salary differentials between the private and public sector do not correspond to training requirements or to social importance of the occupations.

8155 ———. Estudio sobre estratificación social en El Salvador. San Salvador, El Salvador: Publicaciones del Departamento de Sociología y Ciencias Políticas, Universidad Centroamericana José Simeón Cañas, 1979. 504 p.; bibl.; ill.

Report consists of data gathered in 1970–76 from 1,520 households in 15 different socioeconomic neighborhoods in San Salvador. Questionnaire was slightly modified on three occasions and included questions on: house tenancy, income and expenditures, occupational and marital status, number of children, and educational achievement. Statistical treatment of variables did not overcome the theoretical vacuum and design flaws.

8156 Nieves, Isabel. Household arrangements and multiple jobs in San Salvador (UC/S, 5 : 1, Autumn 1979, p. 134–142, tables)

A short article on the role of consanguine households in poor neighborhoods of El Salvador. These households are generally headed by working women. Their economic independence facilitates the formation of social networks upon which relationships of reciprocity, mutual dependence and, in the final analysis, survival is based.

8157 Programa Centroamericano de Desarrollo de las Ciencias Sociales. Estructura demográfica y migraciones internas en Centroamérica. Ciudad Universitaria Rodrigo Facio, Costa Rica: Editorial Universitaria Centroamericana, 1978. 381 p.; 12 leaves of plates; bibl.; ill. (Colección Ciencias sociales)

Study was coordinated by the Central American Social Science Program (CSUCA) and each research team carried out an internal migration study in its country. For comparability purposes, all research groups used a similar format. Flows in interdecennial rural-urban and interdepartmental migration were analyzed using census data from 1950 to the present. Valuable demographic study of interest to the specialist.

8158 Quiroz M., Teresita and **Barbara Larraín E.** Imagen de la mujer que proyectan los medios de comunicación de masas en Costa Rica. San José: Universidad de Costa Rica, Facultad de Ciencias Sociales, Instituto de Investigaciones Sociales, 1978. 344 p.; bibl.; tables (Avances de investigación; 3 : 34)

Empirical study of sex-role images projected by soap opera and advertisement in radio, television and popular magazines. Study explores the socialization role of the media in maintaining and perpetuating the exploitation of women. Part of both authors requirements for their masters degree at the University of Costa Rica, the study is well designed but should have been edited for publication.

8159 Seligson, Mitchell A. Peasants of Costa Rica and the development of agrarian capitalism. Madison: University of Wisconsin Press, 1980. 220 p.; bibl.; ill.; index.

This book searches for reasons that might explain the absence of an agrarian revolution after coffee plantations introduced

agrarian capitalism and poverty to rural Costa Rica. Banana plantations, limited land reform and squatting were channels that diffused political radicalization. Seligson concludes that ethnic homogeneity was an additional factor precluding extreme exploitation of peasants by elites.

8160 Torres Rivas, Edelberto. Elementos para la caracterización de la estructura agraria en Costa Rica (Boletín de Antropología Americana [Instituto Panamericana de Geografía e Historia, México] 1, junio 1980, p. 62–85, ill., tables)

An important contribution to understanding the functions of the state and the role played by social classes in the development of Costa Rica's capitalist agriculture. Using historical materials and studying coffee production, author analyzes the characteristics that distinguish Costa Rica's capitalist evolution from other Latin American countries.

——. Guatemala: crisis and political violence. See item **6204**.

——. Vida y muerte en Guatemala: reflexiones sobre la crisis y la violencia política. See item **6205**.

8161 Ugalde, Antonio. Physicians' control of the health sector: professional values and economic interests. Findings from the Honduran Health System (Social Science and Medicine [Medical anthropology. Pergamon Press, Oxford, UK] v. 14A, 1980, p. 435–444)

Physicians exercise almost total control over decision-making in health matters. Their decisions are not only influenced by their professional values and economic interests but reflect the predominance of the urban sector over the countryside. All these factors contribute to the development of high-technology urban hospitals and emphasis on curative care in a country where the health needs of the population demand primary and preventive interventions.

8162 Vega Carballo, José Luis. Etapas y procesos de la evolución sociopolítica de Costa Rica (SGHG/A, 47 : 1/4, enero/dic. 1974, p. 216–238)

The four-period historical division of postcolonial Costa Rica allows a detailed analysis of the evolution of the country's dependency from Spain to the British Empire and finally to North American capitalism. Includes the role of the oligarchy and its political strategies in inducing foreign dominance. An excellent study.

8163 Winson, Anthony. Class structure and agrarian transition in Central America (LAP, 5[4]: 19, Fall 1978, p. 27–48, table)

After brief examination of the old agrarian structure (1870–1950), author analyzes recent agricultural export trends. Author notes that the following phenomena: the growth of capitalist tenant farmers, the demise of *aparceros* from livestock haciendas, the drastic reduction of permanent-wage agricultural laborers in favor of temporary workers, and the increase of surplus landless peasants are all social class transformations related to capitalist development. A solid piece of research grounded on Poulantzas' theoretical approach.

THE CARIBBEAN AND THE GUIANAS

NELSON P. VALDES, *Associate Professor of Sociology, University of New Mexico*

SOCIOLOGICAL RESEARCH IN THE Caribbean is undergoing changes. As in the past, the favored theoretical approach is Marxist rather than functionalist, as illustrated by the work of the History Task Force of the Centro de Estudios Puertorriqueños (item **8225**). However, demographic studies are now on the decline, and works on internal migration and migration to other countries have come to dominate the discipline. Interest in religion, its values, practices, institutions, and sects, is increasing. Up to now, researchers have concentrated on black / African religions, and these studies are generally more descriptive than analytical. The family continues to attract important research in the region, although there is a shift away from the topics of family-planning and fertility and toward the internal roles and economic functions of the institution. One might say that the emphasis has shifted from the family as a reproductive unit to the family as a production unit.

As in previous years the quantity of studies on women has risen notably, but the quaiity still leaves much to be desired. Interestingly, in this area also the stress is on the economic activities and functions of women. At best, this material is of the testimonial or participant observation variety; at worst, it takes the form of simplistic ideological statements that have much to say about normative predilections but contribute little to scholarship. However, it is noteworthy that scholars are beginning to compile useful, although partial, bibliographies on the subject of women (item **8204**).

Judging by the material made available to the reviewer, the topics of stratification, urban and rural labor, and development are attracting the attention of a growing number of scholars. On the other hand, urban problems, which were so numerous a few years ago, have decreased considerably. Some attempt has been made to consider the social problems of children and the elderly, but for all intents and purposes, these are still uncharted areas. The dependency approach seems to have lost favor, giving way to the world system perspective. More and more authors are struggling with the problem of national identity, particularly in the French and English-speaking islands. This emphasis may be a manifestation of the cultural nationalist current sweeping the region. In spite of this new focus, studies on Puerto Rico are the most numerous in this section, followed closely by those dealing with Cuba, and then Jamaica and the Dominican Republic.

The most original work reviewed here is Ruby Rohrlich-Leavitt's study on culture change and language deviance (item **8237**). Her book is a methodological jewel.

The most notable effort at giving a comparative overview of the Caribbean is the volume on family and kinship edited by Arnaud F. Marks and René A. Römer (in item **8216**). From a theoretical and research standpoint, highest marks go to Fernando I. Ferrán for his provocative discussion of the political power of the tobacco industry in the Dominican Republic (item **8195**).

8164 Aguirre, B.E. and **Jon P. Alston.** Organizational change and religious commitment (PSA/PSR, 23:2, April 1980, p. 171–197, tables)

Original approach to the study of religious organizations in Cuba. Focusing on Jehovah's Witnesses and Seventh-Day Adventists in the period 1938–65, the authors maintain that there is a direct relationship between the size of membership and the degree of activism in religious sects. They argue the need for conceptual refinements in the Church-sect model (which essentially uses the internal dynamics of the organization to explain it), and for the incorporation of collective behavior and social movement approaches into any model of sect studies. Includes a good bibliography of works on Protestant groups in Cuba.

8165 Agyei, William K.A. Modernization and the theory of demographic transition in the developing countries: the case of Jamaica (UWI/SES, 27:1, 1978, p. 44–68)

Studies the effect of social and economic variables on fertility, applying two statistical models, and measuring crude birth rates and fertility rates. From the data used, author maintains that the theory mentioned in the title has been proven correct for Jamaica.

8166 Ahlers, Theodore H. Haitian rural-urban migration: a case study of four small towns. Port-au-Prince: Inter-American Institute of Agricultural Sciences, 1978. 58 p.; bibl.; ill.

Study of the scale and direction of migration and the distinguishing characteristics of in-migrants, out-migrants, and non-migrants in four small towns (Grande Rivière du Nord, Le Borgne, Chardonnières, and Dame Marie) during the period May–Sept. 1976. Contains information on landownership, education, occupation, sex of migrants, and nature of the family; and a short review of migration literature on Haiti.

8167 Albuquerque, Klaus de. Comment on van den Berghe's "The African Diaspora in Mexico, Brazil, and the United States" (SF, 57:1, Sept. 1978, p. 296–300)

Discusses the actual degree of racism in the three societies studied by van den Berghe (Mexico, Brazil and the US). See also item **8248**.

8168 Báez, Leovigildo. Las migraciones internas en República Dominicana: un enfoque teórico conceptual (UNPHU/A, 22:23, julio/dic. 1977, p. 47–60)

Analysis of the causes and consequences of internal migration in the Dominican Republic. Concludes that extent of internal migration is both significant and dysfunctional toward goal of socioeconomic development. Internal migration, Báez concludes, aggravates problems of prostitution, juvenile delinquency and sexual promiscuity. [E. Egginton]

8169 Barbados. National Commission on the Status of Women. Report of the National Commission on the Status of Women in Barbados. St. Michael: Barbados Govt. Print. Off., 1978. 2 v. in 3; bibl.; ill.

This work is the most thorough overview to date on the status of women in Barbados. Well-organized and thoughtfully conceived, the investigation has eight chapters covering the following topics: Historical Background; Traditional Attitudes; Women and the Law (including marriage, maintenance, divorce, guardianship, labor laws, women and criminal law, matrimonial property); Education (covering curriculum, primary and secondary education, the sciences and humanities); Women and Employment (paid and unpaid, unemployment); Health; the Family; and Miscellaneous (Church, politics, media, abortion). Presents 212 recommendations. A very valuable work.

8170 Blumberg, Rae Lesser. The political economy of the mother-child family revisited (*in* Family and kinship in Middle America and the Caribbean: proceedings of the 14th seminar of the Committee on Family Research of the International Sociological Association, Curaçao, September 1975. Arnaud F. Marks, René A. Römer, editors. Willemstad, Netherlands: Institute of Higher Studies in Curaçao, 1978?, p. 526–575, bibl.)

Possibly the most provocative and thoughtful essay in the volume that contains it. The writer challenges various accepted theses on Caribbean matrifocality (e.g., African survivals, levels of modernization, poverty and male marginality, bureaucratic by product, etc.). After examining Guyana, Ghana, the US, Curaçao, Venezuela, Australia and Northern South Wales, she cogently argues that there is a relationship between matrifocality and society's mode of production. Essential reading for anyone interested in the Caribbean family. Contains a good bibliography.

8171 Bondarchuk, Vladimir. El tránsito al socialismo: algunos aspectos socioeconómicos de la experiencia cubana (URSS/AL, 1, 1979, p. 25–40)

Divides revolutionary process into different stages, stressing its economic dimensions. Points out that Cuban system was not feudal in 1959, but does not discuss Cuban model of late 1960s.

8172 Boswell, Thomas D. Inferences concerning intermunicipio migrations in Puerto Rico: 1955–1960 (USM/JTG, 45, Dec. 1977, p. 1–11, bibl., maps, tables)

Using regression-analysis models, author suggests that the availability of economic opportunities influenced migrants in their decision to migrate. Concentrates on the period 1955–60.

8173 Bradford, William Penn. Puerto Rican spiritism: contrasts in the sacred and the profane (UWI/CQ, 24:3/4, Sept./Dec. 1978, p. 48–55, bibl.)

Recollections of a direct observer. Contains a description of some practices but no systematic investigation of the sociological aspects of the phenomenon. Includes a brief bibliography.

8174 Brathwaite, Farley S. Upward mobility and career (value) orientation: an empirical test of the *embourgeoisement* thesis (UPR/CS, 16:3/4, Oct. 1976/Jan. 1977, p. 149–169, tables)

Study of normative reference changes resulting from upward occupational mobility. Author's data suggests that those who are upwardly mobile do absorb the attitudes and behavior traits of those above them. Based on a questionnaire answered by 529 teachers in government and government-assisted secondary schools in Trinidad and Tobago.

8175 Brizan, George I. The Grenadian peasantry and social revolution, 1930–51. Kingston, Jamaica: Institute of Social and Economic Research, 1979. 52 p.; map (Working paper—Institute of Social and Economic Research, University of the West Indies; no. 21)

Describes economic conditions of peasants defined as those who produce for a market, in Grenada. Not a historical treatment, although author deals with the period 1930–51, leading up to the coming to power of E.M. Gairy. Brizan connects Gairy's working-class movement to the peasantry, at times treating the two social categories as if they were identical. Suggests that the 1951 uprising was produced by immiserization (although he notes the size of landholdings increased from 1930–51). Does not discuss the changes that have occurred in Grenada since 1951.

8176 Bruckman, Walter H. Rechazo y atracción como causas de la migración interna en Puerto Rico: un modelo econométrico (UPR/RCS, 20:2, sept. 1978, p. 145–164, bibl., tables)

Puerto Ricans migrate essentially because of push factors within the municipalities of origin. Connects migration to standard of living.

8177 Bruijne, G.A. de. The Lebanese in Suriname (CEDLA/B, 26, junio 1979, p. 15–37, tables)

Knowledgeable treatment of the Lebanese trade minority in Paramaribo. Discusses their migration to Surinam in the late 19th century, their domination of the textile trade, due primarily to a system of mutual aid and support, and their extensive influence on urban society, although they numbered only 300. Data is derived from a survey of 1450 households and interviews conducted in 1966, as well as participant observation.

8178 Cabrera, Lydia. Reglas de Congo: Palo Monte Mayombé. Miami, Fla.: Peninsular Print., 1979. 225 p. (Colección del Chichereku en el exilio)

Leading student of Cuban black religious practices has produced an ethnographic narrative of the beliefs, magical practices, rituals, chants, and designs of the Congolese slaves who lived in Cuba during the 19th century. Author collects the reminiscences of former slaves or their relatives. She also considers the interaction of the Congo tradition with the Lucumís, Mandingas, Araráo and Carabalís. The work suffers from numerous digressions, the lack of a table of contents and index.

8179 Caribbean social relations. Edited by Colin G. Clarke. Liverpool: Centre for Latin-American Studies, University of Liverpool, 1978. 9, 95 p.; bibl.; ill.; maps (Monograph series—Centre for Latin-American Studies, University of Liverpool; no. 8)

Collection of six papers presented at symposium (2–3 May 1975) at University of Liverpool. Papers deal with topics ranging from color, status, urban growth, and social inequality to behavioral patterns, emigration, and migrant adjustment. David Nicholls writes a perceptive piece on "Caste, Class and Colour in Haiti," tracing the clash between blacks and browns on the islands. Stephanie Goodenough, in "Race, Status and Urban Ecology in Port of Spain, Trinidad," affirms that race determines class and place of residence. Bridgett Leach's very original essay, "Activity Space and Social Relations: Young People in Basseterre, St. Kitts," studies recreational behaviors. Two other essays, by Elizabeth M. Thomas-Hope and David Lowenthal discuss migration from the West Indies, upholding the thesis that population pressure produces migration, although they mention other factors as well.

8180 Casal, Lourdes. Race relations in contemporary Cuba (Report [Minority Rights Group, London] 7, 1979, p. 11–27)

One of the best essays on the subject, covering the period pre- and post-1959. Takes issue with prevailing academic views on the degree of racial integration existing in Cuba before 1959, and notes improvements in the situation of the black population on the island. Required reading for anyone interested in Cuba.

8181 Chevannes, Barry. Revivalism: a disappearing religion (UWI/CQ, 24:3/4, Sept./Dec. 1978, p. 1–17)

Discussion of the African Methodist Episcopal Zion Church of Kingston and the process by which it is being absorbed by American evangelical sects. Describes social composition of the membership, internal organization of the Church, basic beliefs and rituals, and the role of healing and testimonials.

Cohen Stuart, Bertie A. Women in the Caribbean: a bibliography. See *HLAS* 42:39.

8182 Conferencia Puertorriqueña de la Mujer, San Juan, P.R., 1977. Documentos de la Conferencia Puertorriqueña de la Mujer: del 10 al 12 de junio de 1977, San Juan, Puerto Rico. Editora, Isabel Picó de Hernández. San Juan: Comité Coordinador, 1977 or 1979. 85 p.; ill.

Contains abstracts of papers presented at conference. Main issues were position of women in the Puerto Rican family; sexual education; women's sexuality; rape; divorce and its consequences; the need for child care centers; and the problem of old-age homes. Conference concluded that regardless of their age, class, or area of residence, women were concerned with similar problems.

8183 Contreras, Brunilda. Ensayo sobre cultura netamente campesina. Santo Domingo: Editora Alfa y Omega, 1979. 144 p.

Not really an essay on peasant culture, this is a collection of sayings author remembers from her childhood in the country about economy, health, lovemaking, religion, and death. Contains only brief descriptions, without analysis or documentation. Lacks table of contents and bibliography.

8184 Conway, Dennis and **Juanita Brown.** Intraurban relocation and structure: low-income migrants in Latin America and the Caribbean (LARR, 15:3, 1980, p. 95–125, bibl., ill., maps, tables)

Challenges Turner thesis of initial settlement into urban areas of Latin America, offering an evolutionary model instead. Authors' main thesis is that evolution of the intraurban structure has influenced cityward migrants' routes.

8185 Crahan, Margaret E. Salvation through Christ or Marx: religion in revolutionary Cuba (SAGE/JIAS, 21:1, Feb. 1979, p. 156–184, bibl., table)

One of the best overviews available on religion in Cuba. Studies the Protestant and Catholic Churches in Cuba since 1959 but excludes Judaism and non-institutionalized African religious practices. Uses sources dating from 1940 and in-depth interviews with 40 Cuban Church leaders. Author posits interesting sociological reasons as to why religion lost influence on the island. Contains a good review of the literature. Recommended reading.

8186 Cristo vivo en Cuba: reflexiones teológicas cubanas. Sergio Arce Martínez et al. Portada, Hugo Díaz. San José, Costa Rica: Departamento Ecuménico de Investigaciones, 1978. 181 p. (Colección Testimonios)

A most unique document from Cuba. Work consists of a compilation of "testimonios" by Christian revolutionaries attempting to develop a theology of revolutionary practice from within the revolutionary process. Authors include Presbyterian, Methodist, Baptist and Episcopal ministers, but no Catholics. Required reading for anyone who wishes to understand how the Revolution and the Protestant Churches began to work together in Cuba.

8187 Cuba. Departamento de Demografía. Características de la divorcialidad cubana. Editores, Mario López Cepero, Ernesto Chávez Alvarez. La Habana: Editorial de Ciencias Sociales, 1976. 113 p.; bibl.; graphs (Demografía)

The Departamento de Demografía of the Junta Central de Planificación sponsored this investigation consisting of five sections: 1) general theoretical overview of the institution of the family and divorce; 2) the legislation on divorce since 1907; 3) historical evolution of divorce from 1907–70; 4) characteristics of divorce (e.g., sex, age, geographic distribution, economic activity, education); 5) relationship of divorce and nuptiality (including duration of marriage, comparison with other countries). The best available study on the subject.

8188 ———. Laws, statutes, etc. Código de familia: Ley No. 1289 de febrero de 1975, *Gaceta Oficial* de 15 de febrero de 1975. La Habana: Ministerio de Justicia, 1975. 69 p.

Family Code approved in Cuba on 15 Feb. 1975, juridically regulates the institution of marriage, its dissolution, and paternal relations. Contains sections on marriage (22 articles), conjugal relations (18), divorce (21), paternal relations (33), adoption (17), kinship (19) and tutelage (30).

8189 Cuba, camino abierto. Compilación de David Barkin y Nita R. Manitzas; traducción de Francisco González Aramburo. 5. ed. en español. México: Siglo Veintiuno Editores, 1979. 342 p.; bibl. (Historia inmediata)

Anthology of articles on the Cuban Revolution "which attempt to describe the country's socioeconomic and political development during recent years and to examine certain fundamental problems" (p. 1). All the articles are annotated separately in this volume and entered under the authors' names (e.g., Nita R. Manitzas; David Barkin; Bertram Silverman; Marvin Leiner; Jorge E. Hardoy; and Richard R. Fagen). [Ed.]

8190 Díaz-Royo, Antonio T. *Dignidad* and *respeto*, two core themes in the traditional Puerto Rican family culture (*in* Family and kinship in Middle America and the Caribbean: proceedings of the 14th seminar of the Committee on Family Research of the International Sociological Association, Curaçao, September 1975. Arnaud F. Marks, René A. Römer, editors. Willemstad, Netherlands: Institute of Higher Studies in Curaçao, 1978?, p. 99–112, bibl.)

A discussion of *dignidad* and *respeto* as independent variables or values that shape the general worldview of Puerto Rican traditionals. According to author, the moral structure of a population determines family relations; he does not take material social conditions into account. The work resulted from participant observation carried out during the period 1972–73. Makes numerous references to other authors who have dealt with same subject.

Doubout, Jean Jacques. Haïti, féodalisme ou capitalisme? Essai sur l'évolution de la formation sociale d'Haïti depuis l'indépendance. See *HLAS 42:2600*.

8191 Edwards, Jay D. The evolution of vernacular architecture in the western Caribbean (*in* Cultural traditions and Caribbean identity: the question of patrimony. Edited by S. Jeffrey K. Wilkerson. Gainesville: Center for Latin American Studies, University of Florida, 1980, p. 291–339, bibl., ill., map, plates, tables)

A most original work, tracing the historical evolution and adaptation of vernacular architecture in Grand Cayman, Utila, Roatan, Guanaja, Providencia, San Andrés and Great Corn Island—all English speaking and Protestant. Author divides history of popular dwellings into four periods, using ethnological approach and historical data.

8192 Encuentro Nacional de Sociología, *1st, Santo Domingo? 1977.* La investigación sociológica en la República Dominicana: una evaluación. Santo Domingo: Asociación para el Desarrollo, 1978. 80 p.

Collection of papers presented at the First National Sociology Congress 1–3 Dec. 1977, discussing the state of sociology as a discipline in the Dominican Republic. Three major themes prevailed: history of sociology, the role of the sociologist in the Dominican Republic, and the significance of the discipline. First paper, by Luis R. del Castillo Morales, is a descriptive institutional history and notes the Dominican Republic produced its first sociologists in 1966. On the role of sociologist, Frederico E. Nadal makes some general statements on objectivity, neutrality and methodology, and calls for investigations related to the rural areas. Review of sociological works by Quisqueya Rivas Jérez is exceedingly sketchy, making no mention of themes or undercurrents. Also includes a piece on Haitian sociology by Bernard Etheart and Françoise B. Molière which is a schematic presentation of Haitian society. Not a very useful volume.

8193 Encuentro Nacional sobre la Investigación Demográfica en la República Dominicana, *Santo Domingo, 1977.* La investigación demográfica en la República Dominicana: una evaluación. Santo Domingo: Asociación para el Desarrollo, 1977. 80 p.; bibl.

Compilation of studies reviewing the literature on demography in the Dominican Republic. The work covers: studies on fertility and family planning (Leovigildo Baez and Nelson Ramírez); 43 studies on population policies (Manuel Ortega); 13 social and economic studies on population (Minerva Breton); demography as a discipline (Francisco A. de Moya and José Miguel Guzmán); internal migration (Pablo J. Tactuk); and morbidity and mortality (Méjixo Angeles).

8194 Ferère, Gérard A. Haitian voodoo: its true face (UWI/CQ, 24:3/4, Sept./Dec. 1978, p. 37–47)

Voodoo has a positive effect on the Haitian masses; it is a mechanism that helps maintain mental health and social happiness under very difficult socioeconomic conditions. Author describes rituals, ceremonies, and gods.

8195 Ferrán, Fernando I. Tabaco y sociedad: la organización del poder en el ecomer-

cado de tabaco dominicano. Santo Domingo: Fondo para el Avance de las Ciencias Sociales, Centro de Investigación y Acción Social, 1976. 209 p.

A work that is logically developed and systematically presented. Author, an anthropologist of the cultural-materialist school, analyzes the social organization of power in the production and distribution of tobacco. He traces the movement of tobacco throughout an entire market system, from petty producer to consumer in the US or Europe. He also looks at the different levels of exchange and how tobacco articulates with those below or above it. The study shows that the exchange of tobacco—its sale or purchase—affects other forms of interaction. A very thoughtful work, highly recommended.

8196 Frucht, Richard. Household in crisis: the failure of petty agricultural production in Nevis, West Indies (*in* Family and kinship in Middle America and the Caribbean: proceedings of the 14th seminar of the Committee on Family Research of the International Sociological Association, Curaçao, September 1975. Arnaud F. Marks, René A. Römer, editores. Willemstad, Netherlands: Institute of Higher Studies in Curaçao, 1978?, p. 405–416)

Petty commodity production of agricultural goods is no longer a viable alternative on the island of Nevis. Author's argument contradicts the thesis of George Beckford on whether a non-capitalist organization or production is possible in a capitalist market.

Fuerza de trabajo y movimientos laborales en América Latina. See item **8016.**

8197 García, Ezequiel. Situación de los asentamientos humanos en la República Dominicana. Santo Domingo: Universidad Nacional Pedro Henriquez Ureña, Centro de Investigaciones, 1976. 132 leaves.

A most informative collection of data on the urban history of the Dominican Republic since colonial times. Contains chapters on regional distribution of the population, impact of land tenure on urban growth, and rural population patterns and agrarian reform. Author also discusses problems of health, housing and urban planning. Descriptive in approach, since the data has not been processed sufficiently as to provide a theoretical understanding of the entire phenomenon. Includes a good bibliographic section.

8198 Gerber, Stanford N. and **Knud Rasmussen.** Further reflection on the concept of matrifocality and its consequences for social science research (*in* Family and kinship in Middle America and the Caribbean: proceedings of the 14th seminar of the Committee on Family Research of the International Sociological Association, Curaçao, September 1975. Arnaud F. Marks, René A. Römer, editors. Willemstad, Netherlands: Institute of Higher Studies in Curaçao, 1978?, p. 576–587)

Authors question the hypothesis that matrifocality is widespread and representative of the West Indian household or domestic group. They also put in doubt the view that matrifocality, even when it exists, produces personality disorders. They stress that the traditional definition of matrifocality is imprecise because it covers any social unit lacking the physical presence of a male. Families with no males can be stable, and even when the male is absent he may make primary decisions. Good general overview of the prevailing schools of thought on the subject.

8199 Gomes, Ralph C. Class, status and privilege: the objective interest of the new elite in Guyana (*in* The Caribbean issues of emergence: socio-economic and political perspectives. Edited by Vincent R. McDonald. Washington: University Press of America, 1980, p. 283–303)

Author maintains there are three major classes in Guyana: 1) old bourgeoisie (also called the oligarchic interests); 2) the middle class (also referred to as the petite bourgeoisie); and 3) the masses. His thesis is that the leadership of the petite bourgeoisie, although comprising a ruling elite, has not served the interests of the masses since it achieved power with independence. Uses a reference group approach.

8200 Gow, David D. The rural power in Haiti: a social analysis. Port-au-Prince, Haiti?: s.n., 1977. 38 leaves; bibl.

Analysis of the actual conditions of the rural poor in Haiti and of some of the reasons for them. Work gives a general overview of landholding, land tenure, income-employment, rural consumption patterns (92 percent of the rural population has a per capita income of less than $40); availability of services (particularly education and health); role of women (they are responsible for marketing agricultural products); the rural populations perception of the root of their problems (need for irrigation, fertilizer, insecticides, roads, health and education); and the lack of political participation. Author offers a good critique of the so-called "fatalism of the peasant thesis." An important contribution, despite its format.

8201 Guevara, Carlos I. and **Myrna J. Sesman.** La madre y el aprendizaje del niño: la experiencia urbana puertorriqueña. Río Piedras: editorial Universitaria, Universidad de Puerto Rico, 1978. 149, 1 p.; bibl.

Identifies the characteristics and behavior patterns of mothers and children from the middle and lower classes in urban San Juan. Sample included 120 children born in 1964, 60 from lower class and 60 from middle class (with each group further disaggregated by sex). Performance on IQ tests was related to educational and income level of parents.

8202 Higman, Barry W. African and Creole slave family patterns in Trinidad (NCFR/JFH, 3:2, 1978, p. 163–180, bibl., tables)

Author maintains that there is a relationship between specific African origins and slave family patterns in Trinidad in 1813. Relied on records kept by the colonial authorities. For historian's comment, see *HLAS* 42:2572.

8203 Hulse, F.S. Migration et selection de groupe: le cas de Cuba (SAP/BM, 6:2, avril/juin 1979, p. 137–146, bibl., tables)

Study in historical anthropology. Author maintains that the majority of Spaniards who went to Cuba in the 16th century were upper-class Andalusians, at least in their family origins. Nature of that migration affected the cultural development and physiognomy of the Cuban population. Basic source is the *Catálogo de pasajeros a Indias durante los siglos XVI, XVII y XVIII.*

8204 Inter-American Center for Documentation and Agriculture Information. Bibliografía, participación de la mujer en el desarrollo rural de América Latina y el Caribe, enero 1980. San José, Costa Rica: OEA, Instituto Interamericano de Ciencias

Agrícolas, Centro Interamericano de Documentación Información Agrícola, 1980. ii, 103, 5 p.; bibl.; index (Serie Documentación e información agrícola; no. 78 0301-438X)

Lists 165 books, pamphlets, articles, position papers, unpublished manuscripts, and official government publications. Material is organized by subject (general, economics-sociology, education, family, legislation, nutrition and health, housing, arts and crafts, development and demography). Also contains a useful author index.

8205 Laguerre, Michel S. The impact of migration on the Haitian family and household organization (*in* Family and kinship in Middle America and the Caribbean: proceedings of the 14th seminar of the Committee on Family Research of the International Sociological Association, Curaçao, September 1975. Arnaud F. Marks, René A. Römer, editors. Willemstad, Netherlands: Institute of Higher Studies in Curaçao, 1978?, p. 446–481, bibl., tables)

Study of efffects of migration (identifying nine phases of adjustment) on family organization of those who do not migrate, but who have migrant relatives. Based on interviews conducted in 1974–75 with members of 78 households in a rural Haitian village with a population of 3,132 inhabitants.

Landis, Joseph B. Commitment to socialism and nonalignment among Guyanese and West Indian leaders. See item **7326.**

8206 Landolfi, Ciriaco. Introducción al estudio de la historia de la cultura dominicana. Santo Domingo: Editora de la Universidad Autónoma de Santo Domingo, 1977. 337 p.; bibl. (Colección Cultura y sociedad; no. 1. Publicaciones de la Universidad Autónoma de Santo Domingo; v. 244)

This work, covering the period 1492 to 1863, applies a phenomenological approach to the topic of *mestizaje*, considered as the key factor in the culture of the Dominican Republic. Author uses flowery, excessively technical language throughout; the text is filled with anecdotes and generalizations, and lacks a unifying theme.

8207 LaPorte, Roy S. Bryce. Migration to the United States: some implication for Caribbean governments and their educators (*in* Caribbean-American perspectives: proceedings and papers from the Caribbean-

American Exchange Program conducted by the Phelps-Stokes Fund. Washington: The Fund, 1978, p. 67–78)

General statement on the need to teach future migrants to the US and elsewhere about the realities of the societies they will encounter. Calls for an updating of linguistic and technical preparation of potential migrants, without indicating how such programs should be financed.

8208 Larose, Serge. The Haitian *lakou*: land, family and ritual (*in* Family and kinship in Middle America and the Caribbean: proceedings of the 14th seminar of the Committee on Family Research of the International Sociological Association, Curaçao, September 1975. Arnaud F. Marks, René A. Römer, editors. Willemstad, Netherlands: Institute of Higher Studies in Curaçao, 1978?, p. 482–512, bibl., ill., map, tables)

Work connects voodoo rituals to land tenure system, and notes that the rituals are an expression of particular social relations of production. The "lakou" (group of interrelated conjugal families) is a mechanism by which families struggle for land. Thoughtful essay, suggestive of new avenues for investigation.

8209 Lasker, Harry M. and Fred L. Strodtbeck. Stratification and ego development in Curaçao (*in* Family and kinship in Middle America and the Caribbean: proceedings of the 14th seminar of the Committee on Family Research of the International Sociological Association, Curaçao, September 1975. Arnaud F. Marks, René A. Römer, editors. Willemstad, Netherlands: Institute of Higher Studies in Curaçao, 1978?, p. 156–180, bibl.)

Uses a mixture of George Foster's limited good model and J. Loevinger's paradigm of ego-development to analyze 301 Curaçaoan males between ages 25–35. Self-protectiveness within the family hinders change. Based on sampling of respondents given sentences they had to complete.

8210 Levine, Robert M. Race and ethnic relations in Latin America and the Caribbean: an historical dictionary and bibliography. Metuchen, N.J.: Scarecrow Press, 1980. 252 p.; index.

This is an alphabetical "dictionary of terms, names and events related to racial and ethnic questions." In most cases, reader is referred to an author whose work appears in the bibliography of 1342 entries. Work is organized in alphabetical order.

8211 Lewis, Maureen Warner. Yoruba religion in Trinidad: transfer and reinterpretation (UWI/CQ, 24:3/4, Sept./Dec. 1978, p. 18–32)

Author relates the world-view of a third generation Yoruba descendant in Trinidad. Information was obtained through interviews. Original piece of work.

8212 Lizardo Barinas, Fradique. Cultura africana en Santo Domingo. Dibujos primarios, Hans Indrikovs Valera; dibujos definitivos, Leonardo Díaz Alvarado. Santo Domingo: Editora Taller, 1979. 103 p.; 2 fold. leaves of plates; bibl.; ill.

Work does not deal with African culture in the Dominican Republic but describes terminology that was generated by racial mixing (known to us since the work of Magnus Mörner), provides a demographic picture of the black population from colonial times to the present, and lists the 72 African ethnic groups that were sent to the island. Work is descriptive, sketchy, and lacking in a thesis. Half of it is a chronology of events related to the black population and covering the period 1500–1978.

8213 Long, Richard. Parameters of information and communication among Afro-Americans and Caribbean peoples (in Caribbean-American perspectives: proceedings and papers from the Caribbean-American Exchange Program conducted by the Phelps-Stokes Fund. Washington: The Fund, 1978, p. 47–53)

General classification of the communities of African origin in this hemisphere into one of three models: US, Jamaican, and Haitian. Compares the three, and notes that each is isolated from the other two.

8214 López Garriga, María M. Estrategias de autoafirmación en mujeres puertorriqueñas (UPR/RCS, 20:3/4, dic. 1978, p. 259–286, bibl.)

Using a model of manipulation strategies developed by Louise Lamphère, author examines Puerto Rican women and their attempts at self-assertion. She notes that manipulative relations are part of a social complex in which social relations are exploitative. Derived from a survey of 80 families

in San Juan, Ponce and Mayagüez. Women from a middle-class background used manipulation much more than working-class women. A perceptive and intelligent study.

8215 Maldonado Denis, Manuel. La ideología: emigración y neomalthusianismo (in Problemas económicos y sociales de América Latina. Raúl Prebisch et al. Bogotá: Ediciones Universidades Simón Bolivar y Libre de Pereira, 1979, p. 323–345)

Critical study of the views of Puerto Rico's dominant class on migration to the US. Author outlines those views and connects them to neo-Malthusian perspectives. The work engages in content-analysis from a Marxist perspective.

8216 Marks, Arnaud F. Institutionalization of marriage and the family in Curaçao (in Family and kinship in Middle America and the Caribbean: proceedings of the 14th seminar of the Committee on Family Research of the International Sociological Association, Curaçao, September 1975. Arnaud F. Marks, René A. Römer, editors. Willemstad, Netherlands: Institute of Higher Studies in Curaçao, 1978?, p. 133–144, bibl.)

Legal monogamous marriages prevail in the lower classes; moreover, those marriages are stable and divorce and concubinage are rare. Author correlates this situation to socioeconomic development, and notes how different Curaçao's situation is from the one that exists in the rest of the Caribbean islands.

8217 ———. Intergroup relationships in the Caribbean: a field of long-range sociological research (CEDLA/B, 26, junio 1979, p. 39–66, bibl.)

Thoughtful review of the literature on inter-group relations in the Caribbean, with special concentration on Afro-Caribbeans and East Indians. Author discusses different theses (including that of the plural society), and organizes the summarized material into macro- and micro-level approaches. As a conclusion, suggests 17 hypotheses to be researched.

8218 Martínez Alier, Juan. La burguesía nacionalista en Cuba: en la década de 1950 (UB/BA, 29, 1979, p. 191–201)

In this critique of Marcos Winocur's book *Las clases olvidadas en la revolución cubana* (Barcelona: Crítica Grijalbo, 1979), author notes that Cuba had a national bourgeoisie (made up of sugar mill owners, among others) who wished to redefine commercial relations with the US, and generally took a nationalist position. Essay stresses the role of these sugar cane growers, which Winocur did not study in depth. Author repeats arguments he has presented elsewhere.

8219 Mathews, Lear and **S.C. Lee.** Matrifocality reconsidered: the case of the rural Afro-Guyanese family (*in* Family and kinship in Middle America and the Caribbean: proceedings of the 14th seminar of the Committee on Family Research of the International Sociological Association, Curaçao, September 1975. Arnaud F. Marks, René A. Römer, editors. Willemstad, Netherlands: Institute of Higher Studies in Curaçao, 1978?, p. 513–525, bibl.)

Authors present the thesis that the matrilineal kinship system of the Akans of West Africa was the cultural archetypes of the rural Afro-Guyanese matrifocal household. They challenge the usual view that the mother-centered family is the product of a plantation system or of slavery.

8220 Mizio, Emelicia. Puerto Rican task force report: project on ethnicity. New York: Family Service Association of America, 1979. 49 p.

This is the product of a research project funded by the National Institute of Mental Health. Its purpose was to develop a model of mental health service delivery systems for the black and Puerto Rican communities in the US. The first of the volume's three sections, dealing with racism in service delivery systems and its relationship to Puerto Rican culture, may be useful to Latin Americanists.

8221 Moncarz Percal, Raúl. The golden cage: Cubans in Miami (La cage d'or: les cubains à Miami; La jaula de oro: cubanos en Miami) (ICEM/IM, 16:3/4, 1978, p. 160–173, bibl., tables)

Studies Cubans' process of adaptation to a new environment (i.e., Miami, Florida). Using a random sample of Cubans over the age of 18 who reported their address to federal authorities, the author correlates education and language to occupation, geographic and income mobility. Concludes that mobility has been minimal, and that Cubans can usually afford to own houses only if women work outside the home.

Moreno, José Antonio. The Dominican revolution revisited. See item **6293**.

8222 Morris, Lydia. Women without men: domestic organization and the welfare state as seen in a coast community of Puerto Rico (BJS, 30:3, Sept. 1979, p. 322–340, tables)

Author argues that alternative household forms are related to socioeconomic status and to the dominant value system. She studies the village of El Bajío, Puerto Rico, and found that male unemployment creates high rates of marital instability. Women with children have different family patterns, depending on whether they receive state assistance or not. When the state aids these women, they set up independent households.

8223 La mujer en Cuba socialista. La Habana: Ministerio de Justicia, 1977. 392 p.

Collection of official documents related to women that the Revolution has issued since 1971. Among the materials included are: Overview of the FMC and its work (issued in 1974); Law establishing the Infancy Institute (1971) and Regulation on Child Care Centers (1973); Maternity Law (1974), FMC Theses and Report (1974); Family Code (1975); Cuban Communist Party's incomplete thesis on Women's Full Participation in the Revolutionary Process (1975); CP Resolution on Women (1975); Declaration on Women Issued in Mexico (1975); General Call to the Women of the World (1975); Berlin Declaration (1975); Communist Party Report on Women and Children (1975), articles of the Cuban Constitution pertaining to Women and Children (1976). The work offers no general analysis, and lacks a bibliography and index.

8224 Mujeres ejemplares. Foto de cubierta, Leonel Constantino. La Habana: Editorial ORBE, 1977. 341 p.; ports.

Collection of journalistic sketches of 33 women (19 of which are Cuban) who have contributed to the development of revolutionary movements throughout the world. Provides no sources or bibliography, or index.

8225 New York (City). **City University of New York. Center for Puerto Rican Studies. History Task Force.** Labor migration under capitalism: the Puerto Rican experience. New York: Monthly Review Press, 1979. 287 p.; bibl.; ill.; index.

A collective work that provides a theoretical and statistical Marxist analysis of the relationship between a capitalist mode of production and the type of labor migration it produces. It is presented within a historical framework covering the period from before 1898 to the present. Upholds the thesis that increases in productivity—resulting from the modernization of the means of production, which in turn improves labor-saving methods—result in a surplus population that is forced to migrate in order to survive. In reviewing other migration studies dealing with Puerto Rico, this study rejects the thesis that migration results from overpopulation. A well-written and logically-presented work.

8226 Paz, Ida. Medios masivos: ideología y propaganda imperialista. La Habana: Unión de Escritores y Artistas de Cuba, 1977. 130 p.; bibl.; ill. (Cuadernos de la revista Unión)

The basic thesis of the author, a Cuban economist, is that the ideological super-structure that rationalizes capitalist exploitation has become more complex as a result of the increased complexity of capitalism itself. She discusses the methods used by capitalist countries to foster a consumer mentality in the Third World; describes the monopolistic control transnational corporations exercise over the mass media in underdeveloped countries, especially Latin America. Chapters discuss "imperialist ideology," "the bourgeois science of propaganda," "information power" (basically, who owns what in the US), and "the mass media and ideological struggle." Lacks specific information on Latin America. Author concludes that under socialism the mass media serve the interests of the masses in their creation of a "New Man."

Pérez, Louis A., Jr. "La Chambelona:" political protest, sugar, and social banditry in Cuba, 1914–1917. See *HLAS 42:2614.*

8227 ———. Cubans in Tampa: from exiles to immigrants, 1892–1901 (FHS/FHQ, 57:2, Oct. 1978, p. 129–140)

Connects development of cigar industry in Tampa with events taking place in Cuba in the 19th century. Shows role of the cigar makers in the war of independence. A

readable essay that uses both primary and secondary sources.

8228 Perkins, Wilmot. If there is a God, He's just gotta be white: ideology as an impediment to development changes (*in* Development issues, Caribbean-American dialogue: proceedings and papers from the Caribbean-American Exchange Program conducted by the Phelps-Stokes Fund. New York: The Fund, 1980, p. 10–20)

Columnist for conservative Jamaican paper *The Daily Gleaner* puts forward thesis that certain countries are developed because development is "a mental condition reflected" in a particular culture (i.e., "developed peoples are those who have achieved their cultures in high degree of problem-solving capability.") This essay represents a return to 19th-century thinking.

8229 Picó de Hernández, Isabel. The quest for race, sex, and ethnic equality in Puerto Rico (UPR/CS, 14:4, Jan. 1975, p. 127–142, table)

First work to determine the extent and scope of discrimination on the basis of sex, race, or national origin that exists in private employment in Puerto Rico. Author surveyed 42 major firms.

8230 Poggie, John J., Jr. Small-scale fishermen's beliefs about success and development: a Puerto Rican case (SAA/HO, 38:1, Spring 1979, p. 6–11, bibl., tables)

Using a cognitive dissonance theory, author compares notions of *perceived* success to *real* success among fishermen of Puerto Real, a barrio of Cabo Robo, on the west coast of Puerto Rico. Based on interviews administered to 50 fishermen, as well as key informant ranking and participant observation.

8231 Pollard, Frank C.R. and J. Wilburg. Family organization in a squatter settlement in Guyana (*in* Family and kinship in Middle America and the Caribbean: proceedings of the 14th seminar of the Committee on Family Research of the International Sociological Association, Curaçao, September 1975. Arnaud F. Marks, René A. Römer, editors. Willemstad, Netherlands: Institute of Higher Studies of Curaçao, 1978?, p. 431–445, bibl., tables)

Survey of 75 households at South Haslington, small rural community 15 miles east of Georgetown. Includes several different types of families (nuclear, extended, joint, composite, female-headed, male-headed). Notes that male-headed families squat first, and that they are less varied than female-headed ones.

8232 The Puerto Rican woman. Edited and with an introduction by Edna Acosta-Belén, with the collaboration of Elia Hidalgo Christensen. New York: Praeger, 1979. 169 p.; bibl.; ill.; index.

Anthology of 11 essays on the history, culture, social and economic status of Puerto Rican women in Puerto Rico and the US. Essays were presented at the 1976 Hispanic American Women Symposium held at the State University of New York at Albany. They are descriptive and multidisciplinary in approach, and cover the following topics: capitalism and women in the labor force; women and equality; Puerto Rican feminism; a profile of the Puerto Rican woman; education and women; the image of women in Puerto Rican literature; cultural reaction to lesbianism; women and racial discrimination. Also presents the success stories of two women.

8233 Puerto Rico, identidad nacional y clases sociales: coloquio de Princeton. Angel G. Quintero Rivera et al. Rio Piedras, P.R.: Ediciones Huracán, 1979. 146 p.

Princeton University held a Colloquium in April 1978 on the National Identity of Puerto Rico and Haiti and this book contains three presentations on Puerto Rico. A.G. Quintero Rivera presents five theses on social classes and national identity on the island focusing on the period 1900–30. Notes that there is no unified and homogeneous national identity; that the very concept is determined by one's class. José Luis González traces the theme of national identity in literature from 1843 to the 1930s. Finally, Ricardo Campos and Juan Flores treat the role of migration in the development of a national culture from the perspective of proletarians. They analyze the literary works of several workers and the working class press. A provocative, highly readable work.

8234 Regalado, Antero. Las luchas campesinas en Cuba. Cubierta, José Salas. La Habana: Editorial Orbe, 1979. 220 p.; bibl.

The first and only attempt by a Cuban revolutionary to write a history of Cuban "peasants" (a term he never defines, but which appears from context to mean cultivators of small parcels of land). This work by an old member of the Cuban Communist Party is not Marxist in its approach, although it uses such terms as "class struggle." Its historical framework is the period from the tobacco growers' revolt of 1717 to the 1960s; and its thesis is that the *latifundia* (which represented anti-Cuban interests) dominated the economy, society and politics of Cuba until 1959. The interests of the peasants, the true representatives of the nation, were finally served with the Revolution. Work contains large amount of data that is useful, but needs further analysis. Author carried out no primary research, nor did he use the work of scholars like Juan Martínez Alier, Brian Pollit, or Lowry Nelson.

8235 Römer, René. Religious syncretism in the Caribbean (*in* Cultural traditions and Caribbean identity: the question of patrimony. Edited by S. Jeffrey K. Wilkerson. Gainesville: Center for Latin American Studies, University of Florida, 1980, p. 247–268, bibl.)

Author explains why the assumption that Caribbean culture is an equal mixture of three cultures does not apply in the religious sphere. In that area, the African tradition has predominated over the indigenous or European. Römer calls for a multidisciplinary study of Caribbean religious systems and their social and psychological components.

8236 Rogler, Lloyd H.; Rosemary Santana Cooney; and **Vilma Ortiz.** Intergenerational change in ethnic identity in the Puerto Rican family (CMS/IMR, 14:2, Summer 1980, p. 193–214, bibl., tables)

Authors argue that "education and age of arrival have significant independent effects upon the ethnic identity of mothers, fathers and children." They studied 100 intergenerationally-linked Puerto Rican nuclear families from New York City.

8237 Rohrlich-Leavitt, Ruby. The Puerto Ricans; culture change and language deviance. Tucson: Published for the Wenner-Gren Foundation for Anthropological Research by University of Arizona Press, 1974. 268 p.; bibl. (Viking Fund publications in anthropology; no. 51)

Author investigated the incidence of stuttering among the children of rural Puerto

Rican migrants living in San Juan and New York City. She uses speech pathology and anthropological methods to test the hypothesis that stuttering is a deviant linguistic response to sociocultural stress. Sample consisted of 10,000 Puerto Rican children attending public school (grades 1–6), most of them from a working-class background. Author's working premise—that acculturation to New York would be much more stressful than to San Juan, with a consequent higher incidence of stuttering among children in New York—was proved false, and the opposite was found to be true. She concludes that upward social mobility, nature of child rearing, and activity in economic, political, social, or religious institutions (i.e., socially-integrated communities) reduce the incidence of stuttering. A very original work.

8238 Romain, Jean-Baptiste. Cultural values: identification, dangers, lines of action (UNESCO/CU, 5:3, 1978, p. 90–109)

Simplistic, undocumented attempt at outlining common Caribbean values, the forces that threaten them, and the measures to be taken to defend those values. Identifies common material values (housing, nutrition, land organization, clothing), social values (the social stratification system, collective work orientation, carnival, etc.), and spiritual values (Creole, oral literature, herbal medicine, dancing, and religious expression) in the region. These are threatened by the replacement of Creole, and the adoption of an American or European education.

8239 Saavedra, José M. Effects of perceived parental warmth and control on the self-evaluation of Puerto Rican adolescent males (HRAF/BSR, 15:1, 1980, p. 41–53)

Author administered questionnaires on parental warmth and control to 208 Puerto Rican youths. Resulting data is correlated to self-esteem and self-adequacy.

8240 Samaroo, Brinsley. The Presbyterian Canadian Mission as an agent of integration in Trinidad during the nineteenth and early twentieth centuries (UPR/CS, 14:4, Jan. 1975, p. 41–55, tables)

Author describes how Canadian missionaries worked to help East Indians in Trinidad become adjusted to a totally different society, one that already faced numerous social strains resulting from the presence

of diverse ethnic groups. Uses historical approach, covering the period 1870–1920.

8241 Sánchez, Antonio. Ensayo sobre las ideas típicas de la pequeña burguesía en la República Dominicana (Realidad Contemporánea [Editora Alfa y Omega, Santo Domingo] 1:3/4, julio/dic. 1976, p. 137–164, tables)

Based on "observations," not a sample, author tries to determine the ideas and sentiments of the petite bourgeoisie that make it receptive to the authority and power of the grande bourgeoisie.

8242 Simmons, Peter. "Red legs:" class and color contradictions in Barbados (RU/SCID, 11:1, 1976, p. 3–24)

Author describes world view of marginal poor whites (descendants of indentured serfs brought over in colonial times) who live in the rural areas of Barbados. He also gives an historical overview of their origins. Based on interviews with approximately 450 persons. For more on the Red legs, see *HLAS 41:1090.*

8243 Simposio sobre las Personas de Mayor Edad: Problemática y Alternativas, *University of Puerto Rico, 1977.* La problemática de los envejecientes de Puerto Rico. Mariano Negrón-Portillo, Nemesio Vargas-Acevedo, Emilio González-Díaz, coordinadores; Rafael Corrada Guerrero, director; editor, Wenceslao Serra Deliz. Río Piedras: Centro de Investigaciones Sociales, Facultad de Ciencias Sociales, Universidad de Puerto Rico, 1978. 132 p.; bibl.

Rich in information, this work provides a model to be applied to other Latin American countries. Contains 11 papers presented at a Symposium on Old Age held Sept. 1977, in Puerto Rico. Topics discussed: 1) impact of modern social changes on old age in Puerto Rico (the elderly becoming marginal as the family becomes nuclear); 2) degree to which elderly form part of poverty cycle (it is estimated that over 50 percent of those over age 65 are poor); 3) demographic changes of Puerto Rican population (population over age 65 has increased 10 times in last 76 years); 4) degree to which elderly have benefitted from human services programs (very little); 5) legal status of the old (favorable in theory but not in practice); 6) problems of the elderly female (loneliness, and an income below that of the elderly male); and 7) attitudes of the young toward the elderly. A very useful work.

8244 Smith, Ashley. Pentecostalism in Jamaica (IJ/JJ, Sept. 1978, p. 2–13, bibl., plates)

Minister of the United Church in Jamaica defines Pentecostalism in Jamaica and describes rites of initiation and their expression, the social ecology of the movement, and the nature and social characteristics of the leadership and followers. Most of the participants are uneducated, poor, ill-housed, and female, and are between adolescence and 30s. Maintains that Pentecostalism is "an escape valve for much of the feelings of anger, disappointment and hopelessness which are quite justifiably built up in the breasts of the large mass of our unprivileged and oppressed people."

8245 Smith, Raymond T. Class differences in West Indian kinship: a genealogical exploration (*in* Family and kinship in Middle America and the Caribbean: proceedings of the 14th seminar of the Committee on Family Research of the International Sociological Association, Curaçao, September 1975. Arnaud F. Marks, René A. Römer, editors. Willemstad, Netherlands: Institute of Higher Studies in Curaçao, 1978?, p. 335–381, tables)

Using sample of 51 individual families from Jamaica and Guyana, author examines family formation and dynamics of family development. Stresses interaction between individual households and more extensive networks of mutual aid found in the Caribbean. Work challenges basic assumptions of functionalist theory about the family, including belief that consensual unions produce erosion of kinship ties or lead to disappearance of males from kinship networks and genealogies. Also notes that there are differences related to social class in the rate of occurrence of mating but not in the systems of mating.

8246 Tata, Robert J. Statistical explanation of the regional variation in growth of median family income in Puerto Rico (PAIGH/G, 88, dic. 1978, p. 79–88, bibl., maps, table)

The thesis of this article is that "the variation in the growth of median family income is positively related to change in the

median number of school years completed for persons over 25 years old," and the "change in absolute population" is also related to family income. Author uses multiple regression analysis.

8247 Techa, Siegfried H. and **Raymond Ph. Römer.** Fertility trends in the Netherlands Antilles (*in* Family and kinship in Middle America and the Caribbean: proceedings of the 14th seminar of the Committee on Family Research of the International Sociological Association, Curaçao, September 1975. Arnaud F. Marks, René A. Römer, editors. Willemstad, Netherlands: Institute of Higher Studies in Curaçao, 1978?, p. 144–155)

Using a fertility model elaborated by Kingsley Davis and Judith Blake, authors trade changes in fertility that have taken place in six islands of the Netherland Antilles. They argue that since 1900 the area has gone through several phases of demographic transition posited by functionalist theory. Cites no sources.

8248 Van den Berghe, Pierre L. Reply to Klaus de Albuquerque (SF, 57:1, Sept. 1978, p. 301–303)

Discusses the degree of racism in Mexico, Brazil and the US. See also item **8167**.

8249 Wall-Malefijt, Annemarie de. Respect patterns and change among the Javanese of Surinam (*in* Family and kinship in Middle America and the Caribbean: proceedings of the 14th seminar of the Committee on Family Research of the International Sociological Association, Curaçao, September 1975. Arnaud F. Marks, René A. Römer, editors. Willemstad, Netherlands: Institute of Higher Studies in Curaçao, 1978?, p. 87–98, bibl.)

Discusses Javanese family respect patterns. Author maintains that tradition of respect toward elders is a mechanism to preserve ethnicity. Work deals with history of Javanese migration to Surinam; importance of status and its terminology; class situation of this particular ethnic group; significance of respect; clash between traditionalism and market-oriented modernization; and breakdown of endogamous patterns of family formation. Field work for the study was done in 1958–59 and 1975.

8250 Wilson, Peter J. Crab antics; the social anthropology of English-speaking

Negro societies of the Caribbean. New Haven: Yale University Press, 1973. 258 p.; bibl.; ill. (Caribbean series; 14)

Ethnographic description of Providencia, a small Colombian island populated by English-speaking Protestant blacks, who have not been integrated into Colombian culture. Author uses field research to study social criteria by which population judges those with power (responsibility) or lack of power (reputation). Work suggests that values of social differentiation provide basis for existing social order; thus, great stress is placed on value patterns as key to understanding this society.

8251 Zuikov, Guennadi. Política social del poder popular (URSS/AL, 1, 1979, p. 41–55, table)

Compares Cuban working conditions, social security, health care, income, standard of living, rationing and housing, before and after 1959.

SOUTH AMERICA: ANDEAN COUNTRIES (Venezuela, Colombia, Ecuador, Peru, Bolivia and Chile)

LISANDRO PEREZ, Associate Professor of Sociology, Louisiana State University
QUENTIN JENKINS, Professor of Sociology, Louisiana State University

THE EMPHASES AND DIRECTIONS noted in the sociological literature on the Andean region reviewed in the proceeding volume, HLAS 41, generally hold true for works annotated in this one. Colombia continues to lead as the prime research setting for sociologists interested in the region, although there is a renewed interest in Peru. This trend may continue for the next few years, spurred by the changes that occurred in Peru's political scene in 1980.

We have noted previously the increasing volume of literature on women, children, and the family. This biennium, the number of works reviewed in these areas reached an astonishing level, and only a fraction of them could be included here (items **8254, 8258, 8261–8262, 8266, 8275** and **8293**). The lack of rigorous analysis of the status of women, a serious gap in the field, is largely due to the fact that most of the literature on the subject has not outgrown the polemic and pamphletary stage. For the first time in recent years works have appeared on the problems of the elderly (items **8252** and **8301**), a subject which, because of the age composition of the region's population, has not received much attention.

The emphasis on cities and their problems, a salient characteristic of the literature reviewed in HLAS 41, is not apparent this year. Instead, there seems to be a resurgence of interest in traditional areas of research that had declined in recent years such as population (items **8259, 8262–8263, 8277, 8280, 8289** and **8305**); rural society and development (items **8253, 8256, 8261, 8265, 8267, 8269, 8276, 8282, 8292, 8294** and **8298**); and social classes and inequality (items **8255, 8281, 8284, 8289** and **8299**). Within the area of population, the emphasis on migration continues, accompanied by a somewhat decreasing interest in fertility and family planning. Unfortunately, mortality appears to be a defunct topic among demographers working on the region.

A return to traditional areas of research has, fortunately, not meant a return to the traditional reliance on a limited range of analytical tools. The literature reviewed for this volume exhibits a wide variety of research approaches, extending beyond the traditional survey of descriptive statistical study. Rigorous analyses using either qualitative or historical methods are much in evidence. In fact, two of the most significant works reviewed for this *HLAS* (items **8264** and **8276**) use the historical approach.

VENEZUELA

8252 Aponte Bolívar, Margarita. El anciano en la sociedad venezolana. Caracas: Universidad Central de Venezuela, Facultad de Ciencias Económicas y Sociales, División de Publicaciones, 1978. 85 p.; bibl.; graphs.

Demographic analysis of elderly in Venezuela that covers the following characteristics: place of birth, age, sex, religion, marital status, educational level, and occupation. Final chapter deals with adequacy of country's social security programs.

8253 Chesterfield, Ray and **Kenneth Ruddle.** Traditional agricultural skill training among peasant farmers in Venezuela (AI/A, 74:3/4, 1979, p. 549–565, bibl., tables)

Detailed and intensive descriptive-analysis of socialization process by which peasant children are taught agricultural skills. A unique and fascinating study.

8254 Colomine Solarte, Feijoó. El menor en situación irregular en Venezuela. Caracas: s.n., 1974 [i.e. 1976]. 181 p.; 2 leaves of plates; bibl.; graphs.

Author's premise: Venezuela's most serious social problem is the neglect and abandonment of children. Covers following topics concisely: legal context; problems' causes and magnitude of; efforts of the Consejo Venezolano del Niño; and reviews existing programs to protect children.

8255 Gil Yepes, José Antonio. El reto de las élites. Madrid: Tecnos, 1978. 292 p.; 1 fold. leaf; bibl.; index (Serie de sociología. Semilla y surco)

Author documents origins and rise of different types of elites within Venezuelan system with emphasis on channels available for access to power. Also analyzes role and effect of elites under four Venezuelan presidential administrations. Challenge faced by elites is how to accelerate development while eliminating distortions that they themselves introduced into the country's political economy. A valuable work that is likely to have a lasting impact on future studies of Latin American elites.

8256 Margolies, Luise and **Maria Matilde Suárez.** The peasant family in the Venezuelan Andes (*in* Family and kinship in Middle America and the Caribbean: proceedings of the 14th seminar of the Committee on Family Research of the International Sociological Association, Curaçao, September 1975. Arnaud F. Marks, René A. Römer, editors. Willemstad, Netherlands: Institute of Higher Studies in Curaçao, 1978, p. 382–404, bibl., map)

Although throughout Latin America the peasants are becoming increasingly urban, this interesting and thoughtful study focuses on the Andean peasants who did not migrate. Authors discuss ways in which "urbanization" has affected the family.

8257 Martin, Richard; Steven J. Chaffee and **Fausto Izcaray.** Media and consumerism in Venezuela (AEJ/JQ, 56:2, Summer 1979, p. 296–304, tables)

Tests Lerner's proposition that rising expectations generated by mass media lead to political alienation. Stimulating restatement of question of desirability of using the media to raise personal consumption aspirations.

8258 Pollak-Eltz, Angelina. The black family in Venezuela (*in* Family and kinship in Middle America and the Caribbean: proceedings of the 14th seminar of the Committee on Family Research of the International Sociological Association, Curaçao, September 1975. Arnaud F. Marks, René A. Römer, editors. Willemstad, Netherlands: Institute of Higher Studies in Curaçao, 1978, p. 417–430, bibl.)

Study of mating patterns and household composition among persons of African ancestry and of lower socioeconomic origins residing in small communities. Unique study, based on author's fieldwork.

———. Indianische Relikte im Volksglauben der Venezolaner. See *HLAS 42:1431.*

8259 Santander Laya, Gustavo and **Rafael Santander Garrido.** Los italianos: forjadores de la nacionalidad y del desarrollo económico de Venezuela. Valencia, Venezuela: Vadell Hermanos Editores, 1978. 284 p.; bibl.; ill.

Noteworthy study, given scarcity of sociological works on European immigrants to Latin America. Authors combine broad overview of contributions of Italians to Venezuelan history and society with biographical studies of prominent Italian immigrants. Emphasizes the latter which gives work a decidedly anecdotal tone that makes for interesting reading. However, authors' exaggerated praise for group in question detracts from study's objectivity.

8260 Schmidt-Relenberg, Norbert; Harmut [sic] **Kärner** and **Volkmar Köhler.** Los pobres de Venezuela: autoorganización de los pobladores: un informe crítico. Traducción de Hugo Yañes; tapa, Luis O. Marsón. Caracas, Venezuela: El Cid Editor, 1979. 173 p.; bibl. (Colección Estudios interdisciplinarios)

Analysis of social and economic marginality in three Venezuelan cities: Barquisimeto, Ciudad Guyana, and Caracas. Authors focus on origins of poverty problem and on assessing concept of "self-help," which they consider a bourgeois solution.

Wright, Winthrop R. Race, nationality, and immigration in Venezuelan thought, 1890 to 1937. See *HLAS 42:3046.*

Zago, Angela. Entre ayer y hoy. See item 6418.

COLOMBIA

8261 Asociación Colombiana para el Estudio de la Población. Mujer y capitalismo agrario: estudio de cuatro regiones colombianas. Magdalena León de Leal, directora de la investigación; Carmen Diana Deere, investigadora asociada; Ingrid Cáceres G. et al., equipo de investigación; foto de la portada, Efraín García "EGAR." Bogotá, Colombia: Asociación Colombiana para el Estudio de la Población, 1980. 295 p.; bibl.; maps.

Interesting and important collection of readings on impact of agricultural capitalist development on sexual division of labor in peasant households. Contrastive analysis encompasses regions of Colombia with different rural socioeconomic structures. Work also provides excellent historical analyses.

8262 Browner, Carole. Toma de decisiones sobre el aborto: algunos hallazgos en Colombia (ACEP/Ep, 4:1/6, enero/junio 1979, p. 16–29, bibl., ill., tables)

Based on interviews with 108 women in Cali who experienced unwanted pregnancies, author investigates why some women seek an abortion while others do not (abortion is illegal but widely practiced). As expected, single and separated women and those in precarious consensual unions were more likely to seek an abortion than other women. Factor of greatest importance in making the decision proved to be the likelihood of economic support from the prospective father.

8263 Cardona Gutiérrez, Ramiro and **Alan B. Simmons.** Destino la metrópoli: un modelo general de las migraciones internas en América Latina. Bogotá: Corporación Centro Regional de Población, 1978. 238 p.; bibl.; ill.

This is one of the best works on general topic of internal migration in Latin America. It concisely brings together knowledge on following topics: general patterns of internal migration in Latin America; socioeconomic context of migration; process of migration to city; selectivity of migration; social mobility of migrants in city; and adaptation of migrants to city life. Most illustrative materials are Colombian, with special emphasis on Bogotá.

8264 Fals-Borda, Orlando. Historia doble de la costa. t. 1, Mompox y Loba. Fotos de Orlando Fals Borda; acuarelas de Edward Mark; dibujos de Iván Chalarca; grabado del papel Periódico Ilustrado. Bogotá: C. Valencia Editores, 1979. 1 v.; ill.

Yet another in Fals Borda's recent series of monographs on the social and agrarian history of the Atlantic Coast (see *HLAS 41:9212–9213*). Like the others, this work is written primarily for a general audience, to help it understand "phenomena which today pass before our eyes without our knowledge of where they originate," and is consistent with his efforts to build in Colombia a "social science of the proletariat" (see also *HLAS 39:9202*). Focusing on the area of Mompox and Loba, this is vol. 1 of a projected multi-volume work on entire coastal region. An interesting feature is that left-hand pages offer descriptions and anecdotes while right-hand pages provide accompanying theoretical interpretations.

8265 Galli, Rosemary. Rural development as social control: international agencies and class struggle in the Colombian countryside (LAP, 5[4]:19, Fall 1978, p. 71–89)

Author is convinced that technology introduced into developing nations during the 1970s was intended to "tie peasants to the land." However, she does not clearly state a position on the proper role of peasants in their respective nations.

8266 El Gamín. v. 1, Su albergue social y su familia. v. 2, Análisis de datos secundarios. Virginia Gutiérrez de Pineda et al.; fotografía portada, Gustavo Perry T. New York?: UNICEF, 1978. 2 v.; bibl.; ill.

The problem of *gamines* in Colombian cities has reached such proportions in recent years that it has engendered a number of studies (see *HLAS 37:9837–9838*). This latest contribution, based on data derived from surveys in Bogotá, Medellín, Cali, Bucaramanga, and Cartagena, is a fairly comprehensive study of characteristics of *gamines* families. Its purpose is to investigate dynamics of setting in which youngsters' initial socialization process takes place.

8267 La Gestión campesina: experiencias de base: selección de los documentos presentados para el Premio Mariano Ospina Pérez 1978. Bogotá: Fundación Mariano Ospina Pérez, 1980. 275 p.; ill. (Publicaciones—Fundación Mariano Ospina Pérez; 8)

Selection of readings on the theme of cooperation in rural areas. Studies highlight successful cooperatives, some of which are agroindustrial entities, located for the most part in Nariño, Cauca, or Antioquia. Of special interest are descriptions of the functioning of dairy cooperatives.

Gilhodès, Pierre. La violence en Colombie: banditisme et guerre sociale. See *HLAS 42:2980.*

8268 Guillén Martínez, Fernando. El poder político en Colombia. Presentación de Alvaro Tirado Mejía. Bogotá: Editorial Punta de Lanza, 1979. 659 p.

Sociological analysis of internal mechanisms that dominant class has used to maintain itself in power from colonial period to present. Author argues that each successive maneuver of the elite to retain power has been followed by a popular reaction realized through formal associations and violent resistance. [D.W. Dent]

8269 Haney, Emil B. and **Wava G. Haney.**
Social and ecological contradictions of community development and rural modernization in a Colombian peasant community (SAA/HO, 37:3, Fall 1978, p. 225–234)

Among best recent analytical case studies of development, this analysis shows how peasants in a village evolve over a period of years and under a number of programs. Authors indicate how action programs effect change and what leaders are learning in the process.

8270 Lynch, Dennis O. Lawyers in Colombia: perspectives on the organization and allocation of legal services (Texas International Law Journal [University of Texas, School of Law, Austin] 13:2, Spring 1978, p. 199–241, tables)

Description of organization, career patterns, and methods of allocating and delivering legal services in Colombia's legal profession, based on 103 interviews conducted in 1974 with a sample of lawyers in Bogotá. Key variables in study include: social origins, legal career pattern; size of bar; cost of legal services; type of clientele; and performance tasks. Elitist nature of the Javeriana and Rosario Law schools is clearly affirmed in the analysis, which states that "the law school a person attends it the most important variable." [D.W. Dent]

8271 Metodología y desarrollo en las ciencias sociales: efectos del crecimiento dependiente sobre la estructura social colombiana. Bogotá: Centro de Estudios sobre Desarrollo Económico, Facultad de Economía, Universidad de los Andes, 1977. 614 p.; bibl.; graphs.

Collection of readings, most of them previously published, intended to raise question (without answering it) of which theoretical orientation is best suited to understanding the central problems of Colombian society. Readings illustrative of four orientations are included, with an emphasis on "structuralism" and the "historical and class focus."

8273 La migración rural urbana: manifestación y agente de un proceso de cambio social. Bogotá: CCRP, Area Distribución Espacial de la Población, 1978. 64 p.; bibl. (Monografía de la Corporación Centro Regional de Población; v. 7)

Corporación Centro Regional de Población in Bogotá has produced numerous works on internal migration and population redistribution, most of them focused on Colombia (see *HLAS 41:5254*). This latest publication is a short and concise work authored primarily by Ramiro Cordona Gutiérrez. Title is misleading, for only in the first 20 pages does author discuss rural-urban migration, urbanization policy, and urban social change. Second edition entitled "Preliminary Guidelines for the Understanding of a Human Settlement as a System," is the result of a study inspired by the HABITAT 76 conference in Vancouver.

8274 Moser, Caroline O.N. Why the poor remain poor: the experience of Bogotá market trades in the 1970s (SAGE/JIAS, 22:3, Aug. 1980, p. 365–387, bibl., tables)

Drawing on specific case studies of self-employment urban market sellers, author examines dynamics, growth potential and constraints on economic expansion of these small-scale enterprises. A micro-level study that attempts to contribute an "apt illustration" for use in the informal sector/petty commodity production debate.

8275 Muñoz Vila, Cecilia and **Martha Palacios V.** El niño trabajador: testimonios. Fotografías, Helena Mogollón. Bogotá: C. Valencia Editores, 1980. 210 p.; ill.

Yet another work on the deprived children (*gamines*) who barely survive in the streets of Colombian cities (see above item **8266** and *HLAS 37:9837–9838*). Work is a compilation of 20 case studies detailing the vicissitudes of children engaged in great variety of very marginal economic activities.

8276 Palacios, Marco. Coffee in Colombia, 1850–1970: an economic, social, and political history. Cambridge; New York: Cambridge University Press, 1980. 338 p.; bibl.; ill.; index (Cambridge Latin American studies; 36)

A landmark work. In author's words: "the aim of this book is to describe and explain the conditions under which Colombia, by becoming an important mono-exporting country of a product characteristic of tropical agriculture, coffee, managed to link its economy solidly with the world market. At the same time the book attempts to show the full effects of such integration on the structure of contemporary Colombia." Author's analysis includes: the making of an oligarchy; the land system of central Colombia; the structure of and living conditions in coffee *haciendas*; and social effects of *antioqueño* colonization. For historian's comment, see *HLAS 42:2989*.

8277 Parada Caicedo, Jorge Humberto. Bibliografía comentada sobre migraciones en Colombia. Bogotá: Instituto Colombiana para el Fomento de la Educación Superior, División de Documentación e Información, Centro de Documentación, 1980. 86 p.

Because of the extensive body of recent literature on Colombian migration (see *HLAS 41*, p. 629), bibliographies on this subject are extremely useful. Unfortunately, this is a rather limited effort, covering only the best-known works. Volume's second half is a rather superficial bibliography of literature on migration in all of Latin America.

8278 Partridge, William L. Banana County in the wake of United Fruit: social and economic linkages (AAA/AE, 6:3, Aug. 1979, p. 491–509)

Author focuses on long-range social impact of multinational corporations, specifically, the withdrawal of United Fruit Company from a community in Colombia. Finds that both "dependency" and "growth-stimulus" theories are inadequate to explain social and economic change at the community level, and defends the "linkage approach," an analytical technique useful for tracing the complex effects of a multinational corporation's production process.

Silva, Renán. Imagen de la mujer en los textos escolares: contribución a un análisis. See item **4444**.

8279 La Situación social en Colombia. Editado por Alejandro Angulo. 4. ed. Bogotá: Editorial CINEP, 1979. 153 p.; bibl.; ill.

Produced under auspices of Centro de Investigación y Educación Popular, this short work covers wide range of topics: population, rural sociology, industrial development, health, political institutions, labor movements, education, and urbanization. While effort is commendable, scope is too ambitious and the analyses are frequently superficial. Furthermore, editor's claim that study focuses on problem of inequality is not borne out in many of the chapters. Nevertheless, work offers a good introduction to Colombian society.

8280 Torales, Ponciano. La dinámica interna de los movimientos migratorios en Colombia. Bogotá: Ministerio de Trabajo y Seguridad Social, 1979. 170 p.; bibl.; ill.; maps; tables.

Contemporary trends in internal migration in Colombia have received considerable attention, but rarely have they been analyzed with a broader historical perspective than in this volume. Making extensive use of graphs, maps, and tables, author generalizes about changing patterns of internal population movements in the country since the 19th century.

ECUADOR

8281 Campo, Esteban del. Crisis de la hegemonía oligárquica, clases populares y populismo en Ecuador (UNAM/RMS, 40[40]: 3, julio/sept. 1978, p. 1101–1118)

In this interesting historical analysis, author applies theories concerning the rise of populism and the crisis of the oligarchy to the Ecuadorian situation. Points out how events in that country have both followed and departed from expected pattern.

The urban poor in Guayaquil, Ecuador: modes correlated, and context of political participation. See item **6432**.

8282 Verduga, César and Gustavo Cosse. El Estado y el agro en el caso ecuatoriano: reflexiones sobre una investigación (UNAM/RMS, 40[40]: 3, julio/sept. 1978, p. 1055–1100, ill., tables)

Rigorous, detailed, and extensive analysis of the formulation and thrust of the Ecuadorian government's programs for rural socioeconomic change in the period 1964–75.

PERU

Aranda, Arturo and Maria Escalante. Lucha de clases en el movimiento sindical cusqueño, 1927–1965. See *HLAS 42:3054*.

8283 Barrig, Maruja. Cinturón de castidad: la mujer de clase media en el Perú. Lima: Mosca Azul, 1979. 210 p.; bibl.

Discusses social factors determining sexual ideology of middle-class Peruvian women. Book's pt. 1 is theoretical; pt. 2 contains three lengthy anonymous statements that illustrate points made in the theoretical section, specifically, the permanence of sexual inhibitions developed during childhood and adolescence.

8284 Bell, W.S. Los desgraciados: aspects of poverty in Peru (JLAS, 21:1, May 1979, p. 223–232)

An excellent summary and critique of studies of Peruvian poverty by Richard Webb, Michael Lipson, Robert Keith and J. Martínez-Alier. Concludes that agrarian reform has not benefited the rural poor.

Bonilla, Heraclio. The War of the Pacific and the national and colonial problem in Peru. See *HLAS 42:3060*.

8285 Centro de Estudios de Población y Desarrollo. Diagnóstico social y jurídico de la mujer en el Perú. Lima, Perú: Centro de Estudios de Población y Desarrollo, 1979. 204 p.

Data concerning roles women play in Peruvian society are very scarce. This work presents data on the health, education, and occupational activities of Peruvian women, including a special section on rural women. A very welcome report.

Claverías, Ricardo. El mercado interno y la espontaneidad de los movimientos campesinos: Puno, 1950–1968. See *HLAS 42:3067*.

Cotler, Julio. Perú: estado oligárquico y reformismo militar. See *HLAS 42:3069*.

8286 Dietz, Henry A. Poverty and problem-solving under military rule: the urban poor in Lima, Peru. Austin: University of Texas Press, 1980. 286 p.; bibl.; ill.; index (Latin American monographs; no. 51)

Welcome addition to limited literature on the reaction of military regimes to political pressures generated by urban poverty and the response of poor to military authority. Includes copy of questionnaire on which the study is based, that researchers will find most valuable.

———— and **Richard J. Moore.** Political participation in a non-electoral setting: the urban poor in Lima, Peru. See item **6452.**

Durand, A.N. Francisco. Movimientos sociales urbanos y problema regional: Arequipa, 1967–1973. See *HLAS 42:3072.*

Flores Galindo, Alberto. Apuntes sobre las ocupaciones de tierras y el sindicalismo agrario: 1945–1964. See *HLAS 42:3076.*

8287 Gilbert, Dennis. Society, politics, and the press: an interpretation of the Peruvian press reform of 1974 (SAGE/JIAS, 21:3, Aug. 1979, p. 369–394, bibl.)
Fascinating, well-documented chronicle of how the Peruvian press, previously dominated by an established ruling class, came under the control of a military regime and its shifting politics.

Graber, Eric S. An annotated bibliography of rural development, urbanization, and levels of living in Peru. See *HLAS 42:43.*

Hünefeldt, Christine. Los negros en Lima: 1800–1830. See *HLAS 42:3085.*

8288 Idígoras, José L. Mirada prospectiva a la religión en el Perú (*in* Perú, identidad nacional. César Arróspide de la Flor et al. Lima: Centro de Estudios para el Desarrollo y la Participación, 1979, p. 403–426 [Serie Realidad nacional])
Perceptive analysis of changes taking place in religion in Peru as a result of development and such secular influences as mass media. discussion of popular Catholicism is especially insightful.

Kaerger, Karl. Condiciones agrarias de la Sierra Sur Peruana: 1899. See *HLAS 42:3086.*

Kapsoli E., Wilfredo. Los movimientos campesinos en el Peru, 1879–1965: ensayos. See *HLAS 42:3088.*

————. Movimientos sociales en Cayaltó: 1915–1919. See *HLAS 42:3089.*

Klaiber, Jeffrey L. Los cholos y los rotos: actitudes raciales durante la Guerra del Pacífico. See *HLAS 42:3091.*

————. Religión y revolución en los Andes en el siglo XIX. See *HLAS 42:3092.*

8289 Laite, A.J. Industrialization, migration and social stratification at the periphery: a case study of mining in the Peruvian Andes (UK/SR, 26:4, new series, Nov. 1978, p. 859–885)
Penetrating analysis of consequences of migratory labor force on class formation. It would be argued, however, that the committed industrial worker and the instrumental migrant complement one another.

8290 Laite, Julian. Miners and national politics in Peru, 1900–1974 (JLAS, 12:2, Nov. 1980, p. 317–340)
Concise treatment of labor movement's history among Peruvian miners in the 20th century. Author contends that because miners' political activity is not institutionalized, history of their interactions with national political structures and issues is cyclical.

Manrique, Nelson. Los movimientos campesinos en la Guerra del Pacífico. See *HLAS 42:3096.*

8291 Matos Mar, José. Las barriadas de Lima, 1957. 2. ed., rev. y aumentada. Lima: Instituto de Estudios Peruanos, 1977. 293 p.; 8 fold. leaves of plates; ill. (Urbanización, migraciones y cambios en la sociedad peruana; 1)
Revised and expanded edition of work first published in 1966 but still relevant because of growth of marginal urban settlements throughout the continent and aggravation of problems associated with them. Few works on the subject, however, are as comprehensive as this one, dealing with Lima. It includes the following: history of each major *barriada*; spatial arrangements of population in a representative settlement; sociodemographic characteristics of inhabitants; action groups within communities; and biographies of some inhabitants. Data are derived primarily from detailed census of Lima's *barriadas* taken in 1957.

Mooney, Mary H. and **Walter C. Soderland.** Clerical attitudes toward political development in Peru. See item **6465.**

Normano, João Frederico and **Antonello Gerbi.** The Japanese in South America: an introductory survey with special reference to Peru. See *HLAS 42:3101.*

Pachas Castilla, Rolando. Economía y sociedad en el Valle de Chincha: 1860–1919. See *HLAS 42:3103.*

Palomino, Abdón. Andahuaylas, 1974: un movimiento de reivindicación campesina dentro del proceso de reforma agraria. See *HLAS 42:3104.*

Peasant cooperation and capitalist expansion in central Peru. See *HLAS 42:3105.*

8292 Plaza J., Orlando. Campesinado, analfabetismo y el problema del voto en el Perú (NSO, 41, marzo/abril 1979, p. 71–82, map, plates, tables)

The 1978 debate on whether to give the vote to illiterates revolved around the fact that 76 percent of those who were reported as being illiterate were *campesinos.*

Reátegui Chávez, Wilson. Explotación agropecuaria y las movilizaciones campesinas en Lauramarca-Cusco. See *HLAS 42:3112.*

Rénique, Gerardo. Comunidades campesinos y "recuperaciones" de tierras: Valle de Mantaro. See *HLAS 42:3113.*

———. Movimientos campesinos en la Sociedad Ganadera del Centro: 1910–1950. See *HLAS 42:3114.*

Rénique, José Luis. Los descentralistas arequipeños en la crisis del 30. See *HLAS 42:-3115.*

Rodríguez Pastor, Humberto. Una rebelión de culíes chinos: Pativilca, 1870. See *HLAS 42:3116.*

———. Los trabajadores chinos culíes en el Perú: artículos históricos. See *HLAS 42:-3117.*

Samaniego L., Carlos and **Bryan Roberts.** El significado de la SAIS de la Sierra Central del Perú: el caso de las SAIS Cahuide. See *HLAS 42:3118.*

Sánchez León, Abelardo and **Julio Calderón Cockburn.** El laberinto de la ciudad: políticas urbanas del estado, 1950–1979. See item **6478.**

8293 Ser mujer en el Perú. Esther Andradi, Ana María Portugal, editoras; hablan, Teresa Dávila et al. Lima: Ediciones Mujer y Autonomía, 1978. 254 p.

Contains 14 interviews with a wide variety of Peruvian women, including a housewife, an educator, a businesswoman, a prostitute, a "vedette," and a fatory worker. Most of the stories poignantly highlight the difficulties faced by Peruvian women.

8294 Smith, Gavin A. Socio-economic differentiation and relations of production among rural-based petty producers in central Peru: 1880–1970 (JPS, 6:3, April 1979, p 286–310, bibl.)

Smith has taken on the very difficult task of examining the development of socio-economic differentiation among a central Peruvian "peasantry." He accomplishes this by analyzing effects of factors such as family relations, migration, population changes, hacienda-community relations, and employment in local mines on the character of petty production over a period of 90 years. For historian's comment, see *HLAS 42:3122.*

Thompson, Stephen I. Assimilation and non-assimilation of Asian-Americans and Asian-Peruvians. See *HLAS 42:3124.*

Tigner, James L. The Ryukyuans in Peru: 1906–1952. See *HLAS 42:3126.*

8295 Tugurización en Lima metropolitana. Abelardo Sánchez León et al. Lima: Centro de Estudios y Promoción del Desarrollo, 1979. 190 p; bibl.

This work, focused on the growth of slum areas (*tugurios*) in the Lima metropolitan area, constitutes yet another example of the increasing emphasis social scientists are placing on the study of urban Latin America. The proliferation of slum areas in the past decade is Lima's most visible social problem, and the authors trace its origins to Lima's housing crisis. They make a useful distinction between two types of *tugurios*: *tugurio interno* (an inner-city slum) and *tugurización en barriadas* (makeshift settlements in fringe areas of the city), and study the characteristics of the population residing in both through a random sample of eight different neighborhoods.

8296 Valderrama, Mariano and **Patricia Ludmann.** La oligarquía terrateniente, ayer y hoy. Lima: Departamento de Ciencias Sociales, P. Universidad Católica del Perú, 1979. 411, 2 p.; annexes; bibl.

Study of Peru's principal agricultural enterprises shows that by the onset of military rule in 1968 the landed oligarchy did not possess the power or wealth generally attributed to them. At the same time, however, their highly cohesive nature and their ties to the urban financial bourgeoisie made them more than mere "puppets of imperialism," as they are defined by some writers. After 1968, peasant movements and agrarian reform significantly curtailed the influence of the landed oligarchy.

Vassallo, Manuel. Rumi Maqui y la nacionalidad quechua. See *HLAS 42:3128*.

8297 Wils, Frits C.M. Industrialization, industrialists, and the nation-state in Peru: a comparative/sociological analysis. Berkeley: Institute of International Studies, University of California, 1979. 273 p.; bibl. (Research series—Institute of International Studies, University of California, Berkeley; no. 41)

As a classical example of a dependent enclave economy in which a few very wealthy families and powerful export companies manage to dominate (until 1968) Peru is an excellent candidate for a study of industrialization. Wils' study increases our knowledge of that process by indicating how industry and industrialists can be studied as "dependent" as well as "independent" variables. His analysis also makes good use of the concept of a "roofless society."

Wong, Bernard. A comparative study of the assimilation of the Chinese in New York City and Lima, Peru. See *HLAS 42:3131*.

Yang, Alexander Chung Yuan. O comércio dos "coolie." See *HLAS 42:3132*.

BOLIVIA

8298 Albó, Xavier. Bodas de plata? o, Requiem por una reforma agraria. Comentarios de Fernando Calderón, Carlos Quiroga, Alfonso Camacho. La Paz: Centro de Investigación y Promoción del Campesinado, 1979. 105 p.; bibl.; ill. (Cuaderno de investigación—CIPCA; 17)

Author evaluates effect of Bolivian agrarian reform program, presumably initiated in 1953. While acknowledging progress in some areas, author concludes that reform has had some undesirable effects on Bolivia's agrarian situation, especially by strengthening large agroindustrial concerns and helping to create unproductive *minifundios*. One of the first works to use the results of the 1976 census.

Costa de la Torre, Arturo. Estirpe y genealogía del protomártir Pedro Domingo Murillo. See *HLAS 42:3148*.

Crespo R., Alberto. Alemanes en Bolivia. See *HLAS 42:3149*.

8299 Lora, Guillermo. Formación de la clase obrera boliviana. La Paz: Ediciones Masas, 1980. 283 p.; bibl.

History of the Bolivian working class from the 19th century to 1979, with an emphasis on unionization efforts and the influence of national political events.

Nash, June. Mi vida en las minas: la autobiografía de una mujer boliviana. See *HLAS 42:3168*.

Sautu, Ruth. The female labor force in Argentina, Bolivia and Paraguay. See item **8329**.

Valencia Vega, Alipio. Simona Josefa Manzaneda: por patrioto, pero "chola," un infamante suplicio acabó con su vida. See *HLAS 42:3184*.

Wainerman, Catalina H.; Ruth Sautu; and Zulma Recchini de Lattes. The participation of women in economic activity in Argentina, Bolivia and Paraguay: a comparative study. See item **8339**.

CHILE

8300 Aram, John D. and Teresa Gana Piraino. The hierarchy of needs theory: an evaluation in Chile (SIP/RIP, 12:2, 1978, p. 179–188, bibl., tables)

Consists of an empirical evaluation of Abraham Maslow's needs hierarchy, using a broad sample from Chile. Results indicate there may be more empirical evidence in support of Maslow's theories—with the exception of "esteem" need—in Latin America than in US.

Barros Lezaeta, Luis and Ximena Vergara Johnson. El modo de ser aristocrático: el caso de la oligarquía chilena hacia 1900. See *HLAS 42:3196*.

Campero Q., Guillermo. Las nuevas condiciones en las relaciones del trabajo y la acción política en Chile. See item **6522**.

Cavarozzi, Marcelo. El orden oligárquico en Chile, 1880–1940. See *HLAS 42:3208*.

8301 Chile. Instituto Nacional de Estadísticas. Perfiles de la población de 65 y más años de edad. Santiago: República de Chile, Instituto Nacional de Estadísticas: Consejo Nacional de la Ancianidad, 1977. 38 p.; bibl.; graphs.

Useful work, chiefly as a data source that consists mostly of statistical materials, presented in both tables and graphs, with very little analysis. Focuses on elderly Chilean population, combining census results with findings of a 1975 national survey of households.

8302 ———. Oficina de Planificación Nacional. A social development experiment in Chile: report. Prepared by the Chilean National Planning Office to be presented to the United Nations General Secretariat. Santiago: National Planning Office, ODEPLAN, 1977. 90 leaves.

Report deals with problem of "extreme poverty" in Chile by mapping where it exists and collecting indicators of human resources, education, training, employment, health and housing. Provides data and useful insights into the rationale for governmental policy.

Gilfeather, Katherine Anne. Women religious, the poor and the institutional Church in Chile. See item **6540**.

8303 Chile: mujer y sociedad. Compiladores, Paz Covarrubias, Rolando Franco. Santiago: Fondo de las Naciones Unidas para la Infancia, 1978. 876 p.; annexes; bibl.; graphs.

Produced by UNICEF, this is a landmark work on Chilean women. Contains 32 previously unpublished essays by more than 45 authors, on the topics of women, feminism and the female role in Chilean society. Essays cover a wide-range of issues (e.g., female labor force participation; fertility and family planning; social-class differences; theological considerations; the male role; motherhood; the feminist movement; the image of women in the mass media; and the legal status of women).

8304 Hartwig, Vera. Grundaspekte der Indianerfrage und ihre Beziehungen zur Agrafrage in Chile bis zum Jahre 1970 (MVL/J, 30, 1975, p. 293–304, map)

Synopsis of doctoral dissertation notes that if Chile's Indians are to be integrated into the nation's agricultural production they must be treated as a unit together with other poor or landless peasants. [R.V. Shaw]

8305 Herold, Joan M. Female migration in Chile: types of moves and socioeconomic characteristics (PAA/D, 16:2, May 1979, p. 257–278, bibl., tables)

"This paper examines inter-provincial female migration in Chile for the 1965–70 period, with a view to describing socioeconomic characteristics of migrant women and to determining differences and similarities in age, educational level, occupation, and type of move (first, return, or repeat) between movers to the capital and to other urban areas. Data are from a five percent sample of the 1970 Chilean census." Perhaps the most interesting find is that recent female migration to urban areas in Chile is more prevalent among upper than the lower strata of society.

Inkeles, Alex. Individual modernity in different ethnic and religious groups: data from a six-nation study. See item **8319**.

8306 Labbé, Octavio and Zbigniew Marcin Kowalewski. La discusión sobre el proletariado en Chile (PAN/ES, 3, 1976, p. 217–230)

Sets forth an analytical framework for assessing changing class-consciousness, specifically, whether or not the proletariat is becoming more "bourgeois." Author then critiques that framework, using data from a recent sociological study of two Chilean enterprises. [A. Hagerman-Johnson]

McCaa, Robert. Chilean social and demographic history. See *HLAS 42:3235*.

Menanteau-Horta, Dario. El sistema educativo y su incidencia en la estratificación social en Chile. See item **4412**.

Monteón, Michael. The *enganche* in the Chilean nitrate sector, 1880–1930. See *HLAS 42:3242*.

Moulian, Tomás. Religion and authoritarianism. See item **6561**.

Petras, James F. The divergence between scientific work and political action. See item **8324**.

Prensa y lucha ideológica en los cordones industriales de Santiago: testimonios. See item **6576**.

Román, Charles G. Pregger. Economic interest groups within the Chilean government, 1851 to 1891: continuity and discontinuity in economic and political evolution. See *HLAS 42:3261*.

Tobler, Hans Werner and **Peter Waldmann.** German colonies in South America: a new Germany in the Cono Sur? See item **8335**.

SOUTH AMERICA: THE RIVER PLATE
(Argentina, Paraguay and Uruguay)

CARLOS H. WAISMAN, *Assistant Professor of Sociology,*
University of California, San Diego

IN ARGENTINA, THE COUNTRY WITH THE LARGEST academic infrastructure in the subregion, social research was disarticulated as a result of the violence of the 1970s that engulfed large segments of the intelligentsia, of the cultural policies of the Isabel Perón administration and, especially, of the authoritarian regime established in 1976. Political upheaval and repression led to cultural decay. A large proportion of the intelligentsia went into exile, social science programs in universities were eliminated, independent research centers closed down, or reduced their activities to a minimum, and, with a few exceptions, publication in the social sciences ceased. The current rulers view sociology and its allied disciplines as intrinsically subversive doctrines, whose practitioners, to repeat the famous charge against Socrates, believe in the gods the state believes in, and also corrupt the young. These charges place social scientists, perhaps undeservedly, in excellent company indeed. It is important to note that most of the studies produced in Argentina report on research that was carried out prior to the 1976 military coup, and that in many cases the authors of these works have since left the country. The southern cone as a whole is becoming an area in which only the least controversial and obtrusive forms of sociological research, such as descriptive demography, can be carried out. Only this type of empirical work is conducted by scientists living in Uruguay and Paraguay.

Most entries in the Argentine subsection correspond to four subject areas: 1) ethnography of rural populations in the country's peripheral regions; 2) historical research on the assimilation of immigrants; 3) quantitative analyses of social structure; and 4) the study of the social basis of politics. The entries exhibit an international division of labor: most pieces in the first and third categories are written by Argentines, while works in the second and fourth group are authored mostly by foreign scholars.

Works on ethnography of the rural periphery fill two existing gaps in Argentine social science, one substantive and the other methodological. Since the urbanization and industrialization of Argentina preceded the development of modern social science, and the main social and political forces are located in the cities, the sociological study of the periphery was neglected. In addition, the two prevailing types of research methodology that evolved were the comparative-historical approach and survey and demographic techniques. Both of these were practiced by Germani, the founder of Argentine sociology. However, in the 1960s and early 1970s, a group of competent ethnographers, who were interested in the study of the rural periphery, emerged. The studies by Archetti and Stolen (item **8308**), Bartolomé (item **8312**), Herrán (item **8318**), Vessuri (item **8336**), and especially the collection of papers edited by Hermitte and Bartolomé (item **8325**), represent the work of this group.

The most original piece on the assimilation of immigrants is Baily's article (item **8311**). Of the several quantitative studies of social structure, the most important, in terms of scope, is Villarreal's book (item **8337**), which combines sophisticated social theory and the analysis of census data. The papers on mobility by Beccaria (item **8313**) and Beccaria and Minujín (item **8314**), and on female participation in the labor force by Sautu (item **8329**), are very competent pieces of work.

Finally, on the social basis of politics, the most significant entry is Rouquié's book (item **8328**), one of the most important contributions to the study of Argentine militarism to date and, in general, one of the most comprehensive surveys of Argentine political development. Schoultz's article on the electoral base of Peronism (item **8332**) is also a significant piece of work.

ARGENTINA

Andrews, George Reid. The Afro-Argentine officers of Buenos Aires Province, 1800–1860. See *HLAS 42:3290.*

———. The Afro-Argentines of Buenos Aires, 1800–1900. See *HLAS 42:3291.*

———. Race versus class association: the Afro-Argentines of Buenos Aires, 1850–1900. See *HLAS 42:3292.*

8307 Archetti, Eduardo P. El proceso de capitalización de campesinos argentinos (UTIEH/C, 28, 1977, p. 123–140, bibl.)

A discussion of process of accumulation of capital in a peasant economy, based on fieldwork conducted in a cotton-producing area in Santa Fe province, Argentina. Author discusses different aspects in development of capitalism: constitution of a class of farmers, effects of this process on agrarian social structure, and consequences for rural organization and political activity (e.g., formation of the "agrarian leagues," in the late 1960s). A sophisticated analysis of social differentiation.

8308 ——— and Kristi Anne Stolen. Economía doméstica, estrategias de herencia y acumulación de capital: la situación de la mujer en el norte de Santa Fe, Argentina (III/AI, 38:2, abril/junio 1978, p. 383–403)

Discussion of status of women in the domestic and agrarian economy in northern Santa Fe, Argentina. Authors analyze changes in three areas during three generations: roles performed by females in the family economy; inheritance patterns, which authors conceptualize as mechanisms for the transfer or "return" of goods and rights; and consequences of the accumulation of capital on the domestic economy. With respect to latter, authors show that female labor became dysfunctional after the replacement of labor forces by capital and of domestic labor by external labor. An interesting analysis of a neglected social category.

8309 Ardila, Rubén. La psicología en Argentina: pasado, presente y futuro (RLP, 21:1, 1979, p. 77–91)

Visiting Colombian psychologist describes the history and current state of his discipline in Argentina. Examines history of academic psychology since colonial times, but focuses on massive clinical psychology programs developed in the 1960s. Author notes four peculiarities of Argentine psychology: 1) quasi-exclusive emphasis on psychoanalytic theory; 2) sensitivity to ideological issues; 3) focus on the profession's "medical" or clinical mode; and 4) relative neglect of experimental research.

8310 Bailey, John P. Inmigración y relaciones étnicas: los ingleses en la Argentina (IDES/DE, 18:72, enero/marzo 1979, p. 539–558, bibl.)

Discussion of British migration to Argentina. Author considers ethnic composition of recipient society, migrants' social characteristics and motivations, and relations between migrants and the Argentine community. Argentine dependency on Britain which helped enhance the migrants' relative power also generated resentment. These two factors led towards the isolation of Argentina's British community from its environment, and facilitated the preservation of ethnic identity.

8311 Baily, Samuel L. Marriage patterns and immigrant assimilation in Buenos Aires: 1882–1923 (HAHR, 60:1, Feb. 1980, p. 32–48, tables)

Baily challenges validity of the melting pot theory in the Argentine case. Process of immigrant assimilation is better understood on the basis of a cultural pluralist model than as an amalgamation of fusion hypothesis. Author's analysis of marriage patterns among Argentines, Italians, and Spaniards in Buenos Aires (1882–1923) reveals that endogamy was dominant: given availability, 70–80 percent of Italians and Spaniards chose spouses of the same national origin.

8312 Bartolomé, Leopoldo J. Populismo y diferenciación social agraria: las ligas agrarias en Misiones, Argentina (UTIEH/C, 28, 1977, p. 141–168, bibl., tables)

Discussion of rural mobilization in the early 1970s in Misiones, Argentina. Author perceives the establishment of corporative organizations therein as an instance of agrarian populism. Mobilization has been strong in areas characterized by recent settlement and by specialization in products affected by recurrent crises. The agrarian movement has more in common, in terms of its social base (a class of farmers rather than a peasantry) and its demands, with farmers' movements in US and Canada than with peasant mobilization in Latin America.

8313 Beccaria, Luis A. Una contribución al estudio de la movilidad social en la Argentina: análisis de los resultados de una encuesta para el Gran Buenos Aires (IDES/DE, 17:68, enero/marzo 1978, p. 593–635, tables)

Analysis of intergenerational social mobility in the greater Buenos Aires area, based on a sample of "chiefs of household" taken in 1969. Young people and women are severely underrepresented in a sample of this type. Author concludes that the mobility rate is comparable to that of more developed countries, but that downward mobility is distinctively high in Argentina. Discusses, in a comparative perspective, effects of structural change on types and rates of mobility. A sophisticated analysis.

8314 ——— and Alberto Minujín. La información dinámica en las estadísticas sociales: comentarios que sugiere la experiencia en la Argentina (IDES/DE, 17:76, oct./dic. 1977, p. 475–495, bibl., tables)

Discusses utilization of household surveys for the analysis of social mobility. Authors consider different methods for the study of social flows, based on input-output matrixes. Article represents a considerable improvement over standard sociological techniques.

8315 Bustamante, Norberto Rodríguez. Sociology and reality in Latin America: the case of Argentina (UN/ISSJ, 31:1, 1979, p. 86–97)

Examines political context of sociology in Argentina, particularly after the military coup of 1966. Author refers to the intellectual debates among sociologists in the 1960s—basically, the acceptance or rejection of theories and methodologies elaborated in the US, and the relationship between theory and radical political practice—and describes the politicization and collapse of the Sociology Department of the University of Buenos Aires after 1966.

8316 Caterina, José U. and Carlos R. Allio. Análisis sociológico y psicosocial de la dependencia. Buenos Aires: Editorial Guadalupe, 1973. 117 p. (Colección La dependencia argentina en el contexto latinoamericano; 5)

Neo-Marxist analysis of Argentina that takes the form of a social, psychological, and political analysis of dependency. Primarily a neo-Marxist analysis of Argentina. [Q. Jenkins]

8317 Fleming, William J. The cultural determinants of entrepreneurship and economic development: a case study of Mendoza province, Argentina; 1861–1914 (EHA/J, 39:1, March 1979, p. 211–224)

Author examines role of cultural factors in Mendoza province's economic development. Curiously, he ignores the structural perspective that prevails in contemporary Latin American sociology, and restricts his attention to two traditional approaches that were popular in the 1950s and 1960s in American social science: the alleged dysfunctionality of the extended family, individualism, and clientelism for development; and the formation of an entrepreneurial class as a consequence of status deprivation. After detailed analysis of Mendoza's economic history, he finds that neither of these theories apply. His conclusions are that entrepreneurship is affected by cultural factors, that local culture will determine extent and nature of opportunities for growth, and that availability of supportive social institutions and public policy is central in determining whether entrepreneurial attempts succeed.

8318 Herrán, Carlos A. Migraciones temporarias y articulación social: el Valle de Santa María, Catamarca (IDES/DE, 19:74, julio/sept. 1979, p. 161–187, bibl., tables)

Study of factors conducive to temporary emigration in rural community of Northwestern Argentina—Santa María Valley, Catamarca, a "labor reserve" of the sugar industry of Tucumán. Peasants hire themselves out as wage laborers for the "zafra" or sugar harvest. Author discusses ecological framework, region's history, characteristics of agrarian economy, forms of social articulation, and migration process. Migration is affected by social differentiation in that the *minifundio* operators are more likely than other peasants to become semiproletarians. Seasonal migration is one of the adaptive strategies open to them, other options being cultivation of their plots, local wage labor, and sharecropping. These forms of articulation exhibit different mixtures of "traditionality" and "modernity."

8319 Inkeles, Alex. Individual modernity in different ethnic and religious groups: data from a six-nation study (NYAS/A, 284, March 18, 1977, p. 539–564, tables)

Analysis of the effect of religion and ethnicity on individual modernity in the six countries of the Inkeles modernization study, which includes Argentina and Chile. The dependent variable is the OM scale. Once factors other than the independent variables are controlled, it is found that religion is not an important determinant. Ethnicity is somewhat more important (e.g., Argentines whose parents are foreign-born are more modern than those whose parents are native, however, only scattered relationships are significant).

8320 Jaramillo, Ana. Movimiento obrero y acumulación de capital: el caso Argentino (UNAM/RMCPS, 23:89, julio/sept. 1977, p. 173–210, tables)

Marxist analysis of relationship between patterns of capital accumulation and working-class mobilization. Author analyzes labor conflicts as a function of models of accumulation implemented in different periods of Argentine economic history, and of labor's productivity level. Those sectors defined by the use of relative surplus value are ones that have greater bargaining power and greater potential for organization and mobilization.

Landi, Oscar. Argentina, 1973–76: la génesis de una nueva crisis política. See item **6607**.

Landi, Oscar. La tercera presidencia de Perón: gobierno de emergencia y crisis política. See *HLAS* 42:3372.

Little, Cynthia Jeffress. Education, philanthropy, and feminism: components of Argentine womanhood, 1860–1926. See *HLAS* 42:3377.

8321 Lepkowski, Tadeusz. La presencia de la emigración polaca en América Latina y la política cultural de Polonia en este continente (PA/ES, 4, 1978, p. 221–232, bibl.)

Discusses Polish communities in Latin America (mainly Brazil and Argentina) and changing policies of the Polish state towards its emigrants. Contains a curious reference to Polish colonialist dreams in the interwar years.

8322 López, Pablo. El antisemitismo en Argentina (AR, 5:18, 1979, p. 24–27)

Journalistic account of anti-Semitic activity in Argentina, with emphasis on period following the 1976 military coup.

8323 Marini, Ana María. Women in contemporary Argentina (LAP, 4:4, Fall 1977, p. 114–120, bibl.)

Report on situation of women in Argentina at the peak of the mid-1970s violence. Based on author's brief visit, an Argentine social scientist living abroad. Discusses authoritarian regime's family policy, traditional ideology regarding women disseminated by government-controlled media, and impact of regime's economic policies on working-class women.

Mechlowicz, Bronislaw and **Zdzislaw Kurnikowski.** Los ucranianos en la Argentina. See *HLAS* 42:3390.

Newton, Ronald C. Social change, cultural crisis and the origins of Nazism within the German-speaking community of Buenos Aires. See *HLAS* 42:3393.

8324 Petras, James F. The divergence between scientific work and political action (NS, 3:5/6, 1978, p. 78–103)

Very interesting discussion of the relationship between theory and praxis by a politically-committed Latin Americanist. Petras discusses the objections to "action research" raised in Latin America by both intellectuals and political figures as well as the consequences of the separation of theory and practice for both social science and political action. To illustrate these issues, author gives political activists' reactions to four projects in Chile and Argentina with which he was involved.

8325 Procesos de articulación social. Greenfield et al.; Esther Hermitte, Leopoleo J. Bartolomé, compiladores. Buenos Aires: Amorrortu, 1977. 338 p.; bibl. (Biblioteca de América Latina)

Collection of 11 research papers written by social anthropologists, most of which deal with Argentina. Their common focus is the study of different processes of social articulation, defined by the editors as the "connective mechanisms that function among the different components of a social system, and which canalize the transmission of social action and the circulation of goods and services" (p. 10). "Social articulation" differs from more common concepts, such as integration, in that it does not "imply necessarily a loss of the differential attributes of the units." Papers deal with following subjects: political brokerage in Brazil (Greenfield); articulating role of landowners in Buenos Aires province in the 19th century (Strickson); weak articulation of Bolivian migrant workers in Salta (Whiteford); informal lawyers in a Bolivian community (Muratorio), interethnic relations in a Misiones border town (Ackerman); functions of inheritance among farmers in Santa Fe (Archetti and Stolen); effects that change in the relations of production have on class-consciousness among Tucumán's rural workers (Vessuri); role of domestic groups and alliances in an agrarian-artisanal community in Catamarca (Hermitte and Herrán); inter-ethnic articulation in a Misiones town (Bartolomé); articulation between Indians and national community in Brazil (Cardoso de Oliveira); and articulation between symbol systems among Chaco's Toba Indians (Miller). Very useful collection.

8326 Queiroz, Maria José de. Perón e o peronismo: uma visão literária (UMG / RBEP, 48, jan. 1979, p. 85–100)

Examination of peronism's effect on Argentine literature. Discusses some characteristics of cultural environment during first Peronist regime (1946–55), and emergence of writers and essayist of the 1950s generation: Viñas, Prieto, Guido, etc.

8327 Quinterno, Carlos Alberto. Militares y populismo: la crisis argentina desde 1966 hasta 1976. Buenos Aires?: Editorial Temas Contemporáneos, 1978. 334 p.

Chronicle of 1966–76 decade, written from the ideological perspective of a supporter of authoritarianism. Author surveys military regime that ruled the country from 1966–73 (the so-called "Argentine Revolution"), populist interlude of 1973–76, which combined mobilization, right and left-wing terrorism, and inefficiency; and military regime established in 1976—the so-called "process of national reorganization."

8328 Rouquié, Alain. Pouvoir militaire et société politique en République Argentine. Paris: Presses de la Fondation Nationale des Sciences Politiques, 1978. 772 p.; bibl.; index.

This is one of the most important works on Argentine militarism published to date, and one of the most comprehensive surveys of Argentine political modernization. After general description of Argentine society and politics, and the development of the professional military, Rouquié examines in detail the intervention of the Armed Forces in political and economic life during 1930–73, and develops a theoretical interpretation of the phenomenon. He discusses intra-organizational processes in the armed forces—the army, in particular. Also systematically explores the relationships between the military and their social environment; influences of social classes, political parties and the state apparatus on the armed forces; as well as the effects of military penetration in different areas of social life. This analysis is carried out for each administration, from Uriburu's authoritarian regime to the self-styled "Argentine Revolution" of the late 1960s and early 1970s. In his attempt to explain the phenomenon of militarism, Rouquié discusses direct political and economic explanations—hypotheses that give causal weight to factors such as mobilization, characteristics of the party system, cyclical variations in the economy, intersectoral transfers, and external blockages—as well as interpretations of the military as the advocates of the industrial bourgeoisie or of the middle classes. Concludes with a variation of the bonapartistic theme: the military exercise a "substitution hegemony," that replaces a divided and wearied ruling class that cannot rule by itself.

8329 Sautu, Ruth. The female labor force in Argentina, Bolivia and Paraguay (LARR, 15:2, 1980, p. 152–161, bibl.)

Analysis of supply and demand factors as determinants of female participation in the labor force. Author concludes that supply of female labor is negatively related to age and socioeconomic positions of the family, and positively related to educational attainment. As for demand for female labor, it is negatively associated with degree of a firm's technological sophistication, and status of occupation, and positively associated with deterioration in the income potential of the occupation. Author also discusses interplay between supply and demand factors. A solid piece of work.

8330 ———. La sociología de la Argentina, 1958–1976 (LARR, 15:3, 1980, p. 199–200)

Reports on work-in-progress in a project aimed at analyzing prevailing areas of research and theoretical orientations in the four major independent centers for research in the social sciences.

8331 Schoultz, Lars. The nature of anti-U.S. sentiment in Latin America: a preliminary analysis with Argentine data (CUNY/CP, 11:4, July 1979, p. 467–481, tables)

Survey analyzes anti-US attitudes in the Argentine population. The sample (N=2,014) and questionnaire are derived from Kirkpatrick's study in 1965. Author constructs an index of anti-US sentiment, based on three items: vote for a candidate who favors Argentine collaboration with the US, vote for a candidate who seeks to strengthen Argentine-US ties, and identification of the US as the country that most tries to create problems for Argentina. This index is correlated with different types of variables: indicators of social disintegration and alienation, class, and urbanization and region; orientations towards political nationalism and economic dependence; and party identification. Three "ideological" variables—attitudes toward economic dependency, political nationalism, and party identification—explain 30 percent of the variations in the sample.

8332 ———. The socio-economic determinants of popular-authoritarian behavior: the case of peronism (APSA/R, 71:4, Dec. 1977, p. 1423–1446, tables)

Analysis of electoral support for Perón in the greater Buenos Aires area, 1948–73. Author examines hypotheses that include following independent variables: social mobilization and a plural party system; class structure; population growth rate; and level of economic satisfaction. Multivariate analysis indicates that two indicators, rate of industrial growth and size of working class, account for 84 percent of total variation in peronist vote.

8333 Stemplowski, Ryszard. Los ucranianos en la Argentina (PAN/ES, 3, 1976, p. 289–307)

Transcription of two dispatches sent by Polish legation in Buenos Aires to the Foreign Affairs Ministry in Warsaw on the Ukrainian minority in Argentina. First dispatch (1935) focuses on Ukrainian nationalism, but contains general description of the Ukrainian immigrant colony (e.g., occupational structure, regional origin in mother country, degree of assimilation, and communal organization). It also expresses concern about anti-Polish activity, and about the possible formation of paramilitary organizations. Second dispatch (1939) deals with German support for anti-Polish Ukrainian groups.

8334 Thomson, Brian A. The periphery and the environment: three case-studies in Argentina and Brazil, 1870–1970 (UN/ISSJ, 30:3, 1978, p. 498–535)

Attempts to develop a historical materialist conceptual framework in area of regional development. Author reinterprets analytical model of social formation in order to apply it to spatial configurations. Following categories are used to describe three cases of regional dependency: in Argentina, Santiago del Estero (1870–1920) and Resistencia (1930–70); and in Brazil, Northwest Paraná (1940–74). In each case, author discusses organization of space and impact of human settlements on ecosystem.

8335 Tobler, Hans Werner and **Peter Waldmann.** German colonies in South America: a new Germany in the Cono Sur? (SAGE/JIAS, 22:2, May 1980, p. 227–245)

Review essay, which discusses four books on German immigration into Argentina, Southern Brazil, and Chile: Blancpain's *Les allemands en Chili*; Newton's *German Buenos Aires*; Roche's *La colonisation allemande et le Rio Grande do Sul*; and Young's *Germans in Chile*. These books examine different aspects of immigration process; patterns of economic organization of German settlers; political and cultural life of German colonies; their degree of assimilation; and long-term influence of German immigrants on host societies. On the basis of their analysis of these works, authors isolate four determinants of adaptation and achievement: 1) immigrants' social origin; 2) characteristics of immigration and settlement process; 3) influence of mother country; and 4) peculiarities of receiver societies. Presents conclusions on extent of economic integration and cultural assimilation of the immigrants, and on their impact on Southern Cone countries.

8336 Vessuri, Hebe M.C. Family, kinship and work among rural proletarians in Tucumán, Argentina (*in* Family and kinship in Middle America and the Caribbean: proceedings of the 14th seminar of the Committee on Family Research of the International Sociological Association, Curaçao, September 1975. Arnaud F. Marks, René A. Römer, editors. Willemstad, Netherlands: Institute of Higher Studies in Curaçao, 1978, p. 181–226, bibl., tables)

Analysis of family organization, kinship ties, and position in the productive process among rural wage laborers in Tucumán, Northwestern Argentina. Study is based on fieldwork conducted in a sugar "finca," among permanent and transient laborers. Author criticizes approaches that view rural world as undifferentiated whole, and fail to pay attention to class differences within it. She finds that, in rural proletarian families, internal solidarity may exist, but it does not lead to constitution of corporate groups or to patriarchal organization. Proletarianization, since it destroys the homogeneity of the peasant community, is associated with individuation. Systematically explores similarities and differences between rural proletarians and peasants on the one hand, and urban wage earners on the other. A solid piece of work.

8337 Villarreal, Juan. El capitalismo dependiente: estudio sobre estructura de clase en Argentina. México: Siglo Veintiuno Editores, 1978. 166 p.; bibl. (Sociología y política)

Analyzes Argentine social formation as an instance of dependent capitalism. Villarreal rejects models that assume either juxtaposition of different modes of production in

dependent social formation, or complete diffusion or capitalist social relations. Rather, he argues, social formation consists of a dominant mode of production (i.e., capitalism) and other relations of production that are articulated with that dominant mode. On the basis of censuses and statistical materials, he discusses major social classes, small mercantile production, regional disparities, internal migration, and marginality. In relation to class structure, he considers the most important trends since 1960 to be centralization of capital, displacement of the working class towards the tertiary, growth of the managerial stratum, and growth of the "independent" sector.

Wainerman, Catalina H. Educación, familia y participación económica femenina en la Argentina. See item **4387.**

8338 ——. Family relations in Argentina: diachrony and synchrony (NCFR/JFH, 3:4, Winter 1978, p. 410–421, bibl., table)

Study of degree of egalitarianism in family relations, through use of linguistic indicator: the pronominal address in dyadic interaction, which in Spanish admits both symmetrical and asymmetrical forms ("tu" or "vos" versus "usted"). Author compares families of different social classes in Buenos Aires and in Catamarca, a traditional province. She finds that inter-generational family relations in Buenos Aires become more egalitarian over time, and that the change began in the upper classes, and later spread downward. On the other hand, egalitarian social relations were more frequent in Buenos Aires than in Catamarca; the pattern in Catamarca is similar to the one found in Buenos Aires 50 years earlier. However, interclass differences in Catamarca are narrower than those existing in Buenos Aires at the beginning of the century.

8339 ——; **Ruth Sautu;** and **Zulma Recchini de Lattes.** The participation of women in economic activity in Argentina, Bolivia and Paraguay: a comparative study (LARR, 15:2, 1980, p. 143–151)

Report on project involving researchers in the three countries mentioned. Study focuses on three areas: 1) intensity and direction of changes in female economic participation since World War II; 2) detailed analysis of the position of women in the occupational structure; and 3) examination of effect of sociological factors, especially education and family status, on female participation. Report includes a summary of findings.

8339a Waisman, Carlos H. Modernization and the working class: the politics of legitimacy. Austin: University of Texas Press, 1982. 244 p.; index (The Dan Danciger publication series)

The incorporation of the working class into the political system is the central issue of this wide-ranging work. Author is particularly interested in how modernization is related to the legitimation of capitalism by the working class. Three cases are examined: Disraelian Britain, Bismarckian Germany, and Peronist Argentina. The emphasis is clearly on Argentina, as the author presents an analysis of data from his field work there. A highly significant work, especially in light of the recent interest in the political sociology of the urban working class in Latin America. [L. Pérez]

Weisbrot, Robert. The Jews of Argentina: from the Inquisition to Perón. See *HLAS 42:3441.*

Wellhofer, E. Spencer. Strategies for party organization and voter mobilization: Britain, Norway, and Argentina. See item **6639.**

8340 Williams, Glyn. Industrialization and ethnic change in the Lower Chubut Valley, Argentina (AAA/AE, 5:3, Aug. 1978, p. 618–631)

Study of effects of social change on the ethnic identity of Welsh settlers in Chubut, Argentina. Anthropologists have analyzed ethnic identity without reference to the structural context. By contrast, Williams focuses on the broader social structure and on the power relationship between the majority and minority cultures. The power of Welsh farmers diminished with the industrialization of Chubut. They adapted by engaging in a cultural division of land use, and by developing mutual aid networks. This power shift affected Welsh ethnic identification: their culture became more secular, and the use of Welsh language declined.

PARAGUAY

Corvalán, Grazziella. Educación técnica de nivel medio y mercado de trabajo: documento de trabajo presentado en la reunión de ECIEL sobre educación técnica, Rio de Janeiro, marzo de 1979. See item **4530.**

Díaz de Arce, Omar. El Paraguay contemporáneo, 1925–1975. See *HLAS 42:3454.*

Domínguez Dibb, Humberto. Presencia y vigencia árabes en el Paraguay. See *HLAS 42:3455.*

8341 Livieres B., Lorenzo N. ¿Para qué ciencias sociales en el Paraguay? (UCNSA/EP, 5:2, dic. 1977, p. 9–20)

Author asks why "modern" social sciences such as sociology and political science are suspect to the elite. After an erudite discussion, which includes an evaluation of Mannheim, he concludes that social sciences are rejected because they are intrinsically critical. The intellectual life that evolved in Paraguay (1870–1936) emphasizes history and law, traditional disciplines that are less prone to generate critical impulses. Author attributes this emphasis to cultural traditions rather than to economic or political structures.

8342 Morínigo A., José Nicolás. El proceso de cambio en la estructura de la población económicamente activa en el Paraguay (UCNSA/EP, 6:2, dic. 1978, p. 121–139, tables)

Sociological study of the out-migration from the agricultural sector during the period 1950–72. Contains no economic analysis, but gives some interesting insights into the migration process. [M.C. Cook]

8343 La Población del Paraguay. Domingo M. Rivarola et al. Asunción: Centro Paraguayo de Estudios Sociológicos, 1974. 194 p.; bibl.; ill.

Describes Paraguay's population and includes sketch of its historical evolution and spatial distribution as well as chapters on birth and mortality rates, emigration, distribution by sex and age, urbanization, internal migration and characteristics of the economically active population. Contains projections by age group for 1960–85, and brief discussion of economic and social effects of population's growth rate.

Sautu, Ruth. The female labor force in Argentina, Bolivia and Paraguay. See item **8329.**

Wainerman, Catalina H.; Ruth Sautu; and Zulma Recchini de Lattes. The participation of women in economic activity in Argentina, Bolivia and Paraguay. See item **8339**.

URUGUAY

Marenales Rossi, Martha and **Guy Bourdé.** L'immigration française et le peuplement de l'Uruguay, 1830–1860. See *HLAS 42:3492*.

8344 Martorelli, Horacio. Ciencias sociales en el Uruguay: sociología (CLAEH, 20, 1978, p. 61–75)

Survey of the development of sociology in Uruguay from its inception in late 1950s to its abrupt decline in mid-1970s, when most courses were suppressed, academic programs were closed down, research centers disappeared and sociological publications halted. Author presents some criteria for the renaissance of sociological studies in the country.

8345 ———. Mujer y sociedad: estudio sobre las diversas situaciones sociales de las mujeres en el medio rural uruguayo. Montevideo: CIEDUR-F.C.U., 1979. 84 p.; 10 leaves of plates (3 fold.); bibl.; ill.

Sociological analysis of Uruguayan women. On the basis of statistical and census materials, author surveys demographic characteristics of female population, participation of women in economy, their education and standard of living, characteristics of the family in different settings, and role of women in rural-urban migration. A competent piece of work.

8346 Prost, Gérard. Structures agraires en Uruguay: l'example du Départment d'Artigas (SGB/COM, 30:118, avril/juin 1977, p. 178–192, maps, tables)

Analysis of agrarian property in an area covering 500,000 hectares in Artigas department, Uruguay. Author examines four maps of the area taken between 1944–75 and a list of proprietors. Area includes units of different sizes, and localization by size is not explained by relief, hydrological characteristics, proximity to cities, or quality of the soil. "Estancias" occupy all types of land, since *latifundio* operators are interested in maximizing the productivity of capital, not land.

Sierra, Gerónimo de. Consolidación y crisis del "capitalismo democrático" en Uruguay. See *HLAS 42:3504*.

8347 Uruguay. Ministerio de Economía y Finanzas. Dirección General de Estadística y Censos. Encuesta de emigración internacional. Encargado de la encuesta, Cesar Güella; planeamiento, procesamiento de datos y análisis descriptivo, Cesar Güella, Nelly N. de Lombardi. Montevideo: La Dirección, 1976 [i.e. 1977]. 50 p.; ill.

Emigration survey, based on data gathered from a sample of households. Due to economic and political factors, large-scale emigration from Uruguay began in the early 1970s. Largest contingent emigrated to Argentina, but there are also significant flows to the US and Australia. Contains basic demographic information on age, sex, marital status, birthplace, education, and occupation of the emigrants.

BRAZIL

SHIRLEY J. HARKESS, *Associate Professor of Sociology, University of Kansas*

THE YEARS SINCE THE PUBLICATION of the previous volume of *HLAS* have witnessed a flowering of sociological literature about, and especially by, Brazilians, particularly as compared to *HLAS 39*. For example, the items annotated below include 24 books and seven articles in Portuguese as compared to six books and 23 articles in English and other languages. Aguiar (item **8348**) has indicated two reasons for this development: the adjustment social scientists in Brazil have made to the control imposed on the conditions and promulgation of their work by regime censorship, and the slight relaxation of the censorship itself. Specifically, in the past few years, a significant number of Brazilian social scientists had to change their place of residence (i.e., leave the country) or their institutional affiliation (e.g., moving from a university to a research center). In addition, many had to modify the method of presentation, if not also the topic, of their work. As Aguiar suggests, such dislocations produced a temporary lull in productivity, a time for reflection and taking stock. I believe the quantity and quality of the works reviewed for this section represent an admirably positive response to that difficult situation.

The major substantive development observed in these works lies in the area of theory and method, and in the integration of the two. First, with regard to theory, we see an increasing sophistication in the use of Marxian analysis. That is to say, researchers are now using selected Marxian concepts which they modify to conform to the nature of the situation under scrutiny (items **8383** and **8399**). The principal concept drawn from Marx is that of the mode of production, which includes both the forces and relations of production as well as the implied changes resulting from a contradiction between them. The general applicability of such concepts to Brazilian society is obvious. What is noteworthy is the sensitive way in which researchers are using these concepts as a guide to understanding rather than as a rigid paradigm which ignores the variations present in even a single social setting (items **8357** and **8362**).

As regards data, a greater variety as well as more detailed reporting are evident in this section. Most of the data are derived from field work (items **8349** and **8353**), historical sources (item **8361**), censuses (item **8355**), and surveys (item **8398**). Researchers still spend considerable time engaging in participant observation but they provide us with little qualitative or quantitative analysis of those observations. However, regardless of the mode of analysis, the intense attention researchers devote to data has resulted in abstract concepts that are grounded in concrete reality thereby achieving a satisfying interplay of theory and method in several works.

Another characteristic of the works reviewed here is that many of them were produced not by sociologists *sensu strictu*, but by researchers identifying themselves as anthropologists. There are several reasons for this phenomena, the main one being that the two disciplines are closely related (and are often integrated into one academic department both in the US and Brazil). Secondly, anthropology may well be a more appropriate tool for analyzing Brazilian society, particularly with respect to the topic of interest to many of the authors in this section: the periphery of the periphery (e.g., the Northeast of Brazil) as viewed from a Marxian perspective (items **5405, 8363, 8393** and **8397**). In contrast to topics such as urbanization, race and ethnicity, the military, and women which do command interest, themes which fall within the traditional purview of sociology (e.g., the family, socialization, education, the polity) are neglected or presented with little quantitative analysis beyond the reporting of percentage distributions.

Finally, it should be pointed out that works included here vary significantly in their emphasis on the uniqueness of Brazil's present situation. Some authors perceive Brazil as a nation like any other whereas others specifically underscore the difference, stressing the need to understand the country's present state as unique (item **8358** and **8388**). Although these opposing interpretations may be a function of the topic (delimitation) and an "objective" approach, switching between the two may be unsettling to the reader.

8348 **Aguiar, Neuma.** Division of labor, technology, and social stratification (*in* The Structure of Brazilian development [see item **8404**] p. 37–70, bibl., tables)

Uses ethnography and survey to analyze different but coexisting forms of social organization involved in the manufacture of the same types of products in Ceará. Shows that occupational status is related to organizational and technological complexity.

Alvaro Moisés, José and **Verena Stolcke.** Urban transport and popular violence: the case of Brazil. See item **6723.**

8349 Alvim, Maria Rosilene Barbosa. A arte do ouro: um estudo sobre os ourives de Juàzeiro do Norte. Brasília: s.n., 1979. 85 p.; bibl. (Pesquisa antropológica; no. 19)

Ethnography of a small group of goldsmiths explores the relations of production and the artisans' representations (or ideology) of that process. Careful linking of participant-observation of single process and conceptualization. National Museum master's thesis in social anthropology.

Azeredo, Paulo Roberto de. Classe social e saúde na cidade no Rio de Janeiro: primeira metade do século XIX. See *HLAS 42:3509.*

8350 Bastide, Roger. The African religions of Brazil: toward a sociology of the interpenetration of civilizations. Translated by Helen Sebba. Baltimore: Johns Hopkins University Press, 1978. 494 p.; bibl.; index (Johns Hopkins studies in Atlantic history and culture)

Skillful English translation of the 1960 comprehensive analysis: *Les réligions afro-brésiliennes.* Critical introduction by Bastide's student D. Monteiro emphasizes sociological significance of the work and Bastide's approach to ideology and superstructure. For historian's comment, see *HLAS 42:3510.*

Beretta, Pier Luigi. Amazzonia Brasiliana: colonizzazione o popolamento?: un contributo informativo e crítico. See item **5319.**

8351 Blay, Eva Alterman. The political participation of women in Brazil: female mayors (UC/S, 5:1, Autumn 1979, p. 42–59, tables)

Basic data and analysis on recent group. In finding that female mayors are elected mainly by poorest, least industrialized, and least urbanized areas, author argues importance of their class origins— whether landowning oligarchy or petite bourgeoisie. Former enter politics as substitutes for men and to maintain family power. For political scientist's comment, see item **6726.**

8352 Brazil, anthropological perspectives: essays in honor of Charles Wagley.

Maxine L. Margolis and William E. Carter, editors. New York: Columbia University Press, 1979. 443 p.; bibl.; ill.; index.

Readable and informative collection of 19 original anthropological articles by Charles Wagley and a group of his former students. Topics include: the Indian, Italian, and the Negro in the Brazilian past; adaptations to varying environments; social structure, especially family and kinship; and political organization. Last two topics of greatest interest to sociologists. Most articles refer specifically to previous literature, in some cases challenging it, and generalize beyond particular phenomenon. See items **8353, 8359, 8363, 8370** and **8396.** For anthropologist's comment see item **1081.**

8353 Brown, Diana. Umbanda and class relations in Brazil (*in* Brazil, anthropological perspectives: essays in honor of Charles Wagley [see item **8352**] p. 270–304)

Well researched chapter includes a survey of 403 practitioners. Demonstrates that Umbanda is not merely a lower-class religion but one which also involves the middle class, whose members participate in patron-client relations as well. In fact, these two national phenomena merge as Umbanda incorporates many elements of such relations.

Cardoso, Fernando Henrique. Les impasses du régime autoritaire: le case brésilien. See item **6730.**

8354 Carvalho, João Carlos Monteiro de. Camponeses do Brasil. Petrópolis, Brasil: Vozes, 1978. 125 p.; bibl.

Introductory study of Brazilian peasantry, which includes conceptualization, brief history, and compilation of comparative data from states of São Paulo and Piauí.

Coelho, Edmundo Campos. Em busca de identidade: o exército e a política na sociedade brasileira. See *HLAS 42:3641.*

Colóquio de Estudos Teuto-Brasileiros, 2d, Recife, 1968. II [i.e. Segundo] Colóquio de Estudos Teuto Brasileiros: trabalhos de intelectuais brasileiros e alemães, vários ligados a universidades e institutos científicos de dois países, sobre aspectos diversos da matéria que motivou o Colóquio. See *HLAS 42:3516.*

8355 Corrêa, Roberto Lobato. Localização inicial do imigrante no cidade: o caso do Rio de Janeiro (IBGE/R, 38:3, julho/set. 1976, p. 116–121, bibl., table)

Using Duncan Index of Dissimilarity with 1970 Census data, author notes that, initially, Rio migrants do not concentrate in the central city but follow residence patterns of the general population.

8356 Current trends in Brazilian social sciences (*in* The Structure of Brazilian development [see item **8404**] p. 1–16, bibl.)

Introduction to volume integrates contributions by relating them to concepts such as mode of production, authoritarianism, and populism and to classic (Marx, Weber, and Durkheim) and contemporary views. Set in context of Brazil's post-1964 intellectual life with its establishment of graduate training on the US model and researchers' reassessment of their product in this context. As author states, "The effects of this are only now beginning to surface," and "assumptions of freedom of research have had to be constantly checked with a two-fold inquiry framework whereby the social scientist conducts his research projects and at the same time analyzes the conditions available for the production of such. The result is always a search for greater rationality and more dispassionate language."

8357 Dias, Gentil Martins. Depois do latifúndio: continuidade e mudança na sociedade rural nordestina. Rio de Janeiro: Tempo Brasileiro, 1978. 248 p.; bibl.; ill. (Biblioteca Tempo universitário; 48)

Social anthropology case study of Bahia's Valença municipio is based on carefully presented field work and set in context of theory and of data for the nation. Stresses importance of commercialization, differences in power between urban elites and rural masses, and nature of social control in approximately 30 years.

Elia, Sílvio Edmundo. A unidade lingüística do Brasil: condicionamentos geoeconômicos. See *HLAS 42:4620*.

8358 Fernandes, Florestan. A condição de sociólogo. Prefácio de Antônio Cândido. São Paulo: HUCITEC, 1978. 168 p.; index (Coleção Estudos brasileiros; 9: Série Depoimentos; 1)

Probing and wide-ranging interview with central figure in development of Brazilian sociology. Thus, this intellectual autobiography is also an intellectual history. Concerns role of sociologist in society

and the debate between functionalism and dialectics.

8359 ———. The Negro in Brazilian society: twenty-five years later (*in* Brazil, anthropological perspectives: essays in honor of Charles Wagley [see item **8352**] p. 96–114)

Overview of contemporary race relations in light of author's and Roger Bastide's previous book *Brancos e negros em São Paulo* (1951). Concludes that although situation in São Paulo has changed dramatically in 25 years, racial inequality continues chiefly because there has never been a Negro protest movement. Underscores lack of activism on part of successful blacks.

———. Slaveholding society in Brazil. See *HLAS 42:3520*.

8360 Fernandes, Heloísa Rodrigues. Os militares como categoria social. Capa, Carlos Clémen. São Paulo: Global Editora, 1978. 267 p.; bibl. (Global universitária; 6: Série História e ciências sociais)

Thorough conceptual and empirical study of the military. Theoretical analysis concerns the class origin and class situation of this social category. Data are based on 1970 study of 424 students in the military police academy of São Paulo. Concludes that the military hierarchy provides class positions for both officers and troops via a unifying channel of individual upward mobility that is ideologically supported (by the state).

8361 ———. Política e segurança: Força Pública do Estado de São Paulo, fundamentos histórico-sociais. Prefácio, Florestan Fernandes. São Paulo: Editora Alfa-Omega, 1974. 259 p.; bibl. (Sociologia; v. 2. Biblioteca Alfa-Omega de ciências sociais: Série 1a.)

Carefully documented historical study of police in state of São Paulo in 19th and early 20th centuries. Fernandes presents the organization of repression in a conceptual context and provides compilation of personnel and budget data. For historian's comment, see *HLAS 42:3653*.

8362 Figueiredo, Vilma. Desenvolvimento dependente brasileiro: industrialização, classes sociais e estado. Rio de Janeiro: Zahar Editores, 1978. 160 p.; bibl. (Biblioteca das ciências sociais: Sociologia e antropologia)

Clearly organized and written sociological analysis of dependent capitalist development in Brazil (1960–70) which emphasizes the nature of industrialization, class structure, and the role of the state. Author's contributions are her classification of fractions of the bourgeoisie and proletariat, relations among these fractions, and changes in these relations over time.

Fleischer, David V. Renovação política-Brasil 1978: eleições parlamentares sob a égide do "Pacote de abril." See item **6668.**

8363 Forman, Shepard and **Joyce F. Riegelhaupt.** The political economy of patron-clientship: Brazil and Portugal compared (*in* Brazil, anthropological perspectives: essays in honor of Charles Wagley [see item **8352**] p. 379–400)

Powerful analysis and plea for studying local politics from perspective of the political economy of the nation-state. Focuses on changing nature of patron-clientship within the context of successive Brazilian and Portuguese political regimes. Argues that patron-clientship is a "moment" on which anthropologists have focused and that, instead, "the process of inclusion of peasants into the national Brazilian polity over time contributed to a radical transformation of inter-class relationships, from [what they term] patron-dependency to patron mobilization and ultimately to class-based organizations which by passed the party structure and gathered a momentum which for a time seemed to threaten the very basis of the Brazilian political system . . . until the 'Revolution of 1964' once more made 'exclusion' and centralization the dominant themes of Brazilian politics." For political scientist's comment, see item **6736.**

8364 Freyre, Gilberto. Obra escolhida: índice remissivo, índice onomástico. Nota editorial, Gilberto Freyre—tradição e modernidade, Antonio Carlos Villaça; cronologia da vida e da obra, bibliografia ativa e passiva, Edson Nery da Fonseca. Rio de Janeiro: Editora Nova Aguilar, 1977. 1090 p.; bibl.; ill.; index (Biblioteca luso-brasileira: Série brasileira; 37)

Republication of three previous works, including the famous *Casa grande e senzala*, with contemporary prefaces by Freyre.

8365 ———. Oh de casa!: em torno da casa brasileira e de sua projeção sobre um tipo nacional de homem. Capa de Studio Ar-

tenova. Recife: Editora Artenova, 1979. 169 p.; 8 leaves of plates; ill. (Série Estudos e pesquisas—Instituto Joaquim Nabuco de Pesquisas Sociais; 13)

Extended contemporary essay on domestic architecture in Brazil restates theme that various types of houses form the context for and the expression of the familial nature of Brazilian society.

8366 Fundação Carlos Chagas. Mulher brasileira: bibliografia anotada. v. 1, História, família, grupos étnicas, feminismo. Capa, Mary. São Paulo: Editora Brasiliense, 1979. 1 v.; index.

Extensive and annotated bibliography of works on the women of Brazil, in Portuguese, Spanish, French, and English and in four sections: 1) women in the family; 2) ethnic women; and two substantial ones; 3) women in Brazilian history; and 4) Brazilian feminism (e.g., laws, organizations, and political participation). Substantive essay introduces each section.

8367 Fundação IBGE. Indicadores sociais para áreas urbanas. Rio de Janeiro: Secretaria de Planejamento da Presidência da República, IBGE, 1977. 162 p.

Tabular presentation of basic data from 1970 Census on urban areas stratified by size and administrative criteria. Data concern population size and migration, housing characteristics, labor force participation, income, and schooling. Introduction accompanies each subsection.

8368 Galvão, Eduardo Enéas. Encontro de sociedades: índios e brancos no Brasil. Prefácio de Darcy Ribeiro; capa, Mário Roberto Corrêa da Silva; baseada em desenho de Hilda Velloso; fotos de autor. Rio de Janeiro: Paz e Terra, 1979. 300 p.; bibl. (Coleção Estudos brasileiros; v. 29)

Convenient republication of major articles of 1950s and 1960s on Indian cultural change by late leading social anthropologist.

8369 Goldman, Frank P. and **Demarisse Machado Goldman.** Problemas brasileiros: alguns aspectos sobre o processo de envelhecer. Piracicaba, Brasil: editora Franciscana do Lar Franciscano de Menores, 1977. 152 p.; bibl.

Consists of an initial assessment of age and ageing in Brazil. Discusses implications of social change for the family, as illustrated in community studies; includes survey of social and economic situation of aged; assesses significance of education, including gerontology, for ageing process.

Gorender, Jacob. Os escravismo colonial. See *HLAS 42:3524.*

8370 Greenfield, Sidney M. Patron-client exchanges in southeastern Minas Gerais (*in* Brazil, anthropological perspectives: essays in honor of Charles Wagley [see item 8352] p. 362–378)

As always with author's work, this is a well told story with a significant anthropological lesson: how patron-client relations mediate the exchange of extra-local resources (e.g., a teaching appointment) for local (votes).

Guimarães, Alba Zaluar. Os movimentos "messiânicos" brasileiros: uma leitura. See *HLAS 42:45.*

Hahner, June E. Women and work in Brazil, 1850–1920: a preliminary investigation. See *HLAS 42:3670.*

Hampl, Zdeněk. A literatura de cordel brasileira como manifestação de participação social e política. See *HLAS 42:1081.*

8371 Heredia, Beatriz Maria Alásia de. A morada da vida: trabalho familiar de pequenos produtories do Nordeste do Brasil. Capa, Mario Roberto Corrêa da Silva. Rio de Janeiro: Paz e Terra, 1979. 164 p.; bibl. (Série Estudos sobre o Nordeste; v. 7)

Primarily a descriptive National Museum case study of domestic production and consumption among peasants of Boa Vista in Pernambuco. Based on qualitative analysis of field work with 20 families.

8372 Ianni, Octávio. Colonização e contra-reforma agrária na Amazônia. Petrópolis: Editora Vozes, 1979. 137 p.; bibl. (Coleção Sociologia brasileira; v. 11)

Documented critique of military regime's Amazon colonization policy since 1964. Concludes that instead of promoting agrarian reform—the stated objection of the regime—its policy resulted in the establishment of capitalism and capitalist relations of production. Brings together government and other descriptive data.

Indice de Ciências Sociais. Ano 1, No. 1, julho 1979– . See *HLAS 42:221.*

Klarner, Izabela. Emigracja z królestwa polskiego do Brazylii, 1890–1914. See *HLAS 42:3680.*

8373 Kluck, Patricia. Small farmers and agricultural development policy: a look at Brazil's land reform statute (SAA/HO, 38:1, Spring 1979, p. 44–51, bibl., tables)

Study of statute, based on data from 60 farm households in southern Brazil classified as marginal *minifundios*, shows they earned substantial income. Therefore, author questions state's classification system.

8374 Lang, James. Portuguese Brazil: the king's plantation. New York: Academic Press, 1979. 266 p.; bibl.; index; maps (Studies in social discontinuity)

Forceful and primarily descriptive overview of colonial Brazil's economic history links secondary sources and includes many in English. Emphasizes importance of export trade as distinguishing feature of Portuguese Brazil. Issues of theory and method remain implicit. For historian's comment, see *HLAS 42:3586.*

Laraia, Roque de Barros. Relações entre negros e brancos no Brasil. See *HLAS 42:49.*

Lepkowski, Tadeusz. La presencia de la emigración polaca en América Latina y la política cultural de Polonia en este continente. See item **8321.**

Lewin, Linda. Some historical implications of kinship organization for family-based politics in the Brazilian Northeast. See *HLAS 42:3689.*

Lima, Danilo. Educação, Igreja e ideologia: uma análise sociológica da elaboração da Lei de Diretrizes e Bases. See item **4615.**

8375 Machado Neto, Zahidé. As meninas: sobre o trabalho da criança e da adolescente na família proletária (SBPC/CC, 32:6, junho 1980, p. 671–683)

Extends analysis of domestic unit to labor of children. Combines field work with Marxian categories in order to demonstrate the considerable and unequal contribution of female children.

8376 ———. Mulher: vida e trabalho, um estudo de caso com mulheres faveladas (SBPC/CC, 31:3, março 1979, p. 280–289)

Presents interesting application of Lomnitz' existence/survival dimension and J. Mitchell's structures (production, reproduction, sexuality, and socialization) to field study of female-headed households in part of a Salvador low-income neighborhood. Includes information on child-care arrangements.

8377 Madeira, Felícia Reicher. El trabajo de la mujer en Fortaleza (CM/DE, 12:1, 1978, p. 46–74)

Despite title, article consists of a general critique of the definition of work as it relates to women in capitalist societies. Develops notion that the official exclusion of women's household labor from production constitutes an ideological effort to camouflage the extent of capitalist exploitation.

8378 Maeyama, Takashi. Ethnicity, secret societies, and associations: the Japanese in Brazil (CSSH, 21:4, Oct. 1979, p. 589–610, bibl.)

Anthropologist analyzes recent Japanese experience. The fact that Japanese Brazilians have weaker kin ties than other Brazilians and weaker vertical ties than the Japanese in Japan, encouraged Japanese Brazilians to establish ties based on ethnicity, fictive kinship, migration experience, and community. These ties served as the foundations of secret societies and later ethnoreligious associations. For historian's comment, see *HLAS 42:3702.*

Mallon, Florencia E. Peasants and rural laborers in Pernambuco: 1955–1964. See *HLAS 42:3704.*

8379 Malloy, James M. The politics of social security in Brazil. Pittsburgh: University of Pittsburgh Press, 1979. 200 p.; bibl.; index (Pitt Latin American series)

Political scientist examines social security under alternating democratic and authoritarian periods of Brazilian government. Author sees policy not as product of social forces, but as action of patrimonial state in delayed dependent capitalist development. Study contributes coherence to a field of political science.

8380 Marconi, Marina de Andrade. Garimpos e garimpeiros em Patrocínio Paulista. São Paulo: Secretaria da Cultura, Ciência e Tecnologia, Conselho Estadual de Artes e Ciências Humanas, 1978. 152 p.; bibl.; ill. (Coleção Folclore; 11)

Concerns 103 diamond miners in a São Paulo município and describes in detail the physical setting, labor and families. Includes tables and graphs for distribution of many variables.

8381 Marcuschi, Luiz Antonio. Linguagem e classes sociais: introdução crítica à teoria dos códigos lingüísticos de Basil Bernstein. Porto Alegre: Editora Movimento, 1975. 83 p.; bibl. (Coleção Augusto Meyer: Ensaios; v. 7)

Critical introduction to Basil Bernstein's theory of linguistic codes. Attacks Bernstein's terminology, lack of consistency, and contradictory evidence, and emphasis on the individual rather than social group.

8382 Marini, Mauro. Las razones del neodesarrollismo: respuesta a F.H. Cardoso y J. Serra (UNAM/RMS, 40:40[E], 1978, p. 57–106, tables)

Passionate response to Serra and Cardoso's critique (see item **8395**) in which Marini angrily denies their charge of economic reductionism. Contends that any analysis of the autonomous role classes and politics play in a society must be grounded in an understanding of the economy: politics is, after all, "concentrated economics." Marini responds in detail to Serra and Cardoso's criticism of his work on dependency in general and the development of Brazil in particular. Often asserts that his critics misunderstand or falsify his argument. [C.H. Waisman]

Martins, José de Souza. Conde Matarazzo, o empresário e o empresa: estudo de sociologia do desenvolvimento. See *HLAS 42:3712.*

8383 ———. Las relaciones de clase y la producción ideológica de la noción de trabajo en Brasil (UNAM/RMS, 40:40[E], 1978, p. 143–159)

Penetrating speculation on the ideology of "free labor." Explores the latter with regard to Italians who, after the abolition of slavery, emigrated to Brazil where they filled the need for similarly docile labor force.

Mattoso, Katia M. de Queiros. Bahia: a cidade do Salvador e seu mercado no século XIX. See *HLAS 42:3713.*

Meios de comunicação, realidade e mito. See item **8038.**

8384 Merrick, Thomas W. Fertility and land availability in rural Brazil (PAA/D, 15:3, 1978, p. 321–344)

Multivariate analysis, based on 1970 Census data, of differences in marital fertility on agricultural frontier and in more settled rural areas. Finds that fertility decreases as settlement increases and that factors such as access to agricultural land are more important than its mere availability, as in US experience.

———— and Douglas H. Graham. Population and economic development in Brazil: 1800 to the present. See HLAS 42:3716.

Moisés, José Alvaro. Greve de massa e crise política: estudo da greve dos 300 mil em São Paulo, 1953/54. See HLAS 42:3718.

8385 Motta, Fernando C. Prestes. Empresários e hegemonia política. Prefácio, Luiz Carlos Bresser Pereira; capa, Silvio Dworecki; revisão, Maria Luíza Alvarenga Correa. São Paulo: Editora Brasiliense, 1979. 146 p.; bibl.
Provides in-depth examination of political stances of business leaders, with some supporting data. Motta's thesis is that their policies reflect their ideology. Concludes that in 1978 their pursuit of policy caused them to break with the military state.

8386 Mudança social no Nordeste: a reprodução da subordinação: estudos sobre trabalhadores urbanos. José Sérgio Leite Lopes et al. Rio de Janeiro: Paz e Terra, 1979. 226 p.; bibl. (Série Estudos sobre o Nordeste; v. 5)
Conceptual and ethnographic articles, by members of National Museum social anthropology research team, analyze the organization of labor of individual workers, their families and households, and the market in the Northeast's urban area.

A mulher no Brasil. See HLAS 42:3542.

8387 Palmeira, Moacir. The aftermath of peasant mobilization: rural conflicts in the Brazilian Northeast since 1964 (in The Structure of Brazilian development [see item 8404] p. 71–98, bibl.)
Analytic statement distinguishes conflicts in Pernambuco cane production in terms of eviction of resident workers and of newer forms of labor exploitation. Traces political implications of union mobilization in an authoritarian context.

Pescatello, Ann M. Music festas and their social role in Brazil: Carnaval in Rio. See HLAS 42:1120.

Pinheiro, Paulo Sérgio and Michael M. Hall. A classe operária no Brasil, 1889–1930: documentos. See HLAS 42:3734.

8388 Portes, Alejandro. Housing policy, urban poverty, and the state: the favelas of Rio de Janeiro, 1972–1976 (LARR, 14:2, 1979, p. 3–24, tables)
Analyzes recent programs of federal and state housing agencies in order to show how they operate to subsidize home ownership for the middle class rather than deprived favela residents. Instructive and inventive application of concept of military oligarchy as a form of the bureaucratic-authoritarian state.

Queiroz, Maria Isaura Pereira de. Cultura, sociedade rural, sociedade urbana no Brasil: ensaios. See HLAS 42:3736.

8389 ————. Uma nova interpretação do Brasil: a contribuição de Roger Bastide à sociologia brasileira (USP/RIEB, 20, 1978, p. 101–121, bibl.)
Analyzes Bastide's approach, especially his conceptualization of interpretation and integration, in terms of its departures from and connections to earlier thinking (e.g., Freyre).

8390 ————. Pecuária de vida pastoril: sua evolução em duas regiões brasileiras (USP/RIEB, 20, 1978, p. 55–78, bibl.)
General comparison of social change, from colonial times to present, in two cattle-producing regions, the Northeast sertão and the South pampa. Suggests that latter society changed relatively slowly because its production was limited to a regional market.

8391 Querino, Manuel Raymundo. The African contribution to Brazilian civilization. Translated with an introduction by E. Bradford Burns. Tempe: Arizona State University, Center for Latin American Studies, 1978. 20 p.; bibl. (Special studies—Arizona State University, Center for Latin American studies; no. 18)
English translation of Querino's 1916 essay establishing the importance of blacks and of their African heritage to Brazilian society. Burns' introduction describes Querino as first Brazilian to state this fact. His essay is little known in Brazil or to English-speaking scholars. Original Portuguese title: O colono prêto como fator da civilização brasileira.

8392 Rattner, Henrique. Recenseamento e pesquisa sociológica da comunidade judaica em São Paulo, 1968 (*in* Nos caminhos da Diáspora. Edited by Henrique Rattner. São Paulo, Brasil: Centro Brasileiro de Estudos Judaicos, 1972, p. 235–256)

Descriptive summary of basic demographic data for 9000 families interviewed.

Ross, Eric B. The evolution of Amazon peasantry. See item **5405**.

8393 Santos, José Vicente Tavares dos. Colonos do vinho: estudo sobre a subordinação do trabalho camponês ao capital. São Paulo: Editora HUCITEC, 1978. 182 p.; 5 leaves of plates (Coleção Ciências sociais: Série Realidade social)

Painstaking study details obvious influences of capitalism in grape-producing community of Italian peasant immigrants. Documents and analyzes connections between system based on family labor and capitalist economy.

Sawyer, Donald R. Colonização de Amazônia: migração do nordestinos para uma frente agrícola no Pará. See item **5411**.

8394 A selection of Brazilian production in the social sciences, 1960–1977 (*in* The Structure of Brazilian development [see item **8404**] p. 223–256)

Extensive, but unannotated, bibliography of Latin American and US sources which includes unpublished ones.

8395 Serra, José and Fernando H. Cardoso. Las desventuras de la dialéctica de la dependencia (UNAM/RMS, 40:40[E], 1978, p. 9–55, bibl., tables)

Harsh critique of R.M. Marini's work, with emphasis on his *La dialéctica de la dependencia*. Authors view Marini as an economic reductionist, who denies the specificity of the political. They review in detail Marini's analysis of dependent development, especially his propositions on stagnation; his discussion of the link between unequal exchange the rate of exploitation; and his discussion of the development of capitalism in Brazil, after the coup of 1964. They claim that Marini's analysis of dependent capitalism is wrong and practically harmful, for it leads to simplistic political choices (see item **8382**). [C.H. Waisman]

8396 Shirley, Robert W. Law in rural Brazil (*in* Brazil, anthropological perspec-

tives: essays in honor of Charles Wagley [see item **8352**] p. 343–361)

Sketches "formal system of the application of written urban laws in Brazil." Offers revealing composite portrait of a rural judge in order to show complex interaction with informal law enforcement represented primarily by the *coroneis*.

8397 Sigaud, Lygia. Os clandestinos e os direitos: estudo sobre trabalhadores da cana-de-açúcar de Pernambuco. São Paulo: Livraria Duas Cidades, 1979. 260 p.; bibl. (Coleção História e sociedade)

Based on field research and theoretical analysis, conducted by National Museum, on subject of separation of sugarcane worker from Pernambuco plantations. Study features very able interplay between the specifics internal to the workers' situation and general operation of class economic and political interests.

8398 Simpósio sobre Marginalidade Social, *Recife, Brazil, 1974.* Cidade, usos & abusos. Daniel J. Hogan et al. São Paulo: Editora Brasiliense, 1978. 166 p; bibl.

Consists of five essays based on a 1974 conference. Two by M. Berlinck and D. Hogan concern a survey of 1000 married men in São Paulo and offer an empirical refutation on the variables/concepts "length of residence" and "culture of poverty" in favor of the structure of industrialization and of classes.

8399 Simpósio Trabalho Produtivo e Classes Sociais, *São Paulo, Brazil, 1977.* Classes sociais e trabalho produtivo. André Villalobos et al. Rio de Janeiro: Paz e Terra, 1978. 143 p.; bibl.

Sophisticated exercises in Marxian theory analyzing the working class and the proletariat, intellectual work and scientific production, and productive work. Succeed in modifying Marxian categories to understand transitional societies.

Smith, Robert J. The ethnic Japanese in Brazil. See item **5417**.

Soares, Glaucio Ary Dillon. Después del milagro. See item **6754**.

8401 Sodré, Muniz. O monopólio da fala: função e linguagem da televisão no Brasil. Petrópolis, Brasil: Editora Vozes, 1977. 155 p.; bibl. (Coleção Vozes do mundo moderno; 16)

Consists of interesting social commentary by television critic (e.g., how television relates to individual, constructs social reality, and homogenizes it). Includes appropriate Brazilian examples.

8402 Souto, Claudio. Sociology of law in Brazil (UW/LBR, 16:1, Summer 1979, p. 53–66)
Summary of incipient stage of this field of sociology.

8403 Souza, Julia Filet-Abreu. Paid domestic service in Brazil (LAP, 7[1]:24, Winter 1980, p. 35–63, ill., tables)
Wide-ranging exploration evaluates various explanations and some aggregate and field in context of women's relationship to peripheral capitalist industrialization. Reviews legal rights, job satisfaction, wages and working conditions, relations with employers, and worker associations. Concludes that: 1) domestic service does not encourage upward social mobility, but 2) does contribute indirectly to process of capital accumulation.

8404 The Structure of Brazilian development. Edited by Neuma Aguiar. New Brunswick, N.J.: Transaction Books, 1979. 1 v.; bibl.; index.
Consists of seven analyses (see items **6664, 6677, 8348, 8356, 8387, 8394** and **8405**) by newly established Brazilian social scientists. Emphasis on rural conditions and on relationships to the state. Substantial bibliography.

Suarez, Maria Teresa S. de Melo. Cassacos e corumbas. See item **5419**.

Thomson, Brian A. The periphery and the environment: three case-studies in Argentina and Brazil, 1870–1970. See item **8334**.

Tobler, Hans Werner and **Peter Waldmann.** German colonies in South America: a new Germany in the Cono Sur? See item **8335**.

Uricoechea, Fernando. The patrimonial foundations of the Brazilian bureaucratic state. See item **6681**.

8405 Velho, Otávio Guilherme. The state and the frontier (*in* The Structure of Brazilian development [see item **8404**] p. 17–36, bibl.)
Essay argues authoritarianism of national state on basis of view that it has assumed the plantation's traditional role of repressing the peasantry and structuring po-

litical participation. Illustrates by comparing the frontier in both Brazil and US.

Vianna, Luiz Werneck. Estudos sobre sindicalismo e movimento operário: resenha de algumas tendências. See *HLAS 42:71*.

8406 Ward, John O. and **John H. Sanders.** Determinantes nutricionais e migração no Nordeste brasileiro: um estudo de caso nas áreas rural e urbana do Ceará (BNB/REN, 11:2, abril/junho 1980, p. 293–324, tables)
Economists' quantitative analysis of Ceará state data shows large "nutritional deficits," which increase with migration to the city and which respond positively to increased income.

8407 Wöhlcke, Manfred. Unterschichtreligiosität in Brasilien (BESPL, 1:4, März/April 1976, p. 18–26)
Author maintains that statistics which establish that 90 percent of Brazilians are Catholic are misleading. In his view, 90 percent of Brazil's rural population practice their own version of "catolicismo popular" which is heavily influenced by "cultos afro-brasileiros" including magic, politheism, and animistic and fetishist beliefs. [R.V. Shaw]

8408 Yoder, Michael L. and **Glenn Fuguitt.** Urbanization frontier growth, and population redistribution in Brazil (UW/LBR, 16:1, Summer 1979, p. 67–90, maps, tables)
Helpful analysis and clear presentation of 1960 and 1970 census data for 361 micro-regions shows that both rural and metropolitan micro-regions grew the fastest and that, although rapid, frontier growth was surpassed by urban growth elsewhere. Latter finding supports policy observation that successful frontier settlement is not equivalent to population deconcentration from "overcrowded" areas.

JOURNAL ABBREVIATIONS SOCIOLOGY

AAA/AE American Ethnologist. American Anthropological Association. Washington.

ACEP/EP Estudios de Población. Asociación Colombiana para el Estudio de la Población. Bogotá.

AEJ/JQ Journalism Quarterly. Association for Education in Journalism *with the* *cooperation of the* American Association of Schools, Depts. of Journalism and Kappa Tau Alpha Society. Univ. of Minnesota. Minneapolis.

AI/A Anthropos. Anthropos-Institut. Psoieux, Switzerland.

AJES The American Journal of Economics and Sociology. Francis Neilson Fund and Robert Schalkenbach Foundation. New York.

APSA/R American Political Science Review. American Political Science Association. Columbus, Ohio.

ASA/ASR American Sociological Review. American Sociological Association. Menasha, Wis.

BESPL Berichte zur Entwicklung in Spanien, Portugal, Lateinamerika. München, FRG.

BJS British Journal of Sociology. London School of Economics and Political Science. London.

BNB/REN Revista Econômica do Nordeste. Banco do Nordeste do Brasil, Depto. de Estudos Econômicos do Nordeste. Fortaleza.

CDAL Cahiers des Amériques Latines. Paris.

CEDLA/B Boletín de Estudios Latinoamericanos. Centro de Estudios y Documentación Latinoamericanos. Amsterdam.

CLAEH Centro Latinoamericano de Economía Humana. Montevideo.

CLAPCS/AL América Latina. Centro Latino-Americano de Pesquisas em Ciências Sociais. Rio de Janeiro.

CM/DE Demografía y Economía. El Colegio de México. México.

CM/FI Foro Internacional. El Colegio de México. México.

CM/HM Historia Mexicana. El Colegio de México. México.

CM/RE Relaciones. Estudios de historia y sociedad. El Colegio de Michoacán. Zamora, México.

CMS/IMR The International Migration Review. Center for Migration Studies. New York.

CNC/RMA Revista del México Agrario. Confederación Nacional Campesina. México.

CPES/RPS Revista Paraguaya de Sociología. Centro Paraguayo de Estudios Sociológicos Asunción.

CSSH Comparative Studies in Society and History. An international quarterly. Society for the Comparative Study of Society and History. The Hague.

CSUCA/ESC Estudios Sociales Centroamericanos. Consejo Superior de Universidades Centroamericanas, Confederación Universitaria Centroamericana, Programa Centroamericana de Ciencias Sociales. San José.

CUA/AQ Anthropological Quarterly. Catholic Univ. of America, Catholic Anthropological Conference. Washington.

CUNY/CP Comparative Politics. The City Univ. of New York, Political Science Program. New York.

CVF/C Cuadernos de la CVF. Corporación Venezolana de Fomento. Caracas.

EHA/J Journal of Economic History. New York Univ., Graduate School of Business Administration *for the* Economic History Association. Rensselaer, N.Y.

FERES/SC Social Compass. International review of socio-religious studies (Revue internationale des études socio-religieuses). International Federation of Institutes for Social and Socio-Religious Research (Fédération Internationale des Instituts de Recherches Sociales et Socio-Religieuses-FERES). The Hague.

FHS/FHQ The Florida Historical Quarterly. The Florida Historical Society. Jacksonville.

FS/CIS Cahiers Internationaux de Sociologie. La Sorbonne École Pratique des Hautes Études. Paris.

HAHR Hispanic American Historical Review. Duke Univ. Press *for the* Conference on Latin American History of the American Historical Association. Durham, N.C.

HRAF/BSR Behavior Science Research. Journal of comparative studies. Human Relations Area Files. New Haven, Conn.

IBGE/R Revista Brasileira de Geografia. Conselho Nacional de Geografia, Instituto Brasileiro de Geografia e Estatística. Rio de Janeiro.

ICEM/IM International Migration (Migrations Internationales = Migraciones Internacionales). Quarterly review of the Intergovernmental Committee for European Migration and the Research Group for European Migration Problems. Geneva, Switzerland.

IDES/DE Desarrollo Económico. Instituto de Desarrollo Económico y Social. Buenos Aires.

IIAS/IRAS International Review of Administrative Sciences. International Institute of Administrative Sciences. Bruxelles.

III/AI América Indígena. Instituto Indigenista Interamericano. México.

IJ/JJ Jamaica Journal. Institute of Jamaica. Kingston.

JDA The Journal of Developing Areas. Western Illinois Univ. Press. Macomb.

JLAS Journal of Latin American Studies. Centers or institutes of Latin American studies at the universities of Cambridge, Glasgow, Liverpool, London and Oxford. Cambridge Univ. Press. London.

JPS The Journal of Peasant Studies. Frank Cass & Co. London.

LAP Latin American Perspectives. Univ. of California. Riverside.

LARR Latin American Research Review. Univ. of North Carolina Press *for the* Latin American Studies Association. Chapel Hill.

MVL/J Jahrbuch des Museums für Völkerkunde zu Leipzig. Berlin.

NCFR/JFH Journal of Family History. Studies in family, kinship and demography. National Council on Family Relations. Minneapolis, Minn.

NIU/JPMS Journal of Political & Military Sociology. Northern Illinois Univ., Dept. of Sociology. DeKalb.

NS NS NorthSouth NordSud NorteSur NorteSul. Canadian journal of Latin American studies. Canadian Association of Latin American Studies. Univ. of Ottawa. Ottawa.

NSO Nueva Sociedad. Revista política y cultural. San José.

NYAS/A Annals of the New York Academy of Sciences. New York.

PAA/D Demography. Population Association of America. Washington.

PAIGH/G Revista Geográfica. Instituto Panamericano de Geografía e Historia, Comisión de Geografía. México.

PAN/ES Estudios Latinoamericanos. Polska Akademia Nauk (Academia de Ciencias de Polonia), Instytut Historii (Instituto de Historia). Warszawa.

PCCLAS/P Proceedings of the Pacific Coast Council on Latin American Studies. Univ. of California. Los Angeles.

PSA/PSR Pacific Sociological Review. Pacific Sociological Association. San Diego State Univ. San Diego, Calif.

RLP Revista Latinoamericana de Psicología. Bogotá.

RU/SCID Studies in Comparative International Development. Rutgers Univ. New Brunswick, N.J.

SAA/HO Human Organization. Society for Applied Anthropology. New York.

SAGE/JIAS Journal of Inter-American Studies and World Affairs. Sage Publication *for the* Center for Advanced International Studies, Univ. of Miami. Coral Gables, Fla.

SAP/BM Bulletins et Mémoires de la Société d'Anthropologie de Paris. Paris.

SBPC/CC Ciência e Cultura. Sociedade Brasileira para o Progresso da Ciência. São Paulo.

SF Social Forces. Univ. of North Carolina Press *by the* Williams & Wilkins Co. Baltimore, Md.

SGB/COM Les Cahiers d'Outre-Mer. Publiée par l'Institut de Géographie de la Faculté des Lettres de Bordeaux, par l'Institut de la France d'Outre-Mer, par la Société de Géographie de Bordeaux *avec le concours du* Centre National de la Recherche Scientifique et de la VI^{ieme} section de l'École Pratique des Hautes Études. Bordeaux, France.

SGHG/A Anales de la Sociedad de Geografía e Historia de Guatemala. Guatemala.

SIP/RIP Revista Interamericana de Psicología (Interamerican Journal of Psychology). Sociedad Interamericana de Psicología (Interamerican Society of Psychology). De Paul Univ., Dept. of Psychology. Chicago, Ill.

SSSP/SP Social Problems. Society for the Study of Social Problems *affiliated with the* American and International Sociological Associations. Kalamazoo, Mich.

UA Urban Anthropology. State Univ. of New York, Dept. of Anthropology. Brockport.

UB/BA Boletín Americanista. Univ. de Barcelona, Facultad de Geografía e Historia, Depto. de Historia de América. Barcelona.

UC/A Anales de la Universidad de Cuenca. Cuenca, Ecuador.

UC/CA Current Anthropology. Univ. of Chicago. Chicago, Ill.

UC/EDCC Economic Development and Cultural Change. Univ. of Chicago, Research Center in Economic Development and Cultural Change. Chicago, Ill.

UC/S Signs. Journal of women in culture and society. The Univ. of Chicago Press. Chicago, Ill.

UCL/CD Cultures et Développement. Revue internationale des sciences du développement. Univ. Catholique de Louvain *avec le concours de la* Fondation Universitaire de Belgique. Louvain, Belgium.

UCNSA/EP Estudios Paraguayos. Univ. Católica Nuestra Señora de la Asunción. Asunción.

UCSD/NS The New Scholar. Univ. of California, Center for Iberian and Latin American Studies and Institute of Chicano Urban Affairs. San Diego.

UJSC/ECA Estudios Centro-Americanos. Revista de extensión cultural. Univ. José Simeón Cañas. San Salvador.

UK/SR The Sociological Review. Univ. of Keele. Staffordshire, England.

UM/JIAS *See* SAGE/JIAS.

UMG/RBEP Revista Brasileira de Estudos Políticos. Univ. de Minas Gerais. Belo Horizonte, Brazil.

UN/ISSJ International Social Science Journal. United Nations Educational, Scientific, and Cultural Organization. Paris.

UNAM/RMCPS Revista Mexicana de Ciencias Políticas y Sociales. Univ. Nacional Autónoma de México, Facultad de Ciencias Políticas y Sociales. México.

UNAM/RMS Revista Mexicana de Sociología. Univ. Nacional Autónoma de México, Instituto de Investigaciones Sociales. México.

UNESCO/CU Cultures. United Nations Educational, Scientific, and Cultural Organization. Paris.

UNPHU/A Aula. Univ. Nacional Pedro Henríquez Ureña. Santo Domingo.

UPR/CS Caribbean Studies. Univ. of Puerto Rico, Institute of Caribbean Studies. Río Piedras.

UPR/RCS Revista de Ciencias Sociales. Univ. de Puerto Rico, Colegio de Ciencias Sociales. Río Piedras.

URSS/AL América Latina. Academia de Ciencias de la URSS (Unión de Repúblicas Soviéticas Socialistas). Moscú.

USB/F Franciscanum. Revista de las ciencias del espíritu. Univ. de San Buenaventura. Bogotá.

USC/SSR Sociology and Social Research. An international journal. Univ. of Southern California. University Park.

USCG/PS Política y Sociedad. Univ. de San Carlos de Guatemala, Facultad de Ciencias Jurídicas y Sociales, Escuela de Ciencias Política, Instituto de Investigaciones Políticas y Sociales. Guatemala.

USM/JTG The Journal of Tropical Geography. Univ. of Singapore and Univ. of Malaya, Depts. of Geography. Singapore.

USP/RIEB Revista do Instituto de Estudos Brasileiros. Univ. de São Paulo, Instituto de Estudos Brasileiros. São Paulo.

UTIEH/C Caravelle. Cahiers du monde hispanique et luso-brésilien. Univ. de Toulouse, Institut d'Études Hispaniques, Hispano-Americaines et Luso-Brésiliennes. Toulouse, France.

UW/LBR   Luso-Brazilian Review. Univ. of Wisconsin Press. Madison.

UWI/CQ   Caribbean Quarterly. Univ. of the West Indies. Mona, Jamaica.

UWI/SES   Social and Economic Studies. Univ. of the West Indies, Institute of Social and Economic Research. Mona, Jamaica.

ZMR   Zeitschrift für Missionswissenschaft und Religionswissenschaft. Lucerne, Switzerland.

INDEXES

ABBREVIATIONS AND ACRONYMS

Except for journal acronyms, which are listed at a) the end of each major disciplinary section (e.g., Anthropology, Economics, etc.), and b) after each serial title in the *Title List of Journal's Indexed,* p. 797.

a	annual
ABC	Argentina, Brazil, Chile
A.C.	antes de Cristo
ACAR	Associação de Crédito e Assistência Rural, Brazil
AD	Anno Domini
A.D.	Acción Democrática, Venezuela
ADESG	Associação dos Diplomados de Escola Superior de Guerra, Brazil
AGI	Archivo General de Indias, Sevilla
AGN	Archivo General de la Nación
AID	Agency for International Development
Ala.	Alabama
ALALC	Asociación Latinoamericana de Libre Comercio
ANAPO	Alianza Nacional Popular, Colombia
ANCARSE	Associação Nordestina de Crédito e Assistência Rural de Sergipe, Brazil
ANCOM	Andean Common Market
ANDI	Asociación Nacional de Industriales, Colombia
AP	Acción Popular
APRA	Alianza Popular Revolucionaria Americana
Arg.	Argentina
Ariz.	Arizona
Ark.	Arkansas
ASA	Association of Social Anthropologists of the Commonwealth, London
ASSEPLAN	Assessoria de Planejamente e Acompanhamento, Recife, Brazil
Assn.	Association
Aufl.	Auflage (edition, edición)
AUFS	American Universities Field Staff Reports, Hanover, N.H.
Aug.	August, Augustan
b.	born (nacido)
B.A.	Buenos Aires
Bar.	Barbados
BBE	Bibliografia Brasileira de Educação
b.c.	indicates dates obtained by radio-carbon methods
BC	Before Christ
bibl.	bibliography
BID	Banco Interamericano de Desarrollo
BNDE	Banco Nacional de Desenvolvimento Econômico, Brazil
BNH	Banco Nacional de Habitação, Brazil
Bol.	Bolivia
BP	before present
b/w	black-and-white
C14	Carbon 14

ca.	circa
C.A.	Centro América, Central America
CACM	Central American Common Market
CADE	Conferencia Anual de Ejecutivos de Empresas, Peru
CAEM	Centro de Altos Estudios Militares, Peru
Calif.	California
CARC	Centro de Arte y Comunicación
CARICOM	Caribbean Common Market
CARIFTA	Caribbean Free Trade Association
CBD	central business district
CD	Christian Democrats, Chile
CDI	Conselho de Desenvolvimento Industrial
CEBRAP	Centro Brasileiro de Análise e Planejamento, São Paulo
CECORA	Central de Cooperativas de la Reforma Agraria, Colombia
CEDAL	Centro de Estudios Democráticos de América Latina, Costa Rica
CEDE	Centro de Estudios sobre Desarrollo Económico, Univ. de los Andes, Bogotá
CEDEPLAR	Centro de Desenvolvimento e Planejamento Region, Belo Horizonte, Brazil
CEDES	Centro de Estudios de Estado y Sociedad, Buenos Aires
CEESTEM	Centro de Estudios Económicos y Sociales del Tercer Mundo, México
CELADE	Centro Latinoamericano de Demografía
CEMLA	Centro de Estudios Monetarios Latinoamericanos, México
CENDES	Centro de Estudios del Desarrollo, Venezuela
CENIDIM	Centro Nacional de Información, Documentación e Investigación Musicales, Mexico
CENIET	Centro Nacional de Información y Estadísticas del Trabajo, México
CEPADE	Centro Paraguayo de Estudios de Desarrollo Económico y Social
CEPA-SE	Comissão Estadual de Planejamento Agrícola, Sergipe, Brazil
CEPAL	*See* ECLA.
CES	constant elasticity of substitution
cf.	compare
CFI	Consejo Federal de Inversiones, B.A.
CGE	Confederación General Económica, Argentina
CGTP	Confederación General de Trabajadores del Perú
ch., chap.	chapter
CHEAR	Council on Higher Education in the American Republics
Cía.	compañía
CIA	Central Intelligence Agency
CIDA	Comité Interamericano de Desarrollo Agrícola
CIDE	Centro de Investigación y Desarrollo de la Educación, Chile
CIE	Centro de Investigaciones Económicas, Buenos Aires
CIP	Conselho Interministerial de Preços
CLACSO	Consejo Latinoamericano de Ciencias Sociales, Secretaría Ejecutiva, Buenos Aires
CLASC	Confederación Latinoamericana Sindical Cristiana
CLE	Comunidad Latinoamericana de Escritores, México
cm	centimeter
CNI	Confederação Nacional da Industria, Brazil
Co.	company
COBAL	Companhia Brasileira de Alimentos
Col.	collection, colección, coleção
Colo.	Colorado
COMCORDE	Comisión Coordinadora para el Desarrollo Económico, Uruguay
comp.	compiler
CONDESE	Conselho de Desenvolvimento Econômico de Sergipe, Brazil
Conn.	Connecticut

COPEI	Comité Organizador Pro-Elecciones Independientes, Venezuela
CORFO	Corporación de Fomento de la Producción, Chile
CORP	Corporación para el Fomento de Investigaciones Económicas, Colombia
Corp.	Corporation
C.R.	Costa Rica
CRIC	Consejo Regional Indígena del Cauca, Colombia
CUNY	City University of New York
CVG	Corporación Venezolana de Guayana
d.	died
DANE	Departamento Nacional de Estadística, Colombia
DC	developed country; Demócratas Cristianos, Chile
d.C.	después de Cristo
Dec.	December, décembre
Del.	Delaware
dept.	department
depto.	departamento
dez.	dezembro
dic.	diciembre
DNOCS	Departamento Nacional de Obras Contra as Sêcas, Brazil
D.R.	Dominican Republic
Dra.	Doctora
ECLA	Economic Comission for Latin America
ECOSOC	UN Dept. of Economic and Social Affairs
Ecua.	Ecuador
ed(s).	edition(s), edición(es), editor(s), redactor(es)
EDEME	Editora Emprendimentos Educacionais Florianópolis, Brazil
Edo.	Estado
EEC	European Economic Community
EFTA	European Free Trade Association
e.g.	exempio gratia [for example]
El Sal.	El Salvador
ELN	Ejército de Liberación Nacional, Colombia
ESG	Escola Superior de Guerra, Brazil
estr.	estrenado
et al	et alia [and others]
ETENE	Escritório Técnico de Estudios Econômicos do Nordeste, Brazil
ETEPE	Escritório Técnico de Planejamento, Brazil
EUDEBA	Editorial Universitaria de Buenos Aires
EWG	Europaische Wirtschaftsgemeinschaft. *See* EEC.
facsim.	facsimile
FAO	Food and Agriculture Organization of the United Nations
FDR	Frente Democrático Revolucionario, El Salvador
feb.	February, febrero
FEDECAFE	Federación Nacional de Cafeteros, Colombia
fev.	fevreiro, février
ff.	following
FFMLN	Frente Farabundo Martí de Liberación Nacional, El Salvador
FGTS	Fundo do Garantia do Tempo de Serviço, Brazil
FGV	Fundação Getúlio Vargas
FIEL	Fundación de Investigaciones Económicas Latinoamericanas, Argentina
film.	filmography
fl.	flourished, floresció
Fla.	Florida
FLACSO	Facultad Latinoamericana de Ciencias Sociales, Buenos Aires
fold. map	folded map

fold. table	folded table
fols.	folios
FRG	Federal Republic of Germany
ft.	foot, feet
FUAR	Frente Unido de Acción Revolucionaria, Colombia
Ga.	Georgia
GAO	General Accounting Office, Washington
GATT	General Agreement on Tariffs and Trade
GDP	gross domestic product
GDR	German Democratic Republic
GEIDA	Grupo Executivo de Irrigação para o Desenvolvimento Agrícola, Brazil
Gen.	General
GMT	Greenwich Meridian Time
GPA	grade point average
GPO	Government Printing Office
Guat.	Guatemala
h.	hijo
ha.	hectares, hectáreas
HLAS	*Handbook of Latin American Studies*
HMAI	*Handbook of Middle American Indians*
Hnos.	Hermanos
Hond.	Honduras
IBBD	Instituto Brasileiro de Bibliografia e Documentação
IBRD	International Bank of Reconstruction and Development
ICA	Instituto Colombiano Agropecuario
ICAIC	Instituto Cubano de Arte de Industria Cinematográficas
ICCE	Instituto Colombiano de Construcción Escolar
ICSS	Instituto Colombiano de Seguridad Social
ICT	Instituto de Crédito Territorial, Colombia
IDB	Inter-American Development Bank
i.e.	id est [that is]
IEL	Instituto Euvaldo Lodi, Brazil
IEP	Instituto de Estudios Peruanos
IERAC	Instituto Ecuatoriano de Reforma Agraria y Colonización
III	Instituto Indigenista Interamericano, Mexico
IIN	Instituto Indigenista Nacional, Guatemala
Ill.	Illinois
illus.	illustration(s)
ILO	International Labour Organization, Geneva
IMES	Instituto Mexicano de Estudios Sociales
in.	inches
INAH	Instituto Nacional de Antropología e Historia, México
INBA	Instituto Nacional de Bellas Artes, México
Inc.	incorporated
INCORA	Instituto Colombiano de Reforma Agraria
Ind.	Indiana
INEP	Instituto Nacional de Estudios Pedagógicos, Brazil
INI	Instituto Nacional Indigenista, Mexico
INIT	Instituto Nacional de Industria Turística, Cuba
INPES/IPEA	Instituto de Planejamento Econômico e Social, Instituto de Pesquisas, Brazil
IPA	Instituto de Pastoral Andina, Univ. de San Antonio de Abad, Seminario de Antropología, Cuzco, Peru
IPEA	Instituto de Pesquisa Econômico-Social Aplicada, Brazil
IPES/GB	Instituto de Pesquisas e Estudos Sociais, Guanabara, Brazil
IPHAN	Instituto de Patrimônio Histórico e Artístico Nacional, Brazil

ir.	irregular
ITT	International Telephone and Telegraph
Jam.	Jamaica
jan.	January, janeiro, Janvier
JLP	Jamaican Labour Party
JUCEPLAN	Junta Central de Planificación, Cuba
Jul.	juli
Jun.	Juni
Kans.	Kansas
km	kilometers, kilómetros
Ky.	Kentucky
l.	leaves, hojas (páginas impresas por una sola cara)
La.	Louisiana
LASA	Latin American Studies Association
LDC	less developed country
Ltda.	Limitada
m	meters, metros, monthly
M	mille, mil, thousand
MAPU	Movimiento de Acción Popular Unitario, Chile
MARI	Middle American Research Institute, Tulane University, New Orleans
Mass.	Massachusetts
MCC	Mercado Común Centro-Americano
MCN	multinational corporation
Md.	Maryland
MDB	Movimiento Democrático Brasileiro
MDC	more developed countries
MEC	Ministério de Educação e Cultura, Brazil
Mex.	Mexico
Mich.	Michigan
mimeo	mimeographed, mimeografiado
min.	minutes, minutos
Minn.	Minnesota
MIR	Movimiento de Izquierda Revolucionaria, Chile
Miss.	Mississippi
MIT	Massachusetts Institute of Technology
MLN	Movimiento de Liberación Nacional
mm.	millimeter
MNR	Movimiento Nacionalista Revolucionario, Bolivia
Mo.	Missouri
MOIR	Movimiento Obrero Independiente y Revolucionario, Colombia
MRL	Movimiento Revolucionario Liberal, Colombia
ms.	manuscript
msl	mean sea level
n.	nacido (born)
N.C.	North Carolina
n.d.	no date
N. Dak.	North Dakota
Nebr.	Nebraska
neubearb.	neurbearbeitet (revised, corregida)
Nev.	Nevada
n.f.	neue Folge
N.H.	New Hampshire
Nic.	Nicaragua
NIEO	new international economic order
NIH	National Institutes of Health, Washington

N.J.	New Jersey
N. Mex.	New Mexico
no(s).	number(s), número(s)
NOSALF	Scandinavian Committee for Research in Latin America
Nov.	noviembre, November, novembre, novembro
n.p.	no place, no publisher
NSF	National Science Foundation
NY	New York
NYC	New York City
OAS	Organization of American States
oct.	October, octubre
ODEPLAN	Oficina de Planificación Nacional, Chile
OEA	Organización de los Estados Americanos
OIT	*See* ILO.
Okla.	Oklahoma
Okt.	Oktober
op.	opus
OPANAL	Organismo para la Proscripción de las Armas Nucleares en América Latina
OPEC	Organization of Petroleum Exporting Countries
OPEP	Organización de Países Exportadores de Petróleo
OPIC	Overseas Investment Corporation
Oreg.	Oregon
ORIT	Organización Regional Interamericana del Trabajo
out.	outubro
p.	page
Pa.	Pennsylvania
Pan.	Panama
PAN	Partido Acción Nacional, Mexico
Par.	Paraguay
PC	partido comunista
PCR	Partido Comunista Revolucionario, Chile and Argentina
PCV	Partido Comunista de Venezuela
PDC	Partido Demócrata Cristiano, Chile
PEMEX	Petróleos Mexicanos
PETROBRAS	Petróleo Brasileiro
PIMES	Programa Integrado de Mestrado em Economia e Sociologia, Brazil
PIP	Partido Independiente de Puerto Rico
PLANAVE	Engenharia e Planejamento Limitada, Brazil
PLANO	Planejamento e Assesoria Limitada, Brazil
PLN	Partido Liberación Nacional, Costa Rica
PNM	People's National Movement, Trinidad and Tobago
PNP	People's National Party, Jamaica
pop.	population
port., ports.	portrait/s
PPP	purchasing power parities
P.R.	Puerto Rico
PRD	Partido Revolucionario Dominicano
PRI	Partido Revolucionario Institucional, Mexico
PROABRIL	Centro de Projetos Industriais, Brazil
Prof.	Professor
PRONAPA	Programa Nacional de Pesquisas Arqueológicas, Brazil
prov.	province, provincia
PS	Partido Socialista, Chile
pseud.	pseudonym, pseudónimo
pt(s).	part(s), parte(s)

PUC	Pontifícia Universidade Católica, Rio
PURSC	Partido Unido de la Revolución Socialista de Cuba
q.	quarterly
R.D.	República Dominicana
rev.	revisada, revista, revised
R.I.	Rhode Island
Rio	Rio de Janeiro
S.a.	semiannual
SALALM	Seminar on the Acquisition of Latin American Library Materials
S.C.	South Carolina
sd.	sound
S. Dak.	South Dakota
SDR	special drawing rights
Sec.	section, sección
SELA	Sistema Económico Latinoamericano
SENAC	Serviço Nacional de Aprendizagem Comerical, Rio
SENAI	Serviço Nacional de Aprendizagem Industrial, São Paulo
Sept.	September, septiembre, septembre
SES	socio-economic status
SESI	Serviço Social de Industria, Brazil
set.	setembre
SIECA	Secretaría Permanente del Tratado General de Integración Centroamericana
SIL	Summer Institute of Linguistics
SINAMOS	Sistema Nacional de Apoyo a la Movilización Social, Peru
S.J.	Society of Jesus
s.l.	sine loco (without place)
s.n.	sine nomine
SNA	Sociedad Nacional de Agricultura, Chile
SPVEA	Superintendência do Plano de Valorização Econômica de Amazônia, Brazil
sq.	square
SUDAM	Superintendência do Desenvolvimento da Amazônia, Brazil
SUDENE	Superintendência do Desenvolvimento do Nordeste, Brazil
SUFRAMA	Superintendência da Zona Franca de Manaus, Brazil
SUNY	State Universities of New York
t.	tomo, tome
T. and T.	Trinidad & Tobago
TAT	Thematic Apperception Test
TB	tuberculosis
Tenn.	Tennessee
Tex.	Texas
TG	transformational generative
TL	Thermoluminescent
TNP	Tratado de No Proliferación
trans.	translator
U.K.	United Kingdom
UN	United Nations
UNAM	Universidad Nacional Autónoma de México
UNCTAD	United Nations Conference on Trade and Development
UNDP	UN Development Programme
UNEAC	Unión de Escritores y Artistas de Cuba
UNESCO	United Nations Educational, Scientific and Cultural Organization
univ.	university, universidad, universidade, université, universität
uniw.	uniwersytet
UP	Unidad Popular, Chile
URD	Unidad Revolucionaria Democrática

URSS	Unión de Repúblicas Soviéticas Socialistas
Uru.	Uruguay
US	United States of America
USIA	Unites States Information Agency, Washington
USSR	Union of Soviet Socialist Republics
UTM	Universal Transverse Mercator
v.; vol.	volume, volumen
Va.	Virginia
Ven.	Venezuela
V.I.	Virgin Islands
viz.	videlicet, that is, namely
vs.	versus
Vt.	Vermont
W.I.	West Indies
Wis.	Wisconsin
Wyo.	Wyoming
yr.	the younger, el joven, year

TITLE LIST OF JOURNALS INDEXED *

Agrociencia. Secretaría de Agricultura y Recursos Hidráulicos, Colegio de Postgraduados de la Escuela Nacional de Agricultura. Chapingo, México. (AGRO)

Alero. Univ. de San Carlos. Guatemala.

Allpanchis. Instituto de Pastoral Andina. Cuzco, Perú. (IPA/A)

Amazonía Peruana. Centro Amazónico de Antropología y Aplicación Práctica, Depto. de Documentación y Publicaciones. Lima. (CAAAP/AP)

América Latina. Academia de Ciencias de la URSS (Unión de Repúblicas Soviéticas Socialistas). Moscú. (URSS/AL)

América Latina. Centro Latino-Americano de Pesquisas em Ciências Sociais. Rio de Janeiro. (CLAPCS/AL)

American Anthropologist. American Anthropological Association. Washington. (AAA/AA)

American Antiquity. The Society for American Archaeology. Menasha, Wis. (SAA/AA)

American Economic Review. Journal of the American Economic Association. Evanston, Ill. (AEA/AER)

American Ethnologist. American Anthropological Association. Washington. (AAA/AE)

The American Journal of Economics and Sociology. Francis Neilson Fund and Robert Schalkenbach Foundation. New York. (AJES)

American Journal of Epidemiology. Johns Hopkins Univ. Baltimore, Md.

American Journal of Human Genetics. The American Society of Human Genetics. Baltimore, Md. (ASHG/J)

American Journal of Physical Anthropology. American Association of Physical Anthropologists and the Wistar Institute of Anatomy and Biology. Philadelphia, Pa. (AJPA)

American Naturalist. Essex Institute. Lancaster, Pa.

American Political Science Review. American Political Science Association. Columbus, Ohio. (APSA/R)

American Sociological Review. American Sociological Association. Menasha, Wis. (ASA/ASR)

Américas. Organization of American States. Washington. (OAS/AM)

The Americas. A quarterly publication of inter-American cultural history. Academy of American Franciscan History. Washington. (AAFH/TAM)

Anais da Biblioteca Nacional. Divisão de Obras Raras e Publicações. Rio de Janeiro. (BRBN/A)

Anales. Administración del Patrimonio Cultural. San Salvador.

Anales. Univ. de Chile. Santiago.

Anales de Antropología. Univ. Nacional Autónoma de México, Instituto de Investigaciones Históricas. México. (UNAM/AA)

Anales de la Academia Nacional de Ciencias Económicas. Buenos Aires. (ANCE/A)

Anales de la Sociedad de Geografía e Historia de Guatemala. Guatemala. (SGHG/A)

Anales de la Universidad de Cuenca. Cuenca, Ecuador. (UC/A)

Anales del Instituto Nacional de Antropología e Historia. Secretaría de Educación Pública. México. (INAH/A)

Analysis & Documentary Information. Ministry of Education and Culture (MEC), Brazilian Literacy Movement Foundation (MOBRAL), Center for Training, Research and Documentation (CEPTEP), Documentation Sector (SEDOC). Rio de Janeiro.

Annales de Géographie. Société de Géographie. Paris. (SG/AG)

Annals. Carnegie Museum of Natural History. Pittsburgh, Pa.

Annals of Human Biology. Taylor and Francis Publishers. London.

Annals of Human Genetics (Annals of Eu-

* Journals that have been included in the *Handbook* as individual items are listed alphabetically by title in the Author Index.

genics). Univ. College, Galton Laboratory. London. (UCGL/AHG)

Annals of the Association of American Geographers. Lawrence, Kan. (AAG/A)

Annals of the New York Academy of Sciences. New York. (NYAS/A)

Annual of Psychoanalysis. Yale Univ. Press. New Haven, Conn.

Annual Report of the Institute of Geoscience. Univ. of Tsukuba. Tsukuba, Japan.

Annual Review of Anthropology. Annual Review, Inc. Palo Alto, Calif.

Annual Review of Genetics. Palo Alto, Calif.

Anthropologica. Canadian Research Centre for Anthropology. St. Paul Univ. Ottawa, Canada. (CRCA/A)

Anthropologica. Research Center for Amerindian Anthropology. Univ. of Ottawa. Ottawa, Canada.

Anthropological Quarterly. Catholic Univ. of America, Catholic Anthropological Conference. Washington. (CUA/AQ)

Anthropology. State Univ. of New York, Dept. of Anthropology. Stony Brook.

Anthropos. Anthropos-Institut. Psoieux, Switzerland. (AI/A)

Antiquitas. Boletín de la Asociación Amigos del Instituto de Arqueología, Facultad de Historia y Letras. Univ. del Salvador. Buenos Aires.

Antiquity. A quarterly review of archaeology. The Antiquity Trust. Cambridge, England. (AT/A)

Antropología Andina. Centro de Estudios Andinos. Cuzco, Peru.

Antropología e Historia de Guatemala. Instituto de Antropología e Historia de Guatemala. Guatemala. (IAHG/AHG)

Antropología Ecuatoriana. Casa de la Cultura Ecuatoriana. Quito.

Antropológica. Fundación La Salle de Ciencias Naturales, Instituto Caribe de Antropología y Sociología. Caracas. (FSCN/A)

Anuário Antropológico. Edições Tempo Brasileiro. Rio de Janeiro.

Anuario de Estudios Centroamericanos. Univ. de Costa Rica. San José. (UCR/AEC)

Anuario de Letras. Univ. Nacional Autónoma de México, Facultad de Filosofía y Letras. México. (UNAM/AL)

Apacheta. Revista de las tradiciones populares de Perú. Francisco Iriarte Brenner. Lima.

Archaeoastronomy. Supplement to Journal of the History of Astronomy. Giles, England.

Archaeology. Archaeological Institute of America. New York. (AIA/A)

Archaeology and Anthropology. Journal of the Walter Roth Museum of Archaeology and Anthropology. Georgetown, Guyana.

Archiv für Völkerkunde. Museum für Völkerkunde in Wien und von Verein Freunde der Völkerkunde. Wien. (MVW/AV)

Archives de Sociologie des Religions. Centre Nationale de la Recherche Scientifique. Paris. (CNRS/ASR)

Archives Européennes de Sociologie. Paris. (AES)

Archivum Historicum Societatis Iesu. Rome. (AHSI)

Areito. Areíto, Inc. New York. (AR)

Argos. División de Ciencias Sociales y Humanidades, Univ. Simón Bolívar. Caracas.

Arqueológicas. Museo Nacional de Antropología y Arqueología. Lima.

Arquivos do Museu de História Natural. Univ. Federal de Minas Gerais. Belo Horizonte, Brazil.

Arstryck. Göteborgs Etnografiska Museum. Göteborgs, Sweden.

Asian Perspectives. Univ. Press of Hawaii. Honolulu.

Assistant Librarian. London.

Atenea. Revista de ciencias, letras y artes. Univ. de Concepción. Concepción, Chile. (UC/AT)

Aula. Univ. Nacional Pedro Henríquez Ureña. Santo Domingo. (UNPHU/A)

Aussenpolitik. Zeitschrift für Internationale Fragen. Deutsche Verlags-Austalt. Hamburg, FRG. (AZIF).

Baessler-Archiv. Museums für Völkerkunde. Berlin. (MV/BA)

Bahia Acervo Bibliográfico. Fundação Centro de Pesquisas e Estudos. Salvador, Brazil.

Bank of London and South America Review. London.

Behavior Science Research. Journal of comparative studies. Human Relations Area Files. New Haven, Conn. (HRAF/BSR)

Beiträge zur Allgemeinen und Vergleichenden Archäologie. Deutsches Archäologisches Institut. Berlin, FRG.

Beiträge zur Romanischen Philologie. Rütten & Loening. Berlin, FRG. (BRP)

Belizean Studies. Belizean Institute of Social Research and Action and St. John's College. Belize City. (BISRA/BS)

Berichte zur Entwicklung in Spanien, Portugal, Lateinamerika. München, FRG. (BESPL)

Bibliografía Médica Venezolana. Ministerio de Sanidad y Asistencia Social. Caracas.

Bibliographie Latinoamericaine d'Articles. Institut des Hautes Êtudes de l'Amérique Latine, Centre de Documentation. Paris.

Bibliotecología y Documentación. Asociación de Bibliotecarios Graduados de la República Argentina. Buenos Aires.

Bijdragen tot de Taal-, Land- en Volkenkunde. Koninklijk Instituut voor Taal-, Land- en Volkenkunde. Leiden, The Netherlands. (KITLV/B)

The Black Scholar. Black World Foundation. Sausalito, Calif.

Bohemia. La Habana.

Boletim Bibliográfico. Secretaria das Minas e Energia, Coordenação da Produção Mineral. Bahia, Brazil.

Boletim Bibliográfico da Biblioteca Nacional. Rio de Janeiro.

Boletim Carioca de Geografia. Associação dos Geógrafos Brasileiros, Secção Regional de São Paulo. São Paulo. (AGB/BCG)

Boletim do Instituto de Arqueologia Brasileira. Rio de Janeiro.

Boletim do Museu Nacional. Compôsto e impresso na Oficina Gráfica da Univ. do Brasil. Rio de Janeiro. (BRMN/B)

Boletim do Museu Paraense Emílio Goeldi. Nova série: antropologia. Conselho Nacional de Desenvolvimento Científico e Tecnológico, Instituto Nacional de Pesquisas da Amazônia. Belém, Brazil. (MPEG/B)

Boletim Geográfico do Estado do Rio Grande do Sul. Diretório Regional de Geografia e da Secção de Geografia. Porto Alegre, Brazil. (DRG/BG)

Boletim Informativo e Bibliográfico de Ciencias Sociais. Instituto Universitário de Pesquisas. Rio de Janeiro.

Boletim Paulista de Geografia. Associação dos Geógrafos Brasileiros, Secção Regional de São Paulo. São Paulo. (AGB/BPG)

Boletín. Museo Arqueológico de La Serena. La Serena, Chile.

Boletín. Museo del Oro, Banco de la República. Bogotá.

Boletín Americanista. Univ. de Barcelona, Facultad de Geografía e Historia, Depto. de Historia de América. Barcelona. (UB/BA)

Boletín Bibliográfico. Banco Central de Nicaragua. Managua.

Boletín Bibliográfico. Instituto Boliviano de Cultura. Instituto Nacional de Historia y Literatura. Depositorio Nacional. La Paz.

Boletín Bibliográfico de Antropología Americana. Instituto Panamericano de Geografía e Historia, Comisión de Historia. México. (BBAA)

Boletín Cultural y Bibliográfico. Banco de la República, Biblioteca Luis-Angel Arango. Bogotá. (CBR/BCB)

Boletín de Antropología Americana. See Boletín Bibliográfico de Antropología Americana.

Boletín de Ciencias Políticas y Sociales. Univ. Nacional de Cuyo, Facultad de Ciencias Políticas y Sociales. Mendoza, Argentina. (UNC/BCPS)

Boletín de Estudios Latinoamericanos. Centro de Estudios y Documentación Latinoamericanos. Amsterdam. (CEDLA/B)

Boletín de Gerencia Administrativa. Negociado de Presupuesto. San Juan? (PRNP/BGA)

Boletín de Historia y Antigüedades. Academia Colombiana de Historia. Bogotá. (ACH/BHA)

Boletín de la Academia de Ciencias Políticas y Sociales. Caracas. (ACPS/B)

Boletín de la Academia Nacional de Ciencias. Córdoba, Argentina. (ANC/B)

Boletín de la Academia Nacional de Historia. Quito. (EANH/B)

Boletín de la Academia Nacional de la Historia. Caracas. (VANH/B)

Boletín de la Academia Panameña de la Historia. Panamá.

Boletín de la Biblioteca Nacional. Lima. (PEBN/B)

Boletín de la Escuela de Ciencias Antropológicas de la Univ. de Yucatán. Mérida, México.

Boletín de la Sociedad Geográfica de Colombia. Bogotá.

Boletín de la Sociedad Geográfica de Lima. Lima. (SGL/B)

Boletín de la Sociedad Geográfica e Histórica Sucre. Sucre, Bolivia. (SGHS/B)

Boletín del Archivo General de la Nación. Secretaría de Gobernación. México. (MAGN/B)

Boletín del Instituto de Estudios Sociales de la Universidad de Guadalajara. Guadalajara, México.

Boletín del Instituto de Geografía. Univ. Nacional Autónoma de México. México.

Boletín del Instituto Nacional de Antropología e Historia. Secretaría de Educación Pública. México. (INAH/B)

Boletín del Museo del Hombre Dominicano. Santo Domingo. (MHD/B)

Boletín del Sistema Bibliotecario de la UNAH. Univ. Nacional Autónoma de Honduras. Tegucigalpa.

Boletín Documental. Univ. del Zulia, Facultad de Humanidades y Educación, Centro de Documentación e Investigación Pedagógica. Maracaibo, Venezuela.

Boletín Indigenista Venezolano. Ministerio de Justicia, Comisión Indigenista. Caracas. (VMJ/BIV)

Boletín Informativo. Centro de Estudios de Población y Desarrollo. Lima.

Boletín Nicaragüense de Bibliografía y Documentación. Banco Central de Nicaragua, Biblioteca. Managua. (BNBD)

Bonner Amerikanistische Studien. Seminar für Volkerkunde. Bonn, FRG.

Brazilian Business. National Association of American Chambers of Commerce in Brazil. Rio de Janeiro.

British Journal of Sociology. London School of Economics and Political Science. London. (BJS)

Bulletin. Société Suisse des Américanistes. Geneva. (SSA/B)

Bulletin de la Société d'Histoire de la Guadaloupe. Archives Départementales *avec le concours du* Conseil Général de la Guadeloupe. Basse-Terre, West Indies. (SHG/B)

Bulletin de l'Académie des Sciences Humaines et Sociales d'Haiti. Port-au-Prince. (ASHSH/B)

Bulletin de l'Association de Géographes Français. Paris. (AGF/B)

Bulletin of Eastern Caribbean Affairs. Univ. of the West Indies, Institute of Social and Economic Research. Cave Hill, Barbados.

Bulletin of the Pan American Health Organization. Washington. (PAHO/B)

Bulletins et Mémoires de la Société d'Anthropologie de Paris. Paris. (SAP/BM)

Business Review. Government Development Bank. San Juan? (GDB/BR)

Cadernos DCP. Univ. Federal de Minas Gerais, Faculdade de Filosofia e Ciências Humanas, Depto. de Ciência Política. Belo Horizonte, Brazil. (UFMG/DCP)

Cahiers des Amériques Latines. Paris. (CDAL)

Les Cahiers d'Outre-Mer. Publiée par l'Institut de Géographie de la Faculté des Lettres de Bordeaux, par l'Institut de la France d'Outre-Mer, par la Société de Géographie de Bordeaux *avec le concours de* Centre National de la Recherche Scientifique et de la VI. section de l'École Pratique des Hautes Études. Bordeaux. (SGB/COM)

Cahiers Internationaux de Sociologie. La Sorbonne, École Pratique des Hautes Études. Paris. (FS/CIS)

The Canadian Review of Sociology and Anthropology. Canadian Sociology and Anthropology Association. Montreal.

Caravelle. Cahiers du monde hispanique et luso-brésilien. Univ. of Toulouse, Institut d'Études Hispaniques, Hispano-Americaines et Luso-Brésiliennes. Toulouse, France. (UTIEH/C)

Caribbean Quarterly. Univ. of the West Indies. Mona, Jamaica. (UWI/CQ)

Caribbean Review. Florida International Univ., Office of Academic Affairs. Miami. (FIU/CR)

Caribbean Studies. Univ. of Puerto Rico, Instituto of Caribbean Studies. Río Piedras. (UPR/CS)

Carta Política. Persona e Persona. Buenos Aires.

Casa de las Américas. Instituto Cubano del Libro. La Habana. (CDLA)

Catholic Historical Review. American Catholic Historical Association. The Catholic Univ. of America Press. Washington. (ACHA/CHR)

Center for Historical Population Studies Newsletter. Univ. of Utah. Salt Lake City.

Central American Accessions at the University of Kansas Libraries. Department for Spain, Portugal and Latin America. Lawrence.

Centro Latinoamericano de Economía Humana. Montevideo. (CLAEH)

CEPAL. Review/Revista de la CEPAL. Naciones Unidas, Comisión Económica para América Latina. Santiago. (CEPAL/R)

Chungara. Univ. del Norte, Depto. de Antropología. Arica, Chile.

Ciência e Cultura. Sociedade Brasileira para o Progresso da Ciência. São Paulo. (SBPC/CC)

Ciencia Interamericana. Organization of American States, Dept. of Scientific Affairs. Washington. (OAS/CI)

Ciencia, Tecnología y Desarrollo. Fondo Colombiano de Investigaciones Científicas y Proyectos Especiales Francisco José de Caldas. Bogotá.

Ciencia y Tecnología. Revista semestral de la Univ. de Costa Rica. San José. (UCR/CT)

Civilisations. International Institute of Differing Civilizations. Bruxelles. (IIDC/C)

Cladindex. Resumen de documentos CEPAL/ILPES. Organización de las Naciones Unidas. Comisión Económica para América Latina (CEPAL). Centro Latinoamericano de Documentación Económica y Social (CLADES). Santiago.

Colección Estudios CIEPLAN. Corporación de Investigaciones Económicas para Latinoamérica. Santiago.

Columbia Journal of Transnational Law. Columbia Univ., School of Law, Columbia Journal of Transnational Law Association. New York.

Comercio Exterior. Banco Nacional de Comercio Exterior. México. (BNCE/CE)

Commentary. American Jewish Committee. New York.

Communications. École des Hautes Études en Sciences Sociales, Centre d'Études Transdisciplinaires. Paris. (EHESS/C)

Comparative Education Review. Comparative Education Society. New York. (CES/CER)

Comparative Political Studies. Northwestern Univ., Evanston, Ill. and Sage Publications, Beverly Hills, Calif. (CPS)

Comparative Politics. The City Univ. of New York, Political Science Program. New York. (CUNY/CP)

Comparative Studies in Society and History. An international quarterly. Society for the Comparative Study of Society and History. The Hague. (CSSH)

Comunicación y Cultura. La comunicación masiva en el proceso político latinoamericano. Editorial Galerna. Buenos Aires y Santiago. (CYC)

Comunicaciones Proyecto Puebla-Tlaxcala. Fundación Alemana para la Investigación Científica. Puebla, México. (FAIC/CPPT)

Comunidades y Culturas Peruanas. Instituto Lingüístico de Verano. Yarinacocha, Peru.

Conjonction. Institut Français d'Haïti. Port-au-Prince. (IFH/C)

Conjuntura Econômica. Fundação Getúlio Vargas, Instituto Brasileiro de Economia. Rio de Janeiro. (FGV/CE)

Criterio. Editorial Criterio. Buenos Aires. (CRIT)

Cuadernos Afro-Americanos. Instituto de Antropología e Historia. Univ. Central de Venezuela. Caracas.

Cuadernos de Economía. Univ. Católica de Chile. Santiago. (UCC/CE)

Cuadernos de la CVF. Corporación Venezolana de Fomento. Caracas. (CVF/C)

Cuadernos Hispanoamericanos. Instituto de Cultura Hispánica. Madrid. (CH)

Cuadernos Políticos. Revista trimestral. Ediciones Era. México. (CP)

Cuadernos Prehispánicos. Seminario Americanista de la Univ., Casa de Colón. Valladolid, Spain.

Cuadrante. Revista del Centro de Estudios Regionales. Buenos Aires.

Cuban Studies/Estudios Cubanos. Univ. of Pittsburgh, Univ. Center for International Studies, Center for Latin American Studies. Pittsburgh, Pa. (UP/CSEC)

Culture, Medicine, and Psychiatry. D. Reidel Dordrecht. The Netherlands.

Cultures. United Nations Educational, Scientific and Cultural Organization. Paris. (UNESCO/CU)

Cultures et Développement. Revue internationale des sciences du développement. Univ. Catholique de Louvain avec le concours de la Fondation Universitaire de Belgique. Louvain, Belgium. (UCL/CD)

Current Anthropology. Univ. of Chicago. Chicago, Ill. (UC/CA)

Current History. A monthly magazine of world affairs. Philadelphia, Pa. (CUH)

Daedalus. Journal of the American Academy of Arts and Sciences. Harvard Univ. Cambridge, Mass. (AAAS/D)

Debates en Antropología. Pontificia Univ. Católica del Perú, Depto. de Ciencias Sociales. Lima. (PUCP/DA)

Defensa Nacional. Revista del Centro de Altos Estudios Militares. Lima.

A Defesa Nacional. Revista de assuntos militares e estudo de problemas brasileiros. Rio de Janeiro. (ADN)

Demografía y Economía. El Colegio de México. México. (CM/DE)

Demography. Population Association of America. Washington. (PAA/D)

Desarrollo Económico. Instituto de Desarrollo Económico y Social. Buenos Aires. (IDES/DE)

Desarrollo Rural en las Américas. Organización de los Estados Americanos. Instituto

Interamericano de Ciencias Agrícolas. Bogotá.

Desarrollo y Sociedad. Univ. de los Andes, Facultad de Economía, Centro de Estudios sobre el Desarrollo Económico. Bogotá. (CEDE/DS)

Deutsche Aussenpolitik. Institut für Internationale Beziehungen. Berlin, GDR. (IIB/DA)

Deutscher Geographentag. Franz Steiner Verlag. Wiesbaden, FRG.

The Developing Economies. The Journal of the Institute of Developing Economies. Tokyo. (IDE/DE)

Development Financing. Semiannual review of the Public Sector Program. Organization of American States, General Secretariat. Washington.

Developmental Medicine and Child Neurology. National Spastics Society, Medical Education and Information Unit. London.

Diálogos. Artes/Letras/Ciencias Humanas. El Colegio de México. México. (CM/D)

Direct from Cuba. Prensa Latina. La Habana.

Docencia. Univ. Autónoma de Guadalajara. Guadalajara, México. (UAG/D)

Docet. CELADEC, Centro de Documentación y Editorial. Lima.

Documentary Relations of the Southwest: Master Indexes. Arizona State Museum. Tucson.

El Dorado. Univ. of Northern Colorado, Museum of Anthropology. Greeley. (UNC/ED)

Die Dritte Welt. Verlag Anton Hain. Meisenheim, FRG. (DDW)

Early Man. Northwestern Archaeology, Inc. Evanston, Ill.

Eastern Economic Journal. Eastern Economic Association. Bloomsbury State College, Dept. of Economics. Bloomsbury, Pa.

Economía. Pontificia Univ. Católica del Perú, Depto. de Economía. Lima. (PUCP/E)

Economía Colombiana. Contraloría General de la República. Bogotá.

Economía de América Latina. Revista de información y análisis de la región. Centro de Investigación y Docencia Económicas (CIDE). México.

Economia Internazionale. Rivista dell'Istituto di Economia Internazionale. Genova, Italy. (IEI/EI)

Economía Mexicana: Análisis y Perspectivas. Centro de Investigación y Docencia Económica. México?

Economía Política. Facultad de Ciencias Económicas. Univ. Autónoma de Honduras. Tegucigalpa.

Economía Política. Instituto Politécnico Nacional, Escuela Superior de Economía. México. (IPN/EP)

Economía y Ciencias Sociales. Univ. Central de Venezuela, Facultad de Economía. Caracas. (UCV/ECS)

Economía y Desarrollo. Univ. de La Habana, Instituto de Economía. La Habana. (UH/ED)

Economic Botany. Devoted to applied botany and plant utilization. Published for The Society for Economic Botany by the New Botanical Garden. New York. (SEB/EB)

Economic Development and Cultural Change. Univ. of Chicago, Research Center in Economic Development and Cultural Change. Chicago, Ill. (UC/EDCC)

Economic Geography. Clark Univ. Worcester, Mass. (CU/EG)

Economic Journal. Quarterly journal of the Royal Economic Society. London. (RES/EJ)

Económica. Univ. Nacional de La Plata, Facultad de Ciencias Económicas, Instituto de Investigaciones Económicas. La Plata, Argentina. (UNLP/E)

Educação e Realidade. Univ. Federal do Rio Grande do Sul, Faculdade de Educação. Porto Alegre, Brazil.

Educação e Sociedade. Revista quadrimestral de ciencias da educação. Centro de Estudos Educação e Sociedad. São Paulo.

La Educación. Revista interamericano de desarrollo educativo. Organization of American States, Secretaría General, Departamento de Asuntos Educativos. Washington. (OAS/LE)

Educación Hoy. Perspectivas Latinoamericanas. Bogotá.

La Educación Superior Contemporánea. Revista internacional de países socialistas. La Habana.

Encontros com a Civilização Brasileira. Rio de Janeiro.

Encuentro. Revista de la Univ. Centroamericana, Instituto Histórico. Managua. (UCA/E)

Ensayos Económicos. Banco Central de la República Argentina. Buenos Aires. (BCRA/EE)

Equinoxe. Revue guyanaise d'histoire et de geographie. Association des Professeurs d'Histoire et de Géographie (A.P.H.G.) de la

Guyane *avec le concours du* Centre Départemental de Documentation Pédagogique (C.D.D.P.). Cayenne.

Die Erde. Zeitschrift der Gesellschaft für Erdkunde zur Berlin. Walter de Gruyter & Co. Berlin. (GEB/E)

Estadística. Journal of the Inter American Statistical Institute. Washington. (IASI/E)

Estados Unidos: Perspectiva Latinoamericana. Cuadernos semestrales. Centro de Investigación y Docencia Económica (CIDE). México. (EEUU/PL)

Estrategia. Instituto Argentino de Estudios Estratégicos y de las Relaciones Internacionales. Buenos Aires. (IAEERI/E)

Estudios. Instituto de Estudios Económicos sobre la Realidad Argentina y Latinoamericana. Córdoba. (IEERAL/E)

Estudios Andinos. Instituto Boliviano de Estudio y Acción Social. La Paz. (IBEAS/EA)

Estudios Andinos. Univ. del Pacífico. Lima.

Estudios Andinos. Univ. of Pittsburgh, Latin American Studies Center. Pittsburgh, Pa. (UP/EA)

Estudios Atacameños. Univ. del Norte, Museo de Arqueología. San Pedro de Atacama, Chile.

Estudios CEDES. Centro Estudios de Estado y Sociedad. Buenos Aires.

Estudios Centro-Americanos. Revista de extensión cultural. Univ. José Simeón Cañas. San Salvador. (UJSC/ECA)

Estudios Contemporáneos. Univ. Autónoma de Puebla. Puebla, México.

Estudios de Cultura Maya. Univ. Nacional Autónoma de México, Centro de Estudios Mayas. México. (CEM/ECM)

Estudios de Economía. Univ. de Chile, Facultad de Ciencias Económicas y·Administrativas, Depto. de Economía. Santiago. (UC/EE)

Estudios de Población. Asociación Colombiana para el Estudio de la Población. Bogotá. (ACEP/EP)

Estudios del Tercer Mundo. Centro de Estudios Económicos y Sociales del Tercer Mundo. México. (EDTM)

Estudios Latinoamericanos. Polska Akademia Nauk (Academia de Ciencias de Polonia), Instytut Historii (Instituto de Historia). Warszawa. (PAN/ES)

Estudios Paraguayos. Univ. Católica Nuestra Señora de la Asunción. Asunción. (UCNSA/EP)

Estudios Rurales Latinoamericanos. Consejo Latinoamericano de Ciencias Sociales, Secretaría Ejecutiva y de la Comisión de Estudios Rurales. Bogotá. (CLACSO/ERL)

Estudios Sociales. Corporación de Promoción Universitaria. Santiago. (CPU/ES)

Estudios Sociales. Univ. Rafael Landívar, Instituto de Ciencias Políticas y Sociales. Guatemala. (URL/ES)

Estudios Sociales Centroamericanos. Consejo Superior de Universidades Centroamericanas, Confederación Universitaria Centroamericana, Programa Centroamericano de Ciencias Sociales. San José. (CSUCA/ECS)

Estudos Baianos. Univ. Federal da Bahia, Centro Editorial e Didático, Núcleo de Publicações. Bahia, Brazil. (UFB/EB)

Estudos Brasileiros. Univ. Federal do Paraná, Setor de Ciências Humanas, Centro de Estudos Brasileiros. Curitiba, Brazil. (UFP/EB)

Estudos Econômicos. Univ. de São Paulo, Instituto de Pesquisas Econômicas. São Paulo. (IPE/EE)

Estudos Leopoldenses. Faculdade de Filosofia, Ciências e Letras. São Leopoldo, Brazil.

Ethnic and Racial Studies. Routledge & Kegan Paul. London. (ERS)

Ethnicity. Academic Press. New York.

Ethnographisch-Archäologische Zeitschrift. Deutscher Verlag Wissenschaften. East Berlin. (EAZ)

Ethnology. Plenum. New York.

Ethnology. Univ. of Pittsburgh. Pittsburgh, Pa. (UP/E)

Ethnomedicine. Arbeits Gemeinschaft Ethnomedizin and H. Buskeverlag. Hamburg, FRG.

Ethnomusicology. Society of Ethnomusicology. Middleton, Conn.

Ethnos. Statens Ethnografiska Museum. Stockholm. (SEM/E)

Ethos. Society for Psychological Anthropology. Washington.

Etnía. Museo Etnográfico Municipal Dámaso Arce. Municipalidad de Olavarría, Provincia de Buenos Aires, Argentina. (MEMDA/E)

Études Littéraires. Press de l'Université Laval. Quebec.

Federal Bar Journal. Federal Bar Association. Washington. (FBA/FBJ)

F.E.P.A. Estudios e Investigaciones. Fundación para el Estudio de los Problemas Argentinos. Buenos Aires. (FEPA/EI)

The Florida Anthropologist. Florida Anthropological Society. Gainesville.

The Florida Historical Quarterly. The Florida Historical Society. Jacksonville. (FHS/FHQ)

Folia Humanística. Ciencias, artes, letras. Editorial Galerna. Barcelona. (FH)

Folklore Americano. Instituto Panamericano de Geografía e Historia, Comisión de Historia, Comité de Folklore. México. (IPGH/FA)

Foreign Affairs. Council on Foreign Relations. New York. (CFR/FA)

Foreign Policy. National Affairs, Inc. and Carnegie Endowment for International Peace. New York. (FP)

Foro Internacional. El Colegio de México. México. (CM/FI)

Forum Educacional. Fundação Getúlio Vargas, Instituto de Estudos Avançados em Educação. Rio de Janeiro.

Freedom at Issue. Freedom House. New York.

Franciscanum. Revista de las ciencias del espíritu. Univ. de San Buenaventura. Bogotá. (USB/F)

Geografiska Annaler. Svenska Sällskapet för Antropologi och Geografi. Stockholm. (SSAG/GA)

The Geographical Magazine. London. (GM)

The Geographical Review. American Geographical Society. New York. (AGS/GR)

Geologische Rundschau. Internationale Zeitschrift für Geologie. Geologische Vereinigung. Ferdinand Enke Verlag. Stuttgart, Germany. (GV/GR)

GeoJournal. Akademische Verlagsgesellschaft. Wiesbaden, FRG.

Geopolítica. Instituto Uruguayo de Estudios Geopolíticos. Montevideo.

Granma. La Habana.

Graphis. International journal of graphic art and applied art. The Graphis Press. Zürich.

Guatemala Indígena. Instituto Indigenista Nacional. Guatemala. (GIIN/GI)

Guyanese National Bibliography. National Library of Guyana. Georgetown.

Hemoglobin. Marcel Dekker Journals. New York.

Hispanic American Historical Review. Duke Univ. Press *for the* Conference on Latin American History of the American Historical Association. Duram, N.C. (HAHR)

Historia. Revista/libro trimestral. Buenos Aires.

Historia Mexicana. El Colegio de México. México. (CM/HM)

Histórica. Pontificia Univ. Católica del Perú, Depto. de Humanidades. Lima. (PUCP/H)

Historiografía y Bibliografía Americanista. Escuela de Estudios Hispanoamericanos de Sevilla. Sevilla. (EEHA/HBA)

L'Homme. Revue française d'anthropologie. La Sorbonne, l'École Pratique des Hautes Études. Paris. (EPHE/H)

Horizonte. Univ. Federal de Paraíba. João Pessoa, Brazil.

Human Biology. Official publication of the Human Biology Council. Wayne State Univ., School of Medicine. Detroit, Mich. (WSU/HB)

Human Ecology. Plenum. New York.

Human Genetics. Excepta Medica Foundation. Amsterdam.

Human Heredity. Basel, Switzerland. (HH)

Human Organization. Society for Applied Anthropology. New York. (SAA/HO)

Ibero Americana. Scandinavian Association for Research on Latin America. Stockholm. (NOSALF/IA)

Ibero-Americana. Univ. of California Press. Berkeley. (UC/I)

Ibero-Americana Pragensia. Univ. Carolina de Praga, Centro de Estudios Ibero-Americanos. Prague. (UCP/IAP)

Ibero-Amerikanisches Archiv. Ibero-Amerikanisches Institut. Berlin, FRG. (IAA)

Indiana. Beiträge zur Volker-und Sprachenkunde, Archäologie und Anthropologie des Indianischen Amerika. Ibero-Amerikanisches Institut. Berlin, FRG. (IAI/I)

Indice de Artículos sobre Capacitación y Adiestramiento. Servicio Nacional de Adiestramiento Rápido de la Mano de Obra en la Industria (ARMO). México.

Indice de Ciências Sociais. Boletim bibliográfico semestral. Instituto Universitário de Pesquisas do Rio de Janeiro. Rio de Janeiro.

Industrial and Labor Relations Review. A publication of the New York School of Industrial and Labor Relations, a Contract College of the State Univ., Cornell Univ. Ithaca. (CU/ILRR)

Information Geographique. Paris. (IG)

Integración Latinoamericana. Instituto para

la Integración de América Latina. Buenos Aires. (INTAL/IL)

Inter-American Economic Affairs. Washington. (IAMEA)

Interciencia. Asociación Interciencia. Caracas. (AI/I)

International Affairs. A monthly journal of political analysis. Moskova. (IA)

International Affairs Bulletin. The South African Institute of International Affairs. Johannesburg.

International Journal. Canadian Institute of International Affairs. Toronto. (CIIA/IJ)

International Journal of Intercultural Relations. Society for Intercultural Education Training and Research. Purdue, Indiana.

International Journal of the Sociology of Law. London.

International Migration (Migrations Internationales = Migraciones Internacionales). Quarterly review of the Intergovernmental Committee for European Migration and the Research Group for European Migration Problems. Geneva, Switzerland. (ICEM/IM)

International Migration Review. Center for Migration Studies. New York. (CMS/IMR)

International Review of Administrative Sciences. International Institute of Administrative Sciences. Bruxelles. (IIAS/IRAS)

International Review of Education. United Nations Educational, Scientific, and Cultural Organization, Institute for Education. Hamburg, FRG. (UNESCO/IRE)

International Social Science Journal. United Nations Educational, Scientific, and Cultural Organization. Paris. (UN/ISSJ)

IREBI. Indices de revistas de bibliotecología. Oficina de Educación Iberoamericana. Madrid.

Islas. Univ. Central de las Villas. Santa Clara, Cuba. (UCLV/I)

Istmo. Revista del pensamiento actual. México. (ISTMO)

Itaytera. Instituto Cultural do Cariri. Crato, Brazil. (ICC/I)

Jahrbuch des Museums für Völkerkunde zu Leipzig. Berlin. (MVL/J)

Jahrbuch des öffentlichen Rechts der Gegenwart. J.C.B. Mohr—Paul Siebeck. Tübingen.

Jahrbuch für Geschichte von Staat, Wirtschaft und Gesellschaft Lateinamerikas. Köln, FRG. (JGSWGL)

Jamaica Journal. Institute of Jamaica. Kingston. (IJ/JJ)

Jamaican National Bibliography. National Library of Jamaica, Institute of Jamaica. Kingston.

The Jewish Journal of Sociology. The World Jewish Community. London. (WJC/JJS)

Journal de la Société des Américanistes. Paris. (SA/J)

Journal of American Folklore. American Folklore Society. Austin, Texas. (AFS/JAF)

Journal of Anthropological Research. Univ. of New Mexico, Dept. of Anthropology. Albuquerque. (UNM/JAR)

Journal of Belizean Affairs. Belize City. (JBA)

Journal of Biosocial Science. Blackwell Scientific Publications. Oxford, England.

Journal of Caribbean Studies. Association of Caribbean Studies. Coral Gables, Fla.

Journal of Common Market Studies. Oxford, England. (JCMS)

Journal of Commonwealth and Comparative Politics. Univ. of London, Institute of Commonwealth Studies. London. (ICS/JCCP)

The Journal of Developing Areas. Western Illinois Univ. Press. Macomb. (JDA)

Journal of Development Economics. North Holland Publishing Co. Amsterdam. (JDE)

The Journal of Development Studies. A quarterly journal devoted to economics, politics and social development. London. (JDS)

Journal of Economic History. New York Univ., Graduate School of Business Administration *for* The Economic History Association. Rensselaer. (EHA/J)

The Journal of Economic Literature. American Economic Association. Nashville, Tenn.

Journal of Economic Studies. Glasgow, Scotland.

Journal of Environmental Health. National Association of Sanitarians. Denver, Colo.

Journal of Ethnic Studies. College of Ethnic Studies, Western Washington State College. Bellingham.

Journal of Ethnopharmacology. Elsevier Sequoia. Lausanne, Switzerland.

Journal of European Economic History. Banco de Roma. Rome.

Journal of Family History. Studies in family, kinship and demography. National Council on Family Relations. Minneapolis, Minn. (NCFR/JFH)

Journal of Field Archaeology. Boston Univ. Boston, Mass.

Journal of Human Evolution. Academic Press. London.

Journal of Information Science, Librarianship and Archives Administration. *See* UNESCO Journal of Information Science, Librarianship and Archives Administration.

Journal of Inter-American Studies and World Affairs. Sage Publications *for the* Center for Advanced International Studies, Univ. of Miami. Coral Gables, Fla. (SAGE/JIAS)

Journal of International Law and Economics. George Washington Univ., The National Law Center. Washington. (GWU/JILE)

The Journal of Japanese Studies. The Society for Japanese Studies. Univ. of Washington. Seattle.

Journal of Latin American Lore. Univ. of California, Latin American Center. Los Angeles. (UCLA/JLAL)

Journal of Latin American Studies. Centers or institutes of Latin American studies at the universities of Cambridge, Glasgow, Liverpool, London and Oxford. Cambridge Univ. Press. London. (JLAS)

Journal of Marriage and the Family. Western Reserve Univ. Cleveland, Ohio. (WRU/JMF)

Journal of Peace Research. Edited at the International Peace Research Institute. Universitetforlaget. Oslo. (JPR)

Journal of Peasant Studies. Frank Cass & Co. London. (JPS)

Journal of Political and Military Sociology. Northern Illinois Univ., Dept. of Sociology. DeKalb. (NIU/JPMS)

Journal of Political Economy. Univ. of Chicago. Chicago, Ill. (JPE)

The Journal of Politics. The Southern Political Science Association *in cooperation with the* Univ. of Florida. Gainesville. (SPSA/JP)

Journal of Psychological Anthropology. Association of Psychohistory. New York.

The Journal of Risk and Insurance. American Risk and Insurance Association. Bloomington, Ill. (ARIAI/JRI)

The Journal of Social and Political Studies. Council on American Affairs. Washington.

The Journal of Taxation. Journal of Taxation, Inc. New York. (JT)

Journal of the Hellenic Diaspora. Pella Publishing Co. New York.

Journal of the Virgin Islands Archaeological Society. Frederickstad, St. Croix.

The Journal of Tropical Geography. Univ. of Singapore and Univ. of Malaya, Depts. of Geography. Singapore. (USM/JTG)

Journalism Quarterly. Association for Education in Journalism *with the cooperation of the* American Association of Schools, Depts. of Journalism and Kappa Tau Alpha Society. Univ. of Minnesota. Minneapolis. (AEJ/JQ)

Katunob. Univ. of Northern Colorado, Museum of Anthropology. Greeley. (UNC/K)

Lateinamerika. Univ. Rostock. Rostock, GDR. (UR/L)

Latin America 1978. Facts on File, Inc. New York.

Latin American Perspectives. Univ. of California. Riverside. (LAP)

Latin American Research Review. Univ. of North Carolina Press *for the* Latin American Studies Association. Chapel Hill. (LARR)

Latinoamérica. Anuario de estudios latinoamericanos. Univ. Nacional Autónoma de México, Facultad de Filosofía y Letras, Centro de Estudios Latinoamericanos. México. (UNAM/L)

Lexis. Revista de lingüística y literatura. Pontificia Univ. Católica del Perú, Lima. (PUC/L)

Lotería. Lotería Nacional de Beneficencia. Panamá. (LNB/L)

Luso Brazilian Review. Univ. of Wisconsin Press. Madison. (US/LBR)

Man. A monthly record of anthropological science. The Royal Anthropological Institute. London. (RAI/M)

Mapocho. Biblioteca Nacional, Extensión Cultural. Santiago. (EC/M)

Marxist Perspectives. Transaction Periodicals Consortium. Rutgers Univ. New Brunswick, N.J. (RU/MP)

Medical Anthropology. Redgrave. Pleasantville, N.Y.

Medical Anthropology Newsletter. Society for Medical Anthropology. Washington.

Mesoamérica. Revista del Centro de Investigaciones Regionales de Mesoamérica. La Antigua, Guatemala.

México Indígena. Organo de Difusión del Instituto Nacional Indigenista. Distribuidor: Porrúa Hnos. México.

Mexicon. Berlin, FRG.

Modern Language Journal. The National Federation of Modern Language Teachers

Association. Univ. of Pittsburgh. Pittsburgh, Pa. (MLTA/MLJ)

Monetaria. Centro de Estudios Monetarios Latinoamericanos. México. (CEMLA/M)

Monthly Labor Review. United States Dept. of Labor. Washington. (USDL/MLR)

Monthly Review. An independent Socialist magazine. New York. (MR)

Mother Jones. Foundation for National Progress. San Francisco.

NACLA: Report on the Americas. North American Congress on Latin America. New York. (NACLA)

NACLA's Latin America & Empire Report. North American Congress on Latin America. New York. (NACLA/LAER)

National Geographic Magazine. National Geographic Society. Washington. (NGS/NGM)

Natural History. American Museum of Natural History. New York. (AMNH/NH)

Nature. A weekly journal of science. Macmillan & Co. London. (NWJS)

Nawpa Pacha. Institute of Andean Studies. Berkeley, Calif. (IAS/NP)

The New Republic. Washington.

The New Scholar. Univ. of California, Center for Iberian and Latin American Studies and Institute of Chicano Urban Affairs. San Diego. (UCSD/NS)

The New York Review of Books. New York. (NYRB)

The New York Times Magazine. New York.

The New Yorker. New York.

Nexos. Sociedad, ciencia, literatura. Centro de Investigación Cultural y Científica. México.

Nicaráuac. Revista bimestral del Ministerio de Cultura. Managua. (NMC/N)

Nieuwe West-Indische Gids. Martinus Nijhoff. The Hague. (NWIG)

Norte Grande. Revista de estudios integrados referentes a comunidades humanas del Norte Grande de Chile, en una perspectiva geográfica e histórica-cultural. Univ. Católica de Chile, Instituto de Geografía, Depto. de Geografía de Chile, Taller Norte Grande. Santiago. (UCC/NG)

Notes et Études Documentaires. Direction de la Documentation. Paris. (FDD/NED)

La Nouvelle Revue des Deux Mondes. Paris. (NRDM)

NS NorthSouth NordSud NorteSur NorteSul. Canadian journal of Latin American studies. Canadian Association of Latin American Studies. Univ. of Ottawa. Ottawa. (NS)

Nueva Sociedad. Revista política y cultural. San José. (NSO)

Numen. International review for the history of religions. International Association for the History of Religions. Leiden, The Netherlands. (IAHR/N)

Oceanus. Oceanographic Institution. Wood Hole, Mass. (OCEANUS)

OCLAE. Revista mensual de la Organización Continental Latinoamericana de Estudiantes. La Habana. (OCLAE)

Omega. Journal of death and dying. Baywood Publishing Co. Farmingdale, N.Y.

Orbis. A journal of world affairs. Foreign Policy Research Institute, Philadelphia, Pa. *in association with the* Fletcher School of Law and Diplomacy, Tufts Univ. Medford, Mass. (FPRI/O)

Ornament. A quarterly of jewelry and personal adornment. Los Angeles.

Oxford Economic Papers. Oxford Univ. Press. London. (OUP/OEP)

Pacific Sociological Review. Pacific Sociological Association. San Diego State Univ. San Diego, Calif. (PSA/PSR)

Paideuma. Mitteilungen zur Kulturkunde. Deutsche Gesellschaft für kulturmorphologie von Frobenius Institut au der Johann Wolfgang Goethe—Universität. Wiesbaden, Germany. (PMK)

El Palacio. School of American Research, the Museum of New Mexico, and the Archaeological Society of New Mexico. Santa Fe. (SAR/P)

Palaeogeography, Palaeoclimatology, Palaeoecology. Elsevier Scientific Publishing Co. New York.

Panorama Anual. Bolsa de Valores, Asesoría Estadística. Montevideo.

Papers in Anthropology. Dept. of Anthropology, Univ. of Oklahoma. Norman.

Past and Present. London. (PP)

Pensamiento y Acción. Editora Lautaro. Santiago.

Pesquisas. Anuário do Instituto Anchietano de Pesquisas. Porto Alegre. (IAP/P)

Petermanns Geographische Mitteilungen. Geographische-Kartoggraphische Anstalt. Gotha, Germany. (PGM)

Philologica Pragensia. Academia Scientiarum Bohemoslovenica. Praha. (ASB/PP)

Plerus. Planificación económica rural urbana y social. Univ. de Puerto Rico. Río Piedras. (UPR/P)

Política y Sociedad. Univ. de San Carlos de Guatemala, Facultad de Ciencias Jurídicas y Sociales, Escuela de Ciencia Política, Instituto de Investigaciones Políticas y Sociales. Guatemala. (USCG/PS)

Population. Institut National d'Études Démographiques. Paris.

Population Studies. London School of Economics, The Population Investigation Committee. London. (LSE/PS)

Prehistoria Bonaerense. Olavarría, Provincia Buenos Aires, Argentina.

Problemas del Desarrollo. Univ. Nacional Autónoma de México, Instituto de Investigaciones Económicas. México. (UNAM/PDD)

Problems of Communism. United States Information Agency. Washington. (USIA/PC)

Proceedings. United States Naval Institute. Annapolis, Md.

Proceedings of the National Academy of Sciences. Washington. (NAS/P)

Proceedings of the Pacific Coast Council on Latin American Studies. Univ. of California. Los Angeles. (PCCLAS/P)

Professional Geographer. Journal of The Association of American Geographers. Washington. (AAG/PG)

Publishers Weekly. New York.

Puntos de Vista. Centro de Estudios Económicos y Sociales. San Luis Potosí.

Purun Pacha. Instituto Andino de Estudios Arqueológicos. Lima.

Quehacer. Realidad nacional: problemas y alternativas. Revista del Centro de Estudios y Promoción del Desarrollo (DESCO). Lima. (DESCO/Q)

Race and Class. A journal of black and Third World liberation. Institute of Race Relations and The Transnational Institute. London. (IRR/RC)

Realidad Contemporánea. Editora Alfa y Omega. Santo Domingo.

Relaciones. Estudios de historia y sociedad. El Colegio de Michoacán. Zamora, México.

Relaciones de la Sociedad Argentina de Antropología. Buenos Aires. (SAA/R)

Relaciones Internacionales. Revista del Centro de Relaciones Internacionales. Univ. Nacional Autónoma de México, Facultad de Ciencias Políticas y Sociales. México. (UNAM/RI)

Report. Minority Rights Group. London.

Res Publica. Claremont Men's College. Claremont, Calif.

Resúmenes Analíticos en Educación. Centro de Investigación y Desarrollo de la Educación. Santiago.

Review of Black Political Economy. National Economic Association and Atlanta Univ. Center. Atlanta, Ga. (NEA/RBPE)

Review of Economics and Statistics. Harvard Univ. Cambridge, Mass. (HU/RES)

Review of Politics. Univ. of Notre Dame. Notre Dame, Ind. (UND/RP)

Revista Brasileira de Cultura. Ministério da Educação e Cultura, Conselho Federal de Cultura. Rio de Janeiro. (CFC/RBC)

Revista Brasileira de Economia. Fundação Getúlio Vargas, Instituto Brasileiro de Economia. Rio de Janeiro. (IBE/RBE)

Revista Brasileira de Estudos Pedagógicos. Instituto Nacional de Estudos Pedagógicos. Centro Brasileiro de Pesquisas Educacionais. Rio de Janeiro. (INEP/RBEP)

Revista Brasileira de Estudos Políticos. Univ. de Minas Gerais. Belo Horizonte, Brazil. (UMG/RBEP)

Revista Brasileira de Geografia. Conselho Nacional de Geografia, Instituto Brasileiro de Geografia e Estatística. Rio de Janeiro. (IBGE/R)

Revista Brasileira de Mercado de Capitais. Instituto Brasileiro de Mercado de Capitais. Rio de Janeiro. (RBMC)

Revista Cartográfica. Instituto Panamericano de Geografía e Historia, Comisión de Cartografía. México. (PAIGH/G)

Revista Centroamericana de Economía. Univ. Nacional Autónoma de Honduras, Programa de Postgrado Centroamericano en Economía y Planificación. Tegucigalpa. (UNAH/RCE)

Revista CERLAL. Bogotá.

Revista Chilena de Antropología. Univ. de Chile, Depto. de Antropología. Santiago.

Revista Chilena de Historia y Geografía. Sociedad Chilena de Historia y Geografía. Santiago. (SCHG/R)

Revista Coahuilense de Historia. Colegio Coahuilense de Investigaciones Históricas. Saltillo, México.

Revista Colombiana de Antropología. Ministerio de Educación Nacional, Instituto Colombiano de Antropología. Bogotá. (ICA/RCA)

Revista Colombiana de Educación. Univ. Pedagógica Nacional, Centro de Investigaciones. Bogotá. (UPN/RCE)

Revista Colombiana de Sociología. Depto. de Sociología, Univ. Nacional. Bogotá.

Revista de Administração Municipal. Instituto Brasileiro de Administração Municipal. Rio de Janeiro.

Revista de Administración Pública. Univ. de Puerto Rico. Río Piedras. (UPR/RAP)

Revista de Antropologia. Univ. de São Paulo, Faculdade de Filosofia, Letras e Ciências Humanas and Associação Brasileira de Antropologia. São Paulo. (USP/RA)

Revista de CEPA. Associação Pró-Ensino em Santa Cruz do Sul, Brazil.

Revista de Ciência Política. Fundação Getúlio Vargas. Rio de Janeiro. (FGV/R)

Revista de Ciencia Política. Instituto de Ciencia Política, Pontificia Univ. Católica de Chile. Santiago.

Revista de Ciencias Sociales. Univ. de Puerto Rico, Colegio de Ciencias Sociales. Río Piedras. (UPR/RCS)

Revista de Colegio de Abogados. Colegio de Abogados de Puerto Rico. San Juan? (CAPR/RCA)

Revista de Economía Latinoamericana. Banco Central de Venezuela. Caracas. (BCV/REL)

Revista de Estudios Agro-Sociales. Instituto de Estudios Agro-Sociales. Madrid. (IEAS/R)

Revista de Historia. Univ. Nacional de Costa Rica, Escuela de Historia. Heredia. (UNCR/R)

Revista de Indias. Instituto Gonzalo Fernández de Oviedo and Consejo Superior de Investigaciones Científicas. Madrid. (IGFO/RI)

Revista de Integración. Banco Interamericano de Desarrollo. Washington. (BID/INTAL)

Revista de la Academia Hondureña de Geografía e Historia. Tegucigalpa. (AHGH/R)

Revista de la CEPAL. *See* CEPAL.

Revista de la Facultad de Derecho. Univ. Nacional Autónoma de México. México. (UNAM/RFD)

Revista de la Universidad de Yucatán. Mérida, México. (UY/R)

Revista de Occidente. Madrid. (RO)

Revista de Oriente. Univ. de Puerto Rico, Colegio Universitario de Humacao. Humacao. (UPR/RO)

Revista de Pré-História. Univ. de São Paulo, Instituto de Pré-História. São Paulo.

Revista del Centro de Investigaciones Arqueológicas de Alta Montaña. San Juan, Argentina.

Revista del Instituto de Antropología. Univ. Nacional de Córdoba. Córdoba, Argentina. (UNCIA/R)

Revista del Instituto de Antropología. Univ. Nacional de Tucumán. San Miguel de Tucumán, Argentina. (UNTIA/R)

Revista del México Agrario. Confederación Nacional Campesina. México. (CNC/RMA)

Revista del Museo de Historia Natural de San Rafael. San Rafael, Argentina.

Revista del Museo de La Plata. Univ. Nacional de La Plata, Facultad de Ciencias Naturales y Museo. La Plata, Argentina. (UNLPM/R)

Revista del Museo Nacional. Casa de la Cultura del Perú, Museo Nacional de la Cultura Peruana. Lima. (PEMN/R)

Revista del Pensamiento Centroamericano. Centro de Investigaciones y Actividades Culturales. Managua. (RCPC)

Revista do Arquivo Municipal. Prefeitura do Município de São Paulo, Depto. Municipal de Cultura. São Paulo. (AM/R)

Revista do Instituto de Estudos Brasileiros. Univ. de São Paulo, Instituto de Estudos Brasileiros. São Paulo. (USP/RIEB)

Revista do Instituto Histórico e Geográfico Brasileiro. Rio de Janeiro. (IHGB/R)

Revista do Museu Paulista. São Paulo. (MP/R)

Revista Dominicana de Antropología e Historia. Univ. Autónoma de Santo Domingo, Facultad de Humanidades, Depto. de Historia y Antropología, Instituto de Investigaciones Antropológicas. Santo Domingo. (UASD/U)

Revista Econômica do Nordeste. Banco do Nordeste do Brasil, Depto. de Estudos Econômicos do Nordeste. Fortaleza, Brazil. (BNB/REN)

Revista Estadística. Comité Estatal de Estadísticas. La Habana.

Revista Geográfica. Instituto Geográfico Militar del Ecuador, Depto. Geográfico. Quito. (IGME/RG)

Revista Geográfica. Instituto Panamericano de Geografía e Historia, Comisión de Geografía. México. (PAIGH/G)

Revista Interamericana. Interamerican Univ. of Puerto Rico. Río Piedras? (IAUPR/RI)

Revista Interamericana de Bibliografía (Inter-American Review of Bibliography). Organization of American States. Washington. (RIB)

Revista Interamericana de Psicología (Inter-american Journal of Psychology). Sociedad Interamericana de Psicología (Inter-american Society of Psychology). De Paul Univ., Dept. of Psychology. Chicago, Ill. (SIP/RIP)

Revista Latinoamericana de Estudios Educativos. Centro de Estudios Educativos. México. (CEE/RL)

Revista Latinoamericana de Psicología. Bogotá. (RLP)

Revista Mexicana de Ciencias Políticas y Sociales. Univ. Nacional Autónoma de México, Facultad de Ciencias Políticas y Sociales. México. (UNAM/RMCPS)

Revista Mexicana de Sociología. Univ. Nacional Autónoma de México, Instituto de Investigaciones Sociales. México. (UNAM/RMS)

Revista Paraguaya de Sociología. Centro Paraguayo de Estudios Sociológicos. Asunción. (CPES/RPS)

Revista/Review Interamericana. Univ. Inter-americana. San Germán, Puerto Rico. (RRI)

Revista Universidad de Sonora. Depto. de Extensión Universitaria, Sección de Publicaciones, Edificio de la Rectoría. Sonora, México.

Revista Universitaria. Anales de la Academia Chilena de Ciencias Naturales. Univ. Católica de Chile. Santiago. (UCC/RU)

Revue Française de Science Politique. Fondation Nationale des Sciences Politiques, l'Association Française de Science Politique *avec le concours du* Centre National de la Recherche Scientifique. Paris. (FNSP/RFSP)

RF Illustrated. The Rockefeller Foundation. New York.

Santiago. Univ. de Oriente. La Habana.

Sapiens. Museo Arqueológico Dr. Osvaldo F.A. Menghin. Chivilcoy, Provincia Buenos Aires, Argentina.

Sarance. Revista del Instituto Otavaleño de Antropología. Otavalo, Ecuador.

Science. American Association for the Advancement of Science. Washington. (AAAS/S)

Science and Society. New York. (SS)

Scientific Yearbook of the School of Law and Economics. Aristotelian Univ. of Salonica. Salonica, Greece.

Signs. Journal of women in culture and society. The Univ. of Chicago Press. Chicago, Ill. (UC/S)

Síntesis Geográfica. Univ. Central de Venezuela, Facultad de Humanidades, Escuela de Geografía. Caracas.

Social and Economic Studies. Univ. of the West Indies, Institute of Social and Economic Research. Mona, Jamaica. (UWI/SES)

Social Biology. Society for the Study of Social Biology. New York.

Social Compass. International review of socio-religious studies (Revue internationale des études socio-religieuses). International Federation of Institutes for Social and Socio-Religious Research (Fédération International des Institutes des Recherches Sociales et Socio-Religieuses [FERES]). The Hague. (FERES/SC)

Social Forces. *Published for the* Univ. of North Carolina Press *by the* Williams & Wilkins Co. Baltimore, Md. (SF)

Social Problems. Society for the Study of Social Problems *affiliated with the* American and International Sociological Associations. Kalamazoo, Mich. (SSSP/SP)

Social Science and Medicine. Medical anthropology. Pergamon Press. Oxford, England.

Social Science and Medicine. New York.

The Social Science Journal. Colorado State Univ., Western Social Science Association. Fort Collins.

Society. Social science and modern society. Transaction, Rutgers—The State Univ. New Brunswick, N.J.

Sociological Review. Univ. of Keele. Staffordshire, England. (UK/SR)

Sociologus. Zeitschrift für empirische Soziologie, sozialpsychologische und ethnologische Forschung (A journal for empirical sociology, social psychology and ethnic research). Berlin. (SOCIOL)

Sociology and Social Research. An international journal. Univ. of Southern Calif. University Park. (USC/SSR)

Southern Economic Journal. Univ. of North Carolina. Chapel Hill.

Soviet Geography: Review and Translation. American Geographical Society. New York. (AGS/SG)

Staff Papers. International Monetary Fund. Washington. (IMF/SP)

Statistical Abstract of Latin America. Univ.

of California, Latin American Center. Los Angeles.

Stichting Surinaams Museum. Paramaribo.

Studia Diplomatica. Chronique de politique etrangère. Institut Royal des Relations Internationales. Bruxelles. (IRRI/SD)

Studies in Comparative Communism. An international interdisciplinary journal. Univ. of Southern California, School of International Relations, Von Klein Smid Institute of International Affairs. Los Angeles. (USC/SCC)

Studies in Comparative International Development. Rutgers Univ. New Brunswick, N.J. (RU/SCID)

Stylo. Revista de ciencia, arte y literatura. Pontificia Univ. Católica de Chile. Temuco.

Suplemento Antropológico. Univ. Católica de Nuestra Señora de la Asunción, Centro de Estudios Antropológicos. Asunción. (UCNSA/SA)

The Tax Magazine. Commerce Clearing House. Chicago, Ill. (CCH/TTM)

Technology and Conservation Magazine. The Technology Organization, Inc. Boston, Mass.

Temas en la Crisis. La Paz.

Texas International Law Journal. Univ. of Texas, School of Law. Austin.

Thesaurus. Boletín del Instituto Caro y Cuervo. Bogotá. (ICC/T)

Thesis. Nueva revista de filosofía y letras. Univ. Nacional Autónoma de México. México.

Tiers Monde. Problèmes des pays sous-développés. Univ. de Paris, Institut d'Etude de Développement Économique et Social. Paris. (UP/TM)

Tijdschrift voor Economische en Sociale Geographie. Netherlands Journal of Economic and Social Geography. Rotterdam. (TESG)

Tlalocan. Revista de fuentes para el conocimiento de las culturas indígenas de México. Univ. Nacional Autónoma de México, Instituto de Investigaciones Antropológicas, Instituto de Investigaciones Históricas. México.

La Torre de Papel. Revista bimestral de literatura, arte, ciencia y filosofía. Buenos Aires.

Trauvaux et Documents de Géographie Tropicale. Centre National de la Recherche Scientifique, Centre d'Études de

Géographie Tropicale. Bordeaux, France.

Tribus. Veröffentlichungen des Linden-Museums. Museum für Länder- und Völkerkunde. Stuttgart, FRG.

El Trimestre Económico. Fondo de Cultura Económica. México. (FCE/TE)

Tropical Agriculture. Univ. of the West Indies, Imperial College of Tropical Agricultura and IPC Science and Technology Press, Ltd. Surrey, England.

UNESCO Journal of Information Science, Librarianship and Archives Administration. United Nations Educational, Scientific, and Cultural Organization. Paris. (UNESCO/JIS)

United States Views of Mexico. A quarterly review of opinion from the United States press and The Congressional Record. Banamex Cultural Foundation. Washington.

Universidad Ponitificia Bolivariana. Medellín, Colombia. (UPB)

Universidades. Unión de Universidades de América Latina. México. (UUAL/U)

Universitas. Ciencias jurídicas y socioeconómicas. Pontificia Univ. Javeriana, Facultad de Derecho y Ciencias Socioeconómicas. Bogotá. (PUJ/U)

Universitas Humanistica. Pontificia Univ. Javeriana, Facultad de Filosofía y Letras. Bogotá. (PUJ/UH)

L'Universo. Rivista bimestrale dell'Istituto Geografico Militare. Firenze, Italy. (IGM/U)

Urban Anthropology. State Univ. of New York, Dept. of Anthropology. Brockport. (UA)

Veritas. Revista. Pontifícia Univ. Católica do Rio Grande do Sul. Porto Alegre, Brazil. (PUC/V)

Vínculos. Revista de antropología. Museo Nacional de Costa Rica. San José. (MNCR/V)

The Washington Post Magazine. Washington.

The Washington Quarterly. A review of strategic and international issues. Georgetown Univ., Center for Strategic and International Studies. Washington.

Weltwirtschaftliches Archiv. Zeitschrift des Instituts für Weltwirtschaft an der Christians-Albrechts-Univ. Kiel. Kiel, FRG. (CAUK/WA)

West Indian Medical Journal. Univ. of the

West Indies. Mona, Jamaica.

West Watch. A report on the Americas and the World. Council for Inter-American Security. Washington.

Westermann Monatschefte. Georg Westermann Verlag. Braunschweig, FRG. (WM)

Western Political Quarterly. Univ. of Utah, Institute of Government *for the* Western Political Science Association; Pacific Northwest Political Science Association; and Southern California Political Science Association. Salt Lake City. (UU/WPQ)

The Wilson Quarterly. Woodrow Wilson International Center for Scholars. Washington. (WQ)

Wirtschaftliche Entwicklung: Paraguay. Bundesstelle für Aussenhandelsinformation. Köln, FRG.

World Affairs. The American Peace Society. Washington. (APS/WA)

World Archaeology. Routledge & Kegan Paul. London.

World Development. Pergamon Press. Oxford, United Kingdom. (WD)

World Politics. A quarterly journal of international relations. Princeton Univ., Center of International Studies. Princeton, N.J. (PUCIS/WP)

Worldview. Council on Religion and International Affairs. New York.

The Writings. A journal of the Young Socialist Movement. Georgetown, Guyana.

Yaxkin. Instituto Hondureño de Antropología e Historia. Tegucigalpa. (YAXKIN)

Yearbook of Physical Anthropology. Wenner Gren Foundation for Anthropological Research. New York.

Yearbook of World Affairs. London Institute of World Affairs. London. (LIWA/YWA)

Zeitschrift für Ethnologie. Deutschen Gesellschaft für Völkerkunde. Braunschweig, FRG. (DGV/ZE)

Zeitschrift für Geomorphologie. Gebrüder Borntraeger. Berlin. (ZG)

Zeitschrift für Kulturaustausch. Institut für Auslandsbeziehungen. Stuttgart, FRG. (IA/ZK)

Zeitschrift für Missionswissenschaft und Religionswissenschaft. Lucerne, Switzerland. (ZMR)

Zeitschrift für Morphologie und Anthropologie. E. Nägele. Stuttgart, Germany. (ZMA)

SUBJECT INDEX

Business Administration. *See also Business;*
Commerce. Antigua, 3165. Barbados,
3165. Saint Kitts, 3165. Saint Lucia, 3165.
Businessmen. *See also Business; Commerce;*
Industry and Industrialization; Mer-
chants. Barbados, 949. Bolivia, 3584. Brazil, 8385. Colombia, 3353, 6367. Peru,
3550, 8297.
Bustamante, Alexander, 6308.

Caacupe, Paraguay (city). Geography, 5622.
Caazapa, Paraguay (department). Geogra-
phy, 5626.
Cabrera, Luis, 6102.
Cacao. *See also Agriculture; Trees.* Bra-
zil, 3778.
CACM. *See Central American Common*
Market.
Caingang (indigenous group), 1609.
Cajamarca, Peru (city). Archaeology, 792.
Ethnology, 1345.
Caldera, Rafael, 6399.
Calendrics. *See also Archaeology; Astron-*
omy; Cosmology. Aztec, 309, 354. Maya,
258, 270, 290, 322, 405, 14262. Otomí,
1426b. Mesoamerica, 265, 367, 405.
Cali, Colombia (city). Economics, 3336–
3337. Physical Anthropology, 1678. Sociol-
ogy, 8262, 8266.
California, United States (state). *See also*
the regions of the Borderlands, South-
west United States. International Rela-
tions, 7161.
Callahuaya (indigenous group), 1250, 1263.
Câmara, Hélder, 28.
Campeche, Mexico (state). Archaeology, 371.
Geography, 5105–5106, 5141.
Campesinos. *See Peasants.*
Campos, Francisco, 6691.
Canada. *See also North America.*
Canada and United States Relations, 7098.
Canadians in Trinidad, 8240.
Canals. *See also Panama Canal; Transporta-*
tion. Brazil, 5583. Central America, 7278.
Maps, 5583. Mesoamerica, 255a.
Canchis, Peru (province). Ethnology,
1377–1378.
Caneca, Joaquim do Amor Divino, 6706.
Canela (indigenous group), 1095, 1119.
Canelos Quichua (indigenous group),
1221, 1327.
Cannibalism. *See also Ethnology.* Aztec,
1503. Yanomami, 1153.
Cap–Haitien, Haiti (city). Geography, 5453.
Capital. *See also Banking and Financial In-*

stitutions; Capitalism; Dependency; Eco-
nomics; Finance; Income; Investments;
Labor and Laboring Classes; Liquidity
(economics); Monopolies; Savings. Argentina, 3676, 3684, 8307–8308, 8320. Brazil,
2921, 3700, 3702, 3714, 3738, 3782, 8393.
Central America, 8151. Chile, 3458. Colombia, 2921. Costa Rica, 8138. Guatemala, 8144. Latin America, 2882, 6521.
Peru, 2921, 3536. Puerto Rico, 3331. Third
World, 8226. Venezuela, 3416.
Capitalism. *See also Capital; Economics;*
Foreign Investments. Argentina, 8337. Bra-
zil, 3732, 6733, 8362, 8395. Central Amer-
ica, 8163. Chile, 3465, 3478, 6556. Costa
Rica, 8159–8160. History, 3478, 3732.
Latin America, 2786, 2807, 2909, 2933,
6054, 7002, 7016, 7123, 8028, 8036. Mex-
ico, 8128–8129, 8134. Panama, 6241. Peru,
3522. Theory, 8036. Third World, 7073.
Venezuela, 3384, 3388.
Capitão Poço, Brazil (city). Geography, 5411.
Caracas, Venezuela (city). Education, 4565.
Geography, 5655. Physical Anthropology,
1526, 1677. Sociology, 8042, 8260.
Carazo Odio, Rodrigo, 6171.
Cardinals. *See also Catholic Church; Clergy.*
Venezuela, 7476.
Cargo Systems. *See Social Structure.*
Carib (indigenous group). *See also*
Black Carib. 411, 431, 453, 943, 1038,
1153, 1202.
CARIBBEAN AREA. *See also Borderlands;*
Commonwealth Caribbean; Greater Anti-
lles; Latin America; Lesser Antilles; West
Indies.
Anthropology, 413.
Archaeology. *See also Mesoamerica.*
408–467, 831.
Ethnology, 955, 960, 970, 993, 998, 1000,
1005, 1014, 1023, 1044, 1050, 1054,
1060, 1064–1065.
Linguistics, 413.
Physical Anthropology, 1528, 1532, 1536,
1538, 1548, 1565–1566, 1593, 1599,
1630, 1675, 1745.
Bibliography, 2, 132, 146, 413, 1054,
1064–1065.
Economics, 1064–1065, 3048, 3058, 3062,
3166, 3168, 3199, 4362, 5430, 8170.
Education, 1064–1065, 4362, 4397–
4402, 8207.
Geography, 413, 5019, 5036–5039,
5430–5433.
Government and Politics, 1064–1065,
6028, 6244–6248, 7327.

1337, 1340, 1342, 1359, 1705–1706. South America, 1706. Venezuela, 1405.

Cochabamba, Bolivia (city). Ethnology, 1259.

Cochabamba, Bolivia (department). Economics, 3573–3574, 6503. Ethnology, 1264, 1269. Geography, 5210. Government and Politics, 5218, 6503. Linguistics, 1467.

Codices. *See also Archaeology; Manuscripts; Paleography.* Dresden, 403. Huichapan Mesoamerica, 1475. Pérez, 1426a. Nuttall, 335. Vaticanus, 399.

Coffee. *See also Agriculture.* Brazil, 3709, 3716, 3729, 3786, 5313, 5343, 5355, 5373, 5427. Colombia, 2895, 3334, 3347, 5244, 8276. Costa Rica, 2898, 3109, 5471, 8159. Haiti, 3159. History, 3334, 3786, 5244, 5343. Latin America, 2895. Maps, 5471. Mexico, 874, 8097. Peru, 3525. Puerto Rico, 3240. Venezuela, 5288.

Cognat, André, 1090.

Colegio Primitivo y Nacional de San Nicolás de Hidalgo, Mexico, 154.

Colima, Mexico (state). Geography, 5512, 5530.

COLOMBIA. *See also the cities of Antioquia, Bogotá, Bucaramanga, Cali, Cartagena, Ipiales, Leticia, Loba, Medellín, Mompox, Puerto Serviez, Ráquira, San Basilio del Palenque, Sutamarchán; the departments and intendancies of Amazonas, Antioquia, Atlántico, Bolívar, Boyacá, Cauca, Cundinamarca, Huila, Nariño, Risaralda, Santander; the commissary of Vaupés; the valleys of Cauca, Orinoco, Vaupés; the islands of Providencia, Salamanca, San Andrés; the regions of Amazonia, Andean Region, Darién, South America.*

Anthropology.
  Archaeology, 492, 597, 655–687, 828.
  Ethnology, 1108, 1127, 1131–1132, 1134, 1136, 1154, 1157, 1190–1191, 1204, 1308–1313.
  Linguistics, 1410, 1436–1440, 1453, 1462, 1465.
  Physical Anthropology, 1523, 1526, 1555, 1598, 1602, 1617, 1632–1633, 1639, 1655, 1668, 1678, 1686, 1702, 1717.
  Bibliography, 3–4, 15, 33–34, 37, 45, 78, 129, 141, 4435, 8277.
  Economics, 37, 129, 1312, 2776, 2778, 2833, 2836, 2852, 2885–2886, 2895, 2907, 2921, 2932, 2935, 2949, 3334–3364, 3373, 5244, 6339, 7459, 8271, 8276, 8278.

Education, 34, 1313, 3343, 4309, 4423–4445, 6363, 8279.

Geography, 5231–5247, 5601–5609.

Government and Politics, 3334, 3339, 3351, 3355, 6005, 6028, 6061, 6338–6375, 8268, 8279.

International Relations, 3358, 7377, 7390, 7458–7459.

Sociology, 45, 192, 3355, 5244, 6339, 8261–8280.

Colombia and Ecuador Relations, 7377.

Colombia and Morocco Relations, 7458.

Colombia and Venezuela Relations, 7390.

Colonization. *See also Cities and Towns; Emigration and Immigration; Internal Migration; Land Settlement.* Amazonia, 8372. Antarctic Regions, 5168. Bibliography, 56. Bolivia, 5216. Brazil, 5374, 8372. Georgias, 5168. Falkland Islands, 5168. Latin America, 56. Orkney Islands, 5168. Patagonia, 5168. Sandwich Islands, 5168. Venezuela, 5303.

Colorado (indigenous group), 1321.

COMECON. *See Council of Mutual Economic Assistance (COMECON).*

Comisión de Inversiones y Desarrollo Económico (Uruguay), 3622.

Comité de Amas de Casa, 1294.

Comités de Defensa de la Revolución, 6259

Commerce. *See also Balance of Trade; Business; Business Administration; Businessmen; Economic Geography; Economics; Finance; Foreign Exchange; Foreign Investments; Foreign Trade; Harbors; Import Substitution; International Finance; Marketing and Product Distribution; Multinational Corporations; Precolumbian Trade; Smuggling; Trademarks; Transportation.* Amazonia, 1184, 5252. Bolivia, 6493. Brazil, 3727, 3755, 3799–3800, 7442. Cuba, 3208. Directories, 3604, 3612. Ecuador, 701. History, 3538. Latin America, 8054. Mexico, 181, 7186, 7192. Paraguay, 3602, 3604. Peru, 1184, 3538. Uruguay, 3612.

Commercial Policy. *See Trade Policy.*

Commercial Treaties. *See Trade Agreements.*

Committee for Political Defense, 7120.

Commodities. *See Agriculture; Industry and Industrialization; names of specific commodities.*

COMMONWEALTH CARIBBEAN. *See also the islands of Anguilla, Antigua, Bahamas, Barbados, Barbuda, British Virgin Islands, Cayman Islands, Dominica, Grenada, Jamaica, Montserrat, Nevis, St.*

Anthropology.
Ethnology, 1056.
Government and Politics, 7322.
Sociology, 8170, 8209, 8216.
Curiel, Henri, 7143.
Customs Administration. *See also Foreign Trade; Public Finance; Smuggling; Tariff; Tourism; Travel.* Costa Rica, 5469. Maps, 5469.
Cuzco, Peru (city). Ethnology, 1348, 1353.
Cuzco, Peru (department). Archaeology, 768. Ethnology, 1370, 1377, 1402. Geography, 5264, 5641.

Dairy Industry. *See also Agricultural Industries; Food Industry and Trade.* Ecuador, 1314. Puerto Rico, 3247. Trinidad and Tobago, 5068.
Dancing. *See also Folklore; Music.* Aguacatec, 849. Belize, 976. Brazil, 112. Caribbean Area, 1060. Carriacou, 1020. Haiti, 971. Kayapó, 1121. Mesoamerica, 849. Mexico, 840. West Indies, 976.
Darién (region). *See also Colombia; Panama.*
Anthropology.
Archaeology, 669.
Economics, 3132, 5101.
Education, 3132.
Geography, 5606.
Sociology, 3132, 5101.
Darwin, Charles Robert, 5229.
Death. *See also Mortality and Morbidity; Mortuary Customs.* Krahō, 1098. Mesoamerica, 298. Mexico, 906. Surinam, 961.
Debray, Régis, 6348.
Debt. *See also Credit; Economics; External Debts; Public Debts.* Brazil, 3706, 3743.
Deception Island. *See also Antarctic Regions.* Geography, 5158.
Deities. *See also Mythology; Religion.* Andean Region, 1235. Brazil, 1058. Cuba, 1058. Haiti, 1058. Mesoamerica, 403, 405. Trinidad and Tobago, 1058.
Democracy. *See also Constitutional History; Constitutional Law; Elections; Federal Government; Political Participation; Political Science; Voting.* Argentina, 6600, 6606, 6612, 6621, 6634. Bolivia, 3586, 6508–6509. Brazil, 6663, 6666–6667, 6678, 6692, 6704, 6725, 6756–6757. Caribbean Area, 6028. Chile, 6531–6532, 6547, 6558, 6564, 6589. Colombia, 6343–6344, 6365, 6372. Congresses, 6401, 6666. Costa Rica, 6169, 6171, 6177, 8146. Ecuador, 6430. Guatemala, 6202. Latin America, 6004, 6010,

6015, 6028, 6042, 6046, 6052, 6059–6060, 6066, 6086, 6535, 6603, 7037, 7067, 7144, 8072. Mexico, 6120, 6128. Peru, 6446–6447, 6462. Uruguay, 6651. Venezuela, 6388, 6399–6400, 6402, 6413–6414.
Demography. *See also Census; Economics; Geopolitics; Human Fertility; Mortality and Morbidity; Population; Population Forecasting; Population Policy.* Brazil, 3735, 3792. Central America, 8150, 8157. Chile, 3473. Costa Rica, 8137, 8140. Cuba, 3209, 5040–5041, 5437. Dominican Republic, 8193, 8212. Ecuador, 1323, 3367. Haiti, 8166. History, 3473, 3735, 8212. Jamaica, 8165. Latin America, 7151, 8002, 8042. Methodology, 5136, 5323. Mesoamerica, 266, 297. Mexico, 8074, 8092, 8113. Panama, 8150. Peru, 8291. Puerto Rico, 8243. Statistics, 3473, 3628. Uruguay, 3628, 8347. Venezuela, 8252.
Demonology. *See also Evil Eye; Witchcraft.* Bolivia, 255b. Colombia, 255b.
Dependency. *See also Capital; Economics; International Relations.* Argentina, 3669, 3694, 8316. Bolivia, 3556, 6508. Brazil, 4580, 4616, 4644, 6748, 8362, 8382, 8395. Caribbean Area, 6245, 6248. Chile, 6556. Costa Rica, 8162. Cuba, 7328. Ecuador, 6421. Guatemala, 3110. Guyana, 3188. Latin America, 2769, 2860, 2903, 2917, 2941, 2971, 6029, 6049, 6054, 7100, 7123, 7149, 8020. Mexico, 7200, 8128. Panama, 6241. Peru, 6447, 6479. Puerto Rico, 6325. Study and Teaching, 4313. Theory, 2868. 2870, 6049, 7067, 7133, 7139. Uruguay, 3634. Venezuela, 3406, 6401.
Desana (indigenous group), 1181–1182.
Devaluation of Currency. *See Monetary Policy.*
Díaz, Porfirio, 7169.
Díaz Ordaz, Gustavo, 6112.
Dictators. *See also Authoritarianism; Corporatism; Military Governments; names of specific dictators; Presidents.* Bolivia, 6512. Central America, 6159–6160. Dominican Republic, 6288. El Salvador, 6180. Guatemala, 6198. Latin America, 6024, 6056, 6059, 7058. Nicaragua, 6229. Paraguay, 6641. Venezuela, 3379, 6389, 6419.
Dictionaries. *See also Dictionaries under specific subjects; Language and Languages; Reference Books.* Chol/Spanish, Spanish/Chol, 1415. Historical Dictionary of Mexico, 128. Place names, 5302. Political Dictionary, 155. Political Dictionary in

Spanish, 6588. Political Lexicon, 6072a. Race and Ethnic Relations, 8210. Rapanui/ Spanish, 1433a. Spanish Dictionary of Botany, 5161. Spanish Dictionary of Zoology, 5161. Trique/Spanish, Spanish/Trique, 1447. Tzotzil/Spanish, Spanish/Tzotzil, 1451.

Diffusion. *See Contact.*

Diplomatic and Consular Service. *See also Diplomatic History; Diplomats; Foreign Policy; International Law; International Relations.* Maps, 5534. United States/ Mexico, 5534.

Diplomatic History. *See also Diplomatic and Consular Service; Diplomats; Foreign Policy, History, International Agreements; International Relations.* Argentina, 7413. Bolivia, 7420. Brazil, 5403, 7430. Colombia, 7458. Cuba, 110. Dominican Republic, 7321. Honduras, 7259. Mexico, 110, 181, 7169, 7172, 7195, 7203. Peru, 7470. South America, 7422. Spain, 7203. Union of the Soviet Socialist Republics, 7172, 7278. United States, 7478. Venezuela, 7477–7478.

Diplomats. *See also Diplomatic and Consular Service; Diplomatic History; Foreign Policy; International Relations; Statesmen.* Bolivia, 6488. Costa Rica, 7240. Mexico, 7187, 7218. Nicaragua, 7256. Peru, 7470. United States, 7237, 7274. Venezuela, 7473.

Disarmament. *See also Armaments; Foreign Policy; International Relations; International Security; Militarism; War.* Mexico, 7186.

Diseases. *See also Alcohol and Alcoholism; Epidemiology, Medical Care; Paleopathology; Physical Anthropology.* Amazonia, 1731. Andean Region, 1639. Anemia, 1491. Anthrax, 968, 1715. Argentina, 1743. Bahamas, 991. Blacking-out, 1059. Blindness, 910. Bolivia, 1639. Brazil, 1572, 1574. Cancer, 1649, 1709, 1752. Cardiovascular, 1649, 1752. Caribbean Area, 1599. Chile, 1587, 1700. Colombia, 1190, 1617, 1639. Costa Rica, 1751. Deafness, 1648. Diabetes, 1615, 1618, 1709. Dominican Republic, 1499. Ecuador, 1315, 1639, 1731. Genetic, 1574, 1580, 1582, 1617. Guatemala, 881, 1733. Haiti, 968. Hemoglobinopathies, 991. Hemophilia, 1587. Hodgkin's, 1720, 1728. Hypertension, 991, 1723, 1753. Hypoglycemia, 1710. Indisposition, 965, 1033, 1059, 1744. Jamaica, 1570. Latin America, 1491, 1580, 1709, 1729. Malaria, 1491.

Maps, 1649. Maya, 1648. Mesoamerica, 908. Mexico, 870, 1580, 1582, 1639, 1648, 1748. Nervous system, 1599. Parasite, 1754. Peru, 1519, 1639. Precolumbian, 1491, 1519. Research, 1639. Sickle cell anemia, 1570. Smallpox, 1739, 5383. South America, 1599. Statistics, 1599, 1615. Susto, 908, 1729, 1733, 1748. Thalessemia, 1582. Venereal, 1499. Waorani, 1731.

Dissertations and Theses. *See also Academic Degrees; Bibliography and General Works; Dissertations and Theses under specific subjects; Universities.* Brazil, 83, 149. Caribbean Area, 146. Latin America, 136, 146. Panama, 19. Peru, 1331, 1368. United Kingdom, 162.

Divorce. *See also Family and Family Relationships; Marriage.* Barbados, 8169. Cuba, 8187–8188. History, 8187. Latin America, 1535. Laws and Legislation, 8187. Puerto Rico, 8182.

Djuka Tribe, 1004.

DOMINICA. *See also Commonwealth Caribbean; Lesser Antilles.*

Anthropology.
    Archaeology, 443.
Economics, 3169, 3200.
Geography, 5441.

DOMINICAN REPUBLIC. *See also the cities of Duvergé, La Concepción de la Vega, Puerto Plata, Santo Domingo; the provinces of Azua, Pedernales; Greater Antilles; Hispaniola.*

Anthropology.
    Archaeology, 414, 442, 445–447, 449–451, 461–462.
    Ethnology, 974, 1057.
    Linguistics, 1467.
    Physical Anthropology, 463, 1494, 1499, 1502, 1655.
Bibliography, 153.
Economics, 3135–3136, 3140–3144, 3148, 3151–3152, 3155–3156, 3158, 5048, 8195.
Education, 4462–4468.
Geography, 5045–5049, 5442–5448.
Government and Politics, 4464, 6028, 6288–6297, 7310.
International Relations, 7310, 7321, 7352, 7357.
Sociology, 3148, 3155, 8168, 8183, 8192–8193, 8195, 8197, 8206, 8241.

Dominican Republic and United States Relations, 6292, 7096, 7310, 7321, 7352, 7357.

Dominican Revolution (1965). *See also Revo-*

4591. Congresses, 4591. Mexico, 4491, 4521. Venezuela, 4555, 4558.

Ejidos. *See also Agricultural Cooperatives; Agriculture; Farms.* 846–847, 861, 863, 2987, 2993, 3005, 3020, 6123, 6131, 8089, 8091, 8117, 8119–8120, 8128.

El Bajío, Mexico (region). Economics, 2993.

El Beni, Bolivia (department). Archaeology, 558. Geography, 5207, 5215.

El Cerrito, Venezuela (city). Economics, 3374.

El Dorado, 658.

El General Valley. *See also Mexico.* Geography, 5082.

EL SALVADOR. *See also the city of San Salvador; the departments of La Paz, San Miguel, Sonsonate; the valley of Lempa, the region of Central America.*
Anthropology.
    Archaeology, *See also Lower Central America.* 476.
    Linguistics, 1470.
    Physical Anthropology, 1555, 1696.
Economics, 3080–3081, 3083, 3094, 3097–3098, 3106, 3113, 3116–3117, 3121, 5477.
Education, 3083, 4338, 4447, 4469, 8155.
Geography, 5088, 5477–5484.
Government and Politics, 6179–6192.
International Relations, 7239, 7244, 7249–7250, 7258, 7265, 7271.
Sociology, 3083, 8152–8152a, 8154–8156.

El Salvador and Honduras Relations, 7239, 7250, 7258.

El Salvador and Mexico Relations, 7265.

El Salvador and United States Relations, 7249, 7271.

Elbrick, C. Burke, 6683, 6717.

Election Law. *See also Elections; Voting.* Mexico, 6113, 6129, 6138, 6157. Peru, 1391.

Elections. *See also Democracy; Election Law; Political Science; Voting.* Argentina, 6607, 6638, 8332. Bolivia, 6486, 6496, 6500. Brazil, 6665, 6668, 6674, 6676. Chile, 5223, 6525, 6543. Colombia, 6340, 6344, 6349, 6352, 6356, 6358, 6366, 6370. Costa Rica, 6170, 6178. Ecuador, 6424. Guatemala, 6194, 6197. Jamaica, 6302, 6307. Latin America, 6093, 8020. Mexico, 181, 6115, 6124, 6137–6138, 6144–6145, 6152, 7173. Peru, 6441, 6483. Venezuela, 6398, 6412–6413.

Elementary Education. *See also Education.* Argentina, 4369, 4371, 4378, 4381. Bolivia,

4392. Brazil, 4609. Chile, 4420. Cuba, 4450, 4460. Curricula, 4626. Haiti, 4479. Latin America, 4324, 4326. Laws and Legislation, 4369. Mexico, 4492. Panama, 4527. Paraguay, 4533. Parental Involvement, 4421. Puerto Rico, 4548, 4551. Venezuela, 4574.

Elites. *See also Leadership; Social Classes; Social Structure; Sociology.* Bolivia, 6046. Brazil, 4645. Cuba, 6046. Ecuador, 6422. Guatemala, 3105. Guyana, 8199. Jamaica, 999, 1043, 6300. Mexico, 6046, 6103, 8082, 8084, 8125. Peru, 6046. Trinidad and Tobago, 962. Venezuela, 8255.

Emerillon (indigenous group), 1614.

Emigration and Immigration. *See also Alien Labor; Assimilation; Colonization; Contact; Human Geography; Internal Migration; names of specific ethnic groups and nationalities; Population Policy; Refugees.* Argentina, 8310, 8321, 8335. Bahamas, 1024. Belize, 1055. Bibliography, 23, 8277. Bolivia, 1432, 5219. Brazil, 1432, 3759, 5417, 7446, 8321, 8335, 8378. Caribbean Area, 411, 1000, 1005, 1538, 7343, 8179, 8207. Central America, 3054. Chile, 3473, 8335. Colombia, 8277. Congresses, 8179. Cuba, 1534, 3209, 8203, 8227. El Salvador, 476. Haiti, 1016, 1024, 1041, 1521. 8205. History, 3473, 3759, 8100, 8203. Jamaica, 964. Latin America, 8042, 8321. Laws and Legislation, 6654. Les Saintes, 958. Mexico, 23, 181, 3015, 3028–3029, 5136, 7178, 7186, 7192, 7197, 7204–7205, 7216, 8074, 8079, 8088, 8095, 8099–8100, 8122. Montserrat, 1034. Panama, 1554. Paraguay, 1432, 8343. Periodicals, 1000. Peru, 1334. Puerto Rico, 3239, 3270–3271, 3281, 3333. Puerto Rico, 8215. Statistics, 3473. Surinam, 8177, 8249. United States, 3028–3029, 5041, 7035, 7178, 7186, 7192, 7197, 7204–7205, 8079, 8088, 8095, 8099, 8122, 8207, 8215, 8225, 8227. Uruguay, 6654, 8347. Venezuela, 8259.

Eminent Domain. *See Expropriation.*

Employment. *See also Economics; Labor and Laboring Classes; Labor Supply; Underemployment; Unemployment.* Andean Region, 2884. Antigua, 3165. Argentina, 2805, 3662–3663, 3683, 3693, 3697–3698. Barbados, 1013, 3165, 8169. Bibliography, 3054. Brazil, 1103, 2805, 3764, 3779. Caribbean Area, 1065, 3195. Central America 2805, 3053–3055, 3059. Chile, 2805, 3456, 3481–3482, 8302–8303. Congresses, 8061.

3783. Andean Region, 2810, 2830, 2887, 2964. Argentina, 3637. Brazil, 3723, 3733, 3743, 3744, 3793–3794, 5349. Caribbean Area, 3058, 3198. Chile, 3451, 3478. Colombia, 3349–3350. Dominican Republic, 6291. El Salvador, 3098. Guyana, 3182. History, 3409, 3478, 3723. Latin America, 2773, 2780, 2812, 2846, 2873, 2890, 2924, 2926, 3416, 7042, 8020. Laws and Legislation, 3037, 3502, 3349, 3451, 7217. Mexico, 3015, 3029, 3033, 3037, 7192, 7217. Nicaragua, 3108. Paraguay, 3595. Peru, 3502, 3504, 3517, 3522, 3537. Policy, 2773. Puerto Rico, 3264–3265, 3283, 3297, 3324. Trinidad and Tobago, 3186. Venezuela, 3409.

Foreign Policy. *See also Armaments; Boundary Disputes; Diplomatic and Consular Service; Diplomatic History; Diplomats; Disarmament; Geopolitics, Good Neighbor Policy; International Agreements; International Economic Relations; International Law; International Relations; International Relations under names of specific countries; Monroe Doctrine; National Security; Nationalism; Refugees.* Andean Region, 2810. Argentina, 7397, 7402, 7405. Barbados, 7317. Brazil, 7433–7434, 7449–7450. Caribbean Area, 7059. Commonwealth Caribbean, 7318. Costa Rica, 7240. Cuba, 7309, 7311, 7329–7330, 7342, 7345. France, 7086. Guyana, 7317. Jamaica, 7317. Latin America, 7052. Mexico, 7189, 7195, 7210, 7212–7213, 7215, 7265. Peru, 7470. Sweden, 7127. Trinidad and Tobago, 7317. United States, 7003, 7008, 7015, 7022, 7028, 7031–7032, 7039, 7043, 7045, 7058–7059, 7067, 7070, 7075, 7078–7079, 7080, 7083, 7091, 7106, 7108, 7121–7122, 7128–7129, 7141, 7153, 7158, 7166, 7182–7183, 7191, 7212–7213, 7219, 7221, 7228, 7249, 7255, 7306, 7403, 7415, 7455. Venezuela, 7473–7475, 7477.

Foreign Relations. *See Foreign Policy; International Relations under names of specific countries.*

Foreign Trade. *See also Balance of Trade; Commerce; Customs Administration; Foreign Exchange; Foreign Investments; Foreign Trade Promotion; Import Substitution; International Economic Relations; International Finance; Multinational Corporations; Tariff; Trade Policy; Transportation.* Africa, 2866. Andean Region, 7370. Argentina, 3672, 3684, 3686. Barbados,

3175. Belize, 3191. Bolivia, 6493. Brazil, 3620, 3686, 3707, 3709–3710, 3727, 3733, 3735, 3755, 3758, 3761, 8374. Central America, 3050, 3052, 3059. Chile, 3447–3448, 3455–3456, 3490. Colombia, 8276. Costa Rica, 3050, 3066, 5471. Cuba, 3201, 3208, 3210, 3212–3213, 3215, 3219, 3222, 3228, 3230, 3232. Czechoslovakia, 7370. Directories, 3447. Dominican Republic, 3142. Europe, 2857. Guyana, 3175. Haiti, 3137, 3146. History, 2925, 3618, 3709, 3735, 8374. Jamaica, 3175. Japan, 2856. Latin America, 2792, 2797, 2855, 2856–2857, 2866–2867, 2910, 2925, 2950, 2953, 2963, 3416. Maps, 5471. Mexico, 181, 2979, 2981, 2989, 2994, 2996, 3007, 3012, 3015–3016, 3045, 7222. Nicaragua, 3050, 3099–3100. Paraguay, 3595, 3601, 3606. Periodicals, 3429. Peru, 3538, 3547. Puerto Rico, 3319, 3328. Research, 2976. Statistics, 3429, 3447–3448, 3684. Theory, 2764, 2766. Third World, 2834. Trinidad and Tobago, 3175. Union of Soviet Socialist Republics, 3215, 3230, 3232. United States, 2844. Uruguay, 3618, 3620. Venezuela, 3373, 3429.

Foreign Trade Promotion. *See also Foreign Exchange; Foreign Trade; Import Substitution; Trade Policy.* Brazil, 3719. Chile, 3457. Latin America, 2826, 2866, 2893, 2973. Mexico, 2985. Puerto Rico, 3326. Uruguay, 3630. Venezuela, 3373.

Forests and Forest Industry. *See also Agriculture; Ecology; Natural Resources; Rubber Industry and Trade; Trees.* Andean Region, 1225. Bibliography, 141, 5398. Brazil, 5321, 5342, 5368, 5398, 5427. Chile, 3447–3448. Colombia, 141. Congress, 1225. Costa Rica, 3078. Dominican Republic, 5444. Latin America, 2961. Maps, 5444, 5621, 5637. Panama, 3132. Paraguay, 3588, 5621. Peru, 5268, 5637. South America, 5163. Statistics, 3447–3448.

Fortaleza, Brazil (city). Sociology, 8377.

Fossil Man. *See also Paleoanthropology; Physical Anthropology.* Argentina, 1486, 1515. Brazil, 1486. Chile, 1486. Dominican Republic, 1494, 1502. Ecuador, 1486. Mexico, 1486, 1508. Panama, 1486. Peru, 1482, 1486, 1490, 1509.

France and United States Relations, 7086.

France and Venezuela Relations, 3409.

Free Trade and Protection. *See also Balance of Trade; Commercial Policy; Economic Policy; Economics; Tariff; Trade Policy.*

Brazil, 3709, 3753, 3761. Latin America, 3032. Mexico, 3029. Third World, 2834.

Freedom of Speech. *See also Civil Rights; Public Opinion.* Chile, 6533.

Freedom of the Press. *See also Censorship; Civil Rights; Journalism; Periodicals; Press; Public Opinion.* Chile, 6519, 6533. Latin America, 6045. Peru, 6436, 6449.

Frei Montalva, Eduardo, 3454, 6531, 6534, 6589.

Freire, Paulo, 4318, 4603, 4613, 4618.

French. in Argentina, 5188. Image of Mexicans, 4515. in Latin America, 29.

FRENCH GUIANA. *See also the Guianas; the regions of Amazonia, South America.*
Anthropology.
   Ethnology, 946.
   Physical Anthropology, 1614.
Economics, 5256.
Geography, 5255–5256.
Government and Politics, 5255.

French Intervention in Mexico (1861–1867), 99.

French Language. *See also Language and Languages.* Guadeloupe, 951. Martinique, 951.

French West Indies. *See Guadeloupe; Martinique.*

Frente Sandinista de Liberación Nacional (Nicaragua). *See Guerrillas; Political Parties.*

Frías, Argentina (city). Geography, 5185.

Fundação Nacional do Indio (FUNAI), 1168, 1172, 1174–1175, 1179.

Gabeira, Fernando, 6716.

Gallegos, Rómulo, 4555.

Games. *See also Folklore.* Barbados, 981. Precolumbian, 807.

Gamines. *See Children.*

García Robles, Alfonso, 7180.

Garfield, James Abram, 7106.

Garifuna. *See Black Carib.*

Garvey, Marcus, 963.

Gê (indigenous group), 1095, 1101, 1118, 1160, 1193, 1209, 1441.

Geisel, Ernesto, 6669, 6679, 6682, 6693–6694, 7449.

Genealogical Society of Utah, 104.

Genealogy. *See also Biography; History.* Latin America, 104.

Generative Grammar. *See Grammar.*

Genetics. *See Human Genetics.*

Genocide. *See also Terrorism.* Amazonia, 1082, 1225. Argentina, 1144. Brazil, 1174.

Ecuador, 1221. Latin America, 8060. Paraguay, 1161.

Geodesy. Ecuador, 5249.

Geographers. *See also Geography.* United States, 4358, 5007, 5025, 5034–5035.

Geographical Names. *See also Geography; Names.* Argentina, 5173. Guyana, 5259. Hispaniola, 5049. Honduras, 5093. Mexico, 5122. Nicaragua, 927. Tierra del Fuego, 5173. Uruguay, 5272. Venezuela, 5294, 5300, 5302.

GEOGRAPHY (items 5001–5655). *See also Atlases; Economic Geography; Ethnology; Geographers; Geographical Names; Geopolitics; Historical Geography; Human Geography; Maps and Cartography; Physical Geography; Regionalism; Social Sciences.* Congresses, 4403. and Development, 5010. Periodicals, 189. Study and Teaching, 4358, 4527–4528, 5033, 5428. Textbooks, 5159. Theory, 5015, 5020–5021.

Geology. *See also Earthquakes; Erosion; Geomorphology; Maps and Cartography; Minerals and Mining Industry; Minerology; Oceanography; Paleontology; Petroleum Industry and Trade; Physical Geography; Science; Soils; Stratigraphy; Volcanoes.* Argentina, 5176, 5551, 5562. Belize, 5466. Bibliography, 54, 87, 5070. Bolivia, 5220, 5564, 5572–5573. Brazil, 87, 5304, 5585, 5592. Central America, 5070, 5073, 5087. Chaco, 5181. Chile, 5226. Colombia, 5608. Congresses, 5027, 5284. Costa Rica, 5082. Ecuador, 688. El Salvador, 5477. Maps, 5466, 5477, 5503, 5516, 5536, 5551, 5562, 5564, 5572–5573, 5592, 5608, 5646. Mesoamerica, 287, 379, 5027. Mexico, 54, 5114, 5516. Panama, 5503. Periodicals, 87. South America, 5154, 5162, 5536. Uruguay, 5646. Venezuela, 5284.

Geomorphology. *See also Erosion; Geology; Glaciers; Karst Hydrology; Physical Geography.* Belize, 5076. Brazil, 584, 5304–5305, 5589. Costa Rica, 5082, 5467–5468. Maps, 5467–5468, 5589. Mexico, 5114–5115, 5125, 5135. Puerto Rico, 5064. Venezuela, 5284.

Geopolitics. *See also Boundary Disputes; Demography; Foreign Policy; Geography; Human Geography; International Relations; Political Science; World Politics.* Amazonia, 5375, 7447. Argentina, 6019, 7399. Bibliogrphy, 21. Bolivia, 6019, 7416–7417, 7423, 7426. Brazil, 3620, 6019, 7408, 7445. Caribbean Area, 5037. Chile, 6019,

Human Population Genetics. *See also Human Genetics; Population.* Amazonia, 1602, 1610. Aymara, 1592. Bibliography, 1600. Black Carib, 1585. Bolivia, 1592. Brazil, 1571, 1581, 1590, 1600, 1602, 1607–1610, 1612. Caingang, 1609. Colombia, 1598, 1602. Cuiva, 1613. Emerillon, 1614. French Guiana, 1614. Gorotire, 1581. Guatemala, 1585, 1589. Kanomari, 1607. Kekchi, 1589. Kraho, 1581, 1608. Mexico, 1584, 1586, 1603. Pano, 1607. Peru, 1602. Research, 1600. South America, 1594, 1596, 1601. Statistics, 1594. Ticuna, 1602, 1610. Venezuela, 1600, 1613. Wayampi, 1614. Wayana, 1614. Xikrin, 1612. Yanomami, 1600.

Human Rights. *See also Civil Rights; Constitutional Law; Political Science; Revolutions and Revolutionary Movements; Violence.* Argentina, 6084, 6633, 7067. Bolivia, 6503. Brazil, 6084, 6669, 6722. Chile, 6084, 6517, 6524, 6528, 6542, 6553, 6580, 6587, 7115. Cuba, 7334. El Salvador, 6186, 8152a. Latin America, 6031, 6048, 7027–7028, 7031, 7043, 7049–7050, 7067, 7069, 7075, 7102, 7104, 7128–7129, 7132, 7153, 7155. Laws and Legislation, 7334. Mexico, 8085. Nicaragua, 6226. Paraguay, 6084, 7115. United States, 7050, 7182. Uruguay, 6652, 7115. Venezuela, 6401.

Human Variation. *See also Biology; Human Adaptation; Human Genetics; Physical Anthropology.* Colombia, 1598. Cuba, 1627.

Humanism. *See also Culture; Philosophy.* 6593.

Hunger Strikes. *See also Strikes and Lockouts.* Bolivia, 6498.

Hunting. Amazonia, 826, 1086, 1204. Andean Region, 759. Argentina, 540, 547. Colombia, 1204. Ecuador, 697. Pampas, 537. Precolumbian, 759, 826. South America, 1653. Venezuela, 1631. Yanomami, 1151.

Hurricanes. *See also Meteorology; Natural Disasters.* Haiti, 3155.

Hydrology. *See also Karst Hydrology; Oceanography; Runoff.* Argentina, 5553. Brazil, 5400, 5421, 5585–5586. Chaco, 5181. El Salvador, 5477. Guatemala, 5486. Guyana, 5618. Jamaica, 5053, 5056. Maps, 5458, 5477, 5486, 5553, 5585–5586, 5618. Mesoamerica, 276. Mexico, 5117, 5128. Peru, 5268. Puerto Rico, 5458. Venezuela, 3432.

Iconography. *See Art; Precolumbian Art.*

Ideology. *See also names of specific ideologies; Philosophy.* Latin America, 6021. Mexico, 6125.

Illegal Trade. *See Drug Trade; Smuggling.*

Illiteracy. *See Literacy and Illiteracy.*

Imbabura, Ecuador (province). Archaeology, 689. Physical Anthropology, 1490.

Immigration. *See Emigration and Immigration.*

Imperialism. *See also International Relations; Militarism; Political Science.* Argentina, 3672. Brazil, 7444. Latin America, 7042, 7080, 7107. Peru, 7466. Union of the Soviet Socialist Republics, 7133. Third World, 8050, 8226. United States, 7056, 7133. Venezuela, 3420, 6411.

Implements. *See also Artifacts; Stone Implements.* Andean Region, 767. Peru, 788.

Import Substitution. *See also Commerce; Foreign Trade; Foreign Trade Promotion; Industrial Promotion; Industry and Industrialization; Trade Policy.* Argentina, 3675. Brazil, 3802. Caribbean Area, 3170. Chile, 3457. Costa Rica, 3088. Latin America, 2754, 2973. Mexico, 2985, 3043. Peru, 3547. Puerto Rico, 3243, 3305, 3328–3329, 3332. Venezuela, 3384.

Imports and Exports. *See Balance of Trade; Foreign Trade.*

Inca. *See also Precolumbian Civilizations.* 498–499, 536, 543, 612, 625, 649, 742, 759, 769, 774–775, 797, 812, 1372, 1379, 1409, 1479, 1488, 1511, 1514, 1742.

Income. *See also Capital; Consumption (economics); Economics; Finance; Income Distribution; Wages.* Argentina, 3650, 3654. Brazil, 3487, 3706, 3710, 3740, 3764, 3790, 5391, 5426, 8367, 8373. Central America, 3059. Chile, 3473, 3487. Colombia, 2885, 3343. Commonwealth Caribbean, 3195. Cuba, 9251. Dominican Republic, 3143. Ecuador, 2885. El Salvador, 3113, 8155. Guatemala, 8148. Guyana, 3187. Haiti, 8200. History, 3743, 3654. Honduras, 3096. Latin America, 2822. Mexico, 8108, 8123. Nicaragua, 3099. Peru, 2885, 3539. Puerto Rico, 3268, 3319, 5066. Statistics, 3473, 3790.

Income Distribution. *See also Economics; Income.* Andean Region, 2964–2965. Argentina, 3652, 3668. Bibliography, 3175. Bolivia, 3581. Brazil, 1527, 3704, 3711, 3715, 3731, 3765, 3775, 3803. Central America, 3053. Chile, 3445, 3462, 3463,

254, 1135, 1202, 1511, 1583, 1594, 1596, 1601, 1633, 1635, 1653. Surinam, 5271. Treatment of, 1132, 1165, 1168, 1175, 1176, 1179, 1222, 6076. Venezuela, 1154, 1631, 5239, 5293.

Industrial Promotion. *See also Import Substitution; Industry and Industrialization.* Argentina, 2935. Brazil, 3788, 3802. Colombia, 2935. Congresses, 2935. Ecuador, 2935. History, 3261. Latin America, 2935. Paraguay, 3599. Peru, 2935. Puerto Rico, 3252, 3261, 3288, 3293. Venezuela, 2935.

Industrial Relations. *See also Industry and Industrialization; Labor and Laboring Classes; Strikes and Lockouts; Trade Unions.* Barbados, 6311. Chile, 6575. Puerto Rico, 3255, 3287. Venezuela, 3425.

Industry and Industrialization. *See also Business; Businessmen; Economic Development; Economic Policy; Economics; Import Substitution; Industrial Promotion; Industrial Relations; Multinational Corporations; Production (economic); specific types of industries; Technical Assistance; Technology.* Argentina, 3636, 3639, 3661, 3670, 3675, 3684, 3693, 3696–3697. Bolivia, 126. Brazil, 3700, 3712, 3720, 3723–3724, 3730, 3732, 3738, 3744, 3762–3763, 3769, 3788, 3790, 3793–3794, 3796, 5334, 5372, 8348, 8362. Caribbean Area, 3198. Central America, 8151. Chile, 3442, 3455, 3458, 3475, 3488, 5221. Colombia, 3353, 8279. Costa Rica, 3070, 3076. Cuba, 3201, 3208, 3210. Directories, 3601, 3604, 3612. Ecuador, 3365, 3367–3368, 5251, 6421. Electric, 3763. Guatemala, 3106. Haiti, 3137, 3146. History, 2986, 3530, 3697, 3720, 3723, 3732, 3744, 3762, 3796. Latin America, 2754, 2767, 2784, 2798, 2831–2832, 2839, 2855, 2875, 2883, 2911, 2928, 2939, 2950, 2961. Laws and Legislation, 3365. Maps, 5621. Mesoamerica, 266. Mexico, 2986, 2989, 2999, 3003, 3012, 3043, 6116, 6156, 8084, 8132. Nicaragua, 3108. Panama, 3126. Paraguay, 3601, 3604, 3606, 5621. Periodicals, 3429. Peru, 1365, 3517, 3527–3528, 3530, 3550, 8289, 8297. Puerto Rico, 3234, 3243, 3250, 3275, 3287–3288, 3308, 3329. Research, 2976. Statistics, 126, 3429, 3488, 3527, 3530, 3790. Trinidad and Tobago, 3193. Uruguay, 3612, 3617, 3626. Venezuela, 3398, 3410, 3414, 3429, 3434.

Inflation. *See also Economic Policy; Finance.* Argentina, 2836, 2840, 2908, 3650, 3650–3651, 3662, 3668, 3678–3679, 3688. Brazil,

2820, 2833, 2840, 2908, 3487, 3705, 3773, 3777, 3787. Central America, 3051, 3057. Chile, 2833, 2840, 2908, 3437, 3487, 3651, 3668. Colombia, 2833, 2840, 3347, 3362. Costa Rica, 2836, 3068. Guatemala, 2836. Guyana, 3184. Industrialized Countries, 2901. Latin America, 2816–2817, 2838, 2840, 2894, 2923, 2958. Mexico, 2820, 2833, 2840, 2983, 2992, 2997, 8112. Peru, 2833, 2840, 3531, 6444. Puerto Rico, 3319. Trinidad and Tobago, 3184. Uruguay, 2840, 2908, 3626–3627, 3651. Venezuela, 3403.

Informal Labor Sector. *See Casual Labor.*

Information Science. *See also Communication; Library Science.* Commonwealth Caribbean, 171. Congresses, 4513. Guyana, 3161. Latin America, 80. Study and Teaching, 80. Venezuela, 77.

Inscriptions. *See also Archaeology; Paleography; Petroglyphs; Pictographs; Stelae; Writing.* Aztec, 406. Brazil, 489. Chile, 489. Maya, 404, 406. Mesoamerica, 400–402. Paraguay, 489.

Institute of Policy Studies, 7454.

Insurance. Maps, 5519. Mexico, 5519. Puerto Rico, 3299.

Intellectuals. Argentina, 5194. Bolivia, 5204. Brazil, 8358. Cuba, 6289. Mexico, 8125. Nicaragua, 6235. Paraguay, 6641. Peru, 172. Venezuela, 6376–6377.

Inter-American Development Bank (IDB), 2782, 2851, 2854, 7343, 7368. Project Evaluation, 2946. Publications, 2842.

Inter-American Institute of Agricultural Sciences, 27.

Inter-American Organizations. *See also names of specific organizations.* Directory, 7101.

Inter-American System. *See Inter-American Organizations; Organization of American States; Pan-Americanism.*

Inter-American Treaty for Reciprocal Assistance, 7174.

Inter-American Tropical Tuna Commission, 7161.

Internal Migration. *See also Agricultural Laborers; Cities and Towns; Colonization; Emigration and Immigration; Land Settlement; Migrant Labor; Population; Rural-urban Migration; Urban-rural Migration.* Amazonia, 1212. Argentina, 5200, 5202–5203, 8337. Bibliography, 45, 8277. Bolivia, 1292–1293. Brazil, 1704, 3759, 5318, 5329, 5353, 5355, 5384, 5419, 6744, 8355, 8372,

Latin Americanists. *See also Latin American Area Studies.* Union of the Soviet Socialist Republics, 125. West Germany, 140.

Law. *See also Courts; International Law; Law and Legislation under specific subjects; Lawyers and Legal Services.* Brazil, 8402. Caribbean Area, 1064. Guyana, 977. Sociology, 8402.

Law of the Sea. *See also International Law; Territorial Waters.* Brazil, 7440, 7442. Congresses, 7014, 7044. Dictionaries, 7154. Peru, 7465.

Lawyers and Legal Services. *See also Law.* Bolivia, 8325. Colombia, 8270.

Leadership. *See also Elites; Sociology.* Amazonia, 1142. Guajiro, 1218. Kagwahiv, 1142. Suyá, 1192.

Lebanese in Surinam, 972, 8177.

Lechín, Juan, 6499.

LEEWARD ISLANDS. *See names of specific islands.*

Legends. *See also Folk Literature; Folklore; Literature; Mythology; Tales.* Aguaruna, 1427. Bororo, 1407. Cuna, 876. Maya, 1466. Mesoamerica, 1466. Mexico, 931. Panama, 876. Peru, 1427.

Legislators. *See also Politicians; Statesmen.* United States. 6317.

Lempa Valley. *See also El Salvador.*
   Anthropology.
      Archaeology, 471, 473.

Lengua (indigenous group), 1732.

LES SAINTES. *See also Guadeloupe.*
   Anthropology.
      Ethnology, 958.

LESSER ANTILLES. *See also the islands of Anguilla, Antigua, Aruba, Barbados, Barbuda, British Virgin Islands, Curaçao, Dominica, Grenada, Guadeloupe, Martinique; Montserrat, Nevis, Saba, Saint Eustatius, Saint Kitts, Saint Lucia, Saint Vincent, Trinidad and Tobago, United States Virgin Islands; the regions of Caribbean Area; West Indies.*
   Anthropology.
      Archaeology, 410–411, 419, 453.
   Bibliography, 29, 42.
   Geography, 5057–5059.
   Government and Politics, 6209–6313.

Letelier, Orlando, 6517, 6546, 6568, 6583, 6590, 7454.

Leticia, Colombia (city). Linguistics, 1411.

Levy, Pablo, 5094.

Lewis, Oscar, 907.

Liberalism. *See also Political Science; Social*

Sciences. Brazil, 6702–6703. Mexico, 6147, 7209.

Liberation Movements. *See Philosophy of Liberation; Revolution and Revolutionary Movements.*

Liberation Theology. *See Philosophy of Liberation.*

Liberty of Speech. *See Freedom of Speech.*

Liberty of the Press. *See Freedom of the Press.*

Libraries and Library Services. *See also Archives; Bibliography; Books; Catalogs; Education.* Bolivia, 152. Brazil, 72–73, 82, 163. Chile, 76, 152. Colombia, 129, 141. Congresses, 79. Ecuador, 152. Jamaica, 68. Latin America, 79. Mexico, 67, 94. Peru, 152. Puerto Rico, 63, 157. Third World, 68. United States, 91, 93, 101. Uruguay, 164. West Germany, 140.

Library Science. *See also Bibliography; Information Science.* Argentina, 71. Bibliography, 81. Colombia, 78. Latin America, 65, 78. Paraguay, 81. Periodicals, 74. Study and Teaching, 65, 71, 78.

Lima, Peru (city). Economics, 1381. Education, 4541, 4543. Ethnology, 1381, 1394, 1397. Geography, 5265, 5630, 5635. Government and Politics, 1397, 6450, 6452, 6463, 6478. Sociology, 8291, 8295.

Limón, Costa Rica (province). Economics, 3074.

Linguistics. *See also Anthropological Linguistics; Grammar; Language and Languages; Loan Words; Mathematical Linguistics; Philologists; Sociolinguistics.* Bibliography, 1465, 1476. Brazil, 40, 8381. Congresses, 1414, 1467. Methodology, 1454–1458, 1467. Periodicals, 184. Study and Teaching, 1467–1468, 1476. Theory, 1467, 1471, 8381.

Lins, Etelvino, 6688.

Lipe (indigenous group), 513.

Liquidity (economics). *See also Banking and Financial Institutions; Capital; Credit; Finance; Monetary Policy.* El Salvador, 3094.

Literacy and Illiteracy. *See also Education.* Argentina, 4344. Bolivia, 1428. Brazil, 3749, 4560, 4577, 4603, 4618, 4622. Caribbean Area, 4400. Congresses, 1391. Costa Rica, 3073, 3104. Honduras, 3111. Latin America, 1467, 4316, 4341, 4344. Mexico, 3008, 4344. Periodicals, 4577. Peru, 1391, 4344, 8292. South America, 1428. Venezuela, 3385, 4560.

Communism and Communist Parties; Political Science; Socialism and Socialist Parties. Acción Democrática (AD, Venezuela), 6376, 6398–6399, 6409. Acción Democrática Nacional (ADN, Bolivia), 6500. Acción Popular (AP, Peru), 6440, 6460, 6472. Alianza Popular Revolucionario Americana (APRA, Peru), 6437, 6444, 6472, 6479. Argentina, 6604, 6606, 6635, 8328. Bibliography, 6122. Bolivia, 6492, 6495, 6500, 6507–6508, 6510–6511. Brazil, 6674, 6696, 6708. Brazilian Labor Party (Brazil), 6069. Caribbean Area, 6246. Chile, 6520, 6588. Colombia, 6352–6353, 6356, 6364, 6372. Congresses, 6506. Costa Rica, 6163, 6174, 8146. Dominican Republic, 6294. Ecuador, 6424, 6427. Frente Amplio de Opositor (FAO, Nicaragua), 6221. Frente Sandinista Liberación Nacional (FSLN, Nicaragua), 6069, 6211–6212, 6215, 6217–6218, 6222, 6229, 6240. Guatemala, 6194–6195, 6201. Jamaica, 6299, 6307. Latin America, 6052, 6066, 8020. Mexico, 6113, 6122, 6129, 6139, 6149, 6157. Movimento Democrático Brasileiro (MDB, Brazil), 6685, 6695. Movimiento de la Izquierda Revolucionaria (MIR, Chile), 6407. Movimiento Electoral del Pueblo (MEP, Venezuela), 6409. Movimiento Nacionalista Revolucionario (MNR, Bolivia), 6487, 6489, 6493. Movimiento Nacionalista Revolucionario Histórico (MNRH, Bolivia), 6509. New Jewel Movement (Grenada), 6069, 6312–6313. Nicaragua, 6220. Partido Acción Democrática (Venezuela), 6394. Partido Aprista Peruano (APRA, Peru), 6458. Partido Conservador (Colombia), 6362. Partido de Liberación Nacional (PLN, Costa Rica), 6171. Partido Democrático Cristiano (El Salvador), 6191. Partido Integralista (Brazil), 6712. Partido Liberal (Colombia), 6362. Partido Nacional (Uruguay), 6653. Partido Nuevo Progresista (PNP, Puerto Rico), 6316. Partido Obrero Revolucionario (POR, Bolivia), 6501, 6506. Partido Popular Cristiano (PPC, Peru), 6472. Partido Popular Democrática (PPD, Puerto Rico), 6316. Partido Revolucionario Auténtico (PRA, Bolivia), 6509. Partido Revolucionario Institucional (PRI, México), 8082. Partido Social Cristiano Comité Organizado Pro Elecciones Independiente (COPEI, Venezuela), 6398–6400, 6414. Partido Social Democrático (PSD, Brazil), 6686. People's National Congress (Guy-

ana), 950. People's National Movement (Trinidad and Tobago), 6329. People's National Party (Jamaica), 6301. People's Political Party (Jamaica), 6302. People's Progressive Party (Guyana), 6333, 6336. Peru, 6445. Trinidad and Tobago, 6327, 6330. União Democrática Nacional (UDN, Brazil), 6063, 6747. Unidad Popular (UP, Chile), 3438, 3464, 6526, 6538–6539, 6544, 6559, 6565–6568, 6571, 6581, 6594. Venezuela, 6379, 6396, 6412.

Political Philosophy. *See also Philosophy; Philosophy of Liberation.* Argentina, 6605. Brazil, 6703–6712. Chile, 6561. Colombia, 6357. Venezuela, 3407.

Political Prisoners. *See also Concentration Camps; Crime and Criminals.* Brazil, 6683, 6714–6715, 6719–6722. Chile, 6576, 6595. Paraguay, 6642.

Political Refugees. *See also Political Asylum; Refugees.* Brazil, 6716. Cuba, 7296. United States, 7351.

POLITICAL SCIENCE (items 6001–6757). *See also Authoritarianism; Bureaucracy; Civil Rights; Civilian Governments; Communism and Communist Parties; Constitutional History; Constitutional Law; Corporatism; Corruption in Politics; Coups d'Etat; Democracy; Elections; Executive Power; Federal Government; Geopolitics; Government and Politics under specific countries and regions; History; Human Rights; Imperialism; Liberalism; Local Government; Military Governments; Nationalism; Nationalization; Oligarchy; Political Boundaries; Political History; Political Parties; Political Sociology; Populism; Public Administration; Public Opinion; Radicalism; Revolutions and Revolutionary Movements; Social Sciences; Socialism and Socialist Parties; the State; Taxation; Voting; World Politics.* Bibliography, 1, 6122, 8032. Congresses, 4464. Dictionaries, 155, 6072a. History, 6710. Institutes, 193. Periodicals, 184, 193. Study and Teaching, 6037. Theory, 6480, 8324.

Political Sociology. *See also Political Participation; Political Science; Sociology.* Argentina, 6604, 8315. Barbados, 949. Chile, 6560. Colombia, 8268. Latin America, 8035. Mexico, 8084, 8112.

Political Violence. *See Violence.*

Politicians. *See also Legislators; Mayors; Presidents; Prime Ministers; Statesmen;*

Totonac (indigenous group), 935, 1448.
Tourism. *See also Customs Administration;
Maps and Cartography; Travel.* Argentina,
5171, 5543, 5549–5550, 5560. Bahamas,
5435. Bermuda, 1021a. Bolivia, 5571. Brazil, 5581. Caribbean Area, 3198. Cayman
Islands, 5436. Chile, 5599–5600. Costa
Rica, 5470, 5473. Cuba, 3208. Dominican
Republic, 5447. Ecuador, 5617. Guides,
5263–5264, 5270, 5447. Haiti, 5452, 5454.
Honduras, 5493. Jamaica, 5455. Machu Picchu, Peru, 5641. Maps, 5435–5436, 5447,
5452, 5454–5455, 5470, 5483, 5493, 5507,
5509–5513, 5515, 5517, 5521–5524, 5526,
5531, 5535, 5543, 5549–5550, 5560, 5571,
5599–5600, 5617, 5632–5633, 5641, 5644,
5647. Mexico, 181, 3015, 5507, 5509–
5513, 5515, 5517, 5521–5524, 5526, 5531,
7192. Peru, 5263–5264, 5270, 5632–5633,
5641. South America, 5535. Surinam,
5644. Trinidad and Tobago, 3193. United
States Virgin Islands, 1028, 5463. Uruguay,
5647. Venezuela, 3374, 5296.
Trade. *See Commerce; Foreign Trade; Precolumbian Trade.*
Trade Agreements. *See also International
Agreements; Trade Policy.* Argentina,
3613. Brazil, 3620. Paraguay, 3606. Uruguay, 3613, 3620.
Trade Barriers. *See Trade Policy.*
Trade Policy. *See also Commerce; Economic
Policy; Foreign Trade Promotion; Foreign
Trade; Free Trade and Protection; Import
Substitution; International Economic Relations; Public Policy; Tariff.* Argentina,
3657. Brazil, 3761, 6671. Colombia, 3351,
3358. Latin America, 2766, 2934, 2953,
2973. Law and Legislation, 2775. Mexico, 3043. Peru, 3538. United States,
2775, 2844.
Trade Unions. *See also Industrial Relations;
Labor and Laboring Classes; Socialism
and Socialist Parties; Strikes and Lockouts; Syndicalism; Teachers Unions.* Argentina, 1242, 3682, 6601, 6609, 6614,
6632. Automotive Workers, 6002, 6095.
Bolivia, 1247, 1278–1279, 6500, 8299. Brazil, 6657, 6680, 6738, 8387. Chemical and
Pharmaceutical Workers, 6680. Chile,
6515, 6522, 6573. Colombia, 6351. Congresses, 4311. El Salvador, 6187. Guyana,
6332. History, 3259, 8299. Jamaica, 3179.
Latin America, 4311, 6002, 6066, 6095,
8016. Metallurgical Workers, 6095. Mexico, 6110, 6116, 6125, 7184, 8116, 8120,

8131. Peru, 6439. Petroleum Workers,
7184. Puerto Rico, 3259, 6315. Trinidad
and Tobago, 3179, 6305. Uruguay, 6646.
Venezuela, 3425, 6401.
Trademarks. *See also Business; Commerce.*
Latin America, 2793. Mexico, 2979.
Transamazon Highways. *See also Highways.*
1082, 5312, 5318.
Transportation. *See also Aeronautics; Automobile Industry and Trade; Canals; Commerce; Communication; Economics;
Foreign Trade; Harbors; Highways; Navigation; Railroads.* Argentina, 5560. Bahamas, 1029. Brazil, 3767, 5339, 5354, 5389,
5413, 5579, 5586, 6723. Caribbean Area,
3198, 5060. Colombia, 5233. Costa Rica,
3076, 3079. Cuba, 3208, 3210. Ecuador,
5251. El Salvador, 3083. Haiti, 5050. Latin
America, 2910. Maps, 5457, 5560, 5579,
5586, 5621, 5631. Mexico, 181. Paraguay,
5621. Patagonia, 5193. Peru, 5631. Precolumbian, 604, 626. Puerto Rico, 5457.
Research, 2976. Trinidad and Tobago, 3193.
Urban, 5579, 5655, 6723. Venezuela, 5655.
Travel. *See also Customs Administration;
Maps and Cartography; Scientific Expedi-
tions; Tourism; Travelers.* Argentina, 5171.
Brazil, 5381, 5390. Chile, 5208, 5224.
Costa Rica, 5472. Cuba, 6253. Ecuador,
5208. Guides, 5381. Latin America, 5005.
Maps, 5472. Panama, 5208. Peru, 5208.
Venezuela, 5280, 5285, 5293.
Travelers. *See also Explorers; Travel.* Andean
Region, 1225, 5165. Brazil, 5310, 5315.
Nicaragua, 5094. Peru, 804. South Amer-
ica, 1107.
Treaties. *See International Agreements;
names of specific treaties.*
Treaty of Tlatelolco, 7109, 7180.
Treaty of Versailles (1919), 7063.
Trees. *See also Botany; Cacao; Forests and
Forest Industry; Plants.* Amazonia, 5368.
Bibliography, 5398. Brazil, 5368, 5398.
Trilateral Commission, 2825, 7015.
TRINIDAD AND TOBAGO. *See also Com-
monwealth Caribbean; Lesser Antilles.*
Anthropology.
    Archaeology, 424–425, 431.
    Ethnology, 960, 962, 969, 1022, 1030–
    1031, 1049, 1058.
    Linguistics, 424.
    Physical Anthropology, 1538, 1559, 1675,
    1757–1758.
Economics, 3172, 3175, 3179, 3184, 3186,
3193, 3395.

Wilson, Woodrow, 7166, 7191.
Windward Islands. *See Lesser Antilles.*
Wit and Humor. Latin America, 7054.
Witchcraft. *See also Demonology; Evil Eye; Folk Healers; Folk Medicine; Folklore; Voodooism.* Mexico, 931.
Women. *See also Feminism; Sociology.* Amahuaca, 1004. Amazonia, 1177. Argentina, 4387, 8308, 8323, 8329, 8339. Barbados, 8169. Bibliography, 16–17, 42, 1064–1065, 8204, 8366. Biographies, 8224. Bolivia, 1247, 1260, 1294, 8329, 8339. Brazil, 16–17, 1072, 3779, 6726, 8351, 8366, 8376–8377, 8403. Caribbean Area, 42, 1064–1065, 3166, 8204. Central America, 3054. Chile, 1540, 6018, 6540, 6549, 6566, 8303, 8305. Colombia, 3348, 4444, 8261–8262. Congresses, 2960, 8182, 8232. Costa Rica, 8158. Cuba, 3225, 8223–8224. Ecuador, 1315. Education, 4325, 4387, 8040, 8232. El Salvador, 8156. Guajiro, 1217–1218, 1313. Guatemala, 1647, 8147–8148. Haiti, 3145, 8200. History, 8169, 8366. Honduras, 3069. Latin America, 2939, 2960, 4325, 6018, 8008, 8040–8041, 8056, 8062, 8067, 8072, 8204. Laws and Legislation, 8223. Mexico, 930, 1676, 6106, 8040, 8077, 8107–8108, 8123. Paraguay, 8329, 8339. Peru, 6018, 6442, 8283, 8285, 8293. in Politics, 6018. Puerto Rico, 3284, 8182, 8214, 8222, 8232. Saint Kitts, 988. Saint Vincent, 996. Statistics, 8108, 8345. Stereotypes, 4444, 8075. Third World, 8008. United States, 8232. Uruguay, 8345. Venezuela, 1217–1218, 6389. Yanomami, 1177, 1199.
World Bank, 7088. Publications, 2843, 2976.
World Politics. *See also Geopolitics; International Relations; Political Science.* 6748, 7024, 7036, 7073, 7087, 7100, 7210, 7455.
World War II, 7406.
Writing. *See also Communication; Inscriptions; Language and Languages; Paleography.* Aztec, 406. Cuna, 879, 912. Maya, 406. Panama, 879.

Xavante (indigenous group), 1111–1113, 1119, 1168, 1213.
Xikri (indigenous group), 1213.
Xikrin (indigenous group), 1612.
Xingú (indigenous group), 1128, 1708.
Xingu Valley. *See also Brazil; Amazonia.*

Anthropology.
Ethnology, 1074, 1078, 1083–1084, 1170, 1193.

Yagua (indigenous group), 1067.
Yale University, New Haven, Connecticut. Library, 107.
Yallah Valley. *See also Jamaica.* Geography, 5052.
Yanomami (indigenous group), 1075, 1085–1086, 1120, 1137, 1151–1153, 1165, 1177–1179, 1199, 1204–1205, 1600, 1661.
Yaqui (indigenous group), 875, 926.
Yaqui Valley. *See also Mexico.* Economics, 3005.
Yatron, Gus, 7150.
Yawalapití (indigenous group), 1170.
Yebamasa (indigenous group), 1717.
Ye'kwana (indigenous group), 1204.
Yemen. *See also Africa.*
Yemen and Cuba Relations, 7336.
Yoruba. *See also Religion.* Trinidad, 8211.
Youth. *See also Children.* Chile, 1643. Mexico, 8112. Puerto Rico, 3291.
Yuca. *See also Agriculture.* Colombia, 672.
Yucatán, Mexico (state). Archaeology, 183, 256, 262, 371, 669. Economics, 183. Ethnology, 837, 846–847, 910, 923. Linguistics, 1426. Geography, 183, 5144, 5524. Government and Politics, 183. Physical Anthropology, 1611, 1648. Sociology, 183.
Yukpa (indigenous group), 1188.
Yuman (indigenous group), 461.
Yungay, Peru (city). Ethnology, 1376.
Yupana, 789.

Zacatecas, Mexico (city). Bibliography, 51, 86.
Zago, Angela, 6418.
Zamuco (indigenous group), 1077.
Zaña Valley. *See also Peru.* Economics, 3512.
Zapatera Island. *See also Nicaragua.*
Anthropology.
Archaeology, 468.
Zapotec. *See also Precolumbian Civilizations.* 335.
Zapotec (present day indigenous group), 1682.
Zoology. *See also Animals; Biology; Birds; Ethnozoology; Paleontology; Science.* Chaco, 5181. Dictionaries, 5161. South America, 5161. Venezuela, 5287.
Zulia, Venezuela (state). Education, 4575.

AUTHOR INDEX

Menezes Bastos, Rafael José de. *See* Bastos, Rafael José de Menezes.

Menget, Patrick, 1164

Menon, Bhashkar P., 2876

Menon, P. K., 5077

Mentz Ribeiro, Pedro Augusto. *See* Ribeiro, Pedro Augusto Mentz.

Mercado Jarrín, Edgardo, 7380

Mercado y dependencia, 2877

Mericle, Ken, 2850

Mérida, México. Universidad de Yucatán. Comisión de Planeación y Fomento de Actividades Académicas, 4511

———. ———. Rectoría, 4512

Merin, Boris M., 6060a

Merino Medina, Antonio, 6560

Merrick, Thomas William, 1550, 3759, 8384

Merryfield, William R., 1106

Mesa Redonda sobre Expresiones de la Cultura Boliviana en el Lapso 1925–74, *La Paz, Bolivia, 1975,* 1273

Mesoamérica, 191

Mesquita, Olindina Vianna, 5377

Messer, Ellen, 1736

Mestriner, A., 1596

Metodología y desarrollo en las ciencias sociales: efectos del crecimiento dependiente sobre la estructura social colombiana, 8271

México. Archivo General de la Nación, 110

———. Comisión Federal Electoral, 6138

———. Comisión Nacional de los Salarios Mínimos, 5525

———. Dirección General de Análise de Inversiones, 5526

———. Dirección General de Estudios del Territorio Nacional, 5527

———. Dirección General de Minas, 5528–5529

———. Dirección General de Oceanografía y Señalamiento Marítimo, 5126

——— (City). Universidad Nacional. Centro de Información Científica y Humanística, 4513

Mexico, realidad política de sus partidos: una investigación psicosocial acerca de los partidos políticos mexicanos, 6139

México, URSS, Bulgaria, 7194

Mexico and the United States: energy, trade, investment, immigration, tourism; the American Assembly, 3015, 7192

México en 500 libros, 148

México Indígena, 897

Mexico-United States relations, 7193

México y Japón en el siglo XIX: la política exterior de México y la co[...] soberanía japonesa, 7195

Mexico's foreign trade in 197[...] prospects, 3016

Mexiko, Brasilien, Argentinier[...]

Meyer-Clason, Curt, 5194

Meyers, Albert, 710–711

Meyers, Glenn D., 3287

Mezhgosudarstvennye otnoshen[...] skoi Amerike, 7082

Mezzalira, Sérgio, 5400

Miasta Gutiérrez, Jaime, 778

Michelini, Zelmar, 6652

Michels, Elizabeth F., 7196

Michels, J. W., 301

Middendorf, Ernest W., 5265

Midgett, Douglas, 1027

Miehlich, Günter, 914

Mieres, Francisco, 3406

Migliazza, Ernesto, 1165

La migración rural urbana: manifesta[...] agente de un proceso de cambio soc[...] 8273

Migración y desigualdad social en la ci[...] de México, 8113

Mihalik, Gary J., 1737

Mikkelsen, Vagn, 6746

Milenky, E. S., 7381

Milkowski, Tadeusz, 6275, 7335

Milenky, Edward S., 6613

Miller, A. G., 285

Miller, Elbert E., 5071

Miller, Elmer S., 1166

Miller, Frank C., 898

Miller, Linda B., 7083

Miller, Tom O., Jr., 1167

Miller Paiva, Ruy. *See* Paiva, Ruy Miller.

Millet, Richard, 7260, 7343

Millones, Luis, 1372

Millor Mauri, Manuel, 7197

Mills, Frank L., 3183

Minello, Nelson, 7084

Minujín, Alberto, 8314

Mirafuentes Galván, José Luis, 5530

Miranda, Avelino Fernandes de, 583

Miranda, Guido A., 5195

Miranda T., Anibal, 3595

Miranda Villaseñor, Luis E., 5127

Mirow, Kurt Rudolf, 7439

Misas Arango, Gabriel, 3351

La Miseria de los partidos, 6356

Misle, Carlos Eduardo, 5292

Mitchell, William P., 1373

Mithun, Marianne, 1454

Mixon, J. Wilson, 3017